THE NATIONWIDE
FOOTBALL ANNUAL
2021–2022

Published by SportsBooks Limited, 9 St Aubyns Place, York, YO24 1EQ
First published in 1887

A CIP catalogue record for this book is available from the British Library.

Editorial compilation by Stuart Barnes

ISBN-13 9781907524622

Front cover shows Chelsea celebrating their Champions League victory. Back cover has
Leicester players hoisting manager Brendan Rodgers after the club's first FA Cup success.
Photos from Alamy/PA Images.

Printed and bound in the UK by CPI Group (UK) Ltd, Croydon CRO 4YY

COMMENT

By Stuart Barnes

The national team came up just short of completing a renaissance under Gareth Southgate, but their performance at Euro 2020 was enough to set the seal on a special year for English football. It confirmed that we are now respected – and feared – in the international game, with every prospect of an exciting build-up to the World Cup. At club level, Chelsea won the Champions League and their midfielder Jorginho went on to complete a notable double success with Italy. Leicester lifted the FA Cup for the first time on an emotional night with a breathtaking goal from Youri Tielemans and world-class goalkeeping from Kasper Schmeichel. Manchester City came from nowhere to become Premier League champions for the third time in four years, while Manchester United reached the final of the Europa League before suffering the same fate as England, albeit in a rather more prolonged penalty shoot-out. The sound of silence still echoed around empty grounds before limited crowds were back at selected matches at the end of the season. Their full return will not come a day too soon.

~

Who would be a goalkeeper? Arguably, it's the most important position in the team, where a single mistake can prove the difference between success and failure. Yet even the best in the business never command the biggest transfer fees and rarely figure in the end-of-season awards lists. England's Jordan Pickford and Manchester United's David de Gea were both left frustrated in their respective finals. But it was Schmeichel who experienced most the pitfalls and the prizes of his profession. After his heroics at Wembley, Leicester were a quarter-of-an-hour away from a Champions League place on the final day of the Premier League campaign when he punched a corner into his own net to present an equaliser to Tottenham, who went on to condemn them to fifth with a 4-2 victory. On to Euro 2020 and Schmeichel was a rock in Denmark's emotional journey to the semi-finals, capping a magnificent performance against England by saving Harry Kane's penalty, before another twist of fate enabled Kane to sweep in the rebound. Scotland's David Marshall, beaten by an outrageous shot from nearly 50 yards by the Czech Republic's Patrik Schick, and Spain's Unai Simon, failing to control a back-pass from almost the same distance against Croatia, were also left cursing their luck in the tournament. But it was all smiles from Liverpool's Brazilian goalkeeper Alisson, who left his manager Jurgen Klopp open-mouthed in amazement with a match-winning, extra-time header from a corner against West Bromwich Albion. And Zander Clark will also never forget his contribution to St Johnstone's trophy double, heading down a corner for Chris Kane to equalise, then saving two penalties in the shoot-out against Rangers in a Scottish FA Cup fifth-round tie.

~

Northern Ireland's international fortunes have been on the wane, failing to qualify for Euro 2020, relegated from their Nations League group and making an indifferent start to the next World Cup. For captain Steven Davis, however, it was a memorable season from a personal perspective. The 36-year-old midfielder became Britain's most-capped player with his 126th appearance against Bulgaria in that qualifying campaign, overtaking Peter Shilton's record which had stood since 1990. England's former goalkeeper sent a message of congratulation to the Rangers player, who made his debut against Canada in February 2005 while playing for Aston Villa. Davis, who also had a spell early in his career with Fulham, achieved the record in the same month that his club clinched their first Scottish title since 2011, denying Celtic a tenth straight success. He featured in all but three of their 38 matches, was the Scottish writers' choice as Footballer of the Year and has signed on for another season at Ibrox.

3

SOUTHGATE ON THE SPOT AS ENGLAND MISS OUT

'We were so close to what was unimaginable at the start. Now we have a new benchmark, a new level of expectation, a new scenario. Many of these players have come of age on the international stage.'

The words of Gareth Southgate after his side's semi-final defeat by Croatia at the 2018 World Cup in Moscow. Fast forward three years and they looked prophetic as England swept into the final of Euro 2020 and led through Luke Shaw after 1 minute and 57 seconds against Italy at an expectant Wembley. Instead, the curse of the penalty shoot-out reared its ugly head again and we were left with a divided debate about missing out on a first major championship victory since the World Cup in 1966. One argument applauded the progress of a vibrant squad with strength in depth and a manager adept at using it fully to suit the occasion and the opposition. Another pointed to how England surrendered control and were forced into their shell after so much positive play for much of the first half against the Italians. The introduction of Marcus Rashford and Jadon Sancho in the final minute of extra-time to supplement the penalty line-up, without the two players given the chance to get a feel of the game, also came under scrutiny. In previous shoot-outs, as Southgate knew full well, even experienced England players succumbed to nerves. So he backed those two, along with Bukayo Saka, on the evidence of work on the training ground and afterwards shouldered all responsibility for the choice. The pressure proved too much for all three after Harry Kane and Harry Maguire both converted with great authority. So we are back to square one, with England's aversion to penalty taking at the highest level remaining unsolved. One felt for Jordan Pickford, who capped a top-drawer tournament with two saves and could not have been far away in the pecking order from his opposite number, Gianluigi Donnarumma, named UEFA's player of the tournament. Maguire and Raheem Sterling were both excellent, while the runs Declan Rice launched from deep in the final suggested a possible future role further forward than one shielding the defence. England certainly need a creative, driving force in midfield to supply Kane and Sterling. Maybe Sancho and Jude Bellingham are eventually the ones to provide it, along with Phil Foden.

Wales did well to finish runners-up in their group under Robert Page, who replaced Ryan Giggs initially for three matches towards the end of 2020 when the manager stepped down to face court charges, then continued through to these finals. His side had to play two matches in distant Baku, but qualified by defeating Turkey and although well beaten by Denmark in the first knockout round, were justified in complaining that the second of the four goals conceded, which really ended their chances, should never not have stood after Kieffer Moore was fouled in the build-up. Scotland, in their first major tournament for 23 years, paid the price for missing chances against the Czech Republic, a 2-0 defeat compounded by the manner of the second goal struck from nearly 50 yards by Patrik Schick. Steve Clarke's team responded resiliently to hold England at Wembley, but had no argument about the defeat by Croatia which left them out in the cold. Apart from the decision to include Azerbaijan in the first tournament to be staged across multiple countries, there was so much to admire throughout the tournament – a record number of goals, surprise results, a high standard of refereeing and, not least, the joy of spectators returning. Few will forget the back-to-back matches which produced scorelines of Croatia 3 Spain 5 and France 3 Switzerland 3.

Schick's spectacular was a leading contender for goal of the tournament, alongside Luka Modric's gem against Scotland and Mikkel Damsgaard's free-kick for Denmark against England. Top assist had to be Joakim Maehle's sublime delivery with the outside of his right boot for Kasper Dolberg to volley in for the Danes against the Czech Republic – a creation to delight Christian Eriksen, watching from home and thankfully recovering from the cardiac arrest suffered in his team's opening match against Finland. And no championship would be complete without a special contribution from Cristiano Ronaldo, the record-breaking Portugal captain who headed clear a Germany corner then sprinted away to put the finishing touch to his team's quick breakaway.

STUART BARNES

EUROPEAN CHAMPIONSHIP FINALS 2020
(title retained for branding purposes)

GROUP A

TURKEY 0 ITALY 3 (Demiral 53 og, Immobile 66, Insigne 79)
Rome (12,916); Friday, June 11
Turkey (4-1-4-1): Cakir, Celik, Demiral, Soyuncu, Meras, Yokuslu (Kahveci 65), Karaman (Dervisoglu 76), Tufan (Ayhan 64), Yazici (Under 46), Calhanoglu. Yilmaz. **Booked**: Soyuncu, Dervisoglu
Italy (4-3-3): Donnarumma, Florenzi (Di Lorenzo 46), Bonucci, Chiellini, Spinazzola, Barella, Jorginho, Locatelli (Crisante 74), Berardi (Bernardeschi 85), Immobile (Belotti 81), Insigne (Chiesa 81)
Referee: Danny Makkelie (Holland). **Half-time**: 0-0

WALES 1 (Moore 74) SWITZERLAND 1 (Embolo 49)
Baku (8,782); Saturday, June 12
Wales (4-2-3-1): Ward, C Roberts, Mepham, Rodon, B Davies, Allen, Morrell, Bale, Ramsey (Ampadu 90+3), James (Brooks 75), Moore. **Booked**: Moore
Switzerland (3-4-1-2): Sommer, Elvedi, Schar, Akanji, Mbabu, Freuler, Xhaka, Rodriguez, Shaqiri (Zakaria 66), Seferovic (Gavranovic 84), Embolo. **Booked**: Schar, Mbabu
Referee: Clement Turpin (France). **Half-time**: 0-0

TURKEY 0 WALES 2 (Ramsey 42, C Roberts 90+5)
Baku (19,762); Wednesday, June 16
Turkey (4-1-4-1): Cakir, Celik, Ayhan, Soyuncu, Meras (Muldur 73), Yokuslu (Demiral 46), Under (Kahveci 83), Tufan (Yazici 46), Calhanoglu, Karaman (Dervisoglu 75), Yilmaz. **Booked**: Calhanoglu, Yilmaz
Wales (4-2-3-1): Ward, C Roberts, Mepham, Rodon, B Davies, Allen (Ampadu 73), Morrell, Bale, Ramsey (Wilson 85), James (N Williams 90+4), Moore. **Booked**: Mepham, B Davies
Referee: Artur Dias (Portugal). **Half-time**: 0-1

ITALY 3 (Locatelli 26, 52, Immobile 89) SWITZERLAND 0
Rome (12,445); Wednesday, June 16
Italy (4-3-3): Donnarumma, Di Lorenzo, Bonucci, Chiellini (Acerbi 24), Spinazzola, Barella (Cristante 86), Jorginho, Locatelli (Pessina 86), Berardi (Toloi 70), Immobile, Insigne (Chiesa 69)
Switzerland (3-4-1-2): Sommer, Elvedi, Schar (Zuber 58), Akanji, Mbabu (Widmer 58), Freuler (Sow 84), Xhaka, Rodriguez, Shaqiri (Vargas 76), Seferovic (Gavranovic 46), Embolo. **Booked**: Gavranovic, Embolo
Referee: Sergey Karasev (Russia). **Half-time**: 1-0

ITALY 1 (Pessina 39) WALES 0
Rome (11,541); Sunday, June 20
Italy (4-3-3): Donnarumma (Siriguat 89), Toloi, Bonucci (Acerbiat 46), Bastoni, Palmieri, Pessina (Castrovilli 86), Jorginho, Crisante, Verratti, Bernardeschi (Raspadori 75), Belotti, Chiesa. **Booked**: Pessina
Wales (3-4-3): Ward, Ampadu, Rodon, Gunter, C Roberts, Allen (Levitt 86), Morrell (Moore 60), N Williams (B Davies 86), Bale (Brooks 86), Ramsey, James (Wilson 63). **Booked**: Allen, Gunter. **Sent off**: Ampadu (55)
Referee: Ovidiu Hategan (Romania). **Half-time**: 1-0

SWITZERLAND 3 (Seferovic 6, Shaqiri 26, 68) TURKEY 1 (Kahveci 62)
Baku (17,138); Sunday, June 20

Switzerland (3-4-1-2): Sommer, Elvedi, Akanji, Rodriguez, Widmer (Mbabu 90), Freuler, Xhaka, Zuber (Benito 85), Shaqiri (Vargas 75), Seferovic (Gavranovic 75), Embolo (Mehmedi 85). **Booked:** Xhaka
Turkey (4-1-4-1): Cakir, Celik, Demiral, Soyuncu, Muldur, Ayhan (Yokuslu 63), Under (Karaman 80), Tufan (Yazici 63), Kahveci (Kokcu 80), Calhanoglu (Tokoz 86) Yilmaz. **Booked:** Calhanoglu, Celik
Referee: Slavko Vincic (Slovenia). **Half-time:** 2-0

	P	W	D	L	F	A	GD	Pts
Italy Q	3	3	0	0	7	0	7	9
Wales Q	3	1	1	1	3	2	1	4
Switzerland Q	3	1	1	1	4	5	-1	4
Turkey	3	0	0	3	1	8	-7	0

GROUP B

DENMARK 0 FINLAND 1 (Pohjanpalo 59)
Copenhagen (13,790); Saturday, June 12
Denmark (4-3-3): Schmeichel, Wass (Stryger Larsen 75), Kjaer (Vestergaard 63), Christensen, Maehle, Eriksen (Jensen 43), Hojbjerg, Delaney (Cornelius 76), Poulsen, Wind (Olsen 63), Braithwaite
Finland (5-3-2): Hradecky, Raitala (Vaisanen 90), Toivio, Arajuuri, O'Shaughnessy, Uronen, Lod, Sparv (Schuller 76), Kamara, Pukki (Kauko 76), Pohjanpalo (Forss 84),. **Booked:** Lod, Sparv
Referee: Anthony Taylor (England). **Half-time:** 0-0

BELGIUM 3 (Lukaku 10, 88, Meunier 34) RUSSIA 0
St Petersburg (26,264); Saturday, June 12
Belgium (3-4-3): Courtois, Alderweireld, Boyata, Vertonghen (Vermaelen 76), Castagne (Meunier 27), Dendoncker, Tielemans, T Hazard, Mertens (E Hazard 72), Lukaku, Carrasco (Praet 77)
Russia (4-2-3-1): Shunin, Mario Fernandes, Semenov, Dzhikiya, Zhirkov, (Karavaev 43), Ozdoev, Barinov (Diveev 46), Zobnin (Mukhin 63), Golovin, Kuzyaev (Cheryshev 29, Miranchuk 63) Dzyuba
Referee: Antonio Lahoz (Spain). **Half-time:** 2-0

FINLAND 0 RUSSIA 1 (Miranchuk 45)
St Petersburg (24,540); Wednesday, June 16
Finland (5-3-2): Hradecky, Raitala (Soiri 75), Toivio (Jensen 84), Arajuuri, O'Shaughnessy, Uronen, Lod, Schuller (Kauko 67), Kamara, Pukki (Lappalainen 75), Pohjanpalo. **Booked:** Kamara, O'Shaughnessy
Russia (3-4-2-1): Safonov, Barinov, Diveev, Dzhikiya, Mario Fernandes, Ozdoev (Zhemaletdinov 61), Zobnin, Kuzyaev, Miranchuk (Mukhin 85), Golovin, Dzyuba (Sobolev 85). **Booked:** Barinov, Ozdoev, Dzhikiya
Referee: Danny Makkelie (Holland). **Half-time:** 0-1

DENMARK 1 (Poulsen 2) BELGIUM 2 (T Hazard 55, De Bruyne 70)
Copenhagen (23,395); Thursday, June 17
Denmark (3-4-3): Schmeichel, Christensen, Kjaer, Vestergaard (Olsen 84), Wass (Stryger Larsen 62), Hojbjerg, Delaney (Jensen 72), Maehle, Braithwaite, Damsgaard (Cornelius 72), Poulsen (Norgaard 62). **Booked:** Wass, Damsgaard, Jensen
Belgium (3-4-3): Courtois, Alderweireld, Denayer, Vertonghen, Meunier, Dendoncker, Tielemans, T Hazard (Vermaelen 90+4), Mertens (De Bruyne 46), Lukaku, Carrasco (E Hazard 59). **Booked:** T Hazard
Referee: Bjorn Kuipers (Holland). **Half-time:** 1-0

FINLAND 0 BELGIUM 2 (Hradecky 74 og, Lukaku 81)
St Petersburg (18,545); Monday, June 21
Finland (5-3-2): Hradecky, Raitala, Toivio, Arajuuri, O'Shaughnessy, Uronen (Alho 70), Lod
(Forss 90+1), Sparv (Schuller 59), Kamara, Pukki (Jensen 90+1), Pohjanpalo (Kauko 70)
Belgium (3-4-2-1): Courtois, Denayer, Boyata, Vermaelen, Trossard (Meunier 75), De Bruyne
(Vanaken 90+1), Witsel, Chadli, Doku (Batshuayi 76), E Hazard, Lukaku (Benteke 84)
Referee: Felix Brych (Germany). **Half-time:** 0-0

**RUSSIA 1 (Dzyuba 70 pen) DENMARK 4 (Damsgaard 38, Poulsen 59, Christensen 79,
Maehle 82)**
Copenhagen (23,644); Monday, June 21
Russia (3-4-2-1): Safonov, Dzhikiya, Diveev, Kudryasov (Karavaev 67), Mario Fernandes,
Ozdoev (Zhemaletdinov 62), Zobnin, Kuzyaev (Mukhin 67), Miranchuk (Sobolev 61)), Golovin,
Dzyuba. **Booked:** Diveev, Kudryashov
Denmark (3-4-3): Schmeichel, Christensen, Kjaer, Vestergaard, Wass (Stryger Larsen 60),
Hojbjerg, Delaney (Jensen 86), Maehle, Braithwaite (Corneluis 85), Damsgaard (Norgaard 72),
Poulsen (Dolberg 60). **Booked:** Delaney
Referee: Clement Turpin (France). **Half-time:** 0-1

Belgium Q	3	3	0	0	7	1	6	9
Denmark Q	3	1	0	2	5	4	1	3
Finland	3	1	0	2	1	3	-2	3
Russia	3	1	0	2	2	7	-5	3

GROUP C

AUSTRIA 3 (Lainer 18, Gregoritsch 78, Arnautovic 89) NORTH MACEDONIA 1 (Pandev 28)
Bucharest (9,082); Sunday, June 13
Austria (3-1-4-2): Bachmann, Dragovic (Lienhart 46), Alaba, Hinteregger, Schlager (Ilsanker
90+4), Lainer, Laimer (Baumgartlinger 90+3), Sabitzer, Ulmer, Kalajdzic (Arnautovic 59),
Baumgartner (Gregoritsch 58): **Booked:** Lainer
North Macedonia (5-3-2): Dimitrievski, Nikolov (Bejtulai 64), S Ristovski, Velkovski, Musliu (M
Ristovski 86), Alioski, Bardhi (Trichkovski 82), Ademi, Elmas, Pandev, Trajovski (Kostadinov
63). **Booked:** Trajovski, Alioski
Referee: Andreas Ekberg (Sweden). **Half-time:** 1-1

**HOLLAND 3 (Wijnaldum 52, Weghorst 58, Dumfries 85) UKRAINE 2 (Yarmolenko, 75,
Yaremchuk 79)**
Amsterdam (15,837); Sunday, June 13
Holland 3-5-2): Stekelenburg, Timber (Veltman 88), De Vrij, Blind (Ake 64), Dumfries, De
Roon, Wijnaldum, F De Jong, Van Aanholt (Wijndal 64), Depay (Malen 90+1), Weghorst (L De
Jong 88)
Ukraine (4-3-3): Bushchan, Karavaev, Zabarnyi, Mativyenko, Mykolenko, Malinovsky,
Sydorchuk, Zinchenko, Yarmolenko, Yaremchuk, Zubkov (Marios 13, Shaparenko 64). **Booked:**
Sydorchuk
Referee: Felix Brych (German). **Half-time:** 0-0

UKRAINE 2 (Yarmolenko 29, Yaremchuk 34) NORTH MACEDONIA 1 (Alisoki 57)
Bucharest (10,001): Thursday, June 17
Ukraine (4-3-3): Bushchan, Karavaev, Zabarnyi, Matviyenko, Mykolenko, Shaparenko
(Sydorchuk 78), Stepanenko, Zinchenko, Yarmolenko (Tsyganov 70), Yaremchuk (Besyedin
70), Malinovsky (Sobil 90 +2). **Booked:** Shaparenko
North Macedonia (5-3-2): Dimitrievski, S Ristovski, Velkovski (Trickovski 85), Musliu, Nikolov
(Trajkovski 46), Ademi (Ristevski 85), Spirovski (Churlinov 46), Bardhi (Avramovski 77),
Alioski, Pandev, Elmas. **Booked:** Velkovski, Avramovski
Referee: Fernando Rapallini (Argentina). **Half-time:** 2-0

HOLLAND 2 (Depay 11 pen, Dumfries 67) AUSTRIA 0
Amsterdam (15,243); Thursday, June 17
Holland (3-4-1-2): Stekelenburg, De Vrij, De Ligt, Blind (Ake 64), Dumfries, De Roon
(Gravenberch 74), F De Jong, Van Aanholt (Wijndal 65), Wijnaldum, Weghorst (Malen 64),
Depay (L De Jong 82). **Booked:** De Roon
Austria (3-1-4-2): Bachmann, Dragovic (Lienhart 85), Alaba, Hinteregger, Schlager (Onisiwo
84), Lainer, Laimer (Grillitsch 62), Sabitzer, Ulmer, Gregoritsch (Kalajdzic 62), Baumgartner
(Lazaro 70). **Booked:** Alaba, Bachmann
Referee: Orel Grinfeeld (Israel). **Half-time:** 1-0

NORTH MACEDONIA 0 HOLLAND 3 (Depay 24, Wijnaldum 51, 58)
Amsterdam (15,227); Monday, June 21
North Macedonia (4-2-3-1): Dimitrievski, S Ristovski, Velkovski, Musliu, Alioski, Ademi
(Nikolov 79), Bardhi (Stojanovski 78), Trickovski (Churlinov 56), Elmas, Trajovski (Hasani 68),
Pandev (Kostadinov 69). **Booked:** S Ristovski, Musliu, Alioski, Kostadinov
Holland (3-4-1-2): Stekelenburg, De Vrij (Timber 46), De Ligt, Blind, Dumfries (Berghuis 46),
F De Jong (Gakpo 79), Gravenberch, Van Aanholt, Wijnaldum, Depay (Weghorst 66), Malen
(Promes 66)
Referee: Istvan Kovacs (Romania). **Half-time:** 0-1

UKRAINE 0 AUSTRIA 1 (Baumgartner 21)
Bucharest (10,472); Monday, June 21
Ukraine (4-3-3): Bushchan, Karavaev, Zabarnyi, Matviyenko, Mykolenko (Besedin 85),
Shaparenko (Marlos 68), Sydorchuk, Zinchenko, Yarmolenko, Yaremchuk, Malinovsky
(Tsygankov 85)
Austria (4-2-3-1): Bachmann, Lainer, Dragovic, Hinteregger, Alaba, Schlager, Grillitsch,
Laimer (Ilsanker 72), Sabitzer, Baumgartner (Schopf 33), Arnautovic (Kalajdzic 90)
Referee: Cuneyt Cakir (Turkey). **Half-time:** 0-1

Holland Q	3	3	0	0	8	2	6	9
Austria Q	3	2	0	1	4	3	1	6
Ukraine Q	3	1	0	2	4	5	-1	3
North Macedonia	3	0	0	3	2	8	-6	0

GROUP D

ENGLAND 1 (Sterling 57) CROATIA 0
Wembley (18,497); Sunday, June 13
England (4-3-3): Pickford, Walker, Stones, Mings, Trippier, Phillips, Rice, Mount, Foden
(Rashford 71), Kane (Bellingham 82), Sterling (Calvert-Lewin 90). **Booked:** Foden
Croatia (4-3-3): Livakovic, Vrsaljko, Vida, Caleta-Car, Gvardiol, Modric, Kovacic (Pasalic 85),
Brozovic (Vlasic 70), Perisic, Kramaric (Brekalo 71), Rebic (Petkovic 79). **Booked:** Caleta-Car,
Brozovic
Referee: Daniele Orsato (Italy). **Half-time:** 0-0

SCOTLAND 0 CZECH REPUBLIC 2 (Schick 42, 52)
Hampden Park (9,847); Monday, June 14
Scotland (3-5-2): Marshall, Hendry (McGregor 67), Hanley, Cooper, O'Donnell (Forrest 79),
McGinn, McTominay, Armstrong (Fraser 67), Robertson, Dykes (Nisbet 79), Christie (Adams
46)
Czech Republic (4-2-3-1): Vaclik, Coufal, Celustka, Kalas, Boril, Soucek, Kral (Holes 67),
Masopust (Vydra 72), Darida (Sevcik 87), Jankto (Hlozek 72), Schick (Krmencik 87)
Referee: Daniel Siebert (Germany). **Half-time:** 0-1

CROATIA 1 (Perisic 47) CZECH REPUBLIC 1 (Schick 37 pen)
Hampden Park (5,607); Friday, June 18

Croatia (4-2-3-1): Livakovic, Vrsaljko, Lovren, Vida, Gvardiol, Modric, Kovacic (Brozovic 87), Perisic, Kramaric (Vlasic 62), Brekalo (Ivanusec 46), Rebic (Perkovic 46). **Booked**: Lovren
Czech Republic (4-2-3-1): Vaclik, Coufal, Celustka, Kalas, Boril, Holes (Kral 63), Soucek, Masopust (Hlozek 63), Darida (Barak 87), Jankto (Sevcik 74), Schick (Krmencik 74). **Booked**: Masopust, Boril, Hlozek
Referee: Carlos del Cerro Grande (Spain). **Half-time**: 0-0

ENGLAND 0 SCOTLAND 0
Wembley (20,306); Friday, June 18

England (4-3-3): Pickford, James, Stones, Mings, Shaw, Phillips, Rice, Mount, Foden (Grealish 63), Kane (Rashford 75), Sterling
Scotland (3-4-1-2): Marshall, McTominay, Hanley, Tierney, O'Donnell, McGregor, McGinn, Gilmour (Armstrong 76), Robertson, Dykes, Adams (Nisbet 86). **Booked**: McGinn, O'Donnell
Referee: Antonio Mateu (Spain)

CROATIA 3 (Vlasic 27, Modric 62, Perisic 77) SCOTLAND 1 (McGregor 42)
Hampden Park (9,896); Tuesday, June 22

Croatia (4-2-3-1): Livakovic, Juranovic, Lovren, Vida, Gvardiol (Barisic 71), Modric, Brozovic, Kovacic, Vlasic (Ivanusec 76), Petkovic (Kramaric 70), Perisic (Rebic 81). **Booked**: Lovren
Scotland (3-5-2): Marshall, McTominay, Hanley (McKenna 33), Tierney, O'Donnell (Patterson 84), McGinn, McGregor, Armstrong (Fraser 70), Robertson, Dykes, Adams (Nisbet 83). **Booked**: McKenna
Referee: Fernando Rapallini (Argentina) **Half-time**: 1-1

CZECH REPUBLIC 0 ENGLAND 1 (Sterling 12)
Wembley (19,104); Tuesday, June 22

Czech Republic (4-2-3-1): Vaclik, Coufal, Celustka, Kalas, Boril, Holes (Vydra 84), Soucek, Masopust (Hlozek 64), Darida (Kral 64), Jankto (Sevcik 46), Schick (Pekhart 75)). **Booked**: Boril
England (4-2-3-1): Pickford, Walker, Stones (Mings 79), Maguire, Shaw, Phillips, Rice (Henderson 46), Saka (Sancho 84), Grealish (Bellingham 68), Sterling (Rashford 67), Kane
Referee: Artur Dias (Portugal). **Half-time**: 1-0

England Q	3	2	1	0	2	0	2	7
Croatia Q	3	1	1	1	4	3	1	4
Czech Rep Q	3	1	1	1	3	2	1	4
Scotland	3	0	1	2	1	5	-4	1

GROUP E

POLAND 1 (Linetty 46) SLOVAKIA 2 (Szczesny 18 og, Skriniar 69)
St Petersburg (12,862); Monday, June 14

Poland (3-1-4-2): Szczesny, Bereszynski, Glik, Bednarek, Krychowiak, Jozwiak, Klich (Moder 85), Linetty (Frankowski 74), Rybus (Puchasz 74), Lewandowski, Zielinski (Swiderski 85). **Booked**: Krychowiak. **Sent off**: Krychowiak (62)
Slovakia (4-2-3-1): Dubravka, Pekarik (Koscelnik 79), Satka, Skriniar, Hubocan, Kucka, Hromada (Hrosovsky 79), Haraslin (Duris 87), Hamsik, Mak (Suslov 87), Duda (Gregus 90+1). **Booked**: Hubocan
Referee: Ovidiu Hategan (Romania). **Half-time**: 0-1

SPAIN 0 SWEDEN 0
Seville (10,559); Monday, June 14

Spain (4-3-3): Simon, Llorente, Aymeric Laporte, Pau Torres, Jordi Alba, Koke (Fabian Ruiz

89), Rodi (Thiago Alcontara 65), Pedri, Ferran Torres (Oyarzabal 74), Alvaro Morata (Sarabia 65), Dani Olmo (Gerard Moreno 74)
Sweden (4-4-2): Olsen, Lustig (Krafth 75), Lindelof, Danielson, Augustinsson, Larsson, Ekdal, Olsson (Cajuste 84), Forsberg (Bengtsson 84), Berg (Quaison 68), Isak (Claesson 69).
Booked: Lustig
Referee: Slavko Vincic (Slovenia)

SWEDEN 1 (Forsberg 77 pen) SLOVAKIA 0
St Petersburg (11,525); Friday, June 18

Sweden (4-4-2): Olsen, Lustig, Lindelof, Danielson, Augustinsson (Bengtsson 88), Larsson Olsson (Claesson 64), Ekdal (Svensson 88), Forsberg (Krafth 90+3), Berg (Quaison 64), Isak.
Booked: Olsson
Slovakia (4-2-3-1): Dubravka, Pekarik (Haraslin 64), Satka, Skriniar, Hubocan (Hancko 85), Kucka, Hrosovsky (Duris 84), Koscelnik, Hamsik (Benes 77), Mak (Weiss 76), Duda. **Booked**: Duda, Dubravka, Weiss
Referee: Daniel Siebert (Germany). **Half-time**: 0-0

SPAIN 1 (Alvaro Morata 25) POLAND 1 (Lewandowski 54)
Seville (11,742); Saturdy, June 19

Spain (4-3-3): Simon, Llorente, Aymeric Laporte, Pau Torres, Jordi Alba, Koke (Sarabia 67), Rodi, Pedri, Gerard Moreno (Ruiz 67), Alvaro Morata (Oyarzabal 87)), Dani Olmo (Ferran Torres 61). **Booked**: Pau Torres, Rodri
Poland (3-1-4-2): Szczesny, Bereszynski, Glik, Bednarek (Dawidowicz 68), Jozwiak, Klich (Kozlowski 55), Zielinski, Moder (Linetty 85), Puchasz, Swiderski (Frankowski 75), Lewandowski. **Booked**: Klich, Moder, Jozwiak, Lewandowski
Referee: Daniele Orsato (Italy). **Half-time**: 1-0

SLOVAKIA 0 SPAIN 5 (Dubravka 30 og, Aymeric Laporte 45, Sarabia 56, Ferran Torres 67, Kucka 71 og)
Seville (11,204); Wednesday, June 23

Slovakia (4-2-3-1): Dubravka, Pekarik, Satka, Skriniar, Hubocan, Kucka, Hromada (Lobotka 46), Haraslin (Suslov 69), Hamsik (Benes 90), Mak (Weiss 69), Duda (Duris 46). **Booked**: Duda, Skriniar
Spain (4-3-3): Simon, Azpilicueta (Oyazarbal 77), Garcia (Pau Torres 71), Aymeric Laporte, Jordi Alba, Koke, Sergio Busquets (Thiago Alcantara 71), Pedri, Sarabia, Alvaro Morata (Ferran Torres 66), Gerard Moreno (Traore 71). **Booked**: Sergio Busquets, Jordi Alba
Referee: Bjorn Kuipers (Holland). **Half-time**: 0-2

SWEDEN 3 (Forsberg 2, 59, Claesson 90+3) POLAND2 (Lewandowski 61, 84)
St Petersburg (14,252); Wednesday, June 23

Sweden (4-4-2): Olsen, Lustig (Krafth 68), Lindelof, Danielson, Augustinsson, Larsson, Olsson, Ekdal, Forsberg (Claesson 78), Quaison (Kulusevski 55), Isak (Berg 68). **Booked**: Danielson
Poland (3-1-4-2): Szczesny, Bereszynski, Glik, Bednarek, Jozwiak (Swierczok 61), Krychowiak (Placheta 78), Klich (Kozlowski 73), Puchasz (Frankowski 46), Zielinski, Swiderski, Lewandowski. **Booked**:Glik, Krychowiak
Referee: Michael Oliver (England). **Half-time**: 1-0

Sweden Q	3	2	1	0	4	2	2	7
Spain Q	3	1	2	0	6	1	5	5
Slovakia	3	1	0	2	2	7	-5	3
Poland	3	0	1	2	4	6	-2	1

GROUP F

HUNGARY 0 PORTUGAL 3 (Guerreiro 84, Cristiano Ronaldo 87, 90+2)
Budapest (55,662); Tuesday, June 15
Hungary (3-5-2): Gulacsi, Botka, Orban, Attila Szalai, Lovrencsics, Kleinheisler (Siger 78),
Nagy (R Varga 89), Schafer (Nego 66), Fiola (K Varga 89), Sallai (Schon 78), Adam Szalai.
Booked: Orban, Nego
Portugal (4-2-3-1): Rui Patricio, Nelson Semedo, Ruben Dias, Pepe, Guerreiro, William
Carvalho (Renato Sanches 81), Danilo, Bernardo Silva (Rafa Silva 71), Bruno Fernandes (Joao
Moutinho 89), Diogo Jota (Andre Silva 81), Cristiano Ronaldo. **Booked**: Ruben Dias
Referee: Cuneyt Cakir (Turkey). **Half-time**: 0-0

FRANCE 1 (Hummels 20 og) GERMANY 0
Munich (13,000); Tuesday, June 15
France (4-3-3): Lloris, Pavard, Varane, Kimpembe, Hernandez, Pogba, Kante, Rabiot (Dembele
90+5), Griezmann, Benzema (Tolisso 89), Mbappe
Germany (3-4-2-1): Neuer, Ginter (Eme Can 87), Hummels, Rudiger, Kimmich, Gundogan,
Kroos, Gosens (Volland 87), Havertz (Sane 74), Muller, Gnabry (Werner 74). **Booked**: Kimmich
Referee: Carlos del Cerro Grande (Spain). **Half-time**: 1-0

HUNGARY 1 (Fiola 45) FRANCE 1 (Griezmann 66)
Budapest (55,998); Saturday, June 19
Hungary (3-5-2): Gulacsi, Botka, Orban, Attila Szalai, Nego, Kleinheisler (Lovrencsics 83),
Nagy, Schafer (Cseri 75), Fiola, Sallai, Adam Szalai (Nikolic 26). **Booked**: Botka
France (4-3-3): Lloris, Pavard, Varane, Kimpembe, Digne, Pogba (Tolisso 75), Kante, Rabiot
(Dembele 57, Lemar 86), Griezmann, Benzema (Giroud 75), Mbappe. **Booked**: Pavard
Referee: Michael Oliver (England). **Half-time**: 1-0

PORTUGAL 2 (Cristiano Ronaldo 15, Diogo Jota 67) GERMANY 4 (Ruben Dias 35 og,
Guerreiro 39 og, Havertz 51, Gosens 60
Munich (12,926); Saturday, June 19
Portugal (4-1-4-1): Rui Patricio, Nelson Semedo, Pepe, Ruben Dias, Guerreiro, Danilo,
Bernardo Silva (Renato Sanches 46), Bruno Fernandes (Joao Moutinho 65), William Carvalho
(Rafa Silva 57), Diogo Jota (Andre Silva 83), Cristiano Ronaldo
Germany (3-4-2-1): Neuer, Ginter, Hummels (Emre Can 62), Rudiger, Kimmich, Gundogan
(Sule 73), Kroos, Gosens (Halstenberg 61), Havertz (Goretzka 73), Muller, Gnabry (Sane 88).
Booked: Ginter, Havertz
Referee: Anthony Taylor (England). **Half-time**: 1-2

GERMANY 2 (Havertz 66, Goretzka 84) HUNGARY 2 (Adam Szalai 11, Schaefer 68)
Munich (12,413); Wednesday, June 23
Germany (3-4-2-1): Neuer, Ginter (Volland 82), Hummels, Rudiger, Kimmich, Gundogan
(Goretzka 58), Kroos, Gosens (Musiala 82), Havertz (Werner 68), Sane, Gnabry (Muller 67).
Booked: Gundogan, Sane
Hungary (5-3-2): Gulacsi, Nego, Botka, Orban, Attila Szalai, Fiola (Nikolic 88), Kleinheisler
(Lovrencsics 89), Nagy, Schafer, Adam Szalai (Varga 82), Sallai (Schon 75). **Booked**: Botka,
Adam Szalai, Fiola
Referee: Sergei Karasev (Russia). **Half-time**: 0-1

PORTUGAL 2 (Cristiano Ronaldo 31 pen, 60 pen) FRANCE 2 (Benzema 45 pen, 47)
Budapest (54,886); Wednesday, June 23
Portugal (4-1-4-1): Rui Patricio, Nelson Semedo (Dalot 72), Pepe, Ruben Dias, Guerreiro,
Danilo (Palhinha 46), Bernardo Silva (Bruno Fernandes 72), Joao Moutinho (Ruben Neves
73), Renato Sanches (Sergio Oliveira 88), Diogo Jota, Cristiano Ronaldo

France (4-2-3-1): Lloris, Kounde, Varane, Kimpembe, Hernandez (Digne 46, Rabiot 52), Pogba, Kante, Tolisso (Coman 66), Griezmann (Sissoko 87), Mbappe, Benzema. **Booked:** Lloris, Hernandez, Griezmann, Kimpembe
Referee: Antonio Mateu (Spain). **Half-time:** 1-1

France Q	3	1	2	0	4	3	1	5
Germany Q	3	1	1	1	6	5	1	4
Portugal Q	3	1	1	1	7	6	1	4
Hungary	3	0	2	1	3	6	-3	2

ROUND OF 16

WALES 0 DENMARK 4 (Dolberg 27, 48, Maehle 88, Braithwaite 90+4)
Amsterdam (14,645); Saturday, June 26
Wales (4-2-3-1): Ward, C Roberts (N Williams 41), Rodon, Mepham, B Davies, Morrell (Wilson 60), Allen, Bale, Ramsey, James (Brooks 78), Moore (T Roberts 78). **Booked:** Rodon, Moore, Brooks, Bale. **Sent off:** Wilson (90)
Denmark (3-4-2-1): Schmeichel, Christensen, Kjaer (Anderson 77), Vestergaard, Stryger Larsen (Boileson 77), Hojbjerg, Delaney (Jensen 60), Maehle, Braithwaite, Damsgaard (Norgaard 60), Dolberg (Cornelius 70)
Referee: Daniel Siebert (Germany). **Half-time:** 0-1

ITALY 2 (Chiesa 95, Pessina 105) AUSTRIA 0 – aet
Wembley (18,910); Saturday, June 26
Italy (4-3-3): Donnarumma, Di Lorenzo, Bonucci, Acerbi, Spinazzola, Barella (Pessina 68), Jorginho, Verratti (Locatelli 68), Berardi (Chiesa 84), Immobile (Belotti 84), Insigne (Cristante 108). **Booked:** Di Lorenzo, Barella
Austria (4-2-3-1): Bachmann, Lainer (Trimmel 114), Dragovic, Hinteregger, Alaba, Schlager (Gregoritsch 105), Grillitsch (Schaub 105), Laimer (Ilsanker 114), Sabitzer, Baumgartner (Schopf 90), Arnautovic (Kalajdzic 97). **Booked:** Arnautovic, Hinteregger, Dragvic
Referee: Anthony Taylor (England). **Half-time** 0-0

HOLLAND 0 CZECH REPUBLIC 2 (Holes 68, Schick 80)
Budapest (52,834); Sunday, June 27
Holland (3-4-1-2): Stekelenburg, De Vrij, De Ligt, Blind (Timber 81), Dumfries, De Roon (Weghorst 73), F De Jong, Van Aanholt (Berghuis 80), Wijnaldum, Depay, Malen (Promes 57). **Booked:** Dumfries, F De Jong. **Sent off:** De Ligt (55)
Czech Republic (4-1-4-1): Vaclik, Coufal, Celustka, Kalas, Kaderabek, Holes (Kral 85), Soucek, Masopust (Janko 79), Barak (Sadilek 90+2), Sevcik (Hlozek 85), Schick (Krmencik (90+2). **Booked:** Coufal
Referee: Sergei Karasev (Russia). **Half-time:** 0-0

BELGIUM 1 (T Hazard 42) PORTUGAL 0
Seville (11,504); Sunday, June 27
Belgium (3-4-2-1): Courtois, Alderweireld, Vermaelen, Vertonghen, Meunier, Tielemans, Witsel, T Hazard (Dendoncker 90+5), De Bruyne (Mertens 48), E Hazard, Lukaku (Carrasco 87). **Booked:** Vermaelen, Alderweireld
Portugal (4-3-3): Rui Patricio, Dalot, Pepe, Ruben Dias, Guerreiro, Joao Moutinho (Joao Felix 55), Palhinha (Danilo 78), Renato Sanches, Bernardo Silva (Bruno Fernandes 55), Cristiano Ronaldo, Diogo Jota (Andre Silva 70). **Booked:** Palhinha, Dalot, Pepe
Referee: Felix Brych (Germany). **Half-time:** 1-0

CROATIA 3 (Pedri 20 og, Orsic 85, Pasalic 90+2) SPAIN 5 (Sarabia 38, Azpilicueta 57, Ferran Torres 77, Alvaro Morata 100, Oyarzabal 103) - aet
Copenhagen (22,771); Monday, June 28

Croatia (4-2-3-1): Livakovic (Brekalo 74), Juranovic, Vida, Caleta-Car, Gvardiol, Modric (Ivanusec 113), Brozovic, Kovacic (Budimir 79), Vlasic (Pasalic 79), Petkovic (Kramaric 46), Rebic (Orsic 67). **Booked**: Brozovic, Caleta-Car
Spain (4-3-3): Simon, Azpilicueta, Garcia (Pau Torres 72), Aymeric Laporte, Gaya (Jordi Alba 78), Koke (Ruiz 78), Sergio Busquets (Rodri 102), Pedri, Ferran Torres (Oyarzabal 88), Alvaro Morata, Sarabia (Olmo 72)
Referee: Cuneyt Cakir (Turkey). **Half-time**: 1-1

FRANCE 3 (Benzema 57, 59, Pogba 75) SWITZERLAND 3 (Seferovic 15, 81, Gavranovic 90)
– aet, Switzerland won 5-4 on pens
Bucharest (22,642); Monday, June 28

France (3-5-2): Lloris, Varane, Lenglet (Coman 46), Thuram 111), Kimpembe, Pavard, Pogba, Kante, Rabiot, Griezmann (Sissoko 88), Benzema (Giroud 94), Mbappe. **Booked**: Varane, Coman, Pavard
Switzerland (3-4-1-2): Sommer, Elvedi, Akanji, Rodriguez (Mehmedi 87), Widmer (Mbabu 73), Freuler, Xhaka, Zuber (Fassnacht 79), Shaqiri (Gavranovic 73), Seferovic (Schar 97), Embolo (Vargas 80). **Booked**: Elvedi, Rodriguez, Xhaka, Akanji
Referee: Fernando Rapalini (Argentina). **Half-time**: 0-1

ENGLAND 2 (Sterling 75, Kane 86) GERMANY 0
Wembley (41,973): Tuesday, June 29

England (3-4-3): Pickford, Walker, Stones, Maguire, Trippier, Phillips, Rice (Henderson 87), Shaw, Saka (Grealish 69), Kane, Sterling. **Booked**: Rice, Phillips, Maguire
Germany (3-4-2-1): Neuer, Ginter (Emre Can 87), Hummels, Rudiger, Kimmich, Kroos, Goretzka, Gosens (Sane 87), Havertz, Muller (Musiala 90+2), Werner (Gnabry 68). **Booked**: Ginter, Gosens
Referee: Danny Makkelie (Holand). **Half-time**: 0-0

SWEDEN 1 (Forsberg 43) UKRAINE 2 (Zinchenko 27, Dovbyk 120+1) - aet
Hampden Park (9,221); Tuesday, June 29

Sweden (4-4-2): Olsen, Lustig (Krafth 83), Lindelof, Danielson, Augustinsson (Bengtsson 83), Larsson (Claesson 97), Olsson (Helander 101), Ekdal, Forsberg, Kulusevski (Quaison 97), Isak (Berg 97). **Booked**: Kulusevski, Forsberg. **Sent off**: Danielsson (99)
Ukraine (3-5-2): Bushchan, Zabarnyi, Kryvtsov, Matviyenko, Karavaev, Sydorchuk (Bezus 118), Stepanenko (Makarenko 95), Shaparenko (Malinovsky 61), Zinchenko, Yarmolenko (Dovbyk 105), Yaremchuk (Besedin 00, Tsyhankov 101). **Booked**: Yarmolenko, Dovbyk
Referee: Daniele Orsato (Italy). **Half-time**: 1-1

QUARTER-FINALS
SWITZERLAND 1 (Shaqiri 68) SPAIN 1 (Zakaria 8 og) – aet, Spain won 3-1 on pens
St Petersburg (24,764); Friday, July 2

Switzerland (3-4-2-1): Sommer, Elvedi, Akanji, Rodriguez, Widmer (Mbabu 100), Freuler, Zakaria (Schar 100), Zuber (Fassnacht 90+2), Shaqiri (Sow 81), Embolo (Vargas 23), Seferovic (Gavranovic 82). **Booked**: Widmer, Gavranovic. **Sent off**: Freuler (77)
Spain (4-3-3): Simon, Azpilicueta, Aymeric Laporte, Pau Torres, (Thiago Alcontara 113), Jordi Alba, Koke (Llorente 90+2), Sergio Busquets, Pedri (Rodri 119), Ferran Torres (Oyarzabal 90), Alvaro Morata (Gerard Moreno 54), Sarabia (Dani Olmo 46). **Booked**: Aymeric Laporte
Referee: Michael Oliver (England). **Half-time**: 0-1

BELGIUM 1 (Lukaku 45 pen) ITALY 2 (Barella 31, Insigne 44)
Munich (12,984); Friday, July 2

Belgium (3-4-2-1): Courtois, Alderweireld, Vermaelen, Vertonghen, Meunier (Chadli 69, Praet 74), Tielemans (Mertens 69), Witsel, T Hazard, De Bruyne, Doku, Lukaku. **Booked**: Tielemans
Italy (4-3-3): Donnarumma, Di Lorenzo, Bonucci, Chiellini, Spinazzola (Emerson 79), Barella,

Jorginho, Verratti (Cristante 75), Chiesa (Toloi 90+1), Immobile (Belotti 75), Insigne (Berardi 79). **Booked**: Verratti, Berardi
Referee: Slavko Vincic (Slovenia). **Half-time**: 1-2

CZECH REPUBLIC 1 (Schick 49) DENMARK 2 (Delaney 5, Dolberg 42)
Baku (16,306); Saturday, July 3
Czech Republic (4-2-3-1): Vaclik, Coufal, Celustka (Brabec 65), Kalas, Boril, Holes (Jankto 46), Soucek, Masopust (Krmencik 46), Barak, Sevcik (Darida 79), Schick (Vydra 79). **Booked**: Krmencik, Kalas
Denmark (3-4-2-1): Schmeichel, Christensen (Andersen 81), Kjaer, Vestergaard, Stryger Larsen (Wass 71), Hojbjerg, Delaney (Jensen 81), Maehle, Damsgaard (Norgaard 60), Braithwaite, Dolberg (Poulsen 59)
Referee: Bjorn Kuipers (Sweden). **Half-time**: 0-2

UKRAINE 0 ENGLAND 4 (Kane 4, 50, Maguire 46, Henderson 63)
Rome (11,880); Saturday, July 3
Ukraine (3-5-2): Bushchan, Zabarnyi, Kryvtsov (Tsygankov 36), Matviyenko, Karavaev, Sydorchuk (Makarenko 64), Shaparenko, Zinchenko, Mykolenko, Yarmolenko, Yaremchuk
England (4-2-3-1): Pickford, Walker, Stones, Maguire, Shaw (Trippier 65), Phillips (Bellingham 65), Rice (Henderson 57), Sancho, Mount, Sterling (Rashford 65), Kane (Calvert-Lewin 73)
Referee: Felix Brych (Germany). **Half-time**: 0-1

SEMI-FINALS

ITALY 1 (Chiesa 60) SPAIN 1 (Alvaro Morata 80) – aet, Italy won 4-2 on pens
Wembley (57,811); Tuesday, July 6
Italy (4-3-3): Donnarumma, Di Lorenzo, Bonucci, Chiellini, Emerson (Toloi 74) Barella (Locatelli 85), Jorginho, Verratti (Pessina 74), Chiesa (Bernardeschi 107), Immobile (Berardi 62), Insigne (Belotti 85). **Booked**: Bonucci, Toloi
Spain (4-3-3): Simon, Azpilicueta (Llorente 85), Garcia (Pau Torres 109), Aymeric Laporte, Jordi Alba, Koke (Rodri 70), Sergio Busquets (Thiago Alcontara 105), Pedri, Oyarzabal, Dani Olmo, Ferran Torres (Alvaro Morata 62). **Booked**: Sergio Busquets
Referee: Felix Brych (Germany). **Half-time**: 0-0

ENGLAND 2 (Kjaer 39 og, Kane 104) DENMARK 1 (Damsgaard 30) - aet
Wembley (64,950; Wednesday, July 7
England (4-2-3-1): Pickford, Walker, Stones, Maguire, Shaw, Phillips, Rice (Henderson 94), Saka (Grealish 68, Trippier 105), Mount (Foden 94), Sterling, Kane. **Booked**: Maguire
Denmark (3-4-3): Schmeichel, Christensen (Andersen 78), Kjaer, Vestergaard (Wind 105), Stryger Larsen (Wass 66), Hojbjerg, Delaney (Jensen 87), Maehle, Braithwaite, Dolberg (Norgaard 66), Damsgaard (Poulsen 66). **Booked**: Wass
Referee: Danny Makkelie (Holland). **Half-time**: 1-1

FINAL

ITALY 1 (Bonucci 67) ENGLAND 1 (Shaw 2) – aet, Italy won 3-2 on pens
Wembley (67,173); Sunday, July 11
Italy (4-3-3): Donnarumma, Di Lorenzo, Bonucci, Chiellini (capt), Emerson (Florenzi 118), Barella (Cristante 54), Jorginho, Verratti (Locatelli 96), Chiesa (Bernardeschi 86), Immobile (Berardi 55), Insigne (Belotti 90). **Subs not used**: Sirigu, Meret, Pessina, Acerbi, Bastoni, Toloi. **Booked**: Barella, Bonucci, Insigne, Chiellini, Jorginho. **Coach**: Roberto Mancini
England (3-4-2-1): Pickford, Walker (Sancho 120), Stones, Maguire, Tripper (Saka 70), Phillips, Rice (Henderson 74, Rashford 120), Shaw, Sterling, Mount (Grealish 99), Kane

(capt). **Subs not used**: Johnstone, Ramsdale, Mings, Coady, Calvert-Lewin, James, Bellingham.
Booked: Maguire. **Manager**: Gareth Southgate
Penalty shoot-out: Italy – scored: Berardi, Bonucci, Bernardeschi; missed – Belotti, Jorginho.
England – scored: Kane, Maguire; missed – Rashford, Sancho, Saka
Referee: Bjorn Kuipers (Holland). **Half-time**: 0-1

EURO 2020 FACTS AND FIGURES

● England have now lost seven of their nine penalty shoot-outs at the World Cup and European Championship.

● Luke Shaw's first international goal, timed at one minute 57 seconds, was the fastest ever scored in the final of the tournament.

● England kept seven consecutive clean sheets for the first time in their history – two in warm-up matches against Austria and Romania and five in the tournament before conceding to Denmark in the semi-finals.

● Jordan Pickford set a record for an England goalkeeper for most minutes without conceding a goal – 725 – overtaking Gordon Banks's total of 720 in 1966.

● Jude Bellingham, at 17 years and 349 days, became the youngest player to feature in a European Championship when he came on for Harry Kane against Croatia. Six days later, Poland's Kacper Kozlowski, aged 17 years and 246 days, claimed the record against Spain.

● Italy's Leonardo Bonucci is now the oldest player to score in a Euro final, aged 34 years and 71 days.

● Aaron Ramsey became the first Wales player to score in two major tournaments, having netted against Russia in Euro 2016.

● UEFA team of the tournament: Donnarumma (Italy), Walker (England), Bonucci (Italy), Maguire (England), Spinazzola (Italy), Hojbjerg (Denmark), Jorginho (Italy), Pedri (Spain), Chiesa (Italy), Lukaku (Belgium), Sterling (England)

● Patrik Schick's goal for the Czech Republic against Scotland, measured at 49.7 yards, was the longest in the history of the Euros. Pedri's own goal in Spain's win over Croatia was just 0.7 of a yard shorter.

● Cristiano Ronaldo continued his record-breaking career. The 36-year-old Portugal captain became the first player to feature in five Euro finals, overtook Michel Platini as the tournament's all-time top scorer with 14 goals and has now scored 21 at the Euros and World Cup, more than anyone else. Ronaldo also drew level with Iran's Ali Daei as the leading marksman in international football on 109 goals.

● Spain's 5-3 victory over Croatia was the second highest scoring match behind Yugoslavia's 5-4 semi-final win over France in 1960. Spain also became the first to score five in successive matches, having beaten Slovakia 5-0 in the group stage

● Euro 2020 delivered a record 142 goals. Leading scorers: 5 Ronaldo (Portugal), Schick (Czech Republic); 4 Benzema (France), Forsberg (Sweden), Kane (England), Lukaku (Belgium)

England squad: Dean Henderson (Manchester Utd), Johnstone (WBA), Pickford (Everton); Chilwell (Chelsea), Coady (Wolves), James (Chelsea), Maguire (Manchester Utd), Mings (Aston Villa), Shaw (Manchester Utd), Stones (Manchester City), Trippier (Atletico Madrid),Walker (Manchester City), White (Brighton); Bellingham (Borussia Dortmund), Foden (Manchester City), Grealish (Aston Villa), Jordan Henderson (Liverpool), Mount (Chelsea), Phillips (Leeds), Rice (West Ham); Calvert-Lewin (Everton), Kane (Tottenham), Rashford (Manchester Utd), Sancho (Borussia Dortmund), Saka (Arsenal), Sterling (Manchester City)

Scotland squad: Gordon (Hearts), McLaughlin (Rangers), Marshall (Derby); Cooper (Leeds), Gallagher (Motherwell), Hanley (Norwich), Hendry (Celtic), McKenna (Nottm Forest), O'Donnell (Motherwell), Patterson (Rangers), Robertson (Liverpool), Taylor (Celtic), Tierney (Arsenal); Armstrong (Southampton), Fleck (Sheffield Utd), Gilmour (Chelsea), McGinn (Aston Villa), McGregor (Celtic), McTominay (Manchester Utd), Turnbull (Celtic); Adams (Southampton), Christie (Celtic), Dykes (QPR), Forrest (Celtic), Fraser (Newcastle), Nisbet (Hibernian)

Wales squad: Hennessey (Crystal Palace), Adam Davies (Stoke), Ward (Leicester); Ampadu (Chelsea), Cabango (Swansea), Ben Davies (Tottenham), Gunter (Charlton), Lockyer (Luton), Mepham (Bournemouth), Norrington-Davies (Sheffield Utd), Connor Roberts (Swansea), Rodon (Tottenham), Neco Williams (Liverpool); Allen (Stoke), Brooks (Bournemouth), Colwill (Cardiff), James (Manchester Utd), Levitt (Manchester Utd), Morrell (Luton), Ramsey (Juventus), Smith (Manchester City), Jonny Williams (Cardiff), Wilson (Liverpool); Bale (Real Madrid), Moore (Cardiff), Tyler Roberts (Leeds)

THE THINGS THEY SAID ...

'The players have run themselves into the ground giving the country some incredible memories. They were a joy to work with and can be proud of what they achieved. We wanted to give the people another fantastic night, but it was not to be. I was responsible for the order of penalties – it was totally my call based on what we did in training. They are a young team who will learn from it and continue to improve. It's hard for me to look that far ahead (to the World Cup). It sems a million miles away. I need a rest' – **Gareth Southgate**, England manager.

'It will hurt for a while, but these boys will grow from it. We got off to the perfect start and did everything we could. It just wasn't our night. We can all hold our heads high' – **Harry Kane**, England captain.

'That was the emotion coming out after achieving something incredible - seeing the players and fans celebrate the result of three years of hard work- - **Roberto Mancini**, Italy's tearful coach who rebuilt the national team after the failure to qualify for the 2018 World Cup.

'It was a big thing for the country. We've a lot to be happy about. We'll make sure it's not 23 years until the next one' – **Steve Clarke**, Scotland manager

'To even get where we did was a big achievement with the players we have not playing domestic football week in week out' – **Robert Page**, Wales caretaker-manager.

'We were suddenly put in a different situation. We needed the love and support and that's what gave us wins' – **Kasper Hjulmand**, Denmark coach, reflecting on Christian Eriksen's cardiac arrest in the opening game against Finland.

DAY-BY-DAY DIARY 2020–21

AUGUST 2020

25 Harry Maguire is given a suspended 21-month prison sentence after being found guilty of assaulting and trying to bribe Greek police on the holiday island of Mykonos. England manager Gareth Southgate drops the Manchester United captain from his squad for Nations League matches against Iceland and Denmark. Maguire instructs his legal team to appeal against the conviction which is nullified pending a retrial.

26 Celtic are knocked out of the Champions League in the second qualifying round, beaten 2-1 at home by Ferencvaros in a one-off tie. Chelsea sign Leicester's Ben Chilwell for £45m. Golden Boot winner Jamie Vardy, Leicester team-mate James Maddison and Manchester United goalkeeper Dean Henderson sign new long-term contracts.

27 In a BBC interview, Harry Maguire continues to plead his innocence and reveals fearing for his career in the alleged brawl. Manchester United's Paul Pogba becomes the highest-profile player to contract COVID.

28 Mark Bowen is replaced as Reading manager by Serbian coach Veljko Paunovic. Former England goalkeeper Tim Flowers is appointed manager of relegated Macclesfield after the departure of Mark Kennedy.

29 Arsenal defeat Liverpool 5-4 on penalties after a 1-1 draw in the FA Community Shield. In a pilot scheme at the Amex Stadium, a crowd of 2,500 watch Brighton's friendly against Chelsea.

30 Promoted Leeds sign Spain striker Rodrigo from Valencia for a club-record £26m.

31 David Silva tests positive for COVID on his first day as a Real Sociedad player after joining the club from Manchester City.

SEPTEMBER 2020

1 Manchester United pay £35m for the Ajax and Holland midfielder Donny van de Beek.

2 Scott Parker signs a new three-year contract after leading Fulham back into the Premier League.

3 Kieffer Moore and Shane Duffy score late goals for Wales and the Republic of Ireland as international football returns after a ten-month break with UEFA Nations League matches. Moore's 80th minute effort, the only one of the game, gives Ryan Giggs's side victory in Finland. Duffy's stoppage-time header earns the Republic a 1-1 draw away to Bulgaria in Stephen Kenny's first match as manager.

4 Ian Baraclough's first game in charge of Northern Ireland also brings a late equaliser – substitute Gavin Whyte's 86th minute header against Romania after his side have Josh Magennis sent off for a second yellow card. Scotland start with a 1-1 draw against Israel. Chelsea pay £71m for Bayer Leverkusen's Germany midfielder Kai Havertz. Lionel Messi decides to remain at Barcelona, ending speculation about a move to Manchester City.

5 Another dismissal, Kyle Walker for a second yellow, is followed by more late drama involving England. Raheem Sterling's penalty puts them ahead in the first minute of stoppage-time in Reykjavik against Iceland, who then waste the chance of equalising when Birkir Bjarnason fires a spot-kick over the bar.

6 Neco Williams heads his first international goal in stoppage-time to give Wales a 1-0 victory over Bulgaria. The Republic of Ireland lose by the same scoreline to Finland. Wolves break their transfer record with the £35.6m signing of 18-year-old striker Fabio Silva from Porto.

7 Two days after making their England debuts against Iceland, Phil Foden and Mason Greenwood are sent home ahead of the game against Denmark for bringing two women back to the team hotel. They are also fined £1,300 by local police for what manager Gareth Southgate describes as an 'unacceptable' breach of COVID rules. Lyndon Dykes scores his first goal for Scotland, who win 2-1 away to the Czech Republic. Northern Ireland are beaten 5-1 by Norway at Windsor Park.

8 Phil Foden and Mason Greenwood issue public apologies for their behaviour. England draw 0-0 in Copenhagen. Kevin De Bruyne is named Manchester City's first PFA Player of the Year.

9 Plans for a partial return of spectators in October are put on hold following new Government COVID restrictions. Aston Villa sign Ollie Watkins from Brentford for £28m – a record fee for both clubs. Leeds are fined £20,000 by the FA for using pyrotechnics while celebrating promotion after their penultimate match of the season at Derby.

10 Claims by Newcastle owner Mike Ashley that the Premier League blocked a proposed takeover of the club are rejected by the governing body.

11 The Premier League warn Government that each month of the season without spectators costs the game across the divisions more than £100m. Leeds manager Marcelo Bielsa signs a new one-year contract. Wigan's administrators appoint John Sheridan as manager on a short-term deal – his seventh Football League club.

12 Liverpool commence their defence of the title with a 4-3 victory over Leeds in a match widely seen as one of the finest openers to a season of modern times. Football League newcomers Harrogate kick-off in style, winning 4-0 at Southend. Barrow, back after 48 years, draw 1-1 against Stevenage.

13 Wolves manager Nuno Espirito Santo signs a new three-year contract.

14 Arsenal captain Pierre-Emerick Aubameyang finally ends speculation about his future by signing a new three-year contract.

15 Jack Grealish, the Aston Villa captain, also decides to stay, signing a new five-year deal with the club.

16 Macclesfield, relegated from League Two to the National League, are forced into liquidation at the High Court over debts of £500,000.

17 Seven years after leaving Tottenham for Real Madrid for a then world-record fee of £85.3m, Gareth Bale returns on a year's loan, at a reported salary of £500,000 a week, after falling out of favour at the Spanish champions.

18 Liverpool pay £41m for Wolves striker Diogo Jota – a record fee for the Molineux club – and £20m for Bayern Munich's Champions League-winning midfielder Thiago Alcontara.

19 Up to 1,000 spectators watch matches at seven clubs – Middlesbrough, Norwich. Blackpool, Charlton, Shrewsbury, Carlisle and Forest Green – under a Government pilot scheme.

20 Tyrone Mings signs a contract extension to 2024 with Aston Villa.

21 Aberdeen and Celtic are fined £30,000 by the SPL after players from both clubs broke Covid rules. A spate of cases at Leyton Orient forces the cancellation of the club's League Cup third round tie against Tottenham.

22 New Government restrictions effectively rule out a return of spectators for another six months – a decision condemned by the Premier League for having 'a devastating impact' on clubs and communities.

23 Premier League clubs come under pressure to give financial aid to those hardest hit in the EFL.

24 Bayern Munich defeat Sevilla 2-1 after extra-time in the UEFA Super Cup, watched by a crowd of 15,180 in Budapest – the first major European match in front of spectators since lockdown.

25 Danish-American businessman Thomas Sandgaard completes his takeover of Charlton from East Street Investments. Tottenham are given a bye into the fourth round of the League Cup after the postponement of their tie against Leyton Orient.

26 Crystal Palace manager Roy Hodgson accuses football's lawmakers of 'killing the game' with the new rigid handball rule.

27 Newcastle's Steve Bruce adds his voice for a change in the law after another controversial decision, saying 'We have lost the plot with it totally.'

28 Manchester City, beaten 5-2 by Leicester in their first Premier League home match of the season, sign Portugal central defender Ruben Dias from Benfica for a club-record £65m.

29 West Ham co-owner David Gold sells the oldest-surviving FA Cup for £759,000 at auction to an anonymous buyer. Macclesfield are expelled from the National League after being liquidated.

30 National League clubs receive emergency Government grants, enabling them to start the season. Swansea coach Alan Tate is given a four-match touchline ban and £920 fine by the FA for grabbing Jon Toral by the throat at half-time in the match against Birmingham. Everton defeat Birmingham 3-0 to reach the Women's FA Cup Final.

OCTOBER 2020

1 Harry Kane scores a hat-trick as Tottenham qualify for the group stage of the Europa League by beating Maccabi Haifa 7-2 in a play-off match. Celtic, Rangers and the Irish side Dundalk also qualify. Manchester City defeat Arsenal 2-1 in the second Women's FA Cup semi-final.

2 Phil Foden and Mason Greenwood, sent home after England's win in Iceland, are left out of the squad for internationals against Wales, Belgium and Denmark. Harry Maguire is recalled pending his re-trial in Greece. Sheffield United pay a club-record £23.5m for Liverpool's Rhian Brewster. Raul Jimenez signs a new four-year contract with Wolves.

3 The National League season starts behind closed doors, with Eastleigh's 5-1 win at Barnet the most eye-catching result.

4 Liverpool are beaten 7-2 by Aston Villa and Manchester United lose 6-1 at home to Tottenham on one of the most eventful days in the history of the Premier League.

5 Arsenal are the biggest spenders on transfer deadline-day, paying £45.3m for Atletico Madrid's Ghana midfielder Thomas Partey. Norwich receive a club-record £25m from Everton for Ben Godfrey. Total spending during the window of £1.24bn is down from £1.41bn the previous window.

6 Sabri Lamouchi becomes the season's first managerial casualty, sacked by Nottingham Forest after four successive defeats follow the collapse of the club's promotion challenge the previous season. He is replaced by Chris Hughton, out of work since his dismissal by Brighton in May 2019. Gerhard Struber leaves Barnsley to take charge of the MLS side New York Red Bulls.

7 England manager Gareth Southgate warns his players that further indiscipline threatens the team's chances of European Championship success after Tammy Abraham, Jadon Sancho and Ben Chilwell are ruled out of the friendly international against Wales for breaking Covid rules when attending a birthday party. Barnsley terminate the contract of defender Bambo Diaby after his two-year FA ban for a doping offence.

8 Steven Davis overtakes Pat Jennings as Northern Ireland's most-capped player with his 120th appearance in a European Championship play-off semi-final against Bosnia-Herzegovina. His side win on penalties and so do Scotland against Israel. The Republic of Ireland lose their shoot-out in Slovakia. Dominic Calvert-Lewin, on his debut, Conor Coady and Danny Ings score their first goals for England, who defeat Wales 3-0 in a friendly.

9 Manchester United's Marcus Rashford is awarded an MBE in the Queen's Birthday Honours after forcing the Government into a U-turn over free school meals during the summer holidays.

10 The Premier League come under pressure to reconsider a £14.95 pay-per-view charge for non-televised matches.

11 A penalty by Marcus Rashford puts England on the way to a 2-1 Nations League victory over the world's No 1 team Belgium. Scotland beat Slovakia 1-0. Northern Ireland, showing ten changes, lose by the same scoreline to Austria, watched by 600 supporters allowed into Windsor Park. The Republic of Ireland have James McClean sent off for a second yellow card in a goalless draw with Wales.

12 Liverpool and Manchester United are revealed to be at the forefront of proposals to reshape English football. 'Project Big Picture' plans include cutting the Premier League from 20 to 18 clubs, giving the big six plus Everton, West Ham and Southampton special voting rights, abolishing the League Cup and Community Shield and delivering a £250m rescue fund to the EFL.

13 The Premier League executive and Government condemn the proposals as damaging the game and creating a closed shop at the top. Arsenal's Eddie Nketiah overtakes Alan Shearer's record of 13 England under-21 goals with the winner against Turkey which ensures qualification for the European Championship finals. Part-owner Paul Scholes takes temporary charge of Salford after manager Graham Alexander is sacked, despite five unbeaten league games at the start of the season.

14 England have two players sent off in the same match for the first time. Harry Maguire receives two yellow cards and Reece James is shown a straight red for confronting the referee at the end of a 1-0 Nations League defeat by Denmark at Wembley. Jonny Williams scores his first goal for Wales, who win away to Bulgaria, while Scotland extend their unbeaten run to eight games – the best for 32 years – with a Ryan Fraser strike against the Czech Republic. Two more 1-0 scorelines deliver defeats for Northern Ireland against Norway and the Republic of Ireland against Finland. Premier League clubs reject 'Project Big Picture.' They agree to a 'strategic' review of the game, offer a £50m rescue package for League One and League Two clubs and consider support for those in the Championship.

15 After an outstanding first season in the Premier League, Allan Saint-Maximin signs a new six-year contract with Newcastle.

16 Relegated Hearts launch the shortened Scottish Championship season with a 6-2 victory over Dundee.

17 The remainder of the Scottish Championship, along with Leagues One and Two, commence their 27-fixture campaigns.

18 Virgil van Dijk is ruled out for the season with knee injury sustained in Liverpool's 2-2 draw at Everton.

19 Burnley's Dwight McNeil signs a new contract through to 2024.

20 A group including former England defender Gary Neville and former FA chairman David Bernstein unveil proposals which they claim will bring financial stability and proper independent governance to football.

21 Financial figures announced by Manchester United show the club's net debt more than doubling to £474m because of the pandemic.

22 Rotherham and Norwich are both fined £5,000 by the FA for a players' confrontation.

23 Valerien Ismael, former Crystal Palace player and coach in Austria and Germany, is appointed Barnsley's new manager.

24 Max Kilman signs a new contract with Wolves through to 2025.

26 Ipswich manager Paul Lambert is given a one-match touchline ban and £1,000 fine by the FA for abusive language after their match against Lincoln. Both clubs are fined for a players' confrontation – Ipswich £2,500 and Lincoln £2,000.

27 Graham Coughlan, manager of Mansfield for ten months, is sacked after nine League Two games without a win.

28 Marcus Rashford scores a hat-trick in Manchester United's 5-0 Champions League group victory over RB Leipzig.

29 UEFA announce an extra Champions League place for Scotland in the 2021–22 season, with the Premiership winners and runners-up both eligible.

30 Mike Jackson, manager of Tranmere for three months, is sacked after a home defeat by Morecambe.

31 Nobby Stiles, World Cup winner with England in 1966 and European Cup winner with Manchester United in 1968, dies aged 78.

NOVEMBER 2020

1 Sir Bobby Charlton has been diagnosed with dementia, his family disclose in a statement in the hope it could help others affected by the condition.

2 Ryan Giggs stands down as Wales manager for their next three matches after being arrested over allegations of assaulting his girlfriend. His assistant, Robert Page, takes temporary charge.

3 Diogo Jota scores a hat-trick in Liverpool's 5-0 Champions League group win over Atalanta. After nearly 30 years, AFC Wimbledon return to the club's 'spiritual' home in Plough Lane in a new 9,000-capacity stadium. They are denied a League One victory by Doncaster's last-minute equaliser.

4 Sheffield Wednesday's deduction of 12 points for breaching financial rules is reduced by half on appeal. Crystal Palace defender Mamadou Sakho accepts 'substantial' damages from the World Anti-Doping Agency over doping allegations.

5 Richie Wellens leaves Swindon to become Salford's new manager. Nigel Clough, former Burton manager, takes charge at Mansfield.

6 UEFA urge FIFA to change the handball law following several controversial penalty awards.

7 The Premier League decide to scrap their controversial pay-per-view method of showing matches.

8 Three Premier League managers, Jurgen Klopp, Pep Guardiola and Ole Gunnar Solskjaer call for changes in weekend match scheduling for clubs with midweek European commitments.

9 Garry Monk is sacked as Sheffield Wednesday manager after a run of one victory in six matches.

10 Greg Clarke resigns as chairman of the FA after referring to 'coloured footballers' while appearing before a parliamentary select committee. He is replaced in the short term by long-serving board member Peter McCormick.

11 Liverpool are hit by another defensive blow when Joe Gomez is ruled out for the season with a knee injury sustained in England training.

12 Scotland reach their first major tournament since 1998 by defeating Serbia on penalties in a European Championship play-off decider. Northern Ireland miss out after a 2-1 extra-time defeat by Slovakia. In friendly internationals, England defeat the Republic of Ireland 3-0 and Wales draw 0-0 with the United States.

13 Tony Pulis is appointed Sheffield Wednesday's new manager – his tenth club. John Sheridan, on a month-to-month contract at Wigan, leaves to take charge at Swindon.

14 Derby, bottom of the Championship, sack manager Phillip Cocu and put Wayne Rooney in temporary charge, alongside three other members of the coaching staff. Ben Garner, manager of Bristol Rovers for 11 months, is dismissed after a 4-1 home defeat by Fleetwood.

15 Ray Clemence, winner of three European Cups and five League titles with Liverpool, dies aged 72. Wales extend their unbeaten record in competitive matches to 11 with a 1-0 Nations League win over the Republic of Ireland who have Jeff Hendrick sent off. England lose 2-0 to Belgium, Northern Ireland face relegation from their group after a 2-1 defeat by Austria and Scotland go down 1-0 to Slovakia.

16 Wrexham's Supporters' Trust agree to a takeover of the National League club by Hollywood actors Ryan Reynolds and Rob McElhenney.

17 EFL clubs are given permission for five substitutes for the remainder of the season.

18 Phil Foden, with a brace, and Declan Rice score their first England goals in a 4-0 win over Iceland which completes a modest Nations League campaign. Wales are promoted to the top tier by beating Finland 3-1, but Scotland miss out after a second successive defeat – 1-0 by Israel. Northern Ireland finish with a 1-1 draw against Romania. The Republic of Ireland fail to score for the seventh successive game – 0-0 with Bulgaria.

19 Manchester City manager Pep Guardiola ends speculation about his future by signing a two-year contract extension through to 2023. Rangers pair Jordan Jones and George Edmundson are banned for seven matches by the Scottish FA for breaches of Covid regulations.

20 Manchester United confirm a 'sophisticated' cyber attack disrupted some of the club's computer systems. Police are investigating. Paul Tisdale, former MK Dons and Exeter manager, takes over at Bristol Rovers.

21 Tranmere appoint Keith Hill, formerly in charge at Rochdale, Barnsley and Bolton, as their new manager.

22 Stephen Kenny stays as manager of the Republic of Ireland after an investigation into a motivational video shown to his players before the friendly against England. The FAI 'accept' the explanation provided.

23 Clubs are told that limited numbers of spectators will be allowed from December 2 unless they are in the Government's high-risk Tier Three category. There are no plans for fans to return in Scotland.

24 Derby appoint former manager Steve McClaren as technical director. Jay Rodriguez and Matej Vydra sign contract extensions to 2022 with Burnley.

25 Diego Maradona, acclaimed as one of the greatest-ever players, dies after a heart attack aged 60. Manchester City qualify for the knockout stage of the Champions League with two group matches to spare. Shrewsbury manager Sam Ricketts is sacked after eight matches without a win leave his side second from bottom.

26 Three days of national mourning for Diego Maradona begin in Argentina. Arsenal and Leicester reach the Europa League knockout stage with two group matches still to play. Celtic fail to qualify. Gary Holt resigns as Livingston manager after a single point from five Scottish Premiership matches

27 Steve Cotterill is appointed the new Shrewsbury manager – his ninth club appointment.

28 Chorley, second from bottom of National League north, spring the surprise of the FA Cup second round, winning 2-1 at Peterborough.

29 Wolves striker Raul Jimenez suffers a fractured skull in an accidental clash of heads with Arsenal's David Luiz. Sunderland manager Phil Parkinson is sacked with his side eighth in League One.

30 Pressure builds on Celtic manager Neil Lennon with his side 11 points behind Rangers and out of the League Cup after a home defeat by Ross County.

DECEMBER 2020

1 Liverpool reach the knockout phase of the Champions League with one match to spare.

2 Olivier Giroud delivers one of the outstanding performances of the season, scoring all four goals in a 4-0 away win over Sevilla which gives Chelsea top spot in their Champions League group. Limited numbers of home spectators are allowed back for EFL matches at Luton, Wycombe, Charlton, Shrewsbury, Cambridge and Carlisle.

3 The Premier League and EFL agree a £250m rescue package for EFL clubs hit financially by the pandemic. Arsenal are the first Premier League club to welcome back supporters, with 2,000 watching the Europa League match against Rapid Vienna. Tottenham and Rangers qualify for the league's knockout stage.

4 Aston Villa against Newcastle becomes the season's first Premier League match to be postponed because of Covid after an outbreak of the virus at the St James' Park club.

5 West Ham's game against Manchester United is the first in the Premier League to have a limited number of supporters. Across the four divisions there are 20 fixtures with up to 2,000 watching.

6 Former Bristol City manager Lee Johnson takes charge at Sunderland.

7 Celtic's board give their backing Neil Lennon after his side fall 13 points behind Rangers, stating that 'progress made' in the new year will be reviewed.

8 Manchester United concede two goals in the opening 13 minutes, lose 3-2 to RB Leipzig and fail to qualify for the Champions League knockout stage.

9 Mohamed Salah scores Liverpool's fastest-ever goal in the Champions League/European Cup after 59 seconds against the Danish side Midtjylland.

10 Trevor Birch, director of football operations at Tottenham, is appointed the EFL's new chief executive.

11 Everton post an annual loss of £139.9m, blaming the impact of the pandemic. John McGinn signs a contract extension to 2025 with Aston Villa.

12 Newcastle's Miguel Almiron scores the fastest goal of the Premier League season so far after 19.9secs against West Bromwich Albion.

13 Two League Two managers are sacked. Stuart McCall, in his third spell at Bradford, leaves after six straight league and cup defeats, having signed a one-year contract extension the previous month. David Dunn, in charge of Barrow for five months, is dismissed after nine games without a win.

14 Gerard Houllier, who led Liverpool to five major trophies between 2001–03, dies aged 73.

15 New Government Covid restrictions for London and the south-east, leave four Premier League clubs with spectators – Brighton, Everton, Liverpool and Southampton. Over the four divisions, 25 of 92 clubs now have fans watching.

16 Slaven Bilic becomes the Premier League's first managerial casualty of the season, sacked by West Bromwich Albion after a single win in 13 games.

17 Sam Allardyce takes over at The Hawthorns, his first appointment since being dismissed by Everton in May 2018. Bayern Munich's Robert Lewandowski is voted the world's best player for 2020. Lucy Bronze of Manchester City wins the women's award. Jurgen Klopp retains the coaching award.

18 Premier League clubs again reject five substitutions. They agree to an increase to nine players on the bench. Michail Antonio signs a new contract with West Ham through to 2023.

19 Vladimir Ivic, manager of Watford for four months, is sacked after leaving fans' favourite Troy Deeney on the bench for a 2-0 defeat at Huddersfield. Stuart Kettlewell, manager of the Scottish Premiership's bottom team Ross County, loses his job.

20 Neil Lennon and Celtic make history in the Scottish Cup Final held over from the previous season. A penalty shoot-out win against Hearts gives Lennon a domestic treble as player and manager. His team complete a clean sweep of trophies for the fourth successive season. Xisco Munoz, coach to the Georgian club Dinamo Tbilisi, becomes Watford's fifth manager in 14 months. Liverpool captain Jordan Henderson is runner-up to Formula One champion Lewis Hamilton for the BBC Sports Personality of the Year award.

21 The League Cup Final is switched from February 28 to April 25 in the hope that spectators will be allowed back to Wembley by then. John Hughes, former Hibernian, Livingston and Inverness manager, takes over at Ross County. David Martindale, Livingston's caretaker-manager, is given the job until the end of the season.

22 Ian Holloway resigns as Grimsby manager, citing an 'inappropriate' approach to him by potential new owners.

23 Everton, Liverpool and seven EFL clubs remain with limited spectators following the latest Government restrictions. Kieran Trippier, Atletico Madrid and England full-back, is given a ten-week, world-wide ban and £70,000 fine for breaching FA betting regulations.

24 Michael Jolley, formerly in charge of Grimsby, is appointed Barrow's new manager.

26 Jim McLean, manager of Dundee United from 1971–93, dies aged 83.

28 Tony Pulis is sacked by Sheffield Wednesday after 45 days, ten games and a single win as manager.

29 Jake Buxton, manager of Burton for seven months, is dismissed with his side six points adrift at the bottom of League One. Paul Hurst returns for a second spell as Grimsby manager, four years after leaving to take over at Shrewsbury.

30 With a new strain of the virus sweeping the county and another Government clampdown imposed, all 92 clubs across the four divisions are again left without spectators.

31 Jimmy Greaves and Ron Flowers, the last surviving members of England's 1966 World Cup-winning squad still to be honoured, receive MBEs. Manchester United's Edinson Cavani is banned for three matches and fined £100,000 by the FA for using the term 'negrito' in a social media post. Tommy Docherty, former Manchester United and Scotland manager, dies aged 92. Burnley are taken over by an American investment group, ALK Capital, for a reported £170m. The group's managing director, Alan Pace, replaces Mike Garlick as chairman.

JANUARY 2021

1 Liverpool and Manchester United go into 2021 level on points at the top of the Premier League. Jimmy Floyd Hasselbaink is appointed Burton manager for the second time, five years after leaving the club to take over at Queens Park Rangers.

2 Wreaths are laid before the Rangers-Celtic match in memory of 66 spectators who died in the Ibrox disaster 50 years ago to the day. Rangers win 1-0 to extend their lead to 19 points from an extra three games played. Thirteen EFL fixtures are postponed – seven Covid-related and six because of frozen pitches.

3 Seven Premier League players apologise and face disciplinary action from their clubs for breaching Covid restrictions over the holiday period – Tottenham's Erik Lamela, Giovani Lo Celso and Sergio Reguilon, Manuel Lanzini (West Ham), Crystal Palace's Luka Milivojevic, Aleksandar Mitrovic (Fulham) and Benjamin Mendy (Manchester City). Former Tottenham manager Mauricio Pochettino takes over at Paris Saint-Germain.

4   Elite football in England and Scotland survives new Government lockdowns. Lower down the pyramid, some leagues are suspended. Fleetwood manager Joey Barton is sacked after a dressing-room altercation with striker Ched Evans. Port Vale dismiss John Askey after a fall from fifth to 17th. Cardiff's Neil Harris, sent off against Wycombe, receives a one-match touchline ban and £2,000 fine from the FA for abusive language.

5   Tottenham reach the League Cup Final by beating Brentford 2-0.

6   Manchester City defeat Manchester United by the same scoreline in the second semi-final. With 52 EFL matches postponed because of Covid, the players' union the PFA commit to twice-weekly tests for all clubs for the rest of the season at a cost of about £5m. Arsenal take out a short-term £120m corporate loan to offset the impact of the pandemic. Wolves manager Nuno Espirito Santo is fined £25,000 by the FA for criticising referee Lee Mason. Sacked West Bromwich Albion manager Slaven Bilic takes over at the Chinese Super League club Beijing Guoan. Former Republic of Ireland manager Mick McCarthy leaves Cypriot champions Apoel Nicosia following four successive defeats.

7   The PFA announce assistance for former players suffering from dementia, along with establishing a dedicated department dealing with the condition. Manchester City owner Sheik Mansoor is revealed to have paid £760,000 for the oldest surviving FA Cup trophy and loaned it indefinitely to the National Football Museum.

8   The Premier League issue a new hardline directive to clubs to try to limit the spread of the virus, warning against hugging, handshakes and shirt-swapping and threatening action against players breaking the rules. Newcastle manager Steve Bruce questions the 'morality' of continuing the season. Aston Villa are forced to field a complete youth side against Liverpool in the FA Cup after an outbreak at the club. Liverpool win 4-1. West Ham sell £45m record-signing Sebastien Haller to Ajax for £20m. Sacked Salford manager Graham Alexander takes over at Motherwell.

9   Derby also have to field a youth team in the third round of the competition against non-league Chorley, who go through 2-0.

10 League Two Crawley deliver the weekend's major FA Cup shock, defeating Leeds 3-0. In the most talked-about tie of the round, eighth-tier Marine go down 5-0 to Tottenham, but secure the club's future through prizemoney, TV fees and selling 30,000 virtual tickets.

11 The Scottish League's One and Two are suspended for three weeks because of increasing cases of the virus. One of the Government's mass vaccination centres opens at Bristol City's Ashton Gate Stadium.

12 Grimsby become the first club to be fined for breaking Covid rules – £4,880 suspended until June – after several breaches by their players.

13 Celtic admit a six-day training trip to Dubai, undertaken by Neil Lennon and his players, was a mistake and offer 'profound apologies.' Scotland's First Minister, Nicola, Sturgeon, tells the club to 'reflect seriously' on what happened.

14 In a joint statement, the FA, Premier League and EFL call on players to abide by the rules at a 'critical period' for the game.

15 Wayne Rooney calls time on a distinguished 18-year playing career after being appointed Derby manager on a two-and-a-half-year contract.

16 Wayne Rooney's first match in charge is a 1-0 home defeat by Rotherham which leaves Derby second from bottom.

17 England women's manager Phil Neville leaves the job early to take over at David Beckham's MLS club Inter Miami.

18 An appeal by his club Atletico Madrid against Kieran Trippier's ten-week worldwide ban for breaking FA betting rules is rejected by FIFA.

19 Newport goalkeeper Tom King scores with a wind-assisted goal-kick in the 1-1 draw against Cheltenham.

20 The FA appoint Norwegian coach Hege Riise interim manager of the England women's team, pending the permanent arrival in September of Holland coach Sarina Wiegman.

21 Manager Neil Lennon admits that a tenth successive title is beyond Celtic with his side 20 points behind Rangers from two fewer games played. Cardiff manager Neil Harris is sacked

after six straight league and cup results.

22 Aston Villa manager Dean Smith is given a one-match touchline ban and £8,000 fine by the FA for using abusive language towards referee Jon Moss after the defeat by Manchester City. Mick McCarthy, former Republic of Ireland manager, takes over at Cardiff until the end of the season. Matches in National League North and South are suspended for a fortnight.

23 Holders Arsenal are beaten 1-0 by Southampton in the FA Cup fourth round. St Johnstone defeat Hibernian 3-0 in the first Scottish League Cup semi-final.

24 Livingston reach the Scottish League Cup Final for the first time by beating St Mirren 1-0.

25 Frank Lampard is sacked after 18 months as Chelsea manager with his side eighth in the Premier League, 11 points adrift of the top spot and effectively out of the title reckoning.

26 A month after his own dismissal by Paris Saint-Germain, Thomas Tuchel becomes Chelsea's 13th manager since Roman Abramovich bought the club in 2003. Ashley Williams, winner of 86 Wales caps, announces his retirement at 36.

27 The Government announce a £10m package for non-elite clubs currently banned from playing.

28 Wolves manager Nuno Espirito Santo donates £250,000 towards tackling poverty in Wolverhampton.

29 Liverpool are left without any fit central defenders after losing Joel Matip for the rest of the season with damaged ankle ligaments. Four Burnley players, Johann Gudmundsson, Kevin Long, Matthew Lowton and Erik Pieters, sign new contracts.

30 AFC Wimbledon manager Glyn Hodges is sacked after a run of two points from 11 matches. Kilmarnock manager Alex Dyer loses his job after two wins in 11 games.

31 Prince William, president of the FA, calls for an end to racist abuse of players, describing it as 'despicable' after Manchester United's Marcus Rashford becomes the latest to be targeted on social media. Simon Grayson is appointed Fleetwood manager until the end of the season – his seventh club.

FEBRUARY 2021

1 Liverpool ease their injury crisis by signing two central defenders – Ben Davies from Preston and Turkey international Ozan Kabak on loan from Schalke – on transfer deadline day. Spending by Premier League clubs of £101m during the winter window is less than half of the previous January total. Rangers striker Alfredo Morelos is banned, retrospectively, by the Scottish FA for three games for stamping on Hibernian's Ryan Porteous in an incident which went unpunished in the match.

2 Manchester United equal the record for the Premier League's biggest win, defeating nine-man Southampton 9-0.

3 Jason Tindall, manager of Bournemouth for six months, is sacked after four successive Championship defeats.

4 Southampton's Jan Bednarek has his red card against Manchester United overturned on appeal.

5 Liverpool captain Jordan Henderson urges 'those with power and authority' – government or social media companies – to intervene in the racial abuse of players.

6 Ole Gunnar Solskjaer, manager of second-place Manchester United, insists his side are defending too poorly to be considered title contenders.

7 Manchester City are installed as odds-on favourites to regain the title after defeating Liverpool 4-1 at Anfield.

8 Referee Mike Dean notifies police of threats and abusive messages to his family following red cards shown to Southampton's Jan Bednarek and West Ham's Tomas Soucek, both overturned on appeal.

9 Hollywood actors Ryan Reynolds and Rob McElhenney complete their takeover of National League Wrexham. Former St Johnstone manager Tommy Wright takes over at Kilmarnock.

10 Everton defeat Tottenham 5-4 after extra-time in an outstanding FA Cup fifth round tie at Goodison Park. Paul Tisdale, manager of Bristol Rovers for three months, is sacked after a run of two points from eight matches.

11 Northampton manager Keith Curle is sacked after one win in 11 leaves his side second from bottom.

12 The FA, Premier League, EFL and PFA unite to demand action from social media companies to tackle on-line abuse.

13 Liverpool manager Jurgen Klopp concedes the title after another defeat – 3-1 by Leicester – but dismisses speculation that he will quit. Sunderland striker Charlie Wyke scores four headed goals against Doncaster, all from crosses by Aiden McGeady.

14 Port Vale appoint Walsall's Darrell Clarke as the new manager after agreeing compensation with their League Two rivals. Coach Brian Dutton is appointed at Walsall until the end of the season.

15 Mason Greenwood signs a new four-year contract with Manchester United.

16 The Champions League resumes, with Liverpool the first to have a match switched because of Covid travel restrictions. They play the away leg of the first knockout round against RB Leipzig in Budapest. Dean Holden, Bristol City manager for six months, is sacked after a sixth successive Championship and FA Cup defeat. Shrewsbury manager Steve Cotterill returns home after 33 days in hospital in Bristol with Covid.

17 Rangers manager Steven Gerrard says he feels 'let down' by five squad players – none of them regulars in the team – who face fines for breaking Covid regulations. Mark Robinson, AFC Wimbledon's interim manager, is given the job on a permanent basis.

18 Frenchman Kyril Louis-Dreyfus, reported to have a trust fund close to £2bn, becomes English football's youngest chairman at the age of 23 after his takeover of Sunderland from Stewart Donald is approved by the EFL.

19 The National League's North and South seasons are abandoned and declared null with no promotion or relegation.

20 Former Middlesbrough manager Jonathan Woodgate takes charge at Bournemouth until the end of the season.

21 Michael Jolley, manager of Barrow for 60 days, is dismissed after one win in his seven League Two matches.

22 Nigel Pearson, formerly in charge at Watford and Leicester, is appointed Bristol City's new manager until the end of the season. Sacked Fleetwood manager Joey Barton takes over at Bristol Rovers. Bradford's interim managers, Mark Trueman and Conor Sellars, are appointed on a permanent basis after accumulating 24 points from 11 games.

23 Clubs in England are given the go-ahead to stage test events in April ahead of the planned return of spectators from May 17 as part of the Government's road map out of lockdown. All non-league football below National League level is abandoned for the second successive season. Jamal Musiala, 17, becomes the youngest English scorer in Champions League history with a goal in Bayern Munich's 4-1 win over Lazio in a last 16, first leg match.

24 Under-pressure Celtic manager Neil Lennon resigns with his side 18 points behind champions-elect Rangers. Tottenham reach the last 16 of the Europa League with an 8-1 aggregate win over Wolfsberger. Steve Ball, manager of Colchester for seven months, is sacked after 13 matches without a win. Scottish clubs approve the use of two concussion substitutes, on a trial basis, until the end of the season.

25 Arsenal, who defeat Benfica 4-3 over the two legs, and Rangers, 9-5 winners against Antwerp, go through in the Europa League. Leicester lose 2-0 at home to Slavia Prague after a goalless first leg.

26 Lucas Digne signs a new contract with Everton through to 2025.

27 Leyton Orient sack manager Ross Embleton after a 3-1 home defeat by Tranmere – the team's seventh match without a win.

28 Paul Lambert loses his job as Ipswich manager after a disagreement with owner Marcus Evans over the direction of the club. St Johnstone lift the Scottish League Cup for the first time, beating Livingston 1-0 in the final.

MARCH 2021

1 Sheffield Wednesday appoint Doncaster's Darren Moore as their new manager. Shrewsbury manager Steve Cotterill is readmitted to hospital with Covid-pneumonia.

2 Ian St John, part of Bill Shankly's successful Liverpool side of the 1960s, dies aged 82.

3 Norwich, bidding for an immediate return to the Premier League, go ten points clear at the top of the Championship.

4 Neil Warnock, 72-year-old Middlesbrough manager, signs a contract extension to the end of the 2021–22 season. Newport receive permission from the EFL to play their next two home games at Cardiff City Stadium because of the poor condition of the club's Rodney Parade pitch.

5 Arsenal post an annual loss of £47.8m. Mick McCarthy, unbeaten in his first ten matches as Cardiff manager, is given a new two-year contract – and takes charge of his 1,000th match, against Huddersfield. The International FA Board, football's lawmakers, rule that accidental handball leading to a goal or scoring chance will no longer be penalised.

6 Newcastle manager Steve Bruce confirms a training-ground confrontation with midfielder Matt Ritchie and promises to seek out whoever leaked the incident, describing the action as 'treason.'

7 Rangers are crowned Scottish champions for the first time since 2011, 20 points ahead of Celtic with six games of the season remaining. Manchester City's record run of 21 successive wins in all competitions is ended by a 2-0 home defeat by Manchester United. Harry Kewell is sacked after seven months as Oldham manager with his side 16th in League Two.

8 Aberdeen's Derek McInnes, appointed in 2013 and the longest-serving manager in the Scottish Premiership, is sacked after one win in ten games. Keith Curle, dismissed by Northampton, is appointed Oldham manager until the end of the season.

9 Liverpool's Jurgen Klopp rules himself out of becoming Germany's new manager after Joachim Low announces he will stand down after the European Championship. West Ham captain Mark Noble signs a one-year contract extension, taking him into his 18th and final season at the club.

10 After two seasons playing home games at St Andrew's, Birmingham, Coventry sign a ten-year contract with Wasps rugby club to return to the Ricoh Arena in season 2021–22. Lukasz Fabianski signs a new one-year contract with West Ham.

11 After six successive Premier League home defeats, Liverpool defeat RB Leipzig 2-0 at Anfield to reach the quarter-finals of the Champions League 4-0 on aggregate. The Welsh FA announce that Robert Page will again be in charge for their next three internationals, against Belgium, the Czech Republic and Mexico, in the continued absence of Ryan Giggs. Referee Darren Drysdale is cleared to officiate again after being given a backdated four-match FA suspension for improper conduct – locking heads with Ipswich's Alan Judge during the game against Northampton.

12 Manager Chris Wilder leaves Sheffield United by mutual consent after long-running disagreements with the board over the future direction of the club. Bournemouth and Watford are each fined £10,000 by the FA for a players' brawl.

13 Salford win their first trophy as an EFL club, defeating Portsmouth on penalties after a goalless draw in the 2020 League Trophy Final, postponed from the previous season.

14 Sunderland defeat Tranmere 1-0 to lift the current League Trophy. Portsmouth dismiss manager Kenny Jackett after their Wembley defeat – and following a single victory in seven League One games.

15 Aitor Karanka, manager of Birmingham for eight months, is sacked after a 3-0 home defeat by Bristol City leaves his side one place above the relegation zone. Lee Bowyer resigns at Charlton manager and takes over at St Andrew's.

16 Manchester City reach the Champions League quarter-finals with a 4-0 aggregate win over Borussia Monchengladbach. Maheta Molango, a 38-year-old Swiss lawyer and former Brighton striker, is named as Gordon Taylor's successor as chief executive of the players union, the PFA. The FA fine Southampton and Sheffield United £20,000 each for a players' confrontation.

17 The FA admit to 'a dark day for football' after an independent report into historical child sex abuse in the game accuses the governing body of leaving young players at risk by delaying introducing protective measures. Several clubs are also criticised – Aston Villa, Chelsea, Crewe, Manchester City, Newcastle, Peterborough, Southampton and Stoke. Chelsea qualify for the last eight of the Champions League with a 3-0 aggregate victory over Atletico Madrid.

18 Manchester United, 2-1 winners over the two legs against AC Milan, and Arsenal, who defeat Olympiacos 3-2, go through to the quarter-finals of the Europa League. Tottenham lose 3-2 to Dinamo Zagreb after winning the first leg 2-0. Rangers have Kemar Roofe and Leon Balogun sent off in the second leg against Slavia Prague and are beaten 3-1 on aggregate. Nigel Adkins, out of management since leaving Hull in the summer of 2019, replaces Lee Bowyer at Charlton.

19 Danny Cowley, former Huddersfield and Lincoln manager, takes charge at Portsmouth, initially until the end of the season.

20 Scottish Leagues One and Two return to action after a break of 11 weeks caused by Covid restrictions.

21 Preston sack manager Alex Neil following a home defeat by Luton and a run of one win in nine matches.

22 Nine days after winning the Football League Trophy at Wembley, Richie Wellens is dismissed by Salford with his team six points adrift of a League Two play-off position. Former Bradford and Blackpool manager Gary Bowyer is appointed until the end of the season. The BBC and Sky announce a three-year broadcasting deal to show live Women's Super League matches.

23 Hearts, beaten finalists for two successive seasons, lose 2-1 to Highland League champions Brora Rangers in a second-round tie – one of the Scottish Cup's biggest-ever upsets. Stephen Glass, head coach of United States club Atlanta, is appointed the new manager of Aberdeen, his first club as a player. Alex Neil, then manager of Preston, is fined £2,000 by the FA after being sent-off during the match against Middlesbrough.

24 Wales, with Robert Page continuing to take charge of the team in the absence of Ryan Giggs, lose 3-1 to Belgium after leading through Harry Wilson in their opening World Cup qualifier. Alan Browne puts the Republic of Ireland in front against Serbia with their first goal in eight games, but two by Fulham's Aleksandar Mitrovic result in a 3-2 defeat. FIFA extend former president Sepp Blatter's ban from football to 2028 and fine him £780,000 after a probe into World Cup bonuses. Crewe chairman John Bowler resigns after criticism of the club in the report into historical child sex abuse.

25 Ollie Watkins scores on his international debut and James Ward-Prowse is also on the mark for the first time for England, who open their qualifying campaign by beating San Marino 5-0. John McGinn's spectacular overhead kick gives Scotland a 2-2 draw with Austria. Northern Ireland go down 2-0 to Italy. England's Under-21 team lose 1-0 to Switzerland in their first match of the European Championship. Interim manager Simon Grayson is appointed on a permanent basis at Fleetwood.

26 Middlesbrough manager Neil Warnock is fined £7,000 by the FA for criticising match officials after the defeat by Swansea. Dover, who ran out of money and failed to fulfil their fixtures, are fined £40,000 and deducted 12 points for season 2021–22 by the National League. The club say they will appeal. The FA announce a £180m investment in grassroots football ahead of the resumption of matches.

27 Chris Gunter becomes the first Wales player to win 100 caps, reaching the milestone in a 1-0 win over Mexico in a friendly international. Republic of Ireland captain Seamus Coleman says his players are 'embarrassed' after one of the worst defeats in the country's history – 1-0 at home to Luxembourg in a World Cup qualifier.

28 Harry Kane, goalless in his previous six internationals, puts England ahead in Albania and sets up a second goal for Mason Mount. Nick Pope becomes the country's first goalkeeper to keep a clean sheet in his first six matches. Scotland draw 1-1 with Israel and Northern Ireland lose a friendly 2-1 to the United States. In the European Under-21 Championship, England go down 2-0 to Portugal.

29 Manchester City announce that record-scorer Sergio Aguero will leave at the end of his contract in the summer after a decade at the club. Three Wales players, Rabbi Matondo, Tyler Roberts and Hal Robson-Kanu are sent back to their clubs for breaking a curfew. Middlesbrough are fined £10,000 by the FA for disorderly behaviour by players after the match against Swansea.

30 Daniel James delivers a first World Cup qualifying win for Wales with an 81st minute header against the Czech Republic. Connor Roberts is sent off for a second yellow card. In a separate incident, Czech striker Patrik Schick is shown a straight red. The Republic of Ireland draw with Qatar in a friendly. Wigan are taken over by a Bahrain-funded consortium. Five Rangers players, including first-team squad members Calvin Bassey, Nathan Patterson and Bongani Zungu are banned for six matches – two suspended – by the Scottish FA for breaking Covid rules.

31 Steven Davis becomes Britain's most-capped player, overtaking former England goalkeeper Peter Shilton's total of 125 in Northern Ireland's goalless World Cup qualifying draw against Bulgaria. Harry Kane becomes England's most prolific penalty-taker with his tenth successful spot-kick in a 2-1 win over Poland. Che Adams scores his first international goal as Scotland defeat the Faroe Islands 4-0. England win their final group match 2-1 against Croatia in the European Under-21 Championship, but fail to reach the knockout stage after conceding a goal in stoppage-time. Chelsea and Manchester City reach the semi-finals of the Women's Champions League.

APRIL 2021

1 Figures show Premier League clubs paying £272m to agents in the past year, an increase of £9m on the previous 12 months. Chelsea (£35.2m), Manchester City (£30.2m) and Manchester United (£29.8m) top the spending list, with West Bromwich Albion (£4.2m) the lowest spenders. Lee Collins, captain of National League side Yeovil, dies aged 32.

3 The FA Cup Final, one semi-final and the League Cup Final are among pilot events announced by the Government ahead of the planned return of spectators.

4 Manchester City post a loss of £126m for the 2019–20 season.

5 Rebecca Welch, 37, the FA's highest-ranked female referee, becomes the first to take charge of a match in England's top four divisions – Harrogate against Port Vale – and is complimented on her performance by respective managers Simon Weaver and Darrell Clarke.

6 Hampden Park receives approval from the Scottish Government for 12,000 spectators to attend European Championship matches this summer.

7 Kevin De Bruyne signs a new four-year contract with Manchester City. Ipswich owner Marcus Evans sells the club to American investment fund ORG. Mel Morris agrees to sell Derby to Spanish businessman Erik Alonso.

8 Mark Molesley, manager of Southend for eight months, is dismissed with his side second from bottom in League Two. Phil Brown, manager from 2013-18, replaces him.

9 Craig Dawson, on loan from Watford, agrees a permanent move to West Ham at the end of the season.

10 Teams throughout the country stand in silence as a mark of respect following the death of the Duke of Edinburgh. The Gill brothers make EFL history as the first South Asians to be part of the same officiating team for a match – Bristol City against Nottingham Forest – with Bhupinder one of two assistant referees and Sunny the fourth official. Hearts return to the Scottish Premiership at the first time of asking as winners of the Championship.

11 Mark Cooper, manager of Forest Green for five years, is sacked after a single point from six matches threatens their chances of promotion from League Two.

12 Wolves striker Pedro Neto is ruled out of Portugal's squad for the European Championship with a knee injury.

13 Chelsea reach the semi-finals of the Champions League with a 2-1 aggregate win over Porto. Holders Bayern Munich are beaten by Paris Saint-Germain on away goals.

14 Manchester City go through 4-2 on aggregate against Borussia Dortmund. Liverpool are knocked out 3-1 by Real Madrid. UEFA ban Slavia Prague's Ondrej Kudela for ten matches for racially abusing Glen Kamara in a stormy Europa League match at Ibrox. The Rangers player is banned for three games for assaulting Kudela after the match and team-mate Kemar Roofe receives a four-match ban for dangerous play. Rangers are fined £7,800 for failing to control their players.

15 Arsenal deliver their best performance of the season to beat Slavia Prague 4-0 away from home in the second leg of their UEFA Cup quarter-final tie and go through 5-1 on aggregate.

Manchester United defeat Granada 4-0 over the two legs. Liverpool are fined £22,000 by UEFA after fans smashed Real Madrid's team coach window and set off flares before the match at Anfield.

16 Rangers midfielder Ryan Jack is ruled out of Scotland's squad for the European Championship with a calf injury. Aidy Boothroyd leaves his job as England Under 21 manager, ahead of the end of his contract, following the team's failure to reach the final stages of the European Championship.

17 Chelsea defeat Manchester City 1-0 in the first FA Cup semi-final. Sheffield United are relegated from the Premier League. Norwich become the first promoted side, returning to the Premier League at the first attempt.

18 The Premier League's 'Big Six' clubs are revealed to have signed up to a breakaway European Super League which threatens to split English football. Arsenal, Chelsea, Liverpool, Manchester City, Manchester United and Tottenham have been joined by AC Milan, Atletico Madrid, Barcelona, Juventus, Inter Milan and Real Madrid. Leicester beat Southampton 1-0 in the second FA Cup semi-final, watched by 4,000 supporters as part of the Government pilot scheme. Rangers continue to dominate Celtic with a 2-0 victory over their rivals in the fourth round of this season's Scottish Cup.

19 The Duke of Cambridge, president of the FA, leads widespread opposition to a European Super League, warning of the damage 'to the game we love.' The Government, UEFA, the Premier League, supporters' organisations and influential former players, including Gary Lineker, Gary Neville and Alan Shearer, denounce the move. Six days before Tottenham contest the League Cup Final, manager Jose Mourinho is sacked, with his team seventh in the table and out of the Europa League. Ryan Mason, 29-year-old head of player development, is appointed caretaker for the rest of the season.

20 Plans for the breakaway league collapse. Bowing to increasing pressure, all six English clubs pull out and their owners apologise publicly for mistakes made. Ed Woodward, resigns as Manchester United's executive chairman.

21 Juventus chairman Andrea Agnelli admits it can no longer go ahead after both Milan clubs and Atletico Madrid withdraw. Ryan Mason becomes the youngest manager to take charge of a Premier League side when leading Tottenham to a 2-1 victory over Southampton.

22 The Government announce a fan-led review of English football, headed by former Sports Minister Tracey Crouch. An extended Champions League, announced by UEFA for the 2024–25 season, is criticised by Manchester City's Germany midfielder Ilkay Gundogan.

23 The Welsh FA announce that Ryan Giggs will not manage the national team at the European Championship after being charged with three offences. His assistant, Robert Page, continues in charge. Wembley is awarded an extra match after the Aviva Stadium loses all four games because the Irish authorities are unable to provide UEFA with minimum capacity guarantees. Dublin's three group games are switched to St Petersburg.

24 Watford, relegated in 2020, make an immediate return to the Premier League.

25 Manchester City win the League Cup for the fourth successive season, beating Tottenham 1-0 in the final watched by a Wembley crowd of nearly 8,000 for one of the Government's test events. Rangers are beaten by St Johnstone on penalties in the fifth round of the Scottish Cup.

26 Fara Williams, 37, announces her forthcoming retirement after a 20-year career and a record 172 caps for the England women's team. Eric Bailly signs a new contract through to 2024 with Manchester United.

27 Liverpool post a loss of £46m in their annual accounts. Grimsby are relegated from the Football League.

28 Alan Shearer and Thierry Henry become the first players to be inducted into the Premier League Hall of Fame.

29 Leicester's Brendan Rodgers turns down an approach from Tottenham to become their new manager. Todd Kane, Queens Park Rangers defender, is banned for seven matches and fined £6,000 by the FA for using insulting language towards Brentford's Sergi Canos. Oxford manager Karl Robinson receives a four-match touchline ban and £4,500 fine for violent conduct during the match at Sunderland which covers his team's play-off games.

30 Football's governing bodies begin a three-day boycott of social media as part of a campaign against on-line abuse.

MAY 2021

1 Southend are relegated after 101 years in the Football League. Norwich clinch the Championship title. Hull win League One.

2 A Premier League game is postponed for the first time because of a protest. Supporters demonstrating against Manchester United's owners, invade the Old Trafford pitch and clash with police outside the stadium before the scheduled fixture against Liverpool. Chelsea reach the final of the women's Champions League with a 5-3 aggregate win over Bayern Munich.

3 Jose Mourinho makes a rapid return to the game as coach of Serie A club Roma.

4 Manchester City reach the Champions League Final for the first time. They defeat Paris Saint-Germain 4-1 on aggregate, with Riyad Mahrez scoring three of the goals.

5 Chelsea set up an all-English final by beating Real Madrid 3-1 over the two legs.

6 Arsenal lose 2-1 on aggregate to Villarreal in the semi-finals of the Europa League and will be out of a major European tournament next season for the first time since 1995-96. Manchester United, 6-2 winners in the first leg against Roma, complete an 8-5 victory. Oxford club captain John Mousinho is elected the Professional Footballers' Association's new chairman.

7 The Government's decision to put Turkey on their travel red list rules out Chelsea and Manchester City supporters watching the Champions League Final in Istanbul.

8 Cheltenham become League Two champions. Interim manager Jon Brady is confirmed in the job at Northampton. Hibernian defeat Dundee United 2-0 to reach the Scottish Cup Final.

9 West Bromwich Albion are relegated from the Premier League. St Johnstone beat St Mirren 2-1 in the second Scottish Cup semi-final. Chelsea retain the Women's Super League title.

10 Fulham go down from the Premier League. Edinson Cavani signs a one-year contract extension with Manchester United. Caretaker Frankie McAvoy is given the Preston manager's job on a permanent basis. Danny Cowley is confirmed as Portsmouth manager.

11 Manchester City are crowned champions of the Premier League for the third time in four seasons. Kenny McLean is ruled out of Scotland's squad for the European Championship with a knee injury. Three days after leading his team into the League Two play-offs, Tranmere manager Keith Hill is sacked.

12 Premier League clubs approve a new £4.5bn, three-year domestic TV deal with Sky, BT and Amazon running from 2022–2025. An extra £100m to lower division and grassroots clubs is included.

13 The Champions League Final is switched from Istanbul to Porto. Former Blackpool and Blackburn manager Gary Bowyer is appointed Salford manager after a spell as caretaker. Hayden Mullins, Colchester's interim manager, gets the job on a permanent basis.

14 The proposed takeover of Derby by Spanish businessman Erik Alonso falls through. Plans for a limited number of spectators at the Scottish Cup Final are scrapped because of rising Covid cases.

15 Leicester win the FA Cup for the first time. Watched by a Wembley crowd of 21,000, they defeat Chelsea 1-0 with a spectacular 28-yard drive by Youri Tielemans and two world-class saves from captain Kasper Schmeichel. Rangers complete an unbeaten title-winning season by beating Aberdeen 4-0 to take their points tally from 38 matches to 102.

16 Steven Gerrard is named Manager of the Year for leading Rangers to the Premiership title by the Scottish League, PFA and football writers. His captain, James Tavernier, wins the PFA's Player of the Year award. Chelsea lose 4-0 to Barcelona in the women's Champions League Final in Gothenburg.

17 Harry Kane tells Tottenham he wants to leave the club. Scottish football writers choose Rangers midfielder Steven Davis as their Player of the Year. Former Salford and Swindon manager Richie Wellens takes over at Doncaster.

18 Roy Hodgson, 73, announces that he will step down as Crystal Palace manager at the end of the season.

19 Three uncapped players are included in Scotland's squad for the European Championship – Rangers defender Nathan Patterson and midfielders Billy Gilmour (Chelsea) and David Turnbull (Celtic). Wes Morgan, Leicester's Premier League title-winning captain and a late substitute in their FA Cup win, calls time on his career at 37. Tottenham youth coach Matt Taylor is appointed Walsall's new manager.

20 Manchester City's Ruben Dias becomes the first defender to be named the English football writers' Footballer of the Year since Liverpool's Steve Nicol in 1989.

21 A second Premier League manager, Nuno Espirito Santo of Wolves, announces he will leave after the final match of the season. Kenny Jackett, former Portsmouth manager, takes charge at Leyton Orient.

22 St Johnstone complete the greatest season in the club's history with a second trophy. They defeat Hibernian 1-0 in the Scottish Cup Final with a goal by Shaun Rooney, their matchwinner in the League Cup victory over Livingston. Hornchurch beat Hereford 3-1 in the FA Trophy Final.

23 Leicester miss out on a top-four place on the last day of the Premier League season for the second successive year, with Liverpool and Chelsea securing the two remaining Champions League spots. Sutton United are promoted to the Football League for the first time in the club's history as champions of the National League. Brechin are relegated after 67 years in the Scottish League, losing the Play-off Final 3-1 on aggregate to Kelty Hearts, a village club from Fife who take their place.

24 Kilmarnock are relegated after 28 years in Scotland's top division, losing 4-2 on aggregate to Dundee in the Play-off Final. John Hughes leaves Ross County after five months as manager.

25 Micky Mellon leaves Dundee United 'by mutual consent' after a year as manager.

26 Manchester United are beaten in a record penalty shoot-out by Villarreal in the Europa League Final. They lose 11-10 after a 1-1 draw, with goalkeeper David de Gea having the decisive spot-kick saved. Former Colchester manager John McGreal takes over at Swindon. Keith Curle is confirmed in the Oldham job. Ross County appoint Malky Mackay, formerly in charge of Warford and Cardiff, as their new manager.

27 Slavisa Jokanovic, former Fulham and Watford manager, takes charge at Sheffield United. Former Wolves and Wales defender Rob Edwards is appointed the new manager of Forest Green.

28 Former Bournemouth manager Eddie Howe turns down the vacant Celtic job. Liverpool make the first major signing of the summer transfer window – central defender Ibrahima Konate from RB Leipzig for £36m. Coventry have a transfer embargo lifted by the EFL. Former Forest Green manager Mark Cooper takes over at Barrow.

29 Chelsea defeat Manchester City 1-0 in the Champions League Final with a goal by Kai Havertz. Brentford qualify for top-flight football for the first time since 1947, beating Swansea 2-0 in the Championship Play-off Final to reach the Premier League. Uncapped Cardiff midfielder Rubin Colwill, 19, is included in the Wales squad for the European Championship.

30 Blackpool win the League One Play-off Final 2-1 against Lincoln. Ian Baraclough wins his first match as Northern Ireland manager in regular time at the 12th attempt – 3-0 against Malta with Jordan Jones and Ali McCann scoring their first international goals.

31 Morecambe defeat Newport 1-0 in the League Two Play-off Final. Luton's Tom Lockyer replaces the injured James Lawrence in the Wales European Championship squad. Micky Mellon returns to Tranmere as manager after his spell with Dundee United.

JUNE 2021

1 Manager Carlo Ancelotti stuns Everton by agreeing to rejoin Real Madrid. Gareth Southgate names four recognised right-backs in England's European Championship squad. Mason Greenwood withdraws with an 'underlying injury.' Sergio Aguero joins Barcelona on a free transfer from Manchester City. Chelsea and Leicester are both fined £22,500 by the FA for a players' brawl in their Premier League match.

2 Bukayo Saka's first goal for England delivers a 1-0 win over Austria in their first warm-up match. Jack Hendry and Kevin Nisbet both score their first for Scotland, who hold Holland to 2-2 despite missing seven players because of Covid restrictions. Neco Williams is sent off for a handling offence as Wales are beaten 3-0 by France. Bournemouth midfielder Jefferson Lerma is banned for six games and fined £40,000 for biting Sheffield Wednesday's Josh Windass.

3 Trent Alexander-Arnold pulls out of the England squad with a thigh injury picked up in the victory over Austria. Manager Derek Adams leaves newly-promoted Morecambe 'to pursue an opportunity elsewhere.' Christian Benteke signs a new two-year contract with Crystal Palace. Stephen Kenny secures his first win as Republic of Ireland manager at the 12th attempt. They beat Andorra 4-1, with Troy Parrott (2) and Jason Knight scoring their first international goals. Northern Ireland lose 1-0 to Ukraine. UEFA confirm Windsor Park in Belfast as the venue for the European Super Cup match between Chelsea and Villarreal on August 11.

4 Thomas Tuchel signs a new contract through to 2024 following Chelsea's Champions League success. Two of his players, Olivier Giroud and Thiago Silva, sign one-year contracts. Derek Adams is appointed Bradford's new manager.

5 Wales are held to a goalless draw by Albania.

6 Marcos Rashford's penalty gives England a 1-0 victory over Romania. Jordan Henderson, playing his first match since February following groin surgery, has a second spot-kick saved and is told off by Gareth Southgate for taking it. Scotland defeat Luxembourg 1-0. Manchester City's Kevin De Bruyne is named PFA Player of the Year for the second successive year.

7 Brighton's Ben White replaces Trent Alexander-Arnold in England's squad. Former Motherwell manager Stephen Robinson takes over at Morecambe. Thomas Courts is promoted from head of tactical performance to Dundee United manager.

8 Former Benfica coach Bruno Lage is appointed Nuno Espirito Santo's successor as Wolves manager. Debbie Hewitt, a business executive, becomes the first woman chairman of the FA.

9 The six Premier League clubs involved in the failed European Super League project agree to a combined 'goodwill' payment of £22m to fund grassroots and community projects. Those who make a further attempt will be fined £25m each and have 30 points deducted.

10 The Scottish League sign a five-year title sponsorship with car retailer cinch spanning all four divisions. Celtic appoint former Australia coach Ange Postecoglou as their new manager. Aston Villa sign Norwich midfielder Emiliano Buendia for £33m – a record fee for both clubs. The Premier League plan thicker lines for VAR offsides in the new season to limit marginal decisions.

11 After a year's delay, the 2020 European Championship gets under way with a 3-0 victory for Italy against Turkey in Rome. Roy Hodgson is awarded a CBE in the Queen's Birthday Honours after a 45-year career in football. Two players receive an MBE - Raheem Sterling for promoting racial equality in sport and Jordan Henderson for services to football and his charity work. West Ham manager David Moyes signs a new three-year contract.

12 Christian Eriksen collapses with a cardiac arrest shortly before half-time of Denmark's opening match against Finland in Copenhagen and undergoes life-saving resuscitation on the pitch. Paramedics spend 13 minutes battling to save the life of the former Tottenham midfielder. He is taken to hospital and UEFA later announce his condition has stabilised. English referee Anthony Taylor restarts the match after a near two-hour suspension, with Finland winning 1-0. Earlier, Kieffer Moore's header earns Wales a 1-1 draw in their first game against Switzerland.

13 Raheem Sterling scores his first goal in a major tournament to give England a winning start – 1-0 against Croatia.

14 Scotland open with a 2-0 defeat by the Czech Republic, whose spectacular second goal from Patrik Schick is scored from nearly 50 yards over the head of backpedalling goalkeeper David Marshall.

15 Dean Henderson pulls out of England's squad with a hip problem and is replaced by Sheffield United's Aaron Ramsdale. Leicester's Timothy Castagne is ruled out of the tournament with a fractured eye socket sustained in Belgium's win over Russia. Dover lose their appeal against a £40,000 fine and 12-point deduction for failing to fulfil National League fixtures.

16 Wales overcome Gareth Bale's penalty miss to defeat Turkey 2-0 with goals from Aaron Ramsey and Connor Roberts.

17 Manchester City captain Fernandinho agrees a new one-year contract.
18 Christian Eriksen is discharged from hospital after an operation to fit a defibrillator implant.
    England and Scotland draw 0-0 at Wembley in their first meeting in a major tournament since
    Euro 96.
19 England captain Harry Kane urges supporters to keep faith with his team after that
    disappointing performance.
20 Wales have Ethan Ampadu shown a straight red card for a dangerous challenge ten minutes
    into the second half and lose 1-0 to Italy. But they qualify for the knockout phase. Hartlepool
    return to the Football League after a four-year absence, beating Torquay on penalties in the
    National League Play-off Final.
21 Scotland's Billy Gilmour tests positive for Covid and is forced to quarantine for ten days.
    England pair Mason Mount and Ben Chilwell are told to isolate after spending time with their
    Chelsea team-mate in the Wembley tunnel. Rebecca Welch becomes the first female referee to
    be appointed to the EFL's National group list for the men's game.
22 Raheem Sterling is again England's matchwinner as they finish on top of Group D by beating
    the Czech Republic 1-0. Scotland go out after losing 3-1 to Croatia at Hampden Park.
23 England are paired in the last 16 with Germany after dramatic final matches in Group F
    on a night when their opponents could also have been France or Portugal. Derby are fined
    £100,000 by an independent tribunal for prohibitive accounting policies.
24 West Bromwich Albion appoint Barnsley's Valerien Ismael as their new manager after a
    compensation package is agreed between the two clubs. UEFA abolish the away goals rule,
    resulting in drawn two-leg European club matches going to extra-time and penalties.
25 Arsenal's Kieran Tierney signs a new five-year contract. John McGreal resigns after 30 days as
    manager of Swindon, a club embroiled in legal proceedings over ownership.
26 Wales are beaten 4-0 by Denmark in the opening match of the round of 16 and have Harry
    Wilson shown a straight red card in the 90th minute for a foul.
27 The Czech Republic spring the first major surprise of the tournament by defeating Holland 2-0.
28 World champions France surrender a 3-1 lead to Switzerland and lose a penalty shoot-out.
    Spain give up the same advantage in another superb match against Croatia, but recover to go
    through 5-3 in extra-time.
29 Raheem Sterling and Harry Kane are on the mark as England defeat Germany in a major
    tournament knockout match for the first time since the 1966 World Cup Final. They win 2-0
    to reach the quarter-finals.
30 Former Liverpool boss Rafael Benitez takes over at Everton – the only manager in modern times
    to have been in charge of both clubs. Tottenham appoint former Wolves manager Nuno Espirito
    Sancho after talks with a number of others failed.

JULY 2021

1   Former Everton and Watford manager Marco Silva Silva is appointed at Fulham. Austrian coach
    Markus Schopp is appointed Barnsley's new manager. Rochdale's Brian Barry-Murphy resigns.
3   England defeat Ukraine 4-0 to reach the semi-finals with goals from Harry Kane (2), Harry
    Maguire, a first by Jordan Henderson and a record seventh successive clean sheet.
4   Former Arsenal captain Patrick Vieira is appointed Crystal Palace's new manager.
6   Italy defeat Spain 4-2 in a penalty shoot-out in the first semi-final.
7   England beat Denmark 2-1 to make it to a major tournament final for the first time since 1966
    when Harry Kane converts the rebound after Kasper Schmeichel saves his extra-time penalty.
8   Former West Bromwich Albion coach Robbie Stockdale is named Rochdale's new manager.
9   UEFA fine the FA £26,600 for incidents during the semi-final - a laser aimed at Schmeichel
    before the penalty, disturbances during the national anthems and fireworks being set off.
11 England lose the final 3-2 on penalties to Italy. Hundreds of people without tickets force their
    way into Wembley and there is violence on the streets before and after the game.
12 Gareth Southgate condemns racist abuse directed on social media at the three players who
    missed penalties – Marcus Rashford, Jadon Sancho and Bukayo Sako.

ENGLISH TABLES 2020–2021

PREMIER LEAGUE

				Home				Away					
		P	W	D	L	F	A	W	D	L	F	A	GD	PTS
1	Man City	38	13	2	4	43	17	14	3	2	40	15	51	86
2	Man Utd	38	9	4	6	38	28	12	7	0	35	16	29	74
3	Liverpool	38	10	3	6	29	20	10	6	3	39	22	26	69
4	Chelsea	38	9	6	4	31	18	10	4	5	27	18	22	67
5	Leicester	38	9	1	9	34	30	11	5	3	34	20	18	66
6	West Ham	38	10	4	5	32	22	9	4	6	30	25	15	65
7	Tottenham	38	10	3	6	35	20	8	5	6	33	25	23	62
8	Arsenal	38	8	4	7	24	21	10	3	6	31	18	16	61
9	Leeds	38	8	5	6	28	21	10	0	9	34	33	8	59
10	Everton	38	6	4	9	24	28	11	4	4	23	20	-1	59
11	Aston Villa	38	7	4	8	29	27	9	3	7	26	19	9	55
12	Newcastle	38	6	5	8	26	33	6	4	9	20	29	-16	45
13	Wolverhampton	38	7	4	8	21	25	5	5	9	15	27	-16	45
14	Crystal Palace	38	6	5	8	20	32	6	3	10	21	34	-25	44
15	Southampton	38	8	3	8	28	25	4	4	11	19	43	-21	43
16	Brighton	38	4	9	6	22	22	5	5	9	18	24	-6	41
17	Burnley	38	4	6	9	14	27	6	3	10	19	28	-22	39
18	Fulham	38	2	4	13	9	28	3	9	7	18	25	-26	28
19	West Brom	38	3	6	10	15	39	2	5	12	20	37	-41	26
20	Sheffield Utd	38	5	1	13	12	27	2	1	16	8	36	-43	23

Manchester City, Manchester United, Liverpool, Chelsea into Champions League group stage; Leicester, West Ham in Europa League group stage; Tottenham into Europa League Conference League play-off round

Prize money/TV revenue (league position = amount received)
1 £154m, 2 £153m, 3 £148m, 4 £151m, 5 £141m, 6 £143m, 7 £139m, 8 £135m, 9 £135m, 10 £134m, 11 £122m, 12 £117m, 13 £120m, 14 £116m, 15 £112m, 16 £107m, 17 £102m, 18 £107m, 19 £102m, 20 £91m
Biggest win: Manchester Utd 9 Southampton 0
Highest aggregate score: Aston Villa 7 Liverpool 2, Manchester Utd 9 Southampton 0
Player of Year: Ruben Dias (Manchester City)
Manager of Year: Pep Guardiola (Manchester City)
Golden Boot: 23 Harry Kane (Tottenham)
Golden Glove: 19 clean sheets Ederson (Manchester City)
Team of Year: Ederson, Joao Cancelo, Stones, Dias (all Manchester City), Shaw (Manchester Utd), De Bruyne (Manchester City), Gundogan (Manchester City), Bruno Fernandes (Manchester Utd), Salah (Liverpool), Kane (Tottenham), Son Heung-min (Tottenham)
Leading league scorers: 23 Kane (Tottenham); 22 Salah (Liverpool); 18 Bruno Fernandes (Manchester Utd); 17 Bamford (Leeds), Son Heung-min (Tottenham); 16 Calvert-Lewin (Everton); 15 Vardy (Leicester); 14 Watkins (Aston Villa); 13 Gundogan (Manchester City), Lacazette (Arsenal); 12 Iheanacho (Leicester), Ings (Southampton), Wilson (Newcastle), Wood (Burnley); 11 Bale (Tottenham), Mane (Liverpool), Pereira (WBA), Rashford (Manchester Utd), Zaha (Crystal Palace); 10 Antonio (West Ham), Aubameyang (Arsenal), Benteke (Crystal Palace), Cavani (Manchester Utd), Pepe (Arsenal), Sterling (Manchester City)

SKY BET CHAMPIONSHIP

			Home				Away						
		P	W	D	L	F	A	W	D	L	F	A	GD	PTS
1	Norwich	46	14	6	3	39	15	15	4	4	36	21	39	97
2	Watford	46	19	2	2	44	12	8	8	7	19	18	33	91
3	Brentford*	46	12	9	2	39	20	12	6	5	40	22	37	87
4	Swansea	46	12	6	5	27	16	11	5	7	29	23	17	80
5	Barnsley	46	12	6	5	30	22	11	3	9	28	28	8	78
6	Bournemouth	46	13	3	7	40	24	9	8	6	33	22	27	77
7	Reading	46	12	4	7	37	27	7	9	7	25	27	8	70
8	Cardiff	46	8	6	9	37	26	10	8	5	29	23	17	68
9	QPR	46	11	4	8	32	27	8	7	8	25	28	2	68
10	Middlesbrough	46	11	4	8	30	25	7	6	10	25	28	2	64
11	Millwall	46	7	10	6	24	24	8	7	8	23	28	-5	62
12	Luton	46	8	9	6	25	23	9	2	12	16	29	-11	62
13	Preston	46	7	5	11	21	24	11	2	10	28	32	-7	61
14	Stoke	46	9	5	9	29	28	6	10	7	21	24	-2	60
15	Blackburn	46	9	7	7	37	28	6	5	12	28	26	11	57
16	Coventry	46	10	7	6	30	22	4	6	13	19	39	-12	55
17	Nott'm Forest	46	6	8	9	21	24	6	8	9	16	21	-8	52
18	Birmingham	46	6	4	13	18	37	7	9	7	19	24	-24	52
19	Bristol City	46	7	3	13	18	30	8	3	12	28	38	-22	51
20	Huddersfield	46	8	7	8	28	23	4	6	13	22	48	-21	49
21	Derby	46	6	7	10	20	26	5	4	14	16	32	-22	44
22	Wycombe	46	7	5	11	17	28	4	5	14	22	41	-30	43
23	Rotherham	46	5	4	14	26	35	6	5	12	18	25	-16	42
24	Sheff Wed	46	8	6	7	22	17	4	3	16	18	44	-21	41

*Also promoted

Biggest win: Norwich 7 Huddersfield 0
Highest aggregate score: Brentford 7 Wycombe 2
Player of Year: Emiliano Buendia (Norwich)
Manager of Year: Daniel Farke (Norwich)
Team of the Year: Begovic (Bournemouth), Aarons (Norwich), Hanley (Norwich), Morrison (Cardiff), Masina (Watford), Buendia (Norwich), Olise (Reading), Mowatt (Barnsley), Danjuma (Bournemouth), Toney (Brentford), Pukki (Norwich)
Leading league scorers: 31 Toney (Brentford); 28 Armstrong (Blackburn); 26 Pukki (Norwich); 20 Moore (Cardiff); 19 Lucas Joao (Reading); 16 Ayew (Swansea); 15 Buendia (Norwich), Danjuma (Bournemouth), Solanke (Bournemouth); 14 Lowe (Swansea); 13 Sarr (Watford); 12 Dykes (QPR), Meite (Reading), Powell (Stoke), Woodrow (Barnsley); 11 Wallace J (Millwall); 10 Collins (Luton), Smith (Rotherham), Stanislas (Bournemouth), Wells (Bristol City)

SKY BET LEAGUE ONE

			Home					Away						
		P	W	D	L	F	A	W	D	L	F	A	GD	PTS
1	Hull	46	14	4	5	32	14	13	4	6	48	24	42	89
2	Peterborough	46	15	5	3	52	22	11	4	8	31	24	37	87
3	Blackpool*	46	12	7	4	30	18	11	4	8	30	19	23	80
4	Sunderland	46	9	8	6	32	25	11	9	3	38	17	28	77
5	Lincoln	46	9	5	9	35	30	13	6	4	34	20	19	77
6	Oxford	46	13	4	6	39	21	9	4	10	38	35	21	74
7	Charlton	46	8	7	8	36	37	12	7	4	34	19	14	74
8	Portsmouth	46	9	5	9	29	24	12	4	7	36	27	14	72
9	Ipswich	46	12	5	6	25	18	7	7	9	21	28	0	69
10	Gillingham	46	10	5	8	31	30	9	5	9	32	30	3	67
11	Accrington	46	10	7	6	31	26	8	6	9	32	42	-5	67
12	Crewe	46	10	7	6	32	30	8	5	10	24	31	-5	66
13	MK Dons	46	10	7	6	36	28	8	4	11	28	34	2	65
14	Doncaster	46	11	4	8	34	32	8	3	12	29	35	-4	64
15	Fleetwood	46	9	8	6	26	17	7	4	12	23	29	3	60
16	Burton	46	7	4	12	32	42	8	8	7	29	31	-12	57
17	Shrewsbury	46	5	8	10	28	31	8	7	8	22	26	-7	54
18	Plymouth	46	11	4	8	31	39	3	7	13	22	41	-27	53
19	AFC Wimbledon	46	7	5	11	32	39	5	10	8	22	31	-16	51
20	Wigan	46	5	6	12	26	42	8	3	12	28	35	-23	48
21	Rochdale	46	4	9	10	27	42	7	5	11	34	36	-17	47
22	Northampton	46	8	5	10	20	26	3	7	13	21	41	-26	45
23	Swindon	46	8	1	14	25	38	5	3	15	30	51	-34	43
24	Bristol Rov	46	7	2	14	23	32	3	6	14	17	38	-30	38

*Also promoted

Biggest win: Peterborough 7 Accrington 0
Highest aggregate score: AFC Wimbledon 4 Plymouth 4, Charlton 4 Rochdale 4
Player of Year: Jonson Clarke-Harris (Peterborough)
Manager of Year: Grant McCann (Hull)
Team of the Year: Burge (Sunderland), O'Nien (Sunderland), Atkinson (Oxford), Beevers (Peterborough), Elder (Hull), Ward (Peterborough), Grant (Lincoln), Honeyman (Hull), McGeady (Sunderland), Clarke-Harris (Peterborough), Wyke (Sunderland)
Leading league scorers: 31 Clarke-Harris (Peterborough); 25 Wyke (Sunderland); 20 Pigott (AFC Wimbledon), Yates (Blackpool); 19 Charles (Accrington), Wilks (Hull); 18 Magennis (Hull), Taylor (Oxford); 17 Oliver (Gillingham); 16 Jephcott (Plymouth), Marquis (Portsmouth); 15 Aneke (Charlton), Hemmings (Burton), Szmodics (Peterborough); 14 Fraser (MK Dons); 13 Grant (Lincoln), Jerome (MK Dons), Lewis-Potter (Hull); 12 Graham (Gillingham)

SKY BET LEAGUE TWO

		P	W	D	L	F	A	W	D	L	F	A	GD	PTS
			Home					Away						
1	Cheltenham	46	13	5	5	37	21	11	5	7	24	18	22	82
2	Cambridge	46	12	5	6	30	20	12	3	8	43	29	24	80
3	Bolton	46	11	5	7	27	23	12	5	6	32	27	9	79
4	Morecambe*	46	13	5	5	38	27	10	4	9	31	31	11	78
5	Newport	46	13	5	5	27	17	7	8	8	30	25	15	73
6	Forest Green	46	10	7	6	31	27	10	6	7	28	24	8	73
7	Tranmere	46	11	5	7	30	22	9	8	6	25	28	5	73
8	Salford	46	11	11	1	36	15	8	3	12	18	19	20	71
9	Exeter	46	11	7	5	38	20	7	9	7	33	30	21	70
10	Carlisle	46	12	5	6	38	25	6	7	10	22	26	9	66
11	Leyton Orient	46	9	7	7	32	25	8	3	12	21	30	-2	61
12	Crawley	46	10	6	7	30	27	6	7	10	26	35	-6	61
13	Port Vale	46	9	5	9	27	25	8	4	11	30	32	0	60
14	Stevenage	46	8	8	7	26	20	6	10	7	15	21	0	60
15	Bradford	46	9	7	7	22	19	7	4	12	26	34	-5	59
16	Mansfield	46	6	10	7	33	31	7	9	7	24	24	2	58
17	Harrogate	46	8	5	10	24	29	8	4	11	28	32	-9	57
18	Oldham	46	6	2	15	31	42	9	7	7	41	39	-9	54
19	Walsall	46	7	6	10	20	27	4	14	5	25	26	-8	53
20	Colchester	46	10	7	6	32	26	1	11	11	12	35	-17	51
21	Barrow	46	7	8	8	32	32	6	3	14	21	27	-6	50
22	Scunthorpe	46	7	6	10	22	28	6	3	14	19	36	-23	48
23	Southend	46	5	6	12	16	29	5	9	9	13	29	-29	45
24	Grimsby	46	5	8	10	17	30	5	5	13	20	39	-32	43

*Also promoted

Biggest win: Exeter 6 Colchester 1, Exeter 5 Tranmere 0, Morecambe 0 Cambridge 5, Scunthorpe 0 Cambridge 5, Tranmere 5 Grimsby 0
Highest aggregate score: Harrogate 5 Cambridge 4, Port Vale 6 Bolton 3
Player of Year: Paul Mullin (Cambridge)
Manager of Year: Michael Duff (Cheltenham)
Team of Year: Hladky (Salford), Knoyle (Cambridge), Boyle (Cheltenham), Tunnicliffe (Crawley), Touray (Salford), Worrall (Port Vale), Hoolahan (Cambridge), Sarcevic (Bolton), Hussey (Cheltenham), Jay (Exeter), Mullin (Cambridge)
Leading league scorers: 32 Mullin (Cambridge); 19 Doyle (Bolton); 18 Jay (Exeter), Vaughan (Tranmere); 17 Henderson (Salford), Johnson (Leyton Orient), McAleny (Oldham); 16 Matt (Forest Green); 15 Mendes Gomes (Morecambe), Muldoon (Harrogate), Quigley (Barrow); 14 Bowman (Exeter), Ironside (Cambridge); 13 Stockton (Morecambe), Watters (Crawley); 12 Wilkinson (Leyton Orient); 11 Mellish (Carlisle), Nichols (Crawley), Rodney (Port Vale) Also: 11 Cook (8 Bradford, 3 Mansfield); 11 Norris (4 Colchester, 7 Stevenage)

PREMIER LEAGUE RESULTS 2020–2021

Home \ Away	Arsenal	Aston Villa	Brighton	Burnley	Chelsea	Crystal Palace	Everton	Fulham	Leeds	Leicester	Liverpool	Man City	Man Utd	Newcastle	Sheffield Utd	Southampton	Tottenham	WBA	West Ham	Wolves
Arsenal	–	0-3	2-0	0-1	3-1	0-0	0-1	1-1	4-2	0-1	0-3	0-1	0-0	3-0	2-1	1-1	2-1	3-1	2-1	1-2
Aston Villa	1-0	–	1-2	0-0	1-2	3-0	3-2	3-1	0-3	1-0	7-2	1-2	1-3	2-0	1-0	3-4	0-2	2-2	1-3	0-0
Brighton	0-1	0-0	–	1-1	1-3	1-2	0-0	0-0	0-0	1-2	1-1	3-2	2-3	3-0	1-1	1-2	1-0	1-1	1-1	3-3
Burnley	1-1	3-2	1-1	–	0-3	1-0	1-1	1-1	0-4	1-1	0-3	0-2	0-1	1-2	1-0	0-1	0-1	0-0	1-2	2-1
Chelsea	0-1	1-1	0-0	2-0	–	4-0	2-0	2-0	3-1	2-1	0-1	1-3	0-0	2-0	4-1	3-3	0-0	2-5	3-0	0-0
Crystal Palace	1-3	3-2	1-1	0-3	1-4	–	1-2	0-0	3-1	1-1	0-7	0-2	0-0	2-0	2-0	1-0	1-1	1-0	3-2	0-0
Everton	2-1	1-2	4-2	1-2	1-0	1-1	–	0-2	2-1	1-1	2-2	1-3	3-3	2-1	2-0	1-0	2-2	5-2	0-1	1-0
Fulham	0-3	0-3	0-0	2-0	0-1	2-1	2-3	–	1-2	0-2	1-1	2-0	1-2	0-2	1-0	1-0	0-1	2-0	0-0	1-0
Leeds	0-0	0-3	0-0	1-0	1-1	2-0	1-2	4-3	–	1-4	1-1	1-1	0-0	5-2	2-1	3-0	3-1	0-0	1-2	1-0
Leicester	1-3	0-1	3-0	4-2	2-0	2-1	0-2	1-2	1-3	–	1-3	0-2	2-2	2-4	5-0	2-0	0-2	3-0	2-1	0-1
Liverpool	3-1	2-1	1-1	0-1	0-1	4-0	2-2	0-1	3-0	3-0	–	1-4	0-0	1-1	2-1	0-1	2-1	1-1	2-1	4-0
Man City	1-0	2-0	1-0	5-0	3-0	4-0	1-1	0-0	1-2	2-5	4-1	–	0-0	2-0	5-2	5-2	3-0	1-1	1-2	4-1
Man Utd	0-1	2-1	2-1	3-1	0-0	1-3	3-3	1-1	6-2	2-1	2-4	0-0	–	3-1	9-0	3-2	1-6	1-0	1-0	1-0
Newcastle	0-2	1-1	0-3	3-1	0-2	2-0	2-1	1-1	1-2	1-2	0-3	3-4	1-4	–	3-1	2-2	2-2	2-1	3-2	1-1
Sheffield Utd	0-3	1-0	1-1	0-1	1-2	0-2	0-1	0-1	0-1	1-2	0-0	0-1	2-3	1-0	–	0-2	1-3	2-1	0-1	0-1
Southampton	1-3	1-0	0-2	3-2	1-1	0-2	2-0	3-1	0-2	1-1	1-0	0-1	2-3	2-0	3-0	–	2-5	3-0	0-0	1-2
Tottenham	2-0	0-2	2-1	4-0	0-1	4-1	0-1	1-1	3-0	2-0	2-1	2-0	1-3	1-1	4-0	2-1	–	2-0	0-0	2-0
WBA	0-4	0-3	1-0	0-0	3-3	1-5	0-1	2-2	1-1	3-0	1-1	0-5	1-1	1-2	3-0	3-0	0-1	–	1-3	1-1
West Ham	3-3	2-1	2-2	2-1	0-1	1-1	0-1	0-0	2-1	3-2	1-3	1-1	1-3	2-0	3-0	3-0	2-1	1-3	–	4-0
Wolves	2-1	0-1	2-1	0-4	2-1	2-0	1-2	1-0	1-0	0-0	1-0	1-3	1-2	1-1	1-0	1-1	1-1	2-3	2-3	–

SKY BET CHAMPIONSHIP RESULTS 2020–2021

Home \ Away	Barnsley	Birmingham	Blackburn	Bournemouth	Brentford	Bristol City	Cardiff	Coventry	Derby	Huddersfield	Luton	Middlesbrough	Millwall	Norwich	Nottm Forest	Preston	QPR	Reading	Rotherham	Sheff Wed	Stoke	Swansea	Watford	Wycombe
Barnsley	–	1-0	0-4	2-2	0-2	0-1	3-0	2-0	0-2	0-1	1-2	2-1	1-1	1-0	1-0	2-0	0-0	0-0	0-1	3-0	2-0	0-2	2-1	1-2
Birmingham	1-2	–	0-2	1-3	0-1	1-0	3-2	0-0	0-1	1-0	1-1	0-0	2-0	1-0	1-1	2-0	2-1	2-1	1-1	1-1	2-1	1-0	0-1	1-2
Blackburn	2-1	5-2	–	0-2	3-2	0-0	0-0	0-4	0-4	5-2	1-1	0-1	0-0	1-1	1-0	3-1	3-1	2-4	2-1	1-2	1-0	1-1	2-3	5-0
Bournemouth	2-3	3-2	0-2	–	1-3	0-0	1-2	1-0	1-0	5-0	2-0	3-1	1-4	2-0	2-0	2-3	0-0	4-2	1-0	3-0	0-2	3-0	1-0	1-0
Brentford	0-2	0-1	2-1	2-1	–	1-0	0-2	2-1	4-0	5-0	2-0	3-1	0-0	1-1	1-1	2-4	2-0	3-1	1-0	0-2	2-1	1-1	2-0	7-2
Bristol City	0-1	0-1	1-2	2-1	1-3	–	0-2	3-1	1-0	2-1	2-3	0-3	0-0	1-3	1-1	2-0	3-1	3-1	1-0	0-2	2-1	1-1	0-0	2-1
Cardiff	3-0	3-2	2-1	1-2	2-3	0-2	–	3-1	4-0	3-0	2-0	3-2	6-1	1-2	2-1	4-0	3-2	1-2	3-1	3-3	0-0	1-1	1-2	2-1
Coventry	2-0	0-0	0-4	1-1	0-2	3-1	1-1	–	1-0	3-0	2-0	1-1	6-1	1-0	0-1	0-1	3-2	3-2	1-2	0-2	0-0	2-0	0-0	0-0
Derby	0-2	1-2	1-3	1-0	3-0	1-0	0-2	1-0	–	2-0	2-0	1-1	0-0	1-2	0-1	0-1	0-1	0-2	0-1	2-0	1-1	0-2	0-1	1-1
Huddersfield	0-1	1-1	1-1	1-2	0-5	1-2	2-1	1-1	2-0	–	2-0	1-3	0-0	0-1	0-1	1-2	1-2	1-2	0-3	0-2	3-0	0-2	2-0	2-3
Luton	1-2	1-1	1-1	1-2	1-4	2-1	0-0	1-1	2-0	2-0	–	3-2	3-1	0-0	2-1	3-0	2-0	2-0	1-0	2-1	1-1	1-1	1-0	2-0
Middlesbrough	2-1	2-0	0-1	1-1	2-0	1-3	0-1	1-1	3-2	1-3	0-0	–	3-0	0-0	0-1	0-2	0-2	0-0	0-3	4-1	0-0	2-0	0-1	0-3
Millwall	1-1	0-0	0-1	2-4	0-0	4-1	2-0	2-0	0-0	0-0	3-1	3-0	–	0-0	0-0	2-2	0-0	1-1	1-0	4-1	0-0	0-1	0-1	0-0
Norwich	1-0	1-2	1-1	1-3	1-3	1-2	0-1	1-1	1-2	0-1	0-0	0-0	2-1	–	2-1	1-2	1-1	1-1	1-2	2-1	1-3	4-1	0-1	2-1
Nottm Forest	0-0	1-0	1-0	1-0	0-0	2-0	2-1	1-0	0-1	0-1	0-0	2-1	3-0	0-1	–	0-2	1-1	2-0	1-1	0-1	1-1	2-0	0-1	0-0
Preston	2-0	0-0	0-3	0-0	0-1	1-2	0-1	2-0	3-0	0-2	0-1	1-2	0-0	2-0	0-1	–	0-0	1-1	1-2	1-0	0-3	1-0	0-1	2-1
QPR	1-3	0-0	1-1	2-1	1-0	3-1	0-1	2-0	2-1	0-0	2-3	2-0	3-2	2-3	1-1	0-2	–	2-1	1-2	1-0	0-1	2-2	1-0	1-0
Reading	2-0	1-2	1-0	3-1	1-2	3-1	0-1	2-0	1-2	4-3	0-0	1-0	3-2	2-3	2-0	0-2	3-1	–	1-2	0-3	1-1	1-3	1-4	1-0
Rotherham	1-2	1-1	0-0	2-2	3-2	2-0	0-1	3-0	1-3	1-2	0-1	1-0	1-2	2-3	1-0	0-2	1-1	0-0	–	1-0	0-1	2-2	1-2	2-0
Sheff Wed	2-2	1-1	2-1	3-1	0-1	1-0	0-1	3-3	0-0	0-2	4-3	1-1	3-2	2-1	0-2	0-2	0-0	1-1	1-2	–	0-0	0-2	2-1	2-0
Stoke	2-0	2-2	0-0	0-0	0-2	1-0	2-0	0-0	1-1	1-2	2-0	0-0	0-0	1-3	1-0	0-0	1-2	0-0	2-0	0-0	–	1-2	2-1	2-0
Swansea	1-0	1-1	2-0	2-1	0-1	2-0	1-1	1-3	2-1	0-2	1-1	1-0	2-1	0-0	0-1	4-1	2-2	1-1	2-0	0-2	1-2	–	1-2	2-2
Watford	1-0	3-0	0-0	1-0	0-2	0-1	0-1	0-0	1-1	2-0	1-0	1-1	0-0	1-2	1-0	0-1	2-0	0-0	2-0	0-0	3-2	1-2	–	2-0
Wycombe	1-3	0-0	3-1	2-1	1-2	0-0	2-1	2-1	1-1	0-0	2-0	0-3	0-0	2-1	0-0	2-0	1-0	1-0	0-3	2-0	2-0	2-2	1-1	–

SKY BET LEAGUE ONE RESULTS 2020-2021

	Wigan	Swindon	Sunderland	Shrewsbury	Rochdale	Portsmouth	Plymouth	Peterborough	Oxford	Northampton	MKDons	Lincoln	Ipswich	Hull	Gillingham	Fleetwood	Doncaster	Crewe	Charlton	Burton	Bristol Rov	Blackpool	AFC Wimbledon	Accrington
Accrington	3-1	2-1	0-2	1-1	2-1	3-3	0-1	2-0	1-4	0-0	2-1	0-0	1-2	2-0	0-1	1-0	2-1	1-0	2-2	2-1	6-1	0-0	1-5	–
AFC Wimbledon	1-1	4-1	0-3	0-1	3-3	1-3	4-4	0-1	2-1	0-0	0-2	2-3	1-2	1-0	1-0	1-0	2-2	1-2	2-2	0-1	2-4	1-0	–	1-1
Blackpool	1-0	0-1	0-1	1-0	2-0	0-1	1-2	1-0	2-0	2-0	2-0	2-3	1-4	0-2	1-0	0-0	2-2	0-1	0-1	1-1	1-0	–	1-1	0-0
Bristol Rov	1-2	0-1	2-1	0-0	2-0	2-1	3-0	2-0	2-0	2-0	1-3	0-2	0-2	1-3	0-2	1-4	2-1	0-1	2-1	4-0	–	2-1	0-0	2-1
Burton	3-4	2-2	0-3	2-4	4-4	2-4	1-1	0-1	1-5	1-3	1-3	0-1	0-0	1-2	0-3	5-2	1-3	2-2	1-2	–	1-0	1-0	5-2	2-1
Charlton	1-0	2-2	0-2	3-2	1-2	0-0	3-3	1-1	0-6	2-1	0-3	0-0	0-1	1-2	2-1	1-0	1-0	2-2	–	4-2	0-2	0-3	1-1	0-2
Crewe	1-0	4-2	2-2	4-1	0-3	2-1	2-1	3-2	3-2	2-1	1-0	2-0	1-1	1-1	1-2	0-2	1-0	–	0-2	1-2	3-2	1-1	1-1	2-0
Doncaster	3-0	2-1	2-2	1-1	1-0	0-0	5-1	1-1	0-1	2-1	0-0	4-1	0-0	1-1	2-1	3-1	–	1-0	0-1	0-3	0-1	3-2	2-0	0-1
Fleetwood	1-4	0-2	1-3	0-2	0-1	1-4	0-1	0-3	3-2	1-1	0-3	0-0	1-2	2-1	0-2	–	2-2	2-2	2-1	2-0	4-1	0-1	0-1	0-1
Gillingham	1-1	1-0	2-2	1-0	2-2	0-0	1-0	1-4	3-1	2-2	4-1	0-1	1-1	1-1	–	0-1	3-1	0-2	1-1	2-0	0-0	2-0	1-1	0-1
Hull	1-0	2-3	2-2	0-0	2-0	0-2	1-0	1-1	2-0	3-0	1-3	0-1	0-0	–	1-0	3-1	2-0	2-0	2-0	2-0	0-0	3-0	2-0	2-0
Ipswich	3-1	2-2	0-1	0-2	2-0	1-3	0-0	1-1	1-1	0-0	4-1	0-2	–	0-3	0-1	3-1	1-1	3-0	0-1	2-1	2-1	2-2	1-1	2-2
Lincoln	2-0	5-0	0-4	1-1	1-2	1-3	3-1	3-4	1-1	2-1	4-0	–	1-0	1-2	0-3	1-2	1-1	3-0	0-1	1-0	3-1	0-1	2-3	1-2
MKDons	2-1	0-1	2-0	2-2	0-2	2-0	4-2	1-1	2-0	4-0	–	1-2	4-0	2-1	3-2	1-1	2-0	0-2	0-6	2-0	2-1	1-2	0-1	2-2
Northampton	2-0	3-1	0-2	3-0	0-0	2-0	0-1	0-2	2-1	–	3-0	2-1	0-0	2-1	1-3	2-3	1-1	2-0	1-1	4-0	0-1	2-2	0-1	0-1
Oxford	0-1	4-2	2-2	1-4	2-0	3-1	1-0	3-4	–	2-0	2-0	1-1	1-0	0-3	1-0	1-2	2-0	3-0	1-0	1-5	2-0	0-3	1-1	1-2
Peterborough	2-1	0-2	0-2	1-0	4-1	0-2	2-2	–	1-1	1-1	2-1	2-1	3-0	1-3	4-3	2-0	3-3	1-0	1-0	2-2	0-2	3-0	2-0	2-2
Plymouth	2-1	2-1	1-0	1-0	1-0	2-2	–	2-0	2-0	4-0	2-1	1-1	2-1	0-4	0-0	2-1	1-1	4-1	0-2	1-2	2-0	0-1	1-0	0-1
Portsmouth	0-2	2-1	0-2	0-2	2-1	–	2-0	0-1	1-1	1-1	2-1	0-2	2-1	0-4	1-1	0-0	3-3	1-2	2-2	1-2	1-2	2-0	1-2	1-0
Rochdale	1-4	1-2	0-2	2-1	–	2-1	2-1	1-2	1-3	1-1	1-2	0-2	0-0	0-3	2-1	2-1	2-0	3-3	0-0	1-2	1-2	3-1	1-0	3-1
Shrewsbury	1-1	2-2	0-2	–	2-2	0-2	0-2	0-1	0-2	2-1	1-1	0-1	2-0	0-3	2-2	0-0	2-0	3-3	0-2	1-1	1-1	1-1	2-1	2-2
Sunderland	1-0	3-3	–	1-0	1-2	1-3	1-3	2-2	2-3	1-1	0-0	0-3	1-1	0-1	0-2	2-1	1-1	2-0	1-0	1-2	1-1	1-1	3-3	3-3
Swindon	1-0	–	1-0	1-0	3-1	3-1	0-2	1-0	3-1	1-1	1-4	1-0	0-0	2-1	1-3	0-1	1-2	2-1	2-2	4-2	1-0	0-2	0-1	0-3
Wigan	–	3-4	2-1	1-1	0-5	1-0	3-0	0-1	1-2	2-3	2-0	0-1	0-1	0-5	2-3	0-0	1-0	2-0	0-1	1-1	1-1	0-0	2-3	4-3

SKY BET LEAGUE TWO RESULTS 2020–2021

	Barrow	Bolton	Bradford	Cambridge	Carlisle	Cheltenham	Colchester	Crawley	Exeter	Forest Green	Grimsby	Harrogate	Leyton Orient	Mansfield	Morecambe	Newport	Oldham	Port Vale	Salford	Scunthorpe	Southend	Stevenage	Tranmere	Walsall
Barrow	–	1-0	1-0	0-2	1-0	0-2	1-1	3-2	2-1	2-2	0-1	0-1	1-1	2-0	1-2	2-1	3-4	0-2	0-1	1-0	1-2	1-1	1-1	2-2
Bolton	3-3	–	1-0	2-1	3-0	0-1	1-1	0-1	2-3	0-1	0-0	2-1	2-0	1-1	1-1	0-2	1-2	3-6	2-0	2-0	3-0	1-0	0-3	2-1
Bradford	2-1	1-1	–	0-0	3-1	1-2	0-0	0-2	1-0	4-1	1-0	2-1	2-1	1-0	2-1	2-1	0-0	0-0	2-0	3-0	3-0	0-1	0-0	1-1
Cambridge	1-1	1-1	1-0	–	1-2	1-1	2-1	0-2	1-4	1-0	3-0	1-2	2-1	1-0	2-1	2-1	1-2	3-1	2-1	0-1	0-0	0-1	0-0	1-0
Carlisle	1-0	3-3	0-1	3-1	–	1-2	3-2	3-1	1-4	1-2	1-1	2-1	0-1	0-0	3-1	3-2	1-3	0-0	2-1	2-0	0-0	0-1	2-3	0-0
Cheltenham	0-2	0-1	0-2	1-1	1-2	–	1-0	1-4	5-3	2-1	1-3	4-1	1-0	0-0	1-2	1-0	0-0	3-2	1-0	1-0	1-0	0-0	4-0	0-0
Colchester	1-1	2-0	1-2	2-1	3-2	1-2	–	2-0	2-0	1-2	2-1	2-1	0-0	2-2	1-2	0-2	3-3	0-1	1-0	0-1	1-0	1-1	2-2	2-1
Crawley	4-2	1-4	2-1	2-1	3-1	1-0	1-0	–	2-1	0-0	1-1	1-3	0-0	2-2	4-0	1-1	1-4	1-3	1-0	1-0	2-0	3-1	4-0	1-1
Exeter	1-1	1-1	3-2	1-4	2-0	0-1	1-0	2-0	–	1-1	3-2	1-2	4-0	2-0	0-2	0-2	1-2	0-2	1-0	3-1	1-1	0-1	5-0	2-1
Forest Green	0-2	0-1	2-2	1-0	2-3	1-2	3-0	0-0	1-1	–	1-1	2-1	2-1	0-2	2-2	1-1	0-0	1-1	0-0	3-2	2-0	1-0	2-1	1-1
Grimsby	1-0	2-1	1-2	3-0	1-1	1-0	3-0	2-3	3-2	1-2	–	1-2	0-1	1-2	0-3	0-0	0-3	4-3	0-1	2-5	1-1	1-0	0-0	0-1
Harrogate	1-0	1-2	2-1	1-0	1-0	1-2	3-0	1-2	0-0	0-1	1-0	–	2-2	1-1	0-2	0-2	0-2	1-1	0-2	1-1	1-1	1-2	0-1	0-2
Leyton Orient	2-0	4-0	1-0	2-4	1-0	0-2	1-0	3-3	1-1	0-1	2-2	2-1	–	1-0	2-1	0-1	2-2	0-2	0-1	4-1	0-1	0-0	1-0	2-3
Mansfield	2-4	2-3	0-3	0-3	3-1	3-1	3-1	3-1	1-2	0-2	1-1	1-0	0-2	–	1-0	1-3	0-0	1-1	2-1	4-0	1-1	1-1	1-0	1-3
Morecambe	1-0	0-1	2-0	0-5	3-1	1-0	3-0	2-3	2-2	1-2	1-0	2-1	0-1	2-1	–	2-1	2-4	4-0	0-0	0-2	1-1	0-0	1-0	0-0
Newport	2-1	1-0	3-1	2-4	1-0	1-3	2-1	2-0	2-1	0-3	1-3	0-0	0-1	2-1	2-1	–	2-4	4-1	2-1	0-1	1-1	1-1	1-0	0-2
Oldham	0-1	0-2	1-2	3-1	1-2	2-0	5-2	2-3	2-1	0-0	1-0	2-0	2-0	0-3	2-4	3-2	–	1-0	1-0	1-1	1-1	0-1	3-4	0-0
Port Vale	0-2	0-1	2-0	0-5	3-1	0-3	1-1	2-0	2-1	1-4	1-1	1-1	2-3	2-3	1-0	1-1	2-0	–	2-1	0-1	5-1	0-1	0-0	1-1
Salford	1-0	0-1	3-0	4-1	2-0	2-1	0-0	0-1	0-2	0-0	3-0	2-2	3-0	0-1	0-0	2-1	1-1	1-1	–	1-1	3-0	2-1	0-0	0-2
Scunthorpe	2-1	0-1	1-3	0-5	2-0	0-0	0-1	2-0	2-2	2-0	1-1	3-1	2-0	2-3	2-1	1-1	1-1	2-0	1-1	–	1-1	0-1	2-0	1-1
Southend	1-0	0-1	0-2	1-2	3-1	1-0	2-0	3-3	2-2	0-1	5-1	0-0	2-0	0-1	1-1	1-0	0-0	1-1	5-1	1-1	–	0-0	2-0	0-0
Stevenage	2-1	1-2	1-2	3-1	1-2	1-1	3-1	1-2	2-1	3-0	0-1	3-2	2-1	0-1	1-1	1-0	2-2	2-1	0-0	3-1	3-0	–	0-0	1-1
Tranmere	1-0	2-1	1-1	1-1	1-0	0-0	2-2	3-2	0-0	2-1	0-0	0-1	0-2	2-1	1-0	1-0	0-0	0-2	0-0	1-2	2-0	0-1	–	1-3
Walsall	0-1	2-1	1-2	0-2	2-1	1-2	2-1	0-1	1-0	0-0	0-0	1-0	2-1	1-1	0-0	0-1	2-2	4-3	0-2	0-0	0-1	1-1	1-0	–

HIGHLIGHTS OF THE PREMIER LEAGUE SEASON 2020–21

SEPTEMBER 2020

12 Liverpool open their title defence with a 4-3 win over Leeds in one of the finest first-day matches of the Premier League era. Three times they lead Leeds, back in the top-flight after a 16-year absence, before Mohamed Salah's second penalty in the 88th minute proves decisive and completes his own hat-trick. Summer-signings Callum Wilson and Jeff Hendrick are both on the mark as Newcastle start with a victory for the first time since 2012 – 2-0 at West Ham. Arsenal centre-half Gabriel also marks his debut with a goal in a 3-0 success away to Fulham in which fellow Brazilian Willian is outstanding after his move from Chelsea. Referee Jonathan Moss shows a red card to new Southampton signing Kyle Walker-Peters for a high challenge on Tyrick Mitchell at Selhurst Park, then downgrades it to yellow after watching the incident on the pitchside monitor. Crystal Palace win 1-0 with a goal from Wilfried Zaha.

13 Timothy Castagne is another debut marksman, paving the way for Leicester's 3-0 defeat of West Bromwich Albion ahead of two penalties from Golden Boot winner Jamie Vardy at The Hawthorns. Jose Mourinho loses on the opening day of a league season for the first time as Tottenham go down 1-0 at home to Dominic Calvert-Lewin's header for Everton.

14 Reece James scores a spectacular first goal for Chelsea – a 25-yard drive in their 3-1 win at Brighton. Two in the first six minutes from Raul Jimenez and Romain Saiss account for Sheffield United 2-0 at Bramall Lane.

19 Dominic Calvert-Lewin sets the pace for a record weekend of Premier League goals with his first senior hat-trick in Everton's 5-2 win over West Bromwich Albion which also includes a first goal for the club by former Columbia World Cup star James Rodriguez. Albion have Kieran Gibbs shown a straight red card on the stroke of half-time for pushing Rodriguez in the face and manager Slaven Bilic is also sent off, for arguing with referee Mike Dean as the teams walk off. Another new signing, Donny van de Beek, opens his account for Manchester United, but it's the only high spot for his team who lose 3-1 at Old Trafford to Crystal Palace. Wilfried Zaha is on the mark twice, his first goal a retaken penalty after David de Gea is penalised for moving off his line to save from Jordan Ayew. Two goals by Helder Costa give Leeds to a 4-1 lead over Fulham, who pull two back as Aleksandar Mitrovic adds to his early penalty. West Ham manager David Moyes admits he is baffled by the rules on handball after VAR fails to award a spot-kick against Arsenal defender Gabriel in his side's 2-1 defeat.

20 Son Heung-min and Harry Kane combine to deadly effective as Tottenham sweep aside Southampton 5-2. Son scores four goals, all set up by the England captain, who nets the fifth himself ahead of a late Danny Ings penalty for the home side, his second of the game. Sadio Mane nets twice as Liverpool prevail 2-0 at Chelsea in the season's first 'heavyweight' match. So does Neal Maupay, whose fourth minute penalty is followed by his second strike three minutes later, setting up Brighton for a 3-0 success at Newcastle, marred by a straight red for Yves Bissouma for a high boot in the face of Jamal Lewis. Jimmy Dunne makes a scoring debut for Burnley in their 4-2 defeat at Leicester in the last of the weekend's eight fixtures, which deliver a total of 39 goals.

21 Emiliano Martinez marks his Aston Villa debut after joining the club from Arsenal by saving John Lundstram's penalty in the 1-0 victory over Sheffield United, who have John Egan shown a straight red for denying Ollie Watkins a scoring opportunity. Manchester City, like Villa playing their first game, win 3-1 at Wolves – Phil Foden scoring their second goal on his first appearance since being sent home from England duty.

26 On a day full of incident and controversy, Manchester United score a winner after the final whistle, Chelsea retrieve a 3-0 deficit and Crystal Palace manager Roy Hodgson warns that the new handball law is 'killing the game.' After hitting the United woodwork five times,

43

Brighton look to have gained a deserved point when Solly March heads a 94th minute equaliser, then clears off the line from Harry Maguire at the other end. But after referee Chris Kavanagh signals time, Maguire protests there has been a handball in the build-up, Kavanagh awards a penalty against Neal Maupay after checking the pitchside monitor and Bruno Fernandes converts it in the 100th minute of the match for 3-2. Chelsea look down and out after two Callum Robinson goals point West Bromwich Albion to a commanding half-time lead. Instead, Frank Lampard rings the changes and his side complete an impressive recovery with Tammy Abraham's 93rd minute equaliser. Hodgson rages after his defender Joel Ward is penalised and Richarlison gives Everton a 2-1 victory from the penalty spot. Golden Boot runner-up Danny Ings delivers Southampton's first three points of the season with a fifth minute goal at Burnley.

27 More heated argument about handball, this time alongside a stunning victory for Leicester against Manchester City. Steve Bruce is grateful for Newcastle's point at Tottenham, earned by Callum Wilson's disputed 97th minute penalty, awarded against Eric Dier. But Bruce admits: 'We have lost the plot with it totally.' Leicester become the first team in Premier League history to score three penalties in a game – two converted by Jamie Vardy on the way to a hat-trick and one from Youri Tielemans. After conceding first, they win 5-2 at the Etihad – the first time a team managed by Pep Guardiola have conceded five goals. Nathan Ake's first for the club is scant consolation. West Ham manager David Moyes, in isolation at home after testing positive for Covid, is boosted by a handsome first success – 4-0 against Wolves with Jarrod Bowen on the mark twice. Patrick Bamford's third in three games gives Leeds the verdict 1-0 away to Sheffield United.

28 Diogo Jota scores on his home debut for Liverpool to round off a 3-1 victory over Arsenal. Fulham manager Scott Parker admits his team need strengthening after a 3-0 home defeat by Aston Villa and ten goals conceded in the opening three fixtures.

OCTOBER 2020

3 Everton beat Brighton 4-2 to record the club's seventh successive win in all competitions at the start of a season for the first time since season 1894-95 and a fourth straight league success for the first time since 1969-70. James Rodriguez nets twice, along with Newcastle's Callum Wilson and Chelsea's Jorginho. Wilson's second in a 3-1 win over Burnley is a penalty. Both Jorginho goals in the 4-0 victory over Crystal Palace come from the spot after Ben Chilwell marks his league debut for the club with the opener, then provides the assist for Kurt Zouma to make it 2-0. Record-signing Rodrigo's first for Leeds earns a 1-1 draw with Manchester City.

4 Liverpool suffer their heaviest defeat for 57 years and Manchester United are hit for six at Old Trafford on one of those astonishing days in Premier League history. Jurgen Klopp admits his side 'lost the plot' when crashing 7-2 at Villa Park to a 'perfect' hat-trick by record-signing Ollie Watkins – left foot, right foot, header – a brace from Jack Grealish and Ross Barkley's debut goal after joining on loan from Chelsea. United are crushed 6-1 by Tottenham after leading through a Bruno Fernandes penalty in the second minute. They also lose Anthony Martial to a straight red card, with the score 2-1, for retaliating against Erik Lamela. Son Heung-min and Harry Kane share four of the goals, Kane's second a penalty. West Ham continue to cheer the recuperating David Moyes as Michail Antonio scores for the fifth successive away league game to launch an impressive 3-0 success at Leicester.

17 Liverpool demand an explanation for two contentious VAR decisions in the Merseyside derby – Jordan Pickford's challenge which puts Virgil van Dijk out for the season and Jordan Henderson's stoppage-time 'winner' disallowed for Sadio Mane being fractionally offside. Everton's Richarlison is shown a straight red card for diving in on Thiago Alcantara in the 2-2 draw. Harry Maguire puts his troubled start to the season behind him with a goal and Aaron Wan-Bissaka opens his account for the club as Manchester United score three times in the final ten minutes for a 4-1 win at Newcastle. Timo Werner, with a brace, and Kai Havertz deliver their first in the Premier League for Chelsea, but Southampton are rewarded for their perseverance at Stamford Bridge, with Jannik Vestergaard's stoppage-time equaliser for 3-3.

18 West Ham become the first team in Premier League history to retrieve a 3-0 deficit going into the 81st minute of a match. Manuel Lanzini completes their comeback from 25 yards in stoppage-time to draw his side level after Tottenham's flying start of three goals in the first quarter-of-an- hour, two of them from Harry Kane. Ross Barkley also strikes from 25 yards in added time as Aston Villa record a fourth successive league win at the start of the season for the first time since 1930-31 – 1-0 away to Leicester. Late drama, too, at Selhurst Park, with substitute Alexis Mac Allister's 90th minute goal earning Brighton a point, then Lewis Dunk shown a straight red for lunging at Crystal Palace's Gary Cahill. Ademola Lookman celebrates his first goal for Fulham, but team-mate Aleksandar Mitrovic has a match to forget, missing a penalty and conceding the spot-kick which Billy Sharp converts to give Sheffield United a point.

23 Patrick Bamford fires a hat-trick in 19 second-half minutes at Villa Park, talking his tally to six goals in the first six games as Leeds end the home team's 100 per cent record 3-0.

24 Michail Antonio submits an early contender for goal of the season with an overhead volley to earn West Ham a 1-1 draw against Manchester City. Jairo Riedewald nets his first for Crystal Palace in a 2-1 win at Fulham, who have Aboubakar Kamara shown a straight red for his tackle on Eberechi Eze. Liverpool come from behind to defeat Sheffield United by the same scoreline.

25 Everton lose their unbeaten record 2-0 at Southampton and have Lucas Digne shown a straight red for his challenge from behind on Kyle Walker-Peters. Jamie Vardy scores his 11th goal in 12 games against Arsenal to give Leicester a 1-0 victory at the Emirates.

30 Rayan Ait-Nouri, 19-year-old loanee from French club Angers, scores on his Wolves debut – a 2-0 success against Crystal Palace, who have Luka Milivojevic shown a straight red for a sliding tackle on Joao Moutinho.

31 Hakim Ziyech scores on his first Premier League start for Chelsea, who are 3-0 winners at Burnley. Diogo Jota continues his bright start at Liverpool with a third goal in successive Premier and Europa League fixtures – an 85th minute strike for 2-1 against West Ham. Kyle Walker chooses not to celebrate his 25-yard winner for Manchester City against Sheffield United – the game's only goal – out of respect for his boyhood club.

NOVEMBER 2020

1 Gareth Bale comes off the bench to score for the first time since his return to Tottenham and deliver a 2-1 win over Brighton, who have Tariq Lamptey on the scoresheet for the first time. Skipper James Ward-Prowse celebrates his 26th birthday with two inch-perfect free-kicks as Southampton overcome Aston Villa 4-3, leading 4-1 going into stoppage-time before the home side restore a measure of pride. Callum Wilson also scores twice – his first goal a penalty – for Newcastle to see off Everton 2-1. Arsenal defeat Manchester United at Old Trafford for the first time since 2006, Pierre-Emerick Aubameyang's penalty separating the teams.

2 Fulham break their duck by beating West Bromwich Albion 2-0, with Ola Aina, on loan from Torino, scoring a spectacular first goal for the club from 20 yards. Two by Youri Tielemans, his second a penalty, point Leicester to a 4-1 success at Leeds.

6 Ahead of the weekend matches, Southampton go top, overcoming the absence of the injured Danny Ings to defeat Newcastle 2-0.

7 Three players score for the first time for their new clubs. Edinson Cavani rounds off Manchester United's 3-1 victory at Everton, adding to two goals from Bruno Fernandes in a performance which eases the pressure on manager Ole Gunnar Solskjaer. Thiago Silva makes his mark in Chelsea's 4-1 defeat of Sheffield United. And Eberechi Eze's delightful free- kick helps Crystal Palace record the same scoreline against Leeds, who are the latest team left bemused by the handball law when Patrick Bamford has a goal ruled out by VAR. West Ham's Tomas Soucek ends stalemate in the London derby with a goal entering stoppage-time. Fulham's Ademola Lookman then wastes the chance to level with the worst penalty of this and many other seasons - a Panenka-style chip scooped into the arms of Lukasz Fabianski.

8 Kevin De Bruyne sends his penalty wide and Manchester City have to be satisfied with a 1-1 draw against Liverpool. Jamie Vardy has his second one of the match against Wolves saved by Rui Patricio, but his first is sufficient for a 1-0 win which leaves his side top on 18 points, Harry Kane's 88th minute goal for the same margin of against West Bromwich Albion puts Tottenham one point behind, alongside Liverpool. Ollie Watkins continues to flourish with a brace for Aston Villa, who outplay Arsenal 3-0 at the Emirates.

21 Tottenham go top by beating Manchester City 2-0, Giovani Lo Celso sealing the points 35 seconds after coming off the bench. Danny Welbeck scores his first goal or Brighton, who win 2-1 at Villa Park despite having Tariq Lamptey sent off for a second yellow card. Michael Oliver changes his mind about awarding Villa a penalty after consulting the pitchside monitor and David Coote also has second thoughts about a spot-kick for West Bromwich Albion at Old Trafford. The referee then awards one to Manchester United, orders a retake when Sam Johnstone moves off his line saving from Bruno Fernandes, who makes no mistake at the second attempt for the only goal of the game.

22 Liverpool make light of the absence of six players through injury and Covid to set a record for the club of 64 unbeaten Premier League games at Anfield by seeing of Leicester 3-0. Two goals from Dominic-Calvert Lewin and a first for the club by Abdoulaye Doucoure deliver a 3-2 success for Everton away to Fulham, who have Ruben Loftus-Cheek on the mark for the first time but waste a penalty when Ivan Cavaleiro fires over after losing his footing. Nicolas Pepe incurs the wrath of his manager for a straight red card for pushing his head into the face of Ezgjan Alioski in Arsenal's goalless draw at Leeds. 'Unacceptable' fumes Mikel Arteta.

23 Chris Wood gives Burnley their first victory of the season with the only goal against Crystal Palace. Theo Walcott's first since returning to Southampton earns a 1-1 result at Wolves.

28 Riyad Mahrez scores a hat-trick and Benjamin Mendy nets his first goal for the club as Manchester City defeat Burnley 5-0 for the fourth time in successive league and cup games at the Etihad. Conor Gallagher, on loan from Chelsea, gets his first for West Bromwich Albion, who record their first victory of the campaign against Sheffield United. So does the Brazilian Raphina for Leeds in another 1-0 scoreline at Everton. James Milner joins Liverpool's injury list and Jurgen Klopp calls for the reintroduction of five substitutes after his side are denied victory at Brighton by a stoppage-time penalty converted by Pascal Gross after Neal Maupay's earlier miss from the spot.

29 Manchester United transform a 2-0 deficit into a 3-2 success at Southampton with two headers from substitute Edinson Cavani, the second in stoppage-time, and a goal for Bruno Fernandes. Wolves overcome the loss of Raul Jimenez with a fractured skull in an accidental collision with Arsenal's David Luiz to prevail 2-1 at the Emirates. Tottenham share a goalless draw at Chelsea to finish the month on top on goal difference from Liverpool. Chelsea are a point behind, while Sheffield United remain bottom, with a single point from ten matches.

30 Fulham break a sequence of three missed penalties with Ivan Cavaleiro's conversion for a 2-1 victory at Leicester. Aston Villa's Ollie Watkins hits he bar with his spot-kick against West Ham, who profit 2-1.

DECEMBER 2020

5 Manchester United maintain their 100 per cent record of coming from behind to win away for the fifth time. In the first Premier League fixture to welcome back a limited number of supporters, they score three second-half goals in 13 minutes, the first a belter from Paul Pogba, to defeat West Ham. Chelsea also secure a 3-1 success after trailing Leeds, Olivier Giroud following up his midweek four-goal Champions League performance against Sevilla with their opener. England manager Gareth Southgate sees his top two goalkeepers, Jordan Pickford and Nick Pope, make eye-catching saves in Burnley's 1-1 draw away at Everton. Manchester City record back-to-back victories for the first time when beating Fulham 2-0.

6 Crystal Palace score five goals away from home for the first time in top-flight football. Wilfried Zaha and Christian Benteke, on his first start of the season, are both on the mark twice after West Bromwich Albion have Matheus Pereira shown a straight red card for kicking out at Patrick van Aanholt and crash 5-1. Harry Kane, with 11 goals, becomes the leading

scorer in north London derbies and Son Heung-min nets his tenth in 11 league games this season as Tottenham overcome Arsenal 2-0. Wolves have a penalty award overturned after Craig Pawson checks his pitchside monitor and concede three second-half goal to lose 4-0 at Liverpool.

12 Miguel Almiron scores the joint fastest goal of the season after 20 seconds and Dwight Gayle marks his first appearance by heading an 82nd minute winner as Newcastle defeat West Bromwich Albion 2-1 on their return to action after a Covid outbreak at the club. Molineux sees two sendings-off and a penalty winner in a frantic finish to the west Midlands derby. Aston Villa lose Douglas Luiz to a second yellow card after 85 minutes, but take the points with Anwar El Ghazi's conversion for the only goal in the fourth minute of stoppage-time. Wolves then lose Joao Moutinho shown a second yellow. Gylfi Sigurdsson's spot-kick for Everton brings to an end Chelsea's 17-match unbeaten run in all competitions. They lose 1-0, while a sterile Manchester derby ends goalless.

13 More problems for Arsenal and their captain Pierre-Emerick Aubameyang. They lose 1-0 to Burnley, the club's fourth successive home league defeat for the first time since 1959, after Aubameyang glances a header into his own net and Granit Xhaka is shown a straight red card for grabbing Ashley Westwood by the throat. Tottenham and Liverpool are held 1-1 by Crystal Palace and Fulham respectively, resulting in all 'big six' clubs dropping points over the weekend. James Maddison keeps Leicester among the leaders with two goals in a 3-0 victory over Brighton.

15 West Bromwich Albion produce a spirited performance for a 1-1 draw away to Manchester City, but it is not enough to prevent Slaven Bilic from the sack after a single win in 13 matches. Wolves come from behind to defeat Chelsea 2-1 with a 95th minute goal by Pedro Neto.

16 Roberto Firmino's 90th minute header gives Liverpool the verdict 2-1 against Tottenham in the meeting of the top two. Jack Harrison's 25-yard drive rounds off a 5-2 success for Leeds against Newcastle and Sebastien Haller strikes another spectacular goal for West Ham. His overhead kick earns a point against Crystal Palace, who have Christian Benteke dismissed after putting them ahead. Arsenal's Gabriel is also shown a second yellow card – the club's third dismissal in five Premier League fixtures – against Southampton in which Pierre-Emerick Aubameyang scores for the first time in open play since the opening day of the season to cancel out Theo Walcott's goal against his old club. Mason Holgate's first in the top-flight seals Everton's 2-0 win at Leicester.

17 Manchester United become the first Premier League team to win six successive away games after conceding first in each of them. They defeat Sheffield United 3-2 with Marcus Rashford on the mark twice. David McGoldrick nets both for the home team.

19 Liverpool ensure top spot at Christmas with a record-breaking 7-0 performance against Crystal Palace. Roberto Firmino and Mohamed Salah both net twice in the club's first top-flight away win by a margin of seven. Palace suffer their worst-ever home defeat. Everton climb to second, albeit for 24 hours, with a 2-1 success against Arsenal, while improving Fulham hold on to a 1-1 scoreline at Newcastle, despite playing for the final half-hour with ten men after Joachim Andersen is shown a straight red card for denying Callum Wilson a scoring opportunity.

20 Scott McTominay scores twice in the opening three minutes to put Manchester United on the way to a 6-2 victory over Leeds. Bruno Fernandes nets a brace, one a penalty, and so does Anwar El Ghazi as Aston Villa brush aside West Bromwich Albion 3-0 to underline the size of the task facing new manager Sam Allardyce at The Hawthorns. His side have Jake Livermore sent off for lunging at Jack Grealish after a VAR review upgrades yellow to red. Sheffield United's John Lundstram suffers the same fate for his challenge on Joel Veltman at Brighton, where a debut goal by Jayden Bogle promises a first win for Chris Wilder's team until Danny Welbeck's 87th minute equaliser. Leicester's 2-0 victory at Tottenham keeps the chasing pack tightly bunched.

21 Two second-half goals in two minutes by Tammy Abraham seal Chelsea's 3-0 win over West Ham.

26 Mikel Arteta makes six changes after Arsenal's worst start to a season since 1974 and is rewarded with a 3-1 success over Chelsea, launched by Alexandre Lacazette's penalty and completed with Bernd Leno's spot-kick save from Jorginho. Manchester United's record-breaking run away from home is ended by Leicester, who twice come from behind to draw 2-2. Aston Villa make light of losing Tyrone Mings to a second yellow card, their ten men scoring twice in the second-half for a 3-0 scoreline against Crystal Palace.

27 West Bromwich Albion chalk up their first point under Sam Allardyce with a dogged defensive performance, rewarded by Semi Ajayi's 82nd minute equaliser for a 1-1 draw against Liverpool at Anfield. Ben Johnson scores for West Ham for the first time in a 2-2 draw against Brighton. Burnley, beaten 1-0 at Leeds, have strong grounds for complaining about an equaliser ruled out for a foul by Ben Mee.

28 Vicente Guaita saves a penalty from Kelechi Iheanacho to earn Crystal Palace a point from a 1-1 draw with Leicester.

29 West Bromwich Albion are back in the doldrums, crushed 5-0 at home by Leeds, who are gifted the lead by a bizarre Romaine Sawyers own goal, then produce ruthless finishing. Marcus Rashford breaks the deadlock in stoppage-time to give Manchester United all three points against Wolves. Arsenal are also 1-0 winners, with a goal by Alexandre Lacazette 21 seconds after coming off the bench at Brighton. So too are Burnley against Sheffield United, with Ben Mee's first at Turf Moor since 2015.

30 Liverpool falter again, held to a goalless draw at Newcastle.

JANUARY 2021

1 Bruno Fernandes converts his seventh penalty of the season in all competitions as Manchester United defeat Aston Villa 2-1 to draw level with Liverpool at the top on 33 points. Leicester and Everton follow on 29. Sheffield United (2), West Bromwich Albion (8) and Fulham (11) fill the bottom three places.

2 A third win in eight days suggests brighter times ahead for Arsenal, with Alexandre Lacazette on the mark twice in a 4-0 success away to West Bromwich Albion. Son Heung-min records his 100th goal for Tottenham, whose 3-0 victory over Leeds is marred by a second yellow card for Matt Doherty. Brighton's Dan Burn concedes an own goal and gives away a penalty against Wolves, but his side recover from a 3-1 deficit to gain a point. Sheffield United are saddled with a Premier League record of 17 games without a victory from the start of the season. They go under 2-0 to Crystal Palace, for whom Eberechi Eze runs from inside his own half for the second goal.

3 After a mixed first half of the season, Manchester City show signs of moving into top gear with three goals in the opening 34 minutes on the way to defeating Chelsea 3-1 at Stamford Bridge. Andy Carroll scores his first Newcastle goal for ten years – since his first spell at the club – but it is not enough to prevent a 2-1 home defeat by Leicester.

4 Liverpool lose to a second-minute Danny Ings goal at Southampton and Jurgen Klopp criticises his players after a third successive game without a win.

12 Sheffield United break their duck at the 18th time of asking, with Billy Sharp's penalty enough to beat Newcastle, who lose Ryan Fraser to a second booking in three minutes. Paul Pogba fires the only goal at Burnley to send Manchester United to the top.

13 Fulham manager Scott Parker describes having to play a rearranged fixture at Tottenham at short notice as 'scandalous,' but his side give a spirited performance to come from behind for a 1-1 draw. Manchester City overcome Raheem Sterling's missed penalty to beat Brighton 1-0.

16 Sam Allardyce relishes his first victory as West Bromwich Albion manager – 3-2 over Wolves in the Black Country derby at Molineux with two penalties by Matheus Pereira. Brighton end a run of nine matches without a win, thanks to the only goal of the game from Neal Maupay at Leeds. It moves them five points clear of third-from-bottom Fulham, who have Antonee Robinson shown a straight red card for his tackle on Cesar Azpilicueta in a 1-0 home defeat by Chelsea. Leicester are up to second, for 24 hours, after beating Southampton 2-0.

17 John Stones, without a Premier League goal in four years at Manchester City, scores two in a

4-0 victory over Crystal Palace. City close in on the top spot after Liverpool and Manchester United share a goalless draw. Tanguy Ndombele seals Tottenham's 3-1 success away to Sheffield United with a brilliant piece of improvisation – a twist of his body and a flick with the outside of his right boot to find the far corner from an angle.

18 Two goals by Pierre-Emerick Aubameyang point Arsenal to a 3-0 victory over Newcastle.

19 Leicester go top for 24 hours after a 2-0 win over Chelsea, launched by Wilfred Ndidi's first goal of the season. It proves to be Frank Lampard's final Premier League match before his dismissal. West Ham reach their best-ever Premier League points tally at the halfway stage of the season – 32 – by beating West Bromwich Albion 2-1.

20 Aston Villa manager Dean Smith is sent off for persistent protests that Bernardo Silva's opening goal in Manchester City's 2-0 victory should have been disallowed for offside. Manchester United come from behind to win 2-1 at Fulham.

21 Liverpool are beaten at home in the Premier League for the first time since April 2017 – a run of 68 games. They lose 1-0 to an Ashley Barnes penalty for Burnley and fall six points behind leaders Manchester United.

26 Manchester City become the ninth team to go top at the end of a day's play, overwhelming West Bromwich Albion 5-0 with Ilkay Gundogan scoring two of the goals. Tomas Soucek nets two as West Ham climb to fourth by beating Crystal Palace 3-2. Arsenal return to St Mary's four days after having their defence of the FA Cup ended and turn the tables on Southampton 3-1 after falling behind.

27 Sheffield United deliver the shock result of the season so far, defeating Manchester United 2-1 at Old Trafford with goals from Kean Bryan, his first for the club, and substitute Oliver Burke, his first in the Premier League. Burnley move further away from the relegation zone by coming from behind twice against Aston Villa, then securing all three points courtesy of Chris Wood's header. Thomas Tuchel's first match as Chelsea manager is a goalless draw against Wolves and he admits the title is already out of reach with his team 11 points adrift.

28 Liverpool are back on song after five league games without a win, the outstanding Sadio Mane sealing a 3-1 scoreline at Tottenham, who have Pierre-Emile Hojbjerg on the scoresheet for the first time but lose Harry Kane with damaged ankles.

30 Manchester City set a club-record of 12 successive victories in all competitions – 1-0 against Sheffield United earned by a first league goal in three months for Gabriel Jesus. Callum Wilson gives Newcastle their first success in 12 league and cup fixtures with two unanswered strikes at Everton. Manchester United drop more points in a goalless draw away to Arsenal.

31 Patrick Bamford and Mohamed Salah share top billing in 3-1 away victories by their teams. Bamford scores one goal and provides assists for two more from Stuart Dallas and Jack Harrison as Leeds overcome a Leicester side missing Jamie Vardy after hernia surgery. Salah's brace is against West Ham. Tottenham's challenge looks to have faded at Brighton, who record their first home league success in 15 matches with the only goal of the game from Leandro Trossard. Marcos Alonso marks his first appearance in four months for Chelsea by sealing a 2-0 win over Burnley – Thomas Tuchel's first as manager. Manchester City (44), Manchester United (41), Liverpool (40) and Leicester (39) occupy the leading positions. Sheffield United (8), West Bromwich Albion (12) and Fulham (14) remain in the relegation places.

FEBRUARY 2021

2 Manchester United equal the Premier League record score against nine-man Southampton, who are swamped 9-0 for the second successive season, having been on the receiving end at home to Leicester in October 2019. This time, they lose 19-year-old Alex Jankewitz 82 seconds into his full debut for lunging at Scott McTominay, then Jan Bednarek for a last-man challenge on two-goal Anthony Martial with the score 6-0 – a dismissal later rescinded on appeal. United have seven different scorers, matching another record. There are also two straight red cards at Molineux, where Wolves come from behind to win for the first time in nine league matches – 2-1 against Arsenal, who lose David Luiz for his penalty box challenge on William Jose and Bernd Leno for handling outside the area. Gary Cahill, 35, becomes

Crystal Palace's oldest Premier League scorer with a header for his first goal for the club at Newcastle. Sheffield United also win by the same scoreline after conceding first against West Bromwich Albion, their decider coming from Billy Sharp, three days before his 35th birthday.

3 Liverpool falter again, this time against Brighton, who prevail at Anfield for the first time for 39 years thanks to Steven Alzate's first Premier League goal for 1-0 which lifts his side ten points clear of the bottom three. Manchester City, meanwhile, sail on serenely by beating Burnley 2-0 at Turf Moor, while West Ham prosper immediately from Jesse Lingard's loan move from Manchester United, his debut marked by two goals in a 3-1 success at Villa Park

4 Jose Mourinho loses back-to-back home league games for the first time in his managerial career as Tottenham go down 1-0 to Jorginho's penalty for Chelsea.

6 Ole Gunnar Solskjaer declares Manchester United are not title contenders after they surrender a two-goal lead to Everton and are eventually pegged back to 3-3 by Dominic Calvert-Lewin in the fifth minute of stoppage-time. Newcastle go down to nine men when Jeff Hendrick's second yellow card is followed by an injury to Fabian Schar, with Steve Bruce having used all his substitutes. But his team hold on to a 3-2 lead against Southampton, established by two goals from Miguel Almiron and one from Arsenal loanee Joe Willock. Southampton's Takumi Minamino, on loan from Liverpool, also scores on his debut. Tomas Soucek's straight red card for an elbow on Aleksandar Mitrovic in West Ham's goalless draw at Fulham is overturned on appeal.

7 Manchester City open a five-point lead at the top with a performance bearing all the hallmarks of champions. They destroy Liverpool 4-1 at Anfield with three second-half goals in 11 minutes, two of them stemming from mistake by goalkeeper Alisson. Ilkay Gundogan nets twice and misses a penalty. Harry Kane returns after injury to spark Tottenham's return to winning ways – 2-0 against West Bromwich Albion – and draws level with Bobby Smith on 208 goals in the club's all-time scoring list.

13 On a day when Jurgen Klopp concedes the title, Ilkay Gundogan continues his prolific form for Manchester City in the 3-0 defeat of Tottenham. Two goals take his tally to 11 in 12 games, the second courtesy of an 80-yard assist from goalkeeper Ederson's clearance. Liverpool are breached three times in seven second-half minutes at Leicester, go down 3-1 and Klopp admits there is no way back after just two wins to show from ten games. Burnley score twice in the first ten minutes at Crystal Palace and Matt Lowton rounds off a 3-0 success with his first top-flight goal for seven years – a spectacular volley.

14 Pierre-Emerick Aubameyang's hat-trick and a two-goal full debut by Josh Maja take pride of place. The Arsenal captain passes 200 goals in Europe's top five leagues in the 4-2 victory over Leeds, who have Pascal Struijk on the mark for the first time. Maja, on loan from Bordeaux, delivers Fulham's first success in 13 matches – 2-0 against Everton – and the club's first-ever in the league at Goodison Park. Galatasaray loanee Mbaye Diagne opens his account for West Bromwich Albion in a 1-1 draw against Manchester United and spurns two further chances to match Aubameyang's treble. Southampton suffer a club-record sixth successive league defeat – 2-1 at home to Wolves, four days after beating them in the FA Cup. Manchester City go ten points clear after a 3-1 success at Everton and become the first team in English top-flight history to win their opening ten games in a calendar year.

20 Everton win the Merseyside derby at Anfield for the first time in 22 years. Goals by Richarlison and Gylfi Sigurdsson with a penalty deliver a 2-0 victory over Liverpool, who lose a fourth successive home league match for the first time since season 1923-24. They also lose Jordan Henderson with a groin injury. Fulham close to within three points of fourth-from-bottom Newcastle with a single goal success against Sheffield United, who look doomed. So do West Bromwich Albion after a goalless draw at Burnley in which last man Semi Ajayi is shown a straight red card for handling.

21 Raheem Sterling's header after 79 seconds is enough to maintain Manchester City's winning ways away to Arsenal. West Ham climb to fourth with a 2-1 win over Tottenham, opening up a nine-point advantage over their rivals, who suffer a fifth defeat in six matches and, like Arsenal, are marooned in mid-table. Bruno Fernandes seals Manchester United's 3-1 victory over Newcastle with his 17th successful penalty in 18 attempts for the club.

22 Jean-Philippe Mateta, on loan from Mainz, scores his first goal for the club and Christian Benetke volleys a 95th minute winner as Crystal Palace overcome Brighton, who have Joel Veltman on the scoresheet for the first time.

27 Manchester City set an English top-flight record of 20 straight wins in all competitions by defeating West Ham 2-1 with goals from centre-backs Ruben Dias, his first for the club, and John Stones. Brighton are left to rue a controversial refereeing decision – and their own wastefulness – after a 1-0 defeat at West Bromwich Albion. Lee Mason rules out a quickly-taken free-kick from Lewis Dunk, then decides the goal should stand and finally disallows it. Amid the chaos, Pascal Gross strikes a penalty against the bar and Danny Welbeck hits a post with his side's second spot-kick.

28 Gareth Bale scores twice and delivers a 60-yard pass for Harry Kane's goal as Tottenham overcome Burnley 4-0. On a successful day for north London, Arsenal come from behind to win 3-1 at Leicester. Manchester United fall further behind after a goalless draw with Chelsea, with Manchester City on 62 points, United on 50, followed by Leicester (49) and West Ham (45). At the bottom, Sheffield United have 11 points, West Bromwich Albion 17 and Fulham 23.

MARCH 2021

2 Manchester City score three goals in the final 13 minutes to defeat Wolves 4-1, Gabriel Jesus netting two of them.

3 Phil Jagielka has a yellow card upgraded to red after a VAR review of his tackle on Aston Villa's Anwar El Ghazi, but Sheffield United hold on to David McGoldrick's goal to record their fourth victory of the season.

4 Liverpool lose another home match, this time to Mason Mount's goal which puts Chelsea back in the mix for a Champions League place.

6 Southampton, with a single point to show from nine matches, halt the slide with a 2-0 victory away to Sheffield United, who have Chris Wilder in charge for the final time before he leaves Bramall Lane. Daniel Amartey's first goal for four-and-a-half years delivers a 2-1 scoreline for Leicester at Brighton, while Chris Wood's bizarre equaliser for Burnley earns a point against Arsenal as Granit Xhaka's wayward pass across the face of goal hits the New Zealander and flies into the net.

7 Bruno Fernandes, with a second-minute penalty, and Luke Shaw call time on Manchester City's record run of 21 successive wins. Manchester United's 2-0 success extends their own unbeaten sequence in Premier League away matches to 22. Two goals each from Gareth Bale and Harry Kane in the 4-1 defeat of Crystal Palace put Tottenham back in the Champions League running. But Liverpool fall further adrift after a sixth successive Anfield loss, this one to resurgent Fulham and their matchwinner Mario Lemina.

8 Thomas Tuchel becomes the first manager in Premier League history to record a clean sheet in his first five home matches as Chelsea defeat Everton 2-0.

10 Kevin De Bruyne and Riyad Mahrez both score twice in Manchester City's 5-2 victory over Southampton.

13 Sergio Aguero, a peripheral figure in Manchester City's season because of injury and illness, scores his first Premier League goal since January 2020 with a penalty to round off a 3-0 win at Fulham. Dwight McNeil's superb 25-yard strike for a 2-1 success at Everton takes Burnley out of immediate relegation trouble.

14 Kelechi Iheanacho records his first hat-trick for Leicester, who strengthen their grip on a Champions League place by beating Sheffield United 5-0. Erik Lamela puts Tottenham ahead at the Emirates with an audacious rabona-style goal, his kicking leg wrapped around his standing leg. The Argentinian is then dismissed for a second yellow card as Arsenal turn things around, thanks to loanee Martin Odegaard's first Premier League goal and Alexandre Lacazette's penalty. Leandro Trossard boosts Brighton's chances of beating the drop with the winner for 2-1 at Southampton.

15 Wolves goalkeeper Rui Patricio is carried off on a stretcher after colliding with team-mate Conor Coady during a 1-0 home defeat by Liverpool.

19 Loanee Joachim Andersen nets his first goal for Fulham, but a 2-1 home defeat by Leeds keeps his side in the bottom three.

20 Leandro Trossard scores another important goal for Brighton, paving the way for a 3-0 victory over Newcastle which puts Steve Bruce's side – and the manager himself – under severe pressure.

21 Jesse Lingard, with the fifth goal of his loan spell, launches West Ham into a 3-0 lead after 32 minutes against Arsenal, who retrieve the deficit for a commendable point with the help of own goals from Tomas Soucek and Craig Dawson. Carlos Vinicius records his first in the Premier League as Tottenham go some way to making up for a midweek Europa League exit – 2-0 away to Aston Villa. With eight matches to play, Manchester City (71) lead Manchester United (57), followed by Leicester (56) and Chelsea (51). At the bottom are Sheffield United (14), West Bromwich Albion (18) and Fulham (26), with Newcastle on 28.

APRIL 2021

3 West Bromwich Albion record an astonishing victory at Stamford Bridge, ending Thomas Tuchel's unbeaten 14-match start in all competitions as Chelsea manager with just two goals conceded. His side have Thiago Silva sent off for a second yellow card, two minutes after leading, and Albion take full advantage with a 5-2 victory to match their goals tally in the previous ten matches. Matheus Pereira and substitute Callum Robinson both score twice. Diogo Jota also comes off the bench to net twice as Liverpool move to within two points of Chelsea by outplaying Arsenal 3-0 at the Emirates. Manchester City sail on serenely as Benjamin Mendy marks a rare start with their first goal in a 2-0 success at Leicester.

4 Nathan Redmond completes Southampton's recovery from two goals down against Burnley for a 3-2 victory which takes them to the brink of safety. Fulham surrender the chance to move out of the bottom three, leading at Villa Park before a brace by substitute Trezeguet points the home side to a 3-1 win. Newcastle benefit thanks to substitute Joe Willock's 85th minute equaliser against Tottenham which comes 52 seconds after Harry Kane is within inches of a hat-trick to make the score 3-1.

9 A 92nd minute goal by Wolves winger Adama Traore, the only one of the match, inflicts a fourth successive defeat on Fulham.

10 Ten-man Leeds score a notable 2-1 victory over Manchester City at the Etihad after captain Liam Cooper is shown a straight red card for catching Gabriel Jesus with a raised boot on the stroke of half-time. Northern Ireland midfielder Stuart Dallas scores both their goals, the winner in stoppage-time. Christian Pulisic also strikes twice as Chelsea beat Crystal Palace 4-1. Trent Alexander-Arnold, dropped from Gareth Southgate's latest squad, impresses the watching England manager at Anfield with Liverpool's winner in added time for 2-1 against Aston Villa.

11 Jesse Lingard and Allan Saint-Maximin deliver outstanding performances in matches at opposite ends of the table. Gareth Southgate sees Lingard continue his prolific form for West Ham with two goals and an assist for Jarrod Bowen. On Mark Noble's 400th appearance for the club, they are 3-2 winners against Leicester, who omit James Maddison, Hamza Choudhury and Ayoze Perez from the squad for a breach of Covid regulations. Kelechi Iheanacho takes his tally to nine in six Premier League and FA Cup games with both their replies. Saint-Maximin puts Newcastle six points clear of the relegation zone with his second goal of a season hit by illness and injury, along with an assist for one by Jacob Murphy. They come from behind at Burnley to end a run of seven games without a victory. Manchester United also trail, but come through strongly in the second-half for a 3-1 success at Tottenham, where Ole Gunnar Solskjaer and Jose Mourinho have a sharp exchange of words after the United manager accuses Son Heung-min of 'conning' his side out of a goal. No arguments at Bramall Lane, where Alexandre Lacazette nets two in Arsenal's 3-0 victory over Sheffield United.

12 West Bromwich Albion follow up their victory at Stamford Bridge by beating Southampton 3-0 to keep alive slim hopes of beating the drop.

16 In Jose Mourinho's last match as Tottenham manager before his dismissal, Harry Kane limps off with an ankle injury after scoring twice in a 2-2 draw at Everton, whose two goals come from Gylfi Sigurdsson, the first a penalty.

17 Sheffield United's relegation is confirmed by a 1-0 defeat against Wolves, who have William Jose on the scoresheet for the first time. Newcastle are all but safe after an 82nd minute header from substitute Joe Willock delivers a 3-2 victory over West Ham, who have Craig Dawson sent off for a second yellow card, before retrieving a 2-0 deficit.

18 Fulham look set for the drop after conceding another late goal, this time in the seventh minute of stoppage-time to substitute Eddie Nketiah which gives Arsenal a 1-1 draw. Two by Mason Greenwood point Manchester United to a 3-1 victory over Burnley.

19 Hundreds of fans protest against plans for a European Super League outside Elland Road, where Leeds score an 87th minute equaliser through Diego Llorente, his first goal for the club, against Liverpool.

20 There are more protests at Stamford Bridge before Chelsea are held to a goalless draw by Brighton.

21 Interim manager Ryan Mason, at 29 the youngest to take charge of a Premier League team, makes a successful start when Son Heung-min's 90th minute penalty gives Tottenham a 2-1 victory over Southampton. Manchester City take another step towards the title by beating Aston Villa by the same scoreline after falling behind to John McGinn's goal in 20 seconds, joint fastest of the season. But City have John Stones ruled out of the League Cup Final when his yellow card for a knee-high challenge on Jacob Ramsey is upgraded to red on a VAR review. Villa's Matty Cash is sent off later for a second yellow.

22 West Bromwich Albion's spurt is ended by Leicester, who have Jamie Vardy back on the mark after seven league games without a goal in a 3-0 victory.

23 Arsenal supporters demonstrating against the club's involvement in the collapsed European Super League let off flares before a 1-0 defeat by Everton.

24 Chelsea's Timo Werner scores the only goal of the game against West Ham, their rivals for a Champions League place. A straight red card for West Ham's Fabian Balbuena for his challenge on Ben Chilwell is later overturned. Loanee Joe Willock comes off the bench to score for the third time for Newcastle, this goal a 95th minute equaliser at Liverpool. Chris Wood becomes the first New Zealander to score a Premier League hat-trick as Burnley record their biggest top-flight away win for 56 years – 4-0 against Wolves. West Bromwich Albion look doomed after Keinan Davis scores in stoppage-time to give Aston Villa a 2-2 draw.

26 Kelechi Iheanacho takes his tally to 14 goals in as many games in all competitions to move Leicester closer to confirming a top-four place with a 2-1 victory over Crystal Palace.

30 Southampton have Jannik Vestergaard shown a straight red card after ten minutes for bringing down Jamie Vardy, but hold Leicester to a 1-1 draw. Leicester remain third on 63 points behind Manchester City (77) and Manchester United (67), with Chelsea fourth on 58. At the bottom Sheffield United have 17, West Bromwich Albion 25 and Fulham 27

MAY 2021

1 Danny Welbeck executes an eye-catching Cruyff-turn to seal Brighton's 2-0 win over Leeds which extends their lead over Fulham to ten points. Scott Parker's side lose by the same scoreline to two Kai Havertz goals for Chelsea. Sergio Aguero, with a reminder of the finishing power which brought him legendary status at the club, puts Manchester City on the way to a 2-0 success at Crystal Palace and to within touching distance of the title.

2 On the day that Manchester United against Liverpool becomes the first Premier League game to be postponed because of protesting fans, Gareth Bale scores his first hat-trick for Tottenham since 2012, during his first spell at the club, in a 4-0 win over Sheffield United. Mohamed Elneny scores his first Premier League goal for Arsenal in their 2-0 victory over Newcastle, who have Fabian Schar shown a straight red card for clattering into Gabriel Martinelli.

3 Michail Antonio returns from injury with both goals in West Ham's 2-1 win at Burnley. Sam Allardyce admits West Bromwich Albion need a miracle to stay up after a 1-1 draw against Wolves.

7 Paul Dummett's first goal for five years, Joe Willock's fourth in four games, then two from Callum Wilson confirm Newcastle are safe with a 4-2 success away to Leicester.

8 Manchester City are presented with the opportunity to clinch the title against Champions League Final opponents Chelsea. But Sergio Aguero's gentle Panenka-style penalty is saved by Edouard Mendy and Chelsea come from behind to win 2-1 with a stoppage-time goal from Marcos Alonso. Thiago Alcantara's first goal for the club, in a 2-0 victory over Southampton, keeps alive Liverpool's chances of a top-four finish. Tottenham look to be out of the running after a 3-1 defeat at Leeds.

9 West Bromwich Albion go down and Sam Allardyce is relegated from the Premier League for the first time after a 3-1 defeat by Arsenal, completed by Willian's first goal for the club. Manchester United, playing the first of three matches in five days, come from behind for a record tenth time to win 3-1 away to Aston Villa, who have Ollie Watkins sent off for two yellow cards, the second for diving.

10 Fulham are relegated after losing 2-0 at home to Burnley, for whom Chris Wood scores his eighth goal in eight games.

11 Manchester City are crowned champions for the third time in four years after Manchester United's 2-1 defeat by Leicester leaves Ole Gunnar Solskjaer's side ten points adrift with three matches remaining. Solskjaer makes ten changes because of United's crowded schedule. Leicester's Luke Thomas, 19, scores his first league goal for Leicester. Danny Ings nets a brace in Southampton's 3-1 victory over Crystal Palace.

12 Chelsea falter in their bid to seal a top-four place, beaten 1-0 at home by Arsenal, who continue a late run for a Europa League spot.

13 Roberto Firmino, without a goal in three-and-a-half-months, nets two as Liverpool beat Manchester United 4-2 in in the clubs' rearranged fixture to press their challenge for a top-four place.

14 Ferran Torres scores a hat-trick as Manchester City set a record for the top four tiers of English football with a 12th successive Premier League away win – 4-3 against Newcastle.

15 Three players score for the first time for their clubs - Nathan Tella in Southampton's 3-1 win over Fulham; 18-year-old Fabio Carvalho with Fulham's consolation on his full debut; Said Benrahma in West Ham's 1-1 draw at Brighton. Rodrigo comes off the bench to net twice in a 4-0 victory for Leeds at Burnley.

16 Liverpool goalkeeper Alisson delivers one of the outstanding moments of the season, heading in Trent Alexander-Arnold's corner in the fifth minute of stoppage-time for a 2-1 victory at West Bromwich Albion. Sheffield United's Daniel Jebbison also has cause to celebrate after scoring the only goal at Everton. At 17 years and 309 days, he becomes the youngest player in Premier League history to score on his first start.

18 On a night when a limited number of spectators are allowed back, Chelsea turn the tables on Leicester after losing in the FA Cup Final, defeating their top-four rivals 2-1 with goals from Antonio Rudiger and Jorginho. Manchester City have Joao Cancelo shown a straight red card for bringing down Danny Welbeck and lose a two-goal lead to Brighton, who beat them 3-2.

19 Selhurst Park bids an emotional farewell to Roy Hodgson following the manager's announcement that he is stepping down at the end of the season. His final home match ends in defeat, with Arsenal continuing their successful late run 3-1. Sam Allardyce takes charge of his last home game for West Bromwich Albion – a 3-1 defeat by West Ham – after turning down the club's offer to stay on. And Harry Kane, having decided to leave Tottenham, makes his last home appearance in a 2-1 defeat by Aston Villa. Nat Phillips heads his first goal for the club as Liverpool win 3-0 at Burnley to return to the top-four at the expense of Leicester, who drop out for the first time. Joe Willock, 21, becomes the youngest Premier League player to score in six successive matches with the only goal against Sheffield United.

23 A dramatic final day of the season brings delight for Liverpool and Chelsea, despair for Kasper Schmeichel and Leicester – and a record-breaking farewell to the Premier League for Sergio Aguero. Jurgen Klopp's side are rewarded for an eighth win in ten matches, Sadio Mane's brace securing third place by a 2-0 win over Crystal Palace in Roy Hodgson's last appearance as Palace manager. Chelsea lose 2-1 at Villa Park and have captain Cesar

Azpilicueta shown a straight red card for catching Jack Grealish in the face. But they finish fourth ahead of Leicester, who are stripped of Champions League football for the second successive campaign. Eight days after their FA Cup triumph, they concede three times in the final 20 minutes to lose 4-2 at home to Tottenham – the first an own goal by Schmeichel attempting to punch away a corner. Harry Kane's 23rd earns him the Golden Boot and Gareth Bale nets twice as Tottenham stay ahead of Arsenal for a place in the new Europa League Conference. Leicester, whose two goals are Jamie Vardy penalties, head for the full Europa League, alongside West Ham, for whom Pablo Fornals is on the mark twice in a 3-0 success against Southampton. Aguero comes off the bench to score twice in Manchester City's 5-0 defeat of Everton and eclipse Wayne Rooney's record 183 goals for a single club. Despite a fifth straight win – 2-0 against Brighton – Arsenal miss out on Europe for the first time since season 1995-96. Joe Willock, one of their players, scores for the seventh successive match on loan at Newcastle – a 2-0 victory against Fulham. Another youngster, Manchester United's Anthony Elanga, records his first for the club in a 2-1 win over Wolves, who have Nuno Espirito Santo in charge for the final time.

HOW MANCHESTER CITY REGAINED THE TITLE

SEPTEMBER 2020

21 Wolves 1 (Raul Jimenez 78) Manchester City 3 (De Bruyne 20 pen, Foden 32, Gabriel Jesus 90+5)
27 Manchester City 2 (Mahrez 4, Ake 84) Leicester 5 (Vardy 37 pen, 54, 58 pen, Maddison 77, Tielemans 88 pen)

OCTOBER 2020

3   Leeds 1 (Rodrigo 59) Manchester City 1 (Sterling 17)
17 Manchester City 1 (Sterling 23) Arsenal 0
24 West Ham 1 (Antonio 18) Manchester City 1 (Foden 51)
31 Sheffield Utd 0 Manchester City 1 (Walker 28)

NOVEMBER 2020

8   Manchester City 1 (Gabriel Jesus 31) Liverpool 1 (Salah 13 pen)
21 Tottenham 2 (Son Heung-min 5, Lo Celso 65) Manchester City 0
27 Manchester City 5 (Mahrez 6, 22, 69, Mendy 41, Torres 66) Burnley 0

DECEMBER 2020

5   Manchester City 2 (Sterling 5, De Bruyne 26 pen) Fulham 0
11 Manchester Utd 0 Manchester City 0
15 Manchester City 1 (Gundogan 30) WBA 1 (Dias 43 og)
19 Southampton 0 Manchester City 1 (Sterling 16)
26 Manchester City 2 (Gundogan 14, Torres 55) Newcastle 0

JANUARY 2021

3   Chelsea 1 (Hudson-Odoi 90+2) Manchester City 3 (Gundogan 18, Foden 21, De Bruyne 34)
13 Manchester City 1 (Foden 72) Brighton 0
17 Manchester City 4 (Stones 26, 68, Gundogan 56, Sterling 88) Crystal Palace 0
20 Manchester City 2 (Bernardo Silva 79, Gundogan 90 pen) Aston Villa 0
26 WBA 0 Manchester City 5 (Gundogan 6, 30, Joao Cancelo 20, Mahrez 45, Sterling 57)
30 Manchester City 1 (Gabriel Jesus 9) Sheffield Utd 0

FEBRUARY 2021

3   Burnley 0 Manchester City 2 (Gabriel Jesus 3, Sterling 38)
7   Liverpool 1 (Salah 63 pen) Manchester City 4 (Gundogan 49, 73, Sterling 76, Foden 83)
13   Manchester City 3 (Rodri 22 pen, Gundogan 50, 66) Tottenham 0
17   Everton 1 (Richarlison 37) Manchester City 3 (Foden 32, Mahrez 63, Bernardo Silva 77)
20   Arsenal 0 Manchester City 1 (Sterling 2)
27   Manchester City 2 (Dias 30, Stones 68) West Ham 1 (Antonio 43)

MARCH 2021

2   Manchester City 4 (Dendoncker 15 og, Gabriel Jesus 80, 90+3, Mahrez 90) Wolves 1 (Coady 61)
7   Manchester City 0 Manchester Utd 2 (Bruno Fernandes 2 pen, Shaw 50)
10   Manchester City 5 (De Bruyne 15, 59, Mahrez 40, 55, Gundogan 45) Southampton 2 (Ward-Prowse 25 pen, Adams 56)
13   Fulham 0 Manchester City 3 (Stones 47, Gabriel Jesus 56, Aguero 60 pen)

APRIL 2021

3   Leicester 0 Manchester City 2 (Mendy 58, Gabriel Jesus 74)
10   Manchester City 1 (Torres 76) Leeds 2 (Dallas 42, 90+1)
21   Aston Villa 1 (McGinn 1) Manchester City 2 (Foden 22, Rodri 40)

MAY 2021

2   Crystal Palace 0 Manchester City 2 (Aguero 57, Torres 59)
8   Manchester City 1 (Sterling 44) Chelsea 2 (Ziyech 63, Marcos Alonso 90+2)
11   Manchester City clinched title, ten points ahead with three games remaining, after Manchester Utd lost to Leicester
14   Newcastle 3 (Krafth 25, Joelinton 45 pen, Willock 62) Manchester City 4 (Joao Cancelo 39, Torres 42, 64, 66)
18   Brighton 3 (Trossard 50, Webster 72, Burn 76) Manchester City 2 (Gundogan 2 Foden 48)
23   Manchester City 5 (De Bruyne 11, Gabriel Jesus 14, Foden 53, Aguero 71, 76) Everton 0

ENGLISH FOOTBALL LEAGUE PLAY-OFFS 2021

Thomas Frank led **Brentford** into the Premier League with a 2-0 victory over Swansea which he believes can inspire more smaller clubs to shoot for the stars. 'There should be a lot of others out there dreaming,' he said. 'Everything is possible if you work hard, have a clear strategy, a top attitude and togetherness.' Frank lost leading scorers Ollie Watkins and Said Benrahma from the side beaten by Fulham in the 2020 Championship final, but his side regrouped in the new Community Stadium, with Ivan Toney proving the ideal replacement. The former Peterborough striker scored 31 Championship goals and put them on the way at Wembley with a tenth minute penalty after goalkeeper Freddie Woodman brought down Bryan Mbeumo. Emiliano Marcondes finished superbly after 20 minutes, Toney struck the crossbar to underline superiority and Swansea's last chance went with a straight red card for Jay Fulton's challenge from behind on Mathias Jensen. It was 30 years since the first of Brentford's nine unsuccessful appearances in previous play-offs – and 74 years since the club last played in the top-flight. 'We have dreamed of this,' said Frank. 'It's a challenge we are now all relishing.' Australian midfielder Kenny Dougall, with a single goal to his name in the regular campaign, scored twice give **Blackpool** a 2-1 win over Lincoln in the League One Final. Both were eye-catching efforts from 20 yards, one with his right foot, the other with his left. They enabled his team to recover from conceding an Ollie Turton own goal after 47 seconds and continue a proud record as the most successful in the history of the play-offs with a sixth success. **Morecambe** reached the third tier for the first time by beating Newport 1-0 with an extra-time penalty from Senegal-born Carlos Mendes Gomes at the end of Derek Adams's first full season as manager. It was one of two controversial decisions by referee Bobby Madley, who turned down Newport appeals after goalkeeper Kyle Letheren collided with Scot Bennett. Some of the gloss was taken off when three days later Adams left to take over at Bradford.

SEMI-FINALS, FIRST LEG

CHAMPIONSHIP
Barnsley 0 **Swansea** 1 (Ayew 39). Att: 3,787. **Bournemouth** 1 (Danjuma55) **Brentford** 0. Att: 2,300

LEAGUE ONE
Lincoln 2 (Hopper 51, Johnson 77) **Sunderland** 0. Att: 3,145. **Oxford** 0 **Blackpool** 3 (Turton 23, Simms 26, 74). Att: 3,204

LEAGUE TWO
Newport 2 (Dolan 31, Collins 56) **Forest Green** 0. Att: 900. **Tranmere** 1 (Clarke 19) **Morecambe** 2 (Knight-Percival 15, McAlinden 45). Att: 3,00

SEMI-FINALS, SECOND LEG

CHAMPIONSHIP
Brentford 3 (Toney 16 pen, Janelt 50, Forss 81) **Bournemout**h 1 (Danjuma 5). Att: 3,830 (Brentford won 3-2 on agg). **Swansea** 1 (Grimes 39) **Barnsley** 1 (Woodrow 71). Att: 3,076 (Swansea won 2-1 on agg)

LEAGUE ONE
Blackpool 3 (Embleton 11, Dougall 13, Yates 54) **Oxford** 3 (Taylor 7, Atkinson 52, Shodipo 74). Att: 4,000 (Blackpool won 6-3 on agg). **Sunderland** 2 (Stewart 13, Wyke 33) **Lincoln** 1 (Hopper 56). Att: 10,000 (Lincoln won 3-2 on agg)

LEAGUE TWO
Forest Green 4 (Adams 7, Collins 8, Cadden 53, Matt 87) **Newport** 3 (Ellison 70, Labadie 76, Maynard 119). Att: 1,100 (aet, Newport won 5-4 on agg). **Morecambe** 1 (Wildig 9) **Tranmere** 1 (Vaughan 53). Att: 1,558 (Morecambe won 3-2 on agg)

FINALS

CHAMPIONSHIP – SATURDAY, MAY 29, 2021
Brentford 2 (Toney 10 pen, Marcondes 20) **Swansea City** 0. Att: 11,689 (Wembley)
Brentford (3-5-2): Raya, Dalsgaard, Jansson (capt) (Reid 79), Pinnock, Roerslev, Jensen, Janelt (Ghoddos 74), Marcondes (Bidstrup 90), Canos (Forss 74), Mbeumo, Toney. **Subs not used:** Daniels, Norgaard, Fosu, Goode, Stevens. **Booked:** Marcondes, Janelt. **Manager:** Thomas Frank
Swansea City (3-1-4-2): Woodman, Naughton (Cullen 60), Cabango, Guehi, Grimes (capt), Roberts, Fulton, Hourihane (Dhanda 63), Bidwell (Manning 82), Ayew, Lowe. **Subs not used:** Hamer, Bennett, Smith, Whittaker, Latibeaudiere, Freeman. **Booked:** Grimes. **Sent off:** Fulton (65). **Manager:** Steve Cooper
Referee: Chris Kavanagh (Lancs). **Half-time:** 2-0

LEAGUE ONE – SUNDAY, MAY 30, 2021
Blackpool 2 (Dougall 34, 54) **Lincoln City** 1 (Turton og 1). Att: 9,751 (Wembley)
Blackpool (4-4-2): Maxwell (capt), Turton, Ballard, Husband, Garbutt, Mitchell (Madine 69), Stewart, Dougall, Anderson (Ward 79), Embleton (Hamilton 79), Yates (Thorniley 90). **Subs not used:** Moore, Gabriel, Ekpiteta. **Booked:** Garbutt, Ballard, Husband, Dougall. **Manager:** Neil Critchley

Lincoln City (4-3-3): Palmer, Poole, Eyoma, Walsh (Montsma 88), Tayo Edun, Bridcutt (capt), McGrandles, Grant (Scully 80), Johnson, Hopper (Morton 63), Rogers. **Subs not used**: Long, Sanders, Bramall, Anderson. **Booked**: Bridcutt. **Manager**: Michael Appleton
Referee: Tony Harrington (Cleveland). **Half-time**: 1-1

LEAGUE TWO – MONDAY, MAY 31, 2021

Morecambe 1 (Mendes Gomes 107 pen) **Newport County** 0. Att: 9,083 (Wembley) – aet
Morecambe (4-1-4-1): Letheren, Cooney, Lavelle (capt), Knight-Percival, Gibson (Mellor 106), Songo'o, McAlinden (Lyons 75), Wildig (O'Sullivan 90), Diagouraga, Mendes Gomes (Kenyon 114), Stockton. **Subs not used**: Halstead, Davis, Pringle. **Booked**: Mendes Gomes, O'Sullivan, Cooney. **Manager**: Derek Adams
Newport County (3-5-2): King, Shephard, Dolan (Hartigan 65), Demetriou, Lewis (Taylor 62), Labadie (capt), Sheehan, Bennett, Haynes (Farquharson 111), Amond (Maynard 80), Collins (Ellison 86). **Subs not used**: Townsend, Ledley. **Booked**: Labadie, Demetrious. **Manager**: Michael Flynn
Referee: Bobby Madley (West Yorks). **Half-time**: 0-0

PLAY-OFF FINALS – HOME & AWAY

1987: Divs 1/2: Charlton beat Leeds 2-1 in replay (Birmingham) after 1-1 agg (1-0h, 0-1a). Charlton remained in Div 1 Losing semi-finalists: Ipswich and Oldham. **Divs 2/3: Swindon** beat Gillingham 2-0 in replay (Crystal Palace) after 2-2 agg (0-1a, 2-1h). Swindon promoted to Div 2. Losing semi-finalists: Sunderland and Wigan; Sunderland relegated to Div 3. **Divs 3/4: Aldershot** beat Wolves 3-0 on agg (2-0h, 1-0a) and promoted to Div 3. Losing semi-finalists: Bolton and Colchester; Bolton relegated to Div 4

1988: Divs 1/2: Middlesbrough beat Chelsea 2-1 on agg (2-0h, 0-1a) and promoted to Div 1; Chelsea relegated to Div 2. Losing semi-finalists: Blackburn and Bradford City. **Divs 2/3: Walsall** beat Bristol City 4-0 in replay (h) after 3-3 agg (3-1a, 0-2h) and promoted to Div 2. Losing semi-finalists: Sheffield Utd and Notts County; Sheffield Utd relegated to Div 3. **Divs 3/4: Swansea** beat Torquay 5-4 on agg (2-1h, 3-3a) and promoted to Div 3. Losing semi-finalists: Rotherham and Scunthorpe.; Rotherham relegated to Div 4

1989: Div 2: Crystal Palace beat Blackburn 4-3 on agg (1-3a, 3-0h). Losing semi-finalists: Watford and Swindon. **Div 3: Port Vale** beat Bristol Rovers 2-1 on agg (1-1a, 1-0h). Losing semi-finalists: Fulham and Preston **Div.4:** Leyton Orient beat Wrexham 2-1 on agg (0-0a, 2-1h). Losing semi-finalists: Scarborough and Scunthorpe

PLAY-OFF FINALS AT WEMBLEY

1990: Div 2: Swindon 1 Sunderland 0 (att: 72,873). Swindon promoted, then demoted for financial irregularities; Sunderland promoted. Losing semi-finalists: Blackburn and Newcastle Utd **Div 3: Notts County** 2 Tranmere 0 (att: 29,252). Losing semi-finalists: Bolton and Bury. **Div 4: Cambridge Utd** 1 Chesterfield 0 (att: 26,404). Losing semi-finalists: Maidstone and Stockport County

1991: Div 2: Notts County 3 Brighton 1 (att: 59,940). Losing semi-finalists: Middlesbrough and Millwall. **Div 3: Tranmere** 1 Bolton 0 (att: 30,217). Losing semi-finalists: Brentford and Bury. **Div 4: Torquay 2** Blackpool 2 – Torquay won 5-4 on pens (att: 21,615). Losing semi-finalists: Burnley and Scunthorpe

1992: Div 2: Blackburn 1 Leicester 0 (att: 68,147). Losing semi-finalists: Derby and Cambridge Utd. **Div 3: Peterborough** 2 Stockport 1 (att: 35,087). Losing semi-finalists: Huddersfield and Stoke. **Div 4: Blackpool** 1 Scunthorpe 1 aet, Blackpool won 4-3 on pens (att: 22,741). Losing semi-finalists: Barnet and Crewe

1993: Div 1: Swindon 4 Leicester 3 (att: 73,802). Losing semi-finalists: Portsmouth and Tranmere. **Div 2: WBA** 3 Port Vale 0 (att: 53,471). Losing semi-finalists: Stockport and

Swansea. **Div 3: York** 1 Crewe 1 aet, York won 5-3 on pens (att: 22,416). Losing semi-finalists: Bury and Walsall

1994: Div 1: Leicester 2 Derby 1 (att: 73,671). Losing semi-finalists: Millwall and Tranmere. **Div 2: Burnley** 2 Stockport 1 (att: 44,806). Losing semi-finalists: Plymouth Argyle and York. **Div 3: Wycombe** 4 Preston 2 (att: 40,109). Losing semi-finalists: Carlisle and Torquay

1995: Div 1: Bolton 4 Reading 3 (att: 64,107). Losing semi-finalists: Tranmere and Wolves. **Div 2: Huddersfield** 2 Bristol Rov 1 (att: 59,175). Losing semi-finalists: Brentford and Crewe. **Div 3: Chesterfield** 2 Bury 0 (att: 22,814). Losing semi-finalists: Mansfield and Preston

1996: Div 1: Leicester 2 Crystal Palace 1 aet (att: 73,573). Losing semi-finalists: Charlton and Stoke. **Div 2: Bradford City** 2 Notts Co 0 (att: 39,972). Losing semi-finalists: Blackpool and Crewe. **Div 3: Plymouth Argyle** 1 Darlington 0 (att: 43,431). Losing semi-finalists: Colchester and Hereford

1997: Div 1: Crystal Palace 1 Sheffield Utd 0 (att: 64,383). Losing semi-finalists: Ipswich and Wolves. **Div 2: Crewe** 1 Brentford 0 (att: 34,149). Losing semi-finalists: Bristol City and Luton. **Div 3: Northampton** 1 Swansea 0 (att: 46,804). Losing semi-finalists: Cardiff and Chester

1998: Div 1: Charlton 4 Sunderland 4 aet, Charlton won 7-6 on pens (att: 77, 739). Losing semi-finalists: Ipswich and Sheffield Utd. **Div 2: Grimsby** 1 Northampton 0 (att: 62,988). Losing semi-finalists: Bristol Rov and Fulham. **Div 3: Colchester** 1 Torquay 0 (att: 19,486). Losing semi-finalists: Barnet and Scarborough

1999: Div 1: Watford 2 Bolton 0 (att: 70,343). Losing semi-finalists: Ipswich and Birmingham. **Div 2: Manchester City** 2 Gillingham 2 aet, Manchester City won 3-1 on pens (att: 76,935). Losing semi-finalists: Preston and Wigan. **Div 3: Scunthorpe** 1 Leyton Orient 0 (att: 36,985). Losing semi-finalists: Rotherham and Swansea

2000: Div 1: Ipswich 4 Barnsley 2 (att: 73,427). Losing semi-finalists: Birmingham and Bolton. **Div 2: Gillingham** 3 Wigan 2 aet (att: 53,764). Losing semi-finalists: Millwall and Stoke. **Div 3: Peterborough** 1 Darlington 0 (att: 33,383). Losing semi-finalists: Barnet and Hartlepool

PLAY-OFF FINALS AT MILLENNIUM STADIUM

2001: Div 1: Bolton 3 Preston 0 (att: 54,328). Losing semi-finalists: Birmingham and WBA. **Div 2: Walsall** 3 Reading 2 aet (att: 50,496). Losing semi-finalists: Stoke and Wigan. **Div 3: Blackpool** 4 Leyton Orient 2 (att: 23,600). Losing semi-finalists: Hartlepool and Hull

2002: Div 1: Birmingham 1 Norwich 1 aet, Birmingham won 4-2 on pens, (att: 71,597). Losing semi-finalists: Millwall and Wolves. **Div 2: Stoke** 2 Brentford 0 (att: 42,523). Losing semi-finalists: Cardiff and Huddersfield. **Div 3: Cheltenham** 3 Rushden & Diamonds 1 (att: 24,368). Losing semi-finalists: Hartlepool and Rochdale

2003: Div 1: Wolves 3 Sheffield Utd 0 (att: 69,473). Losing semi-finalists: Nott'm Forest and Reading. **Div 2: Cardiff** 1 QPR. 0 aet (att: 66,096). Losing semi-finalists: Bristol City and Oldham. **Div 3: Bournemouth** 5 Lincoln 2 (att: 32,148). Losing semi-finalists: Bury and Scunthorpe

2004: Div 1: Crystal Palace 1 West Ham 0 (att: 72,523). Losing semi-finalists: Ipswich and Sunderland. **Div 2: Brighton** 1 Bristol City 0 (att: 65,167). Losing semi-finalists: Hartlepool and Swindon. **Div 3: Huddersfield** 0 Mansfield 0 aet, Huddersfield won 4-1 on pens (att: 37,298). Losing semi-finalists: Lincoln and Northampton

2005: Championship: West Ham 1 Preston 0 (att: 70,275). Losing semifinalists: Derby Co and Ipswich. **League 1: Sheffield Wed** 4 Hartlepool 2 aet (att: 59,808). Losing semi-finalists: Brentford and Tranmere **League 2: Southend** 2 Lincoln 0 aet (att: 19532). Losing semi-finalists: Macclesfield and Northampton

2006: Championship: Watford 3 Leeds 0 (att: 64,736). Losing semi-finalists: Crystal Palace and Preston. **League 1: Barnsley** 2 Swansea 2 aet (att: 55,419), Barnsley won 4-3 on pens.

Losing semi-finalists: Huddersfield and Brentford. **League 2: Cheltenham** 1 Grimsby 0 (att: 29,196). Losing semi-finalists: Wycombe and Lincoln

PLAY-OFF FINALS AT WEMBLEY

2007: Championship: Derby 1 WBA 0 (att: 74,993). Losing semi-finalists: Southampton and Wolves. **League 1: Blackpool** 2 Yeovil 0 (att: 59,313). Losing semi-finalists: Nottm Forest and Oldham. **League 2: Bristol Rov** 3 Shrewsbury 1 (att: 61,589). Losing semi-finalists: Lincoln and MK Dons

2008: Championship: Hull 1 Bristol City 0 (att: 86,703). Losing semi-finalists: Crystal Palace and Watford. **League 1: Doncaster** 1 Leeds 0 (att: 75,132). Losing semi-finalists: Carlisle and Southend. **League 2: Stockport** 3 Rochdale 2 (att: 35,715). Losing semi-finalists: Darlington and Wycombe

2009: Championship: Burnley 1 Sheffield Utd 0 (att: 80,518). Losing semi-finalists: Preston and Reading. **League 1: Scunthorpe** 3 Millwall 2 (att: 59,661). Losing semi-finalists: Leeds and MK Dons. **League 2: Gillingham** 1 Shrewsbury 0 (att: 53,706). Losing semi-finalists: Bury and Rochdale

2010: Championship: Blackpool 3 Cardiff 2 (att: 82,244). Losing semi-finalists: Leicester and Nottm Forest. **League 1: Millwall** 1 Swindon 0 (att:73,108). Losing semi-finalists: Charlton and Huddersfield. **League 2: Dagenham & Redbridge** 3 Rotherham 2 (att: 32,054). Losing semi-finalists: Aldershot and Morecambe

2011: Championship: Swansea 4 Reading 2 (att: 86,581). Losing semi-finalists: Cardiff and Nottm Forest. **League 1: Peterborough** 3 Huddersfield 0 (Old Trafford, att:48,410). Losing semi-finalists: Bournemouth and MK Dons. **League 2: Stevenage** 1 Torquay 0 (Old Trafford, att: 11,484. Losing semi-finalists: Accrington and Shrewsbury

2012: Championship: West Ham 2 Blackpool 1 (att: 78,523). Losing semi-finalists: Birmingham and Cardiff. **League 1: Huddersfield** 0 Sheffield Utd 0 aet, Huddersfield won 8-7 on pens (att: 52,100). Losing semi-finalists: MK Dons and Stevenage. **League 2: Crewe** 2 Cheltenham 0 (att: 24,029). Losing semi-finalists: Southend and Torquay

2013: Championship: Crystal Palace 1 Watford 0 (att: 82,025). Losing semi-finalists: Brighton and Leicester. **League 1: Yeovil** 2 Brentford 1 (att: 41,955). Losing semi-finalists: Sheffield Utd and Swindon. **League 2: Bradford** 3 Northampton 0 (att: 47,127). Losing semi-finalists: Burton and Cheltenham

2014: Championship: QPR 1 Derby 0 (att: 87,348). Losing semi-finalists: Brighton and Wigan. **League 1: Rotherham** 2 Leyton Orient 2 aet, Rotherham won 4-3 on pens (att: 43,401). Losing semi-finalists: Peterborough and Preston. **League 2: Fleetwood** 1 Burton 0 (att: 14,007). Losing semi-finalists: Southend and York

2015: Championship: Norwich 2 Middlesbrough 0 (att: 85,656). Losing semi-finalists: Brentford and Ipswich. **League 1: Preston** 4 Swindon 0 (att: 48,236). Losing semi-finalists: Chesterfield and Sheffield Utd. **League 2: Southend** 1 Wycombe 1 aet, Southend won 7-6 on pens (att: 38,252). Losing semi-finalists: Stevenage and Plymouth

2016: Championship: Hull 1 Sheffield Wed 0 (att 70,189). Losing semi-finalists: Brighton and Derby. **League 1: Barnsley** 3 Millwall 1 (att 51,277). Losing semi-finalists: Bradford and Walsall. **League 2: AFC Wimbledon** 2 Plymouth 0 (att 57,956). Losing semi-finalists: Accrington and Portsmouth)

2017: Championship: Huddersfield 0 Reading 0 aet, Huddersfield won 4-3 on pens (att 76,682). Losing semi-finalists: Fulham and Sheffield Wed. **League 1: Millwall** 1 Bradford 0 (att 53,320. Losing semi-finals: Fleetwood and Scunthorpe. **League 2: Blackpool** 2 Exeter 1 (att 23,380). Losing semi-finalists: Carlisle and Luton

2018: Championship: Fulham 1 Aston Villa 0 (att 85,243). Losing semi-finalists: Derby and Middlesbrough. **League 1: Rotherham** 2 Shrewsbury 1 (att 26,218). Losing semi-finalists: Charlton and Scunthorpe. **League 2: Coventry** 3 Exeter 1. Losing semi-finalists: Lincoln and Notts Co

2019: Championship: Aston Villa 2 Derby 1 (85,826). Losing semi-finalists: Leeds and WBA. **League 1: Charlton** 2 Sunderland 1 (76,155). Losing semi-finalists: Doncaster and Portsmouth. **League 2: Tranmere** 1 Newport 0, aet (25,217 Losing semi-finalists: Forest Green and Mansfield

2020: Championship: Fulham 2 Brentford 1 (no att). Losing semi-finalists: Cardiff and Swansea. **League 1: Wycombe** 2 Oxford 1 (no att). Losing semi-finalists: Fleetwood and Portsmouth. **League 2: Northampton** 4 Exeter 0 (no att). Losing semi-finalists: Cheltenham and Colchester

HISTORY OF THE PLAY-OFFS

Play-off matches were introduced by the Football League to decide final promotion and relegation issues at the end of season 1986-87. A similar series styled 'Test Matches' had operated between Divisions One and Two for six seasons from 1893-98, and was abolished when both divisions were increased from 16 to 18 clubs.

Eighty-eight years later, the play-offs were back in vogue. In the first three seasons (1987-88-89), the Finals were played home-and-away, and since they were made one-off matches in 1990, they have featured regularly in Wembley's spring calendar, until the old stadium closed its doors and the action switched to the Millennium Stadium in Cardiff in 2001.

Through the years, these have been the ups and downs of the play-offs:

1987: Initially, the 12 clubs involved comprised the one that finished directly above those relegated in Divisions One, Two and Three and the three who followed the sides automatically promoted in each section. Two of the home-and-away Finals went to neutral-ground replays, in which **Charlton** clung to First Division status by denying Leeds promotion while **Swindon** beat Gillingham to complete their climb from Fourth Division to Second in successive seasons, via the play-offs, Sunderland fell into the Third and Bolton into Division Four, both for the first time. **Aldershot** went up after finishing only sixth in Division Four; in their Final, they beat Wolves, who had finished nine points higher and missed automatic promotion by one point.

1988: Chelsea were relegated from the First Division after losing on aggregate to **Middlesbrough**, who had finished third in Division Two. So Middlesbrough, managed by Bruce Rioch, completed the rise from Third Division to First in successive seasons, only two years after their very existence had been threatened by the bailiffs. Also promoted via the play-offs: **Walsall** from Division Three and **Swansea** from the Fourth. Relegated, besides Chelsea: Sheffield Utd (to Division Three) and Rotherham (to Division Four).

1989: After two seasons of promotion-relegation play-offs, the system was changed to involve the four clubs who had just missed automatic promotion. That format has remained. Steve Coppell's **Crystal Palace**, third in Division Two, returned to the top flight after eight years, beating Blackburn 4-3 on aggregate after extra time. Similarly, **Port Vale** confirmed third place in Division Three with promotion via the play-offs. For **Leyton Orient**, promotion seemed out of the question in Division Four when they stood 15th on March 1. But eight wins and a draw in the last nine home games swept them to sixth in the final table, and two more home victories in the play-offs completed their season in triumph.

1990: The play-off Finals now moved to Wembley over three days of the Spring Holiday week-end. On successive afternoons, **Cambridge Utd** won promotion from Division Four and **Notts Co** from the Third. Then, on Bank Holiday Monday, the biggest crowd for years at a Football League fixture (72,873) saw Ossie Ardiles' **Swindon** beat Sunderland 1-0 to reach the First Division for the first time. A few weeks later, however, Wembley losers **Sunderland** were promoted instead, by default; Swindon were found guilty of "financial irregularities" and stayed in Division Two.

1991: Again, the season's biggest League crowd (59,940) gathered at Wembley for the First Division Final in which **Notts Co** (having missed promotion by one point) still fulfilled their ambition, beating Brighton 3-1. In successive years, County had climbed from Third Division to First via the play-offs – the first club to achieve double promotion by this route. Bolton were denied automatic promotion in Division Three on goal difference, and lost at Wembley to an extra-time goal by **Tran-**

mere. The Fourth Division Final made history, with Blackpool beaten 5-4 on penalties by **Torquay** – first instance of promotion being decided by a shoot-out. In the table, Blackpool had finished seven points ahead of Torquay.

1992: Wembley that Spring Bank Holiday was the turning point in the history of **Blackburn**. Bolstered by Kenny Dalglish's return to management and owner Jack Walker's millions, they beat Leicester 1-0 by Mike Newell's 45th-minute penalty to achieve their objective – a place in the new Premier League. Newell, who also missed a second-half penalty, had recovered from a broken leg just in time for the play-offs. In the Fourth Division Final **Blackpool** (denied by penalties the previous year) this time won a shoot-out 4-3 against Scunthorpe., who were unlucky in the play-offs for the fourth time in five years. **Peterborough** climbed out of the Third Division for the first time, beating Stockport County 2-1 at Wembley.

1993: The crowd of 73,802 at Wembley to see **Swindon** beat Leicester 4-3 in the First Division Final was 11,000 bigger than that for the FA Cup Final replay between Arsenal and Sheffield Wed Leicester rallied from three down to 3-3 before Paul Bodin's late penalty wiped away **Swindon**'s bitter memories of three years earlier, when they were denied promotion after winning at Wembley. In the Third Division Final, **York** beat Crewe 5-3 in a shoot-out after a 1-1 draw, and in the Second Division decider, **WBA** beat Port Vale 3-0. That was tough on Vale, who had finished third in the table with 89 points – the highest total never to earn promotion in any division. They had beaten Albion twice in the League, too.

1994: Wembley's record turn-out of 158,586 spectators at the three Finals started with a crowd of 40,109 to see Martin O'Neill's **Wycombe** beat Preston 4-2. They thus climbed from Conference to Second Division with successive promotions. **Burnley**'s 2-1 victory in the Second Division Final was marred by the sending-off of two Stockport players, and in the First Division decider **Leicester** came from behind to beat Derby Co and end the worst Wembley record of any club. They had lost on all six previous appearances there – four times in the FA Cup Final and in the play-offs of 1992 and 1993.

1995: Two months after losing the Coca-Cola Cup Final to Liverpool, Bruce Rioch's **Bolton** were back at Wembley for the First Division play-off Final. From two goals down to Reading in front of a crowd of 64,107, they returned to the top company after 15 years, winning 4-3 with two extra-time goals. **Huddersfield** ended the first season at their new £15m. home with promotion to the First Division via a 2-1 victory against Bristol Rov – manager Neil Warnock's third play-off success (after two with Notts Co). Of the three clubs who missed automatic promotion by one place, only **Chesterfield** achieved it in the play-offs, comfortably beating Bury 2-0.

1996: Under new manager Martin O'Neill (a Wembley play-off winner with Wycombe in 1994), **Leicester** returned to the Premiership a year after leaving it. They had finished fifth in the table, but in the Final came from behind to beat third-placed Crystal Palace by Steve Claridge's shot in the last seconds of extra time. In the Second Division **Bradford City** came sixth, nine points behind Blackpool (3rd), but beat them (from two down in the semi-final first leg) and then clinched promotion by 2-0 v Notts County at Wembley. It was City's greatest day since they won the Cup in 1911. **Plymouth Argyle** beat Darlington in the Third Division Final to earn promotion a year after being relegated. It was manager Neil Warnock's fourth play-off triumph in seven seasons after two with Notts County (1990 and 1991) and a third with Huddersfield in 1995.

1997: High drama at Wembley as **Crystal Palace** left it late against Sheffield Utd in the First Division play-off final. The match was scoreless until the last 10 seconds when David Hopkin lobbed Blades' keeper Simon Tracey from 25 yards to send the Eagles back to the Premiership after two seasons of Nationwide action. In the Second Division play-off final, **Crewe** beat Brentford 1-0 courtesy of a Shaun Smith goal. **Northampton** celebrated their first Wembley appearance with a 1-0 victory over Swansea thanks to John Frain's injury-time free-kick in the Third Division play-off final.

1998: In one of the finest games ever seen at Wembley, **Charlton** eventually triumphed 7-6 on penalties over Sunderland. For Charlton, Wearside-born Clive Mendonca scored a hat-trick and Richard Rufus his first career goal in a match that lurched between joy and despair for both sides as it ended 4-4. Sunderland defender Michael Gray's superb performance ill deserved to end with his weakly struck spot kick being saved by Sasa Ilic. In the Third Division, the penalty spot also had a role to play, as **Colchester**'s David Gregory scored the only goal to defeat Torquay, while in the Second Division a Kevin Donovan goal gave **Grimsby** victory over Northampton.

1999: Elton John, watching via a personal satellite link in Seattle, saw his **Watford** side overcome Bolton 2-0 to reach the Premiership. Against technically superior opponents, Watford prevailed with application and teamwork. They also gave Bolton a lesson in finishing through match-winners by Nick Wright and Allan Smart. **Manchester City** staged a remarkable comeback to win the Second Division Final after trailing to goals by Carl Asaba and Robert Taylor for Gillingham. Kevin Horlock and Paul Dickov scored in stoppage time and City went on to win on penalties. A goal by Spaniard Alex Calvo-Garcia earned **Scunthorpe** a 1-0 success against Leyton Orient in the Third Division Final.

2000: After three successive play-off failures, **Ipswich** finally secured a place in the Premiership. They overcame the injury loss of leading scorer David Johnson to beat Barnsley 4-2 with goals by 36-year-old Tony Mowbray, Marcus Stewart and substitutes Richard Naylor and Martijn Reuser. With six minutes left of extra-time in the Second Division Final, **Gillingham** trailed Wigan 2-1. But headers by 38-year-old player-coach Steve Butler and fellow substitute Andy Thomson gave them a 3-2 victory. Andy Clarke, approaching his 33rd birthday, scored the only goal of the Third Division decider for **Peterborough** against Darlington.

2001: **Bolton**, unsuccessful play-off contenders in the two previous seasons, made no mistake at the third attempt. They flourished in the new surroundings of the Millennium Stadium to beat Preston 3-0 with goals by Gareth Farrelly, Michael Ricketts – his 24th of the season – and Ricardo Gardner to reach the Premiership. **Walsall**, relegated 12 months earlier, scored twice in a three-minute spell of extra time to win 3-2 against Reading in the Second Division Final, while **Blackpool** capped a marked improvement in the second half of the season by overcoming Leyton Orient 4-2 in the Third Division Final.

2002: Holding their nerve to win a penalty shoot-out 4-2, **Birmingham** wiped away the memory of three successive defeats in the semi-finals of the play-offs to return to the top division after an absence of 16 years. Substitute Darren Carter completed a fairy-tale first season as a professional by scoring the fourth spot-kick against Norwich. **Stoke** became the first successful team to come from the south dressing room in 12 finals since football was adopted by the home of Welsh rugby, beating Brentford 2-0 in the Second Division Final with Deon Burton's strike and a Ben Burgess own goal. Julian Alsop's 26th goal of the season helped **Cheltenham** defeat League newcomers Rushden & Diamonds 3-1 in the Third Division decider.

2003: Wolves benefactor Sir Jack Hayward finally saw his £60m investment pay dividends when the club he first supported as a boy returned to the top flight after an absence of 19 years by beating Sheffield Utd 3-0. It was also a moment to savour for manager Dave Jones, who was forced to leave his previous club Southampton because of child abuse allegations, which were later found to be groundless. **Cardiff**, away from the game's second tier for 18 years, returned with an extra-time winner from substitute Andy Campbell against QPR after a goalless 90 minutes in the Division Two Final. **Bournemouth**, relegated 12 months earlier, became the first team to score five in the end-of-season deciders, beating Lincoln 5-2 in the Division Three Final.

2004: Three tight, tense Finals produced only two goals, the lowest number since the Play-offs were introduced. One of them, scored by Neil Shipperley, gave **Crystal Palace** victory over West Ham, the much-travelled striker tapping in a rebound after Stephen Bywater parried Andy Johnson's shot. It completed a remarkable transformation for Crystal Palace, who were 19th in the table when Iain Dowie left Oldham to become their manager. **Brighton** made an immediate return to Division One in a poor game against Bristol City which looked set for extra-time until Leon Knight netted his 27th goal of the campaign from the penalty spot after 84 minutes. **Huddersfield** also went back up at the first attempt, winning the Division Three Final in a penalty shoot-out after a goalless 120 minutes against Mansfield.

2005: Goals were few and far between for Bobby Zamora during **West Ham**'s Championship season – but what a difference in the Play-offs. The former Brighton and Tottenham striker scored three times in the 4-2 aggregate win over Ipswich in the semi-finals and was on the mark again with the only goal against Preston at the Millennium Stadium. **Sheffield Wed** were eight minute away from defeat against Hartlepool in the League One decider when Steven MacLean made it 2-2 from the penalty spot and they went on to win 4-2 in extra-time. **Southend**, edged out of an automatic promotion place, won the League Two Final 2-0 against Lincoln, Freddy Eastwood scoring their first in extra-time and making the second for Duncan Jupp. **Carlisle** beat Stevenage 1-0 with a goal by Peter Murphy in the Conference Final to regain their League place 12 months after being relegated.

2006: From the moment Marlon King scored his 22nd goal of the season to set up a 3-0 win over Crystal Palace in the semi-final first leg, **Watford** had the conviction of a team going places. Sure enough, they went on to beat Leeds just as comfortably in the final. Jay DeMerit, who was playing non-league football 18 months earlier, headed his side in front. James Chambers fired in a shot that hit a post and went in off goalkeeper Neil Sullivan. Then Darius Henderson put away a penalty after King was brought down by Shaun Derry, the man whose tackle had ended Boothroyd's playing career at the age of 26. **Barnsley** beat Swansea on penalties in the League One Final, Nick Colgan making the vital save from Alan Tate, while Steve Guinan's goal earned **Cheltenham** a 1-0 win over Grimsby in the League Two Final. **Hereford** returned to the Football League after a nine-year absence with Ryan Green's extra-time winner against Halifax in the Conference Final.

2007: Record crowds, plenty of goals and a return to Wembley for the finals made for some eventful and entertaining matches. Stephen Pearson, signed from Celtic for £650,000 in the January transfer window, took **Derby** back to the Premier League after an absence of five seasons with a 61st minute winner, his first goal for the club, against accounted for West Bromwich Albion. It was third time lucky for manager Billy Davies, who had led Preston into the play-offs, without success, in the two previous seasons. **Blackpool** claimed a place in the game's second tier for the first time for 30 years by beating Yeovil 2-0 – their tenth successive victory in a remarkable end-of-season run. Richard Walker took his tally for the season to 23 with two goals for **Bristol Rov**, who beat Shrewsbury 3-1 in the League Two Final. Sammy McIlroy, who led Macclesfield into the league in 1997, saw his Morecambe side fall behind in the Conference Final against Exeter, but they recovered to win 2-1.

2008: Wembley has produced some unlikely heroes down the years, but rarely one to match 39-year-old Dean Windass. The **Hull** striker took his home-town club into the top-flight for the first time with the only goal of the Championship Final against Bristol City – and it was a goal fit to grace any game. In front of a record crowd for the final of 86,703, Fraizer Campbell, his 20-year-old partner up front, picked out Windass on the edge of the penalty box and a sweetly-struck volley flew into the net. **Doncaster**, who like Hull faced an uncertain future a few years earlier, beat Leeds 1-0 in the League One Final with a header by James Hayter from Brian Stock's corner. Jim Gannon had lost four Wembley finals with **Stockport** as a player, but his first as manager brought a 3-2 win against Rochdale in the League Two Final with goals by Anthony Pilkington and Liam Dickinson and a Nathan Stanton own goal. Exeter's 1-0 win over Cambridge United in the Conference Final took them back into the Football League after an absence of five years.

2009: Delight for Burnley, back in the big time after 33 years thanks to a fine goal from 20 yards by Wade Elliott, and for their town which became the smallest to host Premier League football. Despair for Sheffield Utd, whose bid to regain a top-flight place ended with two players, Jamie Ward and Lee Hendrie, sent off by referee Mike Dean. Martyn Woolford capped a man-of-the-match performance with an 85th minute winner for Scunthorpe, who beat Millwall 3-2 to make an immediate return to the Championship, Matt Sparrow having scored their first two goals. Gillingham also went back up at the first attempt, beating Shrewsbury with Simeon Jackson's header seconds from the end of normal time in the League Two Final. Torquay returned to the Football League after a two-year absence by beating Cambridge United 2-0 in the Conference Final.

2010: Blackpool, under the eccentric yet shrewd Ian Holloway, claimed the big prize two years almost to the day after the manager was sacked from his previous job at Leicester. On a scorching afternoon, with temperatures reaching 106 degrees, they twice came back from a goal down to draw level against Cardiff through Charlie Adam and Gary Taylor-Fletcher, then scored what proved to be the winner through Brett Ormerod at the end of a pulsating first half. **Millwall**, beaten in five previous play-offs, reached the Championship with the only goal of the game against Swindon from captain Paul Robinson. **Dagenham & Redbridge** defeated Rotherham 3-2 in the League Two Final, Jon Nurse scoring the winner 20 minutes from the end. **Oxford** returned to the Football League after an absence of four years with a 3-1 over York in the Conference Final.

2011: Scott Sinclair scored a hat-trick as **Swansea** reached the top flight, just eight years after almost going out of the Football League. Two of his goals came from the penalty spot as Reading were beaten 4-2 in the Championship Final, with Stephen Dobbie netting their other goal. The day after his father's side lost to Barcelona in the Champions League Final, Darren Ferguson led **Peterborough** back to the Championship at the first attempt with goals by Tommy Rowe, Craig Mackail-Smith and Grant McCann in the final 12 minutes against Huddersfield. John Mousinho scored the only one of the League Two Final for **Stevenage**, who won a second successive promotion by beating Torquay. **AFC Wimbledon**, formed by supporters in 2002 after the former FA Cup-winning club relocated to Milton Keynes, completed their rise from the Combined Counties to the Football League by winning a penalty shoot-out against Luton after a goalless draw in the Conference Final.

2012: **West Ham** were third in the Championship and second best to Blackpool in the final. But they passed the post first at Wembley, thanks to an 87th minute goal from Ricardo Vaz Te which gave Sam Allardyce's side a 2-1 victory. Allardyce brought the Portuguese striker to Upton Park from Barnsley for £500,000 – a fee dwarfed by the millions his goal was worth to the club. Goalkeepers took centre stage in the League One Final, with **Huddersfield** and Sheffield United still locked in a marathon shoot-out after a goalless 120 minutes. Alex Smithies put the 21st penalty past his opposite number Steve Simonsen, who then drove over the crossbar to give Huddersfield victory by 8-7. Nick Powell, 18, lit up the League Two Final with a spectacular volley as **Crewe** beat Cheltenham 2-0. **York** regained a Football League place after an absence of eight years by beating Luton 2-1 in the Conference decider.

2013: Veteran Kevin Phillips, a loser in three previous finals, came off the bench to fire **Crystal Palace** into the Premier League with an extra-time penalty. Wilfried Zaha was brought down by Marco Cassetti and 39-year-old Phillips showed nerves of steel to convert the spot-kick. A goalline clearance by Joel Ward then denied Fernando Forestieri as Watford sought an equaliser. **Yeovil** upset the odds by reaching the Championship for the first time. They defeated Brentford 2-1, Paddy Madden scoring his 23rd goal of the season and on-loan Dan Burn adding the second. **Bradford**, back at Wembley three months after their Capital One Cup adventure, swept aside Northampton 3-0 in the League Two Final with goals from James Hanson, Rory McArdle and Nahki Wells. **Newport** returned to the Football League after a 25-year absence by defeating Wrexham 2-0 in the Conference Final.

2014: An immediate return to the Premier League for **Queens Park Rangers** seemed unlikely when Gary O'Neil was sent off for bringing down Derby's Johnny Russell. There was still more than half-an-hour to go of a match Derby had dominated. But Rangers held on and with 90 minutes nearly up Bobby Zamora punished a mistake by captain Richard Keogh to score the only goal. **Rotherham** retrieved a 2-0 deficit against Leyton Orient with two goals by Alex Revell in the League One Final and won the eventual penalty shoot-out 4-3 for a second successive promotion. **Fleetwood** achieved their sixth promotion in ten seasons with a 1-0 victory over Burton, courtesy of a free-kick from Antoni Sarcevic in the League Two Final. Liam Hughes and Ryan Donaldson were on the mark as **Cambridge United** returned to the Football League after a nine-year absence by beating Gateshead 2-1 in the Conference Final, two months after winning the FA Trophy at Wembley

2015: **Norwich** were rewarded for a flying start with a return to the Premier League at the first attempt. Cameron Jerome put them ahead against Middlesbrough after 12 minutes of the Championship Final and Nathan Redmond made it 2-0 three minutes later, a scoreline they maintained without too many problems. Jermaine Beckford's hat-trick put **Preston** on the way to a record 4-0 victory over Swindon in the League One Final. **Southend**, who like Preston were denied automatic promotion on the final day of the regular season, beat Wycombe 7-6 on penalties after the League Two Final ended 1-1. **Bristol Rovers** were also penalty winners, by 5-3 against Grimsby in the Conference decider, so making an immediate return to the Football League.

2016: A goal worthy of winning any game took Hull back to the Premier League at the first attempt. Mohamed Diame, their French-born Senegal international midfielder, curled a 25-yard shot into the top corner after 72 minues for a 1-0 win over Sheffield Wednesday. Another spectacular goal, by Adam Hammill, helped Barnsley beat Millwall 3-1 on their return to Wembley for the League One Final after winning the Johnstone's Paint Trophy. AFC Wimbledon achieved their sixth promotion since being formed by supporters in 2002, defeating favourites Plymouth 2-0 in the League Two

Final. Grimsby ended a six-year absence from the Football League with a 3-1 victory over Forest Green in the National League decider

2017: David Wagner transformed **Huddersfield** from relegation candidates into a Premier League club – with the help of German penalty-taking expertise. After a goalless Championship Play-off Final, they beat Reading 4-3 in a shoot-out clinched by Christopher Schindler'spot-kick. Steve Morison followed up his two goals in **Millwall**'s League One semi-final against Scunthorpe with the only one against Bradford, in the 85th minute at Wembley. Brad Potts and Mark Cullen were on the mark to give **Blackpool** a 2-1 victory over Exeter in the League Two Final. **Forest Green** beat Tranmere 3-1 in the National League Final, on-loan Kaiyne Woolery scoring twice.

2018: **Fulham** overcame the sending-off of central defender Denis Odoi after 70 minutes for a second yellow card to reach the Premier League. They protected the lead established by a goal from captain Tom Cairney, set up by the Championship's Player of the Year, 18-year-old Ryan Sessegnon, to defeat Aston Villa 1-0. There was another captain's performance in the League One Final, Richard Wood scoring both goals in **Rotherham**'s 2-1 win over Shrewsbury. **Coventry** ended years of decline by beating Exeter 3-1 in the League Two Final with goals from Jordan Willis, Jordan Shipley and Jack Grimmer. **Tranmere** had Liam Ridehalgh dismissed after 48 seconds for a two-footed challenge, but were 2-1 winners over Boreham Wood in the National League Final (Andy Cook and James Norwood).

2019: **Aston Villa** made a royal return to the Premier League after a three-year absence by defeating Derby 2-1. Prince William, a supporter of the club, joined the celebrations at Wembley after loanee Anwar El Ghazi and bargain-buy John McGinn scored the goals to complete the club's renaissance under former Brentford manager Dean Smith. **Charlton** recovered from Naby Sarr's bizarre own goal – a back-pass missed by goalkeeper Dillon Phillips – to equalise through Ben Purrington and beat Sunderland with captain Patrick Bauer's goal seconds from time. **Tranmere** made a successful return to the national stadium after winning the National League decider in 2018, scoring the only goal against Newport through Connor Jennings. **Salford**, co-owned by six former Manchester United players, defeated AFC Fylde 3-0 in the National League decider to reach the Football League for the first time.

2020: Full-back Joe Bryan scored both goals as **Fulham** returned to the Premier League at the first attempt with a 2-1 win over Brentford after a goalless 90 minutes in the Championship Final. He deceived goalkeeper David Raya with a low, skidding free-kick, then combined with leading marksman Aleksandar Mitrovic for the second. Henrik Dalsgaard replied in stoppage-time. Two more defenders put unfancied **Wycombe** into the second tier. Anthony Stewart scored from Joe Jacobson's corner and Jacobson converted a penalty to overcome Oxford 2-1 in the League One Final. **Northampton** defeated ten-man Exeter 4-0 in the League Two decider after Dean Moxey was shown a straight red card at 2-0.

Play-off attendances

1987	20	310,000	2005	15	353,330
1988	19	305,817	2006	15	340,804
1989	18	234,393	2007	15	405,278
1990	15	291,428	2008	15	382,032
1991	15	266,442	2009	15	380,329
1992	15	277,684	2010	15	370,055
1993	15	319,907	2011	15	310,998
1994	15	314,817	2012	15	332,930
1995	15	295,317	2013	15	346,062
1996	15	308,515	2014	15	307,011
1997	15	309,085	2015	15	367,374
1998	15	320,795	2016	15	393,145
1999	15	372,969	2017	15	323,727
2000	15	333,999	2018	15	373,295
2001	15	317,745	2019	15	430,025 (record)
2002	15	327,894	2020	No attendances – Covid	
2003	15	374,461	2021	Limited attendances – Covid	
2004	15	388,675			

ENGLISH HONOURS LIST

PREMIER LEAGUE

	First	Pts	Second	Pts	Third	Pts
1992–3*a*	Manchester Utd	84	Aston Villa	74	Norwich	72
1993–4*a*	Manchester Utd	92	Blackburn	84	Newcastle	77
1994–5*a*	Blackburn	89	Manchester Utd	88	Nottm Forest	77
1995–6*b*	Manchester Utd	82	Newcastle	78	Liverpool	71
1996–7*b*	Manchester Utd	75	Newcastle	68	Arsenal	68
1997–8*b*	Arsenal	78	Manchester Utd	77	Liverpool	65
1998–9*b*	Manchester Utd	79	Arsenal	78	Chelsea	75
1999–00*b*	Manchester Utd	91	Arsenal	73	Leeds	69
2000–01*b*	Manchester Utd	80	Arsenal	70	Liverpool	69
2001–02*b*	Arsenal	87	Liverpool	80	Manchester Utd	77
2002–03*b*	Manchester Utd	83	Arsenal	78	Newcastle	69
2003–04*b*	Arsenal	90	Chelsea	79	Manchester Utd	75
2004–05*b*	Chelsea	95	Arsenal	83	Manchester Utd	77
2005–06*b*	Chelsea	91	Manchester Utd	83	Liverpool	82
2006–07*b*	Manchester Utd	89	Chelsea	83	Liverpool	68
2007–08*b*	Manchester Utd	87	Chelsea	85	Arsenal	83
2008–09*b*	Manchester Utd	90	Liverpool	86	Chelsea	83
2009–10*b*	Chelsea	86	Manchester Utd	85	Arsenal	75
2010–11*b*	Manchester Utd	80	Chelsea	71	Manchester City	71
2011–12*b*	Manchester City*	89	Manchester Ud	89	Arsenal	70
2012–13*b*	Manchester Utd	89	Manchester City	78	Chelsea	75
2013–14*b*	Manchester City	86	Liverpool	84	Chelsea	82
2014–15*b*	Chelsea	87	Manchester City	79	Arsenal	75
2015–16*b*	Leicester	81	Arsenal	71	Tottenham	70
2016–17*b*	Chelsea	93	Tottenham	86	Manchester City	78
2017–18*b*	Manchester City	100	Manchester Utd	81	Tottenham	77
2018–19*b*	Manchester City	98	Liverpool	97	Chelsea	72
2019–20*b*	Liverpool	99	Manchester City	81	Manchester Utd	66
2020–21*b*	Manchester City	86	Manchester Utd	74	Liverpool	69

* won on goal difference. Maximum points: *a*, 126; *b*, 114

FOOTBALL LEAGUE

FIRST DIVISION

1992–3	Newcastle	96	West Ham	88	††Portsmouth	88
1993–4	Crystal Palace	90	Nottm Forest	83	††Millwall	74
1994–5	Middlesbrough	82	††Reading	79	Bolton	77
1995–6	Sunderland	83	Derby	79	††Crystal Palace	75
1996–7	Bolton	98	Barnsley	80	††Wolves	76
1997–8	Nottm Forest	94	Middlesbrough	91	††Sunderland	90
1998–9	Sunderland	105	Bradford City	87	††Ipswich	86
1999–00	Charlton	91	Manchester City	89	Ipswich	87
2000–01	Fulham	101	Blackburn	91	Bolton	87
2001–02	Manchester City	99	WBA	89	††Wolves	86
2002–03	Portsmouth	98	Leicester	92	††Sheffield Utd	80
2003–04	Norwich	94	WBA	86	††Sunderland	79

CHAMPIONSHIP

2004–05	Sunderland	94	Wigan	87	††Ipswich	85
2005–06	Reading	106	Sheffield Utd	90	Watford	81
2006–07	Sunderland	88	Birmingham	86	Derby	84
2007–08	WBA	81	Stoke	79	Hull	75

2008–09	Wolves	90	Birmingham	83	††Sheffield Utd	80
2009–10	Newcastle	102	WBA	91	††Nottm Forest	79
2010–11	QPR	88	Norwich	84	Swansea	80
2011–12	Reading	89	Southampton	88	West Ham	86
2012–13	Cardiff	87	Hull	79	††Watford	77
2013–14	Leicester	102	Burnley	93	††Derby	85
2014–15	Bournemouth	90	Watford	89	Norwich	86
2015–16	Burnley	93	Middlesbrough	89	††Brighton	89
2016–17	Newcastle	94	Brighton	93	††Reading	85
2017–18	Wolves	99	Cardiff	90	Fulham	88
2018–19	Norwich	94	Sheffield Utd	89	††Leeds	83
2019–20	Leeds	93	WBA	83	††Brentford	81
2020–21	Norwich	97	Watford	91	Brentford	87

Maximum points: 138 ††Not promoted after play–offs

SECOND DIVISION

1992–3	Stoke	93	Bolton	90	††Port Vale	89
1993–4	Reading	89	Port Vale	88	††Plymouth Argyle	85
1994–5	Birmingham	89	††Brentford	85	††Crewe	83
1995–6	Swindon	92	Oxford Utd	83	††Blackpool	82
1996–7	Bury	84	Stockport	82	††Luton	78
1997–8	Watford	88	Bristol City	85	Grimsby	72
1998–9	Fulham	101	Walsall	87	Manchester City	82
1999–00	Preston	95	Burnley	88	Gillingham	85
2000–01	Millwall	93	Rotherham	91	††Reading	86
2001–02	Brighton	90	Reading	84	††Brentford	83
2002–03	Wigan	100	Crewe	86	††Bristol City	83
2003–04	Plymouth Argyle	90	QPR	83	††Bristol City	82

LEAGUE ONE

2004–05	Luton	98	Hull	86	††Tranmere	79
2005–06	Southend	82	Colchester	79	††Brentford	76
2006–07	Scunthorpe	91	Bristol City	85	Blackpool	83
2007–08	Swansea	92	Nottm Forest	82	Doncaster	80
2008–09	Leicester	96	Peterborough	89	††MK Dons	87
2009–10	Norwich	95	Leeds	86	Millwall	85
2010–11	Brighton	95	Southampton	92	††Huddersfield	87
2011–12	Charlton	101	Sheffield Wed	93	††Sheffield Utd	90
2012–13	Doncaster	84	Bournemouth	83	††Brentford	79
2013–14	Wolves	103	Brentford	94	††Leyton Orient	86
2014–15	Bristol City	99	MK Dons	91	Preston	89
2015–16	Wigan	87	Burton	85	††Walsall	84
2016–17	Sheffield Utd	100	Bolton	86	††Scunthorpe	82
2017–18	Wigan	98	Blackburn	96	††Shrewsbury	87
2018–19	Luton	94	Barnsley	91	Charlton	88
2019–20a	Coventry	67	Rotherham	62	Wycombe	59
2020–21	Hull	89	Peterborough	87	Blackpool	80

a season abandoned – Covid-19; points-per-game decided final positions

Maximum points: 138 †† Not promoted after play–offs

THIRD DIVISION

1992–3a	Cardiff	83	Wrexham	80	Barnet	79
1993–4a	Shrewsbury	79	Chester	74	Crewe	73
1994–5a	Carlisle	91	Walsall	83	Chesterfield	81
1995–6b	Preston	86	Gillingham	83	Bury	79
1996–7b	Wigan	87	Fulham	87	Carlisle	84
1997–8b	Notts Co	99	Macclesfield	82	Lincoln	75
1998–9b	Brentford	85	Cambridge Utd	81	Cardiff	80

1999–00b	Swansea	85	Rotherham	84	Northampton	82
2000–01b	Brighton	92	Cardiff	82	*Chesterfield	80
2001–02b	Plymouth Argyle	102	Luton	97	Mansfield	79
2002–03b	Rushden & D	87	Hartlepool Utd	85	Wrexham	84
2003–04b	Doncaster	92	Hull	88	Torquay	81

* Deducted 9 points for financial irregularities

LEAGUE TWO

2004–05b	Yeovil	83	Scunthorpe	80	Swansea	80
2005–06b	Carlisle	86	Northampton	83	Leyton Orient	81
2006–07b	Walsall	89	Hartlepool	88	Swindon	85
2007–08b	MK Dons	97	Peterborough	92	Hereford	88
2008–09b	Brentford	85	Exeter	79	Wycombe	78
2009–10b	Notts Co	93	Bournemouth	83	Rochdale	82
2010–11b	Chesterfield	86	Bury	81	Wycombe	80
2011–12b	Swindon	93	Shrewsbury	88	Crawley	84
2012–13b	Gillingham	83	Rotherham	79	Port Vale	78
2013–14b	Chesterfield	84	Scunthorpe	81	Rochdale	81
2014–15b	Burton	94	Shrewsbury	89	Bury	85
2015–16b	Northampton	99	Oxford	86	Bristol Rov	85
2016–17b	Portsmouth	87	Plymouth	87	Doncaster	85
2017–18b	Accrington	93	Luton	88	Wycombe	84
2018–19b	Lincoln	85	Bury	79	MK Dons	79
2019–20c	Swindon	69	Crewe	69	Plymouth	68
2020–21b	Cheltenham	82	Cambridge	80	Bolton	79

c season abandoned – Covid 19; points-per-game decided final positions
Maximum points: a, 126; b, 138

FOOTBALL LEAGUE 1888–1992

1888–89a	Preston	40	Aston Villa	29	Wolves	28
1889–90a	Preston	33	Everton	31	Blackburn	27
1890–1a	Everton	29	Preston	27	Notts Co	26
1891–2b	Sunderland	42	Preston	37	Bolton	36

OLD FIRST DIVISION

1892–3c	Sunderland	48	Preston	37	Everton	36
1893–4c	Aston Villa	44	Sunderland	38	Derby	36
1894–5c	Sunderland	47	Everton	42	Aston Villa	39
1895–6c	Aston Villa	45	Derby	41	Everton	39
1896–7c	Aston Villa	47	Sheffield Utd	36	Derby	36
1897–8c	Sheffield Utd	42	Sunderland	39	Wolves	35
1898–9d	Aston Villa	45	Liverpool	43	Burnley	39
1899–1900d	Aston Villa	50	Sheffield Utd	48	Sunderland	41
1900–1d	Liverpool	45	Sunderland	43	Notts Co	40
1901–2d	Sunderland	44	Everton	41	Newcastle	37
1902–3d	The Wednesday	42	Aston Villa	41	Sunderland	41
1903–4d	The Wednesday	47	Manchester City	44	Everton	43
1904–5d	Newcastle	48	Everton	47	Manchester City	46
1905–6e	Liverpool	51	Preston	47	The Wednesday	44
1906–7e	Newcastle	51	Bristol City	48	Everton	45
1907–8e	Manchester Utd	52	Aston Villa	43	Manchester City	43
1908–9e	Newcastle	53	Everton	46	Sunderland	44
1909–10e	Aston Villa	53	Liverpool	48	Blackburn	45
1910–11e	Manchester Utd	52	Aston Villa	51	Sunderland	45
1911–12e	Blackburn	49	Everton	46	Newcastle	44
1912–13e	Sunderland	54	Aston Villa	50	Sheffield Wed	49

Season						
1913–14e	Blackburn	51	Aston Villa	44	Middlesbrough	43
1914–15e	Everton	46	Oldham	45	Blackburn	43
1919–20f	WBA	60	Burnley	51	Chelsea	49
1920–1f	Burnley	59	Manchester City	54	Bolton	52
1921–2f	Liverpool	57	Tottenham	51	Burnley	49
1922–3f	Liverpool	60	Sunderland	54	Huddersfield	53
1923–4f	*Huddersfield	57	Cardiff	57	Sunderland	53
1924–5f	Huddersfield	58	WBA	56	Bolton	55
1925–6f	Huddersfield	57	Arsenal	52	Sunderland	48
1926–7f	Newcastle	56	Huddersfield	51	Sunderland	49
1927–8f	Everton	53	Huddersfield	51	Leicester	48
1928–9f	Sheffield Wed	52	Leicester	51	Aston Villa	50
1929–30f	Sheffield Wed	60	Derby	50	Manchester City	47
1930–1f	Arsenal	66	Aston Villa	59	Sheffield Wed	52
1931–2f	Everton	56	Arsenal	54	Sheffield Wed	50
1932–3f	Arsenal	58	Aston Villa	54	Sheffield Wed	51
1933–4f	Arsenal	59	Huddersfield	56	Tottenham	49
1934–5f	Arsenal	58	Sunderland	54	Sheffield Wed	49
1935–6f	Sunderland	56	Derby	48	Huddersfield	48
1936–7f	Manchester City	57	Charlton	54	Arsenal	52
1937–8f	Arsenal	52	Wolves	51	Preston	49
1938–9f	Everton	59	Wolves	55	Charlton	50
1946–7f	Liverpool	57	Manchester Utd	56	Wolves	56
1947–8f	Arsenal	59	Manchester Utd	52	Burnley	52
1948–9f	Portsmouth	58	Manchester Utd	53	Derby	53
1949–50f	*Portsmouth	53	Wolves	53	Sunderland	52
1950–1f	Tottenham	60	Manchester Utd	56	Blackpool	50
1951–2f	Manchester Utd	57	Tottenham	53	Arsenal	53
1952–3f	*Arsenal	54	Preston	54	Wolves	51
1953–4f	Wolves	57	WBA	53	Huddersfield	51
1954–5f	Chelsea	52	Wolves	48	Portsmouth	48
1955–6f	Manchester Utd	60	Blackpool	49	Wolves	49
1956–7f	Manchester Utd	64	Tottenham	56	Preston	56
1957–8f	Wolves	64	Preston	59	Tottenham	51
1958–9f	Wolves	61	Manchester Utd	55	Arsenal	50
1959–60f	Burnley	55	Wolves	54	Tottenham	53
1960–1f	Tottenham	66	Sheffield Wed	58	Wolves	57
1961–2f	Ipswich	56	Burnley	53	Tottenham	52
1962–3f	Everton	61	Tottenham	55	Burnley	54
1963–4f	Liverpool	57	Manchester Utd	53	Everton	52
1964–5f	*Manchester Utd	61	Leeds	61	Chelsea	56
1965–6f	Liverpool	61	Leeds	55	Burnley	55
1966–7f	Manchester Utd	60	Nottm Forest	56	Tottenham	56
1967–8f	Manchester City	58	Manchester Utd	56	Liverpool	55
1968–9f	Leeds	67	Liverpool	61	Everton	57
1969–70f	Everton	66	Leeds	57	Chelsea	55
1970–1f	Arsenal	65	Leeds	64	Tottenham	52
1971–2f	Derby	58	Leeds	57	Liverpool	57
1972–3f	Liverpool	60	Arsenal	57	Leeds	53
1973–4f	Leeds	62	Liverpool	57	Derby	48
1974–5f	Derby	53	Liverpool	51	Ipswich	51
1975–6f	Liverpool	60	QPR	59	Manchester Utd	56
1976–7f	Liverpool	57	Manchester City	56	Ipswich	52
1977–8f	Nottm Forest	64	Liverpool	57	Everton	55

1978-9f	Liverpool	68	Nottm Forest	60	WBA	59
1979-80f	Liverpool	60	Manchester Utd	58	Ipswich	53
1980-1f	Aston Villa	60	Ipswich	56	Arsenal	53
1981-2g	Liverpool	87	Ipswich	83	Manchester Utd	78
1982-3g	Liverpool	82	Watford	71	Manchester Utd	70
1983-4g	Liverpool	80	Southampton	77	Nottm Forest	74
1984-5g	Everton	90	Liverpool	77	Tottenham	77
1985-6g	Liverpool	88	Everton	86	West Ham	84
1986-7g	Everton	86	Liverpool	77	Tottenham	71
1987-8h	Liverpool	90	Manchester Utd	81	Nottm Forest	73
1988-9j	††Arsenal	76	Liverpool	76	Nottm Forest	64
1989-90j	Liverpool	79	Aston Villa	70	Tottenham	63
1990-1j	Arsenal	83	Liverpool	76	Crystal Palace	69
1991-2g	Leeds	82	Manchester Utd	78	Sheffield Wed	75

Maximum points: *a*, 44; *b*, 52; *c*, 60; *d*, 68; *e*, 76; *f*, 84; *g*, 126; *h*, 120; *j*, 114
*Won on goal average †Won on goal diff ††Won on goals scored No comp 1915-19 -1939-46

OLD SECOND DIVISION 1892-1992

1892-3a	Small Heath	36	Sheffield Utd	35	Darwen	30
1893-4b	Liverpool	50	Small Heath	42	Notts Co	39
1894-5c	Bury	48	Notts Co	39	Newton Heath	38
1895-6c	*Liverpool	46	Manchester City	46	Grimsby	42
1896-7c	Notts Co	42	Newton Heath	39	Grimsby	38
1897-8c	Burnley	48	Newcastle	45	Manchester City	39
1898-9d	Manchester City	52	Glossop	46	Leicester Fosse	45
1899-1900d	The Wednesday	54	Bolton	52	Small Heath	46
1900-1d	Grimsby	49	Small Heath	48	Burnley	44
1901-2d	WBA	55	Middlesbrough	51	Preston	42
1902-3d	Manchester City	54	Small Heath	51	Woolwich Arsenal	48
1903-4d	Preston	50	Woolwich Arsenal	49	Manchester Utd	48
1904-5d	Liverpool	58	Bolton	56	Manchester Utd	53
1905-6e	Bristol City	66	Manchester Utd	62	Chelsea	53
1906-7e	Nottm Forest	60	Chelsea	57	Leicester Fosse	48
1907-8e	Bradford City	54	Leicester Fosse	52	Oldham	50
1908-9e	Bolton	52	Tottenham	51	WBA	51
1909-10e	Manchester City	54	Oldham	53	Hull	53
1910-11e	WBA	53	Bolton	51	Chelsea	49
1911-12e	*Derby	54	Chelsea	54	Burnley	52
1912-13e	Preston	53	Burnley	50	Birmingham	46
1913-14e	Notts Co	53	Bradford PA	49	Woolwich Arsenal	49
1914-15e	Derby	53	Preston	50	Barnsley	47
1919-20f	Tottenham	70	Huddersfield	64	Birmingham	56
1920-1f	*Birmingham	58	Cardiff	58	Bristol City	51
1921-2f	Nottm Forest	56	Stoke	52	Barnsley	52
1922-3f	Notts Co	53	West Ham	51	Leicester	51
1923-4f	Leeds	54	Bury	51	Derby	51
1924-5f	Leicester	59	Manchester Utd	57	Derby	55
1925-6f	Sheffield Wed	60	Derby	57	Chelsea	52
1926-7f	Middlesbrough	62	Portsmouth	54	Manchester City	54
1927-8f	Manchester City	59	Leeds	57	Chelsea	54
1928-9f	Middlesbrough	55	Grimsby	53	Bradford City	48
1929-30f	Blackpool	58	Chelsea	55	Oldham	53
1930-1f	Everton	61	WBA	54	Tottenham	51
1931-2f	Wolves	56	Leeds	54	Stoke	52
1932-3f	Stoke	56	Tottenham	55	Fulham	50

Season						
1933–4f	Grimsby	59	Preston	52	Bolton	51
1934–5f	Brentford	61	Bolton	56	West Ham	56
1935–6f	Manchester Utd	56	Charlton	55	Sheffield Utd	52
1936–7f	Leicester	56	Blackpool	55	Bury	52
1937–8f	Aston Villa	57	Manchester Utd	53	Sheffield Utd	53
1938–9f	Blackburn	55	Sheffield Utd	54	Sheffield Wed	53
1946–7f	Manchester City	62	Burnley	58	Birmingham	55
1947–8f	Birmingham	59	Newcastle	56	Southampton	52
1948–9f	Fulham	57	WBA	56	Southampton	55
1949–50f	Tottenham	61	Sheffield Wed	52	Sheffield Utd	52
1950–1f	Preston	57	Manchester City	52	Cardiff	50
1951–2f	Sheffield Wed	53	Cardiff	51	Birmingham	51
1952–3f	Sheffield Utd	60	Huddersfield	58	Luton	52
1953–4f	*Leicester	56	Everton	56	Blackburn	55
1954–5f	*Birmingham	54	Luton	54	Rotherham	54
1955–6f	Sheffield Wed	55	Leeds	52	Liverpool	48
1956–7f	Leicester	61	Nottm Forest	54	Liverpool	53
1957–8f	West Ham	57	Blackburn	56	Charlton	55
1958–9f	Sheffield Wed	62	Fulham	60	Sheffield Utd	53
1959–60f	Aston Villa	59	Cardiff	58	Liverpool	50
1960–1f	Ipswich	59	Sheffield Utd	58	Liverpool	52
1961–2f	Liverpool	62	Leyton Orient	54	Sunderland	53
1962–3f	Stoke	53	Chelsea	52	Sunderland	52
1963–4f	Leeds	63	Sunderland	61	Preston	56
1964–5f	Newcastle	57	Northampton	56	Bolton	50
1965–6f	Manchester City	59	Southampton	54	Coventry	53
1966–7f	Coventry	59	Wolves	58	Carlisle	52
1967–8f	Ipswich	59	QPR	58	Blackpool	58
1968–9f	Derby	63	Crystal Palace	56	Charlton	50
1969–70f	Huddersfield	60	Blackpool	53	Leicester	51
1970–1f	Leicester	59	Sheffield Utd	56	Cardiff	53
1971–2f	Norwich	57	Birmingham	56	Millwall	55
1972–3f	Burnley	62	QPR	61	Aston Villa	50
1973–4f	Middlesbrough	65	Luton	50	Carlisle	49
1974–5f	Manchester Utd	61	Aston Villa	58	Norwich	53
1975–6f	Sunderland	56	Bristol City	53	WBA	53
1976–7f	Wolves	57	Chelsea	55	Nottm Forest	52
1977–8f	Bolton	58	Southampton	57	Tottenham	56
1978–9f	Crystal Palace	57	Brighton	56	Stoke	56
1979–80f	Leicester	55	Sunderland	54	Birmingham	53
1980–1f	West Ham	66	Notts Co	53	Swansea	50
1981–2g	Luton	88	Watford	80	Norwich	71
1982–3g	QPR	85	Wolves	75	Leicester	70
1983–4g	†Chelsea	88	Sheffield Wed	88	Newcastle	80
1984–5g	Oxford Utd	84	Birmingham	82	Manchester City	74
1985–6g	Norwich	84	Charlton	77	Wimbledon	76
1986–7g	Derby	84	Portsmouth	78	††Oldham	75
1987–8h	Millwall	82	Aston Villa	78	Middlesbrough	78
1988–9j	Chelsea	99	Manchester City	82	Crystal Palace	81
1989–90j	†Leeds	85	Sheffield Utd	85	†† Newcastle	80
1990–1j	Oldham	88	West Ham	87	Sheffield Wed	82
1991–2j	Ipswich	84	Middlesbrough	80	†† Derby	78

Maximum points: *a*, 44; *b*, 56; *c*, 60; *d*, 68; *e*, 76; *f*, 84; *g*, 126; *h*, 132; *j*, 138 * Won on goal average † Won on goal difference †† Not promoted after play-offs

THIRD DIVISION 1958–92

Year						
1958–9	Plymouth Argyle	62	Hull	61	Brentford	57
1959–60	Southampton	61	Norwich	59	Shrewsbury	52
1960–1	Bury	68	Walsall	62	QPR	60
1961–2	Portsmouth	65	Grimsby	62	Bournemouth	59
1962–3	Northampton	62	Swindon	58	Port Vale	54
1963–4	*Coventry	60	Crystal Palace	60	Watford	58
1964–5	Carlisle	60	Bristol City	59	Mansfield	59
1965–6	Hull	69	Millwall	65	QPR	57
1966–7	QPR	67	Middlesbrough	55	Watford	54
1967–8	Oxford Utd	57	Bury	56	Shrewsbury	55
1968–9	*Watford	64	Swindon	64	Luton	61
1969–70	Orient	62	Luton	60	Bristol Rov	56
1970–1	Preston	61	Fulham	60	Halifax	56
1971–2	Aston Villa	70	Brighton	65	Bournemouth	62
1972–3	Bolton	61	Notts Co	57	Blackburn	55
1973–4	Oldham	62	Bristol Rov	61	York	61
1974–5	Blackburn	60	Plymouth Argyle	59	Charlton	55
1975–6	Hereford	63	Cardiff	57	Millwall	56
1976–7	Mansfield	64	Brighton	61	Crystal Palace	59
1977–8	Wrexham	61	Cambridge Utd	58	Preston	56
1978–9	Shrewsbury	61	Watford	60	Swansea	60
1979–80	Grimsby	62	Blackburn	59	Sheffield Wed	58
1980–1	Rotherham	61	Barnsley	59	Charlton	59
†1981–2	**Burnley	80	Carlisle	80	Fulham	78
†1982–3	Portsmouth	91	Cardiff	86	Huddersfield	82
†1983–4	Oxford Utd	95	Wimbledon	87	Sheffield Utd	83
†1984–5	Bradford City	94	Millwall	90	Hull	87
†1985–6	Reading	94	Plymouth Argyle	87	Derby	84
†1986–7	Bournemouth	97	Middlesbrough	94	Swindon	87
†1987–8	Sunderland	93	Brighton	84	Walsall	82
†1988–9	Wolves	92	Sheffield Utd	84	Port Vale	84
†1989–90	Bristol Rov	93	Bristol City	91	Notts Co	87
†1990–1	Cambridge Utd	86	Southend	85	Grimsby	83
†1991–2	Brentford	82	Birmingham	81	††Huddersfield	78

* Won on goal average ** Won on goal difference † Maximum points 138 (previously 92) †† Not promoted after play–offs

FOURTH DIVISION 1958–92

Year								
1958–9	Port Vale	64	Coventry	60	York	60	Shrewsbury	58
1959–60	Walsall	65	Notts Co	60	Torquay	60	Watford	57
1960–1	Peterborough	66	Crystal Palace	64	Northampton	60	Bradford PA	60
1961–2	Millwall	56	Colchester	55	Wrexham	53	Carlisle	52
1962–3	Brentford	62	Oldham	59	Crewe	59	Mansfield	57
1963–4	*Gillingham	60	Carlisle	60	Workington	59	Exeter	58
1964–5	Brighton	63	Millwall	62	York	62	Oxford Utd	61
1965–6	*Doncaster	59	Darlington	59	Torquay	58	Colchester	56
1966–7	Stockport	64	Southport	59	Barrow	59	Tranmere	58
1967–8	Luton	66	Barnsley	61	Hartlepool Utd	60	Crewe	58
1968–9	Doncaster	59	Halifax	57	Rochdale	56	Bradford City	56
1969–70	Chesterfield	64	Wrexham	61	Swansea	60	Port Vale	59
1970–1	Notts Co	69	Bournemouth	60	Oldham	59	York	56
1971–2	Grimsby	63	Southend	60	Brentford	59	Scunthorpe	57
1972–3	Southport	62	Hereford	58	Cambridge Utd	57	Aldershot	56
1973–4	Peterborough	65	Gillingham	62	Colchester	60	Bury	59
1974–5	Mansfield	68	Shrewsbury	62	Rotherham	58	Chester	57
1975–6	Lincoln	74	Northampton	68	Reading	60	Tranmere	58
1976–7	Cambridge Utd	65	Exeter	62	Colchester	59	Bradford City	59
1977–8	Watford	71	Southend	60	Swansea	56	Brentford	59
1978–9	Reading	65	Grimsby	61	Wimbledon	61	Barnsley	61

1979–80	Huddersfield	66	Walsall	64	Newport	61	Portsmouth	60
1980–1	Southend	67	Lincoln	65	Doncaster	56	Wimbledon	55
†1981–2	Sheffield Utd	96	Bradford City	91	Wigan	91	Bournemouth	88
†1982–3	Wimbledon	98	Hull	90	Port Vale	88	Scunthorpe	83
†1983–4	York	101	Doncaster	85	Reading	82	Bristol City	82
†1984–5	Chesterfield	91	Blackpool	86	Darlington	85	Bury	84
†1985–6	Swindon	102	Chester	84	Mansfield	81	Port Vale	79
†1986–7	Northampton	99	Preston	90	Southend	80	††Wolves	79
†1987–8	Wolves	90	Cardiff	85	Bolton	78	††Scunthorpe 77
†1988–9	Rotherham	82	Tranmere	80	Crewe	78	††Scunthorpe 77
†1989–90	Exeter	89	Grimsby	79	Southend	75	††Stockport 74
†1990–1	Darlington	83	Stockport	82	Hartlepool Utd	82	Peterborough 80
1991–2a	Burnley	83	Rotherham	77	Mansfield	77	Blackpool	76

* Won on goal average Maximum points: †, 138; a, 126; previously 92 †† Not promoted after play-offs

THIRD DIVISION – SOUTH 1920–58

1920–1a	Crystal Palace	59	Southampton	54	QPR	53
1921–2a	*Southampton	61	Plymouth Argyle	61	Portsmouth	53
1922–3a	Bristol City	59	Plymouth Argyle	53	Swansea	53
1923–4a	Portsmouth	59	Plymouth Argyle	55	Millwall	54
1924–5a	Swansea	57	Plymouth Argyle	56	Bristol City	53
1925–6a	Reading	57	Plymouth Argyle	56	Millwall	53
1926–7a	Bristol City	62	Plymouth Argyle	60	Millwall	56
1927–8a	Millwall	65	Northampton	55	Plymouth Argyle	53
1928–9a	*Charlton	54	Crystal Palace	54	Northampton	52
1929–30a	Plymouth Argyle	68	Brentford	61	QPR	51
1930–31a	Notts Co	59	Crystal Palace	51	Brentford	50
1931–2a	Fulham	57	Reading	55	Southend	53
1932–3a	Brentford	62	Exeter	58	Norwich	57
1933–4a	Norwich	61	Coventry	54	Reading	54
1934–5a	Charlton	61	Reading	53	Coventry	51
1935–6a	Coventry	57	Luton	56	Reading	54
1936–7a	Luton	58	Notts Co	56	Brighton	53
1937–8a	Millwall	56	Bristol City	55	QPR	53
1938–9a	Newport	55	Crystal Palace	52	Brighton	49
1946–7a	Cardiff	66	QPR	57	Bristol City	51
1947–8a	QPR	61	Bournemouth	57	Walsall	51
1948–9a	Swansea	62	Reading	55	Bournemouth	52
1949–50a	Notts Co	58	Northampton	51	Southend	51
1950–1d	Nottm Forest	70	Norwich	64	Reading	57
1951–2d	Plymouth Argyle	66	Reading	61	Norwich	61
1952–3d	Bristol Rov	64	Millwall	62	Northampton	62
1953–4d	Ipswich	64	Brighton	61	Bristol City	56
1954–5d	Bristol City	70	Leyton Orient	61	Southampton	59
1955–6d	Leyton Orient	66	Brighton	65	Ipswich	64
1956–7d	*Ipswich	59	Torquay	59	Colchester	58
1957–8d	Brighton	60	Brentford	58	Plymouth Argyle	58

THIRD DIVISION – NORTH 1921–58

1921–2b	Stockport	56	Darlington	50	Grimsby	50
1922–3b	Nelson	51	Bradford PA	47	Walsall	46
1923–4a	Wolves	63	Rochdale	62	Chesterfield	54
1924–5a	Darlington	58	Nelson	53	New Brighton	53
1925–6a	Grimsby	61	Bradford PA	60	Rochdale	59
1926–7a	Stoke	63	Rochdale	58	Bradford PA	57
1927–8a	Bradford PA	63	Lincoln	55	Stockport	54
1928–9a	Bradford City	63	Stockport	62	Wrexham	52
1929–30a	Port Vale	67	Stockport	63	Darlington	50
1930–1a	Chesterfield	58	Lincoln	57	Wrexham	54

1931–2c	*Lincoln	57	Gateshead	57	Chester	50
1932–3a	Hull	59	Wrexham	57	Stockport	54
1933–4a	Barnsley	62	Chesterfield	61	Stockport	59
1934–5a	Doncaster	57	Halifax	55	Chester	54
1935–6a	Chesterfield	60	Chester	55	Tranmere	54
1936–7a	Stockport	60	Lincoln	57	Chester	53
1937–8a	Tranmere	56	Doncaster	54	Hull	53
1938–9a	Barnsley	67	Doncaster	56	Bradford City	52
1946–7a	Doncaster	72	Rotherham	64	Chester	56
1947–8a	Lincoln	60	Rotherham	59	Wrexham	50
1948–9a	Hull	65	Rotherham	62	Doncaster	50
1949–50a	Doncaster	55	Gateshead	53	Rochdale	51
1950–1d	Rotherham	71	Mansfield	64	Carlisle	62
1951–2d	Lincoln	69	Grimsby	66	Stockport	59
1952–3d	Oldham	59	Port Vale	58	Wrexham	56
1953–4d	Port Vale	69	Barnsley	58	Scunthorpe	57
1954–5d	Barnsley	65	Accrington	61	Scunthorpe	58
1955–6d	Grimsby	68	Derby	63	Accrington	59
1956–7d	Derby	63	Hartlepool Utd	59	Accrington	58
1957–8d	Scunthorpe	66	Accrington	59	Bradford City	57

Maximum points: a, 84; b, 76; c, 80; d, 92 * Won on goal average

TITLE WINNERS

PREMIER LEAGUE

Manchester Utd	13
Chelsea	5
Manchester City	5
Arsenal	3
Blackburn	1
Leicester	1
Liverpool	1

CHAMPIONSHIP

Newcastle	2
Norwich	2
Reading	2
Sunderland	2
Wolves	2
Bournemouth	1
Burnley	1
Cardiff	1
Leeds	1
Leicester	1
QPR	1
WBA	1

DIV 1 (NEW)

Sunderland	2
Bolton	1
Charlton	1
Crystal Palace	1
Fulham	1
Manchester City	1
Middlesbrough	1
Newcastle	1
Norwich	1
Nottm Forest	1
Portsmouth	1

DIV 1 (ORIGINAL)

Liverpool	18
Arsenal	10
Everton	9
Aston Villa	7
Manchester Utd	7
Sunderland	6
Newcastle	4
Sheffield Wed	4
Huddersfield	3
Leeds	3
Wolves	3
Blackburn	2
Burnley	2
Derby	2
Manchester City	2
Portsmouth	2
Preston	2
Tottenham	2
Chelsea	1
Ipswich	1
Nottm Forest	1
Sheffield Utd	1
WBA	1

LEAGUE ONE

Luton	2
Wigan	2
Brighton	1
Bristol City	1
Charlton	1
Coventry	1
Doncaster	1
Hull	1
Leicester	1
Norwich	1
Scunthorpe	1
Sheffield Utd	1

Southend	1
Swansea	1
Wolves	1

DIV 2 (NEW)

Birmingham	1
Brighton	1
Bury	1
Chesterfield	1
Fulham	1
Lincoln	1
Millwall	1
Plymouth	1
Preston	1
Reading	1
Stoke	1
Swindon	1
Watford	1
Wigan	1
Notts Co	1

DIV 2 (ORIGINAL)

Leicester	6
Manchester City	6
Sheffield Wed	5
Birmingham	4
Derby	4
Liverpool	4
Ipswich	3
Leeds	3
Middlesbrough	3
Notts County	3
Preston	3
Aston Villa	2
Bolton	2
Burnley	2
Chelsea	2
Grimsby	2
Manchester Utd	2

Norwich	2	Crystal Palace	1
Nottm Forest	2	Everton	1
Stoke	2	Fulham	1
Tottenham	2	Huddersfield	1
WBA	2	Luton	1
West Ham	2	Millwall	1
Wolves	2	Newcastle	1
Blackburn	1	Oldham	1
Blackpool	1	Oxford Utd	1
Bradford City	1	QPR	1
Brentford	1	Sheffield Utd	1
Bristol City	1	Sunderland	1
Bury	1		
Coventry	1		

Swindon	2
Accrington	1
Brentford	1
Burton	1
Carlisle	1
Cheltenham	1
Gillingham	1
Lincoln	1
MK Dons	1
Northampton	1
Notts County	1
Portsmouth	1
Walsall	1
Yeovil	1

LEAGUE TWO

Chesterfield	2

APPLICATIONS FOR RE-ELECTION (System discontinued 1987)

14	Hartlepool	4	Norwich	2	Oldham
12	Halifax	3	Aldershot	2	QPR
11	Barrow	3	Bradford City	2	Rotherham
11	Southport	3	Crystal Palace	2	Scunthorpe
10	Crewe	3	Doncaster	2	Southend
10	Newport	3	Hereford	2	Watford
10	Rochdale	3	Merthyr	1	Blackpool
8	Darlington	3	Swindon	1	Brighton
8	Exeter	3	Torquay	1	Bristol Rov
7	Chester	3	Tranmere	1	Cambridge Utd
7	Walsall	2	Aberdare	1	Cardiff
7	Workington	2	Ashington	1	Carlisle
7	York	2	Bournemouth	1	Charlton
6	Stockport	2	Brentford	1	Mansfield
5	Accrington	2	Colchester	1	Port Vale
5	Gillingham	2	Durham	1	Preston
5	Lincoln	2	Gateshead	1	Shrewsbury
5	New Brighton	2	Grimsby	1	Swansea
4	Bradford PA	2	Millwall	1	Thames
4	Northampton	2	Nelson	1	Wrexham

RELEGATED CLUBS (TO 1992)

1892–3	In Test matches, Darwen and Sheffield Utd won promotion in place of Accrington and Notts Co
1893–4	Tests, Liverpool and Small Heath won promotion Darwen and Newton Heath relegated
1894–5	After Tests, Bury promoted, Liverpool relegated
1895–6	After Tests, Liverpool promoted, Small Heath relegated
1896–7	After Tests, Notts Co promoted, Burnley relegated
1897–8	Test system abolished after success of Burnley and Stoke, League extended Blackburn and Newcastle elected to First Division

Automatic promotion and relegation introduced

FIRST DIVISION TO SECOND

1898–9	Bolton, Sheffield Wed
1899–00	Burnley, Glossop
1900–1	Preston, WBA
1901–2	Small Heath, Manchester City
1902–3	Grimsby, Bolton
1903–4	Liverpool, WBA
1904–5	League extended Bury and Notts Co, two bottom clubs in First Division, re-elected
1905–6	Nottm Forest, Wolves
1906–7	Derby, Stoke
1907–8	Bolton, Birmingham
1908–9	Manchester City, Leicester Fosse
1909–10	Bolton, Chelsea
1910–11	Bristol City, Nottm Forest
1911–12	Preston, Bury
1912–13	Notts Co, Woolwich Arsenal
1913–14	Preston, Derby
1914–15	Tottenham, *Chelsea
1919–20	Notts Co, Sheffield Wed

1920–1	Derby, Bradford PA	
1921–2	Bradford City, Manchester Utd	
1922–3	Stoke, Oldham	
1923–4	Chelsea, Middlesbrough	
1924–5	Preston, Nottm Forest	
1925–6	Manchester City, Notts Co	
1926–7	Leeds, WBA	
1927–8	Tottenham, Middlesbrough	
1928–9	Bury, Cardiff	
1929–30	Burnley, Everton	
1930–1	Leeds, Manchester Utd	
1931–2	Grimsby, West Ham	
1932–3	Bolton, Blackpool	
1933–4	Newcastle, Sheffield Utd	
1934–5	Leicester, Tottenham	
1935–6	Aston Villa, Blackburn	
1936–7	Manchester Utd, Sheffield Wed	
1937–8	Manchester City, WBA	
1938–9	Birmingham, Leicester	
1946–7	Brentford, Leeds	
1947–8	Blackburn, Grimsby	
1948–9	Preston, Sheffield Utd	
1949–50	Manchester City, Birmingham	
1950–1	Sheffield Wed, Everton	
1951–2	Huddersfield, Fulham	
1952–3	Stoke, Derby	
1953–4	Middlesbrough, Liverpool	
1954–5	Leicester, Sheffield Wed	
1955–6	Huddersfield, Sheffield Utd	
1956–7	Charlton, Cardiff	
1957–8	Sheffield Wed, Sunderland	
1958–9	Portsmouth, Aston Villa	
1959–60	Luton, Leeds	
1960–61	Preston, Newcastle	
1961–2	Chelsea, Cardiff	
1962–3	Manchester City, Leyton Orient	
1963–4	Bolton, Ipswich	
1964–5	Wolves, Birmingham	
1965–6	Northampton, Blackburn	
1966–7	Aston Villa, Blackpool	
1967–8	Fulham, Sheffield Utd	
1968–9	Leicester, QPR	
1969–70	Sheffield Wed, Sunderland	
1970–1	Burnley, Blackpool	
1971–2	Nottm Forest, Huddersfield	
1972–3	WBA, Crystal Palace	
1973–4	Norwich, Manchester Utd, Southampton	
1974–5	Chelsea, Luton, Carlisle	
1975–6	Sheffield Utd, Burnley, Wolves	
1976–7	Tottenham, Stoke, Sunderland	
1977–8	Leicester, West Ham, Newcastle	
1978–9	QPR, Birmingham, Chelsea	
1979–80	Bristol City, Derby, Bolton	
1980–1	Norwich, Leicester, Crystal Palace	
1981–2	Leeds, Wolves, Middlesbrough	
1982–3	Manchester City, Swansea, Brighton	
1983–4	Birmingham, Notts Co, Wolves	
1984–5	Norwich, Sunderland, Stoke	
1985–6	Ipswich, Birmingham, WBA	
1986–7	Leicester, Manchester City, Aston Villa	
1987–8	Chelsea**, Portsmouth, Watford,	
	Oxford Utd	
1988–9	Middlesbrough, West Ham, Newcastle	
1989–90	Sheffield Wed, Charlton, Millwall	
1990–1	Sunderland, Derby	
1991–2	Luton, Notts Co, West Ham	

* Subsequently re–elected to First Division when League extended after the war

** Relegated after play–offs

SECOND DIVISION TO THIRD DIVISION

1920–1	Stockport
1921–2	Bradford City, Bristol City
1922–3	Rotherham, Wolves
1923–4	Nelson, Bristol City
1924–5	Crystal Palace, Coventry
1925–6	Stoke, Stockport
1926–7	Darlington, Bradford City
1927–8	Fulham, South Shields
1928–9	Port Vale, Clapton Orient
1929–30	Hull, Notts County
1930–1	Reading, Cardiff
1931–2	Barnsley, Bristol City
1932–3	Chesterfield, Charlton
1933–4	Millwall, Lincoln
1934–5	Oldham, Notts Co
1935–6	Port Vale, Hull
1936–7	Doncaster, Bradford City
1937–8	Barnsley, Stockport
1938–9	Norwich, Tranmere
1946–7	Swansea, Newport
1947–8	Doncaster, Millwall
1948–9	Nottm Forest, Lincoln
1949–50	Plymouth Argyle, Bradford PA
1950–1	Grimsby, Chesterfield
1951–2	Coventry, QPR
1952–3	Southampton, Barnsley
1953–4	Brentford, Oldham
1954–5	Ipswich, Derby
1955–6	Plymouth Argyle, Hull
1956–7	Port Vale, Bury
1957–8	Doncaster, Notts Co
1958–9	Barnsley, Grimsby
1959–60	Bristol City, Hull
1960–1	Lincoln, Portsmouth
1961–2	Brighton, Bristol Rov
1962–3	Walsall, Luton
1963–4	Grimsby, Scunthorpe
1964–5	Swindon, Swansea
1965–6	Middlesbrough, Leyton Orient
1966–7	Northampton, Bury
1967–8	Plymouth Argyle, Rotherham
1968–9	Fulham, Bury
1969–70	Preston, Aston Villa
1970–1	Blackburn, Bolton
1971–2	Charlton, Watford
1972–3	Huddersfield, Brighton
1973–4	Crystal Palace, Preston, Swindon
1974–5	Millwall, Cardiff, Sheffield Wed
1975–6	Portsmouth, Oxford Utd, York

1976–7	Carlisle, Plymouth Argyle, Hereford
1977–8	Hull, Mansfield, Blackpool
1978–9	Sheffield Utd, Millwall, Blackburn
1979–80	Fulham, Burnley, Charlton
1980–1	Preston, Bristol City, Bristol Rov
1981–2	Cardiff, Wrexham, Orient
1982–3	Rotherham, Burnley, Bolton
1983–4	Derby, Swansea, Cambridge Utd
1984–5	Notts Co, Cardiff, Wolves
1985–6	Carlisle, Middlesbrough, Fulham
1986–7	Sunderland**, Grimsby, Brighton
1987–8	Sheffield Utd**, Reading, Huddersfield
1988–9	Shrewsbury, Birmingham, Walsall
1989–90	Bournemouth, Bradford City, Stoke
1990–1	WBA, Hull
1991–2	Plymouth Argyle, Brighton, Port Vale

** Relegated after play–offs

THIRD DIVISION TO FOURTH DIVISION

1958–9	Rochdale, Notts Co, Doncaster, Stockport
1959–60	Accrington, Wrexham, Mansfield, York
1960–1	Chesterfield, Colchester, Bradford City, Tranmere
1961–2	Newport, Brentford, Lincoln, Torquay
1962–3	Bradford PA, Brighton, Carlisle, Halifax
1963–4	Millwall, Crewe, Wrexham, Notts Co
1964–5	Luton, Port Vale, Colchester, Barnsley
1965–6	Southend, Exeter, Brentford, York
1966–7	Doncaster, Workington, Darlington, Swansea
1967–8	Scunthorpe, Colchester, Grimsby, Peterborough (demoted)
1968–9	Oldham, Crewe, Hartlepool Utd, Northampton
1969–70	Bournemouth, Southport, Barrow, Stockport
1970–1	Gillingham, Doncaster, Bury, Reading
1971–2	Mansfield, Barnsley, Torquay, Bradford City
1972–3	Scunthorpe, Swansea, Brentford, Rotherham
1973–4	Cambridge Utd, Shrewsbury, Rochdale, Southport
1974–5	Bournemouth, Watford, Tranmere, Huddersfield
1975–6	Aldershot, Colchester, Southend, Halifax
1976–7	Reading, Northampton, Grimsby, York
1977–8	Port Vale, Bradford City, Hereford, Portsmouth
1978–9	Peterborough, Walsall, Tranmere, Lincoln
1979–80	Bury, Southend, Mansfield, Wimbledon

1980–1	Sheffield Utd, Colchester, Blackpool, Hull
1981–2	Wimbledon, Swindon, Bristol City, Chester
1982–3	Reading, Wrexham, Doncaster, Chesterfield
1983–4	Scunthorpe, Southend, Port Vale, Exeter
1984–5	Burnley, Orient, Preston, Cambridge Utd
1985–6	Lincoln, Cardiff, Wolves, Swansea
1986–7	Bolton**, Carlisle, Darlington, Newport
1987–8	Doncaster, York, Grimsby, Rotherham**
1988–9	Southend, Chesterfield, Gillingham, Aldershot
1989–90	Cardiff, Northampton, Blackpool, Walsall
1990–1	Crewe, Rotherham, Mansfield
1991–2	Bury, Shrewsbury, Torquay, Darlington

** Relegated after plays–offs

DEMOTED FROM FOURTH DIVISION TO CONFERENCE

1987	Lincoln
1988	Newport
1989	Darlington
1990	Colchester
1991	No demotion
1992	No demotion

DEMOTED FROM THIRD DIVISION TO CONFERENCE

1993	Halifax
1994–6	No demotion
1997	Hereford
1998	Doncaster
1999	Scarborough
2000	Chester
2001	Barnet
2002	Halifax
2003	Exeter, Shrewsbury
2004	Carlisle, York

DEMOTED FROM LEAGUE TWO TO CONFERENCE/NATIONAL LEAGUE

2005	Kidderminster, Cambridge Utd
2006	Oxford Utd, Rushden & Diamonds
2007	Boston, Torquay
2008	Mansfield, Wrexham
2009	Chester Luton
2010	Grimsby, Darlington
2011	Lincoln, Stockport
2012	Hereford, Macclesfield
2013	Barnet, Aldershot

2014	Bristol Rov, Torquay
2015	Cheltenham, Tranmere
2016	Dagenham, York
2017	Hartlepool, Leyton Orient
2018	Barnet, Chesterfield
2019	Notts Co, Yeovil
2020	Macclesfield
2021	Southend, Grimsby

RELEGATED CLUBS (SINCE 1993)

1993
Premier League to Div 1: Crystal Palace, Middlesbrough, Nottm Forest
Div 1 to Div 2: Brentford, Cambridge Utd, Bristol Rov
Div 2 to Div 3: Preston, Mansfield, Wigan, Chester

1994
Premier League to Div 1: Sheffield Utd, Oldham, Swindon
Div 1 to Div 2: Birmingham, Oxford Utd, Peterborough
Div 2 to Div 3: Fulham, Exeter, Hartlepool Utd, Barnet

1995
Premier League to Div 1: Crystal Palace, Norwich, Leicester, Ipswich
Div 1 to Div 2: Swindon, Burnley, Bristol City, Notts Co
Div 2 to Div 3: Cambridge Utd, Plymouth, Cardiff, Chester, Leyton Orient

1996
Premier League to Div 1: Manchester City, QPR, Bolton
Div 1 to Div 2: Millwall, Watford, Luton
Div 2 to Div 3: Carlisle, Swansea, Brighton, Hull

1997
Premier League to Div 1: Sunderland, Middlesbrough, Nottm Forest
Div 1 to Div 2: Grimsby, Oldham, Southend
Div 2 to Div 3: Peterborough, Shrewsbury, Rotherham, Notts Co

1998
Premier League to Div 1: Bolton, Barnsley, Crystal Palace
Div 1 to Div 2: Manchester City, Stoke, Reading
Div 2 to Div 3: Brentford, Plymouth, Carlisle, Southend

1999
Premier League to Div 1: Charlton, Blackburn, Nottm Forest
Div 1 to Div 2: Bury, Oxford Utd, Bristol City
Div 2 to Div 3: York, Northampton, Lincoln, Macclesfield

2000
Premier League to Div 1: Wimbledon, Sheffield Wed, Watford
Div 1 to Div 2: Walsall, Port Vale, Swindon
Div 2 to Div 3: Cardiff, Blackpool, Scunthorpe, Chesterfield

2001
Premier League to Div 1: Manchester City, Coventry, Bradford City
Div 1 to Div 2: Huddersfield, QPR, Tranmere
Div 2 to Div 3: Bristol Rov, Luton, Swansea, Oxford Utd

2002
Premier League to Div 1: Ipswich, Derby, Leicester
Div 1 to Div 2: Crewe, Barnsley, Stockport
Div 2 to Div 3: Bournemouth, Bury, Wrexham, Cambridge Utd

2003
Premier League to Div 1: West Ham, WBA, Sunderland
Div 1 to Div 2: Sheffield Wed, Brighton, Grimsby
Div 2 to Div 3: Cheltenham, Huddersfield, Mansfield, Northampton

2004
Premier League to Div 1: Leicester, Leeds, Wolves
Div 1 to Div 2: Walsall, Bradford City, Wimbledon
Div 2 to Div 3: Grimsby, Rushden & Diamonds, Notts Co, Wycombe

2005
Premier League to Championship: Crystal Palace, Norwich, Southampton
Championship to League 1: Gillingham, Nottm Forest, Rotherham
League 1 to League 2: Torquay, Wrexham, Peterborough, Stockport

2006
Premier League to Championship: Birmingham, WBA, Sunderland
Championship to League 1: Crewe, Millwall, Brighton
League 1 to League 2: Hartlepool Utd, MK Dons, Swindon, Walsall

2007
Premier League to Championship: Sheffield Utd, Charlton, Watford
Championship to League 1: Southend, Luton, Leeds
League 1 to League 2: Chesterfield, Bradford City, Rotherham, Brentford

2008
Premier League to Championship: Reading, Birmingham, Derby
Championship to League 1: Leicester, Scunthorpe, Colchester
League 1 to League 2: Bournemouth, Gillingham, Port Vale, Luton

2009
Premier League to Championship: Newcastle, Middlesbrough, WBA
Championship to League 1: Norwich, Southampton, Charlton
League 1 to League 2: Northampton, Crewe, Cheltenham, Hereford

2010
Premier League to Championship: Burnley, Hull, Portsmouth
Championship to League 1: Sheffield Wed, Plymouth, Peterborough
League 1 to League 2: Gillingham, Wycombe, Southend, Stockport

2011
Premier League to Championship: Birmingham, Blackpool, West Ham
Championship to League 1: Preston, Sheffield Utd, Scunthorpe
League 1 to League 2: Dagenham & Red bridge, Bristol Rov, Plymouth, Swindon

2012
Premier League to Championship: Bolton, Blackburn, Wolves
Championship to League 1: Portsmouth, Coventry, Doncaster
League 1 to League 2: Wycombe, Chesterfield, Exeter, Rochdale

2013
Premier League to Championship: Wigan, Reading, QPR
Championship to League 1: Peterborough, Wolves, Bristol City
League 1 to League 2: Scunthorpe, Bury, Hartlepool, Portsmouth

2014
Premier League to Championship: Norwich, Fulham, Cardiff
Championship to League 1: Doncaster, Barnsley, Yeovil
League 1 to League 2: Tranmere, Carlisle, Shrewsbury, Stevenage

2015
Premier League to Championship: Hull, Burnley QPR
Championship to League 1: Millwall, Wigan, Blackpool
League 1 to League 2: Notts Co, Crawley, Leyton Orient, Yeovil

2016
Premier League to Championship: Newcastle, Norwich, Aston Villa
Championship to League 1: Charlton, MK Dons, Bolton
League 1 to League 2: Doncaster, Blackpool, Colchester, Crewe

2017
Premier League to Championship: Hull, Middlesbrough, Sunderland
Championship to League 1: Blackburn, Wigan, Rotherham
League 1 to League 2: Port Vale, Swindon, Coventry, Chesterfield

2018
Premier League to Championship: Swansea, Stoke, WBA
Championship to League 1: Barnsley, Burton, Sunderland
League 1 to League 2: Oldham, Northampton, MK Dons, Bury

2019
Premier League to Championship: Cardiff, Fulham, Huddersfield
Championship to League 1: Rotherham, Bolton, Ipswich
League 1 to League 2: Plymouth, Walsall, Scunthorpe, Bradford

2020
Premier League to Championship: Bournemouth, Watford, Norwich
Championship to League 1: Charlton, Wigan, Hull
League 1 to League 2: Tranmere, Southend, Bolton

2021
Premier League to Championship: Fulham, WBA, Sheffield Utd
Championship to League 1: Wycombe, Rotherham, Sheffield Wed
League 1 to League 2: Rochdale, Northampton, Swindon, Bristol Rov

ANNUAL AWARDS

FOOTBALL WRITERS' ASSOCIATION

Footballer of the Year: 1948 Stanley Matthews (Blackpool); **1949** Johnny Carey (Manchester Utd); **1950** Joe Mercer (Arsenal); **1951** Harry Johnston (Blackpool); **1952** Billy Wright (Wolves); **1953** Nat Lofthouse (Bolton); **1954** Tom Finney (Preston); **1955** Don Revie (Manchester City); **1956** Bert Trautmann (Manchester City); **1957** Tom Finney (Preston); **1958** Danny Blanchflower (Tottenham); **1959** Syd Owen (Luton); **1960** Bill Slater (Wolves); **1961** Danny Blanchflower (Tottenham); **1962** Jimmy Adamson (Burnley); **1963** Stanley Matthews (Stoke); **1964** Bobby Moore (West Ham); **1965** Bobby Collins (Leeds); **1966** Bobby Charlton (Manchester Utd); **1967** Jack Charlton (Leeds); **1968** George Best (Manchester Utd); **1969** Tony Book (Manchester City) & Dave Mackay (Derby) – shared; **1970** Billy Bremner (Leeds); **1971** Frank McLintock (Arsenal); **1972** Gordon Banks (Stoke); **1973** Pat Jennings (Tottenham); **1974** Ian Callaghan (Liverpool); **1975** Alan Mullery (Fulham); **1976** Kevin Keegan (Liverpool); **1977** Emlyn Hughes (Liverpool); **1978** Kenny Burns (Nott'm Forest); **1979** Kenny Dalglish (Liverpool); **1980** Terry McDermott (Liverpool); **1981** Frans Thijssen (Ipswich); **1982** Steve Perryman (Tottenham); **1983** Kenny Dalglish (Liverpool); **1984** Ian Rush (Liverpool); **1985** Neville Southall (Everton); **1986** Gary Lineker (Everton); **1987** Clive Allen (Tottenham); **1988** John Barnes (Liverpool); **1989** Steve Nicol (Liverpool); Special award to the Liverpool players for the compassion shown to bereaved families after the Hillsborough Disaster; **1990** John Barnes (Liverpool); **1991** Gordon Strachan (Leeds); **1992** Gary Lineker (Tottenham); **1993** Chris Waddle (Sheffield Wed); **1994** Alan Shearer (Blackburn); **1995** Jurgen Klinsmann (Tottenham); **1996** Eric Cantona (Manchester Utd); **1997** Gianfranco Zola (Chelsea); **1998** Dennis Bergkamp (Arsenal); **1999** David Ginola (Tottenham); **2000** Roy Keane (Manchester Utd); **2001** Teddy Sheringham (Manchester Utd); **2002** Robert Pires (Arsenal); **2003** Thierry Henry (Arsenal); **2004** Thierry Henry (Arsenal); **2005** Frank Lampard (Chelsea); **2006** Thierry Henry (Arsenal); **2007** Cristiano Ronaldo (Manchester Utd); **2008** Cristiano Ronaldo (Manchester Utd); **2009** Steven Gerrard (Liverpool); **2010** Wayne Rooney (Manchester Utd); **2011** Scott Parker (West Ham); **2012** Robin van Persie (Arsenal); **2013** Gareth Bale (Tottenham); **2014** Luis Suarez (Liverpool); **2015** Eden Hazard (Chelsea); **2016** Jamie Vardy (Leicester); **2017** N'Golo Kante (Chelsea); **2018** Mohamed Salah (Liverpool); **2019** Raheem Sterling (Manchester City); **2020** Jordan Henderson (Liverpool); **2021** Ruben Dias (Manchester City)

PROFESSIONAL FOOTBALLERS' ASSOCIATION

Player of the Year: 1974 Norman Hunter (Leeds); **1975** Colin Todd (Derby); **1976** Pat Jennings (Tottenham); **1977** Andy Gray (Aston Villa); **1978** Peter Shilton (Nott'm Forest); **1979** Liam Brady (Arsenal); **1980** Terry McDermott (Liverpool); **1981** John Wark (Ipswich); **1982** Kevin Keegan (Southampton); **1983** Kenny Dalglish (Liverpool); **1984** Ian Rush (Liverpool); **1985** Peter Reid (Everton); **1986** Gary Lineker (Everton); **1987** Clive Allen (Tottenham); **1988** John Barnes (Liverpool); **1989** Mark Hughes (Manchester Utd); **1990** David Platt (Aston Villa); **1991** Mark Hughes (Manchester Utd); **1992** Gary Pallister (Manchester Utd); **1993** Paul McGrath (Aston Villa); **1994** Eric Cantona (Manchester Utd); **1995** Alan Shearer (Blackburn); **1996** Les Ferdinand (Newcastle); **1997** Alan Shearer (Newcastle); **1998** Dennis Bergkamp (Arsenal); **1999** David Ginola (Tottenham); **2000** Roy Keane (Manchester Utd); **2001** Teddy Sheringham (Manchester Utd); **2002** Ruud van Nistelrooy (Manchester Utd); **2003** Thierry Henry (Arsenal); **2004** Thierry Henry (Arsenal); **2005** John Terry (Chelsea); **2006** Steven Gerrard (Liverpool); **2007** Cristiano Ronaldo (Manchester Utd); **2008** Cristiano Ronaldo (Manchester Utd); **2009** Ryan Giggs (Manchester Utd); **2010** Wayne Rooney (Manchester Utd); **2011** Gareth Bale (Tottenham); **2012** Robin van Persie (Arsenal); **2013** Gareth Bale (Tottenham); **2014** Luis Suarez (Liverpool); **2015** Eden Hazard (Chelsea); **2016** Riyad Mahrez (Leicester); **2017** N'Golo Kante (Chelsea); **2018** Mohamed Salah (Liverpool); **2019** Virgil van Dijk (Liverpool); **2020** Kevin De Bruyne (Manchester City); **2021** Kevin De Bruyne (Manchester City)

Young Player of the Year: 1974 Kevin Beattie (Ipswich); **1975** Mervyn Day (West Ham); **1976** Peter Barnes (Manchester City); **1977** Andy Gray (Aston Villa); **1978** Tony Woodcock (Nott'm Forest); **1979** Cyrille Regis (WBA); **1980** Glenn Hoddle (Tottenham); **1981** Gary Shaw (Aston Villa); **1982** Steve Moran (Southampton); **1983** Ian Rush (Liverpool); **1984** Paul Walsh (Luton); **1985** Mark Hughes (Manchester Utd); **1986** Tony Cottee (West Ham); **1987** Tony Adams (Arsenal); **1988** Paul Gascoigne (Newcastle); **1989** Paul Merson (Arsenal); **1990** Matthew Le Tissier (Southampton); **1991** Lee Sharpe (Manchester Utd); **1992** Ryan Giggs (Manchester Utd); **1993** Ryan Giggs (Manchester Utd); **1994** Andy Cole (Newcastle); **1995** Robbie Fowler (Liverpool); **1996** Robbie Fowler (Liverpool); **1997** David Beckham (Manchester Utd); **1998** Michael Owen (Liverpool); **1999** Nicolas Anelka (Arsenal); **2000** Harry Kewell (Leeds); **2001** Steven Gerrard (Liverpool); **2002** Craig Bellamy (Newcastle); **2003** Jermaine Jenas (Newcastle); **2004** Scott Parker (Chelsea); **2005** Wayne Rooney (Manchester Utd); **2006** Wayne Rooney (Manchester Utd); **2007** Cristiano Ronaldo (Manchester Utd); **2008** Cesc Fabregas (Arsenal); **2009** Ashley Young (Aston Villa); **2010** James Milner (Aston Villa); **2011** Jack Wilshere (Arsenal); **2012** Kyle Walker (Tottenham); **2013** Gareth Bale (Tottenham); **2014** Eden Hazard (Chelsea); **2015** Harry Kane (Tottenham); **2016** Dele Alli (Tottenham); **2017** Dele Alli (Tottenham); **2018** Leroy Sane (Manchester City); **2019** Raheem Sterling (Manchester City); **2020** Trent Alexander-Arnold (Liverpool); **2021** Phil Foden (Manchester City)

Merit Awards: 1974 Bobby Charlton & Cliff Lloyd; **1975** Denis Law; **1976** George Eastham; **1977** Jack Taylor; **1978** Bill Shankly; **1979** Tom Finney; **1980** Sir Matt Busby; **1981** John Trollope; **1982** Joe Mercer; **1983** Bob Paisley; **1984** Bill Nicholson; **1985** Ron Greenwood; **1986** England 1966 World Cup–winning team; **1987** Sir Stanley Matthews; **1988** Billy Bonds; **1989** Nat Lofthouse; **1990** Peter Shilton; **1991** Tommy Hutchison; **1992** Brian Clough; **1993** Manchester Utd; **1968** European Champions; Eusebio; **1994** Billy Bingham; **1995** Gordon Strachan; **1996** Pele; **1997** Peter Beardsley; **1998** Steve Ogrizovic; **1999** Tony Ford; **2000** Gary Mabbutt; **2001** Jimmy Hill; **2002** Niall Quinn; **2003** Sir Bobby Robson; **2004** Dario Gradi; **2005** Shaka Hislop; **2006** George Best; **2007** Sir Alex Ferguson; **2008** Jimmy Armfield; **2009** John McDermott; **2010** Lucas Radebe; **2011** Howard Webb; **2012** Graham Alexander; **2013** Eric Harrison/Manchester Utd Class of '92; **2014** Donald Bell (posthumously; only footballer to win Victoria Cross; World War 1); **2015** Steven Gerrard & Frank Lampard; **2016** Ryan Giggs; **2017** David Beckham; **2018** Cyrille Regis (posthumously); **2019** Steph Houghton; **2020** Marcus Rashford; **2021** Gordon Taylor

MANAGER OF THE YEAR 1

(chosen by media and sponsors)

1966 Jock Stein (Celtic); **1967** Jock Stein (Celtic); **1968** Matt Busby (Manchester Utd); **1969** Don Revie (Leeds); **1970** Don Revie (Leeds); **1971** Bertie Mee (Arsenal); **1972** Don Revie (Leeds); **1973** Bill Shankly (Liverpool); **1974** Jack Charlton (Middlesbrough); **1975** Ron Saunders (Aston Villa); **1976** Bob Paisley (Liverpool); **1977** Bob Paisley (Liverpool); **1978** Brian Clough (Nott'm Forest); **1979** Bob Paisley (Liverpool); **1980** Bob Paisley (Liverpool); **1981** Ron Saunders (Aston Villa); **1982** Bob Paisley (Liverpool); **1983** Bob Paisley (Liverpool); **1984** Joe Fagan (Liverpool); **1985** Howard Kendall (Everton); **1986** Kenny Dalglish (Liverpool); **1987** Howard Kendall (Everton); **1988** Kenny Dalglish (Liverpool); **1989** George Graham (Arsenal); **1990** Kenny Dalglish (Liverpool); **1991** George Graham (Arsenal); **1992** Howard Wilkinson (Leeds); **1993** Alex Ferguson (Manchester Utd); **1994** Alex Ferguson (Manchester Utd); **1995** Kenny Dalglish (Blackburn); **1996** Alex Ferguson (Manchester Utd); **1997** Alex Ferguson (Manchester Utd); **1998** Arsene Wenger (Arsenal); **1999** Alex Ferguson (Manchester Utd); **2000** Sir Alex Ferguson (Manchester Utd); **2001** George Burley (Ipswich); **2002** Arsene Wenger (Arsenal); **2003** Sir Alex Ferguson (Manchester Utd); **2004** Arsene Wenger (Arsenal); **2005** Jose Mourinho (Chelsea); **2006** Jose Mourinho (Chelsea); **2007** Sir Alex Ferguson (Manchester Utd); **2008** Sir Alex Ferguson (Manchester Utd); **2009** Sir Alex Ferguson (Manchester Utd); **2010** Harry Redknapp (Tottenham); **2011** Sir Alex Ferguson (Manchester Utd); **2012**: Alan Pardew (Newcastle); **2013** Sir Alex Ferguson (Manchester Utd); **2014** Tony Pulis (Crystal Palace); **2015** Jose Mourinho (Chelsea); **2016** Claudio Ranieri

(Leicester); **2017** Antonio Conte (Chelsea); **2018** Pep Guardiola (Manchester City); **2019** Pep Guardiola (Manchester City); **2020** Jurgen Klopp (Liverpool); **2021** Pep Guardiola (Manchester City)

MANAGER OF THE YEAR 2
(Chosen by the League Managers' Association)

1993 Dave Bassett (Sheffield Utd); **1994** Joe Kinnear (Wimbledon); **1995** Frank Clark (Nott'm Forest); **1996** Peter Reid (Sunderland); **1997** Danny Wilson (Barnsley); **1998** David Jones (Southampton); **1999** Alex Ferguson (Manchester Utd); **2000** Alan Curbishley (Charlton Athletic); **2001** George Burley (Ipswich); **2002** Arsene Wenger (Arsenal); **2003** David Moyes (Everton); **2004** Arsene Wenger (Arsenal); **2005** David Moyes (Everton); **2006** Steve Coppell (Reading); **2007** Steve Coppell (Reading); **2008** Sir Alex Ferguson (Manchester Utd); **2009** David Moyes (Everton); **2010** Roy Hodgson (Fulham); **2011** Sir Alex Ferguson (Manchester Utd); **2012**: Alan Pardew (Newcastle); **2013** Sir Alex Ferguson (Manchester Utd); **2014** Brendan Rodgers (Liverpool); **2015** Eddie Howe (Bournemouth); **2016** Claudio Ranieri (Leicester); **2017** Antonio Conte (Chelsea); **2018** Pep Guardiola (Manchester City); **2019** Chris Wilder (Sheffield Utd); **2020** Jurgen Klopp (Liverpool); **2021** Pep Guardiola (Manchester City)

SCOTTISH FOOTBALL WRITERS' ASSOCIATION
Footballer of the Year: 1965 Billy McNeill (Celtic); **1966** John Greig (Rangers); **1967** Ronnie Simpson (Celtic); **1968** Gordon Wallace (Raith); **1969** Bobby Murdoch (Celtic); **1970** Pat Stanton (Hibernian); **1971** Martin Buchan (Aberdeen); **1972** David Smith (Rangers); **1973** George Connelly (Celtic); **1974** World Cup Squad; **1975** Sandy Jardine (Rangers); **1976** John Greig (Rangers); **1977** Danny McGrain (Celtic); **1978** Derek Johnstone (Rangers); **1979** Andy Ritchie (Morton); **1980** Gordon Strachan (Aberdeen); **1981** Alan Rough (Partick Thistle); **1982** Paul Sturrock (Dundee Utd); **1983** Charlie Nicholas (Celtic); **1984** Willie Miller (Aberdeen); **1985** Hamish McAlpine (Dundee Utd); **1986** Sandy Jardine (Hearts); **1987** Brian McClair (Celtic); **1988** Paul McStay (Celtic); **1989** Richard Gough (Rangers); **1990** Alex McLeish (Aberdeen); **1991** Maurice Malpas (Dundee Utd); **1992** Ally McCoist (Rangers); **1993** Andy Goram (Rangers); **1994** Mark Hateley (Rangers); **1995** Brian Laudrup (Rangers); **1996** Paul Gascoigne (Rangers); **1997** Brian Laudrup (Rangers); **1998** Craig Burley (Celtic); **1999** Henrik Larsson (Celtic); **2000** Barry Ferguson (Rangers); **2001** Henrik Larsson (Celtic); **2002** Paul Lambert (Celtic); **2003** Barry Ferguson (Rangers); **2004** Jackie McNamara (Celtic); **2005** John Hartson (Celtic); **2006** Craig Gordon (Hearts); **2007** Shunsuke Nakamura (Celtic); **2008** Carlos Cuellar (Rangers); **2009** Gary Caldwell (Celtic); **2010** David Weir (Rangers); **2011** Emilio Izaguirre (Celtic); **2012** Charlie Mulgrew (Celtic); **2013** Leigh Griffiths (Hibernian); **2014** Kris Commons (Celtic); **2015** Craig Gordon (Celtic); **2016** Leigh Griffiths (Celtic); **2017** Scott Sinclair (Celtic); **2018** Scott Brown (Celtic); **2019** James Forrest (Celtic); **2020** Odsonne Edouard; **2021** Steven Davis (Rangers)

PROFESSIONAL FOOTBALLERS' ASSOCIATION SCOTLAND
Player of the Year: 1978 Derek Johnstone (Rangers); **1979** Paul Hegarty (Dundee Utd); **1980** Davie Provan (Celtic); **1981** Mark McGhee (Aberdeen); **1982** Sandy Clarke (Airdrieonians); **1983** Charlie Nicholas (Celtic); **1984** Willie Miller (Aberdeen); **1985** Jim Duffy (Morton); **1986** Richard Gough (Dundee Utd); **1987** Brian McClair (Celtic); **1988** Paul McStay (Celtic); **1989** Theo Snelders (Aberdeen); **1990** Jim Bett (Aberdeen); **1991** Paul Elliott (Celtic); **1992** Ally McCoist (Rangers); **1993** Andy Goram (Rangers); **1994** Mark Hateley (Rangers); **1995** Brian Laudrup (Rangers); **1996** Paul Gascoigne (Rangers); **1997** Paolo Di Canio (Celtic) **1998** Jackie McNamara (Celtic); **1999** Henrik Larsson (Celtic); **2000** Mark Viduka (Celtic); **2001** Henrik Larsson (Celtic); **2002** Lorenzo Amoruso (Rangers); **2003** Barry Ferguson (Rangers); **2004** Chris Sutton (Celtic); **2005** John Hartson (Celtic) and Fernando Ricksen (Rangers); **2006** Shaun Maloney (Celtic); **2007** Shunsuke Nakamura (Celtic); **2008** Aiden McGeady (Celtic); **2009** Scott Brown (Celtic); **2010** Steven Davis (Rangers); **2011** Emilio Izaguirre (Celtic); **2012** Charlie Mulgrew (Celtic); **2013** Michael Higdon (Motherwell); **2014** Kris Commons (Celtic); **2015** Stefan Johansen (Celtic); **2016** Leigh Griffiths

(Celtic); **2017** Scott Sinclair (Celtic); **2018** Scott Brown (Celtic); **2019** James Forrest (Celtic); **2020** No Award; **2021** James Tavernier (Rangers)

Young Player of the Year: 1978 Graeme Payne (Dundee Utd); **1979** Ray Stewart (Dundee Utd); **1980** John McDonald (Rangers); **1981** Charlie Nicholas (Celtic); **1982** Frank McAvennie (St Mirren); **1983** Paul McStay (Celtic); **1984** John Robertson (Hearts); **1985** Craig Levein (Hearts); **1986** Craig Levein (Hearts); **1987** Robert Fleck (Rangers); **1988** John Collins (Hibernian); **1989** Billy McKinlay (Dundee Utd); **1990** Scott Crabbe (Hearts); **1991** Eoin Jess (Aberdeen); **1992** Phil O'Donnell (Motherwell); **1993** Eoin Jess (Aberdeen); **1994** Phil O'Donnell (Motherwell); **1995** Charlie Miller (Rangers); **1996** Jackie McNamara (Celtic); **1997** Robbie Winters (Dundee Utd); **1998** Gary Naysmith (Hearts); **1999** Barry Ferguson (Rangers); **2000** Kenny Miller (Hibernian); **2001** Stilian Petrov (Celtic); **2002** Kevin McNaughton (Aberdeen); **2003** James McFadden (Motherwell); **2004** Stephen Pearson (Celtic); **2005** Derek Riordan (Hibernian); **2006** Shaun Maloney (Celtic); **2007** Steven Naismith (Kilmarnock); **2008** Aiden McGeady (Celtic); **2009** James McCarthy (Hamilton); **2010** Danny Wilson (Rangers); **2011:** David Goodwillie (Dundee Utd); **2012** James Forrest (Celtic); **2013** Leigh Griffiths (Hibernian); **2014** Andy Robertson (Dundee Utd); **2015** Jason Denayer (Celtic); **2016** Kieran Tierney (Celtic); **2017** Kieran Tierney (Celticl); **2018** Kieran Tierney (Celtic); **2019** Ryan Kent (Rangers); **2020** No Award; **2021** David Turnbull (Celtic)

SCOTTISH MANAGER OF THE YEAR

1987 Jim McLean (Dundee Utd); **1988** Billy McNeill (Celtic); **1989** Graeme Souness (Rangers); **1990** Andy Roxburgh (Scotland); **1991** Alex Totten (St Johnstone); **1992** Walter Smith (Rangers); **1993** Walter Smith (Rangers); **1994** Walter Smith (Rangers); **1995** Jimmy Nicholl (Raith); **1996** Walter Smith (Rangers); **1997** Walter Smith (Rangers); **1998** Wim Jansen (Celtic); **1999** Dick Advocaat (Rangers); **2000** Dick Advocaat (Rangers); **2001** Martin O'Neill (Celtic); **2002** John Lambie (Partick Thistle); **2003** Alex McLeish (Rangers); **2004** Martin O'Neill (Celtic); **2005** Alex McLeish (Rangers); **2006** Gordon Strachan (Celtic); **2007** Gordon Strachan (Celtic); **2008** Billy Reid (Hamilton); **2009** Csaba Laszlo (Hearts); **2010** Walter Smith (Rangers); **2011:** Mixu Paatelainen (Kilmarnock); **2012** Neil Lennon (Celtic); **2013** Neil Lennon (Celtic); **2014** Derek McInnes (Aberdeen); **2015** John Hughes (Inverness); **2016** Mark Warburton (Rangers); **2017** Brendan Rodgers (Celtic); **2018** Jack Ross (St Mirren); **2019** Steve Clarke (Kilmarnock); **2020** Neil Lennon (Celtic); **2021** Stevn Gerrard (Rangers)

EUROPEAN FOOTBALLER OF THE YEAR

1956 Stanley Matthews (Blackpool); **1957** Alfredo di Stefano (Real Madrid); **1958** Raymond Kopa (Real Madrid); **1959** Alfredo di Stefano (Real Madrid); **1960** Luis Suarez (Barcelona); **1961** Omar Sivori (Juventus); **1962** Josef Masopust (Dukla Prague); **1963** Lev Yashin (Moscow Dynamo); **1964** Denis Law (Manchester Utd); **1965** Eusebio (Benfica); **1966** Bobby Charlton (Manchester Utd); **1967** Florian Albert (Ferencvaros); **1968** George Best (Manchester Utd); **1969** Gianni Rivera (AC Milan); **1970** Gerd Muller (Bayern Munich); **1971** Johan Cruyff (Ajax); **1972** Franz Beckenbauer (Bayern Munich); **1973** Johan Cruyff (Barcelona); **1974** Johan Cruyff (Barcelona); **1975** Oleg Blokhin (Dynamo Kiev); **1976** Franz Beckenbauer (Bayern Munich); **1977** Allan Simonsen (Borussia Moenchengladbach); **1978** Kevin Keegan (SV Hamburg); **1979** Kevin Keegan (SV Hamburg); **1980** Karl-Heinz Rummenigge (Bayern Munich); **1981** Karl-Heinz Rummenigge (Bayern Munich); **1982** Paolo Rossi (Juventus); **1983** Michel Platini (Juventus); **1984** Michel Platini (Juventus); **1985** Michel Platini (Juventus); **1986** Igor Belanov (Dynamo Kiev); **1987** Ruud Gullit (AC Milan); **1988** Marco van Basten (AC Milan); **1989** Marco van Basten (AC Milan); **1990** Lothar Matthaus (Inter Milan); **1991** Jean-Pierre Papin (Marseille); **1992** Marco van Basten (AC Milan); **1993** Roberto Baggio (Juventus); **1994** Hristo Stoichkov (Barcelona); **1995** George Weah (AC Milan); **1996** Matthias Sammer (Borussia Dortmund); **1997** Ronaldo (Inter Milan); **1998** Zinedine Zidane (Juventus); **1999** Rivaldo (Barcelona); **2000** Luis Figo (Real Madrid); **2001** Michael Owen (Liverpool); **2002** Ronaldo (Real Madrid); **2003** Pavel Nedved (Juventus); **2004** Andriy Shevchenko (AC Milan); **2005** Ronaldinho (Barcelona); **2006** Fabio Cannavaro (Real Madrid); **2007** Kaka (AC Milan); **2008** Cristiano Ronaldo (Manchester United); **2009** Lionel Messi (Barcelona)

WORLD FOOTBALLER OF YEAR

1991 Lothar Matthaus (Inter Milan and Germany); **1992** Marco van Basten (AC Milan and Holland); **1993** Roberto Baggio (Juventus and Italy); **1994** Romario (Barcelona and Brazil); **1995** George Weah (AC Milan and Liberia); **1996** Ronaldo (Barcelona and Brazil); **1997** Ronaldo (Inter Milan and Brazil); **1998** Zinedine Zidane (Juventus and France); **1999** Rivaldo (Barcelona and Brazil); **2000** Zinedine Zidane (Juventus and France); **2001** Luis Figo (Real Madrid and Portugal); **2002** Ronaldo (Real Madrid and Brazil); **2003** Zinedine Zidane (Real Madrid and France); **2004** Ronaldinho (Barcelona and Brazil); **2005** Ronaldinho (Barcelona and Brazil); **2006** Fabio Cannavaro (Real Madrid and Italy); **2007** Kaka (AC Milan and Brazil); **2008** Cristiano Ronaldo (Manchester United and Portugal); **2009** Lionel Messi (Barcelona and Argentina)

FIFA BALLON D'OR

(replaces European and World Footballer of the Year)

2010: Lionel Messi (Barcelona). **2011** Lionel Messi (Barcelona); **2012** Lionel Messi (Barcelona); **2013** Cristiano Ronaldo (Real Madrid); **2014**: Cristiano Ronaldo (Real Madrid); **2015** Lionel Messi (Barcelona)

FIFA BEST PLAYER

2016 Cristiano Ronaldo (Real Madrid); **2017** Cristiano Ronaldo (Real Madrid); **2018** Luka Modric (Real Madrid) ; **2019** Lionel Messi (Barcelona); **2020**: Robert Lewandowski (Bayern Munich))

FIFA WORLD COACH OF THE YEAR

2010: Jose Mourinho (Inter Milan). **2011** Pep Guardiola (Barcelona); **2012** Vicente del Bosque (Spain); **2013** Jupp Heynckes (Bayern Munich); **2014** Joachim Low (Germany); **2015** Luis Enrique (Barcelona); **2016** Claudio Ranieri (Leicester); **2017** Zinedine Zidane (Real Madrid); **2018** Didier Deschamps (France); **2019** Jurgen Klopp (Liverpool); **2020** Jurgen Klopp (Liverpool)

THE THINGS THEY SAY...

'It probably won't sink in until I finish my career and look back on what I have achieved' – **Steven Davis** after overtaking Peter Shilton to become Britain's most capped player with his 126th appearance for Northern Ireland.

'This has been a season and a Premier League like no other. It was the hardest and we will always remember it' – **Pep Guardiola**, Manchester City manager, after winning a third title in four years.

'For us to win a final against a great club like Chelsea means everything, particularly with so many people here to see it. This game was about the connection between players and supporters which we have missed so much' – **Brendan Rodgers**, Leicester manager, after their FA Cup Final win.

'We are all united against these disgraceful, self-serving proposals, fuelled above all else by greed' – **Aleksander Ceferin**, UEFA president, on the failed attempt by leading clubs to set up a European Super League.

'To bring forward proposals in the midst of Covid, in the middle of the economic crisis that exists for all clubs, is an absolute scandal' – **Gary Neville**, influential former Manchester United and England defender.

(figures in brackets denote appearances as substitute)

PREMIER LEAGUE

ARSENAL

Five straight wins to finish with were not enough to disguise a disappointing season. For the first time since season 1995-96 there will be no European football to look forward to – and on the evidence of the campaign overall not a great deal of optimism about bridging a growing gap between the top teams. Instead, a potential takeover was a major topic of conversation after the club came under fire for backing plans for a European Super League. Arsenal never rose above the middle reaches of the table once a promising start of three victories in four games gave away to general inconsistency. The defence of the FA Cup ended in round four at Southampton and the opportunity for Europa League success was lost in a goalless draw at the Emirates in the second leg of the semi-final against Villarreal, coached by their former manager Unai Emery, who went on to a record fourth victory in the competition. The emerging talent of Emile Smith Rowe and Bukayo Saka offered promise for the future, while the team's late flourish opened the way to a place in the new Europa League Conference. But while Arsenal were completing a routine win over Brighton in the final round of matches, arch-rivals Tottenham's turnaround at Leicester enabled them to secure seventh place, a single point ahead.

Aubameyang P-E 26 (3)	Luiz D...................... 17 (3)	Runarsson R ....- (1)
Bellerin H 24 (1)	Maitland-Niles A 5 (6)	Ryan M 3
Chambers C 8 (2)	Mari P..........................10	Saka B 30 (2)
Ceballos D 17 (8)	Martinelli G 7 (7)	Smith Rowe E...........18 (2)
Elneny M 17 (6)	Mustafi S .... - (3)	Soares C......................8 (2)
Gabriel 22 (1)	Nelson R .... - (2)	Tierney K 26 (1)
Holding R 28 (2)	Nketiah E 4 (13)	Willian 16 (9)
Kolasinac S................. - (1)	Odegaard M.............. 9 (5)	Willock J 2 (5)
Lacazette A.............. 22 (9)	Partey T 18 (6)	Xhaka G 29 (2)
Leno B 35	Pepe N.................. 16 (13)	

League goals (55): Lacazette 13, Aubameyang 10, Pepe 10, Saka 5, Gabriel 2, Martinelli 2, Nketiah 2, Smith Rowe 2, Bellerin 1, Elneny 1, Luiz 1, Odegaard 1, Tierney 1, Willian 1, Xhaka 1, Opponents 2
FA Cup goals (2): Aubameyang 1, Smith Rowe 1. **League Cup goals** (3): Lacazette 1, Nketiah 1, Opponents 1
Europa League goals (33): Pepe 6, Aubameyang 4, Lacazette 3, Nketiah 3, Willock 3, Balogun 2, Elneny 2, Saka 2, Gabriel 1, Luiz 1, Nelson 1, Odegaard 1, Smith Rowe 1, Tierney 1, Opponents 2
Player of Year: Bukayo Saka

ASTON VILLA

Villa made considerable progress after the previous season's close shave when finishing a point away from an immediate return to the Championship. They made the perfect start with four successive victories, including a memorable a 7-2 rout of Liverpool in which new-signing Ollie Watkins scored a hat-trick. The former Brentford striker netted two more in a 3-0 away victory over Arsenal. And with captain Jack Grealish also winning England recognition for his influential performances, Villa kept on course for a possible European place. Instead, they lost Grealish with a shin injury which kept him out for three months and which had a considerable effect on results. His side lost much of the momentum, developing a costly tendency to surrender points which resulted in fall to just below mid-table on the back of three victories in 13 matches. Grealish' first full appearance back accompanied a 2-1 victory at Tottenham, with Watkins taking his tally for the campaign to 14, to ensure 11th position – an improvement of six on 2020. Villa also finished well by beating Chelsea 2-1, with Bertrand Traore scoring their first goal then winning a penalty converted by Anwar El Ghazi.

Barkley R.................. 18 (6)	Hause K............................7	Ramsey J 6 (16)
Cash M...........................28	Hourihane C 3 (1)	Sanson M....................3 (6)
Chukwuemeka C.......... - (2)	Konsa E 35 (1)	Targett M....................... 38
Davis K..................... 1 (14)	Martinez E....................38	Taylor N .... - (1)
Douglas Luiz 32 (1)	McGinn J 37	Traore B 29 (7)
El Ghazi A 17 (11)	Mings T.........................36	Trezeguet 12 (9)
Elmohamady A 8 (6)	Nakamba M............... 9 (4)	Watkins O.......................37
Grealish J 24 (2)	Philogene-Bidace J........ - (1)	Wesley ....- (3)

League goals (55): Watkins 14, El Ghazi 10, Traore 7, Grealish 6, Barkley 3, McGinn 3, Konsa 2, Mings 2, Trezeguet 2, Davis 1, Hause 1, Hourihane 1, Opponents 3
FA Cup goals (1): BarryL 1. **League Cup goals** (6): Watkins 2, Davis 1, El Ghazi 1, Grealish 1, Traore 1
Player of Year: Emiliano Martinez

BRIGHTON AND HOVE ALBION

Another uncomfortable campaign for the club looked to have eased with significant performances early in the new year. They ended 14 home league games without a win, stretching back to the previous campaign, by defeating Tottenham with a goal from Leandro Trossard. That was followed by another 1-0 success against Liverpool, their first at Anfield for 39 years courtesy of Steven Alzate's first goal in the competition. But a worrying run of five matches yielding just two points left Brighton level on 26 with third-from-bottom Fulham. Relief came in a 2-1 win at Southampton which manager Graham Potter described as giving his side 'renewed belief in avoiding relegation.' Then came a 3-0 success against fellow-strugglers Newcastle which opened up a six-point cushion. Brighton subsequently extended that to 13 by coming from two goals down to defeat ten-man Manchester City as a limited number of spectators returned to the Amex. Potter called it a 'tough season' after his side closed with a 2-0 defeat at Arsenal and finished 16th.

Alzate S.................... 10 (5)	Khadra R.................... - (1)	Ryan M 11
Bernardo.................... 2 (1)	Lallana A................ 16 (14)	Sanchez R..................... 27
Bissouma Y............... 35 (1)	Lamptey T...................11	Tau P.......................... 1 (2)
Burn D 23 (4)	Mac Allister A............ 13 (8)	Trossard L 30 (5)
Connolly A 9 (8)	March S 19 (2)	Veltman J.................. 25 (3)
Dunk L 33	Maupay N 29 (4)	Webster A..................... 29
Gross P 27 (7)	Moder J 7 (5)	Welbeck D................ 17 (7)
Izquierdo J................. - (1)	Molumby J .... - (1)	White B......................... 36
Jahanbakhsh A........ 6 (15)	Propper D 2 (5)	Zeqiri A........................- (9)

League goals (40): Maupay 8, Welbeck 6, Dunk 5, Trossard 5, Gross 3, Connolly 2, March 2, Mac Allister 1, Alzate 1, Bissouma 1, Burn 1, Lallana 1, Lamptey 1, Veltman 1, Webster 1, Opponents 1
FA Cup goals (3): Alzate 1, Bissouma 1, March 1. **League Cup goals** (6): Jahanbakhsh 2, Mac Allister 2, Bernardo 1, Gyokeres 1
Player of Year: Ben White

BURNLEY

Chris Wood's hat-trick at Molineux eased Burnley's relegation worries. It came in a 4-0 win over Wolves, was the club's biggest away from home in the top-flight for 56 years and stretched their lead over the drop zone to nine points. Wood, who became the first New Zealander to score a treble in the Premier League, was on a run of eight goals in eight matches. He finished on 12, almost matching his tally for the previous season. Burnley, however, were down by seven places on 2020. They had a single win to show from the opening ten games, improved when captain Ben Mee returned from injury and went on to record notable victories away at Arsenal, Liverpool and Everton. But home form was a constant problem, with only one victory – 3-2 against Aston Villa – to show from the final 11 games at Turf Moor. Successive defeats to finish with against Leeds (0-4) and Liverpool (0-3) highlighted the problem. Disappointment, too, for England's No 2 goalkeeper Nick Pope, who was ruled out of the European Championship with a knee injury which needed an operation.

Bardsley P 3 (1)	Lowton M 34	Rodriguez J 12 (19)
Barnes A.................. 15 (7)	McNeil D............. 34 (2)	Stephens D................3 (4)
Benson J................... 2 (4)	Mee B...........................30	Tarkowski J...................36
Brady R 12 (7)	Mumbongo J................ - (2)	Taylor C....................28 (1)
Brownhill J.............. 32 (1)	Norris W.........................2	Vydra M................15 (13)
Cork J....................... 15 (1)	Peacock-Farrell B..............4	Westwood A 38
Dunne J..........................3	Pieters E 13 (7)	Wood C 32 (1)
Gudmundsson J B..... 16 (6)	Pope N.........................32	
Long K 7 (1)	Richardson L .... - (2)	

League goals (33): Wood 12, Barnes 3, Vydra 3, Westwood 3, Gudmundsson 2, McNeil 2, Mee 2, Brady 1, Dunne 1, Lowton 1, Rodriguez 1, Tarkowski 1, Opponents 1
FA Cup goals (4): Rodriguez 2, Long 1, Vydra 1. **League Cup goals** (3): Vydra 2, Brownhill 1
Player of Year: Chris Wood

CHELSEA

Chelsea were a spent force in the title race when Frank Lampard was sacked midway through the season and replaced by the former Paris Saint-Germain coach Thomas Tuchel. They were also second best in the FA Cup Final against Leicester – and were clinging on to a top-four place in the Premier League after losing two of the final three games. But their progress in the Champions League was of the highest order, with victories over Atletico Madrid, Porto and Real Madrid setting up a final against Manchester City. The form book favoured Pep Guardiola's team. Previous results between the two teams pointed to Chelsea, who overcame City in their FA Cup semi-final and defeated them again three weeks later in the league at the Etihad. The latter argument prevailed as a Kai Havertz goal in Porto delivered European football's biggest prize to the club for a second time. It was his first goal in the competition and underlined his growing influence after a demanding first season at the club following a £71m move from Bayer Leverkusen. Havertz was part of a £200m summer spending spree which also brought Timo Werner, Hakim Ziyech, Ben Chilwell and Edouard Mendy to the club. Under Lampard, they enjoyed a 17-match unbeaten in all competitions, then stumbled, losing five out of eight league matches. He admitted they were not ready to challenge for the title and Tuchel took over a side down to eighth.

Abraham T............. 12 (10)	Giroud O................... 8 (9)	Mendy E........................31
Arrizabalaga K............ 6 (1)	Havertz K................. 18 (9)	Mount M.................. 32 (4)
Azpilicueta C........... 24 (2)	Hudson-Odoi C....... 10 (13)	Pulisic C 18 (9)
Barkley R................ - (2)	James R 25 (7)	Rudiger A 19
Cabellero W.......................1	Jorginho................ 23 (5)	Thiago Silva 23
Chilwell B 27	Kante N.................. 24 (6)	Tomori F .... - (1)
Christensen A........... 15 (2)	Kovacic M................ 21 (6)	Werner T 29 (6)
Emerson ....– (2)	Loftus-Cheek R.................1	Ziyech H.................. 15 (8)
Gilmour B 3 (2)	Marcos Alonso.......... 11 (2)	Zouma K.................. 22 (2)

League goals (58): Jorginho 7, Abraham 6, Mount 6, Werner 6, Zouma 5, Giroud 4, Havertz 4, Pulisic 4, Chilwell 3, Hudson-Odoi 2, Marcos Alonso 2, Thiago Silva 2, Ziyech 2, Azpilicueta 1,

James 1, Rudiger 1, Opponents 2
FA Cup goals (11): Abraham 4, Ziyech 2, Havertz 1, Hudson-Odoi 1, Mount 1, Werner 1, Opponents 1. **League Cup goals** (7): Havertz 3, Abraham 1, Barkley 1, Giroud 1, Werner 1
Champions League goals (23): Giroud 6, Werner 4, Hudson-Odoi 2, Mount 2, Pulisic 2, Ziyech 2, Abraham 1, Chilwell 1, Emerson 1, Havertz 1, Jorginho 1
Player of Year: Mason Mount

CRYSTAL PALACE

Selhurst Park and Anfield delivered an emotional farewell after Roy Hodgson announced he was stepping down as Palace manager. The 73-year-old was not granted a winning end to his four-year tenure, with Arsenal continuing their late flourish and Liverpool sealing a Champions League place. By then, however, Hodgson had continued to protect his boyhood club's Premier League status with another lower mid-table finish, completed by his side coming from behind in the penultimate home fixture to defeat Aston Villa 3-2. Other highlights from his final campaign included a 3-1 win over Manchester United at Old Trafford, with two goals from Wilfried Zaha and one by Andros Townsend, and a top-flight club record of five goals in an away game, against West Bromwich Albion. Among the low points were a worst-ever 7-0 home defeat by Liverpool, which Hodgson admitted was 'humiliating' and the news that after a successful first season Eberechi Eze would be out for up to eight months with an achilles injury sustained in training. Former Arsenal captain Patrick Vieira succeeded Hodgson.

Ayew J	23 (10)	Guaita V	37	Riedewald J	19 (14)
Batshuayi M	7 (11)	Kelly M	- (1)	Sakho M	3 (1)
Benteke C	21 (9)	Kouyate C	35 (1)	Schlupp J	15 (12)
Butland J	1	Mateta J-P	2 (5)	Tomkins J	6 (2)
Cahill G	20	McArthur J	17 (1)	Townsend A	25 (9)
Clyne N	13	McCarthy J	10 (6)	Ward J	25 (1)
Dann S	15	Milivojevic L	27 (4)	Zaha W	29 (1)
Eze E	29 (5)	Mitchell T	19	Van Aanholt P	20 (2)

League goals (41): Zaha 11, Benteke 10, Eze 4, Batshuayi 2, Riedewald 2, Schlupp 2, Ayew 1, Cahill 1, Dann 1, Kouyate 1, Mateta 1, Milivojevic 1, Mitchell 1, Townsend 1, Opponents 2
FA Cup goals: None. **League Cup goals:** None
Player of Year: Vicente Guaita

EVERTON

A season holding out plenty of promise fell apart amid the club's worst-ever home record. Nine defeats at Goodison Park left Carlo Ancelotti lost for answers and his side marooned in mid-table. They led the division early on after scoring nine goals against West Bromwich Albion and Brighton, with Dominic Calvert-Lewin scoring a hat-trick against the former to go alongside his treble in a League Cup tie against West Ham. Everton twice came from behind for a point against Liverpool, while further victories over Chelsea and Arsenal kept them in the top-four. There was also a classic FA Cup fifth round tie against Tottenham which ended 5-4 after a goal by substitute Bernard seven minutes into stoppage-time. The run was ended by Manchester City in the quarter-finals, by which time Everton were in dire straits at home, losing to Fulham, Burnley, Aston Villa and Sheffield United. They welcomed back supporters with a 1-0 victory over Wolves, courtesy of a towering header from Richarlison and with an impressive performance by Ben Godfrey in front of England manager Gareth Southgate. But a 5-0 drubbing by Manchester City at the Etihad in the final match suggested the club would be active in the summer transfer market. And the club were left stunned when, out of the blue, Ancelotti announced he was returning to Real Madrid. Former Liverpool manager Rafael Benitez replaced him.

Allan	23 (1)	Bernard	3 (9)	Calvert-Lewin D	32 (1)
Andre Gomes	17 (11)	Broadhead N	- (1)	Cenk Tosun	- (5)

Coleman S	18 (7)	Holgate M	26 (2)	Nkounkou N	1 (1)
Davies T	17 (8)	Iwobi A	17 (13)	Olsen R	7
Delph F	2 (6)	Joao Virginia	-(1)	Pickford J	31
Digne L	30	Kean M	- (2)	Richarlison	33 (1)
Doucoure A	29	Keane M	33 (2)	Rodriguez J	21 (2)
Gbamin J-P	- (1)	Kenny J	1 (3)	Sigurdsson G	24 (12)
Godfrey B	29 (2)	King J	- (11)	Walcott T	0 (1)
Gordon A	1 (2)	Mina Y	23 (1)		

League goals (47): Calvert-Lewin 16, Richarlison 7, Rodriguez 6, Sigurdsson 6, Keane 3, Doucoure 2, Mina 2, Bernard 1, Holgate 1, Iwobi 1, Opponents 2
FA Cup goals (10): Richarlison 3, Calvert-Lewin 2, Bernard 1, Doucoure 1, Cenk Tosun 1, Mina 1, Sigurdsson 1. **League Cup goals (12):** Calvert-Lewin 3, Richarlison 3, Kean 2, Bernard 1, Keane 1, Iwobi 1, Sigurdsson 1
Player of Year: Dominic Calvert-Lewin

FULHAM

If there was a crumb of comfort to accompany a second successive relegation from the Premier League, it came with the knowledge that this one did not involve a wasted record spending-spree. Instead of splashing £100m on new signings, as happened last time, the club relied heavily on loanees after some of the players from the 2020 team that went up via the play-offs fell short of the demands of the top-flight. Defensively, Fulham did enough to survive, but an acute shortage of goals kept them in the bottom three for almost the entire campaign. Aleksandar Mitrovic, who led promotion with 26 goals, netted twice early on against Leeds, then found it hard going for the rest of the campaign. One of the loanees, Josh Maja from Bordeaux, scored a brace on his full debut against Everton, but also struggled to add to it. And although Mario Lemina from Southampton delivered a notable victory against Liverpool at Anfield, it proved his side's last one. They failed to win any of the final ten matches, were relegated at Burnley with three remaining and finished 11 points adrift. Manager Scott Parker left by mutual consent in the summer.

Andersen J	30 (1)	Kebano N	1 (4)	Onomah J	4 (7)
Areola A	36	Kongolo T	1	Ream T	7
Bryan J	7 (9)	Le Marchand M	1 (1)	Reed H	26 (5)
Cairney T	9 (1)	Lemina M	19 (9)	Robinson A	24 (4)
Carvalho F	3 (1)	Loftus-Cheek R	21 (9)	Rodak M	2
Decordova-Reid B	28 (5)	Lookman A	31 (3)	Tete K	18 (4)
Francois T	- (1)	Maja J	9 (6)	Adarabioyo T	33
Hector M	3 (1)	Mitrovic A	13 (14)	Zambo-Anguissa F	29 (7)
Ivan Cavaleiro	27 (9)	Odoi J	3		
Kamara A	2 (9)	Aina O	31		

League goals (27): Decordova-Reid 5, Lookman 4, Ivan Cavaleiro 3, Maja 3, Mitrovic 3, Aina 2, Andersen 1, Bryan 1, Cairney 1, Carvalho 1, Lemina 1, Loftus-Cheek 1, Opponents 1
FA Cup goals (2): Decordova-Reid 1, Kebano 1. **League Cup goals (3):** Decordova-Reid 1 Kamara 1, Mitrovic 1.
Player of Year: Alphonse Areola

LEEDS UNITED

Leeds had every reason to be satisfied with their return to the Premier League after a 16-year absence. Ninth place reflected a successful continuation of their adventurous style of play under Marcelo Bielsa which took the club up as champions of the Championship. It made for great entertainment, captured by back-to-back matches approaching Christmas – a 5-2 win over Newcastle followed by a 6-2 defeat by Manchester United. Leeds also put five past West Bromwich Albion and scored four against Fulham and Burnley, while conceding four to Liverpool,

Leicester, Crystal Palace and Arsenal. Best performance came at the Etihad where two Stuart Dallas goals accounted for Manchester City. They also finished on a high, scoring 11 goals in successive victories over Tottenham, Burnley, Southampton and Albion in the final four matches. Patrick Bamford took his tally for the campaign to 17, one more than in the promotion campaign, including a hat-trick early on against Aston Villa.

Alioski E 29 (7)	Harrison J 34 (2)	Phillips K 28 (1)
Ayling L 38	Helder Costa 13 (9)	Poveda I .... - (14)
Bamford P 37 (1)	Hernandez P 3 (13)	Raphinha 26 (4)
Berardi G 1 (1)	Huggins N .... - (1)	Roberts T 14 (13)
Casilla 3	Klich M 28 (7)	Rodrigo 14 (12)
Cooper L 25	Koch R 13 (4)	Shackleton J 3 (10)
Dallas S 38	Llorente D 14 (1)	Struijk P 22 (5)
Davis L .... - (2)	Meslier I 35	

League goals (62): Bamford 17, Dallas 8, Harrison 8, Rodrigo 7, Raphinha 6, Klich 4, Helder Costa 3, Alioski 2, Cooper 1, Llorente 1, Phillips 1, Roberts 1, Struijk 1, Opponents 2
FA Cup goals: None. **League Cup goals (1):** Alioski 1
Player of Year: Stuart Dallas

LEICESTER CITY

Brendan Rodgers and his side experienced delight and despair in the space of eight days at the end of an eventful season. They celebrated the club's first FA Cup triumph with a goal by Youri Tielemans against Chelsea at Wembley good enough to win any final. And there was more champagne ready and waiting for confirmation of a Champions League place they had occupied throughout the campaign. Instead, Chelsea turned the tables 2-1 when the teams reconvened 72 hours later for a league fixture at Stamford Bridge. That result left Leicester fifth going into the final round of matches. On a dramatic afternoon, they looked to be back on track, leading Tottenham in front of expectant supporters at the King Power Stadium with 14 minutes of normal time remaining, while Chelsea were losing at Villa Park. Then came a twist in the tail as Kasper Schmeichel's safe hands, which had been so evident at Wembley, betrayed him. Attempting to clear an inswinging corner, the goalkeeper diverted the ball into his own net and Gareth Bale rubbed it in with two final-day goals for a 4-2 result. So, for the second successive season, Leicester missed out on the final day, having to settle for a return to the Europa League. It was a bitter disappointment, but as Rodgers pointed out, his players could be proud of what they had achieved.

Albrighton M 17 (14)	Gray D .... - (1)	Praet D 10 (5)
Amartey D 8 (4)	Iheanacho K 16 (9)	Schmeichel K 38
Ayoze Perez 15 (10)	Justin J 23	Slimani I .... - (1)
Barnes H 22 (3)	Leshabela T .... - (1)	Soyuncu C 19 (4)
Castagne T 27	Maddison J 24 (7)	Tavares S 1 (1)
Choudhury H 4 (6)	Mendy N 15 (8)	Thomas L 12 (2)
Evans J 28	Morgan W .... - (3)	Tielemans Y 37 (1)
Fofana W 27 (1)	Ndidi W 25 (1)	Under C 1 (8)
Fuchs C 8 (1)	Pereira R 10 (5)	Vardy J 31 (3)

League goals (68): Vardy 15, Iheanacho 12, Barnes 9, Maddison 8, Tielemans 6, Ayoze Perez 2, Castagne 2, Evans 2, Justin 2, Albrighton 1, Amartey 1, Ndidi 1, Praet 1, Soyuncu 1, Thomas 1, Opponents 4
FA Cup goals (13): Iheanacho 4, Tielemans 3, Albrighton 1, Ayoze Perez 1, Barnes 1, Justin 1, Maddison 1, Under 1. **League Cup goals:** None.
Europa League goals (14): Barnes 3, Iheanacho 3, Maddison 2, Vardy 2, Choudhury 1, Praet 1, Thomas 1, Under 1
Player of Year: Youri Tielemans

LIVERPOOL

Liverpool emerged from a bleak midwinter to claim a Champions League place against all the odds. Eight wins and two draws in the final ten matches delivered third place at the end of a season in which their defence of the title was undermined by crippling defensive injuries. They lost Virgil van Dijk after five games, Joe Gomez three weeks later, then Joel Matip midway through. There was more, with Diogo Jota sidelined for three months and finally captain Jordan Henderson missing the last 13 fixtures. Jurgen Klopp patched things up with his young players the odd signing and countless combinations at the back. Somehow, his side went into the new year leading the division, with Mohamed Salah's goals a key factor and the 7-0 rout of Crystal Palace suggesting they were far from a spent force. Then, it all went wrong. An unprecedented six successive home defeats left them seven points adrift of the top-four. There was also defeat by Real Madrid in the quarter-finals of the Champions League. But Jota came off the bench to score twice in a 3-0 away win over Arsenal which Klopp described as a 'statement of intent.' After that they were unstoppable. Liverpool overtook Leicester with a 3-0 win at Burnley in the penultimate fixture and sealed third place on the final day against Crystal Palace with the fans back to see it.

Adrian 3	Keita N 7 (3)	Salah M 34 (3)
Alexander-Arnold T ... 34 (2)	Kelleher C 2	Shaqiri X 5 (9)
Alisson 33	Mane S 31 (4)	Thiago Alcantara 20 (4)
Diogo Jota................ 12 (7)	Matip J 9 (1)	Tsimikas K....................- (2)
Fabinho 28 (2)	Milner J 11 (15)	Wijnaldum G............. 34 (4)
Firmino R 33 (3)	Minamino T 2 (7)	Williams N.................3 (3)
Gomez J 6 (1)	Origi D 2 (7)	Williams R.................7 (2)
Henderson J 20 (1)	Oxlade-Chamberlain A 2 (11)	Van Dijk V 5
Jones C.................. 13 (11)	Phillips N................. 15 (2)	
Kabak O 9	Robertson A....................38	

League goals (68): Salah 22, Mane 11, Diogo Jota 9, Firmino 9, Alexander-Arnold 2, Wijnaldum 2, Alisson 1, Henderson 1, Jones 1, Matip 1, Minamino 1, Oxlade-Chamberlain 1, Phillips 1, Robertson 1, Thiago Alcantara 1, Van Dijk 1, Opponents 3
FA Cup goals (6): Salah 3, Mane 2, Wijnaldum 1. **League Cup goals (7):** Jones 2, Minamino 2, Grujic M 1, Origi 1, Shaqiri 1. **Community Shield goals (1):** Minamino 1.
Champions League goals (15): Salah 6, Diogo Jota 4, Mane 3, Jones 1, Minamino 1
Player of Year: Mohamed Salah

MANCHESTER CITY

They won the Premier League for the third time in four years and League Cup for the fourth successive season. Pep Guardiola also has an FA Cup victory under his belt. But the Champions League remained an elusive target after defeat by Chelsea in the final in Porto. The form book favoured his team. But there were nagging doubts over previous results between the two teams, with Thomas Tuchel having come out on top in their FA Cup semi-final, then in the league three weeks later at the Etihad. And Tuchel continued to outsmart his rival manager with a deserved victory, settled by a goal from Kai Havertz. Amid speculation about the departure of some established players and predictions of major summer signings, City failed to produce the domestic form which took them away from every title challenger after a modest first part of the season. They were down in eighth place going into the new year, with the leadership having repeatedly changed hands and no-one quite sure who might eventually take charge. But as Liverpool faltered and Manchester United dropped points to struggling teams, City delivered 12 successive wins. In all competitions, they had a record 21 victories. A month without the injured Kevin De Bruyne made no difference as Ilkay Gundogan, in the form of his life, scored 11 goals in 12 matches. They were eventually crowned champions with three matches remaining and in his final one Sergio Aguero scored twice against Everton to finish on 184 goals, overtaking Wayne Rooney for the most for a single club.

Aguero S................ 7 (5)	Foden P 17 (11)	Rodri D.................... 31 (3)
Ake N..................... 9 (1)	Gabiel Jesus 22 (7)	Ruben Días.................. 32
Bernardo Silva.......... 24 (2)	Garcia E 3 (3)	Steffen Z......................... 1
Carson S......................1	Gundogan I............. 23 (5)	Sterling R................. 28 (3)
De Bruyne K............. 23 (2)	Joao Cancelo 27 (1)	Stones J........................ 22
Delap L...................... - (1)	Laporte A 14 (2)	Torres F................. 15 (9)
Ederson 36	Mahrez R 23 (4)	Walker K 22 (2)
Fernandinho............ 12 (9)	Mendy B 11 (2)	Zinchenko O............. 15 (5)

League goals (83): Gundogan 13, Sterling 10, Foden 9, Gabriel Jesus 9, Mahrez 9, Torres 7, De Bruyne 6, Agüero 4, Stones 4, Bernardo Silva 2, Joao Cancelo 2, Mendy 2, Rodri 2, Ake 1, Ruben Dias 1, Walker 1, Opponents 1
FA Cup goals (11): Bernardo Silva 2, Foden 2, Gabriel Jesus 2, De Bruyne 1, Gundogan 1, Sterling 1, Torres 1, Walker 1. **League Cup goals (12):** Foden 2, Laporte 2, Sterling 2, Delap 1, Fernandinho 1, Gabriel Jesus 1, Mahrez 1, Stones 1, Torres 1
Champions League goals (25): Mahrez 4, Torres 4, De Bruyne 3, Foden 3, Gundogan 3, Aguero 2, Gabriel Jesus 2, Bernardo Silva 1, Joao Cancelo 1, Sterling 1, Opponents 1
Player of Year: Ruben Dias

MANCHESTER UNITED

Finishing runners-up in the Premier League and Europa League were not enough to satisfy Ole Gunnar Solskjaer, who acknowledged that the club had made progress during the season but could not regard it as a successful one. A dodgy start, too many home defeats and Manchester City's rampant run from new year onwards combined to rule out a title bid. They had a single week at the top when three defeats in the opening six fixtures – including a 6-1 pasting by Tottenham – was followed by a run of 13 unbeaten matches. It was ended by struggling Sheffield United and after that they were left in City's slipstream, despite a record 9-0 rout of Southampton in which seven different players were on the scoresheet. The six losses at Old Trafford were in sharp contrast to the division's only undefeated record away from home. Solskjaer's side also collected un unrivalled 31 points from losing positions overall. They again showed the ability to come from behind in the Europa League Final against Villarreal, but without anything to show for it after a marathon penalty shoot-out ended 11-10 when David de Gea had his spot-kick saved by rival goalkeeper Geronimo Rulli. It was a disappointing end to a season, also clouded by supporters protesting against the club's involvement in plans for a European Super League and calling for a change of ownership.

Bailly E................ 10 (2)	Henderson D............. 12 (1)	Pogba P...................21 (5)
Cavani E................ 13 (13)	Ighalo O .... - (1)	Rashford M...............33 (4)
De Gea D...................26	James D 11 (4)	Shaw L.................30 (2)
Diallo A 2 (1)	Lindelof V........................29	Shoretire S ....- (2)
Elanga A.........................2	Maguire H 34	Telles A.................8 (1)
Bruno Fernandes 35 (2)	Martial A 17 (5)	Tuanzebe A................. 4 (5)
Fish W............................ - (1)	Mata J 6 (3)	Van de Beek D....4 (15)
Fosu-Mensah T.................1	Matic N 12 (8)	Wan-Bissaka A............... 34
Fred 27 (3)	McTominay S 24 (8)	Williams B.................. 2 (2)
Greenwood M 21 (10)	Mejbri N.................... - (1)	

League goals (73): Bruno Fernandes 18, Rashford 11, Cavani 10, Greenwood 7, Martial 4, McTominay 4, James 3, Pogba 3, Maguire 2, Wan-Bissaka 2, Elanga 1, Fred 1, Lindelof 1, Mata 1, Shaw 1, Van de Beek 1, Opponents 3
FA Cup goals (6): Greenwood 2, McTominay 2, Bruno Fernandes 1, Rashford 1. **League Cup goals (8):** Mata 2, Cavani 1, Greenwood 1, Martial 1, McTominay 1, Pogba 1, Rashford 1
Champions League goals (15): Rashford 6, Bruno Fernandes 4, Martial 2, Greenwood 1, James 1, Opponents 1. **Europa League goals (19):** Cavani 6, Bruno Fernandes 5, Pogba 2, Rashford 1, Diallo 1, Greenwood 1, James 1, Opponents 1
Player of Year: Bruno Fernandes

NEWCASTLE UNITED

Steve Bruce found an unlikely saviour towards the end of a troubled season at St James' Park. Joe Willock, a midfielder on loan from Arsenal, scored in seven successive matches to point Newcastle away from the threat of relegation to the security of 12th in the table. In doing he matched the feat, achieved 25 years ago, by Alan Shearer, who was quick to applaud the finishing aplomb of the 21-year-old. The return to fitness of Allan Saint-Maximin and Callum Wilson were also key to the team's recovery from a perilous position one above the drop zone. Injuries, question marks about the commitment of some players and a much-publicised spat between Bruce and midfielder Matt Ritchie accompanied continued talk of a takeover of the club. The turning point was a 2-1 win at Burnley orchestrated by French winger Saint-Maximin, who scored one goal and provided the assist for the other from Jacob Murphy. Newcastle then overcame West Ham with a rare goal from record-signing Joelinton and as Willock grew in confidence with every match, they finished with a commendable record of five victories in the final eight matches.

Almiron M	28 (6)	Gayle D	4 (14)	Manquillo J	10 (3)
Anderson E	- (1)	Hayden I	22 (2)	Murphy J	17 (9)
Carroll A	4 (14)	Hendrick J	17 (5)	Ritchie M	15 (3)
Clark C	21 (1)	Joelinton	23 (8)	Saint-Maximin A	19 (6)
Darlow K	25	Krafth E	14 (2)	Schar F	13 (5)
Dubravka M	13	Lascelles J	19	Shelvey J	29 (1)
Dummett P	14 (1)	Lewis J	20 (4)	Willock J	11 (3)
Fernandez F	24	Longstaff M	4 (1)	Wilson C	23 (3)
Fraser R	9 (9)	Longstaff S	15 (7)	Yedlin D	5 (1)

League goals (46): Wilson 12, Willock 8, Almiron 4, Joelinton 4, Saint-Maximin 3, Hendrick 2, Lascelles 2, Murphy 2, Carroll 1, Clark 1, Dummett 1, Gayle 1, Krafth 1, Schar 1, Shelvey 1, Opponents 2
FA Cup goals: None. **League Cup goals** (9): Joelinton 2, Almiron 1, Fraser 1, Hayden 1, Lascelles 1, Murphy 1, Shelvey 1, Opponents 1
Player of Year: Callum Wilson

SHEFFIELD UNITED

Relegation had been on the cards for months, but the extent of the club's fall from grace was still a shock when defeat at Molineux confirmed the drop with six matches still to play. Chris Wilder's team were a breath of fresh air on their return the previous season to the Premier League which almost brought a place in Europe. This time, they never got off the ground however much the manager chopped and changed his attacking options, which included fruitless attempts to coax goals out of record-signing Rhian Brewster from Liverpool. United had to wait 18 matches for a win – 1-0 against Newcastle courtesy of Billy Sharp's penalty. A glimmer of hope for a sustained revival accompanied one of the season's biggest upsets – a 2-1 victory over Manchester United at Old Trafford with goals from Kean Bryan, his first for the club, and Oliver Burke – followed by the same scoreline against West Bromwich Albion. But Wilder's departure after a prolonged disagreement with the board over the future direction of the club proved the final straw. Paul Heckingbottom's first match as caretaker was a 5-0 reversal against Leicester, part of a run of ten matches yielding just three goals rounded off by that defeat by Wolves. To be fair, it was a rare drubbing, with 15 of the defeats at that stage having been by a single goal margin. Slaviša Jokanović, formerly in charge of Fulham and Watford, became the new permanent manager.

Ampadu E	23 (2)	Bogle J	12 (4)	Egan J	30 (1)
Baldock G	32	Brewster R	12 (15)	Fleck J	29 (1)
Basham C	31	Bryan K	12 (1)	Hackford A	- (1)
Berge S	13 (2)	Burke O	14 (11)	Jagielka P	6 (4)

Jebbison D................. 3 (1)	Mousset L..................... 2 (9)	Ramsdale A.....................38
Lowe M......................... 7 (1)	Ndiaye I...................... - (1)	Robinson J.................. 9 (2)
Lundstram J............. 23 (5)	Norwood O.............. 26 (6)	Sharp B......................... 7 (9)
McBurnie O.............. 12 (11)	O'Connell J 2	Stevens E 30
McGoldrick D.............. 28 (7)	Osborn B 17 (7)	

League goals (20): McGoldrick 8, Sharp 3, Bogle 2, Berge 1, Bryan 1, Burke 1, Jebbison 1, McBurnie 1, Osborn 1, Opponents 1
FA Cup goals (6): Sharp 2, Basham 1, Bogle 1, Burke 1, Opponents 1. **League Cup goals** (1): McGoldrick 1
Player of Year: Aaron Ramsdale

SOUTHAMPTON

Southampton went into the new year with a spring in their step, climbing to sixth after a Danny Ings winner against a Liverpool side who at the time topped the table.. But for the second successive season they were stung by a 9-0 beating, this one by Manchester United at Old Trafford, where 19-year-old Alex Jankewitz was sent off 82 seconds into his full debut and Jan Bednarek followed later, although his red card was later rescinded. It was one of six straight defeats which sent the team plunging. Victory over Bournemouth, which brought a place in the semi-finals of the FA Cup, provided a comforting break from the pressure and was followed by Nathan Redmond's goal which completed a recovery from two down for a 3-2 victory over Burnley. Southampton lost to Leicester by the only goal in the Cup and remained uncomfortably on the fringes of the relegation zone until back-back 3-1 victories over Crystal Palace and Fulham at St Mary's took them well clear. They finished 15th, a fall of four places on 2020.

Adams C.................. 30 (6)	McCarthy A....................30	Tchaptchet A ....- (1)
Armstrong S............ 32 (1)	Minamino T................. 9 (1)	Tella N...................... 7 (11)
Bednarek J....................36	N'Lundulu D........... - (13)	Valery Y....................... 1 (2)
Bertrand R....................29	Obafemi M .... - (4)	Vestergaard J............ 29 (1)
Diallo I 10 (12)	Ramsay K........................1	Vokins J 1
Djenepo M 15 (12)	Redmond N 17 (12)	Walcott T................. 20 (1)
Forster F...........................8	Romeu O.................. 20 (1)	Walker-Peters K 30
Ings D 26 (3)	Salisu M.................. 8 (4)	Ward-Prowse J 38
Jankewitz A................. 1 (1)	Smallbone W 2 (1)	Watts C....................... - (3)
Long S..................... 1 (10)	Stephens J 17 (1)	

League goals (47): Ings 12, Adams 9, Ward-Prowse 8, Armstrong 4, Vestergaard 3, Walcott 3, Minamino 2, Redmond 2, Bednarek 1, Djenepo 1, Romeu 1, Tella 1
FA Cup goals (8): Redmond 2, Armstrong 1, Djenepo 1, Ings 1, N'Lundulu 1, Ward-Prowse 1, Opponents 1. **League Cup goals**: None
Player of Year: James Ward-Prowse

TOTTENHAM HOTSPUR

Tottenham ran into turbulence on and off the pitch after a period of calm which suggested there might be some much-needed silverware on the horizon. A thumping 6-1 win over Manchester United at Old Trafford, together with victories over Manchester City and Arsenal, pointed Jose Mourinho's side to the top of the table, before a lean spell in the run-up to Christmas meant it was just a short stay. They continued to make progress in the League Cup and Europa League before the storm clouds gathered as a 2-0 lead first leg lead was surrendered and eventually overturned by Dinamo Zagreb in a last 16 tie. Then, six days before a Wembley date with Manchester City, Mourinho was sacked after 17 months in charge, leaving head of player development Ryan Mason, 29, in the opposite corner to Pep Guardiola. His side 'escaped' with a 1-0 defeat in a one-sided final. His club's hierarchy, already under fire for backing a European Super League, now had to contend with Harry Kane's request for a move to a club with a greater potential for trophies. Kane ended the season with his third Golden Boot, a 23rd goal coming in a 4-2 victory at Leicester which earned Tottenham a place in the new Europa League Conference. Nuno Espírito Santo succeeded Mourinho, having left Wolves at the end of the season.

Alderweireld T 25	Doherty M 13 (4)	Reguilon S 26 (1)
Alli D......................... 7 (8)	Hojbjerg P 38	Rodon J 8 (4)
Aurier S 19	Kane H 35	Sanchez D 17 (1)
Bale G 10 (12)	Lamela E................ 5 (18)	Scarlett D...................- (1)
Bergwijn S 13 (8)	Lloris H.......................38	Sissoko M 15 (10)
Vinicius C 3 (6)	Lo Celso G 11 (7)	Son Heung-min 36 (1)
Davies B 14 (6)	Lucas Moura........... 14 (16)	Tanganga J 6
Dier E...........................28	Ndombele T............ 28 (5)	Winks H 9 (6)

League goals (68): Kane 23, Son Heung-min 17, Bale 11, Lucas Moura 3, Ndombele 3, Aurier 2, Hojbjerg 2, Alderweireld 1, Bergwijn 1, Vinicius 1, Lamela 1, Lo Celso 1, Opponents 2
FA Cup goals (13): Vinicius 3, Ndombele 2, Sanchez 2, Bale 1, Devine A 1, Kane 1, Lamela 1, Lucas Moura 1, Winks 1. **League Cup goals** (6) : Bale 1, Davies 1, Son Heung-min 1, Kane 1, Lamela 1, Sissoko 1
Europa League goals (37): Kane 8, Vinicius 6, Lucas Moura 5, Lo Celso 4, Son Heung-min 4, Alli 3, Bale 3, Lamela 1, Ndombele 1, Winks 1, Opponents 1
Player of Year: Harry Kane

WEST BROMWICH ALBION

Sam Allardyce put his record of never having been relegated from the Premier League as a manager on the line when replacing Slaven Bilic at The Hawthorns. Albion had a single win to show from the opening 13 matches and a 3-0 home defeat by Aston Villa in Allardyce's first match underlined the size of the task. So did nine goals conceded in back-to-back defeats by Leeds and Arsenal. A first win, 3-2 in the Black Country derby came at Molineux, courtesy of two penalties from Matheus Pereira, and there was a spirited performance for a point against Manchester United. But goals were generally at a premium, until a remarkable 5-2 success against Chelsea at Stamford Bridge, with Pereira and Callum Robinson sharing four of the goals. When Southampton were defeated 3-0 in the follow-up, a glimmer of hope appeared. Instead, it was Albion's last victory. Two points were all they had to show from the final seven matches and the drop was confirmed with three still to play. Allardyce turned down the invitation to stay on, describing himself as a 'short-term manager.' Barnsley's Valerien Ismael took over.

Hegazi A..........................1	Gallagher C............... 28 (2)	O'Shea D...................25 (3)
Ajayi S................... 31 (2)	Gibbs K..................... 9 (1)	Yokuslu O.................15 (1)
Austin C .... - (5)	Grant K 14 (7)	Peltier L.......................3 (1)
Bartley K 28 (2)	Grosicki K 2 (1)	Pereira M 30 (3)
Button D...........................1	Harper R .... - (2)	Phillips M................20 (13)
Diagne M 14 (2)	Ivanovic B 8 (5)	Robinson C 20 (8)
Diangana G 15 (5)	Johnstone S...................37	Robson-Kanu H........2 (17)
Edwards K 1 (4)	Krovinovic F 5 (6)	Sawyers R 17 (2)
Field S .... - (3)	Livermore J 15 (3)	Snodgrass R 6 (2)
Furlong D................ 32 (3)	Maitland-Niles A....... 14 (1)	Townsend C 25

League goals (35): Pereira 11, Robinson 5, Bartley 3, Diagne 3, Ajayi 2, Gallagher 2, Phillips 2, Robson-Kanu 2, Diangana 1, Furlong 1, Grant 1, Opponents 2
FA Cup goals (2): Ajayi 1, Pereira 1. **League Cup goals** (5): Robson-Kanu 3, Harper 1, Robinson 1
Player of Year: Sam Johnstone

WEST HAM UNITED

David Moyes led the club to their highest Premier League position for 22 years, together with a record 65 points. The reward was Europa League football – and with little more than a month of the season remaining, bigger things beckoned. West Ham were within touching distance of a Champions League place, having been reinforced to striking effect by the arrival on loan of Manchester United's Jesse Lingard, who scored nine goals in his first ten appearances. But injuries to Declan Rice and Michail Antonio, back-to-back defeats by Newcastle and Chelsea and a controversial red card – later rescinded – for Fabian Balbuena against the latter, set them back. Antonio returned to score both goals against Burnley. Rice, now the premier English defensive midfielder, came back after missing six matches to seal a 3-0 victory over Southampton in the final round of matches. Two goals earlier from Pablo Fornals had set the scene for sixth place, which Moyes acclaimed as a 'huge achievement and a major step forward for the club.'

Antonio M 24 (2)	Fabianski L.....................35	Masuaku A 12
Balbuena F 13 (1)	Felipe Anderson .... - (2)	Noble M..............8 (13)
Benrahma S........... 14 (16)	Fornals P............... 31 (2)	Ogbonna A 28
Bowen J................... 30 (8)	Fredericks R 6 (8)	Randolph D 3
Coufal V.......................34	Haller S 10 (6)	Rice D .".......................32
Cresswell A 36	Johnson B 5 (9)	Snodgrass R .... - (3)
Dawson C..................22	Lanzini M 5 (12)	Soucek T.......................38
Diop I 15 (3)	Lingard J....................16	Yarmolenko A............1 (14)

League goals (62): Antonio 10, Soucek 10, Lingard 9, Bowen 8, Fornals 5, Dawson 3, Haller 3, Ogbonna 3, Diop 2, Rice 2, Balbuena 1, Benrahma 1, Fredericks 1, Johnson 1, Lanzini 1, Opponents 2
FA Cup goals (5): Afolayan O 1, Dawson 1, Fornals 1, Yarmolenko 1, Opponents 1. **League Cup goals** (9): Haller 4, Snodgrass 2, Yarmolenko 2, Felipe Anderson 1
Player of Year: Tomas Soucek

WOLVERHAMPTON WANDERERS

The loss of leading scorer Raul Jimenez had a profound effect on Wolves' season. The Mexico striker suffered a fractured skull in an accidental collision of heads with Arsenal's David Luiz in their tenth match and was ruled out for the rest of the campaign. With Diogo Jota having joined Liverpool in the summer, it meant that 18-year-old record-signing Fabio Silva had to shoulder extra responsibility, instead of being allowed to adjust gradually to the demands of the Premier League. His new side, consequently, had a single victory to show from the next 11 matches, albeit against Chelsea with a 95th minute goal from Pedro Neto. The youngster had to wait four months for his first from open play, but with Neto enjoying a season of great consistency Wolves picked up in the New Year with three wins out of four against Arsenal, Southampton and Leeds. For Neto, however, there was heartbreak when he sustained a knee injury against Fulham, missed the final seven games and was ruled out of contention for a place in Portugal's squad for the European Championship. His side, seventh in the two previous years, finished 13th.. Two days before the final match against Manchester United, Nuno Espirito Santo announced he was leaving the club after four years as manager. Fellow Portuguese Bruno Lage, former Benfica coach, succeeded him.

Ait Nouri R............... 16 (5)	Hoever K-J 5 (7)	Raul Jimenez 10
Boly W...........................21	Joao Moutinho.......... 28 (5)	Ruben Neves 31 (5)
Buur O .... - (1)	Jonny 7	Ruben Vinagre............. 1 (1)
Coady C.......................37	Kilman M................. 14 (4)	Ruddy J..................... 1 (1)
Corbeanu T .... - (1)	Marcal F 7 (6)	Rui Patricio 37
Cutrone P .... - (2)	Nelson Semedo 34	Saiss R.......................27
Dendoncker L......... 28 (5)	Otasowie O.............. 2 (4)	Traore A 28 (9)
Fabio Silva 11 (21)	Pedro Neto 30 (1)	Vitinha................. 5 (14)
Gibbs-White M 4 (7)	Podence D 22 (2)	William Jose............. 12 (5)

League goals (36): Pedro Neto 5, Ruben Neves 5, Fabio Silva 4, Raul Jimenez 4, Podence 3, Saiss 3, Traore 2, Ait Nouri 1, Boly 1, Coady 1, Dendoncker 1, Gibbs-White 1, Joao Moutinho 1, Nelson Semedo 1, William Jose 1, Opponents 2
FA Cup goals (2): Traore 1, Vitinha 1. **League Cup goals**: None
Player of Year: Pedro Neto

SKY BET CHAMPIONSHIP

BARNSLEY

Former Crystal Palace defender Valerien Ismael led a revival of the club's fortunes all the way to the play-offs before stubborn Swansea ended dreams of a Premier League place. Barnsley survived relegation by a single point in 2020 and seven games without a win to start the new campaign suggested more hard times ahead. Instead, Ismael followed coaching spells in Germany, Greece and Austria by making an instant impact when taking over from Gerhard Struber, who left for New York Red Bulls. A 3-0 victory over Queens Park Rangers set the ball rolling. His side climbed the table steadily, then their season really took off with seven straight wins, featuring an impressive introduction to the Championship by American striker Daryl Dike, on loan from Orlando. Barnsley comfortably held on to a top-six place, but faced a Swansea side who had twice beaten them in the regular campaign and who came away with a 1-0 lead from the first leg of the knockout phase at Oakwell. They conceded a second in the return, but had their opponents hanging on after an equaliser from Cauley Woodrow. Ismael left in the summer to become West Bromwich Albion's new manager. Austrian coach Markus Schopp came in.

Adeboyejo V 9 (23)	Kane H 6 (18)	Schmidt P 2 (6)
Andersen M.................46	Kitching L .... - (1)	Sibbick T 11 (10)
Brittain C.................40	Ludewig K 3 (1)	Simoes E................ 4 (4)
Chaplin C................ 31 (3)	Miller G...................... - (5)	Sollbauer M..............34 (3)
Collins B.....................22	Moon J.................... 1 (2)	Styles C 40 (2)
Dike D 13 (6)	Morris C 6 (17)	Thomas L 7 (12)
Frieser D............ 26 (16)	Mowatt A........................44	Walton J.......................24
Halme A 3 (15)	Oduor C 5 (6)	Williams J 7 (14)
Helik M 43	Palmer R 22 (12)	Woodrow C 41 (1)
James M 13 (2)	Ritzmaier M..................3	

Play-offs – appearances: Andersen 2, Brittain 2, Collins 2, Helik 2, Mowatt 2, Palmer 2, Sibbick 2, Styles 2, Woodrow 2, Adeboyejo 1 (1), Dike 1 (1), Morris 1 (1), Frieser 1, Williams J – (2), Kitching – (1).
League goals (58): Woodrow 12, Dike 9, Mowatt 8, Morris 7, Helik 5, Chaplin 4, Styles 4, Frieser 3, Adeboyejo 2, Andersen 1, Palmer 1, Simoes 1, Opponents 1. **Play-offs – goals** (1): Woodrow 1
FA Cup goals (3): Helik 1, Styles 1, Woodrow 1. **League Cup goals** (3): Schmidt 1, Williams 1, Woodrow 1.
Player of Year: Michal Helik

BIRMINGHAM CITY

As a player, Lee Bowyer made a significant contribution to the club's League Cup triumph, scoring in the semi-final against West Ham and as part of the team that defeated Arsenal at Wembley. Ten years on, he made another major impact as manager by removing the threat of dropping into the third tier. Bowyer left Charlton to replace Aitor Karanka, sacked after a 3-0 home defeat by Bristol City which left his side one place above the drop zone with ten matches remaining. He needed just five of them to steer a course to safety, with three victories establishing a nine-point safety net. Lukas Jutkiewicz and captain Harlee Dean delivered a 2-1 win over Reading, Scott Hogan's penalty accounted for Swansea, then a brace by Jutkiewicz brought a 2-0 success against Stoke. Bowyer insisted there was still work to do. But he needn't have worried. His emphasis on playing to the strength in the air of Jutkiewicz paid further dividends when the striker got two more goals against Derby – four of those five goals coming from headers after he had previously netted just twice all season.

Bela J.......................26 (9)	Clayton A..............10 (4)	Crowley D 1 (2)
Boyd-Munce C.................1	Colin M....................39 (3)	Dacres-Cogley J 5
Clarke-Salter J............ 9 (1)	Cosgrove S 2 (10)	Dean H....................42 (1)

Etheridge N..................43	Jeacock Z 2	Seddon S................... 6 (1)
Friend G 21 (5)	Jutkiewicz L........... 25 (17)	Simmonds K .... - (1)
Gardner G 25 (12)	Kieftenbeld M 8 (2)	Stirk R.................................2
George A...................... - (1)	Leko J 15 (19)	Sunjic I 38 (5)
Gordon N 1 (1)	McGree R 8 (7)	Toral J 10 (6)
Halilovic A 9 (8)	Miller A 2 (3)	Trueman C 1
Harper R................... 11 (7)	Pedersen K 35	Valery Y 2 (5)
Hogan S 28 (5)	Roberts M 29 (7)	
Sanchez I 31 (9)	San Jose M 19 (8)	

League goals (37): Jutkiewicz 8, Hogan 7, Dean 4, Roberts 4, Bela 3, Gardner 2, Sanchez 2, Pedersen 2, Toral 2, Colin 1, Haliklovic 1, McGree 1
FA Cup goals: None. **League Cup goals**: None
Player of Year: Harlee Dean

BLACKBURN ROVERS

With Adam Armstrong in prolific form, Tony Mowbray's side were the Championship's leading scorers going into the new year and looked a decent bet to sustain a promotion challenge. They defeated Wycombe 5-0, with a hat-trick by Armstrong, overcome Derby and Coventry 4-0 and put three past Queens Park Rangers and Preston. There was also the boost of midfielder Bradley Dack returning after a year out with a cruciate ligament injury. But the goals dried up and a run of 15 matches stretching to Easter delivered a single victory – 2-0 at Millwall. Blackburn couldn't buy a win at Ewood Park, while Dack suffered another cruel blow with a similar injury to his other knee which meant another lengthy lay-off. 'Tough times don't last, tough people do' was his encouraging message to supporters. The barren run ended with a 2-1 victory which heaped further pressure on Derby. Armstrong then fired his second hat-trick against Huddersfield and struck a third in another 5-2 victory, this time against Birmingham, to reach 28 for the season, second behind Ivan Toney's 31 for Brentford. Blackburn still finished in the bottom half.

Armstrong A...................40	Dack B....................... 7 (9)	Kaminski T...................43
Ayala D...................... 8 (2)	Davenport J 6 (9)	Lenihan D 41
Bell A 15 (4)	Dolan T.................... 10 (27)	Nyambe R 33 (5)
Bennett E 2 (7)	Douglas B.................. 29 (1)	Pears A 3
Branthwaite J.................10	Downing S................. 2 (16)	Rankin-Costello J 14
Brennan L..................... - (1)	Elliott H 31 (10)	Rothwell J 29 (10)
Brereton B 30 (10)	Evans C..................... 11 (7)	Travis L...................16 (3)
Buckley J................. 7 (21)	Gallagher S............. 24 (15)	Trybull T...................18 (7)
Butterworth D.............. - (1)	Harwood-Bellis T......... 17 (2)	Wharton S 5 (2)
Carter H..................... - (1)	Holtby L.................... 20 (7)	Williams P.....................10
Chapman H.................. - (5)	Johnson B 25 (5)	

League goals (65): Armstrong 28, Gallagher 8, Brereton 7, Elliott 7, Dack 3, Dolan 3, Johnson 3, Rothwell 3, Buckley 1, Davenport 1, Williams 1,
FA Cup goals: None. **League Cup goals** (3): Armstrong 1, Holtby 1, Rankin-Costello 1
Player of Year: Thomas Kaminski

BOURNEMOUTH

Bournemouth surrendered the chance of an immediate return to the Premier League in a madcap second leg of their play-off semi-final at Brentford. They were in a strong position when Arnaut Danjuma ran from inside his own half with barely five minutes on the clock to add to his goal in the team's first meeting and establish a 2-0 overall advantage. But Lloyd Kelly conceded a penalty with outstretched arms, then Chris Mepham was sent off with more than an hour remaining for hauling down Bryan Mbeumo after carelessly being caught in possession. Brentford took full advantage, levelling the tie early in the second-half and scoring again for 3-2 nine minutes from the end of normal time. Bournemouth had secured a top-six place under caretaker Jonathan Woodgate, who came in when Jason Tindall, Eddie Howe's successor, was sacked on the back of four successive defeats in the new year. Seven straight wins and 21 goals scored under the former Middlesbrough manager augured well, although his side lost some momentum through defeats in the final three fixtures of the regular season. Former Fulham manager Scott Parker took over in the summer.

Anthony J .... - (5)	Kelly L 33 (3)	Simpson J 6 (3)
Begovic A 45	Kilkenny G .... - (1)	Smith A 38 (3)
Billing P 23 (11)	King J 5 (7)	Solanke D................. 38 (2)
Brooks D 25 (7)	Lerma J 40 (2)	Stacey J 18 (12)
Burchall A................. - (1)	Long S 4 (7)	Stanislas J 29 (6)
Carter-Vickers C 21	Mepham C 20 (4)	Surridge S 7 (22)
Cook L.........................31	Oforborh N .... - (3)	Travers M 1
Cook S.........................42	Pearson B............... 11 (5)	Wilshere J 9 (5)
Danjuma A 29 (4)	Rico D 23 (9)	Zemura A................. - (2)
Gosling D.................. 7 (8)	Riquelme R 2 (14)	

Play-offs – appearances: Begovic 2, Billing 2, Brooks 2, Carter-Vickers 2, Danjuma 2, Kelly 2, Lerma 2, Pearson 2, Smith A 2, Solanke 2, Mepham 1 (1), Cook 1, Wilshere 1, Stacey – (2), Long – (1), Rico – (1)
League goals (73): Danjuma 15, Solanke 15, Stanislas 10, Billing 8, Brooks 5, Surridge 4, Lerma 3, Gosling 2, Long 2, Carter-Vickers 1, Cook L 1, Kelly 1, Mepham 1, Rico 1, Riquelme 1, Stacey 1, Wilshere 1, Opponents 1. **Play-offs – goals (2)**: Danjuma 2
FA Cup goals (8): King 3, Brooks 1, Riquelme 1, Stanislas 1, Surridge 1, Wilshere 1. **League Cup goals (1)**: Surridge 1
Player of Year: Asmir Begovic

BRENTFORD

The long wait was over – 74 years since they last played in the top-flight and 30 years since the first of nine unsuccessful appearances in the play-offs. Brentford's bid to bring Premier League football to their new Community Stadium failed at the final hurdle against Fulham in 2020. This time they did it in style with two goals in the first 20 minutes, Ivan Toney's penalty followed by a sweet strike by Emiliano Marcondes accounting for Swansea at Wembley. Toney's 31 Championship goals had propelled his side into third place behind Norwich and Watford. It included a hat-trick in the 7-2 defeat of Wycombe and Sergi Canos also scored three, against Cardiff. But it was their mean defence which sealed a season to remember, conceding only twice in the last eight matches. Even so, Brentford, who lost leading marksmen Ollie Watkins and Said Benrahma after that defeat by Fulham, had to come from a 2-0 aggregate deficit in the second leg of the semi-final against Bournemouth. Toney pulled one back with his eighth successful spot-kick and Thomas Frank's side took full advantage when Bournemouth had Chris Mepham sent off, adding further goals from Vitaly Janelt and Marcus Forss. Brentford also reached their first League Cup semi-final, beating Southampton, West Bromwich Albion, Fulham and Newcastle before a 2-0 defeat by Tottenham.

Baptiste S.................. - (1)	Ghoddos S............. 16 (24)	Pressley A ....- (2)
Benrahma S .... - (2)	Haygarth M.................. - (1)	Raya D 42
Bidstrup M............... 1 (3)	Henry R 30	Reid W.......................7 (4)
Canos S 33 (13)	Janelt V................. 36 (5)	Roersley M 10 (7)
Goode A 4 (4)	Jansson P 23 (1)	Sorensen M B 29 (3)
Dalsgaard H 34 (1)	Jensen M 35 (10)	Stevens F ....- (2)
Daniels L.........................4	Marcondes E.......... 12 (19)	Thompson D 1 (3)
Dasilva J 26 (4)	Mbeumo B 37 (7)	Toney I....................44 (1)
Forss M 9 (30)	Norgaard C 15 (2)	Zamburek J .... - (6)
Fosu T 19 (20)	Pinnock E.....................39	

Play-offs – appearances: Canos 3, Janelt 3, Jansson 3, Jensen 3, Pinnock 3, Raya 3, Roersley 3, Toney 3, Dalsgaard 2 (1), Marcondes 2 (1), Mbeumo 2 (1), Forss 1 (2), Fosu 1 (1), Norgaard 1, Ghoddos – (3), Bidstrup – (2), Reid – (1)
League goals (79): Toney 31, Canos 9, Mbeumo 8, Forss 7, Dasilva 5, Fosu-Henry 4, Ghoddos 3, Janelt 3, Sorensen 2, Dalsgaard 2, Jensen 2, Henry 1, Marcondes 1, Pinnock 1. **Play-offs – goals** (5): Toney 2, Forss 1, Janelt 1, Marcondes 1
FA Cup goals (3): Dervisoglu H 1, Ghoddos 1, Sorensen 1. **League Cup goals** (9): Benrahma 2, Da Silva 2, Forss 2, Marcondes 1, Norgaard 1, Pinnock 1
Player of Year: Ivan Toney

BRISTOL CITY

A second successive season offering plenty of promise fell apart, this time amid a dreadful run of results at Ashton Gate. Dean Holden's side were on the fringes of a promotion challenge early in the new year, having defeated Huddersfield 2-1 with a brace from Famara Diedhou. Instead, they plummeted during a club-record seven successive home defeats which yielded a single goal. Neither Holden, sacked after the first two six just months into the job, nor Nigel Pearson who replaced him, could stem the tide. A goalless draw against Nottingham Forest offered some respite, although by then City were in the bottom half of the table. It would have been worse had their away form, in direct contrast, not produced 3-1 victories over Middlesbrough and Swansea – the latter in Pearson's first match in charge – and 3-0 against Birmingham. The former Watford and Leicester manager, appointed initially until the end of the season, was given a three-year contract, but City continued to struggle, surrendering a two-goal lead to Luton in a 3-2 defeat, then going down 3-1 to Brentford – a 13th home defeat.

Adelakun H	2	Janneh S	- (4)	Pearson S	2 (3)
Baker N	2 (1)	Kalas T	38 (2)	Rowe T	27 (4)
Bakinson T	20 (14)	Lansbury H	12 (4)	Scott A	1 (2)
Bell S	1 (3)	Mariappa A	19 (6)	Semenyo A	24 (20)
Bentley D	43	Martin C	20 (6)	Sessegnon S	10 (6)
Britton L	- (1)	Massengo H-N	18 (9)	Simpson D	3 (1)
Brunt C	5 (7)	Mawson A	11	Towler R	3
Conway T	3 (2)	Moore T	16 (6)	Vyner Z	38 (5)
Dasilva J	9 (2)	Nagy A	25 (6)	Walsh L	1 (2)
Diedhiou F	23 (17)	O'Dowda C	14 (5)	Watkins M	- (2)
Edwards Opanin	- (2)	O'Leary M	3	Weimann A	7
Edwards Owuru	1 (2)	Palmer K	16 (7)	Wells N	36 (10)
Hunt J	37 (4)	Paterson J	15 (5)	Williams J	1

League goals (46): Wells 10, Diedhiou 8, Bakinson 4, Paterson 3, Hunt 2, Martin 2, Nagy 2, Palmer 2, Semenyo 2, Vyner 2, Weimann 2, Britton 1, Conway 1, Dasilva 1, Kalas 1, O'Dowda 1, Rowe 1, Opponents 1
FA Cup goals (5): Diedhiou 2, Martin 1, Semenyo 1, Wells 1. **League Cup goals** (6): Palmer 2, Semenyo 2, Martin 1, Paterson 1
Player of Year: Daniel Bentley

CARDIFF CITY

Former Republic of Ireland manager Mick McCarthy transformed the club's fortunes after six successive defeats cost Neil Harris his job. McCarthy also earned himself a new two-year contract, having been appointed initially until the end of the season. In his first match, Cardiff retrieved a two-goal deficit for a point at Barnsley to launch a run of 24 points out of 30 which took them to within two points of a play-off place after a 4-0 victory over Derby. McCarthy reached his 1,000th match as a manager in a goalless draw against Huddersfield, before defeats by Watford and Nottingham Forest, then a 5-0 drubbing by struggling Sheffield Wednesday, effectively ended their promotion challenge. But Cardiff finished strongly, Kieffer Moore scoring twice against Wycombe to reach 20 for the season and Liverpool loanee Harry Wilson firing a hat-trick against Birmingham, which McCarthy rated as good as he had ever seen – a shot with the outside of his left boot and two pin-point free-kicks.

Bacuna L 32 (10)	Harris M 6 (10)	Phillips D 15 (1)
Bagan J 5 (2)	Hoilett J 14 (7)	Ralls J 34 (5)
Bamba S .... - (6)	Moore K 40 (2)	Sang T 8 (1)
Benkovic F .... - (1)	Morrison S 37 (1)	Smithies A 31
Bennett J 28	Murphy J 12 (20)	Tomlin L 1 (4)
Brown C 11 (1)	Nelson C 44	Vaulks W 36 (6)
Colwill R 3 (3)	Ng P 19	Watters M 1 (2)
Cunningham G 3 (2)	Ojo S 25 (16)	Whyte G 1 (6)
Flint A 22	Osi-Tutu J 6 (2)	Williams J 1 (8)
Glatzel R 8 (13)	Pack M 30 (9)	Wilson H 33 (4)

League goals (66): Moore 20, Wilson 7, Morrison 5, Ojo 5, Ralls 5, Vaulks 5, Glatzel 3, Harris 3, Bacuna 2, Hoilett 2, Murphy 2, Pack 2, Bennett 1, Flint 1, Nelson 1, Tomlin 1, Opponents 1
FA Cup goals: None. **League Cup goals**: None
Player of Year: Keiffer Moore

COVENTRY CITY

Coventry ensured a return home as a Championship club with a strong finish to the season. A ten-year agreement with Wasps Rugby, owners of the Ricoh Arena which is now the Coventry Building Society Stadium after a naming rights deal, was followed by four wins in five matches which removed the threat of a dropping straight back into League One. Playing their second season at St Andrew's in Birmingham, they were in danger of being overtaken if Rotherham turned matches in hand to good advantage. The pressure eased with a 3-1 victory over Bristol City in which Leo Ostigard and Viktor Gyokeres, on loan from Brighton, were both on the mark. Then, after a defeat by Bournemouth, Ostigard scored the only goal against Rotherham in what manager Mark Robins described as their best away performance of the campaign. Momentum was maintained with a 2-0 success against promotion-chasing Barnsley and the revival completed when Gyokeres scored the winner at Stoke. Coventry also finished on a high, beating Millwall 6-1.

Allen J 16 (6)	Gyokeres V 7 (12)	O'Hare C 40 (6)
Bakayoko A 2 (12)	Hamer G 36 (6)	Ostigard L 35 (4)
Bapaga W .... - (2)	Hyam D 43	Pask J 6 (11)
Biamou M 20 (14)	James M 19 (4)	Rose M 15 (2)
Burroughs J .... - (2)	Jobello W .... - (3)	Sheaf B 21 (9)
Dabo F 25 (3)	Kastaneer G .... - (2)	Shipley J 15 (12)
Da Costa J 10 (8)	Kelly L 21 (2)	Thompson J .... - (2)
Eccles J 2 (5)	Marosi M 20	Walker T 20 (11)
Giles R 15 (4)	McCallum S 37 (4)	Wilson B 26 (1)
Godden M 18 (5)	McFadzean K 37 (1)	

League goals (49): Walker 7, Godden 6, Biamou 5, Hamer 5, Gyokeres 3, Hyam 3, James 3, O'Hare 3, Shipley 3, Kelly 2, McFadzean 2, Ostigard 2, Allen 1, McCallum 1, Opponents 3
FA Cup goals: None. **League Cup goals** (2): Biamou 1, Walker 1
Player of Year: Callum O'Hare

DERBY COUNTY

Wayne Rooney came through the toughest of managerial baptisms on a nail-biting final day of the season. Despite a single victory in their last 15 matches, Derby preserved Championship status by a single point, thanks to two goals and an assist from Martyn Waghorn against Sheffield Wednesday. For much of the afternoon it looked as if both would be relegated, with fellow-strugglers Rotherham leading at Cardiff. But Rotherham conceded an 88th equaliser which, together with Waghorn's second from the penalty spot for a 3-3 draw, meant Derby survived by a point. Rooney initially shared responsibility alongside fellow coaches Liam Rosenior and Shay Given and academy chief Justin Walker after Phillip Cocu was sacked when his side hit rock bottom. Two months later, he took full control, while calling time on a distinguished playing career. A home defeat by Rotherham was an inauspicious start. Six victories in the next eight games augured well. After that, it proved a struggle all the way – against a background of two failed takeovers and the club facing action for financial misdemeanours.

Baningime B 1 (1)	Gregory L 6 (5)	Roberts P 7 (8)
Bielik K 13	Hector-Ingram J .... - (7)	Rooney W 9 (1)
Bird M 21 (12)	Holmes D 7 (7)	Roos K 13 (1)
Buchanan L 28 (7)	Ibe J .... - (1)	Shinnie G 41
Byrne N 39 (2)	Jozwiak K 30 (11)	Sibley L 10 (20)
Clarke M.....................42	Kazim-Richards C 30 (8)	Stretton J .... - (4)
Cresswell C .... - (1)	Knight J 41 (2)	Te Wierik M 3 (1)
Davies C 11 (2)	Lawrence T 19 (4)	Waghorn M 21 (11)
Ebosele F .... - (3)	MacDonald K 1 (6)	Watson L 1 (8)
Edmundson G 8 (2)	Marriott J 3 (1)	Whittaker M 1 (8)
Evans G 5 (1)	Marshall D......................33	Wisdom A.................36 (2)
Forsyth C 19 (1)	Mengi T 7 (2)	
Gordon K .... - (1)	Mitchell-Lawson J ....:. - (1)	

League goals (36): Kazim-Richards 8, Waghorn 5, Gregory 3, Lawrence 3, Shinnie 3, Bielik 2, Knight 2, Edmundson 1, Holmes 1, Jozwiak 1, Marriott 1, Roberts 1, Rooney 1, Sibley 1, Wisdom 1, Opponents 2
FA Cup goals: None. **League Cup goals** (1): Knight 1
Player of Year: Graeme Shinnie

HUDDERSFIELD TOWN

An uncomfortable first season in charge for Carlos Corberan, right-hand man to Marcelo Bielsa in Leeds's return to the Premier League, threatened to develop into a struggle against relegation when a run of ten matches brought a single victory. It included a 7-0 thrashing by champions-to-be Norwich and left them at the mercy of Rotherham's bid to take advantage of three games in hand during the run-in. Huddersfield were guilty of dropping too many points from winning positions until the boost of 2-0 victory away to Nottingham Forest, earned by Aaron Rowe's second senior goal and a belter by Curacao international Juninho Bacuna, eased the pressure. Huddersfield moved six points clear of the drop zone as Rotherham's backlog of fixtures, caused by Covid postponements, proved too demanding. They maintained that cushion, despite a disappointing finish which included a 5-2 defeat by Blackburn and brought a finishing position of 20th.

Aarons R.................... 5 (5)	Hamer B 15	Pritchard A...............6 (12)
Vallejo A 12 (4)	High S 1 (13)	Rowe A 10 (10)
Bacuna J 37 (6)	Hogg J 37	Sanogo Y....................5 (4)
Brown J 1 (12)	Holmes D 16 (3)	Sarr N 41
Campbell F 35 (5)	Jackson B........................1	Schindler C 10 (2)
Crichlow R 2 (2)	Pereira J.........................2	Schofield R.............29 (1)
Daly M........................ 1 (4)	Keogh R 21	Stearman R 14 (7)
Diakhaby A 7 (9)	Koroma M 19 (1)	Thomas S ....- (7)
Diarra B .... - (1)	Mbenza I 28 (8)	Toffolo H 31
Duhaney D 7 (6)	O'Brien L 39 (3)	Ward D 6 (13)
Edmonds-Green R..... 16 (8)	Phillips K .... - (10)	
Eiting C 17 (5)	Pipa........................ 35 (2)	

League goals (50): Koroma 8, Campbell 7, Bacuna 5, Mbenza 5, Sarr 4, Eiting 3, O'Brien 3, Edmonds-Green 2, Holmes 2, Pipa 2, Toffolo 2, Hogg 1, Rowe 1, Ward 1, Opponents 3
FA Cup goals (2): Crichlow 1, Rowe 1. **League Cup goals:** None
Player of Year: Jonathan Hogg

LUTON TOWN

A remarkable sequence of away performances proved the key to a satisfactory season for Nathan Jones and his players. They won seven 1-0, starting at Barnsley on the opening day of the season and continuing throughout the campaign until an eighth success came at Wycombe by a 3-1 margin. The ninth was arguably the pick of the bunch – retrieving a two-goal deficit against Bristol City to score three times in 15 minutes through James Collins, Elijah Adebayo and Harry Cornick. Luton supplemented this record with adequate form at Kenilworth Road to maintain a position in the middle reaches of the table, an improvement on 2020 when finishing three points above the drop zone. A 3-1 victory over champions Norwich was the high spot, alongside a hat-trick by Collins against Preston, the club's first in the second tier since Kerry Dixon's against Stoke in 1993. Collins also netted three in a League Cup win over Norwich.

Adebayo E............... 15 (3)	Hylton D................... 6 (10)	Norrington-Davies R .. 16 (2)
Berry L 22 (9)	Ince T 3 (4)	Pearson M.................. 38 (2)
Bradley S.................. 36 (1)	Lee E 8 (4)	Pereira D.....................- (1)
Bree J...................... 16 (8)	Lockyer T 18 (2)	Potts D...................... 20 (4)
Clark J.................... 23 (11)	LuaLua K 5 (18)	Rea G 33 (7)
Collins J 29 (13)	Moncur S 10 (11)	Ruddock P 38 (6)
Cornick H 28 (12)	Morrell J..................... 5 (5)	Shea J 7
Cranie M 20 (3)	Naismith K 17 (5)	Sluga S 39
Dewsbury-Hall K...... 36 (3)	Nombe S 1 (10)	Tunnicliffe R............. 17 (7)

League goals (41): Collins 10, Adebayo 5, Dewsbury-Hall 3, Moncur 3, Rea 3, Berry 2, LuaLua 2, Pearson 2, Ruddock 2, Tunnicliffe 2, Bree 1, Clark 1, Cornick 1, Lee 1, Naismith 1, Potts 1, Opponents 1
FA Cup goals (2): Clark 1, Moncur 1. **League Cup goals** (4): Collins 3, Clark 1
Player of Year: Simon Sluga

MIDDLESBROUGH

A ninth promotion proved out of reach, but this was still a season to remember for Neil Warnock. Having recovered from a bout of Covid, the 72-year-old took charge of his 1,500th match as a league manager. It delivered a 2-1 victory over Barnsley, the first of six unbeaten games which netted 14 points and brought him a record 11th Championship Manager-of-the-Month award, this one for October. Middlesbrough were then fifth in what was to be a highly competitive race for play-off places. Four months later, they were still in contention after Warnock signed a contract extension through to the end of the 2021–22 season. But a single point gained from five matches – three of them against serious contenders Bournemouth, Watford and Barnsley in the return fixture – left his side with too much ground to make up. Finishing tenth was still a significant improvement oo 17th place in 2020, although a 3-0 home defeat by relegated Wycombe was a disappointing finish.

Akpom C............... 20 (18)	Coulson H 5 (12)	Hall G...................... 18 (1)
Archer J.............................5	Dijksteel A.....................29	Howson J................. 40 (1)
Assombalonga B...... 19 (12)	Fisher D................... 11 (1)	Johnson M 22 (20)
Bettinelli M....................41	Fletcher A................. 4 (7)	Kebano N 15 (3)
Bola M............................41	Fletcher I............................1	Malley C .... - (3)
Bolasie Y 12 (3)	Folarin S.................... - (2)	McNair P 46
Browne M 1 (4)	Fry D 30 (2)	Mendez-Laing N 2 (7)
Coburn J.................... - (4)	Hackney H .... - (1)	Morsy S 29 (2)

104

Roberts P	4 (5)	Spence D	22 (16)	Wing L	4 (8)
Robinson J	- (1)	Tavernier M	25 (4)	Wood N	2 (2)
Saville G	35 (7)	Watmore D	23 (7)		

League goals (55): Watmore 9, Saville 6, Akpom 5, Assombalonga 5, Bolasie 3, Johnson 3, Tavernier 3, Browne 2, Hall 2, McNair 2, Wing 2, Bola 1, Coburn 1, Fletcher A 1, Fry 1, Howson 1, Kebano 1, Mendez-Laing 1, Morsy 1, Spence 1, Opponents 4
FA Cup goals (1): Folarin 1. **League Cup goals** (4): Fletcher A 2, Johnson 1, Tavernier 1
Player of Year: Paddy McNair

MILLWALL

Millwall flirted with the leading group during a solid start. A 2-0 victory at Preston was particularly encouraging, but a 3-0 home defeat by Huddersfield three days later set the pattern for an up-and-down season. It was the start of a lean run stretching all the way into the new year, with injuries and a lack of depth to the squad contributing to an end to any prospect of a promotion challenge. They fell into the bottom half of the table after a single win in 15 matches, before regaining some momentum, which brought maximum points from successive fixtures against Sheffield Wednesday, Reading and Birmingham. There was another run of success to come, this time against Middlesbrough, Rotherham and Stoke, raising hopes of cementing a healthy position in the table. Instead, a tough run-in against four promotion-minded sides proved too demanding. Millwall ended their home programme on a high, beating Bristol City 4-1, then slipped back again in a 6-1 defeat by Coventry described by manager Gary Rowett as 'embarrassing.'

Bennett M	29 (8)	Kieftenbeld M	8 (3)	Romeo M	30 (5)
Bialkowski B	46	Leonard R	24 (2)	Skalak J	1 (2)
Bodvarsson J D	13 (25)	Mahoney C	4 (10)	Smith M	7 (22)
Bradshaw T	12 (17)	Malone S	37 (4)	Thompson B	16 (14)
Burey T	- (13)	McNamara D	15 (1)	Wallace J	44 (1)
Cooper J	42	Mitchell B	10 (6)	Wallace M	20 (3)
Evans G	19	Muller H	- (2)	Williams S	12 (15)
Ferguson S	2 (11)	Parrott T	7 (4)	Woods R	39 (2)
Hutchinson S	39	Pearce A	20 (4)	Zohore K	10 (7)

League goals (47): Wallace J 11, Bennett 6, Malone 5, Bradshaw 4, Smith 3, Thompson 3, Zohore 2, Bodvarsson 1, Cooper 1, Evans 1, Hutchinson 1, Leonard 1, Mahoney 1, Mitchell 1, Romeo 1, Wallace M 1, Opponents 4
FA Cup goals (2): Hutchinson 1, Zohore 1. **League Cup goals** (6): Smith 2, Leonard 1, Mahoney 1, Malone 1, Opponents 1
Player of Year: Bartosz Bialkowski

NORWICH CITY

Norwich returned to the Premier League as undisputed champions with a commanding performance spearheaded by the prolific Teemu Pukki. The club reaped the reward for keeping faith with Daniel Farke after such a chastening experience in the top-flight the previous season. Farke successfully realigned his defence after losing Ben Godfrey and Jamal Lewis, while making a key loan signing in Tottenham's Oliver Skipp, who alongside Emiliano Buendia provided Pukki with the ammunition to repeat his finishing prowess of the previous promotion success. None of their rivals could keep pace, apart from during a brief wobble early in the new year when Brentford looked capable of a challenging. Norwich were goalless in three successive matches, then powered ahead with nine successive victories, followed over Easter by a 7-0 drubbing of Huddersfield in which Pukki scored a hat-trick. They finished with a club-record 97 points, six clear of Watford. Farke was named Manager-of-the Year, Buendia won the best player award and he and Pukki were in the division's Team of the Year, along with defenders Max Aarons and Grant Hanley.

Aarons M 45	Hugill J 7 (24)	Placheta P............10 (16)
Barden D 1 (1)	Idah A.................. 1 (16)	Pukki T...............39 (2)
Buendia E.................39	Krul T..................36	Rupp L...............15 (8)
Cantwell T............. 30 (3)	Martin J 6 (3)	Skipp O................44 (1)
Dowell K 12 (12)	McAlear R .... - (1)	Sorensen J 20 (12)
Giannoulis D 16	McGovern M 9 (1)	Stiepermann M 12 (6)
Gibson B.............. 26 (1)	McLean K........ 30 (8)	Tettey A........ 5 (14)
Godfrey B 3	Mumba B 1 (3)	Vrancic M......19 (13)
Hanley G..................42	Omobamidele A 8 (1)	Xavi Quintilla................11
Hernandez O 6 (15)	Omotoye T .... - (3)	Zimmermann C......13 (9)

League goals (75): Pukki 26, Buendia 15, Cantwell 6, Dowell 5, Hugill 4, Idah 3, Vrancic 3, Aarons 2, McLean 2, Quintilla 2, Hanley 1, Martin 1, Placheta 1, Skipp 1, Sorensen 1, Stiepermann 1, Opponents 1
FA Cup goals (2): Hugill 1, McLean 1. **League Cup goals** (1): Dowell 1
Player of Year: Emiliano Buendia

NOTTINGHAM FOREST

Chris Hughton introduced a measure of stability at the City Ground after the repercussions of the collapsed promotion bid at the end of the previous season spilled over into the new campaign. Forest lost their opening four fixtures, the club's worst start for 66 years, along with one in the League Cup, and Sabri Lamouchi became the first managerial casualty. Hughton, out of work since his dismissal by Brighton in May 2019, replaced him and started on a successful note, courtesy of Joe Lolley's 90th minute winner at Blackburn. There were also early victories against Coventry and Wycombe, but a run of six defeats in seven, dampened expectation. Forest dropped to the fringes of the relegation zone and subsequently never made it into the top half of the table. Neither were they in danger of being dragged back into trouble after starting the new year with four wins out of six. After that, goals became increasingly scare, with a 3-1 victory over Queens Park Rangers the only match when more than one was scored.

Ameobi S.............. 27 (5)	Gabriel J........................1	Mighten A........... 13 (11)
Arter H 8 (5)	Garner J............... 19 (1)	Murray G............... 8 (8)
Bachirou F .... - (1)	Grabban L.......... 24 (4)	Ribeiro Y................. 24 (1)
Blackett T.............. 9 (5)	Guerrero M A........... 4 (5)	Samba B.................45
Bong G 9 (1)	Ioannou N..............5	Smith J.....................1
Cafu.................. 26 (5)	Jenkinson C 1 (2)	Sow S.................... 12 (3)
Christie C..................44	Knockaert A 24 (10)	Swan W .... - (2)
Colback J 13 (4)	Krovinovic F.............19	Taylor L 15 (24)
Da Costa N............... 1 (1)	Lolley J................ 16 (12)	Worrall J 31
Figueiredo T........... 31 (1)	Mbe Soh L 5 (2)	Yates R 31 (3)
Freeman L ..... 16-(7)	McKenna S 24	

League goals (37): Grabban 6, Garner 4, Taylor 4, Ameobi 3, Mighten 3, Knockaert 2, Murray 2, Yates 2, Freeman 1, Krovinovic 1, Lolley 1, Mbe Soh 1, McKenna 1, Ribeiro 1, Worrall 1, Opponents 4
FA Cup goals (2): Knockaert 1, Taylor 1. **League Cup goals**: None
Player of Year: Joe Worrall

PRESTON NORTH END

All change at Deepdale as players came and went and manager Alex Neil was sacked after a run of one victory in nine matches. It culminated in a home defeat by Luton which left a deflated Neil admitting he had no idea what his best team was. He had lost Ben Davies to Liverpool, Ben Pearson to Bournemouth and Darnell Fisher to Middlesbrough in the winter transfer window.

They were among eight who left the club, with eight others signed. Caretaker Frankie McAvoy started with a point against leaders Norwich, courtesy of a stoppage-time goal from Brad Potts, and victory over another leading side, Swansea. Despite a 5-0 defeat by Brentford, the heaviest at home for 48 years, there was an overall improvement under McAvoy through to the end of the season. Preston defeated Derby, Coventry and Barnsley without conceding a goal, then finished by beating Nottingham Forest 2-1 and the coach was named Neil's permanent replacement.

Barkhuizen T.......... 29 (16)	Gordon A.................... 5 (6)	Potts B.................. 22 (20)
Bauer P 12	Harrop J 1 (4)	Raffety J 14 (7)
Bayliss T.................... 2 (9)	Hughes A 33 (2)	Ripley C 1
Bodin B 1 (3)	Huntington P............ 18 (3)	Jakobsen E R........17 (21)
Browne A 37 (1)	Iversen D.....................23	Rudd D 22
Cunningham G 10 (1)	Johnson D 24 (9)	Sinclair S 33 (4)
Davies B 19	Ledson R................ 31 (5)	Stockley J..............27 (3)
Earl J 4 (1)	Lindsay L 13	Storey J..................27 (3)
Evans C 19 (2)	Maguire S 15 (14)	Whiteman B 20 (3)
Fisher D......................14	Molumby J 7 (8)	Van den Berg S........15 (1)
Gallagher P 6 (7)	Pearson B.................. 8 (1)	

League goals (49): Sinclair 9, Evans 5, Potts 5, Barkhuizen 4, Browne 4, Johnson 4, Maguire 3, Ledson 2, Lindsay 2, Jakobsen 2, Bauer 1, Bayliss 1, Cunningham 1, Fisher 1, Stockley 1, Storey 1, Whiteman 1, Opponents 2
FA Cup goals (1): Jakobsen 1. **League Cup goals** (6): Barkhuizen 2, Bauer 1, Harrop 1, Johnson 1, Maguire 1
Player of Year: Ryan Ledson

QUEENS PARK RANGERS

Rangers came out of the shadows to prove the division's most improved side in the second half of the season. Nine matches without a win had left them two points away from the relegation zone going into the new year. But a run of six wins in seven matches, three of them against promotion-minded Watford, Brentford and Bournemouth, set the course for a rise to the top half of the table. A notable performance against Millwall underlined this recovery – transforming a 2-0 deficit into a 3-2 success with goals from Charlie Austin, back at the club on loan from West Bromwich Albion, Stefan Johansen and Jordy de Wijs. Rangers went on to finish strongly with victory in four of the final five fixtures. It was not enough to break into the leading pack, but a rise to ninth in the table represented the club's best in six years, while offering a good deal of promise for the new campaign.

Adomah A................ 7 (27)	De Wijs J.....................9	Kelman C 1 (10)
Amos L............................5	Dickie R 43	Lumley J 4 (1)
Austin C 19 (2)	Dieng T.........................42	Masterson C 3 (1)
Ball D.................. 24 (15)	Duke-McKenna S .... - (1)	Osayi-Samuel B 20 (1)
Barbet Y......................46	Dykes L.................. 36 (6)	Smyth P......................- (3)
Bettache F .... - (6)	Field S 8 (11)	Thomas G..............5 (12)
Bonne M................ 8 (26)	Hamalainen N.......... 18 (4)	Wallace L 27
Cameron G............ 31 (3)	Johansen S.....................21	Willock C..............20 (18)
Carroll R 19 (3)	Kakay O 23 (5)	
Chair I 43 (2)	Kane T 24 (4)	

League goals (57): Dykes 12, Austin 8, Chair 8, Johansen 4, Bonne 3, Dickie 3, Osayi-Samuel 3, Willock 3, Adomah 2, Barbet 2, Kane 2, Ball 1, De Wijs 1, Field 1, Kakay 1, Wallace 1, Opponents 2
FA Cup goals: None. **League Cup goals** (2): Kakay 1, Manning R 1
Player of Year: Rob Dickie

READING

Reading made a flying start under new manager Veljko Paunovic and retained a promotion place until the business end of the season when succumbing to play-off pressures. The Serbian won his opening four matches, a first for the club since season 1985–86. Yakou Meite's spectacular bicycle-kick against Rotherham was an early contender for goal of the season, while his opener four days later against Blackburn came after just eight seconds. With Lucas Joao also scoring regularly, Reading led the division by seven points at one stage, until eventually overtaken by Norwich and Watford. Successive victories over Rotherham and Blackburn, in the return fixtures, and Sheffield Wednesday maintained a play-off position. Then, a complete loss of momentum proved costly. Defeat by Watford knocked them out of a top-six position, there was a single victory – against Derby – in the final 11 fixtures and Reading were seven points adrift at the finish.

Aluko S..................... 9 (24)	Laurent J.....................45	Rafael Cabral.................45
Araruna F..........................2	Lucas Joao 35 (4)	Richards O 38 (3)
Azeez F...................... - (1)	McIntyre T............. 16 (10)	Rinomhota A.............41(1)
Baldock S 4 (16)	Meite Y 19 (6)	Semedo A............. 24 (15)
Camara M .... - (1)	Moore L 31 (1)	Southwood L....................1
Ejaria O 37 (1)	Morrison M.....................35	Swift J 10 (4)
Esteves T 12 (17)	Olise M 37 (7)	Tetek D 1 (6)
Gibson L....................... 7 (6)	Onen J....................... - (1)	Watson T......................- (1)
Holmes T 30 (9)	Puscas G................. 9 (12)	Yiadom A................ 18 (3)

League goals (62): Lucas Joao 19, Meite 12, Olise 7, Morrison 4, Puscas 4, Ejaria 3, Laurent 3, Aluko 2, McIntyre 2, Semedo 2, Esteves 1, Rinomhota 1, Swift 1, Yiadom 1
FA Cup goals: None. **League Cup goals** (3): Lucas Joao 3
Player of Year: Josh Laurent

ROTHERHAM UNITED

Paul Warne's team came within touching distance of beating the drop against all the odds on a dramatic final day of the season. With time running out at Cardiff, they were holding on to an eighth-minute goal from Middlesbrough loanee Lewis Wing for the victory which would have relegated Derby and Sheffield Wednesday. But an 88th minute equaliser by Marlon Pack sent them down, Derby survived and Warne admitted to being physically and emotionally drained after a fifth successive season of being either relegated or promoted. This time, Rotherham had to contend with a crippling backlog of fixtures after five fixtures were postponed during the course of the season because of Covid. It meant they had to play the final 12 games in 36 days, a demanding task for any club, let alone one struggling against relegation. There was a single victory in that sequence – Rotherham coming from behind to defeat Queens Park Rangers with two goals from Freddie Ladapo. They had chances in other games to have picked up more points, but poor finishing proved costly.

Barlaser D................ 29 (4)	Jones B...................... 3 (2)	Olosunde M 22 (10)
Blackman J.............. 25 (1)	Jozefzoon F 9 (15)	Robertson C............... 11 (5)
Clarke T..................... 1 (8)	Ladapo F................ 23 (19)	Sadlier K...................5 (10)
Crooks M 34 (6)	Lindsay J................. 28 (7)	Smith M................34 (10)
Giles R 12 (11)	MacDonald A............ 36 (3)	Vassell K..................... 6 (6)
Harding W.............. 41 (5)	MacDonald S............ 15 (4)	Wiles B 36 (8)
Hirst G 4 (27)	Mattock J 12 (2)	Wing L 18 (2)
Ihiekwe M....................42	Miller M 6 (3)	Wood R 27 (4)
Johansson V....................21	Ogbene C 6 (5)	

League goals (44): Smith 10, Ladapo 9, Crooks 6, Barlaser 3, Lindsay 3, Giles 2, Ihiekwe 2, Wiles 2, Wing 2, Wood 2, MacDonald A 1, Sadlier 1, Opponents 1
FA Cup goals (1): Olosunde 1. **League Cup goals** (1): Crooks 1
Player of Year: Wes Harding

SHEFFIELD WEDNESDAY

A reduction in the club's punishment for breaching financial rules, a succession of managers and a battling performance on a make-or-break final day of the season were not enough to prevent Wednesday dropping into the third tier. They led twice through Sam Hutchinson and Julian Borner at Derby, where a win would have meant survival. But a penalty conceded in the 78th minute and converted by Martyn Waghorn for a 3-3 draw meant the home side under Wayne Rooney stayed up. Wednesday had made their first change of a turbulent campaign five days after the 12-point deduction was halved on appeal, sacking Garry Monk and bringing in Tony Pulis for his 11th managerial appointment. He was gone after 45 days and a single win in ten games. Caretaker Neil Thompson lifted them out of the bottom three with five victories in seven. But seven successive defeats, including one at Hillsborough by relegation rivals Rotherham in Darren Moore's first match in permanent charge, proved damaging. Adding to their problems, Moore tested positive for Covid and had to take a back seat.

Bannan B 46	Hutchinson S.................22	Penney M.................10 (2)
Borner J..................25 (1)	Iorfa D 9 (1)	Reach A...................38 (6)
Brown I.............. 4 (15)	Kachunga E.............. 9 (18)	Rhodes J...............15 (21)
Dawson C.........................8	Lees T.........................38	Shaw L.....................13 (6)
Dunkley C 10 (2)	Luongo M............... 10 (2)	Urhoghide O 12 (4)
Dele-Bashiru F 2 (6)	Marriott J 4 (8)	Westwood K...................20
Flint A.............................4	Odubajo M 15 (3)	Wildsmith J 18 (1)
Green A 3 (8)	Palmer L 31 (8)	Windass J.................35 (6)
Harris K 30 (8)	Paterson C.............. 34 (9)	Van Aken J 16 (1)
Hunt A 1 (2)	Pelupessy J 24 (15)	

League goals (40): Windass 9, Paterson 8, Rhodes 7, Reach 5, Borner 3, Bannan 2, Hutchinson 1, Lees 1, Palmer 1, Shaw 1, Opponents 2
FA Cup goals (2): Paterson 1, Reach 1. **League Cup goals** (2: Kachunga 1, Windass 1
Player of Year: Barry Bannan

STOKE CITY

Stoke seemed to be gearing up for a promotion challenge approaching the midway point of the season after a run of four wins in six matches. They were up to fifth place, three points off leaders Norwich. But a loss of momentum meant there was a single victory, against Blackburn, to show from the next 13, and they were unable to unable to recover lost ground during an injury-hit second half of the campaign. The one achievement was a total of 21 clean sheets, equalling the club record of Alan Durban's promotion winners in season 1978-79. Only runners-up Watford, with 23, had a better record in the division. It was matched on the final day when Stoke, with 13 players unfit, won 2-0 at Bournemouth, with 19-year-old defender Will Forrester scoring on his debut. The record was balanced by too many goals against in other matches, with three or more conceded on seven occasions. That meant a finishing position of 14th, one higher than the previous season.

Allen J......................15 (3)	Fletcher S 30 (7)	Norton C 2 (4)
Batth D..................27 (2)	Forrester W........................1	Oakley-Boothe T........3 (13)
Brown J 27 (14)	Fox M 20	Powell N 38 (1)
Bursik J 15	Gregory L 3 (3)	Shawcross R.................- (2)
Campbell T 13 (3)	Gunn A 14 (1)	Smith T.......................34 (1)
Chester J 32	Ince T 2 (5)	Souttar H 38
Clarke J 6 (8)	Martins Indi B 2	Taylor C.........................- (1)
Clucas S 18 (6)	Matondo R 5 (5)	Thompson J...............24 (10)
Collins N.................. 19 (3)	McClean J 17 (7)	Tymon J 16 (10)
Cousins J 8 (11)	Mikel J O...............35 (4)	Verlinden T...................- (1)
Davies A......................17	Norrington-Davies R 20	Vokes S 5 (25)

League goals (50): Powell 12, Fletcher 9, Campbell 6, Brown 5, Clucas 2, Collins 2, McClean 2, Smith 2, Batth 1, Forrester 1, Gregory 1, Matondo 1, Norrington-Davies 1, Souttar 1, Thompson 1, Opponents 3
FA Cup goals: None. **League Cup goals** (4): Brown 1, Campbell 1, Vokes 1, Thompson 1
Player of Year: Nick Powell

SWANSEA CITY

Swansea went off the boil when challenging strongly for an automatic promotion place, regained momentum to reach the Play-off Final but paid the price for a below-par performance at Wembley. They were two goals down in 20 minutes, the first a penalty conceded by goalkeeper Freddie Woodman, the Championship's Golden Glove winner with 20 clean sheets to his credit. Leading scorer Andre Ayew's two headers were their only chances of note and Jay Fulton's straight red card for his challenge from behind on Mathias Jensen effectively ended their chances of a comeback. The winter loan signing of Aston Villa's Conor Hourihane had paid dividends – four goals in his first six league games. A fifth at Luton left Swansea tied on 69 points with second-place Watford. But four successive defeats left them nine adrift, before Jamal Lowe sparked a recovery with five goals in as many matches. His side held on to fourth place, Ayew secured victory at Barnsley in the first leg of the semi-final, while a superb Matt Grimes strike consolidated their advantage in the return leg.

Arriola P	- (2)	Fulton J	31 (9)	Morris J	- (4)
Ayew A	41 (2)	Garrick J	- (3)	Naughton K	30
Benda S	1	Gibbs-White M	4 (1)	Palmer K	2 (10)
Bennett R	28	Grimes M	42 (3)	Roberts C	43 (3)
Bidwell J	36 (3)	Gyokeres V	2 (9)	Rodon J	4
Cabango B	28 (2)	Hourihane C	18 (1)	Routledge W	4 (12)
Cooper B	- (1)	Latibeaudiere J	4 (4)	Smith K	27 (10)
Cooper O	- (3)	Lowe J	42 (4)	Whittaker M	3 (9)
Cullen L	6 (7)	Manning R	11 (6)	Woodman F	45
Dhanda Y	14 (12)	Guehi M	40		

Play-offs – appearances: Ayew 3, Bidwell 3, Cabango 3, Fulton 3, Grimes 3, Guehi 3, Hourihane 3, Lowe 3, Naughton 3, Woodman 3, Cullen 1 (1), Roberts 1 (1), Routledge 1 (1), Manning – (1), Smith – (1), Dhanda – (1)
League goals (56): Ayew 16, Lowe 14, Hourihane 5, Roberts 5, Cabango 4, Fulton 3, Grimes 2, Bidwell 1, Cullen 1, Dhanda 1, Gibbs-White 1, Palmer 1, Whittaker 1, Opponents 1. **Play-offs – goals** (2): Ayew 1, Grimes 1
FA Cup goals (8): Cullen 2, Grimes 2, Cooper 1, Gyokeres 1, Routledge 1, Whittaker 1. **League Cup goals**: None
Player of Year: Conner Roberts

WATFORD

Timing their run perfectly, Watford emerged from a pack of promotion hopefuls to return to the Premier League at the first attempt. They won ten out of 11 matches to effectively seal second place behind Norwich by Easter, with five matches still to play. Watford flourished under former Valencia winger and Dinamo Tbilisi coach Xisco Munoz, the club's 13th full-time manager in nine-and-a-half-years. He was appointed the day after Vladimir Ivic was sacked four months into the job after a 2-0 defeat at Huddersfield in which fans' favourite Troy Deeney was left out of the team. Munoz made the perfect start with victory over long-term leaders Norwich. His side still trailed Brentford, Bournemouth and Swansea going into the new year, but a 6-0 win over Bristol City started to reshape the top order. They picked off each of their three rivals for the runners-up spot and by the time record-signing Ismaila Sarr fired two spectacular goals for victory against Reading, they had opened up a 12-point cushion. Promotion was confirmed by Sarr's penalty against Millwall with two fixtures remaining.

Bachmann D 23	Hungbo J 1 (4)	Pussetto I...................- (1)
Capoue E 7 (4)	Joao Pedro 31 (7)	Quina 8 (6)
Cathcart C......... 20 (5)	Kabasele C 19 (10)	Sanchez C 2 (7)
Chalobah N 32 (6)	Kiko.......................... 36 (1)	Sarr I 39
Cleverley T............... 32 (2)	Lazaar A...................... 2 (3)	Sema K..................38 (3)
Deeney T 14 (5)	Navarro M 2 (4)	Sierralta F 24 (2)
Dele-Bashiru T 1 (1)	Masina A 21 (4)	Success I 3 (7)
Foster B...........................23	Murray G 1 (4)	Troost-Ekong W 31 (1)
Garner J................... 12 (8)	Ngakia J................. 18 (7)	Wilmot B 14 (11)
Gosling D.................. 6 (7)	Perica S 2 (14)	Zinckernagel P........9 (11)
Gray A 14 (16)	Phillips D .... - (2)	
Hughes W 21 (9)	Pochettino M.............. - (1)	

League goals (63): Sarr 13, Joao Pedro 9, Deeney 7, Gray 5, Sema 5, Cleverley 4, Chalobah 3, Gosling 2, Hughes 2, Masina 2, Cathcart 1, Kabasele 1, Perica 1, Quina 1, Sierralta 1, Success 1, Troost-Ekong 1, Wilmot 1, Zinckernagel 1, Opponents 2
FA Cup goals: None. **League Cup goals** (2): Penaranda A 1 Sema 1
Player of Year: Ismaila Sarr

WYCOMBE WANDERERS

Gareth Ainsworth worked wonders to take the club into the Championship and never lost faith in the ability of his players to show they were not out of place. That Wycombe went straight back down was perhaps predictable in such a high-profile and competitive division. Nevertheless, Ainsworth ensured the ride was an enjoyable one and only on a couple of occasions were they overwhelmed. A 5-0 drubbing by Blackburn was one of seven successive defeats at the start of the season. A 7-2 thrashing by Brentford proved a harsh lesson in trying to chase a game which was clearly beyond them. For the most part, they competed strongly against some of the biggest names, like Norwich, Watford and Bournemouth, before submitting. Week after week, the manager remained optimistic about a great escape and there was a glint in his eye after a 3-0 victory at Rotherham over Easter. Results elsewhere kept them nine points adrift. But five wins in the final eight matches, rounded off by the 3-0 defeat of Middlesbrough at the Riverside, left Ainsworth a proud man with his side off the foot off the table and a single point away from Derby at the finish.

Adeniran D.............. 18 (3)	Jacobson J 36 (1)	Parker J ....- (3)
Akinfenwa A........... 11 (22)	Kashket S............... 18 (11)	Pattison A 4 (2)
Allsop R..........................29	Knight J 36 (1)	Samuel A 7 (14)
Bloomfield M............ 8 (8)	McCarthy J 22 (2)	Stewart A 31 (1)
Charles D....................5	McCleary G............ 20 (12)	Stockdale D..................17
Freeman N................. 3 (4)	Mehmeti A 18 (11)	Tafazolli R 17 (3)
Gape D 12 (2)	Muskwe A 13 (4)	Thompson C 28 (5)
Grimmer J................ 39 (1)	Obita J...................... 7 (2)	Wheeler D 27 (11)
Horgan A 28 (12)	Ofoborh N 3 (5)	
Ikpeazu U 23 (8)	Onyedinma F 26 (17)	

League goals (39): Ikpeazu 6, Jacobson 4, Kashket 4, McCleary 4, Mehmet 3, Muskwe 3, Onyedinma 3, Wheeler 3, McCarthy 2, Tafazolli 2, Akinfenwa 1, Bloomfield 1, Knight 1, Stewart 1, Opponents 1
FA Cup goals (5): Onyedinma 2, Jacobson 1, Knight 1, Samuel 1. **League Cup goals** (1): Horgan 1
Player of Year: Josh Knight

SKY BET LEAGUE ONE

ACCRINGTON STANLEY

A Dion Charles hat-trick in a 6-1 win over Bristol Rovers put his side in a useful position for a promotion challenge. They were one off sixth place and had games in hand over the sides above them after the postponement of four matches because of Covid. Charles scored two more in a 2-2 draw at Lincoln, his second coming in the 90th minute. But momentum was lost amid a catalogue of injuries which John Coleman rated the worst in his 25 years as a manager. Accrington conceded four in the return fixture with Rovers and were swamped at Peterborough, where a 7-0 defeat was the club's worst since returning to the Football League in 2006. That was followed by a 5-1 home defeat by relegated-threatened AFC Wimbledon, with Coleman calling on his players to stop performing like a 'Jekyll and Hyde' team. It was a point well made as they twice came from behind to earn a point at Sunderland with a superb 85th minute free-kick from Sean McConville – his first goal of the season.

Allan T	1 (3)	Hughes M	36	Rodgers H	27 (1)
Barclay B	23 (3)	Maguire J	5	Russell J	12 (13)
Baxter N	16	Mansell L	- (2)	Sama S	2 (2)
Bishop C	38 (3)	McConville S	26 (5)	Sangare M	1 (1)
Burgess C	42 (2)	Morgan D	9 (7)	Savin T	30 (1)
Butcher M	39 (3)	Nottingham M	41 (1)	Scully T	- (3)
Cassidy R	5 (6)	Perritt H	- (2)	Smyth P	15 (6)
Charles D	42	Phillips A	13 (9)	Sykes R	9
Conneely S	37 (1)	Pritchard J	25 (3)	Uwakwe T	12 (3)
Fenlon R-J	- (2)	Roberts G	- (2)		

League goals (63): Charles 19, Bishop 10, Pritchard 7, Nottingham 4, Burgess 3, Smyth 3, Butcher 2, Cassidy 2, Phillips 2, Russell 2, Barclay 1, Conneely 1, McConville 1, Sykes 1, Uwakwe 1, Opponents 4
FA Cup goals (1): Bishop 1. **League Cup goals** (1): Burgess 1. **League Trophy goals** (12): Uwakwe 3, Burgess 2, Cassidy 2, Pritchard 2, Bishop 1, Charles 1, Mansell 1
Player of Year: TBC

AFC WIMBLEDON

What a difference a week can make. Wimbledon were in danger of being relegated in their first season back at Plough Lane, before finally finding some home comforts with three quick-fire victories. Defeat by Fleetwood had left them third from bottom – their eighth at the new stadium, with manager Glyn Hodges sacked after a particularly painful one by bitter rivals MK Dons. His replacement, coach Mark Robinson, initially struggled to turn things around until his side came from behind to win 5-1 at Accrington, Ollie Palmer and Ayub Assal sharing four of the goals. That was quickly followed by a 3-0 defeat of Ipswich and when two from Joe Pigott came in a 4-1 victory over Swindon, Wimbledon were then five points clear of trouble. Alex Woodyard's first for the club completed another turnround, 2-1 against Oxford, and his side were effectively safe after Pigott's equaliser in the seventh minute of stoppage-time against Rochdale – his 19th goal of the campaign – in the penultimate home game. He finished with 20 to his credit.

Alexander C	18 (11)	Hartigan A	8 (7)	O'Neill L	24 (4)
Assal A	10 (4)	Heneghan B	20 (3)	Oksanen J	12 (15)
Chislett E	12 (15)	Johnson D	11	Osew P	- (10)
Csoka D	20	Kalambayi P	10 (4)	Palmer O	10 (13)
Dobson G	22 (2)	Longman R	35 (9)	Pigott J	45
Guinness-Walker N	25 (6)	McLoughlin S	23 (15)	Reilly C	22 (6)
Harrison S	- (1)	Nightingale W	29 (3)	Robinson Z	- (5)

Roscrow A.................... - (6)   Thomas T................. 17 (2)   Walker S 12
Rudoni J .... 33 (6)   Trueman C 19   Woodyard A.............. 39 (1)
Seddon S................ 15 (1)   Tzanev N 15

League goals (54): Pigott 20, Longman 8, Palmer 5, Assal 4, Rudoni 4, Chislett 2, Heneghan 2, Nightingale 2, Csoka 1, Dobson 1, Guinness-Walker 1, McLoughlin 1, Reilly 1, Seddon 1, Woodyard 1
FA Cup goals (1): Pigott 1. **League Cup goals** (1): Opponents 1. **League Trophy goals** (9): Roscrow 2, Chislett 1, Longman 1, Osew 1, Pigott 1, Robinson 1, Rudoni 1, Thomas 1
Player of Year: Joe Pigott

BLACKPOOL

Kenny Dougall found the scoring touch when it mattered most to fire Blackpool into the Championship. The Australian midfielder, with a single goal to his name in the regular campaign, scored two with identical sweet strikes into the bottom corner from 20 yards at sun-drenched Wembley. They enabled his side to recover from conceding an Ollie Turton own goal after 47 seconds to win 2-1 and continue a proud record as the most successful side in the history of the play-offs. One of the club's six victories, in 2010, earned a place in the Premier League, but recent years were troubled, with supporters boycotting matches in protest against the previous owners. Dougall also scored in the semi-final against Oxford at the end of an impressive first season in charge for Neil Critchley, former manager of Liverpool's Under-23 team. Blackpool started it indifferently, built up a head of steam to win eight out nine games in all competitions, then lost some momentum in mid-winter. A 5-0 win over Wigan proved the turning point. They accumulated 35 points from 16 matches to break into the top-six, with Jerry Yates scoring 12 goals in that productive spell, and went on to finish third behind Hull and Peterborough.

Anderson K .... 11 (6)   Husband J................ 24 (3)   Shaw N ....- (1)
Apter R........................ - (1)   Kaikai S .... 33 (3)   Simms E 17 (4)
Ballard D .... 24 (1)   Kemp D .... 3 (5)   Stewart K 10 (3)
Dougall K .... 32 (2)   Lubala B .... 5 (7)   Thornley J 17 (2)
Ekpiteta M .... 26 (2)   Madine G .... 15 (6)   Turton O 33 (4)
Embleton E............... 14 (4)   Maxwell C.......................43   Virtue M 11 (5)
Gabriel J.................. 18 (9)   Mitchell D .... 13 (19)   Walker S 2
Garbutt L................. 25 (6)   Moore S 1   Ward G.....................29 (7)
Gretarsson D .... 11 (1)   Nottingham M...................3   Williams M 6 (4)
Hamilton C .... 19 (3)   Robson E .... 15 (13)   Woodburn B...............3 (7)
Holmes B.................. 1 (4)   Sarkic O .... 1 (4)   Yates J 41 (3)

Play-offs – appearances: Ballard 3, Dougall 3, Embleton 3, Garbutt 3, Husband 3, Maxwell 3, Stewart 3, Turton 3, Yates 3, Anderson 2 (1), Mitchell 2 (1), Simms 2, Madine – (3), Gabriel – (2), Thornley – (2), Ekpiteta – (1), Hamilton – (1), Ward – (1), Robson – (1)
League goals (60): Yates 20, Simms 8, Kaikai 7, Hamilton 5, Garbutt 4, Madine 4, Anderson 2, Ballard 2, Ekpiteta 2, Virtue 2, Dougall 1, Embleton 1, Mitchell 1, Ward 1. **Play-offs – goals** (8): Dougall 3, Simms 2, Embleton 1, Turton 1, Yates 1
FA Cup goals (10): Madine 4, Yates 2, Gabriel 1, Kemp 1, Ward 1, Opponents 1. **League Cup goals**: None. **League Trophy goals** (4): Anderson 1, Kemp 1, Robson 1, Opponents 1
Player of Year: Chris Maxwell

BRISTOL ROVERS

Three managers tried and failed to arrest the club's slide towards League Two. Ben Garner, in charge for 11 months, was dismissed after a 4-1 home defeat by Fleetwood. Paul Tisdale, previously in charge of MK Dons and Exeter, paid the price for a run of eight matches yielding just two points and including a 6-1 defeat at Accrington. Joey Barton, himself sacked by

Fleetwood the previous month, had three wins to show from 15 matches by the time of a 2-0 home defeat by MK Dons on a night when five other relegation candidates all won. That left Rovers rock bottom, ten points adrift, with the division's lowest goals tally of 40. They were officially relegated after losing to Portsmouth, one of five successive defeats without scoring to end the season. Barton admitted his team did not deserve to stay up. He criticised his two predecessors, the character of some of his players and promised there would be big changes at the club – if he was still manager.

Ayunga J................. 13 (17)	Jaakkola A......................21	Ogogo A 3
Baldwin J................. 32 (6)	Kilgour A.................. 33 (2)	Oztumer E............ 10 (12)
Barrett J .... - (9)	Koiki A....................... 3 (7)	Rodman A 11 (5)
Daly J................... 13 (15)	Leahy L................... 37 (1)	Tutonda D 10 (10)
Day J................................18	Liddle B 1 (2)	Upson E.................... 20 (6)
Ehmer M................. 27 (1)	Little M 2 (3)	Van Stappershoef J....6 (2)
Grant J................... 31 (1)	Martinez P......................8	Walker Z...................4 (7)
Hanlan B 40 (4)	McCormick L 36 (3)	Ward J 1
Hare J 14 (5)	Mehew T................... - (1)	Westbrooke Z..........33 (9)
Hargreaves C............ 3 (10)	Mitchell-Lawson J 3 (2)	Williams G................25 (1)
Harries C 26 (2)	Nicholson S............. 22 (8)	

League goals (40): Leahy 8, Hanlan 7, McCormich 6, Nicholson 6, Daly 3, Ayunga 2, Westbrooke 2, Baldwin 1, Ehmer 1, Grant 1, Kilgour 1, Rodman 1, Upson 1
FA Cup goals (10): Leahy 2, Baldwin 1, Daly 1, Ehmer 1, Hanlan 1, Hare 1, Kilgour 1, Nicholson 1, Oztumer 1. **League Cup goals:** None. **League Trophy goals (9):** Mehew 2, Ayunga 1, Hanlan 1, Hare 1, Koiki 1, Nicholson 1, Sargeant 1, Westbrooke 1
Player of Year: Luke McCormick

BURTON ALBION

Jimmy Floyd Hasselbaink could have been forgiven for wondering what he had let himself in for on his return to the club, five years after leaving to manage Queens Park Rangers. He watched from the stands as Burton were beaten 5-1 at home by Oxford to remain six points adrift at the foot of the table, having conceded 17 goals in four games. A week later, Hasselbaink began to lead a remarkable recovery after taking over from Jake Buxton, sacked seven months into the job. There were nine signings in the winter transfer window, including Jonny Smith on loan from Bristol City, who scored in the 90th minute of his debut for a morale-boosting win against second-place Hull. Burton went on to record six successive victories for the first time in the Football League, completed by a first-half hat-trick by Kane Hemmings at Crewe. Two defeats approaching Easter were taken in their stride and when Mike Fondop and Josh Powell scored either side of half-time for victory over Portsmouth, they were virtually safe, ten points clear, with a superior goal difference and games in hand.

Akins L..............................45	Fox B 5 (4)	Parker J 3 (3)
Barnes D..........................1	Gallacher O 5 (4)	Powell J 23 (16)
Bostwick M 26 (2)	Garratt B 28	Quinn S 21 (1)
Brayford J 40 (1)	Gilligan C 13 (5)	Roles J ....- (2)
Broom R 3 (8)	Hamer T................... 20 (1)	Rowe D 8 (7)
Carter H............................24	Hemmings K........... 26 (10)	Smith J 13 (3)
Clare S 19 (1)	Hewlett T .... - (1)	Taylor T....................6 (10)
Daniel C 17 (2)	Hughes S 14	Varney L ....- (4)
Eardley N................... 9 (1)	Hutchinson R .... - (1)	Vassilev I.....................8 (4)
Earl J 7 (1)	Lawless S 8 (8)	Vernam C 11 (3)
Edwards R 37 (5)	Mancienne M............ 14 (3)	Wallace K...................9 (3)
Ennis N 6 (3)	O'Hara K 17	
Fondop M 8 (9)	O'Toole J-J................ 12 (4)	

League goals (61): Hemmings 15, Akins 9, Powell 6, Brayford 4, Carter 4, Hamer 3, Bostwick 2, Broom 2, Fondop 2, Hughes 2, Smith 2, Vernam 2, Clare 1, Daniel 1, Edwards 1, O'Toole 1, Quinn 1, Opponents 3
FA Cup goals: None. **League Cup goals** (2): Akins 1, Daniel 1. **League Trophy goals** (6): Powell 3, Akins 1, Edwards 1, Lawless 1
Player of Year: Ryan Edwards

CHARLTON ATHLETIC

Nigel Adkins returned to management after a lengthy absence and came so close to leading Charlton into the play-offs. Only goal difference separated his new side from sixth place and the chance of an immediate return to the Championship. Adkins, who left his last job at Hull in the summer of 2019, suffered a single defeat in ten matches after succeeding Lee Bowyer, who resigned to lead Birmingham's bid for Championship survival. He kept Charlton on the fringes of a play-off spot with a 2-1 victory at Sunderland, supervised a club-record-equalling 6-0 away win over Plymouth, then set up a tense last-day finish with a 3-1 success against Lincoln. They could do no more than defeat champions Hull in the last round of fixtures – a 75th minute own goal settling the match. By then, however, Oxford were three goals up against Burton and on the way to completing their own impressive finish to the regular season. Charlton, with a difference of plus-14 compared to their rivals' plus-21, were left to rue too many points dropped previously at home.

Amos B.........................46	Jaiyesimi D................. 7 (7)	Pratley D 33 (6)
Aneke C............. 11 (27)	Lapslie G.................... 1 (1)	Purrington B............. 19 (9)
Barker C 3	Levitt D...........................3	Schwartz R...............3 (13)
Bogle O 12 (5)	Maatsen I 31 (3)	Shinnie A..............18 (11)
Bonne M..........................3	Maddison M 4 (4)	Smith M.....................3 (5)
Doughty A.......................7	Matthews A 22 (5)	Smyth P.....................8 (6)
Famewo A 20 (2)	Millar L 23 (4)	Stockley J...............20 (2)
Forster-Caskey J 32 (2)	Morgan A 14 (14)	Vennings J.........................1
Gilbey A.............. 18 (5)	Oshilaja A............... 16 (1)	Washington C............28 (8)
Gunter C 31 (5)	Oztumer E 2	Watson B..................24 (5)
Inniss R.................. 12 (1)	Pearce J 24 (2)	Williams J 7 (11)

League goals (70): Aneke 15, Washington 11, Stockley 8, Forster-Caskey 6, Gilbey 3, Shinnie 3, Bogle 2, Millar 2, Purrington 2, Williams 2, Doughty 1, Gunter 1, Inniss 1, Jaiyesimi 1, Maatsen 1, Maddison 1, Morgan 1, Oshilaja 1, Pratley 1, Schwartz 1, Smyth 1, Watson 1, Opponents 4
FA Cup goals: None. **League Cup goals** (3): Aneke 1, Barker 1, Bonne 1. **League Trophy goals** (5): Aouachria W 1, Maddison 1, Mingi J 1, Morgan 1, Oztumer 1
Player of Year: Jake Forster-Caskey

CREWE ALEXANDRA

Promoted Crewe were in contention for a play-off place, going into the second half of the season, on the back of a ten-match unbeaten run. They were a point off the leading group and would have broken through had a three-goal lead at Rochdale, established by two from Oliver Finney and one by Owen Dale, not been surrendered. The run ended in a 4-1 defeat at Gillingham and in a highly competitive division they were unable to keep up the pace. A top-half finish still looked within reach, despite the club's worst home defeat for nearly 50 years – 6-0 against Oxford with five goals conceded in 13 minutes either side of half-time. They picked up towards the end, twice coming from behind for a point at Charlton thanks to Dale's second of the match in the sixth minute of stoppage-time. And 12th place was superior to the three other teams who went up from League Two.

Adebisi R................ 11 (4)	Daniels D 11 (4)	Jaaskelainen W................31
Ainley C................ 12 (10)	Evans A 6 (8)	Johnson T 6 (1)
Beckles O 37 (4)	Finney O.................. 19 (7)	Jones B 3
Dale O 32 (11)	Griffiths R .... - (2)	Kirk C.....................41 (1)

Lancashire O 20 (2)	Ng P 15	Richards D 15
Lowery T 30 (7)	Offord L 27 (1)	Walker S 2 (9)
Lundstram J .... - (4)	Pickering H 44	Wintle R 41 (2)
Mandron M 36 (6)	Porter C 14 (21)	Wood N 11 (1)
Murphy L 29 (11)	Powell D 12 (12)	Zanzala O 1 (4)

League goals (56): Dale 11, Mandron 11, Finney 7, Kirk 6, Porter 6, Lowery 3, Pickering 3, Wintle 2, Ainley 1, Beckles 1, Lancashire 1, Ng 1, Offord 1, Powell 1, Walker 1
FA Cup goals (4): Finney 1, Kirk 1, Mandron 1, Porter 1. **League Cup goals** (1): Sass-Davies B 1.
League Trophy goals (7): Mandron 2, Powell 2, Dale 1, Pickering 1, Zanzala 1
Player of Year: Owen Dale

DONCASTER ROVERS

Doncaster lost their captain, their manager and the chance of sustaining a promotion challenge. Nine wins in ten matches had been rewarded with a rise to second place, ahead of a clutch of more fancied teams. It included a 1-0 success against Lincoln during which Ellery Balcombe, on loan from Brentford, saved two penalties. Momentum suffered when midfielder Ben Whiteman moved to Preston in the winter transfer window and Darren Moore accepted the challenge of trying to keep Sheffield Wednesday in the Championship. Defender Andy Butler took over as caretaker of his home-town club and won his first two matches in charge to keep them in a play-off place. After that, Rovers fell right away, with just two points to show from a run of nine games. They retrieved a two-goal deficit for a point away to promotion-chasing Peterborough, but by then were in the bottom half of the table. The season ended with midfielder James Coppinger, 40, making his 695th and final appearance before retiring. Richie Wellens, formerly in charge of Salford and Swindon, was appointed the new manager.

Amos D 4 (4)	Halliday B 34 (3)	Richards T 28 (13)
Anderson T 44	Hasani L .... - (2)	Robertson S 6 (9)
Balcombe E 15	Horton B 9 (2)	Simoes E 7 (1)
Blythe B .... - (1)	James R 42 (1)	Sims J 20 (8)
Bogle O 14 (3)	John C 21 (10)	Taylor J 19 (6)
Bostock J 11 (7)	John-Jules T 13 (5)	Tulloch R 2
Bursik J 10	Jones L 13	Whiteman B 18
Butler A 20	Lokilo J 13 (19)	Williams E .... - (11)
Coppinger J 17 (15)	Lumley J 8	Wright J 36 (4)
Gomes M 11 (11)	Okenabirhie F 30 (9)	
Greaves A 4 (6)	Smith M 37 (3)	

League goals (63): Okenabirhie 11, Richards 10, James 7, John-Jules 5, Whiteman 5, Coppinger 4, Taylor 4, Gomes 3, Anderson 2, Bogle 2, John 2, Wright 2, Halliday 1, Lokilo 1, Smith 1, Sims 1, Opponents 1
FA Cup goals (8): Whiteman 3, Sims 2, Coppinger 1, Okenabirhie 1, Richards 1. **League Cup goals** (2): Gomes 1, Okenabirhie 1. **League Trophy goals** (1): Okenabirhie 1
Player of Year: James Coppinger

FLEETWOOD TOWN

Back-to-back victories over Bristol Rovers (4-1) and Plymouth (5-1) offered an early hint that this might be another successful season for Fleetwood, who reached the play-offs in 2020. The surge, with Callum Camps scoring four of the goals, left them a point off the top-six, two months into the campaign. After that, the goals dried up, with just five scored in 13 matches and a single victory recorded. It proved a recurring problem which ruled out any chance of recovering lost ground. Joey Barton was sacked following a dressing-room altercation with striker Ched Evans and Simon Grayson came in for his eighth managerial appointment, initially until the end of the season. That became a permanent position two months later when a run of four victories in five matches lifted his side into the top-half of the table. They were unable to hold on to it, with a 5-2 defeat by Burton part of a disappointing finish.

Andrew D.....................45	Duffy M.................... 8 (16)	McKay B 15 (11)
Baggley B ....- (2)	Edwards T 10 (1)	Morris J 14 (10)
Batty D.......................17	Evans C 11 (6)	Morris S 1 (4)
Biggins H................. 4 (6)	Finley S 19 (10)	Mulgrew C................22 (1)
Boyes M 2	Garner G 11 (6)	Rossiter J................30 (5)
Burns W 29 (4)	Hill J 24 (4)	Rydel R......................4 (3)
Cairns A......................28	Hilton J...........................2	Saunders H 6 (15)
Camps C 36 (6)	Holgate H 13 (5)	Sheron N.................- (1)
Connolly C 40	Leutwiler J 16	Stubbs S 5
Coutts P 13 (7)	Madden P................24 (8)	Vassell K 24 (2)
Donacien J..............16 (3)	Matete J................. 3 (4)	Whelan C 14 (9)

League goals (49): Camps 9, Madden 7, Burns 5, Evans 5, Vassell 4, Finley 3, Garner 3, Saunders 3, Andrew 2, Connolly 2, McKay 2, Mulgrew 1, Rossiter 1, Stubbs 1, Opponents 1
FA Cup goals: None. **League Cup goals** (7): Evans 2, Morris J 2, Camps 1, Duffy 1, Madden 1.
League Trophy goals (10): Saunders 5, Burns 1, Camps 1, Duffy 1, Madden 1, McKay 1
Player of Year: Danny Andrew

GILLINGHAM

Vadaine Oliver struck a rich seam of goals to propel his side from the bottom half of the table to within sight of a promotion challenge. Eight in eight matches earned him League One's Player of the Month award for March, with Steve Evans taking the managerial prize for five victories. It would have been six had Gillingham not surrendered a two-goal lead established in the opening four minutes against Doncaster, who rallied for a point. They were then two points off a play-off place, needing to maintain momentum in a tightly-packed division. Instead, they paid the penalty for missed chances when held to a goalless draw by Shrewsbury and lost 4-1 against top-six rivals Blackpool – a result Evans had no complaints about, with his side well beaten. He had rather more to say about a 3-2 defeat by Oxford which left his side with too much ground to make up, pointing to a lack of discipline after another two-goal lead was surrendered, this time in the final 20 minutes.

Akinde J 19 (25)	Lee O....................... 19 (6)	Ogilvie C 45
Bonham J 44	Lumley J 2	Oliver V 39 (4)
Coyle T 3 (10)	MacDonald A 22 (15)	Robertson S.............11 (4)
Cundy R 18	Maghoma C 4	Samuel D 15 (7)
Dempsey K 40	McKenzie R 17 (16)	Sithole G...................- (1)
Drysdale D 6 (4)	Medley Z 11 (1)	Slattery C 7
Eccles J................. 10 (2)	Mellis J 7 (1)	Tucker J 42 (1)
Graham J 36 (3)	Morton J.................- (1)	Walsh J ....- (1)
Jackson R 43	O'Connor T 27 (7)	Willock M ....- (11)
Johnson T 1 (6)	O'Keefe S............. 18 (6)	Woods H ....- (4)

League goals (63): Oliver 17, Graham 12, Dempsey 8, Akinde 7, Lee 5, Ogilvie 4, Samuel 3, Coyle 2, Cundy 1, MacDonald 1, McKenzie 1, Mellis 1, Tucker 1
FA Cup goals (5): Samuel 3, Oliver 2. **League Cup goals** (2): Graham 1, Ogilvie 1. **League Trophy goals** (3): Coyle 2, Oliver 1
Player of Year: Kyle Dempsey

HULL CITY

Grant McCann repaid a vote of confidence by leading a title-winning return to the Championship. The club kept faith with the manager after a particularly painful relegation the previous season which included their worst defeat of modern times – 8-0 by Wigan. Hull were one of five teams in contention until an unstoppable run took them clear of the pack. It was launched, ironically, by a 5-0 win over Wigan – who had also gone down – featuring a hat-trick by Mallik Wilks. One by one their rivals fell by the wayside, unable to compete with 11 victories and three draws in 14 matches. Peterborough offered the only real challenge for the top spot with their own productive form, closing to within three points before stalling. Hull never wavered, clinching promotion by beating Lincoln 2-1, then defeating Wigan in the return fixtures 3-1 to establish a five-point cushion with one fixture remaining. Hull scored 48 goals away from home, McCann was named the division's Manager of the Year and two of his players were included in the EFL Team of the Year – defender Callum Elder, midfielder George Honeyman.

Adelakun H.............. 11 (3)	Emmanuel J 21 (7)	Magennis J.............29 (11)
Batty D...................... 2 (4)	Fleming B 3	Mayer T.....................1 (5)
Burke R 31 (3)	Flores J .... - (3)	McLoughlin S ....- (3)
Chadwick B.................- (3)	Greaves J....................39	Samuelsen M...............- (5)
Coyle L 26 (2)	Honeyman G...................42	Scott J 3 (15)
Crowley D 6 (16)	Ingram M.....................38	Slater R 11 (16)
De Wijs J 7	Jones A 27 (4)	Smallwood R 23 (4)
Docherty G.....................44	Jones C .... - (1)	Whyte G 10 (10)
Eaves T.................. 6 (20)	Lewis-Potter K 33 (10)	Wilks M.................42 (2)
Elder C 43 (1)	Long G 8	Wood H ....- (1)

League goals (80): Wilks 19, Magennis 18, Lewis-Potter 13, Docherty 5, Burke 4, Eaves 4, Honeyman 4, Whyte 4, Adelakun 3, Elder 1, Scott 1, Slater 1, Opponents 3
FA Cup goals (3): Burke 1, Eaves 1, Magennis 1. **League Cup goals** (2): Wilks 2. **League Trophy goals** (10): Lewis-Potter 2, Samuelsen 2, Scott 2, Coyle 1, Docherty 1, Jones C 1, Wilks 1
Player of Year: George Honeyman

IPSWICH TOWN

IPSWICH flattered to deceive for the second successive season. They made another strong start, twice led the division and were still in contention approaching Christmas when Covid caused the postponement of four successive fixtures. Struggling to regain momentum on the restart, Paul Lambert's side lost successive home games to lowly Swindon and promotion-contenders Peterborough and Sunderland. Lambert lost his job following a disagreement with owner Marcus Evans over the future direction of the club. His replacement, former Wigan and Portsmouth manager Paul Cook sounded an upbeat note after his first victory in charge, against Plymouth, targeting automatic promotion. But six successive goalless matches, including heavy defeats by AFC Wimbledon and Northampton, ruled that out and eventually any chance of a top-six place. By then Evans had sold the club to an American investment group.

Bennetts K.............. 13 (15)	Holy T........................36	Nydam T.....................- (1)
Bishop E.................. 28 (8)	Huws E 6 (3)	Parrott T.................. 13 (5)
Chambers L...................39	Jackson K................ 12 (13)	Sears F 15 (11)
Cornell D 10	Judge A 29 (5)	Simpson T...................- (1)
Dobra A 8 (9)	Kenlock M................ 17 (4)	Skuse C 1 (3)
Downes F 17 (7)	Lankester J 7 (10)	Thomas L....................4 (1)
Dozzell A 42 (1)	Matheson L.....................2	Vincent-Young K 6 (1)
Drinan A 6 (16)	McGavin B 4 (1)	Ward S 29 (1)
Edwards G 29 (7)	McGuinness M 23 (1)	Wilson J 17
Gibbs L.........................1	Nolan J 11 (2)	Woolfenden L.............24 (1)
Harrop J 3 (12)	Norwood J 19 (7)	
Hawkins O 3 (12)	Nsiala A......................27	

League goals (46): Norwood 9, Edwards 6, Bishop 4, Judge 4, Nolan 3, Chambers 2, Lankester 2, Parrott 2, Wilson 2, Bennetts 1, Drinan 1, Hawkins 1, Huws 1, Jackson 1, McGuinness 1, Sears 1, Woolfenden 1, Opponents 4

FA Cup goals (2): Nolan 1, Norwood 1. **League Cup goals** (3): Sears 2, Chambers 1. **League Trophy goals** (3): Dobra 1, Folami B 1, Nolan 1
Player of Year: James Wilson

LINCOLN CITY

Michael Appleton's team exceeded expectations by making the play-offs – and had a golden chance to go one better by reaching the second tier for the first time for 60 years. Having seen off Sunderland in the semi-finals, they were gifted a dream start against Blackpool at Wembley when Brennan Johnson's cross was turned into his own net by Ollie Turton just 47 seconds on the clock. Had Jorge Grant's shot gone in, instead of clipping the crossbar, they could have had one foot in the Championship. But two goals, both struck from 20 yards by Kenny Dougall, turned the tide and Lincoln were left with the consolation of a fine season's work in Appleton's first full season in charge. When they took over the leadership of a tough division and held it for three weeks in the new year, the manager admitted it was 12 months year ahead of where he expected his rebuilt side to be. Lincoln returned to the top the following month, having won seven successive away games, then faltered. Ten matches delivered a single victory, inviting pressure from rival top-six contenders. Johnson put them back on track with a second-half hat-trick in the space of 11 minutes against MK Dons and they went on to seal a place with a point at Peterborough.

Anderson H............ 14 (15)	Howarth R.................. 4 (7)	Poole R.................... 18 (4)
Archibald T................ - (7)	Jackson A 27 (1)	Rogers M 23 (2)
Bramall C 12 (5)	Johnson B............... 38 (2)	Roughan S.....................6
Bridcutt L................ 22 (1)	Jones J................... 28 (8)	Sanders M 1 (4)
Elbouzedi Z............... - (2)	McGrandles C........... 35 (4)	Scully A.................. 22 (18)
Eyoma T.................. 34 (5)	Melbourne M............. 1 (7)	Soule J...................... - (1)
Gotts R 4 (3)	Montsma L............... 38 (2)	Tayo Edun................ 36 (5)
Grant J 35 (1)	Morton C................. 11 (6)	Walsh J.................. 18 (3)
Hopper T 33 (6)	Palmer A.....................46	

Play-offs – appearances: Bridcutt 3, Eyoma 3, Grant 3, Hopper 3, Johnson 3, Poole 3, Rogers 3, Tayo Edun 3, Scully 2 (1), Palmer 2, McGrandles 1 (2), Montsma 1 (2), Walsh 1 (1), Bursik J 1, Jackson 1, Anderson – (1), Morton – (1)
League goals (69): Grant 13, Scully 11, Johnson 10, Hopper 8, Montsma 6, Rogers 6, McGrandles 4, Anderson 3, Morton 2, Eyoma 1, Howarth 1, Jackson 1, Jones 1, Tayo Edun 1, Opponents 1. **Play-offs – goals** (4): Hopper 2, Johnson 1, Opponents 1
FA Cup goals (6): Grant 2, Scully 2, Johnson 1, Jones 1. **League Cup goals** (9): Montsma 3, Hopper 1, James 1, Morton 1, Scully 1, Tayo Edun 1, Opponents 1. **League Trophy goals** (15): Anderson 3, Scully 3, Elbouzedi 2, Grant 2, Archibald 1, Gotts 1, Howarth 1, Johnson 1, Soule 1
Player of Year: Jorge Grant

MILTON KEYNES DONS

Will Grigg's record-breaking performance, along with three successive wins towards the end of the season, were not enough to secure a top-half finish. The Northern Ireland international, on loan from Sunderland, became the first Dons player to score four goals in a match – the 5-0 win which relegated Swindon. It was their third victory in eight days after maximum points against Portsmouth and Bristol Rovers, but could not compensate for defensive deficiencies which resulted in the worst goals against column of all the leading teams. Three or more goals were conceded in nine games – too many for a club with promotion ambitions. On the bright side, a 2-1 result against Sunderland, courtesy of goals from Cameron Jerome and Scott Fraser with a penalty, ended run of 20 away games without a victory. And evergreen captain Dean Lewington's 800th appearance for the club, which came in a 2-1 away win over resurgent Burton, earned the 36-year-old the EFL's 'Moment of the Season' award.

Bird J .... - (2)
Brittain C 3 (1)
Brown C 1 (19)
Cargill B 7 (4)
Darling H 23
Davies J .... - (1)
Fisher A 39
Fraser S 41 (3)
Freeman J .... - (4)
Gladwin B 12 (14)
Grigg W 14 (6)
Harvie D 18 (13)

Houghton J 9 (10)
Ilunga B .... - (1)
Jerome C 28 (6)
Johnson L .... - (4)
Jules Z 15 (5)
Kasumu D 20 (4)
Keogh R 17 (1)
Laird E 23 (1)
Lewington D 43
Mason J 12 (12)
McEachran J............. 11 (3)
Morris C 14 (4)

Nicholls L 7
Nombe S 2 (2)
O'Hora W 31
O'Riley M 22 (1)
Poole R 14 (6)
Sorenson L 12 (12)
Sorinola M 23 (11)
Surman A 25 (6)
Thompson L 7 (10)
Walker S 5 (7)
Williams G 8

League goals (64): Fraser 14, Jerome 13, Grigg 8, Mason 5, Brown 3, Harvie 3, Morris 3, O'Riley 3, Gladwin 2, O'Hora 2, Surman 2, Walker 2, Cargill 1, Jules 1, Poole 1, Sorinola 1
FA Cup goals (2): Jerome 2. **League Cup goals**: None. **League Trophy goals** (15): Poole 3, Walker 3, Agard K 2, Bird 2, Sorinola 2, Morris 1, Nombe 1, Sorenson 1
Player of Year: Dean Lewington

NORTHAMPTON TOWN

A run of 16 matches yielding a single victory proved costly. It left Northampton at the bottom of the table and despite a subsequent improvement they returned to League Two, 12 months after beating Cheltenham in the Play-off Final. Manager Keith Curle was sacked following a home defeat by fellow-strugglers Wigan – one of six successive games without a goal. The sequence ended under caretaker Jon Brady – a 4-3 defeat by MK Dons after his side led 3-2 going into the final ten minutes. And Northampton boosted their survival chances by winning back-to-back matches for the first time, Ryan Watson scoring four times against Plymouth (2-0) and Portsmouth (4-1). There was also a 3-0 defeat of Ipswich, but it was not enough to counter the way Wigan and AFC Wimbledon raised their performances at a crucial time to climb out of trouble. The drop was confirmed by a 3-0 home defeat by promotion-chasing Blackpool in the penultimate fixture, leaving them four points adrift. Brady was later confirmed in the job.

Adams N 10 (4)
Jones A 4 (5)
Arnold S 11
Ashley-Seal B 7 (16)
Bolger C 26
Chukwuemeka C......... 2 (20)
Cross L .... - (1)
Dyche M 1 (1)
Edmondson R......... 13 (8)
Harriman M 22 (8)
Holmes R 5 (4)
Horsfall F 37 (3)

Hoskins S 44 (2)
Jones L 27
Kioso P 21
Korboa M 5 (11)
Lines C 1 (3)
Marshall M 18 (11)
Martin J 5 (1)
McWilliams S 30 (2)
Miller M 11 (1)
Mills J 27
Missilou C 11 (4)
Mitchell J 35

Morris B 19 (3)
Nuttall J .... - (1)
Racic L 4 (2)
Roberts M .... - (2)
Rose D 23 (16)
Sheehan A............... 12 (2)
Smith H 13 (3)
Sowerby J 26 (2)
Warburton M..................... 4
Watson R 32 (7)

League goals (41): Watson 8, Hoskins 7, Rose 4, Horsfall 3, Kioso 3, Smith 3, Edmondson 2, Korboa 2, Jones 1, Bolger 1, Chukwuemeka 1, Holmes, 1 Lines 1, Marshall 1, Missilou 1, Sheehan 1, Warburton 1
FA Cup goals (1): Hoskins 1. **League Cup goals** (3): Smith 1, Warburton 1, Watson 1. **League Trophy goals** (8): Ashley-Seal 3, Mills 2, Chukwuemeka 1, Marshall 1, Rose 1
Player of Year: Ryan Watson

OXFORD UNITED

No team went into the play-offs with more momentum than Oxford. They won six of the final seven matches, scoring 24 goals, to complete a huge turnaround in the regular season. The run, included a club-record-equalling 6-0 away win over Crewe, transforming a 2-0 deficit to beat Gillingham and the 4-0 defeat of Burton which enabled them to overtake Portsmouth in the last round of fixtures. But it counted for nothing in the knockout phase, with the 2020 beaten finalists losing the first leg 3-0 at home to Blackpool. Manager Karl Robinson refused to give up hope and Matty Taylor cut the deficit seven minutes into the return game. By the quarter-hour mark, however, their opponents had replied twice to seal the tie, leaving Oxford with some consolation for a 3-3 draw. Robinson had to watch from the stands while serving a four-match touchline ban imposed for violent conduct during a stormy match against Sunderland. He had previously led his side away from the bottom of the table, two months into the campaign, on the back of a club-best nine successive victories in league and League Trophy matches.

Agyei D. 11 (28)	Grayson J. 1 (3)	Obita J. 6 (6)
Atkinson R 39	Hall R 1 (8)	Osei Yaw D 1 (2)
Barker B 14 (5)	Hanson J. 9 (15)	Ruffels J 42
Brannagan C 28 (3)	Henry J 34 (3)	Shodipo O 24 (15)
Chambers-Parillon L. .. - (3)	Kelly L 21 (5)	Stevens J 33
Clare S 10 (7)	Lee E....................... 15 (3)	Sykes M 21 (11)
Cooper J .... - (4)	Long S 35 (1)	Taylor M 39 (7)
Eastwood S 13	McGuane M 13 (2)	Winnall S 3 (21)
Forde A................. 18 (17)	Moore E 46	
Gorrin A 28 (7)	Mousinho J 1 (6)	

Play-offs – appearances: Atkinson 2, Barker 2, Brannagan 2, Henry 2, Lee 2, Moore 2, Ruffels 2, Stevens 2, Sykes 2, Taylor 2, Forde 1 (1), Hanson 1, Agyei – (2), Shodipo – (2), Gorrin – (1), Winnall – (1)
League goals (77): Taylor 18, Shodipo 10, Henry 7, Lee 6, Long 6, Ruffels 6, Agyei 5, Moore 5, Winnall 4, Barker 3, Atkinson 1, Brannagan 1, Forde 1, Gorrin 1, Obita 1, Opponents 2. **Play-offs – goals (3):** Atkinson 1, Shodipo 1, Taylor 1
FA Cup goals (1): Ruffels 1. **League Cup goals (2):** Brannagan 1, Hall 1. **League Trophy goals (9):** Osei Yaw 3, Shodipo 2, Winnall 2, Agyei 1, Hall 1
Player of Year: Sam Long

PETERBOROUGH UNITED

Darren Ferguson delivered a fourth promotion for Peterborough and rated it the best of the bunch. In a tough division, his side clinched the runners-up spot behind Hull with a performance which showed why they had the season's best comeback record. Trailing 3-0 to Lincoln, the only team who could overtake them, they replied through Siriki Dembele and Jonson Clarke-Harris, who then converted a penalty in the sixth minute of stoppage-time for the required point. This brought the former Bristol Rovers striker's tally for the season to 31, more than his predecessor Ivan Toney scored the previous season before a summer move to Brentford. It included a 17-minute hat-trick against Rochdale and another treble in the 7-0 victory over Accrington. Dembele hit three against Shrewsbury as Peterborough finished the division's top scorers with 83 goals. They nailed down second place with a run of six successive victories in February, suffered back-to-back defeats by resurgent Burton and Hull, then regained momentum. Defender Mark Beevers and midfielder Joe Ward joined Clarke-Harris in the EFL Team of the Year for League One.

Barker K .... - (1)	Clarke F 2 (2)	Mason N 6 (20)
Beevers M....................45	Clarke-Harris J 45	Nascimento A..............- (1)
Blackmore W............... - (1)	Dembele S 38 (4)	O'Connell C ....- (1)
Blake-Tracy F 3 (6)	Edwards R........................2	Pym C 40
Broom R 5 (10)	Eisa M 6 (21)	Reed L 12 (5)
Brown R 33 (5)	Hamilton E........ 13 (21)	Szmodics S 40 (2)
Burrows H 8 (13)	Jade-Jones R 1 (14)	Taylor J 35 (1)
Bursik J 6	Kanu I 7 (10)	Thompson N.................39
Butler D................. 40 (2)	Kent F.........................45	Ward J.................. 35 (2)

League goals (83): Clarke-Harris 31, Szmodics 15, Dembele 11, Ward 5, Taylor 4, Brown 2, Eisa 2, Kanu 2, Thompson 2, Broom 1, Burrows 1, Butler 1, Jade-Jones 1, Kent 1, Mason 1, Opponents 3
FA Cup goals (3): Taylor 2, Dembele 1. **League Cup goals**: None. **League Trophy goals** (17): Clarke 3, Eisa 3, Clarke-Harris 3, Boyd G 1, Dembele 1, Hamilton 1, Kent 1, Mason 1, Reed 1, Szmodics 1, Tasdemir S 1, Taylor 1
Player of Year: Jonson Clarke-Harris

PLYMOUTH ARGYLE

Luke Jephcott fired Plymouth into the top half of the table, offering his promoted side the chance to challenge for a play-off place in the second half of the season. The Wales under-21 international scored 16 goals in 22 games to underline his rich potential. Jephcott then hit a barren run stretching to the end of the campaign after a brace against Portsmouth, but Plymouth continued to make progress. Manager Ryan Lowe signed a new contract through to the summer of 2024 and when Joe Edwards scored in stoppage-time for a 4-3 victory over Lincoln they were within four points of the leading group. All that good work came to an end with five successive defeats which effectively ended their chances. A return to winnings ways against Bristol Rovers and AFC Wimbledon was followed by another slump, which included a 6-0 defeat at Charlton, the heaviest at Home Park for nearly 65 years, and a finishing position of 18th.

Abraham T	1 (2)	Grant C	34 (4)	Nouble F	12 (12)
Aimson W	39 (1)	Hardie R	26 (17)	Opoku J	30 (3)
Camara P	35 (6)	Jephcott L	31 (10)	Reeves B	5 (23)
Canavan N	10 (2)	Law R	4	Telford D	2 (14)
Cooper G	10 (2)	Lewis A	9 (11)	Tomlinson O	1 (1)
Cooper M	46	Lolos K	- (8)	Watts K	42 (2)
Craske F	- (1)	MacLeod L	10 (5)	Woods S	5 (4)
Edwards J	35 (5)	Mayor D	44	Wootton S	7 (3)
Ennis N	18 (6)	McCormick L	- (2)		
Fornah T	34 (5)	Moore B	16 (22)		

League goals (53): Jephcott 16, Edwards 7, Ennis 6, Hardie 5, Grant 4, Camara 2, Watts 2, Canavan 1, Cooper G 1, Lewis 1, Mayor 1, Moore 1, Nouble 1, Opoku 1, Telford 1, Woods 1, Opponents 2
FA Cup goals (7): Camara 2, Jephcott 2, Edwards 1, Hardie 1, Reeves 1. **League Cup goals** (5): Camara 1, Edwards 1, Mayor 1, Nouble 1, Watts 1. **League Trophy goals** (5): Cooper G 1, Lolos 1, Reeves 1, Telford 1, Opponents 1
Player of Year: Joe Edwards

PORTSMOUTH

Portsmouth fell at the final hurdle and another season of high expectation came to nothing. Victory over Accrington at Fratton Park on the final day of the regular season would have guaranteed a third successive play-off place. Instead, a 1-0 defeat, their ninth at home, enabled fast-finishing Oxford to overtake them, resulting in a familiar inquest for the club, this time conducted by new manager Danny Cowley. He came in after Kenny Jackett was sacked the day after a defeat on penalties in the delayed 2020 League Trophy Final against Salford. Wins in his first four matches restored a play-off place, with every chance of remaining there during a comfortable-looking run-in against none of the leading teams. But Portsmouth failed to take advantage, dropping points to Burton, Crewe, MK Dons, and relegation-bound Swindon and ultimately paying the price. Former Huddersfield and Lincoln manager Cowley and brother Nicky signed new contracts after initially being appointed until the end of the campaign.

Bolton J	8 (5)	Byers G	4 (10)	Close B	13 (9)
Brown L	28 (4)	Cannon A	31 (12)	Curtis R	36 (6)

Daniels C	10 (7)	Johnson C	39 (1)	Pring C	6 (3)
Downing P	2 (1)	MacGillivray C	46	Raggett S	45
Evans G	1	Marquis J	35 (6)	Whatmough J	32 (2)
Harness M	42 (4)	Mnoga H	3 (2)	White H	5 (16)
Harrison E	11 (14)	Morris B	5 (4)	Williams R	33 (8)
Hiwula J	1 (8)	Naylor T	46		
Jacobs M	12 (8)	Nicolaisen R	12 (9)		

League goals (65): Marquis 16, Curtis 10, Harness 7, Naylor 6, Williams 5, Harrison 4, Raggett 3, Brown 2, Cannon 2, Jacobs 2, Whatmough 2, Bolton 1, Close 1, Daniels 1, White 1, Opponents 2
FA Cup goals (10): Naylor 2, Raggett 2, Curtis 1, Harness 1, Harrison 1, Hiwula 1, Johnson 1, Nicolaisen 1. **League Cup goals** (3): Curtis 1, Evans 1, Marquis 1. **League Trophy goals** (9): Curtis 1, Harness 2, Hiwula 2, Harrison 1, Marquis 1, Mnoga 1
Player of Year: Craig MacGillivray

ROCHDALE

Six months without a home win left Rochdale deep in trouble and despite a late rally they were relegated in the penultimate round of matches. The bleak run stretched to 16 matches, contrasting sharply with some excellent performances on their travels – 5-0 against Wigan, 4-0 against Plymouth and a 4-4 draw with Charlton. In addition, there was a rare performance to savour on their own ground when a three-goal deficit was retrieved for a point against Crewe. When two goals by Alex Newby accounted for Bristol Rovers, his side were four points clear of trouble. But a single goal in the next nine matches left them bottom and needing something special during the run-in. Goals by Jimmy Keohane and Conor Grant against Swindon provided the breakthrough at home, followed by further victories over Accrington and Blackpool. The sting in the tail came against AFC Wimbledon, who salvaged a point in the seventh minute of stoppage time to complete their escape – along with that of Wigan – and leave Rochdale adrift.

Baah K	13 (17)	Keohane J	40 (4)	Odoh A	- (2)
Bazunu G	29	Lund M	28 (4)	Osho G	22
Beesley J	27	Lynch J	17	Rathbone O	40
Brierley E	1 (4)	McLaughlin R	23 (11)	Roberts H	24 (2)
Done M	20 (17)	McNulty J	9 (8)	Ryan J	11 (3)
Dooley S	16 (15)	McShane P	18 (1)	Shaughnessy C	14 (4)
Grant C	16 (4)	Morley J	39 (5)	Tavares F	- (12)
Hopper H	- (1)	Newby A	27 (11)	Tolaji Bola	9 (2)
Humphrys S	24 (5)	O'Connell E	39	Vale J	- (3)

League goals (61): Humphrys 11, Lund 11, Keohane 10, Beesley 6, Newby 6, Baah 3, Done 3, Rathbone 3, Morley 2, Dooley 1, Grant 1, O'Connell 1, Osho 1, Shaughnessy 1, Tavares 1
FA Cup goals (1): Lund 1. **League Cup goals** (1): O'Connell 1. **League Trophy goals** (3): Beesley 1, Newby 1, Tavares 1
Player of Year: Jimmy Keohane

SHREWSBURY TOWN

Steve Cotterill was little more than a month into his ninth managerial appointment when he contracted Covid and went into hospital. But it was enough to put his side on course to safety after a single win in 13 matches left them second from bottom. Cotterill, who took over when Sam Ricketts was sacked, engineered 1-0 wins over four promotion-minded teams – Hull, Lincoln, Doncaster and Blackpool. Shrewsbury were then 16th in the table and when he returned to the club four months later, they were just a single place worse off, still well clear of trouble. For much of his absence he kept in touch with assistant manager Aaron Wilbraham and worked remotely with the team. Cotterill, who also had a bout of pneumonia, missed, 24 matches before watching from the directors' box as they led Oxford 2-1 before losing 3-2 to a goal in the 85th minute.

Barnett R 3 (4)	Fossey M 6 (1)	Pugh M 6 (2)
Bloxham T 2 (2)	Golbourne S 6 (4)	Pyke R 2 (10)
Burgoyne H 17 (1)	Goss S 15 (5)	Sarkic M 26
Caton C 1 (2)	High S 8 (4)	Sears R 2 (3)
Chapman H 16 (7)	Iliev D 3	Tracey S 2 (6)
Clarke L 6 (4)	Love D 12 (2)	Udoh D 23 (16)
Cummings J 7 (4)	Main C 14 (6)	Vela J 43 (1)
Daniels C 14	Millar M 9	Walker B 15 (8)
Daniels J 8 (11)	Norburn N 37 (2)	Whalley S 32 (6)
Davis D 14 (7)	Ogbeta N 25	Williams R-S 39 (1)
Ebanks-Landell E 41	Pennington M 18 (1)	Zamburek J 4 (2)
Edwards D 5 (26)	Pierre A 25 (1)	

League goals (50): Whalley 9, Chapman 7, Norburn 4, Pierre 4, Udoh 4, Goss 3, Vela 3, Daniels J 2, Main 2, Ogbeta 2, Pennington 2, Clarke 1, Daniels C 1, Ebanks-Landell 1, Edwards 1, Millar 1, Pugh 1, Walker 1, Opponents 1
FA Cup goals (3): Daniels C 1, Udoh 1, Walker 1. **League Cup goals** (3): Cummings 1, High 1, Pyke 1. **League Trophy goals** (10): Tracey 4, Barnett 2, Cummings 2, High 1, Millar 1
Player of Year: Josh Vela

SUNDERLAND

A familiar failure to cope with promotion pressures left the club facing a fourth season in the third tier. This time, they gave up a strong position in the final month of the season and were then second best to Lincoln in the play-offs. Victory over Tranmere in the League Trophy Final, some consolation with Lyndon Gooch's decider at Wembley, came during a run of 14 games without a defeat. It left them two points behind second-place Peterborough, a game in hand and every incentive for a final push. Instead, three successive defeats, along with two more draws against Hull and Accrington, out of a total of 17, exposed a tendency to surrender winning positions and put paid to going up automatically. Lee Johnson's side retrieved a 2-0 deficit from the first leg of the semi-finals, Aiden McGeady crosses setting up Ross Stewart and leading scorer Charlie Wyke. But they were unable to build on that impressive first 45 minutes, went 3-2 behind and needed a Lee Burge penalty save from Jorge Grant to keep hopes alive. Burge, McGeady, Wyke and Luke O'Nien were all named in the EFL Team of the Season. Johnson had become the club's seventh manager in five years after Phil Parkinson was sacked with Sunderland eighth in late November.

Burge L 41	Jones J 11 (8)	Power M 38 (4)
Curry M .... - (1)	Leadbitter G 30 (10)	Sanderson D 19 (7)
Diamond J 11 (13)	Maguire C 11 (22)	Scowen J 35 (8)
Dobson G 3 (2)	Matthews R 5 (1)	Stewart R 2 (9)
Embleton E 3 (6)	McFadzean C 21 (4)	Vokins J 4
Flanagan T 14 (2)	McGeady A 28 (1)	Willis J 14 (1)
Gooch L 26 (12)	McLaughlin C 22 (3)	Winchester C 12 (8)
Graham D 3 (11)	Neill D .... - (2)	Wright B 33
Grigg W 4 (5)	O'Brien A 22 (10)	Wyke C 40 (3)
Hume D 19 (4)	O'Nien L 34 (4)	Younger O 1

Play-offs – appearances: Burge 2, Gooch 2, McGeady 2, O'Nien 2, Scowen 2, Wright 2, Wyke 2, Flanagan 1 (1), Leadbitter 1 (1), McFadzean 1 (1), Power 1 (1), Stewart 1 (1), Hume 1, Jones 1, Maguire 1, Diamond – (2), O'Brien – (1), Winchester – (1)
League goals (70): Wyke 25, Leadbitter 7, Maguire 5, Power 5, Gooch 4, McGeady 4, O'Brien

4, Jones 3, O'Nien 2, Stewart 2, Wright 2, Diamond 1, Hume 1, McFadzean 1, Sanderson 1, Scowen 1, Winchester 1, Opponents 1. **Play-offs – goals** (2): Stewart 1, Wyke 1
FA Cup goals: None. **League Cup goals**: None. **League Trophy goals** (23): Wyke 5, Maguire 3, McGeady 2, O'Brien 2, Scowen 2, Diamond 1, Dobson 1, Feeney 1, Gooch 1, Graham 1, Hume 1, McFadzean 1, Power 1, Opponents 1
Player of Year: Charlie Wyke

SWINDON TOWN

Swindon lost their two top scorers, two managers and seven of the final nine games to go straight back down. Eoin Doyle and Jerry Yates, whose goals delivered the League Two title, had moved on during the summer, while Richie Wellens resigned two months into the season to take over at Salford. John Sheridan, on a month-to-month contract with Wigan, came in for his 11th managerial appointment and his new team recovered from 2-0 and 3-1 down to draw 3-3 at Shrewsbury in his first match with goals from Joel Grant, Hallam Hope and Matt Smith in stoppage-time. It was an encouraging start, backed up by wins over Bristol Rovers and Oxford. But a single point from six matches left them second from bottom going into the new year. They rallied briefly, with seven points from games against Crewe, Lincoln and Northampton, before dropping back into trouble. Sheridan gave up the struggle with four fixtures remaining and there was little caretaker Tommy Wright could do, apart from bemoan how relegation was confirmed – a 5-0 defeat by MK Dons. John McGreal, formerly in charge at Colchester, was appointed the new manager.

Baudry M.................. 15 (1)	Grounds J.................. 27 (4)	Palmer M 24
Broadbent T............. 11 (7)	Hope H 18 (14)	Parsons H...................- (2)
Caddis P 24 (2)	Hunt R 13 (6)	Payne J....................36 (7)
Camp L...........................11	Iandolo E 5 (3)	Pitman B..............27 (11)
Conroy D 18 (1)	Jaiyesimi D.......... 15 (3)	Smith J.................. 13 (3)
Curran T 3 (8)	Wollacott J 2	Smith M.................. 22 (2)
Donohue D 9 (1)	Kovar M 18	Smith T.................. 15 (8)
Freeman K 2	Lyden J 11 (3)	Stevens J 6 (7)
Fryer J 2	Masterson C 5	Thompson D..........23 (2)
Fryers Z 9 (1)	Matthews A 1	Travers M 8
Garrick J 13 (6)	Missilou C 8 (3)	Trueman C........................4
Grant A 31 (2)	Odimayo A.......... 25 (5)	Twine S..................22 (3)
Grant J 9 (11)	Omotoye T.............. 1 (6)	

League goals (55): Pitman 11, Smith T 7, Twine 7, Hope 5, Jaiyesimi 4, Payne 4, Grant A 3, Garrick 2, Grant J 2, Smith M 2, Baudry 1, Broadbent 1, Caddis 1, Curran 1, Palmer 1, Smith J 1, Stevens 1, Opponents 1
FA Cup goals (1): Pitman 1. **League Cup goals** (1): Smith J 1. **League Trophy goals** (6): Smith T 3, Broadbent 1, Caddis 1, Palmer 1
Player of Year: Akin Odimayo

WIGAN ATHLETIC

Wigan rose from the depths in keeping with the name of their new owners – Phoenix 2021. They were staring at a second successive relegation when three wins in eight days delivered an escape route under caretaker-manager Leam Richardson. A 4-1 success away to Doncaster was the first for the Bahraini-backed consortium who took over the club. A 2-1 victory over promotion-chasing Sunderland ended nearly six months in the bottom four. Then came a 2-0 defeat of Crewe. The points took Wigan four clear of trouble, with work still to do for Richardson, who took over when John Sheridan, on a month-to-month contract, left for Swindon two months into the season. Beating Shrewsbury and gaining a point against revitalised Burton maintained that buffer and earned him the job on a permanent basis. It was a commendable achievement on limited resources which meant relying largely on youngsters and free transfers after the departure of so many senior players during the summer. Supporters also played a crucial role with financial assistance when the club's future looked in doubt.

Aasgaard T 13 (20)	Johnson D 10	Obi E 3 (1)
Cameron N.................... 2	Johnston G 19 (3)	Ojo F 23
Clough Z 4 (9)	Jolley C .... - (2)	Palmer M 10
Crankshaw O 2 (17)	Jones J.......................45	Pearce T...................... 23
Darikwa T 26	Joseph K 12 (6)	Perry A 17 (4)
Dodoo J 12 (8)	Keane W 25 (7)	Proctor J 7 (8)
Evans L 21	Lang C 22 (1)	Roberts G..................... 2
Evans O 1	Long A 10 (3)	Robinson L.............. 20 (5)
Fox D 2	Massey G 13 (3)	Solomon-Otabor V 25 (3)
Gardner D 20 (16)	McHugh H.................. - (1)	Tilt C........................ 36
Garner J....................11	Merrie C 24 (2)	Whelan C 2 (6)
James T....................20	Naismith K 12	Wootton S 12 (1)

League goals (54): Keane 11, Lang 9, Joseph 5, Dodoo 4, Aasgaard 3, Garner 3, James 3, Tilt 3, Evans 2, Naismith 2, Proctor 2, Solomon-Otabor 2, Crankshaw 1, Gardner 1, Johnston 1, Wootton 1, Opponents 1
FA Cup goals (2): Garner 1, James 1. **League Cup goals** (2): Garner 2. **League Trophy goals** (9): Crankshaw 2, Jolley 2, Garner 1, Keane 1, McHugh 1, Naismith 1, Pearce 1

SKY BET LEAGUE TWO

BARROW

Barrow's return to the Football League after an absence of 48 years was a turbulent one until a purple patch with Easter approaching ensured that they stayed there. Before a ball was kicked, Ian Evatt, who took the club up, accepted the challenge of restoring Bolton's faded fortunes. Former Blackburn midfielder and Oldham manager David Dunn replaced him and had to wait nearly two months for a first win, 4-2 at Mansfield. He was sacked after another lean spell, spanning nine games, which brought in former Grimsby manager Michael Jolley, who lasted just 60 days. Jolley's dismissal, after one victory in seven, came with Barrow second from bottom. Assistant Rob Kelly again stepped into the breach and this time things took a turn for the better. Two goals by Patrick Brough delivered the double over Mansfield, followed by maximum points gained against Walsall, Cheltenham and Crawley. When the influential Scott Quigley paved the way for the defeat of Newport, his side were six points clear of trouble, with a superior goal difference and games in hand as further insurance against faltering again. Mark Cooper, formerly in charge of Forest Green, was appointed the new manager.

Andrew C 2 (9)	Donohue D 3 (1)	Ntlhe K 20 (2)
Angus D................ 12 (10)	Eardley N 17 (2)	Platt M........................ 24
Banks O................. 15 (5)	Goodridge M .... - (2)	Quigley S 37 (1)
Barry B 33	Gribbin C .... - (1)	Reid J 2 (8)
Beadling T 19 (10)	Hardcastle L 11 (1)	Sea D........................ - (8)
Biggins H 16 (6)	Hindle L 1 (1)	Taylor C............... 20 (11)
Bramall D .... - (3)	Hird S.......................15	Taylor J 28 (6)
Brough P 39 (4)	James L 33 (11)	Thomas B................ 18 (3)
Brown C 15 (4)	Jones J................ 18 (3)	Wilson S................ 4 (5)
Davies T 12	Jones M 13	Zouma Y........................ 4
Devitt J................... 7 (10)	Kay J 22 (7)	
Dixon J.....................46	Ndjoli M.................... - (2)	

League goals (53): Quigley 15, Brough 6, Kay 5, Angus 4, James 3, Beadling 2, Biggins 2, Jones M 2, Platt 2, Andrew 1, Barry 1, Brown 1, Davies 1, Devit 1, Hardcastle 1, Hird 1, Jones J 1, Taylor C 1, Thomas 1, Opponents 2
FA Cup goals: None. **League Cup goals**: None. **League Trophy goals** (2): Angus 1, Taylor J 1
Player of Year: Scott Quigley

BOLTON WANDERERS

Ian Evatt led Barrow back to the Football League and followed that achievement by lifting Bolton out of the doldrums when switching clubs during the summer. 'We have rebuilt trust in the town and reconnected with the community,' said Evatt after an impressive surge in the second-half of the season regained League One status at the first attempt. It was hard going at first, with his new team fifth from bottom after just two wins in 11 matches. And a significant improvement was interrupted by a bizarre 6-3 home defeat by Port Vale which left them nine points adrift. But with Eoin Doyle continuing to score consistently, Bolton moved into contention with 11 victories in 14 matches. Eight came by a single-goal margin, testament to a highly-competitive division in which nothing could be taken for granted. That was underlined by defeats against rivals Newport and bottom-of-the table Grimsby. Bolton, however, saw off the challenge of Morecambe for the third automatic promotion place with a 4-1 victory at Crawley in the final match in which former Swindon striker Doyle chalked up his 19th goal and like his manager recorded back-to-back promotions.

Afolayan O	19 (2)	Gilks M	35	Williams MJ	21
Amoateng B	- (1)	Gnahoua A	6 (22)	Maddison M	4 (6)
Baptiste A	38 (2)	Gordon L	4 (6)	Mascoll J	2 (5)
Brockbank H	13 (5)	Greenidge R	3 (2)	Miller S	- (20)
Comley B	5 (5)	Hickman J	3 (1)	Santos R	46
Crawford A	17 (4)	Hurford-Lockett F	- (1)	Sarcevic A	29 (3)
Crellin W	11	Isgrove L	21 (11)	Taft G	1
Darcy R	1 (7)	Jackson B	5	Thomason G	18 (6)
Delaney R	20	John D	19 (2)	Tutte A	13 (6)
Delfouneso N	33 (11)	Jones G	37 (1)	White T	4 (5)
Doyle E	43	Kioso P	13		
Elbouzedi Z	2 (12)	Lee K	20		

League goals (59): Doyle 19, Sarcevic 7, Delfouneso 6, Isgrove 3, Jones 3, Kioso 3, Miller 3, Gnahoua 2, John 2, Lee 2, Afolayan 1, Crawford 1, Delaney 1, Jackson 1, Thomason 1, Opponents 4
FA Cup goals (2): Delfouneso 2. **League Cup goals** (1): Sarcevic 1. **League Trophy goals** (6): Delaney 1, Gnahoua 1, Hickman 1, Mascoll 1, Miller 1, Senior A 1
Player of Year: Ricardo Santos

BRADFORD CITY

Alarm bells were ringing when a run of five successive defeats left the club in their lowest league position since 1966. Only goal difference kept them out of the bottom two and Stuart McCall, in his third spell as manager, was dismissed 12 days before Christmas. Coaches Mark Trueman and Conor Sellars, appointed caretakers, initially stemmed the tide, then delivered a complete transformation in fortunes which not only earned them the joint position permanently – or so it seemed – but offered the hint of a most unlikely promotion challenge. Bradford accumulated 34 points in 15 matches to climb to within reach of a play-off place, three of them coming at Grimsby, where Lee Novak's spectacular overhead kick was voted the EFL goal of the season. A lean spell followed in March, before successive victories over Colchester and Forest Green put them back in the hunt. But after completing the double over Grimsby, they fell away, with six defeats in the final seven matches, resulting in the sack for Trueman and Sellars, 78 days after taking charge. Derek Adams came in after leading Morecambe to promotion.

Burrell R..................- (2)	Guthrie K.................. 4 (4)	Pritchard H.............. 11 (5)
Canavan N 15 (1)	Hornby S..................18	Richards-Everton B 9 (1)
Clarke B 20 (9)	Hosanah B 8	Rowe D..................8 (10)
Cook A.................. 16 (5)	Ismail Z 1 (2)	Samuels A..................6 (6)
Cooke C 30 (4)	Levi Sutton J 30 (4)	Scales K..................6 (14)
Cousin-Dawson F 20 (3)	Longridge J............... - (2)	Sikora J..................1
Crankshaw O 11 (8)	Mottley Henry D.......... 4 (7)	Staunton R 8
Donaldson C........... 19 (16)	Novak L 15 (2)	Stevens J 1 (15)
Evans G.................. 19 (8)	O'Connor A..................45	Vernam C 15 (6)
Foulds M ....- (3)	O'Connor P.............. 41 (1)	Watt E.................. 44 (2)
French T 7 (7)	O'Donnell R..................28	Wood C 46

League goals (48): Cook 8, Novak 6, Rowe 5, Donaldson 4, Cooke 3, Watt 3, Clarke 2, Evans 2, O'Connor A 2, O'Connor P 2, Pritchard 2, Levi Sutton 2, Vernam 2, Crankshaw 1, Scales 1, Staunton 1, Wood 1, Opponents 1
FA Cup goals (8): Clarke 2, Donaldson 2, O'Connor A 1, Pritchard 1, Samuels 1, Wood 1. **League Cup goals** (2): Novak 1, Pritchard 1. **League Trophy goals** (2): Donaldson 1, Opponents 1
Player of Year: Paudie O'Connor

CAMBRIDGE UNITED

Paul Mullin and his team upset all the odds to deliver a golden double. Only the most optimistic of supporters could have expected automatic promotion – and for Mullin to finish the highest scorer in all four divisions. They almost had a title to celebrate as well, with Mark Bonner's side pipped at the post by Cheltenham on the final day after the pair had disputed the leadership throughout the second half of the season. Cambridge defeated Grimsby 3-0, but it was not enough to prevent their rivals taking the honours after a 4-1 win over Harrogate. In the club's 50th season in the Football League, Mullin surpassed David Crown's club-record of 24 league goals, set in 1985-86, in 2-1 win at Carlisle. He went on to total 32 as Cambridge scored more goals than any team in the division. Evergreen midfielder Wes Hoolahan played another key role, joining Mullin and defender Kyle Knoyle in the EFL's Team of the Year. Bonner's achievement in his first full season as manager was rewarded with a new three-year contract.

Adesope Okedina J ... 12 (2)	Digby P 34 (1)	Knibbs H.................. 7 (16)
Alese A.................. 1 (1)	Drysdale D.............. 12 (1)	Knoyle K 46
Boateng H.................. 20 (5)	Dunk H 33 (8)	May A.................. 24 (14)
Burton C.................. 26 (1)	El Mizouni I............. 3 (8)	Mitov D 20
Cundy R 14 (3)	Hannant L 38 (5)	Mullin P.................. 45 (1)
Dallas A.................. - (1)	Hoolahan W.............. 30 (4)	O'Neil L 12 (9)
Darling H 15 (1)	Iredale J.............. 26 (12)	Taylor G.................. 46
Davies L 4 (9)	Ironside J.............. 33 (11)	Tracey S 5 (12)

League goals (73): Mullin 32, Ironside 14, Hoolahan 7, Hannant 4, Iredale 4, May 3, Knibbs 2, Knoyle 2, O'Neil 2, Drysdale 1, Tracey 1, Opponents 1
FA Cup goals: None. **League Cup goals** (1): Cundy 1. **League Trophy goals** (9): Hannant 3, Mullin 2, Darling 1, Knibbs 1, Knowles T 1, Worman B 1
Player of Year: Paul Mullin

CARLISLE UNITED

Riding high going into the new year, Carlisle looked a decent bet to maintain a promotion challenge. Manager Chris Beech signed a new contract over Christmas and his side went top with a 2-0 victory over Walsall. They were overtaken during an enforced 28-day lay-off because of a Covid outbreak, faced a backlog of fixtures and struggled to regain momentum. Eight matches produced only two points, pushing them into the bottom half of the table before two goals from Offrande Zanzala set up a 3-1 win over Bradford. Carlisle then made up ground with back-to-back successes against Crawley,

Southend and Scunthorpe, but five draws in six matches during a punishing schedule were not enough to make the breakthrough amid keen competition for play-off places. They retained a place in the top-half, twice coming from behind to beat Leyton Orient 3-2 with a stoppage-time goal from full-back George Tanner. It confirmed an improvement of eight places on the previous season's finish.

Alessandra L 37 (8)	Furman D 7 (10)	Omari P 27 (10)
Anderton N 33 (7)	Guy C 43	Reilly G 3 (13)
Armer J 22 (2)	Hayden A 42 (2)	Riley J 38 (4)
Bell L .... - (1)	Hunt M .... - (2)	Scott C .... - (7)
Bennett R 22 (2)	Kayode J 31 (3)	Tanner G 36 (1)
Charters T 2 (7)	Malley L .... - (3)	Toure C 18 (16)
Devine D 5 (6)	McDonald R 28 (1)	Walker E 3 (13)
Dickenson B 7 (5)	Mellish J 41 (3)	Zanzala O 15 (7)
Dixon J .... - (2)	Norman M 4	
Farman P 42	Obiero M .... - (4)	

League goals (60): Mellish 11, Alessandra 8, Kayode 8, Bennett 5, Hayden 5, Omari 5, Zanzala 5, Tanner 3, Anderton 2, Riley 2, Toure 2, Armer 1, Dickenson 1, Opponents 2
FA Cup goals (3): Mellish 3. **League Cup goals**: None. **League Trophy goals** (7): Mellish 2, Toure 2, Alessandra 1, Obiero 1, Reilly 1
Player of Year: Callum Guy

CHELTENHAM TOWN

Michael Duff's side missed automatic promotion by 0.06 of a point in 2020, losing out to third-place Plymouth when the season was curtailed because of Covid and finishing positions were decided on a points-per-game basis. They then surrendered a two-goal advantage from the first leg of the play-off semi-final, going down 3-2 to Northampton. This time there was no mistake and a fine season was crowned with the title after going head-to-head with Cambridge week after week. Top spot changed hands several times before Cheltenham's greater consistency earned its reward with hard-earned victories over Leyton Orient, Stevenage and Colchester, while their rivals suffered two damaging home defeats. Chris Hussey's free-kick for a 1-1 draw against Carlisle sealed a place in League One. It put them two points clear of Cambridge and that advantage was maintained on the final day with a club-record 24th victory – 4-1 over league newcomers Harrogate. Duff was named Manager of the Season for League Two, with two of his players in the EFL team – defender William Boyle and striker Hussey.

Addai A .... - (10)	Griffiths J 44	Sercombe L 35 (3)
Azaz F 27 (10)	Horton A .... - (1)	Smith S 18 (3)
Blair M 42 (2)	Hussey C 43	Thomas C 35 (3)
Bonds E 3 (2)	Lloyd G 18 (14)	Tozer B 46
Boyle W 29	Long S 18 (4)	Vassilev I ....- (12)
Chapman E 9 (12)	May A 36 (8)	Williams A 20 (25)
Clements C 14 (3)	Raglan C 39 (1)	Wright C 12 (5)
Flinders S 2	Reid R 4 (8)	
Freestone L 9 (5)	Sang T 3 (7)	

League goals (61): May 9, Williams 8, Sercombe 7, Boyle 6, Thomas 5, Smith 4, Wright 4, Blair 2, Lloyd 2, Long 2, Reid 2, Tozer 2, Azaz 1, Clements 1, Hussey 1, Raglan 1, Opponents 3
FA Cup goals (8): May 4, Azaz 1, Boyle 1, Lloyd 1, Sercombe 1. **League Cup goals** (2): Azaz 1, Sercombe 1. **League Trophy goals** (4): Reid 3, Lloyd 1
Player of Year: Ben Tozer

COLCHESTER UNITED

Hayden Mullins led the club away from trouble after the prospect of a promotion challenge turned into the threat of non-league football. A slide from sixth to third from bottom accounted for Steve Ball, sacked after seven months as manager, and his replacement, former Colchester player Wayne Brown. When Mullins, former Crystal Palace and West Ham midfielder, was promoted to interim manager, his side had a single victory to show from 22 matches. He opened with a point away to high-riding Bolton, followed by a 5-2 defeat by Oldham which at least ended a club-record ten successive away games without a goal. Colchester came from behind to defeat Walsall with goals from Michael Folivi and Ryan Clampin. And Folivi was on the mark again, this time alongside captain Harry Pell, in a crucial 2-0 victory over Southend which effectively sent their Essex rivals down. Josh Bohui then scored his first league goal to dent Salford's chances of reaching the play-offs. Mullins was later confirmed in the job.

Bohui J .... - (13)	George S 13 (2)	Sarpong-Wiredu B 19 (1)
Bramall C 23	Gerken D 33	Sayer H .... - (4)
Brown J 28 (12)	Harriott C 33 (3)	Scarlett M 2 (1)
Chilvers N 36 (8)	Lapslie T 6 (7)	Senior C 23 (12)
Clampin R 17 (4)	Marshall M .... - (1)	Smith T 45
Cowan-Hall P 2 (11)	McLeaod S .... - (1)	Sowunmi O 8 (7)
Cracknell B .... - (1)	Norris L 7 (10)	Stagg S .... - (1)
Doherty J 4 (1)	Nouble F 20	Stevenson B 26 (6)
Eastman T 45	Oteh A 4 (9)	Tchamadeu J 8 (3)
Folivi M 12 (15)	Pell H 24 (1)	Welch-Hayes M 35 (3)
Gambin L 6 (5)	Poku K 27 (6)	

League goals (44): Harriott 9, Brown 7, Folivi 5, Norris 4, Nouble 3, Chilvers 2, Eastman 2, Pell 2, Smith 2, Stevenson 2, Bohui 1, Clampin 1, Oteh 1, Sarpong-Wiredu 1, Welch-Hayes 1, Opponents 1
FA Cup goals (1): Pell 1. **League Cup goals (1):** Brown 1. **League Trophy goals (6):** Brown 3, Chilvers 1, Folivi 1, Poku 1
Player of Year: Noah Chilvers

CRAWLEY TOWN

An eye-catching FA Cup run and a promotion challenge made for an eventful season. High spot was the 3-0 victory over Leeds in a third-round tie when Crawley outplayed their Premier League opponents with goals from Nick Tsaroulla, Ashley Nadesan and Jordan Tunnicliffe. The first-round performance against non-league Torquay was also one to remember, with Tom Nichols completing a hat-trick as his side transformed a 5-3 deficit in extra-time into a 6-5 victory. They lost 2-1 to Bournemouth in round four and also lost Max Watters to Cardiff in the winter transfer window after his 13 goals, including a hat-trick against Barrow, brought a rise to fifth in the table. Crawley fell back with a single point from four matches following the cup run, regrouped to beat leaders Cheltenham and stay on the fringes of the leading group. But a 2-0 defeat by Newport meant a six-point gap and the end to hopes of a place in the play-offs.

Adebowale E 1	German R 1 (3)	Powell J 40 (4)
Allarakhia T 8 (9)	Hesketh J 11 (4)	Rodari D 1 (11)
Ashford S 2 (6)	Hassenthaler J 42 (4)	Sesay D 5 (8)
Bulman D 4 (2)	Maguire-Drew J 14 (3)	Tilley J 8 (10)
Craig T 36 (2)	Matthews S 21 (9)	Tsaroulla N 14 (3)
Dallison T 12 (2)	McGill T .... - (1)	Tunnicliffe J 39
Davies A 18 (16)	McNerney J 23 (3)	Watters M 12 (3)
Doherty J 14 (1)	Morris G 45	Wright J 15 (5)
Ferguson N 4 (5)	Nadesan A 30 (10)	Wright M 1
Francomb G 32 (1)	Nelson S 1	
Frost T 10 (13)	Nichols T 42 (1)	

League goals (56): Watters 13, Nichols 11, Francomb 6, Nadesan 5, Powell 3, Tilley 3, Tunnicliffe 3, Dallison 2, Frost 2, Hessenthaler 1, Maguire-Drew 1, Matthews 1, McNerney 1, Rodari 1, Opponents 3

FA Cup goals (12): Nichols 4, Nadesan 3, Tunnicliffe 2, Watters 2, Tsaroulla 1. **League Cup goals** (1): Ashford 1. **League Trophy goals** (4): Galach B 2, Ferguson 1, Watters 1.
Player of Year: Tom Nichols

EXETER CITY

Ryan Bowman scored back-to-back home hat-tricks as Exeter pursued promotion for the fourth time in five seasons. They came in wins over Colchester (6-1) and Tranmere (5-0) when his side were well in contention. But ground was lost over Christmas and the new year, before another treble, this one by Matt Jay against Leyton Orient, restored some momentum. After that, Exeter remained on the fringes of another play-off place, with more inconsistency ruling out a breakthrough. Three successive goalless home draws proved particularly costly. An outstanding performance brought a 4-1 away win over leaders Cambridge. There were also comeback victories over Grimsby and Bolton and they went into the final round of matches still in with a chance. Results elsewhere, however, went against them, along with a 1-1 draw at home to lowly Barrow which left them three points adrift.

Ajose N........................ - (4)	Hartridge A............... 20 (9)	Randall J.................... 26 (4)
Andersson J 29	Jay M....................... 43 (1)	Seymour B 8 (25)
Atangana N............ 11 (17)	Key J....................... 36 (7)	Sparkes J 27 (15)
Bowman R 39 (3)	Kite H....................... 1 (3)	Sweeney P................32 (6)
Caprice J 13 (21)	Law N 4 (14)	Taylor J....................40 (4)
Collins A........................46	Maxted J......................9	Ward L............................8
Dean W..........................2	McArdle R............... 18 (3)	Williams R...............24 (5)
Dyer J....................... - (1)	Page L 26 (6)	Willmott R...............13 (4)
Fisher A................. 3 (15)	Parkes T...................28 (3)	

League goals (71): Jay 18, Bowman 14, Randall 8, Taylor 6, Collins 4, Williams 4, Spakes 3, Sweeney 3, Fisher 2, Kay 1, Law 1, McArdle 1, Parkes 1, Seymour 1, Willmott 1, Opponents 3
FA Cup goals (5): Randall 2, Hartridge 1, Jay 1, Law 1. **League Cup goals:** None. **League Trophy goals** (12): Atangana 2, Kite 2, Seymour 2, Ajose 1, Hartridge 1, Jay 1, Key 1, Law 1, Sparkes 1
Player of Year: Matt Jay

FOREST GREEN ROVERS

An extra-time goal ended Forest Green's promotion chances in a thrilling play-off semi-final against Newport. Trailing 2-0 from the first leg, they scored twice in the first ten minutes of the return match through Ebou Adams and Aaron Collins, then took an overall lead with Nicky Cadden's free-kick. Newport scored twice in six minutes to regain the upper hand, before Jamille Matt sent the tie into overtime with an 87th minute goal – his 17th of the season. With two tired teams anticipating a penalty shoot-out, Nicky Maynard was on the mark in the 119th minute to give Newport the verdict 5-4 on aggregate. Mark Cooper's side had been in the leading group for most of the regular season until running into trouble in the final month when a fifth defeat in six matches cost the manager his job after five years in charge. With two fixtures remaining, they were out of the picture, but wins over Tranmere and Oldham took them back up to sixth. Former Wolves and Wales defender Rob Edwards was appointed the new manager.

Adams E 36 (1)	Hallett L................... - (1)	Stokes C........................34
Allen T 2 (3)	Hutchinson I............ 3 (7)	Sweeney D 16 (5)
Bailey O............... 24 (10)	Kitching L...................15	Thomas L 13
Bernard D 23 (2)	March J.................... 1 (3)	Wagstaff S...............21 (12)
Cadden N 33	Matt J................... 33 (3)	Whitehouse E 18 (9)
Cargill B 23	McCoulsky S............. - (2)	Wilson K...................19 (6)
Collins A 36 (8)	McGee L......................33	Winchester C 16 (2)
Davison J 11 (9)	Moore-Taylor J 28 (1)	Young J 10 (19)
Evans J..................... - (2)	Richardson J........... 15 (17)	
Godwin-Malife U....... 43 (1)	Stevens M .... - (10)	

Play-offs – appearances: Bernard 2, Cargill 2, Collins 2, Godwin-Malife 2, McGee 2, Moore-Taylor 2, Wilson 2, Bailey 1 (1), Cadden 1 (1), Matt 1 (1), Richardson 1 (1), Sweeney 1 (1), Wagstaff 1 (1), Adams 1, Stokes 1, Davison – (2), Young – (1)
League goals (59): Matt 16, Collins 10, Young 6, Bailey 4, Cadden 3, Davison 3, Adams 2, Cargill 2, Moore-Taylor 2, Stevens 2, Stokes 2, Whitehouse 2, Winchester 2, Wagstaff 1, Wilson 1, Opponents 1. **Play-offs – goals** (4): Adams 1, Cadden 1, Collins 1, Matt 1
FA Cup goals (2): Whitehouse 1, Young 1. **League Cup goals** (1): Opponents 1. **League Trophy goals** (6): Stevens 3, Bailey 1, Stokes 1, Young 1
Player of Year: Jamille Matt

GRIMSBY TOWN

The dream of a bright new future under Ian Holloway turned into a nightmare which brought non-league football back to Blundell Park. Less than a year after the game's most surprising managerial appointment, Holloway resigned, citing an 'inappropriate' approach by a potential new owner of the club. Grimsby were already deep in trouble, sixth from bottom, and there was nothing his replacement, Paul Hurst, could do to arrest the slide on his return, four years after leaving to take over at Shrewsbury. Hurst had to wait seven matches for his first victory, 2-1 against Crawley, and a further eight for the next, 1-0 over Barrow. By then, Grimsby, who went down in 2010, were seven points adrift, needing more wins to stand a chance of survival. Instead, they drew seven out of eight fixtures before two sendings-off sealed their fate. Stefan Payne headbutted Filipe Morais during an argument with his team-mate at Bradford and Jay Matete saw red for a reckless challenge when his side were leading at Exeter. Both games were lost and Grimsby went down with two games remaining.

Adams J 3 (3)	Hendrie L 37 (1)	Pollock M 23 (2)
Adlard L .... - (3)	Hewitt E 36 (1)	Preston D 22 (3)
Bennett K 10 (3)	Idehen D 5 (1)	Rose D 19 (3)
Boyd L .... - (1)	Jackson L 7 (13)	Russell S 5
Bunney J 3 (2)	John-Lewis L 14 (6)	Scannell S 5 (6)
Clifton H 30 (5)	Khouri E 6	Sisay A ....- (1)
Coke G 14 (3)	Lamy J 6 (3)	Spokes L 10 (7)
Eastwood J..................7	Matete J 20	Starbuck J ....- (6)
Edwards O 11 (6)	McKeown J 34 (1)	Taylor T 11 (2)
El Mizouni J 6	Menayesse R 21	Tilley A 7 (7)
Gibson M 7 (12)	Mohsni B .... - (1)	Waterfall L 30 (3)
Gomis V .... - (5)	Morais F 13 (3)	Williams G 10 (9)
Green M 17 (11)	Morton J 4 (3)	Windsor O 10 (2)
Haberham S 10 (3)	Ohman L 3	Wright M 4 (2)
Hanson J 16 (7)	Payne S .... 10 ()	

League goals (37): John-Lewis 4, Green 3, Jackson 3, Matete 3, Pollock 3, Clifton 2, Gibson 2, Hanson 2, Hendrie 2, Tilley 2, Williams 2, Adams 1, Edwards 1, Hewitt 1, Morais 1, Payne 1, Spokes 1, Waterfall 1, Windsor 1, Wright 1
FA Cup goals (1): Windsor 1. **League Cup goals** (1): Green 1. **League Trophy goals** (3): Boyd 1, Gibson 1, Pollock 1

HARROGATE TOWN

A thrilling 5-4 victory over second-place Cambridge sealed a satisfactory first season in the Football League for Simon Weaver's side. Brendan Kiernan's hat-trick and Kevin Lokko's 84th minute winner for his first league goal kept them in mid-table. It was a good Bank Holiday weekend for Harrogate, who three days later won the delayed 2020 FA Trophy Final 1-0 against National League South Concord Rangers at Wembley with a goal from captain Josh Falkingham. They started the EFL campaign with a 4-0 victory at Southend, reported to be the biggest by newcomers since 1921. They also won the first match on their own ground, 1-0 against Barrow, after starting out at Doncaster while grass replaced their synthetic pitch. Harrogate had to wait more than three months for the next one, 2-1 against Newport, but a productive away record compensated – 20 points out of a total of 27 at the half-way stage. After that, Harrogate enjoyed improved results at home to dispel any worries about dropping into trouble.

Andrews J .... - (3)	Jones D 18 (3)	Muldoon J 34 (8)
Beck M................ 14 (12)	Kerry L 23 (8)	Power S 11 (2)
Belshaw J 38	Kiernan B 15 (15)	Roberts M 4
Burrell W 39 (4)	Kirby C 10 (6)	Smith W 32
Cracknell J.......................8	Lawlor J 14 (3)	Stead J 8 (11)
Francis E 15 (5)	Lokko K 2 (1)	Thomson G 46
Falkingham J 37 (6)	March J 10 (4)	Walker T 1 (6)
Fallowfield R 26 (5)	Martin A 27 (9)	Williams J 3 (4
Hall C............. 39 (2)	McPake J 22 (1)	
Hondermarck W......... 2 (1)	Miller C 8 (2)	

League goals (52): Muldoon 15, March 5, Martin 5, Beck 4, Kiernan 4, McPake 4, Thomson 3, Kerry 2, Smith 2, Francis 1, Hall 1, Jones 1, Lokko 1, Miller 1, Power 1, Stead 1, Williams 1
FA Cup goals (4): Beck 1, Lawlor 1, Martin 1, Miller 1. **League Cup goals** (1): Kerry 1. **League Trophy goals** (5): Kiernan 2, Jones 1, Lokko 1, Stead 1

LEYTON ORIENT

Danny Johnson's goals kept Orient in the promotion picture until the final few weeks of the season. He had 14 to his credit at the half-way point, including a hat-trick against Harrogate, before a month's absence through injury and a struggle to add to that tally on his return to fitness accompanied his side's run of seven matches without a win. Manager Ross Embleton, sacked after a home defeat by Tranmere, was replaced on an interim basis by player-coach Jobi McAnuff, who revived their fortunes with four successive victories in which Johnson returned to the scoresheet with a brace against Mansfield. Conor Wilkinson was on the mark in victories against Newport, Carlisle and Oldham, enabling Orient to move to within a point of a play-off place. But a single win in the next seven ended their hopes, with seven goals conceded in successive home matches against Cambridge and Carlisle. Former Portsmouth manager Kenny Jackett took over in the summer.

Abrahams T............. 3 (11)	Freeman N 10 (5)	Sweeney J .... - (1)
Akinola O................ 31 (2)	Happe D 38 (2)	Thomas J 1
Angol L...................... 7 (5)	Johnson D 36 (6)	Thompson A 6
Brophy J.......................44	Kemp D 22 (2)	Turley J 15 (3)
Cisse O 40 (2)	Kyprianou H 12 (10)	Vigouroux L 46
Clay C 32 (7)	Ling S................... 27 (3)	Widowson J 21 (5)
Coulson J................. 19 (1)	Maguire-Drew J......... 3 (10)	Wilkinson C 40 (2)
Dayton J 4 (8)	McAnuff J 26 (14)	Wright J..............4 (5)
Dennis L 11 (13)	Sotiriou R................ 8 (14)	Young M.................... - (1)

League goals (53): Johnson 17, Wilkinson 12, Kemp 5, Happe 3, Brophy 2, Maguire-Drew 2, McAnuff 2, Angol 1, Cisse 1, Clay 1, Dennis 1, Sotiriou 1, Turley 1, Wright 1, Opponents 3
FA Cup goals (1): Kyprianou 1. **League Cup goals** (5): Johnson 2, Dennis 1, McAnuff 1, Wilkinson 1. **League Trophy goals** (7): Wilkinson 2, Angol 1, Dennis 1, Johnson 1, Ling 1, Opponents 1
Player of Year: Lawrence Vigouroux

MANSFIELD TOWN

Nigel Clough steadied the ship after the club's worst start to a season in 106 years. They failed to win any of the opening 12 matches in all competitions and manager Graham Coughlan was sacked after a 4-2 home defeat by newly-promoted Barrow. The run stretched to 14 before a

133

1-0 FA Cup victory at Sunderland, with former Burton manager Clough watching from the stand. His arrival sparked a major improvement in league fortunes – 25 points accumulated from his first 13 matches in charge. After five straight wins and 13 goals scored, Mansfield looked to be closing in on a promotion challenge early in the new year. Instead, they slipped back with home defeats by Bolton and Cambridge and from then on form was patchy. It picked up at the end of the campaign, with four wins in five against Stevenage, Scunthorpe, Oldham and Port Vale, but not enough to secure a place in the top-half of the table.

Benning M 25 (7)	Maris G.................... 39 (1)	Reid J...................... 31 (8)
Bowery J................. 38 (5)	Maynard N ....: 9 (8)	Sarkic O ....- (4)
Charles J..................- (2)	McLaughlin S 29 (7)	Sinclair T................ 7 (12)
Charsley H 32 (11)	Menayesse R 10	Smith A ....- (1)
Clarke J 1 (1)	O'Driscoll A 1 (2)	Stech M................. 23 (1)
Clarke O 27 (6)	O'Keefe C 7 (6)	Stone A 22
Cook A..................... 8 (12)	Pardington J............. 1 (1)	Sweeney R 33 (3)
Gordon K 28 (4)	Perch J 31 (1)	Ward K 1 (6)
Lapslie G 27 (2)	Quinn S 21 (2)	Wright J ....- (2)
Law J 12 (5)	Rawson F......................43	

League goals (57): Bowery 10, Lapslie 8, Reid 6, Charsley 4, McLaughlin 4, Clarke O 3, Cook 3, Maynard 3, Perch 3, Sinclair 3, Sweeney 3, Quinn 2, Law 1, Maris 1, Menayesse 1, Opponents 2
FA Cup goals (4): Charsley 1, Lapslie 1, Maynard 1, McLaughlan 1. **League Cup goals**: None.
League Trophy goals (3): Menayesse 1, Reid 1, Sweeney 1
Player of Year: George Lapslie

MORECAMBE

A club more used to celebrating an escape from relegation toasted a place in the third tier for the first time. Senegal-born Carlos Mendes Gomes converted a penalty in extra-time for a 1-0 Play-off Final win over Newport in Derek Adams's first full season as manager. Adams, formerly in charge of Plymouth, led a huge improvement in fortunes which came close to being rewarded with automatic promotion. His matchwinner, spotted while playing for a college team in Manchester, scored his 16th goal of the campaign after Ryan Haynes was penalised for his challenge on John O'Sullivan. It was one of two controversial decisions by referee Bobby Madley, who refused Newport appeals after goalkeeper Kyle Letheren collided with Scot Bennett. Two heavy defeats early on, 5-0 at home by Cambridge and 4-0 at Crawley, hinted at another difficult campaign for Morecambe. Instead, they established a place in the leading group early in the new year and went on to dispute the third promotion spot with Bolton, finishing a point behind their rivals. The consolation for missing out was momentum built up by five victories in the last six matches, along with 15 goals scored, which accounted for Tranmere in their semi-final. Some of the shine was taken off when Adams left to become Bradford's new manager.

Andersson J 2	Knight-Percival N...... 29 (2)	Phillips A 24 (2)
Cooney R 20 (16)	Lavelle S 44 (1)	Price F 2 (9)
Davis H.................... 22 (5)	Leitch-Smith AJ........... 1 (4)	Pringle B...................4 (7)
Denny A 1 (5)	Letheren K 21	Slew J 10 (7)
Diagouraga T 28 (8)	Lyons S 5 (9)	Songo'o Y 34 (4)
Gibson L 21 (2)	McAlinden L 4 (24)	Stockton C 38 (2)
Halstead M 9	Mellor K 29 (3)	Turner J 14
Hendrie S 22 (14)	Mendes Gomes C 43	Wildig A 37
Kenyon A 10 (8)	O'Sullivan J 32 (6)	

Play-offs – appearances: Cooney 3, Diagouraga 3, Knight-Percival 3, Lavelle 3, Letheren 3, McAlinden 3, Mendes Gomes 3, Songo'o 3, Stockton 3, Wildig 3, Gibson 2 (1), Hendrie 1, Lyons – (3), Kenyon – (1), Mellor – (1), O'Sullivan – (1)

134

League goals (69): Mendes Gomes 15, Stockton 13, Phillips 8, Wildig 8, Songo'o 6, O'Sullivan 4, Diagouraga 3, McAlinden 2, Hendrie 1, Kenyon 1, Lavelle 1, Leitch-Smith 1, Lyons 1, Mellor 1, Price 1, Slew 1, Opponents 2. **Play-offs – goals** (4): Knight-Percival 1, McAlinden 1, Mendes Gomes 1, Wildig 1

FA Cup goals (5): Stockton 2, O'Sullivan 1, Phillips 1, Opponents 1. **League Cup goals** (2): Phillips 1, Wildig 1. **League Trophy goals** (5): Cooney 2, Davis 1, Lavelle 1, Price 1
Player of Year: Carlos Mendes Gomes

NEWPORT COUNTY

An eventful season promising so much ended in bitter disappointment in the Play-off Final at Wembley. Newport lost 1-0 to Morecambe in extra-time after two controversial penalty decisions by referee Bobby Madley went against them. Manager Michael Flynn was left calling for VAR in big games after Ryan Haynes was penalised for his challenge on John O'Sullivan, which he insisted was outside the area, and goalkeeper Kyle Letheren escaped when clattering Scot Bennett. Flynn's side had two months leading the division, during which they also reached the League Cup fourth round, beating Swansea and Watford before losing on penalties to Newcastle. Goalkeeper Tom King scored with a wind-assisted goal-kick at Cheltenham, but his side slipped back after having four players red carded in five games. The club also had to play two home matches at the Cardiff City Stadium because of the state of their Rodney Parade pitch. Order was restored on the return home with victory over in-form Bolton. Then, after sealing fifth place, Newport came from behind on aggregate to defeat Forest Green 5-4 in the semi-finals, with Nicky Maynard's goal after 119 minutes.

Abrahams T.............. 15 (8)	Farquharson P 12 (1)	Maynard N 12 (7)
Amond P................. 23 (18)	Gambin L.................. 5 (6)	Proctor J 5 (5)
Baker A 1 (3)	Hartigan A 9 (2)	Scrimshaw J 6 (10)
Bennett S 32 (6)	Haynes R 37	Sheehan J 43
Collins L 8 (8)	Howkins K.....................2	Shephard L....................42
Cooper B................. 18 (1)	Janneh A 4 (4)	Taylor R 15 (10)
Demetriou M 45	King T...................... 8 (1)	Telford D 5 (10)
Devitt J..................... 1 (7)	Labadie J 35 (3)	Townsend N................38
Dolan M.................. 35 (3)	Ledley J 2 (2)	Twine S 18 (1)
Ellison K.................. 2 (21)	Lewis A................... 15 (5)	Willmott R................ 5 (14)
Evans J...................- (1)	Longe-King D 8 (3)	Windsor O ....- (1)

Play-offs – appearances: Amond 3, Bennett 3, Collins 3, Demetriou 3, Dolan 3, Haynes 3, King 3, Sheehan 3, Lewis 3, Shephard 3, Hartigan 2 (1), Labadie 1 (1), Farquharson – (3), Maynard – (3), Taylor – (3), Ellison – (2),

League goals (57): Amond 6, Dolan 6, Twine 6, Abrahams 4, Demetriou 4, Labadie 4, Scrimshaw 3, Sheehan 3, Bennett 2, Ellison 2, Maynard 2, Shephard 2, Taylor 2, Collins 1, Cooper 1, Devitt 1, Gambin 1, Haynes 1, Janneh 1, King 1, Lewis 1, Proctor 1, Telford 1, Opponents 1. **Play-offs – goals (5):** Collins 1, Dolan 1, Ellison 1, Labadie 1, Maynard 1.

FA Cup goals (6): Amond 1, Baker 1, Devitt 1, Janneh 1, Proctor 1, Opponents 1. **League Cup goals** (7): Abrahams 4, Amond 1, Labadie 1, Twine 1. **League Trophy goals** (1): Amond 1
Player of Year: Mickey Demetriou

OLDHAM ATHLETIC

Oldham, never looked like promotion contenders, nor did the threat of relegation ever enter into the equation. It was a modest, middle-of-the-road season in every aspect – bar one. For the club came close to a unique set of statistics. Entering the final round of matches, they had scored more goals (72) and conceded more (78) than any side in League Two. The goals against column bulged with a 3-0 home defeat by Forest Green. But Cambridge overtook them as the leading scorers by beating Grimsby 3-0. Oldham did have one record to show – a club-best seven straight away wins in all competitions which netted 20 goals. At home, it was a different story, poor form resulting in Harry.Kewell's dismissal after seven months as manager with his side on the way to 15 defeats at Boundary Park. Keith Curle, himself sacked by Northampton, became Oldham's eighth manager since 2018. The pattern of the campaign continued – 15 goals scored in four matches against Crawley, Colchester, Morecambe and Harrogate, alongside four conceded in three other games.

Adams N..................... 20 (3)	Diarra R 10 (6)	McAleny C 37 (3)
Badan A 11 (7)	Fage D.................... 22 (12)	McCalmont A 31 (4)
Bahamboula D........ 27 (11)	Garrity B 21 (8)	Ntambwe B 19 (5)
Barnes M 1 (6)	Grant R.................... 18 (5)	Piergianni C 36 (2)
Barnett J.................... 7 (10)	Hamer T 11 (1)	Rowe D 9 (6)
Bilboe L..............................3	Hilssner M 15 (5)	Sutton W .... - (1)
Blackwood G 6 (7)	Jameson K 20 (5)	Tasdemir S................... 4 (3)
Borthwick-Jackson C. 25 (6)	Jombati S 16 (3)	Vaughan H .... - (6)
Chapman M .... - (1)	Kellior-Dunn D 34 (7)	Walker L 13
Clarke M 30 (2)	Lawlor I 30	Whelan C 23 (8)
Dearnley Z 6 (9)	Luamba J................... 1 (1)	

League goals (72): McAleny 17, Kellior-Dunn 10, McCalmont 8, Bahamboula 6, Dearnley 6, Piergianni 5, Rowe 4, Blackwood 3, Grant 3, Borthwick-Jackson 2, Garrity 2, Jameson 2, Clarke 1, Fage 1, Hilssner 1, Opponents 1
FA Cup goals (6): Rowe 2, Bahamboula 1, Garrity 1, Grant 1, McAleny 1. **League Cup goals (3):** Garrity 1, Grant 1, McAleny 1. **League Trophy goals (10):** Grant 2, McAleny 2, McCalmont 2, Rowe 2, Dearnley 1, Kellior-Dunn 1

PORT VALE

An eye-catching 6-3 away win over Bolton put Port Vale back on track after a run of five defeats dampened early optimism of a promotion challenge. Six different scorers represented a notable team effort which closed the gap on the division's leading group. But they were unable to maintain momentum, slipped to 17th and manager John Askey was sacked. Walsall's Darrell Clarke, who replaced him after the two clubs agreed on compensation, had to wait until his eighth match in charge for a win – 2-1 against Newport with goals from Tom Conlon and Devante Rodney. It was the first of eight victories in nine matches, one of which came against Barrow when the first of Conlon's two goals was struck spectacularly from just inside the opposition half. The sequence ended with defeats against relegated Grimsby, then Mansfield, but was enough to secure a finishing position in mid-table after a season of ups and downs.

Amoo D 10 (16)	Gibbons J.................... 8 (3)	Oyeleke E................... 14 (6)
Brisley S 19 (5)	Guthrie K 9 (8)	Pope T 8 (11)
Brown S...............................46	Hurst A 13 (7)	Robinson T............. 15 (14)
Burgess S 18 (6)	Joyce L 40 (1)	Rodney D 35 (5)
Clark M............................11	Legge L 36 (1)	Smith N 44
Conlon T................... 41 (1)	McKirdy H 2 (6)	Swan W 4 (6)
Crookes A 13 (3)	Mills Z 18 (3)	Taylor J 8 (4)
Cullen M..................... 8 (10)	Montano C................. 22 (7)	Whitehead D................... 9 (6)
Fitzpatrick D 18 (4)	Olagunju M................... 2 (4)	Worrall D.................... 35 (2)

League goals (57): Rodney 11, Conlon 10, Worrall 5, Smith 4, Legge 3, Montano 3, Pope 3, Robinson 3, Cullen 2, Oyeleke 2, Amoo 1, Brisley 1, Clark 1, Crookes 1, Guthrie 1 Hurst 1, Swan 1, Taylor 1, Opponents 3
FA Cup goals: None. **League Cup goals (3):** Mills 1, Robinson 1, Whitehead 1. **League Trophy goals (9):** McKirdy 2, Robinson 2, Cullen 1, Hurst 1, Mills 1, Montano 1, Rodney 1
Player of Year: Tom Conlon

SALFORD CITY

The club celebrated EFL silverware for the first time with victory over Portsmouth on penalties after a goalless draw in the delayed 2020 League Trophy Final. But there was no play-off place to go with it after a season of managerial upheaval and too many drawn matches. Graham Alexander, who took the club into the league and secured a top-half finish in their first campaign, was sacked, despite an unbeaten opening five fixtures this time. Part-owner Paul Scholes was in temporary charge before the appointment of Swindon's Richie Wellens, who complained after a ninth home draw against Scunthorpe: 'They are killing us.' He was dismissed nine days after the Wembley victory, with Salford six points adrift, and former Blackpool and Blackburn manager Gary Bowyer took temporary charge through to the end of the campaign. By then, Salford had closed to within two points after four wins in their final five games, earning Bowyer a two-year contract.

Andrade B............... 8 (11)	Eastham A............... 38 (1)	Jones J........................- (1)
Armstrong L 1 (3)	Elliott T................... 3 (11)	Lowe J 44 (1)
Bernard D 27 (3)	Gibson D 4 (1)	Smith M...................... 1 (3)
Boyd G 2 (9)	Golden T 6 (1)	Thomas-Asante B 27 (15)
Burgess L 7 (10)	Gotts R 20 (3)	Threlkeld O............... 29 (6)
Clarke L 27 (5)	Henderson I............ 45 (1)	Touray I................... 45 (1)
Coutts P 14 (5)	Hladky V 46	Towell R 16 (8)
Denny A..................... 4 (5)	Hunter A 37 (4)	Turnbull J................ 35 (7)
Dieseruwve E........... 1 (13)	James T 2 (2)	Wilson J 17 (7)

League goals (54): Henderson 17, Hunter 7, Wilson 7, Thomas-Asante 5, Burgess 3, Gotts 3, Towell 3, Bernard 2, Clarke 2, Eastham 1, Touray 1, Turnbull 1, Opponents 2
FA Cup goals (2): Andrade 1, Dieseruvue 1. **League Cup goals** (1): Henderson 1. **League Trophy goals** (7): Dieseruvue 3, Andrade 1, Hunter 1, Thomas-Asante 1, Wilson 1
Player of Year: Vaclav Hladky

SCUNTHORPE UNITED

Scunthorpe slumped after a new year flourish and were clinging on to their Football League status at the end. Three victories in the space of eight days against local rivals Grimsby, Port Vale and Colchester looked to have transformed a dismal first half of the season. When a backs-to-the-wall performance earned a 1-0 win over Cambridge – particularly satisfying after a 5-0 drubbing at home by the league leaders – they were 12 points clear of trouble and looking to cement a mid-table position. Instead, Neil Cox's side won just one of 16 matches through to the end of the campaign– 2-0 against Bradford and saw that lead disappearing. They were grateful that Grimsby and Southend were unable to take full advantage, but remained in danger after leaking 16 goals over the course of a fortnight in April. Salvation came with a goalless draw in the return fixture with Bradford which took them out of Southend's reach and prevented an anxious final day of the campaign.

Bedeau J 28 (6)	Hippolyte M............ 15 (11)	Olomola O ....- (5)
Beestin A 32 (8)	Hornshaw G................. 7 (1)	Onariase E................ 23 (3)
Brown J 14	Howard M......................34	Pugh T........................- (1)
Butroid L ....- (1)	Howe T 7 (5)	Rowe J 15 (10)
Clarke J 22 (2)	Jarvis A 6 (7)	Spence L................. 30 (11)
Cordner T 10 (2)	Jessop H .... - (3)	Taft G 16
Dunnwald K 1 (4)	Karacan J............... 22 (2)	Taylor J 8 (5)
Eisa A 28 (11)	Loft R 35 (6)	Vincent F..................... 5 (1)
Gilliead A 43 (1)	McAtee J............... 12 (18)	Watson R......................... 12
Green D 23 (13)	McGahey H............... 14 (2)	Van Veen K 14 (5)
Hallam J 3 (10)	O'Malley S............... 27 (2)	

League goals (41): Eisa 9, Loft 8, Beestin 5, Green 3, Hallam 2, Jarvis 2, Onariase 2, Bedeau 1,

Clarke 1, Gilliead 1, Hippolyte 1, McAtee 1, McGahey 1, Rowe 1, Spence 1, Van Veen 1, Opponents 1
FA Cup goals (2): McAtee 1, Van Veen 1. **League Cup goals** (1): Loft 1. **League Trophy goals** (2): Cordner 1, Olomola 1
Player of Year: Alex Gilliead

SOUTHEND UNITED

A second successive relegation brought an end to the club's 101 years in the Football League. Southend never found the cure for an acute shortage of goals, had to wait 12 matches for a first win and spent almost the whole season in the bottom two. A glimmer of hope accompanied four wins out of six against Scunthorpe, Grimsby, Colchester and Barrow approaching the midway point of the campaign. The club also had a transfer embargo lifted. But it proved a false dawn and in a final attempt to stay up with six fixtures remaining, the club sacked Mark Molesley, manager for eight months, and brought back Phil Brown, who was in charge from 2013-18. There was little he could do. Southend, needing to bridge a five-point gap, shared goalless draws against Crawley and Exeter, then lost a potential make-or-break fixture 2-0 to fellow-strugglers Colchester – the 25th match in which they had failed to score. Despite winning 2-1 at Barrow in the penultimate fixture, they went down because of the point Scunthorpe gained in a goalless draw with Bradford. Brown stayed on with a two-year contract.

Acquah E............... 20 (11)	Hackett-Fairchild R ... 21 (4)	Nathaniel-George A . 16 (13)
Akinola S 20 (4)	Halford G 9 (7)	Olayinka J 17 (3)
Bass A.................................1	Hart S 18 (3)	Oxley M............................ 41
Bwomono E................ 38 (3)	Hobson S 41 (3)	Phillips H .... - (1)
Clifford T 22 (6)	Holmes R 8 (6)	Ralph N 7
Coker K .... - (2)	Howard R .... - (2)	Ranger N......................... - (1)
Coker O .... - (1)	Hutchinson I........................2	Rush M 2 (5)
Cordner J 11 (3)	Kelman C 2 (1)	Seaden H .... - (1)
Demetriou J 34 (4)	Kinali E .... - (2)	Sterling K 5 (5)
Dieng T 35 (1)	Klass M .... - (2)	Taylor K.................... 21 (10)
Egbri T 18 (7)	Kyprianou H 2 (3)	Taylor R...................... 4 (8)
Ferguson N 17 (2)	Lennon H 9	Walsh L 2 (3)
Gard L 1 (2)	McCormack A 12 (8)	White J 28
Goodship B 15 (14)	Mellis J .... - (3)	
Green J...............................3	Montgomery J 4	

League goals (29): Clifford 3, Dieng 3, Acquah 2, Akinola 2, Ferguson 2, Hobson 2, Nathaniel-George 2, Olayinka 2, Bwomono 1, Cordner 1, Demetriou 1, Egbri 1, Goodship 1, Hackett-Fairchild 1, Halford 1, Ralph 1, Rush 1, Taylor 1, White 1.
FA Cup goals (3): Egbri 1, Goodship 1, Olayinka 1. **League Cup goals**: None. **League Trophy goals** (2): Humphrys S 1, Sterling 1
Player of Year: Shaun Hobson

STEVENAGE

Stevenage had a narrow escape from relegation in 2020 and the signs at the midway point of this campaign pointed to another struggle to beat the drop. Their reshaped side were a single point away from the relegation zone before a stoppage-time winner by Matty Stevens at Grimsby provided some breathing space. It was the start of an impressive recovery, which not only took them clear of trouble but offered the chance of a place in the top half of the table. Luke Norris, another winter signing, Danny Newton and Elliot Osborne also scored late goals to accumulate more points against Morecambe, Tranmere and Crawley respectively. Victory over the latter was the start of a 12-match unbeaten run, which included a club-record six successive away games without conceding a goal. Three straight defeats meant their target proved out of reach, before Norris was on the mark again with the only goal to dent Cambridge's bid for the title.

Aitchison J............... 17 (9)
Akinwande F 3 (4)
Carter C................... 16 (2)
Coker B 32 (6)
Cumming J 41
Cuthbert S 31 (2)
Dinanga M 5 (1)
Effiong I 3 (6)
Fernandez L....................1
Hector-Ingram J.......... - (1)
Hutton A............... 20 (6)

Iontton A 1 (1)
Lines C............................20
List E 36 (8)
Marsh T................... 4 (6)
Marshall R 10 (5)
Martin J................... 9 (5)
Newton D............ 21 (14)
Norris L 21 (2)
Osborne E............... 20 (6)
Oteh A...................... 7 (6)
Pett T................... 29 (2)

Prosser L 27 (3)
Read A 26 (6)
Roles J 1 (1)
Smith J................... 17 (8)
Stevens M 4 (14)
Stockdale D 5
VanCouten T................29
Vincelot R 14 (12)
Wildin L................. 36 (3)
Williams A .... - (1)

League goals (41): List 9, Norris 7, Newton 4, Oteh 4, Carter 3, Osborne 2, Pett 2, Read 2 Wildin 2, Aitchison 1, Cuthbert 1, Dinanga 1, Effiong 1, Prosser 1, Stevens 1,
FA Cup goals (3): Coker 1, List 1, Newton 1. **League Cup goals (3):** Carter 1, Cuthbert 1, List 1.
League Trophy goals (4): Dinanga 1, Effiong 1, Marsh 1, Opponents 1
Player of Year: Elliot List

TRANMERE ROVERS

Chairman Mark Palios gambled by sacking manager Keith Hill ahead of the play-offs, arguing that it gave the club 'the best chance of being promoted'. The move did not have the desired effect, with Tranmere beaten 2-1 at home by Morecambe in the first leg of their semi-final and held 1-1 in the return. Hill, former Rochdale, Barnsley and Bolton manager, took them into the top-seven with five straight victories early in the new year, a position retained despite winning only two of the final 11 matches. He also secured a place in the final of the League Trophy against Sunderland, who won it 1-0 at Wembley. Palios also dismissed his predecessor, Mike Jackson, three-and-a-half-months into the job, following a home defeat by Morecambe which left Tranmere 18th in the table. Jackson, in turn, had replaced Micky Mellon , who left to take over at Dundee United. After a season in the Scottish Premiership, Mellon returned to his old job at Prenton Park.

Banks O................... 7 (5)
Burton J 1 (1)
Clarke P.........................46
Crawford A............... 4 (5)
Davies S 34
Ellis M.................... 5 (1)
Feeney L.............. 37 (4)
Ferrier M................... 2 (8)
Jolley C.................... - (2)
Khan O................... 29 (6)

Kirby N 2 (4)
Lewis P 33 (7)
Lloyd D 17 (14)
MacDonald C............ 37 (2)
Monthe E 30 (4)
Morris K 29 (13)
Murphy J................ 12 (1)
Nelson S 6 (3)
Nugent D 7 (11)
O'Connor L 28 (5)

Payne S 1 (3)
Ray G.................. 10 (1)
Ridehalgh L........... 15 (9)
Smith S 2 (3)
Spearing J..................43
Taylor C............... 9 (11)
Vaughan J 26 (3)
Walker-Rice D........... - (1)
Woolery K............30 (10)
Young J.................... 4 (1)

Play-offs – appearances: Blackett-Taylor C 2, Clarke 2, Feeney 2, Monthe 2, Morris 2, Murphy 2, O'Connor 2, Ridehalgh 2, Spearing 2, Vaughan 2, Khan 1 (1), Lewis 1 (1), Nugent – (2), Woolery – (2), Lloyd – (1), MacDonald – (1)
League goals (55): Vaughan 18, Woolery 8, Lewis 6, Morris 5, Clarke 3, Feeney 3, Lloyd 3, Khan 2, Nugent 2, MacDonald 1, Ray 1, Spearing 1, Taylor 1, Opponents 1. **Play-offs – goals (2):** Clarke 1, Vaughan 1
FA Cup goals (3): Clarke 1, Taylor 1, Woolery 1. **League Cup goals (1):** Vaughan 1. **League Trophy goals (15):** Lloyd 4, Morris 2, Vaughan 2, Woolery 2, Banks 1, Ferrier 1, Lewis 1, Payne 1, Taylor 1
Player of Year: Jay Spearing

WALSALL

Walsall struck a purple patch in the build-up to Christmas, then fell away. Four successive wins and 12 goals scored pointed to a possible promotion challenge. They included a 4-3 success against Port Vale when twice coming from behind to take the points, with Jake Scrimshaw and Dan Scarr sharing the goals. Walsall were then within goal difference of a play-off place. But the sale of leading scorer Elijah Adebayo to Luton and loss of manager Darrell Clarke to Port Vale, after the two clubs agreed on compensation, hit hard. Coach Brian Dutton, appointed until the end of the season, had to wait 14 matches for his first win, 2-1 against Forest Green with goals from Rory Holden and captain James Clarke. Emmanuel Osadebe's spectacular winner at Tranmere next time out effectively made them safe and Osadebe was on the mark again in a 2-0 victory at Scunthorpe. Tottenham youth coach Matt Taylor was appointed the club's new manager.

Adebayo E	24 (1)	Leak T	4 (2)	Roberts L	31 (1)
Bates A	21 (15)	McDonald W	27 (14)	Rose J	15
Clarke J	30 (1)	Melbourne M	20	Sadler M	23 (3)
Cockerill-Mollett C	5 (6)	Nolan J	2 (7)	Scarr D	34 (1)
Gordon J	31 (5)	Norman C	27 (8)	Scrimshaw J	4 (10)
Guthrie D	7 (7)	Nurse G	9 (1)	Sinclair S	9 (8)
Holden R	19 (2)	Osadebe E	26 (12)	Vincent F	3 (5)
Jules Z	16 (1)	Osei Yaw D	1 (10)	White H	26 (2)
Kinsella L	42 (1)	Perry S	14 (2)	Willis J	- (2)
Lavery C	22 (19)	Reid J	1	Wright T	13 (3)

League goals (45): Adebayo 10, Lavery 6, Gordon 5, Holden 4, Scarr 4, Osadebe 3, Clarke 2, McDonald 2, Scrimshaw 2, Jules 1, Melbourne 1, Nurse 1, Perry 1, Sadler 1, Opponents 2.
FA Cup goals (1): Lavery 1. **League Cup goals**: None. **League Trophy goals** (3): Gordon 1, Jules 1, McDonald 1
Player of Year: Liam Kinsella

THE THINGS THEY SAY ....

'It's a very embarrassing night for us as international players. The criticism will be deserved' – **Seamus Coleman**, Republic of Ireland captain, after a 1-0 home defeat by Luxembourg in a World Cup qualifier.

'What a goal, what a player and what a man. I'm completely in love with him' – **Pep Guardiola**, Manchester City manager, after Sergio Aguero scored against Crystal Palace in one of his final appearances for the club.

'Financially it's right to play on, but for me, morally, it's probably wrong' – **Steve Bruce**, Newcastle manager, on whether football should have stopped at the height of the pandemic.

'I have loved every minute of it. We were so close. Next time we'll get over the line' - **Gareth Ainsworth**, Wycombe manager, after his team were relegated from the Championship by a single point.

'I've been lucky enough to win a lot of trophies in my playing career, but this is right up there with them' – **Barry Ferguson**, former Rangers and Scotland midfielder, after leading Kelty Hearts into the Scottish League as manager.

LEAGUE CLUB MANAGERS 2021–22

Figure in brackets = number of managerial changes at club since the War. †Second spell at club

PREMIER LEAGUE

Arsenal (13)	Mikel Arteta	December 2019
Aston Villa (27)	Dean Smith	October 2018
Brentford (34)	Thomas Frank	October 2018
Brighton (34)	Graham Potter	May 2019
Burnley (24)	Sean Dyche	October 2012
Chelsea (32)	Thomas Tuchel	January 2021
Crystal Palace (44)	Patrick Vieira	July 2021
Everton (22)	Rafael Benitez	June 2021
Leeds (33)	Marcelo Bielsa	June 2018
Leicester (31)	Brendan Rodgers	February 2019
Liverpool (14)	Jurgen Klopp	October 2015
Manchester City (30)	Pep Guardiola	May 2016
Manchester Utd (12)	Ole Gunnar Solskjaer	April 2019
Newcastle (28)	Steve Bruce	July 2019
Norwich (29)	Daniel Farke	May 2017
Southampton (29)	Ralph Hasenhuttl	December 2018
Tottenham (25)	Nuno Espirito Santo	June 2021
Watford (38)	Xisco Munoz	December 2020
West Ham (17)	David Moyes+	December 2019
Wolves (28)	Bruno Lage	June 2021

+Second spell as manager

CHAMPIONSHIP

Barnsley (30)	Markus Schopp	June 2021
Birmingham (32)	Lee Bowyer	March 2021
Blackburn (31)	Tony Mowbray	February 2017
Blackpool (34)	Neil Critchley	March 2020
Bournemouth (26)	Scott Parker	June 2021
Bristol City (28)	Nigel Pearson	February 2021
Cardiff (33	Mick McCarthy	January 2021
Coventry (35)	Mark Robins	March 2017
Derby (29)	Wayne Rooney	January 2021
Fulham (35)	Marco Silva	July 2021
Huddersfield (31)	Carlos Corberan	July 2020
Hull (31)	Grant McCann	June 2019
Luton (4)	Nathan Jones +	May 2020
Middlesbrough (24)	Neil Warnock	June 2020
Millwall (32)	Gary Rowett	October 2019
Nottm Forest (28)	Chris Hughton	October 2020
Peterborough (32)	Darren Ferguson++	January 2019
Preston (30)	Frankie McAvoy	May 2021
QPR (36)	Mark Warburton	May 2019
Reading (26)	Veljko Paunovic	August 2020
Sheffield Utd (39)	Slavisa Jokanovic	May 2021
Stoke (27)	Michael O'Neill	November 2019
Swansea (38)	Steve Cooper	June 2019
WBA (37)	Valerien Ismael	June 2021

Number of changes since elected to Football League: Peterborough 1960. Since returning: Luton 2014.
+ Second spell as manager. ++ Third spell as manager

LEAGUE ONE

Accrington (4)	John Coleman	September 2014
AFC Wimbledon (4)	Mark Robinson	February 2021

Bolton (25)	Ian Evatt	July 2020
Burton (6)	Jimmy Floyd Hasselbaink	January 2021
Cambridge (4)	Mark Bonner	March 2020
Charlton (26)	Nigel Adkins	March 2021
Cheltenham (1)	Michael Duff	September 2018
Crewe (22)	David Artell	January 2017
Doncaster (8)	Richie Wellens	May 2021
Fleetwood (6)	Simon Grayson	January 2021
Gillingham (27)	Steve Evans	May 2019
Ipswich (16)	Paul Cook	March 2021
Lincoln (1)	Michael Appleton	September 2019
MK Dons (19)	Russell Martin	November 2019
Morecambe (3)	Stephen Robinson	June 2021
Oxford (4)	Karl Robinson	March 2018
Plymouth (35)	Ryan Lowe	June 2019
Portsmouth (35)	Danny Cowley	March 2021
Rotherham (28)	Paul Warne	April 2017
Sheffield Wed (34)	Darren Moore	March 2021
Shrewsbury (8)	Steve Cotterill	November 2020
Sunderland (34)	Lee Johnson	December 2020
Wigan (26)	Leam Richardson	April 2021
Wycombe (10)	Gareth Ainsworth	November 2012

Number of changes since elected to Football League: Wigan 1978, Wycombe 1993, Morecambe 2007, Burton 2009, AFC Wimbledon 2011, Fleetwood 2012. Since returning: Doncaster 2003, Shrewsbury 2004, Accrington 2006, Oxford 2010, Cambridge 2014, Cheltenham 2016, Lincoln 2017

LEAGUE TWO

Barrow (3)	Mark Cooper	May 2021
Bradford (41)	Derek Adams	June 2021
Bristol Rov (4)	Joey Barton	February 2021
Carlisle (8)	Chris Beech	November 2019
Colchester (31)	Hayden Mullins	May 2021
Crawley (9)	John Yems	December 2019
Exeter (1)	Matt Taylor	June 2018
Forest Green (1)	Rob Edwards	May 2021
Harrogate (–)	Simon Weaver	May 2009
Hartlepool (–)	Dave Challinor	November 2019
Leyton Orient (3)	Kenny Jackett	May 2021
Mansfield (6)	Nigel Clough	November 2020
Newport (5)	Mike Flynn	May 2017
Northampton (37)	Jon Brady	February 2021
Oldham (38)	Keith Curle	March 2021
Port Vale (29)	Darrell Clarke	February 2021
Rochdale (34)	Robbie Stockdale	July 2021
Salford (2)	Gary Bowyer	May 2021
Scunthorpe (32)	Neil Cox	August 2020
Sutton (–)	Matt Gray	May 2019
Swindon (35)		
Stevenage (7)	Alex Revell	February 2020
Tranmere (3)	Micky Mellon+	May 2021
Walsall (38)	Matt Taylor	May 2021

Number of changes since elected to Football League: Stevenage 2010, Crawley 2011, Forest Green 2017, Salford 2019, Harrogate 2020, Sutton 2021. Since returning: Colchester 1992, Carlisle 2005, Exeter 2008, Mansfield 2013, Newport 2013, Bristol Rov 2015, Tranmere 2018, Leyton Orient 2019, Barrow 2020

MANAGERIAL CHANGES 2020–21

PREMIER LEAGUE

Chelsea:	Out – Frank Lampard (Jan 2021); In – Thomas Tuchel
Crystal Palace:	Out – Roy Hodgson (May 2021); In – Patrick Vieira
Everton:	Out – Carlo Ancelotti (Jun 2021); In– Rafael Benitez
Fulham:	Out – Scott Parker (Jun 2021); In – Marco Silva
Sheffield Utd:	Out – Chris Wilder (Mar 2021); In – Slavisa Jokanovic
Tottenham:	Out – Jose Mourinho (Apr 2021); In– Nuno Espirito Santo
WBA:	Out – Slaven Bilic (Dec 2020); In – Sam Allardyce (Out May 2021); In– Valerien Ismael
Wolves:	Out – Nuno Espirito Santo (May 2021); In– Bruno Lage

CHAMPIONSHIP

Barnsley:	Out – Gerhard Struber (Oct 2020); In – Valerien Ismael (Out Jun 2021); In – Markus Schopp
Birmingham:	Out – Aitor Karanka (Mar 2021); In – Lee Bowyer
Bournemouth:	Out – Jason Tindall (Feb 2021); In– Scott Parker
Bristol City:	Out – Dean Holden (Feb 2021); In – Nigel Pearson
Cardiff:	Out – Neil Harris (Jan 2021); In – Mick McCarthy
Derby:	Out – Phillip Cocu (Nov 2020); In – Wayne Rooney
Nottm Forest:	Out – Sabri Lamouchi (Oct 2020); In – Chris Hughton
Preston:	Out – Alex Neil (Mar 2021); In – Frankie McAvoy
Reading:	Out – Mark Bowen (Aug 2020); In – Veljko Paunovic
Sheffield Wed:	Out – Garry Monk (Nov 2020); In – Tony Pulis (Out Dec 2020); In– Darren Moore
Watford:	Out – Vladimir Ivic (Dec 2020); In – Xisco Munoz

LEAGUE ONE

AFC Wimbledon:	Out – Glyn Hodges (Jan 2021); In – Mark Robinson
Bristol Rov:	Out – Ben Garner (Nov 2021); In – Paul Tisdale; (Out Feb 2021); In – Joey Barton
Burton:	Out – Jake Buxton (Dec 2020); In – Jimmy Floyd Hasselbaink
Charlton:	Out – Lee Bowyer (Mar 2021); In – Nigel Adkins
Doncaster:	Out – Darren Moore (Mar 2021); In – Richie Wellens
Fleetwood:	Out – Joey Barton (Jan 2021); In – Simon Grayson
Ipswich:	Out – Paul Lambert (Feb 2021); In – Paul Cook
Northampton:	Out – Keith Curle (Feb 2021); In – Jon Brady
Portsmouth:	Out – Kenny Jackett (Mar 2021); In – Danny Cowley
Shrewsbury:	Out – Sam Ricketts (Nov 2020); In – Steve Cotterill
Sunderland:	Out – Phil Parkinson (Nov 2020); In – Lee Johnson
Swindon:	Out – Richie Wellens (Nov 2020); In – John Sheridan; (Out Apr 2021); In – John McGreal (Out – Jun 2021)
Wigan:	Out – John Sheridan (Nov 2021); In – Leam Richardson

LEAGUE TWO

Barrow:	Out – David Dunn (Dec 2020); In – Michael Jolley (Out Feb 2021); In– Mark Cooper
Bradford:	Out – Stuart McCall (Dec 2020); In – Conor Sellars/Mark Trueman (Out May 2021); In– Derek Adams
Colchester:	Out – Steve Ball (Feb 2021); In – Hayden Mullins
Forest Green:	Out – Mark Cooper (Apr 2021); In – Rob Edwards
Grimsby:	Out – Ian Holloway (Dec 2020); In – Paul Hurst
Leyton Orient:	Out – Ross Embleton (Feb 2021); In – Kenny Jackett
Mansfield:	Out – Graham Coughlan (Oct 2020); In – Nigel Clough
Morecambe:	Out – Derek Adams (June 2021); In – Stephen Robinson
Oldham:	Out – Harry Kewell (Mar 2021); In – Keith Curle
Port Vale:	Out – John Askey (Jan 2021); In – Darrell Clarke
Salford:	Out – Graham Alexander (Oct 2020); In – Richie Wellens; (Out Mar 2021); In – Gary Bowyer
Southend:	Out – Mark Molesley (Apr 2021); In – Phil Brown
Tranmere:	Out – Mike Jackson (Oct 2020); In – Keith Hill (Out May 2021); In – Micky Mellon
Walsall:	Out – Darrell Clarke (Feb 2021); In – Matt Taylor

EMIRATES FA CUP 2020–21

FIRST ROUND

Non-league sides have a field day with ten victories over EFL opposition. Pride of place goes to Chorley, who overturn a 2-0 deficit at Wigan through Elliot Newbuy, Harry Cardwell and Connor Hall's extra-time strike. Wayne Rooney's younger brother John scores from inside his own half and a second goal from Alex Reid give Stockport victory at Rochdale. Three other teams overcome League One opponents. Two goals from Darlington's Adam Campbell account for Swindon; Oxford City come from behind to defeat Northampton with a James Roberts header and Josh Ashby's penalty; Barnet make light of the dismissal of Matt Preston to see off Burton with the only goal of the tie from Wesley Fonguck. Two penalties converted by Stephen Gleeson, either side of Krystian Pearce's goal, enable Solihull to get the better of Scunthorpe. Scott Wilson's brace and one from Mitch Brundle carry Dagenham and Redbridge to victory over Grimsby, while King's Lynn defeat Port Vale with Sonny Carey on the mark. Through on penalties go Marine against Colchester and Boreham Wood at the expense of Southend. Craziest tie of the round is at Torquay, where Tom Nichols completes a hat-trick as Crawley recover from 5-3 down in extra-time to win 6-5. In the meeting of two former FA Cup winners, Portsmouth beat Ipswich with Sean Raggett's goal in extra-time.

Barrow 0 AFC Wimbledon 0	Havant & Waterlooville 1 Cray Valley 0
(aet, AFC Wimbledon won 4-2 on pens)	Hayes & Yeading 2 Carlisle 2
Banbury 1 Canvey Island 2	(aet, Carlisle won 4-3 on pens)
Barnet 1 Burton 0	Hull 2 Fleetwood 0
Bolton 2 Crewe 3	Ipswich 2 Portsmouth 3 (aet)
Boreham Wood 3 Southend 3	Leyton Orient 1 Newport 2
(aet, Boreham Wood won 4-3 on pens)	Lincoln 6 Forest Green 2
Brackley 3 Bishop's Stortford 3	Maldon & Tiptree 0 Morecambe 1
(aet, Brackley won 3-2 on pens)	Oxford City 2 Northampton 1
Bromley 0 Yeovil 1	Oxford Utd 1 Peterborough 2
Cambridge 0 Shrewsbury 2	Port Vale 0 King's Lynn 1
Charlton 0 Plymouth 1	Rochdale 1 Stockport 2
Cheltenham 3 South Shields 1	Salford 2 Hartlepool 0
Colchester 1 Marine 1	Scunthorpe 2 Solihull 3
(aet, Marine won 5-3 on pens)	Stevenage 2 Concord 2
Dag & Red 3 Grimsby 1	(aet, Stevenage won 5-4 on pens)
Eastbourne 0 Blackpool 3	Sunderland 0 Mansfield 1
Eastleigh 0 MK Dons 0	Swindon 0 Darlington 2
(aet, MK Dons won 4-3 on pens)	Tonbridge 0 Bradford 7
Exeter 2 AFC Fylde 1	Torquay 5 Crawley 6(aet)
FC Utd of Manchester 1 Doncaster 5	Tranmere 2 Accrington 1
Gillingham 3 Woking 2	Walsall 1 Bristol Rov 2
Hampton & Richmond 2 Oldham 3	Wigan 2 Chorley 3 (aet)
Harrogate 4 Skelmersdale 1	

SECOND ROUND

Chorley trail after two minutes at Peterborough, but reach round three for the first time in the club's history with replies from Connor Hall and a deflected Lewis Baines effort. They are joined by Boreham Wood, Marine and Stockport who win all non-league ties. Dagenham and Redbridge are set for a penalty shoot-out at Mansfield until Nicky Maynard's winner for the home side in stoppage-time of extra-time. Oxford City and Solihull also force extra-time before bowing out. Bristol Rovers and Portsmouth both score six.

AFC Wimbledon 1 Crawley 2
Barnet 0 MK Dons 1
Bradford 1 Oldham 2
Bristol Rov 6 Darlington 0
Canvey Island 0 Boreham Wood 3
Carlisle 1 Doncaster 2
Cheltenham 2 Crewe 1 (aet)
Gillingham 2 Exeter 3
Harrogate 0 Blackpool 4
Mansfield 2 Dag & Red 1 (aet)
Marine 1 Havant &Waterlooville 0 (aet)
Morecambe 4 Solihull 2 (aet)

Newport 3 Salford 0
Peterborough 1 Chorley 2
Plymouth 2 Lincoln 0
Portsmouth 6 King's Lynn 1
Shrewsbury 1 Oxford City 0 (aet)
Stevenage 1 Hull 1
(aet, Stevenage won 6-5 on pens)
Stockport 3 Yeovil 2 (aet)
Tranmere 1 Brackley 0

THIRD ROUND

Marine and Crawley deliver the essence of the FA Cup on a day when football is again scarred by
the pandemic. The eighth-tier Merseyside club's tie against Tottenham attracts attention from
around the world and they are within inches of the lead when Neil Kengni's 35-yard shot strikes
the crossbar. The Premier League side eventually take command with a hat-trick in 13 minutes
by Carlos Vinicius and a goal by Alfie Devine which makes him their youngest-ever scorer at 16
years and 163 days. They win 5-0, while Marine's consolation is securing their long-term future
through prizemoney, TV fees and selling 30,000 virtual tickets. League Two Crawley are shock
3-0 winners over Leeds, a margin achieved by only a handful of giant-killing teams down the
years. Nick Tsaroulla, with his first senior goal, and Ashley Nadesan are on the mark in the space
of three second-half minutes, then Jordan Tunnicliffe seals a notable success. Chorley carry
the non-league flag into the last 16 with a 2-0 victory Derby, who field a team of youth players
with the club's senior squad in Covid isolation. Connor Hall and Mike Calverley do the honours.
Another outbreak of the virus forces Aston Villa to rely on their youngsters against Liverpool,
who go through 4-1. There is no respite for struggling West Bromwich Albion, who bow out on
penalties at Blackpool, while two other top division teams need penalties to make progress.
Burnley are thrown a lifeline by Matej Vydra's stoppage-time equaliser against MK Dons. Brighton
are also held 1-1, by Newport. But there is sense of relief for Sheffield United, who record their
first win of the season – 3-2 against Bristol Rovers.

Aston Villa 1 Liverpool 4
Arsenal 2 Newcastle 0 (aet)
Barnsley 2 Tranmere 0
Blackburn 0 Doncaster 1
Blackpool 2 WBA 2
(aet, Blackpool won 3-2 on pens)
Boreham Wood 0 Millwall 2
Brentford 2 Middlesbrough 1
Bristol City 2 Portsmouth 3
Bristol Rov 2 Sheffield Utd 3
Burnley 1 MK Dons 1
(aet, Burnley won 4-3 on pens)
Chelsea 4 Morecambe 0
Cheltenham 2 Mansfield 1 (aet)
Chorley 2 Derby 0
Crawley 3 Leeds 0
Everton 2 Rotherham 1(aet)
Exeter 0 Sheffield Wed 2

Huddersfield 2 Plymouth 3
Luton 1 Reading 0
Manchester City 3 Birmingham 0
Manchester Utd 1 Watford 0
Marine 0 Tottenham 5
Newport 1 Brighton 1
(aet, Brighton won 4-3 on pens)
Norwich 2 Coventry 0
Nottm Forest 1 Cardiff 0
Oldham 1 Bournemouth 4
(played at Bournemouth)
QPR 0 Fulham 2 (aet)
Southampton 2 Shrewsbury 0
Stevenage 0 Swansea 2
Stockport 0 West Ham 1
Stoke 0 **Leicester** 4
Wolves 1 Crystal Palace 0
Wycombe 4 Preston 1

FOURTH ROUND

Cheltenham come closest to the fourth round delivering an upset. The League Two team protect Alfie May's goal until the 81st minute when Phil Foden equalises and Gabriel Jesus and Ferran Torres then see Manchester City through. Chorley proudly fly the non-league flag, restricting Wolves to a single goal by Vitinha, his first for the club, and posing problems throughout for their opponents. So do Crawley against Bournemouth, who have Jack Wilshere on the mark as he bids to resurrect his career at the Championship club. Holders Arsenal go out to an own goal by Gabriel against Southampton. Manchester United and Liverpool provide superb entertainment, in contrast to their goalless Premier League draw a week earlier, with a trademark free-kick from Bruno Fernandes giving United the edge. Tammy Abraham's hat-trick cheers Chelsea, but it's not enough to save Frank Lampard from the sack for indifferent league results.

Barnsley 1 Norwich 0	Fulham 0 Burnley 3
Bournemouth 2 Crawley 1	Manchester Utd 3 Liverpool 2
Brentford 1 **Leicester** 3	Millwall 0 Bristol City 3
Brighton 2 Blackpool 1	Sheffield Utd 2 Plymouth 1
Chelsea 3 Luton 1	Southampton 1 Arsenal 0
Cheltenham 1 Manchester City 3	Swansea 5 Nottm Forest 1
Chorley 0 Wolves 1	West Ham 4 Doncaster 0
Everton 3 Sheffield Wed 0	Wycombe 1 Tottenham 4

FIFTH ROUND

Everton prevail in a nine-goal thriller at Goodison Park after an outstanding performance by Gylfi Sigurdsson. The Iceland midfielder converts a penalty, provides the assist for one of Richarlison's two goals, then lifts a pass over the Tottenham defence for substitute Bernard's extra-time winner. Tammy Abraham also has a major influence on Chelsea's progress, scoring the only goal at Oakwell, then clearing off his own line to deny Barnsley's Michael Sollbauer in Thomas Tuchel's first FA Cup tie as manager. Manchester City's win at Swansea is their 15th in succession in all domestic competitions – a record for an English top-flight club. Bournemouth, under caretaker-manager Jonathan Woodgate, reach the quarter-finals for the first time in 64 years with victory at Turf Moor to keep Championship interest alive in the competition.

Barnsley 0 **Chelsea** 1	Manchester Utd 1 West Ham 0 (aet)
Burnley 0 Bournemouth 2	Sheffield United 1 Bristol City 0
Everton 5 Tottenham 4 (aet)	Swansea 1 Manchester City 3
Leicester 1 Brighton 0	Wolves 0 Southampton 2

SIXTH ROUND

Two goals by Kelechi Iheanacho, taking his tally to seven in four league and cup games, point Leicester to a place in the semi-finals for the first time since 1982 in Brendan Rodgers' 100th game in charge. Nathan Redmond is also on the mark twice, sets up Moussa Djenepo for his side's other goal and Southampton have two more ruled out by VAR in a one-sided tie against Bournemouth. Chelsea keep a clean sheet for the seventh successive match in domestic and European competitions under new manager Thomas Tuchel, sealing their place in the last four with a stoppage-time Hakim Ziyech strike. Manchester City score twice in the final six minutes of normal time through Ilkay Gundogan and Kevin De Bruyne to win at Goodison Park.

Bournemouth 0 Southampton 3	Everton 0 Manchester City 2
Chelsea 2 Sheffield Utd 0	**Leicester** 3 Manchester Utd 1

SEMI-FINALS (both at Wembley)

Hakim Ziyech and Kelechi Iheanacho both score in the 55th minute to send their teams through. Timo Werner's pace set up Ziyech to end Manchester City's bid for an unprecedented quadruple. Iheanacho continues his prolific form to earn Leicester a place in the final for the first time since 1969.

Chelsea 1 Manchester City 0   **Leicester** 1 Southampton 0

FINAL

Great goals, from the likes of Ricky Villa and Steven Gerrard, have graced Wembley finals. So too have memorable goalkeeping performances, none finer perhaps than those from Jim Montgomery and Petr Cech. But rarely in modern times has a combination of both delivered such a dramatic – and emotional – outcome as this one. Leicester's Premier League title win against all the odds in season 2015-16 will always be part of football folklore. This success can take a worthy place alongside that achievement after a wonderful 28-yard strike from Youri Tielemans and two world-class saves by Kasper Schmeichel from Ben Chilwell and Mason Mount. A Chelsea equaliser ruled out by VAR confirmed the club's first victory in the competition on an evening when the game discovered its voice again and found, in the winners, a cheerleader for every club in the country, not just those who wanted to destroy its fabric in a breakaway European Super League. A crowd of 21,000, although less than a quarter of capacity, hopefully signalled the end to empty grounds and soulless matches. Looking down from on high was the face, adorning one of the banners, of the late Leicester owner Vichai Srivaddhanaprabha, who died in the 2018 helicopter crash at the King Power Stadium. His son Top, carrying on the family connection, was a proud onlooker here and, fittingly, was beckoned forward by Schmeichel for the trophy presentation. That moment set the seal on a special occasion. Not a great game overall, but certainly one to remember.

CHELSEA 0 LEICESTER CITY 1 (Tielemans 63)
Wembley (21,000); Saturday, May 15, 2021

Chelsea (3-4-2-1): Arrizabalaga, James, Thiago Silva, Rudiger, Azpilicueta (capt) (Hudson-Odoi 76), Kante, Jorginho (Havertz 75), Marcos Alonso (Chilwell 68), Ziyech (Pulisic 68), Mount, Werner (Giroud 82). **Subs not used**: E Mendy, Zouma, Gilmour, Emerson. **Booked**: Werner. **Manager**: Thomas Tuchel.
Leicester City (3-4-1-2): Schmeichel (capt), Fofana, Evans (Albrighton 34), Soyuncu, Castagne, Tielemans, Ndidi, Thomas (Morgan 82), Ayoze Perez (Choudhury 82), Iheanacho (Maddison 67), Vardy. **Subs not used**: Ward, Amartey, Pereira, N Mendy, Praet. **Booked**: Fofana. **Manager**: Brendan Rodgers
Referee: Michael Oliver (Northumberland). **Half-time**: 0-0

HOW THEY REACHED THE FINAL

Chelsea
Round 3: 4-0 home to Morecambe (Mount, Werner, Hudson-Odoi, Havertz)
Round 4: 3-1 home to Luton (Abraham 11, 17, 74)
Round 5: 1-0 away to Barnsley (Abraham)
Round 6: 2-0 home to Sheffield Utd (Norwood og, Ziyech)
Semi-finals: 1-0 v Manchester City (Ziyech)

Leicester City
Round 3: 4-0 away to Stoke (Justin, Albrighton, Ayoze Perez, Barnes)
Round 4: 3-1 away to Brentford (Under, Tielemans pen, Maddison)
Round 5: 1-0 home to Brighton (Iheanacho)
Round 6: 3-1 home to Manchester Utd (Iheanacho 2, Tielemans)
Semi-finals: 1-0 v Southampton (Iheanacho)

Leading scorers: 4 Abraham (Chelsea), Iheanacho (Leicester), Madine (Blackpool), May (Cheltenham), Nichols (Crawley); 3 Hall (Chorley), King (Bournemouth), Mellish (Carlisle), Nadesan (Crawley), Richarlison (Everton), Salah (Liverpool), Samuel (Gillingham), Vinicius (Tottenham), Whiteman (Doncaster)

FINAL FACTS AND FIGURES

● Leicester lifted the FA Cup for the first time, having lost their four previous finals against Wolves (1949), Tottenham (1961), Manchester United (1963) and Manchester City (1960)

● Jamie Vardy, who started his career with Stocksbridge and Halifax, became the first player to feature in every round of the competition from the preliminary round to the final – 13 stages.

● Brendan Rodgers is the second manager after Sir Alex Ferguson to win the English and Scottish FA Cup, having been successful with Celtic in 2017 and 2018. Sir Alex won four times with Aberdeen and five with Manchester United.

● Youri Tielemans was the third Belgian player to score and win the trophy after Eden Hazard with Chelsea against Manchester United in 2018 and Kevin De Bruyne with Manchester City against Watford in 2019.

● Five of Leicester's match-day squad were part of the club's Premier League title-winning line-up in season 2015-16 – Kasper Schmeichel, Jamie Vardy. Mark Albrighton, Wes Morgan and Daniel Amartey.

● At 37 years and 114 days, Wes Morgan was the oldest outfield player in a final since Teddy Sheringham for West Ham against Liverpool in 2006 aged 40 years and 41 days.

● Kasper Schmeichel followed in the footsteps of his father Peter, a three-time FA Cup winner with Manchester United. He was the first goalkeeper to captain the winning side since Arsenal's David Seaman against Southampton in 2003.

● Chelsea became the first team to lose successive finals since Newcastle were beaten by Arsenal in 1998 and by Manchester United the following year.

● Olivier Giroud appeared in his sixth final in the competition. Only Ashley Cole (8), Ryan Giggs (7) and Roy Keane (7) have appeared in more in modern times.

THE THINGS THEY SAY...

'He is one of the greats of our business. I couldn't have more respect for what he did and how long he did it at this level' – **Jurgen Klopp**, Liverpool manager, on Roy Hodgson stepping down after 45 years in management.

'Today is a dark day for the beautiful game and a critical moment for English football. We must acknowledge the mistakes of the past and ensure that we do everything possible to prevent them from being repeated' – **Mark Bullingham**, chief executive of the FA, after an independent report into historic child sex abuse in the game criticised the governing body for not doing enough to protect youngsters.

FA CUP FINAL SCORES & TEAMS

1872   Wanderers 1 (Betts) Bowen, Alcock, Bonsor, Welch; Betts, Crake, Hooman, Lubbock, Thompson, Vidal, Wollaston. Note: Betts played under the pseudonym 'AH Chequer' on the day of the match **Royal Engineers 0** Capt Merriman; Capt Marindin, Lieut Addison, Lieut Cresswell, Lieut Mitchell, Lieut Renny-Tailyour, Lieut Rich, Lieut George Goodwyn, Lieut Muirhead, Lieut Cotter, Lieut Bogle

1873   Wanderers 2 (Wollaston, Kinnaird) Bowen; Thompson, Welch, Kinnaird, Howell, Wollaston, Sturgis, Rev Stewart, Kenyon-Slaney, Kingsford, Bonsor **Oxford University 0** Kirke-Smith; Leach, Mackarness, Birley, Longman, Chappell-Maddison, Dixon, Paton, Vidal, Sumner, Ottaway. March 29; 3, 000; A Stair

1874 Oxford University 2 (Mackarness, Patton) Neapean; Mackarness, Birley, Green, Vidal, Ottaway, Benson, Patton, Rawson, Chappell-Maddison, Rev Johnson **Royal Engineers 0** Capt Merriman; Major Marindin, Lieut W Addison, Gerald Onslow, Lieut Oliver, Lieut Digby, Lieut Renny-Tailyour, Lieut Rawson, Lieut Blackman Lieut Wood, Lieut von Donop. March 14; 2, 000; A Stair

1875   Royal Engineers 1 (Renny-Tailyour) Capt Merriman; Lieut Sim, Lieut Onslow, Lieut (later Sir) Ruck, Lieut Von Donop, Lieut Wood, Lieut Rawson, Lieut Stafford, Capt Renny-Tailyour, Lieut Mein, Lieut Wingfield-Stratford **Old Etonians 1** (Bonsor) Thompson, Benson, Lubbock, Wilson, Kinnaird, (Sir) Stronge, Patton, Farmer, Bonsor, Ottaway, Kenyon-Slaney. March 13; 2, 000; CW Alcock. aet **Replay – Royal Engineers 2** (Renny-Tailyour, Stafford) Capt Merriman; Lieut Sim, Lieut Onslow, Lieut (later Sir) Ruck, Lieut Von Donop, Lieut Wood, Lieut Rawson, Lieut Stafford, Capt Renny-Tailyour, Lieut Mein, Lieut Wingfield-Stratford **Old Etonians 0** Capt Drummond-Moray; Kinnaird, (Sir) Stronge, Hammond, Lubbock, Patton, Farrer, Bonsor, Lubbock, Wilson, Farmer. March 16; 3, 000; CW Alcock

1876   Wanderers 1 (Edwards) Greig; Stratford, Lindsay, Chappell-Maddison, Birley, Wollaston, C Heron, G Heron, Edwards, Kenrick, Hughes **Old Etonians 1** (Bonsor) Hogg; Rev Welldon, Lyttleton, Thompson, Kinnaird, Meysey, Kenyon-Slaney, Lyttleton, Sturgis, Bonsor, Allene. March 11; 3, 500; WS Rawson aet **Replay – Wanderers 3** (Wollaston, Hughes 2) Greig, Stratford, Lindsay, Chappel-Maddison, Birley, Wollaston, C Heron, G Heron, Edwards, Kenrick, Hughes **Old Etonians 0** Hogg, Lubbock, Lyttleton, Farrer, Kinnaird, (Sir) Stronge, Kenyon-Slaney, Lyttleton, Sturgis, Bonsor, Allene. March 18; 1, 500; WS Rawson

1877   Wanderers 2 (Kenrick, Lindsay) Kinnaird; Birley, Denton, Green, Heron, Hughes, Kenrick, Lindsay, Stratford, Wace, Wollaston **Oxford University 1** (Kinnaird og) Allington; Bain, Dunnell, Rev Savory, Todd, Waddington, Rev Fernandez, Otter, Parry, Rawson. March 24; 3, 000; SH Wright, aet

1878   Wanderers 3 (Kinnaird, Kenrick 2) (Sir) Kirkpatrick; Stratford, Lindsay, Kinnaird, Green, Wollaston, Heron, Wylie, Wace, Denton, Kenrick **Royal Engineers 1** (Morris) Friend; Cowan, (Sir) Morris, Mayne, Heath, Haynes, Lindsay, Hedley, (Sir) Bond, Barnet, Ruck. March 23; 4, 500; SR Bastard

1879   Old Etonians 1 (Clerke) Hawtrey; Edward, Bury, Kinnaird, Lubbock, Clerke, Pares, Goodhart, Whitfield, Chevalier, Beaufoy **Clapham Rovers 0** Birkett; Ogilvie, Field, Bailey, Prinsep, Rawson, Stanley, Scott, Bevington, Growse, Keith-Falconer. March 29; 5, 000; CW Alcock

1880   Clapham Rovers 1 (Lloyd-Jones) Birkett; Ogilvie, Field, Weston, Bailey, Stanley, Brougham, Sparkes, Barry, Ram, Lloyd-Jones **Oxford University 0** Parr; Wilson, King, Phillips, Rogers, Heygate, Rev Childs, Eyre, (Dr) Crowdy, Hill, Lubbock. April 10; 6, 000; Major Marindin

1881   Old Carthusians 3 (Page, Wynyard, Parry) Gillett; Norris, (Sir) Colvin, Prinsep, (Sir) Vintcent, Hansell, Richards, Page, Wynyard, Parry, Todd **Old Etonians 0** Rawlinson; Foley, French, Kinnaird, Farrer, Macauley, Goodhart, Whitfield, Novelli, Anderson, Chevallier. April 9; 4, 000; W Pierce-Dix

1882   Old Etonians 1 (Macauley) Rawlinson; French, de Paravicini, Kinnaird, Foley, Novelli, Dunn, Macauley, Goodhart, Chevallier, Anderson **Blackburn Rov 0** Howarth; McIntyre, Suter, Hargreaves, Sharples, Hargreaves, Avery, Brown, Strachan, Douglas, Duckworth. March 25; 6, 500; JC Clegg

1883   Blackburn Olympic 2 (Matthews, Costley) Hacking; Ward, Warburton, Gibson, Astley, Hunter, Dewhurst, Matthews, Wilson, Costley, Yates **Old Etonians 1** (Goodhart) Rawlinson; French, de Paravicini, Kinnaird, Foley, Dunn, Bainbridge, Chevallier, Anderson, Goodhart, Macauley. March 31; 8, 000; Major Marindin, aet

1884   Blackburn Rov 2 (Sowerbutts, Forrest) Arthur; Suter, Beverley, McIntyre, Forrest, Hargreaves, Brown, Inglis Sowerbutts, Douglas, Lofthouse **Queen's Park 1** (Christie) Gillespie; MacDonald, Arnott, Gow,

Campbell, Allan, Harrower, (Dr) Smith, Anderson, Watt, Christie. March 29; 4, 000; Major Marindin

1885   Blackburn Rov 2 (Forrest, Brown) Arthur; Turner, Suter, Haworth, McIntyre, Forrest, Sowerbutts, Lofthouse, Douglas, Brown, Fecitt **Queen's Park 0** Gillespie; Arnott, MacLeod, MacDonald, Campbell, Sellar, Anderson, McWhammel, Hamilton, Allan, Gray. April 4; 12, 500; Major Marindin

1886   Blackburn Rov 0 Arthur; Turner, Suter, Heyes, Forrest, McIntyre, Douglas, Strachan, Sowerbutts, Fecitt, Brown **WBA 0** Roberts; Green, Bell, Horton, Perry, Timmins, Woodhall, Green, Bayliss, Loach, Bell. April 3; 15, 000; Major Marindin **Replay – Blackburn Rov 2** (Sowerbutts, Brown) Arthur; Turner, Suter, Walton, Forrest, McIntyre, Douglas, Strachan, Sowerbutts, Fecitt, Brown **WBA 0** Roberts; Green, Bell, Horton, Perry, Timmins, Woodhall, Green, Bayliss, Loach, Bell. April 10; 12, 000; Major Marindin

1887   Aston Villa 2 (Hodgetts, Hunter) Warner; Coulton, Simmonds, Yates, Dawson, Burton, Davis, Albert Brown, Hunter, Vaughton, Hodgetts **WBA 0** Roberts; Green, Aldridge, Horton, Perry, Timmins, Woodhall, Green, Bayliss, Paddock, Pearson. April 2; 15, 500; Major Marindin

1888   WBA 2 (Bayliss), Woodhall) Roberts; Aldridge, Green, Horton, Perry, Timmins, Woodhall, Bassett, Bayliss, Wilson, Pearson **Preston 1** (Dewhurst) Mills-Roberts; Howarth, Holmes, Ross, Russell, Gordon, Ross, Goodall, Dewhurst, Drummond, Graham. March 24; 19, 000; Major Marindin

1889   Preston 3 (Dewhurst, Ross, Thomson) Mills-Roberts; Howarth, Holmes, Drummond, Russell, Graham, Gordon, Goodall, Dewhurst, Thompson, Ross **Wolves 0** Baynton; Baugh, Mason, Fletcher, Allen, Lowder, Hunter, Wykes, Brodie, Wood, Knight. March 30; 22, 000; Major Marindin

1890   Blackburn Rov 6 (Lofthouse, Jack Southworth, Walton, Townley 3) Horne; James Southworth, Forbes, Barton, Dewar, Forrest, Lofthouse, Campbell, Jack Southworth, Walton, Townley **Sheffield Wed 1** (Bennett) Smith; Morley, Brayshaw, Dungworth, Betts, Waller, Ingram, Woolhouse, Bennett, Mumford, Cawley. March 29; 20, 000; Major Marindin

1891   Blackburn Rov 3 (Dewar, Jack Southworth, Townley) Pennington; Brandon, Forbes, Barton, Dewar, Forrest, Lofthouse, Walton, Southworth, Hall, Townley **Notts Co 1** (Oswald) Thraves; Ferguson, Hendry, Osborne, Calderhead, Shelton, McGregror, McInnes Oswald, Locker, Daft. March 21; 23, 000; CJ Hughes

1892   WBA 3 (Geddes, Nicholls, Reynolds) Reader; Nicholson, McCulloch, Reynolds, Perry, Groves, Bassett, McLeod, Nicholls, Pearson, Geddes **Aston Villa 0** Warner; Evans, Cox, Devey, Cowan, Baird, Athersmith, Devey, Dickson, Hodgetts, Campbell. March 19; 32, 810; JC Clegg

1893   Wolves 1 (Allen) Rose; Baugh, Swift, Malpass, Allen, Kinsey, Topham, Wykes, Butcher, Griffin, Wood **Everton 0** Williams; Kelso, Howarth, Boyle, Holt, Stewart, Latta, Gordon, Maxwell, Chadwick, Milward. March 25; 45, 000; CJ Hughes

1894   Notts Co 4 (Watson, Logan 3) Toone; Harper, Hendry, Bramley, Calderhead, Shelton, Watson, Donnelly, Logan Bruce, Daft **Bolton 1** (Cassidy) Sutcliffe; Somerville, Jones , Gardiner, Paton, Hughes, Tannahill, Wilson, Cassidy, Bentley, Dickenson. March 31; 37, 000; CJ Hughes

1895   Aston Villa 1 (Chatt) Wilkes; Spencer, Welford, Reynolds, Cowan, Russell, Athersmith Chatt, Devey, Hodgetts, Smith **WBA 0** Reader; Williams, Horton, Perry, Higgins, Taggart, Bassett, McLeod, Richards, Hutchinson, Banks. April 20; 42, 560; J Lewis

1896   Sheffield Wed 2 (Spikesley 2) Massey; Earp, Langley, Brandon, Crawshaw, Petrie, Brash, Brady, Bell, Davis, Spikesley **Wolves 1** (Black) Tennant; Baugh, Dunn, Owen, Malpass, Griffiths, Tonks, Henderson, Beats, Wood, Black. April 18; 48, 836; Lieut Simpson

1897   Aston Villa 3 (Campbell, Wheldon, Crabtree) Whitehouse; Spencer, Reynolds, Evans, Cowan, Crabtree, Athersmith, Devey, Campbell, Wheldon, Cowan **Everton 2** (Bell, Boyle) Menham; Meechan, Storrier, Boyle, Holt, Stewart, Taylor, Bell, Hartley, Chadwick, Milward. April 10; 65, 891; J Lewis

1898   Nottm Forest 3 (Capes 2, McPherson) Allsop; Ritchie, Scott, Forman, McPherson, Wragg, McInnes, Richards, Benbow, Capes, Spouncer **Derby 1** (Bloomer) Fryer; Methven, Leiper, Cox, Goodall, Bloomer, Boag, Stevenson, McQueen. April 16; 62, 017; J Lewis

1899   Sheffield Utd 4 (Bennett, Beers, Almond, Priest) Foulke; Thickett, Boyle, Johnson, Morren, Needham, Bennett, Beers, Hedley, Almond, Priest **Derby 1** (Boag) Fryer; Methven, Staley, Cox, Paterson, May, Arkesden, Bloomer, Boag, McDonald, Allen. April 15; 73, 833; A Scragg

1900   Bury 4 (McLuckie 2, Wood, Plant) Thompson; Darroch, Davidson, Pray, Leeming, Ross, Richards,

150

Wood, McLuckie, Sagar, Plant **Southampton 0** Robinson; Meechan, Durber, Meston, Chadwick, Petrie, Turner, Yates, Farrell; Wood, Milward. April 21; 68, 945; A Kingscott

1901 Tottenham 2 (Brown 2) Clawley; Erentz, Tait, Morris, Hughes, Jones, Smith, Cameron, Brown, Copeland, Kirwan **Sheffield Utd 2** (Priest, Bennett) Foulke; Thickett, Boyle, Johnson, Morren, Needham, Bennett, Field, Hedley, Priest, Lipsham. April 20; 110, 820; A Kingscott **Replay – Tottenham 3** (Cameron, Smith, Brown) Clawley; Erentz, Tait, Morris, Hughes, Jones, Smith, Cameron, Brown, Copeland, Kirwan. **Sheffield Utd 1** (Priest) Foulke; Thickett, Boyle, Johnson, Morren, Needham, Bennett, Field, Hedley, Priest, Lipsham. April 27; 20, 470; A Kingscott

1902 Sheffield Utd 1 (Common) Foulke; Thickett, Boyle, Needham, Wilkinson, Johnson, Bennett, Common, Hedley, Priest, Lipsham **Southampton 1** (Wood) Robinson; Fry, Molyneux, Meston, Bowman, Lee, Turner, Wood Brown, Chadwick, Turner. April 19; 76, 914; T Kirkham. **Replay – Sheffield Utd 2** (Hedley, Barnes) Foulke; Thickett, Boyle, Needham, Wilkinson, Johnson, Barnes, Common, Hedley, Priest, Lipsham **Southampton 1** (Brown) Robinson; Fry, Molyneux, Meston, Bowman, Lee, Turner, Wood, Brown, Chadwick, Turner. April 26; 33, 068; T Kirkham

1903 Bury 6 (Leeming 2, Ross, Sagar, Wood, Plant) Monteith; Lindsey, McEwen, Johnston, Thorpe, Ross, Richards, Wood, Sagar Leeming, Plant **Derby 0** Fryer; Methven, Morris, Warren, Goodall, May, Warrington, York, Boag, Richards, Davis. April 18; 63, 102; J Adams

1904 Manchester City 1 (Meredith) Hillman; McMahon, Burgess, Frost, Hynds, Ashworth, Meredith, Livingstone, Gillespie, Turnbull, Booth **Bolton 0** Davies; Brown, Struthers, Clifford, Greenhalgh, Freebairn, Stokes, Marsh, Yenson, White, Taylor. April 23; 61, 374; AJ Barker

1905 Aston Villa 2 (Hampton 2) George; Spencer, Miles, Pearson, Leake, Windmill, Brawn, Garratty, Hampton, Bache, Hall **Newcastle 0** Lawrence; McCombie, Carr, Gardner, Aitken, McWilliam, Rutherford, Howie, Appleyard, Veitch, Gosnell. April 15; 101, 117; PR Harrower

1906 Everton 1 (Young) Scott; Crelley, Walter Balmer, Makepeace, Taylor, Abbott, Sharp, Bolton, Young, Settle, Hardman **Newcastle 0** Lawrence; McCombie, Carr, Gardner, Aitken, McWilliam, Rutherford, Howie, Orr, Veitch, Gosnell. April 21; 75, 609; F Kirkham

1907 Sheffield Wed 2 (Stewart, Simpson) Lyall; Layton, Burton, Brittleton, Crawshaw, Bartlett, Chapman, Bradshaw, Wilson, Stewart, Simpson **Everton 1** (Sharp) Scott; Walter Balmer, Bob Balmer, Makepeace, Taylor, Abbott, Sharp, Bolton, Young, Settle, Hardman. April 20; 84, 594; N Whittaker

1908 Wolves 3 (Hunt, Hedley, Harrison) Lunn; Jones, Collins, Rev Hunt, Wooldridge, Bishop, Harrison, Shelton, Hedley, Radford, Pedley **Newcastle 1** (Howie) Lawrence; McCracken, Pudan, Gardner, Veitch, McWilliam, Rutherford, Howie, Appleyard, Speedie, Wilson. April 25; 74, 697; TP Campbell

1909 Manchester Utd 1 (Sandy Turnbull) Moger; Stacey, Hayes, Duckworth, Roberts, Bell, Meredith, Halse, J Turnbull, S Turnbull, Wall **Bristol City 0** Clay; Annan, Cottle, Hanlin, Wedlock, Spear, Staniforth, Hardy, Gilligan, Burton, Hilton. April 24; 71, 401; J Mason

1910 Newcastle 1 (Rutherford) Lawrence; McCracken, Whitson, Veitch, Low, McWilliam, Rutherford, Howie, Higgins, Shepherd, Wilson **Barnsley 1** (Tufnell) Mearns; Downs, Ness, Glendinning, Boyle, Utley, Tufnell, Lillycrop, Gadsby, Forman, Bartrop. April 23; 77, 747; JT Ibbotson **Replay – Newcastle 2** (Shepherd 2, 1pen) Lawrence; McCracken, Carr, Veitch, Low, McWilliam, Rutherford, Howie, Higgins, Shepherd, Wilson **Barnsley 0** Mearns; Downs, Ness, Glendinning, Boyle, Utley, Tufnell, Lillycrop, Gadsby, Forman, Bartrop. April 28; 69, 000; JT Ibbotson

1911 Bradford City 0 Mellors; Campbell, Taylor, Robinson, Gildea, McDonald, Logan, Speirs, O'Rourke, Devine, Thompson **Newcastle 0** Lawrence; McCracken, Whitson, Veitch, Low, Willis, Rutherford, Jobey, Stewart, Higgins, Wilson. April 22; 69, 068; JH Pearson **Replay – Bradford City 1** (Speirs) Mellors; Campbell, Taylor, Robinson, Torrance, McDonald, Logan, Speirs, O'Rourke, Devine, Thompson **Newcastle 0** Lawrence; McCracken, Whitson, Veitch, Low, Willis, Rutherford, Jobey, Stewart, Higgins, Wilson. April 26; 58, 000; JH Pearson

1912 Barnsley 0 Cooper; Downs, Taylor, Glendinning, Bratley, Utley, Bartrop, Tufnell, Lillycrop, Travers, Moore **WBA 0** Pearson; Cook, Pennington, Baddeley, Buck, McNeal, Jephcott, Wright, Pailor, Bowser, Shearman. April 20; 54, 556; JR Shumacher **Replay – Barnsley 1** (Tufnell) Cooper; Downs, Taylor, Glendinning, Bratley, Utley, Bartrop, Harry, Lillycrop, Travers, Jimmy Moore **WBA 0** Pearson; Cook, Pennington, Baddeley, Buck, McNeal, Jephcott, Wright, Pailor, Bowser, Shearman. April 24; 38, 555; JR Schumacher. aet

1913 Aston Villa 1 (Barber) Hardy; Lyons, Weston, Barber, Harrop, Leach, Wallace, Halse, Hampton, Stephenson, Bache **Sunderland 0** Butler; Gladwin, Ness, Cuggy, Thomson, Low, Mordue, Buchan,

151

Richardson, Holley, Martin. April 19; 120, 081; A Adams

1914 **Burnley 1** (Freeman) Sewell; Bamford, Taylor, Halley, Boyle, Watson, Nesbit, Lindley, Freeman, Hodgson, Mosscrop **Liverpool 0** Campbell; Longworth, Pursell, Fairfoul, Ferguson, McKinley, Sheldon, Metcalfe, Miller, Lacey, Nicholl. April 25; 72, 778; HS Bamlett

1915 **Sheffield Utd 3** (Simmons, Fazackerly, Kitchen) Gough; Cook, English, Sturgess, Brelsford, Utley, Simmons, Fazackerly, Kitchen, Masterman, Evans **Chelsea 0** Molyneux; Bettridge, Harrow, Taylor, Logan, Walker, Ford, Halse, Thomson, Croal, McNeil. April 24; 49, 557; HH Taylor

1920 **Aston Villa 1** (Kirton) Hardy; Smart, Weston, Ducat, Barson, Moss, Wallace, Kirton, Walker, Stephenson, Dorrell **Huddersfield 0** Mutch; Wood, Bullock, Slade, Wilson, Watson, Richardson, Mann, Taylor, Swann, Islip. April 24; 50, 018; JT Howcroft. aet

1921 **Tottenham 1** (Dimmock) Hunter; Clay, McDonald, Smith, Walters, Grimsdell, Banks, Seed, Cantrell, Bliss, Dimmock **Wolves 0** George; Woodward, Marshall, Gregory, Hodnett, Riley, Lea, Burrill, Edmonds, Potts, Brooks. April 23; 72, 805; S Davies

1922 **Huddersfield 1** (Smith pen) Mutch; Wood, Wadsworth, Slade, Wilson, Watson, Richardson, Mann, Islip, Stephenson, Billy Smith **Preston 0** Mitchell; Hamilton, Doolan, Duxbury, McCall, Williamson, Rawlings, Jefferis, Roberts, Woodhouse, Quinn. April 29; 53, 000; JWP Fowler

1923 **Bolton 2** (Jack, JR Smith) Pym; Haworth, Finney, Nuttall, Seddon, Jennings, Butler, Jack, JR Smith, Joe Smith, Vizard **West Ham 0** Hufton; Henderson, Young, Bishop, Kay, Tresadern, Richards, Brown, Watson, Moore, Ruffell. April 28; 126, 047; DH Asson

1924 **Newcastle 2** (Harris, Seymour) Bradley; Hampson, Hudspeth, Mooney, Spencer, Gibson, Low, Cowan, Harris, McDonald, Seymour **Aston Villa 0** Jackson; Smart, Mort, Moss, Milne, Blackburn, York, Kirton, Capewell, Walker, Dorrell. April 26; 91, 695; WE Russell

1925 **Sheffield Utd 1** (Tunstall) Sutcliffe; Cook, Milton, Pantling, King, Green, Mercer, Boyle, Johnson, Gillespie, Tunstall **Cardiff 0** Farquharson; Nelson, Blair, Wake, Keenor, Hardy, Davies, Gill, Nicholson, Beadles, Evans. April 25; 91, 763; GN Watson

1926 **Bolton 1** (Jack) Pym; Haworth, Greenhalgh, Nuttall, Seddon, Jennings, Butler, JR Smith, Jack, Joe Smith, Vizard **Manchester City 0** Goodchild; Cookson, McCloy, Pringle, Cowan, McMullan, Austin, Browell, Roberts, Johnson, Hicks. April 24; 91, 447; I Baker

1927 **Cardiff 1** (Ferguson) Farquharson; Nelson, Watson, Keenor, Sloan, Hardy, Curtis, Irving, Ferguson, Davies, McLachlan **Arsenal 0** Lewis; Parker, Kennedy, Baker, Butler, John, Hulme, Buchan, Brain, Blythe, Hoar. April 23; 91, 206; WF Bunnell

1928 **Blackburn 3** (Roscamp 2, McLean) Crawford; Hutton, Jones, Healless, Rankin, Campbell, Thornewell, Puddefoot, Roscamp, McLean, Rigby **Huddersfield 1** (Jackson) Mercer; Goodall, Barkas, Redfern, Wilson, Steele, Jackson, Kelly, Brown, Stephenson, Smith. April 21; 92, 041; TG Bryan

1929 **Bolton 2** (Butler, Blackmore) Pym; Haworth, Finney, Kean, Seddon, Nuttall, Butler, McClelland, Blackmore, Gibson, Cook **Portsmouth 0** Gilfillan; Mackie, Bell, Nichol, McIlwaine, Thackeray, Forward, Smith, Weddle, Watson, Cook. April 27; 92, 576; A Josephs

1930 **Arsenal 2** (James, Lambert) Preedy; Parker, Hapgood, Baker, Seddon, John, Hulme, Jack, Lambert, James, Bastin **Huddersfield 0** Turner; Goodall, Spence, Naylor, Wilson, Campbell, Jackson, Kelly, Davies, Raw, Smith. April 26; 92, 488; T Crew

1931 **WBA 2** (WG Richardson 2) Pearson; Shaw, Trentham, Magee, Bill Richardson, Edwards, Glidden, Carter, WG Richardson, Sandford, Wood **Birmingham 1** (Bradford) Hibbs; Liddell, Barkas, Cringan, Morrall, Leslie, Briggs, Crosbie, Bradford, Gregg, Curtis. April 25; 92, 406; AH Kingscott

1932 **Newcastle 2** (Allen 2) McInroy; Nelson, Fairhurst, McKenzie, Davidson, Weaver, Boyd, Richardson, Allen, McMenemy, Lang **Arsenal 1** (John) Moss; Parker, Hapgood, Jones, Roberts, Male, Hulme, Jack, Lambert, Bastin, John. April 23; 92, 298; WP Harper

1933 **Everton 3** (Stein, Dean, Dunn) Sagar; Cook, Cresswell, Britton, White, Thomson, Geldard, Dunn, Dean, Johnson, Stein **Manchester City 0** Langford; Cann, Dale, Busby, Cowan, Bray, Toseland, Marshall, Herd, McMullan, Eric Brook. April 29; 92, 950; E Wood

1934   **Manchester City 2** (Tilson 2) Swift; Barnett, Dale, Busby, Cowan, Bray, Toseland, Marshall, Tilson, Herd, Brook **Portsmouth 1** (Rutherford) Gilfillan; Mackie, Smith, Nichol, Allen, Thackeray, Worrall, Smith, Weddle, Easson, Rutherford. April 28; 93, 258; Stanley Rous

1935   **Sheffield Wed 4** (Rimmer 2, Palethorpe, Hooper) Brown; Nibloe, Catlin, Sharp, Millership, Burrows, Hooper, Surtees, Palethorpe, Starling, Rimmer **WBA 2** (Boyes, Sandford) Pearson; Shaw, Trentham, Murphy, Bill Richardson, Edwards, Glidden, Carter, WG Richardson, Sandford, Wally. April 27; 93, 204; AE Fogg

1936   **Arsenal 1** (Drake) Wilson; Male, Hapgood, Crayston, Roberts, Copping, Hulme, Bowden, Drake, James, Bastin **Sheffield Utd 0** Smith; Hooper, Wilkinson, Jackson, Johnson, McPherson, Barton, Barclay, Dodds, Pickering, Williams. April 25; 93, 384; H Nattrass

1937   **Sunderland 3** (Gurney, Carter, Burbanks) Mapson; Gorman, Hall, Thomson, Johnston, McNab, Duns, Carter, Gurney, Gallacher, Burbanks **Preston 1** (Frank O'Donnell) Burns; Gallimore, Andy Beattie, Shankly, Tremelling, Milne, Dougal, Beresford, Frank O'Donnell, Fagan, Hugh O'Donnell. May 1; 93, 495; RG Rudd

1938   **Preston 1** (Mutch pen) Holdcroft; Gallimore, Andy Beattie, Shankly, Smith, Batey, Watmough, Mutch, Maxwell, Bob Beattie, Hugh O'Donnell **Huddersfield 0** Hesford; Craig, Mountford, Willingham, Young, Boot, Hulme, Issac, MacFadyen, Barclay, Beasley. April 30; 93, 497; AJ Jewell. aet

1939   **Portsmouth 4** (Parker 2, Barlow, Anderson) Walker; Morgan, Rochford, Guthrie, Rowe, Wharton, Worrall, McAlinden, Anderson, Barlow, Parker **Wolves 1** (Dorsett) Scott; Morris, Taylor, Galley, Cullis, Gardiner, Burton, McIntosh, Westcott, Dorsett, Maguire. April 29; 99, 370; T Thompson

1946   **Derby 4** (Stamps 2. Doherty, Bert Turner og) Woodley; Nicholas, Howe, Bullions, Leuty, Musson, Harrison, Carter, Stamps, Doherty, Duncan **Charlton Athletic 1** (Bert Turner) Bartram; Phipps, Shreeve, Bert Turner, Oakes, Johnson, Fell, Brown, Arthur Turner, Welsh, Duffy. April 27; 98, 000; ED Smith. aet

1947   **Charlton Athletic 1** (Duffy) Bartram; Croker, Shreeve, Johnson, Phipps, Whittaker, Hurst, Dawson, Robinson, Welsh, Duffy **Burnley 0** Strong; Woodruff, Mather, Attwell, Brown, Bray, Chew, Morris, Harrison, Potts, Kippax. April 26; 99, 000; JM Wiltshire. aet

1948   **Manchester Utd 4** (Rowley 2, Pearson, Anderson) Crompton; Carey, Aston, Anderson, Chilton, Cockburn, Delaney, Morris, Rowley, Pearson, Mitten **Blackpool 2** (Shimwell pen, Mortensen) Robinson; Shimwell, Crosland, Johnston, Hayward, Kelly, Matthews, Munro, Mortensen, Dick, Rickett. April 24; 99, 000; CJ Barrick

1949   **Wolves 3** (Pye 2, Smyth) Williams; Pritchard, Springthorpe Crook, Shorthouse, Wright, Hancocks, Smyth, Pye, Dunn, Mullen **Leicester 1** (Griffiths) Bradley; Jelly, Scott, Walter Harrison, Plummer, King, Griffiths, Lee, Jimmy Harrison, Chisholm, Adam. April 30; 99, 500; RA Mortimer

1950   **Arsenal 2** (Lewis 2) Swindin; Scott, Barnes, Forbes, Les Compton, Mercer, Cox, Logie, Goring, Lewis, Denis Compton **Liverpool 0** Sidlow; Lambert, Spicer, Taylor, Hughes, Jones, Payne, Baron, Stubbins, Fagan, Liddell. April 29; 100, 000; H Pearce

1951   **Newcastle 2** (Milburn 2) Fairbrother; Cowell, Corbett, Harvey, Brennan, Crowe, Walker, Taylor, Milburn, Jorge Robledo, Mitchell **Blackpool 0** Farm; Shimwell, Garrett, Johnston, Hayward, Kelly, Matthews, Mudie, Mortensen, Slater, Perry. April 28; 100, 000; W Ling

1952   **Newcastle 1** (George Robledo) Simpson; Cowell, McMichael, Harvey, Brennan, Ted Robledo, Walker, Foulkes, Milburn, George Robledo, Mitchell **Arsenal 0** Swindin; Barnes, Smith, Forbes, Daniel Mercer, Cox, Logie, Holton, Lishman, Roper. May 3; 100, 000; A Ellis

1953   **Blackpool 4** (Mortensen 3, Perry) Farm; Shimwell, Garrett, Fenton, Johnston, Robinson, Matthews, Taylor, Mortensen, Mudie, Perry **Bolton 3** (Lofthouse, Moir, Bell) Hanson; Ball, Ralph Banks, Wheeler, Barrass, Bell, Holden, Moir, Lofthouse, Hassall, Langton. May 2; 100, 000; M Griffiths

1954   **WBA 3** (Allen 2 [1pen], Griffin) Sanders; Kennedy, Millard, Dudley, Dugdale, Barlow, Griffin, Ryan, Allen, Nicholls, Lee **Preston 2** (Morrison, Wayman) Thompson; Cunningham, Walton, Docherty, Marston, Forbes, Finney, Foster, Wayman, Baxter, Morrison. May 1; 100, 000; A Luty

1955   **Newcastle 3** (Milburn, Mitchell, Hannah) Simpson; Cowell, Batty, Scoular, Stokoe, Casey, White, Milburn, Keeble, Hannah, Mitchell **Manchester City 1** (Johnstone) Trautmann; Meadows, Little, Barnes, Ewing, Paul, Spurdle, Hayes, Revie, Johnstone, Fagan. May 7; 100, 000; R Leafe

1956   **Manchester City 3** (Hayes, Dyson, Johnstone) Trautmann; Leivers, Little, Barnes, Ewing, Paul, Johnstone, Hayes, Revie, Dyson, Clarke **Birmingham 1** (Kinsey) Merrick; Hall, Green, Newman, Smith, Boyd, Astall, Kinsey, Brown, Murphy, Govan. May 5; 100, 000; A Bond

1957   **Aston Villa 2** (McParland 2) Sims; Lynn, Aldis, Crowther, Dugdale, Saward, Smith, Sewell, Myerscough, Dixon, McParland **Manchester Utd 1** (Tommy Taylor) Wood; Foulkes, Byrne, Colman, Blanchflower, Edwards, Berry, Whelan, Tommy Taylor, Charlton, Pegg. May 4; 100, 000; F Coultas

1958   **Bolton 2** (Lofthouse 2) Hopkinson; Hartle, Tommy Banks, Hennin, Higgins, Edwards, Birch, Stevens, Lofthouse, Parry, Holden **Manchester Utd 0** Gregg; Foulkes, Greaves, Goodwin, Cope, Crowther, Dawson, Ernie Taylor, Charlton, Viollet, Webster. May 3; 100, 000; J Sherlock

1959   **Nottingham Forest 2** (Dwight, Wilson) Thomson; Whare, McDonald, Whitefoot, McKinlay, Burkitt, Dwight, Quigley, Wilson, Gray, Imlach **Luton Town 1** (Pacey) Baynham; McNally, Hawkes, Groves, Owen, Pacey, Bingham, Brown, Morton, Cummins, Gregory. May 2; 100, 000; J Clough

1960   **Wolves 3** (McGrath og, Deeley 2) Finlayson; Showell, Harris, Clamp, Slater, Flowers, Deeley, Stobart, Murray, Broadbent, Horne **Blackburn 0** Leyland; Bray, Whelan, Clayton, Woods, McGrath, Bimpson, Dobing, Dougan, Douglas, McLeod. May 7; 100, 000; K Howley

1961   **Tottenham 2** (Smith, Dyson) Brown; Baker, Henry, Blanchflower, Norman, Mackay, Jones, White, Smith, Allen, Dyson **Leicester 0** Banks; Chalmers, Norman, McLintock, King, Appleton, Riley, Walsh, McIlmoyle, Keyworth, Cheesebrough. May 6; 100, 000; J Kelly

1962   **Tottenham 3** (Greaves, Smith, Blanchflower pen) Brown; Baker, Henry, Blanchflower, Norman, Mackay, Medwin, White, Smith, Greaves, Jones **Burnley 1** (Robson) Blacklaw; Angus, Elder, Adamson, Cummings, Miller, Connelly, McIlroy, Pointer, Robson, Harris. May 5; 100, 000; J Finney

1963   **Manchester Utd 3** (Law, Herd 2) Gaskell; Dunne, Cantwell, Crerand, Foulkes, Setters, Giles, Quixall, Herd, Law, Charlton **Leicester 1** (Keyworth) Banks; Sjoberg, Norman, McLintock, King, Appleton, Riley, Cross, Keyworth, Gibson, Stringfellow. May 25; 100, 000; K Aston

1964   **West Ham 3** (Sissons, Hurst, Boyce) Standen; Bond, Burkett, Bovington, Brown, Moore, Brabrook, Boyce, Byrne, Hurst, Sissons **Preston 2** (Holden, Dawson) Kelly; Ross, Lawton, Smith, Singleton, Kendall, Wilson, Ashworth, Dawson, Spavin, Holden. May 2; 100, 000; A Holland

1965   **Liverpool 2** (Hunt, St John) Lawrence; Lawler, Byrne, Strong, Yeats, Stevenson, Callaghan, Hunt, St John, Smith, Thompson **Leeds 1** (Bremner) Sprake; Reaney, Bell, Bremner, Charlton, Hunter, Giles, Storrie, Peacock, Collins, Johanneson. May 1; 100, 000; W Clements. aet

1966   **Everton 3** (Trebilcock 2, Temple) West; Wright, Wilson, Gabriel, Labone, Harris, Scott, Trebilcock, Young, Harvey, Temple **Sheffield Wed 2** (McCalliog, Ford) Springett; Smith, Megson, Eustace, Ellis, Young, Pugh, Fantham, McCalliog, Ford, Quinn. May 14; 100, 000; JK Taylor

1967   **Tottenham 2** (Robertson, Saul) Jennings; Kinnear, Knowles, Mullery, England, Mackay, Robertson, Greaves, Gilzean, Venables, Saul. Unused sub: Jones **Chelsea 1** (Tambling) Bonetti; Allan Harris, McCreadie, Hollins, Hinton, Ron Harris, Cooke, Baldwin, Hateley, Tambling, Boyle. Unused sub: Kirkup. May 20; 100, 000; K Dagnall

1968   **WBA 1** (Astle) Osborne; Fraser, Williams, Brown, Talbot, Kaye, Lovett, Collard, Astle Hope, Clark Sub: Clarke rep Kaye 91 **Everton 0** West; Wright, Wilson, Kendall, Labone, Harvey, Husband, Ball, Royle, Hurst, Morrissey. Unused sub: Kenyon. May 18; 100, 000; L Callaghan. aet

1969   **Manchester City 1** (Young) Dowd; Book, Pardoe, Doyle, Booth, Oakes, Summerbee, Bell, Lee, Young, Coleman. Unused sub: Connor **Leicester 0** Shilton; Rodrigues, Nish, Roberts, Woollett, Cross, Fern, Gibson, Lochhead, Clarke, Glover. Sub: Manley rep Glover 70. April 26; 100, 000; G McCabe

1970   **Chelsea 2** (Houseman, Hutchinson) Bonetti; Webb, McCreadie, Hollins, Dempsey, Ron Harris, Baldwin, Houseman, Osgood, Hutchinson, Cooke. Sub: Hinton rep Harris 91 **Leeds 2** (Charlton, Jones) Sprake; Madeley, Cooper, Bremner, Charlton, Hunter, Lorimer, Clarke, Jones, Giles, Gray Unused sub: Bates. April 11; 100, 000; E Jennings. aet **Replay – Chelsea 2** (Osgood, Webb) Bonetti; Webb, McCreadie, Hollins, Dempsey, Ron Harris, Baldwin, Houseman, Osgood, Hutchinson, Cooke. Sub: Hinton rep Osgood 105 **Leeds 1** (Jones) Harvey; Madeley, Cooper, Bremner, Charlton, Hunter, Lorimer, Clarke, Jones, Giles, Gray Unused sub: Bates. April 29; 62, 078; E Jennings. aet

1971 **Arsenal 2** (Kelly, George) Wilson; Rice, McNab, Storey, McLintock Simpson, Armstrong, Graham, Radford, Kennedy, George. Sub: Kelly rep Storey 70 **Liverpool 1** (Heighway) Clemence; Lawler, Lindsay, Smith, Lloyd, Hughes, Callaghan, Evans, Heighway, Toshack, Hall. Sub: Thompson rep Evans 70. May 8; 100, 000; N Burtenshaw. aet

1972 **Leeds 1** (Clarke) Harvey; Reaney, Madeley, Bremner, Charlton, Hunter, Lorimer, Clarke, Jones, Giles, Gray. Unused sub: Bates **Arsenal 0** Barnett; Rice, McNab, Storey, McLintock, Simpson, Armstrong, Ball, George, Radford, Graham. Sub: Kennedy rep Radford 80. May 6; 100, 000; DW Smith

1973 **Sunderland 1** (Porterfield) Montgomery; Malone, Guthrie, Horswill, Watson, Pitt, Kerr, Hughes, Halom, Porterfield, Tueart. Unused sub: Young **Leeds 0** Harvey; Reaney, Cherry, Bremner, Madeley, Hunter, Lorimer, Clarke, Jones, Giles, Gray. Sub: Yorath rep Gray 75. May 5; 100, 000; K Burns

1974 **Liverpool 3** (Keegan 2, Heighway) Clemence; Smith, Lindsay, Thompson, Cormack, Hughes, Keegan, Hall, Heighway, Toshack, Callaghan. Unused sub: Lawler **Newcastle 0** McFaul; Clark, Kennedy, McDermott, Howard, Moncur, Smith, Cassidy, Macdonald, Tudor, Hibbitt. Sub: Gibb rep Smith 70. May 4; 100, 000; GC Kew

1975 **West Ham 2** (Alan Taylor 2) Day; McDowell, Tommy Taylor, Lock, Lampard, Bonds, Paddon, Brooking, Jennings, Alan Taylor, Holland. Unused sub: Gould **Fulham 0** Mellor; Cutbush, Lacy, Moore, Fraser, Mullery, Conway, Slough, Mitchell, Busby, Barrett. Unused sub: Lloyd. May 3; 100, 000; P Partridge

1976 **Southampton 1** (Stokes) Turner; Rodrigues, Peach, Holmes, Blyth, Steele, Gilchrist, Channon, Osgood, McCalliog, Stokes. Unused sub: Fisher **Manchester Utd 0** Stepney; Forsyth, Houston, Daly, Brian Greenhoff, Buchan, Coppell, McIlroy, Pearson, Macari, Hill. Sub: McCreery rep Hill 66. May 1; 100, 000; C Thomas

1977 **Manchester Utd 2** (Pearson, J Greenhoff) Stepney; Nicholl, Albiston, McIlroy, Brian Greenhoff, Buchan, Coppell, Jimmy Greenhoff, Pearson, Macari, Hill. Sub: McCreery rep Hill 81 **Liverpool 1** (Case) Clemence; Neal, Jones, Smith, Kennedy, Hughes, Keegan, Case, Heighway, Johnson, McDermott. Sub: Callaghan rep Johnson 64. May 21; 100, 000; R Matthewson

1978 **Ipswich Town 1** (Osborne) Cooper; Burley, Mills, Talbot, Hunter, Beattie, Osborne, Wark, Mariner, Geddis, Woods. Sub: Lambert rep Osborne 79 **Arsenal 0** Jennings; Rice, Nelson, Price, Young, O'Leary, Brady, Hudson, Macdonald, Stapleton, Sunderland. Sub: Rix rep Brady 65. May 6; 100, 000; D Nippard

1979 **Arsenal 3** (Talbot, Stapleton, Sunderland) Jennings; Rice, Nelson, Talbot, O'Leary, Young, Brady, Sunderland, Stapleton, Price, Rix. Sub: Walford rep Rix 83 **Manchester Utd 2** (McQueen, McIlroy) Bailey; Nicholl, Albiston, McIlroy, McQueen, Buchan, Coppell, Jimmy Greenhoff, Jordan, Macari, Thomas. Unused sub: Brian Greenhoff. May 12; 100, 000; R Challis

1980 **West Ham 1** (Brooking) Parkes; Stewart, Lampard, Bonds, Martin, Devonshire, Allen, Pearson, Cross, Brooking, Pike. Unused sub: Brush **Arsenal 0** Jennings; Rice, Devine, Talbot, O'Leary, Young, Brady, Sunderland, Stapleton, Price, Rix. Sub: Nelson rep Devine 61. May 10; 100, 000; G Courtney

1981 **Tottenham 1** (Hutchison og) Aleksic; Hughton, Miller, Roberts, Perryman, Villa, Ardiles, Archibald, Galvin, Hoddle, Crooks. Sub: Brooke rep Villa 68. **Manchester City 1** (Hutchison) Corrigan; Ranson, McDonald, Reid, Power, Caton, Bennett, Gow, Mackenzie, Hutchison Reeves. Sub: Henry rep Hutchison 82. May 9; 100, 000; K Hackett. aet Replay – **Tottenham 3** (Villa 2, Crooks) Aleksic; Hughton, Miller, Roberts, Perryman, Villa, Ardiles, Archibald, Galvin, Hoddle, Crooks. Unused sub: Brooke **Manchester City 2** (Mackenzie, Reeves pen) Corrigan; Ranson, McDonald, Reid, Power, Caton, Bennett, Gow, Mackenzie, Hutchison Reeves. Sub: Tueart rep McDonald 79. May 14; 92, 000; K Hackett

1982 **Tottenham 1** (Hoddle) Clemence; Hughton, Miller, Price, Hazard, Perryman, Roberts, Archibald, Galvin, Hoddle, Crooks. Sub: Brooke rep Hazard 104 **Queens Park Rangers 1** (Fenwick) Hucker; Fenwick, Gillard, Waddock, Hazell, Roeder, Currie, Flanagan, Allen, Stainrod, Gregory. Sub: Micklewhite rep Allen 50. May 22; 100, 000; C White. aet Replay – **Tottenham 1** (Hoddle pen) Clemence; Hughton, Miller, Price, Hazard, Perryman, Roberts, Archibald, Galvin, Hoddle, Crooks. Sub: Brooke rep Hazard 67 **Queens Park Rangers 0** Hucker; Fenwick, Gillard, Waddock, Hazell, Neill, Currie, Flanagan, Micklewhite, Stainrod, Gregory. Sub: Burke rep Micklewhite 84. May 27; 90, 000; C White

1983 **Manchester Utd 2** (Stapleton, Wilkins) Bailey; Duxbury, Moran, McQueen, Albiston, Davies, Wilkins, Robson, Muhren, Stapleton, Whiteside. Unused sub: Grimes **Brighton 2** (Smith, Stevens) Moseley; Ramsey, Gary A Stevens, Pearce, Gatting, Smillie, Case, Grealish, Howlett, Robinson, Smith. Sub: Ryan

155

rep Ramsey 56. May 21; 100, 000; AW Grey, aet **Replay – Manchester Utd 4** (Robson 2, Whiteside, Muhren pen) Bailey; Duxbury, Moran, McQueen, Albiston, Davies, Wilkins, Robson, Muhren, Stapleton, Whiteside. Unused sub: Grimes **Brighton 0** Moseley; Gary A Stevens, Pearce, Foster, Gatting, Smillie, Case, Grealish, Howlett, Robinson, Smith. Sub: Ryan rep Howlett 74. May 26; 100, 000; AW Grey

1984   Everton 2 (Sharp, Gray) Southall; Gary M Stevens, Bailey, Ratcliffe, Mountfield, Reid, Steven, Heath, Sharp, Gray, Richardson. Unused sub: Harper **Watford 0** Sherwood; Bardsley, Price, Taylor, Terry, Sinnott, Callaghan, Johnston, Reilly, Jackett, Barnes. Sub: Atkinson rep Price 58. May 19; 100, 000; J Hunting

1985   Manchester Utd 1 (Whiteside) Bailey; Gidman, Albiston, Whiteside, McGrath, Moran, Robson, Strachan, Hughes, Stapleton, Olsen. Sub: Duxbury rep Albiston 91. Moran sent off 77. **Everton 0** Southall; Gary M Stevens, Van den Hauwe, Ratcliffe, Mountfield, Reid, Steven, Sharp, Gray, Bracewell, Sheedy. Unused sub: Harper. May 18; 100, 000; P Willis. aet

1986   Liverpool 3 (Rush 2, Johnston) Grobbelaar; Lawrenson, Beglin, Nicol, Whelan, Hansen, Dalglish, Johnston, Rush, Molby, MacDonald. Unused sub: McMahon **Everton 1** (Lineker) Mimms; Gary M Stevens, Van den Hauwe, Ratcliffe, Mountfield, Reid, Steven, Lineker, Sharp, Bracewell, Sheedy. Sub: Heath rep Stevens 65. May 10; 98, 000; A Robinson

1987   Coventry City 3 (Bennett, Houchen, Mabbutt og) Ogrizovic; Phillips, Downs, McGrath, Kilcline, Peake, Bennett, Gynn, Regis, Houchen, Pickering. Sub: Rodger rep Kilcline 88. Unused sub: Sedgley **Tottenham 2** (Clive Allen, Mabbutt) Clemence; Hughton Thomas, Hodge, Gough, Mabbutt, Clive Allen, Paul Allen, Waddle, Hoddle, Ardiles. Subs: Gary A Stevens rep Ardiles 91; Claesen rep Hughton 97. May 16; 98, 000; N Midgley. aet

1988   Wimbledon 1 (Sanchez) Beasant; Goodyear, Phelan, Jones, Young, Thorn, Gibson Cork, Fashanu, Sanchez, Wise. Subs: Cunningham rep Cork 56; Scales rep Gibson 63 **Liverpool 0** Grobbelaar; Gillespie, Ablett, Nicol, Spackman, Hansen, Beardsley, Aldridge, Houghton, Barnes, McMahon. Subs: Johnston rep Aldridge 63; Molby rep Spackman 72. May 14; 98, 203; B Hill

1989   Liverpool 3 (Aldridge, Rush 2) Grobbelaar; Ablett, Staunton, Nichol, Whelan, Hansen, Beardsley, Aldridge Houghton, Barnes, McMahon. Subs: Rush rep Aldridge 72; Venison rep Staunton 91 **Everton 2** (McCall 2) Southall; McDonald, Van den Hauwe, Ratcliffe, Watson, Bracewell, Nevin, Steven, Cottee, Sharp, Sheedy. Subs: McCall rep Bracewell 58; Wilson rep Sheedy 77. May 20; 82, 500; J Worrall. aet

1990   Manchester Utd 3 (Robson, Hughes 2) Leighton; Ince, Martin, Bruce, Phelan, Pallister, Robson, Webb, McClair, Hughes, Wallace. Subs: Blackmore rep Martin 88; Robins rep Pallister 93. **Crystal Palace 3** (O'Reilly, Wright 2) Martyn; Pemberton, Shaw, Gray, O'Reilly, Thorn, Barber, Thomas, Bright, Salako, Pardew. Subs: Wright rep Barber 69; Madden rep Gray 117. May 12; 80, 000; A Gunn. aet **Replay – Manchester Utd 1** (Martin) Sealey; Ince, Martin, Bruce, Phelan, Pallister, Robson, Webb, McClair, Hughes, Wallace. Unused subs: Robins, Blackmore **Crystal Palace 0** Martyn; Pemberton, Shaw, Gray, O'Reilly, Thorn, Barber, Thomas, Bright, Salako, Pardew. Subs: Wright rep Barber 64; Madden rep Salako 79. May 17; 80, 000; A Gunn

1991   Tottenham 2 (Stewart, Walker og) Thorstvedt; Edinburgh, Van den Hauwe, Sedgley, Howells, Mabbutt, Stewart, Gascoigne, Samways, Lineker, Paul Allen. Subs: Nayim rep Gascoigne 18; Walsh rep Samways 82. **Nottingham Forest 1** (Pearce) Crossley; Charles, Pearce, Walker, Chettle, Keane, Crosby, Parker, Clough, Glover, Woan. Subs: Hodge rep Woan 62; Laws rep Glover 108. May 18; 80, 000; R Milford. aet

1992   Liverpool 2 (Thomas, Rush) Grobbelaar; Jones, Burrows, Nicol, Molby, Wright, Saunders, Houghton, Rush, McManaman, Thomas. Unused subs: Marsh, Walters **Sunderland 0** Norman; Owers, Ball, Bennett, Rogan, Rush, Bracewell, Davenport, Armstrong, Byrne, Atkinson. Subs: Hardyman rep Rush 69; Hawke rep Armstrong 77. May 9; 80, 000; P Don

1993   Arsenal 1 (Wright) Seaman; Dixon, Winterburn, Linighan, Adams, Jensen, Davis, Parlour, Merson, Campbell, Wright. Subs: Smith rep Parlour 66; O'Leary rep Wright 90. **Sheffield Wed 1** (Hirst) Woods; Nilsson Worthington, Palmer, Hirst, Anderson, Waddle, Warhurst, Bright, Sheridan, Harkes. Subs: Hyde rep Anderson 85; Bart-Williams rep Waddle 112. May 15; 79, 347; K Barratt. aet **Replay – Arsenal 2** (Wright, Linighan) Seaman; Dixon, Winterburn, Linighan, Adams, Jensen, Davis, Smith, Merson, Campbell, Wright. Sub: O'Leary rep Wright 81. Unused sub: Selley **Sheffield Wed 1** (Waddle) Woods; Nilsson, Worthington, Palmer, Hirst, Wilson, Waddle, Warhurst, Bright, Sheridan, Harkes. Subs: Hyde rep Wilson 62; Bart-Williams rep Nilsson 118. May 20; 62, 267; K Barratt. aet

1994 **Manchester Utd 4** (Cantona 2 [2pens], Hughes, McClair) Schmeichel; Parker, Bruce, Pallister, Irwin, Kanchelskis, Keane, Ince, Giggs, Cantona, Hughes. Subs: Sharpe rep Irwin 84; McClair rep Kanchelskis 84. Unused sub: Walsh (gk) **Chelsea 0** Kharine; Clarke, Sinclair, Kjeldberg, Johnsen, Burley, Spencer, Newton, Stein, Peacock, Wise Substitutions Hoddle rep Burley 65; Cascarino rep Stein 78. Unused sub: Kevin Hitchcock (gk) May 14; 79, 634; D Elleray

1995 **Everton 1** (Rideout) Southall; Jackson, Hinchcliffe, Ablett, Watson, Parkinson, Unsworth, Horne, Stuart, Rideout, Limpar. Subs: Ferguson rep Rideout 51; Amokachi rep Limpar 69. Unused sub: Kearton (gk) **Manchester Utd 0** Schmeichel; Gary Neville, Irwin, Bruce, Sharpe, Pallister, Keane, Ince, Brian McClair, Hughes, Butt. Subs: Giggs rep Bruce 46; Scholes rep Sharpe 72. Unused sub: Gary Walsh (gk) May 20; 79, 592; G Ashby

1996 **Manchester Utd 1** (Cantona) Schmeichel; Irwin, Phil Neville, May, Keane, Pallister, Cantona, Beckham, Cole, Butt, Giggs. Subs: Scholes rep Cole 65; Gary Neville rep Beckham 89. Unused sub: Sharpe **Liverpool 0** James; McAteer, Scales, Wright, Babb, Jones, McManaman, Barnes, Redknapp, Collymore, Fowler. Subs: Rush rep Collymore 74; Thomas rep Jones 85. Unused sub: Warner (gk) May 11; 79, 007; D Gallagher

1997 **Chelsea 2** (Di Matteo, Newton) Grodas; Petrescu, Minto, Sinclair, Lebouef, Clarke, Zola, Di Matteo, Newton, Hughes, Wise. Sub: Vialli rep Zola 89. Unused subs: Hitchcock (gk), Myers **Middlesbrough 0** Roberts; Blackmore, Fleming, Stamp, Pearson, Festa, Emerson, Mustoe, Ravanelli, Juninho, Hignett. Subs: Beck rep Ravanelli 24; Vickers rep Mustoe 29; Kinder, rep Hignett 74. May 17; 79, 160; S Lodge

1998 **Arsenal 2** (Overmars, Anelka) Seaman; Dixon, Winterburn, Vieira, Keown, Adams, Parlour, Anelka, Petit, Wreh, Overmars. Sub: Platt rep Wreh 63. Unused subs: Manninger (gk); Bould, Wright, Grimandi **Newcastle 0** Given; Pistone, Pearce, Batty, Dabizas, Howey, Lee, Barton, Shearer, Ketsbaia, Speed. Subs: Andersson rep Pearce 72; Watson rep Barton 77; Barnes rep Ketsbaia 85. Unused subs: Hislop (gk); Albert. May 16; 79, 183; P Durkin

1999 **Manchester Utd 2** (Sheringham, Scholes) Schmeichel; Gary Neville, Johnsen, May, Phil Neville, Beckham, Scholes, Keane, Giggs, Cole, Solskjaer. Subs: Sheringham rep Keane 9; Yorke rep Cole 61; Stam rep Scholes 77. Unused subs: Blomqvist, Van Der Gouw **Newcastle 0** Harper; Griffin, Charvet, Dabizas, Domi, Lee, Hamann, Speed, Solano, Ketsbaia, Shearer. Subs: Ferguson rep Hamann 46; Maric rep Solano 68; Glass rep Ketsbaia 79. Unused subs: Given (gk); Barton. May 22; 79, 101; P Jones

2000 **Chelsea 1** (Di Matteo) de Goey; Melchiot Desailly, Lebouef, Babayaro, Di Matteo, Wise, Deschamps, Poyet, Weah, Zola. Subs: Flo rep Weah 87; Morris rep Zola 90. Unused subs: Cudicini (gk), Terry , Harley **Aston Villa 0** James; Ehiogu, Southgate, Barry, Delaney, Taylor, Boateng, Merson, Wright, Dublin, Carbone. Subs: Stone rep Taylor 79; Joachim rep Carbone 79; Hendrie rep Wright 88. Unused subs: Enckelman (gk); Samuel May 20; 78, 217; G Poll

2001 **Liverpool 2** (Owen 2) Westerveld; Babbel, Henchoz, Hyypia, Carragher, Murphy, Hamann, Gerrard, Smicer, Heskey, Owen. Subs: McAllister rep Hamann 60; Fowler rep Smicer 77; Berger rep Murphy 77. Unused subs: Arphexad (gk); Vignal **Arsenal 1** (Ljungberg) Seaman; Dixon, Keown, Adams, Cole, Ljungberg, Grimandi, Vieira, Pires, Henry, Wilford Subs: Parlour rep Wilford 76; Kanu rep Ljungberg 85; Bergkamp rep Dixon 90. Unused subs: Manninger (gk); Lauren. May 12; 72, 500; S Dunn

2002 **Arsenal 2** (Parlour, Ljungberg) Seaman; Lauren, Campbell, Adams, Cole, Parlour, Wiltord, Vieira, Ljungberg, Bergkamp, Henry Subs: Edu rep Bergkamp 72; Kanu rep Henry 81; Keown rep Wiltord 90. Unused subs: Wright (gk); Dixon **Chelsea 0** Cudicini; Melchiot, Desailly, Gallas, Babayaro, Gronkjaer, Lampard, Petit, Le Saux, Floyd Hasselbaink, Gudjohnsen. Subs: Terry rep Babayaro 46; Zola rep Hasselbaink 68; Zenden rep Melchiot 77. Unused subs: de Goey (gk); Jokanovic. May 4; 73, 963; M Riley

2003 **Arsenal 1** (Pires) Seaman; Lauren, Luzhny, Keown, Cole, Ljungberg, Parlour, Gilberto, Pires, Bergkamp, Henry. Sub: Wiltord rep Bergkamp 77. Unused subs: Taylor (gk); Kanu, Toure, van Bronckhorst **Southampton 0** Niemi; Baird, Svensson, Lundekvam, Bridge, Telfer, Svensson, Oakley, Marsden, Beattie, Ormerod. Subs: Jones rep Niemi 66; Fernandes rep Baird 87; Tessem rep Svensson 75. Unused subs: Williams, Higginbotham. May 17; 73, 726; G Barber

2004 **Manchester Utd 3** (Van Nistelrooy [2, 1 pen], Ronaldo) Howard; Gary Neville, Brown, Silvestre, O'Shea, Fletcher, Keane, Ronaldo, Scholes, Giggs, Van Nistelrooy. Subs: Carroll rep Howard, Butt rep Fletcher, Solskjaer rep Ronaldo 84. Unused subs: P Neville, Djemba-Djemba **Millwall 0** Marshall; Elliott, Lawrence, Ward, Ryan, Wise, Ifill, Cahill, Livermore, Sweeney, Harris. Subs: Cogan rep Ryan, McCammon rep Harris 74 Weston rep Wise 84. Unused subs: Gueret (gk); Dunne. May 22; 71, 350; J Winter

2005 **Arsenal 0** Lehmann; Lauren, Toure, Senderos, Cole, Fabregas, Gilberto, Vieira, Pires, Reyes, Bergkamp Subs: Ljungberg rep Bergkamp 65, Van Persie rep Fabregas 86, Edu rep Pires 105. Unused subs: Almunia (gk); Campbell. Reyes sent off 90. **Manchester Utd 0** Carroll; Brown, Ferdinand, Silvestre, O'Shea, Fletcher, Keane, Scholes, Rooney, Van Nistelrooy, Ronaldo. Subs: Fortune rep O'Shea 77, Giggs rep Fletcher 91. Unused subs: Howard (gk); G Neville, Smith. **Arsenal** (Lauren, Ljungberg, van Persie, Cole, Vieira) beat Manchester Utd (van Nistelrooy, Scholes [missed], Ronaldo, Rooney, Keane) 5-4 on penalties. May 21; 71, 876; R Styles

2006 **Liverpool 3** (Gerrard 2, Cisse) Reina; Finnan, Carragher, Hyypiä, Riise, Gerrard, Xabi, Sissoko, Kewell, Cisse, Crouch. Subs: Morientes rep Kewell 48, Kromkamp rep Alonso 67, Hamman rep Crouch 71. Unused subs: Dudek (gk); Traoré **West Ham 3** (Ashton, Konchesky, Carragher (og)) Hislop; Scaloni, Ferdinand, Gabbidon, Konchesky, Benayoun, Fletcher, Reo-Coker, Etherington, Ashton, Harewood. Subs: Zamora rep Ashton 71, Dailly rep Fletcher, Sheringham rep Etherington 85. Unused subs: Walker (gk); Collins. **Liverpool** (Hamann, Hyypiä [missed], Gerrard, Riise) beat **West Ham** (Zamora [missed], Sheringham, Konchesky [missed], Ferdinand [missed]) 3-1 on penalties. May 13; 71, 140; A Wiley

2007 **Chelsea 1** (Drogba) Cech, Ferreira, Essien, Terry, Bridge, Mikel, Makelele, Lampard, Wright-Phillips, Drogba, Joe Cole Subs: Robben rep J Cole 45, Kalou rep Wright-Phillips 93, A Cole rep Robben 108. Unused subs: Cudicini (gk); Diarra. **Manchester Utd 0** Van der Sar, Brown, Ferdinand, Vidic, Heinze, Fletcher, Scholes, Carrick, Ronaldo, Rooney, Giggs Subs: Smith rep Fletcher 92, O'Shea rep Carrick, Solskjaer rep Giggs 112. Unused subs: Kuszczak (gk); Evra. May 19; 89, 826; S Bennett

2008 **Portsmouth 1** (Kanu) James; Johnson, Campbell, Distin, Hreidarsson, Utaka, Muntari, Mendes, Diarra, Kranjcar, Kanu. Subs: Nugent rep Utaka 69, Diop rep Mendes 78, Baros rep Kanu 87. Unused subs: Ashdown (gk); Pamarot. **Cardiff 0** Enckelman; McNaughton, Johnson, Loovens, Capaldi, Whittingham, Rae, McPhail, Ledley, Hasselbaink, Parry. Subs: Ramsey rep Whittingham 62, Thompson rep Hasselbaink 70, Sinclair rep Rae 87. Unused subs: Oakes (gk); Purse. May 17; 89, 874; M Dean

2009 **Chelsea 2** (Drogba, Lampard) Cech; Bosingwa, Alex, Terry, Ashley Cole, Essien, Mikel, Lampard, Drogba, Anelka, Malouda. Subs: Ballack rep Essien 61. Unused subs: Hilario (gk), Ivanovic, Di Santo, Kalou, Belletti, Mancienne. **Everton 1** (Saha) Howard; Hibbert, Yobo, Lescott, Baines, Osman, Neville, Cahill, Pienaar, Fellaini, Saha. Subs: Jacobsen rep Hibbert 46, Vaughan rep Saha 77, Gosling rep Osman 83. Unused subs: Nash, Castillo, Rodwell, Baxter. May 30; 89, 391; H Webb

2010 **Chelsea 1** (Drogba) Cech; Ivanovic, Alex, Terry, Ashley Cole, Lampard, Ballack, Malouda, Kalou, Drogba, Anelka. Subs: Belletti rep Ballack 44, J Cole rep Kalou 71, Sturridge rep Anelka 90. Unused subs: Hilario (gk), Zhirkov, Paulo Ferreira, Matic. **Portsmouth 0** James; Finnan, Mokoena, Rocha, Mullins, Dindane, Brown, Diop, Boateng, O'Hara, Piquionne. Subs: Utaka rep Boateng 73, Belhadj rep Mullins 81, Kanu rep Diop 81. Unused subs: Ashdown (gk), Vanden Borre, Hughes, Ben Haim. May 15; 88, 335; C Foy

2011 **Manchester City 1** (Y Toure) Hart; Richards, Kompany, Lescott, Kolarov, De Jong, Barry, Silva, Y Toure, Balotelli, Tevez. Subs: Johnson rep Barry73, Zabaleta rep Tevez 87, Vieira rep Silva 90. Unused subs: Given (gk); Boyata, Milner, Dzeko. **Stoke 0** Sorensen; Wilkinson, Shawcross, Huth, Wilson, Pennant, Whelan, Delap, Etherington, Walters, Jones. Subs: Whitehead rep Etherington 62, Carew rep Delap 80, Pugh rep Whelan 84. Unused subs: Nash (gk); Collins, Faye, Diao. May 14; 88, 643; M Atkinson

2012 **Chelsea 2** (Ramires, Drogba) Cech; Bosingwa, Ivanovic, Terry, Ashley Cole, Mikel, Lampard, Ramires, Mata, Kalou, Drogba. Subs: Meireles rep Ramires76, Malouda rep Mata 90. Unused subs: Turnbull (gk); Paulo Ferreira, Essien, Torres, Sturridge. **Liverpool 1** (Carroll) Reina; Johnson, Skrtel, Agger, Luis Enrique, Spearing, Bellamy, Henderson, Gerrard, Downing, Suarez. Subs Carroll rep Spearing 55, Kuyt rep Bellamy 78. Unused subs: Doni (gk), Carragher, Kelly, Shelvey, Rodriguez. May 5; 89, 102; P Dowd

2013 **Wigan 1** (Watson) Robles; Boyce, Alcaraz, Scharner, McCarthy, McArthur, McManaman, Maloney, Gomez, Espinoza, Kone. Subs: Watson rep Gomez 81. Unused subs: Al Habsi (gk), Caldwell, Golobart, Fyvie, Henriquez, Di Santo. **Manchester City 0** Hart, Zabaleta, Kompany, Nastasic, Clichy, Toure, Barry, Silva, Tevez, Nasri, Aguero. Subs: Milner rep Nasri 54, Rodwell rep Tevez 69, Dzeko rep Barry 90. Unused subs: Pantilimon (gk), Lescott, Kolarov, Garcia. Sent off Zabaleta (84). May 11; 86, 254; A Marriner

2014 **Arsenal 3** (Cazorla, Koscielny, Ramsey) Fabianski; Sagna, Koscielny, Mertesacker, Gibbs, Arteta, Ramsey, Cazorla, Ozil, Podolski, Giroud. Subs: Sanogo rep Podolski 61, Rosicky rep Cazorla 106, Wilshire rep Ozil 106. Unused subs: Szczesny (gk); Vermaelen, Monreal, Flamini. **Hull 2** (Chester, Davies) McGregor; Davies, Bruce, Chester, Elmohamady, Livermore, Huddlestone, Meyler, Rosenior,

Quinn, Fryatt. Subs: McShane rep Bruce 67, Aluko rep Quinn 71, Boyd rep Rosenior 102. Unused subs: Harper (gk), Figueroa, Koren, Sagbo. May 17; 89, 345; L Probert. aet

2015   Arsenal 4 (Walcott, Sanchez, Mertesacker, Giroud) Szczesny; Bellerin, Koscielny, Mertesacker, Monreal, Coquelin, Cazorla, Ramsey, Ozil, A Sanchez, Walcott. Subs: Wilshere rep Ozil 77, Giroud rep Walcott 77, Oxlade-Chamberlain rep A Sanchez 90. Unused subs: Ospina (gk), Gibbs, Gabriel, Flamini. **Aston Villa 0** Given; Hutton, Okore, Vlaar, Richardson, Cleverley, Westwood, Delph, N'Zogbia, Benteke, Grealish. Subs: Agbonlahor rep N'Zogbia 53, Bacuna rep Richardson 68, C Sanchez rep Westwood 71. Unused subs: Guzan (gk), Baker, Sinclair, Cole. May 30; 89, 283; J Moss

2016   Manchester Utd 2 (Mata, Lingard) De Gea, Valencia, Smalling, Blind, Rojo, Carrick, Rooney, Fellaini, Mata, Martial, Rashford. Subs: Darmian rep Rojo 65, Young rep Rashford 71, Lingard rep Mata 90. Unused subs: Romero, Jones, Herrera, Schneiderlin. Smalling sent off 105 . **Crystal Palace 1** (Puncheon) Hennessey, Ward, Dann, Delaney, Souare, Cabaye, Jedinak, Zaha, McArthur, Bolasie, Wickham. Unused subs: Speroni, Adebayor, Sako, Kelly. Subs: Puncheon rep Cabaye 72, Gayle rep Wickham 86, Mariappa rep Dann 90 May 21; 88, 619; M Clattenburg

2017   Arsenal 2 (Sanchez, Ramsey) Ospina, Holding, Mertesacker, Monreal, Bellerin, Ramsey, Xhaka, Oxlade-Chamberlain, Sanchez, Ozil, Welbeck. Subs: Giroud rep Welbeck78, Coquelin rep Oxlade-Chamberlain 83, Elneny rep Sanchez 90. Unused subs: Cech (gk), Walcott, Iwobi, Lucas Perez. **Chelsea 1** (Diego Costa) Courtois, Azpilicueta, Luiz, Cahill, Moses, Kante, Matic, Alonso, Pedro, Diego Costa, Hazard. Subs Fabregas rep Matic 62, Willian rep Pedro 72, Batshuayi rep Diego Costa 88. Unused subs: Begovic (gk), Terry, Zouma, Ake, Moses sent off 68. May 27; 89, 472; A Taylor

2018   Chelsea 1 (Hazard pen) Courtois, Azpilicueta, Cahill, Rudiger, Moses, Fabregas, Kante, Bakayoko, Alonso, Hazard, Giroud. Subs: Morata rep Giroud 89, Willian rep Hazard 90. Unused subs: Caballero (gk), Barkley, Pedro, Zappacosta, Chalobah. **Manchester Utd 0** De Gea, Valencia, Smalling, Jones, Young, Herrera, Matic, Pogba, Lingard, Sanchez, Rashford. Subs: Martial rep Lingard 73, Lukaku rep Rashford 73, Mata rep Jones 87. Unused subs: Romero (gk), Bailly, Darmian, McTominay. May 19, 87, 647; M Oliver

2019   Manchester City 6 (Gabriel Jesus 2, Sterling 2, David Silva, De Bruyne) Ederson, Walker, Kompany, Laporte, Zinchenko, Gundogan, David Silva, Bernardo Silva, Mahrez, Gabriel Jesus, Sterling. Subs: De Bruyne rep Mahrez 55, Sane rep Gundogan 73, Stones rep Davi Silva 79. Unused subs: Muric (gk), Danilo, Otamendi, Aguero. **Watford 0** Gomes, Femenia, Mariappa, Cathcart, Holebas, Hughes, Capoue, Doucoure, Pereyra, Deulofeu, Deeney. Subs: Success rep Pereyra 65, Gray rep Deulofeu 65, Cleverley rep Hughes 73. Unused subs: Foster (gk), Janmaat, Masina, Kabasele. May 18; 85, 854; K Friend

2020   Arsenal 2 (Aubameyang 28 pen, 67) Martinez, Holding, Luiz, Tierney, Bellerin, Ceballos, Xhaka, Maitland-Niles, Pepe, Lacazette, Aubameyang. Subs: Nketiah rep Lacazette 82, Sokratis rep Luiz 88, Kolasinac rep Tierney 90. Unused subs: Macey (gk), Torreira. Nelson, Willock, Smith Rowe, Saka. **Chelsea** 1 (Pulisic 5) Caballero, Azpilicueta, Zouma, Rudiger, James, Jorginho, Kovacic, Marcos Alonso, Mount, Pulisic, Giroud. Subs: Christensen rep Azpilicueta 35, Pedro rep Pulisic 49, Hudson-Odoi rep Rudiger 78, Barkley rep Mount 78, Abraham rep Giroud 78. Unused subs: Arrizabalaga (gk), Kante, Tomori, Emerson. August 1; behind closed doors; A Taylor

VENUES

Kennington Oval 1872; **Lillie Bridge** 1873; **Kennington Oval** 1874–1892 (1886 replay at the **Racecourse Ground, Derby**); **Fallowfield**, Manchester, 1893; **Goodison Park** 1894; **Crystal Palace** 1895–1914 (1901 replay at **Burnden Park**; 1910 replay at **Goodison Park**; 1911 replay at **Old Trafford**; 1912 replay at **Bramall Lane**);; **Old Trafford** 1915; **Stamford Bridge** 1920–1922; **Wembley** 1923–2000 (1970 replay at **Old Trafford**; all replays from 1981 at **Wembley**); **Millennium Stadium** 2001–2006; **Wembley** 2007–2021

SUMMARY OF FA CUP WINS

Arsenal	14	Sheffield Wed	3	Clapham Rov	1
Manchester Utd	12	West Ham	3	Coventry	1
Tottenham	8	Bury	2	Derby	1
Chelsea	8	Nottm Forest	2	Huddersfield	1
Aston Villa	7	Old Etonians	2	Ipswich	1
Liverpool	7	Portsmouth	2	Leeds	1
Blackburn Rov	6	Preston	2	Leicester	1
Manchester City	6	Sunderland	2	Notts Co	1
Newcastle	6	Barnsley	1	Old Carthusians	1
Everton	5	Blackburn Olympic	1	Oxford University	1
The Wanderers	5	Blackpool	1	Royal Engineers	1
WBA	5	Bradford City	1	Southampton	1
Bolton	4	Burnley	1	Wigan	1
Sheffield Utd	4	Cardiff	1	Wimbledon	1
Wolves	4	Charlton	1		

APPEARANCES IN FINALS (Figures do not include replays)

Arsenal	21	Portsmouth	5	Notts Co	2
Manchester Utd	20	The Wanderers*	5	Queen's Park (Glasgow)	2
Chelsea	15	West Ham	5	Watford	2
Liverpool	14	Derby	4	Blackburn Olympic*	1
Everton	13	Leeds	4	Bradford City*	1
Newcastle	13	Oxford University	4	Brighton	1
Aston Villa	11	Royal Engineers	4	Bristol City	1
Manchester City	11	Southampton	4	Coventry*	1
WBA	10	Sunderland	4	Fulham	1
Tottenham	9	Blackpool	3	Hull	1
Blackburn Rov	8	Burnley	3	Ipswich*	1
Wolves	8	Cardiff	3	Luton	1
Bolton	7	Nottm Forest	3	Middlesbrough	1
Preston	7	Barnsley	2	Millwall	1
Old Etonians	6	Birmingham	2	Old Carthusians*	1
Sheffield Utd	6	Bury*	2	QPR	1
Sheffield Wed	6	Charlton	2	Stoke	1
Huddersfield	5	Clapham Rov	2	Wigan	1
Leicester	5	Crystal Palace	2	Wimbledon*	1

(* Denotes undefeated)

APPEARANCES IN SEMI-FINALS (Figures do not include replays)

31 Manchester Utd; **30** Arsenal; **26** Everton; **25** Chelsea; **24** Liverpool; **21** Aston Villa, Tottenham; **20** WBA; **18** Blackburn; **17** Newcastle; **16** Sheffield Wed, Manchester City; **15** Wolves; **14** Bolton, Sheffield Utd; **13** Derby, Southampton; **12** Nottm Forest, Sunderland; **10** Preston; **9** Birmingham; **8** Burnley, Leeds, Leicester; **7** Huddersfield, Portsmouth, Watford, West Ham; **6** Fulham, Newcastle Old Etonians, Oxford University; **5** Millwall, Notts Co, The Wanderers; **4** Cardiff, *Crystal Palace, Luton, Queen's Park (Glasgow), Royal Engineers, Stoke; **3** Barnsley, Blackpool, Clapham Rov, Ipswich, Middlesbrough, Norwich, Old Carthusians, Oldham, The Swifts; **2** Blackburn Olympic, Brighton, Bristol City, Bury, Charlton, Grimsby, Hull, Reading, Swansea, Swindon, Wigan, Wimbledon; **1** Bradford City, Cambridge University, Chesterfield, Coventry, Crewe, Darwen, Derby Junction, Marlow, Old Harrovians, Orient, Plymouth Argyle, Port Vale, QPR, Rangers (Glasgow), Shropshire Wand, Wycombe, York

(*A previous and different Crystal Palace club also reached the semi-final in season 1871–72)

CARABAO EFL CUP 2020–21

FIRST ROUND

Barnsley 1 Nottm Forest 0
Birmingham 0 Cambridge 1
Blackburn 3 Doncaster 2
Bolton 1 Bradford 2
Brentford 1 Wycombe 1
(Brentford won 4-2 on pens)
Bristol City 2 Exeter 0
Burton 1 Accrington 1
(Burton won 4-2 on pens)
Crawley 1 Millwall 3
Crewe 1 Lincoln 2
Derby 0 Barrow 0
(Derby won 3-2 on pens)
Fleetwood 3 Wigan 2
Forest Green 1 Leyton Orient 2
Gillingham 1 Southend 0
Grimsby 1 Morecambe 1
(Morecambe won 4-3 on pens)
Huddersfield 0 Rochdale 1
Ipswich 3 Bristol Rov 0
Luton 3 Norwich 1
Middlesbrough 4 Shrewsbury 3
MK Dons 0 Coventry 1

Newport 2 Swansea 0
Northampton 3 Cardiff 0
Oldham 3 Carlisle 0
Oxford 1 Wimbledon 1
(Oxford won 4-3 on pens)
Peterborough 0 Cheltenham 1
Plymouth 3 QPR 2
Preston 4 Mansfield 0
Reading 3 Colchester 1
Salford 1 Rotherham 1
(Salford won 4-2 on pens)
Scunthorpe 1 Port Vale 2
Stevenage 3 Portsmouth 3
(Portsmouth won 3-1 on pens)
Stoke 0 Blackpool 0
(Stoke won 5-4 on pens)
Sunderland 0 Hull 0
(Hull won 5-4 on pens)
Swindon 1 Charlton 3
Tranmere 1 Harrogate 1
(Harrogate won 8-7 on pens)
Walsall 0 Sheffield Wed 0
(Sheffield Wed won 4-2 on pens)

SECOND ROUND

Bournemouth 0 Crystal Palace 0
(Bournemouth won 11-10 on pens)
Bradford 0 Lincoln 5
Brighton 4 Portsmouth 0
Bristol City 4 Northampton 0
Burnley 1 Sheffield Utd 1
(Burnley won 5-4 on pens)
Burton 1 Aston Villa 3
Derby 1 Preston 2
Everton 3 Salford 0
Fleetwood 2 Port Vale 1
Gillingham 1 Coventry 1
(Gillingham won 5-4 on pens)
Ipswich 0 Fulham 1
Leeds 1 Hull 1

(Hull won 9-8 on pens)
Leyton Orient 3 Plymouth 2
Middlesbrough 0 Barnsley 2
Millwall 3 Cheltenham 1
Morecambe 1 Oldham 2
Newcastle 1 Blackburn 0
Newport 1 Cambridge 0
Oxford 1 Watford 1
(Watford won 3-0 on pens)
Reading 0 Luton 1
Rochdale 0 Sheffield Wed 2
Southampton 0 Brentford 2
WBA 3 Harrogate 0
West Ham 3 Charlton 0
Wolves 0 Stoke 1

THIRD ROUND

Bristol City 0 Aston Villa 3
Chelsea 6 Barnsley 0
Fleetwood 2 Everton 5
Fulham 2 Sheffield Wed 0
Leicester 0 Arsenal 2

Leyton Orient v **Tottenham** – postponed
(Tottenham awarded tie)
Lincoln 2 Liverpool 7
Luton 0 Manchester Utd 3
Manchester City 2 Bournemouth 1

Millwall 0 Burnley 2
Morecambe 0 Newcastle 7
Newport 3 Watford 1
Preston 0 Brighton 2

Stoke 1 Gillingham 0
WBA 2 Brentford 2
(Brentford won 5-4 on pens)
West Ham 5 Hull 1

FOURTH ROUND

Aston Villa 0 Stoke 1
Brentford 3 Fulham 0
Burnley 0 **Manchester City** 3
Brighton 0 Manchester Utd 3
Everton 4 West Ham 1
Liverpool 0 Arsenal 1

(Arsenal won 5-4 on pens)
Newport 1 Newcastle 1
(Newcastle won 5-4 on pens)
Tottenham 1 Chelsea 1
(Tottenham won 5-4 on pens)

QUARTER-FINALS

Arsenal 1 Manchester City 4
Brentford 1 Newcastle 0

Everton 0 Manchester Utd 2
Stoke 1 Tottenham 3

SEMI-FINALS (two legs)

Manchester Utd 0 **Manchester City** 2

Tottenham 2 Brentford 0

FINAL

MANCHESTER CITY 1 (Laporte 82) TOTTENHAM HOTSPUR 0
Wembley (7,773); April 25, 2021

Manchester City (4-2-3-1)): Steffen, Walker, Dias, Laporte, Joao Cancelo, Fernandinho (capt) (Rodri 84), Gundogan, Mahrez, De Bruyne (Bernardo Silva 87), Foden, Sterling. **Subs not used:** Ederson, Ake, Gabriel Jesus, Aguero, Zinchenko, Torres, Mendy. **Booked:** Laporte, Fernandinho. **Manager:** Pep Guardiola
Tottenham, Hotspur (4-3-3): Lloris (capt), Aurier (Bergwijn 90), Alderweireld, Dier, Reguilon, Winks, Hojbjerg (Alli 84), Lo Celso (Sissoko 67), Lucas Moura (Bale 67), Kane, Son Heung-min. **Subs not used:** Hart, Tanganga, Sanchez, Lamela, Ndombele. **Booked:** Reguilon. **Manager** (interim): Ryan Mason
Referee: Paul Tierney. **Half-time:** 0-0

For Manchester City an eighth League Cup and a place alongside Liverpool as the competition's most successful club. For Pep Guardiola a record fourth straight victory as manager. For his captain, Fernandinho, an unprecedented sixth winners' medal, the first two having come under Manuel Pellegrini. It was a pertinent reminder of how influential the Brazilian has been, alongside more celebrated players, in the club's rise to prominence. His side should have won more convincingly in a match they dominated from start to finish. Tottenham's only complaint concerned Aymeric Laporte's header from Kevin De Bruyne's 17th assist of the season after 82 minutes. Taken together, Laporte was guilty of two bookable offences for bringing down Lucas Moura. But he escaped a yellow card for the first and interim manager Ryan Mason was honest enough to suggest that had that been shown the central defender would have been unlikely to risk a second foul. Mason, at 29 the youngest to take charge of a Premier League team, handled the pressure commendably just six days after Jose Mourinho's dismissal. He had Harry Kane available after injury, but the England captain was little more than an onlooker in a match which welcomed back a crowd of nearly 8,000 as part of the Government's pilot scheme ahead of a planned full return of spectators. Tottenham were left trophyless since 2008. Of more immediate concern for chairman Daniel Levy was finding the right man to replace Mourinho and whether Kane felt it was now time to seek his first silverware elsewhere.

HOW THEY REACHED THE FINAL

Manchester City
Round 3: 2-1 home to Bournemouth (Delap, Foden)
Round 4: 3-0 away to Burnley (Sterling 2, Torres)
Quarter-finals: 4-1 away to Arsenal (Gabriel Jesus, Mahrez, Foden, Laporte)
Semi-finals: 2-0 away to Manchester Utd (Stones, Fernandinho)

Tottenham Hotspur
Round 3: away to Leyton Orient – awarded tie
Round 4: 1-1 home to Chelsea (Lamela) - won 5-4 on pens
Quarter-finals: 3-1 away to Stoke (Bale, Davies, Kane)
Semi-finals: 2-0 home to Brentford (Sissoko, Son Heung-min)

LEAGUE CUP – COMPLETE RESULTS

LEAGUE CUP FINALS

1961*   Aston Villa beat Rotherham 3-2 on agg (0-2a, 3-0h)
1962   Norwich beat Rochdale 4-0 on agg (3-0a, 1-0h)
1963   Birmingham beat Aston Villa 3-1 o agg (3-1h, 0-0a)
1964   Leicester beat Stoke 4-3 on agg (1-1a, 3-2h)
1965   Chelsea beat Leicester 3-2 on agg (3-2h, 0-0a)
1966   WBA beat West Ham 5-3 on agg (1-2a, 4-1h)

AT WEMBLEY

1967   QPR beat WBA (3-2)
1968   Leeds beat Arsenal (1-0)
1969*   Swindon beat Arsenal (3-1)
1970*   Man City beat WBA (2-1)
1971   Tottenham beat Aston Villa (2-0)
1972   Stoke beat Chelsea (2-1)
1973   Tottenham beat Norwich (1-0)
1974   Wolves beat Man City (2-1)
1975   Aston Villa beat Norwich (1-0)
1976   Man City beat Newcastle (2-1)
1977†*   Aston Villa beat Everton (3-2 after 0-0 and 1-1 draws)
1978††   Nottm Forest beat Liverpool (1-0 after 0-0 draw)
1979   Nottm Forest beat Southampton (3-2)
1980   Wolves beat Nottm Forest (1-0)
1981†††   Liverpool beat West Ham (2-1 after 1-1 draw)

MILK CUP

1982*   Liverpool beat Tottenham (3-1)
1983*   Liverpool beat Man Utd (2-1)
1984**   Liverpool beat Everton (1-0 after *0-0 draw)
1985   Norwich beat Sunderland (1-0)
1986   Oxford Utd beat QPR (3-0)

LITTLEWOODS CUP

1987   Arsenal beat Liverpool (2-1)
1988   Luton beat Arsenal (3-2)
1989   Nottm Forest beat Luton (3-1)
1990   Nottm Forest beat Oldham (1-0)

RUMBELOWS CUP

1991   Sheffield Wed beat Man Utd (1-0)
1992   Man Utd beat Nottm Forest (1-0)

COCA-COLA CUP

1993   Arsenal beat Sheffield Wed (2-1)
1994   Aston Villa beat Man Utd (3-1)
1995   Liverpool beat Bolton (2-1)
1996   Aston Villa beat Leeds (3-0)
1997***   Leicester beat Middlesbrough (*1-0 after *1-1 draw)
1998   Chelsea beat Middlesbrough (2-0)

WORTHINGTON CUP (at Millennium Stadium from 2001)

1999   Tottenham beat Leicester (1-0)
2000   Leicester beat Tranmere (2-1)
2001   Liverpool beat Birmingham (5-4 on pens after *1-1 draw)
2002   Blackburn beat Tottenham (2-1)
2003   Liverpool beat Man Utd (2-0)

CARLING CUP (at Wembley from 2008)

2004   Middlesbrough beat Bolton (2-1)
2005*   Chelsea beat Liverpool (3-2)
2006   Man Utd beat Wigan (4-0)
2007   Chelsea beat Arsenal (2-1)
2008*   Tottenham beat Chelsea (2-1)
2009   Man Utd beat Tottenham (4-1 on pens after *0-0 draw)
2010   Man Utd beat Aston Villa (2-1)
2011   Birmingham beat Arsenal (2-1)
2012   Liverpool beat Cardiff (3-2 on pens after *2-2 draw)

CAPITAL ONE CUP (at Wembley from 2013)

2013	Swansea beat Bradford (5-0)
2014	Manchester City beat Sunderland (3-1)
2015	Chelsea beat Tottenham (2-0)
2016	Manchester City beat Liverpool (3-1 on pens after *1-1 draw)

* After extra time. † First replay at Hillsborough, second replay at Old Trafford. †† Replayed at Old Trafford. ††† Replayed at Villa Park. ** Replayed at Maine Road. *** Replayed at Hillsborough

EFL CUP (at Wembley from 2017)

2017	Manchester Utd beat Southampton (3-2)

CARABAO CUP (at Wembley from 2018)

2018	Manchester City beat Arsenal (3-0)
2019	Manchester City beat Chelsea (4-3 on pens after *0-0 draw)
2020	Manchester City beat Aston Villa (2-1)
2021	Manchester City beat Tottenham 1-0

SUMMARY OF LEAGUE CUP WINNERS

Liverpool	8	Arsenal	2	Oxford Utd	1
Manchester City	8	Birmingham	2	QPR	1
Aston Villa	5	Norwich	2	Sheffield Wed	1
Chelsea	5	Wolves	2	Stoke	1
Manchester Utd	5	Blackburn	1	Swansea	1
Nottm Forest	4	Leeds	1	Swindon	1
Tottenham	4	Luton	1	WBA	1
Leicester	3	Middlesbrough	1		

LEAGUE CUP FINAL APPEARANCES

12 Liverpool; **9**, Aston Villa, Chelsea, Manchester City, Manchester Utd; **8** Arsenal, Tottenham **6** Nottm Forest; **5** Leicester; **4** Norwich; **3** Birmingham, Middlesbrough, WBA; **2** Bolton, Everton, Leeds, Luton, QPR, Sheffield Wed, Southampton, Stoke, Sunderland, West Ham, Wolves; **1** Blackburn, Bradford, Cardiff, Newcastle, Oldham, Oxford Utd, Rochdale, Rotherham, Swansea, Swindon, Tranmere, Wigan (Figures do not include replays)

LEAGUE CUP SEMI-FINAL APPEARANCES

18 Tottenham; **17** Liverpool; **16** Manchester Utd; **15** Arsenal, Aston Villa; **14** Chelsea; **13** Manchester City; **9** West Ham; **6** Blackburn, Leicester, Nottm Forest; **5** Birmingham, Everton, Leeds, Middlesbrough, Norwich; **4** Bolton, Burnley, Crystal Palace, Ipswich, Sheffield Wed, Sunderland, WBA; **3** Bristol City, QPR, Southampton, Stoke, Swindon, Wolves; **2** Cardiff, Coventry, Derby, Luton, Oxford Utd, Plymouth, Sheffield Utd, Tranmere, Watford, Wimbledon; **1** Blackpool, Bradford, Brentford, Burton, Bury, Carlisle, Chester, Huddersfield, Hull, Newcastle, Oldham, Peterborough, Rochdale, Rotherham, Shrewsbury, Stockport, Swansea, Walsall, Wigan, Wycombe. (Figures do not include replays)

THE THINGS THEY SAY...

'What can I say? It's horrible. But we stood up after the first 9-0 (against Leicester) and we have to do that again' – **Ralph Hasenhuttl**, Southampton manager, after his side lost by a record score for the second successive season, this time against Manchester United.

'My unacceptable words were a disservice to our game and to those who watch, play, referee and administer it. I am deeply saddened I have offended those diverse communities' – **Greg Clarke** announcing his resignation as FA chairman after calling black players 'coloured' and making other offensive remarks at a parliamentary select committee.

OTHER COMPETITIONS 2020–21

FA COMMUNITY SHIELD

ARSENAL 1(Aubameyang 12) LIVERPOOL 1 (Minamino 73) (Arsenal won 5-4 on pens)
Wembley (behind closed doors); August 29, 2020

Arsenal (3-4-3): Martinez, Holding, Luiz, Tierney (Kolasinac 83), Bellerin (Soares 59), Xhaka, Elneny, Maitland-Niles, Saka (Willock 82), Nketiah (Nelson 82), Aubameyang (capt). **Subs not used:** Leno, Saliba, Smith Rowe, John-Jules, Olayinka. **Manager:** Mikel Arteta
Liverpool (4-3-3): Alisson, N Williams (Minamino 59), Gomez, Van Dijk, Robertson, Wijnaldum (Brewster 90+2), Fabinho, Milner (capt) (Keita 59), Salah, Firmino, Mane. **Subs not used:** Adrian, Grujic, Tsimikas, Elliott, Koumetio. **Booked:** Milner. **Manager:** Jurgen Klopp
Penalty shoot-out: Arsenal – scored: Nelson, Maitland-Niles, Soares, Luiz, Aubameyang.
Liverpool – scored: Salah, Fabinho, Minamino, Jones; missed: Brewster.
Referee: Andre Marriner (W Midlands). **Half-time:** 1-0

PAPA JOHNS EFL TROPHY

(Three points for a group match win. One point for a drawn game after 90 minutes, then penalties with winners awarded one additional point. Group winners and runners-up through to knockout stage)

NORTHERN SECTION

GROUP A

	P	W	D	L	F	A	Pts
Fleetwood	3	3	0	0	8	2	9
Sunderland	3	2	0	1	14	6	6
Carlisle	3	1	0	2	7	9	3
Aston Villa U21	3	0	0	3	2	14	0

GROUP B

Salford	3	2	0	1	4	7	6
Man Utd U21	3	1	1	1	6	4	5
Rochdale	3	1	1	1	3	3	4
Morecambe	3	1	0	2	5	4	3

GROUP C

Shrewsbury	3	3	0	0	9	4	9
Crewe	3	2	0	1	7	6	6
Bolton	3	1	0	2	6	7	3
Newcastle U21	3	0	0	3	2	7	0

GROUP D

Port Vale	3	2	1	0	7	3	8
Tranmere	3	1	2	0	5	4	6
Wigan	3	1	1	1	9	6	4
Liverpool U21	3	0	0	3	5	13	0

GROUP E

Man City U21	3		1	0	8	1	7
Lincoln	3	1	2	0	5	3	7
Mansfield	3	1	0	2	3	7	3
Scunthorpe	3	0	1	2	2	7	1

GROUP F

Oldham	3	3	0	0	9	1	9
Wolves U21	3	1	1	1	3	6	5
Bradford	3	0	2	1	2	4	2
Doncaster	3	0	1	2	1	4	2

GROUP G

Accrington	3	2	1	0	9	1	8
Blackpool	3	1	2	0	4	1	6
Barrow	3	0	2	1	2	3	3
Leeds U21	3	0	1	2	2	12	1

GROUP H

Hull	3		2	0	1	6	2	6
Leicester U21	3	2	0	1	6	5	6
Harrogate	3	1	1	1	5	5	4
Grimsby	3	0	1	2	3	8	2

SOUTHERN SECTION

GROUP A

West Ham	3	3	0	0	5	1	9
Portsmouth	3	2	0	1	5	1	6
Colchester	3	1	0	2	6	4	3
Southend	3	0	0	3	2	12	0

GROUP B

Arsenal U21	3	2	1	0	5	3	8
Gillingham	3	1	1	1	3	4	4
Crawley	3	1	0	2	4	4	3
Ipswich	3	1	0	2	3	4	3

GROUP C

MK Dons	3	2	0	1	7	5	6
Northampton	3	1	1	1	6	3	5
Stevenage	3	1	1	1	4	4	4
Southampton U21	3	1	0	2	3	8	3

GROUP D

Oxford	3	2	1	0	4	2	8
Bristol Rov	3	1	2	0	7	6	5
Walsall	3	0	2	1	4	4	3
Chelsea U21	3	0	1	2	5	7	2

GROUP E							
Exeter	3	3	0	0	11	5	9
Forest Green	3	1	0	2	5	4	3
Swindon	3	1	0	2	6	7	3
WBA U21	3	1	0	2	3	9	3

GROUP F							
Cheltenham	3	3	0	0	4	0	9
Norwich U21	3	2	0	1	8	3	6
Plymouth	3	1	0	2	5	6	3
Newport	3	0	0	3	1	9	0

GROUP G							
Leyton Orient	3	2	0	1	6	5	6
AFC Wimbledon	3	2	0	1	4	3	6
Charlton	3	1	1	1	5	4	5
Brighton U21	3	0	1	2	3	6	1

GROUP H							
Cambridge	3	2	1	0	7	3	8
Peterborough	3	1	2	0	8	6	6
Burton	3	0	2	1	6	8	3
Fulham U21	3	0	1	2	3	7	1

SECOND ROUND

North: Accrington 3 Manchester Utd U21 2; Fleetwood 0 Blackpool 0 (Fleetwood won 5-4 on pens); Hull 0 Crewe 0 (Hull won 3-2 on pens); Oldham 1 Sunderland 2; Port Vale 2 Wolves U21 1; Salford 3 Leicester U21 3 (Leicester U21 won 6-5 on pens); Shrewsbury 1 Lincoln 4; Tranmere 2 Manchester City U21 1

South: AFC Wimbledon 3 Arsenal U21 0; Cambridge 2 Gillingham 0; Cheltenham 0 Portsmouth 3; Exeter 1 Northampton 2; Leyton Orient 1 Bristol Rov 2; MK Dons 6 Norwich U21 0; Oxford 1 Forest Green 1 (Oxford won 4-1 on pen); Peterborough 3 West Ham U21 0

THIRD ROUND

Bristol Rovers 0 AFC Wimbledon 1; Hull 3 Fleetwood 2; Lincoln 4 Accrington 0; Northampton 0 MK Dons 2; Oxford 1 Cambridge 0; Peterborough 5 Portsmouth 1; Sunderland 2 Port Vale 0; Tranmere 4 Leicester U21 2

QUARTER-FINALS

Hull 1 Lincoln 1 (Lincoln won 4-3 on pens); MK Dons 0 Sunderland 3; Oxford 3 AFC Wimbledon 1; Tranmere 2 Peterborough 1

SEMI-FINALS

Oxford 0 Tranmere 2; Sunderland 1 Lincoln 1 (Sunderland won 5-3 on pens)

FINAL

SUNDERLAND 1 (Gooch 57) TRANMERE ROVERS 0
Wembley; Sunday, March 14, 2021
Sunderland (4-2-2-2): Burge, Power (capt), Flanagan (McLaughlin 44), O'Nien, McFadzean, Leadbitter, Scowen, Maguire (Diamond 63), McGeady, Gooch, Wyke. **Subs not used:** Matthews, Neill, Stewart, Younger, Kimpioka. **Booked:** Power. **Manager:** Lee Johnson
Tranmere Rovers (4-2-3-1): Davies (capt), Khan, Clarke, Ray, MacDonald, Feeney, Spearing, Woolery, Morris (Burton 90+1), Lloyd (Nugent 65), Lewis (Blackett-Taylor 65). **Subs not used:** Murphy, Ridehalgh, Monthe, Kirby. **Manager:** Keith Hill
Referee: Charles Breakspear (Surrey). **Half-time:** 0-0

2019-20 FINAL (postponed from previous season)

PORTSMOUTH 0 SALFORD CITY 0 (aet, Salford City won 4-2 on pens)
Wembley; Saturday, March 13, 2021
Portsmouth (4-4-2): MacGillivray, Bolton, Whatmough, Raggett, Daniels (Brown 46), Williams, Naylor (capt); Byers (Close 73), White (Curtis 46), Hiwula (Harness 46), Marquis (Jacobs 105). **Subs not used:** Ward, Nicolaisen. **Booked:** Bolton, Naylor, Brown. **Manager:** Kenny Jackett
Salford City (4-2-3-1): Hladky, Clarke (Loughlin 115), Eastham (capt), Turnbull, Touray, Lowe,

Threlkeld, Towell (Dieseruvwe 99), Thomas-Asante, Hunter (Andrade 74), Wilson (Burgess 87).
Subs not used: Evans, Fielding, Hawkins. **Booked:** Towell, Lowe, Touray. **Manager:** Richie Wellens
Referee: Carl Boyeson (East Yorks)

BUILDBASE FA TROPHY

THIRD ROUND: Alfreton 1 King's Lynn 3; Altrincham 2 Chester 1; Ashton 1 Kettering 2; Bath 4 Swindon S 0; Boreham Wood w/o v Yeovil; Boston 1 Fylde 1 (Boston won 4-2 on pens); Bromley 2 Hemel Hempstead 0; Chesham 0 Torquay 1; Chesterfield 0 Brackley 0 (Chesterfield won 4-3 on pens); Dag & Red 5 Ebbsfleet 2; Darlington 2 Telford 2 (Darlington won 5-3 on pens); Dartford 0 Haringey 1; Dorking 3 Barnet 1; Dulwich 1 Hornchurch 2; Halifax 3 Hartlepool 3 (Halifax won 4-2 on pens); Havant 1 Braintree 0; Maidstone w/o v Frome; Maldon 1 Gloucester 7; Morpeth 0 Notts Co 3; Nantwich 0 Hereford 1; Oxford City w/o v Truro; Peterborough Sp 3 Bashford 2; Solihull 4 Farsley 0; Spennymoor 2 Southport 2 (Southport won 5-4 on pens); St Albans 0 Sutton 2; Stockport 3 Guiseley 1; Wealdstone 4 Eastleigh 3; Welwyn 1 Aldershot 5; Weymouth 3 Maidenhead 2; Woking 2 Dover 1; Wrexham 0 Leamington 0 (Leamington won 6-5 on pens); Stamford bye

FOURTH ROUND: Aldershot 3 Solihull 2; Bath 0 Peterborough Sp 1; Boreham Wood 0 Torquay 4; Boston 1 Chesterfield 1 (Chesterfield won 4-1 on pens); Bromley 1 Woking 1 (Woking won 7-6 on pens); Halifax 1 Southport 2; Havant w/o v Altrincham; Hornchurch 1 King's Lynn 1 (Hornchurch won 3-0 on pens); Kettering 0 Leamington 3; Maidstone 2 Dorking 1; Oxford City 4 Haringey 2; Stamford 0 Hereford 2; Stockport 1 Notts Co 2; Sutton 3 Dag & Red 1; Wealdstone 3 Gloucester 1; Weymouth 0 Darlington 1

FIFTH ROUND: Aldershot w/o v Chesterfield; Darlington 4 Wealdstone 1; Havant 2 Notts Co 2 (Notts Co won 4-2 on pens); Hereford 1 Leamington 0; Hornchurch 5 Maidstone 4; Oxford City 2 Peterborough Sp 0; Southport 0 Torquay 2; Sutton 0 Woking 1

QUARTER-FINALS: Aldershot 1 Hereford 1 (Hereford won 5-3 on pens); Darlington 1 Hornchurch 2; Notts Co 3 Oxford City 1; Woking 1 Torquay 0

SEMI-FINALS: Hereford 1 Woking 0; Notts Co 3 Hornchurch 3 (Hornchurch won 5-4 on pens)

FINAL

HEREFORD 1 (Owen-Evans 13) HORNCHURCH 3 (Ruff 75, Nash 86, Brown 90+5)
Wembley; Saturday, May 22, 2021
Hereford (4-4-2): Hall, Hodgkiss (capt), Grimes, Butroid, Camwell (McQuilkin 74), Owen-Evans, Haines, Butlin, Finn (Kouhyar 88), Bakare (Klukowski 90), Lloyd. **Subs not used:** White, Pollock, Digie, Jones. **Manager:** Josh Gowling
Hornchurch (4-4-2): Wright, Parcell, Hayles, Muldoon, Sutton, Christou, Clark, Spence (capt) (Ruff 59), Brown, Nash (Stimson 90+1), Higgins (Dickson 60). **Subs not used:** Thackway, Winn, Hassan, Cooper. **Booked:** Hayles, Nash, Brown. **Manager:** Mark Stimson.
Referee: Tony Harrington (Cleveland). **Half-time:** 1-0.

2019–20 BUILDBASE FA TROPHY FINAL

(postponed from previous season)

CONCORD RANGERS 0 HARROGATE TOWN 1 (Falkingham 76)
Wembley; Monday, May 3, 2021
Concord Rangers (5-3-2): Haigh, Pollock, Roast (Sorondo 83), Sterling (capt), Cawley, Payne, Blanchfield (Wall 79), Blackman, Simper, Reynolds, Charles (Barbalola 59). **Subs not used:** McFadden, Wilks, Search, Hernandez. **Manager:** Danny Scopes
Harrogate Town (4-4-2): Cracknell, Burrell, Smith, Hall, Jones (Fallowfield 62), Thomson, Kerry, Falkingham (capt), McPake (Kiernan 67), Muldoon, Stead (Beck 61). **Subs not used:** Belshaw, Francis, Lokko, Williams. **Booked:** Jones. **Manager:** Simon Weaver
Referee: Peter Bankes (Lancs). **Half-time:** 0-0.

FINALS – RESULTS

Associated Members' Cup

1984   (Hull) Bournemouth 2 Hull 1

Freight Rover Trophy – Wembley

1985   Wigan 3 Brentford 1
1986   Bristol City 3 Bolton 0
1987   Mansfield 1 Bristol City 1
         (aet; Mansfield won 5-4 on pens)

Sherpa Van Trophy – Wembley

1988   Wolves 2 Burnley 0
1989   Bolton 4 Torquay 1

Leyland Daf Cup – Wembley

1990   Tranmere 2 Bristol Rov 1
1991   Birmingham 3 Tranmere 2

Autoglass Trophy – Wembley

1992   Stoke 1 Stockport 0
1993   Port Vale 2 Stockport 1
1994   Huddersfield 1 Swansea 1
         (aet; Swansea won 3-1 on pens)

Auto Windscreens Shield – Wembley

1995   Birmingham 1 Carlisle 0
         (Birmingham won in sudden-death overtime)
1996   Rotherham 2 Shrewsbury 1
1997   Carlisle 0 Colchester 0
         (aet; Carlisle won 4-3 on pens)
1998   Grimsby 2 Bournemouth 1
         (Grimsby won with golden goal in extra-time)
1999   Wigan 1 Millwall 0
2000   Stoke 2 Bristol City 1

LDV Vans Trophy – Millennium Stadium

2001   Port Vale 2 Brentford 1
2002   Blackpool 4 Cambridge Utd 1
2003   Bristol City 2 Carlisle 0
2004   Blackpool 2 Southend 0
2005   Wrexham 2 Southend 1

Football League Trophy – Millennium Stadium

2006   Swansea 2 Carlisle 1

Johnstone's Paint Trophy – Wembley

2007   Doncaster 3 Bristol Rov 2 (aet) (Millennium Stadium)
2008   MK Dons 2 Grimsby 0
2009   Luton 3 Scunthorpe 2
2010   Southampton 4 Carlisle 1
2011   Carlisle 1 Brentford 0
2012   Chesterfield 2 Swindon 0
2013   Crewe 2 Southend 0
2014   Peterborough 3 Chesterfield 1
2015   Bristol City 2 Walsall 0
2016   Barnsley 3 Oxford 2

Checkatrade Trophy – Wembley

2017   Coventry 2 Oxford 1
2018   Lincoln 1 Shrewsbury 0
2019   Portsmouth 2 Sunderland 2
         (aet, Portsmouth won 5-4 on pens)

Papa John's Trophy – Wembley

2020   Salford 0 Portsmouth 0
         (aet, Salford won 4-2 on pens)
2021   Sunderland 1 Tranmere 0

FINALS – AT WEMBLEY

Full Members' Cup (Discontinued after 1992)

1985–86   Chelsea 5 Man City 4
1986–87   Blackburn 1 Charlton 0

Simod Cup

1987–88   Reading 4 Luton 1
1988–89   Nottm Forest 4 Everton 3

Zenith Data Systems Cup

1989–90   Chelsea 1 Middlesbrough 0
1990–91   Crystal Palace 4 Everton 1
1991–92   Nottm Forest 3 Southampton 2

Anglo-Italian Cup (Discontinued after 1996
* Home club)

1970   *Napoli 0 Swindon 3
1971   *Bologna 1 Blackpool 2 (aet)
1972   *AS Roma 3 Blackpool 1
1973   *Fiorentina 1 Newcastle 2
1993   Derby 1 Cremonese 3 (at Wembley)
1994   Notts Co 0 Brescia 1 (at Wembley)
1995   Ascoli 1 Notts Co 2 (at Wembley)
1996   Port Vale 2 Genoa 5 (at Wembley)

FA Vase

At Wembley (until 2000 and from 2007)

1975   Hoddesdon 2 Epsom & Ewell 1
1976   Billericay 1 Stamford 0*
1977   Billericay 2 Sheffield 1
         (replay Nottingham after a 1-1 at Wembley)
1978   Blue Star 2 Barton Rov 1
1979   Billericay 4 Almondsbury Greenway 1
1980   Stamford 2 Guisborough Town 0
1981   Whickham 3 Willenhall 2*
1982   Forest Green 3 Rainworth MF Welfare 0
1983   VS Rugby 1 Halesowen 0
1984   Stansted 3 Stamford 2
1985   Halesowen 3 Fleetwood 1
1986   Halesowen 3 Southall 0
1987   St Helens 3 Warrington 2
1988   Colne Dynamoes 1 Emley 0*
1989   Tamworth 3 Sudbury 0 (replay Peterborough after a 1-1 at Wembley)
1990   Yeading 1 Bridlington 0 (replay

	Leeds after 0-0 at Wembley)		
1991	Guiseley 3 Gresley Rov 1 (replay Bramall Lane Sheffield after a 4-4 at Wembley)		
1992	Wimborne 5 Guiseley 3		
1993	Bridlington 1 Tiverton 0		
1994	Diss 2 Taunton 1*		
1995	Arlesey 2 Oxford City 1		
1996	Brigg Town 3 Clitheroe 0		
1997	Whitby Town 3 North Ferriby 0		
1998	Tiverton 1 Tow Law 0		
1999	Tiverton 1 Bedlington 0		
2000	Deal 1 Chippenham 0		
2001	Taunton 2 Berkhamsted 1 (Villa Park)		
2002	Whitley Bay 1 Tiptree 0* (Villa Park)		
2003	Brigg 2 AFC Sudbury 1 (Upton Park)		
2004	Winchester 2 AFC Sudbury 0 (St Andrews)		
2005	Didcot 3 AFC Sudbury 2 (White Hart Lane)		
2006	Nantwich 3 Hillingdon 1 (St Andrews)		
2007	Truro 3 AFC Totton 1		
2008	Kirkham & Wesham (Fylde) 2 Lowestoft 1		
2009	Whitley Bay 2 Glossop 0		
2010	Whitley Bay 6 Wroxham 1		
2011	Whitley Bay 3 Coalville 2		
2012	Dunston 2 West Auckland 0		
2013	Spennymoor 2 Tunbridge Wells 1		
2014	Sholing 1 West Auckland 0		
2015	North Shields 2 Glossop North End 1*		
2016	Morpeth 4 Hereford 1		
2017	South Shields 4 Cleethorpes 0		
2018	Thatcham 1 Stockton 0		
2019	Chertsey 3 Cray Valley 1*		
2020	Hebburn 3 Consett 2		
2021	Warrington Rylands 3 Binfird 2		

* After extra-time

FA Trophy Finals

At Wembley

1970	Macclesfield 2 Telford 0		
1971	Telford 3 Hillingdon 2		
1972	Stafford 3 Barnet 0		
1973	Scarborough 2 Wigan 1*		
1974	Morecambe 2 Dartford 1		
1975	Matlock 4 Scarborough 0		
1976	Scarborough 3 Stafford 2*		
1977	Scarborough 2 Dag & Red 1		
1978	Altrincham 3 Leatherhead 1		
1979	Stafford 2 Kettering 0		
1980	Dag & Red 2 Mossley 1		
1981	Bishop's Stortford 1 Sutton 0		
1982	Enfield 1 Altrincham 0*		

1983	Telford 2 Northwich 1		
1984	Northwich 2 Bangor 1 (replay Stoke after a 1-1 at Wembley)		
1985	Wealdstone 2 Boston 1		
1986	Altrincham 1 Runcorn 0		
1987	Kidderminster 2 Burton 1 (replay WBA after a 0-0 at Wembley)		
1988	Enfield 3 Telford 2 (replay WBA after a 0-0 at Wembley)		
1989	Telford 1 Macclesfield 0*		
1990	Barrow 3 Leek 0		
1991	Wycombe 2 Kidderminster 1		
1992	Colchester 3 Witton 0		
1993	Wycombe 4 Runcorn 1		
1994	Woking 2 Runcorn 1		
1995	Woking 2 Kidderminster 1		
1996	Macclesfield 3 Northwich 1		
1997	Woking 1 Dag & Red & Redbridge 0*		
1998	Cheltenham 1 Southport 0		
1999	Kingstonian 1 Forest Green 0		
2000	Kingstonian 3 Kettering 2		

At Villa Park

2001	Canvey 1 Forest Green 0		
2002	Yeovil 2 Stevenage 0		
2003	Burscough 2 Tamworth 1		
2004	Hednesford 3 Canvey 2		
2005	Grays 1 Hucknall 1* (Grays won 6-5 on pens)		

At Upton Park

2006	Grays 2 Woking 0

At Wembley

2007	Stevenage 3 Kidderminster 2		
2008	Ebbsfleet 1 Torquay 0		
2009	Stevenage 2 York 0		
2010	Barrow 2 Stevenage 1*		
2011	Darlington 1 Mansfield 0 *		
2012	York 2 Newport 0		
2013	Wrexham 1 Grimsby 1 * Wrexham won 4-1 on pens)		
2014	Cambridge Utd 4 Gosport 0		
2015	North Ferriby 3 Wrexham 3* (North Ferriby won 5-4 on pens)		
2016	Halifax 1 Grimsby 0		
2017	York 3 Macclesfield 2		
2018	Brackley 1 Bromley 1		
2019	AFC Fylde 1 Leyton Orient 0		
2020	Harrogate 1 Concord 0		
2021	Hornchurch 3 Hereford 1		

(* Brackley won 5-4 on pens)

(*After extra-time)

FA Youth Cup Winners

Year	Winners	Runners-up	Agg
1953	Man Utd	Wolves	9-3
1954	Man Utd	Wolves	5-4

1955	Man Utd	WBA	7-1	**1991**	Millwall	Sheffield Wed	3-0
1956	Man Utd	Chesterfield	4-3	**1992**	Man Utd	Crystal Palace	6-3
1957	Man Utd	West Ham	8-2	**1993**	Leeds	Man Utd	4-1
1958	Wolves	Chelsea	7-6	**1994**	Arsenal	Millwall	5-3
1959	Blackburn	West Ham	2-1	**1995**	Man Utd	Tottenham	†2-2
1960	Chelsea	Preston	5-2	**1996**	Liverpool	West Ham	4-1
1961	Chelsea	Everton	5-3	**1997**	Leeds	Crystal Palace	3-1
1962	Newcastle	Wolves	2-1	**1998**	Everton	Blackburn	5-3
1963	West Ham	Liverpool	6-5	**1999**	West Ham	Coventry	9-0
1964	Man Utd	Swindon	5-2	**2000**	Arsenal	Coventry	5-1
1965	Everton	Arsenal	3-2	**2001**	Arsenal	Blackburn	6-3
1966	Arsenal	Sunderland	5-3	**2002**	Aston Villa	Everton	4-2
1967	Sunderland	Birmingham	2-0	**2003**	Man Utd	Middlesbrough	3-1
1968	Burnley	Coventry	3-2	**2004**	Middlesbrough	Aston Villa	4-0
1969	Sunderland	WBA	6-3	**2005**	Ipswich	Southampton	3-2
1970	Tottenham	Coventry	4-3	**2006**	Liverpool	Man City	3-2
1971	Arsenal	Cardiff	2-0	**2007**	Liverpool	Man Utd	††2-2
1972	Aston Villa	Liverpool	5-2	**2008**	Man City	Chelsea	4-2
1973	Ipswich	Bristol City	4-1	**2009**	Arsenal	Liverpool	6-2
1974	Tottenham	Huddersfield	2-1	**2010**	Chelsea	Aston Villa	3-2
1975	Ipswich	West Ham	5-1	**2011**	Man Utd	Sheff Utd	6-3
1976	WBA	Wolves	5-0	**2012**	Chelsea	Blackburn	4-1
1977	Crystal Palace	Everton	1-0	**2013**	Norwich	Chelsea	4-2
1978	Crystal Palace	Aston Villa	*1-0	**2014**	Chelsea	Fulham	7-6
1979	Millwall	Man City	2-0	**2015**	Chelsea	Man City	5-2
1980	Aston Villa	Man City	3-2	**2016**	Chelsea	Man City	4-2
1981	West Ham	Tottenham	2-1	**2017**	Chelsea	Man City	6-2
1982	Watford	Man Utd	7-6	**2018**	Chelsea	Arsenal	7-1
1983	Norwich	Everton	6-5	**2019**	Liverpool	Man City	*†††
1984	Everton	Stoke	4-2		1-1		
1985	Newcastle	Watford	4-1	**2020**	Man City	Chelsea	* (asterisk)
1986	Man City	Man Utd	3-1		3-2		
1987	Coventry	Charlton	2-1	**2021**	Aston Villa	Liverpool	2-1
1988	Arsenal	Doncaster	6-1	†††Liverpool won 5-3 on pens			
1989	Watford	Man City	2-1	(*One match only; †Manchester Utd won 4-3			
1990	Tottenham	Middlesbrough	3-2	on pens, ††Liverpool won 4-3 on pens)			

CHARITY/COMMUNITY SHIELD RESULTS (POST WAR)
CHARITY SHIELD

1948	Arsenal	Manchester Utd	4-3
1949	Portsmouth	Wolves	*1-1
1950	England World Cup XI	FA Canadian Tour Team	4-2
1951	Tottenham	Newcastle	2-1
1952	Manchester Utd	Newcastle	4-2
1953	Arsenal	Blackpool	3-1
1954	Wolves	WBA	*4-4
1955	Chelsea	Newcastle	3-0
1956	Manchester Utd	Manchester City	1-0
1957	Manchester Utd	Aston Villa	4-0
1958	Bolton	Wolves	4-1
1959	Wolves	Nottm Forest	3-1
1960	Burnley	Wolves	*2-2
1961	Tottenham	FA XI	3-2
1962	Tottenham	Ipswich Town	5-1

1963	Everton	Manchester Utd	4-0
1964	Liverpool	West Ham	*2-2
1965	Manchester Utd	Liverpool	*2-2
1966	Liverpool	Everton	1-0
1967	Manchester Utd	Tottenham	*3-3
1968	Manchester City	WBA	6-1
1969	Leeds	Manchester City	2-1
1970	Everton	Chelsea	2-1
1971	Leicester	Liverpool	1-0
1972	Manchester City	Aston Villa	1-0
1973	Burnley	Manchester City	1-0
1974	Liverpool	Leeds	1-1

(Liverpool won 6-5 on penalties)

1975	Derby Co	West Ham	2-0
1976	Liverpool	Southampton	1-0
1977	Liverpool	Manchester Utd	*0-0
1978	Nottm Forest	Ipswich	5-0
1979	Liverpool	Arsenal	3-1
1980	Liverpool	West Ham	1-0
1981	Aston Villa	Tottenham	*2-2
1982	Liverpool	Tottenham	1-0
1983	Manchester Utd	Liverpool	2-0
1984	Everton	Liverpool	1-0
1985	Everton	Manchester Utd	2-0
1986	Everton	Liverpool	*1-1
1987	Everton	Coventry	1-0
1988	Liverpool	Wimbledon	2-1
1989	Liverpool	Arsenal	1-0
1990	Liverpool	Manchester Utd	*1-1
1991	Arsenal	Tottenham	*0-0
1992	Leeds	Liverpool	4-3
1993	Manchester Utd	Arsenal	1-1

(Manchester Utd won 5-4 on penalties)

1994	Manchester Utd	Blackburn	2-0
1995	Everton	Blackburn	1-0
1996	Manchester Utd	Newcastle	4-0
1997	Manchester Utd	Chelsea	1-1

(Manchester Utd won 4-2 on penalties)

1998	Arsenal	Manchester Utd	3-0
1999	Arsenal	Manchester Utd	2-1
2000	Chelsea	Manchester Utd	2-0
2001	Liverpool	Manchester Utd	2-1

COMMUNITY SHIELD

2002	Arsenal	Liverpool	1-0
2003	Manchester Utd	Arsenal	1-1

(Manchester Utd won 4-3 on penalties)

2004	Arsenal	Manchester Utd	3-1
2005	Chelsea	Arsenal	2-1
2006	Liverpool	Chelsea	2-1
2007	Manchester Utd	Chelsea	1-1

(Manchester Utd won 3-0 on penalties)

2008	Manchester Utd	Portsmouth	0-0

(Manchester Utd won 3-1 on pens)

2009	Chelsea	Manchester Utd	2-2

(Chelsea won 4-1 on pens)

2010	Manchester Utd	Chelsea	3-1
2011	Manchester Utd	Manchester City	3-2

2012	Manchester City	Chelsea	3-2
2013	Manchester Utd	Wigan	2-0
2014	Arsenal	Manchester City	3-0
2015	Arsenal	Chelsea	1-0
2016	Manchester Utd	Leicester	2-1
2017	Arsenal	Chelsea	1-1
	(Arsenal won 4-1 on pens)		
2018	Manchester City	Chelsea	2-0
2019	Manchester City	Liverpool	1-1
	(Manchester City won 5-4 on pens)		
2020	Arsenal	Liverpool	1-1
	(Arsenal won 5-4 on pens)		

(Fixture played at Wembley 1974–2000 and from 2007); Millennium Stadium 2001–06; Villa Park 2012) * Trophy shared

FOOTBALL'S CHANGING HOMES

Everton followed the appointment of new manager Rafael Benitez by announcing the start of work on a new 53,000 capacity waterfront stadium. Chairman Bill Kenwright hailed a 'momentous' day for the club after years of planning and negotiating for a move from Goodison Park, the club's home since 1892. The target is to be playing in the new ground at Bramley Moore dock by season 2024–25. It is expected to deliver a £1bn regeneration boost, create 15,000 jobs and transform that part of the city. Kenwright said: 'This is a momentous day in the history of the club. Like every Evertonian, Goodison Park has been a massive part of my life. But in moving forward we could not have found a more fitting nor more glorious site for our new stadium – one which will both honour our history and celebrate our future.'

AFC Wimbledon returned to their 'spiritual home' in Plough Lane two months into the 2020-21 season. They initially struggled in the new 9,300-capacity stadium, 250 yards away on the site of a former greyhound track, and were in danger of being relegated from League One until three successive home wins in the final month made them safe. The original Wimbledon left the old ground in 1991 and received FA approval in 2002 to relocate, controversially, to Milton Keynes. AFC were founded, working their way up the football pyramid at Kingsmeadow in Kingston upon Thames and reaching the Football League in 2012.

Brentford had a successful first season in their new Community Stadium near Kew Bridge, winning promotion to the Premier League via the Championship play-offs. After two seasons playing at St Andrew's in Birmingham,

Coventry City returned home in the 2021-22 campaign to the Ricoh Arena, now renamed the Coventry Building Society Arena, after signing a ten-year contract with owners Wasps Rugby. The club still have a long-term ambition to build a new stadium on the south-west edge of the city on land owned by the University of Warwick.

THE THINGS THEY SAY ...

'The technique was absolutely insane. I did not shout stay back. I just let him run' – **Jurgen Klopp**, Liverpool manager, after goalkeeper Alisson's winning header in stoppage-time against West Bromwich Albion.

The message has been lost. It is now not dissimilar to a fancy hashtag or a nice pin badge' – **Les Ferdinand**, Queens Park Rangers' director of football, claiming that players 'taking the knee' became good PR but little more.

SCOTTISH TABLES 2020–2021

PREMIERSHIP

		P	W	D	L	F	A	W	D	L	F	A	Gd	Pts
			Home					Away						
1	Rangers	38	19	0	0	57	4	13	6	0	35	9	79	102
2	Celtic	38	13	4	2	41	11	9	7	3	37	18	49	77
3	Hibernian	38	7	6	6	21	21	11	3	5	27	14	13	63
4	Aberdeen	38	9	5	5	23	18	6	6	7	13	20	-2	56
5	St Johnstone	38	5	6	8	9	15	6	6	7	27	31	-10	45
6	Livingston	38	6	4	9	20	25	6	5	8	22	29	-12	45
7	St Mirren	38	4	8	7	15	23	7	4	8	22	22	-8	45
8	Motherwell	38	6	3	10	20	31	6	6	7	19	24	-16	45
9	Dundee Utd	38	6	6	7	21	24	4	8	7	11	26	-18	44
10	Ross Co	38	5	4	10	19	35	6	2	11	16	31	-31	39
11	Kilmarnock	38	6	5	8	30	27	4	1	14	13	27	-11	36
20	Hamilton	38	4	4	11	13	29	5	3	11	21	38	-33	30

Rangers into Champions League third qualifying round; Celtic into second qualifying round; St Johnstone into Europa League third qualifying round; Hibernian and Aberdeen into Europa Conference League

Play-offs (on agg): Quarter-final: Raith 2 Dunfermline 0. **Semi-final:** Dundee 3 Raith 1. **Final:** Dundee 4 Kilmarnock 2

Player of Year: Allan McGregor (Rangers). **Manager of Year:** Steven Gerrard (Rangers)

Team of Year: McGregor (Rangers), Tavernier (Rangers), Ajer (Celtic), Goldson (Rangers), Barisic (Rangers), Kamara (Rangers), Turnbull (Celtic), Davis (Rangers), Edouard (Celtic), Morelos (Rangers), Kent (Rangers)

Leading league scorers: 18 Edouard (Celtic); 14 Nisbet (Hibernian), Roofe (Rangers); 12 Boyle (Hibernian), Morelos (Rangers), Tavernier (Rangers); 11 Cole (Motherwell); 10 Elyounoussi (Celtic), Kent (Rangers), McGrath (St Mirren)

CHAMPIONSHIP

		P	W	D	L	F	A	W	D	L	F	A	Gd	Pts
			Home					Away						
1	Hearts	27	11	1	2	44	16	6	5	2	19	8	39	57
2	Dundee*	27	8	3	2	25	17	4	6	4	24	23	9	45
3	Raith	27	6	3	4	24	18	6	4	4	21	18	9	43
4	Dunfermline	27	9	3	2	24	13	1	6	6	14	21	4	39
5	Inverness	27	3	8	2	16	13	5	4	5	20	18	5	36
6	Queen of Sth	27	4	3	6	17	24	5	2	7	21	27	-13	32
7	Arbroath	27	5	6	3	16	11	2	3	8	12	23	-6	30
8	Ayr	27	5	4	4	11	12	3	5	6	20	25	-6	29
9	Morton	27	4	5	5	14	18	2	6	5	8	15	-11	29
10	Alloa	27	3	5	6	18	29	2	2	9	12	31	-30	22

*Also promoted

Play-offs (on agg): Semi-finals: Airdrieonians 4 Cove 3; Morton 4 Montrose 3. **Final:** Morton 4 Airdrieonians 0

Player of Year: Liam Boyce (Hearts). **Manager of Year:** James McPake (Dundee)

Team of Year: Gordon (Hearts), Smith (Hearts), Murray (Dunfermline), Obileye (Queen of South), Ashcroft (Dundee), Adam (Dundee), Hendry (Raith), Irving (Hearts), Shields (Queen of South, Boyce (Hearts), Todorov (Inverness)

Leading league scorers: 14 Boyce (Hearts); 9 McManus (Dunfermline), Obileye (Queen of South) Todorov (Inverness), Wighton (Hearts/Dunfermline)' 8 Cummings (Dundee), Hamilton (Arbroath), O'Hara (Dunfermline), Shields (Queen of South), Sow (Dundee)

LEAGUE ONE

			Home				Away						
		P	W	D	L	F	A	W	D	L	F	A	Gd	Pts
1	Partick	22	6	4	1	22	7	5	3	3	18	11	22	40
2	Airdrieonians	22	7	1	3	21	11	5	1	5	14	13	11	38
3	Cove	22	7	1	3	18	10	3	5	3	10	8	10	36
4	Montrose	22	5	3	3	19	14	4	3	4	14	19	0	33
5	Falkirk	22	5	4	2	14	9	4	1	6	15	17	3	32
6	East Fife	22	7	3	1	18	11	3	0	8	12	22	-3	33
7	Peterhead	22	5	1	5	10	12	4	1	6	14	15	-5	29
8	Clyde	22	5	1	5	15	17	3	1	7	12	21	-11	26
9	Dumbarton	22	5	1	5	8	11	2	3	6	6	13	-10	25
10	Forfar	22	1	2	8	10	21	3	3	5	8	16	-19	17

Play-offs (on agg): Semi-finals: Dumbarton 1 Stranraer 0; Edinburgh City 3 Elgin 2. **Final:** Dumbarton 3 Edinburgh City 2
Player of Year: Mitch Megginson (Cove)
Manager of Year: Ian McCall (Partick)
Team of Year: McKenzie (Cove), Ballantyne (Montrose), Brownlie (Partick), Fordyce (Airdrieonians), McCann (Airdrieonians), Webster (Montrose), Brown (Peterhead), Bannigan (Partick), Tiffoney (Partick), Megginson (Cove), Graham (Partick)
Leading scorers: 14 Megginson (Cove); 11 Goodwillie (Clyde), Graham (Partick); 9 Carrick (Airdrieonians); 8 Webster (Montrose); 7 Hamilton (East Fife), McLean (Montrose), Tiffoney (Partick); 6 Connell (Airdrieonians), Gallagher (Airdrieonians), Morrison (Falkirk), Rudden (Partick)

LEAGUE TWO

			Home				Away						
		P	W	D	L	F	A	W	D	L	F	A	Gd	Pts
1	Queen's Park	22	8	2	1	21	5	9	1	1	22	8	30	54
2	Edinburgh	22	5	1	5	18	14	7	1	3	22	13	13	38
3	Elgin	22	7	1	3	23	15	5	1	5	16	13	11	38
4	Stranraer	22	6	1	4	20	13	5	4	2	16	12	11	38
5	Stirling	22	4	3	4	9	9	6	3	2	23	13	10	36
6	Stenhousemuir	22	5	2	4	15	13	2	3	6	10	22	-10	26
7	Albion	22	2	3	6	8	16	5	1	5	17	22	-13	25
8	Annan	22	2	4	5	15	18	3	3	5	10	9	-2	22
9	Cowdenbeath	22	3	2	6	9	19	2	4	5	6	13	-17	21
10	Brechin	22	0	3	8	6	27	2	1	8	7	19	-33	10

Pyramid play-offs (on agg): Semi-final: Kelty 6 Brora 1. **Final:** Kelty 3 Brechin 1
Player of Year: Michael Doyle (Queen's Park)
Manager of Year: Ray McKinnon (Queen's Park)
Team of Year: Muir (Queen's Park), Doyle (Queen's Park), Kilday (Queen's Park), Henderson (Edinburgh City), Stirling (Stranraer), Cameron (Elgin), Gillespie (Queen's Park), Campbell (Edinburgh City), Ryan (Stirling), Hester (Elgin), Orr (Stranraer)
Leading scorers: 15 Hester (Elgin); 10 Aitken (Albion), Ryan (Stirling); 8 Orr (Stranraer); 7 Campbell (Edinburgh City); 6 Biabi (Stenhousemuir), McGuigan (Stenhousemuir), McHugh (Queen's Park), Murray (Queen's Park), Paton (Stranraer)

SCOTTISH LEAGUE RESULTS 2020–2021

PREMIERSHIP

	Aberdeen	Celtic	Dundee Utd	Hamilton	Hibernian	Kilmarnock	Livingston	Motherwell	Rangers	Ross Co	St Johnstone	St Mirren
Aberdeen	–	3-3	0-0	4-2	2-0	1-0	2-1	0-3	0-1	2-0	2-1	2-1
	–	1-1		0-0	0-1	1-0	0-2	2-0	1-2			0-0
Celtic	1-0	–	3-0	5-1	3-0	2-0	3-2	3-0	0-2	2-0	1-1	1-2
	1-0	–		2-0	1-1		0-0	2-1	1-1		4-0	
							6-0					
Dundee Utd	0-0	0-1	–	2-1	0-1	2-0	1-2	1-1	1-2	2-1	1-1	2-1
	1-0	0-0	–		0-2		3-0	2-0		0-2	2-2	1-5
Hamilton	1-1	0-3	1-1	–	0-4	1-0	0-2	3-0	0-2	0-1	3-5	0-1
			0-0	–		0-2		0-1	1-1	1-2	1-1	1-1
			0-1	–								
Hibernian	0-1	2-2	1-1	3-2	–	2-1	0-3	0-0	2-2	0-2	2-2	1-0
	2-0	0-0	2-0		–	2-0	2-1	0-2	0-1		0-1	
Kilmarnock	0-2	1-1	4-0	2-1	0-1	–	1-2	0-1	0-1	3-1	1-2	1-1
		0-4	1-1	2-0		–		4-1		2-2	2-3	3-3
			3-0			–						
Livingston	0-0	2-2	2-0	1-2	1-4	1-3	–	0-2	0-0	1-0	2-0	0-1
	1-2			2-1	1-1	2-0	–		0-1	3-1	1-2	
							–		0-3			
Motherwell	0-0	1-4	0-1	0-1	0-3	0-2	2-2	–	1-5	4-0	1-0	0-1
	2-1	1-4		1-4	2-0	3-1		–	1-1	1-2	0-3	1-0
Rangers	4-0	1-0	4-0	8-0	1-0	2-0	2-0	3-1	–	2-0	3-0	3-0
	4-0	4-1	4-1		2-1	1-0			–	5-0	1-0	3-0
Ross Co	0-3	0-5	1-2	0-2	0-0	2-2	1-1	1-0	0-4	–	1-1	0-2
	4-1	1-0	0-2	2-1	1-2	3-2		1-2		–		1-3
St Johnstone	0-1	0-2	0-0	0-0	0-1	1-0	1-2	1-1	0-3	0-1	–	1-0
	0-0	1-2			1-0		0-0		1-1	1-0	–	1-0
	0-1										–	
St Mirren	1-1	1-2	0-0	1-1	0-3	0-1	1-0	1-1	0-2	1-1	3-2	–
		0-4	0-0	1-2	1-2	2-0	1-1	0-0		1-0		–

	Alloa	Arbroath	Ayr	Dundee	Dunfermline	Greenock Morton	Hearts	Inverness	Queen of South	Raith
Alloa	–	1-1	0-2	3-3	1-4	1-1	1-3	2-1	2-1	2-5
	–		2-2	0-3	1-0			1-1		1-2
Arboath	0-1	–	2-1	1-1	2-0	0-0	0-1	1-1	1-1	1-0
	2-1	–	4-0			0-0	0-0		2-4	
Ayr	4-1	0-1	–	2-0	0-0	1-1	0-1	0-2	2-1	0-0
			–	0-3	1-1				0-0	1-1
Dundee	3-1	1-0	1-3	–	3-3	1-0	3-1	2-1	2-3	1-1
		2-0		–	3-2	1-1				2-1
Dunfermline	2-1	1-0	0-0	0-0	–	1-2	2-1	3-1	3-2	4-1
		4-3			–	1-0	0-0	0-1	3-1	
Greenock Morton	1-0	0-1	3-2	2-2	0-0	–	0-2	2-2	2-0	0-1
	1-1		0-2			–	0-0	1-4	2-1	
Hearts	3-0	3-1	5-3	6-2	1-0	1-1	–	2-1	6-1	2-3
	6-0		2-0	2-1			–	3-0	2-3	
Inverness	2-2	3-1	1-1	2-2	1-1	0-1	1-1	–	0-1	2-0
		1-0	2-2	1-1				–		0-0
Queen of South	2-0	2-2	3-2	1-3	1-0	2-1	1-1	0-3	–	2-5
	2-3			0-2				1-1	–	0-1
Raith	3-1	3-0	0-0	3-1	2-2	5-0	0-4	0-1	0-2	–
		2-2			5-1	1-0	0-4			–

LEAGUE ONE

	Airdrieonians	Clyde	Cove	Dumbarton	East Fife	Falkirk	Forfar	Montrose	Partick	Peterhead
Airdrieonians	–	5-0	1-1	0-2	2-0	2-1	3-1	0-1	2-4	2-0
	–					2-0		2-1		
Clyde	2-4	–	1-1	0-1	1-3	0-3	3-0	3-2	1-0	0-2
		–		2-0	2-1					
Cove	2-0	2-3	–	1-0	3-1	2-0	3-0	1-2	1-0	1-0
	0-2		–						2-2	
Dumbarton	0-1	1-0	1-0	–	2-1	0-3	0-1	0-0	0-2	0-1
				–			1-0			3-2
East Fife	2-0	1-0	0-0	2-1	–	2-1	2-0	2-2	2-2	2-1
				2-1	–					1-3
Falkirk	0-1	2-1	1-0	1-1	2-0	–	1-1	2-0	0-0	2-1
		2-2				–		1-2		
Forfar	1-3	1-3	0-1	0-0	1-2	0-2	–	2-3	0-2	1-1
		2-1			2-3		–			
Montrose	2-2	2-2	1-0	4-0	3-0	1-3	0-0	–	0-1	3-2
		0-2						–	3-2	
Partick	2-1	2-0	1-1	0-0	2-0	2-2	2-2	5-0	–	0-1
	1-0					5-0			–	
Peterhead	1-0	0-2	0-2	1-0	2-1	1-0	0-1	1-1	0-3	–
		3-0					1-2			–

LEAGUE TWO

	Albion	Annan	Brechin	Cowdenbeath	Edinburgh City	Elgin	Queen's Park	Stenhousemuir	Stirling	Stranraer
Albion	– –	1-1 1-0	0-2 1-1	0-0	1-2	3-1	0-3	1-3	0-1	0-2
Annan	2-3	–	3-0	0-0 1-1	0-4	0-3	1-2	5-1 1-1	1-2	1-1
Brechin	2-4	0-0 0-3	–	0-0	1-5	1-2	0-2	1-1 0-1	0-5	1-4
Cowdenbeath	0-1 2-0	0-3	2-0 0-2	–	1-3	1-0	0-3	1-1	1-5	1-1
Edinburgh City	5-2	1-1	2-1	0-1	–	1-0 2-0	2-3	3-1	2-3 0-1	0-1
Elgin	2-5	1-0	3-0	5-2	1-2	–	0-1 3-2	2-0	1-1 3-1	2-1
Queen's Park	2-0	1-0	3-0	3-0	3-3 2-0	0-0	–	3-1	1-0	3-0 0-1
Stenhousemuir	2-0 0-1	1-2	2-1	1-0 0-2	2-0	2-0	1-3	– –	2-2	2-2
Stirling	1-1	1-0	1-0	1-0	0-1	1-2	0-0 1-2	1-0	–	0-1 2-2
Stranraer	4-0	2-0	2-0	2-0	0-1 2-1	1-4 1-4	0-1	4-0	2-2	–

RANGERS IN A CLASS OF THEIR OWN

Steven Gerrard set his players three more targets after they broke Celtic's nine-year stranglehold on the Scottish Premiership title with six games still to play. The Rangers manager asked them to complete the season unbeaten, reach a century of points and break a British defensive record held by Chelsea. In each case they obliged, winning 32 and drawing six of 38 matches to accumulate 102 points. And by conceding just 13 goals – four at Ibrox and nine away from home – they outdid Jose Mourinho's Chelsea, who let in 15 when finishing Premier League champions in 2004–05. In was, in every sense, an outstanding performance – 25 points ahead of Celtic as well as knocking Neil Lennon's side out of the Scottish Cup. Lennon resigned when Celtic were 18 points adrift, although it was certainly not a totally barren season for the club and their manager, who made history in the 2020 Scottish Cup Final, held over from the previous season because of Covid. A 4-3 penalty shoot-out win against Hearts after a 3-3 draw gave Lennon a domestic treble as player and manager and the club a clean sweep of trophies for the fourth successive season.

Gerrard also had to share some of the spotlight with Callum Davidson, who led St Johnstone to the greatest campaign in the club's history with a trophy double. They defeated Livingston 1-0 in the League Cup Final and Hibernian by the same scoreline in the Scottish Cup. The matchwinner each time was wing-back Shaun Rooney and there was another outstanding performance by goalkeeper Zander Clark in the fifth-round victory over Rangers in the latter competition. His downward header from a corner was touched in by Chris Kane for an equaliser in extra-time. Clark then saved from James Tavernier and Kemar Roofe in the resulting penalty shoot-out which St Johnstone won 4-2. They also finished fifth in the Premiership, which saw Kilmarnock relegated after 28 years in the top division by a 4-2 aggregate defeat by Dundee in the play-offs. Brechin's 68 years of league membership came to an end in a 3-1 play-off defeat by up-and-coming Kelty Hearts, a village team from Fife managed by former Rangers and Scotland midfielder Barry Ferguson. Shortly afterwards, Ferguson left to take charge of League One Alloa.

HOW RANGERS HALTED CELTIC'S RUN

AUGUST 2020

1	Aberdeen 0 Rangers 1 (Kent 21)
9	Rangers 3 (McCarthy 23 og, Morelos 69, 74) St Mirren 0
12	Rangers 3 (Barisic 21, Kent 45, Aribo 49) St Johnstone 0
16	Livingston 0 Rangers 0
22	Rangers 2 (Roofe 50, Kent 77) Kilmarnock 0
29	Hamilton 0 Rangers 2 (Hagi 15, Tavernier 20)

SEPTEMBER 2020

12	Rangers 4 (Kent 13, Tavernier 39, Roofe 68, Arfield 87) Dundee Utd 0
19	Hibernian 2 (Wright 22, Doidge 71) Rangers 2 (Morelos 45, Arfield 57)
27	Motherwell 1 (Edmundson 87 og) Rangers 5 (Tavernier 12 pen, 37 pen, Jones 28, Itten 75, 80)

OCTOBER 2020

4	Rangers 2 (Tavernier 17 pen, Barker 88) Ross Co 0
17	Celtic 0 Rangers 2 (Goldson 9, 54)
25	Rangers 2 (Aribo 9, Defoe 16) Livingston 0

NOVEMBER 2020

1	Kilmarnock 0 Rangers 1 (Tavernier 19 pen)

8   Rangers 8 (Arfield 16, Roofe 18, 54, Aribo 19, 36, Barker 62, Tavernier 65 pen, 69) Hamilton 0

22   Rangers 4 (Kent 15, Roofe 29, Arfield 49, Tavernier 53 pen) Aberdeen 0

DECEMBER 2020

6   Ross Co 0 Rangers 4 (Roofe 28, Tavernier 56, Morris 72 og, Defoe 90)
13   Dundee Utd 1 (L Smith 33) Rangers 2 (Tavernier 26, Goldson 44)
19   Rangers 3 (Roofe 73, 90+4, Itten 82) Motherwell 1 (Lang 76)
23   St Johnstone 0 Rangers 3 (Roofe 24, Kamara 31, Hagi 47)
26   Rangers 1 (Hagi 33) Hibernian 0
30   St Mirren 0 Rangers 2 (Roofe 27, Morelos 33)

JANUARY 2021

2   Rangers 1 (McGregor 70 og) Celtic 0
10   Aberdeen 1 (Kennedy 67) Rangers 2 (Morelos 32, 50)
17   Motherwell 1 (Cole 21) Rangers 1 (Itten 72)
23   Rangers 5 (Kent 6, Helander 28, Aribo 37, Jack 66, Goldson 81) Ross Co 0
27   Hibernian 0 Rangers 1 (Morelos 51)

FEBRUARY 2021

3   Rangers 1 (Hagi 52) St Johnstone 0
7   Hamilton 1 (Callachan 90) Rangers 1 (Easton 80 og)
13   Rangers 1 (Jack 38) Kilmarnock 0
21   Rangers 4 (Hagi 35, Kent 38, Aribo 48, Morelos 64) Dundee Utd 1 (McNulty 86)

MARCH 2021

3   Livingston 0 Rangers 1 (Morelos 87)
6   Rangers 3 (Kent 14, Morelos 16, Hagi 46) St Mirren 0
7   Clinched title after Dundee Utd 0 Celtic 0
21   Celtic 1 (Elyounoussi 23) Rangers 1 (Morelos 38)

APRIL 2021

11   Rangers 2 (Aribo 20, Kent 62) Hibernian 1 (Nisbet 78)
21   St Johnstone 1 (Craig 90+5 pen) Rangers 1 (Wright 55)

MAY 2021

2   Rangers 4 (Roofe 26, 57, Morelos 33, Defoe 90+2) Celtic 1 (Edouard 30)
12   Livingston 0 Rangers 3 (Tavernier 42 pen, Kent 57, Hagi 83)
15   Rangers 4 (Lewis 5 og, Roofe 34, 60, Defoe 88) Aberdeen 0

HOW CELTIC MISSED OUT ON A TENTH TITLE

AUGUST 2020

2   Celtic 5 (Edouard 20, 49, 53, Frimpong 31, Klimala 90) Hamilton 1 (Jullien 34 og)
9   Kilmarnock 1 (Burke 24 pen) Celtic 1 (Christie 11)
22   Dundee Utd 0 Celtic 1 (Ajeti 83)
30   Celtic 3 (Forrest 40, Ajeti 74, Jullien 90+2) Motherwell 0

SEPTEMBER 2020

12   Ross Co 0 Celtic 5 (Edouard 4 pen, Ajeti 20, Duffy 59, Ajer 64, Klimala 75)

17	St Mirren 1 (Erwin 3) Celtic 2 (Duffy 21, Forrest 36)
19	Celtic 3 (McGregor 20, Christie 23, Ajeti 52) Livingston 2 (Holt 17 pen, Serrano 78)
27	Celtic 3 (McGregor 7, Ajeti 35, Elyounoussi 79) Hibernian 0

OCTOBER 2020

4	St Johnstone 0 Celtic 2 (Griffiths 90, Klimala 90+3)
17	Celtic 0 Rangers 2 (Goldson 9, 54)
25	Aberdeen 3 (Ferguson 43 pen, 90 pen, Hedges 65) Celtic 3 (McGregor 52, Griffiths 76, Christie 78 pen)

NOVEMBER 2020

| 8 | Motherwell 1 (Gallagher 72) Celtic 4 (Elyounoussi 8, 27, 76, Ntcham 86) |
| 21 | Hibernian 2 (Murphy 52, Nisbet 59) Celtic 2 (Edouard 79 pen, Laxalt 90+1) |

DECEMBER 2020

6	Celtic 1 (Elyounoussi 83) St Johnstone 1 (Kane 79)
13	Celtic 2 (Elyounoussi 58, Duffy 70) Kilmarnock 0
23	Celtic 2 (Turnbull 24, Griffiths 61) Ross Co 0
26	Hamilton 0 Celtic 3 (Edouard 49 pen, Griffiths 54, Turnbull 74)
30	Celtic 3 (Soro 23. Turnbull 40, Edouard 76) Dundee Utd 0

JANUARY 2021

2	Rangers 1 (McGregor 70 og) Celtic 0
11	Celtic 1 (Turnbull 81) Hibernian 1 (Nisbet 90+1)
16	Celtic 0 Livingston 0
20	Livingston 2 (Brown 15, Emmanuel-Thomas 60) Celtic 2 (Elyounoussi 28, Bitton 38)
27	Celtic 2 (Griffiths 12, Edouard 48) Hamilton 0
30	Celtic 1 (Edouard 32) St Mirren 2 (Dennis 18, Durmus 37)

FEBRUARY 2021

2	Kilmarnock 0 Celtic 4 (Brown 29, Edouard 53 pen, 62, Ajeti 86)
6	Celtic 2 (Welsh 2, Edouard 51) Motherwell 1 (Campbell 66)
11	St Mirren 0 Celtic 4 (Rogic 16, Edouard 79 pen, Christie 82, Turnbull 83)
14	St Johnstone 1 (Rooney 50) Celtic 2 (Edouard 60, 62)
17	Celtic 1 (Turnbull 14) Aberdeen 0
21	Ross Co 1 (White 71) Celtic 0
27	Celtic 1 (Edouard 8) Aberdeen 0

MARCH 2021

| 7 | Dundee Utd 0 Celtic 0 – Rangers clinched title |
| 21 | Celtic 1 (Elyounoussi 23) Rangers 1 (Morelos 38) |

APRIL 2021

| 10 | Celtic 6 (Forrest 30, Turnbull 38, Fitzwater 50 og, Elyounoussi 54, 66, Christie 87) Livingston 0 |
| 21 | Aberdeen 1 (Ferguson 17) Celtic 1 (Griffiths 90+3) |

MAY 2021

2	Rangers 4 (Roofe 26, 57, Morelos 33, Defoe 90+2) Celtic 1 (Edouard 30)
12	Celtic 4 (Turnbull 23, Edouard 24, Ajer 79, Dembele 85) St Johnstone 0
15	Hibernian 0 Celtic 0

SCOTTISH HONOURS LIST

PREMIER DIVISION

	First	Pts	Second	Pts	Third	Pts
1975–6	Rangers	54	Celtic	48	Hibernian	43
1976–7	Celtic	55	Rangers	46	Aberdeen	43
1977–8	Rangers	55	Aberdeen	53	Dundee Utd	40
1978–9	Celtic	48	Rangers	45	Dundee Utd	44
1979–80	Aberdeen	48	Celtic	47	St Mirren	42
1980–81	Celtic	56	Aberdeen	49	Rangers	44
1981–2	Celtic	55	Aberdeen	53	Rangers	43
1982–3	Dundee Utd	56	Celtic	55	Aberdeen	55
1983–4	Aberdeen	57	Celtic	50	Dundee Utd	47
1984–5	Aberdeen	59	Celtic	52	Dundee Utd	47
1985–6	*Celtic	50	Hearts	50	Dundee Utd	47
1986–7	Rangers	69	Celtic	63	Dundee Utd	60
1987–8	Celtic	72	Hearts	62	Rangers	60
1988–9	Rangers	56	Aberdeen	50	Celtic	46
1989–90	Rangers	51	Aberdeen	44	Hearts	44
1990–1	Rangers	55	Aberdeen	53	Celtic	41
1991–2	Rangers	72	Hearts	63	Celtic	62
1992–3	Rangers	73	Aberdeen	64	Celtic	60
1993–4	Rangers	58	Aberdeen	55	Motherwell	54
1994–5	Rangers	69	Motherwell	54	Hibernian	53
1995–6	Rangers	87	Celtic	83	Aberdeen	55
1996–7	Rangers	80	Celtic	75	Dundee Utd	60
1997–8	Celtic	74	Rangers	72	Hearts	67

PREMIER LEAGUE

	First	Pts	Second	Pts	Third	Pts
1998–99	Rangers	77	Celtic	71	St Johnstone	57
1999–2000	Rangers	90	Celtic	69	Hearts	54
2000–01	Celtic	97	Rangers	82	Hibernian	66
2001–02	Celtic	103	Rangers	85	Livingston	58
2002–03	*Rangers	97	Celtic	97	Hearts	63
2003–04	Celtic	98	Rangers	81	Hearts	68
2004–05	Rangers	93	Celtic	92	Hibernian	61
2005–06	Celtic	91	Hearts	74	Rangers	73
2006–07	Celtic	84	Rangers	72	Aberdeen	65
2007–08	Celtic	89	Rangers	86	Motherwell	60
2008–09	Rangers	86	Celtic	82	Hearts	59
2009–10	Rangers	87	Celtic	81	Dundee Utd	63
2010–11	Rangers	93	Celtic	92	Hearts	63
2011–12	Celtic	93	**Rangers	73	Motherwell	62
2012–13	Celtic	79	Motherwell	63	St Johnstone	56

Maximum points: 72 except 1986–8, 1991–4 (88), 1994–2000 (108), 2001–10 (114)
* Won on goal difference. **Deducted 10 pts for administration

PREMIERSHIP

	First	Pts	Second	Pts	Third	Pts
2013–14	Celtic	99	Motherwell	70	Aberdeen	68
2014–15	Celtic	92	Aberdeen	75	Inverness	65
2015–16	Celtic	86	Aberdeen	71	Hearts	65
2016–17	Celtic	106	Aberdeen	76	Rangers	67
2017–18	Celtic	82	Aberdeen	73	Rangers	70
2018–19	Celtic	87	Rangers	78	Kilmarnock	67
2019–20C	Celtic	80	Rangers	67	Motherwell	46
2020–21	Rangers	102	Celtic	77	Hibernian	63

C Season curtailed – COVID-19

FIRST DIVISION (Scottish Championship until 1975–76)

	First	Pts	Second	Pts	Third	Pts
1890–1a	††Dumbarton	29	Rangers	29	Celtic	24
1891–2b	Dumbarton	37	Celtic	35	Hearts	30
1892–3a	Celtic	29	Rangers	28	St Mirren	23
1893–4a	Celtic	29	Hearts	26	St Bernard's	22
1894–5a	Hearts	31	Celtic	26	Rangers	21
1895–6a	Celtic	30	Rangers	26	Hibernian	24
1896–7a	Hearts	28	Hibernian	26	Rangers	25
1897–8a	Celtic	33	Rangers	29	Hibernian	22
1898–9a	Rangers	36	Hearts	26	Celtic	24
1899–1900a	Rangers	32	Celtic	25	Hibernian	24
1900–1c	Rangers	35	Celtic	29	Hibernian	25
1901–2a	Rangers	28	Celtic	26	Hearts	22
1902–3b	Hibernian	37	Dundee	31	Rangers	29
1903–4d	Third Lanark	43	Hearts	39	Rangers	38
1904–5a	†Celtic	41	Rangers	41	Third Lanark	35
1905–6a	Celtic	46	Hearts	39	Rangers	38
1906–7f	Celtic	55	Dundee	48	Rangers	45
1907–8f	Celtic	55	Falkirk	51	Rangers	50
1908–9f	Celtic	51	Dundee	50	Clyde	48
1909–10f	Celtic	54	Falkirk	52	Rangers	49
1910–11f	Rangers	52	Aberdeen	48	Falkirk	44
1911–12f	Rangers	51	Celtic	45	Clyde	42
1912–13f	Rangers	53	Celtic	49	Hearts	41
1913–14g	Celtic	65	Rangers	59	Hearts	54
1914–15g	Celtic	65	Hearts	61	Rangers	50
1915–16g	Celtic	67	Rangers	56	Morton	51
1916–17g	Celtic	64	Morton	54	Rangers	53
1917–18f	Rangers	56	Celtic	55	Kilmarnock	43
1918–19f	Celtic	58	Rangers	57	Morton	47
1919–20h	Rangers	71	Celtic	68	Motherwell	57
1920–1h	Rangers	76	Celtic	66	Hearts	56
1921–2h	Celtic	67	Rangers	66	Raith	56
1922–3g	Rangers	55	Airdrieonians	50	Celtic	40
1923–4g	Rangers	59	Airdrieonians	50	Celtic	41
1924–5g	Rangers	60	Airdrieonians	57	Hibernian	52
1925–6g	Celtic	58	Airdrieonians	50	Hearts	50
1926–7g	Rangers	56	Motherwell	51	Celtic	49
1927–8g	Rangers	60	Celtic	55	Motherwell	55
1928–9g	Rangers	67	Celtic	51	Motherwell	50
1929–30g	Rangers	60	Motherwell	55	Aberdeen	53
1930–1g	Rangers	60	Celtic	58	Motherwell	56
1931–2g	Motherwell	66	Rangers	61	Celtic	48
1932–3g	Rangers	62	Motherwell	59	Hearts	50
1933–4g	Rangers	66	Motherwell	62	Celtic	47
1934–5g	Rangers	55	Celtic	52	Hearts	50
1935–6g	Celtic	68	Rangers	61	Aberdeen	61
1936–7g	Rangers	61	Aberdeen	54	Celtic	52
1937–8g	Celtic	61	Hearts	58	Rangers	49
1938–9f	Rangers	59	Celtic	48	Aberdeen	46
1946–7f	Rangers	46	Hibernian	44	Aberdeen	39
1947–8g	Hibernian	48	Rangers	46	Partick	46
1948–9i	Rangers	46	Dundee	45	Hibernian	39
1949–50i	Rangers	50	Hibernian	49	Hearts	43
1950–1i	Hibernian	48	Rangers	38	Dundee	38
1951–2i	Hibernian	45	Rangers	41	East Fife	37
1952–3i	*Rangers	43	Hibernian	43	East Fife	39
1953–4i	Celtic	43	Hearts	38	Partick	35

	First	Pts	Second	Pts	Third	Pts
1954–5f	Aberdeen	49	Celtic	46	Rangers	41
1955–6f	Rangers	52	Aberdeen	46	Hearts	45
1956–7f	Rangers	55	Hearts	53	Kilmarnock	42
1957–8f	Hearts	62	Rangers	49	Celtic	46
1958–9f	Rangers	50	Hearts	48	Motherwell	44
1959–60f	Hearts	54	Kilmarnock	50	Rangers	42
1960–1f	Rangers	51	Kilmarnock	50	Third Lanark	42
1961–2f	Dundee	54	Rangers	51	Celtic	46
1962–3f	Rangers	57	Kilmarnock	48	Partick	46
1963–4f	Rangers	55	Kilmarnock	49	Celtic	47
1964–5f	*Kilmarnock	50	Hearts	50	Dunfermline	49
1965–6f	Celtic	57	Rangers	55	Kilmarnock	45
1966–7f	Celtic	58	Rangers	55	Clyde	46
1967–8f	Celtic	63	Rangers	61	Hibernian	45
1968–9f	Celtic	54	Rangers	49	Dunfermline	45
1969–70f	Celtic	57	Rangers	45	Hibernian	44
1970–1f	Celtic	56	Aberdeen	54	St Johnstone	44
1971–2f	Celtic	60	Aberdeen	50	Rangers	44
1972–3f	Celtic	57	Rangers	56	Hibernian	45
1973–4f	Celtic	53	Hibernian	49	Rangers	48
1974–5f	Rangers	56	Hibernian	49	Celtic	45

*Won on goal average †Won on deciding match ††Title shared. Competition suspended 1940–46 (Second World War)

SCOTTISH TITLE WINS

Rangers	*55	Hibernian	4	Kilmarnock	1
Celtic	51	Dumbarton	*2	Motherwell	1
Aberdeen	4	Dundee	1	Third Lanark	1
Hearts	4	Dundee Utd	1	(*Incl 1 shared)	

FIRST DIVISION (Since formation of Premier Division)

	First	Pts	Second	Pts	Third	Pts
1975–6d	Partick	41	Kilmarnock	35	Montrose	30
1976–7j	St Mirren	62	Clydebank	58	Dundee	51
1977–8j	*Morton	58	Hearts	58	Dundee	57
1978–9j	Dundee	55	Kilmarnock	54	Clydebank	54
1979–80j	Hearts	53	Airdrieonians	51	Ayr	44
1980–1j	Hibernian	57	Dundee	52	St Johnstone	51
1981–2j	Motherwell	61	Kilmarnock	51	Hearts	50
1982–3j	St Johnstone	55	Hearts	54	Clydebank	50
1983–4j	Morton	54	Dumbarton	51	Partick	46
1984–5j	Motherwell	50	Clydebank	48	Falkirk	45
1985–6j	Hamilton	56	Falkirk	45	Kilmarnock	44
1986–7k	Morton	57	Dunfermline	56	Dumbarton	53
1987–8k	Hamilton	56	Meadowbank	52	Clydebank	49
1988–9j	Dunfermline	54	Falkirk	52	Clydebank	48
1989–90j	St Johnstone	58	Airdrieonians	54	Clydebank	44
1990–1j	Falkirk	54	Airdrieonians	53	Dundee	52
1991–2k	Dundee	58	Partick	57	Hamilton	57
1992–3k	Raith	65	Kilmarnock	54	Dunfermline	52
1993–4k	Falkirk	66	Dunfermline	65	Airdrieonians	54
1994–5l	Raith	69	Dunfermline	68	Dundee	68
1995–6l	Dunfermline	71	Dundee Utd	67	Morton	67
1996–7l	St Johnstone	80	Airdrieonians	60	Dundee	58
1997–8l	Dundee	70	Falkirk	65	Raith	60
1998–9l	Hibernian	89	Falkirk	66	Ayr	62
1999–2000l	St Mirren	76	Dunfermline	71	Falkirk	68
2000–01l	Livingston	76	Ayr	69	Falkirk	56
2001–02l	Partick	66	Airdrie	56	Ayr	52

	First	Pts	Second	Pts	Third	Pts
2002–03l	Falkirk	81	Clyde	72	St Johnstone	67
2003–04l	Inverness	70	Clyde	69	St Johnstone	57
2004–05l	Falkirk	75	St Mirren	60	Clyde	60
2005–06l	St Mirren	76	St Johnstone	66	Hamilton	59
2006–07l	Gretna	66	St Johnstone	65	Dundee	53
2007–08l	Hamilton	76	Dundee	69	St Johnstone	58
2008–09l	St Johnstone	65	Partick	55	Dunfermline	51
2009–10l	Inverness	73	Dundee	61	Dunfermline	58
2010–11l	Dunfermline	70	Raith	60	Falkirk	58
2011–12l	Ross	79	Dundee	55	Falkirk	52
2012–13l	Partick	78	Morton	67	Falkirk	53

CHAMPIONSHIP

	First	Pts	Second	Pts	Third	Pts
2013–14l	Dundee	69	Hamilton	67	Falkirk	66
2014–15l	Hearts	91	Hibernian	70	Rangers	67
2015–16l	Rangers	81	Falkirk	70	Hibernian	70
2016–17l	Hibernian	71	Falkirk	60	Dundee Utd	57
2017–18l	St Mirren	74	Livingston	62	Dundee Utd	61
2018–19l	Ross Co	71	Dundee Utd	65	Inverness	56
2019–20C	Dundee Utd	59	Inverness	45	Dundee	41
2020–21m	Hearts	57	Dundee	45	Raith	43

C Season curtailed – COVID-19
Maximum points: a, 36; b, 44; c, 40; d 52; e, 60; f, 68; g, 76; h, 84; i, 60; j, 78; k, 88; l, 108;m, 81
*Won on goal difference

SECOND DIVISION

	First	Pts	Second	Pts	Third	Pts
1921–2a	Alloa	60	Cowdenbeath	47	Armadale	45
1922–3a	Queen's Park	57	Clydebank	52	St Johnstone	50
1923–4a	St Johnstone	56	Cowdenbeath	55	Bathgate	44
1924–5a	Dundee Utd	50	Clydebank	48	Clyde	47
1925–6a	Dunfermline	59	Clyde	53	Ayr	52
1926–7a	Bo'ness	56	Raith	49	Clydebank	45
1927–8a	Ayr	54	Third Lanark	45	King'sPark	44
1928–9b	Dundee Utd	51	Morton	50	Arbroath	47
1929–30a	*LeithAthletic	57	East Fife	57	Albion	54
1930–1a	Third Lanark	61	Dundee Utd	50	Dunfermline	47
1931–2a	*E Stirling	55	St Johnstone	55	Stenhousemuir	46
1932–3c	Hibernian	55	Queen of South	49	Dunfermline	47
1933–4c	Albion	45	Dunfermline	44	Arbroath	44
1934–5c	Third Lanark	52	Arbroath	50	St Bernard's	47
1935–6c	Falkirk	59	St Mirren	52	Morton	48
1936–7c	Ayr	54	Morton	51	St Bernard's	48
1937–8c	Raith	59	Albion	48	Airdrieonians	47
1938–9c	Cowdenbeath	60	Alloa	48	East Fife	48
1946–7d	Dundee Utd	45	Airdrieonians	42	East Fife	31
1947–8e	East Fife	53	Albion	42	Hamilton	40
1948–9e	*Raith	42	Stirling	42	Airdrieonians	41
1949–50e	Morton	47	Airdrieonians	44	St Johnstone	36
1950–1e	*Queen of South	45	Stirling	45	Ayr	36
1951–2e	Clyde	44	Falkirk	43	Ayr	36
1952–3	E Stirling	44	Hamilton	43	Queen's Park	37
1953–4e	Motherwell	45	Kilmarnock	42	Third Lanark	36
1954–5e	Airdrieonians	46	Dunfermline	42	Hamilton	39
1955–6b	Queen's Park	54	Ayr	51	St Johnstone	49
1956–7b	Clyde	64	Third Lanark	51	Cowdenbeath	45
1957–8b	Stirling	55	Dunfermline	53	Arbroath	47

1958–9b	Ayr 60	Arbroath 51	Stenhousemuir 46
1959–60b	St Johnstone 53	Dundee Utd 50	Queen of South 49
1960–1b	Stirling 55	Falkirk 54	Stenhousemuir 50
1961–2b	Clyde 54	Queen of South........53	Morton.................. 44
1962–3b	St Johnstone 55	E Stirling 49	Morton.................. 48
1963–4b	Morton 67	Clyde 53	Arbroath 46
1964–5b	Stirling 59	Hamilton...............50	Queen of South 45
1965–6b	Ayr 53	Airdrieonians..........50	Queen of South 47
1966–7b	Morton 69	Raith..................58	Arbroath 57
1967–8b	St Mirren 62	Arbroath 53	East Fife 49
1968–9b	Motherwell..............64	Ayr 53	East Fife 48
1969–70b	Falkirk.................. 56	Cowdenbeath..........55	Queen of South 50
1970–1b	Partick 56	East Fife 51	Arbroath 46
1971–2b	*Dumbarton 52	Arbroath 52	Stirling 50
1972–3b	Clyde 56	Dunfermline 52	Raith.................. 47
1973–4b	Airdrieonians............ 60	Kilmarnock..........58	Hamilton.............. 55
1974–5b	Falkirk..................... 54	Queen of South........53	Montrose.............. 53

SECOND DIVISION (MODERN)

	First .... Pts	Second ....Pts	Third .... Pts
1975–6d	*Clydebank 40	Raith.....................40	Alloa 35
1976–7f	Stirling.................. 55	Alloa 51	Dunfermline 50
1977–8f	*Clyde 53	Raith.....................53	Dunfermline 48
1978–9f	Berwick 54	Dunfermline 52	Falkirk 50
1979–80f	Falkirk.................. 50	E Stirling 49	Forfar 46
1980–1f	Queen's Park 50	Queen of South.......46	Cowdenbeath........... 45
1981–2f	Clyde 59	Alloa 50	Arbroath 50
1982–3f	Brechin 55	Meadowbank 54	Arbroath 49
1983–4f	Forfar 63	East Fife 47	Berwick 43
1984–5f	Montrose 53	Alloa.....................50	Dunfermline 49
1985–6f	Dunfermline.............. 57	Queen of South........55	Meadowbank 49
1986–7f	Meadowbank............. 55	Raith.....................52	Stirling 52
1987–8f	Ayr 61	St Johnstone 59	Queen's Park 51
1988–9f	Albion 50	Alloa.....................45	Brechin 43
1989–90f	Brechin 49	Kilmarnock..........48	Stirling 47
1990–1f	Stirling.................. 54	Montrose.................46	Cowdenbeath........... 45
1991–2f	Dumbarton 52	Cowdenbeath 51	Alloa................... 50
1992–3f	Clyde 54	Brechin.................53	Stranraer 53
1993–4f	Stranraer 56	Berwick.................48	Stenhousemuir 47
1994–5g	Morton 64	Dumbarton..............60	Stirling 58
1995–6g	Stirling.................. 81	East Fife 67	Berwick 60
1996–7g	Ayr 77	Hamilton.................74	Livingston 64
1997–8g	Stranraer 61	Clydebank..............60	Livingston 59
1998–9g	Livingston 77	Inverness 72	Clyde 53
1999–2000g	Clyde 65	Alloa.....................64	Ross Co 62
2000–01g	Partick 75	Arbroath.................58	Berwick 54
2001–02g	Queen of South 67	Alloa.....................59	Forfar Athletic 53
2002–03g	Raith 59	Brechin.................55	Airdrie 54
2003–04g	Airdrie 70	Hamilton.................62	Dumbarton 60
2004–05g	Brechin 72	Stranraer 63	Morton................ 62
2005–06g	Gretna 88	Morton.................70	Peterhead 57
2006–07g	Morton 77	Stirling.................69	Raith 62
2007–08g	Ross 73	Airdrie.................66	Raith 60
2008–09g	Raith 76	Ayr.....................74	Brechin................ 62
2009–10g	*Stirling 65	Alloa.....................65	Cowdenbeath........... 59
2010–11g	Livingston 82	*Ayr.....................59	Forfar 59
2011–12g	Cowdenbeath 71	Arbroath.................63	Dumbarton 58
2012–13g	Queen of South 92	Alloa.....................67	Brechin................ 61

LEAGUE ONE

	First	Pts	Second	Pts	Third	Pts
2013–14g	Rangers	102	Dunfermline	63	Stranraer	51
2014–15g	Morton	69	Stranraer	67	Forfar	66
2015–16g	Dunfermline	79	Ayr	61	Peterhead	59
2016–17g	Livingston	81	Alloa	62	Airdrieonians	52
2017–18g	Ayr	76	Raith	75	Alloa	60
2018–19g	Arbroath	70	Forfar	63	Raith	60
2019–20C	Raith	53	Falkirk	52	Airdrieonians	48
2020–21h	Partick	40	Airdrieonians	38	Cove	36

C Season curtailed – COVID-19
Maximum points: a, 76; b, 72; c, 68; d, 52e, 60; f, 78; g, 108;h,66 *Won on goal average/goal difference

THIRD DIVISION (MODERN)

	First	Pts	Second	Pts	Third	Pts
1994–5	Forfar	80	Montrose	67	Ross Co	60
1995–6	Livingston	72	Brechin	63	Caledonian Th	57
1996–7	Inverness	76	Forfar	67	Ross Co	77
1997–8	Alloa	76	Arbroath	68	Ross Co	67
1998–9	Ross Co	77	Stenhousemuir	64	Brechin	59
1999–2000	Queen's Park	69	Berwick	66	Forfar	61
2000–01	*Hamilton	76	Cowdenbeath	76	Brechin	72
2001–02	Brechin	73	Dumbarton	61	Albion	59
2002–03	Morton	72	East Fife	71	Albion	70
2003–04	Stranraer	79	Stirling	77	Gretna	68
2004–05	Gretna	98	Peterhead	78	Cowdenbeath	51
2005–06	*Cowdenbeath	76	Berwick	76	Stenhousemuir	73
2006–07	Berwick	75	Arbroath	70	Queen's Park	68
2007–08	East Fife	88	Stranraer	65	Montrose	59
2008–09	Dumbarton	67	Cowdenbeath	63	East Stirling	61
2009–10	Livingston	78	Forfar	63	East Stirling	61
2010–11	Arbroath	66	Albion	61	Queen's Park	59
2011–12	Alloa	77	Queen's Park	63	Stranraer	58
2012–13	Rangers	83	Peterhead	59	Queen's Park	56

LEAGUE TWO

	First	Pts	Second	Pts	Third	Pts
2013–14	Peterhead	76	Annan	63	Stirling	58
2014–15	Albion	71	Queen's Park	61	Arbroath	56
2015–16	East Fife	62	Elgin	59	Clyde	57
2016–17	Arbroath	66	Forfar	64	Annan	58
2017–18	Montrose	77	Peterhead	76	Stirling	55
2018–19	Peterhead	79	Clyde	74	Edinburgh City	67
2019–20C	Cove	68	Edinburgh City	55	Elgin	43
2020–21	Queen's Park	54	Edinburgh City	38	Elgin	38

C Season curtailed – COVID-19. Maximum points: 108 (66 in 2020–21). * Won on goal difference

RELEGATED FROM PREMIER DIVISION/PREMIER LEAGUE/PREMIERSHIP

1975–6	Dundee,	St Johnstone	1985–6	No relegation
1976–7	Kilmarnock,	Hearts	1986–7	Clydebank, Hamilton
1977–8	Ayr,	Clydebank	1987–8	Falkirk, Dunfermline, Morton
1978–9	Hearts,	Motherwell	1988–9	Hamilton
1979–80	Dundee,	Hibernian	1989–90	Dundee
1980–1	Kilmarnock,	Hearts	1990–1	No relegation
1981–2	Partick,	Airdrieonians	1991–2	St Mirren, Dunfermline
1982–3	Morton,	Kilmarnock	1992–3	Falkirk, Airdrieonians
1983–4	St Johnstone,	Motherwell	1993–4	St J'stone, Raith, Dundee
1984–5	Dumbarton,	Morton	1994–5	Dundee Utd

1995–6	Falkirk, Partick	2009–10	Falkirk
1996–7	Raith	2010–11	Hamilton
1997–8	Hibernian	2011–12	Dunfermline, *Rangers
1998–9	Dunfermline	2012–13	Dundee
1999–2000	No relegation	2013–14	Hibernian, **Hearts
2000–01	St Mirren	2014–15	St Mirren
2001–02	St Johnstone	2015–16	Dundee Utd
2002–03	No relegation	2016–17	Inverness
2003–04	Partick	2017–18	Partick, Ross Co
2004–05	Dundee	2018–19	Dundee
2005–06	Livingston	2019–20	Hearts
2006–07	Dunfermline	2020–21	Kilmarnock, Hamilton
2007–08	Gretna		*Following administration, liquidation and new club
2008–09	Inverness		formed. **Deducted 15 points for administration

RELEGATED FROM FIRST DIVISION/CHAMPIONSHIP

1975–6	Dunfermline, Clyde	1999–2000	Clydebank
1976–7	Raith, Falkirk	2000–01	Morton, Alloa
1977–8	Alloa, East Fife	2001–02	Raith
1978–9	Montrose, Queen of South	2002–03	Alloa Athletic, Arbroath
1979–80	Arbroath, Clyde	2003–04	Ayr, Brechin
1980–1	Stirling, Berwick	2004–05	Partick, Raith
1981–2	E Stirling, Queen of South	2005–06	Brechin, Stranraer
1982–3	Dunfermline, Queen's Park	2006–07	Airdrie Utd, Ross Co
1983–4	Raith, Alloa	2007–08	Stirling
1984–5	Meadowbank, St Johnstone	2008–09	*Livingston, Clyde
1985–6	Ayr, Alloa	2009–10	Airdrie, Ayr
1986–7	Brechin, Montrose	2010–11	Cowdenbeath, Stirling
1987–8	East Fife, Dumbarton	2011–12	Ayr, Queen of South
1988–9	Kilmarnock, Queen of South	2012–13	Dunfermline, Airdrie
1989–90	Albion, Alloa	2013–14	Morton
1990–1	Clyde, Brechin	2014–15	Cowdenbeath
1991–2	Montrose, Forfar	2015–16	Livingston, Alloa
1992–3	Meadowbank, Cowdenbeath	2016–17	Raith, Ayr
1993–4	Dumbarton, Stirling, Clyde, Morton, Brechin	2017–18	Dumbarton, Brechin
		2018–19	Falkirk
1994–5	Ayr, Stranraer	2019–20	Partick
1995–6	Hamilton, Dumbarton	2020–21	Alloa
1996–7	Clydebank, East Fife		*relegated to Division Three for breaching insolvency
1997–8	Partick, Stirling		rules
1998–9	Hamilton, Stranraer		

RELEGATED FROM SECOND DIVISION/LEAGUE ONE

1993–4	Alloa, Forfar, E Stirling, Montrose, Queen's Park, Arbroath, Albion, Cowdenbeath	2006–07	Stranraer, Forfar
		2007–08	Cowdenbeath, Berwick
		2008–09	Queen's Park, Stranraer
		2009–10	Arbroath, Clyde
1994–5	Meadowbank, Brechin	2010–11	Alloa, Peterhead
1995–6	Forfar, Montrose	2011–12	Stirling
1996–7	Dumbarton, Berwick	2012–13	Albion
1997–8	Stenhousemuir, Brechin	2013–14	East Fife, Arbroath
1998–9	East Fife, Forfar	2014–15	Stirling
1999–2000	Hamilton	2015–16	Cowdenbeath, Forfar
2000–01	Queen's Park, Stirling	2016–17	Peterhead, Stenhousemuir
2001–02	Morton	2017–18	Queen's Park, Albion
2002–03	Stranraer, Cowdenbeath	2018–19	Stenhousemuir, Brechin
2003–04	East Fife, Stenhousemuir	2019–20	Stranraer
2004–05	Arbroath, Berwick	2020–21	Forfar
2005–06	Dumbarton		

RELEGATED FROM LEAGUE TWO

2015–16	East Stirling	2019–20	No relegation
2018–19	Berwick	2020–21	Brechin

SCOTTISH PREMIERSHIP 2020–2021

(appearances and scorers)

ABERDEEN

Anderson B 1 (5)	Hoban T 35 (2)	Ngwenya K .... - (2)
Bryson C 1 (1)	Hornby F 5 (5)	Ojo F 6 (5)
Campbell D 12 (8)	Kamberi F 11	Ramsey C .... - (4)
Considine A 36	Kennedy M 22 (9)	Ross E .... - (2)
Cosgrove S 9 (5)	Leigh G 6 (2)	McCrorie R 28 (1)
Devlin M .... - (1)	Lewis J 35	Ruth M .... - (1)
Duncan R .... - (1)	Logan S 2 (10)	Taylor A 30 (1)
Edmondson R 3 (11)	MacKenzie J 5 (1)	Virtanen M .... - (2)
Ferguson L 35	Main C 8 (6)	Watkins M 9
Hayes J 34	McGeouch D 7 (8)	Woods G 3
Hedges R 25 (3)	McGinn N 12 (13)	Wright S 14 (3)
Hendry C 5 (7)	McKenna S 4	
Hernandez R 2 (2)	McLennan C 13 (14)	

League goals (36): Ferguson 9, Hedges 5, Cosgrove 3, Edmondson 2, Hayes 2, Hendry 2, Hoban 2, Main 2, Watkins 2, Wright 2, Considine 1, Kennedy 1, McCrorie 1, Taylor 1, Opponents 1
Scottish Cup goals (3): Hendry 1, Kamberi 1, McGinn 1. **League Cup goals (1):** McGinn 1.
Europa League goals (8): Hedges 4, Ferguson 1, Hayes 1, Main 1, McCrorie 1

CELTIC

Ajer K 34 (1)	Elyounoussi M 21 (13)	McGregor C 37
Ajeti A 10 (10)	Forrest J 8 (5)	Montgomery A 1 (1)
Bain S 18	Frimpong J 19 (3)	Okoflex A .... - (2)
Barkas V 15	Griffiths L 7 (15)	Ntcham O 7 (7)
Bitton N 12 (2)	Harper C 1	Ralston A 1
Bolingoli B .... - (1)	Hazard C 5	Rogic T 10 (13)
Brown S 25 (6)	Henderson E .... - (2)	Soro I 11 (8)
Christie R 26 (8)	Johnston M 2 (8)	Taylor G 23 (3)
Dembele K .... - (5)	Jullien C 9	Turnbull D 25 (6)
Duffy S 14 (4)	Kenny J 14	Welsh S 15 (1)
Edouard O 28 (3)	Klimala P 3 (14)	
Elhamed H A 4 (4)	Laxalt D 13 (4)	

League goals (78): Edouard 18, Elyounoussi 10, Turnbull 8, Ajeti 6, Griffiths 6, Christie 5, Duffy 3, Forrest 3, Klimala 3, McGregor 3, Ajer 2, Bitton 1, Brown 1, Dembele 1, Frimpong 1, Jullien 1, Laxalt 1, Ntcham 1, Rogic 1, Soro 1, Welsh 1, Opponents 1
Scottish Cup goals (3): Christie 1, Elyounoussi 1, Forrest 1. **League Cup goals:** None. **Champions League goals (7):** Elyounoussi 2, Christie 1, Edouard 1, Jullien 1, Taylor 1, Opponents 1. **Europa League goals (12):** Elyounoussi 4, Edouard 3, Griffiths 1, Jullien 1, McGregor 1, Rogic 1, Turnbull 1

DUNDEE UNITED

Appere L 11 (11)	Doohan R 2	Harkes I 30 (5)
Bolton L 18 (6)	Edwards R 24	Hoti F 1 (3)
Butcher C 27 (1)	Fotheringham K .... - (1)	McMullan P 3 (5)
Chalmers L 9 (6)	Freeman K 1 (2)	McNulty M 17 (8)
Clark N 24 (7)	Fuchs J 19 (1)	Meekison A 2 (1)
Connolly M 23 (2)	Glass D .... - (1)	Mehmet D 4

Neilson L 7 (2)	Robson J.................. 34 (2)	Smith K...................... 3 (2)
Pawlett P 15 (11)	Shankland L........... 30 (2)	Smith L 28 (2)
Powers D 6 (8)	Siegrist B...................32	Sporle A 15 (9)
Reynolds M.............. 33 (1)	Smith C .... - (4)	Watson D .... - (1)

League goals (32): Clark 8, Shankland 8, Sporle 4, McNulty 3, Edwards 2, Appere 1, Bolton 1, Harkes 1, Meekison 1, Pawlett 1, Reynolds 1, Smith L 1
Scottish Cup goals (6): McNulty 2, Clark 1, Edwards 1, Pawlett 1, Shankland 1. **League Cup goals** (7): Clark 2, Smith C 2, Butcher 1, Edwards 1, Harkes 1

HAMILTON ACADEMICAL

Anderson B 13	Martin A..........................24	Smith C 8 (15)
Callachan R 32 (1)	Martin S 21 (3)	Smith J............................1
Collar W...................... 5 (1)	McKenna C.................. - (1)	Smith L 4 (5)
Easton B.........................24	McMann S......................36	Stanger G 1 (4)
Fjortoft M 1 (1)	Mimnaugh R............ 8 (9)	Stirling B 16 (4)
Fulton R 28	Moyo D 23 (10)	Templeton D 7 (1)
Gourlay K................... 9 (1)	Munro K 9 (7)	Thomas N..................... 3 (7)
Hamilton J............... 21 (6)	Odofin H 37	Trafford C 9 (7)
Hodson L.........................33	Ogkmpoe M 15 (5)	Want S 11
Hughes R.................. 7 (9)	Owolabi T 1 (6)	Winter A................. 10 (12)
Johnson J 1 (4)	Redfern M .... - (1)	

League goals (34): Callachan 9, Moyo 3, Odofin 3, Ogkmpoe 3, Anderson 2, Hughes 2, Munro 2, Smith C 2, Hodson 1, Martin S 1, McMann 1, Templeton 1, Opponents 4
Scottish Cup goals: None. **League Cup goals** (4): McMann 1, Odofin 1, Ogkmpoe 1, Trafford 1

HIBERNIAN

Allan S 3 (5)	Hallberg M 12 (13)	McGinn S.....................- (5)
Barnes D..................... 3 (1)	Hanlon P 36 (1)	McGregor D 8 (2)
Boyle M 35 (1)	Horgan D 4 (1)	Murphy J................14 (5)
Bradley S .... - (2)	Irvine J 14 (1)	Newell J.........................32
Cadden C 8 (2)	Macey M 3	Nisbet K................. 28 (5)
Doidge C 29 (7)	Mackie S.........................2	Porteous R 32 (2)
Doig J 25 (3)	Magennis K 4 (10)	Shanley R.....................- (1)
Gogic A 30 (4)	Mallan S 4 (10)	Stevenson L...........11 (11)
Gray D 1 (1)	Marciano O...................32	Wright D...................11 (9)
Gullan J..................... - (14)	McGinn P 37 (1)	

League goals (48): Nisbet 14, Boyle 12, Doidge 7, McGinn P 3, Doig 1, Gogic 1, Hanlon 1, Magennis 1, Mallan 1, McGinn S 1, McGregor 1, Murphy 1, Newell 1, Porteous 1, Wright 1, Opponents 1
Scottish Cup goals (11): Doidge 5, Boyle 3, Nisbet 2, Irvine 1. **League Cup goals** (13): Mallan 3, Gullan 2, Nisbet 2, Doidge 1, Gray 1, Hallberg 1, Hanlon 1, Murphy 1, Opponents 1

KILMARNOCK

Brindley T .... - (1)	Doyle C..........................11	McGowan A.............. 15 (3)
Broadfoot K.....................31	Eastwood J......................1	McKenzie R 23 (6)
Brophy E 8 (7)	Findlay S 21 (1)	Medley Z.................... 7 (1)
Burke C 28 (9)	Haunstrup B 21 (6)	Millen R 18 (1)
Dabo D 1 (5)	Kabamba N............ 21 (12)	Mulumbu Y 6 (11)
Dicker G 26	Kiltie G 23 (6)	Oakley G 3 (3)
Dikamona C 10 (2)	Lafferty K 8 (1)	Pierrick B 1 (2)

Pinnock M .... 17 (13) Rossi Z .... 11 (3) Whitehall D............. 5 (12)
Power A ....32 Tshibola A 26 (5)
Rogers D................. 26 (1) Waters C 18

League goals (43): Burke 9, Lafferty 8, Kiltie 6, Kabamba 5, Pinnock 4, Tshibola 3, Brophy 2, McKenzie 2, Whitehall 2, Medley 1, Power 1. **Play-offs goals** (2): Haunstrup 1, Lafferty 1
Scottish Cup goals (10): Lafferty 2, Kiltie 2, Millen 1, Oakley 1, Rossie 1, Opponents 1. **League Cup goals** (4): Whitehall 2, Brophy 1, Pinnock 1

LIVINGSTON

Ambrose E .... 17 (5) Hamilton J .... 2 (3) Pittman S................. 37 (1)
Bartley M............... 32 (1) Holt J...................... 27 (3) Poplatnik M......... 5 (14)
Brown C .... 13 (3) Kabia J .... 1 (7) Reilly G 3 (2)
Crawford R................. - (1) Kouider-Aisser S .... - (4) Robinson S 16 (10)
De Vita R ....1 Lawson S .... 7 (8) Serrano J................. 19 (5)
Devlin N .... 35 (1) Lithgow A................. 1 (1) Sibbald C 29 (3)
Diani D .... 2 (2) Lokotsch L .... 2 (2) Souda A ....- (2)
Dykes L ....3 Longridge J................. 8 (1) Stryjek M 22
Emmanuel-Thomas J14 (10) McCrorie R ....16 Taylor-Sinclair A.......... 5 (1)
Fitzwater J ....20 McMillan J .... 4 (4) Tiffoney S.................. 4 (8)
Forrest A .... 21 (9) Mullin J 16 (6)
Guthrie J........................36 Pignatiello C ....- (1)

League goals (42): Pittman 6, Emmanuel-Thomas 5, Guthrie 5, Forrest 4, Robinson 4, Devlin 2, Dykes 2, Mullin 2, Bartley 1, Brown 1, Fitzwater 1, Hamilton 1, Holt 1, Kabia 1, Serrano 1, Sibbald 1, Tiffoney 1, Opponents 3
Scottish Cup goals (4): Emmanuel-Thomas 2, Fitzwater 1, Poplatnik 1. **League Cup goals** (22): Forrest 7, Mullin 3, Emmanuel-Thomas 2, Fitzwater 2, Poplatnik 2, Robinson 2, Lokotsch 1, Sibbald 1, Taylor-Sinclair 1, Oppopnents 1

MOTHERWELL

Archer J..........................4 Hastie J .... 7 (7) Mugabi B 21 (2)
Campbell A ....34 Hylton J .... - (5) O'Donnell S 34
Carroll J .... 14 (1) Johnston M .... 1 (1) O'Hara M 23 (4)
Carson T ....12 Kelly L ....18 Polworth L................. 18 (3)
Chapman A .... 4 (2) Lamie R .... 27 (4) Roberts J.................... 5 (2)
Cole D .... 24 (3) Lang C .... 12 (5) Robinson H ....- (1)
Cornelius D ....- (1) Lawless S .... 3 (4) Seedorf S 6 (4)
Crawford R .... 19 (3) Long C .... 19 (10) Smith H ....- (5)
Donnelly L ....1 MacIver R ....- (1) Turnbull D 5
Foley S .... 3 (1) Magloire T .... 8 (2) Watt T 28 (7)
Gallagher D .... 27 (2) Maguire B .... 14 (10) White J 3 (15)
Grimshaw L .... 12 (2) McGinley N 12 (7)

League goals (39): Cole 11, O'Hara 5, Campbell 4, Long 4, Lang 3, Watt 3, Mugabi 2, Foley 1, Gallagher 1, Maguire 1, O'Donnell 1, Roberts 1, Turnbull 1, Opponents 1
Scottish Cup goals (8): Roberts 2, Campbell 1, Cole 1, Lamie 1, Long 1, O'Donnell 1, Watt 1.
League Cup goals (1): Watt 1. **Europa League goals** (7): Lang 2, Watt 2, Long 1, O'Donnell 1, Polworth 1

RANGERS

Arfield S .... 11 (17) Barisic B ....33 Davis S 29 (6)
Aribo J................. 27 (4) Barker B .... 4 (6) Defoe J 3 (12)
Balogun L .... 15 (4) Bassey C .... 3 (5) Edmundson G ....- (1)

Goldson C 38
Hagi I 23 (10)
Helander F 21 (1)
Itten C................ 5 (22)
Jack R 16 (3)
Jones J 2 (1)
Kamara G 28 (5)

Kent R 36 (1)
Thomson King L .... - (1)
McGregor A.............27
McLaughlan J.............11
Morelos A 26 (3)
Patterson N.............. 3 (4)
Roofe K 18 (6)

Simpson J................. 4 (1)
Stewart G................. - (5)
Tavernier J 33
Wright S 1 (8)
Zungu B 1 (13)

League goals (92): Roofe 14, Morelos 12, Tavernier 12, Kent 10, Aribo 7, Hagi 7, Arfield 4, Defoe 4, Goldson 4, Itten 4, Barker 2, Jack 2, Barisic 1, Helander 1, Jones 1, Kamara 1, Wright 1, Opponents 5
Scottish Cup goals (7): Roofe 2, Davis 1, Defoe 1, Patterson 1, Tavernier 1, Opponents 1. **League Cup goals** (6): Barisic 1, Bassey 1, Davis 1, Defoe 1, Goldson 1, Tavernier 1
Europa League goals (34): Morelos 5, Tavernier 5, Arfield 3, Barisic 3, Goldson 3, Kent 3, Helander 2, Itten 2, Roofe 2, Aribo 1, Defoe 1, Hagi 1, Kamara 1, Patterson 1, Opponents 1

ROSS COUNTY

Andreu T..................... 4 (2)
Charles-Cook R 9 (17)
Donaldson D............... 26 (2)
Doohan R........................5
Draper R 13 (8)
Erwin L..................... 2 (2)
Fuhr Hjelde L.......... 10 (1)
Gardyne M 21 (10)
Grivosti T 3 (2)
Hylton J.................... 7 (11)

Iacovitti A................. 34 (2)
Kelly S 16 (9)
Laidlaw R.........................33
Lakin C 14 (5)
McKay B 14 (14)
Morris C....................12
Mullin J 1 (4)
Naismith J.....................17
Paton S 25 (10)
Randall C 13 (2)

Reid J 17 (3)
Shaw O 12 (13)
Spittal B 7 (2)
Stewart R 19
Tillson J 20 (12)
Tremarco C.................8 (4)
Vigurs I 28 (2)
Watson K.................. 17 (6)
White J 11 (1)
Wright M ....- (2)

League goals (35): Shaw 6, McKay 5, White 4, Lakin 3, Draper 2, Gardyne 2, Iacovitti 2, Stewart 2, Vigurs 2, Donaldson 1, Fuhr Hjelde 1, Grivosti 1, Hylton 1, Paton 1, Spittal 1, Opponents 1
Scottish Cup goals (1): McKay 1. **League Cup goals** (14): Stewart 4, Charles-Cook 2, Iacovitti 2, Shaw 2, Grivosti 1, Lakin 1, McKay 1, Paton 1

ST JOHNSTONE

Booth C 15 (3)
Brown J 4 (1)
Bryson C 12 (8)
Clark Z 27
Conway C 19 (9)
Craig L 18 (5)
Davidson M 14 (7)
Ferguson A................. - (1)
Gilmour C 1 (1)

Gordon L 35 (1)
Hendry C..................... 8 (8)
Kane C 17 (11)
Kerr J...........................31
May S 17 (17)
McCann A 32 (2)
McNamara D.................22
McCart J 37
Melamed G 11 (7)

Middleton G 3 (6)
O'Halloran M 13 (12)
Olaofe I......................... - (2)
Parish E 9
Robertson J .... - (5)
Rooney S 20 (7)
Tanser S 23 (7)
Wotherspoon D...........28 (9)
Zlamal Z 2

League goals (36): May 5, Melamed 5, Kane 4, Conway 3, Craig 3, Wotherspoon 3, McCann 2, Middleton 2, Rooney 2, Tanser 2, Davidson 1, Gordon 1, Kerr 1, McNamara 1, O'Halloran 1
Scottish Cup goals (7): Kane 2, Melamed 2, Middleton 1, O'Halloran 1, Rooney 1. **League Cup goals** (19): May 5, Rooney 3, Wotherspoon 3, Hendry 2, Kane 2, Kerr 2, Conway 1, Davidson 1

ST MIRREN

Alnwick J........................34
Brophy E..................... 4 (2)

Connolly D 18 (11)
Dennis K................... 6 (11)

Doyle-Hayes J............ 21 (1)
Durmus I 23 (8)

Erhahon E............... 28 (3) Lyness D................... 1 (1) Quaner C 2 (4)
Erwin L................ 17 (10) MacPherson C .... 14 (18) Reid D........................ - (1)
Finlayson D................ 2 (1) Mason B .... 5 (2) Shaughnessy J..............33
Flynn R...................... 8 (6) McAllister K .... 12 (23) Sheron N 6 (1)
Foley S .... 10 (1) McCarthy C ....37 Tait R 31 (2)
Fraser M ....37 McGrath J .... 34 (1) Thorvaldsson I .... - (2)
Henderson J............... 4 (1) Morias J................... 7 (7) Zlamal Z 3
Jamieson L .... (2) Obika J................. 21 (13)

League goals (37): McGrath 10, Obika 5, Dennis 3, Durmus 3, Erwin 3, Connolly 2, Erhahon 2, MacPherson 2, Doyle-Hayes 1, Fraser 1, McAllister 1, Quaner 1, Shaughnessy 1, Tait 1, Opponents 1
Scottish Cup goals (9): McGrath 3, Dennis 2, Fraser 1, McCarthy 1, Shaughnessy 1, Opponents 1. **League Cup goals** (13): McGrath 4, Obika 3, Connolly 1, Durmus 1, Fraser 1, McCarthy 1, Tait 1, Opponents 1

THE THINGS THEY SAY ...

'I always say the pat on the back is only a few inches away from a slap on the backside' – **Brendan Rodgers**, Leicester manager, urging caution amid success.

'We've come a long way with this team, but we shouldn't be considered title challengers yet' – **Ole Gunnar Solskjaer**, Manchester United manager.

Football is such a good game, why are we ruining it? We are talking about incidents, rather than the game itself. I'd rather play without it' – **Jordan Henderson**, Liverpool captain, on the trials and tribulations of VAR.

'I do not understand how we in football have allowed this in. It's completely unacceptable and, I have to be honest, it's destroying my enjoyment of the game' – **Roy Hodgson** before stepping down as Crystal Palace manager.

'I don't want to talk about VAR. I have enough problems already' – **Sam Allardyce** during his time managing relegation-bound West Bromwich Albion.

'I asked did they get juggling balls for Christmas?' – **Dean Smith**, Aston Villa manager, on his 'clown' reference to match officials after his side conceded a controversial goal to Manchester City.

BETFRED SCOTTISH LEAGUE CUP 2020–21

Teams awarded three points for a win, one point for a drawn match after 90 minutes, then penalties with winners awarded one additional point. Eight group winners and four best runners-up through to knockout stage to join four sides competing in Europe – Aberdeen, Celtic, Motherwell and Rangers

GROUP A

	P	W	D	L	F	A	Pts
Hearts Q	4	4	0	0	8	3	12
Raith	4	2	1	1	7	7	8
Inverness	4	1	2	1	4	4	6
East Fife	4	1	0	3	3	5	6
Cowdenbeath	4	0	1	3	0	4	1

GROUP B

	P	W	D	L	F	A	Pts
Hibernian Q	4	4	0	0	10	3	12
Dundee Q	4	3	0	1	9	4	9
Cove	4	1	1	2	4	7	5
Brora	4	0	2	2	6	10	2
Forfar	4	0	1	3	3	8	2

GROUP C

	P	W	D	L	F	A	Pts
St Johnstone Q	4	3	1	0	12	2	10
Dundee Utd	4	2	1	1	7	3	8
Peterhead	4	2	1	1	6	5	8
Kelty	4	1	1	2	4	4	4
Brechin	4	0	0	4	3	18	0

GROUP D

	P	W	D	L	F	A	Pts
Ross Co Q	4	3	1	0	12	5	11
Arbroath Q	4	3	0	1	9	4	9
Elgin	4	2	0	2	5	7	6
Stirling	4	1	0	3	3	8	3
Montrose	4	0	1	3	5	10	1

GROUP E

	P	W	D	L	F	A	Pts
Dunfermline Q	4	4	0	0	9	2	12
Falkirk Q	4	3	0	1	9	3	9
Kilmarnock	4	2	0	2	4	6	6
Clyde	4	1	0	3	6	9	3
Dumbarton	4	0	0	4	2	10	0

GROUP F

	P	W	D	L	F	A	Pts
Ayr Q	4	2	1	1	8	5	8
Annan	4	2	1	1	9	4	7
Stranraer	4	1	3	0	6	5	7
Hamilton	4	2	0	2	7	6	6
Albion	4	0	1	3	5	15	2

GROUP G

	P	W	D	L	F	A	Pts
St Mirren Q	4	2	2	0	8	4	10
Queen of South	4	1	3	0	7	5	7
Partick	4	1	2	1	3	4	7
Morton	4	1	3	0	4	3	6
Queen's Park	4	0	0	4	1	7	0

GROUP H

	P	W	D	L	F	A	Pts
Livingston Q	4	4	0	0	15	3	12
Alloa Q	4	3	0	1	9	5	9
Edinburgh City	4	1	1	2	2	5	5
Airdrieonians	4	1	0	3	3	7	3
Stenhousemuir	4	0	1	3	4	12	2

SECOND ROUND: Alloa 1 Hearts 0 (aet); Arbroath 1 Dunfermline 3; Celtic 0 Ross Co 2; Falkirk 0 Rangers 4; Hibernian 1 Dundee 0; Livingston 4 Ayr 0; Motherwell 1 St Johnstone 2; St Mirren 2 Aberdeen 1; **QUARTER-FINALS:** Alloa 1 Hibernian 2; Dunfermline 1 St Johnstone 1 (aet, St Johnstone won 4-3 on pens); Livingston 2 Ross Co 0; St Mirren 3 Rangers 2; **SEMI-FINALS** (both at Hampden Park): Livingston 1 St Mirren 0; St Johnstone 3 Hibernian 0

FINAL
LIVINGSTON 0 ST JOHNSTONE 1 (Rooney 32)
Hampden Park, February 28, 2021

Livingston (4-2-3-1): McCrorie, Devlin, Ambrose, Guthrie, Serrano, Lawson (Sibbald 60), Holt (Emmanuel-Thomas 71), Mullin (Forrest 65), Pittman (Reilly 65), Bartley (capt), Robinson. **Subs not used:** Stryjek, Fitzwater, McMillan, Taylor-Sinclair, Kabia. **Booked:** Bartley, Serrano. **Manager:** David Martindale.

St Johnstone (3-4-2-1): Clark, Kerr (capt), Gordon, McCart, Rooney, McCann, Craig, Booth, Conway, May (77), Wotherspoon, Kane. **Subs not used:** Parish, Brown, Tanser, O'Halloran, Bryson, Gilmour, Melamed. **Booked:** Gordon, Kane. **Manager:** Callum Davidson

Referee: Don Robertson
Referee: W Collum. **Half-time:** 0-1

SCOTTISH LEAGUE CUP FINALS

1946	Aberdeen beat Rangers (3-2)
1947	Rangers beat Aberdeen (4-0)
1948	East Fife beat Falkirk (4-1 after 0-0 draw)
1949	Rangers beat Raith Rov (2-0)
1950	East Fife beat Dunfermline Athletic (3-0)
1951	Motherwell beat Hibernian (3-0)
1952	Dundee beat Rangers (3-2)
1953	Dundee beat Kilmarnock (2-0)
1954	East Fife beat Partick (3-2)
1955	Hearts beat Motherwell (4-2)
1956	Aberdeen beat St Mirren (2-1)
1957	Celtic beat Partick (3-0 after 0-0 draw)
1958	Celtic beat Rangers (7-1)
1959	Hearts beat Partick (5-1)
1960	Hearts beat Third Lanark (2-1)
1961	Rangers beat Kilmarnock (2-0)
1962	Rangers beat Hearts (3-1 after 1-1 draw)
1963	Hearts beat Kilmarnock (1-0)
1964	Rangers beat Morton (5-0)
1965	Rangers beat Celtic (2-1)
1966	Celtic beat Rangers (2-1)
1967	Celtic beat Rangers (1-0)
1968	Celtic beat Dundee (5-3)
1969	Celtic beat Hibernian (6-2)
1970	Celtic beat St Johnstone (1-0)
1971	Rangers beat Celtic (1-0)
1972	Partick beat Celtic (4-1)
1973	Hibernian beat Celtic (2-1)
1974	Dundee beat Celtic (1-0)
1975	Celtic beat Hibernian (6-3)
1976	Rangers beat Celtic (1-0)
1977†	Aberdeen beat Celtic (2-1)
1978†	Rangers beat Celtic (2-1)
1979	Rangers beat Aberdeen (2-1)
1980	Dundee Utd beat Aberdeen (3-0 after 0-0 draw)
1981	Dundee Utd beat Dundee (3-0)
1982	Rangers beat Dundee Utd (2-1)
1983	Celtic beat Rangers (2-1)
1984†	Rangers beat Celtic (3-2)
1985	Rangers beat Dundee Utd (1-0)
1986	Aberdeen beat Hibernian (3-0)
1987	Rangers beat Celtic (2-1)
1988†	Rangers beat Aberdeen (5-3 on pens after 3-3 draw)
1989	Rangers beat Aberdeen (3-2)
1990†	Aberdeen beat Rangers (2-1)
1991†	Rangers beat Celtic (2-1)
1992	Hibernian beat Dunfermline Athletic (2-0)
1993†	Rangers beat Aberdeen (2-1)
1994	Rangers beat Hibernian (2-1)
1995	Raith Rov beat Celtic (6-5 on pens after 2-2 draw)
1996	Aberdeen beat Dundee (2-0)
1997	Rangers beat Hearts (4-3)
1998	Celtic beat Dundee Utd (3-0)
1999	Rangers beat St Johnstone (2-1)
2000	Celtic beat Aberdeen (2-0)
2001	Celtic beat Kilmarnock (3-0)
2002	Rangers beat Ayr (4-0)
2003	Rangers beat Celtic (2-1)
2004	Livingston beat Hibernian (2-0)
2005	Rangers beat Motherwell (5-1)
2006	Celtic beat Dunfermline Athletic (3-0)
2007	Hibernian beat Kilmarnock (5-1)
2008	Rangers beat Dundee Utd (3-2 on pens after 2-2 draw)
2009†	Celtic beat Rangers (2-0)
2010	Rangers beat St Mirren (1-0)
2011†	Rangers beat Celtic (2-1)
2012	Kilmarnock beat Celtic (1-0)
2013	St Mirren beat Hearts (3-2)
2014	Aberdeen beat Inverness Caledonian Thistle (4-2 on pens after 0-0 draw)
2015	Celtic beat Dundee Utd (2-0)
2016	Ross Co beat Hibernian (2-1)
2017	Celtic beat Aberdeen (3-0)
2018	Celtic beat Motherwell (2-0)
2019	Celtic beat Aberdeen (1-0)
2020	Celtic beat Rangers (1-0)
2021	St Johnstone beat Livingston (1-0)

(† After extra time; Skol Cup 1985–93, Coca-Cola Cup 1995–97, Co-operative Insurance Cup 1999 onwards)

SUMMARY OF SCOTTISH LEAGUE CUP WINNERS

Team	Wins	Team	Wins	Team	Wins
Rangers	27	Hibernian	3	Raith	1
Celtic	19	Dundee Utd	2	Ross Co	1
Aberdeen	7	Kilmarnock	1	St Johnstone	1
Hearts	4	Livingston	1	St Mirren	1
Dundee	3	Motherwell	1		
East Fife	3	Partick	1		

SCOTTISH FA CUP 2020–21

FIRST ROUND

Albion 0 Buckie 3
Berwick 0 Stirling 3
Bonnyrigg 5 Bo'ness 2
Brechin 2 Linlithgow 3
Camelon 1 Brora 2
Cowdenbeath 2 Wick 0
Dundonald 1 Queen's Park 3
Edinburgh City 3 Caledonian 1
Elgin 4 Civil Service 0
Gala 1 Annan 2
Haddington 1 Formartine 2

Huntly 3 Cumbernauld 1
Keith 4 Hill of Beath 2
Kelty 2 Jeanfield 1
Lothian 0 Banks O'Dee 3
Nairn 1 Broxburn 1
(Nairn won 4-3 on pens)
Rothes 1 Fraserburgh 3
Stenhousemuir 4 Preston 1
Stranraer 5 Spartans 0
Tranent 4 East Stirling 1

SECOND ROUND

Airdrieonians 0 Edinburgh City 1
Alloa 2 Cove 3
Arbroath 1 Falkirk 2
Brora 2 Hearts 1
Buckie 2 Inverness 3
Dumbarton 4 Huntly 0
Dundee 3 Bonnyrigg 2 (aet)
East Fife 5 Tranent 1
Elgin 0 Ayr 4
Forfar 4 Linlithgow 1 (aet)
Formartine 1 Annan 1

(aet, Formartine won 3-1 on pens)
Fraserburgh 2 Banks O'Dee 1
Keith 0 Clyde 2
Kelty 2 Stranraer 3
Morton 0 Dunfermline 0
(Morton won 6-5 on pens)
Nairn 1 Montrose 7
Partick 3 Cowdenbeath 0
Peterhead 0 Stenhousemuir 1
Queen's Park 0 Queen of South 3
Stirling 0 Raith 2

THIRD ROUND

Ayr 0 Clyde 1
Brora 1 Stranraer 3
Celtic 3 Falkirk 0
Dumbarton 0 Aberdeen 1
Dundee 0 St Johnstone 1
Dundee Utd 2 Partick 1
East Fife 1 Morton 2 (aet)
Forfar 2 Edinburgh City 2
(aet, Forfar won 5-3 on pens)

Formartine 0 Motherwell 5
Fraserburgh 2 Montrose 4
Hamilton 0 St Mirren 3
Livingston 3 Raith 1
Queen of South 1 Hibernian 3
Rangers 4 Cove 0
Ross Co 1 Inverness 3
Stenhousemuir 0 Kilmarnock 4

FOURTH ROUND

Aberdeen 2 Livingston 2
(aet, Aberdeen won 5-3 on pens)
Forfar 0 Dundee Utd 1
Kilmarnock 3 Montrose 1
Motherwell 1 Morton 1
(aet, Motherwell won 5-3 on pens)

Rangers 2 Celtic 0
St Johnstone 2 Clyde 0
St Mirren 2 Inverness 1
Stranraer 0 Hibernian 4

FIFTH ROUND

Aberdeen 0 Dundee Utd 3
Hibernian 2 Motherwell 2
(aet, Hibernian won 4-2 on pens)
Kilmarnock 3 St Mirren 3

(aet, St Mirren won 5-4 on pens)
Rangers 1 St Johnstone 1
(aet, St Johnstone won 4-2 on pens)

SEMI-FINALS

Dundee Utd 0 Hibernian 2

St Mirren 1 St Johnstone 2

ST JOHNSTONE 1 (Rooney 32) **HIBERNIAN 0**
Hampden Park (behind closed doors); Saturday, May 22, 2021
St Johnstone (3-4-2-1): Clark, Kerr (capt), Gordon, McCart, Rooney (Brown 79), McCann, Bryson (Davidson 64), Booth, Middleton (O'Halloran 82), Wotherspoon, Kane. **Subs not used**: Parish, Tanser, Conway, Craig, May, Melamed. **Manager**: Callum Davidson
Hibernian (4-4-2): Macey, McGinn, Porteous, Hanlon, Doig (Stevenson 76), Boyle, Gogic (Murphy 56), Newell (Hallberg 72), Irvine, Doidge, Nisbet. **Subs not used**: Marciano, Gray (capt), McGregor, Wright, Magennis. **Booked**: Irvine, McGinn, Porteous, Boyle. **Manager**: Jack Ross
Referee: Nick Walsh. **Half-time**: 1-0

SCOTTISH FA CUP 2019–20

(Ties postponed from season 2019–20)

Semi-finals: Celtic 2 Aberdeen 0; Hearts 2 Hibernian 1

FINAL

CELTIC 3 (Christie 19, Edouard 29 pen, Griffiths 105) **HEARTS 3** (Boyce 48, Kingsley 67, Ginnelly 111) – aet, Celtic won 4-3 on pens
Hampden Park; Sunday, December 20, 2020
Celtic (4-2-3-1): Hazard, Ajer, Jullien, Duffy (Johnston 91), Taylor (Laxalt 83), Brown (capt) (Soro 106), McGregor, Christie, Turnbull (Rogic 68), Elyounoussi (Frimpong 83), Edouard (Griffiths 97). **Subs not used**: Barkas, Bitton, Klimala. **Booked**: Elyounoussi, Ajer, McGregor, Jullien. **Manager**: Neil Lennon
Hearts (4-2-3-1): Gordon, Smith, Halkett, Berra, Kingsley, Irving (Frear 109), Halliday (Haring 90+1), Walker (Ginnelly 57), Naismith (capt), White (Lee 82), Boyce (Wighton 70). **Subs not used**: Stewart, Popescu, Henderson. **Booked**: Gordon, Halliday, Walker, Naismith, Wighton, Smith. **Manager**: Robbie Neilson. **Referee**: John Beaton. **Half-time**: 2-0

SCOTTISH FA CUP FINALS

1874	Queen's Park beat Clydesdale (2-0)	1891	Hearts beat Dumbarton (1-0)
1875	Queen's Park beat Renton (3-0)	1892	Celtic beat Queen's Park (5-1)
1876	Queen's Park beat Third Lanark (2-0 after 1-1 draw)	1893	Queen's Park beat Celtic (2-1)
		1894	Rangers beat Celtic (3-1)
1877	Vale of Leven beat Rangers (3-2 after 0-0, 1-1 draws)	1895	St Bernard's beat Renton (2-1)
		1896	Hearts beat Hibernian (3-1)
1878	Vale of Leven beat Third Lanark (1-0)	1897	Rangers beat Dumbarton (5-1)
1879	Vale of Leven awarded Cup (Rangers withdrew after 1-1 draw)	1898	Rangers beat Kilmarnock (2-0)
		1899	Celtic beat Rangers (2-0)
1880	Queen's Park beat Thornliebank (3-0)	1900	Celtic beat Queen's Park (4-3)
1881	Queen's Park beat Dumbarton (3-1)	1901	Hearts beat Celtic (4-3)
1882	Queen's Park beat Dumbarton (4-1 after 2-2 draw)	1902	Hibernian beat Celtic (1-0)
		1903	Rangers beat Hearts (2-0 after 0-0, 1-1 draws)
1883	Dumbarton beat Vale of Leven (2-1 after 2-2 draw)	1904	Celtic beat Rangers (3-2)
		1905	Third Lanark beat Rangers (3-1 after 0-0 draw)
1884	Queen's Park awarded Cup (Vale of Leven withdrew from Final)	1906	Hearts beat Third Lanark (1-0)
		1907	Celtic beat Hearts (3-0)
1885	Renton beat Vale of Leven (3-1 after 0-0 draw)	1908	Celtic beat St Mirren (5-1)
		1909	Cup withheld because of riot after two drawn games in final between Celtic and Rangers (2-2, 1-1)
1886	Queen's Park beat Renton (3-1)	
1887	Hibernian beat Dumbarton (2-1)	
1888	Renton beat Cambuslang (6-1)	1910	Dundee beat Clyde (2-1 after 2-2, 0-0 draws)
1889	Third Lanark beat Celtic (2-1)	1911	Celtic beat Hamilton (2-0 after 0-0 draw)
1890	Queen's Park beat Vale of Leven (2-1 after 1-1 draw)	1912	Celtic beat Clyde (2-0)
		1913	Falkirk beat Raith (2-0)

1914	Celtic beat Hibernian (4-1 after 0-0 draw)
1915–19	No competition (World War 1)
1920	Kilmarnock beat Albion (3-2)
1921	Partick beat Rangers (1-0)
1922	Morton beat Rangers (1-0)
1923	Celtic beat Hibernian (1-0)
1924	Airdrieonians beat Hibernian (2-0)
1925	Celtic beat Dundee (2-1)
1926	St Mirren beat Celtic (2-0)
1927	Celtic beat East Fife (3-1)
1928	Rangers beat Celtic (4-0)
1929	Kilmarnock beat Rangers (2-0)
1930	Rangers beat Partick (2-1 after 0-0 draw)
1931	Celtic beat Motherwell (4-2 after 2-2 draw)
1932	Rangers beat Kilmarnock (3-0 after 1-1 draw)
1933	Celtic beat Motherwell (1-0)
1934	Rangers beat St Mirren (5-0)
1935	Rangers beat Hamilton (2-1)
1936	Rangers beat Third Lanark (1-0)
1937	Celtic beat Aberdeen (2-1)
1938	East Fife beat Kilmarnock (4-2 after 1-1 draw)
1939	Clyde beat Motherwell (4-0)
1940–6	No competition (World War 2)
1947	Aberdeen beat Hibernian (2-1)
1948†	Rangers beat Morton (1-0 after 1-1 draw)
1949	Rangers beat Clyde (4-1)
1950	Rangers beat East Fife (3-0)
1951	Celtic beat Motherwell (1-0)
1952	Motherwell beat Dundee (4-0)
1953	Rangers beat Aberdeen (1-0 after 1-1 draw)
1954	Celtic beat Aberdeen (2-1)
1955	Clyde beat Celtic (1-0 after 1-1 draw)
1956	Hearts beat Celtic (3-1)
1957†	Falkirk beat Kilmarnock (2-1 after 1-1 draw)
1958	Clyde beat Hibernian (1-0)
1959	St Mirren beat Aberdeen (3-1)
1960	Rangers beat Kilmarnock (2-0)
1961	Dunfermline beat Celtic (2-0 after 0-0 draw)
1962	Rangers beat St Mirren (2-0)
1963	Rangers beat Celtic (3-0 after 1-1 draw)
1964	Rangers beat Dundee (3-1)
1965	Celtic beat Dunfermline (3-2)
1966	Rangers beat Celtic (1-0 after 0-0 draw)
1967	Celtic beat Aberdeen (2-0)
1968	Dunfermline beat Hearts (3-1)
1969	Celtic beat Rangers (4-0)
1970	Aberdeen beat Celtic (3-1)
1971	Celtic beat Rangers (2-1 after 1-1 draw)
1972	Celtic beat Hibernian (6-1)
1973	Rangers beat Celtic (3-2)

1974	Celtic beat Dundee Utd (3-0)
1975	Celtic beat Airdrieonians (3-1)
1976	Rangers beat Hearts (3-1)
1977	Celtic beat Rangers (1-0)
1978	Rangers beat Aberdeen (2-1)
1979†	Rangers beat Hibernian (3-2 after two 0-0 draws)
1980†	Celtic beat Rangers (1-0)
1981	Rangers beat Dundee Utd (4-1 after 0-0 draw)
1982†	Aberdeen beat Rangers (4-1)
1983†	Aberdeen beat Rangers (1-0)
1984†	Aberdeen beat Celtic (2-1)
1985	Celtic beat Dundee Utd (2-1)
1986	Aberdeen beat Hearts (3-0)
1987†	St Mirren beat Dundee Utd (1-0)
1988	Celtic beat Dundee Utd (2-1)
1989	Celtic beat Rangers (1-0)
1990†	Aberdeen beat Celtic (9-8 on pens after 0-0 draw)
1991†	Motherwell beat Dundee Utd (4-3)
1992	Rangers beat Airdrieonians (2-1)
1993	Rangers beat Aberdeen (2-1)
1994	Dundee Utd beat Rangers (1-0)
1995	Celtic beat Airdrieonians (1-0)
1996	Rangers beat Hearts (5-1)
1997	Kilmarnock beat Falkirk (1-0)
1998	Hearts beat Rangers (2-1)
1999	Rangers beat Celtic (1-0)
2000	Rangers beat Aberdeen (4-0)
2001	Celtic beat Hibernian (3-0)
2002	Rangers beat Celtic (3-2)
2003	Rangers beat Dundee (1-0)
2004	Celtic beat Dunfermline (3-1)
2005	Celtic beat Dundee Utd (1-0)
2006†	Hearts beat Gretna (4-2 on pens after 1-1 draw)
2007	Celtic beat Dunfermline (1-0)
2008	Rangers beat Queen of the South (3-2)
2009	Rangers beat Falkirk (1-0)
2010	Dundee Utd beat Ross Co (3-0)
2011	Celtic beat Motherwell (3-0)
2012	Hearts beat Hibernian (5-1)
2013	Celtic beat Hibernian (3-0)
2014	St Johnstone beat Dundee Utd (2-0)
2015	Inverness beat Falkirk (2-1)
2016	Hibernian beat Rangers (3-2)
2017	Celtic beat Aberdeen (2-1)
2018	Celtic beat Motherwell (2-0)
2019	Celtic beat Hearts (2-1)
2020	Celtic beat Hearts (4-3 on pens after 3-3)
2021	St Johnstone beat Hibernian 1-0
	† After extra time

SUMMARY OF SCOTTISH CUP WINNERS

Celtic 40, Rangers 33, Queen's Park 10, Hearts 8, Aberdeen 7, Clyde 3, Hibernian 3, Kilmarnock 3, St Mirren 3, Vale of Leven 3, Dundee Utd 2, Dunfermline 2, Falkirk 2, Motherwell 2, Renton 2, St Johnstone 2, Third Lanark 2, Airdrieonians 1, Dumbarton 1, Dundee 1, East Fife 1, Inverness 1, Morton 1, Partick 1, St Bernard's 1

VANARAMA NATIONAL LEAGUE 2020–2021

	P	W	D	L	F	A	GD	Pts
Sutton	42	25	9	8	72	36	36	84
Torquay	42	23	11	8	68	39	29	80
Stockport	42	21	14	7	69	32	37	77
Hartlepool*	42	22	10	10	66	43	23	76
Notts Co	42	20	10	12	62	41	21	70
Chesterfield	42	21	6	15	60	43	17	69
Bromley	42	19	12	11	63	53	10	69
Wrexham	42	19	11	12	64	43	21	68
Eastleigh	42	18	12	12	49	40	9	66
Halifax	42	19	8	15	63	54	9	65
Solihull	42	19	7	16	58	48	10	64
Dag & Red	42	17	9	16	53	48	5	60
Maidenhead	42	15	11	16	62	60	2	56
Boreham Wood	42	13	16	13	52	48	4	55
Aldershot	42	15	7	20	59	66	-7	52
Yeovil	42	15	7	20	58	68	-10	52
Altrincham	42	12	11	19	46	60	-14	47
Weymouth	42	11	6	25	45	71	-26	39
Wealdstone	42	10	7	25	49	99	-50	37
Woking	42	8	9	25	42	69	-27	33
King's Lynn	42	7	10	25	50	98	-48	31
Barnet	42	8	7	27	37	88	-51	31

* Also promoted

No relegation from or promotion to this division. Dover record expunged – club stopped playing after 15 matches

Play-offs: Quarter-finals: Hartlepool 3 Bromley 2, Notts Co 3 Chesterfield 2. **Semi-finals:** Stockport 0 Hartlepool 1, Torquay 4 Notts Co 2 (aet). **Final:** Hartlepool 1 Torquay 1 -aet, Hartlepool won 5-4 on pens

Leading scorers: 23 Cheek (Bromley); 19 Orsi-Dadomo (Maidenhead), Tshimanga (Boreham Wood); 17 Reid (Stockport); 16 McCallum (Dag & Red), Rooney (Stockport); 15 Barratt (Maidenhead), Oates (Hartlepool), Wootton (Notts Co); 14 Olaofe (Sutton)

Player of Year: John Rooney (Stockport). **Manager of Year:** Matt Gray (Sutton)

Team of Year: McDonnell (Eastleigh), Sherring (Torquay), John (Sutton), Maguire (Chesterfield), King (Halifax), Young (Wrexham), Rooney (Stockport), Barratt (Maidenhead), Cheek (Bromley), Wootton (Notts Co), Oates (Hartlepool)

CHAMPIONS

1979–80	Altrincham	1995–96	Stevenage	2011–2012*	Fleetwood
1980–81	Altrincham	1996–97*	Macclesfield	2012–13*	Mansfield
1981–82	Runcorn	1997–98*	Halifax	2013–14*	Luton
1982–83	Enfield	1998–99*	Cheltenham	2014–15*	Barnet
1983–84	Maidstone	1999–2000*	Kidderminster	2015–16*	Cheltenham
1984–85	Wealdstone	2000–01*	Rushden	2016–17*	Lincoln
1985–86	Enfield	2001–02*	Boston	2017–18*	Macclesfield
1986–87*	Scarborough	2002–03*	Yeovil	2018–19*	Leyton Orient
1987–88*	Lincoln	2003–04*	Chester	2019–20*	Barrow
1988–89*	Maidstone	2004–05*	Barnet	2020–21*	Sutton
1989–90*	Darlington	2005–06*	Accrington	*Promoted to Football League
1990–91*	Barnet	2006–07*	Dagenham	*Conference – Record attendance:*
1991–92*	Colchester	2007–08*	Aldershot	*11,085 Bristol Rov v Alfreton, April*
1992–93*	Wycombe	2008–09*	Burton	*25, 2015*
1993–94	Kidderminster	2009–10*	Stevenage	
1994–95	Macclesfield	2010–11*	Crawley	

VANARAMA NATIONAL LEAGUE RESULTS 2020–2021

	Aldershot	Altrincham	Barnet	Borham-W	Bromley	Chester	Dag&Red	Dover	Eastleigh	Halifax	Hartlepool	King's Lynn	Maidstone	Notts Co	Solihull	Stockport	Sutton	Torquay	Wealdstone	Weymouth	Woking	Wrexham	Yeovil
Aldershot	–	2-1	3-3	2-3	0-1	2-1	2-1		1-3	1-3	1-3	1-1	0-0	1-0	1-3	1-2	1-2	1-4	2-0	0-2	3-0	3-0	2-0
Altrincham	1-2	–	1-2	2-3	0-1	3-1	0-1		3-2	0-1	1-1	3-0	2-0	2-0	0-2	1-1	0-4	0-2	0-0	0-0	1-0	1-2	4-3
Barnet	3-1	1-2	–	0-3	1-3	0-0	0-2		3-0	5-2	1-0	5-1	3-1	4-2	0-1	2-1	1-0	2-2	1-0	1-3	4-1	0-0	2-0
Borham-W	3-2	0-1	0-0	–	1-1	1-2	0-2		1-0	0-1	0-3	1-4	0-1	0-1	1-1	1-1	2-0	1-1	1-3	2-1	0-0	2-1	1-0
Bromley	2-0	3-1	2-2	1-1	–	1-2	1-0		1-2	1-2	0-0	1-4	2-2	0-2	2-1	0-0	3-2	0-0	3-2	2-1	2-2	1-1	0-1
Chester	0-0	1-0	6-0	0-0	1-2	–	2-1		0-1	1-2	3-1	0-1	2-0	0-1	2-1	2-1	0-1	0-1	3-2	0-1	1-1	1-2	0-1
Dag&Red	0-2	0-1	1-2	2-2	2-2	2-2	–		3-0	2-0	2-0	0-3	2-1	3-1	0-0	1-1	1-1	2-1	0-5	2-1	2-0	0-2	1-0
Dover								–															
Eastleigh	2-2	1-1	3-0	1-0	1-2	0-1	2-0		–	1-0	1-1	0-1	0-1	2-0	1-1	1-0	1-0	2-1	2-0	0-0	0-0	1-1	1-4
Halifax	1-0	3-2	5-2	0-1	1-2	1-2	3-0		3-1	–	1-1	4-2	2-3	1-1	2-0	0-1	2-2	0-5	0-1	3-2	1-0	0-4	0-0
Hartlepool	2-1	1-1	1-0	0-3	0-0	3-1	2-1		0-0	3-1	–	2-0	2-4	2-0	2-0	4-0	0-2	0-5	3-1	1-0	2-3	0-1	0-2
King's Lynn	4-4	2-0	5-1	1-4	1-4	0-1	0-3		2-1	0-3	2-2	–	0-0	0-1	1-1	0-1	2-2	0-1	1-1	2-1	2-1	0-2	2-1
Maidstone	2-4	0-1	3-1	0-1	2-2	2-0	2-1		0-1	2-3	2-4	2-3	–	0-4	0-0	0-0	0-2	0-2	4-0	3-2	1-0	2-2	1-2
Notts Co	0-1	3-1	4-2	0-1	0-2	0-1	3-1		2-0	1-1	0-2	0-4	0-4	–	4-1	1-0	1-2	0-2	3-0	3-0	1-0	1-0	0-2
Solihull	1-0	4-0	0-1	1-1	2-1	2-1	0-0		1-1	2-0	1-1	1-1	3-1	3-1	–	0-5	0-0	4-1	3-1	2-2	1-1	1-0	3-2
Stockport	0-0	2-2	2-1	1-1	0-0	2-1	1-1		1-0	0-1	0-4	0-1	0-3	1-0	0-0	–	1-1	0-1	1-4	2-5	1-1	2-0	1-2
Sutton	3-1	2-2	1-0	2-0	3-2	0-1	1-1		1-0	2-2	0-1	1-0	3-2	0-2	0-0	0-2	–	0-2	0-2	3-3	3-2	1-0	1-2
Torquay	2-1	1-2	2-2	1-1	0-0	0-1	2-1		2-1	0-1	0-5	0-0	3-0	0-1	4-1	1-1	0-1	–	1-1	2-2	0-1	2-1	2-0
Wealdstone	3-4	5-1	1-0	1-3	3-2	3-2	0-5		3-1	1-2	2-7	3-1	0-6	2-2	1-4	1-0	3-3	1-0	–	2-1	0-1	3-1	6-1
Weymouth	0-0	1-0	1-3	2-1	2-1	0-1	2-1		0-0	1-5	2-2	2-1	0-0	0-1	0-0	2-5	0-0	3-4	4-0	–	0-1	4-3	0-2
Woking	0-1	1-1	4-1	0-0	3-4	1-4	2-0		1-1	1-0	2-1	2-1	2-4	2-4	2-1	1-4	2-1	0-2	2-4	2-4	–	0-4	1-1
Wrexham	1-0	0-0	0-0	2-1	3-0	0-0	0-2		2-1	0-4	0-1	2-0	2-1	2-1	2-1	0-3	4-0	2-1	0-0	4-1	2-0	–	3-0
Yeovil	3-0	0-1	2-0	1-0	0-1	0-1	1-0		1-0	0-1	0-1	0-2	3-1	2-2	2-3	0-1	1-2	2-1	0-1	2-1	0-1	0-1	–

VANARAMA NATIONAL LEAGUE NORTH

	P	W	D	L	F	A	GD	PTS
Gloucester	18	10	5	3	36	22	14	35
Fylde	15	9	3	3	26	16	10	30
Chester	17	8	4	5	32	24	8	28
Brackley	16	7	6	3	22	19	3	27
Kidderminster	15	7	4	4	24	17	7	25
Boston	13	6	5	2	20	10	10	23
Chorley	18	6	5	7	21	25	-4	23
York	13	6	4	3	22	17	5	22
Leamington	15	5	7	3	22	20	2	22
Gateshead	14	6	3	5	17	15	2	21
Farsley	17	5	6	6	21	26	-5	21
Hereford	13	5	5	3	20	16	4	20
Spennymoor	13	5	5	3	18	14	4	20
AFC Telford	17	5	4	8	17	23	-6	19
Bradford PA	16	4	6	6	26	30	-4	18
Curzon Ashton	17	4	5	8	18	26	-8	17
Southport	14	4	4	6	16	19	-3	16
Kettering	14	3	6	5	21	23	-2	15
Darlington	11	4	1	6	17	11	6	13
Guiseley	15	3	3	9	17	22	-5	12
Alfreton	15	2	6	7	15	27	-12	12
Blyth	14	1	3	10	10	36	-26	6

Season abandoned – Covid, Results expunged – no promotion or relegation

VANARAMA NATIONAL LEAGUE SOUTH

Dorking	18	12	3	3	40	17	23	39
Dartford	19	10	4	5	26	17	9	34
Eastbourne	19	9	6	4	36	26	10	33
Oxford	17	9	5	3	35	17	18	32
St Albans	15	9	5	1	22	10	12	32
Hampton & R	17	9	2	6	24	16	8	29
Hungerford	19	9	2	8	27	28	-1	29
Ebbsfleet	18	8	4	6	26	24	2	28
Havant & W	14	6	2	6	25	21	4	20
Hemel H	18	6	2	10	28	38	-10	20
Maidstone	13	5	4	4	24	18	6	19
Dulwich	13	4	4	5	15	17	-2	16
Chelmsford	16	4	4	8	21	25	-4	16
Tonbridge	14	5	1	8	16	23	-7	16
Billericay	17	4	4	9	26	35	-9	16
Chippenham	14	4	4	6	13	22	-9	16
Concord	14	3	5	6	16	24	-8	14
Bath	13	4	1	8	16	23	-7	13
Braintree	16	4	1	11	19	34	-15	13
Slough	12	3	3	6	16	24	-8	12
Welling	14	2	6	6	18	30	-12	12

Season abandoned – Covid, Results expunged – no promotion or relegation

OTHER LEAGUES 2020–21

JD WELSH PREMIER LEAGUE

	P	W	D	L	F	A	GD	Pts
Connah's Quay	32	25	4	3	70	20	50	79
New Saints	32	24	5	3	84	17	67	77
Bala	32	18	6	8	67	42	25	60
Penybont	32	13	7	12	42	40	2	46
Barry	32	13	4	15	42	53	-11	43
Caernarfon	32	10	7	15	43	67	-24	37
Newtown	32	12	6	14	57	53	4	42
Cardiff Met	32	11	7	14	47	46	1	40
Haverfordwest	32	10	7	15	38	56	-18	37
Aberystwyth	32	8	9	15	47	53	-6	33
Flint	32	10	2	20	38	58	-20	32
Cefn Druids	32	4	4	24	25	95	-70	16

No relegation

PITCHING IN ISTHMIAN LEAGUE

	P	W	D	L	F	A	GD	Pts
Worthing	8	7	0	1	22	10	12	21
Cheshunt	10	6	1	3	13	14	-1	19
Enfield	10	6	0	4	15	17	-2	18
Carshalton	8	5	1	2	14	10	4	16
Cray	7	5	0	2	21	10	11	15
Kingstonian	9	5	0	4	15	18	-3	15
Bishop's Stortford	6	4	2	0	13	5	8	14
Hornchurch	10	4	2	4	17	12	5	14
Horsham	10	4	2	4	19	15	4	14
Folkestone	9	4	1	4	13	13	0	13
Haringey	8	4	0	4	13	13	0	12
Leatherhead	9	3	3	3	8	15	-7	12
Bowers & Pitsea	5	3	1	1	13	5	8	10
Bognor Regis	7	4	1	2	12	6	6	10
Potters Bar	9	3	1	5	13	11	2	10
Wingate & Finchley	8	3	1	4	18	17	1	10
Corinthian Cas	9	3	1	5	9	13	-4	10
Lewes	8	2	2	4	8	15	-7	8
Brightlingsea	10	2	1	7	11	20	-9	7
Margate	9	1	3	5	6	13	-7	6
East Thurrock	9	1	2	6	10	21	-11	5
Merstham	8	1	1	6	8	18	-10	4

Season abandoned. Results expunged – no promotion or relegation

PITCHING IN NORTHERN PREMIER LEAGUE

	P	W	D	L	F	A	GD	Pts
Mickleover	10	7	1	2	23	11	12	22
Basford	9	6	1	2	15	9	6	19
Buxton	8	5	2	1	22	11	11	17
Warrington	9	5	1	3	16	11	5	16
Witton	7	5	0	2	13	7	6	15
South Shields	9	4	3	2	12	8	4	15
Whitby	9	4	2	3	15	14	1	14
Matlock	6	4	1	1	10	4	6	13
Atherton	8	4	1	3	13	8	5	13
Gainsborough	8	4	0	4	13	12	1	12
Scarborough	8	3	2	3	10	11	-1	11
Lancaster	7	2	4	1	12	10	2	10
United of Manc	7	2	4	1	9	7	2	10
Radcliffe	9	3	1	5	15	23	-8	10
Nantwich	6	2	3	1	9	9	0	9
Morpeth	7	2	3	2	9	10	-1	9
Hyde	6	1	3	2	5	6	-1	6
Stalybridge	9	1	3	5	7	17	-10	6
Ashton	7	1	2	4	5	13	-8	5
Bamber Bridge	9	1	1	7	6	17	-11	4
Grantham	8	0	3	5	5	14	-9	3
Stafford	8	0	1	7	3	15	-12	1

Season abandoned. Results expunged – no promotion or relegation

PITCHING IN SOUTHERN LEAGUE

	P	W	D	L	F	A	GD	Pts
Poole	7	6	1	0	16	7	9	19
Tiverton	7	6	0	1	21	4	17	18
Salisbury	7	5	2	0	17	7	10	17
Truro	8	5	1	2	17	9	8	16
Met Police	8	4	2	2	14	11	3	14
Swindon Super	7	4	0	3	12	10	2	12
Chesham	7	3	3	1	6	4	2	12
Taunton	6	3	2	1	8	5	3	11
Hendon	8	3	2	3	12	10	2	11
Hayes & Yeading	7	2	4	1	11	8	3	10
Gosport	7	2	2	3	11	9	2	8
Walton	6	2	1	3	8	13	-5	7
Wimborne	6	2	1	3	5	12	-7	7
Hartley Wintney	6	1	3	2	5	9	-4	6
Weston SM	6	1	2	3	8	10	-2	5
Harrow	7	1	2	4	11	14	-3	5
Yate	8	1	2	5	8	17	-9	5
Farnborough	8	1	1	6	7	16	-9	4
Dorchester	7	1	1	5	5	17	-12	4
Beaconsfield	7	0	2	5	4	14	-10	2
Merthyr	0	0	0	0	0	0	0	0

Season abandoned. Results expunged – no promotion or relegation

PITCHING IN SOUTHERN CENTRAL LEAGUE

	P	W	D	L	F	A	GD	Pts
Coalville	7	5	2	0	21	5	16	17
Needham Market	7	5	2	0	17	7	10	17
Stratford	8	5	0	3	17	16	1	15
Rushall	8	3	4	1	14	12	2	13
Tamworth	7	3	3	1	13	8	5	12
Redditch	8	3	3	2	14	11	3	12
Stourbridge	8	2	5	1	10	7	3	11
Royston	8	2	5	1	12	11	1	11
Kings Langley	9	2	5	2	11	11	0	11
Hitchin	7	3	1	3	12	14	-2	10
St Ives	6	3	1	2	11	13	-2	10
Peterborough Spts	6	2	3	1	10	5	5	9
Rushden	7	2	3	2	14	11	3	9
Lowestoft	7	2	3	2	8	9	-1	9
Nuneaton	8	2	2	4	14	13	1	8
Biggleswade	8	2	2	4	13	17	-4	8
Alvechurch	9	2	2	5	12	16	-4	8
Banbury	7	2	2	3	9	13	-4	8
Bromsgrove	8	2	2	4	9	17	-8	8
Hednesford	8	2	1	5	12	16	-4	7
Leiston	8	1	2	5	11	21	-10	5
Barwell	7	1	1	5	6	17	-11	4

Season abandoned. Results expunged – no promotion or relegation

BREEDON HIGHLAND LEAGUE

	P	W	D	L	F	A	GD	Pts
Brora	3	3	0	0	20	1	19	9
Fraserburgh	3	3	0	0	16	1	15	9
Buckie	2	2	0	0	8	3	5	6
Formartine	2	2	0	0	7	2	5	6
Inverurie	2	2	0	0	6	2	4	6
Keith	2	1	0	1	2	3	-1	3
Rothes	2	1	0	1	2	5	-3	3
Huntly	3	0	2	1	3	4	-1	2
Lossiemouth	2	0	1	1	2	4	-2	1
Deveronvale	3	0	1	2	2	8	-6	1
Clachnacuddin	1	0	0	1	2	4	-2	0
Nairn	2	0	0	2	1	3	-2	0
Wick	2	0	0	2	3	8	-5	0
Fort William	1	0	0	1	0	10	-10	0
Turriff	2	0	0	2	2	18	-16	0

Season abandoned – Brora declared champions. Forres, Strathspey did not play

LOWLAND LEAGUE

	P	W	D	L	F	A	GD	Pts
Kelty	13	12	0	1	40	4	36	36
BSC Glasgow	13	9	3	1	38	16	22	30
East Kilbride	12	9	2	1	32	6	26	29
Bonnyrigg	12	9	2	1	29	6	23	29
East Stirling	12	8	2	2	30	12	18	26
Stirling Univ	15	7	1	7	31	25	6	22
Gala	12	7	1	4	22	20	2	22
Bo'ness	10	5	3	2	22	13	9	18
Spartans	12	6	0	6	27	22	5	18
Civil Service	14	4	5	5	14	16	-2	17
Berwick	13	5	1	7	12	16	-4	16
Caledonian	14	4	1	9	22	28	-6	13
Cumbernauld	14	3	2	9	17	30	-13	11
Gretna	11	3	1	7	15	25	-10	10
Dalbeattie	10	1	2	7	12	24	-12	5
Edinburgh Univ	15	1	2	12	7	54	-47	5
Vale of Leithen	12	0	0	12	5	58	-53	0

Season abandoned – Kelty declared champions

PREMIER LEAGUE UNDER 23
DIVISION ONE

	P	W	D	L	F	A	GD	Pts
Manchester City	24	17	5	2	79	30	49	56
Chelsea	24	12	6	6	50	36	14	42
Tottenham	24	11	5	8	45	44	1	38
Blackburn	24	10	7	7	48	41	7	37
Everton	24	10	6	8	44	28	16	36
Derby	24	11	3	10	43	49	-6	36
Liverpool	24	10	5	9	48	50	-2	35
Manchester Utd	24	10	4	10	58	59	-1	34
Brighton	24	7	9	8	36	42	-6	30
Arsenal	24	6	8	10	37	43	-6	26
West Ham	24	6	6	12	32	48	-16	24
Leicester	24	6	4	14	41	55	-14	22
Southampton	24	4	4	16	29	65	-36	16

DIVISION TWO

	P	W	D	L	F	A	GD	Pts
Leeds	24	18	2	4	62	29	33	56
Stoke	24	14	3	7	41	30	11	45
Crystal Palace	24	11	3	10	45	41	4	36
Wolves	24	10	6	8	40	36	4	36
Sunderland	24	10	5	9	42	41	1	35
Middlesbrough	24	10	4	10	44	35	9	34
Burnley	24	10	4	10	38	41	-3	34
Reading	24	10	2	12	41	54	-13	32
Aston Villa	24	9	4	11	46	48	-2	31
Fulham	24	9	3	12	38	46	-8	30
Norwich	24	7	4	13	32	40	-8	25
WBA	24	7	4	13	37	49	-12	25
Newcastle	24	7	4	13	31	47	-16	25

Play-offs: Semi-finals: Stoke 0 Sunderland 2; Crystal Palace 3 Wolves 2. **Final:** Crystal Palace 0 Sunderland 0 – Crystal Palace won 5-3 on pens and promoted

WOMEN'S FOOTBALL 2020–21
CHELSEA RETAIN SUPER LEAGUE TITLE

Chelsea held off a strong challenge from Manchester City to retain the Women's Super League title. They defeated Reading 5-0 on the final day of the season, with Melanie Leupolz scoring the fastest goal of the season after 68 seconds and Fran Kirby netting twice. The victory, which maintained a two-point advantage at the top, was the club's fourth success in six seasons. Manager Emma Hayes rated it the most satisfying because of the competition from their rivals. Fara Williams, England's most capped player with 172 international appearances, captained Reading in her final game before retiring. She was denied a farewell goal against her old club by Germany goalkeeper Ann-Katrin Berger, who won the league's golden glove with 12 clean sheets. Kirby also scored twice in Chelsea's 6-0 League Cup Final win over Bristol City and was named the season's best player by football writers and the players' union, the PFA. But the Champions League Final in Gothenburg proved something of an anti-climax against Barcelona, who scored four times in the opening 36 minutes to win 4-0 and become the first club to lift both the men's and women's trophies. Earlier in the season, Manchester City won the FA Cup for the third time in four years, defeating Everton 3-1 in the delayed 2020 final with extra-time goals from Georgia Stanway and Janine Beckie. The final three rounds of the 2021 tournament will be played in the new season, with the final at Wembley on December 5.

● Manchester City defender Lucy Bronze was named the world's best player by FIFA for 2020 at a virtual ceremony in Zurich. She became the first England player to win the award.

SUPER LEAGUE

	P	W	D	L	F	A	GD	Pts
Chelsea	22	18	3	1	69	10	59	57
Manchester City	22	17	4	1	65	13	52	55
Arsenal	22	15	3	4	63	15	48	48
Manchester Utd	22	15	2	5	44	20	24	47
Everton	22	9	5	8	39	30	9	32
Brighton	22	8	3	11	21	41	-20	27
Reading	22	5	9	8	25	41	-16	24
Tottenham	22	5	5	12	18	41	-23	20
West Ham	22	3	6	13	21	39	-18	15
Aston Villa	22	3	6	13	15	47	-32	15
Birmingham*	22	3	6	13	15	44	-29	14
Bristol City	22	2	6	14	18	72	-54	12

*One point deducted

Leading scorers: 21 Kerr (Chelsea); 18 Miedema (Arsenal); 16 Kirby (Chelsea); 10 Foord (Arsenal), Kelly (Manchester City), White (Manchester City); 9 Harder (Chelsea), Toone (Manchester Utd); 8 Kaagman (Brighton), Weir (Manchester City)

Team of the Year: Katrin-Berger (Chelsea), McCabe (Arsenal), Williamson (Arsenal), Eriksson (Chelsea), Mjelde (Chelsea), Mewis (Manchester City), Weir (Manchester City), Kerr (Chelsea), Kelly (Manchester City), Kirby (Chelsea), Hemp (Manchester City)

CHAMPIONSHIP

	P	W	D	L	F	A	GD	Pts
Leicester	20	16	2	2	54	16	38	50
Durham	20	12	6	2	34	15	19	42
Liverpool	20	11	6	3	37	15	22	39
Sheffield Utd	20	11	5	4	37	15	22	38
Lewes	20	8	4	8	19	22	-3	28
London City	20	6	6	8	19	19	0	24
Crystal Place	20	5	5	10	27	36	-9	20
Charlton	20	4	7	9	19	29	-10	19
Blackburn	20	4	6	10	20	31	-11	18
Coventry	20	5	1	14	21	51	-30	16
London Bees	20	3	2	15	14	52	-38	11

IRISH FOOTBALL 2020–21

SSE AIRTRICITY LEAGUE OF IRELAND

PREMIER DIVISION

	P	W	D	L	F	A	Pts
Shamrock Rov	18	15	3	0	44	7	48
Bohemians	18	12	1	5	23	12	37
Dundalk	18	7	5	6	25	23	26
Sligo	18	8	1	9	19	23	25
Waterford	18	7	3	8	17	22	24
St Patrick's	18	5	6	7	14	17	21
Derry City	18	5	5	8	18	18	20
Finn Harps	18	5	5	8	15	24	20
Shelbourne	18	5	4	9	13	22	19R
Cork City	18	2	5	11	10	30	11R

Leading scorer: 10 Patrick Hoban (Dundalk). **Player of Year:** Jack Byrne (Shamrock Rov). **Young Player of Year:** Danny Grant (Bohemians). **Goalkeeper of Year:** Alan Mannus (Shamrock Rov). **Personality of Year:** Jack Byrne (Shamrock Rov)

FIRST DIVISION

	P	W	D	L	F	A	Pts
Drogheda	18	12	3	3	39	17	39P
Bray Wdrs	18	12	2	4	30	13	38
UCD	18	9	3	6	44	29	30
Longford	18	9	2	7	26	23	29P
Galway	18	7	6	5	26	19	27
Cobh	18	8	3	7	22	20	27
Cabinteely	18	7	3	8	22	33	24
Shamrock II	18	4	3	11	21	28	15
Wexford	18	3	4	11	13	39	13
Athlone	18	3	3	12	21	43	12

Leading scorer 15 Yousef Mahdy (UCD). **Player of Year:** Mark Doyle (Drogheda)

Extra.ie FAI CUP FINAL

Dundalk 4 (McMillan 3) Hoare) **Shamrock Rov** 2 (Greene, Lopes) - aet, Aviva Stadium, Dublin, December 6, 2020

Dundalk: Rogers, Gannon (Leahy), Gartland (Hoare), Boyle, Dummigan, McEleney, Shields, Sloggett (Mountney), McEleney, McMillan, Duffy (Kelly)

Shamrock Rov: Mannus, O'Brien (Grace), Lopes, Scales, Kavanagh (Lafferty), Finn (Marshall), Byrne, Burke, McEneff, Watts (Bolger) Greene
Referee: R Harvey (Dublin)

DANSKE BANK PREMIERSHIP

	P	W	D	L	F	A	Pts
Linfield	38	24	6	8	83	38	78
Coleraine	38	21	10	7	57	35	73
Glentoran	38	20	11	7	65	32	71
Larne	38	18	10	10	64	41	64
Cliftonville	38	17	9	12	59	42	60
Crusaders	38	16	6	16	62	50	54
Glenavon	38	18	7	11	10	72	65	62
Ballymena	38	18	7	13	67	44	61
Portadown	38	10	6	22	50	78	36
Warrenpoint	38	9	9	20	38	74	36
Carrick	38	5	8	25	35	92	23
Dungannon	38	4	5	29	22	83	17

League divided after 33 games.
Leading scorer: 23 Shayne Lavery (Linfield). **Player of Year:** Shayne Lavery.
Manager of Year: David Healy (Linfield). **Young Player of Year:** Shayne Lavery

SADLER'S PEAKY BLINDER IRISH CUP FINAL

Linfield 2 (Lavery, Cooper) **Larne** 1 (Hughes). Mourneview Park, Lurgan, May 21, 2021
Linfield: Johns, Haughey, Callacher, Millar, Lavery (Manzinga), Clarke, Mulgrew, Pepper, Quinn, Palmer, Cooper
Larne: Mitchell, Watson, Robinson, Herron, Sule, Hale (McMurray), Donnelly (McDaid), Lynch, (Randall), Cosgrove, Hughes, Jarvis
Referee: A Davey (Bangor)

COUNTY ANTRIM SHIELD FINAL

Glentoran 0 **Larne** 0 (Larne won 4-3 on pens). Seaview, Belfast, December 2, 2020

UEFA CHAMPIONS LEAGUE 2020–21

FIRST QUALIFYING ROUND (single leg)

Celje 3 (Kerin 43, Vizinger 89, Dangubic 90+5) **Dundalk** 0. **Celtic** 6 (Elyounoussi 6, 90+1, Aoalsteinsson 17 og, Jullien 31, Taylor 46, Edouard 71) KR Reykjavik 0. **Connah's Quay** 0 Sarajevo 2 (Tatar 16, 65). Legia Warsaw 1 (Kante 82) **Linfield** 0
Ararat-Armenia 0 Omonia Nicosia 1; Buducnost 1 Ludogorets 3; Dinamo Brest 6 Astana 3; Dinamo Tbilisi 0 Tirana 2; Ferencvaros 2 Djurgarden 0; Flora Tallinn 1 Suduva 1 (aet, Suduva won 4-2 on pens); Floriana 0 CFR Cluj 2; Klaksvikar 3 Slovan Bratislava 0; Maccabi Tel Aviv 2 Riga 0; Molde 5 KuPS 0; Red Star Belgrade 5 Europa 0; Qarabag 4 Sileks 0; Sheriff Tiraspol 2 Fola Esch 0

SECOND QUALIFYING ROUND (single leg))

Celtic 1 (Christie 53) Ferencvaros 2 (Siger 7, Nguen 75). AZ Alkmaar 3 Viktoria Plzen 1; Celje 1 Molde 2; CFR Cluj 2 Dinamo Zagreb 2 (aet, Dinamo Zagreb won 6-5 on pens); Dinamo Brest 2 Sarajevo 1; Legia Warsaw 0 Omonia Nicosia 2; Lokomotiv Zagreb 0 Rapid Vienna 1; Ludogorets 0 Midtjylland 1; PAOK Salonica 1 Besiktas 1; Qarabag 2 Sheriff Tiraspol 1; Suduva 0 Maccabi Tel Aviv 3; Tirana 0 Red Star Belgrade 1; Young Boys 3 Ki Klaksvik 1

THIRD QUALIFYING ROUND (single leg)

Dynamo Kiev 2 AZ Alkmaar 0; Ferencvaros 2 Dinamo Zagreb 1; Gent 2 Rapid Vienna 1; Maccabi Tel Aviv 1 Dinamo Brest 0; Midtjylland 3 Young Boys 0; Omonia Nicosia 1 Red Star Belgrade 1 (aet, Omonia Nicosia won 4-2 on pens); PAOK Salonica 2 Benfica 1; Qarabag 0 Molde 0 (aet, Molde won 6-5 on pens)

QUALIFYING PLAY-OFFS (on aggregate)

Dynamo Kiev 5 Gent 1; Ferencvaros 3 Molde 3 (Ferencvaros won on away goals); Krasnodar 4 PAOK Salonica 2; Midtjylland 4 Slavia Prague 1; Olympiacos 2 Omonia Nicosia 0; Salzburg 5 Maccabi Tel Aviv 2

GROUP A

October 21, 2020
Bayern Munich 4 (Coman 28, 72, Goretzka 41, Tolisso 66) **Atletico Madrid** 0
RB Salzburg 2 (Szoboszlai 45, Junuzovic 50) **Lokomotic Moscow** 2 (Eder 19, Lisakovich 75)

October 27, 2020
Atletico Madrid 3 (Llorente 29, Joao Felix 52, 85) **RB Salzburg** 2 (Szoboszlai 40, Berisha 47)
Lokomotiv Moscow 1 (Miranchuk 70) **Bayern Munich** 2 (Goretzka 13, Kimmich 79)

November 3, 2020
Lokomotiv Moscow 1 (Miranchuk 25 pen) **Atletico Madrid** 1 (Gimenez 18)
RB Salzburg 2 (Berisha 4, Okugawa 66) **Bayern Munich** 6 (Lewandowski 21 pen, 88, Kristensen 44 og, Boateng 79, Sane 83, Hernandez 90+2)

November 25, 2020
Atletico Madrid 0 Lokomotiv Moscow 0
Bayern Munich 3 (Lewandowski 42, Wober 52 og, Sane 68) **RB Salzburg** 1 (Berisha 73)

December 1, 2020
Atletico Madrid 1 (Joao Felix 26) **Bayern Munich** 1 (Muller 86 pen)

Lokomotiv Moscow 1 (Miranchuk 79 pen) **RB Salzburg** 3 (Berisha 28, 41, Adeyemi 81)

December 9, 2020
Bayern Munich 2 (Sule 63, Chopa-Moting 80) **Lokomotiv Moscow** 0
RB Salzburg 0 **Atletico Madrid** 2 (Hermoso 39, Carrasco 86)

	P	W	D	L	F	A	Pts
Bayern Munich Q	6	5	1	0	18	5	16
Atletico Madrid Q	6	2	3	1	5	8	9
RB Salzburg	6	1	1	4	10	17	4
Lokomotiv Moscow	6	0	3	3	5	10	3

GROUP B

October 21, 2020
Inter Milan 2 (Lukaku 49, 90) **Borussia Monchengladbach** 2 (Bensebaini 63 pen, Hofman 85)
Real Madrid 2 (Modrich 54, Vinicius Junior 59) **Shakhtar Donetsk** 3 (Tete 29, Varane 33 og, Solomon 42)

October 27, 2020
Borussia Monchengladbach 2 (Thuram 33, 58) **Real Madrid** 2 (Benzema 87, Casemiro 90+3)
Shakhtar Donetsk 0 **Inter Milan** 0. Att: 10,178

November 3, 2020
Real Madrid 3 (Benzema 25, Sergio Ramos 33, Rodrygo 80) **Inter Milan** 2 (Martinez 35, Perisic 88)
Shakhtar Donetsk 0 **Borussia Monchengladbach** 6 (Plea 8, 26, 78, Bondar 17 og, Bensebaini 44, Stindl 65)

November 25, 2020
Borussia Monchengladbach 4 (Stindl 17 pen, Elvedi 34, Embolo 45, Wendt 77) **Shakhtar Donetsk** 0
Inter Milan 0 **Real Madrid** 2 (Hazard 7 pen, Hakimi 59 og)

December 1, 2020
Borussia Monchengladbach 2 (Plea 45, 75) **Inter Milan** 3 (Darmian 17, Lukaku 64, 73)
Shakhtar Donetsk 2 (Dentinho 57, Solomon 82) **Real Madrid** 0

December 9, 2020
Inter Milan 0 **Shakhtar Donetsk** 0
Real Madrid 2 (Benzema 9, 32) **Borussia Monchengladbach** 0

	P	W	D	L	F	A	Pts
Real Madrid Q	6	3	1	2	11	9	10
Borussia M'gladbach Q	6	2	2	2	16	9	8
Shakhtar Donetsk	6	2	2	2	5	12	8
Inter Milan	6	1	3	2	7	9	6

GROUP C

October 21, 2020
Manchester City 3 (Aguero 20 pen, Gundogan 65, Torres 73) **Porto** 1 (Diaz 14)
Manchester City (4-3-3): Ederson, Walker, Dias, Garcia, Joao Cancelo, Bernardo Silva, Rodri (Fernandinho 85, Stones 90+4), Gundogan (Foden 68), Mahrez, Aguero (Torres 68), Sterling.
Booked: Walker, Bernardo Silva, Joao Cancelo, Garcia, Fernandinho
Olympiacos 1 (Koka 90+1) **Marseille** 0

October 27, 2020
Porto 2 (Vieira 11, Oliveira 85) **Olympiacos** 0
Marseille 0 **Manchester City** 3 (Torres 18, Gundogan 76, Sterling 81)
Manchester City (4-2-3-1): Ederson, Walker, Dias, Laporte (Stones 77), Zinchenko (Joao Cancelo 68), Rodri, Gundogan (Bernardo Silva 78), Sterling, De Bruyne (Palmer 82), Foden, Torres (Mahrez 77). **Booked**: Laporte

November 3, 2020
Manchester City 3 (Torres 12, Gabriel Jesus 81, Joao Cancelo 90) **Olympiacos** 0
Manchester City (4-3-3): Ederson, Walker (Joao Cancelo 82), Stones, Ake, Zinchenko, De Bruyne (Nmecha 85), Gundogan, Foden (Rodri 69), Mahrez (Gabriel Jesus 69), Torres, Sterling (Bernardo Silva 82)
Porto 3 (Marega 4, Sergio Oliveira 28 pen, Diaz 69) **Marseille** 0

November 25, 2020
Marseille 0 **Porto** 2 (Sanusi 39, Sergio Oliveira 72 pen)
Olympiacos 0 **Manchester City** 1 (Foden 36)
Manchester City (4-2-3-1): Ederson, Joao Cancelo, Stones, Dias, Mendy (Zinchenko 78), Rodri (Fernandinho 76), Gundogan (Doyle 86), Sterling (Mahrez 76), Bernardo Silva, Foden, Gabriel Jesus (Aguero 78)

December 1, 2020
Porto 0 **Manchester City** 0
Manchester City (4-2-3-1): Ederson, Joao Cancelo, Dias, Garcia, Zinchenko, Fernandinho, Rodri, Sterling, Bernardo Silva, Foden, Torres (Gabriel Jesus 71). **Booked**: Rodri
Marseille 2 (Payet 55 pen, 75 pen) **Olympiacos** 1 (Camara 33)

December 9, 2020
Manchester City 3 (Torres 48, Aguero 77, Sterling 90) **Marseille** 0
Manchester City (4-2-3-1): Steffen, Walker, Garcia (Stones 26), Laporte, Ake, Fernandinho, Gundogan (Sterling 46), Mahrez (Aguero 66), Bernardo Silva, Foden, Torres
Olympiacos 0 **Porto** 2 (Otavio 10 pen, Uribe 77)

	P	W	D	L	F	A	Pts
Manchester City Q	6	5	1	0	13	1	16
Porto Q	6	4	1	1	10	3	13
Olympiacos	6	1	0	5	2	10	3
Marseille	6	1	0	5	2	13	3

GROUP D

October 21, 2020
Ajax 0 **Liverpool** 1 (Tagliafico 35 og)
Liverpool (4-3-3): Alexander-Arnold, Fabinho, Gomez, Robertson, Jones (Henderson 6), Wijnaldum, Milner (R Williams 90+2), Salah (Shaqiri 60), Firmino (Diogo Jota 60), Mane (Minamino 60). **Booked**: Milner, Alexander-Arnold
Midtjylland 0 **Atalanta** 4 (Zapata 26, Gomez 36, Muriel 42, Miranchuk 89)

October 27, 2020
Atalanta 2 (Zapata 54, 60) **Ajax** 2 (Tadic 30 pen, Traore 38)
Liverpool 2 (Diogo Jota 55, Salah 90+3 pen) **Midtjylland** 0
Liverpool (4-3-3): Alisson, Alexander-Arnold, Fabinho (R Williams 30), Gomez, Robertson, Henderson (Wijnaldum 46), Milner, Shaqiri, Diogo Jota (Firmino 81), Minamino (Mane 60), Origi (Salah 60). **Booked**: Milner

November 3, 2020
Atalanta 0 **Liverpool** 5 (Diogo Jota 16, 33, 54, Salah 47, Mane 49)
Liverpool (4-3-3): Alisson, Alexander-Arnold (N Williams 82), Gomez, R Williams, Robertson (Keita 65), Jones, Henderson (Milner 66), Wijnaldum, Salah, Diogo Jota (Firmino 65), Mane.
Booked: Jones, Wijnaldum
Midtjylland 1 (Dreyer 18) **Ajax** 2 (Antony 1, Tadic 13)

November 25, 2020
Ajax 3 (Gravenberch 47, Mazraoui 49, Neres 66) **Midtjylland** 1 (Mabil 80 pen)
Liverpool 0 **Atalanta** 2 (Ilicic 60 Gosens 64)
Liverpool (4-3-3): Alisson, N Williams, Matip (Minamino 85), R Williams, Tsimikas (Robertson 60), Jones, Wijnaldum (Fabinho 60), Milner, Salah (Firmino 60) Origi (Diogo Jota 60), Mane.
Booked: Tsimikas

December 1, 2020
Atalanta 1 (Romero 79) **Midtjylland** 1 (Scholz 13)
Liverpool 1 (Jones 58) **Ajax** 0
Liverpool (4-3-3): Kelleher, N Williams, Matip, Fabinho, Robertson, Henderson, Wijnaldum, Jones, Diogo Jota (Firmino 68), Mane, Salah (R Williams 90). **Booked:** Wijnaldum, Henderson, Mane

December 9, 2020
Ajax 0 **Atalanta** 1 (Muriel 85)
Midtjylland 1 (Scholz 62 pen) **Liverpool** 1 (Salah 1)
Liverpool (4-2-3-1): Kelleher, Alexander-Arnold, Fabinho (Koumetio 46), R Williams, Tsimikas (Robertson 61), Clarkson, Keita (Henderson 61), Salah, Minamino, Diogo Jota (Mane 87), Origi (Firmino 71). **Booked:** Kelleher

	P	W	D	L	F	A	Pts
Liverpool Q	6	4	1	1	10	3	13
Atalanta Q	6	3	2	1	10	8	11
Ajax	6	2	1	3	7	7	7
Midtjylland	6	0	2	4	4	13	2

GROUP E

October 20, 2020
Chelsea 0 **Sevilla** 0
Chelsea (4-2-3-1): Mendy, James, Thiago Silva, Zouma, Chilwell, Kante, Jorginho (Kovacic 65), Havertz, Mount (Ziyech 62), Pulisic (Hudson-Odoi 90+1), Werner (Abraham 90). **Booked:** Jorginho, Mount, Chilwell
Rennes 1 (Guirassy 56 pen) **Krasnodar** 1 (Ramirez 59)

October 28, 2020
Krasnodar 0 **Chelsea** 4 (Hudson-Odoi 37, Werner 76 pen, Ziyech 79, Pulisic 90). Att: 10,544
Chelsea (4-3-3): Mendy, Azpilicueta, Zouma, Rudiger, Chilwell (Enmerson 81), Kovacic (Pulisic 71), Jorginho (Kante 71), Havertz, Ziyech (Abraham 81), Werner, Hudson-Odoi (Mount 71)
Sevilla 1 (de Jong 55) **Rennes** 0

November 4, 2020
Chelsea 3 (Werner 10 pen, 41 pen, Abraham 50) **Rennes** 0
Chelsea (4-3-3): Mendy, James, Thiago Silva (Rudiger 68), Zouma, Chilwell (Emerson 62), Kante (Kovacic 63), Jorginho, Mount, Ziyech (Hudson-Odoi 75), Abraham (Giroud 63), Werner.
Booked: Kante, Ziyech, Jorginho, Kovacic
Sevilla 3 (Rakitic 42, En-Nesyri 69, 72) **Krasnodar** 2 (Suleymanov 17, Berg 21 pen)

November 24, 2020
Krasnodar 1 (Wanderson 56) **Sevilla** 2 (Rakitic 4, Munier 90)
Rennes 1 (Guirassy 85) **Chelsea** 2 (Hudson-Odoi 22. Giroud 90+1)
Chelsea (4-2-3-1): Mendy, Azpilicueta, Zouma, Thiago Silva, Chilwell, Jorginho, Kovacic (Havertz 76), Hudson-Odoi (Ziyech 75), Mount (Kante 68), Werner (James 90), Abraham (Giroud 69)

December 2, 2020
Krasnodar 1 (Berg 71) **Rennes** 0
Sevilla 0 **Chelsea** 4 (Giroud 8, 54, 74, 83 pen)
Chelsea (4-2-3-3): Mendy, Azpilicueta, Christensen, Rudiger, Emerson, Kovacic (Ziyech 67), Jorginho (Gilmour 85), Hudson-Odoi, Havertz (Kante 67), Pulisic (Mount 67), Giroud (Werner 84). **Booked**: Kovacic, Pulisic, Mount, Ziyech

December 8, 2020
Chelsea 1 (Jorginho 28 pen) **Krasnodar** 1 (Cabella 24)
Chelsea (4-3-3): Arrizabalaga, Azpilicueta, Christensen, Rudiger, Emerson, Gilmour, Jorginho, Kovacic (Kante 75), Havertz (Werner 75), Abraham, Anjorin (Giroud 80). **Booked**: Azpilicueta
Rennes 1 (Rutter 86 pen) **Sevilla** 3 (Kounde 32, En-Nesyri 45, 81)

	P	W	D	L	F	A	Pts
Chelsea Q	6	4	2	0	14	2	14
Sevilla Q	6	4	1	1	9	8	13
Krasnodar	6	1	2	3	6	11	5
Rennes	6	0	1	5	3	11	1

GROUP F

October 20, 2020
Lazio 3 (Immobile 6, Hitz 23 og, Akpa Akpro 76) **Borussia Dortmund** 1 (Haaland 71)
Zenit St Petersburg 1 (Horvath 74 og) **Club Bruges** 2 (Bonaventure 63, De Ketelaere 90)

October 28, 2020
Borussia Dortmund 2 (Sancho 78 pen, Haaland 90) **Zenit St Petersburg** 0
Club Bruges 1 (Vanaken 42 pen) **Lazio** 1 (Correa 14)

November 4, 2020
Club Bruges 0 **Borussia Dortmund** 3 (Hazard 14, Haaland 18, 32)
Zenit St Petersburg 1 (Erokhin 32) **Lazio** 1 (Caicedo 82)

November 24, 2020
Borussia Dortmund 3 (Haaland 18, 60, Sancho 45) **Club Bruges** 0
Lazio 3 (Immobile 3, 55 pen, Parolo 22) **Zenit St Petersburg** 1 (Dzyuba 25)

December 2, 2020
Borussia Dortmund 1 (Guerreiro 44) **Lazio** 1 (Immobile 67 pen)
Club Bruges 3 (De Ketelaere 33, Vanaken 58 pen, Lang 73) **Zenit St Petersburg** 0

December 8, 2020
Lazio 2 (Correa 12, Immobile 27 pen) **Club Bruges** 2 (Vormer 15, Vanaken 76)
Zenit St Petersburg 1 (Driussi 16) **Borussia Dortmund** 2 (Piszczek 68, Witsel 78)

	P	W	D	L	F	A	Pts
Borussia Dortmund Q	6	4	1	1	12	5	13
Lazio Q	6	2	4	0	11	7	10
Club Bruges	6	2	2	2	8	10	8
Zenit St Petersburg	6	0	1	5	4	13	1

GROUP G

October 20, 2020
Barcelona 5 (Messi 27 pen, Fati 42, Coutinho 52, Gonzalez 82, Dembele 89) **Ferencvaros** 1 (Kharatin 70 pen)
Dynamo Kiev 0 **Juventus** 2 (Morata 46, 84)

October 28, 2020
Ferencvaros 2 (Nguen 59, Boli 90) **Dynamo Kiev** 2 (Tsygankov 28 pen, De Pena 41)
Juventus 0 **Barcelona** 2 (Dembele 14, Messi 90 pen)

November 4, 2020
Barcelona 2 (Messi 5 pen, Pique 65) **Dynamo Kiev** 1 (Tsygankov 75)
Ferencvaros 1 (Boli 90) **Juventus** 4 (Morata 7, 60, Dybala 72, Dvali 82 og)

November 24, 2020
Dynamo Kiev 0 **Barcelona** 4 (Dest 52, Braithwaite 57, 70 pen, Griezemann 90+2)
Juventus 2 (Ronaldo 35, Morata 90+2) **Ferencvaros** 1 (Uzuni 19)

December 2, 2020
Ferencvaros 0 **Barcelona** 3 (Griezmann 14, Braithwaite 20, Dembele 28 pen)
Juventus 3 (Chiesa 21, Ronaldo 57, Morata 66) **Dynamo Kiev** 0

December 8, 2020
Barcelona 0 **Juventus** 3 (Ronaldo 13 pen, 52 pen, McKennie 20)
Dynamo Kiev 1 (Popov 60) **Ferencvaros** 0

	P	W	D	L	F	A	Pts
Juventus Q	6	5	0	1	14	4	15
Barcelona Q	6	5	0	1	16	5	15
Dynamo Kiev	6	1	1	4	4	13	4
Ferencvaros	6	0	1	5	5	17	1

GROUP H

October 20, 2020
Paris SG 1 (Martial 55 og) **Manchester Utd** 2 (Bruno Fernandes 23 pen, Rashford 87)
Manchester Utd (3-4-1-2): De Gea, Tuanzebe, Lindelof, Shaw, Wan-Bissaka, Fred, McTominay, Telles (Pogba 67), Bruno Fernandes (Van de Beek 8), Rashford, Martial (James 88) **Booked**: McTominay, Tuanzebe
RB Leipzig 2 (Angelino 16, 20) **Basaksehir** 0

October 28, 2020
Basaksehir 0, **Paris SG** 2 (Kean 64, 69)
Manchester Utd 5 (Greenwood 21, Rashford 74, 78, 90, Martial 87 pen) **RB Leipzig** 0
Manchester Utd (4-1-2-1-2): De Gea, Wan-Bissaka (Tuanzebe 81), Lindelof, Maguire, Shaw, Matic (McTominay 63), Fred, Pogba (Cavani 81), Van de Beek (Bruno Fernandes 68), Greenwood (Rashford 63), Martial. **Booked**: Matic

November 4, 2020
Basaksehir 2 (Demba Ba 13, Visca 40) **Manchester United** 1 (Martial 43)
Manchester United (4-1-2-1-2): Henderson, Wan-Bissaka (Fosu-Mensah 76), Tuanzebe (McTominay 46), Maguire, Shaw, Matic, Van de Beek (Pogba 61), Mata (Cavani 61), Bruno Fernandes, Rashford (Greenwood 76), Martial. **Booked**: Tuanzebe
RB Leipzig 2 (Nkunku 42, Forsberg 57 pen) **Paris SG** 1 (Di Maria 6)

November 24, 2020
Manchester Utd 4 (Bruno Fernandes 7, 19, Rashford 36 pen, James 90+2) **Basaksehir** 0
Manchester Utd (4-2-3-1): De Gea, Wan-Bissaka (Williams 59), Lindelof (Tuanzebe 46), Maguire, Telles, Fred, Van de Beek, Rashford (James 59), Bruno Fernandes (Greenwood 59) Martial (Matic 82), Cavani. **Booked**: Tuanzebe, Maguire
Paris SG 1 (Neymar 11 pen) **RB Leipzig** 0

December 2, 2020
Basaksehir 3 (Kahveci 45, 72, 85) **RB Leipzig** 4 (Poulsen 26, Mukieli 43, Olmo 66, Sorloth 90+2)
Manchester Utd 1 (Rashford 32) **Paris SG** 3 (Neymar 6, 90+1, Marquinhos 69)
Manchester Utd (4-2-3-1): De Gea, Wan-Bissaka (Ighalo 90), Lindelof, Maguire, Telles, McTominay, Fred, Rashford (Pogba 74), Bruno Fernandes, Martial (Greenwood 79), Cavani (Van de Beek 79. **Booked**: Fred, **Sent off**: Fred (70)

December 8, 2020
Paris SG v **Basaksehir** abandoned after 15 minutes – racial incident
RB Leipzig 3 (Angelino 2, Haidara 13, Kluivert 69) **Manchester Utd** 2 (Bruno Fernandes 80 pen, Pogba 82)
Manchester Utd (3-4-1-2): De Gea, Lindelof (Tuanzebe 77), Maguire, Shaw (Williams 61), Wan-Bissaka (Fosu-Mensah 77), McTominay, Matic (Pogba 61), Telles (Van de Beek 46), Bruno Fernandes, Greenwood, Rashford. **Booked**: Bruno Fernandes, Shaw, Maguire, Williams, Lindelof

December 9, 2020
Paris SG 5 (Neymar 21, 37, 50, Mbappe 42 pen, 62) **Basaksehir** 1 (Topal 57)

	P	W	D	L	F	A	Pts
Paris SG Q	6	4	0	2	13	6	12
RB Leipzig Q	6	4	0	2	11	12	12
Manchester Utd	6	3	0	3	15	10	9
Basaksehir	6	1	0	5	7	18	3

ROUND OF 16, FIRST LEG

February 16, 2021
Barcelona 1 (Messi 27 pen) **Paris SG** 4 (Mbappe 32, 65, 85, Kean 70)
RB Leipzig 0 **Liverpool** 2 (Salah 53, Mane 58) – played in Budapest
Liverpool (4-3-3): Alisson, Alexander-Arnold, Kabak, Henderson, Robertson, Thiago Alcantara (Oxlade-Chamberlain 72), Wijnaldum, Jones, Salah (N Williams 90), Firmino (Shaqiri 72), Mane. **Booked**: Kabak, Henderson

February 17, 2021
Sevilla 2 (Suso 7, De Jong 84) **Borussia Dortmund** 3 (Dahoud 19, Haaland 27, 43)
Porto 2 (Taremi 2, Marega 46) **Juventus** 1 (Chiesa 82)

February 23, 2021
Atletico Madrid 0 **Chelsea** 1 (Giroud 68) – played in Bucharest
Chelsea (3-4-2-1): Mendy, Azpilicueta, Christensen, Rudiger, Hudson-Odoi (James 80), Jorginho, Kovacic (Ziyech 74) Marcos Alonso, Mount (Kante 74), Giroud (Havertz 87), Werner (Pulisic 87). **Booked**: Mount, Jorginho
Lazio 0 **Bayern Munich** 4 (Lewandowski 9, Musiala 24, Sane 42, Acerbi 47 og)

February 24, 2021
Atalanta 0 **Real Madrid** 1 (Mendy 86)
Borussia Monchengladbach 0 **Manchester City** 2 (Bernardo Silva 29, Gabriel Jesus 65) – played in Budapest

Manchester City (4-2-3-1): Ederson, Walker, Dias, Laporte, Joao Cancelo, Rodri, Gundogan, Sterling (Mahrez 69), Bernardo Silva, Foden (Torres 80), Gabriel Jesus (Aguero 80)

ROUND OF 16, SECOND LEG

March 9, 2021
Borussia Dortmund 2 (Haaland 35, 54 pen) **Sevilla** 2 (En-Nesyri 68 pen 90) – Borussia Dortmund won 5-4 on agg
Juventus 3 (Chiesa 49, 63, Rabiot 117) **Porto** 2 (Oliveira 19 pen, 115) – aet, agg 4-4, Porto won on away goals

March 10, 2021
Liverpool 2 (Salah 70, Mane 74) **RB Leipzig** 0 – played in Budapest, Liverpool won 4-0 on agg
Liverpool (4-3-3): Alisson, Alexander-Arnold, Phillips, Kabak, Robertson (Tsimikas 89), Thiago Alcantara (Keita 71), Fabinho, Wijnaldum (Milner 82), Jota (Origi 71), Mane (Oxlade-Chamberlain 89), Salah
Paris SG 1 (Mbappe 30 pen) **Barcelona** 1 (Messi 37) – Paris SG won 5-2 on agg

March 16, 2021
Manchester City 2 (De Bruyne 12, Gundogan 18) **Borussia Monchengladbach** 0 – played in Budapest, Manchester City won 4-0 on agg
Manchester City (4-3-3): Ederson, Walker, Dias (Laporte 70), Stones, Joao Cancelo (Zinchenko 64), De Bruyne, Rodri (Fernandinho 63), Gundogan (Sterling 70), Mahrez, Bernardo Silva (Aguero 75), Foden. **Booked**: Joao Cancelo, Fernandinho
Real Madrid 3 (Benzema 34, Sergio Ramos 60 pen, Marco Ascensio 85) **Atalanta** 1 (Muriel 83) – Real Madrid won 4-1 on agg

March 17, 2021
Bayern Munich 2 (Lewandowski 33 pen, Choupo-Moting 73) **Lazio** 1 (Parolo 82) – Bayern Munich won 6-2 on agg
Chelsea 2 (Ziyech 34, Emerson 90+4) **Atletico Madrid** 0 – Chelsea won 3-0 on agg
Chelsea (3-4-3): Mendy, Azpilicueta, Zouma, Rudiger, James, Kante, Kovacic, Marcos Alonso (Chilwell 90+3), Havertz (Emerson 90+3), Werner (Hudson-Odoi 83), Ziyech (Pulisic 77).
Booked: Havertz

QUARTER-FINALS, FIRST LEG

April 6, 2021
Manchester City 2 (De Bruyne 19, Foden 90) **Borussia Dortmund** 1 (Reus 84)
Manchester City (4-1-4-1): Ederson, Walker, Stones, Dias, Joao Cancelo, Rodri, Mahrez, De Bruyne, Gundogan, Foden, Bernardo Silva (Gabriel Jesus 59)
Real Madrid 3 (Vinicius Junior 27, 65, Marco Ascensio 36) **Liverpool** 1 (Salah 51)
Liverpool (4-3-3): Alisson, Alexander-Arnold, Kabak (Shaqiri 81), Phillips, Robertson, Wijnaldum, Fabinho, Keita (Thiago Alcantara 42), Mane, Jota (Firmino 81), Salah. **Booked**: Mane, Thiago Alcantara, Alexander-Arnold

April 7, 2021
Bayern Munich 2 (Choupo-Moting 37, Muller 60) **Paris SG** 3 (Mbappe 3, 68, Marquinhos 28)
Porto 0 **Chelsea** 2 (Mount 32, Chilwell 85) – played in Seville
Chelsea (3-4-2-1): Mendy, Azpilicueta, Christensen, Rudiger, James (Thiago Silva 80), Jorginho, Kovacic (Emerson 90+2), Chilwell, Mount (Kante 80), Werner (Pulisic 65), Havertz (Giroud 65)

QUARTER-FINALS, SECOND LEG

April 13, 2021

Chelsea 0 **Porto** 1 (Taremi 90+3) – played in Seville, Chelsea won 2-1 on agg
Chelsea (3-4-3): Mendy, Azpilicueta, Thiago Silva, Rudiger, James, Jorginho, Kante, Chilwell, Mount (Ziyech 86), Havertz (Giroud 90), Pulisic
Paris SG 0 **Bayern Munich** 1 (Choupo-Moting 40) – agg 3-3, Paris SG won on away goals

April 14, 2021
Borussia Dortmund 1 (Bellingham 15) **Manchester City** 2 (Mahrez 55 pen, Foden 75) – Manchester City won 4-2 on agg
Manchester City (4-1-4-1): Ederson, Walker, Stones, Dias, Zinchenko, Rodri, Mahrez (Sterling 88), De Bruyne, Gundogan, Foden, Bernardo Silva
Liverpool 0 **Real Madrid** 0 – Real Madrid won 3-1 on agg
Liverpool (4-3-3): Alisson, Alexander-Arnold, Phillips, Kabak (Diogo Jota 60), Robertson, Milner (Thiago Alcantara 6), Fabinho, Wijnaldum, Salah, Firmino (Shaqiri 82), Mane (Oxlade-Chamberlain 82). **Booked**: Robertson, Phillips

SEMI-FINALS, FIRST LEG

April 27, 2021
Real Madrid 1 (Benzema 29) **Chelsea** 1 (Pulisic 14)
Chelsea (3-4-3): Mendy, Christensen, Thiago Silva, Rudiger, Azpilicueta (James 66), Kante, Jorginho, Chilwell, Pulisic (Ziyech 66), Werner (Havertz 66), Mount. **Booked**: Pulisic

April 28, 2021
Paris SG 1 (Marquinhos 15) **Manchester City** 2 (De Bruyne 64, Mahrez 71)
Manchester City (4-2-1-3): Ederson, Walker, Stones, Dias, Joao Cancelo, Rodri, Gundogan, Bernardo Silva, Mahrez, De Bruyne, Foden. **Booked**: Joao Cancelo, De Bruyne

SEMI-FINALS, SECOND LEG

May 4, 2021
Manchester City 2 (Mahrez 11, 63) **Paris SG** 0 – Manchester City won 4-1 on agg
Manchester City (4-4-2): Ederson, Walker, Stones, Dias, Zinchenko, Mahrez, Fernandinho, Gundogan, Foden (Aguero 85), De Bruyne (Gabriel Jesus 82), Bernardo Silva (Sterling 82). **Booked**: Zinchenko, De Bruyne

May 5, 2021
Chelsea 2 (Werner 28, Mount 85) **Real Madrid** 0 – Chelsea won 3-1 on agg
Chelsea (3-4-3) Mendy, Christensen, Thiago Silva, Rudiger, Azpilicueta (James 88), Kante, Jorginho, Chilwell, Mount (Ziyech 88), Havertz (Giroud 90+4), Werner (Pulisic 67). **Booked**: Jorginho, Christensen, Mount

FINAL

MANCHESTER CITY 0 CHELSEA 1 (Havertz 42)
Estadio Do Dragao, Porto (14,110); Saturday, May 29, 2021
Manchester City (4-1-2-1-2): Ederson, Walker, Stones, Dias, Zinchenko, Gundogan, Bernardo Silva (Fernandinho 64), Foden, De Bruyne (Gabriel Jesus 60), Sterling (Aguero 77), Mahrez. **Subs not used**: Steffen, Carson, Ake, Laporte, Rodri, Torres, Benjamin Mendy, Joao Cancelo, Garcia. **Booked**: Gundogan, Gabriel Jesus. **Manager**: Pep Guardiola
Chelsea (3-4-3): Edouard Mendy, Azpilicueta, Thiago Silva (Christensen 39), Rudiger, James, Jorginho, Kante, Chilwell, Havertz, Mount (Kovacic 80), Werner (Pulisic 66). **Subs not used**: Arrizabalaga, Caballero, Marcos Alonso, Zouma, Giroud, Hudson-Odoi, Ziyech, Gilmour, Emerson. **Booked**: Rudiger. **Manager**: Thomas Tuchel
Referee: Antonio Mateu Lahoz (Spain): **Half-time**: 0-1

Did Pep Guardiola get his team selection wrong? Were some of his players unsettled by speculation that they might be leaving the club to make way for major summer signings? Are City destined to be undisputed domestic champions but not kings of Europe? Or has Thomas Tuchel found a way to outsmart his rival whenever their paths cross? These were the questions being posed during the inquest into Chelsea's victory in Porto, their third against City in the space of six weeks. They came out on top in the semi-finals of the FA Cup, in the subsequent league fixture at the Eithad and now here in Porto, where Guardiola named his two recognised holding midfielders Fernandinho and Rodri on the bench, while opting for a deeper role for Ilkay Gundogan. By the time he brought on Fernandinho and Gabriel Jesus, Chelsea were rock solid in their protection of Kai Havertz's goal. Sergio Aguero followed them, but he too could make little impression on what was his final appearance before joining Barcelona. Afterwards, Tuchel targeted City's dominance of the Premier League, fortified by the planned acquisition of a top striker. Win or lose, Guardiola had long planned for a replacement for Aguero, while at the same time refreshing other part on his squad. With the return of Liverpool's defensive order, after a season of crippling injuries, and Manchester United also aiming to strengthen, the new season looks rich in promise.

FACTS AND FIGURES

- Chelsea were Champions League winners for the second time, having defeated Bayern Munich on penalties in 2012 with a side captained by Frank Lampard and managed by Roberto Di Matteo

- In the Roman Abramovich era, the club have also won the Europa Lague twice, against Benfica in 2013 and Arsenal in 2019

- Thomas Tuchel is the third German manager to lift the trophy in the last three seasons, following Liverpool's Jurgen Klopp in 2019 and Bayern Munich's Hans-Dieter Flick the following year.

- Bayern's success came against Paris Saint-Germain and Thomas Tuchel, who was sacked four months later.

- Edouard Mendy's nine clean sheets in his 12 Champions League games proved the most by a goalkeeper in their first season in the competition.

- Mason Mount, whose pass sent Kai Havertz through for the only goal, was the first English player to provide an assist in the final since Wes Brown's cross, converted by Cristiano Ronaldo, for Manchester United against Chelsea in 2008.

- Neither side had a shot on target after Havertz scored the matchwinner three minutes before half-time.

- Pep Guardiola has lost more matches (8) in all competitions against Chelsea than against any other club.

Leading scorers: 10 Haaland (Borussia Dortmund); 8 Mbappe (Paris SG); 6 Benzema (Real Madrid), En-Nesyri (Sevilla), Giroud (Chelsea), Morata (Juventus), Neymar (Paris SG), Rashford (Manchester Utd), Salah (Liverpool); 5 Immobile (Lazio), Lewandowski (Bayern Munich), Messi (Barcelona), Oliveira (Porto), Plea (Borussia Monchengladbach)

EUROPEAN CUP/CHAMPIONS LEAGUE FINALS

1956	Real Madrid 4 Reims 3 (Paris)
1957	Real Madrid 2 Fiorentina 0 (Madrid)
1958†	Real Madrid 3 AC Milan 2 (Brussels)
1959	Real Madrid 2 Reims 0 (Stuttgart)
1960	Real Madrid 7 Eintracht Frankfurt 3 (Glasgow)
1961	Benfica 3 Barcelona 2 (Berne)
1962	Benfica 5 Real Madrid 3 (Amsterdam)
1963	AC Milan 2 Benfica 1 (Wembley)
1964	Inter Milan 3 Real Madrid 1 (Vienna)
1965	Inter Milan 1 Benfica 0 (Milan)
1966	Real Madrid 2 Partizan Belgrade 1 (Brussels)
1967	Celtic 2 Inter Milan 1 (Lisbon)
1968†	Manchester Utd 4 Benfica 1 (Wembley)
1969	AC Milan 4 Ajax 1 (Madrid)
1970†	Feyenoord 2 Celtic 1 (Milan)
1971	Ajax 2 Panathinaikos 0 (Wembley)
1972	Ajax 2 Inter Milan 0 (Rotterdam)
1973	Ajax 1 Juventus 0 (Belgrade)
1974	Bayern Munich 4 Atletico Madrid 0 (replay Brussels after a 1-1 draw Brussels)
1975	Bayern Munich 2 Leeds Utd 0 (Paris)
1976	Bayern Munich 1 St. Etienne 0 (Glasgow)
1977	Liverpool 3 Borussia Moenchengladbach 1 (Rome)
1978	Liverpool 1 Brugge 0 (Wembley)
1979	Nottm Forest 1 Malmo 0 (Munich)
1980	Nottm Forest 1 Hamburg 0 (Madrid)
1981	Liverpool 1 Real Madrid 0 (Paris)
1982	Aston Villa 1 Bayern Munich 0 (Rotterdam)
1983	SV Hamburg 1 Juventus 0 (Athens)
1984†	Liverpool 1 AS Roma 1 (Liverpool won 4-2 on penalties) (Rome)
1985	Juventus 1 Liverpool 0 (Brussels)
1986†	Steaua Bucharest 0 Barcelona 0 (Steaua won 2-0 on penalties) (Seville)
1987	Porto 2 Bayern Munich 1 (Vienna)
1988†	PSV Eindhoven 0 Benfica 0 (PSV won 6-5 on penalties) (Stuttgart)
1989	AC Milan 4 Steaua Bucharest 0 (Barcelona)
1990	AC Milan 1 Benfica 0 (Vienna)
1991†	Red Star Belgrade 0 Marseille 0 (Red Star won 5-3 on penalties) (Bari)
1992	Barcelona 1 Sampdoria 0 (Wembley)
1993	Marseille 1 AC Milan 0 (Munich)
1994	AC Milan 4 Barcelona 0 (Athens)
1995	Ajax 1 AC Milan 0 (Vienna)
1996†	Juventus 1 Ajax 1 (Juventus won 4-2 on penalties) (Rome)
1997	Borussia Dortmund 3 Juventus 1 (Munich)
1998	Real Madrid 1 Juventus 0 (Amsterdam)
1999	Manchester Utd 2 Bayern Munich 1 (Barcelona)
2000	Real Madrid 3 Valencia 0 (Paris)
2001	Bayern Munich 1 Valencia 1 (Bayern Munich won 5-4 on penalties) (Milan)
2002	Real Madrid 2 Bayer Leverkusen 1 (Glasgow)
2003†	AC Milan 0 Juventus 0 (AC Milan won 3-2 on penalties) (Manchester)
2004	FC Porto 3 Monaco 0 (Gelsenkirchen)
2005†	Liverpool 3 AC Milan 3 (Liverpool won 3-2 on penalties) (Istanbul)
2006	Barcelona 2 Arsenal 1 (Paris)
2007	AC Milan 2 Liverpool 1 (Athens)

2008†	Manchester Utd 1 Chelsea 1 (Manchester Utd won 6-5 on penalties) (Moscow)
2009	Barcelona 2 Manchester Utd 0 (Rome)
2010	Inter Milan 2 Bayern Munich 0 (Madrid)
2011	Barcelona 3 Manchester Utd 1 (Wembley)
2012†	Chelsea 1 Bayern Munich 1 (Chelsea won 4-3 on pens) (Munich)
2013	Bayern Munich 2 Borussia Dortmund 1 (Wembley)
2014†	Real Madrid 4 Atletico Madrid 1 (Lisbon)
2015	Barcelona 3 Juventus 1 (Berlin)
2016	Real Madrid 1 Atletico Madrid 1 (Real Madrid won 5-3 on pens) (Milan)
2017	Real Madrid 4 Juventus 1 (Cardiff)
2018	Real Madrid 3 Liverpool 1 (Kiev)† aet
2019	Liverpool 2 Tottenham 0 (Madrid)
2020	Bayern Munich 1 Paris Saint-Germain 0 (Lisbon)
2021	Chelsea 1 Manchester City 0 (Porto)

● Champions League since 1993. † after extra time

UEFA EUROPA LEAGUE 2020–21

PRELIMINARY ROUND (single leg, selected results)

Coleraine 1 (McLaughlin 89) La Fiorita 0; **Glentoran** 1 (McDaid 42) HB Torshavn 0; NSI 5 (Olsen 52, 63, 74, Knudsen 67, Lokin 83) **Barry** 1 (McLaggon 88)

FIRST QUALIFYING ROUND (single leg, selected results)

Aberdeen 6 (Ferguson 36, Main 42, Hedges 49, 59, 86 pen, Hayes 63) NSI 0; Fehervar 1 (Nikolic 37 pen) **Bohemians** 1 (Ward 22) – aet, Fehervar won 4-2 on pens; Maribor 1 (Pozeg 65) **Coleraine** 1 (McLaughlin 62) – aet, Coleraine won 5-4 on pens; **Motherwell** 5 (Lang 58, O'Donnell 72, Polworth 75, Watt 78, Long 87) **Glentoran** 1 (McDaid 90 pen); **New Saints** 3 (Robles 56, Smith 100, Cieslewicz 108 pen) Zilina 1 (Mysolovic 77 pen) – aet; Riteriai 3 (Paulauskas 39, 49, Kazlauskas 90+1) **Derry** 2 (Thomson 18, Toal 63); **Shamrock Rov** 2 (Burke 14, Roberto Lopes 78) Ilves Tampere 2 (Ala-Myllymaki 10 pen, Veteli 62) – aet, Shamrock Rov won 12-11 on pens); Valletta 0 **Bala** 1 (Venables 38)

SECOND QUALIFYING ROUND (single leg, selected results)

Coleraine 2 (Doherty 50 pen, 90 pen) **Motherwell** 2 (Lang 17, Watt 38) – aet, Motherwell won 3-0 on pens); **Connah's Quay** 0 Dinamo Tbilisi 1 (Gabedava 90+7 pen); Inter d'Escaldes 0 **Dundalk** 1 (McMillan 14); Lincoln Red Imps 0 **Rangers** 5 (Tavernier 22, Goldson 45, Morelos 68, 89, Defoe 85); **Linfield** 0 Floriana 1 (Garcia 10) Lokomotiv Plovdiv 1 (Minchev 72) **Tottenham** 2 (Kane 81 pen, Ndombele 86); **Shamrock Rov** 0 AC Milan 2 (Ibrahimovic 23, Calhanoglu 67); Standard Liege 2 (Avenatti 19 pen, Amallah 34) **Bala** 0; B36 Torshavn 2 (Przybylski 47, Radosavljevic 120+2) **New Saints** 2 (Smith 80, Ebbe 112) – aet, B36 Torshavn won 5-4 on pens); Viking 0 **Aberdeen** 2 (McCrorie 45, Hedges 79)

THIRD QUALIFYING ROUND (single leg, selected results)

Hapoel Beer Sheva 3 (Vitor 44, Josue 72 pen, Acolatse 83) **Motherwell** 0; Riga 0 **Celtic** 1 (Elyounoussi 90); Sheriff Tiraspol 1 (Posmac 90) **Dundalk** 1 (Murray 45) – aet, Dundalk won 5-3 on pens); Shkendia 1 (Nafiu 55) **Tottenham** 3 (Lamela 5, Son Heung-min 70, Kane 79); Sporting Lisbon 1 (Tomas 8) **Aberdeen** 0; Willem 0 **Rangers** 4 (Tavernier 23 pen, Kent 26, Helander 56, Goldson 72)

QUALIFYING PLAY-OFF ROUND (single leg)

Dundalk 3 (Murray 34, Cleary 49, Kelly 0) Ki Klaksvik 1 (Midtskogen 66); **Rangers** 2 (Arfield 53, Tavernier 60) Galatasaray 1 (Marcao 88); Sarajevo 0 **Celtic** 1 (Edouard 71); **Tottenham** 7 (Kane 2, 56 pen, 74, Lucas Moura 20, Lo Celso 36, 39, Alli 90+1 pen) Maccabi Haifa 2 (Chery 17, Rukavytsya 52 pen)
Other results: AEK Athens 2 Wolfsburg 1; Ararat Armenia 1 Red Star Belgrade 2; Basle 1 CSKA Sofia 3; CFR Cluj 4 KuPS 1; Charleroi 1 Lech Poznan 2; Copenhagen 0 Rijeka 1; Dinamo Brest 0 Ludogorets 2; Dinamo Zagreb 3 Flora Tallinn 1; Hapoel Beer Sheva 1 Viktoria Plzen 0; Legia Warsaw 0 Qarabag 1; Liberec 1 Apoel Nicosia 0; Malmo 1 Granada 1; Rio Ave 2 AC Milan 2 - aet, AC Milan won 9-8 on pens; Rosenborg 0 PSV Eindhoven 2; Sporting Lisbon 1 LASK 4; Standard Liege 3 Fehervar 1

GROUP A

Match-day 1: CSKA Sofia 0 CFR Cluj 2 (Rondon 53, Deac 74 pen). Young Boys 1 (Nsame 14 pen) Roma 2 (Bruno Peres 69, Kumbulla 73)
Match-day 2: CFR Cluj 1 (Rondon 62) Young Boys 1 (Fassnact 67). Roma 0 CSKA Sofia 0
Match-day 3: Roma 5 (Mkhitaryan 1, Ibanez 24, Mayoral 34, 84, Pedro 89). CFR Cluj 0 Young Boys 3 (Mambimbi 2, 32, Sulejmani 18) CSK Sofia 0
Match-day 4: CFR Cluj 0 Roma 2 (Debeljuh 49 og, Veretout 67 pen). CSKA Sofia 0 Young Boys 1 (Nsame 34)
Match-day 5: CFR Cluj 0 CSKA Sofia 0. Roma 3 (Mayoral 44, Calafiori 59, Dzeko 81) Young Boys 1 (Nsame 34)
Match-day 6: CSKA Sofia 3 (Rodrigues 5, Sowe 34, 55) Roma 1 (Milanese 22). Young Boys 2 (Nsame 90+3 pen, Gaudino 90+6) CFR Cluj 1 (Debeljuh 84)

	P	W	D	L	F	A	Pts
Roma Q	6	4	1	1	13	5	13
Young Boys Q	6	3	1	2	9	7	10
CFR Cluj	6	1	2	3	4	10	5
CSKA Sofia	6	1	2	3	3	7	5

GROUP B

Match-day 1: Dundalk 1 (Murray 35), Molde 2 (Hussain 62, Omoijuanfro 72 pen). Rapid Vienna 1 (Fountas 51) **Arsenal** 2 (Luiz 70, Aubameyang 74)
Match-day 2: Arsenal 3 (Nketiah 42, Willock 44, Pepe 46) **Dundalk** 0. Molde 1 (Omoijuanfro 65) Rapid Vienna 0
Match-day 3: Arsenal 4 (Haugen 45 og, Sinyan 62 og, Pepe 69, Willock 88) Molde 1 (Ellingsen 22). Rapid Vienna 4 (Ljubicic 22, Arase 79, Hofmann 87, Demir 90) **Dundalk** 3 (Hoban 7, McMillan 81 pen, 90+6 pen)
Match-day 4: Dundalk 1 (Shields 63 pen) Rapid Vienna 3 (Knasmullner 11, Kara 37, 58). Molde 0 **Arsenal** 3 (Pepe 50, Nelson 55, Balogun 83)
Match-day 5: Arsenal 4 (Lacazette 10, Mari 18, Nketiah 44, Smith Rowe 66) Rapid Vienna 1 (Kitagawa 47). Molde 3 (Eikrem 30, Oloijuanfro 41, Ellingsen 67) **Dundalk** 1 (Flores 90)
Match-day 6: Dundalk 2 (Flores 22, Hoare 85) **Arsenal** 4 (Nketiah 12, Elneny 18, Willock 67, Balogun 80). Rapid Vienna 2 (Ritzmaier 43, Ibrahimoglu 90) Molde 2 (Eikrem 12, 46)

Arsenal Q	6	6	0	0	20	5	18
Molde Q	6	3	1	2	9	11	10
Rapid Vienna	6	2	1	3	11	13	7
Dundalk	6	0	0	6	8	19	0

GROUP C

Match-day 1: Bayer Leverkusen 6 (Amiri 11, Alario 16, Diaby 61, Bellarabi 79, 83, Wirtz 87) Nice 2 (Gouiri 31, Claude Maurice 90). Hapoel Beer Sheva 3 (Agudelo 45, Acolatse 86, 88) Slavia Prague 1 (Provod 75)

Match-day 2: Nice 1 (Gouiri 22) Hapoel Beer Sheva 0. Slavia Prague 1 (Olayinka 80) Bayer Leverkusen 0

Match-day 3: Hapoel Beer Sheva 2 (Acolatse 11, 25) Bayer Leverkusen 4 (Bailey 5, 75, Dadia 39 og, Wirtz 88). Slavia Prague 3 (Kuchta 16, 71, Sima 43) Nice 2 (Gouiri 33, Ndoye 90)

Match-day 4: Bayer Leverkusen 4 (Schick 29, Bailey 48, Demirbay 76, Alario 80) Hapoel Beer Sheva 1 (Shwiro 58). Nice 1 (Gouiri 60) Slavia Prague 3 (Lingr 14, Olayinka 64, Sima 75)

Match-day 5: Nice 2 (Kamara 26, Ndoye 46) Bayer Leverkusen 3 (Diaby 22, Dragovic 32, Baumgartlinger 51). Slavia Prague 3 (Sima 31, Stanciu 36, Twitto 85 og) Hapoel Beer Sheva 0

Match-day 6: Bayer Leverkusen 4 (Bailey 8, 32, Diaby 59, Bellarabi 90+1) Slavia Prague 0. Hapoel Beer Sheva 1 (Gouiri 22) Nice 0

Bayer Leverkusen Q	6	5	0	1	21	8	15
Slavia Prague Q	6	4	0	2	11	10	12
Hapoel Beer Sheva	6	2	0	4	7	13	6
Nice	6	1	0	5	8	16	3

GROUP D

Match-day 1: Lech Poznan 2 (Ishak 15, 48) Benfica 4 (Pizzi 9 pen, Nunez 42, 60, 90+3). Standard Liege 0 Rangers 2 (Tavernier 19 pen, Roofe 90+2)

Match-day 2: Benfica 3 (Pizzi 49 pen, 76, Waldschmidt 66 pen) Standard Liege 0. **Rangers** 1 (Morelos 68) Lech Poznan 0

Match-day 3: Benfica 3 (Goldson 2 og, Rafa Silva 77, Nunez 90) **Rangers** 3 (Goncalves 24 og, Kamara 25, Morelos 51). Lech Poznan 3 (Skoras 14, Ishak 22, 48) Standard Liege 1 (Lestienne 29)

Match-day 4: **Rangers** 2 (Arfield 7, Roofe 69) Benfica 2 (Tavernier 78 og, Pizzi 81). Standard Liege 2 (Tapsoba 63, Laifis 90+3) Lech Poznan 1 (Ishak 60)

Match-day 5: Benfica 4 (Vertonghen 36, Nunez 57, Pizzi 58, Weigl 89) Lech Poznan 0. **Rangers** 3 (Goldson 39, Tavernier 45 pen, Arfield 89) Standard Liege 2 (Lestienne 6, Cop 40)

Match-day 6: Lech Poznan 0 **Rangers** 2 (Itten 31, Hagi 72). Standard Liege 2 (Raskin 12, Tapsoba 60) Benfica 2 (Everton 16, Pizzi 67 pen)

Rangers Q	6	4	2	0	13	7	14
Benfica Q	6	3	3	0	18	9	12
Standard Liege	6	1	1	4	7	14	4
Lech Poznan	6	1	0	5	6	14	3

GROUP E

Match-day 1: PAOK Salonika 1 (Murg 56) Omonia Nicosia 1 (Bautheac 16). PSV Eindhoven 1 (Gotze 45), Granada 2 (Molina 57, Machis 66)

Match-day 2: Granada 0 PAOK Salonika 0. Omonia Nicosia 1 (Jordi Gomez 29) PSV Eindhoven 2 (Malen 40, 90+2)

Match-day 3: Omonia Nicosia 0 Granada 2 (Herrera 4, Suarez 63). PAOK Salonika 4 (Schwab 47, Zivkovic 55, 66, Tzolis 58) PSV Eindhoven 1 (Zahavi 20 pen)

Match-day 4: Granada 2 (Suarez 8, Soro 73) Omonia Nicosia 1 (Asante 60). PSV Eindhoven 3 (Gakpo 20, Madueke 50, Malen 53) PAOK Salonika 2 (Varela 4, Tzolis 13)

Match-day 5: Granada 0 PSV Eindhoven 1 (Malen 38). Omonia Nicosia 2 (Kakoullis 9, Gomez 84 pen) PAOK Salonika 1 (Tzolis 39)

Match-day 6: PAOK Salonika 0 Granada 0. PSV Eindhoven 4 (Malen 35, Dumfries 63 pen, Piroe 90+1, 90+3) Omonia Nicosia 0

PSV Eindhoven Q	6	4	0	2	12	9	12
Granada Q	6	3	2	1	6	3	11
PAOK Salonika	6	1	3	2	8	7	6
Omonia Nicosia	6	1	1	4	5	12	4

GROUP F

Match-day 1: Napoli 0 AZ Alkmaar 1 (De Wit 57). Rijeka 0 Real Sociedad 1 (Bautista 90+3)

Match-day 2: AZ Alkmaar 4 (Koopmeiners 6 pen, Gudmundsson 20, 60, Karlsson 51) Rijeka 1 (Kulenovic 72). Real Sociedad 0 Napoli 1 (Politano 55)

Match-day 3: Real Sociedad 1 (Portu 58) AZ Alkmaar 0. Rijeka 1 (Muric 13) Napoli 2 (Demme 43, Braut 62 og)

Match-day 4: AZ Alkmaar 0 Real Sociedad 0. Napoli 2 (Anastasio 41 og, Lozano 75) Rikeka 0

Match-day 5: AZ Alkmaar 1 (Martins Indi 53) Napoli 1 (Mertens 6). Real Sociedad 2 (Bautista 69, Monreal 79) Rijeka 2 (Velkovski 37, Loncar 73)

Match-day 6: Napoli 1 (Zielinski 34) Real Sociedad 1 (Jose 90+2). Rijeka 2 (Menalo 51, Tomecak 90+3) AZ Alkmaar1 (Wijndal 57)

Napoli Q	6	3	2	1	7	4	11
Real Sociedad Q	6	2	3	1	5	4	9
AZ Alkmaar	6	2	2	2	7	5	8
Rijeka	6	1	1	4	6	12	4

GROUP G

Match-day 1: Braga 3 (Galeno 44, Paulinho 78, Ricardo Horta 88) AEK Athens 0. **Leicester** 3 (Maddison 29, Barnes 45, Iheanacho 67) Zorya 0

Match-day 2: AEK Athens 1 (Tankovic 49) **Leicester** 2 (Vardy 18 pen, Choudhury 39). Zorya 1 (Ivanisenya 90+6) Braga 2 (Paulinho 3, Gaitan 11)

Match-day 3: **Leicester** 4 (Iheanacho 20, 47, Praet 67, Maddison 78) Braga 0. Zorya 1 (Kochergin 81) AEK Athens 4 (Tankovic 6, Mandalos 34, Livaja 54, 81)

Match-day 4: AEK Athens 0 Zorya 3 (Gromov 61, Kabayev 75, Yurchenko 86 pen). Braga 3 (Al Musrati 4, Paulinho 24, Fransergio 90) **Leicester** 3 (Barnes 9, Thomas 78, Vardy 90+5)

Match-day 5: AEK Athens 2 (Oliveira 31, Vasilantonopoulos 89) Braga 4 (Tormena 7, Esgaio 9, Ricardo Horta 45, Galeno 83). Zorya 1 (Sayyadmanesh 84) **Leicester** 0

Match-day 6: Braga 2 (Abu Hanna 61 og, Ricardo Horta 68) Zorya 0. **Leicester** 2 (Under 12, Barnes 14) AEK Athens 0

Leicester Q	6	4	1	1	14	5	13
Braga Q	6	4	1	1	14	10	13
Zorya	6	2	0	4	6	11	6
AEK Athens	6	1	0	5	7	15	3

GROUP H

Match-day 1: Celtic 1 (Elyounoussi 76) AC Milan 3 (Krunic 14, Diaz 42, Hauge 90+2). Sparta Prague 1 (Dockal 46) Lille 4 (Yazici 45, 60, 75, Ikone 66)

Match-day 2: AC Milan 3 (Diaz 24, Leao 57, Dalot 66) Sparta Prague 0. Lille 2 (Celik 67, Ikone 75) **Celtic** 2 (Elyounoussi 28, 32)

Match-day 3: AC Milan 0 Lille 3 (Yazici 22 pen, 55, 58). **Celtic** 1 (Griffiths 65) Sparta Prague 4 (Julis 26, 45, 76, Krejci 90)

Match-day 4: Lille 1 (Bamba 65) AC Milan 1 (Castillejo 46). Sparta Prague 4 (Hancko 27, Julis 38, 80, Plavsic 90+4) **Celtic** 1 (Edouard 15)

Match-day 5: AC Milan 4 (Calhanoglu 24, Castillejo 26, Hauge 50, Diaz 82) **Celtic** 2 (Rogic 7, Edouard 14). Lille 2 (Yilmaz 80, 84) Sparta Prague 1 (Krejci 71)

Match-day 6: **Celtic** 3 (Jullien 22, McGregor 28 pen, Turnbull 75) Lille 2 (Ikone 24, Weah 71). Sparta Prague 0 AC Milan 1 (Hauge 23)

AC Milan Q	6	4	1	1	12	7	13
Lille Q	6	3	2	1	14	8	11
Sparta Prague	6	2	0	4	10	12	6
Celtic	6	1	1	4	10	19	4

GROUP I

Match-day 1: Maccabi Tel Aviv 1 (Cohen 10) Qarabag 0. Villarreal 5 (Kubo 13, Bacca 20, Foyth 57, Alcacer 74, 78) Sivasspor 3 (Kayode 33, Yatabare 43, Gradel 64)

Match-day 2: Qarabag 1 (Kwabena 78) Villarreal 3 (Pin 80, Alcacer 84, 90+6 pen). Sivasspor 1 (Kayode 55) Maccabi Tel Aviv 2 (Biton 68 pen, Dor Peretz 74)

Match-day 3: Sivasspor 2 (Osmanpasa 11, Kayode 88) Qarabag 0. Villarreal 4 (Bacca 4, 52, Baena 71, Nino 81) Maccabi Tel Aviv 0

Match-day 4: Qarabag 2 (Zoubir 8, Matic 51) Sivasspor 3 (Kone 40 pen, 79, Kayode 58). Maccabi Tel Aviv 1 (Pesic 47) Villarreal 1 (Baena 45)

Match-day 5: Qarabag 1 (Romero 37) Maccabi Tel Aviv 1 (Cohen 22 pen). Sivasspor 0 Villarreal 1 (Chukwueze 75)

Match-day 6: Maccabi Tel Aviv 1 (Saborit 66) Sivasspor 0. Villarreal v Qarabag postponed – match awarded 3-0 to Villarreal

Villarreal Q	6	5	1	0	17	5	16
Maccabi Tel Aviv Q	6	3	2	1	6	7	11
Sivasspor	6	2	0	4	9	11	6
Qarabag	6	0	1	5	4	13	1

GROUP J

Match-day 1: Ludogorets 1 (Marin 46) Antwerp 2 (Gerkens 63, Refaelov 70). **Tottenham** 3 (Lucas Moura 18, Andrade 27 og, Son Heung-min 84) LASK 0

Match-day 2: Antwerp 1 (Rafaelov 29) **Tottenham** 0. LASK 4 (Balic 2, Gruber 11, Raguz 34, Verdon 55 og) Ludogorets 3 (Manu 15, 67, 73 pen)

Match-day 3: Antwerp 0 LASK 1 (Eggestein 54). Ludogorets 1 (Keseru 50) **Tottenham** 3 (Kane 13, Lucas Moura 32, Lo Celso 62)

Match-day 4: LASK 0 Antwerp 2 (Refaelov 52, Gerkens 83). **Tottenham** 4 (Vinicius 16, 34, Winks 63, Lucas Moura 73) Ludogorets 0

Match-day 5: Antwerp 3 (Hongla 19, De Laet 72, Benson 87) Ludogorets 1 (Despodov 53). LASK 3 (Michori 42, Eggestein 84, Karamoko 90+3) **Tottenham** 3 (Bale 45 pen, Son Heung-min 56, Alli 86 pen)

Match-day 6: Ludogorets 1 (Manu 46) LASK 3 (Wiesinger 56, Renner 61 pen, Madsen 66). **Tottenham** 2 (Vinicius 56, Lo Celso 71) Antwerp 0

Tottenham Q	6	4	1	1	15	5	13
Antwerp Q	6	4	0	2	8	5	12
LASK	6	3	1	2	11	12	10
Ludogorets	6	0	0	6	7	19	0

GROUP K

Match-day 1: Dinamo Zagreb 0 Feyenoord 0. Wolfsberger 1 (Liendl 42 pen) CSKA Moscow 1 (Gaich 5)

Match-day 2: CSKA Moscow 0 Dinamo Zagreb 0. Feyenoord 1 (Berghuis 53) Wolfsberger 4 (Liendl 4 pen, 13 pen, 60, Joveljic 66 pen)

Match-day 3: Dinamo Zagreb 1 (Atiemwen 76) Wolfsberger 0. Feyenoord 3 (Haps 63, Kokcu 71, Geertruida 72) CSKA Moscow 1 (Senesi 79 og)

Match-day 4: CSKA Moscow 0 Feyenoord 0. Wolfsberger 0 Dinamo Zagreb 3 (Majer 60, Petkovic 75, Ivanusec 90+1)

Match-day 5: CSKA Moscow 0 Wolfsberger 1 (Vizinger 22). Feyenoord 0 Dinamo Zagreb 2 (Petkovic 45 pen, Majer 53)

Match-day 6: Dinamo Zagreb 3 (Gvardiol 28, Orsic 41, Kastratil 75) CSKA Moscow 1 (Bistovic 76). Wolfsberger 1 (Joveljic 31) Feyenoord 0

Dinamo Zagreb Q	6	4	2	0	9	1	14
Wolfsberger Q	6	3	1	2	7	6	10
Feyenoord	6	1	2	3	4	8	5
CSKA Moscow	6	0	3	3	3	8	3

GROUP L

Match-day 1: Hoffenheim 2 (Baumgartner 64, Dabbur 90+3) Red Star Belgrade 0. Liberec 1 (Abdulrahim 29) Gent 0

Match-day 2: Gent 1 (Kleindienst 90+2) Hoffenheim 4 (Belfodil 35 pen, Grillitsch 52, Gacinovic 73, Dabbur 90+3). Red Star Belgrade 5 (Ben Nabouhane 7, 21, Gajic 49, Katai 67, Falcinelli 69) Liberec 1 (Matousek)

Match-day 3: Hoffenheim 5 (Dabbur 22, 29, Grillitsch 59, Adamyan 71, 76) Liberec 0. Red Star Belgrade 2 (Kanga 12, Katai 59) Gent 1 (Odjidja-Ofoe 31

Match-day 4: Gent 0 Red Star Belgrade 2 (Petrovic 1, Milunovic 58). Liberec 0 Hoffenheim 2 (Baumgartner 77, Kramaric 89 pen)

Match-day 5: Gent 1 (Yaremchuk 59) Liberec 2 (Mara 32, Kacharaba 55). Red Star Belgrade 0 Hoffenheim 0

Match-day 6: Hoffenheim 4 (Beier 21, 49, Skov 26, Kramaric 64) Gent 1 (Fortuna 81). Liberec 0 Red Star Belgrade 0

Hoffenheim Q	6	5	1	0	17	2	16
Red Star Belgrade Q	6	3	2	1	9	4	11
Liberec	6	2	1	3	4	13	7
Gent	6	0	0	6	4	15	0

ROUND OF 32, FIRST LEG

Antwerp 3 (Avenatti 45, Refaelov 45 pen, Hongla 66) **Rangers** 4 (Aribo 38, Barisic 59 pen, 90 pen, Kent 84). Benfica 1 (Pizzi 55 pen) **Arsenal** 1 (Saka 57) – played in Rome. Braga 0 Roma 2 (Dzeko 5, Mayoral 86). Dynamo Kiev 1 (Buyalskiy 62) Club Bruges 1 (Mechele 67). Granada 2 (Herrera 19, Kenedy 21) Napoli 0. Krasnador 2 (Berg 28, Claesson 69) Dinamo Zagreb 3 (Petkovic 15, 54, Atiemwen 75). Lille 1 (Weah 72) Ajax 2 (Tadic 87 pen, Brobbey 89). Maccabi Tel Aviv 0 Shakhtar Donetsk 2 (Lourenco 31, Tete 90+2) Molde 3 (Ellingsen 41, Andersen 70, Fofana 74) Hoffenheim 3 (Dabbur 8, 28, Baumgartner 45).
Olympiacos 4 (Bouchalakis 9, M'Vila 37, El Arabi 45, Masouras 83) PSV Eindhoven 2 (Zahavi 14, 39). RB Salzburg 0 Villarreal 2 (Alcacer 41, Nino 71). Red Star Belgrade 2 (Kanga Kaku 52 pen, Pavkov 90+3) AC Milan 2 (Pankov 42 og, Hernandez 61 pen)
Real Sociedad 0 **Manchester Utd** 4 (Bruno Fernandes 27, 57, Rashford 64, James 90) – played in Turin. Slavia Prague 0 **Leicester** 0. Wolfsberger 1 (Liendl 55 pen) **Tottenham** 4 (Son Heung-min 13, Bale 28, Lucas Moura 34, Vinicius 88) – played in Budapest. Young Boys 4 (Fassnacht 3, Siebatcheu 19, 89, Elia 44) Bayer Leverkusen 3 (Schick 49, 52, Diaby 68)

ROUND OF 32, SECOND LEG

AC Milan 1 (Kessie 9 pen) Red Star Belgrade 1 (Ben 24) – agg 3-3, AC Milan won on away goals. Ajax 2 (Klaassen 15, Neres 88) Lille 1 (Yazici 78 pen) – Ajax won 4-2 on agg. **Arsenal** 3 (Aubameyang 21, 87, Tierney 67) Benfica 2 (Goncalves 43, Rafa Silva 61) – played in Athens, Arsenal won 4-3 on agg. Bayer Leverkusen 0 Young Boys 2 (Siebatcheu 47, Fassnacht 86) – Young Boys won 6-3 on agg
Club Bruges 0 Dynamo Kiev 1 (Buyalskiy 83) – Dynamo Kiev won 2-1 on agg. Dinamo Zagreb 1 (Otsic 31) Krasnodar 0 – Dinamo Zagreb won 4-2 on agg. Hoffenheim 0 Molde 2 (Andersen 19, 90) – Molde won 5-3 on agg. **Leicester** 0 Slavia Prague 2 (Provod 49, Sima 79) – Slavia Prague won 2-0 on agg

Manchester Utd 0 Real Sociedad 0 – Manchester Utd won 4-0 on agg. Napoli 2 (Zielinski 3, Fabian 59) Granada 1 (Montoro 25) – Granada won 3-2 on agg. PSV Eindhoven 2 (Zahavi 23, 44) Olympiacos 1 (Kola 88) – PSV Eindhoven won 5-4 on agg. **Rangers** 5 (Morelos 9, Patterson 46, Kent 55, Barisic 79 pen, Itten 90 pen) Antwerp 2 (Refaelov 31, Lamkel Ze 57) – Rangers won 9-5 on agg

Roma 3 (Dzeko 23, Perez 75, Mayoral 90+1) – Roma won 5-1 on agg. Shakhtar Donetsk 1 (Moraes 67 pen) Maccabi Tel Aviv 0 – Shakhtar Donetsk won 3-0 on agg. **Tottenham** 4 (Alli 10, Vinicius 50, 83), Bale 73) Wolfsberger 0 – Tottenham won 8-1 on agg. Villarreal 2 (Gerard 40, 89 pen) RB Salzburg 1 (Berisha 17) – Villarreal won 4-1 on agg

ROUND OF 16, FIRST LEG

Ajax 3 (Klaassen 62, Tadic 82, Brobbey 90) Young Boys 0. Dynamo Kiev 0 Villarreal 2 (Torres 30, Albiol 52). Granada 2 (Jorge Molina 26, Soldado 75) Molde 0. **Manchester Utd** 1 (Diallo 50) AC Milan 1 (Kjaer 90)

Olympiacos 1 (El Arabi 58) **Arsenal** 3 (Odegaard 34, Gabriel 79, Elneny 85). Roma 3 (Pellegrini 23, El Shaarawy 73, Mancini 77) Shakhtar Donetsk 0. Slavia Prague 1 (Stanciu 7) **Rangers** 1 (Helander 36). **Tottenham** 2 (Kane 25, 70) Dinamo Zagreb 0

ROUND OF 16, SECOND LEG

AC Milan 0 **Manchester Utd** 1 (Pogba 48) – Manchester Utd won 2-1 on agg. **Arsenal** 0 Olympiacos 1 (El Arabi 51) – Arsenal won 3-2 on agg. Dinamo Zagreb 3 (Orsic 62, 82, 106) **Tottenham** 0 – aet, Dinamo Zagreb won 3-2 on agg. Molde 2 (Vallejo 29 og, Hestad 90 pen) Granada 1 (Soldado 72) – Granada won 3-2 on agg

Rangers 0 Slavia Prague 2 (Olayinka 14, Stanciu 74) – Slavia Prague won 3-1 on agg. Shakhtar Donetsk 1 (Moraes 59) Roma 2 (Mayoral 48, 72) – Roma won 5-1 on agg. Villarreal 2 (Gerard 13, 36) Dynamo Kiev 0 – Villarreal won 4-0 on agg. Young Boys 0 Ajax 2 (Neres 20, Tadic 49 pen) – Ajax won 5-0 on agg

QUARTER-FINALS, FIRST LEG

Ajax 1 (Klaassen 39) Roma 2 (Pellegrini 57, Ibanez 87). **Arsenal** 1 (Pepe 86) Slavia Prague 1 (Holes 90+3). Dinamo Zagreb 0 Villarreal 1 (Gerard 44 pen). Granada 0 **Manchester Utd** 2 (Rashford 31, Bruno Fernandes 90 pen)

QUARTER-FINALS, SECOND LEG

Manchester Utd 2 (Cavani 6, Vallejo 90 og) Granada 0 – Manchester Utd won 4-0 on agg. Roma 1 (Dzeko 72) Ajax 1 (Brobbey 49) – Roma won 3-2 on agg. Slavia Prague 0 **Arsenal** 4 (Pepe 18, Lacazette 21 pen, 77, Saka 24) – Arsenal won 5-1 on agg. Villarreal 2 (Alcacer 36, Gerard 43) Dinamo Zagreb 1 (Orsic 74) – Villarreal won 3-1 on agg

SEMI-FINALS, FIRST LEG

Manchester Utd 6 (Bruno Fernandes 9, 71 pen, Cavani 48, 64, Pogba 74, Greenwood 86) Roma 2 (Pellegrini 15 pen, Dzeko 33). Villarreal 2 (Trigueros 5, Albiol 23) **Arsenal** 1 (Pepe 73 pen)

SEMI-FINALS, SECOND LEG

Arsenal 0 Villarreal 0 – Villarreal won 2-1 on agg. Roma 3 (Dzeko 57, Cristante 60, Zalewski 83) **Manchester Utd** 2 (Cavani 39, 68) – Manchester Utd won 8-5 on agg

FINAL

VILLARREAL 1 (Gerard Moreno 29) MANCHESTER UNITED 1 (Cavani 55) – aet, Villarreal won 11-10 on pens
Stadion Miejski, Gdansk (9,500); Wednesday, May 26, 2021

Villarreal (4-4-2): Rulli, Foyth (Gaspar 88), Albiol (capt), Torres, Pedraza (Alberto Moreno 88), Pino, Capoue (Raba 120+3), Parejo, Trigueros (Gomez 77), Gerard Moreno, Bacca (Coquelin 60). **Subs not used:** Asenjo, Funes Mori, Estupinan, Pena, Costa, Nino. **Booked:** Capoue, Foyth. **Coach:** Unai Emery

Manchester Utd (4-2-3-1): De Gea, Wan-Bissaka (Mata 120+3), Bailly (Tuanzebe 115), Lindelof, Shaw, McTominay (Telles 120+3), Pogba (James 115), Greenwood (Fred 100), Bruno Fernandes (capt), Rashford, Cavani. **Subs not used:** Henderson, Grant, Maguire, Williams, Diallo, Matic, Van de Beek. **Booked:** Bailly, Cavani. **Manager:** Ole Gunnar Solskjaer

Referee: Clement Turpin (France). **Half-time:** 1-0

Penalty shoot-out: Villarreal scored – Gerard Moreno, Raba, Alcacer, Alberto Moreno, Parejo, Gomez, Albiol, Coquelin, Gaspar, Torres, Rulli. **Manchester United scored** – Mata, Telles, Bruno Fernandes, Rashford, Cavani, Fred, James, Shaw, Tuanzebe, Lindelof; **saved** – De Gea

It had not been an enjoyable season for David de Gea. After nearly a decade with Manchester United, his position came under threat following the return of Dean Henderson from loan at Sheffield United. And after some high-profile errors committed by the Spaniard, Ole Gunnar Solskjaer installed Henderson as his No1 goalkeeper. The man he replaced had to make to do with helping United progress to the final of this competition, although with every chance of collecting a winners' medal. But even that eluded him in a record penalty shoot-out which, unluckily from his point of view, had an unpleasant twist in the tail. De Gea was beaten by all 11 Villarreal spot-kicks, the last of which was taken by his opposite number Geronimo Rulli. He then had his own effort saved, giving the underdogs a first major European trophy and their coach Unai Emery his fourth in the Europa League. Sir Alex Ferguson waited at pitchside to embrace him and offer some sympathy as the pair walked side-by-side down the tunnel. The result left his future in doubt, meant a fourth season for the club without a trophy and put pressure on the manager to bring in new faces in the summer transfer market.

Leading scorers: 7 Gerard Moreno (Villarreal), Mayoral (Roma), Pizzi (Benfica), Yazici (Benfica); 6 Alcacer (Villarreal), Cavani (Manchester Utd), Dabbur (Hoffenheim), Dzeko (Roma), Orsic (Dinamo Zagreb), Pepe (Arsenal), Vinicius (Tottenham)

FINAL FACTS AND FIGURES

- The match produced the most penalties converted in a major UEFA club competition final.
- The longest shoot-out in any UEFA competition was in 2007 when Holland defeated England 13-12 after 32 attempts in their European Under-21 Championship semi-final.
- Unai Emery was the first coach to win either the UEFA Cup or Europa League four times, having previously been successful in this competition with Sevilla in 2014, 2015 and 2016. He surpassed the record of Giovanni Trapattoni with Inter Milan and Juventus
- Villarreal were the first team to win in their first appearance in a major European final since Shakhtar Donetsk in the 2009 UEFA Cup.
- Spanish and English teams have won the Europa League in 11 of the competition's 12 seasons. Porto were the exception in 2011.

- Manchester United's Mason Greenwood made his 52nd appearance of the season, in all competitions, in the final.

EUROPEAN SUPER CUP 2020

BAYERN MUNICH 2 (Goretzka 34, Martinez 104) **SEVILLA 1** (Ocampos 13) –aet
Puskas Arena, Budapest (15,180); September 24, 2020

Bayern Munich (4-2-3-1): Neuer (capt), Pavard, Sule, Alaba (Boateng 112), Hernandez (Martinez 99), Goretzka (Davies 99), Kimmich, Gnabry, Muller, Sane (Tolisso 70), Lewandowski. **Subs not used:** Ulreich, Cuisance, Zirkzee, Fein, Nubel, Tillman, Richards, Musiala. **Booked:** Alaba, Hernandez. **Coach:** Hans-Dieter Flick

Sevilla (4-3-3): Bono, Navas (capt), Kounde, Diego Carlos, Escudero, Jordan (Vazquez 94), Fernando, Rakitic (Torres 56), Suso (Gudelj 73), De Jong (En-Nesyri 56), Ocampos. **Subs not used:** Vaclik, Munir, Gomez, Rodriguez, Acuna, Fernandez, Gil, Diaz. **Booked:** Jordan, Kounder, Fernando, Escudero. **Coach:** Julen Lopetegui
Referee: Anthony Taylor (England). **Half-time:** 1-1

FIFA CLUB WORLD CUP – QATAR 2020

Semi-finals: Palmeiras (Brazil) 0 Tigres (Mexico) 1 (Gignac 54 pen); Al Ahly (Egypt) 0 Bayern Munich 2 (Lewandowski 17, 86). **Final:** Bayerrn Munich 1 (Pavard 56) Tigres 0

UEFA CUP FINALS

1972	Tottenham beat Wolves 3-2 on agg (2-1a, 1-1h)
1973	Liverpool beat Borussia Moenchengladbach 3-2 on agg (3-0h, 0-2a)
1974	Feyenoord beat Tottenham 4-2 on agg (2-2a, 2-0h)
1975	Borussia Moenchengladbach beat Twente Enschede 5-1 on agg (0-0h, 5-1a)
1976	Liverpool beat Brugge 4-3 on agg (3-2h, 1-1a)
1977	Juventus beat Atletico Bilbao on away goals after 2-2 agg (1-0h, 1-2a)
1978	PSV Eindhoven beat Bastia 3-0 on agg (0-0a, 3-0h)
1979	Borussia Moenchengladbach beat Red Star Belgrade 2-1 on agg (1-1a, 1-0h)
1980	Eintracht Frankfurt beat Borussia Moenchengladbach on away goals after 3-3 agg (2-3a, 1-0h)
1981	Ipswich Town beat AZ 67 Alkmaar 5-4 on agg (3-0h, 2-4a)
1982	IFK Gothenburg beat SV Hamburg 4-0 on agg (1-0h, 3-0a)
1983	Anderlecht beat Benfica 2-1 on agg (1-0h, 1-1a)
1984	Tottenham beat Anderlecht 4-3 on penalties after 2-2 agg (1-1a, 1-1h)
1985	Real Madrid beat Videoton 3-1 on agg (3-0a, 0-1h)
1986	Real Madrid beat Cologne 5-3 on agg (5-1h, 0-2a)
1987	IFK Gothenburg beat Dundee Utd 2-1 on agg (1-0h, 1-1a)
1988	Bayer Leverkusen beat Espanol 3-2 on penalties after 3-3 agg (0-3a, 3-0h)
1989	Napoli beat VfB Stuttgart 5-4 on agg (2-1h, 3-3a)
1990	Juventus beat Fiorentina 3-1 on agg (3-1h, 0-0a)
1991	Inter Milan beat AS Roma 2-1 on agg (2-0h, 0-1a)
1992	Ajax beat Torino on away goals after 2-2 agg (2-2a, 0-0h)
1993	Juventus beat Borussia Dortmund 6-1 on agg (3-1a, 3-0h)
1994	Inter Milan beat Salzburg 2-0 on agg (1-0a, 1-0h)
1995	Parma beat Juventus 2-1 on agg (1-0h, 1-1a)
1996	Bayern Munich beat Bordeaux 5-1 on agg (2-0h, 3-1a)
1997	FC Schalke beat Inter Milan 4-1 on penalties after 1-1 agg (1-0h, 0-1a)
1998	Inter Milan beat Lazio 3-0 (one match) – Paris
1999	Parma beat Marseille 3-0 (one match) – Moscow
2000	Galatasaray beat Arsenal 4-1 on penalties after 0-0 (one match) – Copenhagen
2001	Liverpool beat Alaves 5-4 on golden goal (one match) – Dortmund
2002	Feyenoord beat Borussia Dortmund 3-2 (one match) – Rotterdam
2003	FC Porto beat Celtic 3-2 on silver goal (one match) – Seville
2004	Valencia beat Marseille 2-0 (one match) – Gothenburg
2005	CSKA Moscow beat Sporting Lisbon 3-1 (one match) – Lisbon
2006	Sevilla beat Middlesbrough 4-0 (one match) – Eindhoven
2007	Sevilla beat Espanyol 3-1 on penalties after 2-2 (one match) – Hampden Park
2008	Zenit St Petersburg beat Rangers 2-0 (one match) – City of Manchester Stadium
2009†	Shakhtar Donetsk beat Werder Bremen 2-1 (one match) – Istanbul

EUROPA LEAGUE FINALS

2010† Atletico Madrid beat Fulham 2-1 (one match) – Hamburg
2011 Porto beat Braga 1-0 (one match) – Dublin
2012 Atletico Madrid beat Athletic Bilbao 3-0 (one match) – Bucharest
2013 Chelsea beat Benfica 2-1 (one match) – Amsterdam
2014 Sevilla beat Benfica 4-2 on penalties after 0-0 (one match) – Turin
2015 Sevilla beat Dnipro 3-2 (one match) – Warsaw
2016 Sevilla beat Liverpool 3-1 (one match) – Basle
2017 Manchester Utd beat Ajax 2-0 (one match) – Stockholm
2018 Atletico Madrid beat Marseille 3-0 (one match) – Lyon
2019 Chelsea beat Arsenal 4-1 (one match) – Baku
2020 Sevilla beat Inter Milan 3-2 (one match) - Cologne
2021 Villarreal beat Manchester Utd 11-10 on penalties after 1-1 (one match) – Gdansk
(† After extra-time)

FAIRS CUP FINALS
(As UEFA Cup previously known)

1958 Barcelona beat London 8-2 on agg (2-2a, 6-0h)
1960 Barcelona beat Birmingham 4-1 on agg (0-0a, 4-1h)
1961 AS Roma beat Birmingham City 4-2 on agg (2-2a, 2-0h)
1962 Valencia beat Barcelona 7-3 on agg (6-2h, 1-1a)
1963 Valencia beat Dynamo Zagreb 4-1 on agg (2-1a, 2-0h)
1964 Real Zaragoza beat Valencia 2-1 (Barcelona)
1965 Ferencvaros beat Juventus 1-0 (Turin)
1966 Barcelona beat Real Zaragoza 4-3 on agg (0-1h, 4-2a)
1967 Dinamo Zagreb beat Leeds Utd 2-0 on agg (2-0h, 0-0a)
1968 Leeds Utd beat Ferencvaros 1-0 on agg (1-0h, 0-0a)
1969 Newcastle Utd beat Ujpest Dozsa 6-2 on agg (3-0h, 3-2a)
1970 Arsenal beat Anderlecht 4-3 on agg (1-3a, 3-0h)
1971 Leeds Utd beat Juventus on away goals after 3-3 agg (2-2a, 1-1h)

CUP-WINNERS' CUP FINALS

1961 Fiorentina beat Rangers 4-1 on agg (2-0 Glasgow first leg, 2-1 Florence second leg)
1962 Atletico Madrid beat Fiorentina 3-0 (replay Stuttgart, after a 1-1 draw, Glasgow)
1963 Tottenham beat Atletico Madrid 5-1 (Rotterdam)
1964 Sporting Lisbon beat MTK Budapest 1-0 (replay Antwerp, after a 3-3 draw, Brussels)
1965 West Ham Utd beat Munich 1860 2-0 (Wembley)
1966† Borussia Dortmund beat Liverpool 2-1 (Glasgow)
1967† Bayern Munich beat Rangers 1-0 (Nuremberg)
1968 AC Milan beat SV Hamburg 2-0 (Rotterdam)
1969 Slovan Bratislava beat Barcelona 3-2 (Basle)
1970 Manchester City beat Gornik Zabrze 2-1 (Vienna)
1971† Chelsea beat Real Madrid 2-1 (replay Athens, after a 1-1 draw, Athens)
1972 Rangers beat Moscow Dynamo 3-2 (Barcelona)
1973 AC Milan beat Leeds Utd 1-0 (Salonika)
1974 Magdeburg beat AC Milan 2-0 (Rotterdam)
1975 Dynamo Kiev beat Ferencvaros 3-0 (Basle)
1976 Anderlecht beat West Ham Utd 4-2 (Brussels)
1977 SV Hamburg beat Anderlecht 2-0 (Amsterdam)

1978	Anderlecht beat Austria WAC 4-0 (Paris)
1979†	Barcelona beat Fortuna Dusseldorf 4-3 (Basle)
1980†	Valencia beat Arsenal 5-4 on penalties after a 0-0 draw (Brussels)
1981	Dinamo Tbilisi beat Carl Zeiss Jena 2-1 (Dusseldorf)
1982	Barcelona beat Standard Liege 2-1 (Barcelona)
1983†	Aberdeen beat Real Madrid 2-1 (Gothenburg)
1984	Juventus beat Porto 2-1 (Basle)
1985	Everton beat Rapid Vienna 3-1 (Rotterdam)
1986	Dynamo Kiev beat Atletico Madrid 3-0 (Lyon)
1987	Ajax beat Lokomotiv Leipzig 1-0 (Athens)
1988	Mechelen beat Ajax 1-0 (Strasbourg)
1989	Barcelona beat Sampdoria 2-0 (Berne)
1990	Sampdoria beat Anderlecht 2-0 (Gothenburg)
1991	Manchester Utd beat Barcelona 2-1 (Rotterdam)
1992	Werder Bremen beat Monaco 2-0 (Lisbon)
1993	Parma beat Royal Antwerp 3-1 (Wembley)
1994	Arsenal beat Parma 1-0 (Copenhagen)
1995†	Real Zaragoza beat Arsenal 2-1 (Paris)
1996	Paris St Germain beat Rapid Vienna 1-0 (Brussels)
1997	Barcelona beat Paris St Germain 1-0 (Rotterdam)
1998	Chelsea beat VfB Stuttgart 1-0 (Stockholm)
1999	Lazio beat Real Mallorca 2-1 (Villa Park, Birmingham)

(† After extra time)

EUROPEAN SUPER CUP RESULTS

1972*	Ajax beat Rangers 6-3 on agg (3-1, 3-2)
1973	Ajax beat AC Milan 6-1 on agg (0-1, 6-0)
1974	Bayern Munich and Magdeburg did not play
1975	Dynamo Kiev beat Bayern Munich 3-0 on agg (1-0, 2-0)
1976	Anderlecht beat Bayern Munich 5-3 on agg (1-2, 4-1)
1977	Liverpool beat Hamburg 7-1 on agg (1-1, 6-0)
1978	Anderlecht beat Liverpool 4-3 on agg (3-1, 1-2)
1979	Nottm Forest beat Barcelona 2-1 on agg (1-0, 1-1)
1980	Valencia beat Nottm Forest on away goal after 2-2 agg (1-2, 1-0)
1981	Liverpool and Dinamo Tbilisi did not play
1982	Aston Villa beat Barcelona 3-1 on agg (0-1, 3-0 aet)
1983	Aberdeen beat Hamburg 2-0 on agg (0-0, 2-0)
1984	Juventus beat Liverpool 2-0 – one match (Turin)
1985	Juventus and Everton did not play
1986	Steaua Bucharest beat Dynamo Kiev 1-0 – one match (Monaco)
1987	Porto beat Ajax 2-0 on agg (1-0, 1-0)
1988	Mechelen beat PSV Eindhoven 3-1 on agg (3-0, 0-1)
1989	AC Milan beat Barcelona 2-1 on agg (1-1, 1-0)
1990	AC Milan beat Sampdoria 3-1 on agg (1-1, 2-0)
1991	Manchester Utd beat Red Star Belgrade 1-0 – one match (Old Trafford)
1992	Barcelona beat Werder Bremen 3-2 on agg (1-1, 2-1)
1993	Parma beat AC Milan 2-1 on agg (0-1, 2-0 aet)
1994	AC Milan beat Arsenal 2-0 on agg (0-0, 2-0)
1995	Ajax beat Real Zaragoza 5-1 on agg (1-1, 4-0)
1996	Juventus beat Paris St Germain 9-2 on agg (6-1, 3-1)
1997	Barcelona beat Borussia Dortmund 3-1 on agg (2-0, 1-1)
1998	Chelsea beat Real Madrid 1-0 (Monaco)

1999	Lazio beat Manchester Utd 1-0 (Monaco)
2000	Galatasaray beat Real Madrid 2-1 – aet, golden goal (Monaco)
2001	Liverpool beat Bayern Munich 3-2 (Monaco)
2002	Real Madrid beat Feyenoord 3-1 (Monaco)
2003	AC Milan beat Porto 1-0 (Monaco)
2004	Valencia beat Porto 2-1 (Monaco)
2005	Liverpool beat CSKA Moscow 3-1 – aet (Monaco)
2006	Sevilla beat Barcelona 3-0 (Monaco)
2007	AC Milan beat Sevilla 3-1 (Monaco)
2008	Zenit St Petersburg beat Manchester Utd 2-1 (Monaco)
2009	Barcelona beat Shakhtar Donetsk 1-0 – aet (Monaco)
2010	Atletico Madrid beat Inter Milan 2-0 (Monaco)
2011	Barcelona beat Porto 2-0 (Monaco)
2012	Atletico Madrid beat Chelsea 4-1 (Monaco)
2013	Bayern Munich beat Chelsea 5-4 on pens, aet – 2-2 (Prague)
2014	Real Madrid beat Sevilla 2-0 (Cardiff)
2015	Barcelona beat Sevilla 5-4 – aet (Tbilisi)
2016	Real Madrid beat Sevilla 3-2 – aet (Trondheim)
2017	Real Madrid beat Manchester Utd 2-1 (Skopje)
2018	Atletico Madrid beat Real Madrid 4-2 (Tallinn)
2019	Liverpool beat Chelsea 5-4 on pens, aet – 2-2 (Istanbul)
2020	Bayern Munich beat Sevilla 2-1 (Budapest)

*not recognised by UEFA; from 1998 one match

INTER-CONTINENTAL CUP

Year	Winners	Runners-up	Score
1960	Real Madrid (Spa)	Penarol (Uru)	0-0 5-1
1961	Penarol (Uru)	Benfica (Por)	0-1 2-1 5-0
1962	Santos (Bra)	Benfica (Por)	3-2 5-2
1963	Santos (Bra)	AC Milan (Ita)	2-4 4-2 1-0
1964	Inter Milan (Ita)	Independiente (Arg)	0-1 2-0 1-0
1965	Inter Milan (Ita)	Independiente (Arg)	3-0 0-0
1966	Penarol (Uru)	Real Madrid (Spa)	2-0 2-0
1967	Racing (Arg)	Celtic	0-1 2-1 1-0
1968	Estudiantes (Arg)	Manchester Utd	1-0 1-1
1969	AC Milan (Ita)	Estudiantes (Arg)	3-0 1-2
1970	Feyenoord (Hol)	Estudiantes (Arg)	2-2 1-0
1971	Nacional (Uru)	Panathanaikos (Gre)	*1-1 2-1
1972	Ajax (Hol)	Independiente (Arg)	1-1 3-0
1973	Independiente (Arg)	Juventus* (Ita)	1-0 #
1974	Atletico Madrid (Spa)*	Independiente (Arg)	0-1 2-0
1975	Not played		
1976	Bayern Munich (WGer)	Cruzeiro (Bra)	2-0 0-0
1977	Boca Juniors (Arg)	Borussia Mönchengladbach* (WGer)	2-2 3-0
1978	Not played		
1979	Olimpia Asuncion (Par)	Malmö* (Swe)	1-0 2-1
1980	Nacional (Arg)	Nott'm Forest	1-0
1981	Flamengo (Bra)	Liverpool	3-0
1982	Penarol (Uru)	Aston Villa	2-0
1983	Porto Alegre (Bra)	SV Hamburg (WGer)	2-1
1984	Independiente (Arg)	Liverpool	1-0
1985	Juventus (Ita)	Argentinos Juniors (Arg)	2-2 (aet)

	(Juventus won 4-2 on penalties)		
1986	River Plate (Arg)	Steaua Bucharest (Rom)	1-0
1987	Porto (Por)	Penarol (Uru)	2-1 (aet)
1988	Nacional (Uru)	PSV Eindhoven (Hol)	1-1 (aet)
	(Nacional won 7-6 on penalties)		
1989	AC Milan (Ita)	Nacional (Col)	1-0 (aet)
1990	AC Milan (Ita)	Olimpia Asuncion (Par)	3-0
1991	Red Star (Yug)	Colo Colo (Chi)	3-0
1992	Sao Paulo (Bra)	Barcelona (Spa)	2-1
1993	Sao Paulo (Bra)	AC Milan (Ita)	3-2
1994	Velez Sarsfield (Arg)	AC Milan (Ita)	2-0
1995	Ajax (Hol)	Gremio (Bra)	0-0 (aet)
	(Ajax won 4-3 on penalties)		
1996	Juventus (Ita)	River Plate (Arg)	1-0
1997	Borussia Dortmund (Ger)	Cruzeiro (Arg)	2-0
1998	Real Madrid (Spa)	Vasco da Gama (Bra)	2-1
1999	Manchester Utd	Palmeiras (Bra)	1-0
2000	Boca Juniors (Arg)	Real Madrid (Spa)	2-1
2001	Bayern Munich (Ger)	Boca Juniors (Arg)	1-0
2002	Real Madrid (Spa)	Olimpia Ascuncion (Par)	2-0
2003	Boca Juniors (Arg)	AC Milan (Ita)	1-1
	(Boca Juniors won 3-1 on penalties)		
2004	FC Porto (Por)	Caldas (Col)	0-0

(FC Porto won 8-7 on penalties)
Played as a single match in Japan since 1980
* European Cup runners-up # One match only
Summary: 43 contests; South America 22 wins, Europe 23 wins

CLUB WORLD CHAMPIONSHIP

2005	Sao Paulo (Bra) beat Liverpool	1-0
2006	Internacional (Bra) beat Barcelona (Spa)	1-0
2007	AC Milan (Ita) beat Boca Juniors (Arg)	4-2

CLUB WORLD CUP

2008	Manchester Utd beat Liga de Quito (Ecu)	1-0
2009	Barcelona beat Estudiantes (Arg)	2-1 (aet)
2010	Inter Milan (Ita) beat TP Mazembe (DR Congo)	3-0
2011	Barcelona beat Santos (Bra)	4-0
2012	Corinthians (Bra) beat Chelsea	1-0
2013	Bayern Munich (Ger) beat Raja Casablanca (Mar)	2-0
2014	Real Madrid (Spa) beat San Lorenzo (Arg)	2-0
2015	Barcelona beat River Plate (Arg)	3-0
2016	Real Madrid beat Kashima Antlers (Jap)	4-2 (aet)
2017	Real Madrid beat Gremio (Bra)	1-0
2018	Real Madrid beat Al AIN (UAE)	4-1
2019	Liverpool beat Flamengo (Bra)	1-0 (aet)
2020	Bayern Munich (Ger) beat Tigres (Mex)	1-0

EUROPEAN TABLES 2020–2021

FRANCE – LIGUE 1

	P	W	D	L	F	A	GD	Pts
Lille	38	24	11	3	64	23	41	83
Paris SG	38	26	4	8	86	28	58	82
Monaco	38	24	6	8	76	42	34	78
Lyon	38	22	10	6	81	43	38	76
Marseille	38	16	12	10	54	47	7	60
Rennes	38	16	10	12	52	40	12	58
Lens	38	15	12	11	55	54	1	57
Montpellier	38	14	12	12	60	62	-2	54
Nice	38	15	7	16	50	53	-3	52
Metz	38	12	11	15	44	48	-4	47
St Etienne	38	12	10	16	42	54	-12	46
Bordeaux	38	13	6	19	42	56	-14	45
Angers	38	12	8	18	40	58	-18	44
Reims	38	9	15	14	42	50	-8	42
Strasbourg	38	11	9	18	49	58	-9	42
Lorient	38	11	9	18	50	68	-18	42
Brest	38	11	8	19	50	66	-16	41
Nantes	38	9	13	16	47	55	-8	40
Nimes	38	9	8	21	40	71	-31	35
Dijon	38	4	9	25	25	73	-48	21

Leading scorers: 27 Mbappe (Paris SG); 20 Ben Yedder (Monaco), Depay (Lyon); 16 Ajorque (Strasbourg), Laborde (Montpellier), Volland (Monaco), Yilmaz (Lille); 15 Delort (Montpellier); 14 Dia (Reims), Moffi (Lorient)
Cup Final: Paris SG 2 (Icardi 19, Mbappe 81) Monaco 0

HOLLAND – EREDIVISIE

	P	W	D	L	F	A	GD	Pts
Ajax	34	28	4	2	102	23	79	88
PSV Eindhoven	34	21	9	4	74	35	39	72
Alkmaar	34	21	8	5	75	41	34	71
Vitesse Arnhem	34	18	7	9	52	38	14	61
Feyenoord	34	16	11	7	64	36	28	59
Utrecht	34	13	14	7	52	41	11	53
Groningen	34	14	8	12	40	37	3	50
Sparta Rotterdam	34	13	8	13	49	48	1	47
Heracles	34	12	8	14	42	53	-11	44
Twente	34	10	11	13	48	50	-2	41
Fortuna Sittard	34	12	5	17	50	58	-8	41
Heerenveen	34	9	12	13	43	49	-6	39
Zwolle	34	9	11	14	44	53	-9	38
Willem	34	8	7	19	40	68	-28	31
Waalwijk	34	7	9	18	33	55	-22	30
Emmen	34	7	9	18	40	68	-28	30
Venlo	34	6	5	23	43	91	-48	23
Den Haag	34	4	10	20	29	76	-47	22

Leading scorers: 26 Giakoumakis (Venlo); 19 Malen (PSV Eindhoven); 18 Beghuis (Feyenoord); 17 Pereira (Twente); 16 Vloet (Heracles); 15 Boadu (Alkmaar), Koopmeiners (Alkmaar); 14 Tadic (Ajax), Thy (Sparta Rotterdam), Veerman (Heerenveen)
Cup Final: Ajax 2 (Gravenberch 23, Neres 90+1) Vitesse Arnhem 1 (Openda 30)

GERMANY – BUNDESLIGA

Bayern Munich	34	24	6	4	99	44	55	78
RB Leipzig	34	19	8	7	60	32	28	65
Borussia Dortmund	34	20	4	10	75	46	29	64
Wolfsburg	34	17	10	7	61	37	24	61
Eintracht Frankfurt	34	16	12	6	69	53	16	60
Bayer Leverkusen	34	14	10	10	53	39	14	52
Union Berlin	34	12	14	8	50	43	7	50
Borussia M'gladbach	34	13	10	11	64	56	8	49
Stuttgart	34	12	9	13	56	55	1	45
Freiburg	34	12	9	13	52	52	0	45
Hoffenheim	34	11	10	13	52	54	-2	43
Mainz	34	10	9	15	39	56	-17	39
Augsburg	34	10	6	18	36	54	-18	36
Hertha	34	8	11	15	41	52	-11	35
Arminia Bielefeld	34	9	8	17	26	52	-26	35
Cologne	34	8	9	17	34	60	-26	33
Werder Bremen	34	7	10	17	36	57	-21	31
Schalke	34	3	7	24	25	86	-61	16

Leading scorers: 41 Lewandowski (Bayern Munich); 28 Andre Silva (Eintracht Frankfurt); 27 Haaland (Borussia Dortmund); 20 Kramaric (Hoffenheim), Weghorst (Wolfsburg); 16 Kalajdzic (Stuttgart); 14 Stindl (Borussia M'gladbach); 11 Alario (Bayer Leverkusen), Kruse (Union Berlin), Muller (Bayern Munich), Wamangituka (Stuttgart)

Cup Final: Borussia Dortmund 4 (Sancho 5, 45, Haaland 28, 87) RB Leipzig 1 (Olmo 71)

ITALY – SERIE A

Inter Milan	38	28	7	3	89	35	54	91
AC Milan	38	24	7	7	74	41	33	79
Atalanta	38	23	9	6	90	47	43	78
Juventus	38	23	9	6	77	38	39	78
Napoli	38	24	5	9	86	41	45	77
Lazio	38	21	5	12	61	55	6	68
Roma	38	18	8	12	68	58	10	62
Sassuolo	38	17	11	10	64	56	8	62
Sampdoria	38	15	7	16	52	54	-2	52
Verona	38	11	12	15	46	48	-2	45
Genoa	38	10	12	16	47	58	-11	42
Bologna	38	10	11	17	51	65	-14	41
Fiorentina	38	9	13	16	47	59	-12	40
Udinese	38	10	10	18	42	58	-16	40
Spezia	38	9	12	17	52	72	-20	39
Cagliari	38	9	10	19	43	59	-16	37
Torino	38	7	16	15	50	69	-19	37
Benevento	38	7	12	19	40	75	-35	33
Crotone	38	6	5	27	45	92	-47	23
Parma	38	3	11	24	39	83	-44	20

Leading scorers: 29 Ronaldo (Juventus); 24 Lukaku (Inter Milan); 22 Muriel (Atalanta); 21 Vlahovic (Fiorentina); 20 Immobile (Lazio), Nwankwo (Crotone); 19 Insigne (Napol); 17 Berardi (Sassuolo), Martinez (Inter Milan); 16 Joao Pedro (Cagliari)

Cup Final: Juventus 2 (Kulusevski 31, Chiesa 73) Atalanta 1 (Malinovsky 41)

PORTUGAL – PRIMEIRA LIGA

Sporting Lisbon	34	26	7	1	65	20	45	85
Porto	34	24	8	2	74	29	45	80
Benfica	34	23	7	4	69	27	42	76
Sporting Braga	34	19	7	8	53	33	20	64
Pacos de Ferreira	34	15	8	11	40	41	-1	53
Santa Clara	34	13	7	14	44	36	8	46
Guimaraes	34	12	7	15	37	44	-7	43
Moreirense	34	10	13	11	37	43	-6	43
Famalicao	34	10	10	14	40	48	-8	40
Belenenses	34	9	13	12	25	35	-10	40
Gil Vicente	34	11	6	17	33	42	-9	39
Tondela	34	10	6	18	36	57	-21	36
Boavista	34	8	12	14	39	49	-10	36
Portimonense	34	9	8	17	34	41	-7	35
Maritimo	34	10	5	19	27	47	-20	35
Rio Av	34	7	13	14	25	40	-15	34
Farense	34	7	10	17	31	48	-17	31
Nacional	34	6	7	21	30	59	-29	25

Leading scorers; 22 Seferovic (Benfica); 16 Taremi (Porto); 15 Gonzalez (Tondela); 14 Carlos (Santa Clara); 13 Sergio Oliveira (Porto); 11 Beto (Portimonense); 10 Cassierra (Belenenses)
Cup Final: Sporting Braga 2 (Lucas Piazon 45, Ricardo Horta 85) Benfica 0

SPAIN – LA LIGA

Atletico Madrid	38	26	8	4	67	25	42	86
Real Madrid	38	25	9	4	67	28	39	84
Barcelona	38	24	7	7	85	38	47	79
Sevilla	38	24	5	9	53	33	20	77
Real Sociedad	38	17	11	10	59	38	21	62
Real Betis	38	17	10	11	50	50	0	61
Villarreal	38	15	13	10	60	44	16	58
Celta Vigo	38	14	11	13	55	57	-2	53
Granada	38	13	7	18	47	65	-18	46
Athletic Bilbao	38	11	13	14	46	42	4	46
Osasuna	38	11	11	16	37	48	-11	44
Cadiz	38	11	11	16	36	58	-22	44
Valencia	38	10	13	15	50	53	-3	43
Levante	38	9	14	15	46	57	-11	41
Getafe	38	9	11	18	28	43	-15	38
Dep Alves	38	9	11	18	36	57	-21	38
Elche	38	8	12	18	34	55	-21	36
Huesca	38	7	13	18	34	53	-19	34
Valladolid	38	5	16	17	34	57	-23	31
Eibar	38	6	12	20	29	52	-23	30

Leading scorers: 30 Messi (Barcelona); 23 Benzema (Real Madrid), Gerard Moreno (Villarreal); 21 Suarez (Atletico Madrid); 18 En-Nesyri (Sevilla); 17 Isak (Real Sociedad); 14 Iago Aspas (Celta Vigo); 13 Griezmann (Barcelona), Rafa Mir (Huesca), Morales (Levante)
Cup Final: Barcelona 4 (Griezmann 60, De Jong 63, Messi 68, 72) Athletic Bilbao 0

BRITISH AND IRISH INTERNATIONALS
2020–21
(*denotes new cap)

WORLD CUP 2022 QUALIFIYING – EUROPE

GROUP A

SERBIA 3 (Vlahovic 40, A Mitrovic 68, 75) REPUBLIC OF IRELAND 2 (Browne 18, Collins 86)
Belgrade; March 24, 2021
Serbia (3-4-3): Dmitrovic, Milenkovic, S Mitrovic, Pavlovic, Gajic, Lukic, Racic (Maksimovic 62) Mladenovic, Tadic (Gudel 76), Vlahovic (Jovic 81), Djuricic (A Mitrovic 62). **Booked**: Pavlovic
Republic of Ireland (3-5-2): Travers, Coleman, O'Shea, Clark (Brady 79), Doherty, Molumby (Hendrick 61), Cullen, Browne (Collins 79), Stevens, Robinson (McClean 79), Connolly (S Long 66)
Referee: Davide Massa (Italy). **Half-time**: 1-1

REPUBLIC OF IRELAND 0 LUXEMBOURG 1(Rodrigues 85)
Aviva Stadium; March 27, 2021
Republic of Ireland (3-4-1-2): *Bazunu, Coleman, O'Shea, Clark (McClean 61), Doherty (Brady 46), Knight, Cullen (Molumby 88), Stevens, Browne, Collins (Parrott 88), Robinson (S Long 79). **Booked**: Stevens, Cullen
Luxembourg (4-1-4-1): Moris, M Martins, Chanot, Mahmutovic, Jans, C Martins, V Thill (Deville 79), O Thill, Barreiro, Rodrigues, Sinani (Gerson 90+2). **Booked**: O Thill, Sinani, Jans
Referee: Fran Jovic (Croatia). **Half-time**: 0-0

	P	W	D	L	F	A	Pts
Portugal	3	2	1	0	6	3	7
Serbia	3	2	1	0	7	5	7
Luxembourg	2	1	0	1	2	3	3
Republic of Ireland	2	0	0	2	2	4	0
Azerbaijan	2	0	0	2	1	3	0

GROUP C

ITALY 2 (Berardi 14, Immobile 39) NORTHERN IRELAND 0
Parma; March 25, 2021
Italy (4-3-3): Donnarumma, Florenzi, Bonucci, Chiellini, Emerson (Spinazzola 75), Pellegrini (Barella 64), Locatelli (Pessina 84), Verratti, Berardi (Chiesa 75), Immobile, Insigne (Grifo 84)
Northern Ireland (5-3-2): Peacock-Farrell, Smith, Cathcart, J Evans, McNair, Dallas, C Evans (Saville 46), Davis, McCann (Thompson 78), Whyte (Lavery 64), Magennis (Lafferty 78).
Booked: Saville, Thompson
Referee: Ali Palabiyik (Turkey). **Half-time**: 2-0

NORTHERN IRELAND 0 BULGARIA 0
Windsor Park; March 31, 2021
Northern Ireland (4-1-3-2): Peacock-Farrell, Ballard (Smith 74), Cathcart, J Evans, Lewis, Davis, Dallas, McNair, Saville (Kennedy 74), Magennis (Lafferty 82), Whyte (McGinn 64).
Booked: McNair, Saville, Lafferty
(Steven Davis made British record 126th international appearance)
Bulgaria (3-5-2): Naumov, P Hristov, Antov, A Hristov, Yomov (Karagaren 73), Vutov (D Iliev 46), Kostadinov (Vitanov 44), Chochev, Tsvetanov (Zanev 73), Galabinov (A Iliev 73), Despodov. **Booked**: P Hristov, Antov, A Iliev
Referee: Yigal Frid (Israel)

Italy	3	3	0	0	6	0	9
Switzerland	2	2	0	0	4	1	6
Northern Ireland	2	0	1	1	0	2	1
Bulgaria	3	0	1	2	1	5	1
Lithuania	2	0	0	2	0	3	0

GROUP E

BELGIUM 3 (De Bruyne 22, T Hazard 28, Lukaku 73 pen) WALES 1 (Wilson 10)
Leuven; March 24, 2021

Belgium (3-4-2-1): Courtois, Alderweireld, Vermaelen (Denayer 46), Vertonghen, Meunier, Dendoncker, Tielemans, T Hazard (Castagne 84), De Bruyne, Mertens (Trossard 90-3), Lukaku. **Booked:** T Hazard
Wales (3-4-3): Ward, Mepham, Rodon, J Lawrence, C Roberts, Allen (Morrell 8), Ampadu, N Williams, Bale (Moore 84), Wilson (T Roberts 67), James
Referee: Cuneyt Cakir (Turkey). **Half-time:** 2-1

WALES 1 (James 81) CZECH REPUBLIC 0
Cardiff City Stadium; March 30, 2021

Wales (3-4-3): Ward, Mepham (Moore 57), Rodon, J Lawrence, C Roberts, Morrell, Ampadu, N Williams, Bale, Wilson (J Williams 76), James. **Booked:** J Lawrence, C Roberts. **Sent off:** C Roberts (77)
Czech Republic (4-2-3-1): Vaclik, Coufal (Vydra 87), Kudela (Barak 87), Celustka, Boril, Holes (Krmencik 53), Soucek, Provod (Kaderabak 82), Darida, Jankto (Masopust 82), Schick. **Booked:** Jankto. **Sent off:** Schick (48)
Referee: Ovidiu Hategan (Romania). **Half-time:** 0-0

Belgium	3	2	1	0	12	2	7
Czech Republic	3	1	1	1	7	4	4
Wales	2	1	0	1	2	3	3
Belarus	2	1	0	1	4	10	3
Estonia	2	0	0	2	4	10	0

GROUP F

SCOTLAND 2 (Hanley 71, McGinn 85) AUSTRIA 2 (Kalajdzic 55, 80)
Hampden Park; March 25, 2021

Scotland (3-4-2-1): Marshall, Hendry, Hanley, Tierney, O'Donnell, McTominay, McGinn, Robertson, Christie (McLean 88), Armstrong (*Adams 66), Dykes (McGregor 78). **Booked:** Hanley, Christie, Dykes, O'Donnell
Austria (4-4-2): A Schlager, Lainer, Dragovic, Lienhart, Alaba, Baumgartner, Grillitsch, Ilsanker, X Schlager, Kalajdzic, Grbic (Schaub 68). **Booked:** Kalajdzic, Grillitsch, Ilsanker
Referee: Carlos del Cerro Grande (Spain). **Half-time:** 0-0

ISRAEL 1 (Peretz 44) SCOTLAND 1 (Fraser 56)
Tel Aviv; March 28, 2021

Israel (3-4-1-2): Marciano, Elhamed, Tibi, Arad, Dasa, Natcho (Lavi 63), Peretz, Menachem (Kayal 80), Solomon, Weissman (Dabbur 74), Zahavi. **Booked:** Peretz
Scotland (3-4-2-1): Marshall, Hendry (Christie 46), Hanley, Tierney, O'Donnell, McTominay, McGregor, Robertson, McGinn (McLean 74), Fraser (Armstrong 86), Adams (Dykes 75). **Booked:** Hendry
Referee: Deniz Aytekin (Germany). **Half-time:** 1-0

SCOTLAND 4 (McGinn 7, 53, Adams 60, Fraser 70) FAROE ISLANDS 0
Hampden Park; March 31, 2021
Scotland (3-5-2): Gordon, McTominay, Hanley, Tierney (McKenna 79), Fraser (Palmer 79), McGinn, McLean, McGregor (Fleck 73), Robertson, Adams (McBurnie 73), Dykes (Nisbet 68). **Booked**: Nisbet
Faroe Islands (4-4-2): Nielsen, Rolantsson, G Vatnhamar, Nattestad (Baldvinsson 76), Davidsen, S Vatnhamar (Johannesen 69), Hansson, Andreasen (K Olsen 69), Hendriksson, Edmundsson (Vatnsdal 76), M Olsen (Jonsson 76).
Referee: Trustin Farrugia (Malta). **Half-time**: 1-0

Denmark	3	3	0	0	14	0	9
Scotland	3	1	2	0	7	3	5
Israel	3	1	1	1	5	4	4
Austria	3	1	1	1	5	7	4
Faroe Islands	3	0	1	2	2	8	1
Moldova	3	0	1	2	2	13	1

GROUP I

ENGLAND 5 (Ward-Prowse 14, Calvert-Lewin 21, 53, Sterling 31, Watkins 83) SAN MARINO 0
Wembley; March 25, 2021
England (4-3-3): Pope, James (Trippier 46), Stones (Mings 46), Coady, Chilwell, Ward-Prowse, Mount (Bellingham 46), Phillips, Lingard, Calvert-Lewin (*Watkins 63), Sterling (Foden 46). **Booked**: Mings
San Marino (4-4-2): Benedettini, Manuel Battisini, Brolli, Rossi, Grandoni (Ceccaroli 55), Hirsch (Mularoni 55), Lunadel (Giardia 79), Golinucci (Michael Battisini 71), Palazzi, Berardi (D'Addario 79), Nanni
Referee: Kirill Levnikov (Russia). **Half-time**: 3-0

ALBANIA 0 ENGLAND 2 (Kane 38, Mount 63)
Tirana; March 28, 2021
Albania (4-3-3): Berisha, Hysaj, Ismajli, Djimsiti, Veseli, Laci (Ramadani 89), Bare (Memushaj 71), Memolla (Gjasula 59), Cikalleshi (Manaj 59) Broja (Lenjani 59), Uzuni. **Booked**: Bare, Hysaj, Gjasula
England (4-3-3): Pope, Walker, Stones, Maguire, Shaw, Mount, Rice, Phillips (Ward-Prowse 71), Sterling, Kane, Foden (Lingard 81). **Booked**: Walker, Kane
Referee: Orel Grinfeld (Israel). **Half-time**: 0-1

ENGLAND 2 (Kane 19 pen, Maguire 85) POLAND 1 (Moder 58)
Wembley; March 31, 2021
England (4-3-3): Pope, Walker, Stones, Maguire, Chilwell, Phillips, Rice, Mount, Foden (James 86), Kane (Calvert-Lewin 89), Sterling (Lingard 90)
Poland (3-5-2): Szczesny, Helik (Jozwiak 55), Glik, Bednarek, Bereszynski, Zielinski (Grosicki 86), Krychowiak, Moder, Rybus (Reca 86), Piatek (Augustyniak 77), Swiderski (Milik 46). **Booked**: Milik
Referee: Bjorn Kuipers (Holland). **Half-time**: 1-0

England	3	3	0	0	9	1	9
Hungary	3	2	1	0	10	4	7
Albania	3	2	0	1	3	2	6
Poland	3	1	1	1	7	5	4
Andorra	3	0	0	3	1	8	0
San Marino	3	0	0	3	0	10	0

EUROPEAN CHAMPIONSHIP 2020 QUALIFYING

PLAY-OFFS – SEMI-FINALS (one leg)

BOSNIA-HERZEGOVINA 1 (Krunic 13) NORTHERN IRELAND 1 (McGinn 53) – aet, Northern Ireland won 4-3 on pens
Sarajevo; October 8, 2020

Bosnia-Herzegovina (4-3-3): Sehic, Cipetic, Ahmedhodzic, Sanicanin, Kolasinac (Hajradinovic 118), Cimirot (Loncar 105), Hadziahmetovic (Gojak 83), Pjanic, Visca, Dzeko, Krunic (Hotic 88). **Booked:** Hadziahmetovic, Kolasinac, Pjanic

Northern Ireland (4-4-1-1): Peacock-Farrell, Dallas, Cathcart, J Evans, Lewis, C Evans (Whyte 73), Davis, Saville, McGinn (Jones 82) (Washington 120+1), McNair (Thompson 90+3) (Boyce 120+1), Magennis (Lafferty 90+3). **Booked:** Davis

Penalty shoot-out: Bosnia-Herzegovina – scored: Pjanic, Hotic, Dzeko; missed: Hajradinovic, Visca. **Northern Ireland** – scored: Dallas, Lafferty, Washington, Boyce; missed: Saville
Referee: Antonio Mateu (Spain): **Half-time:** 1-0

SCOTLAND 0 ISRAEL 0 – aet, Scotland won 5-3 on pens
Hampden Park, October 8, 2020

Scotland (3-5-2): Marshall, McTominay, Gallagher, Cooper, O'Donnell (McLean 113), Jack (Fraser 83), McGregor, Robertson, McGinn, Dykes (Paterson 91), McBurnie (Shankland 72). **Booked:** McGinn, Fraser, Paterson

Israel (5-3-2): Marciano, Dasa, Bitton, Tibi, Yeina, Elhamed, Golasa (Elmkies 100), Natcho (Abu Fani 68), Solomon, Dabbour (Weissman 83), Zahavi. **Booked:** Natcho, Bitton, Weissman

Penalty shoot-out: Scotland – scored: McGinn, McGregor, McTominay, Shankland, McLean.
Israel – scored: Bitton, Weissman, Abu Fani; missed: Zahavi. **Referee:** Ovidiu Hategan (Romania)

SLOVAKIA 0 REPUBLIC OF IRELAND 0 – aet, Slovakia won 4-2 on pens
Bratislava; October 8, 2020

Slovakia (4-3-3): Rodak, Pekarik, Vavro (Gyomber 112), Valjent, Mazan, Kucka (Gregus 85), Hrosovsky, Hamsik, Rusnak (Mak 85), Duda (Bozenik 107) Mihalik (Haraslin 73). **Booked:** Duda, Hamsik

Republic of Ireland (4-3-3): Randolph, Doherty, Duffy, Egan, Stevens, Hendrick, McCarthy (Browne 60), Hourihane, Robinson (O'Dowda 100), McGoldrick (S Long 112), McClean (Brady 60). **Booked:** Hourihane, McClean, Duffy

Penalty shoot-out: Slovakia – scored: Hamsik, Hrosovsky, Haraslin, Gregus. **Republic of Ireland** – scored: Hourihane, Brady; missed: Browne, Doherty
Referee: Clement Turpin (France)

Other results: Bulgaria 1 Hungary 3; Georgia 1 Belarus 0; Iceland 2 Romania 1; North Macedonia 2 Kosovo 1; Norway 1 Serbia 2 (aet)

FINALS (one leg)

SERBIA 1 (Jovic 90) SCOTLAND 1 (Christie 51) – aet, Scotland won 5-4 on pens
Belgrade; November 12, 2020

Serbia (3-4-2-1): Rajkovic, Milenkovic, S Mitrovic (Spajic 108), Gudelj, Lazovic, Maksimovic (Jovic 70), Lukic, Kostic (Mladenovic 59), Tadic, Milinkovic-Savic (Katai 71), A Mitrovic. **Booked:** Milenkovic, Gudelj

Scotland (3-4-1-2): Marshall, McTominay, Gallagher, Tierney, O'Donnell (Griffiths 116), Jack, McGregor, Robertson, McGinn (McLean 82), Dykes (McBurnie 82), Christie (Paterson 87). **Booked:** Gallagher

Penalty shoot-out: Serbia – scored: Tadic, Jovic, Gudelj, Katai; missed: A Mitrovic. **Scotland** – scored: Griffiths, McGregor, McTominay, McBurnie, McLean
Referee: Antonio Mateu (Spain). **Half-time:** 0-0

NORTHERN IRELAND 1 (Skriniar 87 og) SLOVAKIA 2 (Kucka 17, Duris 110) – aet
Windsor Park; November 12, 2020
Northern Ireland (4-4-2): Peacock-Farrell, Dallas, Cathcart (Flanagan 99), J Evans, Lewis, McGinn (Lafferty 77), McNair (Ferguson 104), Davis, Saville (Thompson 66), Magennis (Boyce 77), Washington (Whyte 66). **Booked:** Boyce
Slovakia (4-1-4-1): Rodak, Pekarik, Satka, Skriniar, Hubocan, Lobotka (Hrosovsky 65), Rusnak (Gyomber 118), Kucka, Hamsik (Gregus 105), Mak (Duris 65), Duda (Mraz 85). **Booked:** Duda, Rodak
Referee: Felix Brych (Germany). **Half-time:** 0-1
Other results: Georgia 0 North Macedonia 1 (Pandev 56); Hungary 2 (Nego 88, Szoboszial 90) Iceland 1 (G Sigurdsson 11)

UEFA NATIONS LEAGUE 2021

LEAGUE A – GROUP 2

ICELAND 0 ENGLAND 1 (Sterling 90+1 pen)
Reykjavik; September 5, 2020
Iceland (4-5-1): Halldorsson, Hermannsson, Arnason, Ingason, Magnusson, Palsson, Traustason (Hallfredsson 76), Bjarnason, Bodvarsson (Fridjonsson 90), Thorsteinsson (Sigurdsson 66), Gudmundsson. **Booked:** Ingason. **Sent off:** Ingason (89)
England (4-3-3): Pickford, Walker, Gomez, Dier, Trippier, Ward-Prowse, Rice, *Foden (Ings 68), Sterling, Kane (*Greenwood 78), Sancho (Alexander-Arnold 73). **Booked:** Walker, Gomez.
Sent off: Walker (70)
Referee: Srdjan Jovanovic (Serbia). **Half-time:** 0-0

DENMARK 0 ENGLAND 0
Copenhagen; September 8, 2020
Denmark (4-3-3): Schmeichel, Wass, Jorgensen, Christensen, Skov, Norgaard (Hojbjerg 73), Eriksen, Delaney, Poulsen, Dolberg (Jensen 76), Braithwaite (Kjaer 82). **Booked:** Braithwaite
England (3-4-3): Pickford, Gomez, *Coady, Dier, Alexander-Arnold (*Maitland-Niles 87), Rice, *Phillips (*Grealish 76), Trippier, Sancho (Mount 60), Kane, Sterling
Referee: Istvan Kovacs (Romania)

ENGLAND 2 (Rashford 39 pen, Mount 64) BELGIUM 1 (Lukaku 16 pen)
Wembley; October 11, 2020
England (3-4-3): Pickford, Walker, Dier, Maguire, Alexander-Arnold (James 79), J Henderson (Phillips 66), Rice, Trippier, Mount (Sancho 89), Calvert-Lewin (Kane 66), Rashford. **Booked:** Rice
Belgium (3-4-3): Mignolet, Alderweireld, Boyata, Denayer, Meunier, Tielemans, Witsel, Castagne, De Bruyne (Verschaeren 73), Lukaku, Carrasco (Doku 83). **Booked:** Meunier
Referee: Tobias Stieler (Germany). **Half-time:** 1-1

ENGLAND 0 DENMARK 1 (Eriksen 35 pen)
Wembley; October 14, 2020
England (3-4-3): Pickford, Walker, Coady, Maguire, James, Phillips, Rice (J Henderson 76), Maitland-Niles (Mings 36), Mount (Sancho 73), Kane, Rashford (Calvert-Lewin 73). **Booked:** Maguire, Henderson, Phillips. **Sent off:** Maguire (31), James (90+4)
Denmark (4-2-3-1): Schmeichel, Wass, Kjaer, Christensen (Jorgensen 46), Skov (Maehle 46), Eriksen, Hojbjerg (Jensen 88), Delaney, Poulsen, Dolberg (Sisto 37), Braithwaite (Vestergaard 73). **Booked:** Christensen, Hojbjerg
Referee: Jesus Gil Mazano (Spain). **Half-time:** 0-1

BELGIUM 2 (Tielemans 10, Mertens 23) ENGLAND 0
Heverlee; November 15, 2020
Belgium (3-4-3): Courtois, Alderweireld, Denayer, Vertonghen, Meunier, Witsel, Tielemans, T

Hazard, De Bruyne, Lukaku, Mertens (Praet 83). **Booked**: Witsel, Alderweireld, Meunier
England (3-4-3): Pickford, Walker, Dier, Mings, Trippier (Sancho 70), J Henderson (Winks 46),
Rice, Chilwell (Saka 38), Mount (Calvert-Lewin 69), Kane, Grealish
Referee: Danny Makkelie (Holland). **Half-time**: 2-0

ENGLAND 4 (Rice 20, Mount 24, Foden 80, 84) ICELAND 0
Wembley; November 18, 2020

England (3-4-3): Pickford, Walker (Mings 64), Dier, Maguire, Trippier (Maitland-Niles 85), Rice,
Mount (Winks 64), Saka, Foden, Kane (Abraham 76), Grealish (Sancho 70). **Booked**: Walker
Iceland (5-3-2): Kristinsson (Halldorsson 46), Saevarsson, Ingason, Arnason, Hermannsson,
Skulason, Palsson, Bjarnason (Johannesson 88), Sigurjonsson (Eyjolfsson 62), Gudmundsson
(Thorsteinsson 73), Bodvarsson (Sigthorsson 73). **Booked**: Saevarsson, Ingason, Arnason. **Sent
off**: Saevarsson (54)
Referee: Fabio Verissimo (Portugal). **Half-time**: 2-0

LEAGUE B – GROUP 1

ROMANIA 1 (Puscas 25) NORTHERN IRELAND 1 (Whyte 86)
Bucharest; September 4, 2020

Romania (4-3-1-2): Tatarusanu, Hanca (Nedelcearu 86), Chiriches, Tosca, Bancu, Stanciu,
Cicaldau (Nistor 74), Maxim, Hagi (Cretu 56), Alibec, Puscas. **Booked**: Hagi, Nistor
Northern Ireland (4-4-1-1): Peacock-Farrell, Dallas, *Ballard (Smith 90+1), Cathcart, Lewis,
Magennis, C Evans (Lafferty 77), Davis, Saville, McNair, Washington (Whyte 65). **Booked**:
Magennis, C Evans. **Sent off**: Magennis (39)
(Ian Baraclough's first match as Northern Ireland manager)
Referee: Francois Letexier (France). **Half-time**: 1-0

NORTHERN IRELAND 1 (McNair 6) NORWAY 5 (Elyounoussi 2, Haaland 7, 58, Sorloth 19, 47)
Windsor Park; September 7, 2020

Northern Ireland (3-5-1-1): Peacock-Farrell, Smith, Ballard (Boyce 46), Cathcart, Dallas,
Davis, Saville (C Evans 71), Thompson, Ferguson, McNair, Washington (Lavery 77). **Booked**:
Ballard, Cathcart
Norway (4-4-2): Jarstein, Elabdellaoui (Svensson 80), Hovland, Ajer, Aleesami (Meling 77),
Johansen (King 71), Henriksen, Normann, Elyounoussi, Sorloth, Haaland. **Booked**: Meling
Referee: Bartosz Frankowski (Poland). **Half-time**: 1-3

NORTHERN IRELAND 0 AUSTRIA 1 (Gregoritsch 42)
Windsor Park; October 11, 2020

Northern Ireland (4-2-3-1): McGovern, C McLaughlin, Cathcart, J Evans, Lewis, Dallas
(Thompson 73), Davis (C Evans 73), Whyte (Boyce 83), McNair (Magennis 83), Jones,
Lafferty (Washington 61). **Booked**: C McLaughlin, Thompson
Austria (4-2-3-1): Pervan, Lainer, Dragovic, Hinteregger, Alaba, Ranftl (Trimmel 73), Ilsanker,
Baumgartlinger, Baumgartner, Gregoritsch (Grbic 80), Schlager. **Booked**: Schlager
Referee: Petr Ardeleanu (Czech Republic). **Half-time**: 0-1

NORWAY 1 (Dallas 67 og) NORTHERN IRELAND 0
Oslo; October 14, 2020

Norway (4-4-2): Hansen, Elabdellaoui, Strandberg, Ajer, Meling, Odegaard (Linnes 78), Berge,
Normann (Midtsjo 65), Elyounoussi, King (Sorloth 65), Haaland (Henriksen 87). **Booked**:
King, Elyounoussi
Northern Ireland (3-5-2): Carson, Smith (Dallas 60), Ballard, J Evans (C McLaughlin
46), Flanagan, Ferguson, Thompson (Davis 85), C Evans, Saville (McNair 61), Magennis,
Washington (Whyte 75)
Referee: Kristo Tohver (Estonia). **Half-time**: 0-0

AUSTRIA 2 (Schaub 81, Grbic 87) NORTHERN IRELAND 1 (Magennis 74)
Vienna; November 15, 2020

Austria (4-2-3-1): Pervan, Lainer, Dragovic (Ranftl 46), Hinteregger, Ulmer (Grbic 87), Baumgartlinger (Schaub 78), Ilsanker, Schlager, Sabitzer, Alaba, Gregoritsch (Arnautovic 63). **Booked**: Dragovic, Sabitzer
Northern Ireland (3-5-2): McGovern, Ballard (Cathcart 83), C McLaughlin, Flanagan, Dallas, Smith, McNair, McCann (Davis 83), Ferguson (Lewis 36), Boyce (Whyte 63), Washington (Magennis 62). **Booked**: Boyce, McGovern
Referee: Maurizio Mariani (Italy). **Half-time**: 0-0

NORTHERN IRELAND 1 (Boyce 56) ROMANIA 1 (Bicfalvi 81)
Windsor Park; November 18, 2020

Northern Ireland (3-5-2): Peacock-Farrell, Ballard, J Evans, Cathcart, Dallas, McNair, Smith (Galbraith 79), McCann, *Kennedy (Lewis 66), Magennis (C McLaughlin 79), Boyce (Washington 67)
Romania (3-4-3): Tatarusanu, Nedelcearu, Cristea, Tosca (Bicfalvi 74), Cretu (Mogos 64), Nistor, Marin, Camora, Man (Maxim 64), Alibec (Baluta 87), Tanase (Ganea 87)
Referee: Sandro Scharer (Switzerland). **Half-time**: 0-0

LEAGUE B – GROUP 2

SCOTLAND 1 (Christie 45 pen) ISRAEL 1 (Zahavi 73)
Hampden Park; September 4, 2020

Scotland (3-5-2): Marshall, McTominay, McKenna, Tierney, Forrest, Jack, McGregor, McGinn (Armstrong 79), Robertson, *Dykes (Burke 74), Christie. **Booked**: Forrest
Israel (5-3-2): Marciano, Dasa, Bitton, Tibi, Elhamed, Tawatha, Dor Peretz (Cohen 72), Natcho, Solomon (Glazer 90), Zahavi, Dabour (Weissman 79). **Booked**: Dor Peretz
Referee: Slavko Vincic (Slovenia). **Half-time**: 1-0

CZECH REPUBLIC 1 (Pesek 11) SCOTLAND 2 (Dykes 27, Christie 52 pen)
Olomouc; September 7, 2020

Czech Republic (4-2-3-1): Mandous, Holes, Hubnik, Jemelka, Zeleny, Janos, Havlik (Rusek 81), Malinski, Budinsky (Breite 55), Pesek (Potocny 76), Tecl. **Booked**: Malinsky, Janos
Scotland (3-5-2): Marshall, McTominay, McKenna, Cooper, Palmer, McLean, Armstrong (McGregor 80), Fleck (McGinn 71), Robertson, Dykes (Paterson 67), Christie. **Booked**: Armstrong, Robertson, McKenna, Palmer
Referee: Serdar Gozubuyuk (Holland). **Half-time**: 1-1

SCOTLAND 1 (Dykes 54) SLOVAKIA 0
Hampden Park; October 11, 2020

Scotland (3-5-2): Marshall, McTominay, Gallagher, *Considine, O'Donnell, Fleck (McGregor 72), McGinn (Jack 87), McLean, Robertson, Dykes (McBurnie 72), Fraser (Paterson 85). **Booked**: Dykes, Fleck, Robertson, McBurnie
Slovakia (4-3-3): Kuciak, Koscelnik. Ninaj, Valjent, Holubek, Bero (Duda 22), Gregus, Hamsik (Kucka 62), Schranz (Mak 62), Bozenik (Safranko 76), Haraslin (Rusnak 76). **Booked**: Hamsik, Haraslin, Kucka
Referee: Davide Massa (Italy). **Half-time**: 0-0

SCOTLAND 1 (Fraser 6) CZECH REPUBLIC 0
Hampden Park; October 14, 2020

Scotland (3-5-2): Marshall, McTominay, Gallagher, Considine, O'Donnell, Jack, McGregor, Taylor (*Hanlon 79), McGinn (Paterson 79), Dykes (McBurnie 65), Fraser (McLean 70). **Booked**: Dykes, Marshall
Czech Republic (4-2-3-1): Vaclik, Coufal, Celustka (Hovorka 20), Kudela, Boril, Soucek, Kral (Kaderabek 77), Masopust (Poznar 65), Darida, Provod, Vydra (Rabusic 77). **Booked**: Boril
Referee: Felix Zwayer (Germany). **Half-time**: 1-0

SLOVAKIA 1 (Gregus 31) SCOTLAND 0
Trnava; November 15, 2020

Slovakia (4-1-4-1): Rodak, Pekarik, Satka, Skriniar, Mazan, Hrosovsky, Duris (Safranko 90+4), Kucka (Lobotka 61), Hamsik (Rusnak 68), Gregus, Duda. **Booked**: Kucka, Pekarik, Skriniar, Duda, Mazan, Rusnak

Scotland (3-4-1-2: Gordon, Considine (Griffiths 68), McKenna, Cooper, Palmer, McGinn, McLean, Tierney, Armstrong (Shankland 87), Christie. McBurnie. **Booked**: Armstrong, McGinn, Christie

Referee: Istvan Kovacs (Romania). **Half-time**: 1-0

ISRAEL 1 (Solomon 44) SCOTLAND 0
Netanya; November 18, 2020

Israel (5-3-2): Marciano, Dasa, Bitton, Tibi, Yeini (Dgani 78), Menachem, Natcho (Golasa 62) Lavi (Abu Fani 78), Solomon (Cohen 84), Weissman, Zahavi. **Booked**: Abu Fani, Marciano, Dgani

Scotland (3-4-1-2): Marshall, McTominay, Gallagher (McKenna 73), Tierney, O'Donnell (Burke 73), Jack, McGregor (McLean 82), Robertson, McGinn (Griffiths 61), Dykes (McBurnie 61), Christie. **Booked**: Jack, Robertson

Referee: Pawel Raczkowski (Poland). **Half-time**: 1-0

LEAGUE B – GROUP 4

BULGARIA 1 (Kraev 56) REPUBLIC OF IRELAND 1 (Duffy 90+3)
Sofia; September 3, 2020

Bulgaria (4-2-3-1): Georgiev, Popov, Dimitrov, Zanev (Galabov 79), Nedyalkov, Malinov, Kostadinov, Delev (Karagaren 76), Nedelev (Tsvetkov 83), Ivanov, Kraev

Republic of Ireland (4-3-3): Randolph, Doherty, Duffy, Egan, Stevens, Hendrick, McCarthy (Brady 70), Hourihane, O'Dowda (Robinson 74), Idah (S Long 77), Connolly. **Booked**: Stevens (Stephen Kenny's first match as Republic of Ireland manager) **Half-time**: 0-0

Referee: Manuel Schuttengruber (Austria). **Half-time**: 0-0

FINLAND 0 WALES 1 (Moore 80)
Helsinki; September 3, 2020

Finland (3-5-2): Hradecky, Vaisanen, Ojala, O'Shaughnessy, Niskanen (Soiri 86), Kamara, Sparv (Lam 76), Kauko (Jensen 70), Uronen, Pukki, Pohjanpalo. **Booked**: Spav, Pukki, Vaisanen

Wales (4-2-3-1): Hennessey, C Roberts, Lockyer, Ampadu, B Davies, *Levitt, Morrell, Bale (Wilson 46), J Williams (*N Williams 60), James (*Cabango (90+1), Moore. **Booked**: Morrell, C Roberts, Wilson, Moore

Referee: Daniel Siebert (Germany). **Half-time**: 0-0

REPUBLIC OF IRELAND 0 FINLAND 1 (Jensen 63)
Aviva Stadium, September 6, 2020

Republic of Ireland (4-3-3): Randolph, Doherty, Duffy, Egan, Stevens, *Molumby, Arter, Brady, O'Dowda (Robinson 59), Idah (McGoldrick 66), Connolly (McClean 77). **Booked**: Molumby, Arter

Finland (5-3-2): Hradecky, Alho, Vaisanen, Ojala, O'Shaughnessy, Hamalainen (Uronen 79), Kamara, Sparv, Taylor, Pukki (Karjalainen 90+1), Pohjanpalo (Jensen 63). **Booked**: O'Shaughnessy

Referee: Fabio Maresca (Italy). **Half-time**: 0-0

WALES 1 (N Williams 90+5) BULGARIA 0
Cardiff City Stadium; September 6, 2020

Wales (4-2-3-1): Hennessey, C Roberts (N Williams 65), Lockyer, Ampadu, B Davies, Smith, Morrell, Bale, Brooks (J Williams 76), James, Moore (Robson-Kanu 61). **Booked**: Smith, N Williams

Bulgaria (4-2-3-1): Georgiev, Cicinho, Dimitrov, Nedyalkov, Goranov, Kostadinov, Karabelyov, Karagaren, Nedelev (Krastev 82), Ivanov (Delev 70), Kraev (Iliev 61). **Booked**: Kostadinov
Referee: Fabio Verissimo (Portugal). **Half-time**: 0-0

REPUBLIC OF IRELAND 0 WALES 0
Aviva Stadium; October 11, 2020
Republic of Ireland (4-2-3-1): Randolph, Doherty, Duffy, K Long (Christie 25), Stevens, Molumby (Cullen 90), Hourihane, Brady (Horgan 73), Hendrick, McClean, S Long (Maguire 74). **Booked**: Christie, McClean. **Sent off**: McClean (83)
Wales (4-2-3-1): Hennessey, C Roberts, Ampadu, Rodon, B Davies, Morrell, Smith (Levitt 67), Wilson (N Williams 67), Ramsey, James (Brooks 77), Moore. **Booked**: Moore, Morrell
Referee: Anastasios Sidiropoulos (Greece)

BULGARIA 0 WALES 1 (J Williams 85)
Sofia; October 14, 2020
Bulgaria (4-2-3-1): Mihaylov, Cicinho, Terzeiv, Dimitrov, Nedyalkov, Malinov (Tsvetkov 46), Nedelev, Despodov (Karagaren 83), Karabelyov, Yomov, Kraev (Isa 75). **Booked**: Cicinho, Karabelyov, Dimitrov
Wales (5-3-2): Hennessey (A Davies 80), *Norrington-Davies, B Davies, Rodon, Mepham, N Williams, Ampadu, Smith (Levitt 72), Wilson (J Williams 72), James, T Roberts. **Booked**: B Davies, Wilson, James, J Williams
Referee: Oliyar Agayev (Azerbaijan). **Half-time**: 0-0

FINLAND 1 (Jensen 66) REPUBLIC OF IRELAND 0
Helsinki; October 14, 2020
Finland (4-4-2): Hradecky, Granlund (Raitala 86), Toivio, Arajuuri, Uronen, Soiri (Niskanen 46), Kamara (Schuller 75), Sparv, Taylor, Jensen (Kauko 86), Pukki (Pohjanpalo 81). **Booked**: Jensen
Republic of Ireland (4-2-3-1): Randolph, Doherty, Duffy, *O'Shea, Stevens, Molumby, Hourihane, Horgan (Curtis 75), Hendrick (Idah 75), Connolly, Maguire (Brady 53). **Booked**: Connolly
Referee: Lionel Tschudi (Switzerland). **Half-time**: 0-0

WALES 1 (Brooks 66) REPUBLIC OF IRELAND 0
Cardiff City Stadium; November 15, 2020
Wales (3-4-3): Ward, Mepham, Rodon, Davies, N Williams, Ampadu, Morrell, Norrington-Davies (Moore 62), Bale, Brooks (T Roberts 88), James. **Booked**: Morrell, Davies, Moore
Republic of Ireland (4-1-4-1): Randolph, Doherty, Duffy, K Long, O'Shea (O'Dowda 81), Hendrick, Horgan (Knight 59), Molumby (Hourihane 76), Brady (Byrne 75), McClean, Idah. **Booked**: Molumby, Hendrick, Knight, Duffy. **Sent off**: Hendrick (90+4)
Referee: Petr Ardeleanu (Czech Republic). **Half-time**: 0-0

WALES 3 (Wilson 29, James 46, Moore 84) FINLAND 1 (Pukki 63)
Cardiff City Stadium; November 18, 2020
Wales (3-4-3): Ward, Mepham, Rodon, J Lawrence (Moore 46), C Roberts, Ampadu, Morrell, Norrington-Davies (Gunter 90+3), Bale (T Lawrence 63), James (T Roberts 89), Wilson (Brooks 89). **Booked**: Ampadu
Finland: Hradecky, Toivio, Arajuuri, O'Shaughnessy, Alho, Schuller (Valakari 73), Taylor, Kamara, Uronen, Pukki (Forss 89), Lod. **Sent off**: Uronen (12)
Referee: Jesus Gil (Spain). **Half-time**: 1-0

REPUBLIC OF IRELAND 0 BULGARIA 0
Aviva Stadium; November 18, 2020
Republic of Ireland (4-3-3): Randolph, O'Shea, Duffy, K Long, *Manning (Christie 86), Knight, Brady (Byrne 78), Hourihane, Curtis (Parrott 86), Collins (Maguire 86), Horgan (Cullen 67). **Booked**: K Long, Manning

Bulgaria (4-2-3-1): Lukov, Popov, Dimitrov, Angelov, Cicinho (Vasilev 60), Malinov, Tsvertkov, Delev (Kovachev 60), Iliev (Aleksandrov 81), Ivanov (Karagaren 60), Kraev. **Booked**: Cicinho, Ivanov. **Referee**: Lawrence Visser (Belgium)

FRIENDLY INTERNATIONALS

ENGLAND 3 (Calvert-Lewin 26, Coady 53, Ings 63) WALES 0
Wembley; October 8, 2020

England (3-4-3): Pope, Gomez (Mings 58), Coady, Keane, Trippier (*James 58), Phillips, Winks (Ward-Prowse 76), *Saka (Maitland-Niles 76), Grealish (*Barnes 76), *Calvert-Lewin (Mount 58), Ings

Wales (4-2-3-1): Hennessey, C Roberts (Gunter 73), Rodon (Cabango 46), Mepham, B Davies, Ampadu (Vaulks 62), Morrell (Levitt 46), T Roberts, J Williams (Smith 73), Matondo, Moore (N Williams 40). **Booked**: C Roberts, Ampadu, Levitt

Referee: Bobby Madden (Scotland). **Half-time**: 1-0

ENGLAND 3 (Maguire 18, Sancho 31, Calvert-Lewin 56 pen) REPUBLIC OF IRELAND 0
Wembley; November 12, 2020

England (3-4-3): Pope (*D Henderson 46), Keane, Maguire, Mings (Maitland-Niles 61), James, Mount (*Bellingham 73), Winks, Saka, Sancho, Calvert-Lewin (Abraham 63), Grealish (Foden 61)

Republic of Ireland (4-2-3-1): Randolph, Christie (K Long 61), Duffy, Egan (O'Shea 14), Doherty, Hendrick, Hourihane (Molumby 71), Horgan (Brady 61), Browne, O'Dowda (McClean 61), Idah (Curtis 71)

Referee: Carlos Del Cerro Grande (Spain). **Half-time**: 2-0

WALES 0 USA 0
Liberty Stadium, Swansea; November 12, 2020

Wales (4-2-3-1): Ward, Gunter, J Lawrence, Lockyer, C Roberts, Levitt (Morrell 80), Smith (*Sheehan 46), Matondo (James 62), Wilson, T Lawrence (Rodon 69), Moore (*Johnson 62)

USA (4-3-3): Steffen, Dest (Cannon 87), Miazga, Brooks, Robinson, Musah (Gioacchini 78), Adams (Cardoso 71), McKennie, Reyna (Weah 78), Lletget (Otasowie 87), De La Fuente (Llanez 71)

Referee: Nick Walsh (Scotland)

WALES 1 (Moore 11) MEXICO 0
Cardiff City Stadium; March 27, 2021

Wales (3-4-2-1): Hennessey, Gunter, Cabango, Norrington-Davies, J Williams (C Roberts 86), Levitt (Sheehan 46), Smith, T Lawrence (N Williams), T Roberts (Johnson 65), Matondo (Bale 81), Moore (Robson-Kanu 46)
(Chris Gunter's 100th cap for Wales)

Mexico (4-2-3-1): Ochoa, Rodriguez (Pizarro 61), Gallardo (Arteaga 79), Salcedo, Montes, Herrera, Alvarez (Lainez 83), Corona, Pineda (Dos Santos 78), Guardado (Sanchez 62), Lozano

Referee: Ian McNabb (Northern Ireland). **Half-time**: 1-0

NORTHERN IRELAND 1 (McGinn 88) USA 2 (Reyna 30, Pulisic 60 pen)
Windsor Park; March 28, 2021

Northern Ireland (3-5-2): Hazard, Ballard (Smith 79), C McLaughlin, Brown, Kennedy (McGinn 67), Thompson, Saville (McCann 60), C Evans (McNair 60), Ferguson (Lewis 60), Lafferty, Lavery (*Charles 60). **Booked**: Saville

USA (3-4-3): Steffen, Long (Richards 63), Miazga, Ream, Dest (Reynolds 46), Acosta (De la Torres 74), Musah (Lletget 46), Robinson, Reyna (Aaronson 63), Siebatcheu, Pulisic

Referee: Rob Jenkins (Wales). **Half-time**: 0-1

QATAR 1 (Muntari 47) REPUBLIC OF IRELAND 1 (McClean 4)
Debrecen (Hungary); March 30, 2021

Qatar (3-5-2): Al Sheeb, Hisham, Khoukhi, Salman, Pedro, Al Heidos (Al Hajri 90+4), Boudiaf, Hatem (Abdulsalam 82), Hassan, Muntari (Youssef 90+1), Ali
Republic of Ireland (3-4-3): Bazunu, Coleman, Duffy, O'Shea, Christie, Molumby (Cullen 83), Hendrick (Browne 83), McClean (Manning 83), Brady (Parrott 21), S Long (Robinson 57), Horgan (Knight 57). **Booked:** Bazunu, Knight
Referee: Balazs Berke (Hungary). **Half-time:** 0-1

MALTA 0 NORTHERN IRELAND 3 (Jones 2, Whyte 53, McCann 55)
Klagenfurt, Austria; May 30, 2021

Malta (3-4-3): Bonello, Apap (Borg 70), Agius, Shaw, Mbong (Xuereb 70), Kristensen (Muscat 82), Teuma (Vella 61), Camenzuli, Satariano (Farrugia 82), Dimech, Montebello (Degabriele 61). **Booked:** Teuma
Northern Ireland (3-5-2): Peacock-Farrell, McNair, Cathcart, Brown, McGinn, McCann (Saville 62), Dallas (*Bradley 86), Thompson (McCalmont 85), Whyte (Ferguson 75), Jones (Boyce 73), Magennis (Charles 62). **Booked:** Thompson
Referee: Sebastian Gishamer (Austria). **Half-time:** 0-1

ENGLAND 1 (Saka 56) AUSTRIA 0
Riverside Stadium, Middlesbrough (7,000); June 2, 2021

England (4-3-1-2): Pickford, Alexander-Arnold, Coady, Mings (Godfrey 62), Trippier, Bellingham, Rice (Ward-Prowse 61), Saka, Grealish (White 71), Lingard (Watkins 61), Kane (Calvert-Lewin 61). **Booked:** Calvert-Lewin, Alexander-Arnold
Austria (4-4-2): Bachmann, Lainer (Trimmel 81), Hinteregger, Dragovic, Friedl, Laimer (Grillitsch 62), Schlager (Baumgartlinger 81), Baumgartner (Schaub 62), Alaba (Schopf 72), Kalajdzic (Gregoritsch 71), Sabitzer. **Booked:** Schlager, Lainer, Hinteregger
Referee: Lawrence Visser (Belgium). **Half-time:** 0-0

HOLLAND 2 (Depay 17, 89) SCOTLAND 2 (Hendry 10, Nisbet 63)
Algarve, Portugal; June 2, 2021

Holland (3-5-2): Krul, Timber (Berghuis 69), De Vrij (L De Jong 85), De Ligt, Dumfries, Wijnaldum (Gravenberch 31), De Roon, F De Jong (Klaassen 31), Wijndal (Van Aanholt 69), Weghorst (Promes 69), Depay. **Booked:** De Ligt
Scotland (3-5-2): Gordon, Hendry, Cooper (Gallagher 60), Tierney (McKenna 69), Forrest (Fraser 60), *Turnbull (*Gilmour 81), McGregor, Armstrong, Robertson (Taylor 69), Christie, Dykes (Nisbet 60)
Referee: Vitor Ferreira (Portugal). **Half-time:** 1-1

FRANCE 3 (Mbappe 34, Griezmann 47, Dembele 79) WALES 0
Nice; June 2, 2021

France (4-1-2-1-2): Lloris, Pavard (Kounde 36), Varane, Kimpembe, Hernandez (Digne 46), Tolisso (Sissoko 64), Pogba (Coman 63), Rabiot, Griezmann (Ben Yedder 84), Benzema, Mbappe (Dembele 73)
Wales (3-4-3): Ward, Mepham (B Davies 59), Rodon, Gunter, C Roberts, Morrell (*Colwill 83), Allen (Levitt 59), N Williams (Moore 59), Bale (Moore 59), Wilson (Ramsey 59), James (Brooks 73). **Booked:** Moore. **Sent off:** N Williams (25)
Referee: Luis Godinho (Portugal). **Half-time:** 1-0

UKRAINE 1 (Zubkov 10) NORTHERN IRELAND 0
Dnipro (15,000); June 3, 2021

Ukraine (4-1-4-1): Bushchan, Karavaev, Zabarnyi, Matvienko, Mykolenko, Sydorchuk (Stepanenko 75), Yarmolenko, Malinovskyi, Shaparenko (Sudakov 72), Zubkov (Marlos 46), Yaremchuk (Besedin 46). **Booked:** Besedin

Northern Ireland (4-4-2): Peacock-Farrell, Ballard, Cathcart, Brown (*McClelland 89), Ferguson (Smyth 46), Dallas (Charles 89), McNair, McCann (Whyte 86), Saville, Magennis (Lafferty 61), McGinn (Thompson 46). **Booked:** McNair
Referee: Szymon Marciniak (Poland). **Half-time:** 1-0

ANDORRA 1 (Vales 52) REPUBLIC OF IRELAND 4 (Parrott 58, 61, Knight 84, Horgan 88)
La Valle; June 3, 2021
Andorra (4-4-2): Iker (Pires 76), San Nicolas, Llovera, Vales, Cervos, Clemente (Martinez 59), Rebes (Garcia 72), Vieira, Martinez (Lima 76), Fernandez (Sanchez 59), Alaez
Republic of Ireland (4-4-2): Bazunu, Doherty, O'Shea (Duffy 86), Egan, McClean (Manning 86), Cullen, Hourihane (Arter 86), Knight, Parrott (*McGrath 82), Curtis (Horgan 66), Collins (Idah 66)
Referee: Javier Estrada (Spain). **Half-time:** 0-0

WALES 0 ALBANIA 0
Cardiff City Stadium (6,500); June 5, 2021
Wales (3-5-2): Hennessey, Ampadu (Moore 46), Mepham, B Davies (Rodon 61), N Williams, Allen (Smith 61), Ramsey (Wilson 61), Levitt, Norrington -Davies, Brooks (J Williams 76), T Roberts (Bale 71). **Booked:** Brooks, Norrington-Davies, Mepham
Albania (3-5-2): Selmani, Ismajli, Kumbulla, Djimsiti, Doka (Veseli 46), Bare (Laci 76), Abrashi, Cekici (Kallaku 76), Lenjani (Trashi 61), Manaj (Sulejmanov 77), Balaj (Cikalleshi (60). **Booked:** Ismajli, Manaj, Abrashi
Referee: Neil Doyle (Republic of Ireland)

ENGLAND 1 (Rashford 68 pen) ROMANIA 0
Riverside Stadium, Middlesbrough; June 6, 2021
England (4-2-3-1): *Johnstone, Godfrey, White, Mings, Shaw (Tripper 75), Ward-Prowse (Rice 65), Phillips (Henderson 46), Sancho (Bellingham 65), Grealish, Rashford (Lingard 75), Calvert-Lewin (Watkins 82)
Romania (4-1-4-1): Nita, Sorescu (Capusa 66), Chiriches, Nedelcearu (Rus 84), Malino Paulinho, Marin, Ivan, Stanciu, Cicaldau (Budescu 80), Paun (Baluta 80), Alibec (Hagi 66). **Booked:** Ivan
Referee: Tiago Martins (Portugal). **Half-time:** 0-0

LUXEMBOURG 0 SCOTLAND 1 (Adams 27)
Josy Barthel; June 6, 2021
Luxembourg (5-3-2): Moris, Jans, Mahmutovic, Selimovic, Carlson, Pinto, Sinani (O Thill 71), Skenderovic (Alves de Mota 84), S Thill (Martins 84), Deville (Bohnert 64), Rodrigues.
Booked: Rodrigues, O Thill. **Sent off:** Selinovic (34)
Scotland (3-5-2): Marshall, Hanley, Gallagher (McKenna 46), Tierney, O'Donnell (*Patterson 64), McGregor (Gilmour 46, Forrest 76), McTominay, McGinn, Robertson (Fraser 64), Adams, Dykes (Nisbet 82)
Referee: Eldorjan Hamiti (Albania). **Half-time:** 0-1

HUNGARY 0 REPUBLIC OF IRELAND 0
Budapest (7,000); June 8, 2021
Hungary (3-5-2): Gulacsi (Bogdan 63), Kecskes, Orban, Attila Szalai, Bolla (Lovrencsics 46), Kleinheisler (Nego 63), Nagy, Schafer, Fiola (Hahn 79), Adam Szalai (Schon 88), R Varga (K Varga 46). **Booked:** Attila Szalai
Republic of Ireland (3-4-1-2): Bazunu (*Kelleher 46), Duffy, Egan, O'Shea, Doherty, Cullen, Hourihane (Molumby 56), McClean (Manning 84), Knight (*Ogbene 89), Parrott (Horgan 56), Idah (Collins 89)
Referee: Daniel Stefanski (Poland)

OTHER BRITISH & IRISH INTERNATIONAL RESULTS

ENGLAND

v ALBANIA
1989	Tirana (WC)	2	0
1989	Wembley (WC)	5	0
2001	Tirana (WC)	3	1
2001	Newcastle (WC)	2	0
2021	Tirana (WC)	2	0

v ALGERIA
2010	Cape Town (WC)	0	0

v ANDORRA
2006	Old Trafford (EC)	5	0
2007	Barcelona (EC)	3	0
2008	Barcelona (WC)	2	0
2009	Wembley (WC)	6	0

v ARGENTINA
1951	Wembley	2	1
1953*	Buenos Aires	0	0
1962	Rancagua (WC)	3	1
1964	Rio de Janeiro	0	1
1966	Wembley (WC)	1	0
1974	Wembley	2	2
1977	Buenos Aires	1	1
1980	Wembley	3	1
1986	Mexico City (WC)	1	2
1991	Wembley	2	2
1998†	St Etienne (WC)	2	2
2000	Wembley	0	0
2002	Sapporo (WC)	1	0
2005	Geneva	3	2

(*Abandoned after 21 mins – rain)
(† England lost 3-4 on pens)

v AUSTRALIA
1980	Sydney	2	1
1983	Sydney	0	0
1983	Brisbane	1	0
1983	Melbourne	1	1
1991	Sydney	1	0
2003	West Ham	1	3
2016	Sunderland	2	1

v AUSTRIA
1908	Vienna	6	1
1908	Vienna	11	1
1909	Vienna	8	1
1930	Vienna	0	0
1932	Stamford Bridge	4	3
1936	Vienna	1	2
1951	Wembley	2	2
1952	Vienna	3	2
1958	Boras (WC)	2	2
1961	Vienna	1	3
1962	Wembley	3	1
1965	Wembley	2	3
1967	Vienna	1	0
1973	Wembley	7	0
1979	Vienna	3	4
2004	Vienna (WC)	2	2
2005	Old Trafford (WC)	1	0
2007	Vienna	1	0
2021	Middlesbrough	1	0

v AZERBAIJAN
2004	Baku (WC)	1	0
2005	Newcastle (WC)	2	0

v BELARUS
2008	Minsk (WC)	3	1
2009	Wembley (WC)	3	0

v BELGIUM
1921	Brussels	2	0
1923	Highbury	6	1
1923	Antwerp	2	2
1924	West Bromwich	4	0
1926	Antwerp	5	3
1927	Brussels	9	1
1928	Antwerp	3	1
1929	Brussels	5	1
1931	Brussels	4	1
1936	Brussels	2	3
1947	Brussels	5	2
1950	Brussels	4	1
1952	Wembley	5	0
1954	Basle (WC)	4	4
1964	Wembley	2	2
1970	Brussels	3	1
1980	Turin (EC)	1	1
1990	Bologna (WC)	1	0
1998*	Casablanca	0	0
1999	Sunderland	2	1
2012	Wembley	1	0
2018	Kaliningrad (WC)	0	1
2018	St Petersburg (WC)	0	2
2020	Wembley (NL)	2	1
2020	Leuven (NL)	0	2

(*England lost 3-4 on pens)

v BOHEMIA

Year	Venue		
1908	Prague	4	0

v BRAZIL

Year	Venue		
1956	Wembley	4	2
1958	Gothenburg (WC)	0	0
1959	Rio de Janeiro	0	2
1962	Vina del Mar (WC)	1	3
1963	Wembley	1	1
1964	Rio de Janeiro	1	5
1969	Rio de Janeiro	1	2
1970	Guadalajara (WC)	0	1
1976	Los Angeles	0	1
1977	Rio de Janeiro	0	0
1978	Wembley	1	1
1981	Wembley	0	1
1984	Rio de Janeiro	2	0
1987	Wembley	1	1
1990	Wembley	1	0
1992	Wembley	1	1
1993	Washington	1	1
1995	Wembley	1	3
1997	Paris (TF)	0	1
2000	Wembley	1	1
2002	Shizuoka (WC)	1	2
2007	Wembley	1	1
2009	Doha	0	1
2013	Wembley	2	1
2013	Rio de Janeiro	2	2
2017	Wembley	0	0

v BULGARIA

Year	Venue		
1962	Rancagua (WC)	0	0
1968	Wembley	1	1
1974	Sofia	1	0
1979	Sofia (EC)	3	0
1979	Wembley (EC)	2	0
1996	Wembley	1	0
1998	Wembley (EC)	0	0
1999	Sofia (EC)	1	1
2010	Wembley (EC)	4	0
2011	Sofia (EC)	3	0
2019	Wembley (EC)	4	0
2019	Sofia (EC)	6	0

v CAMEROON

Year	Venue		
1990	Naples (WC)	3	2
1991	Wembley	2	0
1997	Wembley	2	0
2002	Kobe (Japan)	2	2

v CANADA

Year	Venue		
1986	Vancouver	1	0

v CHILE

Year	Venue		
1950	Rio de Janeiro (WC)	2	0
1953	Santiago	2	1
1984	Santiago	0	0
1989	Wembley	0	0
1998	Wembley	0	2
2013	Wembley	0	2

v CHINA

Year	Venue		
1996	Beijing	3	0

v CIS
(formerly Soviet Union)

Year	Venue		
1992	Moscow	2	2

v COLOMBIA

Year	Venue		
1970	Bogota	4	0
1988	Wembley	1	1
1995	Wembley	0	0
1998	Lens (WC)	2	0
2005	New York	3	2
2018+	Moscow (WC)	1	1

(† England won 4-3 on pens)

v COSTA RICA

Year	Venue		
2014	Belo Horizonte (WC)	0	0
2018	Leeds	2	0

v CROATIA

Year	Venue		
1995	Wembley	0	0
2003	Ipswich	3	1
2004	Lisbon (EC)	4	2
2006	Zagreb (EC)	0	2
2007	Wembley (EC)	2	3
2008	Zagreb (WC)	4	1
2009	Wembley (WC)	5	1
2018	Moscow (WC)	1	2
2018	Rijeka (NL)	0	0
2018	Wembley (NL)	2	1
2021	Wembley (EC)	1	0

v CYPRUS

Year	Venue		
1975	Wembley (EC)	5	0
1975	Limassol (EC)	1	0

v CZECH REPUBLIC

Year	Venue		
1998	Wembley	2	0
2008	Wembley	2	2
2019	Wembley (EC)	5	0
2019	Prague (EC)	1	2
2021	Wembley (EC)	1	0

v CZECHOSLOVAKIA

Year	Venue		
1934	Prague	1	2
1937	White Hart Lane	5	4

1963	Bratislava	4	2
1966	Wembley	0	0
1970	Guadalajara (WC)	1	0
1973	Prague	1	1
1974	Wembley (EC)	3	0
1975*	Bratislava (EC)	1	2
1978	Wembley (EC)	1	0
1982	Bilbao (WC)	2	0
1990	Wembley	4	2
1992	Prague	2	2

(* Aband 0-0, 17 mins prev day – fog)

v DENMARK

1948	Copenhagen	0	0
1955	Copenhagen	5	1
1956	W'hampton (WC)	5	2
1957	Copenhagen (WC)	4	1
1966	Copenhagen	2	0
1978	Copenhagen (EC)	4	3
1979	Wembley (EC)	1	0
1982	Copenhagen (EC)	2	2
1983	Wembley (EC)	0	1
1988	Wembley	1	0
1989	Copenhagen	1	1
1990	Wembley	1	0
1992	Malmo (EC)	0	0
1994	Wembley	1	0
2002	Niigata (WC)	3	0
2003	Old Trafford	2	3
2005	Copenhagen	1	4
2011	Copenhagen	2	1
2014	Wembley	1	0
2020	Copenhagen (NL)	0	0
2020	Wembley (NL)	0	1
2021	Wembley (EC)	2	1

v EAST GERMANY

1963	Leipzig	2	1
1970	Wembley	3	1
1974	Leipzig	1	1
1984	Wembley	1	0

v ECUADOR

1970	Quito	2	0
2006	Stuttgart (WC)	1	0
2014	Miami	2	2

v EGYPT

1986	Cairo	4	0
1990	Cagliari (WC)	1	0
2010	Wembley	3	1

v ESTONIA

2007	Tallinn (EC)	3	0

2007	Wembley (EC)	3	0
2014	Tallinn (EC)	1	0
2015	Wembley (EC)	2	0

v FIFA

1938	Highbury	3	0
1953	Wembley	4	4
1963	Wembley	2	1

v FINLAND

1937	Helsinki	8	0
1956	Helsinki	5	1
1966	Helsinki	3	0
1976	Helsinki (WC)	4	1
1976	Wembley (WC)	2	1
1982	Helsinki	4	1
1984	Wembley (WC)	5	0
1985	Helsinki (WC)	1	1
1992	Helsinki	2	1
2000	Helsinki (WC)	0	0
2001	Liverpool (WC)	2	1

v FRANCE

1923	Paris	4	1
1924	Paris	3	1
1925	Paris	3	2
1927	Paris	6	0
1928	Paris	5	1
1929	Paris	4	1
1931	Paris	2	5
1933	White Hart Lane	4	1
1938	Paris	4	2
1947	Highbury	3	0
1949	Paris	3	1
1951	Highbury	2	2
1955	Paris	0	1
1957	Wembley	4	0
1962	Hillsborough (EC)	1	1
1963	Paris (EC)	2	5
1966	Wembley (WC)	2	0
1969	Wembley	5	0
1982	Bilbao (WC)	3	1
1984	Paris	0	2
1992	Wembley	2	0
1992	Malmo (EC)	0	0
1997	Montpellier (TF)	1	0
1999	Wembley	0	2
2000	Paris	1	1
2004	Lisbon (EC)	1	2
2008	Paris	0	1
2010	Wembley	1	2
2012	Donetsk (EC)	1	1
2015	Wembley	2	0
2017	Paris	2	3

v GEORGIA

1996	Tbilisi (WC)	2	0
1997	Wembley (WC)	2	0

v GERMANY/WEST GERMANY

1930	Berlin	3	3
1935	White Hart Lane	3	0
1938	Berlin	6	3
1954	Wembley	3	1
1956	Berlin	3	1
1965	Nuremberg	1	0
1966	Wembley	1	0
1966	Wembley (WCF)	4	2
1968	Hanover	0	1
1970	Leon (WC)	2	3
1972	Wembley (EC)	1	3
1972	Berlin (EC)	0	0
1975	Wembley	2	0
1978	Munich	1	2
1982	Madrid (WC)	0	0
1982	Wembley	1	2
1985	Mexico City	3	0
1987	Dusseldorf	1	3
1990*	Turin (WC)	1	1
1991	Wembley	0	1
1993	Detroit	1	2
1996†	Wembley (EC)	1	1
2000	Charleroi (EC)	1	0
2000	Wembley (WC)	0	1
2001	Munich (WC)	5	1
2007	Wembley	1	2
2008	Berlin	2	1
2010	Bloemfontein (WC)	1	4
2012	Donetsk (EC)	1	1
2013	Wembley	0	1
2016	Berlin	3	2
2017	Dortmund	0	1
2017	Wembley	0	0
2021	Wembley	2	0
(*England lost 3-4 on pens)			
(† England lost 5-6 on pens)			

v GHANA

2011	Wembley	1	1

v GREECE

1971	Wembley (EC)	3	0
1971	Athens (EC)	2	0
1982	Salonika (EC)	3	0
1983	Wembley (EC)	0	0
1989	Athens	2	1
1994	Wembley	5	0
2001	Athens (WC)	2	0
2001	Old Trafford (WC)	2	2
2006	Old Trafford	4	0

v HOLLAND

1935	Amsterdam	1	0
1946	Huddersfield	8	2
1964	Amsterdam	1	1
1969	Amsterdam	1	0
1970	Wembley	0	0
1977	Wembley	0	2
1982	Wembley	2	0
1988	Wembley	2	2
1988	Dusseldorf (EC)	1	3
1990	Cagliari (WC)	0	0
1993	Wembley (WC)	2	2
1993	Rotterdam (WC)	0	2
1996	Wembley (EC)	4	1
2001	White Hart Lane	0	2
2002	Amsterdam	1	1
2005	Villa Park	0	0
2006	Amsterdam	1	1
2009	Amsterdam	2	2
2012	Wembley	2	3
2016	Wembley	1	2
2018	Amsterdam	1	0
2019	Guimaraes (NL)	1	3

v HONDURAS

2014	Miami	0	0

v HUNGARY

1908	Budapest	7	0
1909	Budapest	4	2
1909	Budapest	8	2
1934	Budapest	1	2
1936	Highbury	6	2
1953	Wembley	3	6
1954	Budapest	1	7
1960	Budapest	0	2
1962	Rancagua (WC)	1	2
1965	Wembley	1	0
1978	Wembley	4	1
1981	Budapest (WC)	3	1
1981	Wembley (WC)	1	0
1983	Wembley (EC)	2	0
1983	Budapest (EC)	3	0
1988	Budapest	0	0
1990	Wembley	1	0
1992	Budapest	1	0
1996	Wembley	3	0
1999	Budapest	1	1
2006	Old Trafford	3	1
2010	Wembley	2	1

v ICELAND

1982	Reykjavik	1	1
2004	City of Manchester	6	1

2016	Nice (EC)	1	2
2020	Reykjavik (NL)	1	0
2020	Wembley (NL)	4	0

v ISRAEL
1986	Tel Aviv	2	1
1988	Tel Aviv	0	0
2006	Tel Aviv (EC)	0	0
2007	Wembley (EC)	3	0

v ITALY
1933	Rome	1	1
1934	Highbury	3	2
1939	Milan	2	2
1948	Turin	4	0
1949	White Hart Lane	2	0
1952	Florence	1	1
1959	Wembley	2	2
1961	Rome	3	2
1973	Turin	0	2
1973	Wembley	0	1
1976	New York	3	2
1976	Rome (WC)	0	2
1977	Wembley (WC)	2	0
1980	Turin (EC)	0	1
1985	Mexico City	1	2
1989	Wembley	0	0
1990	Bari (WC)	1	2
1996	Wembley (WC)	0	1
1997	Nantes (TF)	2	0
1997	Rome (WC)	0	0
2000	Turin	0	1
2002	Leeds	1	2
2012*	Kiev (EC)	0	0
2012	Berne	2	1
2014	Manaus (WC)	1	2
2015	Turin	1	1
2018	Wembley	1	1
2021**	Wembley (EC)	1	1

(*England lost 2-4 on pens)
(*England lost 2-3 on pens)

v JAMAICA
| 2006 | Old Trafford | 6 | 0 |

v JAPAN
1995	Wembley	2	1
2004	City of Manchester	1	1
2010	Graz	2	1

v KAZAKHSTAN
| 2008 | Wembley (WC) | 5 | 1 |
| 2009 | Almaty (WC) | 4 | 0 |

v KOSOVO
| 2019 | Southampton (EC) | 5 | 3 |

| 2019 | Pristina (EC) | 4 | 0 |

v KUWAIT
| 1982 | Bilbao (WC) | 1 | 0 |

v LIECHTENSTEIN
| 2003 | Vaduz (EC) | 2 | 0 |
| 2003 | Old Trafford (EC) | 2 | 0 |

v LITHUANIA
2015	Wembley (EC)	4	0
2015	Vilnius (EC)	3	0
2017	Wembley (WC)	2	0
2017	Vilnius (WC)	1	0

v LUXEMBOURG
1927	Luxembourg	5	2
1960	Luxembourg (WC)	9	0
1961	Highbury (WC)	4	1
1977	Wembley (WC)	5	0
1977	Luxembourg (WC)	2	0
1982	Wembley (EC)	9	0
1983	Luxembourg (EC)	4	0
1998	Luxembourg (EC)	3	0
1999	Wembley (EC)	6	0

v MACEDONIA
2002	Southampton (EC)	2	2
2003	Skopje (EC)	2	1
2006	Skopje (EC)	1	0
2006	Old Trafford (EC)	0	0

v MALAYSIA
| 1991 | Kuala Lumpur | 4 | 2 |

v MALTA
1971	Valletta (EC)	1	0
1971	Wembley (EC)	5	0
2000	Valletta	2	1
2016	Wembley (WC)	2	0
2017	Ta'Qali (WC)	4	0

v MEXICO
1959	Mexico City	1	2
1961	Wembley	8	0
1966	Wembley (WC)	2	0
1969	Mexico City	0	0
1985	Mexico City	0	1
1986	Los Angeles	3	0
1997	Wembley	2	0
2001	Derby	4	0
2010	Wembley	3	1

v MOLDOVA
| 1996 | Kishinev | 3 | 0 |

1997	Wembley (WC)	4	0
2012	Chisinu (WC)	5	0
2013	Wembley (WC)	4	0

v MONTENEGRO

2010	Wembley (EC)	0	0
2011	Podgorica (EC)	2	2
2013	Podgorica (WC)	1	1
2013	Wembley (WC)	4	1
2019	Podgorica (EC)	5	1
2019	Wembley (EC)	7	0
(England's 1,000th international)

v MOROCCO

| 1986 | Monterrey (WC) | 0 | 0 |
| 1998 | Casablanca | 1 | 0 |

v NEW ZEALAND

| 1991 | Auckland | 1 | 0 |
| 1991 | Wellington | 2 | 0 |

v NIGERIA

1994	Wembley	1	0
2002	Osaka (WC)	0	0
2018	Wembley	2	1

v NORWAY

1937	Oslo	6	0
1938	Newcastle	4	0
1949	Oslo	4	1
1966	Oslo	6	1
1980	Wembley (WC)	4	0
1981	Oslo (WC)	1	2
1992	Wembley (WC)	1	1
1993	Oslo (WC)	0	2
1994	Wembley	0	0
1995	Oslo	0	0
2012	Oslo	1	0
2014	Wembley	1	0

v PANAMA

| 2018 | Nizhny Novgorod (WC) | 6 | 1 |

v PARAGUAY

1986	Mexico City (WC)	3	0
2002	Anfield	4	0
2006	Frankfurt (WC)	1	0

v PERU

1959	Lima	1	4
1961	Lima	4	0
2014	Wembley	3	0

v POLAND

1966	Goodison Park	1	1
1966	Chorzow	1	0
1973	Chorzow (WC)	0	2
1973	Wembley (WC)	1	1
1986	Monterrey (WC)	3	0
1989	Wembley (WC)	3	0
1989	Katowice (WC)	0	0
1990	Wembley (EC)	2	0
1991	Poznan (EC)	1	1
1993	Chorzow (WC)	1	1
1993	Wembley (WC)	3	0
1996	Wembley (WC)	2	1
1997	Katowice (WC)	2	0
1999	Wembley (EC)	3	1
1999	Warsaw (EC)	0	0
2004	Katowice (WC)	2	1
2005	Old Trafford (WC)	2	1
2012	Warsaw (WC)	1	1
2013	Wembley (WC)	2	0
2021	Wembley (WC)	2	1

v PORTUGAL

1947	Lisbon	10	0
1950	Lisbon	5	3
1951	Goodison Park	5	2
1955	Oporto	1	3
1958	Wembley	2	1
1961	Lisbon (WC)	1	1
1961	Wembley (WC)	2	0
1964	Lisbon	4	3
1964	Sao Paulo	1	1
1966	Wembley (WC)	2	1
1969	Wembley	1	0
1974	Lisbon	0	0
1974	Wembley (EC)	0	0
1975	Lisbon (EC)	1	1
1986	Monterrey (WC)	0	1
1995	Wembley	1	1
1998	Wembley	3	0
2000	Eindhoven (EC)	2	3
2002	Villa Park	1	1
2004	Faro	1	1
2004*	Lisbon (EC)	2	2
2006†	Gelsenkirchen (WC)	0	0
2016	Wembley	1	0
(† England lost 1–3 on pens)
(*England lost 5–6 on pens)

v REPUBLIC OF IRELAND

1946	Dublin	1	0
1949	Goodison Park	0	2
1957	Wembley (WC)	5	1
1957	Dublin (WC)	1	1

1964	Dublin	3	1
1977	Wembley	1	1
1978	Dublin (EC)	1	1
1980	Wembley (EC)	2	0
1985	Wembley	2	1
1988	Stuttgart (EC)	0	1
1990	Cagliari (WC)	1	1
1990	Dublin (EC)	1	1
1991	Wembley (EC)	1	1
1995*	Dublin	0	1
2013	Wembley	1	1
2015	Dublin	0	0
2020	Wembley	3	0

(*Abandoned 27 mins – crowd riot)

v ROMANIA

1939	Bucharest	2	0
1968	Bucharest	0	0
1969	Wembley	1	1
1970	Guadalajara (WC)	1	0
1980	Bucharest (WC)	1	2
1981	Wembley (WC)	0	0
1985	Bucharest (WC)	0	0
1985	Wembley (WC)	1	1
1994	Wembley	1	1
1998	Toulouse (WC)	1	2
2000	Charleroi (EC)	2	3
2021	Middlesbrough	1	0

v RUSSIA

2007	Wembley (EC)	3	0
2007	Moscow (EC)	1	2
2016	Marseille (EC)	1	1

v SAN MARINO

1992	Wembley (WC)	6	0
1993	Bologna (WC)	7	1
2012	Wembley (WC)	5	0
2013	Serravalle (WC)	8	0
2014	Wembley (EC)	5	0
2015	Serravalle (EC)	6	0
2021	Wembley (WC)	5	0

v SAUDI ARABIA

1988	Riyadh	1	1
1998	Wembley	0	0

v SERBIA-MONTENEGRO

2003	Leicester	2	1

v SLOVAKIA

2002	Bratislava (EC)	2	1
2003	Middlesbrough (EC)	2	1

2009	Wembley	4	0
2016	St Etienne (EC)	0	0
2016	Trnava (WC)	1	0
2017	Wembley (WC)	2	1

v SLOVENIA

2009	Wembley	2	1
2010	Port Elizabeth (WC)	1	0
2014	Wembley (EC)	3	1
2015	Ljubljana (EC)	3	2
2016	Ljubljana (WC)	0	0
2017	Wembley (WC)	1	0

v SOUTH AFRICA

1997	Old Trafford	2	1
2003	Durban	2	1

v SOUTH KOREA

2002	Seoguipo	1	1

v SOVIET UNION (see also CIS)

1958	Moscow	1	1
1958	Gothenburg (WC)	2	2
1958	Gothenburg (WC)	0	1
1958	Wembley	5	0
1967	Wembley	2	2
1968	Rome (EC)	2	0
1973	Moscow	2	1
1984	Wembley	0	2
1986	Tbilisi	1	0
1988	Frankfurt (EC)	1	3
1991	Wembley	3	1

v SPAIN

1929	Madrid	3	4
1931	Highbury	7	1
1950	Rio de Janeiro (WC)	0	1
1955	Madrid	1	1
1955	Wembley	4	1
1960	Madrid	0	3
1960	Wembley	4	2
1965	Madrid	2	0
1967	Wembley	2	0
1968	Wembley (EC)	1	0
1968	Madrid (EC)	2	1
1980	Barcelona	2	0
1980	Naples (EC)	2	1
1981	Wembley	1	2
1982	Madrid (WC)	0	0
1987	Madrid	4	2
1992	Santander	0	1
1996*	Wembley (EC)	0	0
2001	Villa Park	3	0

2004	Madrid	0	1
2007	Old Trafford	0	1
2009	Seville	0	2
2011	Wembley	1	0
2015	Alicante	0	2
2016	Wembley	2	2
(*England won 4-2 on pens)			
2018	Wembley (NL)	1	2
2018	Seville (NL)	3	2

v SWEDEN

1923	Stockholm	4	2
1923	Stockholm	3	1
1937	Stockholm	4	0
1948	Highbury	4	2
1949	Stockholm	1	3
1956	Stockholm	0	0
1959	Wembley	2	3
1965	Gothenburg	2	1
1968	Wembley	3	1
1979	Stockholm	0	0
1986	Stockholm	0	1
1988	Wembley (WC)	0	0
1989	Stockholm (WC)	0	0
1992	Stockholm (EC)	1	2
1995	Leeds	3	3
1998	Stockholm (EC)	1	2
1999	Wembley (EC)	0	0
2001	Old Trafford	1	1
2002	Saitama (WC)	1	1
2004	Gothenburg	0	1
2006	Cologne (WC)	2	2
2011	Wembley	1	0
2012	Kiev (EC)	3	2
2012	Stockholm	2	4
2018	Samara (WC)	2	0

v SWITZERLAND

1933	Berne	4	0
1938	Zurich	1	2
1947	Zurich	0	1
1949	Highbury	6	0
1952	Zurich	3	0
1954	Berne (WC)	2	0
1962	Wembley	3	1
1963	Basle	8	1
1971	Basle (EC)	3	2
1971	Wembley (EC)	1	1
1975	Basle	2	1
1977	Wembley	0	0
1980	Wembley (WC)	2	1
1981	Basle (WC)	1	2
1988	Lausanne	1	0
1995	Wembley	3	1

1996	Wembley (EC)	1	1
1998	Berne	1	1
2004	Coimbra (EC)	3	0
2008	Wembley	2	1
2010	Basle (EC)	3	1
2011	Wembley (EC)	2	2
2014	Basle (EC)	2	0
2015	Wembley (EC)	2	0
2018	Leicester	1	0
2019*	Guimaraes (NL)	0	0
(* England won 6-5 on pens)			

v TRINIDAD & TOBAGO

2006	Nuremberg (WC)	2	0
2008	Port of Spain	3	0

v TUNISIA

1990	Tunis	1	1
1998	Marseille (WC)	2	0
2018	Volgograd (WC)	2	1

v TURKEY

1984	Istanbul (WC)	8	0
1985	Wembley (WC)	5	0
1987	Izmir (EC)	0	0
1987	Wembley (EC)	8	0
1991	Izmir (EC)	1	0
1991	Wembley (EC)	1	0
1992	Wembley (WC)	4	0
1993	Izmir (WC)	2	0
2003	Sunderland (EC)	2	0
2003	Istanbul (EC)	0	0
2016	Etihad Stadium	2	1

v UKRAINE

2000	Wembley	2	0
2004	Newcastle	3	0
2009	Wembley (WC)	2	1
2009	Dnipropetrovski (WC)	0	1
2012	Donetsk (EC)	1	0
2012	Wembley (WC)	1	1
2013	Kiev (EC)	0	0
2012	Rome (EC)	4	0

v URUGUAY

1953	Montevideo	1	2
1954	Basle (WC)	2	4
1964	Wembley	2	1
1966	Wembley (WC)	0	0
1969	Montevideo	2	1
1977	Montevideo	0	0
1984	Montevideo	0	2
1990	Wembley	1	2
1995	Wembley	0	0

2006	Anfield	2	1
2014	Sao Paulo (WC)	1	2

v USA

1950	Belo Horizonte (WC)	0	1
1953	New York	6	3
1959	Los Angeles	8	1
1964	New York	10	0
1985	Los Angeles	5	0
1993	Boston	0	2
1994	Wembley	2	0
2005	Chicago	2	1
2008	Wembley	2	0
2010	Rustenburg (WC)	1	1
2018	Wembley	3	0

v YUGOSLAVIA

1939	Belgrade	1	2
1950	Highbury	2	2
1954	Belgrade	0	1
1956	Wembley	3	0
1958	Belgrade	0	5
1960	Wembley	3	3
1965	Belgrade	1	1
1966	Wembley	2	0
1968	Florence (EC)	0	1
1972	Wembley	1	1
1974	Belgrade	2	2
1986	Wembley (EC)	2	0
1987	Belgrade (EC)	4	1
1989	Wembley	2	1

ENGLAND'S RECORD England's first international was a 0-0 draw against Scotland in Glasgow, on the West of Scotland cricket ground, Partick, on November 30, 1872 The 1,000th was a 7-0 win over Montenegro at Wembley on November 14, 2019. Their complete record at the start of 2020–21 is:

P	W	D	L	F	A
1021	585	245	191	2234	990

ENGLAND B

1937	Stockholm	4	0
1948	Highbury	4	2
1949	Stockholm	1	3
1956	Stockholm	0	0
1959	Wembley	2	3
1965	Gothenburg	2	1
1968	Wembley	3	1
1979	Stockholm	0	0
1986	Stockholm	0	1
1988	Wembley (WC)	0	0
1989	Stockholm (WC)	0	0
1992	Stockholm (EC)	1	2
1995	Leeds	3	3
1998	Stockholm (EC)	1	2
1999	Wembley (EC)	0	0
2001	Old Trafford	1	1
2002	Saitama (WC)	1	1
2004	Gothenburg	0	1
2006	Cologne (WC)	2	2
1949	Finland (A)	4	0
1949	Holland (A)	4	0
1950	Italy (A)	0	5
1950	Holland (H)	1	0
1950	Holland (A)	0	3
1950	Luxembourg (A)	2	1
1950	Switzerland (H)	5	0
1952	Holland (A)	1	0
1952	France (A)	1	7
1953	Scotland (A)	2	2
1954	Scotland (H)	1	1
1954	Germany (A)	4	0

1954	Yugoslavia (A)	1	2
1954	Switzerland (A)	0	2
1955	Germany (H)	1	1
1955	Yugoslavia (H)	5	1
1956	Switzerland (H)	4	1
1956	Scotland (A)	2	2
1957	Scotland (H)	4	1
1978	W Germany (A)	2	1
1978	Czechoslovakia (A)	1	0
1978	Singapore (A)	8	0
1978	Malaysia (A)	1	1
1978	N Zealand (A)	4	0
1978	N Zealand (A)	3	1
1978	N Zealand (A)	4	0
1979	Austria (A)	1	0
1979	N Zealand (H)	4	1
1980	USA (H)	1	0
1980	Spain (A)	1	0
1980	Australia (H)	1	0
1981	Spain (A)	2	3
1984	N Zealand (H)	2	0
1987	Malta (A)	2	0
1989	Switzerland (A)	2	0
1989	Iceland (A) .	2	0
1989	Norway (A)	1	0
1989	Italy (H)	1	1
1989	Yugoslavia (H)	2	1
1990	Rep of Ireland (A)	1	4
1990	Czechoslovakia (H)	2	0
1990	Algeria (A)	0	0
1991	Wales (A)	1	0
1991	Iceland (H)	1	0
1991	Switzerland (H)	2	1
1991	Spanish XI (A)	1	0

1992	France (H)	3	0
1992	Czechoslovakia (A)	1	0
1992	CIS (A)	1	1
1994	N Ireland (H)	4	2
1995	Rep of Ireland (H)	2	0
1998	Chile (H)	1	2
1998	Russia (H)	4	1
2006	Belarus (H)	1	2
2007	Albania	3	1

GB v REST OF EUROPE

| 1947 | at Glsagow | 6-1 |
| 1955 | at Belfast | 1-4 |

SCOTLAND

v ALBANIA
| 2018 | Glasgow (NL) | 2 | 0 |
| 2018 | Shkoder (NL) | 4 | 0 |

v ARGENTINA
1977	Buenos Aires	1	1
1979	Glasgow	1	3
1990	Glasgow	1	0
2008	Glasgow	0	1

v AUSTRALIA
1985*	Glasgow (WC)	2	0
1985*	Melbourne (WC)	0	0
1996	Glasgow	1	0
2000	Glasgow	0	2
2012	Edinburgh	3	1
(* World Cup play-off)			

v AUSTRIA
1931	Vienna	0	5
1933	Glasgow	2	2
1937	Vienna	1	1
1950	Glasgow	0	1
1951	Vienna	0	4
1954	Zurich (WC)	0	1
1955	Vienna	4	1
1956	Glasgow	1	1
1960	Vienna	1	4
1963*	Glasgow	4	1
1968	Glasgow (WC)	2	1
1969	Vienna (WC)	0	2
1978	Vienna (EC)	2	3
1979	Glasgow (EC)	1	1
1994	Vienna	2	1
1996	Vienna (WC)	0	0
1997	Glasgow (WC)	2	0
(* Abandoned after 79 minutes)			
2003	Glasgow	0	2

2005	Graz	2	2
2007	Vienna	1	0
2021	Glasgow (WC)	2	2

v BELARUS
1997	Minsk (WC)	1	0
1997	Aberdeen (WC)	4	1
2005	Minsk (WC)	0	0
2005	Glasgow (WC)	0	1

v BELGIUM
1947	Brussels	1	2
1948	Glasgow	2	0
1951	Brussels	5	0
1971	Liege (EC)	0	3
1971	Aberdeen (EC)	1	0
1974	Brugge	1	2
1979	Brussels (EC)	0	2
1979	Glasgow (EC)	1	3
1982	Brussels (EC)	2	3
1983	Glasgow (EC)	1	1
1987	Brussels (EC)	1	4
1987	Glasgow (EC)	2	0
2001	Glasgow (WC)	2	2
2001	Brussels (WC)	0	2
2012	Brussels (WC)	0	2
2013	Glasgow (WC)	0	2
2018	Glasgow	0	4
2019	Brussels (EC)	0	3
2019	Glasgow (EC)	0	4

v BOSNIA
| 1999 | Sarajevo (EC) | 2 | 1 |
| 1999 | Glasgow (EC) | 1 | 0 |

v BRAZIL
1966	Glasgow	1	1
1972	Rio de Janeiro	0	1
1973	Glasgow	0	1
1974	Frankfurt (WC)	0	0
1977	Rio de Janeiro	0	2
1982	Seville (WC)	1	4
1987	Glasgow	0	2
1990	Turin (WC)	0	1
1998	St Denis (WC)	1	2
2011	Arsenal	0	2

v BULGARIA
1978	Glasgow	2	1
1986	Glasgow (EC)	0	0
1987	Sofia (EC)	1	0
1990	Sofia (EC)	1	1
1991	Glasgow (EC)	1	1
2006	Kobe	5	1

v CANADA
1983	Vancouver	2	0
1983	Edmonton	3	0
1983	Toronto	2	0
1992	Toronto	3	1
2002	Edinburgh	3	1
2017	Edinburgh	1	1

v CHILE
| 1977 | Santiago | 4 | 2 |
| 1989 | Glasgow | 2 | 0 |

v CIS (formerly Soviet Union)
| 1992 | Norrkoping (EC) | 3 | 0 |

v COLOMBIA
1988	Glasgow	0	0
1996	Miami	0	1
1998	New York	2	2

v COSTA RICA
| 1990 | Genoa (WC) | 0 | 1 |
| 2018 | Glasgow | 0 | 1 |

v CROATIA
2000	Zagreb (WC)	1	1
2001	Glasgow (WC)	0	0
2008	Glasgow	1	1
2013	Zagreb (WC)	1	0
2013	Glasgow (WC)	2	0
2021	Glasgow (EC)	1	3

v CYPRUS
1968	Nicosia (WC)	5	0
1969	Glasgow (WC)	8	0
1989	Limassol (WC)	3	2
1989	Glasgow (WC)	2	1
2011	Larnaca	2	1
2019	Glasgow (EC)	2	1
2019	Nicosia (EC)	2	1

v CZECH REPUBLIC
1999	Glasgow (EC)	1	2
1999	Prague (EC)	2	3
2008	Prague	1	3
2010	Glasgow	1	0
2010	Prague (EC)	0	1
2011	Glasgow (EC)	2	2
2016	Prague	1	0
2020	Olomouc (NL)	2	1
2020	Glasgow (NL)	1	0
2021	Glasgow (EC)	0	2

v CZECHOSLOVAKIA
| 1937 | Prague | 3 | 1 |
| 1937 | Glasgow | 5 | 0 |

1961	Bratislava (WC)	0	4
1961	Glasgow (WC)	3	2
1961*	Brussels (WC)	2	4
1972	Porto Alegre	0	0
1973	Glasgow (WC)	2	1
1973	Bratislava (WC)	0	1
1976	Prague (WC)	0	2
1977	Glasgow (WC)	3	1

(*World Cup play-off)

v DENMARK
1951	Glasgow	3	1
1952	Copenhagen	2	1
1968	Copenhagen	1	0
1970	Glasgow (EC)	1	0
1971	Copenhagen (EC)	0	1
1972	Copenhagen (WC)	4	1
1972	Glasgow (WC)	2	0
1975	Copenhagen (EC)	1	0
1975	Glasgow (EC)	3	1
1986	Neza (WC)	0	1
1996	Copenhagen	0	2
1998	Glasgow	0	1
2002	Glasgow	0	1
2004	Copenhagen	0	1
2011	Glasgow	2	1
2016	Glasgow	1	0

v EAST GERMANY
1974	Glasgow	3	0
1977	East Berlin	0	1
1982	Glasgow (EC)	2	0
1983	Halle (EC)	1	2
1986	Glasgow	0	0
1990	Glasgow	0	1

v ECUADOR
| 1995 | Toyama, Japan | 2 | 1 |

v EGYPT
| 1990 | Aberdeen | 1 | 3 |

v ESTONIA
1993	Tallinn (WC)	3	0
1993	Aberdeen	3	1
1996	Tallinn (WC)		

*No result

1997	Monaco (WC)	0	0
1997	Kilmarnock (WC)	2	0
1998	Edinburgh (EC)	3	2
1999	Tallinn (EC)	0	0

(* Estonia absent)

| 2004 | Tallinn | 1 | 0 |
| 2013 | Aberdeen | 1 | 0 |

v FAROE ISLANDS

1994	Glasgow (EC)	5	1
1995	Toftir (EC)	2	0
1998	Aberdeen (EC)	2	1
1999	Toftir (EC)	1	1
2002	Toftir (EC)	2	2
2003	Glasgow (EC)	3	1
2006	Glasgow (EC)	6	0
2007	Toftir (EC)	2	0
2010	Aberdeen	3	0
2021	Glasgow (WC)	4	0

v FINLAND

1954	Helsinki	2	1
1964	Glasgow (WC)	3	1
1965	Helsinki (WC)	2	1
1976	Glasgow	6	0
1992	Glasgow	1	1
1994	Helsinki (EC)	2	0
1995	Glasgow (EC)	1	0
1998	Edinburgh	1	1

v FRANCE

1930	Paris	2	0
1932	Paris	3	1
1948	Paris	0	3
1949	Glasgow	2	0
1950	Paris	1	0
1951	Glasgow	1	0
1958	Orebro (WC)	1	2
1984	Marseilles	0	2
1989	Glasgow (WC)	2	0
1990	Paris (WC)	0	3
1997	St Etienne	1	2
2000	Glasgow	0	2
2002	Paris	0	5
2006	Glasgow (EC)	1	0
2007	Paris (EC)	1	0
2016	Metz	0	3

v GEORGIA

2007	Glasgow (EC)	2	1
2007	Tbilisi (EC)	0	2
2014	Glasgow (EC)	1	0
2015	Tbilisi (EC)	0	1

v GERMANY/WEST GERMANY

1929	Berlin	1	1
1936	Glasgow	2	0
1957	Stuttgart	3	1
1959	Glasgow	3	2
1964	Hanover	2	2
1969	Glasgow (WC)	1	1
1969	Hamburg (WC)	2	3
1973	Glasgow	1	1
1974	Frankfurt	1	2
1986	Queretaro (WC)	1	2
1992	Norrkoping (EC)	0	2
1993	Glasgow	0	1
1999	Bremen	1	0
2003	Glasgow (EC)	1	1
2003	Dortmund (EC)	1	2
2014	Dortmund (EC)	1	2
2015	Glasgow (EC)	2	3

v GIBRALTAR

2015	Glasgow (EC)	6	1
2015	Faro (EC)	6	0

v GREECE

1994	Athens (EC)	0	1
1995	Glasgow	1	0

v HOLLAND

1929	Amsterdam	2	0
1938	Amsterdam	3	1
1959	Amsterdam	2	1
1966	Glasgow	0	3
1968	Amsterdam	0	0
1971	Amsterdam	1	2
1978	Mendoza (WC)	3	2
1982	Glasgow	2	1
1986	Eindhoven	0	0
1992	Gothenburg (EC)	0	1
1994	Glasgow	0	1
1994	Utrecht	1	3
1996	Birmingham (EC)	0	0
2000	Arnhem	0	0
2003*	Glasgow (EC)	1	0
2003*	Amsterdam (EC)	0	6
2009	Amsterdam (WC)	0	3
2009	Glasgow (WC)	0	1
2017	Aberdeen	0	1
2021	Algarve	2	2

(*Qual Round play-off)

v HUNGARY

1938	Glasgow	3	1
1955	Glasgow	2	4
1955	Budapest	1	3
1958	Glasgow	1	1
1960	Budapest	3	3
1980	Budapest	1	3
1987	Glasgow	2	0
2004	Glasgow	0	3
2018	Budapest	1	0

v ICELAND

1984	Glasgow (WC)	3	0
1985	Reykjavik (WC)	1	0
2002	Reykjavik (EC)	2	0

2003 Glasgow (EC) 2 1
2008 Reykjavik (WC) 2 1
2009 Glasgow (WC) 2 1

v IRAN
1978 Cordoba (WC) 1 1

v ISRAEL
1981 Tel Aviv (WC) 1 0
1981 Glasgow (WC) 3 1
1986 Tel Aviv 1 0
2018 Haifa (NL) 1 2
2018 Glasgow (NL) 3 2
2020 Glasgow (NL) 1 1
2020* Glasgow (EC) 0 0
2020 Netanya (NL) 0 1
2021 Tel Aviv (WC) 1 1
(*Scotland won 5-3 on pens)

v ITALY
1931 Rome 0 3
1965 Glasgow (WC) 1 0
1965 Naples (WC) 0 3
1988 Perugia 0 2
1992 Glasgow (WC) 0 0
1993 Rome (WC) 1 3
2005 Milan (WC) 0 2
2005 Glasgow (WC) 1 1
2007 Bari (EC) 0 2
2007 Glasgow (EC) 1 2
2016 Ta'Qali 0 1

v JAPAN
1995 Hiroshima 0 0
2006 Saitama 0 0
2009 Yokohama 0 2

v KAZAKHSTAN
2019 Astana (EC) 0 3
2019 Glasgow (EC) 3 1

v LATVIA
1996 Riga (WC) 2 0
1997 Glasgow (WC) 2 0
2000 Riga (WC) 1 0
2001 Glasgow (WC) 2 1

v LIECHTENSTEIN
2010 Glasgow (EC) 2 1
2011 Vaduz (EC) 1 0

v LITHUANIA
1998 Vilnius (EC) 0 0
1999 Glasgow (EC) 3 0
2003 Kaunus (EC) 0 1
2003 Glasgow (EC) 1 0
2006 Kaunas (EC) 2 1

2007 Glasgow (EC) 3 1
2010 Kaunas (EC) 0 0
2011 Glasgow (EC) 1 0
2016 Glasgow (WC) 1 1
2017 Vilnius (WC) 3 0

v LUXEMBOURG
1947 Luxembourg 6 0
1986 Glasgow (EC) 3 0
1987 Esch (EC) 0 0
2012 Josy Barthel 2 1
2021 Luxembourg 1 0

v MACEDONIA
2008 Skopje (WC) 0 1
2009 Glasgow (WC) 2 0
2012 Glasgow (WC) 1 1
2013 Skopje (WC) 2 1

v MALTA
1988 Valletta 1 1
1990 Valletta 2 1
1993 Glasgow (WC) 3 0
1993 Valletta (WC) 2 0
1997 Valletta 3 2
2016 Ta'Qali (WC) 5 1
2017 Glasgow (WC) 2 0

v MEXICO
2018 Mexico City 0 1

v MOLDOVA
2004 Chisinau (WC) 1 1
2005 Glasgow (WC) 2 0

v MOROCCO
1998 St Etienne (WC) 0 3

v NEW ZEALAND
1982 Malaga (WC) 5 2
2003 Edinburgh 1 1

v NIGERIA
2002 Aberdeen 1 2
2014 Fulham 2 2

v NORWAY
1929 Bergen 7 3
1954 Glasgow 1 0
1954 Oslo 1 1
1963 Bergen 3 4
1963 Glasgow 6 1
1974 Oslo 2 1
1978 Glasgow (EC) 3 2
1979 Oslo (EC) 4 0
1988 Oslo (WC) 2 1
1989 Glasgow (WC) 1 1

1992	Oslo	0	0
1998	Bordeaux (WC)	1	1
2003	Oslo	0	0
2004	Glasgow (WC)	0	1
2005	Oslo (WC)	2	1
2008	Glasgow (WC)	0	0
2009	Oslo (WC)	0	4
2013	Molde	1	0

v PARAGUAY
1958	Norrkoping (WC)	2	3

v PERU
1972	Glasgow	2	0
1978	Cordoba (WC)	1	3
1979	Glasgow	1	1
2018	Lima	0	2

v POLAND
1958	Warsaw	2	1
1960	Glasgow	2	3
1965	Chorzow (WC)	1	1
1965	Glasgow (WC)	1	2
1980	Poznan	0	1
1990	Glasgow	1	1
2001	Bydgoszcz	1	1
2014	Warsaw	1	0
2014	Warsaw (EC)	2	2
2015	Glasgow (EC)	2	2

v PORTUGAL
1950	Lisbon	2	2
1955	Glasgow	3	0
1959	Lisbon	0	1
1966	Glasgow	0	1
1971	Lisbon (EC)	0	2
1971	Glasgow (EC)	2	1
1975	Glasgow	1	0
1978	Lisbon (EC)	0	1
1980	Glasgow (EC)	4	1
1980	Glasgow (WC)	0	0
1981	Lisbon (WC)	1	2
1992	Glasgow (WC)	0	0
1993	Lisbon (WC)	0	5
2002	Braga	0	2
2018	Glasgow	1	3

v QATAR
2015	Edinburgh	1	0

v REPUBLIC OF IRELAND
1961	Glasgow (WC)	4	1
1961	Dublin (WC)	3	0
1963	Dublin	0	1
1969	Dublin	1	1
1986	Dublin (EC)	0	0

1987	Glasgow (EC)	0	1
2000	Dublin	2	1
2003	Glasgow (EC)	0	2
2011	Dublin (CC)	0	1
2014	Glasgow (EC)	1	0
2015	Dublin (EC)	1	1

v ROMANIA
1975	Bucharest (EC)	1	1
1975	Glasgow (EC)	1	1
1986	Glasgow	3	0
1990	Glasgow (EC)	2	1
1991	Bucharest (EC)	0	1
2004	Glasgow	1	2

v RUSSIA
1994	Glasgow (EC)	1	1
1995	Moscow (EC)	0	0
2019	Glasgow (EC)	1	2
2019	Moscow (EC)	0	4

v SAN MARINO
1991	Serravalle (EC)	2	0
1991	Glasgow (EC)	4	0
1995	Serravalle (EC)	2	0
1995	Glasgow (EC)	5	0
2000	Serravalle (WC)	2	0
2001	Glasgow (WC)	4	0
2019	Serravalle (EC)	2	0
2019	Glasgow (EC)	6	0

v SAUDI ARABIA
1988	Riyadh	2	2

v SERBIA
2012	Glasgow (WC)	0	0
2013	Novi Sad (WC)	0	2
2020*	Belgrade (EC)	1	1
(Scotland won 5-4 on pens)			

v SLOVAKIA
2016	Trnava (WC)	0	3
2017	Glasgow (WC)	1	0
2020	Glasgow (NL)	1	0
2020	Trnova (NL)	0	1

v SLOVENIA
2004	Glasgow (WC)	0	0
2005	Celje (WC)	3	0
2012	Koper	1	1
2017	Glasgow (WC)	1	0
2017	Ljubljana (WC)	2	2

v SOUTH AFRICA
2002	Hong Kong	0	2
2007	Aberdeen	1	0

v SOUTH KOREA

2002	Busan	1	4

v SOVIET UNION (see also CIS and RUSSIA)

1967	Glasgow	0	2
1971	Moscow	0	1
1982	Malaga (WC)	2	2
1991	Glasgow	0	1

v SPAIN

1957	Glasgow (WC)	4	2
1957	Madrid (WC)	1	4
1963	Madrid	6	2
1965	Glasgow	0	0
1975	Glasgow (EC)	1	2
1975	Valencia (EC)	1	1
1982	Valencia	0	3
1985	Glasgow (WC)	3	1
1985	Seville (WC)	0	1
1988	Madrid	0	0
2004*	Valencia	1	1

(*Abandoned after 59 mins – floodlight failure)

2010	Glasgow (EC)	2	3
2011	Alicante (EC)	1	3

v SWEDEN

1952	Stockholm	1	3
1953	Glasgow	1	2
1975	Gothenburg	1	1
1977	Glasgow	3	1
1980	Stockholm (WC)	1	0
1981	Glasgow (WC)	2	0
1990	Genoa (WC)	2	1
1995	Solna	0	2
1996	Glasgow (WC)	1	0
1997	Gothenburg (WC)	1	2
2004	Edinburgh	1	4
2010	Stockholm	0	3

v SWITZERLAND

1931	Geneva	3	2
1948	Berne	1	2
1950	Glasgow	3	1
1957	Basle (WC)	2	1
1957	Glasgow (WC)	3	2
1973	Berne	0	1
1976	Glasgow	1	0
1982	Berne (EC)	0	2
1983	Glasgow (EC)	2	2
1990	Glasgow (EC)	2	1
1991	Berne (EC)	2	2
1992	Berne (WC)	1	3
1993	Aberdeen (WC)	1	1
1996	Birmingham (EC)	1	0

2006	Glasgow	1	3

v TRINIDAD & TOBAGO

2004	Hibernian	4	1

v TURKEY

1960	Ankara	2	4

v UKRAINE

2006	Kiev (EC)	0	2
2007	Glasgow (EC)	3	1

v USA

1952	Glasgow	6	0
1992	Denver	1	0
1996	New Britain, Conn	1	2
1998	Washington	0	0
2005	Glasgow	1	1
2012	Jacksonville	1	5
2013	Glasgow	0	0

v URUGUAY

1954	Basle (WC)	0	7
1962	Glasgow	2	3
1983	Glasgow	2	0
1986	Neza (WC)	0	0

v YUGOSLAVIA

1955	Belgrade	2	2
1956	Glasgow	2	0
1958	Vaasteras (WC)	1	1
1972	Belo Horizonte	2	2
1974	Frankfurt (WC)	1	1
1984	Glasgow	6	1
1988	Glasgow (WC)	1	1
1989	Zagreb (WC)	1	3

v ZAIRE

1974	Dortmund (WC)	2	0

WALES

v ALBANIA

1994	Cardiff (EC)	2	0
1995	Tirana (EC)	1	1
2018	Elbasan	0	1
2021	Cardiff	0	0

v ANDORRA

2014	La Vella (EC)	2	1
2015	Cardiff (EC)	2	0

v ARGENTINA

1992	Gifu (Japan)	0	1
2002	Cardiff	1	1

v ARMENIA
2001	Yerevan (WC)	2	2
2001	Cardiff (WC)	0	0

v AUSTRALIA
2011	Cardiff	1	2

v AUSTRIA
1954	Vienna	0	2
1955	Wrexham	1	2
1975	Vienna (EC)	1	2
1975	Wrexham (EC)	1	0
1992	Vienna	1	1
2005	Cardiff	0	2
2005	Vienna	0	1
2013	Swansea	2	1
2016	Vienna (WC)	2	2
2017	Cardiff (WC)	1	0

v AZERBAIJAN
2002	Baku (EC)	2	0
2003	Cardiff (EC)	4	0
2004	Baku (WC)	1	1
2005	Cardiff (WC)	2	0
2008	Cardiff (WC)	1	0
2009	Baku (WC)	1	0
2019	Cardiff (EC)	2	1
2019	Baku (EC)	2	0

v BELARUS
1998	Cardiff (EC)	3	2
1999	Minsk (EC)	2	1
2000	Minsk (WC)	1	2
2001	Cardiff (WC)	1	0
2019	Cardiff	1	0

v BELGIUM
1949	Liege	1	3
1949	Cardiff	5	1
1990	Cardiff (EC)	3	1
1991	Brussels (EC)	1	1
1992	Brussels (WC)	0	2
1993	Cardiff (WC)	2	0
1997	Cardiff (WC)	1	2
1997	Brussels (WC)	2	3
2012	Cardiff (WC)	0	2
2013	Brussels (WC)	1	1
2014	Brussels (EC)	0	0
2015	Cardiff (EC)	1	0
2016	Lille (EC)	3	1
2021	Leuven (WC)	1	3

v BOSNIA-HERZEGOVINA
2003	Cardiff	2	2
2012	Llanelli	0	2
2014	Cardiff (EC)	0	0

2015	Zenica (EC)	0	2

v BRAZIL
1958	Gothenburg (WC)	0	1
1962	Rio de Janeiro	1	3
1962	Sao Paulo	1	3
1966	Rio de Janeiro	1	3
1966	Belo Horizonte	0	1
1983	Cardiff	1	1
1991	Cardiff	1	0
1997	Brasilia	0	3
2000	Cardiff	0	3
2006	White Hart Lane	0	2

v BULGARIA
1983	Wrexham (EC)	1	0
1983	Sofia (EC)	0	1
1994	Cardiff (EC)	0	3
1995	Sofia (EC)	1	3
2006	Swansea	0	0
2007	Bourgas	1	0
2010	Cardiff (EC)	0	1
2011	Sofia (EC)	1	0
2020	Cardiff (NL)	1	0
2020	Sofia (NL)	1	0

v CANADA
1986	Toronto	0	2
1986	Vancouver	3	0
2004	Wrexham	1	0

v CHILE
1966	Santiago	0	2

v CHINA
2018	Nanning	6	0

v COSTA RICA
1990	Cardiff	1	0
2012	Cardiff	0	1

v CROATIA
2002	Varazdin	1	1
2010	Osijek	0	2
2012	Osijek (WC)	0	2
2013	Swansea (WC)	1	2
2019	Osijek (EC)	1	2
2019	Cardiff (EC)	1	1

v CYPRUS
1992	Limassol (WC)	1	0
1993	Cardiff (WC)	2	0
2005	Limassol	0	1
2006	Cardiff (EC)	3	1
2007	Nicosia (EC)	1	3
2014	Cardiff (EC)	2	1
2015	Nicosia	1	0

v CZECHOSLOVAKIA (see also RCS)

1957	Cardiff (WC)	1	0
1957	Prague (WC)	0	2
1971	Swansea (EC)	1	3
1971	Prague (EC)	0	1
1977	Wrexham (WC)	3	0
1977	Prague (WC)	0	1
1980	Cardiff (WC)	1	0
1981	Prague (WC)	0	2
1987	Wrexham (EC)	1	1
1987	Prague (EC)	0	2

v CZECH REPUBLIC

2002	Cardiff	0	0
2006	Teplice (EC)	1	2
2007	Cardiff (EC)	0	0
2021	Cardiff (WC)	1	0

v DENMARK

1964	Copenhagen (WC)	0	1
1965	Wrexham (WC)	4	2
1987	Cardiff (EC)	1	0
1987	Copenhagen (EC)	0	1
1990	Copenhagen	0	1
1998	Copenhagen (EC)	2	1
1999	Anfield (EC)	0	2
2008	Copenhagen	1	0
2018	Aarhus (NL)	0	2
2018	Cardiff (NL)	1	2
2021	Amsterdam (EC)	0	4

v EAST GERMANY

1957	Leipzig (WC)	1	2
1957	Cardiff (WC)	4	1
1969	Dresden (WC)	1	2
1969	Cardiff (WC)	1	3

v ESTONIA

1994	Tallinn	2	1
2009	Llanelli	1	0

v FAROE ISLANDS

1992	Cardiff (WC)	6	0
1993	Toftir (WC)	3	0

v FINLAND

1971	Helsinki (EC)	1	0
1971	Swansea (EC)	3	0
1986	Helsinki (EC)	1	1
1987	Wrexham (EC)	4	0
1988	Swansea (WC)	2	2
1989	Helsinki (WC)	0	1
2000	Cardiff	1	2
2002	Helsinki (EC)	2	0
2003	Cardiff (EC)	1	1
2009	Cardiff (WC)	0	2
2009	Helsinki (WC)	1	2
2013	Cardiff	1	1
2020	Helsinki (NL)	1	0
2020	Cardiff (NL)	3	1

v FRANCE

1933	Paris	1	1
1939	Paris	1	2
1953	Paris	1	6
1982	Toulouse	1	0
2017	Paris	0	2
2021	Nice	0	3

v GEORGIA

1994	Tbilisi (EC)	0	5
1995	Cardiff (EC)	0	1
2008	Swansea	1	2
2016	Cardiff (WC)	1	1
2017	Tbilisi (WC)	1	0

v GERMANY/WEST GERMANY

1968	Cardiff	1	1
1969	Frankfurt	1	1
1977	Cardiff	0	2
1977	Dortmund	1	1
1979	Wrexham (EC)	0	2
1979	Cologne (EC)	1	5
1989	Cardiff (WC)	0	0
1989	Cologne (WC)	1	2
1991	Cardiff (EC)	1	0
1991	Nuremberg (EC)	1	4
1995	Dusseldorf (EC)	1	1
1995	Cardiff (EC)	1	2
2002	Cardiff	1	0
2007	Cardiff (EC)	0	2
2007	Frankfurt (EC)	0	0
2008	Moenchengladbach (WC)	0	1
2009	Cardiff (WC)	0	2

v GREECE

1964	Athens (WC)	0	2
1965	Cardiff (WC)	4	1

v HOLLAND

1988	Amsterdam (WC)	0	1
1989	Wrexham (WC)	1	2
1992	Utrecht	0	4
1996	Cardiff (WC)	1	3
1996	Eindhoven (WC)	1	7
2008	Rotterdam	0	2
2014	Amsterdam	0	2
2015	Cardiff	2	3

v HUNGARY

1958	Sanviken (WC)	1	1
1958	Stockholm (WC)	2	1

1961	Budapest	2	3
1963	Budapest (EC)	1	3
1963	Cardiff (EC)	1	1
1974	Cardiff (EC)	2	0
1975	Budapest (EC)	2	1
1986	Cardiff	0	3
2004	Budapest	2	1
2005	Cardiff	2	0
2019	Budapest (EC)	0	1
2019	Cardiff (EC)	2	0

v ICELAND

1980	Reykjavik (WC)	4	0
1981	Swansea (WC)	2	2
1984	Reykjavik (WC)	0	1
1984	Cardiff (WC)	2	1
1991	Cardiff	1	0
2008	Reykjavik	1	0
2014	Cardiff	3	1

v IRAN

1978	Tehran	1	0

v ISRAEL

1958	Tel Aviv (WC)	2	0
1958	Cardiff (WC)	2	0
1984	Tel Aviv	0	0
1989	Tel Aviv	3	3
2015	Haifa (EC)	3	0
2015	Cardiff (EC)	0	0

v ITALY

1965	Florence	1	4
1968	Cardiff (WC)	0	1
1969	Rome (WC)	1	4
1988	Brescia	1	0
1996	Terni	0	3
1998	Anfield (EC)	0	2
1999	Bologna (EC)	0	4
2002	Cardiff (EC)	2	1
2003	Milan (EC)	0	4
2021	Rome (EC)	0	1

v JAMAICA

1998	Cardiff	0	0

v JAPAN

1992	Matsuyama	1	0

v KUWAIT

1977	Wrexham	0	0
1977	Kuwait City	0	0

v LATVIA

2004	Riga	2	0

v LIECHTENSTEIN

2006	Wrexham	4	0
2008	Cardiff (WC)	2	0
2009	Vaduz (WC)	2	0

v LUXEMBOURG

1974	Swansea (EC)	5	0
1975	Luxembourg (EC)	3	1
1990	Luxembourg (EC)	1	0
1991	Luxembourg (EC)	1	0
2008	Luxembourg	2	0
2010	Llanelli	5	1

v MACEDONIA

2013	Skopje (WC)	1	2
2013	Cardiff (WC)	1	0

v MALTA

1978	Wrexham (EC)	7	0
1979	Valletta (EC)	2	0
1988	Valletta	3	2
1998	Valletta	3	0

v MEXICO

1958	Stockholm (WC)	1	1
1962	Mexico City	1	2
2012	New York	0	2
2018	Pasadena	0	0
2021	Cardiff	1	0

v MOLDOVA

1994	Kishinev (EC)	2	3
1995	Cardiff (EC)	1	0
2016	Cardiff (WC)	4	0
2017	Chisinau (WC)	2	0

v MONTENEGRO

2009	Podgorica	1	2
2010	Podgorica (EC)	0	1
2011	Cardiff (EC)	2	1

v NEW ZEALAND

2007	Wrexham	2	2

v NORWAY

1982	Swansea (EC)	1	0
1983	Oslo (EC)	0	0
1984	Trondheim	0	1
1985	Wrexham	1	1
1985	Bergen	2	4
1994	Cardiff	1	3
2000	Cardiff (WC)	1	1
2001	Oslo (WC)	2	3
2004	Oslo	0	0
2008	Wrexham	3	0
2011	Cardiff	4	1

v PANAMA

2017	Cardiff	1	1

v PARAGUAY

2006	Cardiff	0	0

v POLAND

1973	Cardiff (WC)	2	0
1973	Katowice (WC)	0	3
1991	Radom	0	0
2000	Warsaw (WC)	0	0
2001	Cardiff (WC)	1	2
2004	Cardiff (WC)	2	3
2005	Warsaw (WC)	0	1
2009	Vila-Real (Por)	0	1

v PORTUGAL

1949	Lisbon	2	3
1951	Cardiff	2	1
2000	Chaves	0	3
2016	Lyon (EC)	0	2

v QATAR

2000	Doha	1	0

v RCS (formerly Czechoslovakia)

1993	Ostrava (WC)	1	1
1993	Cardiff (WC)	2	2

v REPUBLIC OF IRELAND

1960	Dublin	3	2
1979	Swansea	2	1
1981	Dublin	3	1
1986	Dublin	1	0
1990	Dublin	0	1
1991	Wrexham	0	3
1992	Dublin	1	0
1993	Dublin	1	2
1997	Cardiff	0	0
2007	Dublin (EC)	0	1
2007	Cardiff (EC)	2	2
2011	Dublin (CC)	0	3
2013	Cardiff	0	0
2017	Dublin (WC)	0	0
2017	Cardiff (WC)	0	1
2018	Cardiff (NL)	4	1
2018	Dublin (NL)	1	0
2020	Dublin (NL)	0	0
2020	Cardiff (NL)	1	0

v REST OF UNITED KINGDOM

1951	Cardiff	3	2
1969	Cardiff	0	1

v ROMANIA

1970	Cardiff (EC)	0	0
1971	Bucharest (EC)	0	2
1983	Wrexham	5	0
1992	Bucharest (WC)	1	5
1993	Cardiff (WC)	1	2

v RUSSIA (See also Soviet Union)

2003*	Moscow (EC)	0	0
2003*	Cardiff (EC)	0	1
2008	Moscow (WC)	1	2
2009	Cardiff (WC)	1	3
2016	Toulouse (EC)	3	0
(*Qual Round play-offs)			

v SAN MARINO

1996	Serravalle (WC)	5	0
1996	Cardiff (WC)	6	0
2007	Cardiff (EC)	3	0
2007	Serravalle (EC)	2	1

v SAUDI ARABIA

1986	Dahran	2	1

v SERBIA

2012	Novi Sad (WC)	1	6
2013	Cardiff (WC)	0	3
2016	Cardiff (WC)	1	1
2017	Belgrade (WC)	1	1

v SERBIA & MONTENEGRO

2003	Belgrade (EC)	0	1
2003	Cardiff (EC)	2	3

v SLOVAKIA

2006	Cardiff (EC)	1	5
2007	Trnava (EC)	5	2
2016	Bordeaux (EC)	2	1
2019	Cardiff (EC)	1	0
2019	Trnava (EC)	1	1

v SLOVENIA

2005	Swansea	0	0

v SOVIET UNION (See also Russia)

1965	Moscow (WC)	1	2
1965	Cardiff (WC)	2	1
1981	Wrexham (WC)	0	0
1981	Tbilisi (WC)	0	3
1987	Swansea	0	0

v SPAIN

1961	Cardiff (WC)	1	2
1961	Madrid (WC)	1	1
1982	Valencia	1	1
1984	Seville (WC)	0	3
1985	Wrexham (WC)	3	0
2018	Cardiff	1	4

v SWEDEN

1958	Stockholm (WC)	0	0
1988	Stockholm	1	4
1989	Wrexham	0	2
1990	Stockholm	2	4
1994	Wrexham	0	2
2010	Swansea	0	1
2016	Stockholm	0	3

v SWITZERLAND

1949	Berne	0	4
1951	Wrexham	3	2
1996	Lugano	0	2
1999	Zurich (EC)	0	2
1999	Wrexham (EC)	0	2
2010	Basle (EC)	1	4
2011	Swansea (EC)	2	0
2021	Baku (EC)	1	1

v TRINIDAD & TOBAGO

2006	Graz	2	1
2019	Wrexham	1	0

v TUNISIA

1998	Tunis	0	4

v TURKEY

1978	Wrexham (EC)	1	0
1979	Izmir (EC)	0	1
1980	Cardiff (WC)	4	0
1981	Ankara (WC)	1	0
1996	Cardiff (WC)	0	0
1997	Istanbul (WC)	4	6
2021	Baku (EC)	2	0

v UKRAINE

2001	Cardiff (WC)	1	1
2001	Kiev (WC)	1	1
2015	Kiev	0	1

v URUGUAY

1986	Wrexham	0	0
2018	Nanning	0	1

v USA

2003	San Jose	0	2
2020	Swansea	0	0

v YUGOSLAVIA

1953	Belgrade	2	5
1954	Cardiff	1	3
1976	Zagreb (EC)	0	2
1976	Cardiff (EC)	1	1
1982	Titograd (EC)	4	4
1983	Cardiff (EC)	1	1
1988	Swansea	1	2

NORTHERN IRELAND

v ALBANIA

1965	Belfast (WC)	4	1
1965	Tirana (WC)	1	1
1983	Tirana (EC)	0	0
1983	Belfast (EC)	1	0
1992	Belfast (WC)	3	0
1993	Tirana (WC)	2	1
1996	Belfast (WC)	2	0
1997	Zurich (WC)	0	1
2010	Tirana	0	1

v ALGERIA

1986	Guadalajara (WC)	1	1

v ARGENTINA

1958	Halmstad (WC)	1	3

v ARMENIA

1996	Belfast (WC)	1	1
1997	Yerevan (WC)	0	0
2003	Yerevan (EC)	0	1
2003	Belfast (EC)	0	1

v AUSTRALIA

1980	Sydney	2	1
1980	Melbourne	1	1
1980	Adelaide	2	1

v AUSTRIA

1982	Madrid (WC)	2	2
1982	Vienna (EC)	0	2
1983	Belfast (EC)	3	1
1990	Vienna (EC)	0	0
1991	Belfast (EC)	2	1
1994	Vienna (EC)	2	1
1995	Belfast (EC)	5	3
2004	Belfast (WC)	3	3
2005	Vienna (WC)	0	2
2018	Vienna (NL)	0	1
2018	Belfast(NL)	1	2
2020	Belfast (NL)	0	1
2020	Vienna (NL)	1	2

v AZERBAIJAN

2004	Baku (WC)	0	0
2005	Belfast (WC)	2	0
2012	Belfast (WC)	1	1
2013	Baku (WC)	0	2
2016	Belfast (WC)	4	0
2017	Baku (WC)	1	0

v BARBADOS

2004	Bridgetown	1	1

v BELARUS

2016	Belfast	3	0
2019	Belfast (EC)	2	1
2019	Borisov (EC)	1	0

v BELGIUM

1976	Liege (WC)	0	2
1977	Belfast (WC)	3	0
1997	Belfast	3	0

v BOSNIA-HERZEGOVINA

2018	Belfast (NL)	1	2
2018	Sarajevo (NL)	0	2
2020*	Sarajevo (EC)	1	1
(*Northern Ireland won 4-3 on pens)			

v BRAZIL

1986	Guadalajara (WC)	0	3

v BULGARIA

1972	Sofia (WC)	0	3
1973	Sheffield (WC)	0	0
1978	Sofia (EC)	2	0
1979	Belfast (EC)	2	0
2001	Sofia (WC)	3	4
2001	Belfast (WC)	0	1
2008	Belfast	0	1
2021	Belfast (WC)	0	0

v CANADA

1995	Edmonton	0	2
1999	Belfast	1	1
2005	Belfast	0	1

v CHILE

1989	Belfast	0	1
1995	Edmonton, Canada	0	2
2010	Chillan	0	1
2014	Valparaiso	0	2

v COLOMBIA

1994	Boston, USA	0	2

v COSTA RICA

2018	San Jose	0	3

v CROATIA

2016	Belfast	0	3

v CYPRUS

1971	Nicosia (EC)	3	0
1971	Belfast (EC)	5	0
1973	Nicosia (WC)	0	1
1973	Fulham (WC)	3	0
2002	Belfast	0	0
2014	Nicosia	0	0

v CZECHOSLOVAKIA/CZECH REP

1958	Halmstad (WC)	1	0
1958	Malmo (WC)	2	1
2001	Belfast (WC)	0	1
2001	Teplice (WC)	1	3
2008	Belfast (WC)	0	0
2009	Prague (WC)	0	0
2016	Prague (WC)	0	0
2017	Belfast (WC)	2	0
2019	Prague	3	2

v DENMARK

1978	Belfast (EC)	2	1
1979	Copenhagen (EC)	0	4
1986	Belfast	1	1
1990	Belfast (EC)	1	1
1991	Odense (EC)	1	2
1992	Belfast (WC)	0	1
1993	Copenhagen (WC)	0	1
2000	Belfast (WC)	1	1
2001	Copenhagen (WC)	1	1
2006	Copenhagen (EC)	0	0
2007	Belfast (EC)	2	1

v ESTONIA

2004	Tallinn	1	0
2006	Belfast	1	0
2011	Tallinn (EC)	1	4
2011	Belfast (EC)	1	2
2019	Belfast (EC)	2	0
2019	Tallinn (EC)	2	1

v FAROE ISLANDS

1991	Belfast (EC)	1	1
1991	Landskrona, Sw (EC)	5	0
2010	Toftir (EC)	1	1
2011	Belfast (EC)	4	0
2014	Belfast (EC)	2	0
2015	Torshavn (EC)	3	1

v FINLAND

1984	Pori (WC)	0	1
1984	Belfast (WC)	2	1
1998	Belfast (EC)	1	0
1999	Helsinki (EC)	1	4
2003	Belfast	0	1
2006	Helsinki	2	1
2012	Belfast	3	3
2015	Belfast (EC)	2	1
2015	Helsinki (EC)	1	1

v FRANCE

1951	Belfast	2	2
1952	Paris	1	3
1958	Norrkoping (WC)	0	4
1982	Paris	0	4

1982	Madrid (WC)	1	4
1986	Paris	0	0
1988	Belfast	0	0
1999	Belfast	0	1

v GEORGIA

2008	Belfast	4	1

v GERMANY/WEST GERMANY

1958	Malmo (WC)	2	2
1960	Belfast (WC)	3	4
1961	Berlin (WC)	1	2
1966	Belfast	0	2
1977	Cologne	0	5
1982	Belfast (EC)	1	0
1983	Hamburg (EC)	1	0
1992	Bremen	1	1
1996	Belfast	1	1
1997	Nuremberg (WC)	1	1
1997	Belfast (WC)	1	3
1999	Belfast (EC)	0	3
1999	Dortmund (EC)	0	4
2005	Belfast	1	4
2016	Paris (EC)	0	1
2016	Hannover (WC)	0	2
2017	Belfast (WC)	1	3
2019	Belfast (EC)	0	2
2019	Frankfurt (EC)	1	6

v GREECE

1961	Athens (WC)	1	2
1961	Belfast (WC)	2	0
1988	Athens	2	3
2003	Belfast (EC)	0	2
2003	Athens (EC)	0	1
2014	Piraeus (EC)	2	0
2015	Belfast (EC)	3	1

v HOLLAND

1962	Rotterdam	0	4
1965	Belfast (WC)	2	1
1965	Rotterdam (WC)	0	0
1976	Rotterdam (WC)	2	2
1977	Belfast (WC)	0	1
2012	Amsterdam	0	6
2019	Rotterdam (EC)	1	3
2019	Belfast (EC)	0	0

v HONDURAS

1982	Zaragoza (WC)	1	1

v HUNGARY

1988	Budapest (WC)	0	1
1989	Belfast (WC)	1	2
2000	Belfast	0	1
2008	Belfast	0	2

2014	Budapest (EC)	2	1
2015	Belfast (EC)	1	1

v ICELAND

1977	Reykjavik (WC)	0	1
1977	Belfast (WC)	2	0
2000	Reykjavik (WC)	0	1
2001	Belfast (WC)	3	0
2006	Belfast (EC)	0	3
2007	Reykjavik (EC)	1	2

v ISRAEL

1968	Jaffa	3	2
1976	Tel Aviv	1	1
1980	Tel Aviv (WC)	0	0
1981	Belfast (WC)	1	0
1984	Belfast	3	0
1987	Tel Aviv	1	1
2009	Belfast	1	1
2013	Belfast (WC)	0	2
2013	Ramat Gan (WC)	1	1
2018	Belfast	3	0

v ITALY

1957	Rome (WC)	0	1
1957	Belfast	2	2
1958	Belfast (WC)	2	1
1961	Bologna	2	3
1997	Palermo	0	2
2003	Campobasso	0	2
2009	Pisa	0	3
2010	Belfast (EC)	0	0
2011	Pescara (EC)	0	3
2021	Parma (WC)	0	2

v LATVIA

1993	Riga (WC)	2	1
1993	Belfast (WC)	2	0
1995	Riga (EC)	1	0
1995	Belfast (EC)	1	2
2006	Belfast (EC)	1	0
2007	Riga (EC)	0	1
2015	Belfast	1	0

v LIECHTENSTEIN

1994	Belfast (EC)	4	1
1995	Eschen (EC)	4	0
2002	Vaduz	0	0
2007	Vaduz (EC)	4	1
2007	Belfast (EC)	3	1

v LITHUANIA

1992	Belfast (WC)	2	2

v LUXEMBOURG

2000	Luxembourg	3	1

2012	Belfast (WC)	1	1
2013	Luxembourg (WC)	2	3
2019	Belfast	1	0

v MALTA
1988	Belfast (WC)	3	0
1989	Valletta (WC)	2	0
2000	Ta'Qali	3	0
2000	Belfast (WC)	1	0
2001	Valletta (WC)	1	0
2005	Valletta	1	1
2013	Ta'Qali	0	0
2021	Klagenfurt	3	0

v MEXICO
| 1966 | Belfast | 4 | 1 |
| 1994 | Miami | 0 | 3 |

v MOLDOVA
| 1998 | Belfast (EC) | 2 | 2 |
| 1999 | Kishinev (EC) | 0 | 0 |

v MONTENEGRO
| 2010 | Podgorica | 0 | 2 |

v MOROCCO
| 1986 | Belfast | 2 | 1 |
| 2010 | Belfast | 1 | 1 |

v NEW ZEALAND
| 2017 | Belfast | 1 | 0 |

v NORWAY
1974	Oslo (EC)	1	2
1975	Belfast (EC)	3	0
1990	Belfast	2	3
1996	Belfast	0	2
2001	Belfast	0	4
2004	Belfast	1	4
2012	Belfast	0	3
2017	Belfast (WC)	2	0
2017	Oslo (WC)	0	1
2020	Belfast (NL)	1	5
2020	Oslo (NL)	0	1

v PANAMA
| 2018 | Panama City | 0 | 0 |

v POLAND
1962	Katowice (EC)	2	0
1962	Belfast (EC)	2	0
1988	Belfast	1	1
1991	Belfast	3	1
2002	Limassol (Cyprus)	1	4
2004	Belfast (WC)	0	3
2005	Warsaw (WC)	0	1
2009	Belfast (WC)	3	2

| 2009 | Chorzow (WC) | 1 | 1 |
| 2016 | Nice (EC) | 0 | 1 |

v PORTUGAL
1957	Lisbon (WC)	1	1
1957	Belfast (WC)	3	0
1973	Coventry (WC)	1	1
1973	Lisbon (WC)	1	1
1980	Lisbon (WC)	0	1
1981	Belfast (WC)	1	0
1994	Belfast (EC)	1	2
1995	Oporto (EC)	1	1
1997	Belfast (WC)	0	0
1997	Lisbon (WC)	0	1
2005	Belfast	1	1
2012	Porto (WC)	1	1
2013	Belfast (WC)	2	4

v QATAR
| 2015 | Crewe | 1 | 1 |

v REPUBLIC OF IRELAND
1978	Dublin (EC)	0	0
1979	Dublin (EC)	1	0
1988	Belfast (WC)	0	0
1989	Dublin (WC)	0	3
1993	Dublin (WC)	0	3
1993	Belfast (WC)	1	1
1994	Belfast (EC)	0	4
1995	Dublin (EC)	1	1
1999	Dublin	1	0
2011	Dublin (CC)	0	5
2018	Dublin	0	0

v ROMANIA
1984	Belfast (WC)	3	2
1985	Bucharest (WC)	1	0
1994	Belfast	2	0
2006	Chicago	0	2
2014	Bucharest (EC)	0	2
2015	Belfast (EC)	0	0
2020	Bucharest (NL)	1	1
2020	Belfast (NL)	1	1

v RUSSIA
| 2012 | Moscow (WC) | 0 | 2 |
| 2013 | Belfast (WC) | 1 | 0 |

v SAN MARINO
2008	Belfast (WC)	4	0
2009	Serravalle (WC)	3	0
2016	Belfast (WC)	4	0
2017	Serravalle (WC)	3	0

v SERBIA & MONTENEGRO
| 2004 | Belfast | 1 | 1 |

v SERBIA
2009	Belfast	0	1
2011	Belgrade (EC)	1	2
2011	Belfast (EC)	0	1

v SLOVAKIA
1998	Belfast	1	0
2008	Bratislava (WC)	1	2
2009	Belfast (WC)	0	2
2016	Trnava	0	0
2020	Belfast (EC)	1	2

v SLOVENIA
2008	Maribor (WC)	0	2
2009	Belfast (WC)	1	0
2010	Maribor (EC)	1	0
2011	Belfast (EC)	0	0
2016	Belfast	1	0

v SOUTH KOREA
2018	Belfast	2	1

v SOVIET UNION
1969	Belfast (WC)	0	0
1969	Moscow (WC)	0	2
1971	Moscow (EC)	0	1
1971	Belfast (EC)	1	1

v SPAIN
1958	Madrid	2	6
1963	Bilbao	1	1
1963	Belfast	0	1
1970	Seville (EC)	0	3
1972	Hull (EC)	1	1
1982	Valencia (WC)	1	0
1985	Palma, Majorca	0	0
1986	Guadalajara (WC)	1	2
1988	Seville (WC)	0	4
1989	Belfast (WC)	0	2
1992	Belfast (WC)	0	0
1993	Seville (WC)	1	3
1998	Santander	1	4
2002	Belfast	0	5
2002	Albacete (EC)	0	3
2003	Belfast (EC)	0	0
2006	Belfast (EC)	3	2
2007	Las Palmas (EC)	0	1

v ST KITTS & NEVIS
2004	Basseterre	2	0

v SWEDEN
1974	Solna (EC)	2	0
1975	Belfast (EC)	1	2
1980	Belfast (WC)	3	0
1981	Stockholm (WC)	0	1
1996	Belfast	1	2

2007	Belfast (EC)	2	1
2007	Stockholm (EC)	1	1

v SWITZERLAND
1964	Belfast (WC)	1	0
1964	Lausanne (WC)	1	2
1998	Belfast	1	0
2004	Zurich	0	0
2010	Basle (EC)	1	4
2017	Belfast (EC)	0	1
2017	Basle (WC)	0	0

v THAILAND
1997	Bangkok	0	0

v TRINIDAD & TOBAGO
2004	Port of Spain	3	0

v TURKEY
1968	Belfast (WC)	4	1
1968	Istanbul (WC)	3	0
1983	Belfast (EC)	2	1
1983	Ankara (EC)	0	1
1985	Belfast (WC)	2	0
1985	Izmir (WC)	0	0
1986	Izmir (EC)	0	0
1987	Belfast (EC)	1	0
1998	Istanbul (EC)	0	3
1999	Belfast (EC)	0	3
2010	Connecticut	0	2
2013	Adana	0	1

v UKRAINE
1996	Belfast (WC)	0	1
1997	Kiev (WC)	1	2
2002	Belfast (EC)	0	0
2003	Donetsk (EC)	0	0
2016	Lyon (EC)	2	0
2021	Dnipro	0	1

v URUGUAY
1964	Belfast	3	0
1990	Belfast	1	0
2006	New Jersey	0	1
2014	Montevideo	0	1

v USA
2021	Belfast	1	2

v YUGOSLAVIA
1975	Belfast (EC)	1	0
1975	Belgrade (EC)	0	1
1982	Zaragoza (WC)	0	0
1987	Belfast (EC)	1	2
1987	Sarajevo (EC)	0	3
1990	Belfast (EC)	0	2
1991	Belgrade (EC)	1	4
2000	Belfast	1	2

REPUBLIC OF IRELAND

v ALBANIA
1992	Dublin (WC)	2	0
1993	Tirana (WC)	2	1
2003	Tirana (EC)	0	0
2003	Dublin (EC)	2	1

v ALGERIA
1982	Algiers	0	2
2010	Dublin	3	0

v ANDORRA
2001	Barcelona (WC)	3	0
2001	Dublin (WC)	3	1
2010	Dublin (EC)	3	1
2011	La Vella (EC)	2	0
2021	La Vella	4	1

v ARGENTINA
1951	Dublin	0	1
1979*	Dublin	0	0
1980	Dublin	0	1
1998	Dublin	0	2
2010	Dublin	0	1

(*Not regarded as full Int)

v ARMENIA
2010	Yerevan (EC)	1	0
2011	Dublin (EC)	2	1

v AUSTRALIA
2003	Dublin	2	1
2009	Limerick	0	3

v AUSTRIA
1952	Vienna	0	6
1953	Dublin	4	0
1958	Vienna	1	3
1962	Dublin	2	3
1963	Vienna (EC)	0	0
1963	Dublin (EC)	3	2
1966	Vienna	0	1
1968	Dublin	2	2
1971	Dublin (EC)	1	4
1971	Linz (EC)	0	6
1995	Dublin (EC)	1	3
1995	Vienna (EC)	1	3
2013	Dublin (WC)	2	2
2013	Vienna (WC)	0	1
2016	Vienna (WC)	1	0
2017	Dublin (WC	1	1

v BELARUS
2016	Cork	1	2

v BELGIUM
1928	Liege	4	2
1929	Dublin	4	0
1930	Brussels	3	1
1934	Dublin (WC)	4	4
1949	Dublin	0	2
1950	Brussels	1	5
1965	Dublin	0	2
1966	Liege	3	2
1980	Dublin (WC)	1	1
1981	Brussels (WC)	0	1
1986	Brussels (EC)	2	2
1987	Dublin (EC)	0	0
1997*	Dublin (WC)	1	1
1997*	Brussels (WC)	1	2
2016	Bordeaux (EC)	0	3

(*World Cup play-off)

v BOLIVIA
1994	Dublin	1	0
1996	East Rutherford, NJ	3	0
2007	Boston	1	1

v BOSNIA HERZEGOVINA
2012	Dublin	1	0
2015	Zenica (EC)	1	1
2015	Dublin (EC)	2	0

v BRAZIL
1974	Rio de Janeiro	1	2
1982	Uberlandia	0	7
1987	Dublin	1	0
2004	Dublin	0	0
2008	Dublin	0	1
2010	Arsenal	0	2

v BULGARIA
1977	Sofia (WC)	1	2
1977	Dublin (WC)	0	0
1979	Sofia (EC)	0	1
1979	Dublin (EC)	3	0
1987	Sofia (EC)	1	2
1987	Dublin (EC)	2	0
2004	Dublin	1	1
2009	Dublin (WC)	1	1
2009	Sofia (WC)	1	1
2019	Dublin	3	1
2020	Sofia (NL)	1	1
2020	Dublin (NL)	0	0

v CAMEROON
2002	Niigata (WC)	1	1

v CANADA
2003	Dublin	3	0

v CHILE
1960	Dublin	2	0
1972	Recife	1	2
1974	Santiago	2	1
1982	Santiago	0	1
1991	Dublin	1	1
2006	Dublin	0	1

v CHINA
| 1984 | Sapporo | 1 | 0 |
| 2005 | Dublin | 1 | 0 |

v COLOMBIA
| 2008 | Fulham | 1 | 0 |

v COSTA RICA
| 2014 | Chester, USA | 1 | 1 |

v CROATIA
1996	Dublin	2	2
1998	Dublin (EC)	2	0
1999	Zagreb (EC)	0	1
2001	Dublin	2	2
2004	Dublin	1	0
2011	Dublin	0	0
2012	Poznan (EC)	1	3

v CYPRUS
1980	Nicosia (WC)	3	2
1980	Dublin (WC)	6	0
2001	Nicosia (WC)	4	0
2001	Dublin (WC)	4	0
2004	Dublin (WC)	3	0
2005	Nicosia (WC)	1	0
2006	Nicosia (EC)	2	5
2007	Dublin (EC)	1	1
2008	Dublin (WC)	1	0
2009	Nicosia (WC)	2	1

v CZECHOSLOVAKIA/CZECH REP
1938	Prague	2	2
1959	Dublin (EC)	2	0
1959	Bratislava (EC)	0	4
1961	Dublin (WC)	1	3
1961	Prague (WC)	1	7
1967	Dublin (EC)	0	2
1967	Prague (EC)	2	1
1969	Dublin (WC)	1	2
1969	Prague (WC)	0	3
1979	Prague	1	4
1981	Dublin	3	1
1986	Reykjavik	1	0
1994	Dublin	1	3
1996	Prague	0	2
1998	Olomouc	1	2
2000	Dublin	3	2

2004	Dublin	2	1
2006	Dublin (EC)	1	1
2007	Prague (EC)	0	1
2012	Dublin	1	1

v DENMARK
1956	Dublin (WC)	2	1
1957	Copenhagen (WC)	2	0
1968*	Dublin (WC)	1	1
1969	Copenhagen (WC)	0	2
1969	Dublin (WC)	1	1
1978	Copenhagen (EC)	3	3
1979	Dublin (EC)	2	0
1984	Copenhagen (WC)	0	3
1985	Dublin (WC)	1	4
1992	Copenhagen (WC)	0	0
1993	Dublin (WC)	1	1
2002	Dublin	3	0
(*Abandoned after 51 mins – fog)			
2007	Aarhus	4	0
2017	Copenhagen (WC)	0	0
2017	Dublin (WC)	1	5
2018	Dublin (NL)	0	0
2018	Aarhus (NL)	0	0
2019	Copenhagen (EC)	1	1
2019	Dublin (EC)	1	1

v ECUADOR
| 2007 | New York | 1 | 1 |

v EGYPT
| 1990 | Palermo (WC) | 0 | 0 |

v ESTONIA
2000	Dublin (WC)	2	0
2001	Tallinn (WC)	2	0
2011	Tallinn (EC)	4	0
2011	Dublin (EC)	1	1

v FAROE ISLANDS
2004	Dublin (WC)	2	0
2005	Torshavn (WC)	2	0
2012	Torshavn (WC)	4	1
2013	Dublin (WC)	3	0

v FINLAND
1949	Dublin (WC)	3	0
1949	Helsinki (WC)	1	1
1990	Dublin	1	1
2000	Dublin	3	0
2002	Helsinki	3	0
2020	Dublin (NL)	0	1
2020	Helsinki (NL)	0	1

v FRANCE
| 1937 | Paris | 2 | 0 |
| 1952 | Dublin | 1 | 1 |

1953	Dublin (WC)	3	5
1953	Paris (WC)	0	1
1972	Dublin (WC)	2	1
1973	Paris (WC)	1	1
1976	Paris (WC)	0	2
1977	Dublin (WC)	1	0
1980	Paris (WC)	0	2
1981	Dublin (WC)	3	2
1989	Dublin	0	0
2004	Paris (WC)	0	0
2005	Dublin (WC)	0	1
2009	Dublin (WC)	0	1
2009	Paris (WC)	1	1
2016	Lyon (EC)	1	2
2018	Paris	0	2

v GEORGIA

2002	Tbilisi (EC)	2	1
2003	Dublin (EC)	2	0
2008	Mainz (WC)	2	1
2009	Dublin (WC)	2	1
2013	Dublin	4	0
2014	Tbilisi (EC)	2	1
2015	Dublin (EC)	1	0
2016	Dublin (WC)	1	0
2017	Tbilisi (WC)	1	1
2019	Dublin (EC)	1	0
2019	Tbilisi (EC)	0	0

v GERMANY/WEST GERMANY

1935	Dortmund	1	3
1936	Dublin	5	2
1939	Bremen	1	1
1951	Dublin	3	2
1952	Cologne	0	3
1955	Hamburg	1	2
1956	Dublin	3	0
1960	Dusseldorf	1	0
1966	Dublin	0	4
1970	Berlin	1	2
1975*	Dublin	1	0
1979	Dublin	1	3
1981	Bremen	0	3
1989	Dublin	1	1
1994	Hanover	2	0
2002	Ibaraki (WC)	1	1
2006	Stuttgart (EC)	0	1
2007	Dublin (EC)	0	0
2012	Dublin (WC)	1	6
2013	Cologne (WC)	0	3
2014	Gelsenkirchen (EC)	1	1
2015	Dublin (EC)	1	0

(*v W Germany 'B')

v GIBRALTAR

2014	Dublin (EC)	7	0
2015	Faro (EC)	4	0
2019	Victoria (EC)	1	0
2019	Dublin (EC)	2	0

v GREECE

2000	Dublin	0	1
2002	Athens	0	0
2012	Dublin	0	1

v HOLLAND

1932	Amsterdam	2	0
1934	Amsterdam	2	5
1935	Dublin	3	5
1955	Dublin	1	0
1956	Rotterdam	4	1
1980	Dublin (WC)	2	1
1981	Rotterdam (WC)	2	2
1982	Rotterdam (EC)	1	2
1983	Dublin (EC)	2	3
1988	Gelsenkirchen (EC)	0	1
1990	Palermo (WC)	1	1
1994	Tilburg	1	0
1994	Orlando (WC)	0	2
1995*	Liverpool (EC)	0	2
1996	Rotterdam	1	3
(*Qual Round play-off)			
2000	Amsterdam (WC)	2	2
2001	Dublin (WC)	1	0
2004	Amsterdam	1	0
2006	Dublin	0	4
2016	Dublin	1	1

v HUNGARY

1934	Dublin	2	4
1936	Budapest	3	3
1936	Dublin	2	3
1939	Cork	2	2
1939	Budapest	2	2
1969	Dublin (WC)	1	2
1969	Budapest (WC)	0	4
1989	Budapest (WC)	0	0
1989	Dublin (WC)	2	0
1992	Gyor	2	1
2012	Budapest	0	0
2021	Budapest	0	0

v ICELAND

1962	Dublin (EC)	4	2
1962	Reykjavik (EC)	1	1
1982	Dublin (EC)	2	0
1983	Reykjavik (EC)	3	0
1986	Reykjavik	2	1
1996	Dublin (WC)	0	0

1997	Reykjavik (WC)	4	2
2017	Dublin	0	1

v IRAN

1972	Recife	2	1
2001*	Dublin (WC)	2	0
2001*	Tehran (WC)	0	1
(*Qual Round play-off)			

v ISRAEL

1984	Tel Aviv	0	3
1985	Tel Aviv	0	0
1987	Dublin	5	0
2005	Tel Aviv (WC)	1	1
2005	Dublin (WC)	2	2

v ITALY

1926	Turin	0	3
1927	Dublin	1	2
1970	Florence (EC)	0	3
1971	Dublin (EC)	1	2
1985	Dublin	1	2
1990	Rome (WC)	0	1
1992	Boston, USA	0	2
1994	New York (WC)	1	0
2005	Dublin	1	2
2009	Bari (WC)	1	1
2009	Dublin (WC)	2	2
2011	Liege	2	0
2012	Poznan (EC)	0	2
2014	Fulham	0	0
2016	Lille (EC)	1	0

v JAMAICA

2004	Charlton	1	0

v KAZAKHSTAN

2012	Astana (WC)	2	1
2013	Dublin (WC)	3	1

v LATVIA

1992	Dublin (WC)	4	0
1993	Riga (WC)	2	0
1994	Riga (EC)	3	0
1995	Dublin (EC)	2	1
2013	Dublin	3	0

v LIECHTENSTEIN

1994	Dublin (EC)	4	0
1995	Eschen (EC)	0	0
1996	Eschen (WC)	5	0
1997	Dublin (WC)	5	0

v LITHUANIA

1993	Vilnius (WC)	1	0
1993	Dublin (WC)	2	0

1997	Dublin (WC)	0	0
1997	Zalgiris (WC)	2	1

v LUXEMBOURG

1936	Luxembourg	5	1
1953	Dublin (WC)	4	0
1954	Luxembourg (WC)	1	0
1987	Luxembourg (EC)	2	0
1987	Luxembourg (EC)	2	1
2021	Dublin (WC)	0	1

v MACEDONIA

1996	Dublin (WC)	3	0
1997	Skopje (WC)	2	3
1999	Dublin (EC)	1	0
1999	Skopje (EC)	1	1
2011	Dublin (EC)	2	1
2011	Skopje (EC)	2	0

v MALTA

1983	Valletta (EC)	1	0
1983	Dublin (EC)	8	0
1989	Dublin (WC)	2	0
1989	Valletta (WC)	2	0
1990	Valletta	3	0
1998	Dublin (EC)	1	0
1999	Valletta (EC)	3	2

v MEXICO

1984	Dublin	0	0
1994	Orlando (WC)	1	2
1996	New Jersey	2	2
1998	Dublin	0	0
2000	Chicago	2	2
2017	New Jersey	1	3

v MOLDOVA

2016	Chisinau (WC)	3	1
2017	Dublin (WC)	2	0

v MONTENEGRO

2008	Podgorica (WC)	0	0
2009	Dublin (WC)	0	0

v MOROCCO

1990	Dublin	1	0

v NEW ZEALAND

2019	Dublin	3	1

v NIGERIA

2002	Dublin	1	2
2004	Charlton	0	3
2009	Fulham	1	1

v NORWAY

Year	Venue		
1937	Oslo (WC)	2	3
1937	Dublin (WC)	3	3
1950	Dublin	2	2
1951	Oslo	3	2
1954	Dublin	2	1
1955	Oslo	3	1
1960	Dublin	3	1
1964	Oslo	4	1
1973	Oslo	1	1
1976	Dublin	3	0
1978	Oslo	0	0
1984	Oslo (WC)	0	1
1985	Dublin (WC)	0	0
1988	Oslo	0	0
1994	New York (WC)	0	0
2003	Dublin	1	0
2008	Oslo	1	1
2010	Dublin	1	2

v OMAN

Year	Venue		
2012	Fulham	4	1
2014	Dublin	2	0
2016	Dublin	4	0

v PARAGUAY

Year	Venue		
1999	Dublin	2	0
2010	Dublin	2	1

v POLAND

Year	Venue		
1938	Warsaw	0	6
1938	Dublin	3	2
1958	Katowice	2	2
1958	Dublin	2	2
1964	Cracow	1	3
1964	Dublin	3	2
1968	Dublin	2	2
1968	Katowice	0	1
1970	Dublin	1	2
1970	Poznan	0	2
1973	Wroclaw	0	2
1973	Dublin	1	0
1976	Poznan	2	0
1977	Dublin	0	0
1978	Lodz	0	3
1981	Bydgoszcz	0	3
1984	Dublin	0	0
1986	Warsaw	0	1
1988	Dublin	3	1
1991	Dublin (EC)	0	0
1991	Poznan (EC)	3	3
2004	Bydgoszcz	0	0
2008	Dublin	2	3
2013	Dublin	2	0

Year	Venue		
2013	Poznan	0	0
2015	Dublin (EC)	1	1
2015	Warsaw (EC)	1	2
2018	Wroclaw	1	1

v PORTUGAL

Year	Venue		
1946	Lisbon	1	3
1947	Dublin	0	2
1948	Lisbon	0	2
1949	Dublin	1	0
1972	Recife	1	2
1992	Boston, USA	2	0
1995	Dublin (EC)	1	0
1995	Lisbon (EC)	0	3
1996	Dublin	0	1
2000	Lisbon (WC)	1	1
2001	Dublin (WC)	1	1
2005	Dublin	1	0
2014	East Rutherford, USA	1	5

v QATAR

Year	Venue		
2021	Debrecen	1	1

v ROMANIA

Year	Venue		
1988	Dublin	2	0
1990*	Genoa	0	0
1997	Bucharest (WC)	0	1
1997	Dublin (WC)	1	1
2004	Dublin	1	0

(*Rep won 5-4 on pens)

v RUSSIA (See also Soviet Union)

Year	Venue		
1994	Dublin	0	0
1996	Dublin	0	2
2002	Dublin	2	0
2002	Moscow (EC)	2	4
2003	Dublin (EC)	1	1
2010	Dublin (EC)	2	3
2011	Moscow (EC)	0	0

v SAN MARINO

Year	Venue		
2006	Dublin (EC)	5	0
2007	Rimini (EC)	2	1

v SAUDI ARABIA

Year	Venue		
2002	Yokohama (WC)	3	0

v SERBIA

Year	Venue		
2008	Dublin	1	1
2012	Belgrade	0	0
2014	Dublin	1	2
2016	Belgrade (WC)	2	2
2017	Dublin (WC)	0	1
2021	Belgrade (WC)	2	3

v SLOVAKIA

2007	Dublin (EC)	1	0
2007	Bratislava (EC)	2	2
2010	Zilina (EC)	1	1
2011	Dublin (EC)	0	0
2016	Dublin	2	2
2020*	Bratislava (EC)	0	0

(* Republic of Ireland lost 4-2 on pens)

v SOUTH AFRICA

2000	New Jersey	2	1
2009	Limerick	1	0

v SOVIET UNION (See also Russia)

1972	Dublin (WC)	1	2
1973	Moscow (WC)	0	1
1974	Dublin (EC)	3	0
1975	Kiev (EC)	1	2
1984	Dublin (WC)	1	0
1985	Moscow (WC)	0	2
1988	Hanover (EC)	1	1
1990	Dublin	1	0

v SPAIN

1931	Barcelona	1	1
1931	Dublin	0	5
1946	Madrid	1	0
1947	Dublin	3	2
1948	Barcelona	1	2
1949	Dublin	1	4
1952	Madrid	0	6
1955	Dublin	2	2
1964	Seville (EC)	1	5
1964	Dublin (EC)	0	2
1965	Dublin (WC)	1	0
1965	Seville (WC)	1	4
1965	Paris (WC)	0	1
1966	Dublin (EC)	0	0
1966	Valencia (EC)	0	2
1977	Dublin	0	1
1982	Dublin (EC)	3	3
1983	Zaragoza (EC)	0	2
1985	Cork	0	0
1988	Seville (WC)	0	2
1989	Dublin (WC)	1	0
1992	Seville (WC)	0	0
1993	Dublin (WC)	1	3
2002*	Suwon (WC)	1	1

(*Rep lost 3-2 on pens)

2012	Gdansk (EC)	0	4
2013	New York	0	2

v SWEDEN

1949	Stockholm (WC)	1	3
1949	Dublin (WC)	1	3
1959	Dublin	3	2
1960	Malmo	1	4
1970	Dublin (EC)	1	1
1970	Malmo (EC)	0	1
1999	Dublin	2	0
2006	Dublin	3	0
2013	Stockholm (WC)	0	0
2013	Dublin (WC)	1	2
2016	Paris (EC)	1	1

v SWITZERLAND

1935	Basle	0	1
1936	Dublin	1	0
1937	Berne	1	0
1938	Dublin	4	0
1948	Dublin	0	1
1975	Dublin (EC)	2	1
1975	Berne (EC)	0	1
1980	Dublin	2	0
1985	Dublin (WC)	3	0
1985	Berne (WC)	0	0
1992	Dublin	2	1
2002	Dublin (EC)	1	2
2003	Basle (EC)	0	2
2004	Basle (WC)	1	1
2005	Dublin (WC)	0	0
2016	Dublin	1	0
2019	Dublin (EC)	1	1
2019	Geneva (EC)	0	2

v TRINIDAD & TOBAGO

1982	Port of Spain	1	2

v TUNISIA

1988	Dublin	4	0

v TURKEY

1966	Dublin (EC)	2	1
1967	Ankara (EC)	1	2
1974	Izmir (EC)	1	1
1975	Dublin (EC)	4	0
1976	Ankara	3	3
1978	Dublin	4	2
1990	Izmir	0	0
1990	Dublin (EC)	5	0
1991	Istanbul (EC)	3	1
1999	Dublin (EC)	1	1
1999	Bursa (EC)	0	0
2003	Dublin	2	2
2014	Dublin	1	2
2018	Antalya	0	1

v URUGUAY

1974	Montevideo	0	2

1986	Dublin	1	1		2000	Foxboro	1	1
2011	Dublin	2	3		2002	Dublin	2	1
2017	Dublin	3	1		2014	Dublin	4	1
					2018	Dublin	2	1

v USA

1979	Dublin	3	2
1991	Boston	1	1
1992	Dublin	4	1
1992	Washington	1	3
1996	Boston	1	2

v YUGOSLAVIA

1955	Dublin	1	4
1988	Dublin	2	0
1998	Belgrade (EC)	0	1
1999	Dublin (EC)	2	1

BRITISH AND IRISH INTERNATIONAL APPEARANCES SINCE THE WAR (1946–2021)

(As at start of season 2021-22; in year shown 2021 = 2020–21. *Also a pre-War international player.
Totals include appearances as substitute)

ENGLAND

Player	Apps
Agbonlahor G (Aston Villa, 2009–10)	3
Abraham T (Chelsea, 2018–21)	6
A'Court A (Liverpool, 1958–59)	5
Adams T (Arsenal, 1987–2001)	66
Alexander-Arnold T (Liverpool, 2018–21)	13
Alli D (Tottenham, 2016–18)	37
Allen A (Stoke, 1960)	3
Allen C (QPR, Tottenham, 1984–88)	5
Allen R (WBA, 1952–55)	5
Anderson S (Sunderland, 1962)	2
Anderson V (Nottm Forest, Arsenal, Manchester Utd, 1979–88)	30
Anderton D (Tottenham, 1994–2002)	30
Angus J (Burnley, 1961)	1
Armfield G (Blackpool, 1959–66)	43
Armstrong D (Middlesbrough, Southampton, 1980–4)	3
Armstrong K (Chelsea, 1955)	1
Ashton D (West Ham, 2008)	1
Astall G (Birmingham, 1956)	2
Astle J (WBA, 1969–70)	5
Aston J (Manchester Utd, 1949–51)	17
Atyeo J (Bristol City, 1956–57)	6
Bailey G (Manchester Utd, 1985)	2
Bailey M (Charlton, 1964–5)	2
Baily E (Tottenham, 1950–3)	9
Baines L (Everton, 2010–15)	30
Baker J (Hibernian, Arsenal, 1960–6)	8
Ball A (Blackpool, Everton, Arsenal, 1965–75)	72
Ball M (Everton, 2001)	1
Banks G (Leicester, Stoke, 1963–72)	73
Banks T (Bolton, 1958–59)	6
Bardsley D (QPR, 1993)	2
Barham M (Norwich, 1983)	2
Barkley R (Everton, Chelsea, 2014–20)	33
Barlow R (WBA, 1955)	1
Barmby N (Tottenham, Middlesbrough, Everton, Liverpool, 1995–2002)	23
Barnes H (Leicester, 2021)	1
Barnes J (Watford, Liverpool, 1983–96)	79
Barnes P (Manchester City, WBA, Leeds, 1978–82)	22
Barrass M (Bolton, 1952–53)	3
Barrett E (Oldham, Aston Villa, 1991–93)	3
Barry G (Aston Villa, Manchester City, 2000–12)	53
Barton J (Manchester City, 2007)	1
Barton W (Wimbledon, Newcastle, 1995)	3
Batty D (Leeds, Blackburn, Newcastle, Leeds, 1991–2000)	42
Baynham R (Luton, 1956)	3
Beardsley P (Newcastle, Liverpool, Newcastle, 1986–96)	59
Beasant D (Chelsea, 1990)	2
Beattie J (Southampton, 2003–04)	5
Beattie K (Ipswich, 1975–58)	9
Beckham D (Manchester Utd, Real Madrid, LA Galaxy, AC Milan 1997–2010)	115
Bell C (Manchester City, 1968–76)	48
Bellingham J (Borussia Dortmund 2021)	7
Bent D (Charlton, Tottenham Sunderland, Aston Villa, 2006–12)	13
Bentley D (Blackburn, 2008–09)	7
Bentley R (Chelsea, 1949–55)	12
Berry J (Manchester Utd, 1953–56)	4
Bertrand R (Chelsea, Southampton, 2013–18)	19
Birtles G (Nottm Forest, 1980–81)	3
Blissett L (Watford, AC Milan, 1983–84)	14
Blockley J (Arsenal, 1973)	1
Blunstone F (Chelsea, 1955–57)	5
Bonetti P (Chelsea, 1966–70)	7
Bothroyd J (Cardiff, 2011)	1
Bould S (Arsenal, 1994)	2
Bowles S (QPR, 1974–77)	5
Bowyer L (Leeds, 2003)	1
Boyer P (Norwich, 1976)	1
Brabrook P (Chelsea, 1958–60)	3
Bracewell P (Everton, 1985–86)	3
Bradford G (Bristol Rov, 1956)	1
Bradley W (Manchester Utd, 1959)	3
Bridge W (Southampton, Chelsea, Manchester City 2002–10)	36

Bridges B (Chelsea, 1965–66) 4
Broadbent P (Wolves, 1958–60) 7
Broadis I (Manchester City, Newcastle, 1952–54) 14
Brooking T (West Ham, 1974–82) 47
Brooks J (Tottenham, 1957) 3
Brown A (WBA, 1971) 1
Brown K (West Ham, 1960) 1
Brown W (Manchester Utd, 1999–2010) 23
Bull S (Wolves, 1989–91) 13
Butcher T (Ipswich, Rangers, 1980–90) 77
Butland D (Birmingham, Stoke, 2013–19) 9
Butt N (Manchester Utd, Newcastle, 1997–2005) 39
Byrne G (Liverpool, 1963–66) 2
Byrne J (Crystal Palace, West Ham, 1962–65) 11
Byrne R (Manchester Utd, 1954–58) 33

Cahill G (Bolton, Chelsea, 2011–18) 61
Callaghan I (Liverpool, 1966–78) 4
Calvert–Lewin D (Everton) 2021) 11
Campbell F (Sunderland, 2012) 1
Campbell S (Tottenham, Arsenal, Portsmouth, 1996–2008) 73
Carragher J (Liverpool, 1999–2010) 38
Carrick M (West Ham, Tottenham, Manchester Utd, 2001–16) 34
Carroll A (Newcastle, Liverpool 2011– 13) 9
Carson S (Liverpool, Aston Villa WBA, Bursaspor 2008–12) 4
*Carter H (Derby, 1947) 7
Caulker S (Tottenham, 2013) 1
Chamberlain M (Stoke, 1983–85) 8
Chalobah N (Watford, 2019) 1
Chambers C (Arsenal, 2015) 3
Channon M (Southampton, Manchester City, 1973–78) 46
Charles G (Nottm Forest, 1991) 2
Charlton, J (Leeds, 1965–70) 35
Charlton, R (Manchester Utd, 1958–70) 106
Charnley R (Blackpool, 1963) 1
Cherry T (Leeds, 1976–80) 27
Chilton A (Manchester Utd, 1951–52) 2
Chilwell B (Leicester, Chelsea, 2019–21) 14
Chivers M (Tottenham, 1971–74) 24
Clamp E (Wolves, 1958) 4
Clapton D (Arsenal, 1959) 1
Clarke A (Leeds, 1970–6) 19
Clarke H (Tottenham, 1954) 1
Clayton R (Blackburn, 1956–60) 35
Clemence R (Liverpool, Tottenham, 1973–84) 61
Clement D (QPR, 1976–7) 5
Cleverley T (Manchester Utd, 2013–14) 13
Clough B (Middlesbrough, 1960) 2
Clough N (Nottm Forest, Liverpool, 1989–93) 14
Clyne N (Southampton, Liverpool, 2015–17) 14
Coady C (Wolves, 2021) 5
Coates R (Burnley, Tottenham, 1970–71) 4
Cockburn H (Manchester Utd, 1947–52) 13
Cohen G (Fulham, 1964–68) 37
Cole Andy (Manchester Utd, 1995–2002) 15
Cole Ashley (Arsenal, Chelsea, 2001–14) 107

Cole C (West Ham, 2009–10) 7
Cole J (West Ham, Chelsea, 2001–10) 56
Collymore S (Nottm Forest, Aston Villa, 1995–97) 3
Compton L (Arsenal, 1951) 2
Connelly J (Burnley, Manchester Utd,1960–66) 20
Cook L (Bournemouth, 2018) 1
Cooper C (Nottm Forest, 1995) 2
Cooper T (Leeds, 1969–75) 20
Coppell S (Manchester Utd, 1978–83) 42
Cork J (Burnley, 2018) 1
Corrigan J (Manchester City, 1976–82) 9
Cottee T (West Ham, Everton, 1987–89) 7
Cowans G (Aston Villa, Bari, Aston Villa, 1983–91) 10
Crawford R (Ipswich, 1962) 2
Cresswell A (West Ham, 2017–18) 3
Crouch P (Southampton, Liverpool, Portsmouth, Tottenham, 2005–11) 42
Crowe C (Wolves, 1963) 1
Cunningham L (WBA, Real Madrid, 1979–81) 6
Curle K (Manchester City, 1992) 3
Currie A (Sheffield Utd, Leeds, 1972–79) 17
Daley T (Aston Villa, 1992) 7
Davenport P (Nottm Forest, 1985) 1
Davies K (Bolton, 2011) 1
Dawson M (Tottenham 2011) 4
Deane B (Sheffield Utd, 1991–93) 3
Deeley N (Wolves, 1959) 2
Defoe J (Tottenham, Portsmouth, Tottenham, Sunderland, 2004–17) 57
Delph F (Aston Villa, Manchester City, 2015–19) 20
Devonshire A (West Ham, 1980–84) 8
Dickinson J (Portsmouth, 1949–57) 48
Dier E (Tottenham, 2016–21) 45
Ditchburn E (Tottenham, 1949–57) 6
Dixon K (Chelsea, 1985–87) 8
Dixon L (Arsenal, 1990–99) 22
Dobson M (Burnley, Everton, 1974–75) 5
Dorigo T (Chelsea, Leeds, 1990–94) 15
Douglas B (Blackburn, 1959–63) 36
Downing S (Middlesbrough, Aston Villa, Liverpool, West Ham, 2005–15) 35
Doyle M (Manchester City, 1976–77) 5
Drinkwater D (Leicester, 2016) 3
Dublin D (Coventry, Aston Villa, 1998–99) 4
Dunk L (Brighton, 2019) 1
Dunn D (Blackburn, 2003) 1
Duxbury, M (Manchester Utd, 1984–85) 10
Dyer K (Newcastle, West Ham, 2000–08) 33
Eastham G (Arsenal, 1963–66) 19
Eckersley W (Blackburn, 1950–54) 17
Edwards D (Manchester Utd, 1955–58) 18
Ehiogu U (Aston Villa, Middlesbrough, 1996–2002) 4
Ellerington W (Southampton, 1949) 2
Elliott W (Burnley, 1952–53) 5
Fantham J (Sheffield Wed, 1962) 1
Fashanu J (Wimbledon, 1989) 2

Fenwick T (QPR, 1984–88) 20
Ferdinand L (QPR, Newcastle, Tottenham, 1993–98) 17
Ferdinand R (West Ham, Leeds, Manchester Utd, 1997–2011) 81
Finney T (Preston, 1947–59) 76
Flanagan J (Liverpool, 2014) 1
Flowers R (Wolves, 1955–66) 49
Flowers T (Southampton, Blackburn, 1993–98) 11
Foden P (Manchester City, 2021) 9
Forster F (Celtic, Southampton, 2014–16) 6
Foster B (Manchester Utd, Birmingham, WBA, 2007–14) 8
Foster S (Brighton, 1982) 3
Foulkes W (Manchester Utd, 1955) 1
Fowler R (Liverpool, Leeds, 1996–2002) 26
Francis G (QPR, 1975–76) 12
Francis T (Birmingham, Nottm Forest, Man City, Sampdoria, 1977–86) 52
Franklin N (Stoke, 1947–50) 27
Froggatt J (Portsmouth, 1950–53) 13
Froggatt R (Sheffield Wed, 1953) 4

Gardner A (Tottenham, 2004) 1
Garrett T (Blackpool, 1952–54) 3
Gascoigne P (Tottenham, Lazio, Rangers, Middlesbrough, 1989–98) 57
Gates E (Ipswich, 1981) 2
George C (Derby, 1977) 1
Gerrard S (Liverpool, 2000–14) 114
Gibbs K (Arsenal, 2011–16) 10
Gidman J (Aston Villa, 1977) 1
Gillard I (QPR, 1975–76) 3
Goddard P (West Ham, 1982) 1
Godfrey B (Everton, 2021) 2
Gomez J (Liverpool, 2018–21) 11
Grainger C (Sheffield Utd, Sunderland, 1956–57) 7
Gray A (Crystal Palace, 1992) 1
Gray M (Sunderland, 1999) 3
Grealish J (Aston Villa, 2021) 12
Greaves J (Chelsea, Tottenham, 1959–67) 57
Green R (Norwich, West Ham 2005–12) 12
Greenhoff B (Manchester Utd, Leeds, 1976–80) 18
Greenwood M (Manchester Utd, 2021) 1
Gregory J (QPR, 1983–84) 6
Guppy S (Leicester, 2000) 1

Hagan J (Sheffield Utd, 1949) 1
Haines J (WBA, 1949) 1
Hall J (Birmingham, 1956–57) 17
Hancocks J (Wolves, 1949–50) 3
Hardwick G (Middlesbrough, 1947–48) 13
Harford M (Luton, 1988–89) 2
Hargreaves O (Bayern Munich, Manchester Utd, 2002–08) 42
Harris G (Burnley, 1966) 1
Harris P (Portsmouth, 1950–54) 2
Hart J (Manchester City, 2010–18) 75
Harvey C (Everton, 1971) 1
Hassall H (Huddersfield, Bolton, 1951–54) 5

Hateley M (Portsmouth, AC Milan, Monaco, Rangers, 1984–92) 32
Haynes J (Fulham, 1955–62) 56
Heaton T (Burnley, 2016–17) 3
Hector K (Derby, 1974) 2
Hellawell M (Birmingham, 1963) 2
Henderson D (Manchester Utd, 2021) 1
Henderson J (Sunderland, Liverpool, 2011–21) 64
Hendrie L (Aston Villa, 1999) 1
Henry R (Tottenham, 1963) 1
Heskey E (Leicester, Liverpool, Birmingham, Wigan, Aston Villa 1999–2010) 62
Hill F (Bolton, 1963) 2
Hill G (Manchester Utd, 1976–78) 6
Hill R (Luton, 1983–86) 3
Hinchcliffe A (Everton, Sheffield Wed, 1997–99) 7
Hinton A (Wolves, Nottm Forest, 1963–65) 3
Hirst D (Sheffield Wed, 1991–92) 3
Hitchens G (Aston Villa, Inter Milan, 1961–62) 7
Hoddle G (Tottenham, Monaco, 1980–88) 53
Hodge S (Aston Villa, Tottenham, Nottm Forest, 1986–91) 24
Hodgkinson A (Sheffield Utd, 1957–61) 5
Holden D (Bolton, 1959) 5
Holliday E (Middlesbrough, 1960) 3
Hollins J (Chelsea, 1967) 1
Hopkinson E (Bolton, 1958–60) 14
Howe D (WBA, 1958–60) 23
Howe J (Derby, 1948–49) 3
Howey S (Newcastle, 1995–96) 4
Huddlestone T (Tottenham, 2010–13) 4
Hudson A (Stoke, 1975) 2
Hudson-Odoi C (Chelsea, 2019–20) 3
Hughes E (Liverpool, Wolves, 1970–80) 62
Hughes L (Liverpool, 1950) 3
Hunt R (Liverpool, 1962–69) 34
Hunt S (WBA, 1984) 2
Hunter N (Leeds, 1966–75) 28
Hurst G (West Ham, 1966–72) 49

Ince P (Manchester Utd, Inter Milan, Liver-ool, Middlesbrough, 1993–2000) 53
Ings D (Liverpool, Southampton, 2016–21) 3

Jagielka P (Everton, 2008–17) 40
James D (Liverpool, Aston Villa, West Ham, Manchester City, Portsmouth, 1997–2010) 53
James R (Chelsea, 2021) 7
Jarvis M (Wolves, 2011) 1
Jeffers F (Arsenal, 2003) 1
Jenas J (Newcastle, Tottenham, 2003–10) 21
Jenkinson C (Arsenal, 2013) 1
Jezzard B (Fulham, 1954–56) 2
Johnson A (Crystal Palace, Everton, 2005–08) 8
Johnson A (Manchester City, 2010–13) 12
Johnson D (Ipswich, Liverpool, 1975–80) 8
Johnson G (Chelsea, Portsmouth, Liverpool, 2004–14) 54
Johnson S (Derby, 2001) 1
Johnstone S (WBA, 2021) 1

Johnston H (Blackpool, 1947–54) 10
Jones M (Leeds, Sheffield Utd, 1965–70) 3
Jones P (Manchester Utd, 2012–18) 27
Jones R (Liverpool, 1992–95) 8
Jones W H (Liverpool, 1950) 2

Kane H (Tottenham, 2015–21) 61
Kay A (Everton, 1963) 1
Keane M (Burnley, Everton, 2017–21) 12
Keegan K (Liverpool, Hamburg,
  Southampton, 1973–82) 63
Kelly, M (Liverpool, 2012) 1
Kennedy A (Liverpool, 1984) 2
Kennedy R (Liverpool, 1976–80) 17
Keown M (Everton, Arsenal,
  1992–2002) 43
Kevan D (WBA, 1957–61) 14
Kidd B (Manchester Utd, 1970) 2
King L (Tottenham, 2002–10) 21
Kirkland C (Liverpool, 2007) 1
Knight Z (Fulham, 2005) 2
Knowles C (Tottenham, 1968) 4
Konchesky P (Charlton, 2003–06) 2

Labone B (Everton, 1963–70) 26
Lallana A (Southampton, Liverpool, 2014–18) 34
Lambert R (Southampton, Liverpool, 2014–15) 11
Lampard F Snr (West Ham, 1973–80) 2
Lampard F Jnr (West Ham, Chelsea, 2000–14) 106
Langley J (Fulham, 1958) 3
Langton R (Blackburn, Preston,
  Bolton, 1947–51) 11
Latchford R (Everton, 1978–9) 12
Lawler C (Liverpool, 1971–72) 4
*Lawton T (Chelsea, Notts Co, 1947–49) 15
Lee F (Manchester City, 1969–72) 27
Lee J (Derby, 1951) 1
Lee R (Newcastle, 1995–99) 21
Lee S (Liverpool, 1983–84) 14
Lennon A (Tottenham, 2006–13) 21
Le Saux G (Blackburn, Chelsea, 1994–2001) 36
Lescott J (Everton, Manchester City, 2008–13) 26
Le Tissier M (Southampton, 1994–97) 8
Lindsay A (Liverpool, 1974) 4
Lineker G (Leicester, Everton, Barcelona,
  Tottenham, 1985–92) 80
Lingard J (Manchester Utd, 2017–21) 29
Little B (Aston Villa, 1975) 1
Livermore J (Tottenham, WBA, 2013–18) 7
Lloyd L (Liverpool, Nottm Forest, 1971–80) 4
Lofthouse N (Bolton, 1951–59) 33
Loftus–Cheek R (Chelsea, 2018–19) 10
Lowe E (Aston Villa, 1947) 3

Mabbutt G (Tottenham, 1983–92) 16
Macdonald M (Newcastle, 1972–76) 14
Madeley P (Leeds, 1971–77) 24
Maddison J (Leicester, 2020) 1
Maguire H (Leicester, Manchester Utd, 2018–21) 37
Maitland–Niles A (Arsenal, 2021) 5
Mannion W (Middlesbrough, 1947–52) 26
Mariner P (Ipswich, Arsenal, 1977–85) 35

Marsh R (QPR, Manchester City, 1972–73) 9
Mason R (Tottenham, 2015) 1
Martin A (West Ham, 1981–87) 17
Martyn N (Crystal Palace, Leeds, 1992–2002) 23
Marwood B (Arsenal, 1989) 1
Matthews R (Coventry, 1956–57) 5
*Matthews S (Stoke, Blackpool, 1947–57) 37
McCann G (Sunderland, 2001) 1
McCarthy A (Southampton, 2019) 1
McDermott T (Liverpool, 1978–82) 25
McDonald C (Burnley, 1958–59) 8
McFarland R (Derby, 1971–77) 28
McGarry W (Huddersfield, 1954–56) 4
McGuinness W (Manchester Utd, 1959) 2
McMahon S (Liverpool, 1988–91) 17
McManaman S (Liverpool, Real Madrid,
  1995–2002) 37
McNab R (Arsenal, 1969) 4
McNeil M (Middlesbrough, 1961–62) 9
Meadows J (Manchester City, 1955) 1
Medley L (Tottenham, 1951–52) 6
Melia J (Liverpool, 1963) 2
Merrick G (Birmingham, 1952–54) 23
Merson P (Arsenal, Middlesbrough,
  Aston Villa, 1992–99) 21
Metcalfe V (Huddersfield, 1951) 2
Milburn J (Newcastle, 1949–56) 13
Miller B (Burnley, 1961) 1
Mills D (Leeds, 2001–04) 19
Mills M (Ipswich, 1973–82) 42
Milne G (Liverpool, 1963–65) 14
Milner J (Aston Villa, Manchester City,
  Liverpool, 2010–16) 61
Milton A (Arsenal, 1952) 1
Mings T (Aston Villa, 2020–21) 13
Moore R (West Ham, 1962–74) 108
Morley A (Aston Villa, 1982–83) 6
Morris J (Derby, 1949–50) 3
Mortensen S (Blackpool, 1947–54) 25
Mount M (Chelsea, 2020–21) 21
Mozley B (Derby, 1950) 3
Mullen J (Wolves, 1947–54) 12
Mullery A (Tottenham, 1965–72) 35
Murphy D (Liverpool, 2002–04) 9

Neal P (Liverpool, 1976–84) 50
Neville G (Manchester Utd, 1995–2009) 85
Neville P (Manchester Utd, Everton,
  1996–2008) 59
Newton K (Blackburn, Everton, 1966–70) 27
Nicholls J (WBA, 1954) 2
Nicholson W (Tottenham, 1951) 1
Nish D (Derby, 1973–74) 5
Norman M (Tottenham, 1962–5) 23
Nugent D (Preston, 2007) 1

O'Grady M (Huddersfield, Leeds, 1963–9) 2
Osgood P (Chelsea, 1970–74) 4
Osman L (Everton, 2013) 2
Osman R (Ipswich, 1980–84) 11
Owen M (Liverpool, Real Madrid,
  Newcastle, 1998–2008) 89

Owen S (Luton, 1954)	3
Oxlade–Chamberlain A (Arsenal, Liverpool, 2012–20)	35
Paine T (Southampton, 1963–66)	19
Pallister G (Middlesbrough, Manchester Utd 1988–97)	22
Palmer C (Sheffield Wed, 1992–94)	18
Parker P (QPR, Manchester Utd, 1989–94)	19
Parker's (Charlton, Chelsea, Newcastle, West Ham, Tottenham, 2004–13)	18
Parkes P (QPR, 1974)	
Parlour R (Arsenal, 1999–2001)	10
Parry R (Bolton, 1960)	2
Peacock A (Middlesbrough, Leeds, 1962–66)	6
Pearce S (Nottm Forest, West Ham, 1987–2000)	78
Pearson Stan (Manchester Utd, 1948–52)	8
Pearson Stuart (Manchester Utd, 1976–78)	15
Pegg D (Manchester Utd, 1957)	1
Pejic M (Stoke, 1974)	4
Perry W (Blackpool, 1956)	3
Perryman S (Tottenham, 1982)	1
Peters M (West Ham, Tottenham, 1966–74)	67
Phelan M (Manchester Utd, 1990)	1
Phillips K (Leeds, 2021)	15
Phillips K (Sunderland, 1999–2002)	8
Phillips L (Portsmouth, 1952–55)	3
Pickering F (Everton, 1964–65)	3
Pickering N (Sunderland, 1983)	1
Pickford J (Everton, 2018–21)	38
Pilkington B (Burnley, 1955)	1
Platt D (Aston Villa, Bari, Juventus, Sampdoria, Arsenal, 1990–96)	62
Pointer R (Burnley, 1962)	3
Pope N (Burnley, 2018–21)	7
Powell C (Charlton, 2001–02)	5
Pye J (Wolves, 1950)	1
Quixall A (Sheffield Wed, 1954–55)	5
Radford J (Arsenal, 1969–72)	2
Ramsey A (Southampton, Tottenham, 1949–54)	32
Rashford M (Manchester Utd, 2016–21)	46
Reaney P (Leeds, 1969–71)	3
Redknapp J (Liverpool, 1996–2000)	17
Redmond N (Southampton 2017)	1
Reeves K (Norwich, Manchester City, 1980)	2
Regis C (WBA, Coventry, 1982–88)	5
Reid P (Everton, 1985–88)	13
Revie D (Manchester City, 1955–57)	6
Rice D (West Ham, 2019–21)	24
Richards, J (Wolves, 1973)	1
Richards M (Manchester City, 2007–12)	13
Richardson K (Aston Villa, 1994)	1
Richardson K (Manchester Utd, 2005–07)	8
Rickaby S (WBA, 1954)	1
Ricketts M (Bolton, 2002)	1
Rimmer J (Arsenal, 1976)	1
Ripley S (Blackburn, 1994–97)	2
Rix G (Arsenal, 1981–84)	17

Robb G (Tottenham, 1954)	1
Roberts G (Tottenham, 1983–84)	6
Robinson P (Leeds, Tottenham, 2003–08)	41
Robson B (WBA, Manchester Utd, 1980–92)	90
Robson R (WBA, 1958–62)	20
Rocastle D (Arsenal, 1989–92)	14
Rodriguez J (Southampton, 2014)	1
Rodwell J (Everton, Manchester City, 2012–13)	3
Rooney W (Everton, Manchester Utd, DC United, 2003–19)	120
Rose D (Tottenham, 2016–20)	29
Rowley J (Manchester Utd, 1949–52)	6
Royle J (Everton, Manchester City, 1971–77)	6
Ruddock N (Liverpool, 1995)	1
Ruddy J (Norwich, 2013)	1
Sadler D (Manchester Utd, 1968–71)	4
Saka B (Arsenal, 2021)	9
Salako J (Crystal Palace, 1991–92)	5
Sancho J (Borussia Dortmund, 2019–21)	22
Sansom K (Crystal Palace, Arsenal, 1979–88)	86
Scales J (Liverpool, 1995)	3
Scholes P (Manchester Utd, 1997–2004)	66
Scott L (Arsenal, 1947–49)	17
Seaman D (QPR, Arsenal, 1989–2003)	75
Sewell J (Sheffield Wed, 1952–54)	6
Shackleton L (Sunderland, 1949–55)	5
Sharpe L (Manchester Utd, 1991–94)	8
Shaw G (Sheffield Utd, 1959–63)	5
Shaw L (Southampton, Manchester Utd, 2014–21)	16
Shawcross, R (Stoke, 2013)	1
Shearer A (Southampton, Blackburn, Newcastle, 1992–2000)	63
Shellito K (Chelsea, 1963)	1
Shelvey J (Liverpool, Swansea, 2013–16)	6
Sheringham E (Tottenham, Manchester Utd, Tottenham, 1993–2002)	51
Sherwood T (Tottenham, 1999)	3
Shilton P (Leicester, Stoke, Nottm Forest, Southampton, Derby, 1971–90)	125
Shimwell E (Blackpool, 1949)	1
Shorey N (Reading, 2007)	2
Sillett P (Chelsea, 1955)	3
Sinclair T (West Ham, Manchester City, 2002–04)	12
Sinton A (QPR, Sheffield Wed, 1992–94)	12
Slater W (Wolves, 1955–60)	12
Smalling C (Manchester Utd, 2012–17)	31
Smith A (Arsenal, 1989–92)	13
Smith A (Leeds, Manchester Utd, Newcastle, 2001–08)	19
Smith L (Arsenal, 1951–53)	6
Smith R (Tottenham, 1961–64)	15
Smith T (Birmingham, 1960)	2
Smith T (Liverpool, 1971)	1
Solanke D (Liverpool, 2018)	1
Southgate G (Aston Villa, Middlesbrough, 1996–2004)	57
Spink N (Aston Villa, 1983)	1

Springett R (Sheffield Wed, 1960–66) 33
Staniforth R (Huddersfield, 1954–55) 8
Statham D (WBA, 1983) 3
Stein B (Luton, 1984) 1
Stepney A (Manchester Utd, 1968) 1
Sterland M (Sheffield Wed, 1989) 1
Sterling R (Liverpool, Manchester City, 2013–21) 68
Steven T (Everton, Rangers, Marseille, 1985–92) 36
Stevens G (Everton, Rangers, 1985–92) 46
Stevens G (Tottenham, 1985–86) 7
Stewart P (Tottenham, 1992) 3
Stiles N (Manchester Utd, 1965–70) 28
Stone S (Nottm Forest, 1996) 9
Stones J (Everton, Manchester City, 2014–21) 49
Storey P (Arsenal, 1971–73) 19
Storey-Moore I (Nottm Forest, 1970) 1
Streten B (Luton, 1950) 1
Sturridge D (Chelsea, Liverpool, 2012–18) 26
Summerbee M (Manchester City, 1968–73) 8
Sunderland, A (Arsenal, 1980) 1
Sutton C (Blackburn, 1997) 1
Swan P (Sheffield Wed, 1960–62) 19
Swift F (Manchester City, 1947–79) 19

Talbot B (Ipswich, Arsenal, 1977–80) 6
Tambling R (Chelsea, 1963–66) 3
Tarkowski J (Burnley, 2018–19) 2
Taylor E (Blackpool, 1954) 1
Taylor J (Fulham, 1951) 2
Taylor P (Liverpool, 1948) 3
Taylor P (Crystal Palace, 1976) 4
Taylor T (Manchester Utd, 1953–58) 19
Temple D (Everton, 1965) 1
Terry J (Chelsea, 2003–13) 78
Thomas D (QPR, 1975–76) 8
Thomas D (Coventry, 1983) 2
Thomas G (Crystal Palace, 1991–92) 9
Thomas M (Arsenal, 1989–90) 2
Thompson A (Celtic, 2004) 1
Thompson Peter (Liverpool, 1964–70) 16
Thompson Phil (Liverpool, 1976–83) 42
Thompson T (Aston Villa, Preston, 1952–57) 2
Thomson R (Wolves, 1964–65) 8
Todd C (Derby, 1972–77) 27
Tomori F (Chelsea, 2020) 1
Towers A (Sunderland, 1978) 3
Townsend A (Tottenham, Newcastle, Crystal Palace, 2014–17) 13
Trippier K (Tottenham, Atletico Madrid, 2017–21) 33
Tueart D (Manchester City, 1975–77) 6

Ufton D (Charlton, 1954) 1
Unsworth D (Everton, 1995) 1
Upson M (Birmingham, West Ham, 2003–10) 21

Vardy (Leicester, 2015–18) 26
Vassell D (Aston Villa, 2002–04) 22
Venables T (Chelsea, 1965) 2
Venison B (Newcastle, 1995) 2
Viljoen C (Ipswich, 1975) 2
Viollet D (Manchester Utd, 1960) 2

Waddle C (Newcastle, Tottenham, Marseille, 1985–92) 62
Waiters A (Blackpool, 1964–65) 5
Walcott T (Arsenal, 2006–17) 47
Walker D (Nottm Forest, Sampdoria, Sheffield Wed, 1989–94) 59
Walker I (Tottenham, Leicester, 1996–2004) 48
Walker K (Tottenham, Manchester City, 2012–21) 61
Wallace D (Southampton, 1986) 1
Walsh P (Luton, 1983–4) 5
Walters M (Rangers, 1991) 1
Ward P (Brighton, 1980) 1
Ward T (Derby, 1948) 2
Ward-Prowse J (Southampton, 2017–21) 8
Warnock S (Blackburn, Aston Villa, 2008–11) 2
Watson D (Sunderland, Manchester City, Werder Bremen, Southampton, Stoke, 1974–82) 65
Watkins O (Aston Villa, 2021) 3
Watson D (Norwich, Everton, 1984–8) 12
Watson W (Sunderland, 1950–1) 4
Webb N (Nottm Forest, Manchester Utd, 1988–92) 26
Welbeck D (Manchester Utd, Arsenal, 2011–19) 42
Weller K (Leicester, 1974) 4
West G (Everton, 1969) 3
Wheeler J (Bolton, 1955) 1
White B (Brighton, 2021) 2
White D (Manchester City, 1993) 1
Whitworth S (Leicester, 1975–76) 7
Whymark T (Ipswich, 1978) 1
Wignall F (Nottm Forest, 1965) 2
Wilcox J (Blackburn, Leeds, 1996–2000) 3
Wilkins R (Chelsea, Manchester Utd, AC Milan, 1976–87) 84
Williams B (Wolves, 1949–56) 24
Williams S (Southampton, 1983–85) 6
Willis A (Tottenham, 1952) 1
Wilshaw D (Wolves, 1954–57) 12
Wilshere J (Arsenal, 2011–16) 34
Wilson C (Bournemouth, 2019–20) 4
Wilson R (Huddersfield, Everton, 1960–8) 63
Winks H (Tottenham, 2018–21) 10
Winterburn N (Arsenal, 1990–93) 2
Wise D (Chelsea, 1991–2001) 21
Withe P (Aston Villa, 1981–85) 11
Wood R (Manchester Utd, 1955–56) 3
Woodcock A (Nottm Forest, Cologne, Arsenal, 1977–86) 42
Woodgate J (Leeds, Newcastle, Middlesbrough, Tottenham, 1999–2008) 8
Woods C (Norwich, Rangers, Sheffield Wed, 1984–93) 43
Worthington F (Leicester, 1974–75) 8
Wright I (Crystal Palace, Arsenal, West Ham, 1991–99) 33
Wright M (Southampton, Derby, Liverpool, 1984–96) 45
Wright R (Ipswich, Arsenal, 2000–02) 2
Wright T (Everton, 1968–70) 11

Wright W (Wolves, 1947–59) 105
Wright–Phillips S (Manchester City,
   Chelsea, Manchester City, 2005–11) 36
Young A (Aston Villa, Manchester Utd, 2008–18) 39
Young G (Sheffield Wed, 1965) 1
Young L (Charlton, 2005) 7
Zaha W (Manchester Utd, 2013–14) 2
Zamora R (Fulham, 2011–12) 2

SCOTLAND

Adam C (Rangers, Blackpool, Liverpool,
   Stoke, 2007–15) 26
Adams C (Southampton, 2021) 7
Aird J (Burnley, 1954) 4
Aitken G (East Fife, 1949–54) 8
Aitken R (Celtic, Newcastle, St Mirren, 1980–92) 57
Albiston A (Manchester Utd, 1982–6) 14
Alexander G (Preston, Burnley, 2002–10) 40
Alexander N (Cardiff, 2006) 3
Allan T (Dundee, 1974) 2
Anderson J (Leicester, 1954) 1
Anderson R (Aberdeen, Sunderland, 2003–08) 11
Anya I (Watford, Derby, 2014–18) 29
Archer J (Millwall, 2018) 1
Archibald S (Aberdeen, Tottenham,
   Barcelona, 1980–86) 27
Armstrong S (Celtic, Southampton, 2017–21) 28
Auld B (Celtic, 1959–60) 3

Bain S (Celtic, 2018–19) 3
Baird H (Airdrie, 1956) 1
Baird S (Rangers, 1957–58) 7
Bannan B (Aston Villa, Crystal Palace,
   Sheffield Wed, 2011–18) 27
Bannon E (Dundee Utd, 1980–86) 11
Bardsley P (Sunderland, 2011–14) 13
Barr D (Falkirk, 2009) 1
Bates D (Hamburger, 2019) 4
Bauld W (Hearts, 1950) 3
Baxter J (Rangers, Sunderland, 1961–68) 34
Beattie C (Celtic, WBA, 2006–08) 7
Bell C (Kilmarnock, 2011) 1
Bell W (Leeds, 1966) 2
Bernard P (Oldham, 1995) 2
Berra C (Hearts, Wolves, Ipswich,
   Hearts, 2008–18) 41
Bett J (Rangers, Lokeren, Aberdeen, 1982–90) 26
Black E (Metz, 1988) 2
Black I (Southampton, 1948) 1
Black I (Rangers, 2013) 1
Blacklaw A (Burnley, 1963–66) 3
Blackley J (Hibernian, 1974–77) 7
Blair J (Blackpool, 1947) 1
Blyth J (Coventry, 1994) 2
Bone J (Norwich, 1972–73) 2
Booth S (Aberdeen, Borussia Dortmund,
   Twente Enschede 1993–2002) 22
Bowman D (Dundee Utd, 1992–94) 6
Boyd G (Peterborough, Hull, 2013–14) 2
Boyd K (Rangers, Middlesbrough, 2006–11) 18
Boyd T (Motherwell, Chelsea, Celtic,
   1991–2002) 72

Brand R (Rangers, 1961–62) 8
Brazil A (Ipswich, Tottenham, 1980–83) 13
Bremner D (Hibernian, 1976) 1
Bremner W (Leeds, 1965–76) 54
Brennan F (Newcastle, 1947–54) 7
Bridcutt L (Brighton, Sunderland, 2013–16) 2
Broadfoot K (Rangers, 2009–11) 4
Brogan J (Celtic, 1971) 4
Brophy E (Kilmarnock, 2019) 1
Brown A (East Fife, Blackpool, 1950–54) 13
Brown H (Partick, 1947) 3
Brown J (Sheffield Utd, 1975) 1
Brown R (Rangers, 1947–52) 5
Brown S (Hibernian, Celtic, 2007–18) 55
Brown W (Dundee, Tottenham, 1958–66) 28
Brownlie J (Hibernian, 1971–76) 7
Bryson C (Kilmarnock, Derby, 2011–16) 3
Buchan M (Aberdeen, Manchester Utd, 1972–8) 34
Buckley P (Aberdeen, 1954–55) 3
Burchill M (Celtic, 2000) 6
Burke C (Rangers, Birmingham, 2006–14) 7
Burke O (Nottm Forest, Leipzig, WBA, 2016–21) 13
Burley C (Chelsea, Celtic, Derby,
   1995–2003) 46
Burley G (Ipswich, 1979–82) 11
Burns F (Manchester Utd, 1970) 1
Burns K (Birmingham, Nottm Forest, 1974–81) 20
Burns T (Celtic, 1981–88) 8

Cadden C (Motherwell, 2018) 2
Caddis P (Birmingham, 2016) 1
Calderwood C (Tottenham, Aston Villa,
   1995–2000) 36
Caldow E (Rangers, 1957–63) 40
Cairney T (Fulham, 2017–18) 2
Caldwell G (Newcastle, Sunderland, Hibernian,
   Wigan, 2002–13) 55
Caldwell S (Newcastle, Sunderland,
   Celtic, Wigan, 2001–11) 12
Callaghan T (Dunfermline, 1970) 2
Cameron C (Hearts, Wolves, 1999–2005) 28
Campbell R (Falkirk, Chelsea, 1947–50) 5
Campbell W (Morton, 1947–48) 5
Canero P (Leicester, 2004) 1
Carr W (Coventry, 1970–73) 6
Chalmers S (Celtic, 1965–67) 5
Christie R (Celtic 2018–21) 20
Clark J (Celtic, 1966–67) 4
Clark R (Aberdeen, 1968–73) 17
Clarke S (Chelsea, 1988–94) 6
Clarkson D (Motherwell, 2008–09) 2
Collins J (Hibernian, Celtic, Monaco,
   Everton, 1988–2000) 58
Collins R (Celtic, Everton, Leeds,
   1951–65) 31
Colquhoun E (Sheffield Utd, 1972–73) 9
Colquhoun J (Hearts, 1988) 2
Combe J (Hibernian, 1948) 3
Commons K (Derby, Celtic, 2009–13) 12
Conn A (Hearts, 1956) 1
Conn A (Tottenham, 1975) 2
Connachan E (Dunfermline, 1962) 2
Connelly G (Celtic, 1974) 2

Gilzean A (Dundee, Tottenham, 1964–71) 22
Glass S (Newcastle Utd 1999) 1
Glavin R (Celtic, 1977) 1
Glen A (Aberdeen, 1956) 2
Goodwillie D (Dundee Utd, Blackburn, 2011–12) 3
Goram A (Oldham, Hibernian, Rangers, 1986–98) 43
Gordon C (Hearts, Sunderland, Celtic, Hearts, 2004–21) 57
Gough R (Dundee Utd, Tottenham, Rangers, 1983–93) 61
Gould J (Celtic, 2000–01) 2
Govan J (Hibernian, 1948–49) 6
Graham A (Leeds, 1978–81) 10
Graham G (Arsenal, Manchester Utd, 1972–73) 12
Gray A (Aston Villa, Wolves, Everton, 1976–85) 20
Gray A (Bradford City, 2003) 2
Gray E (Leeds, 1969–77) 12
Gray F (Leeds, Nottm Forest, 1976–83) 32
Grant J (Hibernian, 1958) 2
Grant P (Celtic, 1989) 2
Green A (Blackpool, Newcastle, 1971–72) 6
Greer G (Brighton, 2014–16) 11
Greig J (Rangers, 1964–76) 44
Griffiths L (Wolves, Celtic, 2013) 22
Gunn B (Norwich, 1990–94) 6

Haddock H (Clyde, 1955–58) 6
Haffey F (Celtic, 1960–61) 2
Hamilton A (Dundee, 1962–66) 24
Hamilton G (Aberdeen, 1947–54) 5
Hamilton W (Hibernian, 1965) 1
Hammell S (Motherwell, 2005) 1
Hanley G (Blackburn, Newcastle, Norwich, 2011–21) 36
Hanlon P (Hibernian, 2021) 1
Hansen A (Liverpool, 1979–87) 26
Hansen J (Partick, 1972) 2
Harper J (Aberdeen, Hibernian, 1973–78) 4
Hartford A (WBA, Manchester City, Everton, 1972–82) 50
Hartley P (Hearts, Celtic, Bristol City, 2005–10) 25
Harvey D (Leeds, 1973–77) 16
Haughney M (Celtic, 1954) 1
Hay D (Celtic, 1970–74) 27
Hegarty P (Dundee Utd, 1979–83) 8
Henderson J (Portsmouth, Arsenal, 1953–59) 7
Henderson W (Rangers, 1963–71) 29
Hendry C (Blackburn, Rangers, Coventry, Bolton, 1994–2001) 51
Hendry J (Celtic, 2018–21) 7
Herd D (Arsenal, 1959–61) 5
Herd G (Clyde, 1958–61) 5
Herriot J (Birmingham, 1969–70) 8
Hewie J (Charlton, 1956–60) 19
Holt D (Hearts, 1963–64) 5
Holt G (Kilmarnock, Norwich, 2001–05) 10
Holton J (Manchester Utd, 1973–75) 15

Hope R (WBA, 1968–69) 2
Hopkin D (Crystal Palace, Leeds, 1997–2000) 7
Houliston W (Queen of the South, 1949) 3
Houston S (Manchester Utd, 1976) 1
Howie H (Hibernian, 1949) 1
Hughes J (Celtic, 1965–70) 8
Hughes R (Portsmouth, 2004–06) 5
Hughes S (Norwich, 2010) 1
Hughes W (Sunderland, 1975) 1
Humphries W (Motherwell, 1952) 1
Hunter A (Kilmarnock, Celtic, 1972–74) 4
Hunter W (Motherwell, 1960–61) 3
Husband J (Partick, 1947) 1
Hutchison D (Everton, Sunderland, West Ham, 1999–2004) 26
Hutchison T (Coventry, 1974–76) 17
Hutton A (Rangers, Tottenham, Aston Villa, 2007–16) 50

Imlach S (Nottm Forest, 1958) 4
Irvine B (Aberdeen, 1991–94) 9
Iwelumo C (Wolves, Burnley, 2009–11) 4

Jack R (Rangers, 2018–21) 10
Jackson C (Rangers, 1975–77) 8
Jackson D (Hibernian, Celtic, 1995–99) 28
Jardine A (Rangers, 1971–80) 38
Jarvie A (Airdrie, 1971) 3
Jess E (Aberdeen, Coventry, Aberdeen, 1993–99) 18
Johnston A (Sunderland, Rangers, Middlesbrough, 1999–2003) 18
Johnston L (Clyde, 1948) 2
Johnston M (Watford, Celtic, Nantes, Rangers, 1984–92) 38
Johnston W (Rangers, WBA, 1966–78) 21
Johnstone D (Rangers, 1973–80) 14
Johnstone J (Celtic, 1965–75) 23
Johnstone R (Hibernian, Manchester City, 1951–56) 17
Jordan J (Leeds, Manchester Utd, AC Milan, 1973–82) 52

Kelly H (Blackpool, 1952) 1
Kelly J (Barnsley, 1949) 2
Kelly L (Kilmarnock, 2013) 1
Kennedy J (Celtic, 1964–65) 6
Kennedy J (Celtic, 2004) 1
Kennedy S (Rangers, 1975) 5
Kennedy S (Aberdeen, 1978–82) 8
Kenneth G (Dundee Utd, 2011) 2
Kerr A (Partick, 1955) 2
Kerr B (Newcastle, 2003–04) 3
Kingsley S (Swansea, 2016) 1
Kyle K (Sunderland, Kilmarnock, 2002–10) 10
Lambert P (Motherwell, Borussia Dortmund, Celtic, 1995–2003) 40
Law D (Huddersfield, Manchester City, Torino, Manchester Utd, 1959–74) 55
Lawrence T (Liverpool, 1963–69) 3
Leggat G (Aberdeen, Fulham, 1956–60) 18
Leighton J (Aberdeen, Manchester Utd, Hibernian, Aberdeen, 1983–99) 91

Lennox R (Celtic, 1967–70) 10
Leslie L (Airdrie, 1961) 5
Levein C (Hearts, 1990–95) 16
Liddell W (Liverpool, 1947–55) 28
Linwood A (Clyde, 1950) 1
Little R (Rangers, 1953) 1
Logie J (Arsenal, 1953) 1
Long H (Clyde, 1947) 1
Lorimer P (Leeds, 1970–76) 21

Macari L (Celtic, Manchester Utd, 1972–78) 24
Macaulay A (Brentford, Arsenal, 1947–48) 7
MacDonald A (Rangers, 1976) 1
MacDougall E (Norwich, 1975–76) 7
Mackail–Smith C (Peterborough, Brighton 2011–12) 7
MacKay D (Celtic, 1959–62) 14
Mackay D (Hearts, Tottenham, 1957–66) 22
Mackay G (Hearts, 1988) 4
Mackay M (Norwich, 2004–05) 5
Mackay-Steven G (Dundee Utd, 2014) 2
MacKenzie J (Partick, 1954–56) 9
Mackie J (QPR, 2011–13) 9
MacLeod J (Hibernian, 1961) 4
MacLeod M (Celtic, Borussia Dortmund, Hibernian, 1985–91) 20
Maguire C (Aberdeen, 2011) 2
Maloney S (Celtic, Aston Villa, Celtic, Wigan, Chicago, Hull, 2006–16) 47
Malpas M (Dundee Utd, 1984–93) 55
Marshall D (Celtic, Cardiff, Hull, Derby, 2005–21) 47
Marshall G (Celtic, 1992) 1
Martin B (Motherwell, 1995) 2
Martin C (Derby, 2014–18) 17
Martin F (Aberdeen, 1954–55) 6
Martin N (Hibernian, Sunderland, 1965–66) 3
Martin R (Norwich, 2011–17) 29
Martis J (Motherwell, 1961) 1
Mason J (Third Lanark 1949–51) 7
Masson D (QPR, Derby, 1976–78) 17
Mathers D (Partick, 1954) 1
Matteo D (Leeds, 2001–02) 6
May S (Sheffield Wed, 2015) 1
McAllister B (Wimbledon, 1997) 3
McAllister G (Leicester, Leeds, Coventry, 1990–99) 57
McAllister J (Livingston, 2004) 1
McArthur J (Wigan, Crystal Palace, 2011–18) 32
McAvennie F (West Ham, Celtic, 1986–88) 5
McBride J (Celtic, 1967) 2
McBurnie O (Swansea, Sheffield Utd, 2018–21) 14
McCall S (Everton, Rangers, 1990–98) 40
McCalliog J (Sheffield Wed, Wolves, 1967–71) 5
McCann N (Hearts, Rangers, Southampton, 1999–2006) 26
McCann R (Motherwell, 1959–61) 5
McClair B (Celtic, Manchester Utd, 1987–93) 30
McCloy P (Rangers, 1973) 1
McCoist A (Rangers, Kilmarnock, 1986–99) 61

McColl I (Rangers, 1950–58) 14
McCormack R (Motherwell, Cardiff, Leeds, Fulham, 2008–16) 13
McCreadie E (Chelsea, 1965–9) 23
McCulloch L (Wigan, Rangers, 2005–11) 18
McDonald J (Sunderland, 1956) 2
McDonald K (Fulham, 2018–19) 5
McEveley, J (Derby, 2008) 3
McFadden J (Motherwell, Everton, Birmingham, 2002–11) 48
McFarlane W (Hearts, 1947) 1
McGarr E (Aberdeen, 1970) 2
McGarvey F (Liverpool, Celtic, 1979–84) 7
McGeoch D (Hibernian, 2018) 2
McGhee M (Aberdeen, 1983–84) 4
McGinlay J (Bolton, 1995–97) 13
McGinn J (Hibernian, Aston Villa, 2016–21) 36
McGrain D (Celtic, 1973–82) 62
McGregor A (Rangers, Besiktas, Hull, Rangers, 2007–19) 42
McGregor C (Celtic, 2018–21) 34
McGrory D (Kilmarnock, 1965–66) 3
McInally A (Aston Villa, Bayern Munich, 1989–90) 8
McInally J (Dundee Utd, 1987–93) 10
McInnes D (WBA, 2003) 2
McKay B (Rangers, 2016) 1
McKean R (Rangers, 1976) 1
McKenna S (Aberdeen, Nottm Forest, 2018–21) 22
McKimmie S (Aberdeen, 1989–96) 40
McKinlay T (Celtic, 1996–98) 22
McKinlay W (Dundee Utd, Blackburn, 1994–99) 29
McKinnon R (Rangers, 1966–71) 28
McKinnon R (Motherwell, 1994–95) 3
McLaren A (Preston, 1947–48) 4
McLaren A (Hearts, Rangers, 1992–96) 24
McLaren A (Kilmarnock, 2001) 1
McLaughlin J (Hearts, Sunderland, 2018–20) 2
McLean G (Dundee, 1968) 1
McLean K (Aberdeen, Norwich, 2016–21) 20
McLean T (Kilmarnock, Rangers,1969–71) 6
McLeish A (Aberdeen, 1980–93) 77
McLintock F (Leicester, Arsenal,1963–71) 9
McManus S (Celtic, Middlesbrough,2007–11) 26
McMillan I (Airdrie, 1952–61) 6
McNamara J (Celtic, Wolves,1997–2006) 33
McNamee D (Livingston, 2004–06) 4
McNaught W (Raith, 1951–55) 5
McNaughton D (Aberdeen, Cardiff, 2002–08) 4
McNeill W (Celtic, 1961–72) 29
McNulty M (Reading, 2019) 2
McPhail J (Celtic, 1950–54) 5
McPherson D (Hearts, Rangers, 1989–93) 27
McQueen G (Leeds, Manchester Utd, 1974–81) 30
McStay P (Celtic, 1984–97) 76
McSwegan G (Hearts, 2000) 2
McTominay S (Manchester Utd, 2018–21) 26
Millar J (Rangers, 1963) 2
Miller C (Dundee Utd, 2001) 1
Miller K (Rangers, Wolves, Celtic, Derby,

Rangers, Bursaspor, Cardiff,
   Vancouver, 2001–14)   69
Miller L (Dundee Utd, Aberdeen 2006–10)   3
Miller W (Celtic, 1946–47)   6
Miller W (Aberdeen, 1975–90)   65
Mitchell R (Newcastle, 1951)   2
Mochan N (Celtic, 1954)   3
Moir W (Bolton, 1950)   1
Moncur R (Newcastle, 1968–72)   16
Morgan L (Celtic, 2018)   2
Morgan W (Burnley, Manchester Utd,
   1968–74)   21
Morris H (East Fife, 1950)   1
Morrison J (WBA, 2008–18)   46
Mudie J (Blackpool, 1957–58)   17
Mulgrew C (Celtic, Blackburn, 2012–20)   44
Mulhall G (Aberdeen, Sunderland, 1960–64)   3
Munro F (Wolves, 1971–75)   9
Munro I (St Mirren, 1979–80)   7
Murdoch R (Celtic, 1966–70)   12
Murphy J (Brighton, 2018)   2
Murray I (Hibernian, Rangers, 2003–06)   5
Murray J (Hearts, 1958)   5
Murray S (Aberdeen, 1972)   1
Murty G (Reading, 2004–08)   4

Naismith S (Kilmarnock, Rangers, Everton,
   Norwich, Hearts, 2007–20)   51
Narey D (Dundee Utd, 1977–89)   35
Naysmith G (Hearts, Everton, Sheffield Utd,
   2000–09)   46
Neilson R (Hearts, 2007)   1
Nevin P (Chelsea, Everton, Tranmere,
   1987–96)   28
Nicholas C (Celtic, Arsenal, Aberdeen,
   1983–89)   20
Nicholson B (Dunfermline, 2001–05)   3
Nicol S (Liverpool, 1985–92)   27
Nisbet K (Hibernian, 2021)   6

O'Connor G (Hibernian, Lokomotiv Moscow,
   Birmingham, 2002–10)   16
O'Donnell P (Motherwell, 1994)   1
O'Donnell S (Kilmarnock, Motherwell,
   2018–21)   22
O'Hare J (Derby, 1970–72)   13
O'Neil B (Celtic, VfL Wolfsburg, Derby,
   Preston, 1996–2006)   7
O'Neil J (Hibernian, 2001)   1
Ormond W (Hibernian, 1954–59)   6
Orr T (Morton, 1952)   2

Parker A (Falkirk, Everton, 1955–56)   15
Parlane D (Rangers, 1973–77)   12
Palmer L (Sheffield Wed, 2019–21)   8
Paterson, C (Hearts, Cardiff, Sheffield Wed,
   2016–21)   17
Paton A (Motherwell, 1952)   2
Patterson N (Rangers, 2021)   2
Pearson S (Motherwell, Celtic, Derby, 2004–07)   10
Pearson T (Newcastle, 1947)   2
Penman A (Dundee, 1966)   1

Pettigrew W (Motherwell, 1976–77)   5
Phillips M (Blackpool, QPR, WBA, 2012–20)   16
Plenderleith J (Manchester City, 1961)   1
Pressley S (Hearts, 2000–07)   32
Provan D (Rangers, 1964–66)   5
Provan D (Celtic, 1980–82)   10

Quashie N (Portsmouth, Southampton,
   WBA, 2004–07)   14
Quinn P (Motherwell, 1961–62)   4

Rae G (Dundee, Rangers, Cardiff, 2001–09)   14
Redpath W (Motherwell, 1949–52)   9
Reilly L (Hibernian, 1949–57)   38
Rhodes J (Huddersfield, Blackburn,
   Sheffield Wed, 2012–17)   14
Ring T (Clyde, 1953–58)   12
Rioch B (Derby, Everton, 1975–78)   24
Riordan D (Hibernian, 2006–10)   3
Ritchie M (Bournemouth, Newcastle, 2015–18)   16
Ritchie P (Hearts, Bolton, 1999–2000)   7
Ritchie W (Rangers, 1962)   1
Robb D (Aberdeen, 1971)   5
Robertson A (Clyde, 1955)   5
Robertson A (Dundee Utd, Hull,
   Liverpool, 2014–21)   48
Robertson D (Rangers, 1992–94)   3
Robertson H (Dundee, 1962)   1
Robertson J (Tottenham, 1964)   1
Robertson J (Nottm Forest, Derby,
   1978–84)   28
Robertson J (Hearts, 1991–96)   16
Robertson S (Dundee Utd, 2009–11)   2
Robinson R (Dundee, 1974–75)   4
Robson B (Celtic, Middlesbrough, 2008–12)   17
Ross M (Rangers, 2002–04)   13
Rough A (Partick, Hibernian, 1976–86)   53
Rougvie D (Aberdeen, 1984)   1
Russell J (Derby, Kansas, 2015–20)   14
Rutherford E (Rangers, 1948)   1

Saunders S (Motherwell, 2011)   1
Schaedler E (Hibernian, 1974)   1
Scott A (Rangers, Everton, 1957–66)   16
Scott J (Hibernian, 1966)   1
Scott J (Dundee, 1971)   2
Scoular J (Portsmouth, 1951–53)   9
Severin S (Hearts, Aberdeen, 2002–07)   15
Shankland, L (Dundee Utd, 2020–21)   4
Sharp G (Everton, 1985–88)   12
Shaw D (Hibernian, 1947–49)   8
Shaw J (Rangers, 1947)   4
Shearer D (Aberdeen, 1994–96)   7
Shearer R (Rangers, 1961)   4
Shinnie A (Inverness, 2013)   1
Shinnie G (Aberdeen, 2018–19)   6
Simpson N (Aberdeen, 1983–88)   5
Simpson R (Celtic, 1967–69)   5
Sinclair J (Leicester, 1966)   1
Smith D (Aberdeen, Rangers, 1966–68)   2
Smith G (Hibernian, 1947–57)   18
Smith H (Hearts, 1988–92)   3

Bradley M (Walsall, 2010) 1
Bradshaw T (Walsall, Barnsley, 2016–18) 3
Brooks D (Sheffield Utd, Bournemouth 2018–21) 21
Brown J (Gillingham, Blackburn, Aberdeen, 2006–12) 3
Browning M (Bristol Rov, Huddersfield, 1996–97) 5
Burgess R (Tottenham, 1947–54) 32
Burton A (Norwich, Newcastle, 1963–72) 9

Cabango B (Swansea, 2021) 3
Cartwright L (Coventry, Wrexham, 1974–79) 7
Charles Jeremy (Swansea City, QPR, Oxford Utd, 1981–87) 19
Charles John (Leeds, Juventus, Cardiff, 1950–65) 38
Charles M (Swansea City, Arsenal, Cardiff, 1955–63) 31
Chester J (Hull, WBA, Aston Villa, 2014–19) 35
Church S (Reading, Nottm Forest, Charlton, MK Dons 2009–16) 38
Clarke R (Manchester City, 1949–56) 22
Coleman C (Crystal Palace, Blackburn, Fulham, 1992–2002) 32
Collins D (Sunderland, Stoke, 2005–11) 12
Collins J (Cardiff, West Ham, Aston Villa, West Ham, 2004–17) 50
Collison J (West Ham, 2008–14) 17
Colwill R (Cardiff, 2021) 1
Cornforth J (Swansea City, 1995) 2
Cotterill D (Bristol City, Wigan, Sheffield Utd, Swansea, Doncaster, Birmingham, 2006–17) 24
Coyne D (Tranmere, Grimsby, Leicester, Burnley, Tranmere, 1996–2008) 16
Crofts A (Gillingham, Brighton, Norwich, Brighton, Scunthorpe, 2006–18) 29
Crossley M (Nottm Forest, Middlesbrough, Fulham, 1997–2005) 8
Crowe V (Aston Villa, 1959–63) 16
Curtis A (Swansea City, Leeds, Southampton, Cardiff, 1976–87) 35

Daniel R (Arsenal, Sunderland, 1951–57) 21
Davies A (Manchester Utd, Newcastle, Swansea City, Bradford City, 1983–90) 13
Davies A (Barnsley, Stoke, 2019–21) 2
Davies A (Yeovil 2006) 1
Davies B (Swansea, Tottenham, 2013–21) 64
Davies C (Charlton, 1972) 1
Davies C (Oxford, Verona, Oldham, Barnsley, Bolton, 2006–14) 7
Davies D (Everton, Wrexham, Swansea City 1975–83) 52
Davies ER (Newcastle, 1953–58) 6
Davies G (Fulham, Chelsea, Manchester City, 1980–86) 16
Davies RT (Norwich, Southampton, Portsmouth, 1964–74) 29
Davies RW (Bolton, Newcastle, Man Utd, Man City, Blackpool, 1964–74) 34
Davies S (Manchester Utd, 1996) 1
Davies S (Tottenham, Everton, Fulham, 2001–10) 58
Davis G (Wrexham, 1978) 3

Deacy N (PSV Eindhoven, Beringen, 1977–79) 12
Delaney M (Aston Villa, 2000–07) 36
Derrett S (Cardiff, 1969–71) 4
Dibble A (Luton, Manchester City, 1986–89) 3
Dorman A (St Mirren, Crystal Palace, 2010–11) 3
Duffy R (Portsmouth, 2006–08) 13
Dummett P (Newcastle, 2014–19) 5
Durban A (Derby, 1966–72) 27
Dwyer P (Cardiff, 1978–80) 10

Eardley N (Oldham, Blackpool, 2008–11) 16
Earnshaw R (Cardiff, WBA, Norwich, Derby, Nottm Forest, Cardiff, 2002–13) 59
Easter J (Wycombe, Crystal Palace, Millwall, 2007–14) 12
Eastwood F (Wolves, Coventry, 2008–11) 11
Edwards C (Swansea City, 1996) 1
Edwards D (Luton, Wolves, Reading, 2007–18) 43
Edwards, G (Birmingham, Cardiff, 1947–50) 12
Edwards, I (Chester, Wrexham, 1978–80) 4
Edwards, L (Charlton, 1957) 2
Edwards, R (Bristol City, 1997–98) 4
Edwards, R (Aston Villa, Wolves, 2003–07) 15
Emmanuel W (Bristol City, 1973) 2
England M (Blackburn, Tottenham, 1962–75) 44
Evans B (Swansea City, Hereford, 1972–74) 7
Evans C (Manchester City, Sheffield Utd, 2008–11) 13
Evans I (Crystal Palace, 1976–78) 13
Evans L (Wolves, Sheffield Utd, Wigan, 2018–19) 4
Evans P (Brentford, Bradford City, 2002–03) 2
Evans R (Swansea City, 1964) 1
Evans S (Wrexham, 2007–09) 7

Felgate D (Lincoln, 1984) 1
Fletcher C (Bournemouth, West Ham, Crystal Palace, 2004–09) 36
Flynn B (Burnley, Leeds, 1975–84) 66
Fon Williams O (Inverness, 2016) 1
Ford T (Swansea City, Sunderland, Aston Villa, Cardiff, 1947–57) 38
Foulkes W (Newcastle, 1952–54) 11
Freeman N (Sheffield Utd, 2019) 1
Freestone R (Swansea City, 2000–03) 1

Gabbidon D (Cardiff, West Ham, QPR, Crystal Palace, 2002–14) 49
Garner G (Leyton Orient, 2006) 1
Giggs R (Manchester Utd, 1992–2007) 64
Giles D (Swansea City, Crystal Palace, 1980–83) 12
Godfrey B (Preston, 1964–65) 3
Goss J (Norwich, 1991–96) 9
Green C (Birmingham, 1965–69) 15
Green R (Wolves, 1998) 2
Griffiths A (Wrexham, 1971–77) 17
Griffiths H (Swansea City, 1953) 1
Griffiths M (Leicester, 1947–54) 11

Sidlow C (Liverpool, 1947–50) 7
Slatter N (Bristol Rov, Oxford Utd, 1983–89) 22
Smallman D (Wrexham, Everton, 1974–6) 7
Smith M (Manchester City, 2018–21) 14
Southall N (Everton, 1982–97) 92
Speed G (Leeds, Everton, Newcastle, 1990–2004) 85
Sprake G (Leeds, Birmingham, 1964–75) 37
Stansfield F (Cardiff, 1949) 1
Stevenson B (Leeds, Birmingham, 1978–82) 15
Stevenson N (Swansea, 1982–83) 4
Stitfall R (Cardiff, 1953–57) 2
Stock B (Doncaster, 2010–11) 3
Sullivan D (Cardiff, 1953–60) 17
Symons K (Portsmouth, Manchester City, Fulham, Crystal Palace, 1992–2004) 37

Tapscott D (Arsenal, Cardiff, 1954–59) 14
Taylor G (Crystal Palace, Sheffield Utd, Burnley, Nottm Forest, 1996–2005) 15
Taylor J (Reading, 2015) 1
Taylor N (Wrexham, Swansea, Aston Villa, 2010–20) 43
Thatcher B (Leicester, Manchester City, 2004–05) 7
Thomas D (Swansea, 1957–58) 2
Thomas G (Leicester, 2018–19) 3
Thomas M (Wrexham, Manchester Utd, Everton, Brighton, Stoke, Chelsea, WBA, 1977–86) 51
Thomas M (Newcastle, 1987) 1
Thomas R (Swindon, Derby, Cardiff, 1967–78) 50
Thomas S (Fulham, 1948–49) 4
Toshack J (Cardiff, Liverpool, Swansea, 1969–80) 40
Trollope P (Derby, Fulham, Northampton, 1997–2003) 9
Tudur Jones O (Swansea, Norwich, Hibernian, 2008–14) 7

Van den Hauwe P (Everton, 1985–89) 13
Vaughan D (Crewe, Real Sociedad, Blackpool, Sunderland, Nottm Forest, 20013–16) 42
Vaughan N (Newport, Cardiff, 1983–85) 10
Vaulks W (Rotherham, Cardiff, 2019–21) 6
Vearncombe G (Cardiff, 1958–61) 2
Vernon R (Blackburn, Everton, Stoke, 1957–68) 32
Villars A (Cardiff, 1974) 3
Vokes S (Wolves, Burnley, Stoke, 2008–20) 64

Walley T (Watford, 1971) 1
Walsh I (Crystal Palace, 1980–82) 18
Ward D (Bristol Rov, Cardiff, 1959–62) 2
Ward D (Notts Co, Nottm Forest, 2000–04) 5
Ward D (Liverpool, Leicester, 2016–21) 17
Watkins M (Norwich, 2018) 2
Webster C (Manchester Utd, 1957–58) 4
Weston R (Arsenal, Cardiff, 2000–05) 7

Williams A (Stockport, Swansea, Everton, 2008–19) 86
Williams A (Reading, Wolves, Reading, 1994–2003) 13
Williams A (Southampton, 1997–98) 2
Williams D (Norwich, 1986–87) 5
Williams G (Cardiff, 1951) 1
Williams G (Derby, Ipswich, 1988–96) 13
Williams G (West Ham, 2006) 2
Williams G (Fulham, 2014–16) 7
Williams GE (WBA, 1960–69) 26
Williams GG (Swansea, 1961–62) 5
Williams HJ (Swansea, 1965–72) 3
Williams HT (Newport, Leeds, 1949–50) 4
Williams J (Crystal Palace, Charlton, 2013–21) 28
Williams N (Liverpool, 2021) 14
Williams S (WBA, Southampton, 1954–66) 43
Wilson H (Liverpool, 2014–21) 29
Wilson J (Bristol City, 2014) 1
Witcomb D (WBA, Sheffield Wed, 1947) 3
Woosnam P (Leyton Orient, West Ham, Aston Villa, 1959–63) 17
Woodburn B (Liverpool, 2018–19) 10

Yorath T (Leeds, Coventry, Tottenham, Vancouver Whitecaps 1970–81) 59
Young E (Wimbledon, Crystal Palace, Wolves, 1990–96) 21

NORTHERN IRELAND

Aherne T (Belfast Celtic, Luton, 1947–50) 4
Anderson T (Manchester Utd, Swindon, Peterborough, 1973–79) 22
Armstrong G (Tottenham, Watford, Real Mallorca, WBA, 1977–86) 63

Baird C (Southampton, Fulham, Burnley, WBA, Derby, 2003–16) 79
Ballard D (Arsenal, 2021) 8
Barr H (Linfield, Coventry, 1962–63) 3
Barton A (Preston, 2011) 1
Best G (Manchester Utd, Fulham, 1964–77) 37
Bingham W (Sunderland, Luton, Everton, Port Vale, 1951–64) 56
Black K (Luton, Nottm Forest, 1988–94) 30
Blair R (Oldham, 1975–76) 5
Blanchflower RD (Barnsley, Aston Villa, Tottenham, 1950–63) 56
Blanchflower J (Manchester Utd, 1954–58) 12
Blayney A (Doncaster, Linfield, 2006–11) 5
Bowler G (Hull, 1950) 3
Boyce L (Werder Bremen, Ross Co, Burton, Hearts, 2011–21) 28
Bradley C (Liverpool, 2021) 1
Braithwaite R (Linfield, Middlesbrough, 1962–65) 10
Braniff K (Portadown, 2010) 2
Brennan R (Luton, Birmingham, Fulham, 1949–51) 5
Briggs W (Manchester Utd, Swansea, 1962–65) 2

Brotherston N (Blackburn, 1980–85) 27
Brown C (Cardiff, 2020–21) 4
Bruce A (Hull, 2013–14) 2
Bruce W (Glentoran, 1961–67) 2
Brunt C (Sheffield Wed, WBA, 2005–18) 65
Bryan, M (Watford, 2010) 2

Camp L (Nottm Forest, 2011–13) 9
Campbell D (Nottm Forest, Charlton, 1987–88) 10
Campbell J (Fulham, 1951) 2
Campbell R (Crusaders, 1963–65) 2
Campbell R (Bradford City, 1982) 2
Campbell W (Dundee, 1968–70) 6
Capaldi A (Plymouth Argyle, Cardiff, 2004–08) 22
Carey J (Manchester Utd, 1947–49) 7
Carroll R (Wigan, Manchester Utd, West Ham, Olympiacos, Notts Co, Linfield, 1997–2017) 45
Carson J (Ipswich, 2011–13) 4
Carson S (Coleraine, 2009) 1
Carson T (Motherwell, 2018–21) 6
Casey T (Newcastle, Portsmouth, 1955–59) 12
Casement C (Ipswich, 2009) 1
Caskey W (Derby, Tulsa, Roughnecks, 1979–82) 7
Cassidy T (Newcastle, Burnley, 1971–82) 24
Cathcart C (Blackpool, Watford, 2011–21) 61
Caughey M (Linfield, 1986) 2
Charles D (Accrington, 2021) 3
Clarke C (Bournemouth, Southampton, QPR, Portsmouth, 1986–93) 38
Cleary J (Glentoran, 1982–85) 5
Clements D (Coventry, Sheffield Wed, Everton, New York Cosmos, 1965–76) 48
Clingan S (Nottm Forest, Norwich, Coventry, Kilmarnock, 2006–15) 39
Clyde, M (Wolves, 2005) 3
Coates C (Crusaders, 2009–11) 6
Cochrane A (Coleraine, Burnley, Middlesbrough, Gillingham, 1976–84) 26
Cochrane D (Leeds, 1947–50) 10
Connell T (Coleraine, 1978) 1
Coote A (Norwich, 1999–2000) 6
Cowan J (Newcastle, 1970) 1
Coyle F (Coleraine, Nottm Forest, 1956–58) 4
Coyle L (Derry City, 1989) 1
Coyle R (Sheffield Wed, 1973–74) 5
Craig D (Newcastle, 1967–75) 25
Craigan S (Partick, Motherwell, 2003–11) 54
Crossan E (Blackburn, 1950–55) 3
Crossan J (Sparta Rotterdam, Sunderland, Manchester City, Middlesbrough, 1960–68) 24
Cunningham W (St Mirren, Leicester, Dunfermline, 1951–62) 30
Cush W (Glenavon, Leeds, Portadown, 1951–62) 26

Dallas S (Crusaders, Brentford, Leeds, 2011–21) 56
D'Arcy S (Chelsea, Brentford, 1952–53) 5
Davis S (Aston Villa, Fulham, Rangers, Southampton, Rangers, 2005–21) 126

Davison A (Bolton, Bradford City, Grimsby, 1996–97) 3
Dennison R (Wolves, 1988–97) 18
Devine J (Glentoran, 1990) 1
Dickson D (Coleraine, 1970–73) 4
Dickson T (Linfield, 1957) 1
Dickson W (Chelsea, Arsenal, 1951–55) 12
Doherty L (Linfield, 1985–88) 2
*Doherty P (Derby, Huddersfield, Doncaster, 1946–50) 6
Doherty T (Bristol City, 2003–05) 9
Donaghy M (Luton, Manchester Utd, Chelsea, 1980–94) 91
Donnelly L (Fulham, Motherwell, 2014–20) 2
Donnelly M (Crusaders, 2009) 1
Dougan D (Portsmouth, Blackburn, Aston Villa, Leicester, Wolves, 1958–73) 43
Douglas J (Belfast Celtic, 1947) 1
Dowd H (Glenavon, 1974) 3
Dowie I (Luton, Southampton, Crystal Palace, West Ham, QPR, 1990–2000) 59
Duff M (Cheltenham, Burnley, 2002–12) 24
Dunlop G (Linfield, 1985–90) 4

Eglington T (Everton, 1947–49) 6
Elder A (Burnley, Stoke, 1960–70) 40
Elliott S (Motherwell, Hull, 2001–08) 38
Evans C (Manchester, Hull, Blackburn, 2009–21) 66
Evans J (Manchester Utd, WBA, Leicester, 2007–21) 91

Farrell P (Everton, 1947–49) 7
Feeney J (Linfield, Swansea, 1947–50) 2
Feeney W (Glentoran, 1976) 1
Feeney W (Bournemouth, Luton, Cardiff, Oldham, Plymouth 2002–12) 46
Ferguson G (Linfield, 1999–2001) 5
Ferguson S (Newcastle, Millwall, 2009–21) 49
Ferguson W (Linfield, 1966–67) 2
Ferris R (Birmingham, 1950–52) 3
Fettis A (Hull, Nottm Forest, Blackburn, 1992–99) 25
Finney T (Sunderland, Cambridge Utd, 1975–80) 14
Flanagan T (Burton, Sunderland, 2017–21) 8
Fleming G (Nottm Forest, Manchester City, Barnsley, 1987–95) 31
Forde J (Ards, 1959–61) 4

Galbraith E (Manchester Utd, 2020–21) 2
Gallogly C (Huddersfield, 1951) 2
Garrett R (Stoke, Linfield, 2009–11) 5
Gaston R (Coleraine, 1969) 1
Gault M (Linfield, 2008) 1
Gillespie K (Manchester Utd, Newcastle, Blackburn, Leicester, Sheffield Utd, 1995–2009) 86
Gorman J (Wolves, 2010–12) 9
Gorman W (Brentford, 1947–48) 4
Graham W (Doncaster, 1951–99) 14
Gray P (Luton, Sunderland, Nancy, Burnley, Oxford Utd, 1993–2001) 25

Gregg H (Doncaster, Manchester Utd 1954–64   25

Griffin D (St Johnstone, Dundee Utd,
Stockport, 1996–2004)   29

Grigg W (Walsall, Brentford, Wigan, 2012–19)   10

Hamill R (Glentoran, 1999)   1

Hamilton B (Linfield, Ipswich, Everton,
Millwall, Swindon, 1969–80)   50

Hamilton G (Glentoran, Portadown,
2003–08)   5

Hamilton W (QPR, Burnley, Oxford Utd, 1978–86)   41

Harkin J (Southport, Shrewsbury,1968–70)   5

Harvey M (Sunderland, 1961–71)   34

Hatton S (Linfield, 1963)   2

Hazard C (Celtic 2018–21)   2

Healy D (Manchester Utd, Preston, Leeds,
Fulham, Sunderland, Rangers,
Bury, 2000–13)   95

Healy F (Coleraine, Glentoran, 1982–83)   4

Hegan D (WBA, Wolves, 1970–73)   7

Hill C (Sheffield Utd, Leicester,
Trelleborg, Northampton, 1990–99)   27

Hill J (Norwich, Everton, 1959–64)   7

Hinton E (Fulham, Millwall, 1947–51)   7

Hodson L (Watford, MK Dons,
Rangers, 2011–18)   24

Holmes S (Wrexham, 2002)   1

Horlock K (Swindon, Manchester City,
1995–2003)   32

Hughes A (Newcastle, Aston Villa, Fulham,
QPR, Brighton, Melbourne,
Hearts, 1997–2018)   112

Hughes J (Lincoln, 2006)   2

Hughes M (Oldham, 2006)   2

Hughes M (Manchester City, Strasbourg,
West Ham, Wimbledon, Crystal Palace,
1992–2005)   71

Hughes P (Bury, 1987)   3

Hughes R (Bolton, 1951)   1

Humphries W (Ards, Coventry, Swansea, 1962–65)14

Hunter A (Blackburn, Ipswich, 1970–80)   53

Hunter B (Wrexham, Reading, 1995–2000)   15

Hunter V (Coleraine, 1962)   2

Ingham M (Sunderland, Wrexham, 2005–07)   3

Irvine R (Linfield, Stoke, 1962–5)   8

Irvine W (Burnley, Preston, Brighton,
1963–72)   23

Jackson T (Everton, Nottm Forest,
Manchester Utd, 1969–77)   35

Jamison J (Glentoran, 1976)   1

Jenkins I (Chester, Dundee Utd, 1997–2000)   6

Jennings P (Watford, Tottenham,
Arsenal, Tottenham, 1964–86)   119

Johnson D (Blackburn, Birmingham, 1999–2010) 56

Johnston W (Glenavon, Oldham, 1962–66)   2

Jones J (Glenavon, 1956–57)   3

Jones J (Kilmarnock, Rangers, 2018–21)   12

Jones S (Crewe, Burnley, 2003–08)   29

Keane T (Swansea, 1949)   1

Kee P (Oxford Utd, Ards, 1990–95)   9

Keith R (Newcastle, 1958–62)   23

Kelly H (Fulham, Southampton, 1950–51)   4

Kelly P (Barnsley, 1950)   1

Kennedy M (Aberdeen, 2021)   2

Kennedy P (Watford, Wigan, 1999–2004)   20

Kirk A (Hearts, Boston, Northampton,
Dunfermline, 2000–10)   11

Lafferty D (Burnley, 2012–16)   13

Lafferty K (Burnley, Rangers, Sion, Palermo,
Norwich, Hearts, Rangers,
Sunderland, Sarpsdorg, Reggina,
Kilmarnock, 2006–21)   83

Lavery S (Everton, Linfield, 2018–21)   7

Lawrie J (Port Vale, 2009–10)   3

Lawther W (Sunderland, Blackburn, 1960–62)   4

Lennon N (Crewe, Leicester, Celtic, 1994–2002) 40

Lewis J (Norwich, Newcastle, 2018–21)   20

Little A (Rangers, 2009–13)   9

Lockhart N (Linfield, Coventry,
Aston Villa, 1947–56)   8

Lomas S (Manchester City, West Ham,
1994–2003)   45

Lund M (Rochdale, 2017)   3

Lutton B (Wolves, West Ham, 1970–4)   6

Magennis J (Cardiff, Aberdeen, Kilmarnock,
Charlton, Bolton, Hull, 2010–21)   61

Magill E (Arsenal, Brighton, 1962–66)   26

Magilton J (Oxford Utd, Southampton,
Sheffield Wed, Ipswich, 1991–2002)   52

Mannus A (Linfield, St Johnstone, 2004–17)   9

Martin C (Glentoran, Leeds, Aston Villa,
1947–50)   6

McAdams W (Manchester City, Bolton,
Leeds, 1954–62)   15

*McAlinden J (Portsmouth, Southend, 1947–49)   2

McArdle R (Rochdale, Aberdeen,
Bradford, 2010–14)   7

McAuley G (Lincoln, Leicester, Ipswich,
WBA, Rangers, 2010–19)   80

McBride S (Glenavon, 1991–92)   4

McCabe J (Leeds, 1949–54)   6

McCalmont A (Leeds, 2020–21)   2

McCann A (St Johnstone, 2021)   6

McCann G (West Ham, Cheltenham, Barnsley,
Scunthorpe, Peterborough, 2002–12)   39

McCartan S (Accrington, Bradford, 2017–18)   2

McCarthy J (Port Vale, Birmingham, 1996–2001) 18

McCartney G (Sunderland, West Ham
Sunderland 2002–10)   34

McCavana T (Coleraine, 1954–55)   3

McCleary J (Cliftonville, 1955)   1

McClelland J (Arsenal, Fulham, 1961–67)   6

McClelland J (Mansfield, Rangers,
Watford, Leeds, 1980–90)   53

McClelland S (Chelsea, 2021)   1

McCourt F (Manchester City, 1952–53)   6

McCourt P (Rochdale, Celtic, Barnsley,
Brighton, Luton, 2002–16)   18

McCoy R (Coleraine, 1987)   1

McCreery D (Manchester Utd, QPR, Tulsa, Newcastle, 1976–90) 67
McCrory S (Southend, 1958) 1
McCullough L (Doncaster, 2014–18) 6
McCullough W (Arsenal, Millwall,1961–67) 10
McCurdy C (Linfield, 1980) 1
McDonald A (QPR, 1986–96) 52
McElhinney G (Bolton, 1984–85) 6
McEvilly L (Rochdale, 2002) 1
McFaul W (Linfield, Newcastle, 1967–74) 6
McGarry J (Cliftonville, 1951) 3
McGaughey M (Linfield, 1985) 1
McGibbon P (Manchester Utd, Wigan, 1995–2000) 7
McGinn N (Derry, Celtic, Aberdeen, 2009–21) 66
McGivern R (Manchester City, Hibernian, Port Vale, Shrewsbury, 2009–17) 24
McGovern M (Ross Co, Hamilton, Norwich, 2010–21) 33
McGrath C (Tottenham, Manchester Utd 1974–79) 21
McIlroy J (Burnley, Stoke, 1952–66) 55
McIlroy S (Manchester Utd, Stoke, Manchester City, 1972–87) 88
McKay W (Inverness, Wigan, 2013–16) 11
McKeag W (Glentoran, 1968) 2
McKenna J (Huddersfield, 1950–52) 7
McKenzie R (Airdrie, 1967) 1
McKinney W (Falkirk, 1966) 1
McKnight A (Celtic, West Ham, 1988–89) 10
McLaughlin C (Preston, Fleetwood, Millwall, Sunderland, 2012–21) 43
McLaughlin J (Shrewsbury, Swansea, 1962–66) 12
McLaughlin R (Liverpool, Oldham, 2014–18) 5
McLean B (Motherwell, 2006) 1
McMahon G (Tottenham, Stoke, 1995–98) 17
McMichael A (Newcastle, 1950–60) 40
McMillan S (Manchester Utd, 1963) 2
McMordie A (Middlesbrough, 1969–73) 21
McMorran E (Belfast Celtic, Barnsley, Doncaster, 1947–57) 15
McNair P (Manchester Utd, Sunderland, Middlesbrough), 2015–21) 47
McNally B (Shrewsbury, 1987–88) 5
McPake J (Coventry, 2012) 1
McParland P (Aston Villa, Wolves, 1954–62) 34
McQuoid J (Millwall, 2011–12) 5
McVeigh P (Tottenham, Norwich, 1999–2005) 20
Montgomery F (Coleraine, 1955) 1
Moore C (Glentoran, 1949) 1
Moreland V (Derby, 1979–80) 6
Morgan S (Port Vale, Aston Villa, Brighton, Sparta Rotterdam, 1972–99) 18
Morrow S (Arsenal, QPR, 1990–2000) 39
Mulgrew J (Linfield, 2010) 2
Mullan G (Glentoran, 1983) 4
Mulryne P (Manchester Utd, Norwich, 1997–2005) 27
Murdock C (Preston, Hibernian, Crewe, Rotherham, 2000–06) 34

Napier R (Bolton, 1966) 1
Neill T (Arsenal, Hull, 1961–73) 59
Nelson S (Arsenal, Brighton, 1970–82) 51
Nicholl C (Aston Villa, Southampton, Grimsby, 1975–83) 51
Nicholl J (Manchester Utd, Toronto, Sunderland, Rangers, WBA, 1976–86) 73
Nicholson J (Manchester Utd, Huddersfield, 1961–72) 41
Nolan I (Sheffield Wed, Bradford City, Wigan, 1997–2002) 18
Norwood O (Manchester Utd, Huddersfield, Reading, Brighton, Sheffield Utd, 2011–19) 57
O'Boyle G (Dunfermline, St Johnstone, 1994–99) 13
O'Connor M (Crewe, Scunthorpe, Rotherham, 2008–14) 11
O'Doherty A (Coleraine, 1970) 2
O'Driscoll J (Swansea, 1949) 3
O'Kane W (Nottm Forest, 1970–75) 20
O'Neill C (Motherwell, 1989–91) 3
O'Neill J (Sunderland, 1962) 1
O'Neill J (Leicester, 1980–86) 39
O'Neill M (Distillery, Nottm Forest, Norwich, Manchester City, Notts Co, 1972–85) 64
O'Neill M (Newcastle, Dundee Utd, Hibernian, Coventry, 1989–97) 31
Owens J (Crusaders, 2011) 1
Parke J (Linfield, Hibernian, Sunderland, 1964–68) 14
Paterson M (Scunthorpe, Burnley, Huddersfield, 2008–14) 22
Paton P (Dundee Utd, St Johnstone, 2014–17) 4
Patterson D (Crystal Palace, Luton, Dundee Utd, 1994–99) 17
Patterson R (Coleraine, Plymouth, 2010–11) 5
Peacock R (Celtic, Coleraine, 1952–62) 31
Peacock-Farrell B (Leeds, Burnley, 2018–21) 23
Penney S (Brighton, 1985–89) 17
Platt J (Middlesbrough, Ballymena, Coleraine, 1976–86) 23
Quinn J (Blackburn, Swindon, Leicester, Bradford City, West Ham, Bournemouth, Reading, 1985–96) 46
Quinn SJ (Blackpool, WBA, Willem 11, Sheffield Wed, Peterborough, Northampton, 1996–2007) 50
Rafferty P (Linfield, 1979) 1
Ramsey P (Leicester, 1984–89) 14
Reeves B (MK Dons, 2015) 2
Rice P (Arsenal, 1969–80) 49
Robinson S (Bournemouth, Luton, 1997–2008) 7
Rogan A (Celtic, Sunderland, Millwall, 1988–97) 18
Ross W (Newcastle, 1969) 1
Rowland K (West Ham, QPR, 1994–99) 19
Russell A (Linfield, 1947) 1
Ryan R (WBA, 1950) 1

Sanchez L (Wimbledon, 1987–89) 3
Saville G (Millwall, Middlesbrough, 2018–21) 31
Scott J (Grimsby, 1958) 2
Scott P (Everton, York, Aldershot, 1976–79) 10
Sharkey P (Ipswich, 1976) 1
Shields J (Southampton, 1957) 1
Shiels D (Hibernian, Doncaster, Kilmarnock,
    Rangers, 2006–13) 14
Simpson W (Rangers, 1951–59) 12
Sloan D (Oxford Utd, 1969–71) 2
Sloan J (Arsenal, 1947) 1
Sloan T (Manchester Utd, 1979) 3
Smith A (Glentoran, Preston, 2003–05) 18
Smith M (Peterborough, Hearts, 2016–21) 17
Smyth P (QPR, 2018–21) 3
Smyth S (Wolves, Stoke, 1948–52) 9
Smyth W (Distillery, 1949–54) 1
Sonner D (Ipswich, Sheffield Wed,
    Birmingham, Nottm Forest,
    Peterborough, 1997–2005) 13
Spence D (Bury, Blackpool,
    Southend, 1975–82) 29
Sproule I (Hibernian, 2006–08) 11
*Stevenson A (Everton, 1947–48) 3
Steele J (New York Bulls, 2014) 3
Stewart A (Glentoran, Derby, 1967–69) 7
Stewart D (Hull, 1978) 1
Stewart I (QPR, Newcastle, 1982–87) 31
Stewart T (Linfield, 1961) 1
Taggart G (Barnsley, Bolton, Leicester,
    1990–2003) 51
Taylor M (Fulham, Birmingham, 1999–2012) 88
Thompson A (Watford, 2011) 2
Thompson J (Rangers, Blackpool,
    Stoke, 2018–21) 16
Thompson P (Linfield, 2006–08) 8
Todd S (Burnley, Sheffield Wed, 1966–71) 11
Toner C (Leyton Orient, 2003) 2
Trainor D (Crusaders, 1967) 1
Tuffey J (Partick, Inverness, 2009–11) 8
Tully C (Celtic, 1949–59) 10
Uprichard W (Swindon, Portsmouth,
    1952–59) 18
Vassell K (Rotherham, 2019) 2
Vernon J (Belfast Celtic, WBA, 1947–52) 17
Walker J (Doncaster, 1955) 1
Walsh D (WBA, 1947–50) 9
Walsh W (Manchester City, 1948–49) 5
Ward J (Derby, Nottm Forest, 2012–19) 35
Washington C (QPR, Shefield, Hearts,
    Charlton, 2016–21) 29
Watson P (Distillery, 1971) 1
Webb S (Ross Co, 2006–07) 4
Welsh E (Carlisle, 1966–67) 4
Whiteside N (Manchester Utd,
    Everton, 1982–90) 38
Whitley Jeff (Manchester City, Sunderland,
    Cardiff, 1997–2006) 20
Whitley Jim (Manchester City, 1998–2000) 3

Williams M (Chesterfield, Watford,
    Wimbledon, Stoke, Wimbledon,
    MK Dons, 1999–2005) 36
Whyte G (Oxford, Cardiff, 2019–21) 19
Williams M (Chesterfield, Watford
    Wimbledon, Stoke, Wimbledon
    MK Dons 1999–2005) 36
Williams P (WBA, 1991) 1
Wilson D (Brighton, Luton,
    Sheffield Wed, 1987–92) 24
Wilson K (Ipswich, Chelsea, Notts Co,
    Walsall, 1987–95) 42
Wilson S (Glenavon, Falkirk, Dundee,
    1962–68) 12
Winchester C (Oldham, 2011) 1
Wood T (Walsall, 1996) 1
Worthington N (Sheffield Wed, Leeds,
    Stoke, 1984–97) 66
Wright T (Newcastle, Nottm Forest, Reading,
    Manchester City, 1989–2000) 31

REPUBLIC OF IRELAND

Aherne T (Belfast Celtic, Luton, 1946–54) 16
Aldridge J (Oxford Utd, Liverpool, Real
    Sociedad, Tranmere, 1986–97) 69
Ambrose P (Shamrock R, 1955–64) 5
Anderson J (Preston, Newcastle, 1980–89) 16
Andrews K (Blackburn, WBA, 2009–13) 35
Arter H (Bournemouth, Nottm Forest, 2015–21) 18

Babb P (Coventry, Liverpool, Sunderland,
    1994–2003) 35
Bailham E (Shamrock R, 1964) 1
Barber E (Bohemians, Birmingham, 1966) 2
Barrett G (Arsenal, Coventry, 2003–05) 6
Bazunu G (Manchester City 2021) 4
Beglin J (Liverpool, 1984–87) 15
Bennett A (Reading, 2007) 2
Best L (Coventry, 2009–10) 7
Braddish S (Dundalk, 1978) 2
Branagan K (Bolton, 1997) 1
Bonner P (Celtic, 1981–96) 80
Boyle A (Preston, 2017) 1
Brady L (Arsenal, Juventus, Sampdoria,
    Inter–Milan, Ascoli, West Ham, 1975–90) 72
Brady R (QPR, 1964) 6
Brady R (Manchester Utd, Hull,
    Burnley, 2013–21) 57
Breen G (Birmingham, Coventry, West Ham,
    Sunderland, 1996–2006) 63
*Breen T (Shamrock R, 1947) 3
Brennan F (Drumcondra, 1965) 1
Brennan S (Manchester Utd, Waterford,
    1965–71) 19
Browne A (Preston, 2017–21) 14
Browne W (Bohemians, 1964) 3
Bruce A (Ipswich, 2007–09) 2
Buckley L (Shamrock R, Waregem, 1984–85) 2
Burke F (Cork Ath, 1952) 1
Burke G (Shamrock Rov, Preston 2018–19) 3
Butler P (Sunderland, 2000) 1

Butler T (Sunderland, 2003) — 2
Byrne A (Southampton, 1970–74) — 14
Byrne J (Shelbourne, 2004–06) — 2
Byrne J (QPR, Le Havre, Brighton, Sunderland, Millwall, 1985–93) — 23
Byrne J (Shamrock Rov, 2020–21) — 4
Byrne P (Shamrock R, 1984–86) — 8

Campbell A (Santander, 1985) — 3
Campbell N (St Patrick's Ath, Fortuna Cologne, 1971–77) — 11
Cantwell N (West Ham, Manchester Utd, 1954–67) — 36
Carey B (Manchester Utd, Leicester, 1992–94) — 3
*Carey J (Manchester Utd, 1946–53) — 21
Carolan J (Manchester Utd, 1960) — 2
Carr S (Tottenham, Newcastle, 1999–2008) — 43
Carroll B (Shelbourne, 1949–50) — 2
Carroll T (Ipswich, 1968–73) — 17
Carsley L (Derby, Blackburn, Coventry, Everton, 1997–2008) — 39
Cascarino A (Gillingham, Millwall, Aston Villa, Chelsea, Marseille, Nancy, 1986–2000) — 88
Chandler J (Leeds, 1980) — 2
Christie C (Derby, Middlesbrough, Fulham, Nottm Forest, 2015–21) — 28
Clark C (Aston Villa, Newcastle, 2011–21) — 36
Clarke C (Stoke, 2004) — 2
Clarke J (Drogheda, 1978) — 1
Clarke K (Drumcondra, 1948) — 2
Clarke M (Shamrock R, 1950) — 1
Clinton T (Everton, 1951–54) — 3
Coad P (Shamrock R, 1947–52) — 11
Coffey T (Drumcondra, 1950) — 1
Colfer M (Shelbourne, 1950–51) — 2
Coleman S (Everton, 2011–21) — 59
Colgan N (Hibernian, 2002–07) — 9
Collins J (Luton, 2020–21) — 10
Conmy O (Peterborough, 1965–70) — 5
Connolly A (Brighton, 2020–21) — 6
Connolly D (Watford, Feyenoord, Excelsior Feyenoord, Wimbledon, West Ham, Wigan, 1996–2006) — 41
Conroy G (Stoke, 1970–77) — 27
Conway J (Fulham, Manchester City, 1967–77) — 20
Corr P (Everton, 1949–50) — 4
Courtney E (Cork Utd, 1946) — 1
Cox S (WBA, Nottm Forest, 2011–14) — 30
Coyle O (Bolton, 1994) — 1
Coyne T (Celtic, Tranmere, Motherwell, 1992–98) — 22
Crowe G (Bohemians, 2003) — 2
Cullen J (West Ham, Anderlecht, 2020–21) — 7
Cummins G (Luton, 1954–61) — 19
Cuneen T (Limerick, 1951) — 1
Cunningham G (Man City, Bristol City, 2010–13) — 4
Cunningham K (Wimbledon, Birmingham, 1996–2006) — 72

Curtis D (Shelbourne, Bristol City, Ipswich, Exeter, 1956–63) — 17
Curtis R (Portsmouth, 2019–21) — 7
Cusack S (Limerick, 1953) — 1
Daish L (Cambridge Utd, Coventry, 1992–96) — 5
Daly G (Manchester Utd, Derby, Coventry, Birmingham, Shrewsbury, 1973–87) — 48
Daly M (Wolves, 1978) — 2
Daly P (Shamrock R, 1950) — 1
Deacy E (Aston Villa, 1982) — 4
Delaney D (QPR, Ipswich, Crystal Palace, 2008–14) — 9
Delap R (Derby, Southampton, 1998–2004) — 11
De Mange K (Liverpool, Hull, 1987–89) — 2
Dempsey J (Fulham, Chelsea, 1967–72) — 19
Dennehy J (Cork Hibernian, Nottm Forest, Walsall, 1972–77) — 11
Desmond P (Middlesbrough, 1950) — 4
Devine J (Arsenal, 1980–85) — 13
Doherty G (Tottenham, Norwich, 2000–06) — 34
Doherty M (Wolves, Tottenham, 2018–21) — 20
Donovan D (Everton, 1955–57) — 5
Donovan T (Aston Villa, 1980) — 2
Douglas J (Blackburn, Leeds, 2004–08) — 8
Doyle C (Shelbourne, 1959) — 1
Doyle C (Birmingham, Bradford, 2007–18) — 4
Doyle K (Reading Wolves, Colorado, 2006–17) — 63
Doyle M (Coventry, 2004) — 1
Duff D (Blackburn, Chelsea, Newcastle, Fulham, 1998–2012) — 100
Duffy B (Shamrock R, 1950) — 1
Duffy S (Everton, Blackburn, Brighton, 2014–21) — 44
Dunne A (Manchester Utd, Bolton,1962–76) — 33
Dunne J (Fulham, 1971) — 1
Dunne P (Manchester Utd, 1965–67) — 5
Dunne R (Everton, Manchester City, Aston Villa, 2000–14) — 80
Dunne S (Luton, 1953–60) — 15
Dunne T (St Patrick's, 1956–57) — 3
Dunning P (Shelbourne, 1971) — 2
Dunphy E (York, Millwall, 1966–71) — 23
Dwyer N (West Ham, Swansea, 1960–65) — 14

Eccles P (Shamrock R, 1986) — 1
Egan J (Brentford, Sheffield Utd, 2017–21) — 14
Eglington T (Shamrock R, Everton, 1946–56) — 24
Elliot R (Newcastle, 2014–16) — 4
Elliott S (Sunderland, 2005–07) — 9
Evans M (Southampton, 1997) — 1

Fagan E (Shamrock R, 1973) — 1
Fagan F (Manchester City, Derby, 1955–61) — 8
Fahey K (Birmingham, 2010–13) — 16
Fairclough M (Dundalk, 1982) — 2
Fallon S (Celtic, 1951–55) — 8
Farrell P (Shamrock R, Everton, 1946–57) — 28
Farrelly G (Aston Villa, Everton, Bolton, 1996–2000) — 6

Kelly P (Wolves, 1961–62) 5

Kelly S (Tottenham, Birmingham, Fulham, Reading, 2006–14) 39

Kenna J (Blackburn, 1995–2000) 27

Kennedy M (Portsmouth, 1986) 2

Kennedy M (Liverpool, Wimbledon, Manchester City, Wolves, 1996–2004) 35

Kenny P (Sheffield Utd, 2004–07) 7

Keogh A (Wolves, Millwall, 2007–14) 30

Keogh J (Shamrock R, 1966) 1

Keogh R (Derby, 2013–20) 26

Keogh S (Shamrock R, 1959) 1

Kernaghan A (Middlesbrough, Manchester City, 1993–96) 22

Kiely D (Charlton, WBA, 2000–09) 11

Kiernan F (Shamrock R, Southampton, 1951–2) 5

Kilbane K (WBA, Sunderland, Everton, Wigan, Hull, 1997–2011) 110

Kinnear J (Tottenham, Brighton, 1967–76) 26

Kinsella M (Charlton, Aston Villa, WBA, 1998–2004) 48

Knight J (Derby 2002) 7

Langan D (Derby, Birmingham, Oxford Utd, 1978–88) 26

Lapira J (Notre Dame, 2007) 1

Lawler R (Fulham, 1953–56) 8

Lawlor J (Drumcondra, Doncaster, 1949–51) 3

Lawlor M (Shamrock R, 1971–73) 5

Lawrence L (Stoke, Portsmouth, 2009–11) 15

Lawrenson M (Preston, Brighton, Liverpool, 1977–88) 39

Lee A (Rotherham, Cardiff, Ipswich, 2003–07) 10

Leech M (Shamrock R, 1969–73) 8

Lenihan D (Blackburn, 2018–19) 2

Long K (Burnley, 2017–21) 17

Long S (Reading, WBA, Hull, Southampton, 2007–21) 88

Lowry D (St Patrick's Ath, 1962) 1

McAlinden J (Portsmouth, 1946) 2

McAteer J (Bolton, Liverpool, Blackburn, Sunderland, 1994–2004) 52

McCann J (Shamrock R, 1957) 1

McCarthy J (Wigan, Everton, Crystal Palace, 2011–21) 43

McCarthy M (Manchester City, Celtic, Lyon, Millwall, 1984–92) 57

McClean J (Sunderland, Wigan, WBA, Stoke, 2012–21) 82

McConville T (Dundalk, Waterford, 1972–73) 6

McDonagh J (Everton, Bolton, Sunderland, Notts Co, 1981–86) 25

McDonagh J (Shamrock R, 1984–85) 3

McEvoy A (Blackburn, 1961–67) 17

McGeady A (Celtic, Spartak Moscow, Everton, Sunderland, 2004–18) 93

McGee P (QPR, Preston, 1978–81) 15

McGoldrick E (Crystal Palace, Arsenal, 1992–95) 15

McGoldrick D (Ipswich, Sheffield Utd, 2015–21) 14

McGowan D (West Ham, 1949) 3

McGowan J (Cork Utd, 1947) 1

McGrath J (St Mirren, 2021) 1

McGrath M (Blackburn, Bradford PA, 1958–66) 22

McGrath P (Manchester Utd, Aston Villa, Derby, 1985–97) 83

Macken J (Manchester City, 2005) 1

Mackey G (Shamrock R, 1957) 3

McLoughlin A (Swindon, Southampton, Portsmouth, 1990–2000) 42

McMillan W (Belfast Celtic, 1946) 2

McNally B (Luton, 1959–63) 3

McPhail S (Leeds, 2000–04) 10

McShane P (WBA, Sunderland, Hull, Reading, 2006–16) 33

Macken A (Derby, 1977) 1

Madden P (Yeovil, 2014) 1

Maguire S (Preston, 2018–21) 11

Mahon A (Tranmere, 2000) 2

Malone G (Shelbourne, 1949) 1

Mancini T (QPR, Arsenal, 1974–75) 5

Manning R (QPR, 2021) 4

Martin C (Glentoran, Leeds, Aston Villa, 1946–56) 30

Martin M (Bohemians, Manchester Utd, 1972–83) 52

Maybury, A (Leeds, Hearts, Leicester, 1998–2005) 10

Meagan M (Everton, Huddersfield, Drogheda, 1961–70) 17

Meyler D (Sunderland, Hull, 2013–19) 26

Miller L (Celtic, Manchester Utd, Sunderland, QPR 2004–10) 21

Milligan M (Oldham, 1992) 1

Molumby J (Brighton, 2021) 9

Mooney J (Shamrock R, 1965) 2

Moore A (Middlesbrough, 1996–97) 8

Moran K (Manchester Utd, Sporting Gijon, Blackburn, 1980–94) 71

Moroney T (West Ham, 1948–54) 12

Morris C (Celtic, Middlesbrough, 1988–93) 35

Morrison C (Crystal Palace, Birmingham, Crystal Palace, 2002–07) 36

Moulson G (Lincoln, 1948–49) 3

Mucklan C (Drogheda, 1978) 1

Mulligan P (Shamrock R, Chelsea, Crystal Palace, WBA, Shamrock R, 1969–80) 50

Munroe L (Shamrock R, 1954) 1

Murphy A (Clyde, 1956) 1

Murphy B (Bohemians, 1986) 1

Murphy D (Sunderland, Ipswich, Newcastle, Nottm Forest, 2007–18) 33

Murphy J (Crystal Palace, 1980) 3

Murphy J (Scunthorpe, 2009–10) 2

Murphy J (WBA, 2004) 1

Murphy P (Carlisle, 2007) 1

Murray T (Dundalk, 1950) 1

Newman W (Shelbourne, 1969) 1

Nolan E (Preston, 2009–10) 3

Tuohy L (Shamrock R, Newcastle, Shamrock R, 1956–65) — 8
Turner A (Celtic, 1963) — 2

Vernon J (Belfast Celtic, 1946) — 2

Waddock G (QPR, Millwall, 1980–90) — 21
Walsh D (WBA, Aston Villa, 1946–54) — 20
Walsh J (Limerick, 1982) — 1
Walsh M (Blackpool, Everton, QPR, Porto, 1976–85) — 21
Walsh M (Everton, Norwich, 1982–83) — 4
Walsh W (Manchester City, 1947–50) — 9

Walters J (Stoke, Burnley, 2011–19) — 54
Ward S (Wolves, Burnley, 2011–19) — 50
Waters J (Grimsby, 1977–80) — 2
Westwood K (Coventry, Sunderland, Sheffield Wed, 2009–17) — 21
Whelan G (Stoke, Aston Villa, 2009–20) — 91
Whelan R (St Patrick's Ath, 1964) — 2
Whelan R (Liverpool, Southend, 1981–95) — 53
Whelan L (Manchester Utd, 1956–57) — 4
Whittaker R (Chelsea, 1959) — 1
Williams D (Blackburn, 2018) — 3
Williams S (Millwall, 2018–19) — 3
Wilson M (Stoke, Bournemouth, 2011–17) — 25

INTERNATIONAL GOALSCORERS 1946–2021

(start of season 2021–2022)

ENGLAND

Rooney	53	Gascoigne	10	Hitchens	5
Charlton R	49	Lee F	10	Johnson D	5
Lineker	48	Milburn	10	Latchford	5
Greaves	44	Wilshaw	10	Neal	5
Owen	40	Beardsley	9	Pearce	5
Kane	38	Bell	9	Pearson Stan	5
Finney	30	Bentley	9	Pearson Stuart	5
Lofthouse	30	Hateley	9	Pickering F	5
Shearer	30	Wright I	9	Barmby	4
Lampard Frank jnr	29	Ball	8	Barnes P	4
Platt	27	Broadis	8	Bent	4
Robson B	26	Byrne J	8	Bull	4
Hurst	24	Hoddle	8	Calvert-Lewin	4
Mortensen	23	Kevan	8	Dixon K	4
Crouch	22	Sturridge	8	Hassall	4
Channon	21	Walcott	8	Lingard	4
Gerrard	21	Anderton	7	Maguire	4
Keegan	21	Connelly	7	Mount	4
Defoe	20	Coppell	7	Revie	4
Peters	20	Fowler	7	Robson R	4
Haynes	18	Heskey	7	Steven	4
Hunt R	18	Oxlade-Chamberlain	7	Watson Dave (Sunderland)	4
Beckham	17	Paine	7	Alli	3
Sterling	17	Vardy	7	Baker	3
Lawton	16	Young A	7	Blissett	3
Taylor T	16	Barkley	6	Butcher	3
Woodcock	16	Charlton J	6	Currie	3
Welbeck	16	Macdonald	6	Dier	3
Scholes	14	Mullen	6	Elliott	3
Chivers	13	Rowley	6	Francis G	3
Mariner	13	Terry	6	Grainger	3
Smith R	13	Vassell	6	Jagielka	3
Francis T	12	Waddle	6	Kennedy R	3
Rashford	12	Wright-Phillips S	6	Lallana	3
Barnes J	11	Adams	5	Lambert	3
Douglas	11	Atyeo	5	McDermott	3
Mannion	11	Baily	5	McManaman	3
Sheringham	11	Brooking	5	Matthews S	3
Clarke A	10	Cahill	5	Merson	3
Cole J	10	Carter	5	Morris	3
Flowers R	10	Edwards	5	O'Grady	3
		Ferdinand L	5	Peacock	3

Ramsey	3	
Sancho	3	
Sewell	3	
Townsend	3	
Webb	3	
Wilkins	3	
Wright W	3	
Allen R	2	
Anderson	2	
Barry	2	
Bradley	2	
Broadbent	2	
Brooks	2	
Carroll	2	
Cowans	2	
Eastham	2	
Ferdinand R	2	
Foden	2	
Froggatt J	2	
Froggatt R	2	
Haines	2	
Hancocks	2	
Hunter	2	
Ince	2	
Johnson A	2	
Keown	2	
Lee R	2	
Lee S	2	
Moore	2	
Perry	2	
Pointer	2	
Richardson	2	
Royle	2	
Smith A (1989–92)	2	
Southgate	2	
Stone	2	
Stones	2	
Taylor P	2	
Tueart	2	
Upson	2	
Wignall	2	
Wilshere	2	
Worthington	2	
Abraham	1	
A'Court	1	
Alexander-Arnold	1	
Astall	1	
Baines	1	
Beattie K	1	
Bertrand	1	
Bowles	1	
Bradford	1	
Bridge	1	
Bridges	1	
Brown	1	
Campbell	1	
Caulker	1	
Chamberlain	1	
Coady	1	

Cole Andy	1
Crawford	1
Dixon L	1
Ehiogu	1
Goddard	1
Henderson	1
Hirst	1
Hughes E	1
Ings	1
Jeffers	1
Jenas	1
Johnson G	1
Kay	1
Keane	1
Kidd	1
King	1
Langton	1
Lawler	1
Lee J	1
Lescott	1
Le Saux	1
Mabbutt	1
Marsh	1
Medley	1
Melia	1
Milner	1
Mullery	1
Murphy	1
Nicholls	1
Nicholson	1
Nugent	1
Palmer	1
Parry	1
Redknapp	1
Rice	1
Richards	1
Saka	1
Sansom	1
Shackleton	1
Shaw	1
Smalling	1
Smith A (2001–5)	1
Stiles	1
Summerbee	1
Tambling	1
Thompson Phil	1
Trippier	1
Viollet	1
Wallace	1
Walsh	1
Ward-Prowse	1
Watkins	1
Weller	1
Wilson	1
Winks	1
Wise	1
Withe	1
Wright M	1

SCOTLAND

Dalglish	30
Law	30
Reilly	22
McCoist	19
Miller K	18
McFadden	15
Johnston M	14
Collins J	12
Gilzean	12
Steel	12
Jordan	11
Collins R	10
Fletcher S	10
Johnstone R	10
McGinn	10
Naismith	10
Wilson D	10
Gallacher	9
McStay	9
Mudie	9
St John	9
Stein	9
Brand	8
Gemmill A	8
Leggat	8
Robertson J (1978–84)	8
Boyd K	7
Dodds	7
Durie	7
Gray A	7
Maloney	7
Snodgrass	7
Wark	7
Booth	6
Brown A	6
Cooper	6
Dailly	6
Gough	6
Hutchison D	6
Liddell	6
Murdoch	6
Rioch	6
Waddell	6
Fletcher D	5
Forrest J (2011-20)	5
Hartford	5
Henderson W	5
Macari	5
Masson	5
McAllister G	5
McQueen	5
Nevin	5
Nicholas	5
O'Hare	5
Scott A	5
Strachan	5
Young A	5
Archibald	4

Berra ... 4
Brown S ... 4
Caldow ... 4
Christie ... 4
Crawford ... 4
Fraser R ... 4
Griffiths ... 4
Hamilton ... 4
Jackson D ... 4
Johnstone J ... 4
Lorimer ... 4
Mackay D ... 4
Mason ... 4
McArthur ... 4
McGinlay ... 4
McKinlay W ... 4
McLaren ... 4
O'Connor ... 4
Smith G ... 4
Souness ... 4
Anya ... 3
Baxter ... 3
Bremner W ... 3
Burley C ... 3
Chalmers ... 3
Ferguson B ... 3
Gibson ... 3
Graham G ... 3
Gray E ... 3
Greig ... 3
Hendry C ... 3
Herd D ... 3
Lennox ... 3
MacDougall ... 3
McCann ... 3
McInally A ... 3
McNeill ... 3
McPhail ... 3
Martin C ... 3
Morris ... 3
Morrison ... 3
Mulgrew ... 3
Rhodes ... 3
Ritchie M ... 3
Robertson A (2014–20) ... 3
Robertson J (1991–5) ... 3
Sturrock ... 3
Thompson ... 3
White ... 3
Adams ... 2
Armstrong ... 2
Baird S ... 2
Bauld ... 2
Burke C ... 2
Caldwell G ... 2
Cameron ... 2
Commons ... 2
Dykes ... 2
Flavell ... 2

Fleming ... 2
Graham A ... 2
Hanley ... 2
Harper ... 2
Hewie ... 2
Holton ... 2
Hopkin ... 2
Houliston ... 2
Jess ... 2
Johnston A ... 2
Johnstone D ... 2
Mackie ... 2
McClair ... 2
McCormack ... 2
McGhee ... 2
McMillan ... 2
McManus ... 2
Ormond ... 2
Pettigrew ... 2
Ring ... 2
Robertson A (1955) ... 2
Shearer D ... 2
Aitken R ... 1
Bannon ... 1
Beattie ... 1
Bett ... 1
Bone ... 1
Boyd T ... 1
Brazil ... 1
Broadfoot ... 1
Buckley ... 1
Burke O ... 1
Burns ... 1
Calderwood ... 1
Campbell R ... 1
Clarkson ... 1
Combe ... 1
Conn A (1956) ... 1
Craig J ... 1
Curran ... 1
Davidson ... 1
Dickov ... 1
Dobie ... 1
Docherty ... 1
Duncan D ... 1
Elliott ... 1
Fernie ... 1
Findlay ... 1
Freedman ... 1
Goodwillie ... 1
Gray F ... 1
Gemmill S ... 1
Gemmill T (1966–71) ... 1
Gemmell T (1955) ... 1
Hartley ... 1
Henderson J ... 1
Hendry J ... 1
Herd G ... 1
Holt ... 1

Howie ... 1
Hughes J ... 1
Hunter W ... 1
Hutchison T ... 1
Jackson C ... 1
Jardine ... 1
Johnston L ... 1
Kyle ... 1
Lambert ... 1
Linwood ... 1
Mackail-Smith ... 1
Mackay G ... 1
MacLeod ... 1
MacKenzie ... 1
McAvennie ... 1
McCall ... 1
McCalliog ... 1
McCulloch ... 1
McGregor C ... 1
McKimmie ... 1
McKinnon ... 1
McLean K ... 1
McLean T ... 1
McLintock ... 1
McSwegan ... 1
Miller W ... 1
Mitchell ... 1
Morgan ... 1
Mulhall ... 1
Murray J ... 1
Narey ... 1
Naysmith ... 1
Nisbet ... 1
Orr ... 1
Parlane ... 1
Phillips ... 1
Provan D (1980–82) ... 1
Quashie ... 1
Ritchie P ... 1
Russell ... 1
Sharp ... 1
Shankland ... 1
Stewart R ... 1
Thornton ... 1
Wallace I ... 1
Webster ... 1
Weir A ... 1
Weir D ... 1
Wilkie ... 1
Wilson Danny ... 1

WALES

Bale ... 33
Rush ... 28
Allchurch I ... 23
Ford ... 23
Saunders ... 22
Bellamy ... 19
Ramsey ... 17

McCarthy 2
McLoughlin 2
O'Connor (1968–73 2
O'Farrell 2
Parrott 2
Pearce 2
Reid S 2
Whelan G 2
Ambrose 1
Anderson 1
Burke G 1
Carroll 1
Coleman 1
Dempsey 1
Doherty M 1
Elliott 1
Fitzgerald F 1
Fullam 1
Galvin 1
Gibson 1
Gleeson 1
Glynn 1

Gibson 1
Green 1
Grimes 1
Healy 1
Horgan 1
Holmes 1
Hourihane 1
Hughton 1
Hunt S 1
Judge 1
Kavanagh 1
Keogh R 1
Kernaghan 1
Knight 1
Long K 1
Mancini 1
McCann 1
Maguire 1
McGoldrick 1
McPhail 1
Miller 1
Mooney 1

Moroney 1
Mulligan 1
O'Brien Aiden 1
O'Brien Andy 1
O'Dea 1
O'Callaghan K 1
O'Keefe 1
O'Leary 1
O'Neill F 1
O'Reilly J 1
Pilkington 1
Robinson C 1
Ryan G 1
Slaven 1
Sloan 1
Strahan 1
Waters 1
Williams D 1
Williams S 1
Wilson 1

HOME INTERNATIONAL RESULTS

Note: In the results that follow, WC = World Cup, EC = European Championship, CC = Carling Cup
TF = Tournoi de France For Northern Ireland read Ireland before 1921

ENGLAND v SCOTLAND

Played 115; England won 49; Ireland 41; drawn 25 Goals: England 203, Ireland 174

		E	S				
1872	Glasgow	0	0	1898	Glasgow	3	1
1873	The Oval	4	2	1899	Birmingham	2	1
1874	Glasgow	1	2	1900	Glasgow	1	4
1875	The Oval	2	2	1901	Crystal Palace	2	2
1876	Glasgow	0	3	1902	Birmingham	2	2
1877	The Oval	1	3	1903	Sheffield	1	2
1878	Glasgow	2	7	1904	Glasgow	1	0
1879	The Oval	5	4	1905	Crystal Palace	1	0
1880	Glasgow	4	5	1906	Glasgow	1	2
1881	The Oval	1	6	1907	Newcastle	1	1
1882	Glasgow	1	5	1908	Glasgow	1	1
1883	Sheffield	2	3	1909	Crystal Palace	2	0
1884	Glasgow	0	1	1910	Glasgow	0	2
1885	The Oval	1	1	1911	Goodison Park	1	1
1886	Glasgow	1	1	1912	Glasgow	1	1
1887	Blackburn	2	3	1913	Stamford Bridge	1	0
1888	Glasgow	5	0	1914	Glasgow	1	3
1889	The Oval	2	3	1920	Sheffield	5	4
1890	Glasgow	1	1	1921	Glasgow	0	3
1891	Blackburn	2	1	1922	Birmingham	0	1
1892	Glasgow	4	1	1923	Glasgow	2	2
1893	Richmond	5	2	1924	Wembley	1	1
1894	Glasgow	2	2	1925	Glasgow	0	2
1895	Goodison Park	3	0	1926	Manchester	0	1
1896	Glasgow	1	2	1927	Glasgow	2	1
1897	Crystal Palace	1	2	1928	Wembley	1	5

Year	Venue	E	S	Year	Venue	E	S
1929	Glasgow	0	1	1968	Glasgow (EC)	1	1
1930	Wembley	5	2	1969	Wembley	4	1
1931	Glasgow	0	2	1970	Glasgow	0	0
1932	Wembley	3	0	1971	Wembley	3	1
1933	Glasgow	1	2	1972	Glasgow	1	0
1934	Wembley	3	0	1973	Glasgow	5	0
1935	Glasgow	0	2	1973	Wembley	1	0
1936	Wembley	1	1	1974	Glasgow	0	2
1937	Glasgow	1	3	1975	Wembley	5	1
1938	Wembley	0	1	1976	Glasgow	1	2
1939	Glasgow	2	1	1977	Wembley	1	2
1947	Wembley	1	1	1978	Glasgow	1	0
1948	Glasgow	2	0	1979	Wembley	3	1
1949	Wembley	1	3	1980	Glasgow	2	0
1950	Glasgow (WC)	1	0	1981	Wembley	0	1
1951	Wembley	2	3	1982	Glasgow	1	0
1952	Glasgow	2	1	1983	Wembley	2	0
1953	Wembley	2	2	1984	Glasgow	1	1
1954	Glasgow (WC)	4	2	1985	Glasgow	0	1
1955	Wembley	7	2	1986	Wembley	2	1
1956	Glasgow	1	1	1987	Glasgow	0	0
1957	Wembley	2	1	1988	Wembley	1	0
1958	Glasgow	4	0	1989	Glasgow	2	0
1959	Wembley	1	0	1996	Wembley (EC)	2	0
1960	Glasgow	1	1	1999	Glasgow (EC)	2	0
1961	Wembley	9	3	1999	Wembley (EC)	0	1
1962	Glasgow	0	2	2013	Wembley	3	2
1963	Wembley	1	2	2014	Glasgow	3	1
1964	Glasgow	0	1	2016	Wembley (WC)	3	0
1965	Wembley	2	2	2017	Glasgow (WC)	2	2
1966	Glasgow	4	3	2021	Wembledy (EC)	0	0
1967	Wembley (EC)	2	3				

ENGLAND v WALES

Played 103; England won 68; Wales 14; drawn 21; Goals: England 250 Wales 91

Year	Venue	E	W	Year	Venue	E	W
1879	The Oval	2	1	1896	Cardiff	9	1
1880	Wrexham	3	2	1897	Bramall Lane	4	0
1881	Blackburn	0	1	1898	Wrexham	3	0
1882	Wrexham	3	5	1899	Bristol	4	0
1883	The Oval	5	0	1900	Cardiff	1	1
1884	Wrexham	4	0	1901	Newcastle	6	0
1885	Blackburn	1	1	1902	Wrexham	0	0
1886	Wrexham	3	1	1903	Portsmouth	2	1
1887	The Oval	4	0	1904	Wrexham	2	2
1888	Crewe	5	1	1905	Anfield	3	1
1889	Stoke	4	1	1906	Cardiff	1	0
1890	Wrexham	3	1	1907	Fulham	1	1
1891	Sunderland	4	1	1908	Wrexham	7	1
1892	Wrexham	2	0	1909	Nottingham	2	0
1893	Stoke	6	0	1910	Cardiff	1	0
1894	Wrexham	5	1	1911	Millwall	3	0
1895	Queens Club, London	1	1	1912	Wrexham	2	0
				1913	Bristol	4	3

Year	Venue	E	W		Year	Venue	E	W
1914	Cardiff	2	0		1959	Cardiff	1	1
1920	Highbury	1	2		1960	Wembley	5	1
1921	Cardiff	0	0		1961	Cardiff	1	1
1922	Anfield	1	0		1962	Wembley	4	0
1923	Cardiff	2	2		1963	Cardiff	4	0
1924	Blackburn	1	2		1964	Wembley	2	1
1925	Swansea	2	1		1965	Cardiff	0	0
1926	Selhurst Park	1	3		1966	Wembley (EC)	5	1
1927	Wrexham	3	3		1967	Cardiff (EC)	3	0
1927	Burnley	1	2		1969	Wembley	2	1
1928	Swansea	3	2		1970	Cardiff	1	1
1929	Stamford Bridge	6	0		1971	Wembley	0	0
1930	Wrexham	4	0		1972	Cardiff	3	0
1931	Anfield	3	1		1972	Cardiff (WC)	1	0
1932	Wrexham	0	0		1973	Wembley (WC)	1	1
1933	Newcastle	1	2		1973	Wembley	3	0
1934	Cardiff	4	0		1974	Cardiff	2	0
1935	Wolverhampton	1	2		1975	Wembley	2	2
1936	Cardiff	1	2		1976	Wrexham	2	1
1937	Middlesbrough	2	1		1976	Cardiff	1	0
1938	Cardiff	2	4		1977	Wembley	0	1
1946	Maine Road	3	0		1978	Cardiff	3	1
1947	Cardiff	3	0		1979	Wembley	0	0
1948	Villa Park	1	0		1980	Wrexham	1	4
1949	Cardiff (WC)	4	1		1981	Wembley	0	0
1950	Sunderland	4	2		1982	Cardiff	1	0
1951	Cardiff	1	1		1983	Wembley	2	1
1952	Wembley	5	2		1984	Wrexham	0	1
1953	Cardiff (WC)	4	1		2004	Old Trafford (WC)	2	0
1954	Wembley	3	2		2005	Cardiff (WC)	1	0
1955	Cardiff	1	2		2011	Cardiff (EC)	2	0
1956	Wembley	3	1		2011	Wembley (EC)	1	0
1957	Cardiff	4	0		2016	Lens (EC)	2	1
1958	Villa Park	2	2		2020	Wembley	3	0

ENGLAND v N IRELAND
Played 98; England won 75; Ireland 7; drawn 16 Goals: England 323, Ireland 81

Year	Venue	E	I		Year	Venue	E	I
1882	Belfast	13	0		1896	Belfast	2	0
1883	Aigburth, Liverpool	7	0		1897	Nottingham	6	0
1884	Belfast	8	1		1898	Belfast	3	2
1885	Whalley Range	4	0		1899	Sunderland	13	2
1886	Belfast	6	1		1900	Dublin	2	0
1887	Bramall Lane	7	0		1901	Southampton	3	0
1888	Belfast	5	1		1902	Belfast	1	0
1889	Goodison Park	6	1		1903	Wolverhampton	4	0
1890	Belfast	9	1		1904	Belfast	3	1
1891	Wolverhampton	6	1		1905	Middlesbrough	1	1
1892	Belfast	2	0		1906	Belfast	5	0
1893	Perry Barr	6	1		1907	Goodison Park	1	0
1894	Belfast	2	2		1908	Belfast	3	1
1895	Derby	9	0		1909	Bradford PA	4	0
					1910	Belfast	1	1

1911	Derby	2	1		1958	Belfast	3	3
1912	Dublin	6	1		1959	Wembley	2	1
1913	Belfast	1	2		1960	Belfast	5	2
1914	Middlesbrough	0	3		1961	Wembley	1	1
1919	Belfast	1	1		1962	Belfast	3	1
1920	Sunderland	2	0		1963	Wembley	8	3
1921	Belfast	1	1		1964	Belfast	4	3
1922	West Bromwich	2	0		1965	Wembley	2	1
1923	Belfast	1	2		1966	Belfast (EC)	2	0
1924	Goodison Park	3	1		1967	Wembley (EC)	2	0
1925	Belfast	0	0		1969	Belfast	3	1
1926	Anfield	3	3		1970	Wembley	3	1
1927	Belfast	0	2		1971	Belfast	1	0
1928	Goodison Park	2	1		1972	Wembley	0	1
1929	Belfast	3	0		1973	*Goodison Park	2	1
1930	Bramall Lane	5	1		1974	Wembley	1	0
1931	Belfast	6	2		1975	Belfast	0	0
1932	Blackpool	1	0		1976	Wembley	4	0
1933	Belfast	3	0		1977	Belfast	2	1
1935	Goodison Park	2	1		1978	Wembley	1	0
1935	Belfast	3	1		1979	Wembley (EC)	4	0
1936	Stoke	3	1		1979	Belfast	2	0
1937	Belfast	5	1		1979	Belfast (EC)	5	1
1938	Old Trafford	7	0		1980	Wembley	1	1
1946	Belfast	7	2		1982	Wembley	4	0
1947	Goodison Park	2	2		1983	Belfast	0	0
1948	Belfast	6	2		1984	Wembley	1	0
1949	Maine Road (WC)	9	2		1985	Belfast (WC)	1	0
1950	Belfast	4	1		1985	Wembley (WC)	0	0
1951	Villa Park	2	0		1986	Wembley (EC)	3	0
1952	Belfast	2	2		1987	Belfast (EC)	2	0
1953	Goodison Park (WC)	3	1		2005	Old Trafford (WC)	4	0
1954	Belfast	2	0		2005	Belfast (WC)	0	1
1955	Wembley	3	0					
1956	Belfast	1	1					
1957	Wembley	2	3					

(*Switched from Belfast because of political situation)

SCOTLAND v WALES

Played 107; Scotland won 61; Wales 23; drawn 23; Goals: Scotland 243, Wales 124

		s	w				s	w
1876	Glasgow	4	0		1890	Paisley	5	0
1877	Wrexham	2	0		1891	Wrexham	4	3
1878	Glasgow	9	0		1892	Edinburgh	6	1
1879	Wrexham	3	0		1893	Wrexham	8	0
1880	Glasgow	5	1		1894	Kilmarnock	5	2
1881	Wrexham	5	1		1895	Wrexham	2	2
1882	Glasgow	5	0		1896	Dundee	4	0
1883	Wrexham	3	0		1897	Wrexham	2	2
1884	Glasgow	4	1		1898	Motherwell	5	2
1885	Wrexham	8	1		1899	Wrexham	6	0
1886	Glasgow	4	1		1900	Aberdeen	5	2
1887	Wrexham	2	0		1901	Wrexham	1	1
1888	Edinburgh	5	1		1902	Greenock	5	1
1889	Wrexham	0	0		1903	Cardiff	1	0
					1904	Dundee	1	1

Year	Venue	S	I	Year	Venue	S	I
1905	Wrexham	1	3	1955	Glasgow	2	0
1906	Edinburgh	0	2	1956	Cardiff	2	2
1907	Wrexham	0	1	1957	Glasgow	1	1
1908	Dundee	2	1	1958	Cardiff	3	0
1909	Wrexham	2	3	1959	Glasgow	1	1
1910	Kilmarnock	1	0	1960	Cardiff	0	2
1911	Cardiff	2	2	1961	Glasgow	2	0
1912	Tynecastle	1	0	1962	Cardiff	3	2
1913	Wrexham	0	0	1963	Glasgow	2	1
1914	Glasgow	0	0	1964	Cardiff	2	3
1920	Cardiff	1	1	1965	Glasgow (EC)	4	1
1921	Aberdeen	2	1	1966	Cardiff (EC)	1	1
1922	Wrexham	1	2	1967	Glasgow	3	2
1923	Paisley	2	0	1969	Wrexham	5	3
1924	Cardiff	0	2	1970	Glasgow	0	0
1925	Tynecastle	3	1	1971	Cardiff	0	0
1926	Cardiff	3	0	1972	Glasgow	1	0
1927	Glasgow	3	0	1973	Wrexham	2	0
1928	Wrexham	2	2	1974	Glasgow	2	0
1929	Glasgow	4	2	1975	Cardiff	2	2
1930	Cardiff	4	2	1976	Glasgow	3	1
1931	Glasgow	1	1	1977	Glasgow (WC)	1	0
1932	Wrexham	3	2	1977	Wrexham	0	0
1933	Edinburgh	2	5	1977	Anfield (WC)	2	0
1934	Cardiff	2	3	1978	Glasgow	1	1
1935	Aberdeen	3	2	1979	Cardiff	0	3
1936	Cardiff	1	1	1980	Glasgow	1	0
1937	Dundee	1	2	1981	Swansea	0	2
1938	Cardiff	1	2	1982	Glasgow	1	0
1939	Edinburgh	3	2	1983	Cardiff	2	0
1946	Wrexham	1	3	1984	Glasgow	2	1
1947	Glasgow	1	2	1985	Glasgow (WC)	0	1
1948	Cardiff (WC)	3	1	1985	Cardiff (WC)	1	1
1949	Glasgow	2	0	1997	Kilmarnock	0	1
1950	Cardiff	3	1	2004	Cardiff	0	4
1951	Glasgow	0	1	2009	Cardiff	0	3
1952	Cardiff (WC)	2	1	2011	Dublin (CC)	3	1
1953	Glasgow	3	3	2012	Cardiff (WC)	1	2
1954	Cardiff	1	0	2013	Glasgow (WC	1	2

SCOTLAND v NORTHERN IRELAND

Played 96; Scotland won 64; Northern Ireland 15; drawn 17; Goals: Scotland 258, Northern Ireland 80

Year	Venue	S	I	Year	Venue	S	I
1884	Belfast	5	0	1895	Glasgow	3	1
1885	Glasgow	8	2	1896	Belfast	3	3
1886	Belfast	7	2	1897	Glasgow	5	1
1887	Belfast	4	1	1898	Belfast	3	0
1888	Belfast	10	2	1899	Glasgow	9	1
1889	Glasgow	7	0	1900	Belfast	3	0
1890	Belfast	4	1	1901	Glasgow	11	0
1891	Glasgow	2	1	1902	Belfast	5	1
1892	Belfast	3	2	1902	Belfast	3	0
1893	Glasgow	6	1	1903	Glasgow	0	2
1894	Belfast	2	1	1904	Dublin	1	1
				1905	Glasgow	4	0

Year	Venue			Year	Venue		
1906	Dublin	1	0	1954	Glasgow	2	2
1907	Glasgow	3	0	1955	Belfast	1	2
1908	Dublin	5	0	1956	Glasgow	1	0
1909	Glasgow	5	0	1957	Belfast	1	1
1910	Belfast	0	1	1958	Glasgow	2	2
1911	Glasgow	2	0	1959	Belfast	4	0
1912	Belfast	4	1	1960	Glasgow	5	1
1913	Dublin	2	1	1961	Belfast	6	1
1914	Belfast	1	1	1962	Glasgow	5	1
1920	Glasgow	3	0	1963	Belfast	1	2
1921	Belfast	2	0	1964	Glasgow	3	2
1922	Glasgow	2	1	1965	Belfast	2	3
1923	Belfast	1	0	1966	Glasgow	2	1
1924	Glasgow	2	0	1967	Belfast	0	1
1925	Belfast	3	0	1969	Glasgow	1	1
1926	Glasgow	4	0	1970	Belfast	1	0
1927	Belfast	2	0	1971	Glasgow	0	1
1928	Glasgow	0	1	1972	Glasgow	2	0
1929	Belfast	7	3	1973	Glasgow	1	2
1930	Glasgow	3	1	1974	Glasgow	0	1
1931	Belfast	0	0	1975	Glasgow	3	0
1932	Glasgow	3	1	1976	Glasgow	3	0
1933	Belfast	4	0	1977	Glasgow	3	0
1934	Glasgow	1	2	1978	Glasgow	1	1
1935	Belfast	1	2	1979	Glasgow	1	0
1936	Edinburgh	2	1	1980	Belfast	0	1
1937	Belfast	3	1	1981	Glasgow (WC)	1	1
1938	Aberdeen	1	1	1981	Glasgow	2	0
1939	Belfast	2	0	1981	Belfast (WC)	0	0
1946	Glasgow	0	0	1982	Belfast	1	1
1947	Belfast	0	2	1983	Glasgow	0	0
1948	Glasgow	3	2	1984	Belfast	0	2
1949	Belfast	8	2	1992	Glasgow	1	0
1950	Glasgow	6	1	2008	Glasgow	0	0
1951	Belfast	3	0	2011	Dublin (CC)	3	0
1952	Glasgow	1	1	2015	Glasgow	1	0
1953	Belfast	3	1				

WALES v NORTHERN IRELAND

Played 97; Wales won 45; Northern Ireland won 27; drawn 25; Goals: Wales 191 Northern Ireland 132

Year	Venue	W	I	Year	Venue		
1882	Wrexham	7	1	1895	Belfast	2	2
1883	Belfast	1	1	1896	Wrexham	6	1
1884	Wrexham	6	0	1897	Belfast	3	4
1885	Belfast	8	2	1898	Llandudno	0	1
1886	Wrexham	5	0	1899	Belfast	0	1
1887	Belfast	1	4	1900	Llandudno	2	0
1888	Wrexham	11	0	1901	Belfast	1	0
1889	Belfast	3	1	1902	Cardiff	0	3
1890	Shrewsbury	5	2	1903	Belfast	0	2
1891	Belfast	2	7	1904	Bangor	0	1
1892	Bangor	1	1	1905	Belfast	2	2
1893	Belfast	3	4	1906	Wrexham	4	4
1894	Swansea	4	1	1907	Belfast	3	2
				1908	Aberdare	0	1

1909	Belfast	3	2		1957	Belfast	0	0
1910	Wrexham	4	1		1958	Cardiff	1	1
1911	Belfast	2	1		1959	Belfast	1	4
1912	Cardiff	2	3		1960	Wrexham	3	2
1913	Belfast	1	0		1961	Belfast	5	1
1914	Wrexham	1	2		1962	Cardiff	4	0
1920	Belfast	2	2		1963	Belfast	4	1
1921	Swansea	2	1		1964	Swansea	2	3
1922	Belfast	1	1		1965	Belfast	5	0
1923	Wrexham	0	0		1966	Cardiff	1	4
1924	Belfast	1	0		1967	Belfast (EC)	0	0
1925	Wrexham	0	0		1968	Wrexham (EC)	2	0
1926	Belfast	0	3		1969	Belfast	0	0
1927	Cardiff	2	2		1970	Swansea	1	0
1928	Belfast	2	1		1971	Belfast	0	1
1929	Wrexham	2	2		1972	Wrexham	0	0
1930	Belfast	0	7		1973	*Goodison Park	0	1
1931	Wrexham	3	2		1974	Wrexham	1	0
1932	Belfast	0	4		1975	Belfast	0	1
1933	Wrexham	4	1		1976	Swansea	1	0
1934	Belfast	1	1		1977	Belfast	1	1
1935	Wrexham	3	1		1978	Wrexham	1	0
1936	Belfast	2	3		1979	Belfast	1	1
1937	Wrexham	4	1		1980	Cardiff	0	1
1938	Belfast	0	1		1982	Wrexham	3	0
1939	Wrexham	3	1		1983	Belfast	1	0
1947	Belfast	1	2		1984	Swansea	1	1
1948	Wrexham	2	0		2004	Cardiff (WC)	2	2
1949	Belfast	2	0		2005	Belfast (WC)	3	2
1950	Wrexham (WC)	0	0		2007	Belfast	0	0
1951	Belfast	2	1		2008	Glasgow	0	0
1952	Swansea	3	0		2011	Dublin (CC)	2	0
1953	Belfast	3	2		2016	Cardiff	1	1
1954	Wrexham (WC)	1	2		2016	Paris (EC)	1	0
1955	Belfast	3	2		(*Switched from Belfast because of political			
1956	Cardiff	1	1		situation)			

THE THINGS THEY SAY ...

'The way the game is going, it's getting a little sterile. Sooner or later there will be no need for shinpads' – **Scott Parker** on a controversial red card for West Ham's Tomas Soucek against his Fulham side.

'I had goosebumps' – **Jurgen Klopp**, Liverpool manager, after fans returning – briefly – to Anfield sang 'You'll never walk alone.'

'I leave with my head held high' – **Slaven Bilic** after being sacked as West Bromwich Albion manager.

'We don't look after these players. They are not robots, they are human beings' – **Ole Gunnar Solskjaer**, Manchester United manager, claiming the Premier League weekend match scheduling for clubs with European commitments is 'a joke.'

YOUNG ENGLAND OUT AFTER STOPPAGE-TIME GOAL

For the fifth time in six tournaments, England failed to advance beyond the group stage of the European Under 21 Championship. Aidy Boothroyd's side lost to Switzerland and Portugal in the first two matches and were then denied by a stoppage-time goal, just when it seemed they would qualify for the knockout phase by winning the third game against Croatia by the required two-goal margin in Slovenia. A penalty from Eberechi Eze was followed by a fine strike by Curtis Jones, but England conceded in the 91st minute and their opponents went through. Tempers frayed at the final whistle, with Jones sent off during a scuffle with Croatia players. Germany defeated Portugal 1-0 in the final with a goal by Manchester City's Lukas Nmecha. After five years as manager, Boothroyd did not have his contract renewed by the FA.

GROUP STAGE – MARCH 24–31, 2021

(Hungary and Slovenia)

GROUP A

	P	W	D	L	F	A	Pts
Holland Q	3	1	2	0	8	3	5
Germany Q	3	1	2	0	4	1	5
Romania	3	1	2	0	3	2	5
Hungary	3	0	0	3	2	11	0

Results: Hungary 0 Germany 3, Romania 1 Holland 1, Hungary 1 Romania 2, Germany 1 Holland 1, Germany 0 Romania 0, Holland 6 Hungary 1

GROUP B

	P	W	D	L	F	A	Pts
Spain Q	3	2	1	0	5	0-	7
Italy Q	3	1	2	0	5	1	5
Czech Republic	3	0	2	1	2	4	2
Slovenia	3	0	1	2	1	8	1

Results: Czech Republic 1 Italy 1, Slovenia 0 Spain 3, Slovenia 1 Czech Republic 1, Spain 0 Italy 0, Spain 2 Czech Republic 0, Italy 4 Slovenia 0

GROUP C

	P	W	D	L	F	A	Pts
Denmark Q	3	3	0	0	6	0	9
France Q	3	2	0	1	4	1	6
Russia	3	1	0	2	4	6	3
Iceland	3	0	0	3	1	8	0

Results: France 0 Denmark 1, Russia 4 Iceland 1, Russia 0 France 2, Iceland 0 Denmark 2, Icerland 0 France 2, Denmark 3 Russia 0

GROUP D

	P	W	D	L	F	A	Pts
Portugal Q	3	3	0	0	6	0	9
Croatia Q	3	1	0	2	4	5	3
Switzerland	3	1	0	2	3	6	3
England	3	1	0	2	2	4	3

Match-day 1
England 0 **Switzerland** 1 (Ndoye 77) – Koper
England (3-4-2-1) : Ramsdale, Godfrey, Guehi, Kelly, Aarons, Skipp, Davies (Jones 66) McNeil (R Sessegnon 76), Hudson-Odoi, Smith Rowe (Eze 66), Nketiah (Brewster 76).
Booked: Guehi, Hudson-Odoi, Skipp
Other result: Portugal 1 Croatia 0

Match-day 2
Portugal 2 (Mota 64, Trincao 74 pen) **England** 0 – Ljubljana
England (4-2-3-1): Ramsdale, Tanganga, Godfrey, Guehi, S Sessegnon (Brewster 83), Davies (Gallagher 72), Skipp, Madueke (Jones 72), Smith Rowe (Eze 46), R Sessegnon (McNeil 55), Nketiah. **Booked**: Godfrey
Other result: Croatia 3 Switzerland 2

Matchday-day 3
Croatia 1 (Bradaric 90+1) **England** 2 (Eze 12 pen, Jones 74) - Koper
England (4-2-3-1): Ramsdale, Aarons, Tanganga, Wilmot, Kelly, Skipp, Gallagher (Cantwell 72), Jones, Eze, McNeil (S Sessegnon 89), Nketiah (Brewster 71). **Booked**: Kelly, Jones, Tanganga, Skipp. **Sent off**: Jones (90+8):
Other result: Switzerland 0 Portugal 3

KNOCKOUT PHASE – MAY 31–JUNE 6, 2021

(Hungary and Slovenia)

Quarter-finals: Denmark 2 Germany 2 (aet, Germany won 6-5 on pens), Holland 2 France 1, Portugal 5 Italy 3, Spain 2 Croatia 1

Semi-finals: Holland 1 Germany 2, Spain 0 Portugal 1

Final: Germany 1 (Nmecha 459) Portugal 0

England squad: Bursik (Stoke), Griffiths (WBA), Ramsdale (Sheffield Utd); Aarons (Norwich), Godfrey (Everton), Guehi (Chelsea), Kelly (Bournemouth), R Sessegnon (Tottenham), S Sessegnon (Fulham), Tanganga (Tottenham), Wilmot (Watford); Davies (Everton), Eze (Crystal Palace), Gallagher (Chelsea), Jones (Liverpool), McNeil (Burnley), Skipp (Tottenham); Brewster (Sheffield Utd), Hudson-Odoi (Chelsea), Madueke (PSV Eindhoven), Nketiah (Arsenal), Smith Rowe (Arsenal)

BRITISH AND IRISH UNDER 21 INTERNATIONALS 2020–21 EUROPEAN CHAMPIONSHIP QUALIFYING

GROUP ONE

ITALY 2 REPUBLIC OF IRELAND 0
Pisa; October 13, 2020
Republic of Ireland: Bazunu, L O'Connor, Collins, Masterson, Leahy, Taylor (Mandroiu 75), Coventry, Smallbone, Ronan (Grant 75), Elbouzedi, Obafemi (Afolabi 74). **Booked**: L O'Connor
Scorers – Italy: Sottil (43), Cutrone (62). **Half-time**: 1-0

REPUBLIC OF IRELAND 1 ICELAND 2
Tallaght Stadium, Dublin; November 15, 2020
Republic of Ireland: McGinty, L O'Connor, Collins, Masterson, Scales, Taylor, Coventry (T O'Connor 83), Ronan (Mandroiu 74) Scully (Parrott 46), Elbouzedi (Grant 83), Obafemi (Odaye 74). **Booked**: Scales, Kayode. **Sent off**: Collins (88)
Scorers – Republic of Ireland: Leifsson (75 og). **Iceland**: Gudjohnsen (25), Ingimundarson (90+3). **Half-time**: 0-1

LUXEMBOURG 1 REPUBLIC OF IRELAND 2
November 18, 2020
Republic of Ireland: McGinty, McNamara, Leahy, Masterson, McGuinness, T O'Connor (Lennon

46), Mandroiu, Ronan, Scully (Grant 71), Elbouzedi (Obafemi 78), Kayode (Ferry 78). **Booked:** Ronan, Mandroiu

Scorers – Luxembourg: Avdusinovic (84). **Republic of Ireland:** Kayode (35), Lennon (65). **Half-time:** 0-1

	P	W	D	L	F	A	Pts
Italy Q	10	8	1	1	27	5	25
Iceland Q	10	7	0	3	19	12	21
Republic of Ireland	10	6	1	3	15	8	19
Sweden	10	6	0	4	31	12	18
Armenia	10	1	0	9	4	33	3
Luxembourg	10	1	0	9	3	29	3

GROUP THREE

KOSOVO 0 ENGLAND 6
Pristina; September 4, 2020

England: Ramsdale, Godfrey, Guehi, Aarons, Kelly, Davies (Bellingham 62), Gallagher (R Sessegnon 71), Cantwell (Nelson 63), Skipp, Saka (Hudson-Odoi 63), Nketiah (Brewster 73)

Scorers – England: Nketiah (51, 55, 61 pen), Nelson (66), R Sessegnon (82), Bellingham (85). **Half-time:** 0-0

AUSTRIA 1 ENGLAND 2
Ried im Innkreis; September 8, 2020

England: Ramsdale, Lamptney (Aarons 71), Godfrey, Guehi, Justin, Bellingham, Skipp (Davies 80), R Sessegnon (Dasilva 66), Nelson (Cantwell 80), Hudson-Odoi, Nketiah (Brewster 81)

Scorers – Austria: Schmidt (60). **England:** Nketiah (27), Godfrey (49). **Half-time:** 0-1

ANDORRA 3 ENGLAND 3
La Vella; October 7, 2020

England: Ramsdale, Aarons, R Williams, Panzo, B Williams, Dasilva (Bellingham 72), Davies, Jones (Hudson-Odoi 74), Eze, McNeil (R Sessegnon 77), Surridge (Nketiah 72). **Booked:** Jones, R Williams

Scorers – Andorra: Fernandez (28, 76), Garcia (90+1). **England:** Davies (45), Dasilva (69), Nketiah (83). **Half-time:** 1-1

ENGLAND 2 TURKEY 1
Molineux; October 13, 2020

England: Ramsdale, Aarons, Godfrey, Guehi, Justin, Bellingham, Dasilva (Eze 63), Skipp, Hudson-Odoi (McNeil 85), Nketiah, R Sessegnon. **Booked:** Skipp, Bellingham

Scorers – England: Turkmen (17 og), Nketiah (88). **Turkey:** Dervisoglu (90+2). **Half-time:** 1-0

ENGLAND 3 ANDORRA 1
Molineux; November 13, 2020

England: Ramsdale, Lamptey, Wilmot, Williams, Panzo, Jones (Musiala 72), Gallagher, Da Silva, Hudson-Odoi (Eze 72), Brewster (Nketiah 72), McNeil (Buchanan 82)

Scorers – England: Jones (27), Wilmot (48), Hudson-Odoi (65 pen). **Andorra:** Garcia (45 pen). **Half-time:** 1-1

ENGLAND 5 ALBANIA 0
Molineux; November 17, 2020

England: Bursik, Wilmot, Godfrey, Kelly, Justin, Musiala (Jones 61), Skipp (Da Silva 76), Davies, Buchanan (McNeil 76), Hudson-Odoi (Gallagher 61), Nketiah. **Booked:** Nketiah

Scorers – England: Hudson-Odoi (5), Justin (26), Musiala (36), Nketiah (52, 86). **Half-time:** 3-0

England Q	10	9	1	0	34	9	28
Austria	10	6	0	4	24	16	18
Albania	10	4	2	4	16	21	14
Turkey	10	4	1	5	15	18	13
Kosovo	10	3	0	7	9	20	9
Andorra	10	1	2	7	10	24	5

GROUP FOUR

LITHUANIA 0 SCOTLAND 1
Vilnius; September 8, 2020
Scotland: Doohan, Harvie, Porteous, Johnston, Campbell, Ferguson, McCrorie, Patterson (McLennan 85), Middleton (Mayo 80), Turnbull (Scott 60), Hornby. **Booked**: Patterson, Middleton, McCrorie, Porteous
Scorer – Scotland: Campbell (81). **Half-time**: 0-0

SCOTLAND 2 CZECH REPUBLIC 0
Tynecastle Park, Edinburgh; October 9, 2020
Scotland: Doohan, Ashby (McLennan 84), Harvie, Mayo, McIntyre, Campbell, Patterson (Maguire 72), Reading, Ferguson, McCrorie, Hornby. **Booked**: Campbell, Reading, Ashby
Scorers – Scotland: Hornby (25), McCrorie (82). **Half-time**: 1-0

SAN MARINO 0 SCOTLAND 7
Serravalle; October 13, 2020
Scotland: Doohan (Wright 57), McIntyre, Harvie, Mayo, Patterson (Chalmers 71), Turnbull (Kelly 57), Irving (McInroy 71), Maguire, Middleton, Hornby (Ashby 57), McLennan. **Booked**: Middleton
Scorers – Scotland: Hornby (20 pen, 50, 51), Turnbull (39), Maguire (43), McLennan (70), Ashby (75). **Half-time**: 0-3

SCOTLAND 2 CROATIA 2
Tynecastle Park, Edinburgh; November 12, 2020
Scotland: Doohan, Reading (McLennan 63), Harvie, Porteous, Johnston, Campbell, Patterson (Middleton 46), Hornby, Maguire, Ferguson (Gilmour 63), McCrorie. **Booked**: Johnson, Reading, McCrorie, Porteous. **Sent off**: Gilmour (71)
Scorers – Scotland: Middleton (54), McLennan (70). **Croatia**: Morro (19), Bistrovic (24). **Half-time**: 0-2

GREECE 1 SCOTLAND 0
Athens; November 17, 2020
Scotland: Doohan, Harvie, Porteous, Johnston, McCrorie, Campbell, Maguire (Turnbull 72), Ferguson, Middleton (Fiorini 72), McLennan, Hornby. **Booked**: McCrorie, McLennan
Scorer – Greece: Christopoulos (26). **Half-time**: 1-0

Czech Republic Q	10	6	3	1	20	4	21
Croatia Q	10	6	2	2	37	7	20
Scotland	10	5	3	2	16	5	18
Greece	10	5	1	4	10	11	16
Lithuania	10	3	1	6	9	15	10
San Marino	10	0	0	10	0	50	0

GROUP EIGHT

MALTA 0 NORTHERN IRELAND 2
Ta'Qali; September 4, 2020
Northern Ireland: Hazard, Kerr, Toal, Marron, Amos, McCann (McClean 80), McCalmont (Gallagher 80), Galbraith, Parkhouse (O'Neill 90), Boyce-Munce (Dunwoody 63), Larkin (Balmer 89). **Booked**: Boyd Munce
Scorers – Northern Ireland: Larkin (57), Parkhouse (67). **Half-time**: 0-0

NORTHERN IRELAND 0 DENMARK 1
Showgrounds, Ballymena; September 8, 2020
Northern Ireland: Hazard, Marron, Amos (Scott 54), Larkin, Toal, Galbraith, Kerr, McCalmont, Dunwoody (Parkhouse 65), McCann, Lavery (O'Neill 84). **Booked**: Larkin, Galbraith
Scorer – Denmark: Olsen (75). **Half-time**: 0-0

NORTHERN IRELAND 2 FINLAND 3
Showgrounds, Ballymena; October 9, 2020
Northern Ireland: Hazard, Marron, Brown, Amos, (Burns 61), Toal, Kerr, McCalmont (Scott 79), Boyd-Munce, McKiernan (Bonis 46), O'Neill, Dunwoody. **Booked**: McKiernan, McCalmont
Scorers – Northern Ireland: O'Neill (23, 59). **Finland**: Stavitski (44), Soisalo (62), Skytta (68). **Half-time**: 1-1

NORTHERN IRELAND 1 UKRAINE 0
Showgrounds, Ballymena; October 13, 2020
Northern Ireland: Hazard, Marron,. Brown, Amos, Toal, Kerr, Galbraith, Bansal-McNulty (McKiernan 76), Boyd-Munce, O'Neill (Bonis 76), Dunwoody. **Booked**: Bansal-McNulty, Dunwoody, Hazard, O'Neill
Scorer – Northern Ireland: O'Neill (61). **Half-time**: 0-0

UKRAINE 3 NORTHERN IRELAND 0
Kovalivka; November 17, 2020
Northern Ireland: Webber, Marron, Amos, Brown, Toal, Bansal-McNulty, Boyd-Munce, McCalmont, Hume, O'Neill, Lavery. **Booked**: Toal, Boyd-Munce, Marron, Bansal-McNulty, McCalmont

Scorers – Ukraine: Baboglo (67), Isaenko (70), Kukharevych (74). **Half-time**: 0-0

Denmark Q	10	8	2	0	21	9	26
Romania Q	10	6	2	2	22	7	20
Ukraine	10	5	1	4	17	11	16
Finland	10	4	1	5	14	15	13
Northern Ireland	10	2	3	5	7	13	9
Malta	10	0	1	9	4	30	1

GROUP NINE

BOSNIA HERZEGOVINA 1 WALES 0
Zenica; September 4, 2020
Wales: Przybek, A Lewis, Boyes, Evans, Poole, B Cooper, Cullen (Waite 80), Burton (O Cooper 80), Harris (Jephcott 80), Taylor (Clifton 82), Broadhead (Stirk 82). **Booked**: A Lewis, Poole, Jephcott
Scorer – Bosnia-Herzegovina: Resic (74). **Half-time**: 0-0

BELGIUM 5 WALES 0
Leuven; October 9, 2020
Wales: Przybek, Coxe, Boyes, Stirk, Poole, B Cooper, Cullen (Pearson 81), Bowen (Williams 74), Harris (Touray 73), Spence (Adams 54). Waite (Collins 54). **Booked**: Harris, Bowen
Scorers – Belgium: Tresor (17 pen), Lokonga (20, 33), Bataille (77), Openda (82 pen). **Half-time**: 3-0

WALES 3 MOLDOVA 0
Racecourse Ground, Wrexham; November 13, 2020
Wales: Ratcliffe, Poole, Coxe, B Cooper, Boyes, Clifton, Taylor, Broadhead (O Cooper 90), Cullen, Spence (A Lewis 82), Jephcott (Touray 90)
Scorers – Wales: Taylor (61), Broadhead (77 pen), Touray (90+3). **Half-time**: 0-0

GERMANY 2 WALES 1
Braunschweig; November 17, 2020
Wales: Ratcliffe, Poole, Coxe, Cooper (J Lewis 86), Boyes, Taylor, Clifton, Broadhead, Cullen (A Lewis 68), Harris (Touray 86), Jephcott (Spence 73). **Booked**: Broadhead, Cullen, Coxe, Poole
Scorers – Germany: Nmecha (17 pen), Burkardt (26). **Wales**: Harris (35). **Half-time**: 2-1

Germany Q	8	6	0	2	22	10	18
Belgium	8	4	1	3	18	9	13
Bosnia-Herz	8	3	2	3	9	7	11
Wales	8	3	0	5	8	15	9
Moldova	8	2	1	5	6	22	7

EUROPEAN CHAMPIONSHIP 2023 QUALIFYING

GROUP FIVE

WALES 0 MOLDOVA 0
Stebonheath Park, Llanelli; June 4 2021
Wales: Barden, Stevens, Jones, Stirk, Sass-Davies, Boyes, Huggins (Pearson 63), Taylor, Jephcott (Collins 89), Spence, Adams. **Booked**: Spence, Jones. **Sent off**: Spence (73)

FRIENDLY INTERNATIONALS

WALES 1 REPUBLIC OF IRELAND 2
Colliers Park, Wrexham; March 26, 2021
Wales: Webb (Shepperd 46), Stevens, Sass-Davies, Boyes, Jones, Stirk, Taylor (Bowen 72), Huggins, Adams (Colwill 81), Spence (Pearson 61), Jephcott (Norton 61)
Republic of Ireland: Maher, O'Connor, McGuinness, Omobamidele, O'Malley (Kilkenny 68), Connell, Noss, Watson (Grant 73), Ferry, Gilbert (Wright 68), Afolabi (Varian 86)
Scorers – Wales: Adams (11). **Republic of Ireland**: Afolabi (75), Boyes (76 og). **Half-time**: 1-0

SCOTLAND 1 NORTHERN IRELAND 2
C&G Systems Stadium, Dumbarton; June 2, 20-21
Scotland: Slicker (Kinnear 66), Burroughs, Welsh, Deas, Harper (Bowie 86), Banks (Chalmers 66), Kelly, Erhahon (Clayton 66), Middleton, Joseph (Makcay 66), Urain (Rudden 77)
Northern Ireland: Mee, Scott (Hume 68), Finlayson, Balmer, Donnelly, Baggley (McCann 72), Palmer, Boyd-Munce, Stewart, Conn-Clarke (Johnson 68), Taylor (Smyth 72)
Scorers – Scotland: Middleton (35 pen). **Northern Ireland**: Taylor (9), Baggley (44). **Half-time**: 1-2

SCOTLAND 3 NORTHERN IRELAND 2
C&G Systems Stadium, Dumbarton, June 5, 2021
Scotland: Mair (Kinnear 67), Burroughs, Welsh (Deas 70), Mayo, Banks (Middleton 67), Kelly, Williamson (Urain 67), Clayton, Chalmers (Erhahon 75), Mackay, McPake (MacGregor 72)
Northern Ireland: Mee, Hume, Balmer, Cousin-Dawson, Donnelly (Finlayson 63), Stewart (Scott 70), Boyd-Munce (Boyle 46), Smyth, Johnson, Taylor (McCann 58), Wylie (Waide 58)
Scorers – Scotland: Clayton (21), Williamson (42), Middleton (82 pen). **Northern Ireland**: Wylie (24), Waide (70). **Half-time**: 2-1

TRANSFER TRAIL

Player	From	To	Date	£
Philippe Coutinho	Liverpool	Barcelona	1/18	142,000,000
Paul Pogba	Juventus	Manchester Utd	8/16	89,300,000
Eden Hazard	Chelsea	Real Madrid	6/19	89,000,000
Gareth Bale	Tottenham	Real Madrid	8/13	85,300,000
Cristiano Ronaldo	Manchester Utd	Real Madrid	7/09	80,000,000
Harry Maguire	Leicester	Manchester Utd	8/19	80,000,000
Romelu Lukaku	Everton	Manchester Utd	7/17	75,000,000
Virgil van Dijk	Southampton	Liverpool	1/18	75,000,000
Romelu Lukaku	Manchester Utd	Inter Milan	8/19	74,000,000
Nicolas Pepe	Lille	Arsenal	8/19	72,000,000
Kepa Arrizabalaga	Athletic Bilbao	Chelsea	8/18	71,600,000
Kai Havertz	Bayer Leverekusen	Chelsea	9/20	71,000,000
Luis Suarez	Liverpool	Barcelona	7/14	65,000,000
Alisson	Roma	Liverpool	7/18	65,000,000
Ruben Dias	Benfica	Manchester City	9/20	65,000,000
Rodri	Atletico Madrid	Manchester City	7/19	62,800,000
Riyad Mahrez	Leicester	Manchester City	7/18	60,000,000
Joao Cancelo	Juventus	Manchester City	8/19	60,000,000
Angel di Maria	Real Madrid	Manchester Utd	8/14	59,700,000
Alvaro Morata	Chelsea	Atletico Madrid	7/20	58,300,000
Christian Pulisic	Borussia Dortmund	Chelsea	7/19	58,000,000
Alvaro Morata	Real Madrid	Chelsea	7/17	57,200,000
Diego Costa	Chelsea	Atletico Madrid	1/18	57,000,000
Aymeric Laporte	Athletic Bilbao	Manchester City	1/18	57,000,000
Pierre-Emerick Aubameyang	Borussia Dortmund	Arsenal	1/18	56,000,000
Kevin De Bruyne	Wolfsburg	Manchester City	8/15	54,500,000
Tanguy Ndombele	Lyon	Tottenham	7/19	53,800,000
Oscar	Chelsea	Shanghai Shenhua	1/17	52,000,000
Benjamin Mendy	Monaco	Manchester City	7/17	52,000,000
Fred	Shaktar Donetsk	Manchester Utd	6/18	52,000,000
Fernando Torres	Liverpool	Chelsea	1/11	50,000,000
David Luiz	Chelsea	Paris SG	6/14	50,000,000
Jorginho	Napoli	Chelsea	7/18	50,000,000
Aaron Wan-Bissaka	Crystal Palace	Manchester Utd	6/19	50,000,000
Raheem Sterling	Liverpool	Manchester City	7/15	49,000,000
Naby Keita	Leipzig	Liverpool	7/18	48,000,000
John Stones	Everton	Manchester City	8/16	47,500,000
Alexandre Lacazette	Lyon	Arsenal	7/17	46,500,000
Bruno Fernandes	Sporting Lisbon	Manchester Utd	1/20	47,000,000
Gylfi Sigurdsson	Swansea	Everton	8/17	45,000,000
Kyle Walker	Tottenham	Manchester City	7/17	45,000,000
Sebastien Haller	Eintracht Frankfurt	West Ham	7/19	45,000,000
Ben Chilwell	Leicester	Chelsea	8/20	45,000,000
Leroy Sane	Manchester City	Bayern Munich	7/20	44,700,000
Angel di Maria	Manchester Utd	Paris SG	8/15	44,300,000
Fabinho	Monaco	Liverpool	5/8	43,700,000
Bernardo Silva	Monaco	Manchester City	6/17	43,000,000
Mesut Ozil	Real Madrid	Arsenal	9/13	42,400,000
Davinson Sanchez	Ajax	Tottenham	8/17	42,000,000
Diogo Jota	Wolves	Liverpool	9/20	41,000,000
Nemanja Matic	Chelsea	Manchester Utd	7/17	40,000,000

Name	From	To	Date	Fee
Richarlison	Watford	Everton	7/18	40,000,000
Youri Tielemans	Monaco	Leicester	7/19	40,000,000
Mateo Kovacic	Real Madrid	Chelsea	7/19	40,000,000
Nathan Ake	Bournemouth	Manchester City	8/20	40,000,000
Joelinton	Hoffenheim	Newcastle	7/19	40,000,000
Tiemoue Bakayoko	Monaco	Chelsea	7/17	39,700,000
Sergio Aguero	Atletico Madrid	Manchester City	7/11	38,500,000
Thibaut Courtois	Chelsea	Real Madrid	8/18	38,000,000
Hakim Ziyech	Ajax	Chelsea	6/00	37,800,000
Amad Diallo	Atalanta	Manchester Utd	1/21	37,200,000
Juan Mata	Chelsea	Manchester Utd	1/14	37,100,000
Leroy Sane	Schalke	Manchester City	7/16	37,000,000
Anthony Martial	Monaco	Manchester Utd	9/15	36,000,000
Felipe Anderson	Lazio	West Ham	7/18	36,000,000
Fabio Silva	Porto	Wolves	9/20	35,600,000
Andy Carroll	Newcastle	Liverpool	1/11	35,000,000
Cesc Fabregas	Arsenal	Barcelona	8/11	35,000,000
Alexis Sanchez	Barcelona	Arsenal	7/14	35,000,000
Granit Xhaka	Borussia M'gladbach	Arsenal	6/16	35,000,000
Shkodran Mustafi	Valencia	Arsenal	8/16	35,000,000
Alex Oxlade-Chamberlain	Arsenal	Liverpool	8/17	35,000,000
Danny Drinkwater	Leicester	Chelsea	8/17	35,000,000
Donny van de Beek	Ajax	Manchester Utd	9/20	35,000,000
Ibrahima Konate	RB Leipzig	Liverpool	6/21	35,000,000
Ederson	Benfica	Manchester City	6/17	34,900,000
Mohamed Salah	Roma	Liverpool	7/17	34,300,000
Danilo	Manchester City	Juventus	8/19	34,100,000
Sadio Mane	Southampton	Liverpool	6/16	34,000,000
Michy Batshuayi	Marseille	Chelsea	7/16	33,000,000
Emiliano Buendia	Norwich	Aston Villa	6/21	33,000,000
Robinho	Real Madrid	Manchester City	9/08	32,500,000
Christian Benteke	Aston Villa	Liverpool	7/15	32,500,000
Eden Hazard	Lille	Chelsea	6/12	32,000,000
Diego Costa	Atletico Madrid	Chelsea	7/14	32,000,000
N'Golo Kante	Leicester	Chelsea	7/16	32,000,000
David Luiz	Paris SG	Chelsea	8/16	32,000,000
Eliaquim Mangala	Porto	Manchester City	8/14	31,900,000
Wesley Fofana	St Etienne	Leicester	10/20	31,500,000
Ismaila Sarr	Rennes	Watford	8/19	31,000,000
Dimitar Berbatov	Tottenham	Manchester Utd	9/08	30,750,000
Victor Lindelof	Benfica	Manchester Utd	6/17	30,700,000
Andriy Shevchenko	AC Milan	Chelsea	5/06	30,800,000
Xabi Alonso	Liverpool	Real Madrid	8/09	30,000,000
Fernandinho	Shakhtar Donetsk	Manchester City	6/13	30,000,000
Willian	Anzhi Makhachkala	Chelsea	8/13	30,000,000
Erik Lamela	Roma	Tottenham	8/13	30,000,000
Luke Shaw	Southampton	Manchester Utd	6/14	30,000,000
Eric Bailly	Villarreal	Manchester Utd	6/16	30,000,000
Moussa Sissoko	Newcastle	Tottenham,	8/16	30,000,000
Ayoze Perez	Newcastle	Leicester	7/19	30,000,000
Idrissa Gueye	Everton	Paris SG	7/19	30,000,000
Islam Slimani	Sporting Lisbon	Leicester	8/16	29,700,000
Rio Ferdinand	Leeds	Manchester Utd	7/02	29,100,000
Antonio Rudiger	Roma	Chelsea	7/17	29,000,000

Ander Herrara	Athletic Bilbao	Manchester Utd	6/14	28,800,000
Nicolas Otamendi	Valencia	Manchester City	8/15	28,500,000
Juan Sebastian Veron	Lazio	Manchester Utd	7/01	28,100,000
Yaya Toure	Barcelona	Manchester City	7/10	28,000,000
Romelu Lukaku	Chelsea	Everton	7/14	28,000,000
Wilfried Bony	Swansea	Manchester City	1/15	28,000,000
Roberto Firmino	Hoffenheim	Liverpool	6/15	28,000,000
Ollie Watkins	Brentford	Aston Villa	9/20	28,000,000
Nelson Semedo	Barcelona	Wolves	9/20	27,600,000
Marouane Fellaini	Everton	Manchester Utd	9/13	27,500,000
Yerry Mina	Barcelona	Everton	8/18	27,200,000
Wayne Rooney	Everton	Manchester Utd	8/04	27,000,000
Edin Dzeko	Wolfsburg	Manchester City	1/11	27,000,000
Luka Modric	Tottenham	Real Madrid	8/12	27,000,000
Cesc Fabregas	Barcelona	Chelsea	6/14	27,000,000
Gabriel Jesus	Palmeiras	Manchester City	7/16	27,000,000
Christian Benteke	Liverpool	Crystal Palace	8/16	27,000,000
Cenk Tosun	Besiktas	Everton	1/18	27,000,000
William Saliba	Saint-Etienne	Arsenal	7/19	27,000,000
Steven Bergwijn	PSV Eindhoven	Tottenham	1/20	27,000,000
Giovani Lo Celso	Real Betis	Tottenham	1/20	27,000,000
Danilo	Real Madrid	Manchester City	7/17	26,500,000
Roberto Soldado	Valencia	Tottenham	8/13	26,000,000
Henrikh Mkhitaryan	Borussua Dortmund	Manchester Utd	7/16	26,000,000
Mamadou Sakho	Liverpool	Crystal Palace	8/17	26,000,000
Lucas Torreira	Sampdoria	Arsenal	7/18	26,000,000
Rodrigo	Valencia	Leeds	8/20	26,000,000

BRITISH RECORD TRANSFERS FROM FIRST £1,000 DEAL

Player	From	To	Date	£
Alf Common	Sunderland	Middlesbrough	2/1905	1,000
Syd Puddefoot	West Ham	Falkirk	2/22	5,000
Warney Cresswell	South Shields	Sunderland	3/22	5,500
Bob Kelly	Burnley	Sunderland	12/25	6,500
David Jack	Bolton	Arsenal	10/28	10,890
Bryn Jones	Wolves	Arsenal	8/38	14,500
Billy Steel	Morton	Derby	9/47	15,000
Tommy Lawton	Chelsea	Notts Co	11/47	20,000
Len Shackleton	Newcastle	Sunderland	2/48	20,500
Johnny Morris	Manchester Utd	Derby	2/49	24,000
Eddie Quigley	Sheffield Wed	Preston	12/49	26,500
Trevor Ford	Aston Villa	Sunderland	10/50	30,000
Jackie Sewell	Notts Co	Sheffield Wed	3/51	34,500
Eddie Firmani	Charlton	Sampdoria	7/55	35,000
John Charles	Leeds	Juventus	4/57	65,000
Denis Law	Manchester City	Torino	6/61	100,000
Denis Law	Torino	Manchester Utd	7/62	115,000
Allan Clarke	Fulham	Leicester	6/68	150,000
Allan Clarke	Leicester	Leeds	6/69	165,000
Martin Peters	West Ham	Tottenham	3/70	200,000
Alan Ball	Everton	Arsenal	12/71	220,000
David Nish	Leicester	Derby	8/72	250,000
Bob Latchford	Birmingham	Everton	2/74	350,000

Player	From	To	Date	£
Graeme Souness	Middlesbrough	Liverpool	1/78	352,000
Kevin Keegan	Liverpool	Hamburg	6/77	500,000
David Mills	Middlesbrough	WBA	1/79	516,000
Trevor Francis	Birmingham	Nottm Forest	2/79	1,180,000
Steve Daley	Wolves	Manchester City	9/79	1,450,000
Andy Gray	Aston Villa	Wolves	9/79	1,469,000
Bryan Robson	WBA	Manchester Utd	10/81	1,500,000
Ray Wilkins	Manchester Utd	AC Milan	5/84	1,500,000
Mark Hughes	Manchester Utd	Barcelona	5/86	2,300,000
Ian Rush	Liverpool	Juventus	6/87	3,200,000
Chris Waddle	Tottenham	Marseille	7/89	4,250,000
David Platt	Aston Villa	Bari	7/91	5,500,000
Paul Gascoigne	Tottenham	Lazio	6/92	5,500,000
Andy Cole	Newcastle	Manchester Utd	1/95	7,000,000
Dennis Bergkamp	Inter Milan	Arsenal	6/95	7,500,000
Stan Collymore	Nottm Forest	Liverpool	6/95	8,500,000
Alan Shearer	Blackburn	Newcastle	7/96	15,000,000
Nicolas Anelka	Arsenal	Real Madrid	8/99	22,500,000
Juan Sebastian Veron	Lazio	Manchester Utd	7/01	28,100,000
Rio Ferdinand	Leeds	Manchester Utd	7/02	29,100,000
Andriy Shevchenko	AC Milan	Chelsea	5/06	30,800,000
Robinho	Real Madrid	Manchester City	9/08	32,500,000
Cristiano Ronaldo	Manchester Utd	Real Madrid	7/09	80,000,000
Gareth Bale	Tottenham	Real Madrid	9/13	85,300,000
Paul Pogba	Juventus	Manchester Utd	8/16	89.300,000
Philippe Coutinho	Liverpool	Barcelona	1/18	142,000,000

• World's first £1m transfer: GuiseppeSavoldi, Bologna to Napoli, July 1975

TOP FOREIGN SIGNINGS

Player	From	To	Date	£
Neymar	Barcelona	Paris SG	8/17	198,000,000
Kylian Mbappe	Monaco	Paris SG	8/17	165,700,000
Ousmane Dembele	Borussia Dortmund	Barcelona	8/17	134,000,000
Joao Felix	Benfica	Atletico Madrid	7/19	113,000,000
Antoine Griezmann	Atletico Madrid	Barcelona	7/19	107,000,000
Cristiano Ronaldo	Real Madrid	Juventus	7/18	99,200,000
Gonzalo Higuain	Napoli	Juventus	7/16	75,300,000
Lucas Hernandez	Atletico Madrid	Bayern Munich	7/19	68,000,000
Matthijs de Ligt	Ajax	Juventus	7/19	67,500,000
Arthur	Barcelona	Juventus	7/20	66,000,000
Frenkie de Jong	Ajax	Barcelona	1/19	65,000,000
Luka Jovic	Eintracht Frankfurt	Real Madrid	6/19	62,000,000
Zlatan Ibrahimovic	Inter Milan	Barcelona	7/09	60,300,000
James Rodriguez	Monaco	Real Madrid	7/14	60,000,000
Kaka AC	Milan	Real Madrid	6/08	56,000,000

WORLD'S MOST EXPENSIVE TEENAGER

£165,700,000: Kylian Mbappe, 19, Monaco to Paris SG, August 2017

WORLD RECORD FOR 16-YEAR-OLD

£39,600,000: Vinicius Junior, Flamengo to Real Madrid, July 2018

RECORD TRIBUNAL FEE
£6.5m: Danny Ings, Burnley to Liverpool, Jun 2016

RECORD FEE BETWEEN SCOTTISH CLUBS
£4.4m: Scott Brown, Hibernian to Celtic, May 2007

RECORD NON-LEAGUE FEE
£1m: Jamie Vardy, Fleetwood to Leicester, May 2012

RECORD FEE BETWEEN NON-LEAGUE CLUBS
£275,000: Richard Brodie, York to Crawley, Aug 2010

MILESTONES

1848: First code of rules compiled at Cambridge University.
1857: Sheffield FC, world's oldest football club, formed.
1862: Notts Co (oldest League club) formed.
1863: Football Association founded – their first rules of game agreed.
1871: FA Cup introduced.
1872: First official International: Scotland 0 England 0. Corner-kick introduced.
1873: Scottish FA formed; Scottish Cup introduced.
1874: Shinguards introduced.
1875: Crossbar introduced (replacing tape).
1876: FA of Wales formed.
1877: Welsh Cup introduced.
1878: Referee's whistle first used.
1880: Irish FA founded; Irish Cup introduced.
1883: Two-handed throw-in introduced.
1885: Record first-class score (Arbroath 36 Bon Accord 0 – Scottish Cup). Professionalism legalised.
1886: International Board formed.
1887: Record FA Cup score (Preston 26 Hyde 0).
1888: Football League founded by William McGregor. First matches on Sept 8.
1889 Preston win Cup and League (first club to complete Double).
1890: Scottish League and Irish League formed.
1891: Goal-nets introduced. Penalty-kick introduced.
1892: Inter-League games began. Football League Second Division formed.
1893: FA Amateur Cup launched.
1894: Southern League formed.
1895: FA Cup stolen from Birmingham shop window – never recovered.
1897: First Players' Union formed. Aston Villa win Cup and League.
1898: Promotion and relegation introduced.
1901: Maximum wage rule in force (£4 a week). Tottenham first professional club to take FA Cup south. First six-figure attendance (110,802) at FA Cup Final.
1902: Ibrox Park disaster (25 killed). Welsh League formed.
1904: FIFA founded (7 member countries).
1905: First £1,000 transfer (Alf Common, Sunderland to Middlesbrough).
1907: Players' Union revived.
1908: Transfer fee limit (£350) fixed in January and withdrawn in April.
1911: New FA Cup trophy – in use to 1991. Transfer deadline introduced.
1914: King George V first reigning monarch to attend FA Cup Final.

1916: Entertainment Tax introduced.

1919: League extended to 44 clubs.

1920: Third Division (South) formed.

1921: Third Division (North) formed.

1922: Scottish League (Div II) introduced.

1923: Beginning of football pools. First Wembley Cup Final.

1924: First International at Wembley (England 1 Scotland 1). Rule change allows goals to be scored direct from corner-kicks.

1925: New offside law.

1926: Huddersfield complete first League Championship hat-trick.

1927: First League match broadcast (radio): Arsenal v Sheffield United. First radio broadcast of Cup Final (winners Cardiff City). Charles Clegg, president of FA, becomes first knight of football.

1928: First £10,000 transfer – David Jack (Bolton to Arsenal). WR ('Dixie') Dean (Everton) creates League record – 60 goals in season. Britain withdraws from FIFA.

1930: Uruguay first winners of World Cup.

1931: WBA win Cup and promotion.

1933: Players numbered for first time in Cup Final (1-22).

1934: Sir Frederick Wall retires as FA secretary; successor Stanley Rous. Death of Herbert Chapman (Arsenal manager).

1935: Arsenal equal Huddersfield's Championship hat-trick record. Official two-referee trials.

1936: Joe Payne's 10-goal League record (Luton 12 Bristol Rov 0).

1937: British record attendance: 149,547 at Scotland v England match.

1938: First live TV transmission of FA Cup Final. Football League 50th Jubilee. New pitch marking – arc on edge of penalty-area. Laws of Game re-drafted by Stanley Rous. Arsenal pay record £14,500 fee for Bryn Jones (Wolves).

1939: Compulsory numbering of players in Football League. First six-figure attendance for League match (Rangers v Celtic 118,567). All normal competitions suspended for duration of Second World War.

1945: Scottish League Cup introduced.

1946: British associations rejoin FIFA. Bolton disaster (33 killed) during FA Cup tie with Stoke. Walter Winterbottom appointed England's first director of coaching.

1947: Great Britain beat Rest of Europe 6-1 at Hampden Park, Glasgow. First £20,000 transfer – Tommy Lawton, Chelsea to Notts Co

1949: Stanley Rous, secretary FA, knighted. England's first home defeat outside British Champ. (0-2 v Eire).

1950: Football League extended from 88 to 92 clubs. World record crowd (203,500) at World Cup Final, Brazil v Uruguay, in Rio. Scotland's first home defeat by foreign team (0-1 v Austria).

1951: White ball comes into official use.

1952: Newcastle first club to win FA Cup at Wembley in successive seasons.

1953: England's first Wembley defeat by foreign opponents (3-6 v Hungary).

1954: Hungary beat England 7-1 in Budapest.

1955: First FA Cup match under floodlights (prelim round replay): Kidderminster v Brierley Hill Alliance.

1956: First FA Cup ties under floodlights in competition proper. First League match by floodlight (Portsmouth v Newcastle). Real Madrid win first European Cup.

1957: Last full Football League programme on Christmas Day. Entertainment Tax withdrawn.

1958: Manchester United air crash at Munich. League re-structured into four divisions.

1960: Record transfer fee: £55,000 for Denis Law (Huddersfield to Manchester City). Wolves win Cup, miss Double and Championship hat-trick by one goal. FA recognise Sunday football. Football League Cup launched.

1961: Tottenham complete the first Championship–FA Cup double this century. Maximum wage (£20 a week) abolished in High Court challenge by George Eastham. First British

£100-a-week wage paid (by Fulham to Johnny Haynes). First £100,000 British transfer – Denis Law, Manchester City to Torino. Sir Stanley Rous elected president of FIFA

1962: Manchester United raise record British transfer fee to £115,000 for Denis Law.

1963: FA Centenary. Season extended to end of May due to severe winter. First pools panel. English 'retain and transfer' system ruled illegal in High Court test case.

1964: Rangers' second great hat-trick – Scottish Cup, League Cup and League. Football League and Scottish League guaranteed £500,000 a year in new fixtures copyright agreement with Pools. First televised 'Match of the Day' (BBC2): Liverpool 3 Arsenal 2.

1965: Bribes scandal – ten players jailed (and banned for life by FA) for match-fixing 1960–63. Stanley Matthews knighted in farewell season. Arthur Rowley (Shrewsbury) retires with record of 434 League goals. Substitutes allowed for injured players in Football League matches (one per team).

1966: England win World Cup (Wembley).

1967: Alf Ramsey, England manager, knighted; OBE for captain Bobby Moore. Celtic become first British team to win European Cup. First substitutes allowed in FA Cup Final (Tottenham v Chelsea) but not used.

1968: First FA Cup Final televised live in colour (BBC2 – WBA v Everton). Manchester United first English club to win European Cup.

1970: FIFA/UEFA approve penalty shoot-out in deadlocked ties.

1971: Arsenal win League Championship and FA Cup. Sixty-six supporters die in the Ibrox Stadium disaster.

1973: Football League introduce 3-up, 3-down promotion/relegation between Divisions 1, 2 and 3 and 4-up, 4-down between Divisions 3 and 4.

1974: First FA Cup ties played on Sunday. League football played on Sunday for first time. Last FA Amateur Cup Final. Joao Havelange (Brazil) succeeds Sir Stanley Rous as FIFA president.

1975: Scottish Premier Division introduced.

1976: Football League introduce goal difference (replacing goal average) and red/yellow cards.

1977: Liverpool achieve the double of League Championship and European Cup. Don Revie defects to United Arab Emirates when England manager – successor Ron Greenwood.

1978: Freedom of contract for players accepted by Football League. PFA lifts ban on foreign players in English football. Viv Anderson (Nottm Forest) first black player to win a full England cap.

1979: First all-British £500,000 transfer – David Mills, Middlesbrough to WBA. First British million pound transfer (Trevor Francis – Birmingham to Nottm Forest). Andy Gray moves from Aston Villa to Wolves for a record £1,469,000 fee.

1981: Tottenham win 100th FA Cup Final. Liverpool first British side to win European Cup three times. Three points for a win introduced by Football League. Death of Bill Shankly, manager–legend of Liverpool 1959–74. Record British transfer – Bryan Robson (WBA to Manchester United), £1,500,000.

1982: Aston Villa become sixth consecutive English winners of European Cup. Tottenham retain FA Cup – first club to do so since Tottenham 1961 and 1962. Football.

1983: Liverpool complete League Championship–Milk Cup double for second year running. Manager Bob Paisley retires. Aberdeen first club to do Cup-Winners' Cup and domestic Cup double. Football League clubs vote to keep own match receipts. Football League agree two-year contract for live TV coverage of ten matches per season (5 Friday night, BBC, 5 Sunday afternoon, ITV).

1984: Aberdeen take Scottish Cup for third successive season, win Scottish Championship, too. Tottenham win UEFA Cup on penalty shoot-out. Liverpool win European Cup on penalty shoot-out to complete unique treble with Milk Cup and League title (as well as Championship hat-trick). N Ireland win the final British Championship. France win European Championship – their first honour. Britain's biggest score this century: Stirling Alb 20 Selkirk 0 (Scottish Cup).

1985: Bradford City fire disaster – 56 killed. First £1m receipts from match in Britain (FA Cup Final). Kevin Moran (Manchester United) first player to be sent off in FA Cup Final. Celtic win 100th Scottish FA Cup Final. European Cup Final horror (Liverpool v Juventus, riot in Brussels) 39 die. UEFA ban all English clubs indefinitely from European competitions. No TV coverage at start of League season – first time since 1963 (resumption delayed until January 1986). Sept: first ground-sharing in League history – Charlton Athletic move from The Valley to Selhurst Park (Crystal Palace).

1986: Liverpool complete League and Cup double in player-manager Kenny Dalglish's first season in charge. Swindon (4th Div Champions) set League points record (102). League approve reduction of First Division to 20 clubs by 1988. Two substitutes in FA Cup and League (Littlewoods) Cup. Two-season League/TV deal (£6.2m):- BBC and ITV each show seven live League matches per season, League Cup semi-finals and Final. Luton first club to ban all visiting supporters; as sequel are themselves banned from League Cup. Oldham and Preston install artificial pitches, making four in Football League (following QPR and Luton).

1987: League introduce play-off matches to decide final promotion/relegation places in all divisions. Re-election abolished – bottom club in Div 4 replaced by winners of GM Vauxhall Conference. Two substitutes approved for Football League 1987–8. Red and yellow disciplinary cards (scrapped 1981) re-introduced by League and FA Football League sponsored by Barclays. First Div reduced to 21 clubs.

1988: Football League Centenary. First Division reduced to 20 clubs.

1989: Soccer gets £74m TV deal: £44m over 4 years, ITV; £30m over 5 years, BBC/BSB. Hillsborough disaster: 95 die at FA Cup semi-final (Liverpool v Nottm Forest). Arsenal win closest-ever Championship with last kick.

1990: Both FA Cup semi-finals played on Sunday and televised live. Play-off finals move to Wembley; Swindon win place in Div 1, then relegated back to Div 2 (breach of financial regulations) – Sunderland promoted instead. Peter Shilton retires as England goalkeeper with 125 caps (world record). Graham Taylor (Aston Villa) succeeds Bobby Robson as England manager. English clubs back in Europe (Manchester United and Aston Villa) after 5-year exile.

1991: First FA Cup semi-final at Wembley (Tottenham 3 Arsenal 1). Bert Millichip (FA chairman) and Philip Carter (Everton chairman) knighted. End of artificial pitches in Div 1 (Luton, Oldham). Scottish League reverts to 12-12-14 format (as in 1987–8). Penalty shoot-out introduced to decide FA Cup ties level after one replay.

1992: FA launch Premier League (22 clubs). Football League reduced to three divisions (71 clubs). Record TV-sport deal: BSkyB/BBC to pay £304m for 5-year coverage of Premier League. ITV do £40m, 4-year deal with Football League. FIFA approve new back-pass rule (goalkeeper must not handle ball kicked to him by team-mate).

1993: For first time both FA Cup semi-finals at Wembley (Sat, Sun). Arsenal first club to complete League Cup/FA Cup double. FA in record British sports sponsorship deal (£12m over 4 years) with brewers Bass for FA Carling Premiership, from Aug. Brian Clough retires after 18 years as Nottm Forest manager; as does Jim McLean (21 years manager of Dundee Utd). Premier League introduce squad numbers with players' names on shirts. Graham Taylor resigns as England manager after World Cup exit. Bobby Moore (51), England World Cup winning captain, dies.

1994: Death of Sir Matt Busby. Terry Venables appointed England coach. Last artificial pitch in English football goes – Preston revert to grass, summer 1994. Bobby Charlton knighted. Scottish League format changes to four divisions of ten clubs. FA announce first sponsorship of FA Cup – Littlewoods Pools (4-year, £14m deal, plus £6m for Charity Shield).

1995: First England match abandoned through crowd trouble (v Republic of Ireland, Dublin). Premiership reduced to 20 clubs. Starting season 1995–6, teams allowed to use 3 substitutes per match, not necessarily including a goalkeeper. European Court of Justice upholds Bosman ruling, barring transfer fees for players out of contract and removing limit on number of foreign players clubs can field.

1996: Death of Bob Paisley (77), ex-Liverpool, most successful manager in English Football. FA appoint Chelsea manager Glenn Hoddle to succeed Terry Venables as England coach after

Euro 96. Manchester United first English club to achieve Double twice (and in 3 seasons). Football League completes £125m, 5-year TV deal with BSkyB starting 1996–7. England stage European Championship, reach semi-finals, lose on pens to tournament winners Germany. Linesmen become known as 'referees' assistants'. Alan Shearer football's first £15m player (Blackburn to Newcastle). Peter Shilton first player to make 1,000 League appearances.

1997: Howard Wilkinson appointed English football's first technical director. England's first home defeat in World Cup (0–1 v Italy). Ruud Gullit (Chelsea) first foreign coach to win FA Cup. Rangers equal Celtic's record of 9 successive League titles. Manchester United win Premier League for fourth time in 5 seasons. New record World Cup score: Iran 17, Maldives 0 (qualifying round). Season 1997–8 starts Premiership's record £36m, 4-year sponsorship extension with brewers Bass (Carling).

1998: In French manager Arsene Wenger's second season at Highbury, Arsenal become second English club to complete the Double twice. In breakaway from Scottish League, top ten clubs form new Premiership under SFA, starting season 1998–9. Football League celebrates its 100th season, 1998–9. New FA Cup sponsors – French insurance giants AXA (25m, 4-year deal).

1999: FA buy Wembley Stadium (£103m) for £320m, plan rebuilding (Aug 2000–March 2003) as new national stadium. Scotland's new Premier League takes 3-week mid-season break in January. Sky screen Oxford Utd v Sunderland (Div 1) as first pay-per-view match on TV. FA sack England coach Glenn Hoddle; Fulham's Kevin Keegan replaces him. Sir Alf Ramsey, England's World Cup-winning manager, dies aged 79. With effect 1999, FA Cup Final to be decided on day (via penalties, if necessary). Hampden Park re-opens for Scottish Cup Final after £63m refit. Alex Ferguson knighted after Manchester United complete Premiership, FA Cup, European Cup treble. End of Cup-Winners' Cup (merged into 121-club UEFA Cup). FA allow holders Manchester United to withdraw from FA Cup to participate in FIFA's inaugural World Club Championship. Chelsea first British club to field an all-foreign line-up – at Southampton (Prem). FA vote in favour of streamlined 14-man board of directors to replace its 92-member council.

2000: Wales move to Cardiff's £125m Millennium Stadium (v Finland). Brent Council approve plans for new £475m Wembley Stadium (completion target spring 2003); demolition of old stadium to begin after England v Germany (World Cup qual.). FA Premiership and Nationwide League to introduce (season 2000–01) rule whereby referees advance free-kick by 10 yards and caution player who shows dissent, delays kick or fails to retreat 10 yards. Scottish football increased to 42 League clubs in 2000–01 (12 in Premier League and 3 divisions of ten; Peterhead and Elgin elected from Highland League). France win European Championship – first time a major international tournament has been jointly hosted (Holland/ Belgium). England manager Kevin Keegan resigns after World Cup defeat by Germany in Wembley's last International. Sven-Goran Eriksson agrees to succeed him.

2001: Scottish Premier League experiment with split into two after 33 matches. ITV, after winning auction against BBC's Match of the Day, begin £183m, 3-season contract for highlights of Premiership matches; BSkyB's live coverage (66 matches per season) for next 3 years will cost £1.1bn. BBC and BSkyB pay £400m (3-year contract) for live coverage of FA Cup and England home matches. ITV and Ondigital pay £315m to screen Nationwide League and Worthington Cup matches. In new charter for referees, top men can earn up to £60,000 a season in Premiership. Real Madrid break world transfer record, buying Zinedine Zidane from Juventus for £47.2m. FA introduce prize money, round by round, in FA Cup.

2002: Scotland appoint their first foreign manager, Germany's former national coach Bertie Vogts replacing Craig Brown. Collapse of ITV Digital deal, with Football League owed £178m, threatens lower-division clubs. Bobby Robson knighted. New record British transfer and world record for defender, £29.1m Rio Ferdinand (Leeds to Manchester United). Transfer window introduced to British football. FA Charity Shield renamed FA Community Shield. After 2-year delay, demolition of Wembley Stadium begins. October:

2003: FA Cup draw (from 4th Round) reverts to Monday lunchtime. Scottish Premier League decide to end mid-winter shut-down. For first time, two Football League clubs demoted (replaced by two from Conference). July: David Beckham becomes record British export (Manchester United to Real Madrid, £23.3m). Biggest takeover in British football history – Roman Abramovich buys control of Chelsea for £150m Wimbledon become England's first franchised club in 68-mile move to Milton Keynes.

2004: Arsenal first club to win Premiership with unbeaten record.. Trevor Brooking knighted. Wimbledon change name to Milton Keynes Dons. Greece beat hosts Portugal to win European Championship as biggest outsiders (80-1 at start). Div 1 rebranded as Football League Championship, with 2nd and 3rd Divisions, becoming Leagues 1 and 2. All-time League record of 49 unbeaten Premiership matches set by Arsenal.

2005: Liverpool lift European Cup on penalties after trailing 0-3 in Champions League Final. Wigan, a League club since only 1978, promoted to Premiership. In new record British-club take-over, American tycoon Malcolm Glazer buys Manchester United for £790m George Best dies aged 59.

2006: Steve Staunton succeeds Brian Kerr as Republic of Ireland manager. Sven-Goran Eriksson steps down as England coach. Steve McClaren replaces him. The Premier League announce a new 3-year TV deal worth £1.7 billion under which Sky lose their monopoly of coverage.

2007: Walter Smith resigns as Scotland manager to return to Rangers and is replaced by Alex McLeish. The new £800m Wembley Stadium is completed. World Cup-winner Alan Ball dies aged 61. Lawrie Sanchez resigns as Northern Ireland manager to take over at Fulham. Nigel Worthington succeeds him. Steve McClaren is sacked after England fail to qualify for the European Championship Finals and is replaced by Fabio Capello. The Republic of Ireland's Steve Staunton also goes. Scotland's Alex McLeish resigns to become Birmingham manager.

2008: The Republic of Ireland follow England's lead in appointing an Italian coach – Giovanni Trapattoni. George Burley leaves Southampton to become Scotland manager. Manchester United beat Chelsea in the first all-English Champions League Final.

2009: Sky secure the rights to five of the six Premier League packages from 2010–13 with a bid of £1.6bn. David Beckham breaks Bobby Moore's record number of caps for an England outfield player with his 109th appearance. A British league record for not conceding a goal ends on 1,311 minutes for Manchester United's Edwin van der Sar. AC Milan's Kaka moves to Real Madrid for a world record fee of £56m. Nine days later, Manchester United agree to sell Cristiano Ronaldo to Real for £80m. Sir Bobby Robson dies aged 76. Shay Given and Kevin Kilbane win their 100th caps for the Republic of Ireland. The Premier League vote for clubs to have eight home-grown players in their squads. George Burley is sacked as Scotland manager and replaced by Craig Levein.

2010: Portsmouth become the first Premier League club to go into administration. John Toshack resigns as Wales manager and is replaced by former captain Gary Speed. England are humiliated in the vote for the 2018 World Cup which goes to Russia, with the 2022 tournament awarded to Qatar.

2011: Seven club managers are sacked in a week. The transfer record between British clubs is broken twice in a day, with Liverpool buying Newcastle's Andy Carroll for £35m and selling Fernando Torres to Chelsea for £50m. Football League clubs vote to reduce the number of substitutes from seven to five. Nigel Worthington steps down as Northern Ireland manager and is succeeded by Michael O'Neill. Sir Alex Ferguson completes 25 years as Manchester United manager. Huddersfield set a Football League record of 43 successive unbeaten league games. Football mourns Gary Speed after the Wales manager is found dead at his home.

2012: Chris Coleman is appointed the new Wales manager. Fabio Capello resigns as manager after John Terry is stripped of the England captaincy for the second time. Roy Hodgson takes over. Rangers are forced into liquidation by crippling debts and a newly-formed club are demoted from the Scottish Premier League to Division Three. Manchester City become champions for the first time since 1968 after the tightest finish to a Premier League season. Chelsea win a penalty shoot-out against Bayern Munich in the Champions League Final. Steven Gerrard (England) and Damien Duff (Republic of Ireland) win their 100th caps. The FA's new £120m National Football Centre at Burton upon Trent is opened. Scotland manager Craig Levein is sacked.

2013: Gordon Strachan is appointed Scotland manager. FIFA and the Premier League announce the introduction of goal-line technology. Sir Alex Ferguson retires after 26 years as Manchester United manager. Wigan become the first club to lift the FA Cup and be relegated in the same season. Chelsea win the Europa League. Ashley Cole and Frank Lampard win their 100th England caps. Robbie Keane becomes the most capped player in the British Isles on his 126th appearance for the Republic of Ireland. Scottish Football League clubs agree to merge with the Scottish Premier League. Real Madrid sign Tottenham's Gareth Bale for £85.3m. Giovanni Trapatonni is replaced as Republic of Ireland manager by Martin O'Neill.

2014: Sir Tom Finney dies aged 91. England experience their worst-ever World Cup, finishing bottom the group with a single point. Germany record one of the most remarkable scorelines in World Cup history – 7-1 against Brazil in the semi-finals. England's Wayne Rooney and the Republic of Ireland's John O'Shea win their 100th caps.

2015: The Premier League sell live TV rights for 2016-19 to Sky and BT for a record £5.13bn. FIFA president Sepp Blatter resigns as a bribery and corruption scandal engulfs the world governing body. Blatter and suspended UEFA president Michel Platini are banned for eight years, reduced on appeal to six years.

2016: An inquest jury rules that the 96 Liverpool fans who died in the Hillsborough disaster of 1989 were unlawfully killed. Leicester, 5,000-1 outsiders become Premier League champions in one of the game's biggest-ever surprises. Aaron Hughes wins his 100th cap for Northern Ireland. FA Cup quarter-final replays are scrapped. England manager Roy Hodgson resigns. He is replaced by Sam Allardyce, who is forced out after one match for 'inappropriate conduct' and succeeded by Gareth Southgate.

2017: Paris Saint-Germain sign Barcelona's Neymar for a world record £198m. Managers Gordon Strachan (Scotland) and Chris Coleman (Wales) resign. Steven Davis reaches a century of Northern Ireland caps. Manchester United win the Europa League. Celtic are champions without losing a game. Arsenal win a record 13th FA Cup, Arsene Wenger for a record seventh time. Wayne Rooney retires from international football as England's record scorer with 53 goals.

2018: Manchester City become the first English champions to total 100 points. Celtic are the first in Scotland to win back-to-back domestic trebles. Alex McLeish (Scotland) and Ryan Giggs (Wales) are appointed. Arsene Wenger leaves Arsenal after 22 years as manager. A helicopter crash outside Leicester's King Power Stadium claims the lives of club owner Vichai Srivaddhanaprabha, the pilot and three others on board. Martin O'Neill is sacked as Republic of Ireland manager and replaced by Mick McCarthy, his second time in charge.

2019: **World Cup-winner G**ordon Banks dies aged 81. Tottenham open their new £1bn stadium. Manchester City achieve an unprecedented domestic treble. Celtic also make history with a third successive Scottish treble. Scotland manager Alex McLeish is sacked and replaced by Kilmarnock's Steve Clarke. For the first time, English clubs occupy all four places in the European finals - Liverpool defeating Tottenham in the Champions League and Chelsea beating Arsenal to win the Europa League. Bury are expelled from the EFL for financial mismanagement. England play their 1,000th international, against Montenegro. World Cup winner Martin Peters dies aged 76.

2020 Coronavirus forces the English League's One and Two and all four Scottish divisions to be abandoned, with a points-per-game system settling promotion and relegation issues, The Premier League and Championship complete the season, after a three-month break, with Liverpool title winners for the first time since 1990. Euro 2020 is postponed for a year. England lose two more World Cup winners - Jack Charlton (85) and Nobby Stiles (78). FA Cup replays are scrapped. Ian Baraclough succeeds Michael O'Neill as Northern Ireland manager. Stephen Kenny replaces Mick McCarthy in charge of the Republic of Ireland.

2021 Northern Ireland captain Steven Davis becomes Britain's most capped player, overtaking Peter Shilton's record of 125. Chelsea win the Champions League. Rangers deny Celtic a tenth successive Scottish title.

FINAL WHISTLE – OBITUARIES 2020–21

AUGUST 2020

PAT McCLUSKEY, 68, won six domestic honours during seven years with Celtic under Jock Stein. The versatile under-23 international, who was comfortable in defensive and midfield roles, accumulated three championship medals. He lifted the Scottish Cup twice, scoring the clinching goal from the penalty spot in a 3-1 victory over Airdrieonians in the 1975 final, and played in the 6-3 League Cup success against Hibernian. McCluskey moved on to Dumbarton following the emergence of Roy Aitken and signing of Pat Stanton and later had spells with Airdrieonians and Queen of the South.

SEPTEMBER 2020

REG HARRISON, 97, was the oldest surviving FA Cup winner, having played in Derby's 4-1 win over Charlton after extra-time in the 1946 final. He was understudy that season to England winger Sammy Crooks, but came into the side when Crooks was injured in an earlier round. Harrison spent 11 years at his home-town club, in addition to guesting for Sheffield United, Notts County and Charlton during the War. He then joined non-league Boston United and was in the team that defeated his old club 6-1 in a major FA Cup second round upset at the Baseball Ground in 1955. After retiring, he spent many years coaching schoolchildren and in 2018 was made a Freeman of Derby for services to the community.

FRED DAVIES, 81, made nearly 400 league appearances in goal for Wolves, Cardiff and Bournemouth. He was mentored by Molyneux legend Bert Williams and helped the club regain top-flight status as runners-up to Coventry in season 1966–67. After moving into management, Davies led Shrewsbury to the 1993–94 Third Division title, then took them to Wembley for the first time – the 1996 Auto Windscreens Shield Final which they lost 2-1 to Rotherham.

ALBERT CHEESEBROUGH, 85, joined Leicester from home-town club Burnley for £20,000 and was part of the team beaten 2-0 by double-winners Tottenham in the 1961 FA Cup Final. The inside-forward, an England under-23 international, had two more seasons at Filbert Street before moving to Port Vale, then played for Mansfield, where a broken leg ended his career.

PETER HAMPTON, 66, was part of the Leeds squad that reached the European Cup Final in 1975. He was an unused substitute in the 2-0 defeat by Bayern Munich and for much of his time at the club had to face strong competition for the left-back position. After leaving, Hampton was a regular during four seasons with Stoke. He then had spells at Burnley, Rochdale and Carlisle and managed Workington.

TONY VILLARS, 68, won three Wales caps in the Home International Championship in season 1973–74. The winger was selected against England, Scotland and Northern Ireland during his time with Cardiff. He also played for Newport.

KEITH JOBLING, 86, led Grimsby back to the old Second Division as runners-up to Portsmouth in season 1961–62. The centre-half made 450 Football League appearances during 16 years service, a club record until John McDermott overtook his total in 2000. After leaving Blundell Park in 1969, he was player-manager at Boston.

ALAN WELSH, 73, was an inside-forward who started and finished his Football League career with Millwall. In between, he had spells with Torquay, Plymouth and Bournemouth and also played in South Africa.

OCTOBER 2020

NOBBY STILES, 78, captured the nation's joy with his celebration of England's World Cup triumph in 1966. Clutching the Jules Rimet Trophy in one hand and his dentures in the other, he danced a jig of delight alongside captain Bobby Moore on the Wembley pitch after the 4-2 victory over West Germany. With front teeth missing and hair receding he made for an unlikely hero. But Alf Ramsey later spelled out how influential the Manchester United wing-half had been. England's manager said he had five world-class players – and Nobby was one of them. Those words were echoed by Bobby Charlton, a team-mate for club and country, who like Ramsey was subsequently knighted. Charlton insisted there was much more to his game than just winning the ball for others to use; he was a skilled, creative player in his own right. Stiles, who won the first of 28 caps against Scotland in 1965, had also played a key role in the semi-final against Portugal, nullifying the great Eusebio as two goals by Charlton delivered a 2-1 win. Two years later, the United pair again had the better of Eusebio, this time in the European Cup Final at Wembley which brought a 4-1 success against Benfica. Stiles, who was christened Norbert, made 395 appearances between 1960–71 for United, who were champions in 1965, on goal average from Leeds, and again two years later, four points clear of Nottingham Forest. He later played for Middlesbrough and Preston, managed the Deepdale club and returned to Old Trafford as youth team coach, helping to develop a new generation of stars including David Beckham, Nicky Butt and Paul Scholes. His achievements were finally recognised with an MBE in 2000, but there was no great financial reward to show for a distinguished career and in 2010 he auctioned his World Cup winner's medal, his Wembley shirt and European Cup medal for £311,000. He died after a long illness, the seventh member of that famous England side to pass away.

GORDON ASTALL, 93, was the oldest living England international. The right-winger won two caps in 1956, scoring against Finland (5-1) and featuring against West Germany (3-1) six days later. He was called up soon after playing for Birmingham in the 3-1 FA Cup Final defeat by Manchester City. Astall also played in both legs of the 1960 Inter-Cities Fairs Cup Final which Birmingham lost 4-1 to Barcelona on aggregate. He joined the club from Plymouth, who won the Division Three South title in season 1951–52, and finished his career at Torquay.

RICHIE BARKER, 80, started his career at Burton in their non-league days. The inside-forward then played for Derby, helped Notts County become Division Four champions in season 1970–71 and had a spell with Peterborough. His managerial career embraced Shrewsbury, Stoke, where he broke the club's transfer record to sign Sammy McIlroy from Manchester United for £350,000, and clubs in Greece and Egypt.

TOMMY ROBSON, 76, was an England youth international forward who played for Northampton, Chelsea and Newcastle. He then joined Peterborough in 1968 and over 13 years made a club-record 559 appearances, scoring 128 goals. Robson later managed their youth team, was a sponsor's matchday host and raised thousands of points for good causes. In July 2020, he was given the freedom of the city.

MARIUS ZALIUKAS, 36, captained Hearts to a 5-1 win over Hibernian in the 2012 all-Edinburgh Scottish Cup Final. He spent seven years at Tynecastle before spells with Leeds and Rangers. The centre-back then returned to Lithuania, where he played 25 times for the national team.

BOB WILSON, 77, helped Cardiff reach the semi-finals of the League Cup in 1966 and the last four of the European Cup Winners' Cup two years later. Signed from Aston Villa, the goalkeeper spent six seasons at Ninian Park, then had a brief spell with Bristol City before playing for six years for Exeter.

SAM BURTON, 93, spent his entire career with home-town club Swindon. He signed professional forms in 1948, became first choice goalkeeper two years later and went on to make 509 appearances, the last of which was two days before his 35th birthday.

JIM TOWNSEND, 75, helped St Johnstone win the old Scottish Second Division title in season 1962–63. The wing-half then spent two years with Middlesbrough after a £20,000 move, returned to the Perth club and finished his career at Hearts and home-town side Morton.

HUGH MORROW, 90, was a right-winger who played for West Bromwich Albion in 1948,

Northampton in 1956 and non-league Leamington, Nuneaton and Kettering. He also managed Tamworth.

NOVEMBER 2020

DIEGO MARADONA, 60, became one of the world's greatest players – and one of the most controversial. Both sides of his career and character were captured in equal measures in Argentina's 1986 World Cup quarter-final against England in Mexico City. His first goal was a clear-cut case of cheating with what became known as the 'Hand of God' which directed the ball past goalkeeper Peter Shilton, who otherwise would have cleared it to safety. The second, a run from inside his own half which carved open the England defence, was widely considered the finest in World Cup history. He went on to captain his side to a 3-2 victory over West Germany and claim the Golden Ball as the tournament's outstanding player. Four years later, the Germans had their revenge, 1-0 in the final. Maradona, who made his international debut at 16 and scored his first goal against Scotland at Hampden Park, had two other involvements as a player. In 1982, Argentina went out at the second group stage. In 1994, he was sent home in disgrace from the United States after testing positive for the banned substance ephedrine. There was one further involvement, this time as manager of the national team, who lost in the quarter-finals to Germany in 2010. Maradona's club career also embraced success and scandal after starting out at Argentinos and Boca Juniors. He won three domestic cups with Barcelona, then delivered two Serie A titles and the UEFA Cup at Napoli. A 15-month ban for cocaine use was followed by a spell at Sevilla, before a return to club football at home and eventual retirement in 1997 on his 37th birthday after 628 appearances and 340 goals. Maradona later coached in Dubai, Mexico and at the Argentine club Gimnasia, where he was still active at the time of his to his death from a heart attack.

RAY CLEMENCE, 72, was one of the finest and most decorated goalkeepers of his generation. Five League titles, three European Cups, two UEFA Cups, an FA Cup and a League Cup were testament to his enduring quality in a Liverpool jersey. With England, he won 61 caps at a time of having to contend and compete with the prodigious talent of his great rival and friend Peter Shilton. Initially, Clemence had to bide his time after Bill Shankly paid Scunthorpe £18,000 to bring him to Anfield in 1967, spending two-and-a-half years in the reserves before succeeding Tommy Lawrence as the club's No 1. Under Shankly and then Bob Paisley, Liverpool became Europe's dominant force throughout the 1970s. Season 1978–79 was particularly special for Clemence, who conceded just 16 goals in 42 games on the way to a fourth domestic title. Two years later, victory over Real Madrid brought a third success in Europe's premier club competition. It also marked the last of 665 appearances for the goalkeeper, who decided it was time to move on and joined Tottenham for a £300,000 fee. His first season there brought more FA Cup success, against Queens Park Rangers, leading eventually to another 330 club appearances, along with a continuation of his international rivalry with Shilton. England manager Ron Greenwood rotated the two players before Shilton was given the nod for the 1982 World Cup and went on to a record 125 caps for his country. Clemence retired with a knee injury in 1987, having joined the elite ranks of players with more than 1,000 appearances, and received an MBE for services to the game. He worked as a goalkeeping coach for Tottenham and England, managed Barnet for two years and took on a development role with the FA. He died after a long illness and tributes were led by Shilton, his room-mate for ten years on England duty, and Sir Kenny Dalglish.

MAURICE SETTERS, 83, was an FA Cup winner with Manchester United and Jack Charlton's right-hand man during the Republic of Ireland's emergence on the international stage. The combative England under-23 wing-half signed from West Bromwich Albion for £30,000 in 1960, proved a key player in a transitional period for United following the Munich air crash. They defeated Leicester 3-1 at Wembley in 1963 and were runners-up to champions Liverpool the following season. Setters, who started his career at Exeter, spent five years at Old Trafford, moving on to Stoke following the emergence of Nobby Stiles, then playing for Coventry and

Charlton. After managing Doncaster, he linked up with Charlton, first at Sheffield Wednesday, then with the Republic, who reached the 1988 European Championship finals and two subsequent World Cups.

TONY WAITERS, 83, won five England caps and was included in Alf Ramsey's initial 40-strong squad for the 1966 World Cup. The Blackpool goalkeeper did not make the final 22, with Ron Springett and Peter Bonetti named as back-up to Gordon Banks. Waiters started out as an amateur with Bishop Auckland, made more than 250 appearances for Blackpool, then played for Burnley. He managed Plymouth to the semi-finals of the League Cup in 1973-74 and promotion from Division Three the following season as runners-up to Blackburn. He also led Canada to their first World Cup finals in 1986 in the first of two spells as national coach.

ALBERT QUIXALL, 87, was Manchester United's first signing after the 1958 Munich air crash which claimed the lives of eight players. Sir Matt Busby, rebuilding his team, paid a then British record fee of £45,000 for the inside-forward who had won five England caps with Sheffield Wednesday. He helped United win the FA Cup in 1963 (3-1 against Leicester) and Sir Bobby Charlton credited him with creating many of his goals for the club. Quixall had six years at Old Trafford and later played for Oldham and Stockport.

PAPA BOUBA DIOP, 42, was part of Portsmouth's 2008 FA Cup-winning squad, coming off the bench in the 1-0 victory over Cardiff at Wembley. The 6ft 5in Senegal midfielder also helped West Ham back to the Premier League in season 2011-12, played for Fulham following a £6m move from the French club Lens and had a short-term contract with Birmingham. Diop made 63 international appearances, scoring the opening goal of the 2002 World Cup when Senegal upset defending champions France 1-0. He died after a long illness.

CAMPBELL FORSYTH, 86, helped Kilmarnock become Scottish champions for the first, and so far, only time in their history. They defeated Hearts 2-0 at Tynecastle in a title decider on the final day of the 1964-65 season to finish top on goal average after both teams had 50 points. Kilmarnock were also runners-up to Rangers three times during the goalkeeper's five years at the club. Forsyth won four Scottish caps during that time, making his debut in a 1-0 British Championship victory over England in front of a 133,000 crowd at Hampden Park in 1964. He joined the club from St Mirren and finished his career with Southampton.

DOUG WRAGG, 86, was part of the West Ham squad that won the old Division Two title, a point ahead of Blackburn, in season 1957-58. The England schoolboy right-winger had seven years at the club before leaving for Mansfield with competition for places intense. He played for Rochdale in the 1962 League Cup Final against Norwich (0-4) and had a spell at Chesterfield.

MATT TEES, 81, had none of the physical attributes associated with most centre-forwards of his era. He weighed just over 10st, but was a prolific scorer in two spells with Grimsby, scoring 110 goals in 228 appearances. The second, under manager Lawrie McMenemy, brought his side the Division Four title in season 1971-72. In between, Tees played for Charlton and helped Luton to promotion from the Third Division. He started his career in Scotland with Airdrie and finished it at Boston.

JOHN POOLE, 87, was Port Vale's goalkeeper for an FA Cup fifth-round tie against Aston Villa which attracted the club's record crowd of 49,768 in 1960. He spent eight years at the club and also played for Macclesfield.

STAN TRAFFORD,74, came through Port Vale's youth ranks and made a dozen Football League appearances. He then had a spell with Macclesfield before giving up football in 1966 to concentrate on a cricketing career with Staffordshire in the Minor Counties.

HARRY HOLMAN, 62, was an England schoolboy international who started as an apprentice at Chelsea before following in the footsteps of his father and signing for home-town club Exeter. The forward made 37 league appearances in the 1977-78 season, but was then restricted by a knee injury which eventually ended his career after joining Peterborough.

GWYN JONES, 85, made a handful of appearances for Wolves during back-to-back League title-winning seasons in the late 1950s. He eventually left the club because of strong competition for places and while playing for Bristol Rovers was a whistle-blower in football's betting scandal after refusing an offer to help throw a game.

JOHN ROWLAND, 79, equalled Port Vale's club record when scoring in seven successive league matches during season 1965–66. The England youth international, who played right-wing before switching to centre-forward, joined the club from Nottingham Forest and later had spells with Mansfield and Tranmere.

DECEMBER 2020

TOMMY DOCHERTY, 92, was a charismatic often controversial manager who joked that he had 'more clubs than Jack Nicklaus.' There were 12 of them in all, plus his time in charge of Scotland, with five years at Manchester United arguably the best remembered. Docherty was on course to take the national team to the World Cup when he was persuaded to succeed Frank O'Farrell at Old Trafford in 1972. He led United back to the top division, suffered a shock defeat by Southampton in the 1976 FA Cup Final, then returned to Wembley the following year to dash Liverpool's hopes of the Treble. Two months later, he was sacked over an affair with the wife of United physio Laurie Brown. Previously, The Doc as he was known in the game, won the League Cup with Chelsea – where he had ended his playing career – and spent 28 days in charge of Queens Park Rangers. He also managed Rotherham, Aston Villa, Porto in Portugal, Derby, Sydney Olympic, Preston, South Melbourne, Wolves and Altrincham. Docherty began his career as a right-half with Celtic, then made more than 300 appearances for Preston, who were twice runners-up in the old First Division Two and FA Cup finalists in 1954 against West Bromwich Albion (2-3). He had a spell with Arsenal and won 25 Scotland caps.

GERARD HOULLIER, 73, led Liverpool out of the shadow of Manchester United and Arsenal after becoming the club's first foreign manager in 1998. Having initially shared the role for three months with Roy Evans, he supervised major changes on and off the field during five-and-a-half-years years at Anfield, laying some of the foundations for the club's present-day success. The former Paris Saint-Germain and France coach, won five major trophies, three of them in season 2000–01 when Liverpool lifted the FA Cup by beating Arsenal, the League Cup against Birmingham and UEFA Cup by beating the Portuguese club Alaves after knocking out Roma, Porto and Barcelona en route. Houllier added the European Super Cup against Bayern Munich, but that year had 11 hours of life-saving heart surgery after falling ill during a match against Leeds. He returned to win a second League Cup, against Manchester United, and he and Arsenal's Arsene Wenger were each awarded an honorary OBE for services to the game. But the final two years of his tenure were mixed and he was replaced by Rafael Benitez in 2004. After that, he won the French title with Lyon and had a season back in the Premier League with Aston Villa. He died after another heart operation.

JIM MCLEAN, 83, led Dundee United to league and cup success during a 30-year involvement with the club. A tough, no-nonsense manager of the old school, he delivered their first and only top-flight title in season 1982–83, one point ahead of Celtic and Aberdeen. With Alex Ferguson's Aberdeen champions for the next two years, the pair interrupted the domestic dominance exercised by Celtic and Rangers. McLean twice won the League Cup, took his team to two other finals in that competition and also lost six finals in the Scottish FA Cup. They reached the 1987 UEFA Cup Final, beaten over two legs by Gothenburg, and a European Cup semi-final. He stepped down in 1993 after 22 years as manager, having latterly been chairman as well. He resigned from that position in 2000, following an altercation with a journalist, and sold his stake in the club two years later. McLean, who had a spell as part-time assistant to Scotland manager Jock Stein, spent his playing career as an inside-forward with Hamilton, Clyde, the other Tayside team Dundee and Kilmarnock.

PAOLO ROSSI, 64, described his World Cup-winning performances in 1982 as a 'personal redemption.' A three-year ban for being implicated in a match-fixing scandal would have left him on the sidelines had it not been reduced by a year on appeal. Rossi, who maintained his innocence, took his place in Italy's team and scored a hat-trick in their 3-2 win over Brazil to reach the semi-finals in a match rated one of the finest in World Cup history. He delivered both goals which defeated Poland, then netted the first in Italy' 3-1 victory over West Germany in the final in Madrid. The tournament's top scorer was voted its best player and he later became European Footballer of the Year. Rossi achieved major domestic and European club success with Juventus, who twice won Serie A and defeated Liverpool amid tragedy at the 1985 European Cup Final when 39 spectators died at the Heysel Stadium in Brussels. They also won the Cup-Winners' Cup and Super Cup. Rossi's other clubs were Vicenza, Perugia, Milan and Verona.

JOHN FITZPATRICK, 74, played alongside George Best in Manchester United's FA Youth Cup-winning team in 1964 and made his senior debut the following season in place of the injured Nobby Stiles. That year, he became the club's first substitute in a league match, replacing Denis Law at Tottenham. Fitzpatrick, comfortable at full-back or wing-half, played twice in United's European Cup-winning season of 1967–68 against Sarajevo and the Polish club Gornik Zabrze. He went on to establish a first-team place, but was forced to retire at the age of 26 with an arthritic knee after 147 appearances.

ALEJANDRO 'ALEX' SABELLA, 66, joined Sheffield United from River Plate for £160,000 in 1978 when manager Harry Haslam flew to Argentina looking for talent after the country's World Cup victory. The midfielder was unable to prevent the club from relegation from the old Second Division and after 88 appearances was sold to Leeds for £400,000. He made 27 at Elland Road before returning home to join Estudiantes. Sabella played for his country eight times and coached the national team to the 2014 World Cup Final, stepping down after the 1-0 extra-time defeat by Germany.

BOBBY WISHART, 87, was one of the few players in Scottish football to win the title with two clubs, apart from those at Rangers and Celtic. He helped Aberdeen become champions for the first time in season 1954–55 and was part of Dundee's one success in 1961–62. Wishart, a wing-half or inside-forward, also lifted the League Cup with Aberdeen (2-1 v St Mirren). Later in his career, he played for Airdrieonians and Raith Rovers.

DAVIE SNEDDON, 84, put Kilmarnock on the way to becoming Scottish champions for the first and only time. He scored their first goal in a 2-0 win over Hearts at Tynecastle in a title decider on the final day of the 1964–65 season. Having finished runners-up in four of the previous five years, they were 0.04 of a goal ahead of their rivals after both totalled 50 points. Sneddon, an under-23 international inside-forward, had another match to remember in that campaign, Kilmarnock retrieving a 4-0 deficit to beat Eintracht Frankfurt 5-4 on aggregate in the Inter-Cities Fairs Cup, forerunner of the UEFA Cup. During five years at Rugby Park, he also became the club's first substitute in a League Cup tie against Dunfermline. He previously played for Preston and Dundee, later served Raith Rovers and managed Kilmarnock and Stranraer. In 2014, Sneddon received an MBE for services to football and the community.

MIKE SUTTON, 76, began his league career with home-town club Norwich in 1962. The half-back moved to Chester, then on to Carlisle before having to retire with a knee injury at 28. He suffered from dementia for the last decade of his life and son Chris, who also played for Norwich, is a leading campaigner for a greater awareness of the condition in former players.

GEORGE HUDSON, 83, played a key role in Coventry's transformation from a struggling Third Division club into a force to be reckoned with under manager Jimmy Hill. Signed from Peterborough for a then club-record £21,000, the centre-forward scored a hat-trick on his debut against Halifax in 1963. He netted 28 goals the following season, including the title-clinching winner against Colchester, then 25 in the higher division. Hudson's tally was 75 in 129 appearances before he was sold to Northampton for £22,000 after a dip in form. He finished at Tranmere, his sixth club after starting out with Blackburn and Accrington.

COLIN WITHERS, 80, was a goalkeeper with Aston Villa during one of the most difficult periods in the club's history. They were relegated from the old First Division in 1967, but Withers, an England schoolboy international who signed from Birmingham, remained a popular figure with the supporters. He spent five years at Villa Park before moving on to play for Lincoln and the Dutch side Go Ahead.

BILL HOLMES, 94, scored on his Blackburn debut against Queens Park Rangers in 1952 and in his next four appearances. The England amateur international centre-forward ended the season with 19 goals in 25 appearances, then left to rejoin non-league Morecambe and finished his career at Bradford City and Southport. He started it with Wolves, followed by a spell with Doncaster, and was part of the Great Britain squad for the Helsinki Olympics in 1952.

JOHN MCSEVENEY, 89, was a left-winger who started his career in Scotland with Hamilton in 1948 and went on to play for Sunderland, Cardiff, Newport and Hull. He then managed Barnsley and the Irish club Waterford, was assistant manager at Nottingham Forest and was part of the backroom staff at Sheffield United and Rotherham.

GEORGE SHARPLES, 77, joined Everton straight from school and made his senior debut aged 17, deputising for Jimmy Gabriel against West Bromwich Albion in 1960. The England youth international wing-half had limited first-team opportunities and moved on to Blackburn, where he spent four years. After recovering from a broken leg, he joined Southport, having to retire at 28 when a specialist diagnosed arthritis.

CHIC MCLELLAND, 63, made 212 appearances for Aberdeen between 1973–79 and after his career ended he returned to Pittodrie to head up the club's youth development programme. The Scotland under-23 international left-back also played for Motherwell and Dundee and was part of the Montrose Division Two title-winning squad of season 1984–85.

TOM DOCHERTY, 96, was a left-winger who started his career with Lincoln in 1947 and went on to play for Norwich, Reading and Newport.

JANUARY 2021

COLIN BELL, 74, achieved legendary status during 13 years at Manchester City, a stylish, skilful, goalscoring midfielder from the same mould as the club's current shining light Kevin De Bruyne. Sir Tom Finney once said he was as good a player as he had ever seen. Bell made 501 appearances, netted 153 goals after a £45,000 move from Bury in 1966 and would almost certainly have collected more silverware but for a knee injury which cut short his career at 29. He immediately helped City back to the top tier as Division Two winners. Two seasons later they were English champions, ahead of Manchester United and Liverpool, with a team also featuring the talents of Mike Summerbee, Francis Lee and Neil Young. More domestic and European honours followed – the 1969 FA Cup (1-0 v Leicester), two League Cups and the Cup-Winners' Cup with victory over the Polish side Gornik Zabrze. Bell made his international debut against Brazil in the Maracana, played in the 1970 World Cup and won 48 caps. He sustained the injury in a Manchester derby in 1975, returned after a two-year period of recovery, but was not the same player again and had to call it a day. He was awarded an MBE in 2004 and had a stand named after him at the Etihad Stadium.

PETER SWAN, 84, came through the ranks at Sheffield Wednesday, featured in the side that finished runners-up to Tottenham's Double winners in 1960–61 and became England's established centre-half. Illness ruled him out of the 1962 World Cup, but he was earmarked for a place alongside Bobby Moore in Alf Ramsey's team for the next tournament. Instead, he was implicated in a betting scandal that rocked the game, along with club-mates Tony Kay and David Layne and seven other players. Swan, who won 19 international caps in a row, was jailed for four months in 1965 and banned for life by the FA. The ban was lifted in 1972 and he returned to Hillsborough for a season, taking his appearances for the club to 301. He went on to play for Bury and as player-manager led Matlock to victory in the 1975 FA Trophy Final at Wembley.

JOHN MORTIMORE, 86, enjoyed success at home and abroad as player and manager. During a decade at Chelsea, the centre-half was an ever-present in their promotion from Division Two as runners-up to Stoke in 1962–63, featured in the League Cup Final victory over Leicester two seasons later and was part of the club's introduction to European competition in the Fairs Cup – forerunner of the UEFA Cup. After 279 appearances, he joined Queens Park Rangers, then moved into management at Portsmouth, spending 16 months before making way for the former Liverpool centre-forward Ian St John. Mortimore led Benfica to two league titles and two Portuguese cups and also coached in Greece and Spain. Later, he became Southampton president after coaching and scouting for the club.

DR JOZEF VENGLOS, 84, became the first manager of an English top-flight club from outside the UK and Ireland. He had one season, 1990–91, with Aston Villa, who finished 17th then replaced him with Ron Atkinson. Venglos, who held a doctorate in physical recreation, also spent a single campaign at Celtic, who were runners-up to Rangers in 1998–99. He was assistant to Vaclav Jezek when Czechoslovakia were crowned European champions in 1976, had two spells in charge of the national team and also coached Slovakia, Australia and Oman. At club level, he served Fenerbahce and Sporting Lisbon. As a player, he spent 12 years with Slovan Bratislava.

EDDIE CONNACHAN, 85, played a key role in Dunfermline's first Scottish Cup win under Jock Stein in 1961. The goalkeeper defied Celtic with fine saves in a goalless draw followed by a 2-0 victory in the replay. He was part of the team that reached the quarter-finals of the European Cup-Winners' Cup the following season and won two Scotland caps during six years at the club, against Czechoslovakia and Uruguay. Connachan later had spells with Middlesbrough and Falkirk before ending his career in South Africa.

CLINT BOULTON, 72, set three records during his time with Port Vale. The wing-half made his debut at Hull on Boxing Day 1964 aged 16 years and 364 days – at the time the club's youngest-ever in the Football League. At 17 years and 110 days, he became their youngest scorer, against Walsall, and that mark still stands. At 18 he was made captain by general manager Sir Stanley Matthews. Boulton was an ever-present as Vale won promotion from Division Four in season 1969–70 and made 267 appearances before being sold to Torquay for £10,000 because the club needed money for new floodlights. There, he played 286 times.

TOSH CHAMBERLAIN, 86, was an England youth international who spent 11 seasons at Fulham. He was part of the team that reached the semi-finals of the FA Cup in 1958 and won promotion to the old First Division, as runners-up to Sheffield Wednesday, the following year. The outside-left had a powerful kick and on one occasion a back pass to Tony Macedo left the goalkeeper with broken ribs. Chamberlain made 204 appearances and scored 64 goals before ending his career at Dover and Gravesend.

GEOFF BARNETT, 74, won the FA Youth Cup with Everton, but first-team opportunities were limited in Harry Catterick's successful 1960s side which had two fine goalkeepers in Gordon West and Andy Rankin. He joined Arsenal when Bob Wilson suffered a broken arm and was able to play more senior matches there, including the 1972 FA Cup Final against Leeds which his side lost 1-0. Barnett finished his career in the United States with Minnesota.

JOHN JEFFERS, 52, turned professional with Liverpool under Kenny Dalglish, but with John Barnes occupying the left-wing spot there was little opportunity to break into the team. He moved to Port Vale for £30,000 in 1988 and twice won promotion from the third tier in seven seasons there. Jeffers also went up with his next club, Stockport, in 1997 when they also reached the League Cup semi-finals, stretching Middlesbrough to a 2-1 aggregate win. Jeffers finished his career at non-league Hednesford.

JOHNNY WILLIAMS, 73, made 419 appearances in 11 years with Watford. They embraced a Third Division title win in season 1968–69 when his side finished ahead of Swindon on goal average after both totalled 64 points. The left-back was also part of the team that reached the semi-finals of the FA Cup against Chelsea (1-5) in 1970. He later played for Colchester and non-league Margate.

BOBBY KELLARD, 77, became Southend's youngest-ever player when he made his debut against Bradford City, aged 16 years and 208 days, in 1959. The wing-half went on to have two spells with Crystal Palace and Portsmouth, along with time at Ipswich, Bristol City, Leicester. Hereford and Torquay and with Cape Town in South Africa. Kellard was also player-manager at Chelmsford.

TONY GREGORY, 83, spent four years with home-town club Luton and was part of the team beaten 2-1 by Nottingham Forest in the 1959 FA Cup Final. The England youth international left-winger moved on to Watford, helping secure promotion from Division Four, and later played non-league football.

LUTON SHELTON, 35, was a Jamaican international striker who joined Sheffield United under Neil Warnock from the Swedish club Helsingborgs in 2007. He made his full debut against Manchester United and played 25 times over two seasons before leaving for the Norwegian side Valerenga. Shelton also had spells in Denmark, Turkey and Russia and scored a record 35 goals in 75 appearances for his national team. He died from a form of motor neurone disease.

RON RAFFERTY, 86, scored 145 goals in 264 matches for Grimsby, 34 of them in their Third Division promotion season of 1961–62. The inside-forward joined the club from Portsmouth and went on to play for Hull and Aldershot.

JOHN GRANT, 89, made over 300 appearances in a decade with Hibernian. They included the 1958 Scottish Cup Final when his side lost 1-0 to Clyde and, two seasons earlier, the semi-final of the inaugural European Cup – when clubs were invited to compete – against the French side Reims (0-3 on agg). Grant, a right-back, won two Scotland caps, against Wales and Northern Ireland in the Home International Championship. He also played for Raith Rovers.

BARRIE MITCHELL, 73, was part of Dunfermline's Scottish Cup-winning squad in 1967–68. He signed from Arbroath for £13,000 – a record for a Division Two player – and spent five years at the club. Mitchell, who occupied most forward positions, helped Tranmere to promotion from Division Four in 1975–76 and also had spells with Aberdeen, Preston, York, Morton, Wigan and Vancouver.

JOHNNY GIBBONS, 95, was Ipswich's oldest surviving player. The centre-forward signed from Queens Park Rangers in 1949 and later joined Tottenham.

PETER GILLOTT, 85, made a handful of appearances for his home-town club Barnsley in the mid-1950s. The England youth international full-back spent most of his career in non-league football, notably at Chelmsford where he played 376 matches.

FEBRUARY 2021

GLENN ROEDER, 65, commanded respect throughout the game as player and manager in a career spanning nearly 40 years. The central defender led Queens Park Rangers to the 1982 FA Cup Final, which Tottenham won in a replay, and to the old Second Division title a year later when they finished ahead of Wolves and Leicester. He then helped Newcastle to promotion to the top division behind Chelsea and Sheffield Wednesday in his first season at St James' Park. After starting out in the youth ranks at Arsenal, Roeder also played for Leyton Orient twice, Notts County, Watford and Gillingham, making 561 senior appearances alongside seven for the England B team. He started out in management at Gillingham, followed by spells at Watford, West Ham, Newcastle and Norwich, together with coaching under Glenn Hoddle with England. Roeder died after a long battle with a brain tumour.

TONY COLLINS, 94, was the Football League's first black manager. He had seven years in charge at Rochdale – where he finished his playing career - leading the club to the 1962 League Cup Final against Norwich, who won it 4-0 on aggregate over the two legs. Collins later became chief scout for Manchester United. The left-winger also played for Watford in two spells, York, Norwich, Torquay and Crystal Palace.

DAI DAVIES, 72, made 52 appearances for Wales in a seven-year international career. He was their most capped goalkeeper until that total was overtaken by Neville Southall and later by Wayne Hennessey. Davies spent a large part of his club career at Everton, including the 1974–75 season when the title beckoned until they slipped up during the run-in and finished fourth, three points behind champions Derby. He had three spells with Swansea, two at Wrexham – including a Division Three title win – and also played for Tranmere and Bangor.

PETER HINDLEY, 76, was a mainstay in the Nottingham Forest team that finished runners-up to Manchester United in the old First Division in season 1966–67. The England under-23 right-back made 368 league appearances in 11 years at the City Ground and later played for Coventry and Peterborough.

KEN ROBERTS, 84, made his debut for Wrexham in 1951 aged 15 years and 158 days, equalling the Football League record of Bradford Park Avenue's Albert Geldard from 1929. The record stood until 2008 when Reuben Noble-Lazarus played for Barnsley aged 15 years and 45 days. It was the only senior appearance right-winger Roberts made for the club before joining Aston Villa. As manager, he led Chester to promotion from Division Four in 1974–75 and took his side to the semi-finals of the League Cup that season – a run which included a 3-0 victory over defending League champions Leeds.

JOHN JAMES, 72, won promotion from Division Four with three clubs – Port Vale (1969–70), Chester (1974–75) and Tranmere (1975–76). That season with Chester, his team also reached the semi-finals of the League Cup, defeating Preston, Leeds and Newcastle before losing to Aston Villa 5-4 on aggregate in the two-leg tie. The forward played 429 games during his Football League career – including 229 for Port Vale – and scored 122 goals.

ALAN WOAN, 90, helped Crystal Palace to promotion from the Fourth Division as runners-up to Peterborough in season 1960–61. His contribution included a hat-trick in a 9-2 win over Accrington. The inside-forward, whose son Ian played for Nottingham Forest and went on to become No 2 to Burnley manager Sean Dyche, began his career at Norwich and also played for Northampton and Aldershot.

JOHN KIRKHAM, 79, won the FA Youth Cup with Wolves in 1958 and was part of the senior squad that finished runners-up for the League Championship in season 1959–60, one point behind Burnley. The England under-23 wing-half spent the first nine years of his career at Molineux, then played for Peterborough and Exeter.

JOHN MANNING, 80, started in the youth ranks at Liverpool and went on to play for seven Football League clubs. The centre-forward had two spells with both Tranmere and Crewe and was also with Shrewsbury, Norwich, Bolton, Walsall and Barnsley. He then coached at Crewe and scouted for Birmingham, Brighton and Middlesbrough.

JOHN BOLTON, 79, helped Morton become Scottish Second Division champions in season 1966–67. They finished ahead of Raith Rovers, the club where the central defender began his career and later had a second spell. He also played for Ipswich and Dumbarton.

WHELAN WARD, 91, was a 5ft 3in inside-forward who played for both Bradford clubs in the Football League. He was top scorer with 12 goals for City in the 1951–52 season, spent six years at the club, then after a spell with King's Lynn returned to have three seasons at Bradford Park Avenue.

GRAHAM DAY, 67, played in central defence for home-town club Bristol Rovers from 1974–78, then had six years in the United States with Portland.

HARRY CLARK, 88, was an inside-forward who played for Darlington and Hartlepool in the 1960s, sandwiched by a short spell at Sheffield Wednesday.

MARCH 2021

IAN ST JOHN, 82, played a key role in Liverpool rise to prominence under Bill Shankly which set the standard for the club's success in future years. He made an immediate impact after a £37,500 move from Motherwell in 1961 – a hat-trick on his debut against Everton in the Liverpool Senior Cup and 18 goals as the club returned to the top-flight as Second Division winners. With Roger Hunt alongside him in attack and Ron Yeats the team's new defensive rock, Liverpool became League champions in 1964, four points ahead of Manchester United, and again two seasons later, six points clear of Leeds. In between, St John delivered their first FA Cup with a flying header for an extra-time winner against Leeds at Wembley. In a decade at Anfield, he scored 118 goals in 425 appearances – alongside nine in 21 games for Scotland – before Shankly started rebuilding his first great team. After brief spells at Coventry and Tranmere, St John managed home-town team Motherwell and Portsmouth. Later, he teamed up with Jimmy Greaves for the popular *Saint and Greavsie* Saturday show which ran for seven years on ITV.

PETER LORIMER, 74, started his career as Leeds' youngest-ever player and finished it as the club's all-time record goalscorer. In between, he won domestic and European honours as Don Revie's team became a dominant force in English football. The attacking midfielder, who had one of the most powerful shots in the game, made his debut against Southampton in 1962 aged 15 years and 289 days. His goals helped them become champions in 1969 and 1974, ahead of Liverpool each time, and finish runners-up five times. Leeds defeated Arsenal to win the 1972 FA Cup, lost two more finals to Chelsea and Sunderland, and had one League Cup success, again overcoming Arsenal. There were two victories in the Inter-Cities Fairs Cup, forerunner of the UEFA Cup, against Ferencvaros and Juventus, alongside defeats in the two major tournaments. Lorimer had a goal controversially disallowed in the 1975 European Cup Final against Bayern Munich, who won it 2-0. Two years earlier, they lost to the only goal of the Cup-Winners' Cup Final against AC Milan. Lorimer left Elland Road in 1979 for spells with Toronto and Vancouver in Canada and York City. He returned to play for another two seasons, taking his record to 238 goals in 705 appearances. The Dundee-born player won 21 Scotland caps, featuring in all three matches at the 1974 World Cup and scoring in a 2-0 victory over Zaire. After retiring, he retained links with Leeds as a director and club ambassador. Lorimer became their fourth player of that era to pass away in 12 months after Norman Hunter, Jack Charlton and Trevor Cherry.

FRANK WORTHINGTON, 72, was football's travelling showman, a flamboyant figure on and off the pitch whose career was captured by a goal for Bolton against Ipswich at the old Burnden Park Stadium in 1979. Juggling the ball with his back to goal on the edge of the penalty area, he flicked it over his head, evaded defenders and volleyed low into the cornet of the net. Worthington was the First Division's top scorer that season with 24 goals, three more than Liverpool's Kenny Dalglish. It also marked the start of a nomadic existence after the first decade of his career at just two clubs – Huddersfield, Second Division champions in 1970, and Leicester, where he won eight England caps. There might have been more international recognition had a record £150,000 transfer to Bill Shankly's Liverpool not fallen through on medical grounds. After leaving Bolton, Worthington played for Birmingham, Leeds, Sunderland, Southampton, who were runners-up to Liverpool for the title in 1984, Brighton, Tranmere, Preston and Stockport. In 22 consecutive Football League seasons, he made 882 appearances in all competitions, scoring 266 goals. They were accompanied by loan spells in the United States and Sweden and followed by time at five non-league clubs. Worthington also managed Tranmere and coached at home-town team Halifax.

DEREK UFTON, 92, was the oldest surviving England international, winning one cap in a match against a team from the Rest of Europe which ended 4-4 at Wembley in 1953. The centre-half was a one-club man, making 277 appearances in a decade at Charlton. During that time he dislocated his shoulder 20 times, most notably during an epic match against Huddersfield at The Valley in 1957 when his side transformed a 5-1 deficit into a 7-6 victory. Ufton was a director of the club for 25 years and also managed Plymouth from 1965–68. He was an all-round sportsman, who played county cricket for Kent, making 149 appearances as a wicketkeeper-batsman.

ALAN SLOUGH, 73, was part of his home-town club's rise to prominence in the late 1960s. Luton were Division Four champions in 1967–68, runners-up in the Third Division two years later and finished sixth in the second tier the following season. The versatile midfielder, who was comfortable in several other positions, made 312 appearances before joining his old manager Alec Stock at Fulham. There, Slough featured in all the team's marathon 1974–75 FA Cup campaign which spanned 12 matches, including two replays against Hull, three against Nottingham Forest and one in the semi-final with Birmingham. In the final, he lined up alongside Bobby Moore and Alan Mullery in a 2-0 defeat by West Ham. During a spell at Peterborough, Slough scored a hat-trick of penalties in a 4-3 defeat by Chester. He finished his Football League career with Millwall.

DEREK HAWKSWORTH, 93, made 286 appearances and scored 103 goals during eight years with Sheffield United. They included the Division Two title-winning season of 1952–53 and a 7-3 victory in a local derby against Sheffield Wednesday in which he netted twice. Hawksworth, a left-winger, also had spells at Huddersfield, Lincoln, Bradford City and Bradford Park Avenue and played for the England B team.

PHIL CHISNALL, 78, was an England under-23 international inside-forward who came through the youth system at Manchester United and spent six years at Old Trafford. He signed for Liverpool in 1964 – the last player to move directly between the rival clubs – and later played for Southend and Stockport.

MICKEY LEWIS, 56, joined Oxford United in 1988 after playing for Derby and West Bromwich Albion and had a 27-year association with the club. The midfielder played 351 games, was assistant manager to Chris Wilder, had two spells as caretaker-manager and was also youth coach.

WILLIE WHIGHAM, 81, helped relegated Middlesbrough make an immediate return to the old Second Division as runners up to Queens Park Rangers in season 1966–67. The Scottish goalkeeper made 214 appearances in six years at the club after starting his career with Albion and Falkirk. He later played for Dumbarton and Darlington.

STEVE JAGIELKA, 43, was part of memorable performances by two clubs in the lower divisions. The elder brother of former Everton and England defender Phil Jagielka helped Shrewsbury escape from dropping into non-league football with a 2-1 victory at Exeter on the final day of the 1999–2000 season. In 2003, he was involved in shock 2-1 win over Everton in the third round of the FA Cup. Three years later, the midfielder was part of Accrington's return to the Football League, after an absence of 44 years, as Conference champions.

MICK BROWN, 76, joined Millwall from Fulham in February 1965 to supplement their Fourth Division promotion bid. They finished runners-up to Brighton and were promoted again the following season, second to Hull. The inside-forward moved on to Luton, then played for Colchester.

ALEX KIDDIE, 93, was a winger and believed to be Aberdeen's oldest surviving player and the only one from the club's first senior trophy win, 3-2 against Rangers in the Southern League Cup in front of a 130,000 crowd at Hampden Park in 1946.

RON PHOENIX, 91, scored on his debut for Manchester City against Arsenal in 1952. But his career was interrupted by a complicated broken leg, sustained against Newcastle, which kept him out for two years. The full-back later played for Rochdale and non-league Altrincham.

TERRY MELLING, 81, was a late starter in league football after playing for minor teams and then unable to break through at Newcastle. The forward made his debut for Watford, aged 26, in 1966, followed by spells with Newport, Mansfield, Rochdale and Darlington.

LEN FLETCHER, 91, helped Ipswich win the Third Division South title in season 1953–54. Following the death of Johnny Gibbons in January, he was the club's oldest surviving player. The wing-half also played for Falkirk.

LEE COLLINS, 32, was the captain of National League side Yeovil. He died two months after his last appearance for the club against Stockport. The centre-half began his career in the youth ranks at Wolves, then played for Hereford, Port Vale, Barnsley, Shrewsbury, Northampton, Mansfield and Forest Green.

JIM STEVENSON, 74, was a Scottish schoolboy international wing-half who had four seasons at Hibernian and also played for Southend before concentrating on a career in non-league football.

BOB GRAVES, 78, joined Lincoln in 1959 and had five seasons in goal for the club. He then played county rugby for Lincolnshire.

APRIL 2021

DOUG HOLDEN, 90, was the last surviving player of the famous 1953 FA Cup Final in which his side Bolton were beaten 4-3 by Blackpool, who retrieved a 3-1 deficit through the magic of Stanley Matthews and Stan Mortensen's hat-trick. Holden, who was on the right wing that day, returned to Wembley in 1958, this time on the left flank, when Bolton defeated Manchester United 2-0. He made 463 appearances in 11 seasons at the club and won five England caps, the first against Scotland at the age of 28. Holden then joined Preston and played in another FA Cup Final, scoring his side's first goal from the left side in their 3-2 defeat by West Ham in 1964. He also played and coached in Australia.

COLIN BAKER, 86, spent his entire 14-year career with home-town club Cardiff, making 340 appearances and playing a key role in promotion to the old First Division in season 1959–60 when they finished runners-up to Aston Villa. The wing-half was also their first to be substituted when replaced by David Summerhayes after being injured against Bury in the 1965–66 campaign. Baker won the first of seven Wales caps against Mexico (1-1) in a World Cup group match in 1958.

FRANK BROGAN, 78, helped Ipswich win the old Second Division title in season 1967–68 with 59 points, one ahead of Queens Park Rangers and Blackpool. A pacy winger, he was leading scorer for Bill McGarry's side with 17 goals. Brogan joined the club from Celtic, where he scored their 5,000th league goal, against Partick, in 1962, and had seven years at Portman Road. He later played for Morton, on loan, and Halifax.

IAN HAMILTON, 80, was the only player to score a league hat-trick for Bristol Rovers and finish on the losing side. They lost 6-3 at Southend during the 1964–65 season when he scored 21 goals in 33 matches. In the previous campaign, Hamilton netted four in League Cup tie against Shrewsbury. The inside-forward spent 12 years at the club and also had spells with Exeter and Newport.

PETER GELSON, 79, came through the youth ranks at Brentford, made his league debut in 1961 and went on to make 516 appearances for the club. The wing-half, initially a part-timer, played more than 40 matches in eight out of ten seasons when he was a regular. Gelson was part of two Fourth Division promotion-winning sides and had two testimonials. He was still a season ticket holder in the club's final season at Griffin Park - 2019–20.

STEVE PERKS, 58, made 292 appearances in a decade in goal for Shrewsbury. They included the club's highest-ever finish of eighth in the old Second Division.

PETER GOY, 82, came through the youth ranks at Arsenal and made two senior appearances. The goalkeeper moved to Southend in 1960 and also played for Watford and Huddersfield.

WALTER BORTHWICK, 73, started his career with Morton in 1965 and went on to play for four other Scottish clubs – St Mirren (twice), St Johnstone, East Fife and Dunfermline. He was then coach and assistant manager at Hearts and manager at Arbroath.

WAYNE TALKES, 68, began at Southampton, had a spell on loan with Doncaster, then joined Bournemouth, where his career was cut short, at the age of 22, by an ankle injury.

MAY 2021

COLIN APPLETON, 85, was at the heart of a golden era for Leicester in the 1960s. It included the club's first trophy, the League Cup, with a 4-3 aggregate victory over Stoke. Appleton, who formed a formidable half-back line alongside Frank McLintock and Ian King, led his side to the two-leg final again the following year, this time losing 3-2 to Chelsea. They reached two FA Cup Finals, against Tottenham (0-2) and Manchester United (1-3), and were a force to be reckoned with in the old First Division. Appleton made 333 appearances over 12 years, then played for Charlton, before returning to home-town club Scarborough, where he was involved in three FA Trophy wins. Later, he managed Swansea, Exeter and Hull.

ALAN MCLOUGHLIN, 54, scored the goal which took the Republic of Ireland to the 1994 World Cup in the United States. His equaliser earned a 1-1 draw against Northern Ireland at Windsor Park, one of 42 international appearances under Jack Charlton and Mick McCarthy. McLoughlin was also in the Republic squad for the 1990 finals in Italy and was their Player of the Year in 1996. The midfielder, a former Manchester United apprentice, made 361 appearances in seven-and-a-half-years at Portsmouth. He also played for Swindon, Southampton, Wigan and Rochdale, along with loan spells at Torquay and Aston Villa.

CHRIS CHILTON, 77, scored a club-record 222 goals in 477 appearances for his home-town club Hull between 1960–71. He formed a prolific strike partnership with Ken Wagstaff which brought the Division Three title in season 1965–66 when Hull scored 109 goals under manager Cliff Britton. Chilton also had one season at Coventry before a back injury ended his league career. He returned to Boothferry Park as part of the coaching staff, also filled caretaker and assistant manager roles and was involved in two promotions – from Division Four in 1983 and Division Three two years later.

LEN BADGER, 75, was an England under-23 international and part of Alf Ramsey's World Cup 'shadow squad' in 1966. That same year, the right-back became Sheffield United's youngest-ever captain, aged 21, and he went on to make 541 appearances in nearly 14 years at his hometown club. It included promotion to the top division, as runners-up to Leicester, in season 1970–71 under manager John Harris. Badger finished his career at Chesterfield.

ERIC WINSTANLEY, 76, made 461 appearances for home-town Barnsley between 1962–73. He was an England youth international who developed into a highly-rated central defender, attracting the attention of some big clubs before a serious knee injury. Winstanley came back to help Barnsley win promotion from Division Four in season 1967–68 and the following year scored a hat-trick against Watford. He also played for Chesterfield, then returned to coach at Oakwell, bringing through a generation of talented young players. He was assistant manager when they reached the Premier League in 1997, had two spells as caretaker and coached in South Africa, Zambia and St Kitts.

STEVE CONROY, 64, spent most of his goalkeeping career in South Yorkshire. He had two spells with Rotherham after starting out at Sheffield United, where the highlight was an outstanding performance in a 1978 League Cup win over Liverpool. Conroy also had a spell at Rochdale.

JOHN SLUDDEN, 56, was a Scottish schoolboy international who made a single appearance for Celtic. The forward then played for St Johnstone, Airdrieonians, Ayr, Kilmarnock, East Fife, Clydebank, Clyde and Stenhousemuir and was a youth coach at Celtic.

JUNE 2021

JOHN ANGUS, 82, was a key player in a golden era for Burnley, who were crowned League champions in season 1959–60. The right-back missed only one match that season when his side finished a point ahead of Wolves, with Tottenham in third place. They were runners-up to Ipswich two seasons later when also reaching the FA Cup Final, losing 3-1 to Tottenham. Angus, who signed for the club as a 16-year-old amateur in 1954, featured in two European campaigns and went on to make 521 appearances, more than any outfield player at Turf

Moor, before retiring in 1972. He won a single England cap, against Austria, largely because of the form of Blackpool's Jimmy Armfield.

ALAN MILLER, 51, won the FA Youth Cup with Arsenal in 1988 and was part of the senior squad that lifted the FA Cup, League Cup and Cup-Winners' Cup in the early 1990s. After a handful of senior appearances, the England under 21 goalkeeper helped Middlesbrough reach the Premier League and was on the bench when Blackburn beat Tottenham to win the League Cup in 2002. He also played for West Bromwich Albion and during his career went on loan to Plymouth, Birmingham, Grimsby, Bristol City, Coventry and St Johnstone.

JOCK AIRD, 94, was Burnley's oldest surviving player and the club's only dual international. During seven years at Turf Moor, he won four Scotland caps – two of them in group defeats by Austria and Uruguay at the 1954 World Cup in Switzerland. After emigrating to New Zealand, the Fife-born full-back played twice for their national team.

PAUL CAHILL, 65, was an England youth international defender who, at the age of 21, became Portsmouth's youngest captain during three years at the club. He also played for Aldershot, Tranmere and Stockport before finishing his career in the United States.

SPENCER WHELAN, 49, made nearly 250 appearances in eight years at Chester after starting his career as a Liverpool apprentice. They included the 1993–94 season when his side finished runners-up to Shrewsbury in the old Third Division. The central defender moved Shrewsbury in 1998, but had his career cut short by injury at the age of 29.

JACK BERTOLINI, 87, spent six years at Workington in their Football League days, then made 279 appearances for Brighton between 1958–66. They included 193 successive matches before a knee injury ended the full-back's career.

JULY 2021

PAUL MARINER, 68, was one of finest centre-forwards of his era, playing 35 times for England and winning domestic and European trophies under Bobby Robson at Ipswich. He combined skill, strength and aerial power to score 135 goals in 339 appearances after joining the club from Plymouth in 1976. Mariner helped them defeat Arsenal 1-0 in the 1978 FA Cup Final and scored in the first leg of the 1981 UEFA Cup Final in which Ipswich defeated the Dutch side Alkmaar 5-4 on aggregate. They were runners-up to Aston Villa in the old First Division that year and second to Liverpool 12 months later, in addition to finishing third on two other occasions. Mariner scored 13 international goals, one of them in a 3-1 victory over France at the 1982 World Cup in Spain. He played in the two other group successes against Czechoslovakia and Kuwait, then in both goalless draws against West Germany and Spain in the second group phase. After leaving Portman Road in 1984, he had spells at Arsenal and Portsmouth, finished his career in the United States, then managed Plymouth and Toronto in Canada.

JIMMY GABRIEL, 80, played a key role in Everton's league and cup success during seven years with the club. They were champions in season 1962–63, ahead of Tottenham and Burnley, and defeated Sheffield Wednesday 3-2 after trailing 2-0 in the FA Cup Final three years later. The wing-half, who signed from home-town Dundee, made 303 appearances and won two Scotland caps at a time when there was strong competition for places in the national side. He then played for Southampton, Bournemouth, Swindon and Brentford before ending his career in the United States. Gabriel returned to Everton as assistant to manager Colin Harvey and had two spells as caretaker-manager.

CHARLIE GALLAGHER, 80, was part of Celtic's squad that won the European Cup in 1967. The inside-forward did not feature when they defeated Inter Milan 2-1 in Lisbon, but played an important part in their progress to the final and during 12 years at the club won three league titles, the Scottish Cup and League Cup. He also became the first Scot to play for the Republic of Ireland, winning two caps.

RECORDS SECTION

GOALSCORING
(†Football League pre-1992–93)

Highest: Arbroath 36 Bon Accord (Aberdeen) 0 in Scottish Cup 1, Sep 12, 1885. On same day, also in Scottish Cup 1, Dundee Harp beat Aberdeen Rov 35-0.

Internationals: France 0 England 15 in Paris, 1906 (Amateur); Ireland 0 England 13 in Belfast Feb 18, 1882 (record in UK); England 9 Scotland 3 at Wembley, Apr 15, 1961; Biggest England win at Wembley: 9-0 v Luxembourg (Euro Champ), Dec 15, 1982.

Other record wins: Scotland: 11-0 v Ireland (Glasgow, Feb 23, 1901); **Northern Ireland:** 7-0 v Wales (Belfast, Feb 1, 1930); **Wales:** 11-0 v Ireland (Wrexham, Mar 3, 1888); **Rep of Ireland:** 8-0 v Malta (Euro Champ, Dublin, Nov 16, 1983).

Record international defeats: England: 1-7 v Hungary (Budapest, May 23, 1954); **Scotland:** 3-9 v England (Wembley, Apr 15, 1961); **Ireland:** 0-13 v England (Belfast, Feb 18, 1882); **Wales:** 0-9 v Scotland (Glasgow, Mar 23, 1878); **Rep of Ireland:** 0-7 v Brazil (Uberlandia, May 27, 1982).

World Cup: Qualifying round – Australia 31 American Samoa 0, world record international score (Apr 11, 2001); Australia 22 Tonga 0 (Apr 9, 2001); Iran 19 Guam 0 (Nov 25, 2000); Maldives 0 Iran 17 (Jun 2, 1997). **Finals – highest scores:** Hungary 10 El Salvador 1 (Spain, Jun 15, 1982); Hungary 9 S Korea 0 (Switzerland, Jun 17, 1954); Yugoslavia 9 Zaire 0 (W Germany, Jun 18, 1974).

European Championship: Qualifying round – highest scorers: San Marino 0 Germany 13 (Serravalle, Sep 6, 2006). **Finals – highest score:** Holland 6 Yugoslavia 1 (quarter-final, Rotterdam, Jun 25, 2000).

Biggest England U-21 win: 9-0 v San Marino (Shrewsbury, Nov 19, 2013).

FA Cup: Preston 26 Hyde 0 1st round, Oct 15, 1887.

League Cup: West Ham 10 Bury 0 (2nd round, 2nd leg, Oct 25, 1983); Liverpool 10 Fulham 0 (2nd round, 1st leg, Sep 23, 1986). **Record aggregates:** Liverpool 13 Fulham 2 (10-0h, 3-2a), Sep 23, Oct 7, 1986; West Ham 12 Bury 1 (2-1a, 10-0h), Oct 4, 25, 1983; Liverpool 11 Exeter 0 (5-0h, 6-0a), Oct 7, 28, 1981.

League Cup – most goals in one match: 12 Reading 5 Arsenal 7 aet (4th round, Oct 30, 2012). Dagenham & Redbridge 6 Brentford 6 aet (Brentford won 4-2 on pens; 1st round, Aug 12, 2014)

Premier League (beginning 1992–93): Manchester Utd 9 Ipswich 0, Mar 4, 1995; Manchester Utd 9 Southampton 0, Feb 2, 2021. **Record away win:** Southampton 0 Leicester 9, Oct 25, 2019.

Highest aggregate scores in Premier League – 11: Portsmouth 7 Reading 4, Sep 29, 2007; **10:** Tottenham 6 Reading 4, Dec 29, 2007; Tottenham 9 Wigan 1, Nov 22, 2009; Manchester Utd 8 Arsenal 2, Aug 28, 2011; Arsenal 7 Newcastle 3, Dec 29, 2012; WBA 5 Manchester Utd 5, May 19, 2013.

Big back-to-back wins: Manchester City became the first Premier League team to score five or more goals in three successive matches in the same season – beating Liverpool 5-0, Watford 6-0 and Crystal Palace 5-0 in September 2017. Chelsea also scored heavily in the last game of the 2009-10 season (Wigan 8-0) and in the first two fixtures of the following campaign (WBA 6-0, Wigan 6-0).

†Football League (First Division): Aston Villa 12 Accrington 2, Mar 12, 1892; Tottenham 10 Everton 4, Oct 11, 1958 (highest Div 1 aggregate that century); WBA 12 Darwen 0, Apr 4, 1892; Nottm Forest 12 Leicester Fosse 0, Apr 21, 1909. **Record away win:** Newcastle 1 Sunderland 9, Dec 5, 1908; Cardiff 1 Wolves 9, Sep 3, 1955; Wolves 0 WBA 8, Dec 27, 1893.

New First Division (beginning 1992–93): Bolton 7 Swindon 0, Mar 8, 1997; Sunderland 7 Oxford Utd 0, Sep 19, 1998. **Record away win:** Stoke 0 Birmingham 7, Jan 10, 1998; Oxford Utd 0 Birmingham 7, Dec 12, 1998. **Record aggregate:** Grimsby 6 Burnley 5, Oct 29, 2002; Burnley 4 Watford 7, Apr 5, 2003.

Championship (beginning 2004–05): Birmingham 0 Bournemouth 8, Oct 25, 2014. **Record away win:** Birmingham 0 Bournemouth 8, Oct 25, 2014. **Record aggregate:** Leeds 6 Preston 6, Sep 29, 2010; Leeds 3 Nottm Forest 7, Mar 20, 2012; Bristol City 5 Hull 5, Apr 21, 2018. Aston Villa 5 Nottm Forest 5, Nov 28, 2018.

†Second Division: Newcastle 13 Newport Co 0, Oct 5, 1946; Small Heath 12 Walsall Town Swifts 0, Dec 17, 1892; Darwen 12 Walsall 0, Dec 26, 1896; Woolwich Arsenal 12 Loughborough 0, Mar 12, 1900; Small Heath 12 Doncaster 0, Apr 11, ˜1903. **Record away win:** *Burslem Port Vale 0 Sheffield Utd 10, Dec 10, 1892. **Record aggregate:** Manchester City 11 Lincoln 3, Mar 23, 1895.

New Second Division (beginning 1992–93): Hartlepool 1 Plymouth Argyle 8, May 7, 1994; Hartlepool 8 Grimsby 1, Sep 12, 2003.

New League 1 (beginning 2004–05): MK Dons 7 Oldham 0, Dec 20, 2014; Oxford 0 Wigan 7, Dec 23, 2017; Peterborough 7 Accrington 0, Mar 27, 2021. **Record aggregate:** Hartlepool 4 Wrexham 6, Mar 5, 2005; Wolves 6 Rotherham 4, Apr 18, 2014; Bristol City 8 Walsall 2, May 3, 2015.

†Third Division: Gillingham 10 Chesterfield 0, Sep 5, 1987; Tranmere 9 Accrington 0, Apr 18, 1959; Brentford 9 Wrexham 0, Oct 15, 1963. **Record away win:** Halifax 0 Fulham 8, Sep 16, 1969. **Record aggregate:** Doncaster 7 Reading 5, Sep 25, 1982.

New Third Division (beginning 1992–93): Barnet 1 Peterborough 9, Sep 5, 1998. **Record aggregate:** Hull 7 Swansea 4, Aug 30, 1997.

New League 2 (beginning 2004–05): Peterborough 7 Brentford 0, Nov 24, 2007 Shrewsbury 7 Gillingham 0, Sep 13, 2008; Crewe 7 Barnet 0, Aug 21, 2010; Crewe 8 Cheltenham 1, Apr 2, 2011; Cambridge 7 Morecambe 0, Apr 19, 2016; Luton 7 Cambridge 0, Nov 18, 2017. **Record away win:** Boston 0 Grimsby 6, Feb 3, 2007; Macclesfield 0 Darlington 6, Aug 30, 2008; Lincoln 0 Rotherham 6, Mar 25, 2011. **Record aggregate:** Burton 5 Cheltenham 6, Mar 13, 2010; Accrington 7 Gillingham 4, Oct 2, 2010.

†Third Division (North): Stockport 13 Halifax 0 (still joint biggest win in Football League – see Div 2) Jan 6, 1934; Tranmere 13 Oldham 4, Dec 26, 1935. (17 is highest Football League aggregate score). **Record away win:** Accrington 0 Barnsley 9, Feb 3, 1934.

†Third Division (South): Luton 12 Bristol Rov 0, Apr 13, 1936; Bristol City 9 Gillingham 4, Jan 15, 1927; Gillingham 9 Exeter 4, Jan 7, 1951. **Record away win:** Northampton 0 Walsall 8, Apr 8, 1947.

†Fourth Division: Oldham 11 Southport 0, Dec 26, 1962. **Record away win:** Crewe 1 Rotherham 8, Sep 8, 1973. **Record aggregate:** Hartlepool 10 Barrow 1, Apr 4, 1959; Crystal Palace 9 Accrington 2, Aug 20, 1960; Wrexham 10 Hartlepool 1, Mar 3, 1962; Oldham 11 Southport 0, Dec 26, 1962; Torquay 3 Newport 7, Oct 19, 1963; Shrewsbury 7 Doncaster 4, Feb 1, 1975; Barnet 4 Crewe 7, Aug 17, 1991.

Scottish Premier – Highest aggregate: 12: Motherwell 6 Hibernian 6, May 5, 2010; **11:** Celtic 8 Hamilton 3, Jan 3, 1987; Motherwell 5 Aberdeen 6, Oct 20, 1999. **Other highest team scores:** Aberdeen 8 Motherwell 0 (Mar 26, 1979); Hamilton 0 Celtic 8 (Nov 5, 1988); Celtic 9 Aberdeen 0 (Nov 6, 2010).

Scottish League Div 1: Celtic 11 Dundee 0, Oct 26, 1895. **Record away win:** Hibs 11 *Airdrie 1, Oct 24, 1959.

Scottish League Div 2: Airdrieonians 15 Dundee Wanderers 1, Dec 1, 1894 (biggest win in history of League football in Britain).

Record modern Scottish League aggregate: 12 – Brechin 5 Cowdenbeath 7, Div 2, Jan 18, 2003.

Record British score since 1900: Stirling 20 Selkirk 0 (Scottish Cup 1, Dec 8, 1984). Winger Davie Thompson (7 goals) was one of 9 Stirling players to score.

346

LEAGUE GOALS – BEST IN SEASON (Before restructure in 1992)

Div		Goals	Games
1	WR (Dixie) Dean, Everton, 1927–28	60	39
2	George Camsell, Middlesbrough, 1926–27	59	37
3(S)	Joe Payne, Luton, 1936–37	55	39
3(N)	Ted Harston, Mansfield, 1936–37	55	41
3	Derek Reeves, Southampton, 1959–60	39	46
4	Terry Bly, Peterborough, 1960–61	52	46

(Since restructure in 1992)

Div		Goals	Games
1	Guy Whittingham, Portsmouth, 1992–93	42	46
2	Jordan Rhodes Huddersfield 2011-12	36	40
3	Andy Morrell, Wrexham, 2002–03	34	45

Premier League – BEST IN SEASON
Andy Cole **34 goals** (Newcastle – 40 games, 1993–94); Alan Shearer **34 goals** (Blackburn – 42 games, 1994–95).

FOOTBALL LEAGUE – BEST MATCH HAULS

(Before restructure in 1992)

Div	Goals	
1	Ted Drake (Arsenal), away to Aston Villa, Dec 14, 1935	7
	James Ross (Preston) v Stoke, Oct 6, 1888	7
2	*Neville (Tim) Coleman (Stoke) v Lincoln, Feb 23, 1957	7
	Tommy Briggs (Blackburn) v Bristol Rov, Feb 5, 1955	7
3(S)	Joe Payne (Luton) v Bristol Rov, Apr 13, 1936	10
3(N)	Robert ('Bunny') Bell (Tranmere) v Oldham, Dec 26, 1935 he also missed a penalty	9
3	Barrie Thomas (Scunthorpe) v Luton, Apr 24, 1965	5
	Keith East (Swindon) v Mansfield, Nov 20, 1965	5
	Steve Earle (Fulham) v Halifax, Sep 16, 1969	5
	Alf Wood (Shrewsbury) v Blackburn, Oct 2, 1971	5
	Tony Caldwell (Bolton) v Walsall, Sep 10, 1983	5
	Andy Jones (Port Vale) v Newport Co., May 4, 1987	5
4	Bert Lister (Oldham) v Southport, Dec 26, 1962	6

*Scored from the wing

(Since restructure in 1992)

Div Goals

1 4 in match – John Durnin (Oxford Utd v Luton, 1992–93); Guy Whittingham (Portsmouth v Bristol Rov 1992–93); Craig Russell (Sunderland v Millwall, 1995–96); David Connolly (Wolves at Bristol City 1998–99); Darren Byfield (Rotherham at Millwall, 2002–03); David Connolly (Wimbledon at Bradford City, 2002–03); Marlon Harewood (Nottm Forest v Stoke, 2002–03); Michael Chopra (Watford at Burnley, 2002–03); Robert Earnshaw (Cardiff v Gillingham, 2003–04). **5** in match – Paul Barnes (Burnley v Stockport, 1996–97); Robert Taylor (all 5, Gillingham at Burnley, 1998–99); Lee Jones (all 5, Wrexham v Cambridge Utd, 2001–02).

3 5 in match – Tony Naylor (Crewe v Colchester, 1992–93); Steve Butler (Cambridge Utd v Exeter, 1993–4); Guiliano Grazioli (Peterborough at Barnet, 1998–99).

Champ 4 in match – Garath McCleary (Nottm Forest at Leeds 2011–12); Nikola Zigic (Birmingham at Leeds 2011–12; Craig Davies (Barnsley at Birmingham 2012–13; Ross McCormack (Leeds at Charlton 2013–14), Jesse Lingard (Birmingham v Sheffield Wed 2013–14); Odion Ighalo (Watford v Blackpool, 2014-15); Leon Clarke (all 4, Sheffield Utd v Hull, 2017–18); Tammy Abraham (Aston Villa v Nottm Forest, 2018–19); Yakou Meite (Reading at Luton, 2019–20).

Lge 1   4 in match – Jordan Rhodes (all 4, Huddersfield at Sheffield Wed, 2011–12); Ellis
Harrison (Bristol Rov v Northampton, 2016–17); James Vaughan (Bury v Peterborough,
2016–17); Will Grigg (MK Dons v Swindon, 2020-21); Charlie Wyke (Sunderland v
Doncaster, 2020–21).
5 in match – Juan Ugarte (Wrexham at Hartlepool, 2004–05); Jordan Rhodes
(Huddersfield at Wycombe, 2011–12).

Last player to score 6 in English League match: Geoff Hurst (West Ham 8 Sunderland 0, Div 1
Oct 19,1968.

PREMIER LEAGUE – BEST MATCH HAULS

5 goals in match: Andy Cole (Manchester Utd v Ipswich, Mar 4, 1995); Alan Shearer
(Newcastle v Sheffield Wed, Sep 19, 1999); Jermain Defoe (Tottenham v Wigan, Nov 22,
2009); Dimitar Berbatov (Manchester Utd v Blackburn, Nov 27, 2010), Sergio Aguero
(Manchester City v Newcastle, Oct 3, 2015).

SCOTTISH LEAGUE

Div		Goals
Prem	Gary Hooper (Celtic) v Hearts, May 13, 2012	5
	Kris Boyd (Rangers) v Dundee Utd, Dec 30, 2009	5
	Kris Boyd (Kilmarnock) v Dundee Utd, Sep 25, 2004	5
	Kenny Miller (Rangers) v St Mirren, Nov 4, 2000	5
	Marco Negri (Rangers) v Dundee Utd, Aug. 23, 1997	5
	Paul Sturrock (Dundee Utd) v Morton, Nov 17, 1984	5
1	Jimmy McGrory (Celtic) v Dunfermline, Jan 14, 1928	8
1	Owen McNally (Arthurlie) v Armadale, Oct 1, 1927	8
2	Jim Dyet (King's Park) v Forfar, Jan 2, 1930 on his debut for the club	8
2	John Calder (Morton) v Raith, Apr 18, 1936	8
2	Norman Haywood (Raith) v Brechin, Aug. 20, 1937	8

SCOTTISH LEAGUE – BEST IN SEASON

Prem	Brian McClair (Celtic, 1986–87)	35
	Henrik Larsson (Celtic, 2000–01)	35
1	William McFadyen (Motherwell, 1931–32)	53
2	*Jimmy Smith (Ayr, 1927–28 – 38 appearances)	66
	(*British record)	

CUP FOOTBALL

Scottish Cup: John Petrie (Arbroath) v Bon Accord, at Arbroath, 1st round, Sep 12, 1885		13
FA Cup: Ted MacDougall (Bournemouth) v Margate, 1st round, Nov 20,1971		9
FA Cup Final: Billy Townley (Blackburn) v Sheffield Wed, at Kennington Oval, 1890; Jimmy Logan (Notts Co) v Bolton, at Everton, 1894; Stan Mortensen (Blackpool) v Bolton, at Wembley, 1953		3
League Cup: Frank Bunn (Oldham) v Scarborough (3rd round), Oct 25, 1989		6
Scottish League Cup: Willie Penman (Raith) v Stirling, Sep 18, 1948		6

Scottish Cup: Most goals in match since war: 10 by **Gerry Baker** (St Mirren) in 15-0 win (1st
round) v Glasgow Univ, Jan 30, 1960; 9 by his brother **Joe Baker** (Hibernian) in 15-1 win
(2nd round) v Peebles, Feb 11, 1961.

AGGREGATE LEAGUE SCORING RECORDS

	Goals
*Arthur Rowley (1947–65, WBA, Fulham, Leicester, Shrewsbury)	434
†Jimmy McGrory (1922–38, Celtic, Clydebank)	410
Hughie Gallacher (1921–39, Airdrieonians, Newcastle, Chelsea, Derby, Notts Co, Grimsby, Gateshead)	387

William ('Dixie') Dean (1923–37, Tranmere, Everton, Notts Co) **379**
Hugh Ferguson (1916–30, Motherwell, Cardiff, Dundee) **362**
● Jimmy Greaves (1957–71, Chelsea, Tottenham, West Ham) **357**
Steve Bloomer (1892–1914, Derby, Middlesbrough, Derby) **352**
George Camsell (1923–39, Durham City, Middlesbrough) **348**
Dave Halliday (1920–35, St Mirren, Dundee, Sunderland, Arsenal,
    Manchester City, Clapton Orient) **338**
John Aldridge (1979–98, Newport, Oxford Utd, Liverpool, Tranmere) **329**
Harry Bedford (1919–34, Nottm Forest, Blackpool, Derby, Newcastle,
    Sunderland, Bradford PA, Chesterfield) **326**
John Atyeo (1951–66, Bristol City) **315**
Joe Smith (1908–29, Bolton, Stockport) **315**
Victor Watson (1920–36, West Ham, Southampton) **312**
Harry Johnson (1919–36, Sheffield Utd, Mansfield) **309**
Bob McPhail (1923–1939, Airdrie, Rangers) **306**

(*__Rowley__ scored 4 for WBA, 27 for Fulham, 251 for Leicester, 152 for Shrewsbury.
● **Greaves'** 357 is record top-division total (he also scored 9 League goals for AC Milan).
Aldridge also scored 33 League goals for Real Sociedad. †**McGrory** scored 397 for Celtic, 13
for Clydebank).

Most League goals for one club: 349 – Dixie Dean (Everton 1925–37); **326** – George Camsell
(Middlesbrough 1925–39); **315** – John Atyeo (Bristol City 1951–66); **306** – Vic Watson
(West Ham 1920–35); **291** – Steve Bloomer (Derby 1892–1906, 1910–14); **259** – Arthur
Chandler (Leicester 1923–35); **255** – Nat Lofthouse (Bolton 1946–61); **251** – Arthur Rowley
(Leicester 1950–58).

More than 500 goals: Jimmy McGrory (Celtic, Clydebank and Scotland) scored a total of **550**
goals in his first-class career (1922–38).

More than 1,000 goals: Brazil's **Pele** is reputedly the game's all-time highest scorer with **1,283**
goals in **1,365** matches (1956–77), but many of them were scored in friendlies for his club,
Santos. He scored his 1,000th goal, a penalty, against Vasco da Gama in the Maracana
Stadium, Rio, on Nov 19, 1969. ● Pele (born Oct 23, 1940) played regularly for Santos from
the age of 16. During his career, he was sent off only once. He played 95 'A' internationals
for Brazil and in their World Cup-winning teams in 1958 and 1970. † Pele (Edson Arantes do
Nascimento) was subsequently Brazil's Minister for Sport. He never played at Wembley, apart
from being filmed there scoring a goal for a commercial. Aged 57, Pele received an 'honorary
knighthood' (Knight Commander of the British Empire) from the Queen at Buckingham
Palace on Dec 3, 1997.

Romario (retired Apr, 2008, aged 42) scored more than 1,000 goals for Vasco da Gama,
Barcelona, PSV Eindhoven, Valencia and Brazil (56 in 73 internationals).

MOST LEAGUE GOALS IN SEASON: DEAN'S 60

WR ('Dixie') Dean, Everton centre-forward, created a League scoring record in 1927–28 with 60
in 39 First Division matches. He also scored three in FA Cup ties, and 19 in representative
games, totalling 82 for the season.

George Camsell, of Middlesbrough, previously held the record with 59 goals in 37 Second
Division matches in 1926–27, his total for the season being 75.

SHEARER'S RECORD 'FIRST'

Alan Shearer (Blackburn) is the only player to score more than 30 top-division goals in 3
successive seasons since the War: 31 in 1993–94, 34 in 1994–95, 31 in 1995–96.

Thierry Henry (Arsenal) is the first player to score more than 20 Premier League goals in five
consecutive seasons (2002–06). **David Halliday** (Sunderland) topped 30 First Division goals
in 4 consecutive seasons with totals of 38, 36, 36 and 49 from 1925–26 to 1928–29.

MOST GOALS IN A MATCH

Sep 12, 1885: John Petrie set the all-time British individual record for a first-class match when, in Arbroath's 36-0 win against Bon Accord (Scottish Cup 1), he scored **13.**

Apr 13, 1936: Joe Payne set the still-existing individual record on his debut as a centre-forward, for Luton v Bristol Rov (Div 3 South). In a 12-0 win he scored **10.**

ROWLEY'S ALL-TIME RECORD

Arthur Rowley is English football's top club scorer with a total of 464 goals for WBA, Fulham, Leicester and Shrewsbury (1947–65). There were 434 in the League, 26 FA Cup, 4 League Cup.

Jimmy Greaves is second with a total of 420 goals for Chelsea, AC Milan, Tottenham and West Ham, made up of 366 League, 35 FA Cup, 10 League Cup and 9 in Europe. He also scored nine goals for AC Milan.

John Aldridge retired as a player at the end of season 1997–98 with a career total of 329 League goals for Newport, Oxford Utd, Liverpool and Tranmere (1979–98). In all competitions for those clubs he scored 410 in 737 appearances. He also scored 45 in 63 games for Real Sociedad.

MOST GOALS IN INTERNATIONAL MATCHES

13 by **Archie Thompson** for Australia v American Samoa in World Cup (Oceania Group qualifier) at Coff's Harbour, New South Wales, Apr 11, 2001. Result: 31-0.

7 by **Stanley Harris** for England v France in Amateur International in Paris, Nov 1, 1906. Result: 15-0.

6 by **Nat Lofthouse** for Football League v Irish League, at Wolverhampton, Sep 24, 1952. Result: 7-1.

    Joe Bambrick for Northern Ireland against Wales (7-0) in Belfast, Feb 1, 1930 – a record for a Home Nations International. **WC Jordan** in Amateur International for England v France, at Park Royal, Mar 23, 1908. Result: 12-0. **Vivian Woodward** for England v Holland in Amateur International, at Chelsea, Dec 11,1909. Result: 9-1.

5 by **Howard Vaughton** for England v Ireland (Belfast) Feb 18, 1882. Result: 13-0.

    Steve Bloomer for England v Wales (Cardiff) Mar 16, 1896. Result: 9-1.

    Hughie Gallacher for Scotland against Ireland (Belfast), Feb 23, 1929. Result: 7-3.

    Willie Hall for England v Northern Ireland, at Old Trafford, Nov 16, 1938. Five in succession (first three in 3·5 mins – fastest international hat-trick). Result: 7-0.

    Malcolm Macdonald for England v Cyprus (Wembley) Apr 16, 1975. Result: 5-0.

    Hughie Gallacher for Scottish League against Irish League (Belfast) Nov 11, 1925. Result: 7-3.

    Barney Battles for Scottish League against Irish League (Firhill Park, Glasgow) Oct 31, 1928. Result: 8-2.

    Bobby Flavell for Scottish League against Irish League (Belfast) Apr 30, 1947. Result: 7-4.

    Joe Bradford for Football League v Irish League (Everton) Sep 25, 1929. Result: 7-2.

    Albert Stubbins for Football League v Irish League (Blackpool) Oct 18, 1950. Result: 6-3.

    Brian Clough for Football League v Irish League (Belfast) Sep 23, 1959. Result: 5-0.

LAST ENGLAND PLAYER TO SCORE ...

3 goals: Harry Kane v Bulgaria (4-0) Euro Champ qual, Wembley, Sept 7, 2019; Harry Kane v Montenegro (7-0) Euro Champ qual, Wembley, Nov 14. 2019 (England's 1,000th international).

4 goals: Ian Wright v San Marino (7-1), World Cup qual, Bologna, Nov 17, 1993.

5 goals: Malcolm Macdonald v Cyprus (5-0), Euro Champ qual, Wembley, Apr 16, 1975.

INTERNATIONAL TOP SHOTS

		Goals	Games
England	Wayne Rooney (2003–2019)	53	120

		Goals	Games
N Ireland	David Healy (2000–13)	36	95
Scotland	Denis Law (1958–74)	30	55
	Kenny Dalglish (1971–86)	30	102
Wales	Gareth Bale (2006–21)	33	96
Rep of Ire	Robbie Keane (1998–2017)	68	146

ENGLAND'S TOP MARKSMEN

(As at start of season 2021–22)

	Goals	Games
Wayne Rooney (2003–17)	53	120
Bobby Charlton (1958–70)	49	106
Gary Lineker (1984–92)	48	80
Jimmy Greaves (1959–67)	44	57
Michael Owen (1998–2008)	40	89
Harry Kane (2015–2021)	38	61
Tom Finney (1946–58)	30	76
Nat Lofthouse (1950–58)	30	33
Alan Shearer (1992–2000)	30	63
Vivian Woodward (1903–11)	29	23
Frank Lampard (2003–14)	29	106
Steve Bloomer (1895–1907)	28	23
David Platt (1989–96)	27	62
Bryan Robson (1979–91)	26	90
Geoff Hurst (1966–72)	24	49
Stan Mortensen (1947–53)	23	25
Tommy Lawton (1938–48)	22	23
Peter Crouch (2005–11)	22	42
Mike Channon (1972–77)	21	46
Steven Gerrard (2000–14)	21	114
Kevin Keegan (1972–82)	21	63

ROONEY'S ENGLAND RECORD

Wayne Rooney reached 50 international goals with a penalty against Switzerland at Wembley on September 8, 2015 to become England's record scorer, surpassing Bobby Charlton's mark. Charlton's record was set in 106 games, Rooney's tally on 107.

CONSECUTIVE GOALS FOR ENGLAND

Steve Bloomer scored in **10** consecutive appearances (19 goals) between Mar 1895 and Mar 1899.
Jimmy Greaves scored **11** goals in five consecutive matches from the start of season 1960–61.

ENGLAND'S TOP FINAL SERIES MARKSMEN

Gary Lineker with 6 goals at 1986 World Cup in Mexico.
Harry Kane with 6 goals at 2018 World Cup in Russia.

MOST ENGLAND GOALS IN SEASON

13 – **Jimmy Greaves** (1960–61 in 9 matches); **12 – Dixie Dean** (1926–27 in 6 matches); **11 – Harry Kane** (2017-18 in 11 matches); **10 – Gary Lineker** (1990–91 in 10 matches); **10 – Wayne Rooney** – (2008–09 in 9 matches); **Harry Kane** (2019–20 in six matches).

MOST ENGLAND HAT-TRICKS

Jimmy Greaves 6; **Gary Lineker** 5, **Bobby Charlton** 4, **Vivian Woodward** 4, **Stan Mortensen** 3; **Harry Kane** 3.

MOST GOALS FOR ENGLAND U-21s

14 – Eddie Nketiah (12 apps), **13** – Alan Shearer (11 apps), Francis Jeffers (13 apps).

GOLDEN GOAL DECIDERS

The Football League, in an experiment to avoid penalty shoot-outs, introduced a new golden goal system in the 1994–95 **Auto Windscreens Shield** to decide matches in the knock-out stages of the competition in which scores were level after 90 minutes. The first goal scored in overtime ended play.

Iain Dunn (Huddersfield) became the first player in British football to settle a match by this sudden-death method. His 107th-minute goal beat Lincoln 3-2 on Nov 30, 1994, and to mark his 'moment in history' he was presented with a golden football trophy.

The AWS Final of 1995 was decided when Paul Tait headed the only goal for Birmingham against Carlisle 13 minutes into overtime – the first time a match at Wembley had been decided by the 'golden goal' formula.

First major international tournament match to be decided by sudden death was the Final of the **1996 European Championship** at Wembley in which Germany beat Czech Rep 2-1 by **Oliver Bierhoff's** goal in the 95th minute.

In the **1998 World Cup Finals** (2nd round), host country France beat Paraguay 1-0 with **Laurent Blanc's** goal (114).

France won the **2000 European Championship** with golden goals in the semi-final, 2-1 v Portugal (Zinedine Zidane pen, 117), and in the Final, 2-1 v Italy (David Trezeguet, 103).

Galatasaray (Turkey) won the **European Super Cup** 2-1 against Real Madrid (Monaco, Aug 25, 2000) with a 103rd minute golden goal, a penalty.

Liverpool won the **UEFA Cup** 5-4 against Alaves with a 117th-min golden goal, an own goal, in the Final in Dortmund (May 19, 2001).

In the **2002 World Cup Finals**, 3 matches were decided by Golden Goals: in the 2nd round Senegal beat Sweden 2-1 (Henri Camara, 104) and South Korea beat Italy 2-1 (Ahn Jung-hwan, 117); in the quarter-final, Turkey beat Senegal 1-0 (Ilhan Mansiz, 94).

France won the 2003 **FIFA Confederations Cup Final** against Cameroon (Paris, Jun 29) with a 97th-minute golden goal by Thierry Henry.

Doncaster won promotion to Football League with a 110th-minute golden goal winner (3-2) in the Conference Play-off Final against Dagenham at Stoke (May 10, 2003).

Germany won the **Women's World Cup Final** 2-1 v Sweden (Los Angeles, Oct 12, 2003) with a 98th-minute golden goal.

GOLD TURNS TO SILVER

Starting with the 2003 Finals of the UEFA Cup and Champions League/European Cup, UEFA introduced a new rule by which a silver goal could decide the winners if the scores were level after 90 minutes.

Team leading after 15 minutes' extra time win match. If sides level, a second period of 15 minutes to be played. If still no winner, result to be decided by penalty shoot-out.

UEFA said the change was made because the golden goal put too much pressure on referees and prompted teams to play negative football.

Although both 2003 European Finals went to extra-time, neither was decided by a silver goal. The new rule applied in the 2004 European Championship Finals, and Greece won their semi-final against the Czech Republic in the 105th minute.

The **International Board** decided (Feb 28 2004) that the golden/silver goal rule was 'unfair' and that from July 1 competitive international matches level after extra-time would, when necessary, be settled on penalties.

PREMIER LEAGUE TOP SHOTS (1992–2021)

Alan Shearer	260	Nicolas Anelka	125
Wayne Rooney	208	Dwight Yorke	123
Andy Cole	187	Steven Gerrard	120

Sergio Aguero	184	Jamie Vardy	118
Frank Lampard	177	Romelu Lukaku	113
Thierry Henry	175	Ian Wright	113
Harry Kane	166	Dion Dublin	111
Robbie Fowler	163	Emile Heskey	110
Jermain Defoe	162	Ryan Giggs	109
Michael Owen	150	Peter Crouch	108
Les Ferdinand	149	Paul Scholes	107
Teddy Sheringham	146	Darren Bent	106
Robin van Persie	144	Didier Drogba	104
Jimmy Floyd Hasselbaink	127	Matt Le Tissier	100
Robbie Keane	126		

LEAGUE GOAL RECORDS

The highest goal-scoring aggregates in the Football League, Premier and Scottish League are:

For

	Goals	Games	Club	Season
Prem	106	38	Manchester City	2017–18
Div 1	128	42	Aston Villa	1930–31
New Div 1	108	46	Manchester City	2001–02
New Champ	99	46	Reading	2005–06
Div 2	122	42	Middlesbrough	1926–27
New Div 2	89	46	Millwall	2000–01
New Lge 1	106	46	Peterborough	2010–11
Div 3(S)	127	42	Millwall	1927–28
Div 3(N)	128	42	Bradford City	1928–29
Div 3	111	46	QPR	1961–62
New Div 3	96	46	Luton	2001–02
New Lge 2	96	46	Notts Co	2009–10
Div 4	134	46	Peterborough	1960–61
Scot Prem	105	38	Celtic	2003–04
Scot L 1	132	34	Hearts	1957–58
Scot L 2	142	34	Raith Rov	1937–38
Scot L 3 (Modern)	130	36	Gretna	2004–05
Against				
Prem	100	42	Swindon	1993–94
Div 1	125	42	Blackpool	1930–31
New Div 1	102	46	Stockport	2001–02
New Champ	86	46	Crewe	2004–05
Div 2	141	34	Darwen	1898–99
New Div 2	102	46	Chester	1992–93
New Lge 1	98	46	Stockport	2004–05
Div 3(S)	135	42	Merthyr T	1929–30
Div 3(N)	136	42	Nelson	1927–28
Div 3	123	46	Accrington Stanley	1959–60
New Div 3	113	46	Doncaster	1997–98
New Lge 2	96	46	Stockport	2010–11
Div 4	109	46	Hartlepool Utd	1959–60
Scot Prem	100	36	Morton	1984–85
Scot Prem	100	44	Morton	1987–88
Scot L 1	137	38	Leith A	1931–32
Scot L 2	146	38	Edinburgh City	1931–32
Scot L 3 (Modern)	118	36	East Stirling	2003–04

BEST DEFENSIVE RECORDS *Denotes under old offside law

Div	Goals Agst	Games	Club	Season
Prem	15	38	Chelsea	2004–05
1	16	42	Liverpool	1978–79
1	*15	22	Preston	1888–89
New Div 1	28	46	Sunderland	1998–99
New Champ	30	46	Preston	2005–06
2	18	28	Liverpool	1893–94
2	*22	34	Sheffield Wed	1899–1900
2	24	42	Birmingham	1947–48
2	24	42	Crystal Palace	1978–79
New Div 2	25	46	Wigan	2002–03
New Lge 1	32	46	Nottm Forest	2007–08
3(S)	*21	42	Southampton	1921–22
3(S)	30	42	Cardiff	1946–47
3(N)	*21	38	Stockport	1921–22
3(N)	21	46	Port Vale	1953–54
3	30	46	Middlesbrough	1986–87
New Div 3	20	46	Gillingham	1995–96
New Lge 2	31	46	Notts Co	2009–10
4	25	46	Lincoln	1980–81

SCOTTISH LEAGUE

Div	Goals Agst	Games	Club	Season
Prem	13	38	Rangers	2020–21
1	*12	22	Dundee	1902–03
1	*14	38	Celtic	1913–14
2	20	38	Morton	1966–67
2	*29	38	Clydebank	1922–23
2	29	36	East Fife	1995–96
New Div 3	21	36	Brechin	1995–96

TOP SCORERS (LEAGUE ONLY)

		Goals	Div
2020–21	Paul Mullin (Cambridge)	32	Lg 2
2019–20	Aleksandar Mitrovic (Fulham)	26	Champ
2018–19	Teemu Pukki (Norwich)	29	Champ
	James Norwood (Tranmere)	29	Lge 2
2017–18	Mohamed Salah (Liverpool)	32	Prem
2016–17	Billy Sharp (Sheffield Utd)	30	Lge 1
2015–16	Matt Taylor (Bristol Rov)	27	Lge 2
2014–15	Daryl Murphy (Ipswich)	27	Champ
2013–14	Luis Suarez (Liverpool)	31	Prem
2012–13	Tom Pope (Port Vale)	31	Lge 2
2011–12	Jordan Rhodes (Huddersfield)	36	Lge 1
2010–11	Clayton Donaldson (Crewe)	28	Lge 2
2009–10	Rickie Lambert (Southampton)	31	Lge 1
2008–09	Simon Cox (Swindon)		
	Rickie Lambert (Bristol Rov)	29	Lge 1
2007–08	Cristiano Ronaldo (Manchester Utd)	31	Prem
2006–07	Billy Sharp (Scunthorpe)	30	Lge 1
2005–06	Thierry Henry (Arsenal)	27	Prem
2004–05	Stuart Elliott (Hull)	27	1
	Phil Jevons (Yeovil)	27	2
	Dean Windass (Bradford City)	27	1

2003–04	Thierry Henry (Arsenal)	30	Prem
2002–03	Andy Morrell (Wrexham)	34	3
2001–02	Shaun Goater (Manchester City)	28	1
	Bobby Zamora (Brighton)	28	2
2000–01	Bobby Zamora (Brighton)	28	3
1999–00	Kevin Phillips (Sunderland)	30	Prem
1998–99	Lee Hughes (WBA)	31	1
1997–98	Pierre van Hooijdonk (Nottm Forest)	29	1
	Kevin Phillips (Sunderland)	29	1
1996–97	Graeme Jones (Wigan)	31	3
1995–96	Alan Shearer (Blackburn)	31	Prem
1994–95	Alan Shearer (Blackburn)	34	Prem
1993–94	Jimmy Quinn (Reading)	35	2
1992–93	Guy Whittingham (Portsmouth)	42	1
1991–92	Ian Wright (Crystal Palace 5, Arsenal 24)	29	1
1990–91	Teddy Sheringham (Millwall)	33	2
1989–90	Mick Quinn (Newcastle)	32	2
1988–89	Steve Bull (Wolves)	37	3
1987–88	Steve Bull (Wolves)	34	4
1986–87	Clive Allen (Tottenham)	33	1
1985–86	Gary Lineker (Everton)	30	1
1984–85	Tommy Tynan (Plymouth Argyle)	31	3
	John Clayton (Tranmere)	31	4
1983–84	Trevor Senior (Reading)	36	4
1982–83	Luther Blissett (Watford)	27	1
1981–82	Keith Edwards (Hull 1, Sheffield Utd 35)	36	4
1980–81	Tony Kellow (Exeter)	25	3
1979–80	Clive Allen (Queens Park Rangers)	28	2
1978–79	Ross Jenkins (Watford)	29	3
1977–78	Steve Phillips (Brentford)	32	4
	Alan Curtis (Swansea City)	32	4
1976–77	Peter Ward (Brighton)	32	3
1975–76	Dixie McNeil (Hereford)	35	3
1974–75	Dixie McNeil (Hereford)	31	3
1973–74	Brian Yeo (Gillingham)	31	4
1972–73	Bryan (Pop) Robson (West Ham)	28	1
1971–72	Ted MacDougall (Bournemouth)	35	3
1970–71	Ted MacDougall (Bournemouth)	42	4
1969–70	Albert Kinsey (Wrexham)	27	4
1968–69	Jimmy Greaves (Tottenham)	27	1
1967–68	George Best (Manchester Utd)	28	1
	Ron Davies (Southampton)	28	1
1966–67	Ron Davies (Southampton)	37	1
1965–66	Kevin Hector (Bradford PA)	44	4
1964–65	Alick Jeffrey (Doncaster)	36	4
1963–64	Hugh McIlmoyle (Carlisle)	39	4
1962–63	Jimmy Greaves (Tottenham)	37	1
1961–62	Roger Hunt (Liverpool)	41	2
1960–61	Terry Bly (Peterborough)	52	4

100 LEAGUE GOALS IN SEASON

Manchester City, First Div Champions in 2001–02, scored 108 goals.

Bolton, First Div Champions in 1996–97, reached 100 goals, the first side to complete a century in League football since 103 by **Northampton** (Div 4 Champions) in 1986–87.

Last League Champions to reach 100 League goals: **Manchester City** (106 in 2017–18). Last century of goals in the top division: 111 by runners-up **Tottenham** in 1962–63.

Clubs to score a century of Premier League goals in season: **Manchester City** 106 in 2017-18, **Chelsea** 103 in 2009–10, Manchester City (102) and Liverpool (101) in 2013–14.

Wolves topped 100 goals in four successive First Division seasons (1957–58, 1958–59, 1959–60, 1960–61).

In **1930–31**, the top three all scored a century of League goals: 1 Arsenal (127), 2 Aston Villa (128), 3 Sheffield Wed (102).

Latest team to score a century of League goals: Peterborough with 106 in 2010–11 (Lge 1).

100 GOALS AGAINST

Swindon, relegated with 100 goals against in 1993–94, were the first top-division club to concede a century of League goals since **Ipswich** (121) went down in 1964. Most goals conceded in the top division: 125 by **Blackpool** in 1930–31, but they avoided relegation.

MOST LEAGUE GOALS ON ONE DAY

A record of 209 goals in the four divisions of the Football League (43 matches) was set on **Jan 2, 1932:** 56 in Div 1, 53 in Div 2, 57 in Div 3 South and 43 in Div 3 North.

There were two 10-goal aggregates: Bradford City 9, Barnsley 1 in Div 2 and Coventry City 5, Fulham 5 in Div 3 South.

That total of 209 League goals on one day was equalled on **Feb 1, 1936** (44 matches): 46 in Div 1, 46 in Div 2, 49 in Div 3 South and 69 in Div 3 North. Two matches in the Northern Section produced 23 of the goals: Chester 12, York 0 and Crewe 5, Chesterfield 6.

MOST GOALS IN TOP DIV ON ONE DAY

This record has stood since **Dec 26, 1963,** when 66 goals were scored in the ten First Division matches played.

MOST PREMIER LEAGUE GOALS ON ONE DAY

47, in nine matches on **May 8, 1993** (last day of season). For the first time, all 20 clubs scored in the Premier League programme over the weekend of Nov 27-28, 2010.

FEWEST PREMIER LEAGUE GOALS IN ONE WEEK-END

10, in 10 matches on **Nov 24/25, 2001.**

FEWEST FIRST DIV GOALS ON ONE DAY

For full/near full programme: **Ten goals,** all by home clubs, in ten matches on Apr 28, 1923 (day of Wembley's first FA Cup Final).

SCORER OF LEAGUE'S FIRST GOAL

Kenny Davenport (2 mins) for Bolton v Derby, Sep 8, 1888.

VARDY'S RECORD

Jamie Vardy set a Premier League record by scoring in 11 consecutive matches for Leicester (Aug-Nov 2015). The all-time top division record of scoring in 12 successive games was set by **Jimmy Dunne** for Sheffield Utd in the old First Division in season 1931-32. **Stan Mortensen** scored in 15 successive matches for Blackpool (First Division) in season 1950-51, but that sequence included two injury breaks.

LUTON GOAL FEAST

Luton set a Football League record in season 2017–18 by scoring seven or more goals in three games before Christmas – beating Yeovil 8-2 on the opening day of the season, Stevenage 7-1 and Cambridge 7-0.

SCORERS FOR 7 PREMIER LEAGUE CLUBS

Craig Bellamy (Coventry, Newcastle, Blackburn, Liverpool, West Ham, Manchester City, Cardiff).

SCORERS FOR 6 PREMIER LEAGUE CLUBS

Les Ferdinand (QPR, Newcastle, Tottenham, West Ham, Leicester, Bolton); **Andy Cole** (Newcastle, Manchester Utd, Blackburn, Fulham, Manchester City, Portsmouth); **Marcus Bent** (Crystal Palace, Ipswich, Leicester, Everton, Charlton, Wigan); **Nick Barmby** (Tottenham, Middlesbrough, Everton, Liverpool, Leeds, Hull); **Peter Crouch** (Tottenham, Aston Villa, Southampton, Liverpool, Portsmouth, Stoke); **Robbie Keane** (Coventry, Leeds, Tottenham, Liverpool, West Ham, Aston Villa); **Nicolas Anelka** (Arsenal, Liverpool, Manchester City, Bolton, Chelsea, WBA); **Darren Bent** (Ipswich, Charlton, Tottenham, Sunderland, Aston Villa, Fulham).

SCORERS FOR 5 PREMIER LEAGUE CLUBS

Stan Collymore (Nottm Forest, Liverpool, Aston Villa, Leicester, Bradford); **Mark Hughes** (Manchester Utd, Chelsea, Southampton, Everton, Blackburn); **Benito Carbone** (Sheffield Wed, Aston Villa, Bradford, Derby, Middlesbrough); **Ashley Ward** (Norwich, Derby, Barnsley, Blackburn Bradford); **Teddy Sheringham** (Nottm Forest, Tottenham, Manchester Utd, Portsmouth, West Ham); **Chris Sutton** (Norwich, Blackburn, Chelsea, Birmingham, Aston Villa).

SCORERS IN MOST CONSECUTIVE LEAGUE MATCHES

Arsenal broke the record by scoring in 55 successive Premier League fixtures: the last match in season 2000–01, then all 38 games in winning the title in 2001–02, and the first 16 in season 2002–03. The sequence ended with a 2-0 defeat away to Manchester Utd on December 7, 2002.
Chesterfield previously held the record, having scored in 46 consecutive matches in Div 3 (North), starting on Christmas Day, 1929 and ending on December 27, 1930.

HEADING FOR VICTORY

When **Oxford Utd** beat Shrewsbury 6-0 (Div 2) on Apr 23, 1996, all six goals were headers. Charlie Wyke scored four headed goals, all from Aiden McGeady crosses, when Sunderland beat Doncaster 4-1 (Lge 1) on Feb 13, 2021.

ALL–ROUND MARKSMEN

Alan Cork scored in four divisions of the Football League and in the Premier League in his 18-season career with Wimbledon, Sheffield Utd and Fulham (1977–95).
Brett Ormerod scored in all four divisions (2, 1, Champ and Prem Lge) for Blackpool in two spells (1997–2002, 2008–11). **Grant Holt** (Sheffield Wed, Rochdale, Nottm Forest, Shrewsbury, Norwich) has scored in four Football League divisions and in the Premier League.

CROUCH AHEAD OF THE GAME

Peter Crouch holds the record for most headed goals in the Premier League with a total of 53, ahead of Alan Shearer (46) and Dion Dublin (45).

MOST CUP GOALS

FA Cup – most goals in one season: 20 by Jimmy Ross (Preston, runners-up 1887–88); 15 by Alex (Sandy) Brown (Tottenham, winners 1900–01).
Most FA Cup goals in individual careers: 49 by Harry Cursham (Notts Co 1877–89); 20th century: 44 by Ian Rush (39 for Liverpool, 4 for Chester, 1 for Newcastle 1979–98). Denis Law was the previous highest FA Cup scorer in the 20th century with 41 goals for Huddersfield Town, Manchester City and Manchester Utd (1957–74).
Most FA Cup Final goals by individual: 5 by Ian Rush for Liverpool (2 in 1986, 2 in 1989, 1 in 1992).

HOTTEST CUP HOT-SHOT

Geoff Hurst scored 21 cup goals in season 1965–66: 11 League Cup, 4 FA Cup and 2 Cup-Winners' Cup for West Ham, and 4 in the World Cup for England.

SCORERS IN EVERY ROUND

Twelve players have scored in every round of the FA Cup in one season, from opening to Final inclusive: **Archie Hunter** (Aston Villa, winners 1887); **Sandy Brown** (Tottenham, winners 1901); **Harry Hampton** (Aston Villa, winners 1905); **Harold Blackmore** (Bolton, winners 1929); **Ellis Rimmer** (Sheffield Wed, winners 1935); **Frank O'Donnell** (Preston, beaten 1937); **Stan Mortensen** (Blackpool, beaten 1948); **Jackie Milburn** (Newcastle, winners 1951); **Nat Lofthouse** (Bolton, beaten 1953); **Charlie Wayman** (Preston, beaten 1954); **Jeff Astle** (WBA, winners 1968); **Peter Osgood** (Chelsea, winners 1970).

Blackmore and the next seven completed their 'set' in the Final at Wembley; Osgood did so in the Final replay at Old Trafford.

Tony Brown became the first player to score in every round of the **League Cup**, including one in the final which WBA won 5-3 on aggregate against West Ham in 1966. The following season, the first to be contested in a single match at Wembley, Albion's Clive Clark also scored in every round, netting both goals in the 3-2 defeat by QPR in the final.

TEN IN A ROW

Dixie McNeill scored for Wrexham in ten successive FA Cup rounds (18 goals): 11 in Rounds 1-6, 1977–78; 3 in Rounds 3-4, 1978–79; 4 in Rounds 3-4, 1979–80.

Stan Mortensen (Blackpool) scored 25 goals in 16 FA Cup rounds out of 17 (1946–51).

TOP MATCH HAULS IN FA CUP

Ted MacDougall scored nine goals, a record for the competition proper, in the FA Cup first round on Nov 20, 1971, when Bournemouth beat Margate 11-0. On Nov 23, 1970 he had scored six in an 8-1 first round replay against Oxford City.

Other six-goal FA Cup scorers include **George Hilsdon** (Chelsea v Worksop, 9-1, 1907–08), **Ronnie Rooke** (Fulham v Bury, 6-0, 1938–39), **Harold Atkinson** (Tranmere v Ashington, 8-1, 1952–53), **George Best** (Manchester Utd v Northampton 1969–70, 8-2 away), **Duane Darby** (Hull v Whitby, 8-4, 1996–97).

Denis Law scored all six for Manchester City at Luton (6-2) in an FA Cup 4th round tie on Jan 28, 1961, but none of them counted – the match was abandoned (69 mins) because of a waterlogged pitch. He also scored City's goal when the match was played again, but they lost 3-1.

Tony Philliskirk scored **five** when Peterborough beat Kingstonian 9-1 in an FA Cup 1st round replay on Nov 25, 1992, but had them wiped from the records.

With the score at 3-0, the Kingstonian goalkeeper was concussed by a coin thrown from the crowd and unable to play on. The FA ordered the match to be replayed at Peterborough behind closed doors, and Kingstonian lost 1-0.

● Two players have scored **ten goals** in FA Cup preliminary round matches: **Chris Marron** for South Shields against Radcliffe in Sep 1947; **Paul Jackson** when Sheffield-based club Stocksbridge Park Steels beat Oldham Town 17-1 on Aug 31, 2002. He scored 5 in each half and all ten with his feet – goal times 6, 10, 22, 30, 34, 68, 73, 75, 79, 84 mins.

QUICKEST GOALS AND RAPID SCORING

A goal in **4 sec** was claimed by **Jim Fryatt**, for Bradford PA v Tranmere (Div 4, Apr 25, 1965), and by **Gerry Allen** for Whitstable v Danson (Kent League, Mar 3,1989). **Damian Mori** scored in **4 sec** for Adelaide v Sydney (Australian National League, December 6, 1995).

Goals after **6 sec** – **Albert Mundy** for Aldershot v Hartlepool, Oct 25, 1958; **Barrie Jones** for Notts Co v Torquay, Mar 31, 1962; **Keith Smith** for Crystal Palace v Derby, Dec 12, 1964.

9.6 sec by **John Hewitt** for Aberdeen at Motherwell, 3rd round, Jan 23, 1982 (fastest goal in Scottish Cup history).

Colin Cowperthwaite reputedly scored in **3.5 sec** for Barrow v Kettering (Alliance Premier League) on Dec 8, 1979, but the timing was unofficial.

Phil Starbuck for Huddersfield **3 sec** after entering the field as 54th min substitute at home to Wigan (Div 2) on Easter Monday, Apr 12, 1993. Corner was delayed, awaiting his arrival and he scored with a header.

Malcolm Macdonald after **5 sec** (officially timed) in Newcastle's 7-3 win in a pre-season friendly at St Johnstone on Jul 29, 1972.

World's fastest goal: 2.8 sec, direct from kick-off, Argentinian **Ricardo Olivera** for Rio Negro v Soriano (Uruguayan League), December 26, 1998.

Fastest international goal: 7 sec, Christian Benteke for Belgium v Gibraltar (World Cup qual, Faro), Oct 10, 2016.

Fastest England goals: 17 sec, Tommy Lawton v Portugal in Lisbon, May 25, 1947. **27 sec, Bryan Robson** v France in World Cup at Bilbao, Spain on Jun 16, 1982; **37 sec, Gareth Southgate** v South Africa in Durban, May 22, 2003; **30 sec, Jack Cock** v Ireland, Belfast, Oct 25, 1919; **30 sec, Bill Nicholson** v Portugal at Goodison Park, May 19, 1951. **38 sec, Bryan Robson** v Yugoslavia at Wembley, Dec 13, 1989; **42 sec, Gary Lineker** v Malaysia in Kuala Lumpur, Jun 12, 1991.

Fastest international goal by substitute: 5 sec, John Jensen for Denmark v Belgium (Euro Champ), Oct 12, 1994.

Fastest goal by England substitute: 10 sec, Teddy Sheringham v Greece (World Cup qualifier) at Old Trafford, Oct 6, 2001.

Fastest FA Cup goal: 4 sec, Gareth Morris (Ashton Utd) v Skelmersdale, 1st qual round, Sep 15, 2001.

Fastest FA Cup goal (comp proper): 9.7 sec, Jimmy Kebe for Reading v WBA, 5th Round, Feb 13, 2010.

Fastest FA Cup Final goal: 25 sec, Louis Saha for Everton v Chelsea at Wembley, May 30, 2009.

Fastest goal by substitute in FA Cup Final: 96 sec, Teddy Sheringham for Manchester Utd v Newcastle at Wembley, May 22, 1999.

Fastest League Cup Final goal: 45 sec, John Arne Riise for Liverpool v Chelsea, 2005.

Fastest goal on full League debut: 7.7 sec, Freddy Eastwood for Southend v Swansea (Lge 2), Oct 16, 2004. He went on to score hat-trick in 4-2 win.

Fastest goal in cup final: 4.07 sec, 14-year-old Owen Price for Ernest Bevin College, Tooting, beaten 3-1 by Barking Abbey in Heinz Ketchup Cup Final at Arsenal on May 18, 2000. Owen, on Tottenham's books, scored from inside his own half when the ball was played back to him from kick-off.

Fastest Premier League goals: 7.69 sec, Shane Long for Southampton v Watford, Apr 23, 2019 **9.82 sec, Ledley King** for Tottenham away to Bradford, Dec 9, 2000; **10.52 sec, Alan Shearer for** Newcastle v Manchester City, Jan 18, 2003: **10.54 sec Christian Eriksen** for Tottenham v Manchester Utd, Jan 31, 2018; **11.9 sec, Mark Viduka** for Leeds v Charlton, Mar 17, 2001, **11.90 sec. James Beattie** for Southampton at Chelsea, Aug 28, 2004; **13 sec, Chris Sutton** for Blackburn at Everton, Apr 1, 1995; **13 sec, Dwight Yorke** for Aston Villa at Coventry, Sep 30, 1995; **13 sec Asmir Begovic** (goalkeeper) for Stoke v Southampton, Nov 2, 2013; **13 sec Jay Rodriguez** for Southampton at Chelsea, Dec 1, 2013.

Fastest top-division goal: 7 sec, Bobby Langton for Preston v Manchester City (Div 1), Aug 25, 1948.

Fastest goal in Champions League: 10 sec, Roy Makaay for Bayern Munich v Real Madrid (1st ko rd), Mar 7, 2007.

Fastest Premier League goal by substitute: 9 sec, Shaun Goater, Manchester City's equaliser away to Manchester Utd (1-1), Feb 9, 2003. In Dec, 2011, Wigan's **Ben Watson** was brought off the bench to take a penalty against Stoke and scored.

Fastest goal on Premier League debut: 36 sec, Thievy Bifouma on as sub for WBA away to Crystal Palace, Feb 8, 2014.

Fastest Scottish Premiership goal: 10 sec, Kris Boyd for Kilmarnock v Ross Co, Jan 28, 2017.

Fastest-ever hat-trick: 90 sec, credited to 18-year-old **Tommy Ross** playing in a Highland match for Ross County against Nairn County on Nov 28, 1964.

Fastest goal by goalkeeper in professional football: 13 sec, Asmir Begovic for Stoke v Southampton (Prem Lge), Nov 2, 2013.

Fastest goal in Olympic Games: 14 sec, Neymar for Brazil in semi-finals v Honduras, Aug 17, 2016, Rio de Janeiro.

Fastest goal in women's football: 7 sec, Angie Harriott for Launton v Thame (Southern League, Prem Div), season 1998–99.

Fastest hat-trick in League history: 2 min 20 sec, Bournemouth's 84th-minute substitute **James**

Hayter in 6-0 home win v Wrexham (Div 2) on Feb 24, 2004 (goal times 86, 87, 88 mins).

Fastest First Division hat-tricks since war: Graham Leggat, 3 goals in 3 minutes (first half) when Fulham beat Ipswich 10-1 on Boxing Day, 1963; **Nigel Clough,** 3 goals in **4 minutes** (81, 82, 85 pen) when Nottm Forest beat QPR 4-0 on Dec 13, 1987.

Fastest Premier League hat-trick: 2 min 56 sec (13, 14, 16) by **Sadio Mane** in Southampton 6, Aston Villa 1 on May 16, 2015.

Fastest international hat-trick: 2 min 35 sec, Abdul Hamid Bassiouny for Egypt in 8-2 win over Namibia in Abdallah, Libya, (African World Cup qual), Jul 13, 2001.

Fastest international hat-trick in British matches: 3.5 min, Willie Hall for England v N Ireland at Old Trafford, Manchester, Nov 16, 1938. (Hall scored 5 in 7-0 win); **3min 30 sec, Arif Erdem** for Turkey v N Ireland, European Championship qualifier, at Windsor Park, Belfast, on Sep 4, 1999.

Fastest FA Cup hat-tricks: In 3 min, Billy Best for Southend v Brentford (2nd round, Dec 7, 1968); **2 min 20 sec,** Andy Locke for Nantwich v Droylsden (1st Qual round, Sep 9, 1995).

Fastest Scottish hat-trick: 2 min 30 sec, Ian St John for Motherwell away to Hibernian (Scottish League Cup), Aug 15, 1959.

Fastest hat-trick of headers: Dixie Dean's 5 goals in Everton's 7-2 win at home to Chelsea (Div 1) on Nov 14, 1931 included 3 headers between **5th** and **15th-min.**

Scored first kick: Billy Foulkes (Newcastle) for Wales v England at Cardiff, Oct 20, 1951, in his first international match.

Preston scored six goals in **7 min** in record 26-0 FA Cup 1st round win v Hyde, Oct 15, 1887.

Notts Co scored six second-half goals in **12 min** (Tommy Lawton 3, Jackie Sewell 3) when beating Exeter 9-0 (Div 3 South) at Meadow Lane on Oct 16, 1948.

Arsenal scored six in **18 min** (71-89 mins) in 7-1 home win (Div 1) v Sheffield Wed, Feb 15, 1992.

Tranmere scored six in first **19 min** when beating Oldham 13-4 (Div 3 North), December 26, 1935.

Sunderland scored eight in **28 min** at Newcastle (9-1 Div 1), December 5, 1908. Newcastle went on to win the title.

Southend scored all seven goals in **29 min** in 7-0 win at home to Torquay (Leyland Daf Cup, Southern quarter-final), Feb 26, 1991. Score was 0-0 until 55th minute.

Plymouth scored five in first **18 min** in 7-0 home win v Chesterfield (Div 2), Jan 3, 2004.

Five in 20 min: Frank Keetley in Lincoln's 9-1 win over Halifax in Div 3 (North), Jan 16, 1932; **Brian Dear** for West Ham v WBA (6-1, Div 1) Apr 16, 1965. **Kevin Hector** for Bradford PA v Barnsley (7-2, Div 4), Nov 20, 1965.

Four in 5 min: John McIntyre for Blackburn v Everton (Div 1), Sep 16, 1922; **WG (Billy) Richardson** for WBA v West Ham (Div 1), Nov 7, 1931.

Three in 2˙5 min: Jimmy Scarth for Gillingham v Leyton Orient (Div 3S), Nov 1, 1952.

Three in three minutes: Billy Lane for Watford v Clapton Orient (Div 3S), December 20, 1933; **Johnny Hartburn** for Leyton Orient v Shrewsbury (Div 3S), Jan 22, 1955; **Gary Roberts** for Brentford v Newport, (Freight Rover Trophy, South Final), May 17, 1985; **Gary Shaw** for Shrewsbury v Bradford City (Div 3), December 22, 1990.

Two in 9 sec: Jamie Bates with last kick of first half, **Jermaine McSporran** 9 sec into second half when Wycombe beat Peterborough 2-0 at home (Div 2) on Sep 23, 2000.

Premier League – fastest scoring: Four goals in 4 min 44 sec, Tottenham home to Southampton on Sunday, Feb 7, 1993.

Premier League – fast scoring away: When Aston Villa won 5-0 at Leicester (Jan 31, 2004), all goals scored in **18 second-half min** (50-68).

Four in 13 min by Premier League sub: Ole Gunnar Solskjaer for Manchester Utd away to Nottm Forest, Feb 6, 1999.

Five in 9 mins by substitute: Robert Lewandowski for Bayern Munich v Wolfsburg (5-1, Bundesliga), Sep 22, 2015.

FASTEST GOALS IN WORLD CUP FINAL SERIES

10.8 sec, Hakan Sukur for Turkey against South Korea in 3rd/4th-place match at Taegu, Jun 29, 2002; **15 sec, Vaclav Masek** for Czechoslovakia v Mexico (in Vina, Chile, 1962); **27 sec, Bryan Robson** for England v France (in Bilbao, Spain, 1982).

TOP MATCH SCORES SINCE WAR

By English clubs: 13-0 by Newcastle v Newport (Div 2, Oct 1946); 13-2 by Tottenham v Crewe (FA Cup 4th. Rd replay, Feb 1960); 13-0 by Chelsea v Jeunesse Hautcharage, Lux. (Cup-Winners' Cup 1st round, 2nd leg, Sep 1971).

By Scottish club: 20-0 by Stirling v Selkirk (E. of Scotland League) in Scottish Cup 1st round. (Dec 1984). That is the highest score in British first-class football since Preston beat Hyde 26-0 in FA Cup, Oct 1887.

MOST GOALS IN CALENDAR YEAR

91 by Lionel Messi in 2012 (79 Barcelona, 12 Argentina).

ROONEY'S DOUBLE TOP

Wayne Rooney ended season 2016–17 as top scorer for England (53) and Manchester Utd (253).

PREMIER LEAGUE LONGEST-RANGE GOALS BY OUTFIELD PLAYERS

66 yards: Charlie Adam (Stoke at Chelsea, Apr 4, 2015)
64 yards: Xabi Alonso (Liverpool v Newcastle, Sep 20, 2006)
62 yards: Maynor Figueroa (Wigan at Stoke, Dec 12, 2009)
60 yards: Wayne Rooney (Everton v West Ham, Nov 29, 2017)
59 yards: David Beckham (Manchester Utd at Wimbledon, Aug 17, 1996)
55 yards: Wayne Rooney (Manchester Utd at West Ham, Mar 22, 2014)

GOALS BY GOALKEEPERS

(Long clearances unless stated)

Pat Jennings for Tottenham v Manchester Utd (goalkeeper Alex Stepney), Aug 12, 1967 (FA Charity Shield).

Peter Shilton for Leicester v Southampton (Campbell Forsyth), Oct 14, 1967 (Div 1).

Ray Cashley for Bristol City v Hull (Jeff Wealands), Sep 18, 1973 (Div 2).

Steve Sherwood for Watford v Coventry (Raddy Avramovic), Jan 14, 1984 (Div 1).

Steve Ogrizovic for Coventry v Sheffield Wed (Martin Hodge), Oct 25, 1986 (Div 1).

Andy Goram for Hibernian v Morton (David Wylie), May 7, 1988 (Scot Prem Div).

Andy McLean, on Irish League debut, for Cliftonville v Linfield (George Dunlop), Aug 20, 1988.

Alan Paterson Glentoran v Linfield (George Dunlop), Nov 30, 1988 (Irish League Cup Final – only instance of goalkeeper scoring winner in a senior cup final in UK).

Ray Charles for East Fife v Stranraer (Bernard Duffy), Feb 28, 1990 (Scot Div 2).

Iain Hesford for Maidstone v Hereford (Tony Elliott), Nov 2, 1991 (Div 4).

Chris Mackenzie for Hereford v Barnet (Mark Taylor), Aug 12, 1995 (Div 3).

Peter Schmeichel for Manchester Utd v Rotor Volgograd, Sep 26, 1995 (header, UEFA Cup 1).

Mark Bosnich (Aston Villa) for Australia v Solomon Islands, Jun 11, 1997 (penalty in World Cup qual – 13-0).

Peter Keen for Carlisle away to Blackpool (goalkeeper John Kennedy), Oct 24, 2000 (Div 3).

Steve Mildenhall for Notts Co v Mansfield (Kevin Pilkington), Aug 21, 2001 (free-kick inside own half, League Cup 1).

Peter Schmeichel for Aston Villa v Everton (Paul Gerrard), Oct 20, 2001 (volley, first goalkeeper to score in Premier League).

Mart Poom for Sunderland v Derby (Andy Oakes), Sep 20, 2003 (header, Div 1).

Brad Friedel for Blackburn v Charlton (Dean Kiely), Feb 21, 2004 (shot, Prem).

Paul Robinson for Leeds v Swindon (Rhys Evans), Sep 24, 2003 (header, League Cup 2).

Andy Lonergan for Preston v Leicester (Kevin Pressman), Oct 2, 2004 (Champ).

Matt Glennon for St Johnstone away to Ross Co (Joe Malin), Mar 11, 2006 (shot, Scot Div 1).

Gavin Ward for Tranmere v Leyton Orient (Glenn Morris), Sep 2, 2006 (free-kick Lge 1).

Mark Crossley for Sheffield Wed v Southampton (Kelvin Davis), Dec 23, 2006 (header, Champ).

Paul Robinson for Tottenham v Watford (Ben Foster), Mar 17, 2007 (Prem).

Adam Federici for Reading v Cardiff (Peter Enckelman), Dec 28, 2008 (shot, Champ).

Chris Weale for Yeovil v Hereford (Peter Gulacsi), Apr 21, 2009 (header, Lge 1).
Scott Flinders for Hartlepool v Bournemouth (Shwan Jalal), Apr 30, 2011 (header, Lge 1).
Iain Turner for Preston v Notts Co (Stuart Nelson), Aug 27 2011 (shot, Lge 1).
Andy Leishman for Auchinleck v Threave (Vinnie Parker), Oct 22, 2011 (Scot Cup 2).
Tim Howard for Everton v Bolton (Adam Bogdan), Jan 4, 2012 (Prem).
Asmir Begovic for Stoke v Southampton (Artur Boruc), Nov 2, 2013 (Prem).
Mark Oxley for Hibernian v Livingston (Darren Jamieson), Aug 9, 2014 (Scot Champ).
Jesse Joronen for Stevenage v Wycombe (Matt Ingram), Oct 17, 2015 (Lge 2).
Barry Roche for Morecambe v Portsmouth (Ryan Fulton), Feb 2, 2016 (header, Lge 2).
Lewis McMinn for Brechin v Stirling (Blair Currie), Dec 7, 2019 (Scot Lge 2).
Tom King for Newport v Cheltenham (Josh Griffiths), Jan 19, 2021 (Lge 2)
Alisson for Liverpool v WBA (Sam Johnstone), May 16, 2021 (header, Prem)

MORE GOALKEEPING HEADLINES

Arthur Wilkie, sustained a hand injury in Reading's Div 3 match against Halifax on Aug 31, 1962, then played as a forward and scored twice in a 4-2 win.
Alex Stepney was Manchester Utd's joint top scorer for two months in season 1973–74 with two penalties.
Dundee Utd goalkeeper Hamish McAlpine scored three penalties in a ten-month period between 1976–77, two against Hibernian, home and away, and one against Rangers at Ibrox.
Alan Fettis scored twice for Hull in 1994–95 Div 2 season, as a substitute in 3-1 home win over Oxford Utd (Dec 17) and, when selected outfield, with last-minute winner (2-1) against Blackpool on May 6.
Roger Freestone scored for Swansea with a penalty at Oxford Utd (Div 2, Apr 30, 1995) and twice from the spot the following season against Shrewsbury (Aug 12) and Chesterfield (Aug 26).
Jimmy Glass, on loan from Swindon, kept Carlisle in the Football League on May 8, 1999. With ten seconds of stoppage-time left, he went upfield for a corner and scored the winner against Plymouth that sent Scarborough down to the Conference instead.
Paul Smith, Nottm Forest goalkeeper, was allowed to run through Leicester's defence unchallenged and score direct from the kick-off of a Carling Cup second round second match on Sep 18, 2007. It replicated the 1-0 score by which Forest had led at half-time when the original match was abandoned after Leicester defender Clive Clarke suffered a heart attack. Leicester won the tie 3-2.
Tony Roberts (Dagenham), is the only known goalkeeper to score from open play in the FA Cup, his last-minute goal at Basingstoke in the fourth qualifying round on Oct 27, 2001 earning a 2-2 draw. Dagenham won the replay 3-0 and went on to reach the third round proper.
The only known instance in first-class football in Britain of a goalkeeper scoring direct from a goal-kick was in a First Division match at Roker Park on Apr 14, 1900. The kick by Manchester City's **Charlie Williams** was caught in a strong wind and Sunderland keeper J. E Doig fumbled the ball over his line.
Jose Luis Chilavert, Paraguay's international goalkeeper, scored a hat-trick of penalties when his club Velez Sarsfield beat Ferro Carril Oeste 6-1 in the Argentine League on Nov 28, 1999. In all, he scored 8 goals in 72 internationals. He also scored with a free-kick from just inside his own half for Velez Sarsfield against River Plate on Sep 20, 2000.
Most goals by a goalkeeper in a League season: 5 (all penalties) by **Arthur Birch** for Chesterfield (Div 3 North), 1923–24.
When Brazilian goalkeeper **Rogerio Ceni** (37) converted a free-kick for Sao Paulo's winner (2-1) v Corinthians in a championship match on Mar 27, 2011, it was his 100th goal (56 free-kicks, 44 pens) in a 20-season career.

OWN GOALS

Most goals by player in one season: 5 by **Robert Stuart** (Middlesbrough) in 1934–35.
Three in match by one team: Sheffield Wed's **Vince Kenny**, **Norman Curtis** and **Eddie Gannon** in 5-4 defeat at home to WBA (Div 1) on Dec 26, 1952; Rochdale's **George Underwood**, **Kenny**

Boyle and Danny Murphy in 7-2 defeat at Carlisle (Div 3 North), Dec 25, 1954; Sunderland's Stephen Wright and Michael Proctor (2) at home to Charlton (1-3, Prem), Feb 1, 2003; Brighton's Liam Bridcutt (2) and Lewis Dunk in 6-1 FA Cup 5th rd defeat at Liverpool, Feb 19, 2012.; Sunderland's Santiago Vergini, Liam Bridcutt and Patrick van Aanholt in 8-0 defeat at Southampton (Prem), Oct 18, 2014.

One-man show: Chris Nicholl (Aston Villa) scored all four goals in 2-2 draw away to Leicester (Div 1), Mar 20, 1976 – two for his own side and two own goals.

Fastest own goals: 8 sec by Pat Kruse of Torquay, for Cambridge Utd (Div 4), Jan 3, 1977; in First Division, **16 sec** by Steve Bould (Arsenal) away to Sheffield Wed, Feb 17, 1990.

Late own-goal man: Frank Sinclair (Leicester) put through his own goal in the 90th minute of Premier League matches away to Arsenal (L1-2) and at home to Chelsea (2-2) in Aug 1999.

Half an own goal each: Chelsea's second goal in a 3-1 home win against Leicester on December 18, 1954 was uniquely recorded as 'shared own goal'. Leicester defenders Stan Milburn and Jack Froggatt, both lunging at the ball in an attempt to clear, connected simultaneously and sent it rocketing into the net.

Match of 149 own goals: When Adama, Champions of Malagasy (formerly Madagascar) won a League match 149-0 on Oct 31, 2002, all 149 were own goals scored by opponents Stade Olympique De L'Emryne. They repeatedly put the ball in their own net in protest at a refereeing decision.

MOST SCORERS IN MATCH

Liverpool set a Football League record with **eight** scorers when beating Crystal Palace 9-0 (Div 1) on Sep 12, 1989. Marksmen were: Steve Nicol (7 and 88 mins), Steve McMahon (16), Ian Rush (45), Gary Gillespie (56), Peter Beardsley (61), John Aldridge (67 pen), John Barnes (79), Glenn Hysen (82).

Fifteen years earlier, **Liverpool** had gone one better with **nine** different scorers when they achieved their record win, 11-0 at home to Stromsgodset (Norway) in the Cup-Winners' Cup 1st round, 1st leg on Sep 17, 1974.

Eight players scored for **Swansea** when they beat Sliema, Malta, 12-0 in the Cup-Winners' Cup 1st round, 1st leg on Sep 15, 1982.

Nine Stirling players scored in the 20-0 win against Selkirk in the Scottish Cup 1st Round on December 8, 1984.

Premier League record: **Seven Chelsea** scorers in 8-0 home win over Aston Villa, Dec 23, 2012. An eighth player missed a penalty.

LONG SCORING RUNS

Tom Phillipson scored in 13 consecutive matches for Wolves (Div 2) in season 1926–27, which is still an English League record. In the same season, **George Camsell** scored in 12 consecutive matches for Middlesbrough (Div 2). **Bill Prendergast** scored in 13 successive League and Cup appearances for Chester (Div 3 North) in season 1938–39.

Dixie Dean scored in 12 consecutive games (23 goals) for Everton in Div 2 in 1930–31.

Danish striker **Finn Dossing** scored in 15 consecutive matches (Scottish record) for Dundee Utd (Div 1) in 1964–65.

50-GOAL PLAYERS

With **52** goals for **Wolves** in 1987–78 (34 League, 12 Sherpa Van Trophy, 3 Littlewoods Cup, 3 FA Cup), **Steve Bull** became the first player to score 50 in a season for a League club since **Terry Bly** for Div 4 newcomers Peterborough in 1960–61. Bly's 54 comprised 52 League goals and 2 in the FA Cup, and included 7 hat-tricks, still a post-war League record. Bull was again the country's top scorer with 50 goals in season 1988–89: 37 League, 2 Littlewoods Cup and 11 Sherpa Van Trophy. Between Bly and Bull, the highest individual scoring total for a season was 49 by two players: **Ted MacDougall** (Bournemouth 1970–71, 42 League, 7 FA Cup) and **Clive Allen** (Tottenham 1986–87, 33 League, 12 Littlewoods Cup, 4 FA Cup).

HOT SHOTS

Jimmy Greaves was top Div 1 scorer (League goals) six times in 11 seasons: 32 for Chelsea (1958–59), 41 for Chelsea (1960–61) and, for Tottenham, 37 in 1962–63, 35 in 1963–64, 29 in 1964–65 (joint top) and 27 in 1968–69.

Brian Clough (Middlesbrough) was leading scorer in Div 2 in three successive seasons: 40 goals in 1957–58, 42 in 1958–59 and 39 in 1959–60.

John Hickton (Middlesbrough) was top Div 2 scorer three times in four seasons: 24 goals in 1967–68, 24 in 1969–70 and 25 in 1970–71.

MOST HAT-TRICKS

Nine by George Camsell (Middlesbrough) in Div 2, 1926–27, is the record for one season. Most League hat-tricks in career: 37 by Dixie Dean for Tranmere and Everton (1924–38).

Most top division hat-tricks in a season since last War: six by **Jimmy Greaves** for Chelsea (1960–61). **Alan Shearer** scored five hat-tricks for Blackburn in the Premier League, season 1995–96.

Frank Osborne (Tottenham) scored three consecutive hat-tricks in Div 1 in Oct–Nov 1925, against Liverpool, Leicester (away) and West Ham.

Tom Jennings (Leeds) scored hat-tricks in three successive Div 1 matches (Sep–Oct, 1926): 3 goals v Arsenal, 4 at Liverpool, 4 v Blackburn. Leeds were relegated that season.

Jack Balmer (Liverpool) scored his three hat-tricks in a 17-year career in successive Div 1 matches (Nov 1946): 3 v Portsmouth, 4 at Derby, 3 v Arsenal. No other Liverpool player scored during that 10-goal sequence by Balmer.

Gilbert Alsop scored hat-tricks in three successive matches for Walsall in Div 3 South in Apr 1939: 3 at Swindon, 3 v Bristol City and 4 v Swindon.

Alf Lythgoe scored hat-tricks in three successive games for Stockport (Div 3 North) in Mar 1934: 3 v Darlington, 3 at Southport and 4 v Wrexham.

TRIPLE HAT-TRICKS

There have been at least three **instances of 3 hat-tricks being scored for one team in a Football League match:**

Apr 21, 1909: Enoch West, Billy Hooper and **Alfred Spouncer** for Nottm Forest (12-0 v Leicester Fosse, Div 1).

Mar 3, 1962: Ron Barnes, Wyn Davies and **Roy Ambler** in Wrexham's 10-1 win against Hartlepool (Div 4).

Nov 7, 1987: Tony Adcock, Paul Stewart and **David White** for Manchester City in 10-1 win at home to Huddersfield (Div 2).

For the first time in the Premier League, **three** hat-tricks were completed on one day (Sep 23, 1995): **Tony Yeboah** for Leeds at Wimbledon; **Alan Shearer** for Blackburn v Coventry; **Robbie Fowler** with 4 goals for Liverpool v Bolton.

In the FA Cup, **Jack Carr, George Elliott** and **Walter Tinsley** each scored 3 in Middlesbrough's 9-3 first round win against Goole in Jan, 1915. **Les Allen** scored 5, **Bobby Smith** 4 and **Cliff Jones** 3 when Tottenham beat Crewe 13-2 in a fourth-round replay in Feb 1960.

HAT-TRICKS v THREE 'KEEPERS

When West Ham beat Newcastle 8-1 (Div 1) on Apr 21, 1986 **Alvin Martin** scored 3 goals against different goalkeepers: Martin Thomas injured a shoulder and was replaced, in turn, by outfield players Chris Hedworth and Peter Beardsley.

Jock Dodds of Lincoln had done the same against West Ham on Dec 18, 1948, scoring past Ernie Gregory, Tommy Moroney and George Dick in 4-3 win.

David Herd (Manchester Utd) scored against Sunderland's Jim Montgomery, Charlie Hurley and Johnny Parke in 5-0 First Division home win on Nov 26, 1966.

Brian Clark, of Bournemouth, scored against Rotherham's Jim McDonagh, Conal Gilbert and Michael Leng twice in 7-2 win (Div 3) on Oct 10, 1972.

On Oct 16, 1993 (Div 3) **Chris Pike** (Hereford) scored a hat-trick in 5-0 win over Colchester, who became the first team in league history to have two keepers sent off in the same game.

On Dec 18, 2004 (Lge 1), in 6-1 defeat at Hull, Tranmere used **John Achterberg** and **Russell Howarth,** both retired injured, and defender **Theo Whitmore.**

On Mar 9, 2008, Manchester Utd had three keepers in their 0-1 FA Cup quarter-final defeat by Portsmouth. **Tomasz Kuszczak** came on at half-time for **Edwin van der Sar** but was sent off when conceding a penalty. **Rio Ferdinand** went in goal and was beaten by Sulley Muntari's spot-kick.

Derby used three keepers in a 4-1 defeat at Reading (Mar 10, 2010, Champ). **Saul Deeney,** who took over when **Stephen Bywater** was injured, was sent off for a foul and **Robbie Savage** replaced him.

EIGHT-DAY HAT-TRICK TREBLE

Joe Bradford, of Birmingham, scored three hat-tricks in eight days in Sep 1929–30 v Newcastle (won 5-1) on the 21st, 5 for the Football League v Irish League (7-2) on the 25th, and 3 in his club's 5-7 defeat away to Blackburn on the 28th.

PREMIER LEAGUE DOUBLE HAT-TRICK

Robert Pires and **Jermaine Pennant** each scored 3 goals in Arsenal's 6-1 win at home to Southampton (May 7, 2003).

TON UP – BOTH ENDS

Manchester City are the only club to score and concede a century of League goals in the same season. When finishing fifth in the 1957–58 season, they scored 104 and gave away 100.

TOURNAMENT TOP SHOTS

Most individual goals in a World Cup Final series: 13 by **Just Fontaine** for France, in Sweden 1958. Most in European Championship Finals: 9 by **Michel Platini** for France, in France 1984.

MOST GOALS ON CLUB DEBUT

Jim Dyet scored eight in King's Park's 12-2 win against Forfar (Scottish Div 2, Jan 2, 1930). **Len Shackleton** scored six times in Newcastle's 13-0 win v Newport (Div 2, Oct 5, 1946) in the week he joined them from Bradford Park Avenue.

MOST GOALS ON LEAGUE DEBUT

Five by **George Hilsdon,** for Chelsea (9-2) v Glossop, Div 2, Sep 1, 1906. **Alan Shearer,** with three goals for Southampton (4-2) v Arsenal, Apr 9, 1988, became, at 17, the youngest player to score a First Division hat-trick on his full debut.

FOUR-GOAL SUBSTITUTE

James Collins (Swindon), sub from 60th minute, scored 4 in 5-0 home win v Portsmouth (Lge 1) on Jan 1, 2013.

CLEAN-SHEET RECORDS

On the way to promotion from Div 3 in season 1995–96, Gillingham's ever-present goalkeeper **Jim Stannard** set a clean-sheet record. In 46 matches. He achieved 29 shut-outs (17 at home, 12 away), beating the 28 by **Ray Clemence** for Liverpool (42 matches in Div 1, 1978–79) and the previous best in a 46-match programme of 28 by Port Vale (Div 3 North, 1953–54). In conceding only 20 League goals in 1995–96, Gillingham created a defensive record for the lower divisions.

Chris Woods, Rangers' England goalkeeper, set a British record in season 1986–87 by going 1,196 minutes without conceding a goal. The sequence began in the UEFA Cup match against Borussia Moenchengladbach on Nov 26, 1986 and ended when Rangers were sensationally beaten 1-0 at home by Hamilton in the Scottish Cup 3rd round on Jan 31, 1987 with a 70th-minute goal by **Adrian Sprott.** The previous British record of 1,156 minutes without a goal conceded was held by Aberdeen goalkeeper **Bobby Clark** (season 1970–01).

Manchester Utd set a new Premier League clean-sheet record of 1,333 minutes (including 14 successive match shut-outs) in season 2008–09 (Nov 15–Feb 21). **Edwin van der Sar's** personal British league record of 1,311 minutes without conceding ended when United won 2-1 at Newcastle on Mar 4, 2009.

Most clean sheets in season in top English division: **28** by **Liverpool** (42 matches) in 1978–79; **25** by **Chelsea** (38 matches) in 2004–05.

There have been three instances of clubs keeping 11 consecutive clean sheets in the Football League: **Millwall** (Div 3 South, 1925–26), **York** (Div 3, 1973–74) and **Reading** (Div 4, 1978–79). In his sequence, Reading goalkeeper **Steve Death** set the existing League shut-out record of 1,103 minutes.

Sasa Ilic remained unbeaten for over 14 hours with 9 successive shut-outs (7 in Div 1, 2 in play-offs) to equal a Charlton club record in Apr/May 1998. He had 12 clean sheets in 17 first team games after winning promotion from the reserves with 6 successive clean sheets.

Sebastiano Rossi kept a clean sheet in 8 successive away matches for AC Milan (Nov 1993–Apr 1994).

A world record of 1,275 minutes without conceding a goal was set in 1990–01 by **Abel Resino**, the Atletico Madrid goalkeeper. He was finally beaten by Sporting Gijon's Enrique in Atletico's 3-1 win on Mar 19, 1991.

In international football, the record is held by **Dino Zoff** with a shut-out for Italy (Sep 1972 to Jun 1974) lasting 1,142 minutes.

LOW SCORING

Fewest goals by any club in season in Football League: 18 by **Loughborough** (Div 2, 34 matches, 1899–1900); in 38 matches 20 by **Derby** (Prem Lge, 2007–08); in 42 matches, 24 by **Watford** (Div 2, 1971–72) and by **Stoke** (Div 1, 1984–85)); in 46-match programme, 27 by **Stockport** (Div 3, 1969–70).

Arsenal were the lowest Premier League scorers in its opening season (1992–93) with 40 goals in 42 matches, but won both domestic cup competitions. In subsequent seasons the lowest Premier League scorers were **Ipswich** (35) in 1993–94, **Crystal Palace** (34) in 1994–95, **Manchester City** (33) in 1995–96 and **Leeds** (28) in 1996–97 until **Sunderland** set the Premier League's new fewest-goals record with only 21 in 2002–03. Then, in 2007–08, **Derby** scored just 20.

LONG TIME NO SCORE

The world international non-scoring record was set by **Northern Ireland** when they played 13 matches and 1,298 minutes without a goal. The sequence began against Poland on Feb 13, 2002 and ended 2 years and 5 days later when David Healy scored against Norway (1-4) in Belfast on Feb 18, 2004.

Longest non-scoring sequences in Football League: 11 matches by **Coventry** in 1919–20 (Div 2); 11 matches in 1992–93 (Div 2) by **Hartlepool**, who after beating Crystal Palace 1-0 in the FA Cup 3rd round on Jan 2, went 13 games and 2 months without scoring (1 FA Cup, 1 Autoglass Trophy). The sequence ended after 1,227 blank minutes with a 1-1 draw at Blackpool (League) on Mar 6.

In the Premier League (Oct–Jan season 1994–95) **Crystal Palace** failed to score in nine consecutive matches.

The British non-scoring club record is held by **Stirling**: 14 consecutive matches (13 League, 1 Scottish Cup) and 1,292 minutes play, from Jan 31 1981 until Aug 8, 1981 (when they lost 4-1 to Falkirk in the League Cup).

In season 1971–72, **Mansfield** did not score in any of their first nine home games in Div 3. They were relegated on goal difference of minus two.

FA CUP CLEAN SHEETS

Most consecutive FA Cup matches without conceding a goal: 11 by **Bradford City**. The sequence spanned 8 rounds, from 3rd in 1910–11 to 4th. Round replay in 1911–12, and included winning the Cup in 1911.

GOALS THAT WERE WRONGLY GIVEN

Tottenham's last-minute winner at home to Huddersfield (Div 1) on Apr 2, 1952: Eddie Baily's corner-kick struck referee WR Barnes in the back, and the ball rebounded to Baily, who crossed for Len Duquemin to head into the net. Baily had infringed the Laws by playing the ball twice, but the result (1-0) stood. Those two points helped Spurs to finish Championship runners-up; Huddersfield were relegated.

The second goal (66 mins) in **Chelsea's** 2-1 home win v Ipswich (Div 1) on Sep 26, 1970: Alan Hudson's shot hit the stanchion on the outside of goal and the ball rebounded on to the pitch. But instead of the goal-kick, referee Roy Capey gave a goal, on a linesman's confirmation. TV pictures proved otherwise. The Football League quoted from the Laws of the Game: 'The referee's decision on all matters is final.'

When **Watford's** John Eustace and **Reading's** Noel Hunt challenged for a 13th minute corner at Vicarage Road on Sep 20, 2008, the ball was clearly diverted wide. But referee Stuart Attwell signalled for a goal on the instruction of his assistant and it went down officially as a Eustace own goal. The Championship match ended 2-2.

Sunderland's 1-0 Premier League win over **Liverpool** on Oct 17, 2009 was decided by one of the most bizarre goals in football history when Darren Bent's shot struck a red beach ball thrown from the crowd and wrong-footed goalkeeper Jose Reina. Referee Mike Jones wrongly allowed it to stand. The Laws of the Game state: 'An outside agent interfering with play should result in play being stopped and restarted with a drop ball.'

Blackburn's 59th minute equaliser (2-2) in 3-3 draw away to Wigan (Prem) on Nov 19, 2011 was illegal. Morten Gamst Pedersen played the ball to himself from a corner and crossed for Junior Hoilett to net.

The Republic of Ireland were deprived of the chance of a World Cup place in the second leg of their play-off with France on Nov 18, 2009. They were leading 1-0 in Paris when Thierry Henry blatantly handled before setting up William Gallas to equalise in extra-time time and give his side a 2-1 aggregate victory. The FA of Ireland's call for a replay was rejected by FIFA.

• The most notorious goal in World Cup history was fisted in by Diego Maradona in **Argentina's** 2-1 quarter-final win over England in Mexico City on Jun 22, 1986.

ATTENDANCES

GREATEST WORLD CROWDS

World Cup, Maracana Stadium, Rio de Janeiro, Jul 16, 1950. Final match (Brazil v Uruguay) attendance 199,850; receipts £125,000.

Total attendance in three matches (including play-off) between Santos (Brazil) and AC Milan for the Inter-Continental Cup (World Club Championship) 1963, exceeded 375,000.

BRITISH RECORD CROWDS

Most to pay: 149,547, Scotland v England, at Hampden Park, Glasgow, Apr 17, 1937. This was the first all-ticket match in Scotland (receipts £24,000).

At Scottish FA Cup Final: 146,433, Celtic v Aberdeen, at Hampden Park, Apr 24, 1937. Estimated another 20,000 shut out.

For British club match (apart from a Cup Final): 143,470, Rangers v Hibernian, at Hampden Park, Mar 27, 1948 (Scottish Cup semi-final).

FA Cup Final: 126,047, Bolton v West Ham, Apr 28, 1923. Estimated 150,000 in ground at opening of Wembley Stadium.

New Wembley: 89,874, FA Cup Final, Cardiff v Portsmouth, May 17, 2008.

World Cup Qualifying ties: 120,000, Cameroon v Morocco, Yaounde, Nov 29, 1981; 107,580, Scotland v Poland, Hampden Park, Oct 13, 1965.

European Cup: 135,826, Celtic v Leeds (semi-final, 2nd leg) at Hampden Park, Apr 15, 1970.

European Cup Final: 127,621, Real Madrid v Eintracht Frankfurt, at Hampden Park, May 18, 1960.

European Cup-Winners' Cup Final: 100,000, West Ham v TSV Munich, at Wembley, May 19, 1965.

Scottish League: 118,567, Rangers v Celtic, Jan 2, 1939.

Scottish League Cup Final: 107,609, Celtic v Rangers, at Hampden Park, Oct 23, 1965.
Football League old format: First Div: 83,260, Manchester Utd v Arsenal, Jan 17, 1948 (at Maine Road); **Div 2** 70,302 Tottenham v Southampton, Feb 25, 1950; **Div 3S:** 51,621, Cardiff v Bristol City, Apr 7, 1947; **Div 3N:** 49,655, Hull v Rotherham, Dec 25, 1948; **Div 3:** 49,309, Sheffield Wed v Sheffield Utd, Dec 26, 1979; **Div 4:** 37,774, Crystal Palace v Millwall, Mar 31, 1961.
Premier League: 83,222, Tottenham v Arsenal (Wembley), Feb 10, 2018
Football League – New Div 1: 41,214, Sunderland v Stoke, Apr 25, 1998; **New Div 2:** 32,471, Manchester City v York, May 8, 1999; **New Div 3:** 22,319, Hull v Hartlepool Utd, Dec 26, 2002. **New Champs:** 52,181, Newcastle v Ipswich, Apr 24, 2010; **New Lge 1:** 46,039, Sunderland v Bradford, Dec 26, 2018; **New Lge 2:** 28,343, Coventry v Accrington, Feb 10, 2018.
In English Provinces: 84,569, Manchester City v Stoke (FA Cup 6), Mar 3, 1934.
Record for Under-21 International: 55,700, England v Italy, first match at New Wembley, Mar 24, 2007.
Record for friendly match: 104,679, Rangers v Eintracht Frankfurt, at Hampden Park, Glasgow, Oct 17, 1961.
FA Youth Cup: 38,187, Arsenal v Manchester Utd, at Emirates Stadium, Mar 14, 2007.
Record Football League aggregate (season): 41,271,414 (1948–49) – 88 clubs.
Record Football League aggregate (single day): 1,269,934, December 27, 1949, previous day, 1,226,098.
Record average home League attendance for season: 75,691 by Manchester Utd in 2007–08.
Long-ago League attendance aggregates: 10,929,000 in 1906–07 (40 clubs); 28,132,933 in 1937–38 (88 clubs).
Last 1m crowd aggregate, League (single day): 1,007,200, December 27, 1971.
Record Amateur match attendance: 100,000 for FA Amateur Cup Final, Pegasus v Harwich & Parkeston at Wembley, Apr 11, 1953.
Record Cup-tie aggregate: 265,199, at two matches between Rangers and Morton, in Scottish Cup Final, 1947–48.
Abandoned match attendance records: In England – 63,480 at Newcastle v Swansea City FA Cup 3rd round, Jan 10, 1953, abandoned 8 mins (0-0), fog.
In Scotland: 94,596 at Scotland v Austria (4-1), Hampden Park, May 8, 1963. Referee Jim Finney ended play (79 minutes) after Austria had two players sent off and one carried off.
Colchester's record crowd (19,072) was for the FA Cup 1st round tie v Reading on Nov 27, 1948, abandoned 35 minutes (0-0), fog.

SMALLEST CROWDS

Smallest League attendances: 450 Rochdale v Cambridge Utd (Div 3, Feb 5, 1974); 469, Thames v Luton (Div 3 South, December 6, 1930).
Only 13 people paid to watch Stockport v Leicester (Div 2, May 7, 1921) at Old Trafford, but up to 2,000 stayed behind after Manchester Utd v Derby earlier in the day. Stockport's ground was closed.
Lowest Premier League crowd: 3,039 for Wimbledon v Everton, Jan 26, 1993 (smallest top-division attendance since War).
Lowest Saturday post-war top-division crowd: 3,231 for Wimbledon v Luton, Sep 7, 1991 (Div 1).
Lowest Football League crowds, new format – Div 1: 849 for Wimbledon v Rotherham, (Div 1) Oct 29, 2002 (smallest attendance in top two divisions since War); 1,054 Wimbledon v Wigan (Div 1), Sep 13, 2003 in club's last home match when sharing Selhurst Park; **Div 2:** 1,077, Hartlepool Utd v Cardiff, Mar 22, 1994; **Div 3:** 739, Doncaster v Barnet, Mar 3, 1998.
Lowest top-division crowd at a major ground since the war: 4,554 for Arsenal v Leeds (May 5, 1966) – fixture clashed with live TV coverage of Cup-Winners' Cup Final (Liverpool v Borussia Dortmund).
Smallest League Cup attendances: 612, Halifax v Tranmere (1st round, 2nd leg) Sep 6, 2000; 664, Wimbledon v Rotherham (3rd round), Nov 5, 2002.
Smallest League Cup attendance at top-division ground: 1,987 for Wimbledon v Bolton (2nd Round, 2nd Leg) Oct 6, 1992.

Smallest Wembley crowds for England matches: 15,628 v Chile (Rous Cup, May 23, 1989 – affected by Tube strike); 20,038 v Colombia (Friendly, Sep 6, 1995); 21,432 v Czech. (Friendly, Apr 25, 1990); 21,142 v Japan (Umbro Cup, Jun 3, 1995); 23,600 v Wales (British Championship, Feb 23, 1983); 23,659 v Greece (Friendly, May 17, 1994); 23,951 v East Germany (Friendly, Sep 12, 1984); 24,000 v N Ireland (British Championship, Apr 4, 1984); 25,756 v Colombia (Rous Cup, May 24, 1988); 25,837 v Denmark (Friendly, Sep 14, 1988).

Smallest international modern crowds: 221 for Poland v N Ireland (4-1, friendly) at Limassol, Cyprus, on Feb 13, 2002. Played at neutral venue at Poland's World Cup training base. 265 (all from N Ireland) at their Euro Champ qual against Serbia in Belgrade on Mar 25, 2011. Serbia ordered by UEFA to play behind closed doors because of previous crowd trouble.

Smallest international modern crowds at home: N Ireland: 2,500 v Chile (Belfast, May 26, 1989 – clashed with ITV live screening of Liverpool v Arsenal Championship decider); Scotland: 7,843 v N Ireland (Hampden Park, May 6, 1969); Wales: 2,315 v N Ireland (Wrexham, May 27, 1982).

Smallest attendance for post-war England match: 2,378 v San Marino (World Cup) at Bologna (Nov 17, 1993). Tie clashed with Italy v Portugal (World Cup) shown live on Italian TV.

Lowest England attendance at New Wembley: 40,181 v Norway (friendly), Sep 3, 2014

Smallest paid attendance for British first-class match: 29 for Clydebank v East Stirling, CIS Scottish League Cup 1st round, Jul 31, 1999. Played at Morton's Cappielow Park ground, shared by Clydebank. Match clashed with the Tall Ships Race which attracted 200,000 to the area.

FA CUP CROWD RECORD (OUTSIDE FINAL)

The first FA Cup-tie shown on closed-circuit TV (5th round, Saturday, Mar 11, 1967, kick-off 7pm) drew a total of 105,000 spectators to Goodison Park and Anfield. At Goodison, 64,851 watched the match 'for real', while 40,149 saw the TV version on eight giant screens at Anfield. Everton beat Liverpool 1-0.

LOWEST SEMI-FINAL CROWD

The smallest FA Cup semi-final attendance since the War was 17,987 for the Manchester Utd–Crystal Palace replay at Villa Park on Apr 12, 1995. Palace supporters largely boycotted tie after a fan died in car-park clash outside pub in Walsall before first match.

Previous lowest: 25,963 for Wimbledon v Luton, at Tottenham on Apr 9, 1988.

Lowest quarter-final crowd since the war: 8,735 for Chesterfield v Wrexham on Mar 9, 1997.

Smallest FA Cup 3rd round attendances for matches between League clubs: 1,833 for Chester v Bournemouth (at Macclesfield) Jan 5, 1991; 1,966 for Aldershot v Oxford Utd, Jan 10, 1987.

PRE-WEMBLEY CUP FINAL CROWDS

AT CRYSTAL PALACE

1895	42,560	1902	48,036	1908	74,967
1896	48,036	Replay	33,050	1909	67,651
1897	65,891	1903	64,000	1910	76,980
1898	62,017	1904	61,734	1911	69,098
1899	73,833	1905	101,117	1912	54,434
1900	68,945	1906	75,609	1913	120,028
1901	110,802	1907	84,584	1914	72,778

AT OLD TRAFFORD

1915   50,000

AT STAMFORD BRIDGE

1920	50,018	1921	72,805	1922	53,000

England women's record crowd: 77,768 v Germany, 1-2 (Wembley, Nov 9, 2019).

INTERNATIONAL RECORDS

MOST APPEARANCES

Steven Davis became the most capped British player when captaining Northern Ireland in a World Cup qualifier against Bulgaria at Windsor Park on Mar 31, 2021. The 36-year-old Rangers midfielder overtook former England goalkeeper **Peter Shilton**'s record of 125 appearances which had stood since 1990. Davis won his first cap against Canada in 2005, when playing for Aston Villa, and was made captain by manager Nigel Worthington in his 50th international in 2011.

Nine players have completed a century of appearances in full international matches for England. **Billy Wright** of Wolves, was the first, retiring in 1959 with a total of 105 caps. **Bobby Charlton**, of Manchester Utd, beat Wright's record in the World Cup match against West Germany in Leon, Mexico, in Jun 1970 and **Bobby Moore**, of West Ham, overtook Charlton's 106 caps against Italy in Turin, in Jun 1973. Moore played 108 times for England, a record that stood until **Shilton** reached 109 against Denmark in Copenhagen (Jun 7, 1989). In season 2008–09, **David Beckham** (LA Galaxy/AC Milan) overtook Moore as England's most-capped outfield player. In the vastly different selection processes of their eras, Moore played 108 full games for his country, whereas Beckham's total of 115 to the end of season 2009–10, included 58 part matches, 14 as substitute and 44 times substituted. **Steven Gerrard** won his 100th cap against Sweden in Stockholm on Nov 14, 2012 and **Ashley Cole** reached 100 appearances against Brazil at Wembley on Feb 6, 2013. **Frank Lampard** played his 100th game against Ukraine in Kiev (World Cup qual) on Sep 10, 2013. **Wayne Rooney**'s 100th appearance was against Slovenia at Wembley (Euro Champ qual) on Nov 15, 2014.

Robbie Keane won his 126th Republic of Ireland cap, overtaking Shay Given's record, In a World Cup qualifier against the Faroe Islands on Jun 7, 2013. Keane scored all his team's goals in a 3-0 win.

Kenny Dalglish became Scotland's first 100-cap international v Romania (Hampden Park, Mar 26, 1986).

World's most-capped player: Ahmed Hassan, 184 for Egypt (1995–2012).

Most-capped European player: Vitalijs Astafjevs, 167 for Latvia (1992–2010).

Most-capped European goalkeeper: Thomas Ravelli, 143 Internationals for Sweden (1981–97).

BRITAIN'S MOST-CAPPED PLAYERS

(As at start of season 2021–22)

England		Alex McLeish	77	Pat Jennings	119
Peter Shilton	125	Paul McStay	76	Aaron Hughes	112
Wayne Rooney	120	Tommy Boyd	72	David Healy	95
David Beckham	115			Mal Donaghy	91
Steven Gerrard	114	**Wales**		Jonny Evans	91
Bobby Moore	108	Chris Gunter	102	Sammy McIlroy	88
Ashley Cole	107	Gareth Bale	96	Maik Taylor	88
Bobby Charlton	106	Wayne Hennessey	96		
Frank Lampard	106	Neville Southall	92	**Republic of Ireland**	
Billy Wright	105	Ashley Williams	86	Robbie Keane	146
		Gary Speed	85	Shay Given	134
Scotland		Craig Bellamy	78	John O'Shea	118
Kenny Dalglish	102	Joe Ledley	77	Kevin Kilbane	110
Jim Leighton	91			Steve Staunton	102
Darren Fletcher	80	**Northern Ireland**		Damien Duff	1002
		Steven Davis	126		

ENGLAND'S MOST-CAPPED PLAYER (either gender)

Fara Williams made 172 appearances for the England women's team. The midfielder played in three World Cups and four European Championships in a 20-year career. She retired, aged 37, at the end of the 2020–21 season.

MOST ENGLAND CAPS IN ROW

Most consecutive international appearances: 70 by **Billy Wright,** for England from Oct 1951 to May 1959. He played 105 of England's first 108 post-war matches.

England captains most times: Billy Wright and **Bobby Moore,** 90 each.

England captains – 4 in match (v Serbia & Montenegro at Leicester Jun 3, 2003): **Michael Owen** was captain for the first half and after the interval the armband passed to **Emile Heskey** (for 15 minutes), **Phil Neville** (26 minutes) and substitute **Jamie Carragher** (9 minutes, including time added).

MOST SUCCESSIVE ENGLAND WINS

10 (Jun 1908–Jun 1909. Modern: 8 (Oct 2005–Jun 2006).

ENGLAND'S LONGEST UNBEATEN RUN

19 matches (16 wins, 3 draws), Nov 1965–Nov 1966.

ENGLAND'S TALLEST

At **6ft 7in,** Peter Crouch became England's tallest-ever international when he made his debut against Colombia in New Jersey, USA on May 31, 2005.

MOST PLAYERS FROM ONE CLUB IN ENGLAND SIDES

Arsenal supplied seven men (a record) to the England team v Italy at Highbury on Nov 14, 1934. They were: Frank Moss, George Male, Eddie Hapgood, Wilf Copping, Ray Bowden, Ted Drake and Cliff Bastin. In addition, Arsenal's Tom Whittaker was England's trainer.

Since then until 2001, the most players from one club in an England team was six from **Liverpool** against Switzerland at Wembley in Sep 1977. The side also included a Liverpool old boy, Kevin Keegan (Hamburg).

Seven **Arsenal** men took part in the England – France (0-2) match at Wembley on Feb 10, 1999. Goalkeeper David Seaman and defenders Lee Dixon, Tony Adams and Martin Keown lined up for England. Nicolas Anelka (2 goals) and Emmanuel Petit started the match for France and Patrick Vieira replaced Anelka.

Manchester Utd equalled Arsenal's 1934 record by providing England with seven players in the World Cup qualifier away to Albania on Mar 28, 2001. Five started the match – David Beckham (captain), Gary Neville, Paul Scholes, Nicky Butt and Andy Cole – and two went on as substitutes: Wes Brown and Teddy Sheringham.

INTERNATIONAL SUBS RECORDS

Malta substituted all 11 players in their 1-2 home defeat against England on Jun 3, 2000. Six substitutes by England took the total replacements in the match to 17, then an international record.

Most substitutions in match by **England:** 11 in second half by Sven-Goran Eriksson against Holland at Tottenham on Aug 15, 2001; 11 against Italy at Leeds on Mar 27, 2002; Italy sent on 8 players from the bench – the total of 19 substitutions was then a record for an England match; 11 against Australia at Upton Park on Feb 12, 2003 (entire England team changed at half-time); 11 against Iceland at City of Manchester Stadium on Jun 5, 2004.

Forty three players, a record for an England match, were used in the international against Serbia & Montenegro at Leicester on Jun 3, 2003. England sent on 10 substitutes in the second half and their opponents changed all 11 players.

The **Republic of Ireland** sent on 12 second-half substitutes, using 23 players in all, when they beat Russia 2-0 in a friendly international in Dublin on Feb 13, 2002.

First England substitute: Wolves winger **Jimmy Mullen** replaced injured Jackie Milburn (15 mins) away to Belgium on May 18, 1950. He scored in a 4-1 win.

ENGLAND'S WORLD CUP-WINNERS

At Wembley, Jul 30, 1966, 4-2 v West Germany (2-2 after 90 mins), scorers Hurst 3, Peters. Team: Banks; Cohen, Wilson, Stiles, Jack Charlton, Moore (capt), Ball, Hurst, Bobby Charlton, Hunt, Peters. Manager **Alf Ramsey** fielded that same eleven in six successive matches (an

England record): the World Cup quarter-final, semi-final and Final, and the first three games of the following season. England wore red shirts in the Final and The Queen presented the Cup to Bobby Moore. The players each received a £1,000 bonus, plus £60 World Cup Final appearance money, all less tax, and Ramsey a £6,000 bonus from the FA The match was shown live on TV (in black and white).

England's non-playing 'reserves' – there were no substitutes – also received the £1,000 bonus, but no medals. That remained the case until FIFA finally decided that non-playing members and staff of World Cup-winning squads should be given replica medals. England's 'forgotten heroes' received theirs at a reception in Downing Street on June 10, 2009 and were later guests of honour at the World Cup qualifier against Andorra at Wembley. The 11 'reserves' were: Springett, Bonetti, Armfield, Byrne, Flowers, Hunter, Paine, Connelly, Callaghan, Greaves, Eastham. Jimmy Greaves played in all three group games, against Uruguay, Mexico and France. John Connelly was in the team against Uruguay, Terry Paine against Mexico and Ian Callaghan against France.

BRAZIL'S RECORD RUN

Brazil hold the record for the longest unbeaten sequence in international football: 45 matches from 1993–97. The previous record of 31 was held by Hungary between Jun 1950 and Jul 1954.

ENGLAND MATCHES ABANDONED

May 17, 1953 v **Argentina** (Friendly, Buenos Aires) after 23 mins (0-0) – rain.
Oct 29, 1975 v **Czechoslovakia** (Euro Champ qual, Bratislava) after 17 mins (0-0) – fog. Played next day.
Feb 15, 1995 v **Rep of Ireland** (Friendly, Dublin) after 27 mins (1-0) – crowd disturbance.

ENGLAND POSTPONEMENTS

Nov 21, 1979 v **Bulgaria** (Euro Champ qual, Wembley, postponed for 24 hours – fog; Aug 10, 2011 v **Holland** (friendly), Wembley, postponed after rioting in London.
Oct 16, 2012 v **Poland** (World Cup qual, Warsaw) postponed to next day – pitch waterlogged.
The friendly against **Honduras** (Miami, Jun 7, 2014) was suspended midway through the first half for 44 minutes – thunderstorm.

ENGLAND UNDER COVER

England played indoors for the first time when they beat Argentina 1-0 in the World Cup at the Sapporo Dome, Japan, on Jun 7, 2002.

ALL-SEATED INTERNATIONALS

The first **all-seated crowd** (30,000) for a full international in Britain saw **Wales** and **West Germany** draw 0-0 at Cardiff Arms Park on May 31, 1989. The terraces were closed.
England's first all-seated international at Wembley was against Yugoslavia (2-1) on December 13, 1989 (attendance 34,796). The terracing behind the goals was closed for conversion to seating.
The first **full-house all-seated** international at Wembley was for England v Brazil (1-0) on Mar 28, 1990, when a capacity 80,000 crowd paid record British receipts of £1,200,000.

MOST NEW CAPS IN ENGLAND TEAM

6, by Sir Alf Ramsey (v Portugal, Apr 3, 1974) and **by Sven-Goran Eriksson** (v Australia, Feb 12, 2003; 5 at half-time when 11 changes made).

PLAYED FOR MORE THAN ONE COUNTRY

Multi-nationals in senior international football include: **Johnny Carey** (1938–53) – caps Rep of Ireland 29, N Ireland 7; **Ferenc Puskas** (1945–62) – caps Hungary 84, Spain 4; **Alfredo di Stefano** (1950–56) – caps Argentina 7, Spain 31; **Ladislav Kubala** (1948–58) – caps, Hungary 3, Czechoslovakia 11, Spain 19, only player to win full international honours with 3 countries. Kubala also played in a fourth international team, scoring twice for FIFA v England at Wembley in 1953. Eleven players, including **Carey**, appeared for both N Ireland and the Republic of Ireland in seasons directly after the last war.

Cecil Moore, capped by N Ireland in 1949 when with Glentoran, played for USA v England in 1953.

Hawley Edwards played for England v Scotland in 1874 and for Wales v Scotland in 1876.

Jack Reynolds (Distillery and WBA) played for both Ireland (5 times) and England (8) in the 1890s.

Bobby Evans (Sheffield Utd) had played 10 times for Wales when capped for England, in 1910–11. He was born in Chester of Welsh parents.

In recent years, several players have represented USSR and one or other of the breakaway republics. The same applies to Yugoslavia and its component states. **Josip Weber** played for Croatia in 1992 and made a 5-goal debut for Belgium in 1994.

THREE-GENERATION INTERNATIONAL FAMILY

When Bournemouth striker **Warren Feeney** was capped away to Liechtenstein on Mar 27, 2002, he became the third generation of his family to play for Northern Ireland. He followed in the footsteps of his grandfather James (capped twice in 1950) and father Warren snr. (1 in 1976).

FATHERS & SONS CAPPED BY ENGLAND

George Eastham senior (pre-war) and **George Eastham junior**; **Brian Clough** and **Nigel Clough**; **Frank Lampard snr** and **Frank Lampard jnr**; **Mark Chamberlain** and **Alex Oxlade-Chamberlain**; **Ian Wright** and **Shaun Wright-Phillips**.

FATHER & SON SAME-DAY CAPS

Iceland made father-and-son international history when they beat Estonia 3-0 in Tallin on Apr 24, 1996. **Arnor Gudjohnsen** (35) started the match and was replaced (62 mins) by his 17-year-old son **Eidur**.

LONGEST UNBEATEN START TO ENGLAND CAREER

Steven Gerrard, 21 matches (W16, D5) 2000–03.

SUCCESSIVE ENGLAND HAT-TRICKS

The last player to score a hat-trick in consecutive England matches was **Dixie Dean** on the summer tour in May 1927, against Belgium (9-1) and Luxembourg (5-2).

MOST GOALS BY PLAYER v ENGLAND

4 by Zlatan Ibrahimovic (Sweden 4 England 2, Stockholm, Nov 14, 2012).

POST-WAR HAT-TRICKS v ENGLAND

Nov 25, 1953, **Nandor Hidegkuti** (England 3, Hungary 6, Wembley); May 11, 1958, **Aleksandar Petakovic** (Yugoslavia 5, England 0, Belgrade); May 17, 1959, **Juan Seminario** (Peru 4, England 1, Lima); Jun 15, 1988, **Marco van Basten** (Holland 3, England 1, European Championship, Dusseldorf). Six other players scored hat-tricks against England (1878–1930).

NO-SAVE GOALKEEPERS

Chris Woods did not have one save to make when England beat San Marino 6-0 (World Cup) at Wembley on Feb 17, 1993. He touched the ball only six times.

Gordon Banks had a similar no-save experience when England beat Malta 5-0 (European Championship) at Wembley on May 12, 1971. Malta did not force a goal-kick or corner, and the four times Banks touched the ball were all from back passes.

Robert Green was also idle in the 6-0 World Cup qualifying win over Andorra at Wembley on Jun 10, 2009.

Joe Hart was untroubled in England's 5-0 win over San Marino in a World Cup qualifier at Wembley on Oct 12, 2012.

WORLD/EURO MEMBERS

FIFA has 211 member countries, **UEFA** 55

NEW FIFA PRESIDENT

The 18-year reign of FIFA president **Sepp Blatter** ended in December 2015 amid widespread allegations of corruption. He was replaced in February 2016 by Gianni Infantino, a 45-year-old Swiss-Italian lawyer, who was previously general secretary of UEFA. Under new rules, he will serve four years.

FIFA WORLD YOUTH CUP (UNDER-20)

Finals: 1977 (Tunis) Soviet Union 2 Mexico 2 (Soviet won 9-8 on pens.); **1979** (Tokyo) Argentina 3 Soviet Union 1; **1981** (Sydney) W Germany 4 Qatar 0; **1983** (Mexico City) Brazil 1 Argentina 0; **1985** (Moscow) Brazil 1 Spain 0; **1987** (Santiago) Yugoslavia 1 W Germany 1 (Yugoslavia won 5-4 on pens.); **1989** (Riyadh) Portugal 2 Nigeria 0; **1991** (Lisbon) Portugal 0 Brazil 0 (Portugal won 4-2 on pens.); **1993** (Sydney) Brazil 2 Ghana 1; **1995** (Qatar) Argentina 2 Brazil 0; **1997** (Kuala Lumpur) Argentina 2 Uruguay 1; **1999** (Lagos) Spain 4 Japan 0; **2001** (Buenos Aires) Argentina 3 Ghana 0; **2003** (Dubai) Brazil 1 Spain 0; **2005** (Utrecht) Argentina 2 Nigeria 1; **2007** (Toronto) Argentina 2 Czech Republic 1; **2009** (Cairo) Ghana 0 Brazil 0 (aet, Ghana won 4-3 on pens); **2011** (Bogota) Brazil 3 Portugal 2 (aet); **2013** (Istanbul) France 0 Uruguay 0 (aet, France won 4-1 on pens), **2015** (Auckland) Serbia 2 Brazil 1 (aet); **2017** (Suwon) England 1 Venezuela 0; **2019** (Lodz) Ukraine 3 South Korea 1. **2021** Tournament cancelled.

FAMOUS CLUB FEATS

Manchester City won the 2017–18 Premier League title under Pep Guardiola in record style. They became England's first champions to total 100 points and had the longest winning streak, 18 matches, in top-flight history. There were other new Premier League marks for goals scored (106), goal difference (79), overall wins (32), away victories (16), and for a 19-point gap to second-place. In season 2018–19, City made history with a domestic treble, winning the Premier League, FA Cup and League Cup. On their way to the 2020–21 title, City set a top-flight record of 21 straight wins in all competitions and a record for the top four tiers of English football with a 12 successive Premier League away victories.

Arsenal created an all-time English League record sequence of 49 unbeaten Premier League matches (W36, D13), spanning 3 seasons, from May 7, 2003 until losing 2-0 away to Manchester Utd on Oct 24, 2004. It included all 38 games in season 2003–04.

The Double: There have been 11 instances of a club winning the Football League/Premier League title and the FA Cup in the same season. Preston 1888–89; Aston Villa 1896–97; **Tottenham** 1960–61; **Arsenal** 1970–71, 1997–98, 2001–02; **Liverpool** 1985–86; **Manchester Utd** 1993–94, 1995–96, 1998–99; **Chelsea** 2009–10.

The Treble: Liverpool were the first English club to win three major competitions in one season when in 1983–84, Joe Fagan's first season as manager, they were League Champions, League Cup winners and European Cup winners.

Sir Alex Ferguson's **Manchester Utd** achieved an even more prestigious treble in 1998–99, completing the domestic double of Premier League and FA Cup and then winning the European Cup. In season 2008–09, they completed another major triple success – Premier League, Carling Cup and World Club Cup.

Liverpool completed a unique treble by an English club with three cup successes under Gerard Houllier in season 2000–01: the League Cup, FA Cup and UEFA Cup.

Liverpool the first English club to win five major trophies in one calendar year (Feb– Aug 2001): League Cup, FA Cup, UEFA Cup, Charity Shield, UEFA Super Cup.

As Champions in season 2001–02, **Arsenal** set a Premier League record by winning the last 13 matches. They were the first top-division club since Preston in the League's inaugural season (1888–89) to maintain an unbeaten away record.

(See Scottish section for treble feats by Rangers and Celtic).

Record Home Runs: Liverpool went 85 competitive first-team games unbeaten at home between losing 2-3 to Birmingham on Jan 21, 1978 and 1-2 to Leicester on Jan 31, 1981. They comprised 63 in the League, 9 League Cup, 7 in European competition and 6 FA Cup.

Chelsea hold the record unbeaten home League sequence of 86 matches (W62, D24) between losing 1-2 to Arsenal, Feb 21, 2004, and 0-1 to Liverpool, Oct 26, 2008.

Third to First: Charlton, in 1936, became the first club to advance from the Third to First Division in successive seasons. **Queens Park Rangers** were the second club to achieve the feat in 1968, and **Oxford Utd** did it in 1984 and 1985 as Champions of each division. Subsequently, **Derby** (1987), **Middlesbrough** (1988), **Sheffield Utd** (1990) and **Notts Co** (1991) climbed from Third Division to First in consecutive seasons.

Watford won successive promotions from the modern Second Division to the Premier League in 1997–98, 1998–99. **Manchester City** equalled the feat in 1998–99, 1999–2000. **Norwich** climbed from League 1 to the Premier League in seasons 2009–10, 2010–11. **Southampton** did the same in 2010–11 and 2011–12.

Fourth to First: Northampton, in 1965 became the first club to rise from the Fourth to the First Division. **Swansea** climbed from the Fourth Division to the First (three promotions in four seasons), 1977–78 to 1980–81. **Wimbledon** repeated the feat, 1982–83 to 1985–86 **Watford** did it in five seasons, 1977–8 to 1981–82. **Carlisle** climbed from Fourth Division to First, 1964–74.

Non-League to First: When **Wimbledon** finished third in the Second Division in 1986, they completed the phenomenal rise from non-League football (Southern League) to the First Division in nine years. Two years later they won the FA Cup.

Tottenham, in 1960–61, not only carried off the First Division Championship and the FA Cup for the first time that century but set up other records by opening with 11 successive wins, registering most First Division wins (31), most away wins in the League's history (16), and equalling Arsenal's First Division records of 66 points and 33 away points. They already held the Second Division record of 70 points (1919–20).

Arsenal, in 1993, became the first club to win both English domestic cup competitions (FA Cup and League Cup) in the same season. **Liverpool** repeated the feat in 2001. **Chelsea** did it in 2007.

Chelsea achieved the FA Cup/Champions League double in May 2012.

Preston, in season 1888–89, won the first League Championship without losing a match and the FA Cup without having a goal scored against them. Only other English clubs to remain unbeaten through a League season were **Liverpool** (Div 2 Champions in 1893–94) and **Arsenal** (Premier League Champions 2003–04).

Bury, in 1903, also won the FA Cup without conceding a goal.

Everton won Div 2, Div 1 and the FA Cup in successive seasons, 1930–31, 1931–32, 1932–33.

Wolves won the League Championship in 1958 and 1959 and the FA Cup in 1960.

Liverpool won the title in 1964, the FA Cup in 1965 and the title again in 1966. In 1978 they became the first British club to win the European Cup in successive seasons. Nottm Forest repeated the feat in 1979 and 1980.

Liverpool won the League Championship six times in eight seasons (1976–83) under **Bob Paisley's** management.

Sir Alex Ferguson's **Manchester Utd** won the Premier League in 13 of its 21 seasons (1992–2013). They were runners-up five times and third three times.

FA CUP/PROMOTION DOUBLE

WBA are the only club to achieve this feat in the same season (1930–31).

COVENTRY UNIQUE

Coventry are the only club to have played at every top level – the Premier League, Championship, League's One and Two, the old Divisions One, Two, Three and Four and the old Division Three North and South.

FAMOUS UPS & DOWNS

Sunderland: Relegated in 1958 after maintaining First Division status since their election to the Football League in 1890. They dropped into Division 3 for the first time in 1987.

Aston Villa: Relegated with Preston to the Third Division in 1970.

Arsenal up: When the League was extended in 1919, Woolwich Arsenal (sixth in Division Two in 1914–15, last season before the war) were elected to Division One. Arsenal have been in the top division ever since.

Tottenham down: At that same meeting in 1919 Chelsea (due for relegation) retained their place in Division One but the bottom club (Tottenham) had to go down to Division Two.

Preston and **Burnley down:** Preston, the first League Champions in season 1888–89, dropped into the Fourth Division in 1985. So did Burnley, also among the League's original members in 1888. In 1986, Preston had to apply for re-election.

Wolves' fall: Wolves, another of the Football League's original members, completed the fall from First Division to Fourth in successive seasons (1984–85–86).

Lincoln out: Lincoln became the first club to suffer automatic demotion from the Football League when they finished bottom of Div 4, on goal difference, in season 1986–87. They were replaced by Scarborough, champions of the GM Vauxhall Conference. Lincoln regained their place a year later.

Swindon up and down: In the 1990 play-offs, Swindon won promotion to the First Division for the first time, but remained in the Second Division because of financial irregularities.

MOST CHAMPIONSHIP WINS

Manchester Utd have been champions of England a record 20 times (7 Football League, 13 Premier League).

LONGEST CURRENT MEMBERS OF TOP DIVISION

Arsenal (since 1919), **Everton** (1954), **Liverpool** (1962), **Manchester Utd** (1975).

CHAMPIONS: FEWEST PLAYERS

Liverpool used only **14** players (five ever-present) when they won the League Championship in season 1965–66. **Aston Villa** also called on no more than 14 players to win the title in 1980–81, with seven ever-present.

UNBEATEN CHAMPIONS

Only two clubs have become Champions of England with an unbeaten record: **Preston** as the Football League's first winners in 1888–89 (22 matches) and **Arsenal**, Premier League winners in 2003–04 (38 matches).

LEAGUE HAT-TRICKS

Huddersfield created a record in 1924–25–26 by winning the League Championship three years in succession.

Arsenal equalled this hat-trick in 1933–34–35, **Liverpool** in 1982–83–84 and **Manchester Utd** in 1999–2000–01. Sir Alex Ferguson's side became the first to complete two hat-tricks (2007–08–09).

'SUPER DOUBLE' WINNERS

Since the War, there have been three instances of players appearing in and then managing FA Cup and Championship-winning teams:

Joe Mercer: Player in Arsenal Championship teams 1948, 1953 and in their 1950 FA Cup side; manager of Manchester City when they won Championship 1968, FA Cup 1969.

Kenny Dalglish: Player in Liverpool Championship-winning teams 1979, 1980, 1982, 1983, 1984, player-manager 1986, 1988, 1990: player-manager when Liverpool won FA Cup (to complete Double) 1986; manager of Blackburn, Champions 1995.

George Graham: Played in Arsenal's Double-winning team in 1971, and as manager took them to Championship success in 1989 and 1991 and the FA Cup – League Cup double in 1993.

ORIGINAL TWELVE

The original 12 members of the Football League (formed in 1888) were: **Accrington, Aston Villa, Blackburn, Bolton, Burnley, Derby, Everton, Notts Co, Preston, Stoke, WBA** and **Wolves.**

Results on the opening day (Sep 8, 1888): Bolton 3, Derby 6; Everton 2, Accrington 1; Preston 5, Burnley 2; Stoke 0, WBA 2; Wolves 1, Aston Villa 1. Preston had the biggest first-day crowd: 6,000. Blackburn and Notts Co did not play that day. They kicked off a week later (Sep 15) – Blackburn 5, Accrington 5; Everton 2, Notts Co 1.

Accrington FC resigned from the league in 1893 and later folded. A new club, Accrington Stanley, were members of the league from 1921 until 1962 when financial problems forced their demise. The current Accrington Stanley were formed in 1968 and gained league status in 2007.

FASTEST CLIMBS

Three promotions in four seasons by two clubs – **Swansea City**: 1978 third in Div 4; 1979 third in Div 3; 1981 third in Div 2; **Wimbledon**: 1983 Champions of Div 4; 1984 second in Div 3; 1986 third in Div 2.

MERSEYSIDE RECORD

Liverpool is the only city to have staged top-division football – through Everton and/or Liverpool – **in every season** since League football began in 1888.

EARLIEST PROMOTIONS TO TOP DIVISION POST-WAR

Mar 23, 1974, **Middlesbrough**; Mar 25, 2006, **Reading**.

EARLIEST RELEGATIONS POST-WAR

From top division: **QPR** went down from the old First Division on Mar 29, 1969; **Derby** went down from the Premier League on Mar 29, 2008, with 6 matches still to play. From modern First Division: **Stockport** on Mar 16, 2002, with 7 matches still to play; **Wimbledon** on Apr 6, 2004, with 7 matches to play.

LEAGUE RECORDS

CHAMPIONS OF ENGLAND 1888–2021

Football League and Premier league

Manchester Utd 20, Liverpool 19, Arsenal 13, Everton 9, Aston Villa 7, Manchester City 7, Chelsea 6, Sunderland 6, Newcastle 4, Sheffield Wed 4, Blackburn 3, Huddersfield 3, Leeds 3, Wolves 3, Burnley 2, Derby 2, Portsmouth 2, Preston 2, Tottenham 2, Ipswich 1, Leicester 1, Nottm Forest 1, Sheffield Utd 1, WBA 1

DOUBLE CHAMPIONS

Nine men have played in and managed League Championship-winning teams:

Ted Drake Player – Arsenal 1934, 1935, 1938. Manager – Chelsea 1955.
Bill Nicholson Player – Tottenham 1951. Manager – Tottenham 1961.
Alf Ramsey Player – Tottenham 1951. Manager – Ipswich 1962.
Joe Mercer Player – Everton 1939, Arsenal 1948, 1953. Manager – Manchester City 1968.
Dave Mackay Player – Tottenham 1961. Manager – Derby 1975.
Bob Paisley Player – Liverpool 1947. Manager – Liverpool 1976, 1977, 1979, 1980, 1982, 1983.
Howard Kendall Player – Everton 1970. Manager – Everton 1985, 1987.
Kenny Dalglish Player – Liverpool 1979, 1980, 1982, 1983, 1984. Player-manager – Liverpool 1986, 1988, 1990. Manager – Blackburn 1995.
George Graham Player – Arsenal 1971. Manager – Arsenal 1989, 1991.

CANTONA'S FOUR-TIMER

Eric Cantona played in four successive Championship-winning teams: Marseille 1990–01, Leeds 1991–92, Manchester Utd 1992–93 and 1993–94.

ARRIVALS AND DEPARTURES

The following are the Football League arrivals and departures since 1923:

Year	In	Out
1923	Doncaster	Stalybridge Celtic
	New Brighton	
1927	Torquay	Aberdare Athletic
1928	Carlisle	Durham
1929	York	Ashington
1930	Thames	Merthyr Tydfil
1931	Mansfield	Newport Co
	Chester	Nelson
1932	Aldershot	Thames
	Newport Co	Wigan Borough
1938	Ipswich	Gillingham
1950	Colchester, Gillingham	
	Scunthorpe, Shrewsbury	
1951	Workington	New Brighton
1960	Peterborough	Gateshead
1962	Oxford Utd	Accrington (resigned)
1970	Cambridge Utd	Bradford PA
1972	Hereford	Barrow
1977	Wimbledon	Workington
1978	Wigan	Southport
1987	Scarborough	Lincoln
1988	Lincoln	Newport Co
1989	Maidstone	Darlington
1990	Darlington	Colchester
1991	Barnet	
1992	Colchester	Aldershot, Maidstone (resigned)
1993	Wycombe	Halifax
1997	Macclesfield	Hereford
1998	Halifax	Doncaster
1999	Cheltenham	Scarborough
2000	Kidderminster	Chester
2001	Rushden	Barnet
2002	Boston	Halifax
2003	Yeovil, Doncaster	Exeter, Shrewsbury
2004	Chester, Shrewsbury	Carlisle, York
2005	Barnet, Carlisle	Kidderminster, Cambridge Utd
2006	Accrington, Hereford	Oxford Utd, Rushden & Diamonds
2007	Dagenham, Morecambe	Torquay, Boston
2008	Aldershot, Exeter	Wrexham, Mansfield
2009	Burton, Torquay	Chester, Luton
2010	Stevenage, Oxford Utd	Grimsby, Darlington
2011	Crawley, AFC Wimbledon	Lincoln, Stockport
2012	Fleetwood, York	Hereford, Macclesfield
2013	Mansfield, Newport	Barnet, Aldershot
2014	Luton, Cambridge Utd	Bristol Rov, Torquay
2015	Barnet, Bristol Rov	Cheltenham, Tranmere
2016	Cheltenham, Grimsby	Dagenham & Redbridge, York
2017	Lincoln, Forest Green	Hartlepool, Leyton Orient
2018	Macclesfield, Tranmere	Barnet, Chesterfield
2019	Leyton Orient, Salford	Notts Co Yeovil
2020	Barrow, Harrogate	Macclesfield
2021	Sutton, Hartlepool	Southend, Grimsby

Leeds City were expelled from Div 2 in Oct, 1919; Port Vale took over their fixtures.

EXTENSIONS TO FOOTBALL LEAGUE

Clubs	Season	Clubs	Season
12 to 14	1891–92	44 to 66†	1920–21
14 to 28*	1892–93	66 to 86†	1921–22
28 to 31	1893–94	86 to 88	1923–24
31 to 32	1894–95	88 to 92	1950–51
32 to 36	1898–99	92 to 93	1991–92
36 to 40	1905–06	(Reverted to 92 when Aldershot closed, Mar 1992)	

*Second Division formed. † Third Division (South) formed from Southern League clubs.
‍† Third Division (North) formed.
Football League reduced to 70 clubs and three divisions on the formation of the FA Premier League in 1992; increased to 72 season 1994–95, when Premier League reduced to 20 clubs.

RECORD RUNS

Arsenal hold the record unbeaten sequence in the English League – 49 Premier League matches (36 wins, 13 draws) from May 7, 2003 until Oct 24, 2004 when beaten 2-0 away to Manchester Utd. The record previously belonged to **Nottm Forest** – 42 First Division matches (21 wins, 21 draws) from Nov 19, 1977 until beaten 2-0 at Liverpool on December 9, 1978.
Huddersfield set a new Football League record of 43 League 1 matches unbeaten from Jan 1, 2011 until Nov 28, 2011 when losing 2-0 at Charlton.
Best debuts: Ipswich won the First Division at their first attempt in 1961–62.
Peterborough in their first season in the Football League (1960–01) not only won the Fourth Division but set the all-time scoring record for the League of 134 goals. **Hereford** were promoted from the Fourth Division in their first League season, 1972–73.
Wycombe were promoted from the Third Division (via the play-offs) in their first League season, 1993–94. **Stevenage** were promoted from League 2 (via the play-offs) in their first League season, 2010–11. **Crawley** gained automatic promotion in their first season in 2011–12.
Record winning sequence in a season: 18 consecutive League victories by Manchester City, 2017-18, and Liverpool, 2019-20, longest in English top-flight.
Best winning start to League season: 13 successive victories in Div 3 by **Reading**, season 1985–86.
Best starts in 'old' First Division: 11 consecutive victories by **Tottenham** in 1960–61; 10 by **Manchester Utd in** 1985–86. In 'new' First Division, 11 consecutive wins by **Newcastle** in 1992–93 and by **Fulham** in 2000–01.
Longest unbeaten sequence (all competitions): 40 by **Nottm Forest,** Mar–December 1978. It comprised 21 wins, 19 draws (in 29 League matches, 6 League Cup, 4 European Cup, 1 Charity Shield).
Longest unbeaten starts to League season: 38 matches (26 wins, 12 draws) in **Arsenal's** undefeated Premier League season, 2003–04; 29 matches – **Leeds,** Div 1 1973–74 (19 wins, 10 draws); **Liverpool,** Div 1 1987–88 (22 wins, 7 draws).
Most consecutive League matches unbeaten in a season: 38 **Arsenal** Premier League season 2003–04 (see above); 33 **Reading** (25 wins, 8 draws) 2005–06.
Longest winning sequence in Div 1: 13 matches by **Tottenham** – last two of season 1959–60, first 11 of 1960–61.
Longest unbeaten home League sequence in top division: 86 matches (62 wins, 24 draws) by **Chelsea** (Mar 2004–Oct 2008).
League's longest winning sequence with clean sheets: 9 matches by **Stockport** (Lge 2, 2006–07 season).
Premier League – best starts to season: Arsenal, 38 games, 2003–04; **Manchester City,** 14 games, 2011–12.
Best winning start to Premier League season: 9 consecutive victories by **Chelsea** in 2005–06.
Premier League – most consecutive home wins: 20 by **Manchester City** (last 5 season 2010–11, first 15 season 2011–12).
Most consecutive away League wins in top flight: 12 by **Manchester City** in 2020–21.
Premier League – longest unbeaten away run: 27 matches (W17, D10) by **Arsenal** (Apr 5, 2003 – Sep 25, 2004).

Record home-win sequences: Bradford Park Avenue won 25 successive home games in Div 3 North – the last 18 in 1926–27 and the first 7 the following season. Longest run of home wins in the top division is 21 by **Liverpool** – the last 9 of 1971–72 and the first 12 of 1972–73.

British record for successive League wins: 25 by **Celtic** (Scottish Premier League), 2003–04.

WORST SEQUENCES

Cambridge Utd had the previous worst of 31 in 1983–84 (21 lost, 10 drawn). They were bottom of Div 2.

Longest sequence without home win: Sunderland, in the Championship, went an English record 21 games in all competitions without a victory in front of their own supporters (Dec 2016–Nov 2017).

Worst losing start to a League season : 12 consecutive defeats by **Manchester Utd** (Div 1), 1930–31.

Worst Premier League start: QPR 16 matches without win (7 draws, 9 defeats), 2012–13.

Premier League – most consecutive defeats: 20 **Sunderland** last 15 matches, 2002–03, first five matches 2005–06.

Longest non-winning start to League season: 25 matches (4 draws, 21 defeats) by **Newport**, Div 4. Worst no-win League starts since then: 16 matches by **Burnley** (9 draws, 7 defeats in Div 2, 1979–80); 16 by **Hull** (10 draws, 6 defeats in Div 2, 1989–90); 16 by **Sheffield Utd** (4 draws, 12 defeats in Div 1, 1990–91).

Most League defeats in a season: 18 by Cambridge Utd (Div 3, 1984–85) and by Leyton Orient (Lg 2, 2016–17).

Fewest League wins in a season: 1 by **Loughborough** (Div 2, season 1899–1900). They lost 27, drew 6, goals 18-100 and dropped out of the League. (See also Scottish section.) 1 by **Derby** (Prem Lge, 2007–08). They lost 29, drew 8, goals 20-89.

Most consecutive League defeats in season: 18 by **Darwen** (Div 1, 1898–99); 17 by **Rochdale** (Div 3 North, 1931–32).

Fewest home League wins in season: 1 by **Loughborough** (Div 2, 1899–1900), **Notts Co** (Div 1, 1904–05), **Woolwich Arsenal** (Div 1, 1912–13), **Blackpool** (Div 1, 1966–67), **Rochdale** (Div 3, 1973–74), **Sunderland** (Prem Lge, 2005–06); **Derby** (Prem Lge, 2007–08).

Away League defeats record: 24 in row by **Crewe** (Div 2) – all 15 in 1894–95 followed by 9 in 1895–96; by **Nelson** (Div 3 North) – 3 in Apr 1930 followed by all 21 in season 1930–31. They then dropped out of the League.

Biggest defeat in Champions' season: During **Newcastle's** title-winning season in 1908–09, they were beaten 9-1 at home by Sunderland on December 5.

WORST START BY EVENTUAL CHAMPIONS

Sunderland took only 2 points from their first 7 matches in season 1912–13 (2 draws, 5 defeats). They won 25 of the remaining 31 games to clinch their fifth League title.

DISMAL DERBY

Derby were relegated in season 2007–08 as the worst-ever team in the Premier League, having recorded the fewest wins (1), fewest points (11) and fewest goals (20). They experienced the longest run without a victory in League history – 32 games from Sept 22 to the end of the campaign. The sequence extended to 36 at the start of the following season. Macclesfield also went 36 matches without winning, 23 up to the end of their relegation season 2011–12 and 13 after returning to League Two in 2018–19.

UNBEATEN LEAGUE SEASON

Only three clubs have completed an English League season unbeaten: **Preston** (22 matches in 1888–89, the League's first season), **Liverpool** (28 matches in Div 2, 1893–94) and **Arsenal** (38 matches in Premier League, 2003–04).

100 PER CENT HOME RECORDS

Six clubs have won every home League match in a season: **Sunderland** (13 matches)' in 1891–92 and four teams in the old Second Division: **Liverpool** (14) in 1893–94, **Bury** (15) in

1894–95, **Sheffield Wed** (17) in 1899–1900 and **Small Heath,** subsequently **Birmingham** (17) in 1902–03. The last club to do it, **Brentford,** won all 21 home games in Div 3 South in 1929–30. **Rotherham** just failed to equal that record in 1946–47. They won their first 20 home matches in Div 3 North, then drew the last 3-3 v Rochdale.

BEST HOME LEAGUE RECORDS IN TOP FLIGHT

Sunderland, 1891–92 (P13, W13); **Newcastle,** 1906–07 (P19, W18, D1); **Chelsea,** 2005–06 (P19, W18, D1); **Manchester Utd,** 2010–11 (P19, W18, D1); **Manchester City,** 2011–12 (P19, W18, D1); **Liverpool,** 2019-20 (P19, W18, D1)

MOST CONSECUTIVE CLEAN SHEETS

Premier League – 14: **Manchester Utd** (2008–09); **Football League** – 11: **Millwall** (Div 3 South 1925–26); **York** (Div 3 1973–74); **Reading** (Div 4, 1978–79).

WORST HOME RUNS

Most consecutive home League defeats: 14 **Rochdale (**Div 3 North) seasons 1931–32 and 1932–33; 10 **Birmingham** (Div 1) 1985–86; 9 **Darwen** (Div 2) 1897–98; 9 **Watford** (Div 2) 1971–72.
Between Nov 1958 and Oct 1959 **Portsmouth** drew 2 and lost 14 out of 16 consecutive home games.
West Ham did not win in the Premier League at Upton Park in season 2002–03 until the 13th home match on Jan 29.

MOST AWAY WINS IN SEASON

Doncaster won 18 of their 21 away League fixtures when winning Div 3 North in 1946–47.

A100 PER CENT HOME WINS ON ONE DAY

Div 1 – All 11 home teams won on Feb 13, 1926 and on Dec 10, 1955. **Div 2** – All 12 home teams won on Nov 26, 1988. **Div 3,** all 12 home teams won in the week-end programme of Oct 18–19, 1968.

NO HOME WINS IN DIV ON ONE DAY

Div 1 – 8 away wins, 3 draws in 11 matches on Sep 6, 1986. **Div 2** – 7 away wins, 4 draws in 11 matches on Dec 26, 1987. **Premier League** – 6 away wins, 5 draws in 11 matches on Dec 26, 1994.
The weekend **Premier League** programme on Dec 7–8–9, 1996 produced no home win in the ten games (4 aways, 6 draws). There was again no home victory (3 away wins, 7 draws) in the week-end **Premier League** fixtures on Sep 23–24, 2000.

MOST DRAWS IN A SEASON (FOOTBALL LEAGUE)

23 by **Norwich** (Div 1, 1978–79), **Exeter** (Div 4, 1986–87). **Cardiff** and **Hartlepool** (both Div 3, 1997–98). **Norwich** played 42 matches, the others 46.

MOST DRAWS IN PREMIER LEAGUE SEASON

18 (in 42 matches) by **Manchester City** (1993–94), **Sheffield Utd** (1993–94), **Southampton** (1994–95).

MOST DRAWS IN ONE DIV ON ONE DAY

On Sep 18, 1948 **nine** out of 11 First Division matches were drawn.

MOST DRAWS IN PREMIER DIV PROGRAMME

Over the week-ends of December 2–3–4, 1995, and Sep 23–24, 2000, **seven** out of the ten matches finished level.

FEWEST DRAWS IN SEASON

In 46 matches: 3 by **Reading** (Div 3 South, 1951–52); **Bradford Park Avenue** (Div 3 North, 1956–57); **Tranmere** (Div 4, 1984–85); **Southend** (Div 3, 2002–03); in 42 matches: 2 by **Reading** (Div 3 South, 1935–36); **Stockport** (Div 3 North, 1946–47); in 38 matches: 2 by **Sunderland** (Div 1, 1908–09).

HIGHEST-SCORING DRAWS IN LEAGUE

Leicester 6, **Arsenal** 6 (Div 1 Apr 21, 1930); **Charlton** 6, **Middlesbrough** 6 (Div 2. Oct 22, 1960)
Latest **6-6** draw in first-class football was between **Tranmere** and **Newcastle** in the Zenith Data Systems Cup 1st round on Oct 1, 1991. The score went from 3-3 at 90 minutes to 6-6 after extra time, and Tranmere won 3-2 on penalties. In Scotland: **Queen of the South** 6, **Falkirk** 6 (Div 1, Sep 20, 1947).
Most recent **5-5** draws in top division: **Southampton** v **Coventry** (Div 1, May 4, 1982); **QPR** v **Newcastle** (Div 1, Sep 22, 1984); **WBA** v **Manchester Utd** (Prem Lge, May 19, 2013).

DRAWS RECORDS

Most consecutive drawn matches in Football League: 8 by Torquay (Div 3, 1969–70), **Middlesbrough** (Div 2, 1970–71), **Peterborough** (Div 4, 1971–72), **Birmingham** (Div 3 (1990–91), **Southampton** (Champ, 2005–06), **Chesterfield** (Lge 1, 2005–06), **Swansea** (Champ, 2008–09).
Longest sequence of draws by the same score: six 1-1 results by **QPR** in season 1957–58. **Tranmere** became the first club to play **five consecutive 0-0 League draws**, in season 1997–98. Relegated **Chesterfield** drew nine successive National League games in season 2018–19.

IDENTICAL RECORDS

There is only **one instance** of two clubs in one division finishing a season with identical records. In 1907–08, **Blackburn** and **Woolwich Arsenal** were bracketed equal 14th in the First Division with these figures: P38, W12, D12, L14, Goals 51-63, Pts. 36.
The total of **1195 goals** scored in the Premier League in season 1993–94 was repeated in 1994–95.

DEAD LEVEL

Millwall's record in Division Two in season 1973–74 was P42, W14, D14, L14, F51, A51, Pts 42.

CHAMPIONS OF ALL DIVISIONS

Wolves, Burnley and **Preston** are the only clubs to have won titles in the old Divisions 1, 2, 3 and 4. Wolves also won the Third Division North and the new Championship.

POINTS DEDUCTIONS

2000–01: Chesterfield 9 for breach of transfer regulations and falsifying gate receipts.
2002–03: Boston 4 for contractual irregularities.
2004–05: Wrexham, Cambridge Utd 10 for administration.
2005–06: Rotherham 10 for administration.
2006–07: Leeds, Boston 10 for administration; **Bury** 1 for unregistered player.
2007–08: Leeds 15 over insolvency rules; **Bournemouth, Luton, Rotherham** 10 for administration.
2008–09: Luton 20 for failing Insolvency rules, 10 over payments to agents; **Bournemouth, Rotherham** 17 for breaking administration rules; **Southampton, Stockport** 10 for administration – **Southampton** with effect from season 2009–10 **Crystal Palace** 1 for ineligible player.
2009–10: Portsmouth 9, **Crystal Palace** 10 for administration; **Hartlepool** 3 for ineligible player.
2010–11: Plymouth 10 for administration; **Hereford** 3, **Torquay** 1, each for ineligible player
2011–12: Portsmouth and **Port Vale** both 10 for administration – Portsmouth from following season.
2013–14: Coventry 10 for administration; **AFC Wimbledon** 3 for ineligible player.

2014–15: Rotherham 3 for ineligible player.
2015–16: Bury 3 for ineligible player.
2018–19: Birmingham 9 for financial irregularities; **Bolton** 12 for administration, triggered in season 2019–20.

Among previous points penalties imposed:
Nov 1990: Arsenal 2, **Manchester Utd** 1 following mass players' brawl at Old Trafford.
Dec 1996: Brighton 2 for pitch invasions by fans.
Jan 1997: Middlesbrough 3 for refusing to play Premier League match at Blackburn because of injuries and illness.
Jun 1994: Tottenham 12 (reduced to 6) and banned from following season's FA Cup for making illegal payments to players. On appeal, points deduction annulled and club re-instated in Cup.
2019–20: Bury 12 for insolvency (club later expelled); **Wigan** 12 into administration; **Macclesfield** 17 for breaches of regulations; 12 **Sheffield Wed** for breaking spending rules, triggered in season 2020–21 and later reduced by half.

NIGHTMARE STARTS
Most goals conceded by a goalkeeper on League debut: 13 by Steve Milton when Halifax lost 13-0 at Stockport (Div 3 North) on Jan 6, 1934.
Post-war: 11 by Crewe's new goalkeeper **Dennis Murray** (Div 3 North) on Sep 29, 1951, when Lincoln won 11-1.

RELEGATION ODD SPOTS
None of the Barclays Premier League relegation places in season 2004–05 were decided until the last day (Sunday, May 15). **WBA** (bottom at kick-off) survived with a 2-0 home win against Portsmouth, and the three relegated clubs were **Southampton** (1-2 v Manchester Utd), **Norwich** (0-6 at Fulham) and **Crystal Palace** (2-2 at Charlton).
In season 1937–38, **Manchester City** were the highest-scoring team in the First Division with 80 goals (3 more than Champions Arsenal), but they finished in 21st place and were relegated – a year after winning the title. They scored more goals than they conceded (77).
That season produced the **closest relegation battle** in top-division history, with only 4 points spanning the bottom 11 clubs in Div 1. **WBA** went down with **Manchester City**.
Twelve years earlier, in 1925–26, City went down to Division 2 despite totalling 89 goals – still the most scored in any division by a relegated team. Manchester City also scored 31 FA Cup goals that season, but lost the Final 1-0 to Bolton Wanderers.
Cardiff were relegated from Div 1 in season 1928–29, despite conceding fewest goals in the division (59). They also scored fewest (43).
On their way to relegation from the First Division in season 1984–85, **Stoke** twice lost ten matches in a row.

RELEGATION TREBLES
Two Football League clubs have been relegated three seasons in succession. **Bristol City** fell from First Division to Fourth in 1980–81–82 and **Wolves** did the same in 1984–85–86.

OLDEST CLUBS
Oldest Association Football Club is **Sheffield FC** (formed in 1857). The oldest Football League clubs are **Nottm Forest**, 1865; and **Sheffield Wed**, 1866.

NOTTS COUNTY RELEGATED
Notts County, formed in 1862 and the world's oldest professional club, were relegated from the Football League for the first time in season 2018–19.

FOUR DIVISIONS
In **May, 1957**, the Football League decided to re-group the two sections of the Third Division into Third and Fourth Divisions in **season 1958–59**.

The Football League was reduced to three divisions on the formation of the Premier League in **1992**. In season 2004–05, under new sponsors Coca-Cola, the titles of First, Second and Third Divisions were changed to League Championship, League One and League Two.

THREE UP – THREE DOWN

The Football League annual general meeting of Jun 1973 agreed to adopt the promotion and relegation system of three up and three down.

The **new system** came into effect in **season 1973–74** and applied only to the first three divisions; four clubs were still relegated from the Third and four promoted from the Fourth.

It was the first change in the promotion and relegation system for the top two divisions in 81 years.

MOST LEAGUE APPEARANCES

Players with more than 700 English League apps (as at end of season 2019–20)

1005   Peter Shilton 1966–97 (286 Leicester, 110 Stoke, 202 Nottm Forest, 188 Southampton, 175 Derby, 34 Plymouth Argyle, 1 Bolton, 9 Leyton Orient).

931   Tony Ford 1975–2002 (423 Grimsby, 9 Sunderland, 112 Stoke, 114 WBA, 5 Bradford City, 76 Scunthorpe, 103 Mansfield, 89 Rochdale).

840   Graham Alexander 1991–2012 (159 Scunthorpe, 152 Luton, 372 Preston, 157 Burnley)

824   Terry Paine 1956–77 (713 Southampton, 111 Hereford).

795   Tommy Hutchison 1968–91 (165 Blackpool, 314 Coventry City, 46 Manchester City, 92 Burnley, 178 Swansea). In addition, 68 Scottish League apps for Alloa 1965–68, giving career League app total of 863.

791   David James 1988–2013 (89 Watford, 217 Liverpool, 67 Aston Villa, 91 West Ham, 93 Manchester City, 134 Portsmouth, 81 Bristol City, 19 Bournemouth).

790   Neil Redfearn 1982–2004 (35 Bolton, 100 Lincoln, 46 Doncaster, 57 Crystal Palace, 24 Watford, 62 Oldham, 292 Barnsley, 30 Charlton, 17 Bradford City, 22 Wigan, 42 Halifax, 54 Boston, 9 Rochdale).

782   Robbie James 1973–94 (484 Swansea, 48 Stoke, 87 QPR, 23 Leicester, 89 Bradford City, 51 Cardiff).

777   Alan Oakes 1959–84 (565 Manchester City, 211 Chester, 1 Port Vale).

773   Dave Beasant 1980–2003 (340 Wimbledon, 20 Newcastle, 6 Grimsby, 4 Wolves, 133 Chelsea, 88 Southampton, 139 Nottm F, 27 Portsmouth, 16 Brighton).

770   John Trollope 1960–80 (all for Swindon, record total for one club).

764   Jimmy Dickinson 1946–65 (all for Portsmouth).

761   Roy Sproson 1950–72 (all for Port Vale).

760   Mick Tait 1974–97 (64 Oxford Utd, 106 Carlisle, 33 Hull, 240 Portsmouth, 99 Reading, 79 Darlington, 139 Hartlepool Utd).

758   Billy Bonds 1964–88 (95 Charlton, 663 West Ham).

758   Ray Clemence 1966–88 (48 Scunthorpe, 470 Liverpool, 240 Tottenham).

757   Pat Jennings 1963–86 (48 Watford, 472 Tottenham, 237 Arsenal).

757   Frank Worthington 1966–88 (171 Huddersfield Town, 210 Leicester, 84 Bolton, 75 Birmingham, 32 Leeds, 19 Sunderland, 34 Southampton, 31 Brighton, 59 Tranmere, 23 Preston, 19 Stockport).

755   Wayne Allison 1986–2008 (84 Halifax, 7 Watford, 195 Bristol City, 103 Swindon, 76 Huddersfield, 102 Tranmere, 73 Sheffield Utd, 115 Chesterfield).

749   Ernie Moss 1968–88 (469 Chesterfield, 35 Peterborough, 57 Mansfield, 74 Port Vale, 11 Lincoln, 44 Doncaster, 26 Stockport, 23 Scarborough, 10 Rochdale).

746   Les Chapman 1966–88 (263 Oldham, 133 Huddersfield Town, 70 Stockport, 139 Bradford City, 88 Rochdale, 53 Preston).

744   Asa Hartford 1967–90 (214 WBA, 260 Manchester City, 3 Nottm Forest, 81 Everton, 28 Norwich, 81 Bolton, 45 Stockport, 7 Oldham, 25 Shrewsbury).

743   Alan Ball 1963–84 (146 Blackpool, 208 Everton, 177 Arsenal, 195 Southampton, 17 Bristol Rov).

743   John Hollins 1963–84 (465 Chelsea, 151 QPR, 127 Arsenal).
743   Phil Parkes 1968–91 (52 Walsall, 344 QPR, 344 West Ham, 3 Ipswich).
737   Steve Bruce 1979–99 (205 Gillingham, 141 Norwich, 309 Manchester Utd 72 Birmingham, 10 Sheffield Utd).
734   Teddy Sheringham 1983–2007 (220 Millwall, 5 Aldershot, 42 Nottm Forest, 104 Manchester Utd, 236 Tottenham, 32 Portsmouth, 76 West Ham, 19 Colchester)
732   Mick Mills 1966–88 (591 Ipswich, 103 Southampton, 38 Stoke).
731   Ian Callaghan 1959–81 (640 Liverpool, 76 Swansea, 15 Crewe).
731   David Seaman 1982–2003 (91 Peterborough, 75 Birmingham, 141 QPR, 405 Arsenal, 19 Manchester City).
725   Steve Perryman 1969–90 (655 Tottenham, 17 Oxford Utd, 53 Brentford).
722   Martin Peters 1961–81 (302 West Ham, 189 Tottenham, 207 Norwich, 24 Sheffield Utd).
718   Mike Channon 1966–86 (511 Southampton, 72 Manchester City, 4 Newcastle, 9 Bristol Rov, 88 Norwich, 34 Portsmouth).
716   Ron Harris 1961–83 (655 Chelsea, 61 Brentford).
716   Mike Summerbee 1959–79 (218 Swindon, 357 Manchester City, 51 Burnley, 3 Blackpool, 87 Stockport).
714   Glenn Cockerill 1976–98 (186 Lincoln, 26 Swindon, 62 Sheffield Utd, 387 Southampton, 90 Leyton Orient, 40 Fulham, 23 Brentford).
705   Keith Curle 1981–2003 (32 Bristol Rov, 16 Torquay, 121 Bristol City, 40 Reading, 93 Wimbledon, 171 Manchester City, 150 Wolves, 57 Sheffield Utd, 11 Barnsley, 14 Mansfield.
705   Phil Neal 1968–89 (186 Northampton, 455 Liverpool, 64 Bolton).
705   John Wile 1968–86 (205 Peterborough, 500 WBA).
703   Rob Lee 1983-2006 (298 Charlton, 303 Newcastle, 48 Derby, 16 West Ham, 38 Wycombe).
703   Andy Melville 1986-2005 (175 Swansea, 135 Oxford, 204 Sunderland, 6 Bradford City, 153 Fulham, 17 West Ham, 13 Nottm F).
701   Neville Southall 1980–2000 (39 Bury, 578 Everton, 9 Port Vale, 9 Southend, 12 Stoke, 53 Torquay, 1 Bradford City).
● **Stanley Matthews** made 701 League apps 1932–65 (322 Stoke, 379 Blackpool), incl. 3 for Stoke at start of 1939–40 before season abandoned (war).
● Goalkeeper **John Burridge** made a total of 771 League appearances in a 28-season career in English and Scottish football (1968–96). He played 691 games for 15 English clubs (Workington, Blackpool, Aston Villa, Southend, Crystal Palace, QPR, Wolves, Derby, Sheffield Utd, Southampton, Newcastle, Scarborough, Lincoln, Manchester City and Darlington) and 80 for 5 Scottish clubs (Hibernian, Aberdeen, Dumbarton, Falkirk and Queen of the South).

LONGEST LEAGUE APPEARANCE SEQUENCE

Harold Bell, centre-half of Tranmere, was ever-present for the first nine post-war seasons (1946–55), achieving a League record of 401 consecutive matches. Counting FA Cup and other games, his run of successive appearances totalled 459.

The longest League sequence since Bell's was 394 appearances by goalkeeper **Dave Beasant** for Wimbledon, Newcastle and Chelsea. His nine-year run began on Aug 29, 1981 and was ended by a broken finger sustained in Chelsea's League Cup-tie against Portsmouth on Oct 31, 1990. Beasant's 394 consecutive League games comprised 304 for Wimbledon (1981–88), 20 for Newcastle (1988–89) and 70 for Chelsea (1989–90).

Phil Neal made 366 consecutive First Division appearances for Liverpool between December 1974 and Sep 1983, a remarkable sequence for an outfield player in top-division football.

MOST CONSECUTIVE PREMIER LEAGUE APPEARANCES

310 by goalkeeper **Brad Friedel** (152 Blackburn, 114 Aston Villa, 44 Tottenham, May 2004–Oct 2012). He played in 8 **ever-present seasons** (2004–12, Blackburn 4, Villa 3, Tottenham 1).

EVER-PRESENT DEFENCE

The **entire defence** of **Huddersfield** played in all 42 Second Division matches in season 1952–53, namely, Bill Wheeler (goal), Ron Staniforth and Laurie Kelly (full-backs), Bill McGarry, Don McEvoy and Len Quested (half-backs). In addition, Vic Metcalfe played in all 42 League matches at outside-left.

FIRST SUBSTITUTE USED IN LEAGUE

Keith Peacock (Charlton), away to Bolton (Div 2) on Aug 21, 1965.

FROM PROMOTION TO CHAMPIONS

Clubs who have become Champions of England a year after winning promotion: **Liverpool** 1905, 1906; **Everton** 1931, 1932; **Tottenham** 1950, 1951; **Ipswich** 1961, 1962; **Nottm Forest** 1977, 1978. The first four were placed top in both seasons: Forest finished third and first.

PREMIER LEAGUE'S FIRST MULTI-NATIONAL LINE-UP

Chelsea made history on December 26, 1999 when starting their Premier League match at Southampton without a single British player in the side.

Fulham's Unique XI: In the Worthington Cup 3rd round at home to Bury on Nov 6, 2002, Fulham fielded 11 players of 11 different nationalities. Ten were full Internationals, with Lee Clark an England U–21 cap.

On Feb 14, 2005 **Arsenal** became the first English club to select an all-foreign match squad when Arsene Wenger named 16 non-British players at home to Crystal Palace (Premier League).

Fifteen nations were represented at Fratton Park on Dec 30, 2009 (Portsmouth 1 Arsenal 4) when, for the first time in Premier League history, not one Englishman started the match. The line-up comprised seven Frenchmen, two Algerians and one from each of 13 other countries.

Players from 22 nationalities (subs included) were involved in the Blackburn–WBA match at Ewood Park on Jan 23, 2011.

PREMIER LEAGUE'S FIRST ALL-ENGLAND LINE-UP

On Feb 27, 1999 **Aston Villa** (at home to Coventry) fielded the first all-English line up seen in the Premier League (starting 11 plus 3 subs).

ENTIRE HOME-GROWN TEAM

Crewe Alexandra's starting 11 in the 2-0 home win against Walsall (Lge 1) on Apr 27, 2013 all graduated from the club's academy.

THREE-NATION CHAMPIONS

David Beckham won a title in four countries: with Manchester Utd six times (1996–97–99–2000–01–03), Real Madrid (2007), LA Galaxy (2011 and Paris St Germain (2013).

Trevor Steven earned eight Championship medals in three countries: two with Everton (1985, 1987); five with Rangers (1990, 1991, 1993, 1994, 1995) and one with Marseille in 1992.

LEEDS NO WIN AWAY

Leeds, in 1992–93, provided the first instance of a club failing to win an away League match as reigning Champions.

PIONEERS IN 1888 AND 1992

Three clubs among the twelve who formed the Football League in 1888 were also founder members of the Premier League: **Aston Villa, Blackburn** and **Everton.**

CHAMPIONS (MODERN) WITH TWO CLUBS – PLAYERS

Francis Lee (Manchester City 1968, Derby 1975); **Ray Kennedy** (Arsenal 1971, Liverpool 1979, 1980, 1982); **Archie Gemmill** (Derby 1972, 1975, Nottm Forest 1978); **John McGovern**

(Derby 1972, Nottm Forest 1978) **Larry Lloyd** (Liverpool 1973, Nottm Forest 1978); **Peter Withe** (Nottm Forest 1978, Aston Villa 1981); **John Lukic** (Arsenal 1989, Leeds 1992); **Kevin Richardson** (Everton 1985, Arsenal 1989); **Eric Cantona** (Leeds 1992, Manchester Utd 1993, 1994, 1996, 1997); **David Batty** (Leeds 1992, Blackburn 1995), **Bobby Mimms** (Everton 1987, Blackburn 1995), **Henning Berg** (Blackburn 1995, Manchester Utd 1999, 2000); **Nicolas Anelka** (Arsenal 1998, Chelsea 2010); **Ashley Cole** (Arsenal 2002, 2004, Chelsea 2010); **Gael Clichy** (Arsenal 2004, Manchester City 2012); **Robert Huth** (Chelsea 2005, 2006, Leicester 2016); **Kolo Toure** (Arsenal 2004, Manchester City 2012); **Carlos Tevez** (Manchester Utd 2008, 2009, Manchester City 2012, **James Milner** (Manchester City 2012, 2014, Liverpool 2020); **N'Golo Kante** (Leicester 2016, Chelsea 2017), **Riyad Mahrez** (Leicester 2016, Manchester City 2019).

TITLE TURNABOUTS

In Jan 1996, **Newcastle** led the Premier League by 13 points. They finished runners-up to Manchester Utd.

At Christmas 1997, **Arsenal** were 13 points behind leaders Manchester Utd and still 11 points behind at the beginning of Mar 1998. But a run of 10 wins took the title to Highbury.

On Mar 2, 2003, **Arsenal**, with 9 games left, went 8 points clear of Manchester Utd, who had a match in hand. United won the Championship by 5 points.

In Mar 2002, **Wolves** were in second (automatic promotion) place in Nationwide Div 1, 11 points ahead of WBA, who had 2 games in hand. They were overtaken by Albion on the run-in, finished third, then failed in the play-offs. A year later they won promotion to the Premier League via the play-offs.

CLUB CLOSURES

Five clubs have left the Football League in mid-season: **Leeds City** (expelled Oct 1919); **Wigan Borough** (Oct 1931, debts of £20,000); **Accrington Stanley** (Mar 1962, debts £62,000); **Aldershot** (Mar 1992, debts £1.2m). **Maidstone**, with debts of £650,000, closed Aug 1992, on the eve of the season; **Bury** (expelled Aug 2019, financial mismanagement).

FOUR-DIVISION MEN

In season 1986–87, goalkeeper **Eric Nixon**, became the first player to appear in **all four divisions** of the Football League **in one season**. He served two clubs in Div 1: Manchester City (5 League games) and Southampton (4); in Div 2 Bradford City (3); in Div 3 Carlisle (16); and in Div 4 Wolves (16). Total appearances: 44.

Harvey McCreadie, a teenage forward, played in four divisions over two seasons inside a calendar year – from Accrington (Div 3) to Luton (Div 1) in Jan 1960, to Div 2 with Luton later that season and to Wrexham (Div 4) in Nov.

Tony Cottee played in all four divisions in season 2000–01, for Leicester (Premier League), Norwich (Div 1), Barnet (Div 3, player-manager) and Millwall (Div 2).

FATHERS AND SONS

When player-manager **Ian** (39) and **Gary** (18) **Bowyer** appeared together in the **Hereford** side at Scunthorpe (Div 4, Apr 21, 1990), they provided the first instance of father and son playing in the same team in a Football League match for 39 years. Ian played as substitute, and Gary scored Hereford's injury-time equaliser in a 3-3 draw.

Alec (39) and **David** (17) **Herd** were among previous father-and-son duos in league football – for Stockport, 2-0 winners at Hartlepool (Div 3 North) on May 5, 1951.

When Preston won 2-1 at Bury in Div 3 on Jan 13, 1990, the opposing goalkeepers were brothers: **Alan Kelly** (21) for Preston and **Gary** (23) for Bury. Their father, **Alan** (who kept goal for Preston in the 1964 FA Cup Final and won 47 Rep of Ireland caps) flew from America to watch the sons he taught to keep goal line up on opposite sides.

Other examples: **Bill Dodgin Snr** (manager, Bristol Rov) faced son **Bill Jnr** (manager of Fulham) four times between 1969 and 1971. On Apr 16, 2013 (Lge 1), Oldham, under **Lee Johnson**, won 1-0 at home to Yeovil, managed by his father **Gary.**

George Eastham Snr (manager) and son **George Eastham Jnr** were inside-forward partners for Ards in the Irish League in season 1954–55.

FATHER AND SON REFEREE PLAY-OFF FINALS

Father and son refereed two of the 2009 Play-off Finals. **Clive Oliver,** 46, took charge of Shrewsbury v Gillingham (Lge 2) and **Michael Oliver,** 26, refereed Millwall v Scunthorpe (Lge 1) the following day.

FATHER AND SON BOTH CHAMPIONS

John Aston snr won a Championship medal with Manchester Utd in 1952 and **John Aston jnr** did so with the club in 1967. **Ian Wright** won the Premier League title with Arsenal in 1998 and **Shaun Wright-Phillips** won with Chelsea in 2006.

FATHER AND SON RIVAL MANAGERS

When **Bill Dodgin snr** took Bristol Rov to Fulham for an FA Cup 1st Round tie in Nov 1971, the opposing manager was his son, **Bill jnr.** Rovers won 2-1. Oldham's new manager, **Lee Johnson,** faced his father **Gary's** Yeovil in a Lge 1 match in April, 2013. Oldham won 1-0.

FATHER AND SON ON OPPOSITE SIDES

It happened for the first time in FA Cup history (1st Qual Round on Sep 14, 1996) when 21-year-old **Nick Scaife** (Bishop Auckland) faced his father **Bobby** (41), who played for Pickering. Both were in midfield. Home side Bishops won 3-1.

THREE BROTHERS IN SAME SIDE

Southampton provided the first instance for 65 years of three brothers appearing together in a Div 1 side when **Danny Wallace** (24) and his 19-year-old twin brothers **Rodney** and **Ray** played against Sheffield Wed on Oct 22, 1988. In all, they made 25 appearances together for Southampton until Sep 1989.

A previous instance in Div 1 was provided by the Middlesbrough trio, **William, John** and **George Carr** with 24 League appearances together from Jan 1920 to Oct 1923.

The **Tonner** brothers, **Sam, James** and **Jack,** played together in 13 Second Division matches for Clapton Orient in season 1919–20.

Brothers **David, Donald** and **Robert Jack** played together in Plymouth's League side in 1920.

TWIN TEAM-MATES (see also Wallace twins above)

Twin brothers **David** and **Peter Jackson** played together for three League clubs (Wrexham, Bradford City and Tranmere) from 1954–62. The **Morgan** twins, **Ian** and **Roger,** played regularly in the QPR forward line from 1964–68. WBA's **Adam** and **James Chambers,** 18, were the first twins to represent England (v Cameroon in World Youth Championship, Apr 1999). They first played together in Albion's senior team, aged 19, in the League Cup 2nd. Round against Derby in Sep 2000. Brazilian identical twins **Rafael** and **Fabio Da Silva** (18) made first team debuts at full-back for Manchester Utd in season 2008– 09. Swedish twins **Martin** and **Marcus Olsson** played together for Blackburn in season 2011–12. **Josh** and **Jacob Murphy,** 19, played for Norwich in season 2013–2014.

SIR TOM DOES THE HONOURS

Sir Tom Finney, England and Preston legend, opened the Football League's new headquarters on their return to Preston on Feb 23, 1999. Preston had been the League's original base for 70 years before the move to Lytham St Annes in 1959.

SHORTENED MATCHES

The 0-0 score in the **Bradford City v Lincoln** Third Division fixture on May 11, 1985, abandoned through fire after 40 minutes, was subsequently confirmed as a result. It is the shortest officially- completed League match on record, and was the fourth of only five instances in Football League history of the score of an unfinished match being allowed to stand.

The other occasions: **Middlesbrough 4, Oldham 1** (Div 1, Apr 3, 1915), abandoned after 55 minutes when Oldham defender Billy Cook refused to leave the field after being sent off; **Barrow 7, Gillingham 0** (Div 4, Oct 9, 1961), abandoned after 75 minutes because of bad light, the match having started late because of Gillingham's delayed arrival.

A crucial **Manchester** derby (Div 1) was abandoned after 85 minutes, and the result stood, on Apr 27, 1974, when a pitch invasion at Old Trafford followed the only goal, scored for City by Denis Law, which relegated United, Law's former club.

The only instance of a first-class match in England being abandoned **'through shortage of players'** occurred in the First Division at Bramall Lane on Mar 16, 2002. Referee Eddie Wolstenholme halted play after 82 minutes because **Sheffield Utd** were reduced to 6 players against **WBA**. They had had 3 men sent off (goalkeeper and 2 substitutes), and with all 3 substitutes used and 2 players injured, were left with fewer than the required minimum of 7 on the field. Promotion contenders WBA were leading 3-0, and the League ordered the result to stand.

The last 60 seconds of **Birmingham v Stoke** (Div 3, 1-1, on Feb 29, 1992) were played behind locked doors. The ground had been cleared after a pitch invasion.

A First Division fixture, **Sheffield Wed v Aston Villa** (Nov 26, 1898), was abandoned through bad light after 79 mins with Wednesday leading 3-1. The Football League ruled that the match should be completed, and the remaining 10.5 minutes were played four months later (Mar 13, 1899), when Wednesday added another goal to make the result 4-1.

SIX TRANSFER RECORDS

Sheffield Utd broke their transfer record six times during 2019-20, signing Luke Freeman (£5m), Callum Robinson (£8m), Lys Mousset £10m), Oliver McBurnie (£20m), Sander Berge (£22m) and Rhian Brewster (£23.5m)

FA CUP RECORDS

(See also Goalscoring section)

CHIEF WINNERS

14 Arsenal; **12** Manchester Utd; **8** Tottenham, Chelsea; **7** Aston Villa, Liverpool; **6** Blackburn, Manchester City, Newcastle.

Three times in succession: The Wanderers (1876–77–78) and Blackburn (1884–85–86).

Trophy handed back: The FA Cup became the Wanderers' absolute property in 1878, but they handed it back to the Association on condition that it was not to be won outright by any club.

In successive years by professional clubs: Blackburn (1890 and 1891); Newcastle (1951 and 1952); Tottenham (1961 and 1962); Tottenham (1981 and 1982); Arsenal (2002 and 2003); Chelsea (2009 and 2010); Arsenal (2014 and 2015).

Record Final-tie score: Bury 6, Derby 0 (1903); Manchester City 6 Watford 0 (2019)

Most FA Cup Final wins at Wembley: Arsenal 11, Manchester Utd 10, Chelsea 8, Tottenham 6, Liverpool 5, Manchester City 5, Newcastle 5.

SECOND DIVISION WINNERS

Notts Co (1894), **Wolves** (1908), **Barnsley** (1912), **WBA** (1931), **Sunderland** (1973), **Southampton** (1976), **West Ham** (1980). When **Tottenham** won the Cup in 1901 they were a Southern League club.

'OUTSIDE' SEMI-FINALISTS

Sheffield Utd, in 2014, became the ninth team from outside the top two divisions to reach the semi-finals, following **Millwall** (1937), **Port Vale** (1954), **York** (1955), **Norwich** (1959), **Crystal Palace** (1976), **Plymouth** (1984), **Chesterfield** (1997) and **Wycombe** (2001). None reached the Final. .

FOURTH DIVISION QUARTER-FINALISTS

Oxford Utd (1964), Colchester (1971), Bradford City (1976), Cambridge Utd (1990).

FOURTH ROUND – NO REPLAYS

No replays were necessary in the 16 fourth round ties in January 2008 (7 home wins, 9 away). This had not happened for 51 years, since 8 home and 8 away wins in season 1956–57.

FIVE TROPHIES

The trophy which Arsenal won in 2014 was the fifth in FA Cup history. These were its predecessors:
1872–95: First Cup stolen from shop in Birmingham while held by Aston Villa. Never seen again.
1910: Second trophy presented to Lord Kinnaird on completing 21 years as FA president.
1911–91: Third trophy used until replaced ('battered and fragile') after 80 years' service.
1992–2013 Fourth FA Cup lasted 21 years – now retained at FA headquarters at Wembley Stadium.
Traditionally, the Cup stays with the holders until returned to the FA in March.

FINALISTS RELEGATED

Six clubs have reached the FA Cup Final and been relegated. The first five all lost at Wembley – **Manchester City** 1926, **Leicester** 1969, **Brighton** 1983, **Middlesbrough** 1997 and **Portsmouth** 2010. **Wigan**, Cup winners for the first time in 2013, were relegated from the Premier League three days later.

FA CUP – TOP SHOCKS

1922 (1)	Everton	0	Crystal Palace	6
1933 (3)	Walsall	2	Arsenal	0
1939 (F)	Portsmouth	4	Wolves	1
1948 (3)	Arsenal	0	Bradford PA	1
1948 (3)	Colchester	1	Huddersfield	0
1949 (4)	Yeovil	2	Sunderland	1
1954 (4)	Arsenal	1	Norwich	2
1955 (5)	York	2	Tottenham	1
1957 (4)	Wolves	0	Bournemouth	1
1957 (5)	Bournemouth	3	Tottenham	1
1958 (4)	Newcastle	1	Scunthorpe	3
1959 (3)	Norwich	3	Manchester Utd	0
1959 (3)	Worcester	2	Liverpool	1
1961 (3)	Chelsea	1	Crewe	2
1964 (3)	Newcastle	1	Bedford	2
1965 (4)	Peterborough	2	Arsenal	1
1971 (5)	Colchester	3	Leeds	2
1972 (3)	Hereford	2	Newcastle	1R
1973 (F)	Sunderland	1	Leeds	0
1975 (3)	Burnley	0	Wimbledon	1
1976 (F)	Southampton	1	Manchester Utd	0
1978 (F)	Ipswich	1	Arsenal	0
1980 (3)	Chelsea	0	Wigan	1
1980 (3)	Halifax	1	Manchester City	0
1980 (F)	West Ham	1	Arsenal	0
1981 (4)	Exeter	4	Newcastle	0R
1984 (3)	Bournemouth	2	Manchester Utd	0
1985 (4)	York	1	Arsenal	0
1986 (3)	Birmingham	1	Altrincham	2
1988 (F)	Wimbledon	1	Liverpool	0
1989 (3)	Sutton	2	Coventry	1

1991 (3)	WBA	2	Woking	4
1992 (3)	Wrexham	2	Arsenal	1
1994 (3)	Liverpool	0	Bristol City	1R
1994 (3)	Birmingham	1	Kidderminster	2
1997 (5)	Chesterfield	1	Nottm Forest	0
2001 (4)	Everton	0	Tranmere	3
2003 (3)	Shrewsbury	2	Everton	1
2005 (3)	Oldham	1	Manchester City	0
2008 (6)	Barnsley	1	Chelsea	0
2009 (2)	Histon	1	Leeds	0
2010 (4)	Liverpool	1	Reading	2R
2011 (3)	Stevenage	3	Newcastle	1
2012 (3)	Macclesfield	2	Cardiff	1
2013 (4)	Norwich	0	Luton	1
2013 (4)	Oldham	3	Liverpool	2
2013 (F)	Wigan	1	Manchester City	0
2014 (3)	Rochdale	2	Leeds	0
2015 (4)	Chelsea	2	Bradford City	4
2015 (5)	Bradford City	2	Sunderland	0
2016 (3)	Oxford	3	Swansea	2
2017 (5)	Burnley	0	Lincoln	1
2018 (5)	Wigan	1	Manchester City	0
2019 (3)	Fulham	1	Oldham	2
2019 (3)	Gillingham	1	Cardiff	0
2019 (3)	Newport	2	Leicester	1
2019 (3)	Sheffield Utd	0	Barnet	1
2019 (4)	AFC Wimbledon	4	West Ham	2
2020 (3)	Tranmere	2	Watford	1R
2021 (3)	Crawley	3	Leeds	0

YEOVIL TOP GIANT-KILLERS

Yeovil's victories over Colchester and Blackpool in season 2000–01 gave them a total of 20 FA Cup wins against League opponents. They set another non-League record by reaching the third round 13 times.

This was Yeovil's triumphant (non-League) Cup record against League clubs: 1924–25 Bournemouth 3-2; 1934–35 Crystal Palace 3-0, Exeter 4-1; 1938–39 Brighton 2-1; 1948–49 Bury 3-1, Sunderland 2-1; 1958–59 Southend 1-0; 1960–61 Walsall 1-0; 1963–64 Southend 1-0, Crystal Palace 3-1; 1970–71 Bournemouth 1-0; 1972–73 Brentford 2-1; 1987–88 Cambridge Utd 1-0; 1991–92 Walsall 1-0; 1992–93 Torquay 5-2, Hereford 2-1; 1993–94 Fulham 1-0; 1998–99 Northampton 2-0; 2000–01 Colchester 5-1, Blackpool 1-0.

NON-LEAGUE BEST

Since League football began in 1888, three non-League clubs have reached the FA Cup Final. **Sheffield Wed** (Football Alliance) were runners-up in 1890, as were **Southampton** (Southern League) in 1900 and 1902. **Tottenham** won the Cup as a Southern League team in 1901.

Lincoln won 1-0 at Burnley on Feb 18, 2017, to become the first non-league club to reach the last eight in 103 years. Two non-league sides – **Lincoln** and **Sutton** – had reached the last 16 for the first time.

Otherwise, the furthest progress by non-League clubs has been to the 5th round on 7 occasions: **Colchester** 1948, **Yeovil** 1949, **Blyth** 1978, **Telford** 1985, **Kidderminster** 1994, **Crawley** 2011, **Luton** 2013.

Greatest number of non-League sides to reach the **3rd round** is 8 in 2009: **Barrow, Blyth, Eastwood, Forest Green, Histon, Kettering, Kidderminster** and **Torquay**.

Most to reach **Round 4: 3** in 1957 (**Rhyl, New Brighton, Peterborough**) and 1975 (**Leatherhead, Stafford** and **Wimbledon**).

Five non-League clubs reaching round 3 in 2001 was a Conference record. They were **Chester, Yeovil, Dagenham, Morecambe** and **Kingstonian**.

In season 2002–03, **Team Bath** became the first University-based side to reach the FA Cup 1st Round since **Oxford University** (Finalists in 1880).

NON-LEAGUE 'LAST TIMES'

Last time no non-League club reached round 3: 1951. Last time only one did so: 1969 (**Kettering**).

TOP-DIVISION SCALPS

Victories in FA Cup by non-League clubs over top-division teams since 1900 include: 1900–01 (Final, replay): **Tottenham** 3 Sheffield Utd 1 (Tottenham then in Southern League); 1919–20 **Cardiff** 2, Oldham 0; Sheffield Wed 0, **Darlington** 2; 1923–24 **Corinthians** 1, Blackburn 0; 1947–48 **Colchester** 1, Huddersfield 0; 1948–9 **Yeovil** 2, Sunderland 1; 1971–72 **Hereford** 2, Newcastle 1; 1974–75 Burnley 0, **Wimbledon** 1; 1985–86 Birmingham 1, **Altrincham** 2; 1988–89 **Sutton** 2, Coventry 1; 2012–13 Norwich 0, **Luton** 1, 2016–17 Burnley 0 **Lincoln** 1.

MOST WINNING MEDALS

Ashley Cole has won the trophy seven times, with (Arsenal 2002–03–05) and Chelsea (2007–09–10–12). **The Hon Arthur Kinnaird** (The Wanderers and Old Etonians), **Charles Wollaston** (The Wanderers) and **Jimmy Forrest** (Blackburn) each earned five winners' medals. Kinnaird, later president of the FA, played in nine of the first 12 FA Cup Finals, and was on the winning side three times for The Wanderers, in 1873 (captain), 1877, 1878 (captain), and twice as captain of Old Etonians (1879, 1882).

MANAGERS' MEDALS BACKDATED

In 2010, the FA agreed to award Cup Final medals to all living managers who took their teams to the Final before 1996 (when medals were first given to Wembley team bosses). Lawrie McMenemy had campaigned for the award since Southampton's victory in 1976.

MOST WINNERS' MEDALS AT WEMBLEY

4 – **Mark Hughes** (3 for Manchester Utd, 1 for Chelsea), **Petr Cech, Frank Lampard, John Terry, Didier Drogba, Ashley Cole** (all Chelsea) **Olivier Giroud** (3 for Arsenal, 1 for Chelsea).

3 – **Dick Pym** (3 clean sheets in Finals), **Bob Haworth, Jimmy Seddon, Harry Nuttall, Billy Butler** (all Bolton); **David Jack** (2 Bolton, 1 Arsenal); **Bob Cowell, Jack Milburn, Bobby Mitchell** (all Newcastle); **Dave Mackay** (Tottenham); **Frank Stapleton** (1 Arsenal, 2 Manchester Utd); **Bryan Robson** (3 times winning captain); **Arthur Albiston, Gary Pallister** (all Manchester Utd); **Bruce Grobbelaar, Steve Nicol, Ian Rush** (all Liverpool); **Roy Keane, Peter Schmeichel, Ryan Giggs** (all Manchester Utd); **Dennis Wise** (1 Wimbledon, 2 Chelsea).

Arsenal's **David Seaman** and **Ray Parlour** have each earned 4 winners' medals (2 at Wembley, 2 at Cardiff) as have Manchester Utd's **Roy Keane** and **Ryan Giggs** (3 at Wembley, 1 at Cardiff).

MOST WEMBLEY FINALS

Olivier Giroud appeared in his sixth FA Cup Final when he came off the bench in Chelsea's 1-0 defeat by Leicester in May 2021 – three for Arsenal and three for Chelsea.

MOST WEMBLEY/CARDIFF FINAL APPEARANCES

8 Ashley Cole (Arsenal, Chelsea), 7 Roy Keane (Nottm Forest, Manchester Utd), Ryan Giggs (Manchester Utd); 6 Paul Scholes (Manchester Utd), Olivier Giroud (Arsenal, Chelsea).

BIGGEST FA CUP SCORE AT WEMBLEY

6-0 by Manchester City v Watford (final, May 18, 2019).

WINNING GOALKEEPER-CAPTAINS

1988 **Dave Beasant** (Wimbledon); 2003 **David Seaman** (Arsenal).

MOST WINNING MANAGERS

7 Arsene Wenger (Arsenal) 1998, 2002, 2003, 2005, 2014, 2015, 2017; **6 George Ramsay** (Aston Villa) 1887, 1895, 1897, 1905, 1913, 1920; **5 Sir Alex Ferguson** (Manchester Utd) 1990, 1994, 1996, 1999, 2004.

PLAYER-MANAGERS IN FINAL

Kenny Dalglish (Liverpool, 1986); **Glenn Hoddle** (Chelsea, 1994); **Dennis Wise** (Millwall, 2004).

DEBUTS IN FINAL

Alan Davies (Manchester Utd v Brighton, 1983); **Chris Baird** (Southampton v Arsenal, 2003); **Curtis Weston** (Millwall sub v Manchester Utd, 2004).

SEMI-FINALS AT WEMBLEY

1991 Tottenham 3 Arsenal 1; **1993** Sheffield Wed 2 Sheffield Utd 1, Arsenal 1 Tottenham 0; **1994** Chelsea 2 Luton 0, Manchester Utd 1 Oldham 1; **2000** Aston Villa beat Bolton 4-1 on pens (after 0-0), Chelsea 2 Newcastle 1; **2008** Portsmouth 1 WBA 0, Cardiff 1 Barnsley 0; **2009** Chelsea 2 Arsenal 1, Everton beat Manchester Utd 4-2 on pens (after 0-0); **2010** Chelsea 3 Aston Villa 0, Portsmouth 2 Tottenham 0; **2011** Manchester City 1 Manchester Utd 0, Stoke 5 Bolton 0; **2012** Liverpool 2 Everton 1, Chelsea 5 Tottenham 1; **2013** Wigan 2 Millwall 0, Manchester City 2 Chelsea 1; **2014** Arsenal beat Wigan 4-2 on pens (after 1-1), Hull 5 Sheffield Utd 3; **2015** Arsenal 2 Reading 1, Aston Villa 2 Liverpool 1; **2016** Manchester Utd 2 Everton 1, Crystal Palace 2 Watford 1; **2017** Arsenal 2 Manchester City 1, Chelsea 4 Tottenham 2; **2018** Chelsea 2 Southampton 0, Manchester Utd 2 Tottenham 1; **2019** Manchester City 1 Brighton 0, Watford 3 Wolves 2; **2020** Arsenal 2 Manchester City 0, Chelsea 3 Manchester Utd 1; **2021** Chelsea 1 Manchester City 0, Leicester 1 Southampton 0

CHELSEA'S FA CUP MILESTONES

Their victory over Liverpool in the 2012 Final set the following records:
Captain **John Terry** first player to lift the trophy four times for one club; **Didier Drogba** first to score in four Finals; **Ashley Cole** first to earn seven winner's medals (Arsenal 3, Chelsea 4); **Roberto Di Matteo** first to score for and manage the same winning club (player for Chelsea 1997, 2000, interim manager 2012).
Chelsea's four triumphs in six seasons (2007–12) the best winning sequence since Wanderers won five of the first seven competitions (1872–78) and Blackburn won five out of eight (1884–91).

FIRST ENTRANTS (1871–72)

Barnes, Civil Service, Crystal Palace, Clapham Rov, Donnington School (Spalding), Hampstead Heathens, Harrow Chequers, Hitchin, Maidenhead, Marlow, Queen's Park (Glasgow), Reigate Priory, Royal Engineers, Upton Park and Wanderers. Total 15.

LAST ALL-ENGLISH WINNERS

Manchester City, in 1969, were the last club to win the final with a team of all English players.

FA CUP FIRSTS

Out of country: Cardiff, by defeating Arsenal 1-0 in the 1927 Final at Wembley, became the first and only club to take the FA Cup out of England.
All-English Winning XI: First club to win the FA Cup with all-English XI: Blackburn Olympic in 1883. Others since: WBA in 1888 and 1931, Bolton (1958), Manchester City (1969), West Ham (1964 and 1975).
Non-English Winning XI: Liverpool in 1986 (Mark Lawrenson, born Preston, was a Rep of Ireland player).
Won both Cups: Old Carthusians won the FA Cup in 1881 and the FA Amateur Cup in 1894 and 1897. **Wimbledon** won Amateur Cup in 1963, FA Cup in 1988.

MOST GAMES NEEDED TO WIN

Barnsley played a record 12 matches (20 hours' football) to win the FA Cup in season 1911–12. All six replays (one in round 1, three in round 4 and one in each of semi-final and Final) were brought about by goalless draws.

Arsenal played 11 FA Cup games when winning the trophy in 1979. Five of them were in the 3rd round against Sheffield Wed.

LONGEST TIES

6 matches: (11 hours): Alvechurch v Oxford City (4th qual round, 1971–72). Alvechurch won 1-0.

5 matches: (9 hours, 22 mins – record for competition proper): Stoke v Bury (3rd round, 1954–55). Stoke won 3-2.

5 matches: Chelsea v Burnley (4th round, 1955–56). Chelsea won 2-0.

5 matches: Hull v Darlington (2nd round, 1960–61). Hull won 3-0.

5 matches: Arsenal v Sheffield Wed (3rd round, 1978–79). Arsenal won 2-0.

Other marathons (qualifying comp, all 5 matches, 9 hours): Barrow v Gillingham (last qual round, 1924–25) – winners Barrow; Leyton v Ilford (3rd qual round, 1924–25) – winners Leyton; Falmouth v Bideford (3rd qual round, 1973–74) – winners Bideford.

End of Cup Final replays: The FA decided that, with effect from 1999, there would be no Cup Final replays. In the event of a draw after extra-time, the match would be decided on penalties. This happened for the first time in 2005, when Arsenal beat Manchester Utd 5-4 on penalties after a 0-0 draw. A year later, Liverpool beat West Ham 3-1 on penalties after a 3-3 draw.

FA Cup marathons ended in season 1991–92, when the penalty shoot-out was introduced to decide ties still level after one replay and extra-time.

In 1932–33 **Brighton** (Div 3 South) played 11 FA Cup games, including replays, and scored 43 goals, without getting past round 5. They forgot to claim exemption and had to play from 1st qual round.

LONGEST ROUND

The longest round in FA Cup history was the **3rd round** in **1962–63**. It took 66 days to complete, lasting from Jan 5 to Mar 11, and included 261 postponements because of bad weather.

LONGEST UNBEATEN RUN

23 matches by Blackburn In winning the Cup in three consecutive years (1884–05–06), they won 21 ties (one in a replay), and their first Cup defeat in four seasons was in a first round replay of the next competition.

RE-STAGED TIES

Sixth round, Mar 9, 1974: Newcastle 4, Nottm Forest 3. Match declared void by FA and ordered to be replayed following a pitch invasion after Newcastle had a player sent off. Forest claimed the hold-up caused the game to change its pattern. The tie went to two further matches at Goodison Park (0-0, then 1-0 to Newcastle).

Third round, Jan 5, 1985: Burton 1, Leicester 6 (at Derby). Burton goalkeeper Paul Evans was hit on the head by a missile thrown from the crowd and continued in a daze. The FA ordered the tie to be played again, behind closed doors at Coventry (Leicester won 1-0).

First round replay, Nov 25, 1992: Peterborough 9 (Tony Philliskirk 5), Kingstonian 1. Match expunged from records because, at 3-0 after 57 mins, Kingstonian were reduced to ten men when goalkeeper Adrian Blake was concussed by a 50 pence coin thrown from the crowd. The tie was re-staged on the same ground behind closed doors (Peterborough won 1-0).

Fifth round: Within an hour of holders Arsenal beating Sheffield Utd 2-1 at Highbury on Feb 13, 1999, the FA took the unprecedented step of declaring the match void because an unwritten rule of sportsmanship had been broken. With United's Lee Morris lying injured, their goalkeeper Alan Kelly kicked the ball into touch. Play resumed with Arsenal's Ray Parlour throwing it in the direction of Kelly, but Nwankwo Kanu took possession and centred for Marc Overmars to score the 'winning' goal. After four minutes of protests by manager Steve Bruce and his players, referee Peter Jones confirmed the goal. Both managers absolved Kanu of cheating but Arsenal's Arsene Wenger offered to replay the match. With the FA immediately approving, it was re-staged at Highbury ten days later (ticket prices halved) and Arsenal again won 2-1.

PRIZE FUND

The makeover of the FA Cup competition took off in 2001–02 with the introduction of round-by-round prize-money.

FA CUP FOLLIES

1999–2000 The FA broke with tradition by deciding the 3rd round be moved from its regular Jan date and staged before Christmas. Criticism was strong, gates poor and the 3rd round in 2000–01 reverted to the New Year. By allowing the holders Manchester Utd to withdraw from the 1999–2000 competition in order to play in FIFA's inaugural World Club Championship in Brazil in Jan, the FA were left with an odd number of clubs in the 3rd round. Their solution was a 'lucky losers' draw among clubs knocked out in round 2. Darlington, beaten at Gillingham, won it to re-enter the competition, then lost 2-1 away to Aston Villa.

HAT-TRICKS IN FINAL

There have been three in the history of the competition: **Billy Townley** (Blackburn, 1890), **Jimmy Logan** (Notts Co, 1894) and **Stan Mortensen** (Blackpool, 1953).

MOST APPEARANCES

88 by **Ian Callaghan** (79 for Liverpool, 7 for Swansea City, 2 for Crewe); 87 by **John Barnes** (31 for Watford, 51 for Liverpool, 5 for Newcastle); 86 by **Stanley Matthews** (37 for Stoke, 49 for Blackpool); 84 by **Bobby Charlton** (80 for Manchester Utd, 4 for Preston); 84 by **Pat Jennings** (3 for Watford, 43 for Tottenham, 38 for Arsenal); 84 by **Peter Shilton** for seven clubs (30 for Leicester, 7 for Stoke, 18 for Nottm Forest, 17 for Southampton, 10 for Derby, 1 for Plymouth Argyle, 1 for Leyton Orient); 82 by **David Seaman** (5 for Peterborough, 5 for Birmingham, 17 for QPR, 54 for Arsenal, 1 for Manchester City).

THREE-CLUB FINALISTS

Five players have appeared in the FA Cup Final for three clubs: **Harold Halse** for Manchester Utd (1909), Aston Villa (1913) and Chelsea (1915); **Ernie Taylor** for Newcastle (1951), Blackpool (1953) and Manchester Utd (1958); **John Barnes** for Watford (1984), Liverpool (1988, 1989, 1996) and Newcastle (1998); **Dennis Wise** for Wimbledon (1988), Chelsea (1994, 1997, 2000), Millwall (2004); **David James** for Liverpool (1996), Aston Villa (2000) and Portsmouth (2008, 2010).

CUP MAN WITH TWO CLUBS IN SAME SEASON

Stan Crowther, who played for Aston Villa against Manchester Utd in the 1957 FA Cup Final, appeared for both Villa and United in the 1957–58 competition. United signed him directly after the Munich air crash and, in the circumstances, he was given dispensation to play for them in the Cup, including the Final.

CAPTAIN'S CUP DOUBLE

Martin Buchan is the only player to have captained Scottish and English FA Cup-winning teams – Aberdeen in 1970 and Manchester Utd in 1977.

MEDALS BEFORE AND AFTER

Two players appeared in FA Cup Final teams before and after the Second World War: **Raich Carter** was twice a winner (Sunderland 1937, Derby 1946) and **Willie Fagan** twice on the losing side (Preston 1937, Liverpool 1950).

DELANEY'S COLLECTION

Scotland winger **Jimmy Delaney** uniquely earned Scottish, English, Northern Ireland and Republic of Ireland Cup medals. He was a winner with Celtic (1937), Manchester Utd (1948) and Derry City (1954) and a runner-up with Cork City (1956).

STARS WHO MISSED OUT

Internationals who never won an FA Cup winner's medal include: Tommy Lawton, Tom Finney, Johnny Haynes, Gordon Banks, George Best, Terry Butcher, Peter Shilton, Martin Peters, Nobby Stiles, Alan Ball, Malcolm Macdonald, Alan Shearer, Matthew Le Tissier, Stuart Pearce, Des Walker, Phil Neal, Ledley King.

CUP WINNERS AT NO COST

Not one member of **Bolton**'s 1958 FA Cup-winning team cost the club a transfer fee. Each joined the club for a £10 signing-on fee.

11-NATIONS LINE-UP

Liverpool fielded a team of 11 different nationalities in the FA Cup 3rd round at Yeovil on Jan 4, 2004.

HIGH-SCORING SEMI-FINALS

The **record team score** in FA Cup semi-finals is **6**: 1891–92 WBA 6, Nottm Forest 2; 1907–08 Newcastle 6, Fulham 0; 1933–34 Manchester City 6, Aston Villa 1.

Most goals in semi-finals (aggregate): 17 in 1892 (4 matches) and 1899 (5 matches). In modern times: 15 in 1958 (3 matches, including Manchester Utd 5, Fulham 3 – highest-scoring semi-final since last war); 16 in 1989–90 (Crystal Palace 4, Liverpool 3; Manchester Utd v Oldham 3-3, 2-1. All **16 goals** in those three matches were scored by **different players**.

Stoke's win against Bolton at Wembley in 2011 was the first 5-0 semi-final result since Wolves beat Grimsby at Old Trafford in 1939. In 2014, Hull defeated Sheffield Utd 5-3.

Last hat-trick in an FA Cup semi-final was scored by **Alex Dawson** for Manchester Utd in 5-3 replay win against Fulham at Highbury in 1958.

SEMI-FINAL VENUES

Villa Park has staged more such matches (55 including replays) than any other ground. Next is Hillsborough (33).

ONE IN A HUNDRED

The 2008 semi-finals included only one top-division club, Portsmouth, for the first time in 100 years – since Newcastle in 1908.

FOUR SPECIAL AWAYS

For the only time in FA Cup history, **all four quarter-finals** in season 1986–87 were won by the away team. -

DRAWS RECORD

In season 1985–86, **seven** of the eight 5th round ties went to replays – a record for that stage of the competition.

SHOCK FOR TOP CLUBS

The fourth round on Jan 24, 2015 produced an astonishing set of home defeats for leading clubs. The top three in the Premier League, Chelsea, Manchester City and Southampton were all knocked out and sixth-place Tottenham also lost at home. Odds against this happening were put at 3825-1.

LUCK OF THE DRAW

In the FA Cup on Jan 11, 1947, eight of **London**'s ten Football League clubs involved in the 3rd round were drawn at home (including Chelsea v Arsenal). Only Crystal Palace played outside the capital (at Newcastle).

In the 3rd round in Jan 1992, Charlton were the only London club drawn at home (against Barnet), but the venue of the Farnborough v West Ham tie was reversed on police instruction. So Upton Park staged Cup ties on successive days, with West Ham at home on the Saturday and Charlton (who shared the ground) on Sunday.

Arsenal were drawn away in every round on the way to reaching the Finals of 1971 and 1972. **Manchester Utd** won the Cup in 1990 without playing once at home.

The 1999 finalists, **Manchester Utd** and **Newcastle**, were both drawn at home every time in Rounds 3–6.

On their way to the semi-finals of both domestic Cup competitions in season 2002–03, **Sheffield Utd** were drawn at home ten times out of ten and won all ten matches – six in the League's Worthington Cup and four in the FA Cup.

On their way to winning the Cup in 2014, **Arsenal** did not play once outside London. Home draws in rounds 3, 4, 5 and 6 were followed by the semi-final at Wembley.

ALL TOP-DIVISION VICTIMS

The only instance of an FA Cup-winning club meeting top-division opponents in every round was provided by Manchester Utd in 1947–48. They beat Aston Villa, Liverpool, Charlton, Preston, then Derby in the semi-final and Blackpool in the Final.

In contrast, these clubs have reached the Final without playing top-division opponents on the way: West Ham (1923), Bolton (1926), Blackpool (1948), Bolton (1953), Millwall (2004).

WON CUP WITHOUT CONCEDING GOAL

1873 **The Wanderers** (1 match; as holders, exempt until Final); 1889 **Preston** (5 matches); 1903 **Bury** (5 matches). In 1966 **Everton** reached Final without conceding a goal (7 matches), then beat Sheffield Wed 3-2 at Wembley.

HOME ADVANTAGE

For the first time in FA Cup history, all eight ties in the 1992–93 5th round were won (no replays) by the **clubs drawn at home**. Only other instance of eight home wins at the last 16 stage was in 1889–90, in what was then the 2nd round.

NORTH-EAST WIPE-OUT

For the first time in 54 years, since the 4th round in Jan, 1957, the North-East's 'big three' were knocked out on the same date, Jan 8, 2011 (3rd round). All lost to lower-division opponents – Newcastle 3-1 at Stevenage, **Sunderland** 2-1 at home to Notts County and **Middlesbrough** 2-1 at Burton.

FEWEST TOP-DIVISION CLUBS IN LAST 16 (5TH ROUND)

5 in 1958; **6** in 1927, 1970, 1982; **7** in 1994, 2003; **8** in 2002, 2004.

SIXTH-ROUND ELITE

For the first time in FA Cup 6th round history, dating from 1926 when the format of the competition changed, all **eight quarter-finalists** in 1995–96 were from the top division.

SEMI-FINAL – DOUBLE DERBIES

There have been three instances of both FA Cup semi-finals in the same year being local derbies: **1950** Liverpool beat Everton 2-0 (Maine Road), Arsenal beat Chelsea 1-0 after 2-2 draw (both at Tottenham); **1993** Arsenal beat Tottenham 1-0 (Wembley), Sheffield Wed beat Sheffield Utd 2-1 (Wembley); **2012** Liverpool beat Everton 2-1 (Wembley), Chelsea beat Tottenham 5-1 (Wembley).

TOP CLUB DISTINCTION

Since the Football League began in 1888, there has never been an FA Cup Final in which **neither club** represented the top division.

CLUBS THROWN OUT

Bury expelled (Dec 2006) for fielding an ineligible player in 3-1 2nd rd replay win at Chester. **Droylsden** expelled for fielding a suspended player in 2-1 2nd rd replay win at home to Chesterfield (Dec 2008).

SPURS OUT – AND IN

Tottenham were banned, pre-season, from the 1994–95 competition because of financial irregularities, but were re-admitted on appeal and reached the semi-finals.

FATHER & SON FA CUP WINNERS

Peter Boyle (Sheffield Utd 1899, 1902) and **Tommy Boyle** (Sheffield Utd 1925); **Harry Johnson Snr** (Sheffield Utd 1899, 1902) and **Harry Johnson Jnr** (Sheffield Utd 1925); **Jimmy Dunn Snr** (Everton 1933) and **Jimmy Dunn Jnr** (Wolves 1949); **Alec Herd** (Manchester City 1934) and **David Herd** (Manchester Utd 1963); **Frank Lampard Snr** (West Ham 1975, 1980) and **Frank Lampard Jnr** (Chelsea 2007, 2009, 2010, 2012).

BROTHERS IN FA CUP FINAL TEAMS (modern times)

1950 **Denis and Leslie Compton** (Arsenal); 1952 **George and Ted Robledo** (Newcastle); 1967 **Ron and Allan Harris** (Chelsea); 1977 **Jimmy and Brian Greenhoff** (Manchester Utd); 1996 and 1999 **Gary and Phil Neville** (Manchester Utd).

FA CUP SPONSORS

Littlewoods Pools became the first sponsors of the FA Cup in season 1994–95 in a £14m, 4-year deal. French insurance giants **AXA** took over (season 1998–99) in a sponsorship worth £25m over 4 years. German energy company **E.ON** agreed a 4-year deal worth £32m from season 2006–07 and extended it for a year to 2011. American beer company **Budweiser** began a three-year sponsorship worth £24m in season 2011–12. The **Emirates** airline became the first title sponsor (2015-18) in a reported £30m deal with the FA. This sponsorship was extended for a further three years.

FIRST GOALKEEPER-SUBSTITUTE IN FINAL

Paul Jones (Southampton), who replaced injured Antti Niemi against Arsenal in 2003.

LEAGUE CUP RECORDS

(See also Goalscoring section)

Most winning teams: 8 Liverpool, Manchester City; 5 Aston Villa, Chelsea, Manchester Utd.
Most winning managers: 4 Brian Clough (Nottm Forest), Sir Alex Ferguson (Manchester Utd), Jose Mourinho (3 Chelsea, 1 Manchester Utd), Pep Guardiola (Manchester City, record four successive years, 2018–21)
Highest scores: West Ham 10-0 v Bury (2nd round, 2nd leg 1983–84; agg 12-1); Liverpool 10-0 v Fulham (2nd round, 1st leg 1986–87; agg 13-2).
Most League Cup goals (career): 49 Geoff Hurst (43 West Ham, 6 Stoke, 1960–75); 49 Ian Rush (48 Liverpool, 1 Newcastle, 1981–98).
Highest scorer (season): 12 Clive Allen (Tottenham 1986–87 in 9 apps).
Most goals in match: 6 Frank Bunn (Oldham v Scarborough, 3rd round, 1989–90).
Most winners' medals: 6 Fernandinho (Manchester City)
Most appearances in Final: 6 Kenny Dalglish (Liverpool 1978–87), Ian Rush (Liverpool 1981–95), Emile Heskey (Leicester 1997, 1999, 2000), Liverpool (2001, 2003), Aston Villa (2010), Fernandinho (Manchester City 2014–21).
Biggest Final win: Swansea City 5 Bradford City 0 (2013).
League Cup sponsors: Milk Cup 1981–86, Littlewoods Cup 1987–90, Rumbelows Cup 1991–92, Coca-Cola Cup 1993–98. Worthington Cup 1999–2003, Carling Cup 2003–12; Capital One Cup from season 2012–16; Carabao 2017–22.

Up for the cup, then down: In 2011, Birmingham became only the second club to win a major trophy (the Carling Cup) and be relegated from the top division. It previously happened to Norwich in 1985 when they went down from the old First Division after winning the Milk Cup.

Rush record: Ian Rush was the first to play in 8 winning teams in Cup Finals at Wembley, all with Liverpool (FA Cup 1986–89–92); League Cup 1981–82–83–84–95)

Britain's first under-cover Cup Final: Worthington Cup Final between Blackburn and Tottenham at Cardiff's Millennium Stadium on Sunday, Feb 24, 2002. With rain forecast, the retractable roof was closed on the morning of the match.

Record penalty shoot-out: Liverpool beat Middlesbrough 14-13 (3rd round, Sep 23, 2014) after 2-2. Derby beat Carlisle 14-13 (2nd round, Aug 23, 2016) after 1-1.

DISCIPLINE

SENDINGS-OFF

Season 2003–04 set an **all-time record** of 504 players sent off in English domestic football competitions. There were 58 in the Premier League, 390 Nationwide League, 28 FA Cup (excluding non-League dismissals), 22 League Cup, 2 in Nationwide play-offs, 4 in LDV Vans Trophy.

Most sendings-off in Premier League programme (10 matches): 9 (8 Sat, 1 Sun, Oct 31–Nov 1, 2009).

The 58 Premier League red cards was 13 fewer than the record English **top-division** total of 71 in 2002–03. **Bolton** were the only club in the English divisions without a player sent off in any first-team competition that season.

Worst day for dismissals in English football was Boxing Day, 2007, with **20 red cards** (5 Premier League and 15 Coca-Cola League). Three players, Chelsea's Ashley Cole and Ricardo Carvalho and Aston Villa's Zat Knight were sent off in a 4-4 draw at Stamford Bridge. Luton had three men dismissed in their game at Bristol Rov, but still managed a 1-1 draw.

Previous worst day was Dec 13, 2003, with **19 red cards** (2 Premier League and the 17 Nationwide League).

In the entire first season of post-war League football (1946–47) only 12 players were sent off, followed by 14 in 1949–50, and the total League dismissals for the first nine seasons after the War was 104.

The worst pre-War total was 28 in each of seasons 1921–22 and 1922–23.

ENGLAND SENDINGS-OFF

England had two players sent off in the same match for the first time on Oct 14, 2020 when losing 1-0 to Denmark in the Nations League at Wembley. Harry Maguire was dismissed for two yellow cards and Reece James shown a straight red for confronting Spanish referee Jesus Gil Manzano after the final whistle.

Jun 5, 1968	**Alan Mullery**	v Yugoslavia (Florence, Euro Champ)
Jun 6, 1973	**Alan Ball**	v Poland (Chorzow, World Cup qual)
Jun 12, 1977	**Trevor Cherry**	v Argentina (Buenos Aires, friendly)
Jun 6, 1986	**Ray Wilkins**	v Morocco (Monterrey, World Cup Finals)
Jun 30, 1998	**David Beckham**	v Argentina (St Etienne, World Cup Finals)
Sep 5, 1998	**Paul Ince**	v Sweden (Stockholm, Euro Champ qual)
Jun 5, 1999	**Paul Scholes**	v Sweden (Wembley, Euro Champ qual)
Sep 8, 1999	**David Batty**	v Poland (Warsaw, Euro Champ qual)
Oct 16, 2002	**Alan Smith**	v Macedonia (Southampton, Euro Champ qual)
Oct 8, 2005	**David Beckham**	v Austria (Old Trafford, World Cup qual)
Jul 1, 2006	**Wayne Rooney**	v Portugal (Gelsenkirchen, World Cup Finals)
Oct 10, 2009	**Robert Green**	v Ukraine (Dnipropetrovsk, World Cup qual)
Oct 7, 2011	**Wayne Rooney**	v Montenegro (Podgorica, Euro Champ qual)
Sep 11, 2012	**Steven Gerrard**	v Ukraine (Wembley, World Cup qual)
Jun 4, 2014	**Raheem Sterling**	v Ecuador (Miami, friendly)

Sep 5, 2020 **Kyle Walker** v Iceland (Reykjavik, Nations Lge)

Oct 14, 2020 **Harry Maguire** and **Reece James** v Denmark (Wembley, Nations Lge)

Other countries: Most recent sendings-off of players representing other Home Countries:

N Ireland – Josh Magennis (Nations Lge v Romania, Bucharest, Sep 4, 2020).

Scotland – John Souttar (Nations Lge v Israel, Haifa, Oct 11, 2018).

Wales – Ethan Ampadu (European Champ v Italy, Rome, Jun 20,2021; Harry Wilson (European Champ v Denmark, Amsterdam, Jun 26,2021)

Rep of Ireland – Jeff Hendrick (Nations Lge v Wales, Cardiff, Nov 15, 2020)

England dismissals at other levels:

U-23: Stan Anderson (v Bulgaria, Sofia, May 19, 1957); **Alan Ball** (v Austria, Vienna, Jun 2, 1965); **Kevin Keegan** (v E Germany, Magdeburg, Jun 1, 1972); **Steve Perryman** (v Portugal, Lisbon, Nov 19, 1974).

U-21: Sammy Lee (v Hungary, Keszthely, Jun 5, 1981); **Mark Hateley** (v Scotland, Hampden Park, Apr 19, 1982); **Paul Elliott** (v Denmark, Maine Road, Manchester, Mar 26, 1986); **Tony Cottee** (v W Germany, Ludenscheid, Sep 8, 1987); **Julian Dicks** (v Mexico, Toulon, France, Jun 12, 1988); **Jason Dodd** (v Mexico, Toulon, May 29, 1991; 3 Mexico players also sent off in that match); **Matthew Jackson** (v France, Toulon, May 28, 1992); **Robbie Fowler** (v Austria, Kafkenberg, Oct 11, 1994); **Alan Thompson** (v Portugal, Oporto, Sep 2, 1995); **Terry Cooke** (v Portugal, Toulon, May 30, 1996); **Ben Thatcher** (v Italy, Rieti, Oct 10, 1997); **John Curtis** (v Greece, Heraklion, Nov 13, 1997); **Jody Morris** (v Luxembourg, Grevenmacher, Oct 13, 1998); **Stephen Wright** (v Germany, Derby, Oct 6, 2000); **Alan Smith** (v Finland, Valkeakoski, Oct 10, 2000); **Luke Young** and **John Terry** (v Greece, Athens, Jun 5, 2001); **Shola Ameobi** (v Portugal, Rio Maior, Mar 28, 2003); **Jermaine Pennant** (v Croatia, Upton Park, Aug 19, 2003); **Glen Johnson** (v Turkey, Istanbul, Oct 10, 2003); **Nigel Reo-Coker** (v Azerbaijan, Baku, Oct 12, 2004); **Glen Johnson** (v Spain, Henares, Nov 16, 2004); **Steven Taylor** (v Germany, Leverkusen, Oct 10, 2006); **Tom Huddlestone** (v Serbia & Montenegro, Nijmegen, Jun 17, 2007); **Tom Huddlestone** (v Wales, Villa Park, Oct 14, 2008); **Michael Mancienne** (v Finland, Halmstad, Jun 15, 2009); **Fraizer Campbell** (v Sweden, Gothenburg, Jun 26, 2009); **Ben Mee** (v Italy, Empoli, Feb 8, 2011); **Danny Rose** (v Serbia, Krusevac, Oct 16, 2012); **Andre Wisdom** (v Finland, Tampere, Sep 9, 2013); **Jack Stephens** (v Bosnia-Herz, Sarajevo, Nov 12, 2015; **Jordon Ibe** (vSwitzerland, Thun, Mar 26, 2016); **Curtis Jones** (v Croatia, Koper, Mar 31, 2021).

England 'B' (1): **Neil Webb** (v Algeria, Algiers, Dec 11, 1990).

MOST DISMISSALS IN INTERNATIONAL MATCHES

19 (10 Chile, 9 Uruguay), Jun 25, 1975; **6** (2 Mexico, 4 Argentina), 1956; **6** (5 Ecuador, 1 Uruguay), Jan 4, 1977 (4 Ecuadorians sent off in 78th min, match abandoned, 1-1); **5** (Holland 3, Brazil 2), Jun 6, 1999 in Goianio, Brazil.

INTERNATIONAL STOPPED THROUGH DEPLETED SIDE

Portugal v Angola (5-1), friendly international in Lisbon on Nov 14, 2001, abandoned (68 mins) because Angola were down to 6 players (4 sent off, 1 carried off, no substitutes left).

MOST 'CARDS' IN WORLD CUP FINALS MATCH

20 in Portugal v Holland quarter-final, Nuremberg, Jun 25, 2006 (9 yellow, 2 red, Portugal; 7 yellow, 2 red, Holland).

FIVE OFF IN ONE MATCH

For the first time since League football began in 1888, five players were sent off in one match (two Chesterfield, three Plymouth) in Div 2 at Saltergate on **Feb 22, 1997**. Four were dismissed (two from each side) in a goalmouth brawl in the last minute. Five were sent off on Dec 2, 1997 (4 Bristol Rov, 1 Wigan) in Div 2 match at Wigan, four in the 45th minute. The third instance occurred at Exeter on **Nov 23, 2002** in Div 3 (three Exeter, two Cambridge United) all in the last minute. On **Mar 27, 2012** (Lge 2) three Bradford players and two from Crawley were shown red cards in the dressing rooms after a brawl at the final whistle at Valley Parade.

Matches with **four** Football League club players being sent off in one match:

Jan 8, 1955: Crewe v Bradford City (Div 3 North), two players from each side.

Dec 13, 1986: Sheffield Utd (1 player) v Portsmouth (3) in Div 2.

Aug 18, 1987: Port Vale v Northampton (Littlewoods Cup 1st Round, 1st Leg), two players from each side.

Dec 12, 1987: Brentford v Mansfield (Div 3), two players from each side.

Sep 6, 1992: First instance in British first-class football of four players from one side being sent off in one match. Hereford's seven survivors, away to Northampton (Div 3), held out for a 1-1 draw.

Mar 1, 1977: Norwich v Huddersfield (Div 1), two from each side.

Oct 4, 1977: Shrewsbury (1 player), Rotherham (3) in Div 3.

Aug 22, 1998: Gillingham v Bristol Rov (Div 2), two from each side, all after injury-time brawl.

Mar 16, 2001: Bristol City v Millwall (Div 2), two from each side.

Aug 17, 2002: Lincoln (1 player), Carlisle (3) in Div 3.

Aug 26, 2002: Wycombe v QPR (Div 2), two from each side.

Nov 1, 2005: Burnley (1 player) v Millwall (3) in Championship.

Nov 24, 2007: Swindon v Bristol Rov (Lge 1), two from each side.

Mar 4, 2008: Hull v Burnley (Champ) two from each side.

Four Stranraer players were sent off away to Airdrie (Scottish Div 1) on Dec 3, 1994, and that Scottish record was equalled when four Hearts men were ordered off away to Rangers (Prem Div) on Sep 14, 1996. Albion had four players sent off (3 in last 8 mins) away to Queen's Park (Scottish Div 3) on Aug 23, 1997.

In the **Island Games** in Guernsey (Jul 2003), five players (all from Rhodes) were sent off against Guernsey for violent conduct and the match was abandoned by referee Wendy Toms.

Most dismissals one team, one match: Five players of America Tres Rios in first ten minutes after disputed goal by opponents Itaperuna in Brazilian cup match in Rio de Janeiro on Nov 23, 1991. Tie then abandoned and awarded to Itaperuna.

Eight dismissals in one match: Four on each side in South American Super Cup quarter-final (Gremio, Brazil v Penarol, Uruguay) in Oct 1993.

Five dismissals in one season – Dave Caldwell (2 with Chesterfield, 3 with Torquay) in 1987–88.

First instance of four dismissals in Scottish match: three Rangers players (all English – Terry Hurlock, Mark Walters, Mark Hateley) and Celtic's Peter Grant in Scottish Cup quarter-final at Parkhead on Mar 17, 1991 (Celtic won 2-0).

Four players (3 Hamilton, 1 Airdrie) were sent off in Scottish Div 1 match on Oct 30, 1993.

Four players (3 Ayr, 1 Stranraer) were sent off in Scottish Div 1 match on Aug 27, 1994.

In Scottish Cup first round replays on Dec 16, 1996, there were two instances of three players of one side sent off: Albion Rov (away to Forfar) and Huntly (away to Clyde).

FASTEST SENDINGS-OFF

World record – 10 sec: Giuseppe Lorenzo (Bologna) for striking opponent in Italian League match v Parma, Dec 9, 1990. Goalkeeper **Preston Edwards** (Ebbsfleet) for bringing down opponent and conceding penalty in Blue Square Premier League South match v Farnborough, Feb 5, 2011.

World record (non-professional) – 3 sec: David Pratt (Chippenham) at Bashley (British Gas Southern Premier League, Dec 27, 2008).

Domestic – 13 sec: Kevin Pressman (Sheffield Wed goalkeeper at Wolves, Div 1, Sunday, Aug 14, 2000); **15 sec: Simon Rea** (Peterborough at Cardiff, Div 2, Nov 2, 2002). **19 sec: Mark Smith** (Crewe goalkeeper at Darlington, Div 3, Mar 12, 1994). **Premier League – 72 sec: Tim Flowers** (Blackburn goalkeeper v Leeds Utd, Feb 1, 1995).

In World Cup – 55 sec: Jose Batista (Uruguay v Scotland at Neza, Mexico, Jun 13, 1986).

In European competition – 90 sec: Sergei Dirkach (Dynamo Moscow v Ghent UEFA Cup 3rd round, 2nd leg, Dec 11, 1991).

Fastest FA Cup dismissal – 52 sec: Ian Culverhouse (Swindon defender, deliberate hand-ball on goal-line, away to Everton, 3rd Round, Sunday Jan 5, 1997).

Fastest League Cup dismissal – 33 sec: Jason Crowe (Arsenal substitute v Birmingham, 3rd Round, Oct 14, 1997). Also fastest sending off on debut.

Fastest Sending-off of substitute – 0 sec: Walter Boyd (Swansea City) for striking opponent before ball in play after he went on (83 mins) at home to Darlington, Div 3, Nov 23, 1999. **15 secs: Keith Gillespie** (Sheffield Utd) for striking an opponent at Reading (Premier League), Jan 20, 2007. **90 sec: Andreas Johansson** (Wigan), without kicking a ball, for shirt-pulling (penalty) away to Arsenal (Premier League), May 7, 2006.

MOST SENDINGS-OFF IN CAREER

21 **Willie Johnston** , 1964–82 (Rangers 7, WBA 6, Vancouver Whitecaps 4, Hearts 3, Scotland 1)
21 **Roy McDonough**, 1980–95 (13 in Football League – Birmingham, Walsall, Chelsea, Colchester, Southend, Exeter, Cambridge Utd plus 8 non-league)
13 **Steve Walsh** (Wigan, Leicester, Norwich, Coventry)
13 **Martin Keown** (Arsenal, Aston Villa, Everton)
13 **Alan Smith** (Leeds, Manchester Utd, Newcastle, England U–21, England)
12 **Dennis Wise** (Wimbledon, Chelsea, Leicester, Millwall)
12 **Vinnie Jones** (Wimbledon, Leeds, Sheffield Utd, Chelsea, QPR)
12 **Mark Dennis** (Birmingham, Southampton, QPR)
12 **Roy Keane** (Manchester Utd, Rep of Ireland)
10 **Patrick Vieira** (Arsenal)
10 **Paul Scholes** (Manchester Utd, England)
Most Premier League sendings-off: Patrick Vieira 9, Duncan Ferguson 8, Richard Dunne 8, Vinnie Jones 7, Roy Keane 7, Alan Smith 7. Lee Cattermole 7.

● **Carlton Palmer** holds the unique record of having been sent off with each of his five Premier League clubs: Sheffield Wed, Leeds, Southampton, Nottm Forest and Coventry.

FA CUP FINAL SENDINGS-OFF

Kevin Moran (Manchester Utd) v Everton, Wembley, 1985; **Jose Antonio Reyes** (Arsenal) v Manchester Utd, Cardiff, 2005; **Pablo Zabaleta** (Manchester City) v Wigan, Wembley 2013; **Chris Smalling** (Manchester Utd) v Crystal Palace , Wembley, 2016; **Victor Moses** (Chelsea) v Arsenal, Wembley, 2017. **Mateo Kovacic** (Chelsea) v Arsenal, Wembley 2020.

WEMBLEY SENDINGS-OFF

Aug 1948	**Branko Stankovic** (Yugoslavia) v Sweden, Olympic Games
Jul 1966	**Antonio Rattin** (Argentina captain) v England, World cup quarter-final
Aug 1974	**Billy Bremner** (Leeds) and **Kevin Keegan** (Liverpool), Charity Shield
Mar 1977	**Gilbert Dresch** (Luxembourg) v England, World Cup
May 1985	**Kevin Moran** (Manchester Utd) v Everton, FA Cup Final
Apr 1993	**Lee Dixon** (Arsenal) v Tottenham, FA Cup semi-final
May 1993	**Peter Swan** (Port Vale) v WBA, Div 2 Play-off Final
Mar 1994	**Andrei Kanchelskis** (Manchester Utd) v Aston Villa, League Cup Final
May 1994	**Mike Wallace, Chris Beaumont** (Stockport) v Burnley, Div 2 Play-off Final
Jun 1995	**Tetsuji Hashiratani** (Japan) v England, Umbro Cup
May 1997	**Brian Statham** (Brentford) v Crewe, Div 2 Play-off Final
Apr 1998	**Capucho** (Portugal) v England, friendly
Nov 1998	**Ray Parlour** (Arsenal) and **Tony Vareilles** (Lens), Champions League
Mar 1999	**Justin Edinburgh** (Tottenham) v Leicester, League Cup Final
Jun 1999	**Paul Scholes** (England) v Sweden, European Championship qual
Feb 2000	**Clint Hill** (Tranmere) v Leicester, League Cup Final
Apr 2000	**Mark Delaney** (Aston Villa) v Bolton, FA Cup semi-final
May 2000	**Kevin Sharp** (Wigan) v Gillingham, Div 2 Play-off Final
Aug 2000	**Roy Keane** (Manchester Utd captain) v Chelsea, Charity Shield
May 2007	**Marc Tierney** (Shrewsbury) v Bristol Rov, Lge 2 Play-off Final
May 2007	**Matt Gill** (Exeter) v Morecambe, Conf Play-off Final
May 2009	**Jamie Ward** (Sheffield Utd) and **Lee Hendrie** (Sheffield Utd) v Burnley, Champ Play-off Final (Hendrie after final whistle)

May 2009	**Phil Bolland** (Cambridge Utd) v Torquay, Blue Square Prem Lge Play-off Final
May 2010	**Robin Hulbert** (Barrow) and **David Bridges** (Stevenage), FA Trophy Final
Apr 2011	**Paul Scholes** (Manchester Utd) v Manchester City, FA Cup semi-final
Apr 2011	**Toumani Diagouraga** (Brentford) v Carlisle, Johnstone's Paint Trophy Final
Sep 2012	**Steven Gerrard** (England) v Ukraine, World Cup qual
Feb 2013	**Matt Duke** (Bradford) v Swansea, League Cup Final
May 2013	**Pablo Zabaleta** (Manchester City) v Wigan, FA Cup Final
Mar 2014	**Joe Newell** (Peterborough) v Chesterfield, Johnstone's Paint Trophy Final
May 2014	**Gary O'Neil** (QPR) v Derby, Champ Play-off Final
May 2016	**Chris Smalling** (Manchester Utd) v Crystal Palace, FA Cup Final
May 2017	**Victor Moses** (Chelsea) v Arsenal, FA Cup Final
Aug 2017	**Pedro** (Chelsea) v Arsenal, Community Shield
Sep 2017	**Jan Vertonghen** (Tottenham) v Borussia Dortmund, Champions League
May 2018	**Liam Ridehalgh** (Tranmere) v Boreham Wood, National League Play-off Final – after 48 secs
May 2018	**Denis Odoi** (Fulham) v Aston Villa, Championship Play-off Final
May 2019	**Mark O'Brien** (Newport) v Tranmere, Lge 2 Play-off Final
Jun 2020	**Dean Moxey** (Exeter) v Northampton, Lge 2 Play-off Final
Aug 2020	**Mateo Kovacic** (Chelsea) v Arsenal, FA Cup Final
Oct 2020	**Harry Maguire, Reece James** (England) v Denmark, Nations Lge
May 2021	**Jay Fulton** (Swansea) v Brentford, Champ Play-off Final

WEMBLEY'S SUSPENDED CAPTAINS

Suspension prevented four **club captains** playing at Wembley in modern finals, in successive years. Three were in FA Cup Finals – **Glenn Roeder** (QPR, 1982), **Steve Foster** (Brighton, 1983), **Wilf Rostron** (Watford, 1984). Sunderland's **Shaun Elliott** was banned from the 1985 Milk Cup Final. Roeder was banned from QPR's 1982 Cup Final replay against Tottenham, and Foster was ruled out of the first match in Brighton's 1983 Final against Manchester Utd.

RED CARD FOR KICKING BALL-BOY

Chelsea's **Eden Hazard** was sent off (80 mins) in the League Cup semi-final, second leg at Swansea on Jan 23, 2013 for kicking a 17-year-old ball-boy who refused to hand over the ball that had gone out of play. The FA suspended Hazard for three matches.

BOOKINGS RECORDS

Most players of one Football League club booked in one match is **TEN** – members of the Mansfield team away to Crystal Palace in FA Cup second round, Nov 1962. Most yellow cards for one team in Premier League match – **9** for Tottenham away to Chelsea, May 2, 2016.

Fastest bookings – 3 seconds after kick-off, **Vinnie Jones** (Chelsea, home to Sheffield Utd, FA Cup fifth round, Feb 15, 1992); 5 seconds after kick-off: **Vinnie Jones** (Sheffield Utd, away to Manchester City, Div 1, Jan 19, 1991). He was sent-off (54 mins) for second bookable offence.

FIGHTING TEAM-MATES

Charlton's **Mike Flanagan** and **Derek Hales** were sent off for fighting each other five minutes from end of FA Cup 3rd round tie at home to Southern League Maidstone on Jan 9, 1979.

Bradford City's **Andy Myers** and **Stuart McCall** had a fight during the 1-6 Premier League defeat at Leeds on Sunday, May 13, 2001.

On Sep 28, 1994 the Scottish FA suspended Hearts players **Graeme Hogg** and **Craig Levein** for ten matches for fighting each other in a pre-season 'friendly' v Raith.

Blackburn's England players **Graeme Le Saux** and **David Batty** clashed away to Spartak Moscow (Champions League) on Nov 22, 1995. Neither was sent off.

Newcastle United's England Internationals **Lee Bowyer** and **Kieron Dyer** were sent off for fighting each other at home to Aston Villa (Premier League on Apr 2, 2005).

Arsenal's **Emmanuel Adebayor** and **Nicklas Bendtner** clashed during the 5-1 Carling Cup semi-final 2nd leg defeat at Tottenham on Jan 22, 2008. Neither was sent off; each fined by their club.

Stoke's **Ricardo Fuller** was sent off for slapping his captain, Andy Griffin, at West Ham in the Premier League on Dec 28, 2008.

Preston's **Jermaine Beckford** and **Eoin Doyle** clashed in the Championship game against Sheffield Wednesday on Dec 3, 2016, and were sent off.

St Johnstone's **Richard Foster** and **Danny Swanson** were dismissed for brawling in the Scottish Premier League match with Hamilton on Apr 1, 2017.

FOOTBALL'S FIRST BETTING SCANDAL

A Football League investigation into the First Division match which ended Manchester Utd 2, Liverpool 0 at Old Trafford on Good Friday, Apr 2, 1915 proved that the result had been 'squared' by certain players betting on the outcome. Four members of each team were suspended for life, but some of the bans were lifted when League football resumed in 1919 in recognition of the players' war service.

PLAYERS JAILED

Ten professional footballers found guilty of conspiracy to fraud by 'fixing' matches for betting purposes were given prison sentences at Nottingham Assizes on Jan 26, 1965.

Jimmy Gauld (Mansfield), described as the central figure, was given four years. Among the others sentenced, **Tony Kay** (Sheffield Wed, Everton & England), **Peter Swan** (Sheffield Wed & England) and **David 'Bronco' Layne** (Sheffield Wed) were suspended from football for life by the FA.

DRUGS BANS

Abel Xavier (Middlesbrough) was the first Premier League player found to have taken a performance-enhancing drug. He was banned by UEFA for 18 months in Nov 2005 after testing positive for an anabolic steroid. The ban was reduced to a year in Jul 2006 by the Court of Arbitration for Sport. **Paddy Kenny** (Sheffield Utd goalkeeper) was suspended by an FA commission for 9 months from July, 2009 for failing a drugs test the previous May. Kolo Toure (Manchester City) received a 6-month ban in May 2011 for a doping offence. It was backdated to Mar 2.

LONG SUSPENSIONS

The longest suspension (8 months) in modern times for a player in British football was imposed on two Manchester Utd players. First was **Eric Cantona** following his attack on a spectator as he left the pitch after being sent off at Crystal Palace (Prem League) on Jan 25, 1995. The club immediately suspended him to the end of the season and fined him 2 weeks' wages (est £20,000). Then, on a disrepute charge, the FA fined him £10,000 (Feb 1995) and extended the ban to Sep 30 (which FIFA confirmed as world-wide). A subsequent 2-weeks' jail sentence on Cantona for assault was altered, on appeal, to 120 hours' community service, which took the form of coaching schoolboys in the Manchester area.

On **Dec 19, 2003** an FA Commission, held at Bolton, suspended **Rio Ferdinand** from football for 8 months (plus £50,000 fine) for failing to take a random drug test at the club's training ground on Sep 23. The ban operated from Jan 12, 2004.

Aug 1974: Kevin Keegan (Liverpool) and **Billy Bremner** (Leeds) both suspended for 10 matches and fined £500 after being sent off in FA Charity Shield at Wembley.

Jan 1988: Mark Dennis (QPR) given 8-match ban after 11th sending-off of his career.

Oct 1988: Paul Davis (Arsenal) banned for 9 matches for breaking the jaw of Southampton's Glenn Cockerill.

Oct 1998: Paolo Di Canio (Sheff Wed) banned for 11 matches and fined £10,000 for pushing referee Paul Alcock after being sent off at home to Arsenal (Prem), Sep 26.

Mar 2005: David Prutton (Southampton) banned for 10 matches (plus 1 for red card) and fined £6,000 by FA for shoving referee Alan Wiley when sent off at home to Arsenal (Prem), Feb 26.

Aug 2006: Ben Thatcher (Manchester City) banned for 8 matches for elbowing Pedro Mendes (Portsmouth).

Sep 2008: Joey Barton (Newcastle) banned for 12 matches (6 suspended) and fined £25,000 by FA for training ground assault on former Manchester City team-mate Ousmane Dabo.

May 2012: Joey Barton (QPR) suspended for 12 matches and fined £75,000 for violent conduct when sent off against Manchester City on final day of Premier League season.

Mar 2014: Joss Labadie (Torquay) banned for 10 matches and fined £2,000 for biting Chesterfield's Ollie Banks (Lge 2) on Feb 15, 2014.

Seven-month ban: Frank Barson, 37-year-old Watford centre-half, sent off at home to Fulham (Div 3 South) on Sep 29, 1928, was suspended by the FA for the remainder of the season.

Twelve-month ban: Oldham full-back Billy Cook was given a 12-month suspension for refusing to leave the field when sent off at Middlesbrough (Div 1), on Apr 3, 1915. The referee abandoned the match with 35 minutes still to play, and the score (4-1 to Middlesbrough) was ordered to stand.

Long Scottish bans: Sep 1954: Willie Woodburn, Rangers and Scotland centre-half, suspended for rest of career after fifth sending-off in 6 years.

Billy McLafferty, Stenhousemuir striker, was banned (Apr 14) for 8 and a half months, to Jan 1, 1993, and fined £250 for failing to appear at a disciplinary hearing after being sent off against Arbroath on Feb 1.

Twelve-match ban: On May 12, 1994 Scottish FA suspended Rangers forward Duncan Ferguson for 12 matches for violent conduct v Raith on Apr 16. On Oct 11, 1995, Ferguson (then with Everton) sent to jail for 3 months for the assault (served 44 days); Feb 1, 1996 Scottish judge quashed 7 matches that remained of SFA ban on Ferguson.

On Sep 29, 2001 the SFA imposed a **17-match suspension** on Forfar's former Scottish international Dave Bowman for persistent foul and abusive language when sent off against Stranraer on Sep 22. As his misconduct continued, he was shown **5 red cards** by the referee.

On Apr 3, 2009, captain Barry Ferguson and goalkeeper Allan McGregor were banned for life from playing for Scotland for gestures towards photographers while on the bench for a World Cup qualifier against Iceland.

On Dec 20, 2011 Liverpool and Uruguay striker Luis Suarez was given an 8-match ban and fined £40,000 by the FA for making 'racially offensive comments' to Patrice Evra of Manchester Utd (Prem Lge, Oct 15).

On Apr 25, 2013 Luis Suarez was given a 10-match suspension by the FA for 'violent conduct' – biting Chelsea defender Branislav Ivanovic, Prem Lge, Apr 21. The Liverpool player was also fined £200,000 by Liverpool. His ban covered the last 4 games of that season and the first 6 of 2013–14. On Jun 26, 2014, Suarez, while still a Liverpool player, received the most severe punishment in World Cup history – a four-month ban from 'all football activities' and £66,000 fine from FIFA for biting Giorgio Chiellini during Uruguay's group game against Italy.

On Nov 4, 2016 Rochdale's Calvin Andrew was banned by the FA for 12 matches – reduced to 9 on appeal – for elbowing Peter Clarke (Oldham) in the face.

On Apr 16, 2017 Joey Barton was banned by the FA for 18 months and fined £30,000 for breaching betting rules. The Burnley player admitted placing 1,260 bets on matches.

TWO-YEAR EUROPEAN BAN OVERTURNED

Manchester City received a two-season European ban and £25m fine in February 2020 after being charged with breaking UEFA's Financial Fair Play rules. The club lodged an appeal with the Court of Arbitration for Sport and the ban was quashed in July 2020. The fine, for not co-operating with UEFA, was reduced to £9m.

TOP FINES

Clubs: **£49,000,000** (World record) Manchester City: May 2014 for breaking UEFA Financial Fair Play rules (**£32,600,000** suspended subject to City meeting certain conditions over two seasons). **£42m** settlement Queens Park Rangers: Jul 2018, breaching Financial Fair Play rules; **£7.6m** Bournemouth: May 2016, for breaking Financial Fair Play rules; **£5,500,000** West Ham: Apr 2007, for breaches of regulations involving 'dishonesty and deceit' over Argentine signings Carlos Tevez and Javier Mascherano; **£3.95m** Watford: Aug 2017, forged banking letter; **£1,500,000** (increased from original £600,000) Tottenham: Dec 1994, financial irregularities; **£875,000** QPR: May 2011 for breaching rules when signing Argentine Alejandro Faurlin; **£500,000** (plus 2-year academy signings ban) Everton: Nov 2018, breaking recruitment rules; **£460,000** plus signings ban in two transfer windows (reduced on appeal to £230,000 and one transfer window) Chelsea: breaching rules relating to under-18 foreign players; **£390,000** FA: Feb 2019, failing to police recruitment of young players; **£375,000** (reduced to £290,000 on appeal) Chelsea: May 2016, players brawl v Tottenham; **£315,000** Manchester City: Aug 2019, breaching rules on signing youth players; **£300,000** (reduced to £75,000 on appeal) Chelsea: Jun 2005, illegal approach to Arsenal's Ashley Cole; **£300,000** (plus 2-year ban on signing academy players, part suspended) Manchester City: May 2017, approaching young players; **£225,000** (reduced to £175,000 on appeal) Tottenham: May 2016, players brawl v Chelsea; **£200,000** Aston Villa: May 2015 for fans' pitch invasion after FA Cup quarter-final v WBA; **£200,000** Leeds: Feb 2019, spying on other clubs' training sessions; **£200,000** (half suspended): Liverpool: Oct 2019, ineligible player, League Cup v MK Dons; **£175,000** Arsenal: Oct 2003, players' brawl v Manchester Utd; **£150,000** Leeds: Mar 2000, players' brawl v Tottenham; **£150,000** Tottenham: Mar 2000, players brawl v Leeds; **£145,000** Hull: Feb 2015, breaching Financial Fair Play rules; **£115,000** West Ham: Aug 2009, crowd misconduct at Carling Cup; v Millwall; **£105,000** Chelsea: Jan 1991, irregular payments; **£100,000** Boston Utd: Jul 2002, contract irregularities; **£100,000** Arsenal and Chelsea: Mar 2007 for mass brawl after Carling Cup Final; **£100,000** (including suspended fine) Blackburn: Aug 2007, poor disciplinary record; **£100,000** Sunderland: May 2014, breaching agents' regulations; **£100,000** Reading: Aug 2015, pitch invasion, FA Cup tie v Bradford (reduced to £40,000 on appeal); **£100,000** Chelsea: Dec 2016, players brawl v Manchester City; **£100,000** (plus 2-year ban on signing academy players, part suspended) Liverpool: Apr 2017, approaching young player; **£100,000** West Ham: Jan 2019, pitch invasions v Burnley; **£100,000** Derby: Jun 2021, prohibitive accounting policies;

£90,000 Brighton: Feb 2015, breaching rules on agents; **£71,000** West Ham: Feb 2015 for playing Diafra Sakho in FA Cup 4th round tie against Bristol City after declaring him unfit for Senegal's Africa Cup of Nations squad; **£65,000** Chelsea: Jan 2016, players brawl v WBA; **£62,000** Macclesfield: Dec 2005, funding of a stand at club's ground.

Players: £220,000 (plus 4-match ban) John Terry (Chelsea): Sep 2012, racially abusing Anton Ferdinand (QPR); **£150,000** Roy Keane (Manchester Utd): Oct 2002, disrepute offence over autobiography; **£150,000** plus 4-month ban (increased from £75,000 and two-week ban after appeal by FA) Daniel Sturridge (ex-Liverpool): Mar 2020, breaching betting rules; **£100,000** (reduced to £75,000 on appeal) Ashley Cole (Arsenal): Jun 2005, illegal approach by Chelsea; **£100,000 (plus 5-match ban)** Jonjo Shelvey (Newcastle): Dec 2016, racially abusing Romain Saiss (Wolves); **£100,000 (plus 3-match ban)** Edinson Cavani (Manchester Utd): Dec 2020, offensive social media post; **£70,000** (plus world-wide 10-week ban Kieran Trippier (Atletico Madrid and England): Dec 2020, breaching FA betting rules; **£90,000** Ashley Cole (Chelsea): Oct 2012, offensive Tweet against FA; **£80,000 (plus 5-match ban)** Nicolas Anelka (WBA): Feb 2014, celebrating goal at West Ham with racially-offensive 'quenelle' gesture; **£75,000 (plus 12-match ban)** Joey Barton (QPR): May 2012, violent conduct v Manchester City; **£60,000 (plus 3-match ban)** John Obi Mikel (Chelsea): Dec 2012, abusing referee Mark Clattenburg after Prem Lge v Manchester Utd); **£60,000** Dexter Blackstock (Nottm Forest): May 2014, breaching betting rules; **£60,000** (plus 8-match ban) Kiko Casilla (Leeds): Feb 2020, racially abusing Jonathan Leko (Charlton);**£50,000** Cameron Jerome (Stoke): Aug 2013, breaching FA betting rules; **£50,000** Benoit Assou-Ekotto (Tottenham): Sep 2014, publicly backing Nicolas Anelka's controversial 'quenelle' gesture; **£50,000** (plus 1-match ban) Bernardo Silva (Manchester City): Nov 2019, offensive social media message to team-mate Benjamin Mendy; **£50,000** (plus 1-match ban) Dele Alli (Tottenham): Jun 2020, offensive social media post; **£45,000** Patrick Vieira (Arsenal): Oct 1999, tunnel incidents v West Ham; **£45,000** Rio Ferdinand (Manchester Utd): Aug 2012, improper comments about Ashley Cole on Twitter; **£40,000** Lauren (Arsenal): Oct 2003, players' fracas v Manchester Utd; **£40,000 (plus 8-match ban)** Luis Suarez (Liverpool): Dec 2011, racially abusing Patrice Evra (Manchester Utd); **£40,000 (plus 3-match ban)** Dani Osvaldo (Southampton): Jan 2014, violent conduct, touchline Newcastle; **£40,000** Bacary Sagna (Manchester City): Jan 2017, questioning integrity of referee Lee Mason; **£40,000**

(plus 4-match ban) Eric Dier (Tottenham): Jul 2020, confronting spectator in the stand.

*In eight seasons with Arsenal (1996–2004) **Patrick Vieira** was fined a total of £122,000 by the FA for disciplinary offences.

Managers: £200,000 (reduced to £75,000 on appeal) Jose Mourinho (Chelsea): Jun 2005, illegal approach to Arsenal's Ashley Cole; **£60,000 (plus 7-match ban)** Alan Pardew (Newcastle): head-butting Hull player David Meyler (also fined £100,000 by club); **£60,000** Rafael Benitez (Newcastle): Oct 2018, talking about match referee ahead of fixture; **£60,000** Rafael Benitez (Newcastle): Oct 2018, talking about match referee ahead of fixture; **£58,000** Jose Mourinho (Manchester Utd): Nov 2016, misconduct involving referees Mark Clattenburg and Anthony Taylor; **£50,000** Jose Mourinho (Chelsea): Oct 2015, accusing referees of bias; **£45,000** Jurgen Klopp (Liverpool): Feb 2019, questioning integrity of referee Kevin Friend; **£40,000 (plus 1 match stadium ban)** Jose Mourinho (Chelsea): Nov 2015, abusive behaviour towards referee Jon Moss v West Ham; **£40,000 (plus 3-match Euro ban)** Arsene Wenger (Arsenal): Jan 2018, abuse towards referee Mike Dean v WBA; **£33,000 (plus 3-match Euro ban)** Arsene Wenger: Mar 2012, criticising referee after Champions League defeat by AC Milan; **£30,000** Sir Alex Ferguson (Manchester Utd): Mar 2011 criticising referee Martin Atkinson v Chelsea; **£30,000 (plus 6-match ban ((plus 6-match ban reduced to 4 on appeal)**; Rui Faria (Chelsea assistant): May 2014, confronting match officials v Sunderland.

• Jonathan Barnett, Ashley Cole's agent was fined **£100,000** in Sep 2006 for his role in the 'tapping up' affair involving the player and Chelsea.

• Gillingham and club chairman Paul Scally each fined **£75,000** in Jul 2015 for 'racial victimisation' towards player Mark McCammon. Club fine reduced to £50,000 on appeal.

• Leyton Orient owner Francesco Becchetti fined £40,000 and given six-match stadium ban in Jan 2016 for violent conduct towards assistant manager Andy Hessenthaler.

***£68,000** FA: May 2003, pitch invasions and racist chanting by fans during England v Turkey, Sunderland.

£50,000 FA: Dec 2014, for Wigan owner-chairman Dave Whelan, plus six-week ban from all football activity, for remarks about Jewish and Chinese people in newspaper interview.

***£250,000** FA: Dec 2016, for Leeds owner Massimo Cellino, plus 18-month ban, for breaking agent regulations (reduced to £100,000 and one year on appeal). Club fined £250,000 (reduced to £200,000 on appeal). Agent Derek Day fined £75,000 and banned for 18 months (11 months suspended).

MANAGERS

INTERNATIONAL RECORDS
(As at start of season 2021–2022

	P	W	D	L	F	A
Gareth Southgate (England appointed Sep 2016)	61	39	12	10	122	40
Steve Clarke (Scotland – appointed May 2019)	24	9	7	8	31	31
Ryan Giggs (Wales – appointed Jan 2018)	24	12	4	8	28	20
Robert Page (Wales – caretaker)	12	5	3	4	10	13
Ian Baraclough (Northern Ireland – appointed Jun 2020)	13	1	4	8	10	19
Stephen Kenny (Republic of Ireland – appointed Apr 2020)	13	1	6	6	8	13

ENGLAND MANAGERS

		P	W	D	L
1946–62	**Walter Winterbottom**	139	78	33	28
1963–74	**Sir Alf Ramsey**	113	69	27	17
1974	**Joe Mercer**, caretaker	7	3	3	1
1974–77	**Don Revie**	29	14	8	7
1977–82	**Ron Greenwood**	55	33	12	10
1982–90	**Bobby Robson**	95	47	30	18

1990–93	Graham Taylor	38	18	13	7
1994–96	Terry Venables	23	11	11	1
1996–99	Glenn Hoddle	28	17	6	5
1999	Howard Wilkinson, caretaker	1	0	0	1
1999–2000	Kevin Keegan	18	7	7	4
2000	Howard Wilkinson, caretaker	1	0	1	0
2000	Peter Taylor, caretaker	1	0	0	1
2001–06	Sven–Goran Eriksson	67	40	17	10
2006–07	Steve McClaren	18	9	4	5
2007–12	Fabio Capello	42	28	8	6
2012	Stuart Pearce, caretaker	1	0	0	1
2012–16	Roy Hodgson	56	33	15	8
2016	Sam Allardyce	1	1	0	0

INTERNATIONAL MANAGER CHANGES

England: Walter Winterbottom 1946–62 (initially coach); **Alf Ramsey** (Feb 1963–May 1974); **Joe Mercer** (caretaker May 1974); **Don Revie** (Jul 1974–Jul 1977); **Ron Greenwood** (Aug 1977–Jul 1982); **Bobby Robson** (Jul 1982–Jul 1990); **Graham Taylor** (Jul 1990–Nov 1993); **Terry Venables**, coach (Jan 1994–Jun 1996); **Glenn Hoddle**, coach (Jun 1996–Feb 1999); **Howard Wilkinson** (caretaker Feb 1999); **Kevin Keegan** coach (Feb 1999–Oct 2000); **Howard Wilkinson** (caretaker Oct 2000); **Peter Taylor** (caretaker Nov 2000); **Sven–Goran Eriksson** (Jan 2001–Aug 2006); **Steve McClaren** (Aug 2006–Nov 2007); **Fabio Capello** (Dec 2007–Feb 2012); **Roy Hodgson** (May 2012– Jun 2016); **Sam Allardyce** (Jul-Sep 2016); **Gareth Southgate** (Sep-Nov 2016 interim, then permanent appointment).

Scotland (modern): Bobby Brown (Feb 1967–Jul 1971); **Tommy Docherty** (Sep 1971–Dec 1972); **Willie Ormond** (Jan 1973–May 1977); **Ally MacLeod** (May 1977–Sep 1978); **Jock Stein** (Oct 1978–Sep 1985); **Alex Ferguson** (caretaker Oct 1985–Jun 1986); **Andy Roxburgh**, coach (Jul 1986–Sep 1993); **Craig Brown** (Sep 1993–Oct 2001); **Berti Vogts** (Feb 2002–Oct 2004); **Walter Smith** (Dec 2004–Jan 2007); **Alex McLeish** (Jan 2007–Nov 2007); **George Burley** (Jan 2008–Nov 2009); **Craig Levein** (Dec 2009–Nov 2012); **Billy Stark** (caretaker Nov–Dec 2012); **Gordon Strachan** (Jan 2013-Oct 2017); **Malky Mackay**, (caretaker Nov 2017); **Alex McLeish** (Feb 2018–Apr 2019); **Steve Clarke** (since May 2019).

Northern Ireland (modern): Peter Doherty (1951–62); **Bertie Peacock** (1962–67); **Billy Bingham** (1967–Aug 1971); **Terry Neill** (Aug 1971–Mar 1975); **Dave Clements** (player-manager Mar 1975–1976); **Danny Blanchflower** (Jun 1976–Nov 1979); **Billy Bingham** (Feb 1980–Nov 1993); **Bryan Hamilton** Feb 1994–Feb 1998); **Lawrie McMenemy** (Feb 1998–Nov 1999); **Sammy McIlroy** (Jan 2000–Oct 2003); **Lawrie Sanchez** (Jan 2004–May 2007); **Nigel Worthington** (May 2007–Oct 2011); **Michael O'Neill** (Oct 2011–Apr 2020); **Ian Baraclough** (since Jun 2020).

Wales (modern): Mike Smith (Jul 1974–Dec 1979); **Mike England** (Mar 1980–Feb 1988); **David Williams** (caretaker Mar 1988); **Terry Yorath** (Apr 1988–Nov 1993); **John Toshack** (Mar 1994, one match); **Mike Smith** (Mar 1994–Jun 1995); **Bobby Gould** (Aug 1995–Jun 1999); **Mark Hughes** (Aug 1999 – Oct 2004); **John Toshack** (Nov 2004–Sep 2010); Brian Flynn (caretaker Sep–Dec 2010); **Gary Speed** (Dec 2010–Nov 2011); **Chris Coleman** (Jan 2012-Nov 2017); **Ryan Giggs** (since Jan 2018).

Republic of Ireland (modern): Liam Tuohy (Sep 1971–Nov 1972); **Johnny Giles** (Oct 1973–Apr 1980, initially player-manager); **Eoin Hand** (Jun 1980–Nov 1985); **Jack Charlton** (Feb 1986–Dec 1995); **Mick McCarthy** (Feb 1996–Oct 2002); **Brian Kerr** (Jan 2003–Oct 2005); **Steve Staunton** (Jan 2006–Oct 2007); **Giovanni Trapattoni** (May 2008–Sep 2013); **Martin O'Neill** (Nov 2013–Nov 2018); **Mick McCarthy** (Nov 2018–Apr 2020); **Stephen Kenny** (since Apr 2020).

WORLD CUP-WINNING MANAGERS

1930 Uruguay (Alberto Suppici); 1934 and 1938 Italy (Vittorio Pozzo); 1950 Uruguay (Juan Lopez Fontana); 1954 West Germany (Sepp Herberger); 1958 Brazil (Vicente Feola); 1962

Brazil (Aymore Moreira); 1966 England (Sir Alf Ramsey); 1970 Brazil (Mario Zagallo); 1974 West Germany (Helmut Schon); 1978 Argentina (Cesar Luis Menotti); 1982 Italy (Enzo Bearzot); 1986 Argentina (Carlos Bilardo); 1990 West Germany (Franz Beckenbauer); 1994 Brazil (Carlos Alberto Parreira); 1998 France (Aimee Etienne Jacquet); 2002 Brazil (Luiz Felipe Scolari); 2006 Italy (Marcello Lippi); 2010 Spain (Vicente Del Bosque); 2014 Germany (Joachim Low); 2018 France (Didier Deschamps).

Each of the 21 winning teams had a manager/coach of that country's nationality.

YOUNGEST LEAGUE MANAGERS

Ivor Broadis, 23, appointed player-manager of Carlisle, Aug 1946; **Chris Brass**, 27, appointed player-manager of York, Jun 2003; **Terry Neill**, 28, appointed player manager of Hull, Jun 1970; **Graham Taylor**, 28, appointed manager of Lincoln, Dec 1972.

LONGEST-SERVING LEAGUE MANAGERS – ONE CLUB

Fred Everiss, secretary–manager of WBA for 46 years (1902–48); **George Ramsay**, secretary–manager of Aston Villa for 42 years (1884–1926); **John Addenbrooke**, Wolves, for 37 years (1885–1922). Since last war: **Sir Alex Ferguson** at Manchester Utd for 27 seasons (1986–2013); **Sir Matt Busby**, in charge of Manchester Utd for 25 seasons (1945–69, 1970–71); **Dario Gradi** at Crewe for 26 years (1983–2007, 2009–11); **Jimmy Seed** at Charlton for 23 years (1933–56); **Brian Clough** at Nottm Forest for 18 years (1975–93); **Arsene Wenger** at Arsenal for 22 years (1996-2018).

LAST ENGLISH MANAGER TO WIN CHAMPIONSHIP

Howard Wilkinson (Leeds), season 1991–92.

MANAGERS WITH MORE THAN 1000 MATCHES

Sir Alex Ferguson, Sir Bobby Robson, Sir Matt Busby, Arsene Wenger, Roy Hodgson, Harry Redknapp, Alec Stock, Brian Clough, Jim Smith, Graham Taylor, Dario Gradi, Tony Pulis, Dave Bassett, Lennie Lawrence, Alan Buckley, Denis Smith, Joe Royle, Ron Atkinson, Brian Horton, Neil Warnock, Len Ashurst, Lawrie McMenemy, Graham Turner, Steve Coppell, John Toshack, Rafael Benitez, Sven-Goran Eriksson, Claudio Ranieri and Carlo Ancelotti, Sam Allardyce, Danny Wilson, Mick McCarthy

SHORT-TERM MANAGERS

Departed

3 days	Bill Lambton (Scunthorpe)	Apr 1959
6 days	Tommy McLean (Raith Rov)	Sep 1996
7 days	Tim Ward (Exeter)	Mar 1953
7 days	Kevin Cullis (Swansea City)	Feb 1996
8 days	Billy McKinlay (Watford)	Oct 2014
10 days	Dave Cowling (Doncaster)	Oct 1997
10 days	Peter Cormack (Cowdenbeath)	Dec 2000
13 days	Johnny Cochrane (Reading)	Apr 1939
13 days	Micky Adams (Swansea City)	Oct 1997
16 days	Jimmy McIlroy (Bolton)	Nov 1970
19 days	Martin Allen (Barnet)	Apr 2011
20 days	Paul Went (Leyton Orient)	Oct 1981
27 days	Malcolm Crosby (Oxford Utd)	Jan 1998
27 days	Oscar Garcia (Watford)	Sep 2014
28 days	Tommy Docherty (QPR)	Dec 1968
28 days	Paul Hart (QPR)	Jan 2010
29 days	Carl Fletcher (Leyton Orient)	Nov 2019
29 days	John McGreal (Swindon)	Jun 2021
31 days	Paul Scholes (Oldham)	Mar 2019

32 days	Steve Coppell (Manchester City)	Nov 1996
32 days	Darko Milanic (Leeds)	Oct 2014
34 days	Niall Quinn (Sunderland)	Aug 2006
36 days	Steve Claridge (Millwall)	Jul 2005
39 days	Paul Gascoigne (Kettering)	Dec 2005
39 days	Kenny Jackett (Rotherham)	Nov 2016
40 days	Alex McLeish (Nottm Forest)	Feb 2013
41 days	Steve Wicks (Lincoln)	Oct 1995
41 days	Les Reed (Charlton)	Dec 2006
43 days	Mauro Milanese (Leyton Orient)	Dec 2014
44 days	Brian Clough (Leeds)	Sep 1974
44 days	Jock Stein (Leeds)	Oct 1978
45 days	Tony Pulis (Sheffield Wed)	Dec 2020
45 days	Paul Murray (Hartlepool)	Dec 2014
48 days	John Toshack (Wales)	Mar 1994
48 days	David Platt (Sampdoria coach)	Feb 1999
49 days	Brian Little (Wolves)	Oct 1986
49 days	Terry Fenwick (Northampton)	Feb 2003
52 days	Alberto Cavasin (Leyton Orient)	Nov 2016
54 days	Craig Levein (Raith Rov)	Oct 1996
54 days	Chris Lucketti (Bury)	Jan 2018
56 days	Martin Ling (Swindon)	Dec 2015
57 days	Henning Berg (Blackburn)	Dec 2012
59 days	Kevin Nugent (Barnet)	Apr 2017
60 days	Michael Jolley (Barrow)	Feb 2021
61 days	Bill McGarry (Wolves)	Nov 1985
63 days	Graham Westley (Stevenage)	Feb 2020

● In May 1984, Crystal Palace named **Dave Bassett** as manager, but he changed his mind four days later, without signing the contract, and returned to Wimbledon.
● In May 2007, **Leroy Rosenior** was reportedly appointed manager of Torquay after relegation and sacked ten minutes later when the club came under new ownership.
● **Brian Laws** lost his job at Scunthorpe on Mar 25, 2004 and was reinstated three weeks later.
● In an angry outburst after a play-off defeat in May 1992, Barnet chairman Stan Flashman sacked manager **Barry Fry** and re-instated him a day later.

EARLY-SEASON MANAGER SACKINGS

2012: Andy Thorn (Coventry) 8 days; John Sheridan (Chesterfield) 10 days; **2011:** Jim Jefferies (Hearts) 9 days; **2010** Kevin Blackwell (Sheffield Utd) 8 days; **2009** Bryan Gunn (Norwich) 6 days; **2007:** Neil McDonald (Carlisle) 2 days; Martin Allen (Leicester) 18 days; **2004:** Paul Sturrock (Southampton) 9 days; **2004:** Sir Bobby Robson (Newcastle) 16 days; **2003:** Glenn Roeder (West Ham) 15 days; **2000:** Alan Buckley (Grimsby) 10 days; **1997:** Kerry Dixon (Doncaster) 12 days; **1996:** Sammy Chung (Doncaster) on morning of season's opening League match; **1996:** Alan Ball (Manchester City) 12 days; **1994:** Kenny Hibbitt (Walsall) and Kenny Swain (Wigan) 20 days; **1993:** Peter Reid (Manchester City) 12 days; **1991:** Don Mackay (Blackburn) 14 days; **1989:** Mick Jones (Peterborough) 12 days; **1980:** Bill McGarry (Newcastle) 13 days; **1979:** Dennis Butler (Port Vale) 12 days; **1977:** George Petchey (Leyton O) 13 days; **1977:** Willie Bell (Birmingham) 16 days; **1971:** Len Richley (Darlington) 12 days.

DOUBLE DISMISSAL

Mark Hughes became the first manager to be sacked by two Premier League clubs in the same calendar year (2018) – Stoke in January and Southampton in December.

FOUR GAMES AND OUT

Frank de Boer was sacked as Crystal Palace manager after his first four Premier League matches at the start of the 2017–18 season – the competition's shortest reign in terms of games.

BRUCE'S FOUR-TIMER

Steve Bruce is the only manager to win four promotions to the Premier League – with Birmingham
in 2002 and 2007 and with Hull in 2013 and 2016.

RECORD START FOR MANAGER

Russ Wilcox, appointed by Scunthorpe in Nov 2013, remained unbeaten in his first 28 league
matches (14 won, 14 drawn) and took the club to promotion from League Two. It was the
most successful start to a managerial career In English football, beating the record of 23
unbeaten games by Preston's William Sudell in 1889.

RECORD TOP DIVISION START

Arsenal were unbeaten in 17 league matches from the start of season 1947-48 under new
manager **Tom Whittaker**.

SACKED, REINSTATED, FINISHED

Brian McDermott was sacked as Leeds manager on Jan 31, 2014. The following day, he was reinstated.
At the end of the season, with the club under new ownership, he left by 'mutual consent.'

CARETAKER SUPREME

As Chelsea's season collapsed, Andre Villas-Boas was sacked in March 2012 after eight months
as manager, 2012. Roberto Di Matteo was appointed caretaker and by the season's end his
team had won the FA Cup and the Champions League.

MANAGER DOUBLES

Four managers have won the League Championship with different clubs: **Tom Watson**, secretary-
manager with Sunderland (1892–93–95) and **Liverpool** (1901); **Herbert Chapman** with
Huddersfield (1923–24, 1924–25) and Arsenal (1930–31, 1932–33); **Brian Clough** with
Derby (1971–72) and Nottm Forest (1977–78); **Kenny Dalglish** with Liverpool (1985–86,
1987–88, 1989–90) and Blackburn (1994–95).

Managers to win the FA Cup with different clubs: **Billy Walker** (Sheffield Wed 1935, Nottm Forest
1959); **Herbert Chapman** (Huddersfield 1922, Arsenal 1930).

Kenny Dalglish (Liverpool) and **George Graham** (Arsenal) completed the Championship/FA Cup
double as both player and manager with a single club. **Joe Mercer** won the title as a player
with Everton, the title twice and FA Cup as a player with Arsenal and both competitions as
manager of Manchester City.

CHAIRMAN–MANAGER

On Dec 20, 1988, after two years on the board, Dundee Utd manager **Jim McLean** was elected
chairman, too. McLean, Scotland's longest-serving manager (appointed on Nov 24, 1971),
resigned at end of season 1992–93 (remained chairman).

Ron Noades was chairman-manager of Brentford from Jul 1998–Mar 2001. **John Reames** did
both jobs at Lincoln from Nov 1998–Apr 2000)

Niall Quinn did both jobs for five weeks in 2006 before appointing Roy Keane as manager of
Sunderland.

TOP DIVISION PLAYER–MANAGERS

Les Allen (QPR 1968–69); **Johnny Giles** (WBA 1976–77); **Howard Kendall** (Everton 1981–82);
Kenny Dalglish (Liverpool, 1985–90); **Trevor Francis** (QPR, 1988–89); **Terry Butcher** (Coventry,
1990–91), **Peter Reid** (Manchester City, 1990–93), **Trevor Francis** (Sheffield Wed, 1991–94),
Glenn Hoddle, (Chelsea, 1993–95), **Bryan Robson** (Middlesbrough, 1994–97), **Ray Wilkins**
(QPR, 1994–96), **Ruud Gullit** (Chelsea, 1996–98), **Gianluca Vialli** (Chelsea, 1998–2000).

FIRST FOREIGN MANAGER IN ENGLISH LEAGUE

Uruguayan **Danny Bergara** (Rochdale 1988–89).

COACHING KINGS OF EUROPE

Five coaches have won the European Cup/Champions League with two different clubs: **Ernst Happel** with Feyenoord (1970) and Hamburg (1983); **Ottmar Hitzfeld** with Borussia Dortmund (1997) and Bayern Munich (2001); **Jose Mourinho** with Porto (2004) and Inter Milan (2010); **Jupp Heynckes** with Real Madrid (1998) and Bayern Munich (2013); **Carlo Ancelotti** with AC Milan (2003, 2007) and Real Madrid (2014).

FOREIGN TRIUMPH

Former Dutch star **Ruud Gullit** became the first foreign manager to win a major English competition when Chelsea took the FA Cup in 1997.

Arsene Wenger and **Gerard Houllier** became the first foreign managers to receive recognition when they were awarded honorary OBEs in the Queen's Birthday Honours in Jun 2003 'for their contribution to English football and Franco–British relations'.

MANAGERS OF POST-WAR CHAMPIONS (*Double winners)

1947 George Kay (Liverpool); **1948** Tom Whittaker (Arsenal); **1949** Bob Jackson (Portsmouth).
1950 Bob Jackson (Portsmouth); **1951** Arthur Rowe (Tottenham); **1952** Matt Busby (Manchester Utd); **1953** Tom Whittaker (Arsenal); **1954** Stan Cullis (Wolves); **1955** Ted Drake (Chelsea); **1956** Matt Busby (Manchester Utd); **1957** Matt Busby (Manchester Utd); **1958** Stan Cullis (Wolves); **1959** Stan Cullis (Wolves).
1960 Harry Potts (Burnley); **1961** *Bill Nicholson (Tottenham); **1962** Alf Ramsey (Ipswich); **1963** Harry Catterick (Everton); **1964** Bill Shankly (Liverpool); **1965** Matt Busby (Manchester Utd); **1966** Bill Shankly (Liverpool); **1967** Matt Busby (Manchester Utd); **1968** Joe Mercer (Manchester City); **1969** Don Revie (Leeds).
1970 Harry Catterick (Everton); **1971** *Bertie Mee (Arsenal); **1972** Brian Clough (Derby); **1973** Bill Shankly (Liverpool); **1974** Don Revie (Leeds); **1975** Dave Mackay (Derby); **1976** Bob Paisley (Liverpool); **1977** Bob Paisley (Liverpool); **1978** Brian Clough (Nottm Forest); **1979** Bob Paisley (Liverpool).
1980 Bob Paisley (Liverpool); **1981** Ron Saunders (Aston Villa); **1982** Bob Paisley (Liverpool); **1983** Bob Paisley (Liverpool); **1984** Joe Fagan (Liverpool); **1985** Howard Kendall (Everton); **1986** *Kenny Dalglish (Liverpool – player/manager); **1987** Howard Kendall (Everton); **1988** Kenny Dalglish (Liverpool – player/manager); **1989** George Graham (Arsenal).
1990 Kenny Dalglish (Liverpool); **1991** George Graham (Arsenal); **1992** Howard Wilkinson (Leeds); **1993** Alex Ferguson (Manchester Utd); **1994** *Alex Ferguson (Manchester Utd); **1995** Kenny Dalglish (Blackburn); **1996** *Alex Ferguson (Manchester Utd); **1997** Alex Ferguson (Manchester Utd); **1998** *Arsene Wenger (Arsenal); **1999** *Alex Ferguson (Manchester Utd).
2000 Sir Alex Ferguson (Manchester Utd); **2001** Sir Alex Ferguson (Manchester Utd); **2002** *Arsene Wenger (Arsenal); **2003** Sir Alex Ferguson (Manchester Utd); **2004** Arsene Wenger (Arsenal); **2005** Jose Mourinho (Chelsea); **2006** Jose Mourinho (Chelsea); **2007** Sir Alex Ferguson (Manchester Utd); **2008** Sir Alex Ferguson (Manchester Utd); **2009** Sir Alex Ferguson (Manchester Utd); **2010** *Carlo Ancelotti (Chelsea); **2011** Sir Alex Ferguson (Manchester Utd); **2012** Roberto Mancini (Manchester City); **2013** Sir Alex Ferguson (Manchester Utd); **2014** Manuel Pellegrini (Manchester City); **2015** Jose Mourinho (Chelsea) **2016** Claudio Ranieri (Leicester); **2017** Antonio Conte (Chelsea); **2018** Pep Guardiola (Manchester City); **2019** Pep Guardiola (Manchester City); **2020** Jurgen Klopp (Liverpool); **2021** Pep Guardiola (Manchester City.

WORLD NO 1 MANAGER

When **Sir Alex Ferguson**, 71, retired in May 2013, he ended the most successful managerial career in the game's history. He took Manchester United to a total of 38 prizes – 13 Premier League titles,

5 FA Cup triumphs, 4 League Cups, 10 Charity/Community Shields (1 shared), 2 Champions League wins, 1 Cup-Winners' Cup, 1 FIFA Club World Cup, 1 Inter-Continental Cup and 1 UEFA Super Cup. Having played centre-forward for Rangers, the Glaswegian managed 3 Scottish clubs, East Stirling, St Mirren and then Aberdeen, where he broke the Celtic/Rangers duopoly with 9 successes: 3 League Championships, 4 Scottish Cups, 1 League Cup and 1 UEFA Cup. Appointed at Old Trafford in November 1986, when replacing Ron Atkinson, he did not win a prize there until his fourth season (FA Cup 1990), but thereafter the club's trophy cabinet glittered with silverware. His total of 1,500 matches in charge ended with a 5-5 draw away to West Bromwich Albion. The longest-serving manager in the club's history, he constructed 4 triumphant teams. Sir Alex was knighted in 1999 and in 2012 he received the FIFA award for services to football. On retirement from management, he became a director and club ambassador. United maintained the dynasty of long-serving Scottish managers (Sir Matt Busby for 24 seasons) by appointing David Moyes, who had been in charge at Everton for 11 years.

WENGER'S LEGACY

Arsene Wenger was a virtually unknown French manager when taking over Arsenal in 1996. He left 22 years later as the most successful in the club's history. Wenger led them to three Premier League titles, including the unbeaten season in 2003-04 achieved by the team known as the 'Invincibles.' There were seven FA Cup successes, one in 2002 when Arsenal completed the Double. He was also closely involved in planning the move from Highbury to the Emirates Stadium in 2006.

THE PROMOTION MAN

Neil Warnock set a record of eight promotions when he took Cardiff back to the Premier League in 2018. In 38 years as a manager, he was also successful with Scarborough, Notts County twice, Plymouth, Huddersfield, Sheffield United and Queens Park Rangers. Warnock's achievements were marked by a special award from the League Managers' Association.

MANAGERS' EURO TREBLES

Two managers have won the European Cup/Champions League three times. **Bob Paisley** did it with Liverpool (1977,78, 81).

Carlo Ancelotti's successes were with AC Milan in 2003 and 2007 and with Real Madrid in 2014.

WINNER MOURINHO

In winning the Premier League and League Cup in 2015, Jose Mourinho embellished his reputation as Chelsea's most successful manager. Those achievements took his total of honours in two spells at the club to 8: 3 Premier League, 3 League Cup, 1 FA Cup, 1 Community Shield. Joining from Portuguese champions Porto, Mourinho was initially with Chelsea from June 2004 to September 2007. He then successfulty coached Inter Milan and Real Madrid before returning to Stamford Bridge in June 2013. His Premier League triumph in 2015 was his eighth title In 11 years in four countries (England 3, Portugal 2, Italy 2, Spain 1). In his first season with Manchester Utd (2016–17), he won three trophies – League Cup, Europa League and Community Shield.

WENGER'S CUP AGAIN

Arsenal's win against Aston Villa in the 2015 Final was a record 12th success for them in the FA Cup and a sixth triumph in the competition for manager Arsene Wenger, equalling the record of George Ramsay for Villa (1887-1920). With his sixth victory in seven Finals, Wenger made history as the first manager to win the Cup in successive seasons twice (previously in 2002 and 2003). He won it for a record seventh time – in eight finals – in 2017.

FATHER AND SON MANAGERS WITH SAME CLUB

Fulham: Bill Dodgin Snr 1949–53; Bill Dodgin Jnr 1968–72. **Brentford:** Bill Dodgin Snr 1953–57; Bill Dodgin Jnr 1976–80. **Bournemouth:** John Bond 1970–73; Kevin Bond 2006–08. **Derby:** Brian Clough 1967–73; Nigel Clough 2009–2013. **Bristol City:** Gary Johnson 2005–10; Lee Johnson 2016-present.

SIR BOBBY'S HAT-TRICK

Sir Bobby Robson, born and brought up in County Durham, achieved a unique hat-trick when he received the Freedom of Durham in Dec 2008. He had already been awarded the Freedom of Ipswich and Newcastle. He died in July 2009 and had an express loco named after him on the East Coast to London line.

MANAGERS WITH MOST FA CUP SUCCESSES

7 Arsene Wenger (Arsenal); **6 George Ramsay** (Aston Villa); **5 Sir Alex Ferguson** (Manchester Utd); **3 Charles Foweraker** (Bolton), **John Nicholson** (Sheffield Utd), **Bill Nicholson** (Tottenham).

RELEGATION 'DOUBLES'

Managers associated with two clubs relegated in same season: **John Bond** in 1985–86 (Swansea City and Birmingham); **Ron Saunders** in 1985–86 (WBA – and their reserve team – and Birmingham); **Bob Stokoe** in 1986–87 (Carlisle and Sunderland); **Billy McNeill** in 1986–87 (Manchester City and Aston Villa); **Dave Bassett** in 1987–88 (Watford and Sheffield Utd); **Mick Mills** in 1989–90 (Stoke and Colchester); **Gary Johnson** in 2014-15 (Yeovil and Cheltenham)

THREE FA CUP DEFEATS IN ONE SEASON

Manager **Michael Appleton** suffered three FA Cup defeats in season 2012-13, with Portsmouth (v Notts Co, 1st rd); Blackpool (v Fulham, 3rd rd); Blackburn (v Millwall, 6th rd).

WEMBLEY STADIUM

NEW WEMBLEY

A new era for English football began in March 2007 with the completion of the new national stadium. The 90,000-seater arena was hailed as one of the world's finest – but came at a price. Costs soared, the project fell well behind schedule and disputes involving the FA, builders Multiplex and the Government were rife. The old stadium, opened in 1923, cost £750,000. The new one, originally priced at £326m in 2000, ended up at around £800m. The first international after completion was an Under-21 match between England and Italy. The FA Cup Final returned to its spiritual home after being staged at the Millennium Stadium in Cardiff for six seasons. Then, England's senior team were back for a friendly against Brazil.

DROGBA'S WEMBLEY RECORD

Didier Drogba's FA Cup goal for Chelsea against Liverpool in May 2012 meant that he had scored in all his 8 competitive appearances for the club at Wembley. (7 wins, 1 defeat) They came in: 2007 FA Cup Final (1-0 v Manchester Utd); 2008 League Cup Final (1-2 v Tottenham); 2009 FA Cup semi-final (2-1 v Arsenal); 2009 FA Cup Final (2-1 v Everton); 2010 FA Cup semi-final (3-0 v Aston Villa); 2010 FA Cup Final (1-0 v Portsmouth); 2012 FA Cup semi-final (5-1 v Tottenham); 2012 FA Cup Final (2-1 v Liverpool).

INVASION DAY

Memorable scenes were witnessed at the first **FA Cup Final at Wembley**, Apr 28, 1923, between **Bolton** and **West Ham**. An accurate return of the attendance could not be made owing to thousands breaking in, but there were probably more than 200,000 spectators present. The match was delayed for 40 minutes by the crowd invading the pitch. Official attendance was 126,047. Gate receipts totalled £27,776. The two clubs and the FA each received £6,365 and the FA refunded £2,797 to ticket-holders who were unable to get to their seats. Cup Final admission has since been by ticket only.

REDUCED CAPACITY

Capacity of the all-seated Wembley Stadium was 78,000. The last 100,000 attendance was for the 1985 FA Cup Final between Manchester Utd and Everton. Crowd record for New Wembley: 89,874 for 2008 FA Cup Final (Portsmouth v Cardiff).

WEMBLEY'S FIRST UNDER LIGHTS

Nov 30, 1955 (England 4, Spain 1), when the floodlights were switched on after 73 minutes (afternoon match played in damp, foggy conditions).
First Wembley international played throughout under lights: England 8, N Ireland 3 on evening of Nov 20, 1963 (att: 55,000).

MOST WEMBLEY APPEARANCES

59 by **Tony Adams** (35 England, 24 Arsenal); **57** by **Peter Shilton** (52 England, 3 Nottm Forest, 1 Leicester, 1 Football League X1).

WEMBLEY HAT-TRICKS

Three players have scored hat-tricks in major finals at Wembley: **Stan Mortensen** for Blackpool v Bolton (FA Cup Final, 1953), **Geoff Hurst** for England v West Germany (World Cup Final, 1966) and **David Speedie** for Chelsea v Manchester City (Full Members Cup, 1985).

ENGLAND'S WEMBLEY DEFEATS

England have lost 26 matches to foreign opponents at Wembley:

Nov 1953	3-6 v Hungary	**Jun 1995**	1-3 v Brazil
Oct 1959	2-3 v Sweden	**Feb 1997**	0-1 v Italy
Oct 1965	2-3 v Austria	**Feb 1998**	0-2 v Chile
Apr 1972	1-3 v W Germany	**Feb 1999**	0-2 v France
Nov 1973	0-1 v Italy	**Oct 2000**	0-1 v Germany
Feb 1977	0-2 v Holland	**Aug 2007**	1-2 v Germany
Mar 1981	1-2 v Spain	**Nov 2007**	2-3 v Croatia
May 1981	0-1 v Brazil	**Nov 2010**	1-2 v France
Oct 1982	1-2 v W Germany	**Feb 2012**	2-3 v Holland
Sep 1983	0-1 v Denmark	**Nov 2013**	0-2 v Chile
Jun 1984	0-2 v Russia	**Nov 2013**	0-1 v Germany
May 1990	1-2 v Uruguay	**Mar 2016**	1-2 v Holland
Sep 1991	0-1 v Germany	**Oct 2020**	0-1 v Denmark

A further defeat came in **Euro 96**. After drawing the semi-final with Germany 1-1, England went out 6-5 on penalties.

FASTEST GOALS AT WEMBLEY

In first-class matches: **25 sec** by **Louis Saha** for Everton in 2009 FA Cup Final against Chelsea; **38 sec** by **Bryan Robson** for England's against Yugoslavia in 1989; **42 sec** by **Roberto Di Matteo** for Chelsea in 1997 FA Cup Final v Middlesbrough; **44 sec** by **Bryan Robson** for England v Northern Ireland in 1982.
Fastest goal in **any** match at Wembley: **20 sec** by **Maurice Cox** for Cambridge University against Oxford in 1979.

FOUR WEMBLEY HEADERS

When **Wimbledon** beat Sutton 4-2 in the FA Amateur Cup Final at Wembley on May 4, 1963, Irish centre-forward **Eddie Reynolds** headed all four goals.

WEMBLEY ONE-SEASON DOUBLES

In 1989, **Nottm Forest** became the first club to win two Wembley Finals in the same season (Littlewoods Cup and Simod Cup).
In 1993, **Arsenal** made history there as the first club to win the League (Coca-Cola) Cup and the FA Cup in the same season. They beat Sheffield Wed 2-1 in both finals.
In 2012, **York** won twice at Wembley in nine days at the end of the season, beating Newport 2-0 in the FA Trophy Final and Luton 2-1 in the Conference Play-off Final to return to the Football League.

SUDDEN-DEATH DECIDERS

First Wembley Final decided on sudden death (first goal scored in overtime): Apr 23, 1995 – **Birmingham** beat Carlisle (1-0, Paul Tait 103 mins) to win Auto Windscreens Shield.

First instance of a golden goal deciding a major international tournament was at Wembley on Jun 30, 1996, when **Germany** beat the Czech Republic 2-1 in the European Championship Final with Oliver Bierhoff's goal in the 95th minute.

WEMBLEY'S MOST ONE-SIDED FINAL (in major domestic cups)

Manchester City 6 **Watford** 0 (FA Cup, May 18, 2019).

FOOTBALL TRAGEDIES

DAYS OF TRAGEDY – CLUBS

Season 1988–89 brought the worst disaster in the history of British sport, with the death of 96 Liverpool supporters (200 injured) at the **FA Cup semi-final** against Nottm Forest at **Hillsborough, Sheffield**, on Saturday, Apr 15. The tragedy built up in the minutes preceding kick-off, when thousands surged into the ground at the Leppings Lane end. Many were crushed in the tunnel between entrance and terracing, but most of the victims were trapped inside the perimeter fencing behind the goal. The match was abandoned without score after six minutes' play. The dead included seven women and girls, two teenage sisters and two teenage brothers. The youngest victim was a boy of ten, the oldest 67-year-old Gerard Baron, whose brother Kevin played for Liverpool in the 1950 Cup Final. (*Total became 96 in Mar 1993, when Tony Bland died after being in a coma for nearly four years). A two-year inquest at Warrington ended on April 26, 2016 with the verdict that the 96 were 'unlawfully killed.' It cleared Liverpool fans of any blame and ruled that South Yorkshire Police and South Yorkshire Ambulance Service 'caused or contributed' to the loss of life.

The two worst disasters in one season in British soccer history occurred at the end of 1984–85. On May 11, the last Saturday of the League season, 56 people (two of them visiting supporters) were burned to death – and more than 200 taken to hospital – when fire destroyed the main stand at the **Bradford City–Lincoln** match at Valley Parade.

The wooden, 77-year-old stand was full for City's last fixture before which, amid scenes of celebration, the club had been presented with the Third Division Championship trophy. The fire broke out just before half-time and, within five minutes, the entire stand was engulfed.

Heysel Tragedy

Eighteen days later, on May 29, at the European Cup Final between **Liverpool** and **Juventus** at the Heysel Stadium, Brussels, 39 spectators (31 of them Italian) were crushed or trampled to death and 437 injured. The disaster occurred an hour before the scheduled kick-off when Liverpool supporters charged a Juventus section of the crowd at one end of the stadium, and a retaining wall collapsed. The sequel was a 5-year ban by UEFA on English clubs generally in European competition, with a 6-year ban on Liverpool.

On May 26 1985 ten people were trampled to death and 29 seriously injured in a crowd panic on the way into the **Olympic Stadium, Mexico City** for the Mexican Cup Final between local clubs National University and America.

More than 100 people died and 300 were injured in a football disaster at **Nepal's national stadium** in Katmandu in Mar 1988. There was a stampede when a violent hailstorm broke over the capital. Spectators rushed for cover, but the stadium exits were locked, and hundreds were trampled in the crush.

In South Africa, on Jan 13 1991 40 black fans were trampled to death (50 injured) as they tried to escape from fighting that broke out at a match in the gold-mining town of Orkney, 80 miles from Johannesburg. The friendly, between top teams **Kaiser Chiefs** and **Orlando Pirates**, attracted a packed crowd of 20,000. Violence erupted after the referee allowed Kaiser Chiefs a disputed second-half goal to lead 1-0.

Disaster struck at the French Cup semi-final (May 5, 1992), with the death of 15 spectators and 1,300 injured when a temporary metal stand collapsed in the Corsican town of Bastia. The tie between Second Division **Bastia** and French Champions **Marseille** was cancelled. Monaco, who won the other semi-final, were allowed to compete in the next season's Cup-Winners' Cup.

A total of 318 died and 500 were seriously injured when the crowd rioted over a disallowed goal at the National Stadium in Lima, Peru, on May 24, 1964. **Peru** and **Argentina** were competing to play in the Olympic Games in Tokyo.

That remained **sport's heaviest death** toll until Oct 20, 1982, when (it was revealed only in Jul 1989) 340 Soviet fans were killed in Moscow's Lenin Stadium at the UEFA Cup second round first leg match between **Moscow Spartak** and **Haarlem** (Holland). They were crushed on an open stairway when a last-minute Spartak goal sent departing spectators surging back into the ground.

Among other crowd disasters abroad: Jun, 1968 – 74 died in Argentina. Panic broke out at the end of a goalless match between River Plate and Boca Juniors at Nunez, Buenos Aires, when Boca supporters threw lighted newspaper torches on to fans in the tiers below.

Feb 1974 – 49 killed in **Egypt** in crush of fans clamouring to see Zamalek play Dukla Prague.

Sep 1971 – 44 died in **Turkey**, when fighting among spectators over a disallowed goal (Kayseri v Siwas) led to a platform collapsing.

The then worst disaster in the history of British football, in terms of loss of life, occurred at Glasgow Rangers' ground at **Ibrox Park**, Jan 2 1971. Sixty-six people were trampled to death (100 injured) as they tumbled down Stairway 13 just before the end of the **Rangers v Celtic** New Year's match. That disaster led to the 1975 Safety of Sports Grounds legislation.

The Ibrox tragedy eclipsed even the Bolton disaster in which 33 were killed and about 500 injured when a wall and crowd barriers collapsed near a corner-flag at the **Bolton v Stoke** FA Cup sixth round tie on Mar 9 1946. The match was completed after half an hour's stoppage.

In a previous crowd disaster at **Ibrox** on Apr 5, 1902, part of the terracing collapsed during the Scotland v England international and 25 people were killed. The match, held up for 20 minutes, ended 1-1, but was never counted as an official international.

Eight leading players and three officials of **Manchester Utd** and eight newspaper representatives were among the 23 who perished in the air crash at **Munich** on Feb 6, 1958, during take-off following a European Cup-tie in Belgrade. The players were Roger Byrne, Geoffrey Bent, Eddie Colman, Duncan Edwards, Mark Jones, David Pegg, Tommy Taylor and Liam Whelan, and the officials were Walter Crickmer (secretary), Tom Curry (trainer) and Herbert Whalley (coach). The newspaper representatives were Alf Clarke, Don Davies, George Follows, Tom Jackson, Archie Ledbrooke, Henry Rose, Eric Thompson and Frank Swift (former England goalkeeper of Manchester City).

On May 14, 1949, the entire team of Italian Champions **Torino**, 8 of them Internationals, were killed when the aircraft taking them home from a match against Benfica in Lisbon crashed at Superga, near Turin. The total death toll of 28 included all the club's reserve players, the manager, trainer and coach.

On Feb 8, 1981, 24 spectators died and more than 100 were injured at a match in **Greece**. They were trampled as thousands of the 40,000 crowd tried to rush out of the stadium at Piraeus after Olympiacos beat AEK Athens 6-0.

On Nov 17, 1982, 24 people (12 of them children) were killed and 250 injured when fans stampeded at the end of a match at the Pascual Guerrero stadium in **Cali, Colombia**. Drunken spectators hurled fire crackers and broken bottles from the higher stands on to people below and started a rush to the exits.

On Dec 9, 1987, the 18-strong team squad of **Alianza Lima**, one of Peru's top clubs, were wiped out, together with 8 officials and several youth players, when a military aircraft taking them home from Puccalpa crashed into the sea off Ventillana, ten miles from Lima. The only survivor among 43 on board was a member of the crew.

On Apr 28, 1993, 18 members of **Zambia's international squad** and 5 ZFA officials died when the aircraft carrying them to a World Cup qualifying tie against Senegal crashed into the Atlantic soon after take-off from Libreville, Gabon.

On Oct 16 1996, 81 fans were crushed to death and 147 seriously injured in the 'Guatemala **Disaster'** at the World Cup qualifier against Costa Rica in Mateo Flores stadium. The tragedy happened an hour before kick-off, allegedly caused by ticket forgery and overcrowding – 60,000 were reported in the 45,000-capacity ground – and safety problems related to perimeter fencing.

On Jul 9, 1996, 8 people died, 39 injured in riot after derby match between **Libya's two top clubs** in Tripoli. Al-Ahli had beaten Al-Ittihad 1-0 by a controversial goal.

On Apr 6, 1997, 5 spectators were crushed to death at **Nigeria's national stadium** in Lagos after the 2-1 World Cup qualifying victory over Guinea. Only two of five gates were reported open as the 40,000 crowd tried to leave the ground.

It was reported from the **Congo** (Oct 29, 1998) that a bolt of lightning struck a village match, killing all 11 members of the home team Benatshadi, but leaving the opposing players from Basangana unscathed. It was believed the surviving team wore better-insulated boots.

On Jan 10, 1999, eight fans died and 13 were injured in a stampede at **Egypt's Alexandria Stadium**. Some 25,000 spectators had pushed into the ground. Despite the tragedy, the cup-tie between Al-Ittihad and Al-Koroum was completed.

Three people suffocated and several were seriously injured when thousands of fans forced their way into **Liberia's national stadium** in Monrovia at a goalless World Cup qualifying match against Chad on Apr 23, 2000. The stadium (capacity 33,000) was reported 'heavily overcrowded'.

On Jul 9, 2000, 12 spectators died from crush injuries when police fired tear gas into the 50,000 crowd after South Africa scored their second goal in a World Cup group qualifier against Zimbabwe in **Harare**. A stampede broke out as fans scrambled to leave the national stadium. Players of both teams lay face down on the pitch as fumes swept over them. FIFA launched an investigation and decided that the result would stand, with South Africa leading 2-0 at the time of the 84th-minute abandonment.

On Apr 11, 2001, at one of the biggest matches of the South African season, 43 died and 155 were injured in a crush at **Ellis Park, Johannesburg**. After tearing down a fence, thousands of fans surged into a stadium already packed to its 60,000 capacity for the Premiership derby between top Soweto teams Kaizer Chiefs and Orlando Pirates. The match was abandoned at 1-1 after 33 minutes. In Jan 1991, 40 died in a crowd crush at a friendly between the same clubs at Orkney, 80 miles from Johannesburg.

On Apr 29, 2001, seven people were trampled to death and 51 injured when a riot broke out at a match between two of Congo's biggest clubs, Lupopo and Mazembe at **Lubumbashi**, southern Congo.

On May 6, 2001, two spectators were killed in Iran and hundreds were injured when a glass fibre roof collapsed at the over-crowded Mottaqi Stadium at Sari for the match between Pirouzi and Shemshak Noshahr.

On May 9, 2001, in Africa's worst football disaster, 123 died and 93 were injured in a stampede at the national stadium in **Accra, Ghana**. Home team Hearts of Oak were leading 2-1 against Asante Kotoko five minutes from time, when Asanti fans started throwing bottles on to the pitch. Police fired tear gas into the stands, and the crowd panicked in a rush for the exits, which were locked. It took the death toll at three big matches in Africa in Apr/May to 173.

On Aug 12, 2001, two players were killed by lightning and ten severely burned at a **Guatemala** Third Division match between Deportivo Culquimulilla and Pueblo Nuevo Vinas.

On Nov 1, 2002, two players died from injuries after lightning struck Deportivo Cali's training ground in **Colombia**.

On Mar 12 2004, five people were killed and more than 100 injured when spectators stampeded shortly before the Syrian Championship fixture between Al-Jihad and Al-Fatwa in **Qameshli**, Northern Syria. The match was cancelled.

On Oct 10, 2004, three spectators died in a crush at the African Zone World Cup qualifier between **Guinea** and **Morocco** (1-1) at Conakry, Guinea.

On Mar 25, 2005, five were killed as 100,000 left the Azadi Stadium, **Tehran**, after Iran's World Cup qualifying win (2-1) against Japan.

On Jun 2, 2007, 12 spectators were killed and 46 injured in a crush at the Chillabombwe Stadium, **Zambia**, after an African Nations Cup qualifier against Congo.

On Mar 29, 2009, 19 people died and 139 were injured after a wall collapsed at the Ivory Coast stadium in **Abidjan** before a World Cup qualifier against Malawi. The match went ahead, Ivory

Coast winning 5-0 with two goals from Chelsea's Didier Drogba. The tragedy meant that, in 13 years, crowd disasters at club and internationals at ten different grounds across Africa had claimed the lives of 283 people.

On Jan 8, 2010, terrorists at **Cabinda**, Angola machine-gunned the Togo team buses travelling to the Africa Cup of Nations. They killed a driver, an assistant coach and a media officer and injured several players. The team were ordered by their Government to withdraw from the tournament.

On Oct 23, 2010, seven fans were trampled to death when thousands tried to force their way into the Nyayo National Stadium in **Nairobi** at a Kenya Premier League match between the Gor Mahia and AFC Leopards clubs.

On Feb 1, 2012, 74 died and nearly 250 were injured in a crowd riot at the end of the Al-Masry v Al-Ahly match in **Port Said** – the worst disaster in Egyptian sport.

On Nov 28, 2016, 71 died in the worst air crash in world football history when a charter flight carrying players, officials and staff of leading Brazilian club Chapecoense from **Bolivia** to **Colombia** hit a mountain ridge at 8,500 feet. The victims included 65 people from the club.

On Feb 8, 2019, ten young players died when fire engulfed a dormitory at the youth team training centre of one of Brazil's biggest clubs, Flamengo in Rio de Janeiro.

DAYS OF TRAGEDY – PERSONAL

Sam Wynne, Bury right-back, collapsed five minutes before half-time in the First Division match away to Sheffield Utd on Apr 30, 1927, and died in the dressing-room.

John Thomson, Celtic and Scotland goalkeeper, sustained a fractured skull when diving at an opponent's feet in the Rangers v Celtic League match on Sep 5, 1931, and died the same evening.

Sim Raleigh (Gillingham), injured in a clash of heads at home to Brighton (Div 3 South) on Dec 1, 1934, continued to play but collapsed in second half and died in hospital the same night.

James Thorpe, Sunderland goalkeeper, was injured during the First Division match at home to Chelsea on Feb 1, 1936 and died in a diabetic coma three days later.

Derek Dooley, Sheffield Wed centre-forward and top scorer in 1951–52 in the Football League with 46 goals in 30 matches, broke a leg in the League match at Preston on Feb 14, 1953, and, after complications set in, had to lose the limb by amputation.

John White, Tottenham's Scottish international forward, was killed by lightning on a golf course at Enfield, North London in Jul, 1964.

Tony Allden, Highgate centre-half, was struck by lightning during an Amateur Cup quarter-final with Enfield on Feb 25, 1967. He died the following day. Four other players were also struck but recovered.

Roy Harper died while refereeing the York v Halifax (Div 4) match on May 5, 1969.

Jim Finn collapsed and died from a heart attack while refereeing Exeter v Stockport (Div 4) on Sep 16, 1972.

Scotland manager **Jock Stein**, 62, collapsed and died at the end of the Wales-Scotland World Cup qualifying match (1-1) at Ninian Park, Cardiff on Sep 10, 1985.

David Longhurst, York forward, died after being carried off two minutes before half-time in the Fourth Division fixture at home to Lincoln on Sep 8, 1990. The match was abandoned (0-0). The inquest revealed that Longhurst suffered from a rare heart condition.

Mike North collapsed while refereeing Southend v Mansfield (Div 3) on Apr 16, 2001 and died shortly afterwards. The match was abandoned and re-staged on May 8, with the receipts donated to his family.

Marc-Vivien Foe, on his 63rd appearance in Cameroon's midfield, collapsed unchallenged in the centre circle after 72 minutes of the FIFA Confederations Cup semi-final against Colombia in Lyon, France, on Jun 26, 2003, and despite the efforts of the stadium medical staff he could not be revived. He had been on loan to Manchester City from Olympique Lyonnais in season 2002–03, and poignantly scored the club's last goal at Maine Road.

Paul Sykes, Folkestone Invicta (Ryman League) striker, died on the pitch during the Kent Senior Cup semi-final against Margate on Apr 12, 2005. He collapsed after an innocuous off-the-ball incident.

Craig Gowans, Falkirk apprentice, was killed at the club's training ground on Jul 8, 2005 when he came into contact with power lines.

Peter Wilson, Mansfield goalkeeping coach, died of a heart attack after collapsing during the warm-up of the League Two game away to Shrewsbury on Nov 19, 2005.

Matt Gadsby, Hinckley defender, collapsed and died while playing in a Conference North match at Harrogate on Sep 9, 2006.

Phil O'Donnell, 35-year-old Motherwell captain and Scotland midfield player, collapsed when about to be substituted near the end of the SPL home game against Dundee Utd on Dec 29, 2007 and died shortly afterwards in hospital.

Vichai Srivaddhanaprabha, Leicester owner, died in a helicopter crash following the club's Premier League match against West Ham. The pilot and three others on board also died in the crash outside the King Power Stadium, seconds after the helicopter's take-off from the pitch on Oct 27, 2018

Emiliano Sala, Argentine striker, died in a plane crash in the English Channel on Jan 21, 2019 two days after signing for Cardiff from Nantes. The pilot of the light aircraft also died.

Justin Edinburgh, Leyton Orient manager, suffered a cardiac arrest and died five days later on Apr 8, 2019

GREAT SERVICE

'For services to Association Football', **Stanley Matthews** (Stoke, Blackpool and England), already a CBE, became the first professional footballer to receive a knighthood. This was bestowed in 1965, his last season. Before he retired and five days after his 50th birthday, he played for Stoke to set a record as the oldest First Division footballer (v Fulham, Feb 6, 1965).

Over a brilliant span of 33 years, he played in 886 first-class matches, including 54 full Internationals (plus 31 in war time), 701 League games (including 3 at start of season 1939–40, which was abandoned on the outbreak of war) and 86 FA Cup-ties, and scored 95 goals. He was never booked in his career.

Sir Stanley died on Feb 23, 2000, three weeks after his 85th birthday. His ashes were buried under the centre circle of Stoke's Britannia Stadium. After spending a number of years in Toronto, he made his home back in the Potteries in 1989, having previously returned to his home town, Hanley in Oct, 1987 to unveil a life-size bronze statue of himself. The inscription reads: 'Sir Stanley Matthews, CBE. Born Hanley, 1 Feb 1915.

His name is symbolic of the beauty of the game, his fame timeless and international, his sportsmanship and modesty universally acclaimed. A magical player, of the people, for the people.' On his home-coming in 1989, Sir Stanley was made President of Stoke, the club he joined as a boy of 15 and served as a player for 20 years between 1931 and 1965, on either side of his spell with Blackpool.

In Jul 1992 FIFA honoured him with their 'Gold merit award' for outstanding services to the game.

Former England goalkeeper **Peter Shilton** has made more first-class appearances (1,387) than any other footballer in British history. He played his 1,000th League game in Leyton Orient's 2-0 home win against Brighton on Dec 22, 1996 in his final season. He retired from international football after the 1990 World Cup in Italy with 125 caps, then a world record. Shilton kept a record 60 clean sheets for England.

Shilton's career spanned 32 seasons, 20 of them on the international stage. He made his League debut for Leicester in May 1966, two months before England won the World Cup.

His 1,387 first-class appearances comprise a record 1,005 in the Football League, 125 Internationals, 102 League Cup, 86 FA Cup, 13 for England U-23s, 4 for the Football League and 52 other matches (European Cup, UEFA Cup, World Club Championship, Charity Shield, European Super Cup, Full Members' Cup, Play-offs, Screen Sports Super Cup, Anglo-Italian Cup, Texaco Cup, Simod Cup, Zenith Data Systems Cup and Autoglass Trophy).

Shilton appeared 57 times at Wembley, 52 for England, 2 League Cup Finals, 1 FA Cup Final, 1 Charity Shield match, and 1 for the Football League. He passed a century of League appearances with each of his first five clubs: Leicester (286), Stoke (110), Nottm Forest

(202), Southampton (188) and Derby (175) and subsequently played for Plymouth, Bolton and Leyton Orient.

He was awarded the MBE and OBE for services to football. At the Football League Awards ceremony in March 2013, he received the League's Contribution award.

Six other British footballers have made more than 1,000 first-class appearances:

Ray Clemence, formerly with Tottenham, Liverpool and England, retired through injury in season 1987–88 after a goalkeeping career of 1,119 matches starting in 1965–66.

Clemence played 50 times for his first club, Scunthorpe; 665 for Liverpool; 337 for Tottenham; his 67 representative games included 61 England caps.

A third great British goalkeeper, **Pat Jennings**, ended his career (1963–86) with a total of 1,098 first-class matches for Watford, Tottenham, Arsenal and N Ireland. They were made up of 757 in the Football League, 119 full Internationals, 84 FA Cup appearances, 72 League/Milk Cup, 55 European club matches, 2 Charity Shield, 3 Other Internationals, 1 Under-23 cap, 2 Texaco Cup, 2 Anglo-Italian Cup and 1 Super Cup. Jennings played his 119th and final international on his 41st birthday, Jun 12, 1986, against Brazil in Guadalajara in the Mexico World Cup.

Yet another outstanding 'keeper, **David Seaman**, passed the 1,000 appearances milestone for clubs and country in season 2002–03, reaching 1,004 when aged 39, he captained Arsenal to FA Cup triumph against Southampton.

With Arsenal, Seaman won 3 Championship medals, the FA Cup 4 times, the Double twice, the League Cup and Cup-Winners' Cup once each. After 13 seasons at Highbury, he joined Manchester City (Jun 2003) on a free transfer. He played 26 matches for City before a shoulder injury forced his retirement in June 2004, aged 40.

Seaman's 22-season career composed 1,046 first-class matches: 955 club apps (Peterborough 106, Birmingham 84, QPR 175, Arsenal 564, Manchester City 26); 75 senior caps for England, 6 'B' caps and 10 at U-21 level.

Defender **Graeme Armstrong**, 42-year-old commercial manager for an Edinburgh whisky company and part-time assistant-manager and captain of Scottish Third Division club Stenhousemuir, made the 1000th first team appearance of his career in the Scottish Cup 3rd Round against Rangers at Ibrox on Jan 23, 1999. He was presented with the Man of the Match award before kick-off.

Against East Stirling on Boxing Day, he had played his 864th League game, breaking the British record for an outfield player set by another Scot, Tommy Hutchison, with Alloa, Blackpool, Coventry, Manchester City, Burnley and Swansea City.

Armstrong's 24-year career, spent in the lower divisions of the Scottish League, began as a 1-match trialist with Meadowbank Thistle in 1975 and continued via Stirling Albion, Berwick Rangers, Meadowbank and, from 1992, Stenhousemuir.

Tony Ford became the first English outfield player to reach 1000 senior appearances in Rochdale's 1-0 win at Carlisle (Auto Windscreens Shield) on Mar 7, 2000. Grimsby-born, he began his 26-season playing career with Grimsby and played for 7 other League clubs: Sunderland (loan), Stoke, WBA, Bradford City, Scunthorpe, Mansfield and Rochdale. He retired, aged 42, in 2001 with a career record of 1072 appearances (121 goals) and his total of 931 League games is exceeded only by Peter Shilton's 1005.

On Apr 16, 2011, **Graham Alexander**, reached 1,000 appearances when he came on as a sub for Burnley at home to Swansea. Alexander, 40, ended a 22-year career with the equaliser for Preston against Charlton (2-2, Lge 1) on Apr 28, 2012 – his 1,023rd appearance. He also played for Luton and Scunthorpe and was capped 40 times by Scotland.

RECORD FOR BARRY

Gareth Barry surpassed Ryan Giggs's record of 632 Premier League appearances in West Bromwich Albion's 2-0 defeat by Arsenal in the 2017–18 season.

GIGGS RECORD COLLECTION

Ryan Giggs (Manchester Utd) has collected the most individual honours in English football with a total of 34 prizes. They comprise: 13 Premier League titles, 4 FA Cups, 3 League Cups, 2 European Cups, 1 UEFA Super Cup, 1 Inter-Continental Cup, 1 World Club Cup, 9 Charity Shields/Community Shields. One-club man Giggs played 24 seasons for United, making a record 963 appearances. He won 64 Wales caps and on retiring as a player, aged 40, in May 2014, became the club's assistant manager. He ended a 29-year association with the club in June 2016.

KNIGHTS OF SOCCER

Players, managers and administrators who have been honoured for their services to football: **Charles Clegg** (1927), **Stanley Rous** (1949), **Stanley Matthews** (1965), **Alf Ramsey** (1967), **Matt Busby** (1968), **Walter Winterbottom** (1978) **Bert Millichip** (1991), **Bobby Charlton** (1994), **Tom Finney** (1998), **Geoff Hurst** (1998), **Alex Ferguson** (1999), **Bobby Robson** (2002), **Trevor Brooking** (2004), **Dave Richards** (2006), **Doug Ellis** (2011), **Kenny Dalglish** (2018).

● On Nov 6, 2014, **Karren Brady**, vice-chairman of West Ham, was elevated to the Lords as Karren, Baroness Brady, OBE, of Knightsbridge, life peer

PENALTIES

The **penalty-kick** was introduced to the game, following a proposal to the Irish FA in 1890 by William McCrum, son of the High Sheriff for Co Omagh, and approved by the International Football Board on Jun 2, 1891.

First penalty scored in a first-class match in England was by John Heath, for Wolves v Accrington Stanley (5-0 in Div 1, Sep 14, 1891).

The greatest influence of the penalty has come since the 1970s, with the introduction of the shoot-out to settle deadlocked ties in various competitions.

Manchester Utd were the first club to win a competitive match in British football via a shoot-out (4-3 away to Hull, Watney Cup semi-final, Aug 5, 1970); in that penalty contest, George Best was the first player to score, Denis Law the first to miss.

The shoot-out was adopted by FIFA and UEFA the same year (1970).

In season 1991–92, penalty shoot-outs were introduced to decide FA Cup ties still level after one replay and extra time.

Wembley saw its first penalty contest in the 1974 Charity Shield. Since then many major matches across the world have been settled in this way, including:

1976	**European Championship Final (Belgrade):** Czechoslovakia beat West Germany 5-3 (after 2-2)
1980	**Cup-Winners' Cup Final (Brussels):** Valencia beat Arsenal 5-4 (after 0-0)
1984	**European Cup Final (Rome):** Liverpool beat Roma 4-2 (after 1-1)
1984	**UEFA Cup Final:** Tottenham (home) beat Anderlecht 4-3 (2-2 agg)
1986	**European Cup Final (Seville):** Steaua Bucharest beat Barcelona 2-0 (after 0-0).
1987	**Freight Rover Trophy Final (Wembley):** Mansfield beat Bristol City 5-4 (after 1-1)
1987	**Scottish League Cup Final (Hampden Park):** Rangers beat Aberdeen 5-3 (after 3-3)
1988	**European Cup Final (Stuttgart):** PSV Eindhoven beat Benfica 6-5 (after 0-0)
1988	**UEFA Cup Final:** Bayer Leverkusen (home) beat Espanyol 3-2 after 3-3 (0-3a, 3-0h)
1990	**Scottish Cup Final (Hampden Park):** Aberdeen beat Celtic 9-8 (after 0-0)
1991	**European Cup Final (Bari):** Red Star Belgrade beat Marseille 5-3 (after 0-0)
1991	**Div 4 Play-off Final (Wembley):** Torquay beat Blackpool 5-4 (after 2-2)
1992	**Div 4 Play-off Final (Wembley):** Blackpool beat Scunthorpe 4-3 (after 1-1)
1993	**Div 3 Play-off Final(Wembley):** York beat Crewe 5-3 (after 1-1)
1994	**Autoglass Trophy Final (Wembley):** Swansea City beat Huddersfield 3-1 (after 1-1)
1994	**World Cup Final (Los Angeles):** Brazil beat Italy 3-2 (after 0-0)
1994	**Scottish League Cup Final (Ibrox Park):** Raith beat Celtic 6-5 (after 2-2)
1995	**Copa America Final (Montevideo):** Uruguay beat Brazil 5-3 (after 1-1)
1996	**European Cup Final (Rome):** Juventus beat Ajax 4-2 (after 1-1)

1996	**European U-21 Champ Final (Barcelona):** Italy beat Spain 4-2 (after 1-1)
1997	**Auto Windscreens Shield Final (Wembley):** Carlisle beat Colchester 4-3 (after 0-0)
1997	**UEFA Cup Final:** FC Schalke beat Inter Milan 4-1 (after 1-1 agg)
1998	**Div 1 Play-off Final (Wembley):** Charlton beat Sunderland 7-6 (after 4-4)
1999	**Div 2 Play-off Final (Wembley):** Manchester City beat Gillingham 3-1 (after 2-2)
1999	**Women's World Cup Final (Pasedena):** USA beat China 5-4 (after 0-0)
2000	**African Nations Cup Final (Lagos):** Cameroon beat Nigeria 4-3 (after 0-0)
2000	**UEFA Cup Final (Copenhagen):** Galatasaray beat Arsenal 4-1 (after 0-0)
2000	**Olympic Final (Sydney):** Cameroon beat Spain 5-3 (after 2-2)
2001	**League Cup Final (Millennium Stadium):** Liverpool beat Birmingham 5-4 (after 1-1)
2001	**Champions League Final (Milan):** Bayern Munich beat Valencia 5-4 (after 1-1)
2002	**Euro U-21 Champ Final (Basle):** Czech Republic beat France 3-1 (after 0-0)
2002	**Div 1 Play-off Final (Millennium Stadium):** Birmingham beat Norwich 4-2 (after 1-1)
2003	**Champions League Final (Old Trafford):** AC Milan beat Juventus 3-2 (after 0-0)
2004	**Div 3 Play-off Final (Millennium Stadium):** Huddersfield beat Mansfield 4-1 (after 0-0)
2004	**Copa America Final (Lima):** Brazil beat Argentina 4-2 (after 2-2)
2005	**FA Cup Final (Millennium Stadium):** Arsenal beat Manchester Utd 5-4 (after 0-0)
2005	**Champions League Final (Istanbul):** Liverpool beat AC Milan 3-2 (after 3-3)
2006	**African Cup of Nations Final (Cairo):** Egypt beat Ivory Coast 4-2 (after 0-0)
2006	**FA Cup Final (Millennium Stadium):** Liverpool beat West Ham 3-1 (after 3-3)
2006	**Scottish Cup Final (Hampden Park):** Hearts beat Gretna 4-2 (after 1-1)
2006	**Lge 1 Play-off Final (Millennium Stadium):** Barnsley beat Swansea City 4-3 (after 2-2)
2006	**World Cup Final (Berlin):** Italy beat France 5-3 (after 1-1)
2007	**UEFA Cup Final (Hampden Park):** Sevilla beat Espanyol 3-1 (after 2-2)
2008	**Champions League Final (Moscow):** Manchester Utd beat Chelsea 6-5 (after 1-1)
2008	**Scottish League Cup Final (Hampden Park):** Rangers beat Dundee Utd 3-2 (after 2-2)
2009	**League Cup Final (Wembley):** Manchester Utd beat Tottenham 4-1 (after 0-0)
2011	**Women's World Cup Final (Frankfurt):** Japan beat USA 3-1 (after 2-2)
2012	**League Cup Final (Wembley):** Liverpool beat Cardiff 3-2 (after 2-2)
2012	**Champions League Final (Munich):** Chelsea beat Bayern Munich 4-3 (after 1-1)
2012	**Lge 1 Play-off Final (Wembley):** Huddersfield beat Sheffield Utd 8-7 (after 0-0)
2012	**Africa Cup of Nations Final (Gabon):** Zambia beat Ivory Coast 8-7 (after 0-0)
2013	**FA Trophy Final (Wembley):** Wrexham beat Grimsby 4-1 (after 1-1)
2013	**European Super Cup (Prague):** Bayern Munich beat Chelsea 5-4 (after 2-2)
2014	**Scottish League Cup Final (Celtic Park):** Aberdeen beat Inverness 4-2 (after 0-0)
2014	**Lge 1 Play-off Final (Wembley):** Rotherheam beat Leyton Orient 4-3 (after 2-2)
2014	**Europa Lge Final (Turin):** Sevilla beat Benfica 4-2 (after 0-0)
2015	**Africa Cup of Nations Final (Equ Güinea):** Ivory Coast beat Ghana 9-8 (after 0-0)
2015	**Conference Play-off Final (Wembley):** Bristol Rov beat Grimsby 5-3 (after 1-1)
2015	**Lge 2 Play-off Final (Wembley):** Southend beat Wycombe 7-6 (after 1-1)
2015	**FA Trophy Final (Wembley)** North Ferriby beat Wrexham 5-4 (after3-3)
2015	**Euro U-21 Champ Final (Prague):** Sweden beat Portugal 4-3 (after 0-0)
2015	**Copa America Final (Santiago):** Chile beat Argentina 4-1 (after 0-0)
2016	**League Cup Final (Wembley):** Manchester City beat Liverpool 3-1 (after 1-1)
2016	**Champions League Final (Milan):** Real Madrid beat Atletico Madrid 5-3 (after 1-1)
2016	**Olympic Men's Final (Rio de Janeiro):** Brazil beat Germany 5-4 (after 1-1)
2017	**Champ Play-off Final (Wembley):** Huddersfield beat Reading 4-3 (after 0-0)
2017	**Community Shield (Wembley):** Arsenal beat Chelsea 4-1 (after 1-1)
2019	**League Cup Final (Wembley):** Manchester City beat Chelsea 4-3 (after 0-0)
2019	**Football League Trophy Final (Wembley):** Portsmouth beat Sunderland 5-4 (after 2-2)
2019	**Community Shield (Wembley):** Manchester City beat Liverpool 5-4 (after 1-1)
2020	**Community Shield (Wembley):** Arsenal beat Liverpool 5-4 (after 1-1)
2020	**Euro 2020 Qualifying Play-off Final (Belgrade):** Scotland beat Serbia 5-4 (after 1-1)

| 2020 | **League Trophy Final (Wembley):** Salford beat Portsmouth 4-1 (after 0-0) |
| 2021 | **Europa League Final (Godansk):** Villarreal beat Manchester Utd 11-10 (after 1-1) |

In South America in 1992, in a 26-shot competition, **Newell's Old Boys** beat America 11-10 in the Copa Libertadores.

Longest-recorded penalty contest in first-class matches was in Argentina in 1988 – from 44 shots, **Argentinos Juniors** beat Racing Club 20-19. Genclerbirligi beat Galatasaray 17-16 in a Turkish Cup-tie in 1996. Only one penalty was missed.

Highest-scoring shoot-outs in international football: **North Korea** beat Hong Kong 11-10 (after 3-3 draw) in an Asian Cup match in 1975; and **Ivory Coast** beat Ghana 11-10 (after 0-0 draw) in African Nations Cup Final, 1992.

Most penalties needed to settle an adult game in Britain: **44** in Norfolk Primary Cup 4th round replay, Dec 2000. Aston Village side **Freethorpe** beat Foulsham 20-19 (5 kicks missed). All 22 players took 2 penalties each, watched by a crowd of 20. The sides had drawn 2-2, 4-4 in a tie of 51 goals.

Penalty that took 24 days: That was how long elapsed between the award and the taking of a penalty in an Argentine Second Division match between **Atalanta** and Defensores in 2003. A riot ended the original match with 5 minutes left. The game resumed behind closed doors with the penalty that caused the abandonment. Lucas Ferreiro scored it to give Atalanta a 1-0 win.

INTERNATIONAL PENALTIES, MISSED

Four penalties out of five were missed when **Colombia** beat Argentina 3-0 in a Copa America group tie in Paraguay in Jul 1999. Martin Palmermo missed three for Argentina and Colombia's Hamilton Ricard had one spot-kick saved.

In the European Championship semi-final against Italy in Amsterdam on Jun 29, 2000, **Holland** missed five penalties – two in normal time, three in the penalty contest which Italy won 3-1 (after 0-0). Dutch captain Frank de Boer missed twice from the spot.

ENGLAND'S SHOOT-OUT RECORD

1990	(World Cup semi-final, Turin) 3-4 v West Germany after 1-1.
1996	(Euro Champ quarter-final, Wembley) 4-2 v Spain after 0-0.
1996	(Euro Champ semi-final, Wembley) 5-6 v Germany after 1-1.
1998	(World Cup 2nd round., St Etienne) 3-4 v Argentina after 2-2.
2004	(Euro Champ quarter-final, Lisbon) 5-6 v Portugal after 2-2.
2006	(World Cup quarter-final, Gelsenkirchen) 1-3 v Portugal after 0-0.
2007	(Euro U-21 Champ semi-final, Heerenveen) 12-13 v Holland after 1-1.
2009	(Euro U-21 Champ semi-final, Gothenburg) 5-4 v Sweden after 3-3.
2012	(Euro Champ quarter-final, Kiev) 2-4 v Italy after 0-0.
2017	(Euro-21 Champ semi-final, Tychy) 3-4 v Germany after 2-2.
2018	(World Cup round of 16, Moscow) 4-3 v Colombia after 1-1.
2019	(Nations Lge, third-place play-off, Guimaraes) 6-5 v Switzerland after 0-0
2019	(Euro Champ final, Wembley) 2-3 v Italy after 1-1

FA CUP SHOOT-OUTS

First penalty contest in the FA Cup took place in 1972. In the days of the play-off for third place, the match was delayed until the eve of the following season when losing semi-finalists Birmingham and Stoke met at St Andrew's on Aug 5. The score was 0-0 and Birmingham won 4-3 on penalties.

Highest-scoring: Preliminary round replay (Aug 30, 2005): Tunbridge Wells beat Littlehampton 16-15 after 40 spot-kicks (9 missed).

Competition proper: Scunthorpe beat Worcester 14-13 in 2nd round replay (Dec 17, 2014) after 1-1 (32 kicks).

Shoot-out abandoned: The FA Cup 1st round replay between Oxford City and Wycombe at Wycombe on Nov 9, 1999 was abandoned (1-1) after extra-time. As the penalty shoot-out was about to begin, a fire broke out under a stand. Wycombe won the second replay 1-0 at Oxford Utd's ground.

First FA Cup Final to be decided by shoot-out was in 2005 (May 21), when Arsenal beat Manchester Utd 5-4 on penalties at Cardiff's Millennium Stadium (0-0 after extra time). A year later (May 13) Liverpool beat West Ham 3-1 (3-3 after extra-time).

ENGLISH RECORD SHOOT-OUT

Total of 34 spot-kicks: Football League Trophy group match, Nov 8, 2016, won 13-12 by Chelsea under-23 v Oxford United. Also: Southern League Challenge Cup 2nd rd, Nov 20, 2019, won 12-11 by Taunton v Truro.

SHOOT-OUT RECORD WINNERS AND LOSERS

When **Bradford** beat Arsenal 3-2 on penalties in a League Cup fifth round tie, it was the club's ninth successive shoot-out victory in FA Cup, League Cup and Johnstone's Paint Trophy ties between Oct 2009 and Dec 2012.

Tottenham's 4-1 spot-kick failure against Basel in the last 16 of the Europa League was their seventh successive defeat in shoot-outs from Mar 1996 to Apr 2013 (FA Cup, League Cup, UEFA Cup, Europa League)

MISSED CUP FINAL PENALTIES

John Aldridge (Liverpool) became the first player to miss a penalty in an FA Cup Final at Wembley when Dave Beasant saved his shot in 1988 to help Wimbledon to a shock 1-0 win. Seven penalties before had been scored in the Final at Wembley.

Previously, **Charlie Wallace**, of Aston Villa, had failed from the spot in the 1913 Final against Sunderland at Crystal Palace, which his team won 1-0

Gary Lineker (Tottenham) had his penalty saved by Nottm Forest's Mark Crossley in the 1991 FA Cup Final.

For the first time, two spot-kicks were missed in an FA Cup Final. In 2010, Petr Cech saved from Portsmouth's **Kevin-Prince Boateng** while Chelsea's **Frank Lampard** put his kick wide.

Another miss at Wembley was by Arsenal's **Nigel Winterburn**, Luton's Andy Dibble saving his spot-kick in the 1988 Littlewoods Cup Final, when a goal would have put Arsenal 3-1 ahead. Instead, they lost 3-2.

Winterburn was the third player to fail with a League Cup Final penalty at Wembley, following **Ray Graydon** (Aston Villa) against Norwich in 1975 and **Clive Walker** (Sunderland), who shot wide in the 1985 Milk Cup Final, also against Norwich who won 1-0. Graydon had his penalty saved by Kevin Keelan, but scored from the rebound and won the cup for Aston Villa (1-0).

Derby's Martin Taylor saved a penalty from **Eligio Nicolini** in the Anglo-Italian Cup Final at Wembley on Mar 27, 1993. Cremonese won 3-1.

LEAGUE PENALTIES RECORD

Most penalties in Football League match: Five – 4 to Crystal Palace (3 missed), 1 to Brighton (scored) in Div 2 match at Selhurst Park on Mar 27 (Easter Monday), 1989. Crystal Palace won 2-1. Three of the penalties were awarded in a 5-minute spell. The match also produced 5 bookings and a sending-off. Other teams missing 3 penalties in a match: Burnley v Grimsby (Div 2), Feb 13, 1909; Manchester City v Newcastle (Div 1), Jan 17, 1912.

HOTTEST MODERN SPOT-SHOTS

Matthew Le Tissier ended his career in season 2001–02 with the distinction of having netted 48 out of 49 first-team penalties for Southampton. He scored the last 27 after his only miss when Nottm Forest keeper Mark Crossley saved in a Premier League match at The Dell on Mar 24, 1993.

Graham Alexander scored 78 out of 84 penalties in a 22-year career (Scunthorpe, Luton, Preston twice and Burnley) which ended in 2012.

SPOT-KICK HAT-TRICKS

Right-back **Joe Willetts** scored three penalties when Hartlepool beat Darlington 6-1 (Div 3N) on Good Friday 1951.

Danish international **Jan Molby**'s only hat-trick in English football, for Liverpool in a 3-1 win at home to Coventry (Littlewoods Cup, 4th round replay, Nov 26, 1986) comprised three goals from the penalty spot.

It was the first such hat-trick in a major match for two years – since **Andy Blair** scored three penalties for Sheffield Wed against Luton (Milk Cup 4th round, Nov 20 1984).

Portsmouth's **Kevin Dillon** scored a penalty hat-trick in the Full Members Cup (2nd round) at home to Millwall (3-2) on Nov 4, 1986.

Alan Slough scored a hat-trick of penalties in an away game, but was on the losing side, when Peterborough were beaten 4-3 at Chester (Div 3, Apr 29, 1978).

Josh Wright's three penalties in the space of 11 minutes enabled Gillingham to come from 2-0 down to defeat his former club Scunthorpe 3-2 in League One on Mar 11, 2017

Penalty hat-tricks in **international football: Dimitris Saravakos** (in 9 mins) for Greece v Egypt in 1990. He scored 5 goals in match. **Henrik Larsson**, among his 4 goals in Sweden's 6-0 home win v Moldova in World Cup qualifying match, Jun 6, 2001.

MOST PENALTY GOALS (LEAGUE) IN SEASON

13 out of 13 by **Francis Lee** for Manchester City (Div 1) in 1971–72. His goal total for the season was 33. In season 1988–89, **Graham Roberts** scored 12 League penalties for Second Division Champions Chelsea. In season 2004–05, **Andrew Johnson** scored 11 Premier League penalties for Crystal Palace, who were relegated.

PENALTY-SAVE SEQUENCES

Ipswich goalkeeper **Paul Cooper** saved eight of the ten penalties he faced in 1979–80. **Roy Brown** (Notts Co) saved six in a row in season 1972–73.

Andy Lomas, goalkeeper for Chesham (Diadora League) claimed a record eighth **consecutive** penalty saves – three at the end of season 1991–92 and five in 1992–93.

Mark Bosnich (Aston Villa) saved five in two consecutive matches in 1993–94: three in Coca-Cola Cup semi-final penalty shoot–out v Tranmere (Feb 26), then two in Premier League at Tottenham (Mar 2).

MISSED PENALTIES SEQUENCE

Against Wolves in Div 2 on Sep 28, 1991, **Southend** missed their seventh successive penalty (five of them the previous season).

RANGERS SPOT-ON

Rangers were awarded four penalties in their 4-0 win Scottish Premiership win over St Mirren on Feb 2, 2019, converting three of them.

SCOTTISH RECORDS

(See also under 'Goals' & 'Discipline')

CELTIC SUPREME

In winning the Treble for the fourth time in 2016–17, **Celtic** rewrote the Scottish records. In the first season under **Brendan Rodgers**, previously Liverpool manager, they did not lose a domestic match, the first to stay unbeaten in the league since Rangers in 1899. They set new records for points (106), goals (106), victories (34) and for a 30-point winning margin. In 2017–18, Celtic became the first in Scotland to win back-to-back domestic trebles and stretched an unbeaten run to a British record 69 games in domestic competitions. Their 25 consecutive victories in season 2003–04 also represents a British best, while the 1966–67 record was the most successful by a British side in one season. They won the Treble and became the first to win the European Cup. Under Jock Stein, there were nine titles in a row (1966–74). In season 2018–19, Celtic completed a third successive domestic treble, this one under **Brendan Rodgers** and **Neil Lennon**, who took over when Rodgers left to become Leicester manager in late February. After a ninth straight title in the curtailed 2019–20 season Celtic set their sights on a record tenth in the new campaign. **Rangers** ended the run, but Celtic and Lennon still made history with victory over Hearts in the delayed 2020 Scottish Cup Final. It gave the club a fourth straight domestic treble and the manager a domestic treble as player and manager.

RANGERS BACK ON TOP

Rangers denied arch-rivals Celtic a record tenth straight title with a runaway triumph under Steven Gerrard in season 2020–21. They finished 25 points ahead, were unbeaten in their 38 matches and set a new British defensive record by conceding only 13 goals.

RANGERS' MANY RECORDS

Rangers' record-breaking feats include:

League Champions: 55 times (once joint holders) – world record.

Winning every match in Scottish League (18 games, 1898–99 season).

Major hat-tricks: Rangers have completed the domestic treble (League Championship, League Cup and Scottish FA Cup) a record seven times (1948–49, 1963–64, 1975–76, 1977–78, 1992–93, 1998–99, 2002–03).

League & Cup double: 17 times.

Nine successive Championships (1989–97). Four men played in all nine sides: Richard Gough, Ally McCoist, Ian Ferguson and Ian Durrant.

116 major trophies: Championships 55, Scottish Cup 33, League Cup 27, Cup-Winners' Cup 1.

UNBEATEN SCOTTISH CHAMPIONS

Celtic and **Rangers** have each won the Scottish Championship with an unbeaten record: Celtic in 1897–98 (P18, W15, D3), Rangers in 1898–99 (P18, W18).

FORSTER'S SHUT-OUT RECORD

Celtic goalkeeper **Fraser Forster** set a record in Scottish top-flight football by not conceding a goal for 1,256 consecutive minutes in season 2013–14.

TRIO OF TOP CLUBS MISSING

Three of Scotland's leading clubs were missing from the 2014–15 Premiership season. With **Hearts** finishing bottom and **Rangers** still working their way back through the divisions after being demoted, they were joined in the second tier by **Hibernian**, who lost the play-off final on penalties to Hamilton.

SCOTTISH CUP HAT-TRICKS

Aberdeen's feat of winning the Scottish FA Cup in 1982–83–84 made them only the third club to achieve that particular hat-trick. **Queen's Park** did it twice (1874–75–76 and 1880–81–82), and **Rangers** have won the Scottish Cup three years in succession on three occasions: 1934–35–36, 1948–49–50 and 1962–63–64.

SCOTTISH CUP FINAL DISMISSALS

Five players have been sent off in the Scottish FA Cup Final: **Jock Buchanan** (Rangers v Kilmarnock, 1929); **Roy Aitken** (Celtic v Aberdeen, 1984); **Walter Kidd** (Hearts captain v Aberdeen, 1986); **Paul Hartley** (Hearts v Gretna, 2006); **Pa Kujabi** (Hibernian v Hearts, 2012); **Carl Tremarco** (Inverness v Falkirk, 2015).

HIGHEST-SCORING SHOOT-OUT

In Scottish football's highest-scoring penalty shoot-out, **Stirling Albion** beat junior club Hurlford 13-12 after 28 spot-kicks in a third round replay. The tie, on Nov 8, 2014, had ended 2-2 after extra-time.

RECORD SEQUENCES

Celtic hold Britain's League record of 62 matches undefeated, from Nov 13, 1915 to Apr 21,

1917, when Kilmarnock won 2-0 at Parkhead. They won 49, drew 13 (111 points) and scored 126 goals to 26.

Greenock Morton in 1963–64 accumulated 67 points out of 72 and scored 135 goals.

Queen's Park did not have a goal scored against them during the first seven seasons of their existence (1867–74, before the Scottish League was formed).

EARLIEST PROMOTIONS IN SCOTLAND

Dundee promoted from Div 2, Feb 1, 1947; **Greenock Morton** promoted from Div 2, Mar 2, 1964; **Gretna** promoted from Div 3, Mar 5, 2005; **Hearts** promoted from Championship, Mar 21, 2015.

WORST HOME SEQUENCE

After gaining promotion to Div 1 in 1992, **Cowdenbeath** went a record 38 consecutive home League matches without a win. They ended the sequence (drew 8, lost 30) when beating Arbroath 1-0 on Apr 2, 1994, watched by a crowd of 225.

ALLY'S RECORDS

Ally McCoist became the first player to complete 200 goals in the Premier Division when he scored Rangers' winner (2-1) at Falkirk on Dec 12, 1992. His first was against Celtic in Sep 1983, and he reached 100 against Dundee on Boxing Day 1987.

When McCoist scored twice at home to Hibernian (4-3) on Dec 7, 1996, he became Scotland's record post-war League marksman, beating Gordon Wallace's 264.

Originally with St Johnstone (1978–81), he spent two seasons with Sunderland (1981–83), then joined Rangers for £200,000 in Jun 1983.

In 15 seasons at Ibrox, he scored 355 goals for Rangers (250 League), and helped them win 10 Championships (9 in succession), 3 Scottish Cups and earned a record 9 League Cup winner's medals. He won the European Golden Boot in consecutive seasons (1991–92, 1992–93).

His 9 Premier League goals in three seasons for Kilmarnock gave him a career total of 281 Scottish League goals when he retired at the end of 2000–01. McCoist succeeded Walter Smith as manager of Rangers in May 2011.

SCOTLAND'S MOST SUCCESSFUL MANAGER

Bill Struth, 30 trophies for Rangers, 1920–54 (18 Championships, 10 Scottish Cups, 2 League Cups.

SMITH'S IBROX HONOURS

Walter Smith, who retired in May, 2011, won a total of 21 trophies in two spells as Rangers manager (10 League titles, 5 Scottish Cups, 6 League Cups).

RANGERS PUNISHED

In April 2012, **Rangers** (in administration) were fined £160,000 by the Scottish FA and given a 12-month transfer ban on charges relating to their finances. The ban was later overturned in court. The club had debts estimated at around £135m and on June 12, 2012 were forced into liquidation. A new company emerged, but Rangers were voted out of the Scottish Premier League and demoted to Division Three for the start of the 2012-13 season. They returned to the top division in 2016 via three promotions in four seasons.

FIVE IN A MATCH

Paul Sturrock set an individual scoring record for the Scottish Premier Division with 5 goals in Dundee Utd's 7-0 win at home to Morton on Nov 17, 1984. **Marco Negri** equalled the feat with all 5 when Rangers beat Dundee Utd 5-1 at Ibrox (Premier Division) on Aug 23, 1997, and **Kenny Miller** scored 5 in Rangers' 7-1 win at home to St Mirren on Nov 4, 2000. **Kris Boyd** scored all Kilmarnock's goals in a 5-2 SPL win at home to Dundee Utd on Sep 25, 2004. **Boyd** scored another 5 when Rangers beat Dundee Utd 7-1 on Dec 30, 2009. That took his total of SPL goals to a record 160. **Gary Hooper** netted all Celtic's goals in 5-0 SPL win against Hearts on May 13, 2012

NEGRI'S TEN-TIMER

Marco Negri scored in Rangers' first ten League matches (23 goals) in season 1997–98, a Premier Division record. The previous best was 8 by **Ally MacLeod** for Hibernian in 1978.

DOUBLE SCOTTISH FINAL

Rangers v Celtic drew **129,643** and **120,073** people to the Scottish Cup Final and replay at Hampden Park, Glasgow, in 1963. Receipts for the two matches totalled £50,500.

MOST SCOTTISH CHAMPIONSHIP MEDALS

13 by **Sandy Archibald** (Rangers, 1918–34). Post-war record: 10 by **Bobby Lennox** (Celtic, 1966–79).

Alan Morton won **nine** Scottish Championship medals with Rangers in 1921–23–24–25–27–28–29–30–31. **Ally McCoist** played in the Rangers side that won nine successive League titles (1989–97).

Between 1927 and 1939 **Bob McPhail** helped Rangers win nine Championships, finish second twice and third once. He scored 236 League goals but was never top scorer in a single season.

TOP SCOTTISH LEAGUE SCORERS IN SEASON

Raith Rovers (Div 2) 142 goals in 1937–38; **Morton** (Div 2) 135 goals in 1963–64; **Hearts** (Div 1) 132 goals in 1957–58; **Falkirk** (Div 2) 132 goals in 1935–36; **Gretna** (Div 3) 130 goals in 2004–05.

SCOTTISH CUP – NO DECISION

The **Scottish FA** withheld their Cup and medals in 1908–09 after Rangers and Celtic played two drawn games in the Final. Spectators rioted.

FEWEST LEAGUE WINS IN SEASON

In modern times: 1 win by **Ayr** (34 matches, Div 1, 1966–67); **Forfar** (38 matches, Div 2, 1973–74); **Clydebank** (36 matches, Div 1, 1999–2000).

Vale of Leven provided the only instance of a British team failing to win a single match in a league season (Div 1, 18 games, 1891–92).

HAMPDEN'S £63M REDEVELOPMENT

On completion of redevelopment costing £63m **Hampden Park**, home of Scottish football and the oldest first-class stadium in the world, was re-opened full scale for the Rangers-Celtic Cup Final on May 29, 1999.

Work on the 'new Hampden' (capacity 52,000) began in 1992. The North and East stands were restructured (£12m); a new South stand and improved West stand cost £51m. The Millennium Commission contributed £23m and the Lottery Sports Fund provided a grant of £3.75m.

FIRST FOR INVERNESS

Inverness Caledonian Thistle won the Scottish Cup for the Highlands for the first time when beating Falkirk 2-1 in the Final on May 30, 2015.

FASTEST GOALS IN SPL

10.4 sec by **Kris Boyd** for Kilmarnock in 3-2 win over Ross Co, Jan 28, 2017; 12.1 sec by **Kris Commons** for Celtic in 4-3 win over Aberdeen, Mar 16, 2013; 12.4 sec by **Anthony Stokes** for Hibernian in 4-1 home defeat by Rangers, Dec 27, 2009.

YOUNGEST SCORER IN SPL

Fraser Fyvie, aged 16 years and 306 days, for Aberdeen v Hearts (3-0) on Jan 27, 2010.

12 GOALS SHARED

There was a record aggregate score for the SPL on May 5, 2010, when **Motherwell** came from 6-2 down to draw 6-6 with **Hibernian**.

25-POINT DEDUCTION

Dundee were deducted 25 points by the Scottish Football League in November 2010 for going into administration for the second time. It left the club on minus 11 points, but they still managed to finish in mid-table in Division One.

GREAT SCOTS

In Feb 1988, the Scottish FA launched a national **Hall of Fame**, initially comprising the first 11 Scots to make 50 international appearances, to be joined by all future players to reach that number of caps. Each member receives a gold medal, invitation for life at all Scotland's home matches, and has his portrait hung at Scottish FA headquarters in Glasgow.

MORE CLUBS IN 2000

The **Scottish Premier League** increased from 10 to 12 clubs in season 2000–01. The **Scottish Football League** admitted two new clubs – Peterhead and Elgin City from the Highland League – to provide three divisions of 10 in 2000–01.

FIRST FOR EDINBURGH CITY

In May 2016, **Edinburgh City** became the first club to be promoted to Scottish League Two through the pyramid system with a 2-1 aggregate play-off aggregate win over East Stirling, whose 61 years in senior football came to an end.

NOTABLE SCOTTISH 'FIRSTS'

- The father of League football was a Scot, **William McGregor**, a draper in Birmingham. The 12-club Football League kicked off in Sep 1888, and McGregor was its first president.
- **Hibernian** were the first British club to play in the European Cup, by invitation. They reached the semi-final when it began in 1955–56.
- **Celtic** were Britain's first winners of the European Cup, in 1967.
- Scotland's First Division became the **Premier Division** in season 1975–76.
- Football's **first international** was staged at the West of Scotland cricket ground, Partick, on Nov 30, 1872: Scotland 0, England 0.
- Scotland introduced its **League Cup** in 1945–46, the first season after the war. It was another 15 years before the Football League Cup was launched.
- Scotland pioneered the use in British football of **two subs** per team in League and Cup matches.
- The world's **record football score** belongs to Scotland: Arbroath 36, Bon Accord 0 (Scottish Cup 1st rd) on Sep 12, 1885.
- The Scottish FA introduced the penalty **shoot-out** to their Cup Final in 1990.
- On Jan 22, 1994 all six matches in the **Scottish Premier Division** ended as draws.
- Scotland's new Premier League introduced a **3-week shut-down** in Jan 1999 – first instance of British football adopting the winter break system that operates in a number of European countries. The SPL ended its New Year closure after 2003. The break returned from season 2016–17.
- **Rangers** made history at home to St Johnstone (Premier League, 0-0, Mar 4, 2000) when fielding a team entirely without Scottish players.
- **John Fleck**, aged 16 years, 274 days, became the youngest player in a Scottish FA Cup Final when he came on as a substitute for Rangers in their 3-2 win over Queen of the South at Hampden Park on May 24, 2008

SCOTTISH CUP SHOCK RESULTS

1885–86	(1)	Arbroath 36 Bon Accord 0
1921–22	(F)	Morton 1 Rangers 0
1937–38	(F)	East Fife 4 Kilmarnock 2 (replay, after 1-1)
1960–61	(F)	Dunfermline 2 Celtic 0 (replay, after 0-0)
1966–67	(1)	Berwick 1 Rangers 0
1979–80	(3)	Hamilton 2 Keith 3

1984–85	(1)	Stirling 20 Selkirk 0
1984–85	(3)	Inverness 3 Kilmarnock 0
1986–87	(3)	Rangers 0 Hamilton 1
1994–95	(4)	Stenhousemuir 2 Aberdeen 0
1998–99	(3)	Aberdeen 0 Livingston 1
1999–2000	(3)	Celtic 1 Inverness 3
2003–04	(5)	Inverness 1 Celtic 0
2005–06	(3)	Clyde 2 Celtic 1
2008–09	(6)	St Mirren 1 Celtic 0
2009–10	(SF)	Ross Co 2 Celtic 0
2013–14	(4)	Albion 1 Motherwell 0
2020–21	(2)	Brora 2 Hearts 1

Scottish League (Coca-Cola) Cup Final

1994–95	Raith 2, Celtic 2 (Raith won 6-5 on pens)

Europa League first qualifying round

2017–18	Progres Niederkorn (Luxembourg) 2 Rangers 1 (on agg)
2019–20	Connah's Quay (Wales) 3 Kilmarnock 2 (on agg)

MISCELLANEOUS

NATIONAL ASSOCIATIONS FORMED

FA	1863
FA of Wales	1876
Scottish FA	1873
Irish FA	1904
Federation of International Football Associations (FIFA)	1904

NATIONAL & INTERNATIONAL COMPETITIONS LAUNCHED

FA Cup	1871
Welsh Cup	1877
Scottish Cup	1873
Irish Cup	1880
Football League	1888
Premier League	1992
Scottish League	1890
Scottish Premier League	1998
Scottish League Cup	1945
Football League Cup	1960
Home International Championship	1883–84
World Cup	1930
European Championship	1958
European Cup	1955
Fairs/UEFA Cup	1955
Cup-Winners' Cup	1960
European Champions League	1992
Olympic Games Tournament, at Shepherd's Bush	1908

INNOVATIONS

Size of Ball: Fixed in **1872**.

Shinguards: Introduced and registered by Sam Weller Widdowson (Nottm Forest & England) in **1874**.

Referee's whistle: First used on Nottm Forest's ground in **1878**.

Professionalism: Legalised in England in the summer of **1885** as a result of agitation by Lancashire clubs.

Goal-nets: Invented and patented in **1890** by Mr JA Brodie of Liverpool. They were first used in the North v South match in Jan, **1891**.

Referees and linesmen: Replaced umpires and referees in Jan, **1891**.

Penalty-kick: Introduced at Irish FA's request in the season **1891–92**. The penalty law ordering the goalkeeper to remain on the goal-line came into force in Sep, **1905**, and the order to stand on his goal-line until the ball is kicked arrived in **1929–30**.

White ball: First came into official use in **1951**.

Floodlighting: First FA Cup-tie (replay), Kidderminster Harriers v Brierley Hill Alliance, **1955**. First Football League match: Portsmouth v Newcastle (Div 1), **1956**.

Heated pitch to beat frost tried by Everton at Goodison Park in **1958**.

First soccer closed-circuit TV: At Coventry ground in Oct **1965** (10,000 fans saw their team win at Cardiff, 120 miles away).

Substitutes (one per team) were first allowed in Football League matches at the start of season **1965–66**. Three substitutes (one a goalkeeper) allowed, two of which could be used, in Premier League matches, **1992–93**. The Football League introduced three substitutes for **1993–94**.

Three points for a win: Introduced by the Football League in **1981–82**, by FIFA in World Cup games in **1994**, and by the Scottish League in the same year.

Offside law amended, player 'level' no longer offside, and 'professional foul' made sending-off offence, **1990**.

Penalty shoot-outs introduced to decide FA Cup ties level after one replay and extra time, **1991–92**.

New back-pass rule: goalkeeper must not handle ball kicked to him by team-mate, **1992**.

Linesmen became 'referees' assistants', **1998**.

Goalkeepers not to hold ball longer than 6 seconds, **2000**.

Free-kicks advanced by ten yards against opponents failing to retreat, **2000**. This experimental rule in England was scrapped in 2005).

YOUNGEST AND OLDEST

Youngest Caps

Harry Wilson (Wales v Belgium, Oct 15, 2013)	**16 years 207 days**
Norman Whiteside (N Ireland v Yugoslavia, Jun 17, 1982)	**17 years 41 days**
Theo Walcott (England v Hungary, May 30, 2006)	**17 years 75 days**
Johnny Lambie (Scotland v Ireland, Mar 20, 1886)	**17 years 92 days**
Jimmy Holmes (Rep of Ireland v Austria, May 30, 1971)	**17 years 200 days**

Youngest England scorer: Wayne Rooney (17 years, 317 days) v Macedonia, Skopje, Sep 6, 2003.

Youngest scorer on England debut: Marcus Rashford (18 years, 208 days) v Australia, Sunderland, May 27, 2016.

Youngest England hat-trick scorer: Theo Walcott (19 years, 178 days) v Croatia, Zagreb, Sep 10, 2008.

Youngest England captains: Bobby Moore (v Czech., Bratislava, May 29, 1963), 22 years, 47 days; Michael Owen (v Paraguay, Anfield, Apr 17, 2002), 22 years, 117 days.

Youngest England goalkeeper: Jack Butland (19 years, 158 days) v Italy, Bern, Aug 15, 2012

Youngest England players to reach 50 caps: Michael Owen (23 years, 6 months) v Slovakia at Middlesbrough, Jun 11, 2003; Bobby Moore (25 years, 7 months) v Wales at Wembley, Nov 16, 1966.

Youngest player in World Cup Final: Pele (Brazil) aged 17 years, 237 days v Sweden in Stockholm, Jun 12, 1958.

Youngest player to appear in World Cup Finals: Norman Whiteside (N Ireland v Yugoslavia in Spain – Jun 17, 1982, age 17 years and 42 days.

Youngest First Division player: Derek Forster (Sunderland goalkeeper v Leicester, Aug 22, 1964) aged 15 years, 185 days.

Youngest First Division scorer: At 16 years and 57 days, schoolboy Jason Dozzell (substitute after 30 minutes for Ipswich at home to Coventry on Feb 4, 1984). Ipswich won 3-1 and Dozzell scored their third goal.

Youngest Premier League player: Harvey Elliott (Fulham on loan from Liverpool, sub away to Wolves, May 4, 2019), 16 years and 30 days.

Youngest Premier League scorer: James Vaughan (Everton, home to Crystal Palace, Apr 10, 2005), 16 years, 271 days.

Youngest Premier League scorer on first start: Daniel Jebbison (Sheffield Utd away to Everton, May 16, 2021) aged 17 years, 309 days.

Youngest Premier League captain: Lee Cattermole (Middlesbrough away to Fulham, May 7, 2006) aged 18 years, 47 days.

Youngest player sent off in Premier League: Wayne Rooney (Everton, away to Birmingham, Dec 26, 2002) aged 17 years, 59 days.

Youngest First Division hat-trick scorer: Alan Shearer, aged 17 years, 240 days, in Southampton's 4-2 home win v Arsenal (Apr 9, 1988) on his full debut. Previously, Jimmy Greaves (17 years, 309 days) with 4 goals for Chelsea at home to Portsmouth (7-4), Christmas Day, 1957.

Youngest to complete 100 Football League goals: Jimmy Greaves (20 years, 261 days) when he did so for Chelsea v Manchester City, Nov 19, 1960.

Youngest players in Football League: Reuben Noble-Lazarus (Barnsley 84th minute sub at Ipswich, Sep 30, 2008, Champ) aged 15 years, 45 days; Mason Bennett (Derby at Middlesbrough, Champ, Oct 22, 2011) aged 15 years, 99 days; Albert Geldard (Bradford PA v Millwall, Div 2, Sep 16, 1929) aged 15 years, 158 days; Ken Roberts (Wrexham v Bradford Park Avenue, Div 3 North, Sep 1, 1951) also 15 years, 158 days.

Youngest Football League scorer: Ronnie Dix (for Bristol Rov v Norwich, Div 3 South, Mar 3, 1928) aged 15 years, 180 days.

Youngest player in Scottish League: Goalkeeper Ronnie Simpson (Queens Park) aged 15 in 1946.

Youngest player in FA Cup: Andy Awford, Worcester City's England Schoolboy defender, aged 15 years, 88 days when he substituted in second half away to Boreham Wood (3rd qual round) on Oct 10, 1987.

Youngest player in FA Cup proper: Luke Freeman, Gillingham substitute striker (15 years, 233 days) away to Barnet in 1st round, Nov 10, 2007.

Youngest FA Cup scorer: Sean Cato (16 years, 25 days), second half sub in Barrow Town's 7-2 win away to Rothwell Town (prelim rd), Sep 3, 2011.

Youngest Wembley Cup Final captain: Barry Venison (Sunderland v Norwich, Milk Cup Final, Mar 24, 1985 – replacing suspended captain Shaun Elliott) – aged 20 years, 220 days.

Youngest FA Cup-winning captain: Bobby Moore (West Ham, 1964, v Preston), aged 23 years, 20 days.

Youngest FA Cup Final captain: David Nish aged 21 years and 212 days old when he captained Leicester against Manchester City at Wembley on Apr 26, 1969.

Youngest FA Cup Final player: Curtis Weston (Millwall sub last 3 mins v Manchester Utd, 2004) aged 17 years, 119 days.

Youngest FA Cup Final scorer: Norman Whiteside (Manchester Utd v Brighton, 1983 replay, Wembley), aged 18 years, 19 days.

Youngest FA Cup Final managers: Stan Cullis, Wolves (32) v Leicester, 1949; Steve Coppell, Crystal Palace (34) v Manchester Utd, 1990; Ruud Gullit, Chelsea (34) v Middlesbrough, 1997.

Youngest player in Football League Cup: Chris Coward (Stockport) sub v Sheffield Wed, 2nd Round, Aug 23, 2005, aged 16 years and 31 days.

Youngest Wembley scorer: Norman Whiteside (Manchester Utd v Liverpool, Milk Cup Final, Mar 26, 1983) aged 17 years, 324 days.

Youngest Wembley Cup Final goalkeeper: Chris Woods (18 years, 125 days) for Nottm Forest v Liverpool, League Cup Final on Mar 18, 1978.

Youngest Wembley FA Cup Final goalkeeper: Peter Shilton (19 years, 219 days) for Leicester v Manchester City, Apr 26, 1969.

Youngest senior international at Wembley: Salomon Olembe (sub for Cameroon v England, Nov 15, 1997), aged 16 years, 342 days.

Youngest winning manager at Wembley: Stan Cullis, aged 32 years, 187 days, as manager of Wolves, FA Cup winners on April 30 1949.

Youngest scorer in full international: Mohamed Kallon (Sierra Leone v Congo, African Nations

Cup, Apr 22, 1995), reported as aged 15 years, 192 days.

Youngest English player to start a Champions League game: Phil Foden (Manchester City v Shakhtar Donetsk, Dec 6, 2017) aged 17 years, 192 days.

Youngest English scorer in Champions League: Alex Oxlade-Chamberlain (Arsenal v Olympiacos, September 28 2011) aged 18 years, 1 month 13 days.

Youngest player sent off in World Cup Final series: Rigobert Song (Cameroon v Brazil, in USA, Jun 1994) aged 17 years, 358 days.

Youngest FA Cup Final referee: Kevin Howley, of Middlesbrough, aged 35 when in charge of Wolves v Blackburn, 1960.

Youngest player in England U-23 team: Duncan Edwards (v Italy, Bologna, Jan 20, 1954), aged 17 years, 112 days.

Youngest player in England U-21 team: Theo Walcott (v Moldova, Ipswich, Aug 15, 2006), aged 17 years, 152 days.

Youngest player in Scotland U-21 team: Christian Dailly (v Romania, Hampden Park, Sep 11, 1990), aged 16 years, 330 days.

Youngest player in senior football: Cameron Campbell Buchanan, Scottish-born outside right, aged 14 years, 57 days when he played for Wolves v WBA in War-time League match, Sep 26, 1942.

Youngest player in peace-time senior match: Eamon Collins (Blackpool v Kilmarnock, Anglo-Scottish Cup quarter-final 1st leg, Sep 9, 1980) aged 14 years, 323 days.

World's youngest player in top division match: Centre-forward Fernando Rafael Garcia, aged 13, played for 23 minutes for Peruvian club Juan Aurich in 3-1 win against Estudiantes on May 19, 2001.

Oldest player to appear in Football League: New Brighton manager Neil McBain (51 years, 120 days) as emergency goalkeeper away to Hartlepool (Div 3 North, Mar 15, 1947).

Other oldest post-war League players: Sir Stanley Matthews (Stoke, 1965, 50 years, 5 days); Peter Shilton (Leyton Orient 1997, 47 years, 126 days); Kevin Poole (Burton, 2010, 46 years, 291 days); Dave Beasant (Brighton 2003, 44 years, 46 days); Alf Wood (Coventry, 1958, 43 years, 199 days); Tommy Hutchison (Swansea City, 1991, 43 years, 172 days).

Oldest Football League debutant: Andy Cunningham, for Newcastle at Leicester (Div 1) on Feb 2, 1929, aged 38 years, 2 days.

Oldest post-war debut in English League: Defender David Donaldson (35 years, 7 months, 23 days) for Wimbledon on entry to Football League (Div 4) away to Halifax, Aug 20, 1977.

Oldest player to appear in First Division: Sir Stanley Matthews (Stoke v Fulham, Feb 6, 1965), aged 50 years, 5 days – on that his last League appearance, the only 50-year-old ever to play in the top division.

Oldest players in Premier League: Goalkeepers John Burridge (Manchester City v QPR, May 14, 1995), 43 years, 5 months, 11 days; Alec Chamberlain (Watford v Newcastle, May 13, 2007) 42 years, 11 months, 23 days; Steve Ogrizovic (Coventry v Sheffield Wed, May 6, 2000), 42 years, 7 months, 24 days; Brad Friedel (Tottenham v Newcastle, Nov 10, 2013) 42 years, 4 months, 22 days; Neville Southall (Bradford City v Leeds, Mar 12, 2000), 41 years, 5 months, 26 days. Outfield: Teddy Sheringham (West Ham v Manchester City, Dec 30, 2006), 40 years, 8 months, 28 days; Ryan Giggs (Manchester Utd v Hull, May 6, 2014), 40 years, 5 months, 7 days; Gordon Strachan (Coventry City v Derby, May 3, 1997), 40 years, 2 months, 24 days.

Oldest player for British professional club: John Ryan (owner-chairman of Conference club Doncaster, played as substitute for last minute in 4-2 win at Hereford on Apr 26, 2003), aged 52 years, 11 months, 3 weeks.

Oldest FA Cup Final player: Walter (Billy) Hampson (Newcastle v Aston Villa on Apr 26, 1924), aged 41 years, 257 days.

Oldest captain and goalkeeper in FA Cup Final: David James (Portsmouth v Chelsea, May 15, 2010) aged 39 years, 287 days.

Oldest FA Cup Final scorers: Bert Turner (Charlton v Derby, Apr 27, 1946) aged 36 years, 312 days. Scored for both sides. Teddy Sheringham (West Ham v Liverpool, May 13, 2006) aged 40 years, 41 days. Scored in penalty shoot-out.

Oldest FA Cup-winning team: Arsenal 1950 (average age 31 years, 2 months). Eight of the players were over 30, with the three oldest centre-half Leslie Compton 37, and skipper Joe

Mercer and goalkeeper George Swindin, both 35.

Oldest World Cup-winning captain: Dino Zoff, Italy's goalkeeper v W Germany in 1982 Final, aged 40 years, 92 days.

Oldest player capped by England: Stanley Matthews (v Denmark, Copenhagen, May 15, 1957), aged 42 years, 103 days.

Oldest England scorer: Stanley Matthews (v N Ireland, Belfast, Oct 6, 1956), aged 41 years, 248 days.

Oldest British international player: Billy Meredith (Wales v England at Highbury, Mar 15, 1920), aged 45 years, 229 days.

Oldest 'new caps': Goalkeeper Alexander Morten, aged 41 years, 113 days when earning his only England Cap against Scotland on Mar 8, 1873; Arsenal centre-half Leslie Compton, at 38 years, 64 days when he made his England debut in 4-2 win against Wales at Sunderland on Nov 15, 1950. **For Scotland:** Goalkeeper Ronnie Simpson (Celtic) at 36 years, 186 days v England at Wembley, Apr 15, 1967.

Oldest scorer in Wembley Final: Chris Swailes, 45, for Morpeth in 4-1 win over Hereford (FA Vase), May 22, 2016.

Longest Football League career: This spanned 32 years and 10 months, by Stanley Matthews (Stoke, Blackpool, Stoke) from Mar 19, 1932 until Feb 6, 1965.

Shortest FA Cup-winning captain: 5ft 4in – Bobby Kerr (Sunderland v Leeds, 1973).

KANTE'S PEAK

N'Golo Kante became the first player in English football to win back-to-back titles with different clubs while playing a full season with each – Leicester (2015-16), Chelsea (2016–17).

EURO FIRST FOR REFEREE

Liverpool's defeat of Chelsea on penalties in the Super Cup on Aug 14, 2019, was refereed by Stephanie Frappart, of France, who became the first woman to take charge of a major European men's match.

SHIRT NUMBERING

Numbering players in Football League matches was made compulsory in 1939. Players wore numbered shirts (1-22) in the FA Cup Final as an experiment in 1933 (Everton 1-11 v Manchester City 12-22).

Squad numbers for players were introduced by the Premier League at the start of season 1993–94. They were optional in the Football League until made compulsory in 1999–2000.

Names on shirts: For first time, players wore names as well as numbers on shirts in League Cup and FA Cup Finals, 1993.

SUBSTITUTES

In **1965**, the Football League, by 39 votes to 10, agreed that **one substitute** be allowed for an injured player at any time during a League match. First substitute used in Football League: Keith Peacock (Charlton), away to Bolton in Div 2, Aug 21, 1965.

Two substitutes per team were approved for the League (Littlewoods) Cup and FA Cup in season 1986–87 and two were permitted in the Football League for the first time in 1987–88.

Three substitutes (one a goalkeeper), two of which could be used, introduced by the Premier League for 1992–93. The Football League followed suit for 1993–94.

Three substitutes (one a goalkeeper) were allowed at the World Cup Finals for the first time at US '94.

Three substitutes (any position) introduced by Premier League and Football League in 1995–96.

Five named substitutes (three of which could be used) introduced in Premier League in 1996–97, in FA Cup in 1997–98, League Cup in 1998–99 and Football League in 1999–2000.

Seven named substitutes for Premier League, FA Cup and League Cup in 2008–09. Still only three to be used. Football League adopted this rule for 2009–10, reverted to five in 2011–12 and went back to seven for the 2012–13 season.

First substitute to score in FA Cup Final: Eddie Kelly (Arsenal v Liverpool, 1971). The **first recorded use** of a substitute was in 1889 (Wales v Scotland at Wrexham on Apr 15) when

Sam Gillam arrived late – although he was a Wrexham player – and Allen Pugh (Rhostellyn) was allowed to keep goal until he turned up. The match ended 0-0.

When **Dickie Roose**, the Welsh goalkeeper, was injured against England at Wrexham, Mar 16, 1908, **Dai Davies** (Bolton) was allowed to take his place as substitute. Thus Wales used 12 players. England won 7-1.

END OF WAGE LIMIT

Freedom from the maximum wage system – in force since the formation of the Football League in 1888 – was secured by the Professional Footballers' Association in 1961. About this time Italian clubs renewed overtures for the transfer of British stars and Fulham's **Johnny Haynes** became the first British player to earn £100 a week.

THE BOSMAN RULING

On Dec 15, 1995 the **European Court of Justice** ruled that clubs had no right to transfer fees for out-of-contract players, and the outcome of the 'Bosman case' irrevocably changed football's player-club relationship. It began in 1990, when the contract of 26-year-old **Jean-Marc Bosman**, a midfield player with FC Liege, Belgium, expired. French club Dunkirk wanted him but were unwilling to pay the £500,000 transfer fee, so Bosman was compelled to remain with Liege. He responded with a lawsuit against his club and UEFA on the grounds of 'restriction of trade', and after five years at various court levels the European Court of Justice ruled not only in favour of Bosman but of all professional footballers.

The end of restrictive labour practices revolutionised the system. It led to a proliferation of transfers, rocketed the salaries of elite players who, backed by an increasing army of agents, found themselves in a vastly improved bargaining position as they moved from team to team, league to league, nation to nation. Removing the limit on the number of foreigners clubs could field brought an increasing ratio of such signings, not least in England and Scotland.

Bosman's one-man stand opened the way for footballers to become millionaires, but ended his own career. All he received for his legal conflict was 16 million Belgian francs (£312,000) in compensation, a testimonial of poor reward and martyrdom as the man who did most to change the face of football.

By 2011, he was living on Belgian state benefits, saying: 'I have made the world of football rich and shifted the power from clubs to players. Now I find myself with nothing.'

INTERNATIONAL SHOCK RESULTS

1950	USA 1 England 0 (World Cup).
1953	England 3 Hungary 6 (friendly).
1954	Hungary 7 England 1 (friendly)
1966	North Korea 1 Italy 0 (World Cup).
1982	Spain 0, Northern Ireland 1; Algeria 2, West Germany 1 (World Cup).
1990	Cameroon 1 Argentina 0; Scotland 0 Costa Rica 1; Sweden 1 Costa Rica 2 (World Cup).
1990	Faroe Islands 1 Austria 0 (European Champ qual).
1992	Denmark 2 Germany 0 (European Champ Final).
1993	USA 2 England 0 (US Cup tournament).
1993	Argentina 0 Colombia 5 (World Cup qual).
1993	France 2 Israel 3 (World Cup qual).
1994	Bulgaria 2 Germany 1 (World Cup).
1994	Moldova 3 Wales 2; Georgia 5 Wales 0 (European Champ qual).
1995	Belarus 1 Holland 0 (European Champ qual).
1996	Nigeria 4 Brazil 3 (Olympics).
1998	USA 1 Brazil 0 (Concacaf Gold Cup).
1998	Croatia 3 Germany 0 (World Cup).
2000	Scotland 0 Australia 2 (friendly).

2001	Australia 1 France 0; Australia, 1, Brazil 0 (Confederations Cup).
2001	Honduras 2 Brazil 0 (Copa America).
2001	Germany 1 England 5 (World Cup qual).
2002	France 0 Senegal 1; South Korea 2 Italy 1 (World Cup).
2003:	England 1 Australia 3 (friendly).
2004:	Portugal 0 Greece 1 (European Champ Final).
2005:	Northern Ireland 1 England 0 (World Cup qual).
2014:	Holland 5 Spain 1 (World Cup).
2014:	Brazil 1 Germany 7 (World Cup).
2016	England 1 Iceland 2 (European Champ)
2018	South Korea 2 Germany 0 (World Cup)

GREAT RECOVERIES – DOMESTIC FOOTBALL

On Dec 21, 1957, **Charlton** were losing 5-1 against Huddersfield (Div 2) at The Valley with only 28 minutes left, and from the 15th minute, had been reduced to ten men by injury, but they won 7-6, with left-winger Johnny Summers scoring five goals. Huddersfield (managed by Bill Shankly) remain the only team to score six times in a League match and lose. On Boxing Day, 1927 in Div 3 South, **Northampton** won 6-5 at home to Luton after being 1-5 down at half-time.

Season 2010–11 produced a Premier League record for **Newcastle**, who came from 4-0 down at home to Arsenal to draw 4-4. Previous instance of a team retrieving a four-goal deficit in the top division to draw was in 1984 when Newcastle trailed at QPR in a game which ended 5-5.

In the 2012-13 League Cup, **Arsenal** were 0-4 down in a fourth round tie at Reading, levelled at 4-4 and went on to win 7-5 in extra-time.

MATCHES OFF

Worst day for postponements: Feb 9, 1963, when 57 League fixtures in England and Scotland were frozen off. Only 7 Football League matches took place, and the entire Scottish programme was wiped out.

Other weather-hit days:

Jan 12, 1963 and Feb 2, 1963 – on both those Saturdays, only 4 out of 44 Football League matches were played.

Jan 1, 1979 – 43 out of 46 Football League fixtures postponed.

Jan 17, 1987 – 37 of 45 scheduled Football League fixtures postponed; only 2 Scottish matches survived.

Feb 8–9, 1991 – only 4 of the week-end's 44 Barclays League matches survived the freeze-up (4 of the postponements were on Friday night). In addition, 11 Scottish League matches were off.

Jan 27, 1996 – 44 Cup and League matches in England and Scotland were frozen off.

On the weekend of Jan 9, 10, 11, 2010, 46 League and Cup matches in England and Scotland were victims of the weather. On the weekend of Dec 18-21, 2010, 49 matches were frozen off in England and Scotland.

Fewest matches left on one day by postponements was during the Second World War – Feb 3, 1940 when, because of snow, ice and fog only one out of 56 regional league fixtures took place. It resulted Plymouth Argyle 10, Bristol City 3.

The Scottish Cup second round tie between Inverness Thistle and Falkirk in season 1978–79 was **postponed 29 times** because of snow and ice. First put off on Jan 6, it was eventually played on Feb 22. Falkirk won 4-0.

Pools Panel's busiest days: Jan 17, 1987 and Feb 9, 1991 – on both dates they gave their verdict on 48 postponed coupon matches.

FEWEST 'GAMES OFF'

Season 1947–48 was the best since the war for English League fixtures being played to schedule. Only six were postponed.

LONGEST SEASON

The latest that league football has been played in a season was **July 26, 2020**, following a three-month shutdown from the middle of March caused by the coronavirus pandemic. The

Premier League and Championship were completed, with Leagues One and Two curtailed and final positions decided on a points-per-game basis. This system was used in Scotland, where all four divisions were cut short. The FA Cup was completed on August 1, Arsenal defeating Chelsea 2-1. The Scottish Cup, paused after the quarter-finals, was completed in the 2020-21 season.

Worst winter hold-up was in season 1962–63. The Big Freeze began on Boxing Day and lasted until Mar, with nearly 500 first-class matches postponed. The FA Cup 3rd round was the longest on record – it began with only three out of 32 ties playable on Jan 5 and ended 66 days and 261 postponements later on Mar 11. The Lincoln–Coventry tie was put off 15 times. The Pools Panel was launched that winter, on Jan 26, 1963.

HOTTEST DAYS

The Nationwide League kicked off season 2003–04 on Aug 9 with pitch temperatures of 102 degrees recorded at Luton v Rushden and Bradford v Norwich. On the following day, there was a pitch temperature of 100 degrees for the Community Shield match between Manchester Utd and Arsenal at Cardiff's Millennium Stadium. Wembley's pitch-side thermometer registered 107 degrees for the 2009 Chelsea–Everton FA Cup Final.

FOOTBALL LEAGUE NAME CHANGE

From the start of the 2016-17 season, the Football League was renamed the English Football League, as part of a corporate and competition rebranding.

FOOTBALL ASSOCIATION SECRETARIES/CHIEF EXECUTIVES

1863–66 Ebenezer Morley; 1866–68 Robert Willis; 1868–70 RG Graham; 1870–95 Charles Alcock (paid from 1887); 1895–1934 Sir Frederick Wall; 1934–62 Sir Stanley Rous; 1962–73 Denis Follows; 1973–89 Ted Croker (latterly chief executive); 1989–99 Graham Kelly (chief executive); 2000–02 Adam Crozier (chief executive); 2003–04 Mark Palios (chief executive); 2005–08: Brian Barwick (chief executive); 2009–10 Ian Watmore (chief executive); 2010-15 Alex Horne (chief executive); 2015–19 Martin Glenn (chief executive); 2019 Mark Bullingham (chief executive).

FOOTBALL'S SPONSORS

Football League: Canon 1983–86; Today Newspaper 1986–87; Barclays 1987–93; Endsleigh Insurance 1993–96; Nationwide Building Society 1996–2004; Coca-Cola 2004–10; npower 2010–14; Sky Bet from 2014.

League Cup: Milk Cup 1982–86; Littlewoods 1987–90; Rumbelows 1991–92; Coca-Cola 1993–98; Worthington 1998–2003; Carling 2003–12; Capital One 2012–16; Carabao from 2017.

Premier League: Carling 1993–2001; Barclaycard 2001–04; Barclays 2004–16.

FA Cup: Littlewoods 1994–98; AXA 1998–2002; E.ON 2006–11; Budweiser 2011–15; Emirates (title sponsor) from 2015.

NEW HOMES FOR CLUBS

Newly-constructed League grounds in England since the war: 1946 Hull (Boothferry Park); 1950 Port Vale (Vale Park); 1955 Southend (Roots Hall); 1988 Scunthorpe (Glanford Park); 1990 Walsall (Bescot Stadium); 1990 Wycombe (Adams Park); 1992 Chester (Deva Stadium); 1993 Millwall (New Den); 1994 Huddersfield (McAlpine Stadium); 1994 Northampton (Sixfields Stadium); 1995 Middlesbrough (Riverside Stadium); 1997 Bolton (Reebok Stadium); 1997 Derby (Pride Park); 1997 Stoke (Britannia Stadium); 1997 Sunderland (Stadium of Light); 1998 Reading (Madejski Stadium); 1999 Wigan (JJB Stadium); 2001 Southampton (St Mary's Stadium); 2001 Oxford Utd (Kassam Stadium); 2002 Leicester (Walkers Stadium); 2002 Hull (Kingston Communications Stadium); 2003 Manchester City (City of Manchester Stadium); 2003 Darlington (New Stadium); 2005 Coventry (Ricoh Arena); Swansea (Stadium of Swansea, Morfa); 2006 Arsenal (Emirates Stadium); 2007 Milton Keynes Dons (Stadium: MK); 2007 Shrewsbury (New Meadow); Doncaster (Keepmoat

Stadium); 2008 Colchester (Community Stadium); 2009 Cardiff City Stadium; 2010 Chesterfield (b2net Stadium), Morecambe (Globe Arena); 2011 Brighton (American Express Stadium); 2012 Rotherham (New York Stadium). 2016 West Ham (Olympic Stadium); 2020 Brentford (Community Stadium); AFC Wimbledon (Plough Lane Stadium).

NATIONAL FOOTBALL CENTRE

The FA's new £120m centre at St George's Park, Burton upon Trent, was opened on Oct 9, 20012 by the Duke of Cambridge, president of the FA. The site covers 330 acres, has 12 full-size pitches (5 with undersoil heating and floodlighting). There are 5 gyms, a 90-seat lecture theatre, a hydrotherapy unit with swimming pool for the treatment of injuries and two hotels. It is the base for England teams, men and women, at all levels.

GROUND-SHARING

Manchester Utd played their home matches at **Manchester City's** Maine Road ground for 8 years after Old Trafford was bomb-damaged in Aug 1941. **Crystal Palace** and **Charlton** shared Selhurst Park (1985–91); **Bristol Rov** and **Bath City** (Twerton Park, Bath, 1986–96); **Partick Thistle** and **Clyde** (Firhill Park, Glasgow, 1986–91; in seasons 1990–01, 1991–92 **Chester** shared **Macclesfield's** ground (Moss Rose).

Crystal Palace and **Wimbledon** shared Selhurst Park, from season 1991–92, when **Charlton** (tenants) moved to rent Upton Park from **West Ham**, until 2003 when Wimbledon relocated to Milton Keynes. **Clyde** moved to Douglas Park, **Hamilton Academical's** home, in 1991–92. **Stirling Albion** shared Stenhousemuir's ground, Ochilview Park, in 1992–93. In 1993–94, **Clyde** shared **Partick's** home until moving to Cumbernauld. In 1994–95, **Celtic** shared Hampden Park with **Queen's Park** (while Celtic Park was redeveloped); **Hamilton** shared **Partick's** ground. **Airdrie** shared **Clyde's** Broadwood Stadium. **Bristol Rov** left **Bath City's** ground at the start of season 1996–97, sharing Bristol Rugby Club's Memorial Ground. **Clydebank** shared **Dumbarton's** Boghead Park from 1996–97 until renting **Greenock Morton's** Cappielow Park in season 1999–2000. **Brighton** shared **Gillingham's** ground in seasons 1997–98, 1998–99. **Fulham** shared **QPR's** home at Loftus Road in seasons 2002–03, 2003–04, returning to Craven Cottage in Aug 2004. **Coventry** played home fixtures at Northampton in season 2013–14, returning to their own ground, the Ricoh Arena, in Sept 2014**Coventry** were unable to agree terms to play at the Ricoh Arena in season 2019–20 and moved home games to Birmingham's St Andrew's Stadium. Coventry returned home for season 2021–22, with the Ricoh Arena having been renamed the Coventry Building Society Stadium.

Inverness Caledonian Thistle moved to share **Aberdeen's** Pittodrie Stadium in 2004–05 after being promoted to the SPL; **Gretna's** home matches on arrival in the SPL in 2007–08 were held at Motherwell and Livingston. Stenhousemuir (owners) share Ochilview with East Stirling (tenants).

ARTIFICIAL TURF

QPR were the first British club to install an artificial pitch, in 1981. They were followed by **Luton** in 1985, and **Oldham** and **Preston** in **1986**. QPR reverted to grass in 1988, as did Luton and promoted Oldham in season 1991–92 (when artificial pitches were banned in Div 1). **Preston** were the last Football League club playing 'on plastic' in 1993–94, and their Deepdale ground was restored to grass for the start of 1994–95.

Stirling were the **first Scottish club** to play on plastic, in season 1987–88.

DOUBLE RUNNERS-UP

There have been nine instances of clubs finishing runner-up in **both the League Championship** and **FA Cup** in the same season: 1928 Huddersfield; 1932 Arsenal; 1939 Wolves; 1962 Burnley; 1965 and 1970 Leeds; 1986 Everton; 1995 Manchester Utd; 2001 Arsenal.

CORNER-KICK RECORDS

Not a single corner-kick was recorded when **Newcastle** drew 0-0 at home to **Portsmouth** (Div 1) on Dec 5, 1931.

The record for **most corners** in a match for one side is believed to be **Sheffield Utd's 28** to **West Ham's 1** in Div 2 at Bramall Lane on Oct 14, 1989. For all their pressure, Sheffield Utd lost 2-0.

Nottm Forest led **Southampton** 22-2 on corners (Premier League, Nov 28, 1992) but lost the match 1-2.

Tommy Higginson (Brentford, 1960s) once passed back to his own goalkeeper from a corner kick.

When **Wigan** won 4-0 at home to Cardiff (Div 2) on Feb 16, 2002, all four goals were headed in from corners taken by N Ireland international **Peter Kennedy**.

Steve Staunton (Rep of Ireland) is believed to be the only player to score direct from a corner in **two** Internationals.

In the 2012 Champions League Final, **Bayern Munich** forced 20 corners without scoring, while **Chelsea** scored from their only one.

SACKED AT HALF-TIME

Tottenham sacked **Martin Jol** after a poor start to the 2007-08 season, with the manager learning of his fate at half-time of a UEFA Cup group match against the Spanish side Getafe at White Hart Lane on the night of October 25.

Leyton Orient sacked **Terry Howard** on his 397th appearance for the club – at half-time in a Second Division home defeat against Blackpool (Feb 7, 1995) for 'an unacceptable performance'. He was fined two weeks' wages, given a free transfer and moved to Wycombe.

Bobby Gould resigned as **Peterborough's** head coach at half-time in their 1-0 defeat in the LDV Vans Trophy 1st round at Bristol City on Sep 29, 2004.

Harald Schumacher, former Germany goalkeeper, was sacked as Fortuna Koln coach when they were two down at half-time against Waldhof Mannheim (Dec 15, 1999). They lost 5-1.

MOST GAMES BY 'KEEPER FOR ONE CLUB

Alan Knight made 683 League appearances for Portsmouth, over 23 seasons (1978–2000), a record for a goalkeeper at one club. The previous holder was Peter Bonetti with 600 League games for Chelsea (20 seasons, 1960–79).

PLAYED TWO GAMES ON SAME DAY

Jack Kelsey played full-length matches for both club and country on Wednesday Nov 26, 1958. In the afternoon he kept goal for Wales in a 2-2 draw against England at Villa Park, and he then drove to Highbury to help Arsenal win 3-1 in a prestigious floodlit friendly against Juventus.

On the same day, winger **Danny Clapton** played for England (against Wales and Kelsey) and then in part of Arsenal's match against Juventus.

On Nov 11, 1987, **Mark Hughes** played for Wales against Czechoslovakia (European Championship) in Prague, then flew to Munich and went on as substitute that night in a winning Bayern Munich team, to whom he was on loan from Barcelona.

On Feb 16, 1993 goalkeeper **Scott Howie** played in Scotland's 3-0 U-21 win v Malta at Tannadice Park, Dundee (ko 1.30pm) and the same evening played in Clyde's 2-1 home win v Queen of South (2).

Ryman League **Hornchurch**, faced by end-of-season fixture congestion, played **two matches** on the same night (May 1, 2001). They lost 2-1 at home to Ware and drew 2-2 at Clapton.

FIRST 'MATCH OF THE DAY'

BBC TV (recorded highlights): Liverpool 3, Arsenal 2 on Aug 22, 1964. **First complete match to be televised:** Arsenal 3, Everton 2 on Aug 29, 1936. **First League match televised in colour:** Liverpool 2, West Ham 0 on Nov 15, 1969.

'MATCH OF THE DAY' – BIGGEST SCORES

Football League: Tottenham 9, Bristol Rov 0 (Div 2, 1977–78). **Premier League:** Nottm Forest 1, Manchester Utd 8 (1998–99); Portsmouth 7 Reading 4 (2007–08).

FIRST COMMENTARY ON RADIO

Arsenal 1 Sheffield Utd 1 (Div 1) broadcast on BBC, Jan 22, 1927.

OLYMPIC FOOTBALL WINNERS

1908 Great Britain (in London); **1912** Great Britain (Stockholm); **1920** Belgium (Antwerp); **1924** Uruguay (Paris); **1928** Uruguay (Amsterdam); **1932** No soccer in Los Angeles Olympics; **1936** Italy (Berlin); **1948** Sweden (London); **1952** Hungary (Helsinki); **1956** USSR (Melbourne); **1960** Yugoslavia (Rome); **1964** Hungary (Tokyo); **1968** Hungary (Mexico City); **1972** Poland (Munich); **1976** E Germany (Montreal); **1980** Czechoslovakia (Moscow); **1984** France (Los Angeles); **1988** USSR (Seoul); **1992** Spain (Barcelona); **1996** Nigeria (Atlanta); **2000** Cameroon (Sydney); **2004** Argentina (Athens); **2008** Argentina (Beijing); **2012** Mexico (Wembley); **2016** Brazil (Rio de Janeiro).

Highest scorer in Final tournament: Ferenc Bene (Hungary) 12 goals, 1964.
Record crowd for Olympic Soccer Final: 108,800 (France v Brazil, Los Angeles 1984).

MOST AMATEUR CUP WINS

Bishop Auckland set the FA Amateur Cup record with 10 wins, and in 1957 became the only club to carry off the trophy in three successive seasons. The competition was discontinued after the Final on Apr 20, 1974. (Bishop's Stortford 4, Ilford 1, at Wembley).

FOOTBALL FOUNDATION

This was formed (May 2000) to replace the **Football Trust**, which had been in existence since 1975 as an initiative of the Pools companies to provide financial support at all levels, from schools football to safety and ground improvement work throughout the game.

SEVEN-FIGURE TESTIMONIALS

The first was **Sir Alex Ferguson**'s at Old Trafford on Oct 11, 1999, when a full-house of 54,842 saw a Rest of the World team beat Manchester Utd 4-2. United's manager pledged that a large percentage of the estimated £1m receipts would go to charity.

Estimated receipts of £1m and over came from testimonials for **Denis Irwin** (Manchester Utd) against Manchester City at Old Trafford on Aug 16, 2000 (45,158); **Tom Boyd** (Celtic) against Manchester Utd at Celtic Park on May 15, 2001 (57,000) and **Ryan Giggs** (Manchester Utd) against Celtic on Aug 1, 2001 (66,967).

Tony Adams' second testimonial (1-1 v Celtic on May 13, 2002) two nights after Arsenal completed the Double, was watched by 38,021 spectators at Highbury. Of £1m receipts, he donated £500,000 to Sporting Chance, the charity that helps sportsmen/women with drink, drug, gambling problems.

Sunderland and a Republic of Ireland XI drew 0-0 in front of 35,702 at the Stadium of Light on May 14, 2002. The beneficiary, **Niall Quinn**, donated his testimonial proceeds, estimated at £1m, to children's hospitals in Sunderland and Dublin, and to homeless children in Africa and Asia.

A record testimonial crowd of 69,591 for **Roy Keane** at Old Trafford on May 9, 2006 netted more than £2m for charities in Dublin, Cork and Manchester. Manchester Utd beat Celtic 1-0, with Keane playing for both teams.

Alan Shearer's testimonial on May 11, 2006, watched by a crowd of 52,275 at St James' Park, raised more than £1m. The club's record scorer, in his farewell match, came off the bench in stoppage time to score the penalty that gave Newcastle a 3-2 win over Celtic. Total proceeds from his testimonial events, £1.64m, were donated to 14 charities in the north-east.

Ole Gunnar Solskjaer, who retired after 12 years as a Manchester Utd player, had a crowd of 68,868, for his testimonial on Aug 2, 2008 (United 1 Espanyol 0). He donated the estimated receipts of £2m to charity, including the opening of a dozen schools In Africa.

Liverpool's **Jamie Carragher** had his testimonial against Everton (4-1) on Sep 4, 2010. It was watched by a crowd of 35,631 and raised an estimated £1m for his foundation, which supports community projects on Merseyside.

Gary Neville donated receipts of around £1m from his testimonial against Juventus (2-1) in front of 42,000 on May 24, 2011, to charities and building a Supporters' Centre near Old Trafford.

Paul Scholes had a crowd of 75,000 for his testimonial, Manchester United against New York Cosmos, on Aug 5, 2011. Receipts were £1.5m.

Steven Gerrard, Liverpool captain, donated £500,000 from his testimonial to the local Alder Hey Children's Hospital after a match against Olympiacos was watched by a crowd of 44,362 on Aug 3, 2013. Gerrard chose the Greek champions because he scored a special goal against them in the season Liverpool won the 2005 Champions League.

Wayne Rooney's match against Everton on Aug 3, 2016, raised £1.2m, which the Manchester United captain donated to local children's charities.

WHAT IT USED TO COST

Minimum admission to League football was one shilling in 1939 After the war, it was increased to 1s 3d in 1946; 1s 6d in 1951; 1s 9d in 1952; 2s in 1955; 2s 6d; in 1960; 4s in 1965; 5s in 1968; 6s in 1970; and 8s (40p) in 1972 After that, the fixed minimum charge was dropped.

Wembley's first Cup Final programme in 1923 cost three pence (1¼p in today's money). The programme for the 'farewell' FA Cup Final in May, 2000 was priced £10.

FA Cup Final ticket prices in 2011 reached record levels – £115, £85, £65 and £45.

WHAT THEY USED TO EARN

In the 1930s, First Division players were on £8 a week (£6 in close season) plus bonuses of £2 win, £1 draw. The maximum wage went up to £12 when football resumed post-war in 1946 and had reached £20 by the time the limit was abolished in 1961.

EUROPEAN TROPHY WINNERS

European Cup/Champions League: 13 Real Madrid; **7** AC Milan; **6** Liverpool, Bayern Munich; **5** Barcelona; **4** Ajax; **3** Inter Milan, Manchester Utd; **2** Benfica, Chelsea, Juventus, Nottm Forest, Porto; **1** Aston Villa, Borussia Dortmund, Celtic, Feyenoord, Hamburg, Marseille, PSV Eindhoven, Red Star Belgrade, Steaua Bucharest

Cup-Winners' Cup: 4 Barcelona; **2** Anderlecht, Chelsea, Dynamo Kiev, AC Milan; **1** Aberdeen, Ajax, Arsenal, Atletico Madrid, Bayern Munich, Borussia Dortmund, Dynamo Tbilisi, Everton, Fiorentina, Hamburg, Juventus, Lazio, Magdeburg, Manchester City, Manchester Utd, Mechelen, Paris St Germain, Parma, Rangers, Real Zaragoza, Sampdoria, Slovan Bratislava, Sporting Lisbon, Tottenham, Valencia, Werder Bremen, West Ham.

UEFA Cup: 3 Barcelona, Inter Milan, Juventus, Liverpool, Valencia; **2** Borussia Moenchengladbach, Feyenoord, Gothenburg, Leeds, Parma, Real Madrid, Sevilla, Tottenham; **1** Anderlecht, Ajax, Arsenal, Bayer Leverkusen, Bayern Munich, CSKA Moscow, Dynamo Zagreb, Eintracht Frankfurt, Ferencvaros, Galatasaray, Ipswich, Napoli, Newcastle, Porto, PSV Eindhoven, Real Zaragoza, Roma, Schalke, Shakhtar Donetsk, Zenit St Petersburg.

Europa League: 4 Sevilla; **3** Atletico Madrid; **2** Chelsea; **1** Manchester Utd, Porto, Villarreal

● The Champions League was introduced into the European Cup in 1992–93 to counter the threat of a European Super League. The UEFA Cup became the Europa League, with a new format, in season 2009–10.

BRITAIN'S 38 TROPHIES IN EUROPE

Euro Cup/Champs Lge (15)	Cup-Winners' Cup (10)	Fairs/UEFA Cup/Europa Lge (13)
1967 Celtic	1963 Tottenham	1968 Leeds
1968 Manchester Utd	1965 West Ham	1969 Newcastle
1977 Liverpool	1970 Manchester City	1970 Arsenal
1978 Liverpool	1971 Chelsea	1971 Leeds
1979 Nottm Forest	1972 Rangers	1972 Tottenham
1980 Nottm Forest	1983 Aberdeen	1973 Liverpool
1981 Liverpool	1985 Everton	1976 Liverpool
1982 Aston Villa	1991 Manchester Utd	1981 Ipswich
1984 Liverpool	1994 Arsenal	1984 Tottenham
1999 Manchester Utd	1998 Chelsea	2001 Liverpool
2005 Liverpool		2013 Chelsea
2008 Manchester Utd		2017 Manchester Utd

2012 Chelsea
2019 Liverpool
2021 Chelsea

2019 Chelsea

ENGLAND'S EUROPEAN RECORD

England had an unprecedented clean sweep of finalists in the two European club competitions in season 2018–19, with Liverpool defeating Tottenham in the Champions League and Chelsea beating Arsenal in the Europa League.

END OF CUP-WINNERS' CUP

The **European Cup-Winners' Cup**, inaugurated in 1960–61, terminated with the 1999 Final. The competition merged into a revamped **UEFA Cup**.

From its inception in 1955, the **European Cup** comprised only championship-winning clubs until 1998–99, when selected runners-up were introduced. Further expansion came in 1999–2000 with the inclusion of clubs finishing third in certain leagues and fourth in 2002.

EUROPEAN CLUB COMPETITIONS – SCORING RECORDS

European Cup – record aggregate: 18-0 by Benfica v Dudelange (Lux) (8-0a, 10-0h), prelim rd, 1965–66.

Record single-match score: 11-0 by Dinamo Bucharest v Crusaders (rd 1, 2nd leg, 1973-74 (agg 12-0).

Champions League – record single-match score: Liverpool 8-0 v Besiktas, Group A qual (Nov 6, 2007).

Highest match aggregate: 13 – Bayern Munich 12 Sporting Lisbon 1 (5-0 away, 7-1 at home, 1st ko rd, 2008–09)

Cup-Winners' Cup – *record aggregate: 21-0 by Chelsea v Jeunesse Hautcharage (Lux) (8-0a, 13-0h), 1st rd, 1971–72.

Record single-match score: 16-1 by Sporting Lisbon v Apoel Nicosia, 2nd round, 1st leg, 1963–64 (aggregate was 18-1).

UEFA Cup (prev Fairs Cup) – *Record aggregate: 21-0 by Feyenoord v US Rumelange (Lux) (9-0h, 12-0a), 1st round, 1972–73.

Record single-match score: 14-0 by Ajax Amsterdam v Red Boys (Lux) 1st rd, 2nd leg, 1984–85 (aggregate also 14-0).

Record British score in Europe: 13-0 by **Chelsea** at home to Jeunesse Hautcharage (Lux) in Cup-Winners' Cup 1st round, 2nd leg, 1971–72. Chelsea's overall 21-0 win in that tie is highest aggregate by British club in Europe.

Individual scoring record for European tie (over two legs): 10 goals (6 home, 4 away) by **Kiril Milanov** for Levski Spartak in 19-3 agg win Cup-Winners' Cup 1st round v Lahden Reipas, 1976–77. Next highest: **8 goals** by **Jose Altafini** for AC Milan v US Luxembourg (European Cup, prelim round, 1962–63, agg 14-0) and by **Peter Osgood** for Chelsea v Jeunesse Hautcharage (Cup-Winners' Cup, 1st round 1971–72, agg 21-0). Altafini and Osgood each scored 5 goals at home, 3 away.

Individual single-match scoring record in European competition: **6** by **Mascarenhas** for Sporting Lisbon in 16-1 Cup-Winner's Cup 2nd round, 1st leg win v Apoel, 1963–64; and by **Lothar Emmerich** for Borussia Dortmund in 8-0 CWC 1st round, 2nd leg win v Floriana 1965–66; and by **Kiril Milanov** for Levski Spartak in 12-2 CWC 1st round, 1st leg win v Lahden Reipas, 1976–77.

Most goals in single European campaign: 15 by **Jurgen Klinsmann** for Bayern Munich (UEFA Cup 1995–96).

Most goals by British player in European competition: 30 by **Peter Lorimer** (Leeds, in 9 campaigns).

Most individual goals in Champions League match: 5 by **Lionel Messi** (Barcelona) in 7-1 win at home to Bayer Leverkusen in round of 16 second leg, 2011–12.

Most European Cup goals by individual player: 49 by **Alfredo di Stefano** in 58 apps for Real Madrid (1955–64).

(*Joint record European aggregate)

First European treble: **Clarence Seedorf** became the first player to win the European Cup with three clubs: Ajax in 1995, Real Madrid in 1998 and AC Milan in 2003.

EUROPEAN FOOTBALL – BIG RECOVERIES

In the most astonishing Final in the history of the European Cup/Champions League, **Liverpool** became the first club to win it from a 3-0 deficit when they beat AC Milan 3-2 on penalties after a 3-3 draw in Istanbul on May 25, 2005. Liverpool's fifth triumph in the competition meant that they would keep the trophy.

The following season, **Middlesbrough** twice recovered from three-goal aggregate deficits in the UEFA Cup, beating Basel 4-3 in the quarter finals and Steaua Bucharest by the same scoreline in the semi-finals. In 2010, **Fulham** beat Juventus 5-4 after trailing 1-4 on aggregate in the second leg of their Europa League, Round of 16 match at Craven Cottage.

Two Scottish clubs have won a European tie from a 3-goal, first leg deficit: **Kilmarnock** 0-3, 5-1 v Eintracht Frankfurt (Fairs Cup 1st round, 1964–65); **Hibernian** 1-4, 5-0 v Napoli (Fairs Cup 2nd round, 1967–68).

English clubs have three times gone out of the **UEFA** Cup after leading 3-0 from the first leg: 1975–76 (2nd Rd) **Ipswich** lost 3-4 on agg to Bruges; 1976–77 (quarter-final) **QPR** lost on penalties to AEK Athens after 3-3 agg; 1977–78 (3rd round) **Ipswich** lost on penalties to Barcelona after 3-3 agg.

On Oct 16, 2012, Sweden recovered from 0-4 down to draw 4-4 with Germany (World Cup qual) in Berlin.

● In the **1966 World Cup quarter-final** (Jul 23) at Goodison Park, North Korea led Portugal 3-0, but Eusebio scored 4 times to give **Portugal** a 5-3 win.

RONALDO'S EURO CENTURY

Cristiano Ronaldo became the first player to reach a century of goals in European club competitions when scoring twice for Real Madrid away to Bayern Munich on Apr 12, 2017. He reached the hundred in 143 matches (84 for Real, 16 for Manchester Utd) in the Champions League (97), UEFA Super Cup (2) and Champions League qualifying round (1).

RECORD COMEBACK

The greatest turnaround in Champions League history took place in a round of 16 match on Mar 8, 2017. **Barcelona**, 0-4 down to Paris St Germain, won the return leg 6-1, scoring three goals in the last seven minutes.

HEAVIEST ENGLISH-CLUB DEFEATS IN EUROPE

(Single-leg scores)

Champions League: Porto 5 Leicester 0 (group, Dec 6, 2016); Tottenham 2 Bayern Munich 7 (group, Oct 1, 2019)

European Cup: Artmedia Bratislava 5, **Celtic** 0 (2nd qual round), Jul 2005 (agg 5-4); Ajax 5, **Liverpool** 1 (2nd round), Dec 1966 (agg 7-3); Real Madrid 5, **Derby** 1 (2nd round), Nov 1975 (agg 6-5).

Cup-Winners' Cup: Sporting Lisbon 5, **Manchester Utd** 0 (quarter-final), Mar 1964 (agg 6-4).

Fairs/UEFA Cup: Bayern Munich 6, **Coventry** 1 (2nd round), Oct 1970 (agg 7-3). **Combined London** team lost 6-0 (agg 8-2) in first Fairs Cup Final in 1958. Barcelona 5, **Chelsea** 0 in Fairs Cup semi-final play-off, 1966, in Barcelona (after 2-2 agg).

SHOCK ENGLISH CLUB DEFEATS

1968–69 (Eur Cup, 1st round): **Manchester City** beaten by Fenerbahce, 1-2 agg.
1971–72 (CWC, 2nd round): **Chelsea** beaten by Atvidaberg on away goals.
1993–94 (Eur Cup, 2nd round): **Manchester Utd** beaten by Galatasaray on away goals.
1994–95 (UEFA Cup, 1st round): **Blackburn** beaten by Trelleborgs, 2-3 agg.
2000–01 (UEFA Cup, 1st round): **Chelsea** beaten by St Gallen, Switz 1-2 agg.

RECORD MEDAL SALES

At Sotherby's in London on Nov 11, 2014, the FA Cup winner's medal which **Sir Stanley**

Matthews earned with Blackpool in 1953 was sold for £220,000 – the most expensive medal in British sporting history. At the same auction, **Ray Wilson's** 1966 World Cup winner's medal fetched £136,000, while **Jimmy Greaves**, who was left out of the winning England team, received £44,000 for the medal the FA belatedly awarded him in 2009

West Ham bought (Jun 2000) the late **Bobby Moore's** collection of medals and trophies for £1.8m at Christie's auction. It was put up for sale by his first wife Tina and included his World Cup-winner's medal.

A No. 6 duplicate red shirt made for England captain **Bobby Moore** for the 1966 World Cup Final fetched £44,000 at an auction at Wolves' ground in Sep, 1999. Moore kept the shirt he wore in that Final and gave the replica to England physio Harold Shepherdson.

Sir Geoff Hurst's 1966 World Cup-winning shirt fetched a record £91,750 at Christie's in Sep, 2000. His World Cup Final cap fetched £37,600 and his Man of the Match trophy £18,800. Proceeds totalling £274,410 from the 129 lots went to Hurst's three daughters and charities of his choice, including the Bobby Moore Imperial Cancer Research Fund.

In Aug, 2001, Sir Geoff sold his World Cup-winner's medal to his former club West Ham Utd (for their museum) at a reported £150,000.

'The **Billy Wright** Collection' – caps, medals and other memorabilia from his illustrious career – fetched over £100,000 at Christie's in Nov, 1996.

At the sale in Oct 1993, trophies, caps and medals earned by **Ray Kennedy**, former England, Arsenal and Liverpool player, fetched a then record total of £88,407. Kennedy, suffering from Parkinson's Disease, received £73,000 after commission. The PFA paid £31,080 for a total of 60 lots – including a record £16,000 for his 1977 European Cup winner's medal – to be exhibited at their Manchester museum. An anonymous English collector paid £17,000 for the medal and plaque commemorating Kennedy's part in the Arsenal Double in 1971.

Previous record for one player's medals, shirts etc collection: £30,000 (**Bill Foulkes**, Manchester Utd in 1992). The sale of **Dixie Dean's** medals etc in 1991 realised £28,000.

In Mar, 2001, **Gordon Banks'** 1966 World Cup-winner's medal fetched a new record £124,750. TV's Nick Hancock, a Stoke fan, paid £23,500 for **Sir Stanley Matthews's** 1953 FA Cup-winner's medal. He also bought one of Matthews's England caps for £3,525 and paid £2,350 for a Stoke Div 2 Championship medal (1963).

Dave Mackay's 1961 League Championship and FA Cup winner's medals sold for £18,000 at Sotherby's. Tottenham bought them for their museum.

A selection of England World Cup-winning manager **Sir Alf Ramsey's** memorabilia – England caps, championship medals with Ipswich etc. – fetched more than £80,000 at Christie's. They were offered for sale by his family, and his former clubs Tottenham and Ipswich were among the buyers.

Ray Wilson's 1966 England World Cup-winning shirt fetched £80,750. Also in Mar, 2002, the No. 10 shirt worn by **Pele** in Brazil's World Cup triumph in 1970 was sold for a record £157,750 at Christies. It went to an anonymous telephone buyer.

In Oct, 2003, **George Best's** European Footballer of the Year (1968) trophy was sold to an anonymous British bidder for £167,250 at Bonham's. It was the then most expensive item of sporting memorabilia ever auctioned in Britain.

England captain **Bobby Moore's** 1970 World Cup shirt, which he swapped with Pele after Brazil's 1-0 win in Mexico, was sold for £60,000 at Christie's in Mar, 2004.

Sep, 2004: England shirt worn by tearful **Paul Gascoigne** in 1990 World Cup semi-final v Germany sold at Christie's for £28,680. At same auction, shirt worn by Brazil's **Pele** in 1958 World Cup Final in Sweden sold for £70,505.

May, 2005: The **second FA Cup** (which was presented to winning teams from 1896 to 1909) was bought for £420,000 at Christie's by Birmingham chairman David Gold, a world record for an item of football memorabilia. It was presented to the National Football Museum, Preston. At the same auction, the World Cup-winner's medal earned by England's **Alan Ball** in 1966 was sold for £164,800.

Oct, 2005: At auction at Bonham's, the medals and other memorabilia of Hungary and Real Madrid legend **Ferenc Puskas** were sold for £85,000 to help pay for hospital treatment.

Nov, 2006: A ball used in the 2006 World Cup Final and signed by the winning **Italy** team was sold for £1.2m (a world record for football memorabilia) at a charity auction in Qatar. It was bought by the Qatar Sports Academy.

Feb, 2010: A pair of boots worn by **Sir Stanley Matthews** in the 1953 FA Cup Final was sold at Bonham's for £38,400.

Oct, 2010: Trophies and memorabilia belonging to **George Best** were sold at Bonham's for £193,440. His 1968 European Cup winner's medal fetched £156,000.

Oct–Nov 2010: **Nobby Stiles** sold his 1966 World Cup winner's medal at an Edinburgh auction for a record £188,200. His old club, Manchester Utd, also paid £48,300 for his 1968 European Cup medal to go to the club's museum at Old Trafford. In London, the shirt worn by Stiles in the 1966 World Cup Final went for £75,000. A total of 45 items netted £424,438. **George Cohen** and **Martin Peters** had previously sold their medals from 1966.

Oct 2011: **Terry Paine** (who did not play in the Final) sold his 1966 World Cup medal for £27,500 at auction.

Mar 2013: **Norman Hunter** (Leeds and England) sold his honours' collection on line for nearly £100,000

Nov 2013: A collection of **Nat Lofthouse's** career memorabilia was sold at auction for £100,000. Bolton Council paid £75,000 for items including his 1958 FA Cup winner's medal to go on show at the local museum.

LONGEST UNBEATEN CUP RUN

Liverpool established the longest unbeaten Cup sequence by a Football League club: 25 successive rounds in the League/Milk Cup between semi-final defeat by Nottm Forest (1-2 agg) in 1980 and defeat at Tottenham (0-1) in the third round on Oct 31, 1984. During this period Liverpool won the tournament in four successive seasons, a feat no other Football League club has achieved in any competition.

BIG HALF-TIME SCORES

Tottenham 10, Crewe 1 (FA Cup 4th round replay, Feb 3, 1960; result 13-2); Tranmere 8, Oldham 1 (Div 3N., Dec 26, 1935; result 13-4); **Chester City 8, York 0** (Div 3N., Feb 1, 1936; result 12-0; believed to be record half-time scores in League football).

Nine goals were scored in the first half – **Burnley 4, Watford 5** in Div 1 on Apr 5, 2003. Result: 4-7.

Stirling Albion led Selkirk 15-0 at half-time (result 20-0) in the Scottish Cup 1st round, Dec 8, 1984.

World record half-time score: **16-0** when **Australia** beat **American Samoa** 31-0 (another world record) in the World Cup Oceania qualifying group at Coff's Harbour, New South Wales, on Apr 11 2001.

• On Mar 4 1933 **Coventry** beat QPR (Div 3 South) 7-0, having led by that score at half-time. This repeated the half-time situation in Bristol City's 7-0 win over Grimsby on Dec 26, 1914.

TOP SECOND-HALF TEAM

Most goals scored by a team in one half of a League match is **11. Stockport** led Halifax 2-0 at half-time in Div 3 North on Jan 6 1934 and won 13-0.

FIVE NOT ENOUGH

Last team to score **5** in League match and lose: **Burton**, beaten 6-5 by Cheltenham (Lge 2, Mar 13, 2010).

LONG SERVICE WITH ONE CLUB

Bill Nicholson, OBE, was associated with Tottenham for 67 years – as a wing-half (1938–55), then the club's most successful manager (1958–74) with 8 major prizes, subsequently chief advisor and scout. He became club president, and an honorary freeman of the borough, had an executive suite named after him at the club, and the stretch of roadway from Tottenham High Road to the main gates has the nameplate Bill Nicholson Way. He died, aged 85, in Oct 2004.

Ted Bates, the Grand Old Man of Southampton with 66 years of unbroken service to the club, was awarded the Freedom of the City in Apr, 2001. He joined Saints as an inside-forward from Norwich in 1937, made 260 peace-time appearances for the club, became reserve-team trainer in 1953 and manager at The Dell for 18 years (1955–73), taking Southampton into the top division in 1966. He was subsequently chief executive, director and club president. He died in Oct 2003, aged 85.

Bob Paisley was associated with Liverpool for 57 years from 1939, when he joined them from Bishop Auckland, until he died in Feb 1996. He served as player, trainer, coach, assistant-manager, manager, director and vice-president. He was Liverpool's most successful manager, winning 13 major trophies for the club (1974–83).

Dario Gradi, MBE, stepped down after completing 24 seasons and more than 1,000 matches as manager of Crewe (appointed Jun 1983). Never a League player, he previously managed Wimbledon and Crystal Palace. At Crewe, his policy of finding and grooming young talent has earned the club more than £20m in transfer fees. He stayed with Crewe as technical director, and twice took charge of team affairs again following the departure of the managers who succeeded him, Steve Holland and Gudjon Thordarson.

Ronnie Moran, who joined Liverpool in as a player 1952, retired from the Anfield coaching staff in season 1998–99.

Ernie Gregory served West Ham for 52 years as goalkeeper and coach. He joined them as boy of 14 from school in 1935, retired in May 1987.

Ryan Giggs played 24 seasons for Manchester Utd (1990-2014), then became assistant manager under Louis van Gaal.

Ted Sagar, Everton goalkeeper, 23 years at Goodison Park (1929–52, but only 16 League seasons because of war).

Alan Knight, goalkeeper, played 23 seasons (1977–2000) for his only club, Portsmouth.

Sam Bartram was recognised as one of the finest goalkeepers never to play for England, apart from unofficial wartime games. He was with Charlton from 1934–56

Jack Charlton, England World Cup winner, served Leeds from 1952–73.

Roy Sproson, defender, played 21 League seasons for his only club, Port Vale (1950–71).

John Terry had a 22-year association with Chelsea from 1994–2017.

TIGHT AT HOME

Fewest home goals conceded in League season (modern times): 4 by **Liverpool** (Div 1, 1978–9); 4 by **Manchester Utd** (Premier League, 1994–95) – both in 21 matches.

TRANSFER WINDOW

This was introduced to Britain in Sep 2002 via FIFA regulations to bring uniformity across Europe (the rule previously applied in a number of other countries).

The transfer of contracted players is restricted to two periods: Jun 1–Aug 31 and Jan 1–31).

On appeal, Football League clubs continued to sign/sell players (excluding deals with Premier League clubs).

PROGRAMME PIONEERS

Chelsea pioneered football's magazine-style programme by introducing a 16-page issue for the First Division match against Portsmouth on Christmas Day 1948. It cost sixpence (2.5p). A penny programme from the 1909 FA Cup Final fetched £23,500 at a London auction in May, 2012.

WORLD'S OLDEST FOOTBALL ANNUAL

Now in its 135th edition, this publication began as the 16-page Athletic News Football Supplement & Club Directory in 1887. From the long-established Athletic News, it became the Sunday Chronicle Annual in 1946, the Empire News in 1956, the News of the World & Empire News in 1961 and the News of the World Annual from 1965 until becoming the Nationwide Annual in 2008.

PREMIER LEAGUE CLUB DETAILS AND SQUADS 2021–22

(at time of going to press)

ARSENAL

Ground: Emirates Stadium, Highbury, London, N5 IBU. **Telephone:** 0207 619 5003. **Club nickname:** Gunners. **Capacity:** 60,260. **Colours:** Red and white. **Main sponsor:** Emirates
Record transfer fee: £72m to Lille for Nicolas Pepe, Aug 2019. **Record fee received:** £35m from Barcelona for Cesc Fabregas, Aug 2011; £35m from Liverpool for Alex Oxlade-Chamberlain, Aug 2017. **Record attendance:** Highbury: 73,295 v Sunderland (Div 1) Mar 9, 1935. Emirates Stadium: 60,161 v Manchester Utd (Prem Lge) Nov 3, 2007. Wembley: 73,707 v Lens (Champ Lge) Nov 25, 1998. **League Championship:** Winners 1930–31, 1932–33, 1933–34, 1934–35, 1937–38, 1947–48, 1952–53, 1970–71, 1988–89, 1990–91, 1997–98, 2001–02, 2003–04
FA Cup: Winners 1930, 1936, 1950, 1971, 1979, 1993, 1998, 2002, 2003, 2005, 2014, 2015, 2017, 2020. **League Cup:** Winners 1987, 1993. **European competitions:** Winners Fairs Cup 1969-70; Cup-Winners' Cup 1993–94
Finishing positions in Premier League: 1992–93 10th, 1993–94 4th, 1994–95 12th, 1995–96 5th, 1996–97 3rd, 1997–98 1st, 1998–99 2nd, 1999–2000 2nd, 2000–01 2nd, 2001–02 1st, 2002–03 2nd, 2003–04 1st, 2004–05 2nd, 2005–06 4th, 2006–07 4th, 2007–08 3rd, 2008–09 4th, 2009–10 3rd, 2010–11 4th, 2011–12 3rd, 2012–13 4th, 2013–14 4th, 2014–15 3rd, 2015–16 2nd, 2016–17 5th, 2017–18 6th, 2018–19 5th, 2019-20 8th, 2020-21 8th
Biggest win: 12-0 v Loughborough (Div 2) Mar 12, 1900. **Biggest defeat:** 0-8 v Loughborough (Div 2) Dec 12, 1896. **Highest League scorer in a season:** Ted Drake 42 (1934–35). **Most League goals in aggregate:** Thierry Henry 175 (1999–2007) (2012). **Longest unbeaten League sequence:** 49 matches (2003–04). **Longest sequence without a League win:** 23 matches (1912–13). **Most capped player:** Thierry Henry (France) 81

Name	Height ft in	Previous club	Birthplace	Birthdate
Goalkeepers				
Iliev, Dejan	6.4	Belastica	Strumica, Mace	25.02.95
Leno, Bernd	6.3	Bayer Leverkusen	Bietighem-Bissingen, Ger	04.03.92
Runarsson, Runar Alex	6.1	Dijon	Reykjavik, Ice	18.02.95
Defenders				
Bellerin, Hector	5.10	Barcelona	Barcelona, Sp	19.03.95
Cedric Soares	5.8	Southampton	Singen, Ger	31.08.91
Chambers, Calum	6.0	Southampton	Petersfield	20.01.95
Gabriel	6.3	Lille	Sao Paulo, Br	19.12.97
Holding, Rob	6.0	Bolton	Tameside	12.09.95
Kolasinac, Sead	6.0	Schalke	Karlsruhe, Ger	20.06.93
Mari, Pablo	6.4	Flamengo	Valencia, Sp	31.08.93
Saliba, William	6.4	Saint-Etienne	Bondy, Fr	24.03.01
Nuno Tavares	6.0	Benfica	Lisbon Por	26.01.00
Tierney, Kieran	5.10	Celtic	Douglas, IOM	05.06.97
Midfielders				
Elneny, Mohamed	5.11	Basle	El-Mahalla, Egy	11.07.92
Guendouzi, Matteo	6.1	Lorient	Poissy, Fr	14.04.99
Maitland-Niles, Ainsley	5.10	–	Goodmayes	29.08.97
Partey, Thomas	6.1	Atletico Madrid	Krobo Odumase, Gha	13.06.93
Pepe, Nicolas	5.10	Lille	Mantes-la-Jolie, Fr	29.05.95
Smith Rowe, Emile	6.0	–	Croydon	28.07.00

Torreira, Lucas	5.6	Sampdoria	Fray Bentos, Uru	11.02.96
Willian	5.9	Chelsea	Ribeirao Pires, Br	09.08.88
Willock, Joe	5.10	–	Waltham Forest	20.08.99
Xhaka, Granit	6.1	Borussia M'gladbach	Basle, Swi	27.09.92
Forwards				
Aubameyang, Pierre-Emerick	6.2	Borussia Dortmund	Laval, Fr	18.06.89
Balogun, Folarin	5.10	–	New York, US	03.07.01
Lacazette, Alexandre	5.9	Lyon	Lyon, Fr	28.05.91
Martinelli, Gabriel	5.11	Ituano	Guarulhos, Br	18.06.01
Nelson, Reiss	5.9	–	Elephant and Castle	10.12.99
Nketiah, Eddie	5.9	–	Lewisham	30.05.99
Saka, Bukayo	5.10	–	Ealing	05.09.01

ASTON VILLA

Ground: Villa Park, Trinity Road, Birmingham, B6 6HE. **Telephone:** 0333 323 1874. **Club nickname:** Villans. **Capacity:** 42,682. **Colours:** Claret and blue. **Main sponsor:** Cazoo. **Record transfer fee:** £33m to Norwich for Emiliano Buendia, Jun 2021. **Record fee received:** £32.5m from Liverpool for Christian Benteke, Jul 2015. **Record attendance:** 76,588 v Derby (FA Cup 6) Mar 2, 1946. **League Championship:** Winners 1893–94, 1895–96, 1896–97, 1898–99,. 1899–1900, 1909–10, 1980–81. **FA Cup:** Winners 1887, 1895, 1897, 1905, 1913, 1920, 1957. **League Cup:** Winners 1961, 1975, 1977, 1994, 1996. **European competitions:** Winners European Cup 1981–82; European Super Cup 1982

Finishing positions in Premier League: 1992–93 2nd, 1993–94 10th, 1994–95 18th, 1995–96 4th, 1996–97 5th, 1997–98 7th, 1998–99 6th, 1999–2000 6th, 2000–01 8th, 2001–02 8th, 2002–03 16th, 2003–04 6th,2004–05 10th, 2005–06 16th, 2006–07 11th, 2007–08 6th, 2008–09 6th, 2009–10 6th, 2010–11 9th, 2011–12 16th, 2012–13th 15th, 2013–14 15th,2014–15 17th, 2015–16 20th 2019–20 17th, 2020–21 11th

Biggest win: 12-2 v Accrington (Div 1) Mar 12, 1892; 11-1 v Charlton (Div 2) Nov 24, 1959; 10-0 v Sheffield Wed (Div 1) Oct 5, 1912, v Burnley (Div 1) Aug 29, 1925. Also: 13-0 v Wednesbury (FA Cup 1) Oct 30, 1886. **Biggest defeat:** 0-8 v Chelsea (Prem Lge) Dec 23, 2012. **Highest League scorer in a season:** 'Pongo' Waring 49 (1930–31). **Most League goals in aggregate:** Harry Hampton 215 (1904–15). **Longest unbeaten League sequence:** 15 matches (1897, 1909–10 and 1949. **Longest sequence without a League win:** 19 matches (2015–16). **Most capped player:** Steve Staunton (Republic of Ireland) 64

Goalkeepers				
Martinez, Emiliano	6.4	Arsenal	Mar del Plata, Arg	02.09.92
Steer, Jed	6.3	Norwich	Norwich	23.09.92
Defenders				
Cash, Matty	6.1	Nottm Forest	Slough	07.08.97
Guilbert, Frederic	5.10	Caen	Valognes, Fr	24.12.94
Hause, Kortney	6.3	Wolves	Goodmayes	16.07.95
Konsa, Ezri	6.0	Brentford	Newham	23.10.97
Mings, Tyrone	6.3	Bournemouth	Bath	13.03.93
Young, Ashley	5.9	Inter Milan	Stevenage	09.07.85
Midfielders				
Buendia, Emiliano	5.8	Norwich	Mar del Plata, Arg	25.12.96
Douglas Luiz	5.9	Manchester City	Rio de Janeiro, Br	09.05.98
El Ghazi, Anwar	6.2	Lille	Barendrecht, Hol	03.05.95
Grealish, Jack	5.9	–	Solihull	10.09.95
Hourihane, Conor	6.0	Barnsley	Cork, Ire	02.02.91
Marvelous Nakamba	5.10	Club Bruges	Hwange, Zim	19.01.94
McGinn, John	5.10	Hibernian	Glasgow	18.10.94
Ramsey, Jacob	5.11	–	Birmingham	28.05.01

Sanson, Morgan	6.0	Marseille	Saint-Doulchard, Fr	18.08.94
Targett, Matt	6.0	Southampton	Eastleigh	18.09.95
Traore, Bertrand	5.11	Lyon	Burkina Faso	06.09.95
Trezeguet	5.10	Kasimpasa	Kafr el-Sheikh, Egy	01.10.94
Vassilev, Indiana	5.9	–	Savannah, US	16.02.01
Forwards				
Davis, Keinan	6.3	–	Stevenage	13.02.98
Watkins, Ollie	5.10	Brentford	Torbay	30.12.95
Wesley	6.2	Club Bruges	Juiz de Fora, Br	26.11.96

BRENTFORD

Ground: Community Stadium, Lionel Road, Brentford TW8 7BW. **Telephone:** 0208 847 2511. **Club nickname:** Bees. **Capacity:** 17,250. **Colours:** Red, white and black. **Shirt sponsor:** Utilita. **Record attendance:** Griffin Park: 38,678 v Leicester (FA Cup 6) Feb 26, 1949. **Record transfer fee:** £10m to Peterborough for Ivan Toney, Aug 2020. **Record fee received:** £28m from Aston Villa for Ollie Watkins, Sep 2020. **League Championship:** 5th 1935–36. **FA Cup:** 6th rd 1938, 1946, 1949, 1989. **League Cup:** Semi-finals 2021. **European competitiopns:** Semi-finals Anglo-Italian Cup 1992–93. **Biggest win:** 9-0 v Wrexham (Div 3) Oct 15, 1963. **Biggest defeat:** 0-7 v Swansea (Div 3 south) Nov 8, 1924; 0-7 v Walsall (Div 3 South) Jan 19, 1957; 0-7 v Peterborough (Lg 2) Nov 24, 2007. **Highest League scorer in a season:** Jack Holliday 38 (1932–33). **Most League goals in aggregate:** Jim Towers 153 (1954–61). **Longest unbeaten League sequence:** 26 matches (1999). **Longest sequence without a League win:** 16 (1994). **Most capped player:** Henrik Dalsgaard (Denmark) 22

Goalkeepers				
Raya, David	6.0	Blackburn	Barcelona, Sp	15.09.95
Defenders				
Goode, Charlie	6.5	Northampton	Watford	03.08.95
Henry, Rico	5.8	Walsall	Birmingham	08.07.97
Jansson, Pontus	6.5	Leeds	Arlov, Swe	13.02.91
Pinnock, Ethan	6.2	Barnsley	Lambeth	29.05.93
Roersley, Mads	6.0	FC Copenhagen	Copenhagen, Den	24.06.99
Sorensen, Mads Bech	6.2	AC Horsens	Horsens, Den	07.01.99
Midfielders				
Baptiste, Shandon	5.10	Oxford	Grenada	08.04.98
Dasilva, Josh	6.0	Arsenal	Ilford	23.10.98
Fosu-Henry, Tarique	5.11	Oxford	Wandsworth	05.11.95
Ghoddos, Saman	5.10	Amiens	Malmo, Swer	06.09.93
Janelt, Vitaly	6.1	Bochum	Hamburg, Ger	10.05.98
Jensen, Mathias	5.10	Celta Vigo	Jerslev, Den	01.01.96
Mbeumo, Bryan	5.7	Troyes	Avallon, Fr	07.08.99
Norgaard, Christian	6.1	Fiorentina	Copenhagen, Den	10.03.94
Zamburek, Jan	6.0	Slavia Prague	Czech	13.02.01
Forwards				
Canos, Sergi	5.9	Norwich	Nules, Sp	02.02.97
Forss, Marcus	6.0	–	Turku, Fin	18.06.99
Toney, Ivan	5.10	Peterborough	Northampton	16.03.96

BRIGHTON AND HOVE ALBION

Ground: Amex Stadium, Village Way, Brighton BN1 9BL. **Telephone:** 0344 324 6282. **Club nickname:** Seagulls. **Capacity:** 30,666. **Colours:** Blue and white. **Main sponsor:** American Express. **Record transfer fee:** £20m to Bristol City for Adam Webster, Aug 2019; £20m to Brentford for Neal Maupay, Aug 2019. **Record fee received:** £15m from Fulham for Anthny

Knockaert, Jul 2020. **Record attendance:** Goldstone Ground: 36,747 v Fulham (Div 2) Dec 27, 1958; Withdean Stadium: 8,729 v Manchester City (League Cup 2) Sep 24, 2008; Amex Stadium: 30,634 v Liverpool (Prem Lge) Dec 2, 2017. **League Championship:** 13th 1981–82. **FA Cup:** Runners-up 1983. **League Cup:** Fifth round 1979. **Finishing position in Premier League:** 2017–18 15th, 2018–19 17th, 2019–20 15th, 2020–21 16th. **Biggest win:** 10-1 v Wisbech (FA Cup 1) Nov 13, 1965. **Biggest defeat:** 0-9 v Middlesbrough (Div 2) Aug 23, 1958. **Highest League scorer in a season:** Peter Ward 32 (1976–77). **Most League goals in aggregate:** Tommy Cook 114 (1922–29). **Longest unbeaten League sequence:** 22 matches (2015). **Longest sequence without a League win:** 15 matches (1972–73). **Most capped player:** Shane Duffy (Republic of Ireland) 39

Goalkeepers

Sanchez, Robert	6.6	–	Cartagena, Sp	18.11.97
Steele, Jason	6.2	Sunderland	Newton Aycliffe	18.08.90

Defenders

Bernardo	6.1	Leipzig	Sao Paulo, Bra	14.05.95
Burn, Dan	6.7	Wigan	Blyth	09.05.92
Duffy, Shane	6.4	Blackburn	Derry	01.01.92
Dunk, Lewis	6.4	–	Brighton	01.11.91
Lamptey, Tariq	5.6	Chelsea	Hillingdon	30.09.00
Veltman, Joel	6.0	Ajax	Ijmuiden, Hol	15.01.92
Webster, Adam	6.3	Bristol City	Chichester	04.01.95
White, Ben	6.1	Southampton	Poole	08.10.97

Midfielders

Alzate, Steven	5.11	Leyton Orient	Camden	08.09.98
Bissouma, Yves	6.0	Lille	Issia, Iv C	30.08.96
Caicedo, Moises	5.10	Ind del Valle	Santo Domingo, Ec	02.11.01
Gross, Pascal	6.0	Ingolstadt	Mannheim, Ger	15.06.91
Lallana, Adam	5.10	Liverpool	Bournemouth	10.05.8
Mac Alliste, Alexis	5.9	Argentinos	La Pampa, Arg	24.12.98
March, Solly	5.11	–	Eastbourne	20.07.94
Moder, Jakub	6.3	Lech Poznan	Szczecinek, Pol	07.04.99
Mwepu, Enock	6.0	Salzburg	Lusaka, Zam	01.01.98

Forwards

Andone, Florin	5.11	Dep La Coruna	Botosani, Rom	11.04.93
Connolly, Aaron	5.10	Mervue	Galway, Ire	28.01.00
Jahanbakhsh, Alireza	5.11	Alkmaar	Jirandeh, Ira	11.08.93
Maupay, Neal	5.7	Brentford	Versailles, Fr	14.08.96
Trossard, Leandro	5.8	Genk	Waterschei, Bel	04.12.94
Welbeck, Danny	5.10	Watford	Manchester	26.11.90
Zeqiri, Andi	6.1	Lausanne	Lausanne, Switz	22.06.99

BURNLEY

Ground: Turf Moor, Harry Potts Way, Burnley BB10 4BX. **Telephone:** 0871 221 1882. **Club nickname:** Clarets. **Capacity:** 21,944. **Colours:** Claret and blue. **Main sponsor:** LoveBet. **Record transfer fee:** £15m to Leeds for Chris Wood, Aug 2017, £15m to Middlesbrough for Ben Gibson, Aug 2018. **Record fee received:** £25m from Everton for Michael Keane, Jul 2017. **Record attendance:** 54,775 v Huddersfield (FA Cup 3) Feb 23, 1924. **League Championship:** Winners 1920–21, 1959–60. **FA Cup:** Winners 1914. **League Cup:** Semi-finals 1961, 1969, 1983, 2009. **European competitions:** European Cup quarter-finals 1960–61. **Finishing positions in Premier League:** 2014–15 19th, 2016–17 16th, 2017–18 7th, 2018–19 15th, 2019–20 10th, 2020–21 17th. **Biggest win:** 9-0 v Darwen (Div 1) Jan 9, 1892, v Crystal Palace (FA Cup 2) Feb 10, 1909, v New Brighton (FA Cup 4) Jan 26, 1957, v Penrith (FA Cup 1) Nov 17, 1984. **Biggest defeat:** 0-10 v Aston Villa (Div 1) Aug 29, 1925, v Sheffield Utd (Div 1) Jan 19,

1929. **Highest League scorer in a season:** George Beel 35 (1927–28). **Highest League scorer in aggregate:** George Beel 178 (1923–32). **Longest unbeaten League sequence:** 30 matches (1920–21). **Longest sequence without a League win:** 24 matches (1979). **Most capped player:** Jimmy McIlroy (Northern Ireland) 51

Goalkeepers

Norris, Will	6.4	Wolves	Watford	12.08.93
Pope, Nick	6.3	Charlton	Cambridge	19.04.92
Peacock-Farrell, Bailey	6.2	Leeds	Darlington	29.10.96

Defenders

Bardsley, Phil	5.11	Stoke	Salford	28.06.85
Collins, Nathan	6.4	Stoke	Leixlip, Ire	30.04.01
Long, Kevin	6.2	Cork	Cork, Ire	18.08.90
Lowton, Matthew	5.11	Aston Villa	Chesterfield	09.06.89
Mee, Ben	5.11	Man City	Sale	23.09.89
Pieters, Erik	6.1	Stoke	Tiel, Hol	07.08.88
Tarkowski, James	6.1	Brentford	Manchester	19.11.92
Taylor, Charlie	5.9	Leeds	York	18.09.93

Midfielders

Benson, Josh	5.10	Arsenal	Brentwood	05.12.99
Brownhill, Josh	5.10	Bristol City	Warrington	19.12.95
Cork, Jack	6.1	Swansea	Carshalton	25.06.89
Gudmundsson, Johann Berg	6.1	Charlton	Reykjavik, Ice	27.10.90
McNeil, Dwight	6.1	–	Rochdale	22.11.99
Stephens, Dale	5.7	Brighton	Bolton	12.06.89
Westwood, Ashley	5.7	Aston Villa	Nantwich	01.04.90

Forwards

Barnes, Ashley	6.0	Brighton	Bath	31.10.89
Rodriguez, Jay	6.1	WBA	Burnley	29.07.89
Vydra, Matej	5.11	Derby	Chotebor, Cz	01.05.92
Wood, Chris	6.3	Leeds	Auckland, NZ	07.12.91

CHELSEA

Ground: Stamford Bridge Stadium, London SW6 1HS. **Telephone:** 0371 811 1955. **Club nickname:** Blues. **Capacity:** 40,853. **Colours:** Blue. **Main sponsor:** Three. **Record transfer fee:** £71.6m to Athletic Bilbao for Kepa Arrizabalaga, Aug 2018. **Record fee received:** £88.5m from Real Madrid for Eden Hazard, Jun 2019. **Record attendance:** 82,905 v Arsenal (Div 1) Oct 12, 1935. **League Championship:** Winners 1954–55, 2004–05, 2005–06, 2009–10, 2014–15, 2016–17. **FA Cup:** Winners 1970, 1997, 2000, 2007, 2009, 2010, 2012, 2018. **League Cup:** Winners 1965, 1998, 2005, 2007, 2015. **European competitions:** Winners Champions League 2011–12, 2020–21; Cup-Winners' Cup 1970–71, 1997–98; Europa League 2012–13, 2018–19; European Super Cup 1998

Finishing positions in Premier League: 1992–93 11th, 1993–94 14th, 1994–95 11th, 1995–96 11th, 1996–97 6th, 1997–98 4th, 1998–99 3rd, 1999–2000 5th, 2000–01 6th, 2001–02 6th, 2002–03 4th, 2003–04 2nd, 2004–05 1st, 2005–06 1st, 2006–07 2nd, 2007–08 2nd, 2008–09 3rd, 2009–10 1st, 2010–11 2nd, 2011–12 6th, 2012–13 3rd, 2013–14 3rd, 2014–15 1st, 2015–16 10th, 2016–17 1st, 2017–18 5th, 2018–19 3rd, 2019–20 4th, 2020–21 4th

Biggest win: 8-0 v Aston Villa (Prem Lge) Dec 23, 2012. Also: 13-0 v Jeunesse Hautcharage, (Cup-Winners' Cup 1) Sep 29, 1971. **Biggest defeat:** 1-8 v Wolves (Div 1) Sep 26, 1953; 0-7 v Leeds (Div 1) Oct 7, 1967, v Nottm Forest (Div 1) Apr 20, 1991. **Highest League scorer in a season:** Jimmy Greaves 41 (1960–61). **Most League goals in aggregate:** Bobby Tambling 164 (1958–70). **Longest unbeaten League sequence:** 40 matches (2004–05). **Longest sequence without a League win:** 21 matches (1987–88). **Most capped player:** Frank Lampard (England) 104

Goalkeepers

Arrizabalaga, Kepa	6.2	Athletic Bilbao	Ondarroa. Sp	03.10.94
Mendy, Edouard	6.6	Rennes	Montivilliers, Fr	01.03.92

Defenders

Azpilicueta, Cesar	5.10	Marseille	Pamplona, Sp	28.08.89
Chilwell, Ben	5.10	Leicester	Milton Keynes	21.12.96
Christensen, Andreas	6.2	Brondby	Lillerod, Den	10.04.96
Emerson	5.9	Roma	Santos, Br	03.08.94
James, Reece	6.0	–	Redbridge	08.12.99
Rudiger, Antonio	6.3	Roma	Berlin, Ger	03.03.93
Thiago Silva	6.0	Paris SG	Rio de Janeiro, Br	22.09.84
Zouma, Kurt	6.3	St Etienne	Lyon, Fr	27.10.94

Midfielders

Barkley, Ross	6.2	Everton	Liverpool	05.12.93
Hudson-Odoi, Callum	6.0	–	Wandsworth	07.11.00
Jorginho	5.11	Napoli	Imbituba, Bra	20.12.91
Kante, N'Golo	5.7	Leicester	Paris, Fr	29.03.91
Kovacic, Mateo	5.10	Real Madrid	Linz, Aut	06.05.94
Havertz, Kai	6.2	Bayer Leverkusen	Aachen, Ger	11.06.99
Loftus-Cheek, Ruben	6.3	–	Lewisham	23.01.96
Marcos Alonso	6.2	Fiorentina	Madrid, Sp	28.12.90
Mount, Mason	5.10	–	Portsmouth	10.01.99
Ziyech, Hakim	5.11	Ajax	Dronten, Hol	19.03.93

Forwards

Abraham, Tammy	6.3	–	Camberwell	02.10.97
Batshuayi, Michy	6.0	Marseille	Brussels, Bel	02.10.93
Giroud, Olivier	6.4	Arsenal	Chambery, Fr	30.09.86
Pulisic, Christian	5.8	Borussia Dortmund	Hershey, US	18.09.98
Werner, Timo	5.11	Leipzig	Stuttgart, Ger	06.03.96

CRYSTAL PALACE

Ground: Selhurst Park, Whitehorse Lane, London SE25, 6PU. **Telephone:** 0208 768 6000.
Club nickname: Eagles. **Capacity:** 25,486. **Colours:** Red and blue. **Main sponsor:** W888. **Record transfer fee:** £27m to Liverpool for Christian Benteke, Aug 2016. **Record fee received:** £50m from Manchester Utd for Aaron Wan-Bissaka, Jun 2019. **Record attendance:** 51,482 v Burnley (Div 2), May 11, 1979. **League Championship:** 3rd 1990–91. **FA Cup:** Runners-up 1990, 2016. **League Cup:** Semi-finals 1993, 1995, 2001, 2012. **Finishing positions in Premier League:** 1992–93 20th, 1994–95 19th, 1997–98 20th,. 2004–05 18th, 2013–14 11th, 2014–15 10th, 2015–16 15th, 2016–17 14th, 2017–18 11th, 2018–19 12th, 2019–20 14th, 2020–21 14th. **Biggest win:** 9-0 v Barrow (Div 4) Oct 10, 1959. **Biggest defeat:** 0-9 v Liverpool (Div 1) Sep 12, 1989. Also: 0-9 v Burnley (FA Cup 2 rep) Feb 10, 1909. **Highest League scorer in a season:** Peter Simpson 46 (1930–31). **Most League goals in aggregate:** Peter Simpson 153 (1930–36). **Longest unbeaten League sequence:** 18 matches (1969). **Longest sequence without a League win:** 20 matches (1962). **Most capped player:** Wayne Hennessey (Wales) 50

Goalkeepers

Butland, Jack	6.4	Stoke	Bristol	10.03.93
Guaita, Vicente	6.3	Getafe	Torrente, Sp	10.01.87
Henderson, Stephen	6.3	Nottingham Forest	Dublin, Ire	02.05.88

Defenders

Ferguson, Nathan	5.11	WBA	Birmingham	06.10.00
Kelly, Martin	6.3	Liverpool	Whiston	27.04.90
Kouyate, Cheikhou	6.4	West Ham	Dakar, Sen	21.12.89
Mitchell, Tyrick	5.9	–	Brent	01.09.99

Riedewald, Jairo	6.0	Ajax	Haarlem, Hol	09.09.96
Schlupp, Jeffrey	5.8	Leicester	Hamburg, Ger	23.12.92
Tomkins, James	6.3	West Ham	Basildon	29.03.89
Midfielders				
McArthur, James	5.7	Wigan	Glasgow	07.10.87
Milivojevic, Luka	6.0	Olympiacos	Kragujevac, Serb	07.04.91
Olise, Michael	6.2	Reading	Hammersmith	12.12.01
Forwards				
Ayew, Jordan	6.0	Swansea	Marseille, Fr	11.09.91
Benteke, Christian	6.3	Liverpool	Kinshasa, DR Cong	03.12.90
Eze, Eberechi	5.8	QPR	Greenwich	29.06.98
Zaha, Wilfried	5.10	Man Utd	Abidjan, Iv C	10.11.92

EVERTON

Ground: Goodison Park, Liverpool L4 4EL. **Telephone:** 0151 556 1878. **Club nickname:** Toffees. **Capacity:** 39,221. **Colours:** Blue and white. **Main sponsor:** Cazoo. **Record transfer fee:** £45m to Swansea for Gylfi Sigurdsson, Aug 2017. **Record fee received:** £75m from Manchester Utd for Romelu Lukaku, Jul 2017. **Record attendance:** 78,299 v Liverpool (Div 1) Sep 18, 1948. **League Championship:** Winners 1890–91, 1914–15, 1927–28, 1931–31, 1938–39,, 1962–63, 1969–70, 1984–85, 1986–87. **FA Cup:** Winners 1906, 1933, 1966, 1984, 1995. **League Cup:** Runners-up 1977, 1984. **European competitions:** Winners Cup-Winners' Cup 1984–85
Finishing positions in Premier League: 1992–93 13th, 1993–94 17th, 1994–95 15th, 1995–96 6th 1996–97 15th 1997–98 17th 1998–99 14th, 1999–2000 13th, 2000–01 16th, 2001–02 15th, 2002–03 7th, 2003–04 17th, 2004–05 4th, 2005–06 11th, 2006–07 6th, 2007–08 5th, 2008–09 5th, 2009–10 8th, 20010–11 7th, 2011–12 7th, 2012–13 6th, 2013–14 5th, 2014–15 11th, 2015–16 11th, 2016–17 7th, 2017–18 8th, 2018–19 8th, 2019–20 12th, 2020–21 10th
Biggest win: 9-1 v Manchester City (Div 1) Sep 3, 1906, v Plymouth (Div 2) Dec 27, 1930. Also: 11-2 v Derby (FA Cup 1) Jan 18, 1890. **Biggest defeat:** 0-7 v Portsmouth (Div 1) Sep 10, 1949, v Arsenal (Prem Lge) May 11, 2005. **Highest League scorer in a season:** Ralph 'Dixie' Dean 60 (1927–28). **Most League goals in aggregate:** Ralph 'Dixie' Dean 349 (1925–37). **Longest unbeaten League sequence:** 20 matches (1978). **Longest sequence without a League win:** 14 matches (1937). **Most capped player:** Neville Southall (Wales) 92

Goalkeepers				
Joao Virginia	6.3	–	Faro Por	10.09.99
Pickford, Jordan	6.1	Sunderland	Washington, Co Dur	07.03.94
Defenders				
Coleman, Seamus	5.10	Sligo	Donegal, Ire	11.10.88
Digne, Lucas	5.10	Barcelona	Meaux, Fr	20.07.93
Godfrey, Ben	6.0	Norwich	York	1501.98
Holgate, Mason	5.11	Barnsley	Doncaster	22.10.96
Keane, Michael	6.3	Burnley	Stockport	11.01.93
Kenny Jonjoe	5.9	–	Liverpool	15.03.97
Mina, Yerry	6.4	Barcelona	Guachene, Col	23.09.94
Nkounkou, Niels	5.11	Marseille	Pontoise, Fr	01.11.00
Midfielders				
Allan	5.9	Napoli	Rio de Janeiro, Br	08.01.91
Bernard	5.5	Shakhtar Donetsk	Belo Horizonte, Br	08.09.92
Davies, Tom	5.11	–	Liverpool	30.06.98
Delph, Fabian	5.9	Manchester City	Bradford	21.11.89
Doucoure, Abdoulaye	6.0	Watford	Meulan, Fr	01.01.93
Gomes, Andre	6.2	Barcelona	Grijo, Por	30.07.93

James Rodriguez	5.11	Real Madrid	Cucuta, Col	12.07.91
Sigurdsson, Gylfi	6.1	Swansea	Hafnarfjordur, Ice	08.09.89
Forwards				
Calvert-Lewin, Dominic	6.2	Sheffield Utd	Sheffield	16.03.97
Gordon, Anthony	5.10	–	Liverpool	24.02.01
Iwobi, Alex	5.11	Arsenal	Lagos, Nig	03.05.96
Kean, Moise	6.0	Juventus	Vercelli, It	28.02.00
Richarlison	5.10	Watford	Nova Venecia, Br	10.05.97
Cenk Tosun	6.0	Besiktas	Wetzlar, Ger	07.06.91

LEEDS UNITED

Ground: Elland Road, Leeds LS11 0ES. **Telephone:** 0871 334 1919. **Club nickname:** Whites. **Capacity:** 37,890. **Colours:** White. **Main sponsor:** Sbotop. **Record transfer fee:** £26m to Valencia for Rodrigo, Aug 2020. **Record fee received:** £29.1m from Manchester Utd for Rio Ferdinand, Jul 2002. **Record attendance:** 57,892 v Sunderland (FA Cup 5 rep) Mar 15, 1967. **League Championship:** Winners 1968–69, 1973–74, 1991–92. **FA Cup:** Winner 1972. **League Cup:** Winners 1968. **European competitions:** Winners Fairs Cup 1967–68, 1970–71. **Finishing positions in Premier League:** 1992–93 17th, 1993–94 5th, 1994–95 5th, 1995–96 13th, 1996–97 11th, 1997–98 5th, 1998–99 4th, 1999–2000 3rd, 2000–01 4th, 2001–02 5th, 2002–03 15th, 2003–04 19th, 2020–21 9th. **Biggest win:** 8-0 v Leiceter (Div 1) Apr 7, 1934. **Biggest defeat:** 1-8 v Stoke (Div 1) Aug 27, 1934. **Highest League scorer in a season:** John Charles 43 (1953–54). **Most League goals in aggregate:** Peter Lorimer 168 (1965–79, 1983–86). **Longest unbeaten League sequence:** 34 matches (1968–69). **Longest sequence without a League win:** 17 matches (1947). **Most capped player:** Billy Bremner (Scotland) 54

Goalkeepers				
Meslier, Illan	6.5	Lorient	Lorient Fr	02.03.00
Defenders				
Ayling, Luke	6.1	Bristol City	Lambeth	25.08.91
Cooper, Liam	6.0	Chesterfield	Hull	30.08.91
Drameh, Cody	5.8	Fulham	London	08.12.01
Junior Firpo	6.0	Barcelona	Santo Domingo, Dom Rep 22.08.96	
Koch, Robin	6.3	Freiburg	Kaiserslautern, Ger	17.07.96
Llorente, Diego	6.1	Real Sociedad	Madrid, Sp	16.08.93
Struijk, Pascal	6.3	Ajax	Deurne, Bel	11.08.99
Midfielders				
Alioski, Ezgjan	5.8	Lugano	Prilep, Maced	12.02.92
Dallas, Stuart	6.0	Brentford	Cookstown	19.04.91
Forshaw, Adam	6.1	Middlesbrough	Liverpool	08.10.91
Harrison, Jack	5.9	Manchester City	Stoke	20.11.96
Klich, Mateusz	6.0	FC Twente	Tarnow, Pol	13.06.90
Phillips, Kalvin	5.10	–	Leeds	02.12.95
Poveda, Ian	5.6	Manchester City	Southwark	09.02.00
Raphinha	5.9	Rennes	Porto Alegre, Br	14.12.96
Shackleton, Jamie	5.7	–	Leeds	08.10.99
Forwards				
Bamford, Patrick	6.1	Middlesbrough	Grantham	05.09.93
Gelhardt, Joe	5.10	Wigan	Liverpool	04.05.92
Helder Costa	5.10	Wolves	Luandra, Ang	12.01.94
Roberts, Tyler	5.11	WBA	Gloucester	12.01.99
Rodrigo	6.0	Valencia	Rio de Janeiro, Br	06.03.91

LEICESTER CITY

Ground: King Power Stadium, Filbert Way, Leicester, LE2 7FL. **Telephone:** 0344 815 5000. **Club nickname:** Foxes. **Capacity:** 32,273. **Colours:** Blue and white. **Main sponsor:** FBS. **Record transfer fee:** £40m to Monaco for Youri Tielemans, Jul 2019. **Record fee received:** £80m from Manchester United for Harry Maguire, Aug 2019. **Record attendance:** Filbert Street: 47,298 v. Tottenham (FA Cup 5) Feb 18, 1928; King Power Stadium: 32,148 v Newcastle (Prem Lge) Dec 26, 2003. Also: 32,188 v Real Madrid (friendly) Jul 30, 2011. **League Championship:** Winners 2015–16. **FA Cup:** Winners 2020–21. **League Cup:** Winners 1964, 1997, 2000. **European competitions:** Champions League quarter-finals 2016–17. **Finishing positions in Premier League:** 1994–95 21st, 1996–97 9th, 1997–98 10th, 1998–99 10th, 1999–2000 8th, 2000–01 13th, 2001–02 20th, 2003–04 18th, 2014–15 14th, 2015–16 1st, 2016–17 12th, 2017–18 9th, 2018–19 9th, 2019–2020 5th, 2020–21 5th. **Biggest win:** 10-0 v Portsmouth (Div 1) Oct 20, 1928. Also: 13-0 v Notts Olympic (FA Cup) Oct 13, 1894. **Biggest defeat (while Leicester Fosse):** 0-12 v Nottm Forest (Div 1) Apr 21, 1909. **Highest League scorer in a season:** Arthur Rowley 44 (1956–57). **Most League goals in aggregate:** Arthur Chandler 259 (1923–35). **Longest unbeaten League sequence:** 23 matches (2008–09). **Longest sequence without a League win:** 19 matches (1975). **Most capped player:** Andy King (Wales) 50

Goalkeepers				
Jakupovic, Eldin	6.3	Hull	Sarajevo, Bos	02.10.84
Schmeichel, Kasper	6.0	Leeds	Copenhagen, Den	05.11.86
Ward, Danny	6.4	Liverpool	Wrexham	22.06.93
Defenders				
Benkovic, Filip	6.4	Dinamo Zagreb	Zagreb, Cro	13.07.97
Caglar Soyuncu	6.1	Freiburg	Izmir, Tur	23.05.96
Castagne, Timothy	6.1	Atalanta	Arlon, Bel	05.12.95
Evans, Jonny	6.2	WBA	Belfast	02.01.88
Fofana, Wesley	6.3	St Etienne	Marseille, Fr	17.12.00
Justin, James	6.3	Luton	Luton	11.07.97
Ricardo Pereira	5.9	Porto	Lisbon, Por	06.10.93
Thomas, Luke	5.11	–	Syston	10.06.01
Midfielders				
Albrighton, Mark	6.1	Aston Villa	Tamworth	18.11.89
Amartey, Daniel	6.0	Copenhagen	Accra, Gh	01.12.94
Choudhury, Hamza	5.10	–	Loughborough	01.10.97
Maddison, James	5.10	Norwich	Coventry	23.11.96
Mendy, Nampalys	5.6	Nice	La Seyne, Fr	23.06.92
Ndidi, Wilfred	6.0	Genk	Lagos, Nig	16.12.96
Praet, Dennis	5.11	Sampdoria	Leuven, Bel	14.05.94
Soumare, Boubakary	6.2	Lille	Noisy-le-Sec, Fr	27.02.99
Tielemans, Youri	5.10	Monaco	Sint-Pieters, Bel	07.05.97
Forwards				
Ayoze Perez	5.11	Newcastle	Santa Cruz, Ten	23.07.93
Barnes, Harvey	5.9	–	Burnley	09.12.97
Daka, Patson	6.1	RB Salzburg	Kafue, Zam	09.10.98
Hirst, George	6.3	Leuven	Sheffield	15.02.99
Iheanacho, Kelechi	6.2	Man City	Owerri, Nig	03.10.96
Vardy, Jamie	5.10	Fleetwood	Sheffield	11.01.87

LIVERPOOL

Ground: Anfield, Liverpool L4 0TH. **Telephone:** 0151 263 2361. **Club nickname:** Reds or Pool. **Capacity:** 53,394. **Colours:** Red. **Main sponsor:** Standard Chartered. **Record transfer fee:** £75m to Southampton for Virgil van Dijk, Jan 2018. **Record fee received:** £142m from Barcelona

for Philippe Coutinho, Jan 2018. **Record attendance:** 61,905 v Wolves, (FA Cup 4), Feb 2, 1952. **League Championship:** Winners 1900–01, 1905–06, 1921–22, 1922–23, 1946–47, 1963–64, 1965–66, 1972–73, 1975–76, 1976–77, 1978–79, 1979–80, 1981–82, 1982–83,1983–84, 1985–86, 1987–88, 1989–90, 2019–20 1st, 2020–21. **FA Cup:** Winners 1965, 1974, 1986, 1989, 1992, 2001, 2006. **League Cup:** Winners 1981, 1982, 1983, 1984, 1995, 2001, 2003, 2012. **European competitions:** Winners European Cup/Champions League 1976–77, 1977–78,1980–81, 1983–84, 2004–05, 2018–19; UEFA Cup 1972–73, 1975–76, 2000–01; European Super Cup 1977, 2001, 2005
Finishing positions in Premier League: 1992–93 6th, 1993–94 8th, 1994–95 4th, 1995–96 3rd, 1996–97 4th, 1997–98 3rd, 1998–99 7th, 1999–2000 4th, 2000–01 3rd, 2001–02 2nd, 2002–03 5th, 2003–04 4th, 2004–05 5th, 2005–06 3rd, 2006–07 3rd, 2007–08 4th, 2008–09 2nd, 2009–10 7th, 2010–11 6th, 2011–12 8th, 2012–13 7th, 2013–14 2nd, 2014–15 6th, 2015–16 8th, 2016–17 4th, 2017–18 4th, 2018–19 2nd, 2019–20 1st, 2020–21 3rd
Biggest win: 10-1 v Rotherham (Div 2) Feb 18, 1896. Also: 11-0 v Stromsgodset (Cup-Winners' Cup 1) Sep 17, 1974. **Biggest defeat:** 1-9 v Birmingham (Div 2) Dec 11, 1954. **Highest League scorer in a season:** Roger Hunt 41 (1961–62). **Most League goals in aggregate:** Roger Hunt 245 (1959–69). 31 matches (1987–88)). **Longest unbeaten League sequence:** 44 matches (2019–20). **Longest sequence without a League win:** 14 matches (1953–54)). **Most capped player:** Steven Gerrard (England) 114

Goalkeepers

Adrian	6.3	West Ham	Seville, Sp	03.01.87
Alisson	6.4	Roma	Novo Hamburgo, Bra	02.10.92
Kelleher, Caoimhin	6.2	–	Cork, Ire	23.11.98

Defenders

Alexander-Arnold, Trent	5.10	–	Liverpool	07.10.98
Davies, Ben	5.11	Preston	Barrow	11.08.95
Gomez, Joe	6.1	Charlton	Catford	23.05.97
Konate, Ibrahima	6.4	RB Leipzig	Paris, Fr	25.05.99
Matip, Joel	6.5	Schalke	Bochum, Ger	08.08.91
Phillips, Nat	6.3	–	Bolton	21.03.97
Robertson, Andrew	5.10	Hull	Glasgow	11.03.94
Van Dijk, Virgil	6.4	Southampton	Breda, Hol	08.07.91
Williams, Neco	6.0	–	Wrexham	13.04.01
Williams, Rhys	6.5	–	Preston	03.02.01

Midfielders

Diogo Jota	5.10	Wolves	Porto, Por	04.12.96
Fabinho	6.2	Monaco	Campinas, Bra	23.10.93
Henderson, Jordan	5.10	Sunderland	Sunderland	17.06.90
Jones, Curtis	6.0	–	Liverpool	30.01.01
Keita, Naby	5.8	Leipzig	Conakry, Guin	10.02.95
Milner, James	5.11	Man City	Leeds	04.01.86
Oxlade-Chamberlain, Alex	5.11	Arsenal	Portsmouth	15.08.93
Shaqiri, Xherdan	5.7	Stoke	Gjilan, Kos	10.10.91
Thiago Alcantara	5.9	Bayern Munich	San Pietro, It	11.04.91

Forwards

Firmino, Roberto	6.0	Hoffenheim	Maceio, Br	02.10.91
Mane, Sadio	5.9	Southampton	Sedhiou, Sen	10.04.92
Minamino, Takumi	5.9	Sazburg	Osaka, Jap	16.01.95
Origi, Divock	6.1	Lille	Ostend, Bel	18.04.95
Salah, Mohamed	5.9	Roma	Basyoun, Egy	15.06.92
Woodburn, Ben	5.11	–	Nottingham	15.10.99

MANCHESTER CITY

Ground: Etihad Stadium, Etihad Campus, Manchester M11 3FF. **Telephone:** 0161 444 1894.
Club nickname: City. **Capacity:** 55,017. **Colours:** Sky blue and white. **Main sponsor:** Etihad.
Record transfer fee: £65m to Benfica for Ruben Dias, Sep 2020. **Record fee received:** £25m
from Leicester for Kelechi Iheanacho, Jul 2017. **Record attendance:** Maine Road: 84,569 v
Stoke (FA Cup 6) Mar 3, 1934 (British record for any game outside London or Glasgow). Etihad
Stadium: 54,693 v Leicester (Prem Lge) February 6, 2016. **League Championship:** Winners
1936–37, 1967–68, 2011–12, 2013–14, 2017–18, 2018–19, 2020–21. **FA Cup:** Winners
1904, 1934, 1956, 1969, 2011, 2019. **League Cup:** Winners 1970, 1976, 2014, 2016,
2018, 2019, 2020, 2021. **European competitions:** Winners Cup-Winners' Cup 1969–70v
Finishing positions in Premier League: 1992–93 9th, 1993–94 16th, 1994–95 17th,
1995–96 18th, 2000–01: 18th, 2002–03 9th, 2003–04 16th, 2004–05 8th, 2005–06
15th, 2006–07 14th, 2007–08 9th, 2008–09 10th, 2009–10 5th, 2010–11 3rd, 2011–12
1st, 2012–13 2nd, 2013–14 1st, 2014–15 2nd, 2015–16 4th, 2016–17 3rd, 2017–18 1st,
2018–19 1st, 2019–20 2nd, 2020–21 1st
Biggest win: 10-1 v Huddersfield (Div 2) Nov 7, 1987. Also: 10-1 v Swindon (FA Cup 4) Jan 29,
1930. **Biggest defeat:** 1-9 v Everton (Div 1) Sep 3, 1906. **Highest League scorer in a season:**
Tommy Johnson 38 (1928–29). **Most League goals in aggregate:** Tommy Johnson, 158
(1919–30). **Longest unbeaten League sequence:** 22 matches (1946–47) and (2017–18).
Longest sequence without a League win: 17 matches (1979–80). **Most capped player:** Joe Hart
(England) 63

Goalkeepers

Ederson	6.2	Benfica	Osasco, Br	17.08.93
Steffen, Zack	6.3	Columbus Crew	Coatesville, US	02.04.95

Defenders

Ake, Nathan	5.11	Bournemouth	The Hague, Hol	18.02.95
Dias, Ruben	6.2	Benfica	Amadora, Por	14.05.97
Joao Cancelo	6.0	Juventus	Barrreiro, Por	27.05.94
Laporte, Aymeric	6.3	Athletic Bilbao	Agen, Fr	27.05.94
Mendy, Benjamin	6.0	Monaco	Longjumeau, Fr	17.07.94
Stones, John	6.2	Everton	Barnsley	28.05.94
Walker, Kyle	6.0	Tottenham	Sheffield	28.05.90
Zinchenko, Oleksandr	5.9	FC Ufa	Radomyshi, Ukr	15.12.96

Midfielders

Bernardo Silva, Bernardo		Monaco	Lisbon, Por	10.08.94
De Bruyne, Kevin	5.11	Wolfsburg	Drongen, Bel	28.06.91
Doyle, Tommy	5.8	–	Manchester	17.10.01
Fernandinho	5.10	Shakhtar Donetsk	Londrina, Br	04.05.85
Foden, Phil	5.7	–	Stockport	28.05.00
Gundogan, Ilkay	5.11	Borussia Dortmund	Gelsenkirchen, Ger	24.10.90
Mahrez, Riyad	5.10	Leicester	Sarcelles, Fr	21.02.91
Rodri	6.3	Atletico Madrid	Madrid, Sp	23.06.96

Forwards

Delap, Liam	6.1	Derby	Winchester	08.02.03
Ferran Torres	6.0	Valencia	Foios, Sp	29.02.00
Gabriel Jesus	5.9	Palmeiras	Sao Paulo, Br	03.04.97
Sterling, Raheem	5.7	Liverpool	Kingston, Jam	08.12.94

MANCHESTER UNITED

Ground: Old Trafford Stadium, Sir Matt Busby Way, Manchester, M16 0RA. **Telephone:** 0161
868 8000. **Club nickname:** Red Devils. **Capacity:** 74,879. **Colours:** Red and white. **Main sponsor:** TeamViewer. **Record transfer fee:** £89.3m to Juventus for Paul Pogba, Aug 2016. **Record
fee received:** £80m from Real Madrid for Cristiano Ronaldo, Jun 2009. **Record attendance:**

75,811 v Blackburn (Prem Lge), Mar 31, 2007. Also: 76,962 Wolves v Grimsby (FA Cup semi-final) Mar 25, 1939. Crowd of 83,260 saw Manchester Utd v Arsenal (Div 1) Jan 17, 1948 at Maine Road – Old Trafford out of action through bomb damage. **League Championship:** Winners 1907–08, 1910–11, 1951–52, 1955–56, 1956–7, 1964–65, 1966–67, 1992–93, 1993–94, 1995–96, 1996–97, 1998–99, 1999–2000, 2000–01, 2002–03, 2006–07, 2007–08, 2008–09, 2010–11, 2012–13. **FA Cup:** Winners 1909, 1948, 1963, 1977, 1983, 1985, 1990, 1994, 1996, 1999, 2004, 2016. **League Cup:** Winners 1992, 2006, 2009, 2010, 2017. **European competitions:** Winners European Cup/Champions League 1967–68, 1998–99, 2007–08; Cup-Winners' Cup 1990–91; European Super Cup 1991; Europa League 2016–17. **World Club Cup:** Winners 2008
Finishing positions in Premier League: 1992–93 1st, 1993–94 1st, 1994–95 2nd, 1995–96 1st, 1996–97 1st, 1997–98 2nd, 1998–99 1st, 1999–2000 1st, 2000–01 1st, 2001–02 3rd, 2002–03 1st, 2003–04 3rd, 2004–05 3rd, 2005–06 2nd, 2006–07 1st, 2007–08 1st, 2000–09 1st, 2009–10 2nd, 2010–11 1st, 2011–12 2nd, 2012–13 1st, 2013–14 7th, 2014–15 4th, 2015–16 5th, 2016–17 6th, 2017–18 2nd, 2018–19 6th, 2019–20 3rd, 2020–21 2nd
Biggest win: As Newton Heath: 10-1 v Wolves (Div 1) Oct 15, 1892. As Manchester Utd: 9-0 v Ipswich (Prem Lge), Mar 4, 1995;. 9-0 v Southampton (Prem Lge), Feb 2, 2021. Also: 10-0 v Anderlecht (European Cup prelim rd) Sep 26, 1956. **Biggest defeat:** 0-7 v Blackburn (Div 1) Apr 10, 1926, v Aston Villa (Div 1) Dec 27, 1930, v Wolves (Div 2) 26 Dec, 1931. **Highest League scorer in a season:** Dennis Viollet 32 (1959–60). **Most League goals in aggregate:** Sir Bobby Charlton 199 (1956–73). **Longest unbeaten League sequence:** 29 matches (1998–99). **Longest sequence without a League win:** 16 matches (1930). **Most capped player:** Sir Bobby Charlton (England) 106

Goalkeepers
De Gea, David	6.4	Atletico Madrid	Madrid, Sp	07.11.90
Henderson, Dean	6.3		Whitehaven	12.03.97
Heaton, Tom	6.1	Aston Villa	Chester	15.04.86

Defenders
Bailly, Eric	6.1	Villarreal	Bingerville, Iv C	12.04.94
Jones, Phil	5.11	Blackburn	Blackburn	21.02.92
Lindelof, Victor	6.2	Benfica	Vasteras, Swe	17.07.94
Maguire, Harry	6.2	Leicesterl	Sheffield	05.03.93
Shaw, Luke	6.1	Southampton	Kingston upon Thames	12.07.95
Telles, Alex	5.11	Porto	Caxias do Sul, Br	15.12.92
Tuanzebe, Axel	6.1	–	DR Cong	14.11.97
Wan-Bissaka, Aaron	6.0	Crystal Palace	Croydon	26.11.97
Williams, Brandon	5.8	–	Manchester	03.09.00

Midfielders
Bruno Fernandes	5.8	Sporting Lisbon	Maia, Por	08.09.84
Diallo, Amad	5.8	Atalanta	Abidjan, Iv C	11.07.02
Fred	5.7	Shakhtar Donetsk	Belo Horizonte, Bra	05.03.93
James, Daniel	5.8	Swansea	Beverley	10.11.97
Mata, Juan	5.7	Chelsea	Burgos, Sp	28.04.88
Matic, Nemanja	6.4	Chelsea	Sabac, Serb	01.08.88
McTominay, Scott	6.4	–	Lancaster	08.12.96
Pogba, Paul	6.3	Juventus	Lagny-sur-Marne, Fr	15.03.93
Van de Beek, Donny	6.1	Ajax	Nijkerkerveen, Hol	18.04.97

Forwards
Cavani, Edinson	6.1	Paris SG	Salto, Uru	14.02.87
Greenwood, Mason	5.11	–	Bradford	01.10.01
Lingard, Jesse	6.2	–	Warrington	15.12.92
Martial, Anthony	5.11	Monaco	Massy, Fr	05.12.95
Rashford, Marcus	6.0	–	Wythensawe	31.10.97

NEWCASTLE UNITED

Ground: St James' Park, Newcastle-upon-Tyne, NE1 4ST. **Telephone:** 0844 372 1892. **Club nickname:** Magpies. **Capacity:** 52,305. **Colours:** Black and white. **Main sponsor:** Fun88. **Record attendance:** 68,386 v Chelsea (Div 1) Sep 3, 1930. **Record transfer fee:** £40m to Hoffenheim for Joelinton, Jul 2019. **Record fee received:** £35m from Liverpool for Andy Carroll, Jan 2011. **League Championship:** Winners 1904–05, 1906–07, 1908–09, 1926–27. **FA Cup:** Winners: 1910, 1924, 1932, 1951, 1952,1955. **League Cup:** Runners-up 1976. **European competitions:** Winners Fairs Cup 1968–69; Anglo-Italian Cup 1972–73
Finishing positions in Premier League: 1993–94 3rd, 1994–95 6th, 1995–96 2nd, 1996–97 2nd, 1997–98 13th, 1998–99 13th, 1999–2000 11th, 2000–01 11th, 2001–02 4th, 2002–03 3rd, 2003–04 5th, 2004–05 14th, 2005–06 7th, 2006–07 13th, 2007–08 12th, 2008–09 18th, 2010–11 12th, 2011–12 5th, 2012–13 16th, 2013–14 10th, 2014–15 15th, 2015–16 18th, 2017–18 10th, 2018–19 13th, 2019–20 13th, 2020–21 12th
Biggest win: 13-0 v Newport (Div 2) Oct 5, 1946. **Biggest defeat:** 0-9 v Burton (Div 2) Apr 15, 1895. **Highest League scorer in a season:** Hughie Gallacher 36 (1926–27). **Most League goals in aggregate:** Jackie Milburn 177 (1946–57). **Longest unbeaten League sequence:** 14 matches (1950). **Longest sequence without a League win:** 21 matches (1978). **Most capped player:** Shay Given (Republic of Irelnd) 83

Goalkeepers				
Darlow, Karl	6.1	Nottm Forest	Northampton	08.10.90
Dubravka, Martin	6.3	Sparta Prague	Zilina, Slovak	15.01.89
Gillespie, Mark	6.3	Motherwell	Newcastle	27.03.92
Defenders				
Clark, Ciaran	6.2	Aston Villa	Harrow	26.09.89
Dummett, Paul	6.0	–	Newcastle	26.09.91
Fernandez, Federico	6.3	Swansea	Tres Algarrobos, Arg	21.02.89
Krafth, Emil	6.1	Amiens	Stockholm, Swe	02.08.94
Lascelles, Jamaal	6.2	Nottm Forest	Derby	11.11.93
Lewis, Jamal	5.10	Norwch	Luton	25.01.98
Manquillo, Javier	6.0	Atletico Madrid	Madrid, Sp	05.05.94
Schar, Fabian	6.2	Dep La Coruna	Wil, Switz	20.12.91
Yedlin, DeAndre	5.9	Tottenham	Seattle, US	09.07.93
Midfielders				
Almiron, Miguel	5.9	Atlanta	Asuncion, Par	10.02.94
Fraser, Ryan	5.4	Bournemouth	Aberdeen	24.02.94
Hayden, Isaac	6.1	Arsenal	Chelmsford	22.03.95
Hendrick, Jeff	6.1	Burnley	Dublin, Ire	31.01.92
Longstaff, Matty	5.8	–	Rotherham	21.03.00
Longstaff, Sean	5.1	–	North Shields	30.10.97
Murphy, Jacob	5.10	Norwich	Wembley	24.02.95
Ritchie, Matt	5.8	Bournemouth	Gosport	10.09.89
Saint-Maximin, Allan	5.9	Nice	Chatenay-Malabry, Fr	12.03.97
Shelvey, Jonjo	6.0	Swansea	Romford	27.02.92
Forwards				
Gayle, Dwight	5.10	Crystal Palace	Walthamstow	20.10.90
Joelinton	6.1	Hoffenheim	Alianca, Br	14.08.96
Wilson, Callum	5.11	Bournemouth	Coventry	27.02.92

NORWICH CITY

Ground: Carrow Road, Norwich NR1 1JE. **Telephone:** 01603 760760. **Club nickname:** Canaries. **Capacity:** 27,244. **Colours:** Yellow and green. **Main sponsor:** Lotus Cars. **Record signing:** £8.5m to Everton for Steven Naismith, Jan 2016. **Record fee received:** £33m from Aston Villa for Emiliano Buendia, June 2021. **Record attendance:** 43,984 v Leicester (FA Cup 6), Mar 30, 1963. **League Championship:** 3rd1993. **FA Cup:** Semi-finals 1959, 1989, 1992. **League Cup:** Winners 1962, 1985. **European competitions:** UEFA Cup rd 3 1993–94. **Finishing positions in Premier League:** 1992–93 3rd, 1993–94 12th,1994–95 20th, 2004–05 19th, 2011–12 12th, 2012–13 11th, 2013–14 18th, 2015–16 19th, 2019–20 20th. **Biggest win:** 10-2 v Coventry (Div3S) Mar 15, 1930. **Biggest defeat:** 2-10 v Swindon (Southern Lge) Sep 5, 1908. **Highest League scorer in a season:** Ralph Hunt 31 (1955–56). **Most League goals in aggregate:** Johnny Gavin 122 (1945–54, 55–58). **Longest unbeaten League sequence:** 20 matches (1950). **Longest sequence without a League win:** 25 matches (1956–57). **Most capped player:** Wes Hoolahan (Republic of Ireland) 42

Goalkeepers

Gunn, Angus	6.5	Southampton	Norwich	22.01.96
Krul, Tim	6.3	Brighton	Den Haag, Hol	03.04.88
McGovern, Michael	6.3	Hamilton	Enniskillen	12.07.84

Defenders

Aarons, Max	5.10	Luton	Hammersmith	04.01.00
Byram, Sam	5.11	West Ham	Thurrock	16.09.93
Hanley, Grant	6.2	Newcastle	Dumfries	20.11.91
Zimmermann, Christoph	6.4	Borussia Dortmund	Dusseldorf, Ger	12.01.93

Midfielders

Cantwell, Todd	6.0	–	Dereham	27.02.98
Gilmour, Billy	5.6	Chelsea (loan)	Glasgow	11.06.01
Hernandez, Onel	5.8	Braunschweig	Moron, Cub	01.12.93
Dowell, Kieran	6.0	Everton	Ormskirk	10.10.97
Lees-Melou, Pierre	6.1	Nice	Langon, Fe	25.05.93
McLean, Kenny	6.0	Aberdeen	Rutherglen	08.01.92
Placheta, Przemyslaw	5.10	Slask Wroclaw	Lowicz, Pol	23.03.98
Sinani, Daniel	6.1	Dudelange	Belgrade, Serb	05.04.97
Sorensen, Jacob	6.0	Esbjerg	Esbjerg, Den	03.03.98
Thompson, Louis	5.11	Swindon	Bristol	19.12.94
Trybull, Tom	5.11	Den Haag	Berlin, Ger	09.03.93

Forwards

Drmic, Josip	6.0	Borussia M'gladbach	Freienbach, Switz	08.08.92
Hugill, Jordan	6.0	West Ham	Middlesbrough	04.06.92
Idah, Adam	6.3	College Corinthians	Cork, Ire	11.02.01
Pukki, Teemu	5.11	Brondby	Kotka, Fin	29.03.90

SOUTHAMPTON

Ground: St Mary's Stadium, Britannia Road, Southampton, SO14 5FP. **Telephone:** 0845 688 9448. **Club nickname:** Saints. **Capacity:** 32,384. **Colours:** Red and white. **Main sponsor:** Sportsbet. **Record transfer fee:** £20m to Liverpool for Danny Ings, Jul 2019. **Record fee received:** £75m from Liverpool for Virgil van Dijk, Jan 2018. **Record attendance:** The Dell: 31,044 v Manchester Utd (Div 1) Oct 8, 1969. St Mary's:. 32,363 v Coventry (Champ) Apr 28, 2012. **League Championship:** Runners-up 1983–84. **FA Cup:** Winners 1976. **League Cup:** Runners-up 1979, 2017. **European competitions:** Fairs Cup rd 3 1969–70; Cup-Winners' Cup rd 3 1976–77. **Finishing positions in Premier League:** 1992–93 18th, 1993–94 18th, 1994–5 10th, 1995–96 17th, 1996–97 16th, 1997–98 12th, 1998–99 17th, 1999–200 15th, 2000–01 10th, 2001–02 11th, 2002–03 8th, 2003–04 12th, 2004–05 20th, 2012–13 14th, 2013–14 8th, 2014–15 7th, 2015–16 6th, 2016–17 8 th, 2017–18 17th, 2018–19 16th, 2019–20 11th, 2020–21 15th. **Biggest win:** 8-0 v Northampton (Div 3S) Dec 24, 1921, v Sunderland (Prem Lge) Oct 18, 2014. **Biggest defeat:** 0-9 v Leicester (Prem Lge) Oct 25, 2019; 0-9 v Manchester Utd (Prem Lge) Feb 2, 2021. **Highest League scorer in a season:** Derek Reeves 39 (1959–60). **Most League goals in aggregate:** Mick Channon 185 (1966–82).

Longest unbeaten League sequence: 19 matches (1921). **Longest sequence without a League win:** 20 matches (1969). **Most capped player:** Steven Davis (Northern Ireland)) 59

Goalkeepers

Forster, Fraser	6.7	Celtic	Hexham	17.03.88
McCarthy, Alex	6.4	Crystal Palace	Guildford	03.12.89

Defenders

Bednarek, Jan	6.2	Lech Poznan	Slupca, Pol	12.04.96
Perraud, Romain	5.8	Brest	Toulouse, Fr	22.09.97
Stephens, Jack	6.1	Plymouth	Torpoint	27.01.94
Valery, Yan	5.11	Rennes	Champigny, Fr	22.02.99
Vestergaard, Jannik	6.6	Borussia M'gladbach	Copenhagen, Den	03.08.92
Walker-Peters, Kyle	5.8	Tottenham	Edmonton	13.04.97

Midfielders

Armstrong, Stuart	6.0	Celtic	Inverness	30.03.92
Diallo, Ibrahima	5.10	Brest	Tours, Fr	08.03.99
Djenepo, Moussa	5.10	Standard Liege	Bamako, Mali	15.06.98
Lemina, Mario	6.1	Juventus	Libreville, Gab	01.09.93
Redmond, Nathan	5.8	Norwich	Birmingham	06.03.94
Romeu, Oriol	6.0	Chelsea	Ulldecona, Sp	24.09.91
Salisu, Mohammed	6.3	Valladolid	Accra, Gh	17.04.99
Smallbone, Will	5.8	–	Basingstoke	21.02.00
Ward-Prowse, James	5.8	–	Portsmouth	01.11.94

Forwards

Adams, Che	5.10	Birmingham	Leicester	13.07.96
Ings, Danny	5.10	Liverpool	Winchester	16.03.92
Long, Shane	5.11	Hull	Gortnahoe, Ire	22.01.87
Nlundulu, Dan	6.1	Chelsea	France	05.02.99
Obafemi, Michael	5.7	–	Dublin, Ire	06.07.00
Tella, Nathan	5.9	Arsenal	Stevenage	05.07.99
Walcott, Theo	5.8	Everton	Newbury	16.03.89

TOTTENHAM HOTSPUR

Ground: Tottenham Hotspur Stadium, High Road, Tottenham N17 0BX. **Telephone:** 0344 499 5000. **Club nickname:** Spurs. **Capacity:** 62,062. **Colours:** White. **Main sponsor:** AIA. **Record transfer fee:** £54m to Lyon for Tanguy Ndombele, Jul 2019. **Record fee received:** £85.3m from Real Madrid for Gareth Bale, Aug 2013. **Record attendance:** White Hart Lane: 75,038 v Sunderland (FA Cup 6) Mar 5, 1938. Wembley: 85,512 v Bayer Leverkusen (Champs Lge group) Nov 2, 2016. Tottenham Hotspur Stadium: 60,043 v Ajax (Champs Lge semi-final) Apr 29, 2019. **League Championship:** Winners 1950–51, 1960–61. **FA Cup:** Winners 1901, 1921, 1961, 1962, 1967, 1981, 1982, 1991. **League Cup:** Winners 1971, 1973, 1999, 2008. **European competitions:** Winners Cup-Winners' Cup 1962–63; UEFA Cup 1971–72, 1983–84 **Finishing positions in Premier League:** 1992–93 8th, 1993–94 15th, 1994–95 7th, 1995–96 8th, 1996–97 10th, 1997–98 14th, 1998–99 11th, 1999–2000 10th, 2000–01 12th, 2001–02 9th, 2002–03 10th, 2003–04 14th, 2004–05 9th, 2005–06 5th, 2006–07 5th, 2007–08 11th, 2008–09 8th, 2009–10 4th, 2010–11 5th, 2011–12 4th, 2012–13 5th, 2013–14 6th, 2014–15 5th, 2015–16 3rd, 2016–17 2nd, 2017–18 3rd, 2018–19 4th, 2019–20 6th, 2020–21 7th
Biggest win: 9-0 v Bristol Rov (Div 2) Oct 22, 1977. Also: 13-2 v Crewe (FA Cup 4 replay) Feb 3, 1960. **Biggest defeat:** 0-7 v Liverpool (Div 1) Sep 2, 1979. Also: 0-8 v Cologne (Inter Toto Cup) Jul 22, 1995. **Highest League scorer in season:** Jimmy Greaves 37 (1962–63). **Most League goals in aggregate:** Jimmy Greaves 220 (1961–70). **Longest unbeaten League sequence:** 22 matches (1949). **Longest sequence without a League win:** 16 matches (1934–35). **Most capped player:** Pat Jennings (Northern Ireland) 74

Goalkeepers

Hart, Joe	6.3	Burnley	Shrewsbury	19.04.87
Lloris, Hugo	6.2	Lyon	Nice, Fr	26.12.86

Defenders

Alderweireld, Toby	6.2	Atletico Madrid	Antwerp, Bel	02.03.89
Aurier, Serge	5.9	Paris SG	Ouragahio, Iv C	24.12.92
Davies, Ben	5.6	Swansea	Neath	24.04.93
Dier, Eric	6.2	Sporting Lisbon	Cheltenham	15.01.94
Doherty, Matt	5.11	Wolves	Dublin, Ire	16.01.92
Reguilon, Sergio	5.10	Real Madrid	Madrid, Sp	16.12.96
Rodon, Joe	6.4	Swansea	Llangyfelach	22.10.97
Sanchez, Davinson	6.2	Ajax	Caloto, Col	12.06.96
Tanganga, Japhet	6.1	–	Hackney	31.03.99

Midfielders

Alli, Dele	6.1	MK Dons	Milton Keynes	11.04.96
Hojbjerg, Pierre-Emile	6.1	Soutyhampton	Copenhagen, Den	05.08.95
Lamela, Erik	6.0	Roma	Buenos Aires, Arg	04.03.92
Lo Celso, Giovani	5.10	Real Betis	Rosario, Arg	09.04.96
Ndombele, Tanguy	5.11	Lyon	Longjumeau, Fr	28.12.96
Sessegnon, Ryan	5.10	Fulham	Roehampton	18.05.00
Sissoko, Moussa	6.2	Newcastle	Le Blanc-Mesnil, Fr	16.08.89
Winks, Harry	5.10	–	Hemel Hempstead	02.02.96

Forwards

Bergwijn, Steven	5.10	PSV Eiondhoven	Amsterdam, Hol	08.10.97
Kane, Harry	6.2	–	Walthamstow	28.07.93
Lucas Moura	5.8	Paris SG	Sao Paulo, Br	13.08.92
Son Heung-Min	6.1	Bayer Leverkusen	Chuncheon, S Kor	08.07.92

WATFORD

Ground: Vicarage Road Stadium, Vicarage Road, Watford WD18 OER. **Telephone:** 01923 496000. **Club nickname:** Hornets. **Capacity:** 21,000. **Colours:** Yellow and black. **Main sponsor:** Sportsbet. **Record transfer fee:** £31m to Rennes for Ismaila Sarr, Aug 2019. **Record fee received:** £40m from Everton for Richarlsion, July 2018. **Record attendance:** 34,099 v Manchester Utd (FA Cup 4 rep) Feb 3, 1969. **League Championship:** Runners-up 1982–83. **FA Cup:** Runners-up 1984. **League Cup:** Semi-finals 1979, 2005. **European competitions:** UEFA Cup rd 3 1983–84. **Finishing positions in Premier League:** 1999–2000 20th, 2006–07 20th, 2015–16 13th, 2016–17 17th, 2017–18 14th, 2018–19 11th, 2019–20 19th. **Biggest win:** 8-0 v Sunderland (Div 1) Sep 25, 1982. Also: 10-1 v Lowestoft (FA Cup 1) Nov 27, 1926. **Biggest defeat:** 0-10 v Wolves (FA Cup 1 replay) Jan 24, 1912. **Highest League scorer in a season:** Cliff Holton 42 (1959–60). **Most League goals in aggregate:** Luther Blissett 148 (1976–83, 1984–88, 1991–92). **Longest unbeaten League sequence:** 22 matches (1996–97). **Longest sequence without a League win:** 19 matches (1971–72). **Most capped players:** John Barnes (England) 31, Kenny Jackett (Wales) 31.

Goalkeepers

Bachmann, Daniel	6.3	Stoke	Vienna, Aut	09.07.94
Elliot, Rob	6.3	Newcastle	Chatham	30.04.86
Foster, Ben	6.2	WBA	Leamington	03.04.83

Defenders

Cathcart, Craig	6.2	Blackpool	Belfast	06.02.89
Kabasele, Christian	6.1	Genk	Lubumbashi, DR Cong	24.01.91
Kiko	5.9	Alaves	Sanet Negrals, Sp	02.02.91
Masina, Adam	6.2	Bologna	Khouribga, Mor	02.01.94
Navarro, Marc	6.2	Espanyol	Barcelona, Sp	02.07.95

Ngakia, Jeremy	6.1	Wst Ham	Lewisham	07.09.00
Rose, Danny	5.8	Tottenham	Doncaster	02.07.90
Sierralta, Francisco	6.4	Udinese	Las Condes Chil	06.05.97
Troost-Ekong, William	6.3	Udinese	Haarlem, Hol	01.09.93
Midfielders				
Chalobah, Nathaniel	6.1	Chelsea	Freetown, SLeone	12.12.94
Cleverley, Tom	5.10	Everton	Basingstoke	12.08.89
Dele-Bashiru, Tom	6.0	Manchester City	Manchester	17.09.99
Etebo, Peter	5.9	Stoke (loan)	Warri, Nig	09.11.95
Gosling, Dan	5.10	Bournemouth	Brixham	02.02.90
Hughes, Will	6.1	Derby	Weybridge	07.04.95
Sema, Ken	5.10	Ostersunds	Norrkoping, Swe	30.09.93
Zinckernagel, Philip	–	Bodo/Glint	Copenhagen, Den	16.12.94
Forwards				
Baah, Kwadwo	6.0	Rochdale	Stuttgart	27.01.03
Deeney, Troy	6.0	Walsall	Birmingham	29.06.88
Dennis, Emmanuel	5.10	Club Bruges	Yola, Nig	15.11.97
Fletcher, Ashley	6.1	Middlesbrough	Keighler	02.10.95
Gray, Andre	5.10	Burnley	Wolverhampton	26.06.91
Joao Pedro	6.0	Fluminense	Ribeirao Preto, Br	26.09.01
King, Joshua	6.2	Everton	Oslo, Nor	15.01.92
Mebude, Dapo	5.9	Rangers	London	29.07.01
Perica, Stipe	6.4	Udinese	Skabrnja, Cro	07.07.95
Sarr, Ismaila	6.1	Rennes	Saint-Louis, Sen	25.02.98
Success, Isaac	6.0	Granada	Benin City, Nig	07.01.96

WEST HAM UNITED

Ground: London Stadium, Olympic Park, London E20 2ST. **Telephone:** 0208 548 2748. **Club nickname:** Hammers. **Capacity:** 60,000. **Colours:** Claret and blue. **Main sponsor:** Betway. **Record transfer fee:** £45m to Eintracht Frankfurt for Sebastien Haller, Jul 2019. **Record fee received:** £25m from Marseille for Dimitri Payet, Jan 2017. **Record attendance:** Upton Park: 43,322 v Tottenham (Div 1) Oct 17, 1970. London Stadium: 59.988 v Everton (Prem Lge) Mar 30, 2019. **League Championship:** 3rd 1985–86. **FA Cup:** Winners 1964, 1975, 1980. **League Cup:** Runners-up 1966, 1981. **European competitions:** Winners Cup-Winners' Cup 1964–65. **Finishing positions in Premier League:** 1993–94 13th, 1994–95 14th, 1995–96 10th, 1996–97 14th, 1997–98 8th, 1998–99 5th, 1999–2000 9th, 2000–01 15th, 2001–02 7th, 2002–03 18th, 2005–06 9th, 2006–07 15th, 2007–08 10th, 2008–09: 9th, 2009–10 17th, 2010–11 20th, 2012–13 10th, 2013–14 13th, 2014–15 12th, 2015–16 7th, 2016–17 11th, 2017–18 13th, 2018–19 10th, 2019–20 16th, 2020–21 6th
Biggest win: 8-0 v Rotherham (Div 2) Mar 8, 1958, v Sunderland (Div 1) Oct 19, 1968. Also: 10-0 v Bury (League Cup) Oct 25, 1983. **Biggest defeat:** 0-7 v Barnsley (Div 2) Sep 1, 1919, v Everton (Div 1) Oct 22, 1927, v Sheffield Wed (Div 1) Nov 28, 1959. **Highest League scorer in a season:** Vic Watson 42 (1929–30). **Most League goals in aggregate:** Vic Watson 298 (1920–35). **Longest unbeaten League sequence:** 27 matches (1980–81). **Longest sequence without a League win:** 17 matches (1976). **Most capped player:** Bobby Moore (England) 108.

Goalkeepers

Fabianski, Lukasz	6.3	Swansea	Kostrzyn, Pol	18.04.85
Martin, David	6.2	Millwall	Romford	22.01.86
Randolph, Darren	6.1	Middlesbrough	Bray, Ire	12.05.87
Defenders				
Coufal, Vladimir	5.10	Slavia Prague	Ostrava, Cz	22.08.92
Cresswell, Aaron	5.7	Ipswich	Liverpool	15.12.89
Dawson, Craig	6.2	Watford	Rochdale	06.05.90

Diop, Issa	6.4	Toulouse	Toulouse	09.01.97
Fredericks, Ryan	5.8	Fulham	Potters Bar	10.10.92
Johnson, Ben	5.9	–	Waltham Forest	24.01.00
Masuaku, Arthur	5.11	Olympiacos	Lille, Fr	07.11.93
Ogbonna, Angelo	6.3	Juventus	Cassino, It	23.05.88
Midfielders				
Fornals, Pablo	5.10	Villarreal	Castellon, Sp	22.02.96
Lanzini, Manuel	5.6	Al Jazira	Ituzaingo, Arg	15.02.93
Noble, Mark	5.11	–	West Ham	08.05.87
Rice, Declan	6.1	–	London	14.01.99
Snodgrass, Robert	6.0	Hull	Glasgow	07.09.87
Soucek, Tomas	6.3	Slavia Prague	Havlicku Brod, Cz	27.02.95
Forwards				
Antonio, Michail	5.11	Nottm Forest	Wandsworth	28.03.90
Benrahma, Said	5.8	Brentford	Temouchent, Alg	10.08.95
Bowen, Jarrod	5.10	Hull	Leominster	20.12.96
Yarmolenko, Andriy	6.2	Borussia Dortmund	St Petersburg, Rus	23.10.89

WOLVERHAMPTON WANDERERS

Ground: Molineux Stadium, Waterloo Road, Wolverhampton WV1 4QR. **Telephone:** 0871 222 1877. **Club nickname:** Wolves. **Capacity:** 32,050. **Colours:** Yellow and black. **Main sponsor:** ManBetX. **Record attendance:** 61,315 v Liverpool (FA Cup 5) Feb 11, 1939. **Record transfer fee:** £35.6m to Porto for Fabio Silva, Sep 2020. **Record fee received:** £41m from Liverpool for Diogo Jota, Sep 2020. **Record attendance:** 61,315 v Liverpool (FA Cup 5), Feb 11, 1935. **League Championship:** Winners 1953–54, 1957–58, 1958–59. **FA Cup:** Winners 1893, 1908, 1949, 1960. **League Cup:** Winners 1974, 1980. **European competitions:** UEFA Cup runners-up 1971–72. **Finishing positions in Premier League:** 2003–04 20th, 2009–10 15th, 2003–04 20th, 2011–12 20th, 2018–19 7th, 2019–20 7th, 2020–21 13th. **Biggest win:** 10-1 v Leicester (Div 2) Apr 15, 1938. Also: 14-0 v Crosswell's Brewery (FA Cup 2) Nov 13, 1886. **Biggest defeat:** 1-10 v Newton Heath (Div 1) Oct 15, 1892. **Highest League scorer in a season:** Dennis Westcott 38 (1946–47). **Most League goals in aggregate:** Steve Bull 250 (1986–90). **Longest unbeaten League sequence:** 20 matches (1923–24). **Longest sequence without a League win:** 19 matches (1984–85). **Most capped player:** Billy Wright (England) 105.

Goalkeepers				
Ruddy, John	6.4	Norwich	St Ives, Camb	24.10.86
Defenders				
Ait-Nouri, Rayan	5.10	Angers	Montreuil, Fr	06.06.01
Boly, Willy	6.2	Porto	Melun, Fr	03.02.91
Coady, Conor	6.1	Huddersfield	St Helens	25.02.93
Hoever, Ki-Jana	5.11	Liverpool	Amsterdam, Hol	18.01.02
Jonny	5.9	Atletico Madrid	Vigo, Sp	03.03.94
Kilman, Max	5.10	Maidenhead	Kensington	23.05.97
Marcal	5.10	Lyon	Sao Paulo, Br	19.02.89
Nelson Semedo	5.10	Barcelona	Lisbon, Por	16.11.93
Ruben Vinagre	5.9	Monaco	Charneca, Por	09.04.99
Midfielders				
Dendoncker, Leander	6.2	Anderlecht	Passendale, Bel	15.04.95
Gibbs-White, Morgan	5.11	–	Stafford	27.01.00
Joao Moutinho	5.7	Monaco	Portimao, Por	08.09.86
Ruben Neves	6.0	Porto	Mozelos, Por	13.03.97
Saiss, Romain	6.3	Angers	Bourg-de-Peage, Fr	26.03.90
Forwards				
Cutrone, Patrick	6.0	AC Milan	Como, It	03.01.98

Fabio Silva	6.1	Porto	Porto, Por	19.07.02
Pedro Neto	5.8	Braga	Viana do Castelo, Por	09.03.00
Raul Jimenez	6.2	Benfica	Tepeji del Rio, Mex	05.05.91
Traore, Adama	5.10	Middlesbrough	L'Hospitalet, Sp	25.01.96
Trincao, Francisco	6.0	Barcelona (loan)	Viana do Castelo, Por	29.12.99

ENGLISH FOOTBALL LEAGUE

(At time of going to press)

CHAMPIONSHIP

BARNSLEY

Ground: Oakwell Stadium, Barnsley S71 1ET. **Telephone:** 01226 211211. **Club nickname:** Tykes. **Colours:** Red and white. **Capacity:** 23,287. **Record attendance:** 40,255 v Stoke (FA Cup 5) Feb 15, 1936

Goalkeepers
| Collins, Brad | 6.0 | Chelsea | Southampton | 18.02.97 |
| Walton, Jack | 6.1 | – | Bury | 23.04.98 |

Defenders
Andersen, Mads	6.4	Horsens	Albertsund, Den	27.12.97
Brittain, Callum	5.10	MK Dons	Bedford	12.03.98
Halme, Aapo	6.5	Leeds	Helsinki, Fin	22.05.98
Helik, Michal	6.3	Cracovia	Chorzow, Pol	09.09.95
Kitching, Liam	6.1	Forest Green	Harrogate	01.10.99
Moon, Jasper	6.1	Leicester	Coventry	24.11.00
Oduor, Clarke	5.10	Leeds	Siaya, Ken	25.06.99
Sibbick, Toby	6.0	AFC Wimbledon	Isleworth	23.05.99
Williams, Jordan	5.10	Huddersfield	Huddersfield	22.10.99

Midfielders
Frieser, Dominik	5.9	LASK	Graz, Aut	09.09.93
Kane, Herbie	5.8	Liverpool	Bristol	23.11.98
Palmer, Romal	5.11	Manchester City	Manchester	30.09.98
Ritzmaier, Marcel	5.10	Wolfsberger	Knittelfeld, Aut	22.04.93
Styles, Callum	5.6	Burnley	Bury	28.03.00

Forwards
Adeboyejo, Victor	5.11	Leyton Orient	Ibadan, Nig	12.01.98
Chaplin, Conor	5.10	Coventry	Worthing	16.02.97
Cole, Devante	6.1	Motherwell	Alderley Edge	10.05.95
Miller, George	5.10	Middlesbrough	Bolton	11.08.98
Morris, Carlton	6.2	Norwich	Cambridge	16.12.95
Woodrow, Cauley	6.1	Fulham	Hemel Hempstead	02.12.94

BIRMINGHAM CITY

Ground: St Andrew's, Birmingham B9 4NH. **Telephone:** 0844 557 1875. **Club nickname:** Blues. **Colours:** Blue and white. **Capacity:** 29,409. **Record attendance:** 66,844 v Everton (FA Cup 5) Feb 11, 1939

Goalkeepers
Etheridge, Neil	6.3	Cardiff	Enfield	07.02.90
Prieto, Andres	6.4	Espanyol	Alicante, Sp	17.10.93
Trueman, Connal	6.1	–	Birmingham	26.03.96

Defenders

Castillo, Juan	5.9	Chelsea (loan)	Amsterdam, Hol	13.01.00
Colin, Maxime	5.11	Brentford	Arras, Fr	15.11.91
Dean, Harlee	5.10	Brentford	Basingstoke	26.07.91
Friend, George	6.0	Middlesbrough	Barnstaple	19.10.87
Graham, Jordan	6.0	Gillingham	Coventry	05.03.95
Pedersen. Kristian	6.2	Union Berlin	Ringsted, Den	04.08.94
Roberts, Marc	6.0	Barnsley	Wakefield	26.07.90
Midfielders				
Boyd-Munce Caolan	5.10	Glentoran	Belfast	26.01.00
Chong, Tahith	6.1	Manchester Utd (loan)	Willemstad, Hol	04.12.99
Clayton, Adam	5.9	Middlesbrough	Manchester	14.01.89
Gardner, Gary	6.2	Aston Villa	Solihull	29.06.92
Halilovic, Alen	5.7	Dinamo Zagreb	Dubrovnik, Cro	18.06.96
McGree, Riley	5.10	Charlotte (loan)	Gawler, Aus	02.11.98
Sanchez, Ivan	5.9	Elche	Campillo, Sp	23.09.92
Sunjic, Ivan	6.0	Dinamo Zagreb	Zenica, Bos	09.10.96
Woods, Ryan	5.8	Stoke	Norton Canes	13.12.93
Forwards				
Aneke, Chuks	6.3	Charlton	Newham	03.07.93
Bela, Jeremy	5.9	Albacete	08.04.93Melun, Fr	
Cosgrove, Sam	6.2	Aberdeen	Beverley	02.12.96
Hogan, Scott	5.1	Aston Villa	Salford	13.04.92
Jutkiewicz, Lukas	6.1	Burnley	Southampton	20.03.89
Leko, Jonathan	6.0	WBA	Kinshasa, DR Cong	24.04.99

BLACKBURN ROVERS

Ground: Ewood Park, Blackburn BB2 4JF. **Telephone:** 0871 702 1875. **Club nickname:** Rovers. **Colours:** Blue and white. **Capacity:** 31,367. **Record attendance:** 62,522 v Bolton (FA Cup 6) Mar 2, 1929

Goalkeepers				
Kaminski, Thomas	6.3	Gent	Dendermonde, Bel	23.10.92
Pears, Aynsley	6.1	Middlesbrough	Durham	23.04.98
Defenders				
Ayala, Daniel	6.3	Middlesbrough	El Saucejo, Sp	07.11.90
Lenihan, Darragh	5.10	Belvedere	Dunboyne, Ire	16.03.94
Nyambe, Ryan	6.0	–	Katima, Nam	04.12.97
Wharton, Scott	–	–	Blackburn	03.10.97
Midfielders				
Bennett, Elliott	5.10	Norwich	Telford	18.12.88
Buckley, John	5.8	–	Manchester	13.10.99
Dack, Bradley	5.8	Gillingham	Greenwich	31.12.93
Davenport, Jacob	5.10	Manchester City		28.12.98
Dolan, Tyrhys	5.8	Preston	Manchester	28.12.01
Johnson, Bradley	5.10	Derby	Hackney	28.04.87
Rankin-Costello, Joe	6.0	Manchester Utd	–	26.07.99
Rothwell, Joe	6.1	Oxford	Manchester	11.01.95
Travis, Lewis	6.0	Liverpool	Whiston	16.10.97
Forwards				
Armstrong, Adam	5.8	Newcastle	Newcastle	10.02.97
Brereton, Ben	6.0	Nottm Forest	Blythe Bridge	18.04.99
Gallagher, Sam	6.4	Southampton	Crediton	15.09.95

BLACKPOOL

Ground: Bloomfield Road, Blackpool FY1 6JJ. Telephone: 0871 622 1953. Club nickname: Seasiders. Colours: Tangerine and white. Capacity: 17,338. Record attendance: 38,098 v Wolves (Div 1) Sep 17, 1955

Goalkeepers

Maxwell, Chris	6.1	Preston	St Asaph	30.07.90
Grimshaw, Daniel	6.1	Manchester City	Salford	16.01.98

Defenders

Casey, Oliver	6.2	Leeds	Leeds	14.10.00
Connolly, Callum	6.1	Everton	Liverpool	23.09.97
Ekpiteta, Marvin	6.4	Leyton Orient	Enfield	26.08.95
Garbutt, Luke	5.11	Everton	Harrogate	21.05.93
Gretarsson, Daniel	6.1	Aalesunds	Keflavik, Ice	02.10.95
Howe, Teddy	5.11	Reading	Oxford	09.10.98
Husband, James	5.11	Norwich	Leeds	03.01.94
Mitchell, Demetri	5.11	Manchester Utd	Manchester	11.01.97
Thorniley, Jordan	5.11	Sheffield Wed	Warrington	24.11.96

Midfielders

Bowler, Josh	5.9	Everton	Chertsey	05.03.99
Carey, Sonny	6.1	King's Lynn	Norwich	20.01.01
Dougall, Kenny	6.0	Barnsley	Brisbane, Aus	07.05.93
Hamilton CJ	5.7	Mansfield	Harrow	23.03.95
Stewart, Kevin	5.7	Hull	Enfield	07.09.93
Virtue, Matty	5.10	Liverpool	Epsom	02.05.97
Ward, Grant	5.10	Ipswich	Lewisham	05.12.94

Forwards

Anderson, Keshi	5.10	Swindon	Luton	06.04.95
Madine, Gary	6.3	Cardiff	Gateshead	24.08.90
Lavery, Shayne	5.11	Linfield	Aghagallon	08.12.98
Lubula, Bez	5.10	Crawley	DR Congo	08.01.98
Nuttall, Joe	6.0	Blackburn	Bury	27.11.97
Sarkic, Oliver	6.0	Burton	Grimsby	23.07.97
Yates, Jerry	5.10	Rotherham	Doncaster	10.11.96

BOURNEMOUTH

Ground: Vitality Stadium, Dean Court, Bournemouth BH7 7AF. Telephone: 0344 576 1910. Club nickname: Cherries. Colours: Red and black. Capacity: 11,329. Record attendance: 28,799 v Manchester Utd (FA Cup 6) Mar 2, 1957

Goalkeepers

Begovic, Asmir	6.5	Chelsea	Trebinje, Bos	20.06.87
Travers, Mark	6.3	Shamropck Rov	Maynooth, Ire	18.05.99

Defenders

Cook, Steve	6.1	Brighton	Hastings	19.04.91
Kelly, Lloyd	5.10	Bristol City	Bristol	01.10.98
Mepham, Chris	6.3	Brentford	Hammersmith	05.11.97
Rico, Diego	6.0	Leganes	Burgos, Sp	23.02.93
Smith, Adam	5.11	Tottenham	Leystonstone	29.04.91
Stacey, Jack	5.11	Luton	Bracknell	06.04.96
Zemura, Jordan	5.9	Charlton	Lambeth	14.11.99

Midfielders

Billing, Philip	6.4	Huddersfield	Esbjerg, Den	11.06.96

Brooks, David	5.8	Sheffield Utd	Warrington	08.07.97
Cook, Lewis	5.9	Leeds	Leeds	03.02.97
Danjuma, Arnaut	5.10	Club Bruges	Lagos, Nig	31.01.97
Kilkenny, Gavin	5.7	–	Dublin, Ire	01.02.00
Lerma, Jefferson	5.10	Levante	Cerrito, Col	25.10.94
Marcondes, Emiliano	6.0	Brentford	Hvidovre, Den	09.03.95
Pearson, Ben	5.5	Preston	Oldham	04.01.95
Stanislas, Junior	6.0	Burnley	Eltham	26.11.89
Forwards				
Anthony, Jaidon	6.0	Arsenal	Hackney	01.12.99
Solanke, Dominic	6.1	Liverpool	Reading	14.09.97
Surridge, Sam	6.3	–	Slough	28.07.98

BRISTOL CITY

Ground: Ashton Gate, Bristol BS3 2EJ. **Telephone:** 0871 222 6666. **Club nickname:** Robins. **Colours:** Red and white. **Capacity:** 27,000. **Record attendance:** 43,335 v Preston (FA Cup 5) Feb 16, 1935

Goalkeepers				
Bentley, Daniel	6.2	Brentford	Basildon	13.07.93
O'Leary, Max	6.1	–	Bath	10.10.96
Defenders				
Atkinson, Rob	6.4	Oxford	Chesterfield	13.07.98
Baker, Nathan	6.2	Aston Villa	Worcester	23.04.91
Cundy, Robbie	6.2	Bath	Oxford	30.05.97
Dasilva, Jay	5.7	Chelsea	Luton	22.04.98
Kalas, Tomas	6.0	Chelsea	Olomouc, Cz	15.05.93
Moore, Taylor	6.1	Lens	Walthamstow	12.05.97
Simpson, Danny	5.9	Huddersfield	Eccles	04.01.87
Vyner, Zak	6.2	–	London	14.05.97
Midfielders				
James, Matty	5.11	Leicester	Bacup	22.07.91
King, Andy	6.0	Leuven	Barnstaple	29.10.88
Massengo, Han-Noah	5.9	Monaco	Villepinte, Fr	07.07.01
Nagy, Adam	5.10	Bologna	Budapest, Hun	17.06.95
O'Dowda, Callum	5.11	Oxford	Oxford	23.04.95
Palmer, Kasey	5.8	Chelsea	Lewisham	09.11.96
Semenyo, Antoine	5.10	–	Chelsea	07.01.00
Williams, Joe	5.10	Wigan	Liverpool	08.12.96
Forwards				
Martin, Chris	5.10	Derby	Beccles	04.11.88
Weimann, Andreas	6.2	Derby	Vienna, Aut	05.08.91
Wells, Nahki	5.8	Burnley	Hamilton, Berm	01.06.90

CARDIFF CITY

Ground: Cardiff City Stadium, Leckwith Road, Cardiff CF11 8AZ. **Telephone:**0845 365 1115. **Club nickname:** Bluebirds. **Colours:** Blue and white. **Capacity:** 33,280. **Record attendance:** Ninian Park: 62,634 Wales v England, Oct 17, 1959; Club: 57,893 v Arsenal (Div 1) Apr 22, 1953, Cardiff City Stadium: 33,280 (Wales v Belgium) Jun 12, 2015. Club: 33,082 v Liverpool (Prem Lge) Apr 21, 2019

| **Goalkeepers** | | | | |
| Phillips, Dillon | 6.2 | Charlton | Hornchurch | 11.06.95 |

Smithies, Alex	6.3	QPR	Huddersfield	05.03.90
Defenders				
Bagan, Joel	6.3	Southampton	Basingstoke	03.09.01
Flint, Aden	6.2	Middlesbrough	Pinxton	11.07.89
McGuinness, Mark	6.4	Arsenal	Slough	05.01.01
Morrison, Sean	6.1	Reading	Plymouth	08.01.91
Nelson, Curtis	6.0	Oxford	Newcastle-under-Lyme	21.05.93
Ng, Perry	5.11	Crewe	Liverpool	27.04.96
Midfielders				
Bacuna, Leandro	6.2	Reading	Groningen, Hol	21.08.91
Colwill, Rubin	5.8	–	Neath	27.04.02
Giles, Ryan	6.0	Wolves (loan)	Telford	26.01.00
Harris, Mark	6.0	–	Swansea	29.12.98
Murphy, Josh	5.9	Norwich	Wembley	24.02.95
Pack, Marlon	6.2	Bristol City	Portsmouth	25.03.91
Ralls, Joe	6.0	–	Aldershot	13.10.93
Vaulks, Will	5.11	Rotherham	Wirral	13.09.93
Whyte, Gavin	5.8	Oxford	Belfast	31.01.96
Wintle, Ryan	5.6	Crewe	Newcastle-under-Lyme	13.06.97
Forwards				
Moore, Keiffer	6.45	Wigan	Torquay	08.08.92
Tomlin, Lee	5.11	Bristol City	Leicester	12.01.89
Vassell, Isaac	5.8	Birmingham	Newquay	09.09.93

COVENTRY CITY

Ground: Coventry Building Society Arena, Phoenix Way, Coventry CV6 6GE. **Telephone:** 02476 991987. **Club nickname:** Sky Blues. **Colours:** Sky blue. **Capacity:** 32,500. **Record attendance:** Highfield Road: 51,455 v Wolves (Div 2) Apr 29, 1967. Coventry Building Society Arena: 31,407 v Chelsea (FA Cup 6), Mar 7, 2009.

Goalkeepers				
Moore, Simon	6.3	Sheffield Utd	Sandown IOW	19.05.90
Wilson, Ben	6.1	Bradford	Stanley	09.08.92
Defenders				
Dabo, Fankaty	5.11	Chelsea	Southwark	11.10.95
Dacosta, Julien	6.0	Niort	Marseille	29.05.96
Drysdale, Declan	6.2	Tranmere	Birkenhead	14.11.99
Hyam, Dominic	6.2	Reading	Dundee	20.12.95
Mason, Brandon	5.9	Watford	Westminster	30.09.97
McFadzean, Kyle	6.1	Burton	Sheffield	28.02.87
Pask, Josh	6.2	West Ham	Waltham Forest	01.11.97
Rose, Michael	5.11	Ayr	Aberdeen	11.10.95
Midfielders				
Allen, Jamie	5.11	Burton	Rochdale	29.01.95
Eccles, Josh	6.0	–	Coventry	02.04.00
Hamer, Gustavo	5.7	Zwolle	Itajai, Br	24.06.97
Hilssner, Marcel	6.0	Paderborn	Leipzig, Ger	30.01.96
Jobello, Wesley	5.10	Ajaccio	Gennebilliers, Mart	23.01.94
Kelly, Liam	5.10	Leyton Orient	Milton Keynes	10.02.90
O'Hare, Callum	5.9	–	Solihull	01.05.98
Sheaf, Ben	6.1	Arsenal	Dartford	05.02.98
Shipley, Jordan	6.0	–	Leamington Spa	26.09.97
Forwards				
Enobakhare, Bright	5.11	East Bengal	Benin City, Nig	08.02.98

Godden, Matt	6.1	Peterborough	Canterbury	29.07.91
Gyokeres, Viktor	6.2	Brighton	Stockholm, Swe	04.06.98
Kastaneer, Gervane	6.2	Breda	Rotterdam, Hol	09.06.96
Tavares, Fabio	5.11	Rochdale	Porto, Por	22.01.01
Waghorn, Martyn	5.10	Derby	South Shields	23.01.93
Walker, Tyler	5.11	Nottm Forest	Nottingham	17.10.96

DERBY COUNTY

Ground: Pride Park, Derby DE24 8XL. **Telephone:** 0871 472 1884. **Club nickname:** Rams.
Colours: White and black. **Capacity:** 33,597. **Record attendance:** Baseball Ground: 41,826 v Tottenham (Div 1) Sep 20, 1969; Pride Park: 33,597 (England v Mexico) May 25, 2011; Club: 33,475 v Rangers (Ted McMinn testimonial) May 1, 2006

Goalkeepers
| Marshall, David | 6.3 | Wigan | Glasgow | 05.03.85 |
| Roos, Kelle | 6.5 | Nuneaton | Rijkevoort, Hol | 31.05.92 |

Defenders
Bielik, Krystian	6.2	Arsenal	Konin, Pol	04.01.98
Buchanan, Lee	5.9	–	Mansfield	07.03.01
Byrne, Nathan	5.11	Wigan	St Albans	05.06.92
Davies, Curtis	6.2	Hull	Waltham Forest	15.03.85
Forsyth, Craig	6.0	Watford	Carnoustie	24.02.89
Wisdom, Andre	6.1	Liverpool	Leeds	09.05.93

Midfielders
Bird, Max	6.0	–	Burton	08.09.00
Brown, Jordan	5.11	–	Stoke	21.06.01
Jozwiak, Kamil	5.9	Lech Poznan	Miedzyrzecz, Pol	22.04.98
Knight, Jason	5.9	Cabinteely	Dublin, Ire	13.02.01
Lawrence, Tom	5.10	Leicester	Wrexham	13.01.94
Shinnie, Graeme	5.9	Aberdeen	Aberdeen	04.08.91
Sibley, Louie	5.11	–	Birmingham	13.09.01

Forwards
| Kazim-Richards, Colin | 6.1 | Panucha | Leytonstone | 26.08.86 |

FULHAM

Ground: Craven Cottage, Stevenage Road, Lndon SW6 6HH. **Telephone:** 0870 442 1222.
Club nickname: Cottagers. **Colours:** White and black. **Capacity:** 19,359 (reduced). **Record attendance:** 49,335 v Millwall (Div 2) Oct 8, 1938

Goalkeepers
| Rodak, Marek | 6.5 | – | Kosice, Slovak | 13.2.96 |

Defenders
Adarabioyo, Tosin	6.5	Manchester City	Manchester	24.09.97
Bryan, Joe	5.7	Bristol City	Bristol	17.09.93
Christie, Cyrus	6.2	Middlesbrough	Coventry	30.09.92
Hector, Michael	6.4	Chelsea	East Ham	19.07.92
Kongolo, Terence	6.2	Huddersfield	Fribourg, Switz	14.02.94
Le Marchand, Maxime	5.11	Nice	Saint-Malo, Fr	11.10.89
Mawson, Alfie	6.2	Swansea	Hillingdon	19.01.94
Odoi, Denis	5.10	Lokeren	Leuven, Bel	27.05.88
Ream, Tim	6.1	Bolton	St Louis, US	05.10.87
Robinson, Antonee	6.0	Wigan	Milton Keynes	08.08.97
Tete, Kenny	5.11	Lyon	Amsterdam, Hol	09.10.95

Midfielders

Cairney, Tom	6.0	Blackburn	Nottingham	20.01.91
Fabio Carvalho	5.8	–	Torres Vedras, Por	30.08.02
Ivan Cavaleiro	5.9	Wolves (loan)	Vila Franca de Xira, Por	18.10.93
Kebano, Neeskens	5.11	Genk	Montereau, Fr	10.03.92
Onomah, Josh	5.11	Tottenham	Enfield	27.04.97
Reed, Harrison	5.11	Southampton	Worthing	27.01.95
Zambo Anguissa, Andre-Frank	6.1	Marseille	Yaounde, Cam	16.11.95

Forwards

Decordova-Reid, Bobby	5.8	Carfdiff	Bristol	02.02.93
Kamara, Aboubakar	5.10	Amiens	Gonesse, Fr	07.03.95
Mitrovic, Aleksandar	6.3	Newcastle	Smederevo, Serb	16.09.94

HUDDERSFIELD TOWN

Ground: John Smith's Stadium, Huddersfield HD1 6PX. **Telephone:**0870 444 4677. **Club nickname:** Terriers. **Colours:** Blue and white. **Capacity:** 24,121. **Record attendance:** Leeds Road: 67,037 v Arsenal (FA Cup 6) Feb 27, 1932; John Smith's Stadium: 24,426 v Manchester Utd (Prem Lge), Oct 21, 2017

Goalkeepers

Nicholls, Lee	6.3	MK Dons	Huyton	05.10.92
Schofield, Ryan	6.3	–	Huddersfield	11.12.99

Defenders

Colwill, Levi	6.2	Chelsea (loan)	Southampton	26.02.03
Edmonds-Green, Rarmani	6.0	–	Peckham	14.04.00
Pearson, Matty	6.3	Luton	Keighley	03.08.93
Pipa	5.9	Espanyol	Esparreguera, Sp	26.01.98
Sarr, Naby	6.5	Charlton	Marseille, Fr	13.08.93
Toffolo, Harry	6.0	Lincoln	Welwyn Garden City	19.08.95
Turton, Ollie	5.11	Blackpool	Manchester	06.12.92

Midfielders

Aarons, Rolando	5.10	Newcastle	Kingston, Jam	16.11.95
Bacuna, Juninho	5.10	Groningen	Groningen, Hol	07.08.97
Brown, Reece	5.9	Forest Green	Derby	03.03.96
High, Scott	5.10	-	Dewsbury	15.02.01
Hogg, Jonathan	5.7	Watford	Middlesbrough	06.12.88
Holmes, Duane	5.6	Derby	Columbus, US	06.11.94
O'Brien, Lewis	5.8	–	Colchester	14.10.98
Rowe, Aaron	5.11	–	Hackney	07.09.00
Ruffels, Josh	5.10	Oxford	Oxford	23.10.93
Thomas, Sorba	6.1	Boreham Wood	Newham	25.01.99
Vallejo, Alex	6.3	Fuenlabrada	Vitoria-Gasteiz, Sp	16.01.92

Forwards

Campbell, Fraizer	5.8	Hull	Huddersfield	13.09.87
Koroma, Josh	5.10	Leyton Orient	Southwark	09.11.98
Mbenza, Isaac	6.2	Montpellier	Saint-Dennis, Fr	08.03.96
Rhodes, Jordan	6.1	Sheff Wed	Oldham	05.02.90

HULL CITY

Ground: KCOM Stadium, Anlaby Road, Hull, HU3 6HU. **Telephone:** 01482 504 600. **Club nickname:** Tigers. **Capacity:** 25,586. **Colours:** Amber and black. **Record attendance:** Boothferry Park: 55,019 v Manchester Utd (FA Cup 6) Feb 26, 1949. KC Stadium: 25,030 v Liverpool (Prem Lge) May 9, 2010. Also: 25,280 (England U21 v Holland) Feb 17, 2004

Goalkeepers

Baxter, Nathan	6.3	Chelsea (loan)	Westminster	08.11.98
Ingram, Matt	6.3	QPR	High Wycombe	18.12.93

Defenders

Coyle, Lewie	5.8	Fleetwood	Hull	15.10.95
Elder, Callum	5.11	Leicester	Sydney, Aus	23.01.95
Emmanuel, Josh	6.0	Bolton	London	18.08.97
Fleming, Brandon	5.10	–	Dewsbury	03.12.9
Greaves, Jacob	–	–	Cottingham	12.09.00
Jones, Alfie	6.3	Southampton	Bristol	07.10.97
McLoughlin, Sean	Cork City		Cork, Ire	13.11.96

Midfielders

Cannon, Andy	5.10	Portsmouth	Tameside	14.03.96
Docherty, Greg	5.10	Rangers	Milngavie	10.09.96
Honeyman, George	5.8	Sunderland	Prudhoe	02.09.94
Longman, Ryan	5.11	Brighton (loan)	Redhill	06.11.00
Mayer, Thoms	5.8	Lustenau	Linz, Aut	23.08.95
Moncur, George	5.9	Luton	Swindon	18.08.93
Samuelsen, Martin	6.2	West Ham	Haugesund, Nor	17.04.97
Smallwood, Richie	5.11	Blackburn	Redcar	29.12.90
Williams, Randell	5.9	Exeter	Lambeth	30.12.96

Forwards

Eaves, Tom	6.4	Gillingham	Liverpool	14.01.92
Lewis-Potter, Keane	5.11	–	Hull	22.02.01
Magennis, Josh	6.2	Bolton	Bangor, NI	15.08.90
Scott, James	6.2	Motherwell	Glasgow	30.08.00
Wilks, Mallik	5.11	Barnsley	Leeds	15.12.98

LUTON TOWN

Ground: Kenilworth Road, Maple Road, Luton LU4 8AW. **Telephone:** 01582 411622. **Club nickname:** Hatters. **Colours:** Orange and black. **Capacity:** 10,073. **Record attendance:** 30,069 v Blackpool (FA Cup 6) Mar 4, 1959

Goalkeepers

Shea, James	5.11	AFC Wimbledon	Islington	16.06.91
Sluga, Simon	6.3	Rijeka	Porec, Cro	17.03.93

Defenders

Bell, Amari'i	5.11	Blackburn	Burton	05.05.94
Bradley, Sonny	6.4	Plymouth	Hull	13.09.91
Bree, James	5.10	Aston Villa	Wakefield	11.10.97
Burke, Reece	6.2	Hull	Newham	02.09.96
Cranie, Martin	6.0	Sheffield Utd	Yeovil	26.09.86
Kioso, Peter	6.0	Hartlepool	Dublin, Ire	15.08.99
Lockyer, Tom	6.1	Charlton	Cardiff	03.12.94
Potts, Dan	5.8	West Ham	Romford	13.04.94

Midfielders

Berry, Luke	5.9	Cambridge	Cambridge	12.07.92
Campbell, Allan	5.9	Motherwell	Glasgow	04.07.98
Clark, Jordan	6.0	Accrington	Hoyland	22.09.93
Lansbury, Henri	6.0	Bristol City	Enfield	12.10.90
Morrrell, Joe	5.8	Bristol City	Ipswich	03.01.97
Naismith, Kai	6.1	Wigan	Glasgow	18.12.92
Ruddock, Pelly	5.9	West Ham	Hendon	17.07.93
Rea, Glen	6.1	Brighton	Brighton	03.09.94

Forwards

Adebayo, Elijah	6.4	Walsall	Brent	07.01.98
Collins, James	6.2	Crawley	Coventry	01.12.90
Cornick, Harry	5.11	Bournemouth	Poole	06.03.95
Jerome, Cameron	6.1	MK Dons	Huddersfield	14.08.86
Hylton, Danny	6.0	Oxford	Camden	25.02.89
Lee, Elliot	5.11	Barnsley	Durham	16.12.94
Mendes Gomes, Carlos	5.10	Morecambe	Yeumbeul, Sen	14.11.98
Oyedinma, Fred	6.1	Wycombe	Plumstead	24.11.96

MIDDLESBROUGH

Ground: Riverside Stadium, Middlesbrough, TS3 6RS. **Telephone:** 0844 499 6789. **Club nickname:** Boro. **Capacity:** 34,742. **Colours:** Red. **Record attendance:** Ayresome Park: 53,596 v Newcastle (Div 1) Dec 27, 1949; Riverside Stadium: 35,000 (England v Slovakia) Jun 11, 2003. Club: 34,836 v Norwich (Prem Lge) Dec 28, 2004

Goalkeepers

Lumley, Joe	6.4	QPR	Harlow	15.02.95
Stojanovic, Dejan	6.5	St Gallen	Fieldkirch, Aut	19.07.93
Defenders				
Bola, Marc	6.1	Blackpool	Greenwich	09.12.97
Coulson, Hayden	5.11	–	Gateshead	17.06.98
Dijksteel, Anfernee	6.0	Charlton	Amsterdam, Hol	27.10.96
Fisher, Darnell	5.9	Preston	Reading	04.04.94
Fry, Dael	6.0	–	Middlesbrough	30.08.97
Hall, Grant	6.4	QPR	Brighton	29.10.91
Peltier, Lee	5.11	WBA	Toxteth	11.12.86
Spence, Djed	6.1	Fulham	London	09.08.00
Wood, Nathan	6.2	–	Ingleby-Barwick	31.05.02
Midfielders				
Ameobi, Sammy	6.4	Nottm Forest	Newcastle	01.05.92
Browne, Marcus	5.10	West Ham	London	18.12.97
Howson, Jonny	5.11	Norwich	Leeds	21.05.88
McNair, Paddy	6.0	Sunderland	Ballyclare	27.04.95
Morsy, Sam	5.9	Wigan	Wolverhampton	10.09.91
Tavernier, Marcus	5.10	Newcastle	Leeds	22.03.99
Wing, Lewis	6.1	Shildon	Newton Aycliffe	23.05.95
Forwards				
Akpom, Chuba	6.0	PAOK Salonica	Canning Town	09.10.95
Ikpeazu, Uche	6.2	Wycombe	Harrow	28.02.95
Whatmore, Duncan	5.10	Sunderland	Manchester	08.03.94

MILLWALL

Ground: The Den, Zampa Road, London SE16 3LN. **Telephone:** 0207 232 1222. **Club nickname:** Lions. **Colours:** Blue. **Capacity:** 20,146. **Record attendance:** The Den: 48,672 v Derby (FA Cup 5) Feb 20, 1937. New Den: 20,093 v Arsenal (FA Cup 3) Jan 10, 1994

Goalkeepers

Bialkowski, Bartosz	6.0	Ipswich	Braniewo, Poil	06.07.87
Long, George	6.4	Hull	Sheffield	05.11.93
Defenders				
Ballard, Daniel	6.2	Arsenal (loan)	Stevenage	22.09.99
Cooper, Jake	6.4	Reading	Bracknell	03.02.95
Hutchinson, Shaun	6.2	Fulham	Newcastle	23.11.90

Malone, Scott	6.2	Derby	Rowley Regis	25.03.91
McNamara, Danny	5.11	–	Sidcup	27.12.98
Pearce, Alex	6.2	Derby	Wallingford	09.11.88
Romeo, Mahlon	5.10	Gillingham	Westminster	19.09.95
Wallace, Murray	6.2	Scunthorpe	Glasgow	10.01.93

Midfielders

Evans, George	6.1	Derby	Cheadle	13.12.94
Kieftenbeld, Maikel	5.11	Birmingham	Lemelerveld, Hol	26.06.90
Leonard, Ryan	6.1	Sheffield Utd	Plymouth	24.05.92
Mahoney, Connor	5.9	Bournemouth	Blackburn	12.02.97
Mitchell, Billy	5.9	–	Orpington	07.04.01
Saville, George	5.9	Wolves	Camberley	01.06.93
Thompson, Ben	5.10	–	Sidcup	03.10.95
Wallace, Jed	5.10	Wolves	Reading	26.03.94
Woods, Ryan	5.8	Stoke	Norton Canes	13.12.93

Forwards

Afobe, Benik	6.0	Stoke (loan)	Waltham Forest	12.02.93
Bennett, Mason	5.10	Derby	Shirebrook	15.07.96
Bodvarsson, Jon Dadi	6.3	Reading	Selfoss, Ice	25.05.92
Bradshaw, Tom	5.10	Barnsley	Shrewsbury	27.07.92
Smith, Matt	6.6	QPR	Birmingham	07.06.89

NOTTINGHAM FOREST

Ground: City Ground, Pavilion Road, Nottingham NG2 5FJ. **Telephone:** 0115 982 4444. **Club nickname:** Forest. **Colours:** Red and white. **Capacity:** 30,445. **Record attendance:** 49,946 v Manchester Utd (Div 1) Oct 28, 1967

Goalkeepers

| Samba, Brice | 6.1 | Caen | Linzola Cong | 25.04.94 |
| Smith, Jordan | 6.1 | – | South Normanton | 08.12.94 |

Defenders

Blackett, Tyler	6.1	Reading	Manchester	02.04.94
Bong, Gaetan	6.2	Brighton	Sakbayeme, Cam	25.04.88
Figueiredo, Tobias	6.2	Sporting CP	Satao, Por	02.02.94
Jenkinson, Carl	6.1	Arsenal	Harlow	08.02.92
Mbe Soh, Loic	6.2	Paris SG	Nanga, Cam	13.06.01
McKenna, Scott	6.2	Aberdeen	Kirriemuir	12.11.96
Worrall, Joe	6.4	–	Hucknall	10.01.97

Midfielders

Arter, Harry	5.9	Bournemouth	Eltham	28.12.89
Colback, Jack	5.10	Newcastle	Killingworth	24.10.89
Joao Carvalho	5.8	Benfica	Castanheira, Por	09.03.97
Lolley, Joe	5.10	Huddersfield	Redditch	25.08.92
Yates, Ryan	6.3	–	Lincoln	21.11.97

Forwards

Grabban, Lewis	6.0	Bournemouth	Croydon	12.01.88
Mighten, Alex	5.9	–	Nottingham	11.04.02
Taylor, Lyle	6.2	Charlton	Greenwich	29.03.90

PETERBOROUGH UNITED

Ground: Western Homes Stadium, London Road, Peterborough PE2 8AL. **Telephone:** 01733 563947. **Club nickname:** Posh. **Colours:** Blue and white. **Capacity:** 15,314. **Record attendance:** 30,096 v Swansea (FA Cup 5) Feb 20, 1965

Goalkeepers

Cornell, David	6.2	Ipswich	Waunarlwydd	28.03.91
Pym, Christy	5.11	Exeter	Exeter	24.04.95

Defenders

Beevers, Mark	6.4	Bolton	Barnsley	21.11.89
Butler, Dan	5.9	Newport	Cowes	26.08.94
Edwards, Ronnie	5.11	Barnet	Harlow	28.03.03
Kent, Frankie	6.2	Colchester	Romford	21.11.95
Knight, Josh	6.1	Leicester	Fleckney	07.09.97
Thompson, Nathan	5.10	Portsmouth	Chester	22.04.91

Midfielders

Broom, Ryan	5.10	Cheltenham	Newport	04.09.96
Burrows, Harrison	5.10	–	Murrow	12.01.02
Grant, Jorge	5.10	Lincoln	Banbury	19.12.94
Hamilton, Ethan	6.2	Manchester Utd	Edinburgh	18.10.98
Jade-Jones, Ricky	6.0	–	Peterborough	08.11.02
Szmodics, Sammie	5.7	Bristol City	Colchester	24.09.95
Tasdemir, Serhat	5.11	Fylde	Blackburn	21.07.00
Taylor, Jack	6.1	Barnet	Hammersmith	23.06.98
Ward, Joe		Woking	Chelmsford	22.08.95

Forwards

Clarke-Harris, Jonson	6.0	Bristol Rov	Leicester	20.07.94
Dembele, Siriki	5.8	Grimsby	Ivory Coast	07.09.96
Eisa, Mo	6.0	Bristol City	Khartoum, Sud	12.07.94
Kanu, Idris	6.0	Aldershot	London	05.12.99
Marriott, Jack	5.9	Derby	Beverley	09.09.84

PRESTON NORTH END

Ground: Deepdale, Sir Tom Finney Way, Preston PR1 6RU. **Telephone:** 0844 856 1964. **Club nickname:** Lilywhites. **Colours:** White and navy. **Capacity:** 23,404. **Record attendance:** 42,684 v Arsenal (Div 1) Apr 23, 1938

Goalkeepers

Ripley, Connor	6.3	Middlesbrough	Middlesbrough	13.02.93
Rudd, Declan	6.3	Norwich	Diss	16.01.91

Defenders

Bauer, Patrick	6.4	Charlton	Backnang, Ger	28.10.92
Cunningham, Greg	6.0	Cardiff	Galway, Ire	31.01.91
Earl, Josh	6.4	–	Southport	24.10.98
Hughes, Andrew	5.11	Peterborough	Cardiff	05.06.92
Huntington, Paul	6.2	Yeovil	Carlisle	17.09.87
Lindsay, Liam	6.3	Stoke	Paisley	12.10.95
Olosunde, Matthew	6.1	Rotherham	Philadelphia, US	07.03.98
Rafferty, Joe	6.0	Rochdale	Liverpool	06.10.93
Storey, Jordan	6.2	Exeter	Yeovil	02.09.97
Van den Berg, Sepp	6.2	Liverpool (loan)	Zwolle, Hol	20.12.01

Midfielders

Bayliss, Tom	6.0	Coventry	Leicester	06.04.99
Brown, Izzy	6.0	Chelsea	Peterborough	07.01.97
Browne, Alan	5.8	Cork	Cork, Ire	15.04.95
Johnson, Daniel	5.8	Aston Villa	Kingston, Jam	08.10.92
Ledson, Ryan	5.9	Oxford	Liverpool	19.08.97
Potts, Brad	6.2	Barnsley	Hexham	07.03.94
Sinclair, Scott	5.8	Celtic	Bath	25.03.89

Whiteman, Ben	6.0	Doncaster	Rochdale	17.06.96
Forwards				
Barkhuizen, Tom	5.11	Preston	Blackpool	04.07.93
Evans, Ched	6.0	Fleetwood	St Asaph	28.12.88
Jakobsen, Emil Riise	6.3	Randers	Hobro, Denmark	24.06.98
Maguire, Sean	5.9	Cork	Luton	01.05.94

QUEENS PARK RANGERS

Ground: Kiyan Prince Foundation Stadium, South Africa Road, London W12 7PA. **Telephone:** 0208 743 0262. **Club nickname:** Hoops. **Colours:** Blue and white. **Capacity:** 18,439. **Record attendance:** 35,353 v Leeds (Div 1) 27 Apr, 1974

Goalkeepers				
Archer, Jordan	6.2	Middlesbrough	Walthamstow	12.04.93
Dieng, Seny	6.4	Duisburg	Zurich, Switz	23.11.94
Defenders				
Ball, Dominic	6.1	Rotherham	Welwyn Garden City	02.08.95
Barbet, Yoann	62	Brentford	Libourne, Fr	10.05.93
De Wijs, Jordy	6.2	Hull	Kortrijk, Bel	08.01.95
Dickie, Rob	6.4	Oxford	Wokingham	03.03.96
Dunne, Jimmy	6.0	Burnley	Dundalk, Ire	19.10.97
Hamalainen, Niko	5.9	Dallas	West Palm Beach, US	05.03.97
Kakay, Osman	5.11	–	Westminster	25.08.97
Kane, Todd	5.11	Chelsea	Huntingdon	17.09.93
Masterson, Conor	6.1	Liverpool	Cellbridge, Ire	08.09.98
McCallum, Sam	5.10	Norwich (loan)	Canterbury	02.09.00
Wallace, Lee	6.1	Rangers	Edinburgh	01.08.87
Midfielders				
Adomah, Albert	6.1	Notttm Forest	Lambeth	13.12.87
Amos, Luke	5.11	Tottenham (loan)	Welwyn Garden City	23.02.97
Carroll, Tom	5.10	Swansea	Watford	28.05.92
Chair, Ilias	5.4	Lierse	Antwerp, Bel	14.06.96
Dozzell, Andre	5.10	Ipswich	Ipswich	02.05.99
Field, Sam	5.11	WBA	Stourbridge	08.05.98
Shodipo, Olamide	5.10	–	Leixlip, Ire	05.07.97
Forwards				
Austin, Charlie	6.2	WBA	Hungerford	05.07.89
Dykes, Lyndon	6.2	Livingston	Gold Coast, Aus	07.10.95
Kelman, Charlie	5.11	Southend	Basildon	02.11.01
Willock, Chris	5.11	Benfica	Waltham Forest	31.01.98

READING

Ground: Madejski Stadium, Junction 11 M4, Reading RG2 OFL. **Telephone:** 0118 968 1100. **Club nickname:** Royals. **Colours:** Blue and white. **Capacity:** 24,161. **Record attendance:** Elm Park: 33,042 v Brentford (FA Cup 5) Feb 19, 1927; Madejski Stadium: 24,184 v Everton (Prem Lge) Nov 17, 2012

Goalkeepers				
Rafael Cabral	6.1	Sampdoria	Sorocaba, Br	20.05.90
Southwood, Luke			Oxford	06.12.97
Defenders				
Holmes, Tom	6.1	–	London	12.03.00
McIntyre, Tom	6.1	–	Reading	06.11.98

Moore, Liam	6.1	Leicester	Leicester	31.01.93
Morrison, Michael	6.1	Birmingham	Bury St Edmunds	03.03.88
Yiadom, Andy	5.11	Barnsley	Holloway	02.12.91
Midfielders				
Ejaria, Ovie	6.0	Liverpool	Southwark	18.11.97
Felipe Araruna	5.9	Sao Paulo	Porto Alegre, Br	12.03.96
Laurent, Josh	6.2	Shrewsbury	Leytonstone	06.05.95
Rinomhota, Andy	5.9	Portchester	Leeds	21.04.97
Tetek, Dejan	5.11	–	Oxford	24.09.02
Swift, John	6.0	Chelsea	Portsmouth	23.06.95
Forwards				
Lucas Joao	6.4	Sheffield Wed	Lisbon, por	04/09.93
McNulty, Marc	5.10	Coventry	Edinburgh	14.09.92
Meite, Yakou	6.1	Paris SG	Paris, Fr	11.02.96
Puscas, George	6.2	Inter Milan	Marghita, Rom	08.04.96

SHEFFIELD UNITED

Ground: Bramall Lane, Sheffield S2 4SU. **Telephone:** 0114 253 7200. **Club nickname:** Blades. **Colours:** Red and white. **Capacity:** 32,702. **Record attendance:** 68,287 v Leeds (FA Cup 5) Feb 15, 1936

Goalkeepers				
Foderingham, Wes	6.1	Rangers	Hammersmith	14.01.91
Ramsdale, Aaron	6.2	Bournemouth	Stoke	14.05.98
Defenders				
Baldock, George	5.9	MK Dons	Buckingham	09.03.93
Basham, Chris	5.11	Blackpool	Hebburn	18.02.88
Bogle, Jayden	5.10	Derby	Reading	27.07.00
Bryan, Kean	6.1	Manchester City	Manchester	01.11.96
Egan, John	6.2	Brentford	Cork, Ire	20.10.92
Lowe, Max	5.9	Derby	Birmingham	11.05.97
Norrington-Davies, Rhys	6.0	–	Riyadh, Saudi	22.04.99
O'Connell, Jack	6.3	Brentford	Liverpool	29.03.94
Robinson, Jack	5.7	Nottm Forest	Warrington	01.09.93
Stevens, Enda	6.0	Portsmouth	Dublin, Ire	09.07.90
Midfielders				
Berge, Sander	6.4	Genk	Baerum, Nor	14.02.98
Burke, Oliver	6.2	WBA	Kircaldy	07.04.97
Fleck, John	5.7	Coventry	Glasgow	24.08.91
Jebbison, Daniel	6.3	–	Oakville, Can	11.07.03
Norwood, Oliver	5.11	Brighton	Burnley	12.04.91
Osborn, Ben	5.10	Nottm Forest	Derby	05.08.94
Forwards				
Brewster, Rhian	5.11	Liverpool	Chadwell Heath	01.04.00
McBurnie, Oliver	6.2	Swansea	Leeds	04.06.96
McGoldrick, David	6.1	Ipswich	Nottingham	29.11.87
Mousset, Lys	6.0	Bournemouth	Montivilliers, Fr	08.12.96
Sharp, Billy	5.9	Leeds	Sheffield	05.02.86

STOKE CITY

Ground: bet365 Stadium, Stanley Matthews Way, Stoke-on-Trent ST4 7EG. **Telephone:** 01782 367598. **Club nickname:** Potters. **Colours:** Red and white. **Capacity:** 30,089. **Record attendance:** Victoria Ground: 51,380 v Arsenal (Div 1) Mar 29, 1937. bet365 Stadium: 30,022 v Everton (Prem Lge) Mar 17, 2018

Goalkeepers

Bonham, Jack	6.4	Gillingham	Stevenage	14.09.93
Bursik, Josef	6.2	AFC Wimbledon	Lambeth	12.07.00
Davies, Adam	6.1	Barnsley	Rintein, Ger	17.07.92

Defenders

Batth, Danny	6.3	Wolves	Brierley Hill	21.09.90
Chester, James	5.11	Aston Villa	Warrington	23.01.89
Smith, Tommy	6.1	Huddersfield	Warrington	14.04.92
Souttar, Harry	6.6	Dundee Utd	Aberdeen	22.10.98
Tymon, Josh	5.10	Hull	Hull	22.05.99
Wilmot, Ben	6.2	Watford	Stevenage	04.11.99

Midfielders

Allen, Joe	5.7	Liverpool	Carmarthen	14.03.90
Brown, Jacob	5.1	Barnsley	Halifax	10.04.98
Clucas, Sam	5.10	Swansea	Lincoln	25.09.90
Doughty, Alfie	6.0	Charlton	Hatfield	21.12.99
Fox, Morgan	6.1	Sheffield Wed	Chelmsford	21.09.93
Ince, Tom	5.10	Huddersfield	Stockport	30.01.92
McClean, James	5.11	WBA	Derry	22.04.89
Powell, Nick	6.0	Wigan	Crewe	23.03.94
Thompson, Jordan	5.9	Blackpool	Belfast	03.01.97
Vrancic, Mario	6.1	Norwich	Slavonski Brod, Cro	23.05.89

Forwards

Campbell, Tyrese	6.0	Manchester City	Cheadle Hulme	28.12.99
Fletcher, Steven	6.1	Sheffield Wed	Shrewsbury	26.03.87
Gregory, Lee	6.2	Millwall	Sheffield	26.08.88
Vokes, Sam	5.11	Burnley	Lymington	21.10.89

SWANSEA CITY

Ground: Liberty Stadium, Morfa, Swansea SA1 2FA. **Telephone:** 01792 616600. **Club nickname:** Swans. **Colours:** White. **Capacity:** 21,088. **Record attendance:** Vetch Field: 32,796 v Arsenal (FA Cup 4) Feb 17, 1968. Liberty Stadium: 20,972 v Liverpool (Prem Lge) May 1, 2016

Goalkeepers

Benda, Steven	6.3	1860 Munich	Stuttgart, Ger	01.10.98
Hamer, Ben	6.4	Huddersfield	Chard	20.11.87

Defenders

Bennett, Ryan	6.2	Wolves	Orsett	06.03.90
Bidwell, Jake	6.1	QPR	Southport	21.03.93
Cabango, Ben	6.1	Newport	Cardiff	30.05.00
Latibeaudiere, Joel	5.11	Manchester City	Doncaster	06.01.00
Naughton, Kyle	5.10	Tottenham	Sheffield	11.11.88
Roberts, Connor	5.10	–	Neath	23.09.95

Midfielders

Dhanda, Yan	5.8	Liverpool	Birmingham	14.12.98
Fulton, Jay	5.10	Falkirk	Bolton	04.04.94
Grimes, Matt	5.10	Exeter	Exeter	15.07.95
Manning, Ryan	5.11	QPR	Galway, Ire	14.06.96
Routledge, Wayne	5.7	Newcastle	Sidcup	07.01.85
Smith, Korey	5.10	Bristol City	Hatfield	31.01.91
Walsh, Liam	5.8	Bristol City	Huyton	15.09.97

Forwards

Cullen, Liam	5.10	–	Kilgetty	23.04.99
Garrick, Jordan	5.11	–	Jamaica	15.07.98

Lowe, Jamal	6.0	Wigan	Harrow	21.07.94
Piroe, Joel	5.11	PSV Eindhoven	Wijchen, Hol	02.08.99
Whittaker, Morgan	6.0	Derby	Derby	07.01.01

WEST BROMWICH ALBION

Ground: The Hawthorns, Halfords Lane, West Bromwich B71 4LF. **Telephone:** 0871 271 1100.
Club nickname: Baggies. **Colours:** Blue and white. **Capacity:** 26,500. **Record attendance:**
64,815 v Arsenal (FA Cup 6) Mar 6, 1937

Goalkeepers

| Button, David | 6.3 | Brighton | Stevenage | 27.02.89 |
| Johnstone, Sam | 6.4 | Man Utd | Preston | 25.03.93 |

Defenders

Ajayi, Semi	6.4	Rotherham	Crayford	09.11.93
Bartley, Kyle	6.1	Swansea	Stockport	22.05.91
Clarke, Matt	6.1	Brighton (loan)	Barham	22.09.96
Furlong, Darnell	5.11	QPR	Luton	31.10.95
Gibbs, Kieran	5.10	Arsenal	Lambeth	26.09.89
O'Shea Dara	6.2	–	Dublin, Ire	04.03.99`
Townsend, Conor	5.6	Scunthorpe	Hessle	04.03.93

Midfielders

Diangana, Grady	5.11	West Ham	DR Congo	19.04.98
Livermore, Jake	6.0	Hull	Enfield	14.11.89
Mowatt, Alex	5.10	Barnsley	Doncaster	13.02.95
Pereira, Matheus	5.9	Sporting Lisbon	Belo Horizonte, Br	05.05.96
Phillips, Matt	6.0	QPR	Aylesbury	13.03.91
Sawyers, Romaine	5.9	Brentford	Birmingham	02.11.91
Snodgrass, Robert	6.0	West Ham	Glasgow	07.09.87

Forwards

| Grant, Karlan | 6.0 | Huddersfield | Greenwich | 19.12.97 |
| Robinson, Callum | 5.10 | Sheffield Utd | Northampton | 02.02.95 |

LEAGUE ONE

ACCRINGTON STANLEY

Ground: Wham Stadium, Livingstone Road, Accrington BB5 5BX. **Telephone:** 0871 434 1968.
Club nickname: Stanley. **Colours:** Red. **Capacity:** 5,450. **Record attendance:** 5,397 v Derby (FA
Cup 4) Jan 26, 2019

Goalkeepers

| Savin, Toby | 6.4 | Crewe | – | 26.05.00 |

Defenders

Barclay, Ben	6.2	Brighton	Altrincham	07.10.96
Burgess, Cameron	6.4	Scunthorpe	Aberdeen	21.10.95
Conneely, Seamus	6.1	Sligo	Lambeth	09.07.88
Nottingham, Michael	6.4	Blackpool	Birmingham	14.04.89
Procter, Archie	5.10	AFC Wimbldon	Blackburn	13.11.01
Rodgers, Harvey	5.11	Fleetwood	York	20.10.96
Sama, Stephen	6.2	Heracles	Bamenda, Cam	05.03.93
Sykes, Ross	6.5	–	Burnley	26.03.99

Midfielders

| Butcher, Matt | 6.2 | Bournemouth | Portsmouth | 14.05.97 |

Coyle, Liam	–	Liverpool	Liverpool	06.12.99
Fenlon, Rhys	5.9	Burnley	Salford	02.11.01
McConville, Sean	5.11	Chester	Burscough	06.03.89
Morgan, David	5.8	Southport	Belfast	04.07.94
O'Sullivan, John	5.11	Morecambe	Dublin, Ire	18.09.93
Pell, Harry	6.4	Colchester	Tilbury	21.10.91
Pritchard, Joe	5.8	Bolton	Watford	10.09.96
Scully, Tom	6.0	Norwich	Liverpool	01.10.99
Forwards				
Bishop, Colby	5.11	Leamington	Nottingham	04.11.96
Charles, Dion	6.0	Southport	Preson	07.10.95
Hardy, Joe	5.8	Liverpool	Wirral	26.09.98
Mansell, Lewis	6.2	Partick	Burnley	20.09.97

AFC WIMBLEDON

Ground: Plough Lane, London SW17 ONR. **Telephone:** 0208 547 3528. **Club nickname:** Dons. **Colours:** Blue. **Capacity:** 9,300

Goalkeepers				
Cox, Matthew	6.0	–	Sutton	02.05.03
Tzanev, Nik	6.5	Brentford	Wellington, NZ	23.12.96
Defenders				
Alexander, Cheye	5.8	Barnet	Newham	06.01.95
Charles, Darius	6.1	Wycombe	Ealing	10.12.87
Guinness-Walker, Nesta	5.11	Met Police	London	14.09.99
Csoka, Daniel	6.2	Wolves	Zalaegerszeg, Hun	04.04.00
Heneghan, Ben	6.3	Sheffield Utd	Manchester	19.09.93
Kalambay, Paul	6.0	–	Dulwich	09.07.99
Madelin, Jack	6.1	–	London	19.04.02
Nightingale, Will	6.1	–	Wandsworth	02.08.95
Osew, Paul	5.7	Brentford	London	25.11.00
Midfielders				
Assai, Ayoub	5.9	–	Maidstone	21.01.02
Chislett, Ethan	5.10	Aldershot	Guildford	22.02.00
Hartigan, Anthony	5.10	–	Kingston upon Thames	27.01.00
Marsh, George	5.11	Tottenham	Pembury	05.11.98
McCormick, Luke	5.9	Chelsea	Bury St Edmunds	21.01.99
Woodyard, Alex	5.9	Peterborough	Gravesend	03.05.93
Forwards				
Cosgrave, Aaron	6.0	Lewes	Shenfield	17.07.99
Harrison, Shayon	6.0	Almere	Hornsey	13.07.97
Palmer, Ollie	6.6	Crawley	Epsom	21.01.92
Robinson, Zach	6.2	–	Lambeth	11.06.02
Rudoni, Jack	6.1	–	Carshalton	14.06.01

BOLTON WANDERERS

Ground: University of Bolton Stadium, Burnden Way, Lostock, Bolton BL6 6JW. **Telephone:** 0844 871 2932. **Club nickname:** Trotters. **Colours:** White and navy. **Capacity:** 28,723. **Record attendance:** Burnden Park: 69,912 v Manchester City (FA Cup 5) Feb 18, 1933. University of Bolton Stadium: 28,353 v Leicester (Prem Lge) Dec 28, 2003

| **Goalkeepers** | | | | |
| Alexander, Matt | | Newcastle | Newcastle upon Tyne | 07.05.02 |

Dixon, Joel	6.4	Barrow	Middlesbrough	09.12.93

Defenders

Aimson, Will	5.10	Plymouth	Christchurch	01.01.94
Baptiste, Alex	5.11	Doncaster	Sutton-in-Ashfield	31.01.86
Brockbank, Harry	5.11	–	Bolton	26.09.98
Edwards, Liam	6.3	Stoke	Crewe	02.10.96
Gordon, Liam	6.1	Dagenham	Croydon	15.05.99
Greenidge, Reiss	6.6	Arendal	Enfield	08.02.96
John, Declan	5.10	Swansea	Merthyr Tydfil	30.06.95
Johnston, George	6.0	Feyenoord	Manchester	01.09.98
Jones, Gethin	5.10	Carlisle	Perth, Aus	13.20.95
Santos, Ricardo	6.6	Barnet	Almada, Por	18.06.95
Senior, Adam	6.0	–	Bolton	20.01.02

Midfielders

Amaechi, Xavier	5.10	Hamburg (loan)	Bath	05.01.01
Comley, Brandon	5.11	Colchester	Islington	18.11.95
Crawford, Ali	5.8	Doncaster	Lanark	30.07.91
Lee, Kieran	6.1	Sheffield Wed	Stalybridge	22.06.88
Politic, Dennis	5.10	Manchester Utd	Brasov, Rom	05.03.00
Sarcevic, Antoni	6.0	Plymouth	Manchester	13.03.92
Sheehan, Josh	6.0	Newport	Pembrey	30.03.95
Tutte, Andrew	5.9	Morecambe	Liverpool	21.09.90
Williams MJ	6.0	Blackpool	Bangor, Wal	06.11.95

Forwards

Bakayoko, Amadou	6.3	Coventry	Kenema, SL	01.01.96
Delfouneso, Nathan	6.1	Blackpool	Birmingham	02.02.91
Doyle, Eoin	6.0	Swindon	Dublin, Ire	12.03.88
Isgrove, Lloyd	5.10	Swindon	Yeovil	12.01.93

BURTON ALBION

Ground: Pirelli Stadium, Princess Way, Burton upon Trent DE13 AR. **Telephone:** 01283 565938. **Club nickname:** Brewers. **Colours:** Yellow and black. **Capacity:** 6,912. **Record attendance:** 6,746 v Derby (Champ), Aug 26, 2016

Goalkeepers

Garratt, Ben	6.1	Crewe	Market Drayton	25.04.94
O'Hara, Kieran	6.3	Manchester Utd	Manchester	22.04.96

Defenders

Blake-Tracy, Frazer	6.0	Peterborough	Dereham	10.09.95
Borthwick-Jackson, Cameron	6.0	Oldham	Mancheter	02.02.97
Bostwick, Michael	6.3	Lincoln	Eltham	17.05.88
Brayford, John	5.8	Sheffield Utd	Stoke	29.12.87
Hamer, Tom	6.2	Oldham	Bolton	16.11.99
Mancienne, Michael	6.0	New England	Feltham	08.01.88
O'Connor, Thomas	5.11	Southampton	Kilkenny, Ire	21.04.99
Oshilaja, Deji	6.0	Charlton	Bermondsey	16.07.93
Shaughnessy, Conor	6.3	Rochdale	Galway, Ire	30.06.96
Wallace, Kieran	6.1	Matlock	Nottingham	26.01.95

Midfielders

Maddox, Jacob	5.10	Guimaraes (loan)	Bristol	03.11.98
Morris, Bryn	6.0	Portsmotuh	Hartlepool	25.04.96
Powell, Joe	5.11	West Ham	Newham	30.10.98
Smith, Jonny	5.10	Bristol City	Liverpool	28.07.97
Taylor, Terry	6.1	Wolves	Irvine	29.06.01

Forwards

Akins, Lucas	6.0	Stevenage	Huddersfield	25.02.89
Hemmings, Kane	6.1	Dundee	Burton	08.04.91
Moult, Lewis	6.0	Preston	Stoke	14.05.92
Patrick, Omari	6.1	Carlisle	Slough	24.05.96
Parker, Josh	5.11	Wycombe	Slough	01.12.90
Rowe, Danny	6.0	Ipswich	Wythenshawe	09.03.92

CAMBRIDGE UNITED

Ground: Abbey Stadium, Newmarket Road, Cambridge CB5 8LN. **Telephone:** 01223 566500. **Club nickname:** U's. **Colours:** Yellow and black. **Capacity:** 8,217. **Record attendance:** 14,000 v Chelsea (friendly) May 1, 1970

Goalkeepers

McKenzie-Lyle, Kai	6.7	Barnet	Haringey	30.11.97
Mitov, Dimitar	6.2	Charlton	–	22.01.97

Defenders

Brophy, James	5.10	Leyton Orient	Brent	25.07.94
Davies, Leon	5.11	–	Cambridge	22.11.99
Iredale, Jack	6.1	Carlisle	Greenock	02.05.96
Jones, Lloyd	6.3	Northampton	Plymouth	07.10.95
Taylor, Greg	6.1	Luton	Bedford	15.01.90
Williams, George	5.9	Bristol Rov	Hillingdon	14.04.93

Midfielders

Digby, Paul	6.3	Stevenage	Sheffield	02.02.95
Dunk, Harrison	6,0	Bromley	London	25.10.90
Hannant, Luke	5.11	Port Vale	Great Yarmouth	04.11.93
Hoolahan, Wes	5.7	Newcastle Jets	Dublin, Ire	20.05.82
Lankester, Jack	5.10	Ipswich	Bury St Edmunds	19.01.00
May, Adam	6.0	Portsmouth	Southampton	06.12.97
O'Neil, Liam	5.11	Chesterfield	Cambridge	31.07.93
Tracey, Shilow	5.10	Tottenham	Newham	29.04.98
Weir, Jensen	6.1	Brighton (loan)	Warrington	31.01.02
Worman, Ben	5.8	–	Cambridge	30.08.01

Forwards

Dallas, Andy	5.10	Rangers	–	22.07.99
Ironside, Joe	5.11	Macclesfield	Middlesbrough	16.10.93
Knibbs, Harvey	6.1	Aston Villa	–	26.04.99
Smith, Sam	6.0	Reading	Manchester	08.03.98

CHARLTON ATHLETIC

Ground: The Valley, Floyd Road, London SE7 8BL. **Telephone:** 0208 333 4000. **Club nickname:** Addicks. **Colours:** Red and white. **Capacity:** 27,111. **Record attendance:** 75,031 v Aston Villa (FA Cup 5) Feb 12, 1938

Goalkeepers

MacGillivray, Craig	6.2	Portsmouth	Harrogate	12.01.93

Defenders

Famewo, Akin	6.2	Norwich (loan)	Lewisham	09.11.98
Gunter, Chris	5.11	Reading	Newport	21.07.89
Inniss, Ryan	6.5	Crystal Palace	Penge	05.06.956
Matthews, Adam	5.10	Sunderland	Swansea	13.01.92
Morgan, Albie	5.11	–	Rochester	02.02.00

Pearce, Jason	5.11	Wigan	Hillingdon	06.12.87
Purrington, Ben	5.9	Rotherham	Exeter	05.05.96
Midfielders				
Dobson, George	6.1	Sunderlandl	Harold Wood	15.11.97
Forster-Caskey, Jake	5.10	Brighton	Southend	05.04.94
Gilbey, Alex	6.0	MK Dons	Dagenham	09.12.94
Jaiyesimi, Diallang	6.0	Swindon	Southwark	07.05.98
Watson, Ben	5.10	Nottm Forest	Camberwell	09.07.85
Forwards				
Schwartz, Ronnie	6.0	Midtjylland	Aalborg, Den	29.08.89
Stockley, Jayden	6.3	Preston	Poole	15.09.93
Washington, Conor	5.11	Hearts	Chatham	18.05.92

CHELTENHAM TOWN

Ground: Jonny-Rocks Stadium, Whaddon Road, Cheltenham GL52 5NA. **Telephone:** 01242 573558. **Club nickname:** Robins. **Colours:** Red and white. **Capacity:** 7,066. **Record attendance:** 8,326 v Reading (FA Cup 1) Nov 17, 1956

Goalkeepers				
Evans, Owen	6.2	Wigan	Newport	28.11.96
Flinders, Scott	6.4	Macclesfield	Rotherham	12.06.86
Harris, Max	6.2	Oxford	Gloucester	14.09.99
Defenders				
Boyle, Will	6.2	Huddersfield	Garforth	01.09.95
Freestone, Lewis	5.9	Brighton	King's Lynn	26.10.99
Hussey, Chris	6.0	Sheffield Utd	Hammersmith	02.01.89
Long, Sean	5.10	Lincoln	Dublin	02.05.95
Raglan, Charlie	6.0	Oxford	Wythenshawe	28.04.93
Midfielders				
Blair, Matty	5.10	Doncaster	Warwick	30.11.87
Bonds, Elliot	5.10	Hull	Brent	23.03.00
Chapman, Ellis	6.3	Leicester	Lincoln	08.01.01
Sercombe, Liam	5.10	Bristol Rov	Exeter	25.04.90
Thomas, Conor	6.1	ATK	Coventry	29.10.93
Tozer, Ben	6.1	Newport	Plymouth	01.03.90
Forwards				
Lloyd, George	5.8	–	Gloucester	11.02.00
May, Alfie	5.10	Doncaster	Gravesend	02.07.93
Williams, Andy	5.10	Northampton	Hereford	14.08.86

CREWE ALEXANDRA

Ground: Alexandra Stadium, Gresty Road, Crewe CW2 6EB. **Telephone:** 01270 213014. **Club nickname:** Railwaymen. **Colours:** Red and white. **Capacity:** 10,153. **Record attendance:** 20,000 v Tottenham (FA Cup 4) Jan 30, 1960

Goalkeepers				
Jaaskelainen, Will	6.0	Bolton	Bolton	25.07.98
Richards, David	6.0	Bristol City	Abergavenny	31.12.93
Defenders				
Adebisi, Rio	5.10	–	Croydon	27.09.00
Daniels, Donervon	6.1	Luton	Montserratt	24.11.93
Hoban, Tommie	6.2	Aberdeen	Walthamstow	24.01.94
Oford, Luke	5.7	–	Chichester	19.11.99

Ramsay, Kayne	5.10	Southampton (loan)	Hackney	10.10.00
Sass-Davies, Billy	6.1	–	Abergele	17.02.00
Midfielders				
Ainley, Callum	5.8	–	Middlewich	02.11.97
Finney, Oliver	5.7	–	Stoke	15.12.97
Griffiths, Regan	5.11	–	Liverpool	01.05.00
Kirk, Charlie	5.7	–	Winsford	24.12.97
Lowery, Tom	–	–	Holmes Chapel	31.12.97
Lundstram, Josh	5.9	–	Stoke	19.02.99
MacDonald, Shaun	6.1	Rotherham	Swansea	17.06.88
Murphy, Luke	6.2	Bolton	Macclesfield	21.10.89
Forwards				
Mandron, Mikael	6.3	Gillingham	Boulogne, Fr	11.01.94
Dale, Owen	5.9	–	Warrington	01.11.98
Long, Chris	5.11	Motherwell	Huyton	25.02.95
Porter, Chris	6.1	Colchester	Wigan	12.12.83

DONCASTER ROVERS

Ground: Keepmoat Stadium, Stadium Way, Doncaster DN4 5JW. **Telephone:** 01302 764664. **Club nickname:** Rovers. **Colours:** Red and white. **Capacity:** 15,231. **Record attendance:** Belle Vue: 37,149 v Hull (Div 3 N) Oct 2, 1948. Keepmoat Stadium: 15,001 v Leeds (Lge 1) Apr 1, 2008

Goalkeepers				
Jones, Louis	6.1	–	Doncaster	12.10.98
Defenders				
Anderson, Tom	6.3	Burnley	Burnley	02.09.93
Horton, Branden	5.10	–	Doncaster	09.09.00
John, Cameron	5.11	Wolves	Havering	24.08.99
Knoyle, Kyle	5.10	Cambridge	Newham	24.09.96
Seaman, Charlie	5.8	Bournemouth	–	30.09.99
Williams, Ro-Shaun	6.0	Shrewsbury	Manchester	03.09.98
Wright, Joe	6.4	Huddersfield	Monk Fryston	26.02.95
Midfielders				
Bostock, John	6.2	Toulouse	Camberwell	15.11.92
Close, Ben	5.9	Portsmouth	Portsmouth	08.08.96
Hasani, Lirak	6.0	–	Cantley	25.06.02
Rowe, Tommy	5.11	Bristol City	Wythenshawe	24.09.88
Smith, Matt	5.9	Arsenal (loan)	Harlow	05.10.00
Williams, Ed	5.8	Kidderminster	Cheltenham	20.07.95
Forwards				
Bogle, Omar	6.3	Charlton	Sandwell	26.07.93
Hiwula, Jordy	5.11	Portsmouth	Manchester	21.09.94
Okenabirhie, Feiiri	5.10	Shrewsbury	Hendon	25.02.96
Taylor, Jon	5.11	Rotherham	Liverpool	20.07.92

FLEETWOOD TOWN

Ground: Highbury Stadium, Park Avenue, Fleetwod FY7 6TX. **Telephone:** 01253 775080. **Club nickname:** Fishermen. **Colours:** Red and white. **Capacity:** 5,327. **Record attendance:** 5,194 v York (Lge 2 play-off semi-final, 2nd leg) May 16, 2014

| **Goalkeepers** | | | | |
| Cairns, Alex | 6.0 | Rotherham | Doncaster | 04.01.93 |

Czajor, Szymon	6.2	–	Poznan, Pol	19.09.01

Defenders

Andrew, Danny	5.11	Doncaster	Holbeach	23.12.90
Clark, Max	5.11	Hull	Hull	19.01.96
Clarke, Tom	5.11	Salford	Halifax	21.12.87
Hill, James	6.1	–	Bristol	10.01.02
Holgate, Harrison	6.1	–	Leeds	01.07.00

Midfielders

Baggley, Barry	5.9	Glentoran	Belfast	11.01.02
Batty, Dan	5.11	Hull	Pontefract	10.12.97
Biggins, Harrison	5.10	Stocksbridge	Sheffield	15.03.96
Boyle, Dylan	5.9	–	Belfast	15.01.02
Camps, Callum	5.11	Rochdale	Stockport	14.03.96
Johnston, Carl	5.10	Linfield	Belfast	30.03.02
Matete, Jay	–	Reading	Lambeth	11.02.01
Morris, Shayden	6.0	Southend	Newham	03.11.02
Rossiter, Jordan	5.10	Rangers (loan)	Liverpool	24.03.97

Forwards

Edmondson, Ryan	6.2	Leeds (loan)	Harrogate	20.05.01
Garner, Gerard	6.2	–	Liverpool	02.11.98

GILLINGHAM

Ground: Mems Priestfield Stadium, Redfern Avenue, Gillingham ME7 4DD. **Telephone:** 01634 300000. **Club nickname:** Gills. **Colours:** Blue and white. **Capacity:** 11,582. **Record attendance:** 23,002 v QPR. (FA Cup 3) Jan 10, 1948

Goalkeepers

Chapman, Aaron	6.7	Motherwell	Rotherham	29.05.90

Defenders

Ehmer, Max	6.2	Bristol Rov	Frankfurt, Ger	03.02.92
Jackson, Ryan	5.9	Colchester	Streatham	31.07.90
McKenzie, Robbie	6.1	Hull	Hull	25.09.98
Maghoma, Christian	6.1	Arka Gdynia	Lubumbashi, DR Con	08.11.97
Tucker, Jack	6.2	–	Whiotstable	12.11.99
Tutonda, David	5.11	Bristol Rov	Kinshasa, Zai	11.10.95

Midfielders

Dempsey, Kyle	5.10	Fleetwood	Whitehaven	19.9.95
Lee, Olly	5.11	Hearts	Hornchurch	11.07.91
Lloyd, Danny	5.8	Tranmere	Liverpool	03.12.91
MacDonald, Alex	5.7	Mansfield	Nottingham	14.04.90
O'Keefe, Stuart	5.8	Cardiff	Norwich	04.03.91
Reeves, Ben	5.10	Plymouth	Verwood	19.11.91

Forwards

Akinde, John	6.2	Lincoln	Gravesend	08.07.89
Oliver, Vadaine	6.1	Northampton	Sheffield	21.10.91

IPSWICH TOWN

Ground: Portman Road, Ipswich IP1 2DA. **Telephone:** 01473 400500. **Club nickname:** Blues/ Town. **Colours:** Blue and white. **Capacity:** 30,311. **Record attendance:** 38,010 v Leeds (FA Cup 6) Mar 8, 1975

Goalkeepers

Hladky, Vaclav	6.2	Salford	Bron, Cz	14.11.90
Holy, Tomas	6.9	Gillingham	Rychnov, Cz	10.12.91

Defenders

Donacien, Janoi	6.0	Accrington	Castries, St Luc	03.11.93
Kenlock, Myles	6.1	–	Croydon	29.11.96
Ndaba, Corrie	6.2	–	Dublin, Ire	25.12.99
Nsiala, Toto	6.4	Shrewsbury	Kinshasa, DR Cong	25.03.92
Penney, Matt	5.8	Sheffield Wed	Chesterfield	11.02.98
Vincent-Young, Kane	5.11	Colchester	Camden	15.03.96
Woolfenden, Luke	6.1	–	Ipswich	21.10.98

Midfielders

Bishop, Teddy	5.11	–	Cambridge	15.07.96
Dobra, Armando	5.8	–	Redbridge	14.04.01
Downes, Flynn	5.10	–	Brentwood	20.01.99
El Mizouni, Idris	5.10	–	Paris, Fr	26.09.00
Evans, Lee	6.1	Wigan	Newport	24.07.94
Harper, Rekeem	6.0	WBA	Birmingham	08.03.00
Nolan, Jon	5.10	Shrewsbury	Huyton	22.04.92
Tunnicliffe, Ryan	6.0	Luton	Heywood	30.12.92

Forwards

Bonne, Macauley	5.11	QPR (loan)	Ipswich	26.10.95
Burns, Wes	5.8	Fleetwood	Cardiff	23.11.94
Hawkins, Oli	6.4	Portsmouth	Ealing	08.04.92
Jackson, Kayden	5.11	Accrington	Bradford	22.02.94
Norwood, James	5.10	Tranmere	Eastbourne	05.09.90
Pigott, Joe	6.2	AFC Wimbledon	Maidstone	24.11.93

LINCOLN CITY

Ground: LNER Stadium, Lincoln LN5 8LD. **Telephone:** 01522 880011. **Club nickname:** Imps. **Colours:** Red and white. **Capacity:** 10,300. **Record attendance:** 23,196 v Derby (League Cup 4) Nov 15, 1967

Goalkeepers

Long, Sam	6.0	Crystal Palace	Redbridge	12.11.02

Defenders

Bramall, Cohen	5.9	Colchester	Crewe	02.04.96
Jackson, Adam	6.2	Hibernian	Darlington	18.05.94
Melbourne, Max	5.10	WBA	Solihull	24.10.98
Montsma, Lewis	6.3	Dordrecht	Amsterdam, Hol	25.04.98
Poole, Regan	6.0	MK Dons	Cardiff	18.06.98
Walsh, Joe	5.11	MK Dons	Cardiff	13.05.92

Midfielders

Archibald, Theo	6.1	Macclesfield	Glasgow	05.03.98
Bridcutt, Liam	5.9	Nottm Florest	Reading	08.05.89
Elbouzedi, Zack	6.1	Waterford	Dublin, Ire	05.04.98
Fiorini, Lewis	5.10	Manchester City (loan)	Manchester	17.05.02
Jones, Jamie	5.9	Crewe	Winsford	01.02.96
Maguire, Chris	5.8	Sunderland	Bellshill	16.01.89
McGrandles, Conor	6.0	MK Dons	Falkirk	24.09.95
Sanders, Max	5.9	Brighton	Horsham	04.01.99
Tayo Edun	5.10	Fulham	Islington	14.05.98

Forwards

Hopper, Tom	6.1	Southend	Boston	14.12.93
Howarth, Remy	5.11	Cefn Druids	Manchester	14.09.97
Scully, Anthony	5.10	West Ham	London	19.04.99

MILTON KEYNES DONS

Ground: stadiummk, Stadium Way West, Milton Keynes MK1 1ST. **Telephone:** 01908 622922.
Club nickname: Dons. **Colours:** White. **Capacity:** 30,500. **Record attendance:** 28,127 v Chelsea
(FA Cup 4) Jan 31, 2016

Goalkeepers

Fisher, Andrew	6.0	Blackburn	Wigan	12.02.98
Ravizzoli, Franco	6.1	Eastbourne	Mar del Plata, Arg	09.07.97

Defenders

Darling, Harry	5.11	Cambridge	Cambridge	08.08.99
Jules, Zak	6.3	Walsall	Islington	02.07.97
Harvie, Daniel	6.0	Ayr	Glasgow	14.07.98
Lewington, Dean	5.11	Wimbledon	Kingston upon Thames	18.05.84

Midfielders

Fraser, Scott	6.0	Burton	Dundee	30.03.95
Gladwin, Ben	6.3	Blackburn	Reading	08.06.92
Kasumu, David	5.11	–	Lambert	05.10.99
Martin, Josh	5.9	Norwich (loan)	Luton	09.09.01
O'Riley, Matt	6.2	Fulham	London	
Robson, Ethan	6.0	Blackpool (loan)	Houghton-le-Spring	25.10.96
Surman, Andrew	5.10	Bournemouth	Johannesburg, SA	20.08.86

Forwards

Bird, Jay	6.0	–	Milton Keynes	13.09.00
Brown, Charlie	6.1	Chelsea	Ipswich	23.09.99
Twine, Scott	5.9	Swindon	Swindon	14.07.99
Watters, Max	5.11	Cardiff (loan)	Camden	23.03.99

MORECAMBE

Ground: Mazuma Stadium, Christie Way, Westgate, Morecambe LA4 4TB. **Telephone:** 01524
411797. **Club nickname:** Shrimps. **Colours:** Red. **Capacity:** 6,476. **Record attendance:** Christie
Park: 9,234 v Weymouth (FA Cup 3) Jan 6, 1962. Mazuma Stadium: 5,003 v Burnley (League
Cup 2) Aug 24, 2010

Goalkeepers

Letheren, Kyle	6.2	Chesterfield	Llanelli	26.12.87

Defenders

Cooney, Ryan	5.10	Burnley	Manchester	26.02.00
Delaney, Ryan	6.0	Bolton	Wexford, Ire	06.09.96
Gibson, Liam	6.1	Newcastle	Stanley	25.04.97
Lavelle, Sam	6.0	Bolton	Blackpool	03.10.96
Leigh, Greg	5.11	Aberdeen	Sale	30.09.94
Mellor, Kelvin	6,2	Bradford	Crewe	25.01.91

Midfielders

Diagouraga, Toumani	6.2	Swindon	Paris, Fr	10.06.87
Jones, Callum	5.9	Hull (loan)	Birkenhead	05.04.01
McAlmont, Alfie	5.9	Leeds (loan)	Thirsk	25.03.00
McDonald, Wes	5.9	Walsall	Lambeth	04.05.97
McPake, Josh	6.1	Rangers	Coatbridge	31.08.01
Price, Freddie	5.11	–	Stafford	12.05.02
Wildig, Aaron	5.9	Shrewsbury	Hereford	15.04.92

Forwards

Gnahoua, Arthur	5.11	Bolton	London	18.09.92
Obika, Jonathan	6.0	St Mirren	Enfield	12.09.90
Stockton, Cole	6.1	Tranmere	Huyton	13.03.94

OXFORD UNITED

Ground: Kassam Stadium, Grenoble Road, Oxford OX4 4XP. **Telephone:** 01865 337500.
Club nickname: U's. **Colours:** Yellow and black. **Capacity:** 12,500. **Record attendance:** Manor
Ground: 22,750 v Preston (FA Cup 6) Feb 29, 1964. Kassam Stadium: 12,243 v Leyton Ori-
ent (Lge 2) May 6, 2006

Goalkeepers

Eastwood, Simon	6.2	Blackburn	Luton	26.06.89
Stevens, Jack	6.2	–	–	02.08.97

Defenders

Elechi, Michael	6.1	Manchester Utd	Westminster	10.10.00
Lofthouse, Kyran	5.11	–	Oxford	21.10.00
Long, Sam	5.10	–	Oxford	16.01.95
Moore, Elliott	6.5	Leicester	Coalville	16.03.97
Mousinho, John	6.1	Burton	Isleworth	30.04.86

Midfielders

Brannagan, Cameron	5.11	Liverpool	Manchester	09.05.96
Clare, Sean	6.3	Hearts	Hackney	18.09.96
Cooper, Joel	5.11	Linfield	Ballyclare	29.02.96
Forde, Anthony	6.1	Rotherham	Ballingarry, Ire	16.11.93
Gorrin, Alex	6.0	Motherwell	Tenerife, Sp	01.08.93
Hanson, Jamie	6.3	Derby	Burton upon Trent	10.11.95
Henry, James	6.1	Wolves	Reading	10.06.89
McGuane, Marcus	5.10	Nottm Forest	Greenwich	02.12.99
Sykes, Mark	6.0	Glenavon	Belfast	04.08.97
Williams, Ryan	5.8	Portsmouth	Perth, Aus	28.10.93

Forwards

Agyei, Dan	6.0	Burnley	Kingston upon Thames	01.06.97
Bodin, Billy	5.11	Preston	Swindon	24.03.92
Osei, Derick	6.2	Brest	Toulouse, Fr	10.09.98
Taylor, Matty	5.9	Bristol City	OxfoOrd	30.03.90
Winnall, Sam	5.10	Barnsley	Wolverhampton	19.01.91

PLYMOUTH ARGYLE

Ground: Home Park, Plymouth PL2 3DQ. **Telephone:** 01752 562561. **Club nickname:** Pilgrims
Colours: Green and white. **Capacity:** 18,600. **Record attendance:** 43,596 v Aston Villa (Div 2)
Oct 10, 1936

Goalkeepers

Burton, Callum	6.2	Cambridge	Newport, Salop	15.08.96
Cooper, Michael	6.1	–	Exeter	08.10.99

Defenders

Bolton, James	6.0	Portsmouth	Stone	13.08.94
Gillesphey, Macaulay	5.11	Brisbane	Ashington	24.11.95
Law, Ryan	5.10	–	Kingsteignton	08.09.99
Sawyer, Gary	6.0	Leyton Orient	Bideford	05.07.85
Scarr, Dan	6.2	Walsall	Bromsgrove	24.12.94
Wilson, James	6.2	Lincoln	Newport	26.02.89

Midfielders

Camara, Panutche	6.1	Crawley	Guin-Bass	28.02.97
Cooper, George	5.9	Peterborough	Warrington	30.10.96
Edwards, Joe	5.9	Walsall	Gloucester	31.10.90
Grant, Conor	5.9	Everton	Fazakerley	18.04.95

Houghton, Jordan	6.0	MK Dons	Chertsey	09.11.95
Jephcott, Luke	5.10	–	Truro	26.01.00
Mayor, Danny	6.0	Bury	Leyland	18.10.90
Randell, Adam	5.9	–	Plymouth	01.10.00
Forwards				
Ennis, Niall	5.10	Wolves	Wolverhampton	20.05.99
Hardie, Ryan	6.2	Blackpool	Stranraer	17.03.97

PORTSMOUTH

Ground: Fratton Park, Frogmore Road, Portsmouth, PO4 8RA. **Telephone:** 0239 273 1204.
Club nickname: Pompey. **Colours:** Blue and white. **Capacity:** 21,000. **Record attendance:**
51,385 v Derby (FA Cup 6) Feb 26, 1949

Goalkeepers				
Bass, Alex	6.2	–	Southampton	01.04.98
Bazunu, Gavin	6.2	Manchester City (loan)	Dublin, Ire	20.02.02
Defenders				
Brown, Lee	6.0	Bristol Rov	Farnborough	10.08.90
Downing, Paul	6.1	Blackburn	Taunton	26.10.91
Freeman, Kieron	5.10	Swansea	Arnold	21.03.92
Johnson, Callum	5.11	Accrington	Yarm	23.10.96
Mnoga, Haji	6.1	–	Portsmouth	16.04.02
Raggett, Sean	6.6	Norwich	Gillingham	25.01.94
Robertson, Clark	6.2	Rotherham	Aberdeen	05.09.93
Vincent, Liam	5.8	Bromley	Bromley	11.02.03
Midfielders				
Curtis, Ronan	6.0	Derry	Donegal, Ire	29.03.96
Harness, Marcus	6.0	Burton	Coventry	01.08.94
Jacobs, Michael	5.9	Wigan	Rothwell	04.11.91
Williams, Shaun	6.0	Millwall	Dublin, Ire	19.09.86
Forwards				
Hackett-Fairchild, Reeco	6.3	Bromley	Redbridge	09.01.98
Harrison, Ellis	5.11	Ipswich	Newport	29.01.94
Marquis, John	6.1	Doncaster	Leisham	16.05.92

ROTHERHAM UNITED

Ground: New York Stadium, New York Way, Rotherham S60 1AH. **Telephone:** 08444 140733.
Club nickname: Millers. **Colours:** Red and white. **Capacity:** 12,021. **Record attendance:**
Millmoor: 25,170 v Sheffield Wed (Div 2) Jan 26, 1952 and v Sheffield Wed (Div 2) Dec 13,
1952; Don Valley Stadium: 7,082 v Aldershot (Lge 2 play-off semi-final, 2nd leg) May 19,
2010; New York Stadium: 11,758 v Sheffield Utd (Lge 1) Sep 7, 2013

Goalkeepers				
Johansson, Viktor	6.1	Leicester	Sweden	14.09.98
Vickers, Josh	6.4	Lincoln	Brentwood	01.12.95
Defenders				
Harding, Wes	5.11	Birmingham	Leicester	20.10.96
Ihiekwe, Michael	6.1	Tranmere	Liverpool	29.11.92
MacDonald, Angus	6.3	Hull	Wincheter	15.10.92
Mattock, Joe	6.0	Sheffield Wed	Leicester	15.05.90
Tilt, Curtis	6.4	Blackpool	Walsall	04.08.91
Wood, Richard	6.3	Charlton	Ossett	05.07.85

Midfielders

Barlaser, Dan	5.10	Newcastle	Gateshead	18.01.97
Crooks, Matt	6.1	Northampton	Leeds	20.01.94
Lindsay, Jamie	6.0	Ross Co	Rutherglen	11.10.95
Ogbene, Chiedozie	5.11	Brentford	Lagos, Nig	01.05.97
Sadlier, Kieran	6.0	Doncaster	Haywards Heath	14.09.94
Wiles, Ben	5.8	–	Rotherham	17.04.99

Forwards

Gratton, Jacob	6.0	–	Mansfield	05.01.02
Kayode, Joshua	6.3	–	Lagos, Nig	04.05.00
Ladapo, Freddie	6.0	Plymouth	Romford	01.02.93
Miller, Mickel	5.8	Hamilton	Croydon	02.12.95
Smith, Michael	6.4	Bury	Wallsend	17.10.91

SHEFFIELD WEDNESDAY

Ground: Hillsborough, Sheffield, S6 1SW. **Telephone:** 0871 995 1867. **Club nickname:** Owls. **Colours:** Blue and white. **Capacity:** 39,732. **Record attendance:** 72,841 v Manchester City (FA Cup 5) Feb 17, 1934

Goalkeepers

Dawson, Cameron	6.0	Sheffield Utd	Sheffield	07.07.95
Wildsmith, Joe	6.2	–	Sheffield	28.12.95

Defenders

Borner, Julian	6.2	Arminia Bielefeld	Weimar, Ger	21.01.91
Brennan, Ciaran	6.2	Waterford	Kilkenny, Ire	05.05.00
Dunkley, Chey	6.2	Wigan	Wolverhampton	13.02.92
Iorfa, Dominic	6.4	Wolves	Southend	24.06.95
Palmer, Liam	6.2	–	Worksop	19.09.91

Midfielders

Adeniran, Dennis	5.11	Everton	Southwark	02.01.99
Bannan, Barry	5.11	Crystal Palace	Airdrie	01.12.89
Dele-Bashiru, Fisayo	5.10	Manchester City	Hamburg, Ger	06.02.01
Green, Andre	5.11	Aston Villa	Solihull	26.07.98
Hunt, Alex	5.9	–	Sheffield	29.05.00
Hutchinson, Sam	6.0	Pafos	Windsor	31.08.89
Luongo, Massimo	5.10	QPR	Sydney, Aus	25.09.92

Forwards

Paterson, Callum	6.0	Cardiff	–	13.10.94
Windass, Josh	5.9	Wigan	Hull	09.01.94

SHREWSBURY TOWN

Ground: Montgomery Waters Meadow, Oteley Road, Shrewsbury SY2 6ST. **Telephone:** 01743 289177. **Club nickname:** Shrews. **Colours:** Blue and yellow. **Capacity:** 9,875. **Record attendance:** Gay Meadow: 18,917 v Walsall (Div 3) Apr 26, 1961. Montgmery Waters Meadow: 10,210 v Chelsea (Lge Cup 4) Oct 28, 2014

Goalkeepers

Burgoyne, Harry	6.4	Wolves	Ludlow	28.12.96
Gregory, Cameron	6.3	–	Sutton Coldfield	20.01.00
Marosi, Marko	6.3	Coventry	Slovakia	23.10.93

Defenders

Bennett, Elliott	5.10	Blackburn	Telford	18.12.88
Ebanks-Landell, Ethan	6.2	Wolves	West Bromwich	16.12.92

Name	Height	Previous Club	Birthplace	DOB
Leahy, Luke	5.10	Bristol Rov	Coventry	19.11.92
Ogbeta, Nathaniel	6.0	Manchester City	Salford	28.04.01
Pennington, Matthew	6.1	Everton	Warrington	06.10.94
Pierre, Aaron	6.1	Northampton	Southall	17.02.93
Midfielders				
Daniels, Josh	5.10	Glenavon	Derry	22.02.96
Davis, David	5.10	Birmingham	Smethwick	20.02.91
Norburn, Ollie	6.1	Tranmere	Bolton	26.10.92
Vela, Josh	5.11	Hibernian	Salford	14.12.93
Forwards				
Bowman, Ryan	6.2	Exeter	Carlisle	30.11.91
Pyke, Rekeil	6.2	Huddersfield	Leeds	01.09.97
Udoh, Daniel	6.1	AFC Telord	Lagos, Nig	30.08.96
Whalley, Shaun	5.9	Luton	Whiston	07.08.87

SUNDERLAND

Ground: Stadium of Light, Sunderland SR5 1SU. **Telephone:** 0871 911 1200. **Club nickname:** Black Cats. **Capacity:** 49,400. **Colours:** Red and white. **Record attendance:** Roker Park: 75,118 v Derby (FA Cup 6 rep) Mar 8, 1933. Stadium of Light: 48,353 v Liverpool (Prem Lge) Apr 13, 2002

Name	Height	Previous Club	Birthplace	DOB
Goalkeepers				
Burge, Lee	6.0	Coventry	Hereford	09.01.93
Defenders				
Arbenit Xhemajli	6.3	Neuchatel	Brugg, Switz	23.04.98
Flanagan, Tom	6.2	Burton	Hammersmith	21.10.91
Hume, Denver	5.10	–	Newbiggin	11.08.98
Willis, Jordan	5.11	Coventry	Coventry	24.08.94
Wright, Bailey	5.10	Bristol City	Mebourne, Aus	28.07.92
Midfielders				
Diamond, Jack	5.9	–	Gateshead	12.01.00
Embleton, Elliot	5.8	–	Durham	02.04.99
Gooch, Lyndon	5.8	–	Santa Cruz, US	24.12.95
McGeady, Aiden	5.11	Everton	Paisley	04.04.86
O'Nien, Luke	5.9	Wycombe	Hemel Hempstead	21.11.94
Pritchard, Alex	5.9	Huddersfield	Orsett	03.05.93
Winchester, Carl	6.0	Forest Green	Belfast	12.04.93
Forwards				
Grigg, Will	5.11	Wigan	Solihull	03.07.91
O'Brien, Aiden	5.9	Millwall	Islington	04.10.93
Stewart, Ross	6.2	Ross Co	Irvine	11.07.96

WIGAN ATHLETIC

Ground: DW Stadium, Robin Park, Wigan WN5 0UZ. **Telephone:** 01942 774000. **Club nickname:** Latics. **Colours:** Blue. **Capacity:** 25,138. **Record attendance:** Springfield Park: 27,526 v Hereford (FA Cup 2) Dec 12, 1953; DW Stadium: 25,133 v Manchester Utd (Prem Lge) May 11, 2008

Name	Height	Previous Club	Birthplace	DOB
Goalkeepers				
Amos, Ben	6.3	Charlton	Macclesfield	10.04.90
Jones, Jamie	6.2	Stevenage	Kirkby	18.02.89
Defenders				
Darikwa, Tendayi	6.2	Nottm Forest	Nottingham	13.12.91

Naylor, Tom	6.2	Portsmouth	Kirkby-in-Ashfield	28.06.91
Pearce, Tom	6.1	Leeds	Ormskirk	12.04.98
Whatmough, Jack	6.0	Portsmouth	Gosport	19.08.96
Midfielders				
Edwards, Gwion	5.9	Ipswich	Lampeter	01.03.93
McGurk, Sean	5.10	–	Liverpool	15.03.03
Power, Max	5.11	Sunderland	Birkenhead	27.07.93
Solomon-Otabor, Viv	5.9	CSKA Sofia	London	02.01.96
Forwards				
Dodoo, Joe	6.0	Ankara	Kumasi, Gh	29.06.95
Humphrys, Stephen	6.1	Rochdale	Oldham	15.09.97
Joseph, Kyle	6.1	–	Barnet	10.09.01
Keane, Will	6.2	Ipswich	Stockport	11.01.93
Lang, Callum	6.0	Liverpool	Liverpool	08.09.98
Massey, Gavin	5.10	Leyton Orient	Watford	14.10.92
Wyke, Charlie	5.11	Sunderland	Middlesbrough	06.12.92

WYCOMBE WANDERERS

Ground: Adams Park, Hillbottom Road, High Wycombe HP12 4HJ. **Telephone:** 01494 472100.
Club nickname: Chairboys. **Colours:** Light and dark blue. **Capacity:** 10,137. **Record attendance:**
10,000 v Chelsea (friendly) July 13, 2005

Goalkeepers				
Stockdale, David	6.3	Birmingham	Leeds	20.09.85
Defenders				
Grimmer, Jack	6.1	Coventry	Aberdeen	25.01.94
Jacobson, Joe	5.11	Shrewsbury	Cardiff	17.11.86
McCarthy, Jason	6.1	Millwall	Southampton	07.11.95
McCleary, Garath	6.0	Reading	Oxford	15.05.87
Stewart, Anthony	6.0	Crewe	Lambeth	18.09.92
Tafazolli, Ryan	6.5	Hull	Sutton	28.09.91
Midfielders				
Bloomfield, Matt	5.8	Ipswich	Felixstowe	08.02.84
Freeman, Nick	5.11	Biggleswade	Stevenage	07.11.95
Gape, Dominic	5.11	Southampton	Burton Bradstock	09.09.94
Horgan, Daryl	5.8	Hibernian	Galway, Ire	10.08.92
Mehmeti, Anis	Woodford		Islington	09.01.01
Obita, Jordan	5.11	Oxford	Oxford	08.12.93
Wheeler, David	5.11	QPR	Brighton	04.10.90
Scowen, Josh	5.10	Sunderland	Enfield	28.03.93
Thompson, Curtis	5.7	Notts Co	Nottingham	02.09.93
Forwards				
Akinfenwa, Adebayo	6.0	Wimbledon	Islington	10.05.82
Kashket, Scott	5.9	Leyton Orient	Chigwell	25.02.96
Samuel; Alex	5.9	Stevenage	Neath	20.09.95

LEAGUE TWO

BARROW

Ground: Progession Solicitors Stadium, Wilkie Road, Barrow LA14 5UW. **Telephone:** 01229 666010. **Club nickname:** Bluebirds. **Colours:** Blue and white. **Capacity:** 5,045. **Record attendance:** 16,874 v Swansea (FA Cup 3) Jan 9, 1954

Goalkeepers
Farman, Paul	6.5	Carlisle	North Shields	02.11.89
Lillis, Josh	6.2	Rochdale	Derby	24.06.87

Defenders
Beadling, Tom	6.1	Dunfermline	Barrow 16.01.96	
Brough, Patrick	6.3	Falkirk	Carlisle	20.02.96
Brown, Connor	5.9	York	Sheffield	02.10.91
Burns, Bobby	5.9	Hearts	Antrim	07.10.99
Ellis, Mark	6.2	Tranmere	Plymouth	30.09.88
Hutton, Remeao	5.10	Birmingham	Walsall	28.09.98
Jones, James	6.0	Altrincham	Wrexham	13.03.97
Ntlhe, Kgosi	5.9	Scunthorpe	Pretoria, SA	21.02.94
Platt, Matty	6.0	Blackburn	Knowsley	03.10.97

Midfielders
Banks, Ollie	6.3	Tranmere	Rotherham	21.09.92
Devitt, Jamie	5.10	Blackpool	Dublin, Ire	06.07.90
Grayson, Joe	5.10	Blackburn	Leicester	26.03.99
James, Luke	5.11	Hartlepool	Amble	04.01.94
Jones, Mike	6.0	Carlisle	Birkenhead	15.08.87
Kay, Josh	6.0	Chesterfield	Blackpool	30.01.97
Taylor, Jason	6.1	Eastleigh	Droylsden	28.01.87
White, Tom	5.10	Blackburn	–	09.05.97

Forwards
Gordon, Josh	5.10	Walsall	Stoke	19.01.95
Quigley, Scott	6.4	Blackpool	Shrewsbury	02.09.92
Sea, Dimitri	5.11	Aston Villa	Paris, Fr	28.08.01
Zanzala, Offrande	6.1	Carlisle	Brazzaville, Rep Con	08.11.96

BRADFORD CITY

Ground: Utilita Energy Stadium, Valley Parade, Bradford BD8 7DY. **Telephone:** 01274 773355. **Club nickname:** Bantams. **Colours:** Claret and amber. **Capacity:** 25,136. **Record attendance:** 39,146 v Burnley (FA Cup 4) Mar 11, 1911

Goalkeepers
Hornby, Sam	6.3	Port Vale	Birmingham	02.02.95
O'Donnell, Richard	6.2	Northampton	Sheffield	12.09.88

Defenders
Canavan, Niall	6.3	Plymouth	Leeds	11.04.91
Cousin-Dawson, Finn	6.0	–	Stockton	04.07.02
Evans, Gareth	5.10	Portsmouth	Macclesfield	26.04.88
Foulds, Matty	5.10	Como	Bradford	17.02.98
Kelleher, Fiacre	6.3	Wrexham	Cork, Ire	10.03.96
O'Connor, Paudie	6.3	Leeds	Limerick, Ire	14.07.97
Ridehalgh, Liam	5.10	Tranmere	Halifax	20.04.91
Sikora, Jorge	6.2	–	Bradford	29.03.02

Songo'o, Yann	6.1	Morecambe	Toulon, Fr	19.11.91
Staunton, Reece	6.0	–	Bradford	10.12.01
Threlkeld, Oscar	6.0	Salford	Radcliffe	15.12.94

Midfielders

Cooke, Callum	5.9	Peterborough	Peterlee	21.02.97
Crankshaw, Ollie	5.0	Wigan	Preston	12.08.98
Gilliead, Alex	6.0	Scunthorpe	Shotley Bridge	11.02.96
Scales, Kian	5.11	–	Leeds	10.05.02
Sutton, Levi	5.11	Scunthorpe	Scunthorpe	24.03.96
Watt, Elliot	5.11	Wolves	Preston	11.03.00

Forwards

Angol, Lee	6.2	Leyton Orieny	Sutton	04.08.94
Cook, Andy	6.1	Mansfield	Bishop Auckland	18.10.90
Eisa, Abou	5.11	Scunthorpe	Khartoum, Sud	05.01.96
Vernam, Charles	5.9	Burton	Lincoln	08.10.96

BRISTOL ROVERS

Ground: Memorial Stadium, Filton Avenue, Horfield, Bristol BS7 OBF. **Telephone:** 0117 909 6648. **Club nickname:** Pirates. **Colours:** Blue and white. **Capacity:** 12,300. **Record attendance:** Eastville: 38,472 v Preston (FA Cup 4) Jan 30, 1960. Memorial Stadium: 12,011 v WBA (FA Cup 6) Mar 9, 2008

Goalkeepers

Jaakkola, Anssi	6.5	Reading	Kemi, Fin	13.03.87

Defenders

Baldwin, Jack	6.1	Sunderland	Barking	30.06.93
Clarke, Trevor	5.9	Rotherham	Dublin, Ire	26.03.98
Grant, Josh	6.1	Chelsea	Brixton	11.10.98
Harries, Cian	6.1	Swansea	Birmingham	01.04.97
Kilgour, Alfie	5.10	–	Bath	18.05.98
Martinez, Pablo	6.1	WBA	Oxford	11.10.00
Westbrooke, Zain	5.11	Coventry	Chertseyy	28.10.96

Midfielders

Anderson, Harry	5.9	Lincoln	Slough	09.01.97
Barrett, Josh	5.11	Reading	Oxford	21.06.98
Hargreaves, Cameron	5.10	Exeter	Plymouth	01.12.98
Liddle, Ben	5.7	Middlesbrough	Durham	21.09.98
Nicholson, Sam	5.10	Colorado	Edinburgh	20.01.95
Thomas, Luke	5.8	Barnsley (loan)	Soudley	19.02.99
Walker, Zain	5.8	–	Wandsworth	08.01.02

Forwards

Ayunga, Jonah	6.1	Havant	Beaminster	24.04.97
Collins, Aaron	6.1	Forest Green	Newport	27.05.97
Hanlan, Brandon	6.0	Gillingham	Chelsea	31.05.97
Phillips, Kieran	5.11	–	Bristol	13.08.02
Rodman, Alex	6.2	Shrewsbury	Sutton Coldfield	15.12.87
Saunders, Harvey	5.10	Fleetwood	Wolverhampton	20.07.97

CARLISLE UNITED

Ground: Brunton Park, Warwick Road, Carlisle CA1 1LL. **Telephone:** 01228 526237. **Club nickname:** Cumbrians. **Colours:** Blue. **Capacity:** 17,949. **Record attendance:** 27,500 v Birmingham City (FA Cup 3) Jan 5, 1957, v Middlesbrough (FA Cup 5) Jan 7, 1970

Goalkeepers

Norman, Magnus	6.4	Fulham	London	19.01.97

Defenders

Armer, Jack	6.1	Preston	Preston	16.04.01
Bennett, Reece	6.3	Peterborough	Bolton	01.09.91
Feeney, Morgan	6.3	Sunderland	Bootle	05.02.99
Hayden, Aaron	6.1	Wolves	Croydon	16.01.97
McDonald, Rod	6.3	AFC Wimbledon	Crewe	11.04.92
Mellish, Jon	6.2	Gateshead	South Shields	19.09.97
Tanner, George	5.11	Manchester Utd	Blackpool	16.11.99
Whelan, Corey	6.0	Wigan	Chester	12.12.97

Midfielders

Charters, Taylor	6.1	–	Whitehaven	02.10.01
Devine, Danny	5.11	Bradford	Bradford	04.09.97
Dickenson, Brennan	6.0	Exeter	Ferndown	26.02.93
Dixon, Josh	5.11	–	-	07.02.01
Guy, Callum	5.10	Blackpool	Nottingham	25.11.96
Riley, Joe	5.10	Bradfprd	Blackpool	06.12.96

Forwards

Abrahams, Tristan	6.1	Newport	Lewisham	29.12.98
Alessandra, Lewis	5.10	Morecambe	Heywood	08.02.89
Clough, Zach	5.8	Wigan	Denton	08.03.95
Toure, Gime	6.3	Hartlepool	France	07.05.94

COLCHESTER UNITED

Ground: JobServe Community Stadium, United Way, Colchester CO4 5HE. **Telephone:** 01206 755100. **Club nickname:** U's. **Colours:** Blue and. **Capacity:** 10,105. **Record attendance:** Layer Road:19,072 v Reading (FA Cup 1) Nov 27, 1948.
Community Stadium: 10,064 v Norwich (Lge 1) Jan 16, 2010

Goalkeepers

George, Shamal	6.3	Liverpool	Wirral	06.01.98
Gerken, Dean	6.2	Ipswich	Southend	04.08.85

Defenders

Chambers, Luke	5.11	Ipswich	Kettering	29.08.85
Clampin, Ryan	5.11	–	Colchester	29.01.99
Coxe, Cameron	6.1	Solihull (loan)	Merthyr Tydfil	18.12.98
Eastman, Tom	6.3	Ipswich	Colchester	21.10.91
Smith, Tommy	6.2	Sunderland	Macclesfield	31.03.90
Welch-Hayes, Miles	5.11	Macclesfield	Oxford	25.10.96

Midfielders

Chilvers, Noah	5.8	–	Chelmsford	22.02.01
Hannant, Luke	5.11	Cambridge	Great Yarmouth	04.11.93
Hasanally, Andree	5.10	–	Waltham Forest	10.02.02
Judge, Alan	6.0	Ipswich	Dublin, Ire	11.11.88
Poku, Kwame	5.9	Worthing	Croydon	11.08.01
Skuse, Cole	5.9	Ipswich	Bristol	29.03.86

Forwards

Nouble, Frank	6.3	Plymouth	Lewisham	24.09.91
Sears, Freddie	5.10	Ipswich	Hornchurch	27.11.89

CRAWLEY TOWN

Ground: People's Pension Stadium, Winfield Way, Crawley RH11 9RX. **Telephone:** 01293

410000. **Club nickname:** Reds. **Colours:** Red. **Capacity:** 6,134. **Record attendance:** 5,880 v Reading (FA Cup 3) Jan 5, 2013

Goalkeepers
Jones, Alfie	6.0	MK Dons	–	02.10.00
Morris, Glenn	6.0	Gillingham	Woolwich	20.12.83

Defenders
Adebowale, Emmanuel	6.5	Eastbourne	Stratford	19.09.97
Craig, Tony	6.0	Bristol Rov	Greenwich	20.04.85
Dallison, Tom	6.1	Falkirk	Romford	02.02.96
Davies, Archie	6.0	Brighton	St Leonards	07.10.98
Gallacher, Owen	-	Burton	Newcastle	06.04.99
Ransom, Harry	–	Millwall	Uckfield	01.10.99
Tsaroulla, Nick	5.10	Brentford	Bristol	29.03.99
Tunnicliffe, Jordan	6.1	AFC Fylde	Nuneaton	13.20.93
Young, Lewis	5.9	Bury	Stevenage	27.09.89

Midfielders
Al-Hussaini, Zaid	5.11	Hampton	Lodon	07.06.00
Bulman, Dannie	5.8	AFC Wimbledon	Ashford, Surrey	24.01.79
Francomb, George	6.0	AFC Wimbledon	Hackney	08.09.91
Frost, Tyler	5.9	Reading	Reading	07.07.99
Grego-Cox, Reece	5.7	Woking	Hammersmith	02.11.96
Hessenthaler, Jake	5.10	Grimsby	Gravesend	20.04.90
Mathews, Sam	5.10	Bristol Rov	Poole	01.03.97
Powell, Jack	5.10	Maidstone	Canning Town	29.01.94
Wright, Josh	6.0	Leyton Orient	Bethnal Green	06.11.89

Forwards
Ashford, Sam	5.11	Hemel Hempstead	Chelmsford	21.12.95
German, Ricky	5.11	Hendon	Harlesden	13.01.99
Nadesan, Ashley	6.2	Fleetwood	Redhill	09.09.94
Nichols, Tom	5.10	Bristol Rov	Taunton	28.08.93
Rodari, Davide	–	Hastings	Switzerland	23.06.99
Tilley, James	5.10	Grimsby	Billingshurst	13.06.98

EXETER CITY

Ground: St James Park, Stadium Way, Exeter EX4 6PX. **Telephone:** 01392 411243. **Club nickname:** Grecians. **Colours:** Red and white. **Capacity:** 8,696. **Record attendance:** 20,984 v Sunderland (FA Cup 6 replay) Mar 4, 1931

Goalkeepers
Brown, Scott	6.0	Port Vale	Wolverhampton	26.04.85

Defenders
Caprice, Jake	5.11	Tranmere	Lambeth	11.11.92
Hartridge, Alex	6.1	–	Torquay	09.03.99
Page, Lewis	5.10	Charlton	Enfield	20.05.96
Ray, George	6.0	Tranmere	Warrington	03.10.93
Rowe, Callum	–	Aston Villa	Leicester	02.09.99
Stubbs, Sam	6.0	Fleetwood	Liverpool	20.11.98
Sweeney, Pierce	6.0	Swindon	Dublin, Ire	11.09.94

Midfielders
Atangana, Nigel	6.2	Cheltenham	Corbeil-Essonnes, Fr	09.09.89
Brown, Jevani	5.9	Colchester	Letchworth	16.10.94
Coley, Josh	5.10	Maidenhead	Stevenage	24.07.98
Collins, Archie	5.9	–	Taunton	31.08.99

Key, Josh	5.1	Torquay	Exeter	19.11.99
Randall, Joel	5.10	–	Salisbury	01.11.99
Sparkes, Jack	5.9	–	Exeter	29.09.00
Taylor, Jake	5.10	Reading	Ascot	01.12.91
Forwards				
Jay, Matt	5.10	–	Torbay	27.02.96
Nombe, Sam	5.11	MK Dons	Croydon	22.10.98
Seymour, Ben	6.0	–	Watford	16.04.99

FOREST GREEN ROVERS

Ground: New Lawn, Another Way, Nailsworth GL6 OFG. **Telephone:** 01453 835291. **Club nickname:** Green Devils. **Colours:** Green. **Capacity:** 5,140. **Record attendance:** 4,836 v Derby (FA Cup 3, Jan 3, 2009)

Goalkeepers				
McGee, Luke	6.2	Portsmouth	Edgware	02.09.95
Thomas, Lewis	6.1	Swansea	Swansea	20.09.97
Defenders				
Bernard, Dom	6.0	Birmingham	Gloucester	29.03.97
Cargill, Baily	6.2	MK Dons	Winchester	05.07.95
Evans, Jack	5.8	Blackburn	Warrington	10.08.00
Moore-Taylor, Jordan	5.10	MK Dons	Exeter	21.01.94
Udoka Godwin-Malife	5.11	Oxford City	–	09.05.00
Wilson, Kane	5.10	WBA	Birmingham	11.03.00
Midfielders				
Adams, Ebou	5.11	Ebbsfleet	Greenwich	15.01.96
Aitchison, Jack	5.9	Barnsley (loan)	Fauldhouse	05.03.00
Bunker, Harvey	5.11	Southampton	Portsmouth	15.04.03
Cadden, Nicky	5.10	Morton	Bellshill	19.09.96
Covil, Vaughn	5.10	Southampton	San Diego, US	26.07.03
Diallo, Sadou	6.2	Wolves	Guin	10.06.99
Edwards, Opi	5.8	Bristol City	Bristol	30.04.99
Hendry, Regan	5.10	Raith Rov	Edinburgh	21.01.98
Stevenson, Ben	6.0	Colchester	Leicester	23.03.97
Sweeney, Dan	6.3	Barnet	Kingston upon Thames	25.04.94
Whitehouse, Elliott	5.11	Grimsby	Worksop	27.10.93
Forwards				
Allen, Taylor	5.10	Nuneaton	Walsall	16.06.00
March, Josh	5.10	Leamington	Stourbridge	18.03.97
Matt, Jamille	6.1	Newport	Kingston, Jam	20.10.89
Stevens, Matty	5.11	Peterborough	Guildford	12.02.98
Young, Jake	5.11	Sheffield Utd	Huddersfield	22.07.02

HARROGATE TOWN

Ground: EnviroVent Stadium, Wetherby Road, Harrogate, HG2 7SA. Telephone: 01423 210600. Club nickname: Town. Colours: Yellow and black. Capacity: 4,108. Record attendance: 4,280 v Harrogate Railway (Whitworth Cup Final, 1949-50)

Goalkeepers				
Belshaw, James	6.3	Tamworth	Nottingham	12.10.90
Cracknell, Joe	6.0	Bradford	Hull	28.09.94
Oxley, Mark	6.2	Southend	Sheffield	28.09.90

Defenders

Burrell, Warren	6.1	Buxton	Sheffield	03.06.90
Fallowfield, Ryan	5.9	North Ferriby	Hull	03.01.96
Hall, Connor	6.4	Brackley	Slough	23.05.93
Lokko, Kevin	6.2	Dover	Whitechapel	03.11.95
McArdle, Rory	6.1	Exeter	Sheffield	01.05.87
Smith, Will	6.1	Barnsley	Leeds	04.11.98

Midfielders

Falkingham, Josh	5.7	Darlington	Leeds	25.08.90
Kerry, Lloyd	5.6	Tamworth	Chesterfield	22.07.88
Kirby, Connor	5.10	Sheffield Wed	Barnsley	10.09.98
Pattison, Alex	6.0	Wycombe	Darlington	06.09.97
Thomson, George	FC United		Sheffield	19.05.92
Walker, Tom	6.0	AFC Fylde	Salfordq12.12.95	

Forwards

Armstrong, Luke	6.1	Salford	Durham	02.07.96
Beck, Mark	6.5	Darlington	Sunderland	02.02.94
Leesley, Joe	6.0	Alfreton	Sheffield	29.03.94
Martin, Aaron	6.0	Guisely	Sheffield	06.07.9
Muldoon, Jack	5.10	AFC Fylde	Scunthorpe	19.05.89
Orsi, Danilo	6.2	Maidenhead	Camden	19.04.96
Power, Simon	5.10	Norwich	Greystones, Ire	13.05.98

HARTLEPOOL UNITED

Ground: Victoria Park, Clarence Road, Hartlepool TS24 8BZ. Telephone: 01429 272584.
Club nickname: Pool. Colours: Blue and white. Capacity: 7,865. Record attendance: 17,426 v
Manchester Utd (FA Cup 3) Jan 5,1957

Goalkeepers

Killip, Ben	6.2	Braintree	Isleworth	24.11.95
Young, Brad	6.3	–	Sunderland	05.05.02

Defenders

Ferguson, David	5.10	York	Sunderland	07.06.94
Francis-Angol, Zaine	5.9	Brentwood	Walthamstow	30.06.93
Liddle, Gary	6.1	Walsall	Middlesbrough	15.06.86
Odusina, Timi	6.1	Norwich	Croydon	28.10.99
Ogle, Reagan	5.9	Accrington	Wollongong, Aus	29.03.99
Sterry, Jamie	5.11	South Shields	Newcastle	21.11.95

Midfielders

Campbell, Adam	6.2	–	–	28.05.03
Crawford, Tom	6.1	Notts Co	Chester	30.05.99
Donaldson, Ryan	5.9	Plymouth	Newcastle	01.05.91
Featherstone, Nicky	5.8	Harrogate	Goole	22.09.88
Holohan, Gavan	5.11	Waterford	Kilkenny, Ire	15.12.91
MacDonald, Josh	6.0	Halifax	Stockton	07.02.95
Molyneux, Luke	5.1	Sunderland	Bishop Auckland	29.03.98
Shelton, Mark	6.0	Salford	Nottingham	12.09.96

Forwards

Grey, Joe	5.9	–	Newcastle	04.05.03

LEYTON ORIENT

Ground: Breyer Group Stadium, Brisbane Road, London E10 5NF. Telephone: 0208 926 1111.
Club nickname: O's. Colours: Red. Capacity: 9,271. Record attendance: 34,345 v West Ham
(FA Cup 4) Jan 25, 1964

Goalkeepers

Sargeant, Sam	6.0	–	Greenwich	23.09.97
Vigouroux, Lawrence	6.4	Everton de Vina	Camden	19.11.93

Defenders

Beckles, Omar	6.3	Crewe	Kettering	19.10.91
Happe, Dan	6.5	–	Tower Hamlets	28.09.98
Kemp, Dan	5.7	West Ham	Sidcup	11.01.99
Ogie, Shadrach	6.1	–	Limerick, Ire	26.08.01
Sweeney, Jayden	5.10	–	Camden	04.12.01
Thompson, Adam	6.1	Rotherham	Harlow	28.09.92
Wood, Connor	5.11	Bradford	Harlow	17.07.96

Midfielders

Cisse, Ousseynou	6.5	Gillingham	Suresnes, Fr	07.04.91
Clay, Craig	5.11	Motherwell	Nottingham	05.05.92
Kyprianou, Hector	6.1	Tottenham	Enfield	27.05.01
Pratley, Darren	6.0	Charlton	Barking	22.04.85

Forwards

Drinan, Aaron	6.0	Ipswich	Cork, Ire	06.05.98
Smith, Harry	6.5	Northampton	Chatham	18.05.95
Smyth, Paul	5.8	QPR	Belfast	10.09.97
Sotiriou, Ruel	5.11	–	Edmonton	24.08.00

MANSFIELD TOWN

Ground: One Call Stadium, Quarry Lane, Mansfield NG18 5DA. **Telephone:** 01623 482482.
Club nickname: Stags. **Colours:** Amber and blue. **Capacity:** 9,186. **Record attendance:** 24,467
v Nottm Forest (FA Cup 3) Jan 10, 1953

Goalkeepers

Bishop, Nathan	6.1	Manchester Utd (loan)	Hillingdon	15.10.99
Shelvey, George	6.2	Nottm Forest (loan)	Nottingham	22.04.01
Stech, Marek	6.5	Luton	Prague, Cz	28.01.90

Defenders

Burke, Ryan	5.11	Birmingham	Dublin, Ire	23.11.00
Clarke, James	6.0	Burnley	Birkenhead	02.04.00
Hewitt, Elliott	5.11	Grimsby	Bodelwyddan	30.05.94
Menayesse, Rollin	6.3	Bristol Rov	Kinshasa, DR Con	04.12.97
O'Driscoll, Aaron	6.2	Southampton	Dublin, Ire	04.04.99
Perch, James	6.0	Scunthorpe	Mansfield	28.09.85
Rawson, Farrend	6.2	Forest Green	Nottingham	11.07.96

Midfielders

Charsley, Harry	5.10	Everton	Birkenhead	01.11.96
Clarke, Ollie	5.11	Bristol Rov	Bristol	29.06.92
Gordon, Kellan	.11	Derby	Burton	25.12.97
Lapslie, George	5.9	Charlton	Waltham Forest	05.09.97
Maris, George	5.11	Cambridge	Sheffield	06.03.96
McLaughlin, Stephen	5.10	Southend	Donegal, Ire	14.06.90
O'Keefe, Corey	6.0	Birmingham	Birmingham	05.06.98
Quinn, Stephen	5.6	Burton	Dublin, Ire	01.04.86
Sinclair, Tyrese	5,9	Blackburn	Kingston upon Thames	04.02.01

Forwards

Bowery, Jordan	6.1	MK dons	Nottingham	02.07.91
Hawkins, Oli	6.4	Ipswich	Ealing	08.04.92
Johnson, Danny	5.10	Leyton Orient	Middlesbrough	28.02.93
Knowles, Jimmy	6.0	Nottm Forest	Sutton-in-Ashfield	25.01.02

| Law, Jason | 5.10 | Carlton | Nottingham | 26.04.99 |
| Oates, Rhys | 6.0 | Hartlepool | Pontefract | 04.12.94 |

NEWPORT COUNTY

Ground: Rodney Parade, Newport NP19 0UU. **Telephone:** 01633 670690. **Club nickname:** Exiles. **Colours:** Amber and black. **Capacity:** 7,850. **Record attendance:** Somerton Park: 24,268 v Cardiff (Div 3S) Oct 16, 1937. Rodney Parade: 9,836 v Tottenham (FA Cup 4) Jan 27, 2018.

Goalkeepers
| Day, Joe | 6.1 | Cardiff | Brighton | 13.08.90 |
| Townsend, Nick | 5.11 | Barnsley | Solihull | 01.11.94 |

Defenders
Bennett, Scott	5.10	Notts Co	Newquay	30.11.90
Clarke, James	6.0	Walsall	Aylesbury	17.11.89
Demetriou, Mickey	6.2	Shrewsbury	Dorrington	12.03.90
Farquharson, Priestley	6.3	Connah's Quay	London	15.03.97
Norman, Cameron	6.2	Walsall	Norwih	12.10.95
Haynes, Ryan	6.1	Shrewsbury	Northampton	27.09.95
Upson, Ed	5.10	Bristol Rov	Bury St Edmunds	21.11.89

Midfielders
Collins, Lewis	5.10	–	Newport	09.05.01
Dolan, Matt	5.9	Yeovil	Hartlepool	11.02.93
Ellison, Kevin	6.0	Morecambe	Liverpool	23.02.79
Missilou, Christopher	5.11	Swindon	Auxerre, Fr	18.07.92
Willmott, Robbie	5.9	Chelmsford	Harlow	16.05.90

Forwards
Amond, Padraig	5.11	Hartlepool	Carlow, Ire	15.04.88
Baker-Richardson, Courtney	6.2	Barrow	Coventry	05.12.95
Hylton, Jermaine	5.10	Ross Co	Birmingham	28.06.93
Telford, Dom	5.9	Plymouth	Burnley	05.12.96

NORTHAMPTON TOWN

Ground: Sixfields Stadium, Upton Way, Northampton NN5 5QA. **Telephone:** 01604 683700. **Club nickname:** Cobblers. **Colours:** Claret and white. **Capacity:** 7,789. **Record attendance:** County Ground: 24,523 v Fulham (Div 1) Apr 23, 1966. Sixfields Stadium: 7,798 v Manchester Utd (Lge Cup 3) Sep 21, 2016

Goalkeepers
| Maxted, Jonny | 6.0 | Exeter | Tadcaster | 26.10.93 |
| Roberts, Liam | 6.0 | Walsall | Walsall | 24.11.94 |

Defenders
Bolger, Cian	6.4	Lincoln	Cellbridge, Ire	12.03.92
Guthrie, Jon	6.3	Livingston	Devizes	29.07.92
Harriman, Michael	5.7	Wycombe	Chichester	23.10.92
Horsfall, Fraser	6.3	Macclesfield	Huddersfield	12.11.96
McGowan, Aaron	6.0	Kilmarnock	Liverpool	24.07.96
Mills, Joseph	5.9	Forest Green	Swindon	30.10.89
Nelson, Sid	6.1	Tranmere	Lewisham	01.01.96

Midfielders
Connolly, Dylan	5.9	St Mirren	Dublin, Ire	02.05.95
Flores, Jordan	5.11	Hull (loan)	Wigan	04.10.95
Hoskins, Sam	5.8	Yeovil	Dorchester	04.02.93
Lewis, Paul	6.1	Tranmere	Liverpool	17.12.94
McWilliams, Shaun	5.11	–	Northampton	14.08.98

Pinnock, Mitch	6.1	Kilmarnock	Gravesend	12.12.94
Pollock, Scott	5.10	–	Northampton	12.03.01
Roberts, Morgan	5.10	–	Northampton	20.12.00
Sowerby, Jack	5.9	Fleetwood	Preston	23.03.95
Forwards				
Ashley-Seal, Benny	6.1	Wolves	Southwark	21.11.98
Rose, Danny	5.9	Mansfield	Barnsley	10.12.93

OLDHAM ATHLETIC

Ground: Boundary Park, Oldham OL1 2PA. **Telephone:** 0161 624 4972. **Club nickname:** Latics. **Colours:** Blue and white. **Capacity:** 13,513. **Record attendance:** 47,761 v Sheffield Wed (FA Cup 4) Jan 25, 1930

Goalkeepers				
Leutwiler, Jayson	6.4	Huddersfield	Neuchatel, Switz	25.04.89
Defenders				
Badan, Andrea	5.10	Hellas Verona	Monselice, It	21.03.98
Clarke, Jordan	6.0	Scunthorpe	Coventry	19.11.91
Diarra, Raphael	6.1	Rouen	Paris, Fr	27.05.95
Hart, Sam	5.11	Southend	Bolton	10.09.96
Jameson, Kyle	6.0	AFC Fylde	Urmston	11.09.98
McGahey, Harrison	6.1	Scunthorpe	Preston	26.09.95
Piergianni, Carl	6.1	Salford	Peterborough	03.05.92
Midfielders				
Adans, Nicky	5.10	Northampton	Bolton	16.10.86
Bahamboula, Dylan	6.1	Tsarsko Selo	Corbeil-Essonnes, Fr	22.05.95
Fage, Dylan	5.0	Auxerre	Paris, Fr	18.03.99
Keillor-Dunn, Davis	5.11	Wrexham	Sunderland	02.11.97
Whelan, Callum	5.9	Watford	Barnsley	24.09.98
Forwards				
Blackwood, Geoge	6.2	Adelaide	Berowra, Aus	04.06.97
Dearnley, Zak	5.11	New Mills	Sheffield	28.09.98
Hope, Hallam	5.11	Swindon	Manchester	17.03.94

PORT VALE

Ground: Vale Park, Hamil Road, Burslem, Stoke-on-Trent ST6 1AW. **Telephone:** 01782 655800. **Club nickname:** Valiants. **Colours:** White and black. **Capacity:** 19,052. **Record attendance:** 49,768 v Aston Villa (FA Cup 5) Feb 20, 1960

Goalkeepers				
Covolan, Lucas	6.4	Torquay	Curitiba, Br	06.06.91
Stone, Aidan	6.1	Mansfield	Stafford	20.07.99
Defenders				
Benning, Mal	5.10	Mansfield	Sandwell	02.11.93
Cass, Lewis	6.1	Newcastle (loan)	North Shields	27.02.00
Gibbons, James	5.9	–	Stoke	16.03.98
Johnson, Ryan	6.2	Hartlepool	Birmingham	02.10.96
Jones, Dan	6.0	Salford	Bishop Auckland	14.12.94
Legge, Leon	6.1	Cambridge	Hastings	28.04.85
Martin, Aaron	6.3	Hamilton	Newport, IOW	29.09.89
Smith, Nathan	6.0	–	Madeley	03.04.96
Midfielders				
Amoo, David	5.10	Cambridge	Southwark	13.04.91
Burgess, Scott	5.10	Bury	Warrington	12.08.97

Conlon, Tom	5.9	Stevenage	Stoke	03.02.96
Garrity, Ben	6.0	Blackpool	Liverpool	21.02.97
Hurst, Alex	5.8	Bradford PA	Stoke	06.10.99
Pett, Tom	5.8	Stevenage	Potters Bar	03.12.91
Taylor, Jake	5.10	Nottm Forest	Manchester	08.09.98
Walker, Brad	6.1	Shrewsbury	Billingham	25.04.96
Whitehead, Danny	5.10	Salford	Manchester	23.10.93
Worrall, David	6.0	Millwall	Manchester	12.06.90
Forwards				
Proctor, Jamie	6.2	Wigasn	Preston	25.03.92
Robinson, Theo	5.10	Southend	Birmingham	22.01.89
Rodney, Devante	5.10	Salford	Manchester	19.05.98
Wilson, James	6.1	Salford	Biddulph	01.12.95

ROCHDALE

Ground: Crown Oil Arena, Wilbutts Lane, Rochdale OL11 5DS. **Telephone:** 01706 644648.
Club nickname: Dale. **Colours:** Blue and black. **Capacity:** 10,249. **Record attendance:** 24,231
v Notts Co (FA Cup 2) Dec 10, 1949

Goalkeepers				
Lynch, Jay	6.2	AFC Fylde	Salford	31.03.93
Wade, Bradley	6.2	–	Gloucester	03.07.00
Defenders				
McNulty, Jim	6.0	Bury	Liverpool	13.02.85
Dunne, Joe	6.0	–	Stafford	25.10.0
Midfielders				
Done, Matt	5.10	Sheffield Utd	Oswestry	22.07.88
Dooley, Stephen	5.11	Coleraine	Ballymoney	19.10.91
Grant, Conor	5.10	Sheffield Wed	Dublin, Ire	18.12.97
Keohane, Jimmy	5.11	Cork	Aylesbury	22.01.91
Morley, Aaron	5.10	–	Bury	27.02.00
Newby, Alex	5.0	Chorley	Barrow	21.11.95
Odoh, Abraham	5.7	Charlton	Lambeth	25.06.00
Rathbone, Oliver	5.11	Man Utd	Blackburn	10.10.96
Forwards				
Beesley, Jake	6.1	Solihull	Sheffield	02.12.96

SALFORD CITY

Ground: Peninsula Stadium, Moor Lane, Salford M7 3PZ. **Telephone:** 0161 792 6287. **Club
nickname:** Ammies. **Colours:** Red and white. **Capacity:** 5,106. **Record attendance:** 4,518 v
Leeds (League Cup 1) Aug 13, 2019

Goalkeepers				
King, Tom	6.1	Newport	Plymouth	09.03.95
Defenders				
Eastham, Ashley	6.3	Fleetwood	Preston	22.03.91
Shephard, Liam	5.10	Newport	Pentre	22.11.94
Touray, Ibou	5.10	Nantwich	Liverpool	24.12.94
Turnbull, Jordan	6.1	Northampton	Trowbridge	30.10.94
Midfielders				
Burgess, Luke	5.10	Wigan	Liverpool	03.03.99
Lowe, Jason	5.10	Bolton	Wigan	02.09.91
Lund, Matty	6.0	Rochdale	Manchester	21.11.90
Morris, Josh	5.10	Fleetwood	Preston	30.09.91

Forwards

Bruno Andrade	5.10	Lincoln	Viseu, Port	02.10.93
Elliott, Tom	6.4	Millwall	Leeds	09.11.90
Henderson, Ian	5.10	Rochdale	Thetford	24.01.85
Hunter, Ashley	5.10	Fleetwood	Derby	29.09.95
McAleny, Conor	5.10	Oldham	Liverpool	12.08.92
Thomas-Asante, Brandon	5.11	Ebbsfleet	Milton Keynes	29.12.98
Touray, Momodou	5.11	Newport	Gambia	30.07.99

SCUNTHORPE UNITED

Ground: Sands Venue Stadium, Doncaster Road, Scunthorpe DN15 8TD. **Telephone:** 0871 221 1899. **Club nickname:** Iron. **Colours:** Claret and blue. **Capacity:** 9,088. **Record attendance:** Old Show Ground: 23,935 v Portsmouth (FA Cup 4) Jan 30, 1954. Sands Venue Stadium: 8,921 v Newcastle (Champ) Oct 20, 2009

Goalkeepers

Collins, Tom	6.4	–	Scunthorpe	04.08.02
Watson, Rory	6.3	Hull	York	05.02.96

Defenders

Davis, Harry	6.2	Morecambe	Burnley	24.09.91
Millen, Ross	6.2	Kilmarnock	Glasgow	28.09.94
O'Malley, Mason	5.10	Huddersfield	Leeds	08.06.01
Onariasse, Manny	6.2	Dagenham	Croydon	21.10.96
Taft, George	6.3	Bolton	Leicester	29.07.93
Rowe, Jai	5.11	Barwell	Nuneaton	08.08.01

Midfielders

Beestin, Alfie	5.10	Doncaster	Leeds	01.10.97
Hallam, Jordan	5.8	Sheffield Utd	Sheffield	06.10.98
Hippolyte, Myles	6.0	Yeovil	Harrow	09.11.94
Kenyon, Alex	6.0	Morecambe	Euxton	17.07.92
Pugh, Tom	5.7	Leeds	Doncaster	27.09.00
Spence, Lewis	6.0	Ross Co	Kirkcaldy	28.01.96

Forwards

Dunnwald-Turan, Kenan	6.2	Bonner SC	Dusseldorf, Ger	14.11.95
Green, Devarn	5.9	Southport	Sandwell	26.08.96
Jarvis, Aaron	6.2	Luton	Basingstoke	24.01.98
Loft, Ryan	6.3	Leicester	Gravesend	14.09.87
McAtee, John	5.11	Shrewsbury	Salford	23.07.99

STEVENAGE

Ground: Lamex Stadium, Broadhall Way, Stevenage SG2 8RH. **Telephone:** 01438 223223. **Club nickname:** Boro. **Colours:** White and red. **Capacity:** 7,318. **Record attendance:** 8,040 v Newcastle (FA Cup 4) January 25, 1998

Goalkeepers

Anang, Joseph	6.0	West Ham (loan)	Ghana	08.06.00
Johnson, Billy	6.1	Norwich	Great Yarmouth	25.09.99

Defenders

Barry, Brad	6.0	Barrow	Hastings	13.02.95
Coker, Ben	5.11	Lincoln	Hatfield	17.06.89
Cuthbert, Scott	6.2	Luton	Alexandria, Scot	15.06.87
Fernandez, Luis	6.4	–	Enfield	28.09.01
Prosser, Luke	6.3	Colchester	Enfield	28.09.01
Vancooten, Terence	6.1	Reading	Kingston upon Thames	29.12.97

Wildin, Luther	5.10	Nuneaton	Leicester	03.12.97
Midfielders				
Carter, Charlie	6.1	Chesterfield	London	25.10.96
Lines, Chris	6.2	Northampton	Bristol	30.11.85
List, Elliott	5.10	Gillingham	Camberwell	12.05.97
Marshall, Ross	6.1	Maidstone	–	09.10.99
Osborne, Elliot	6.0	Stockport	Stoke	16.05.96
Read, Arthur	5.10	Brentford	Camden	03.11.99
Reeves, Jake	5.8	Notts Co	Lewisham	30.05.93
Taylor, Jake	5.10	Exeter	Ascot	01.12.91
Forwards				
Daly, James	5.11	Bristol Rov	Brighton	12.01.00
Norris, Luke	6.1	Colchester	Stevenage	03.06.93

SUTTON UNITED

Ground: Gander Green Lane, Sutton SM1 2EY. **Telephone:** 0208 644 444:. **Colours:** Amber and brown. **Capacity:** 5,013. **Record attendance:** 14,000 v Leeds (FA Cup 4) Jan 24, 1970

Goalkeepers				
Bouzanis, Dean	6.2	Melbourne	Sydney, Aus	02.10.90
House, Brad	6.2	Horsham	Worthing	19.10.98
Defenders				
Goodliffe, Ben	6.2	Wolves	Watford	19.06.99
John, Louis	6.3	Cambridge Utd	Croydon	19.04.94
Kizzi, Joe	6.4	Bromley	Enfield	24.06.93
Milsom, Rob	5.10	Notts Co	Redhill	02.01.87
Rowe, Coby	6.3	Haringey	Waltham Forest	02.10.95
Wyatt, Ben	5.8	St Albans	Norwich	04.02.96
Midfielders				
Barden, Jon	6.0	St Louis	Harrow	09.11.92
Beautyman, Harry	5.10-	Stevenage	Newham	01.04.92
Boldewijn, Enzio	6.1	Notts Co	Almere, Hol	17.11.92
Davis, Kenny	5.8	Boreham Wood	Camden	17.04.88
Dundas, Craig	–	Hampton & Richmond	–	16.02.81
Eastmond, Craig	6.0	Yeovil	Wandsworth	09.12.90
Lovatt, Adam	–	Hastings	–	11.05.99
Randall, Will	5.11	Newport	Swindon	02.05.97
Smith, Alistair	6.2	Altrincham	Beverley	19.05.99
Forwards				
Ajiboye, David	–	Worthing	Bromley	28.09.98
Bennett, Richie	6.3	Stockport	Oldham	03.03.91
Browne, Rhys	5.10	Wealdstone	Romford	16.11.95
Bugiel, Omar	6.1	Bromley	Berlin, Ger	03.01.94
Sho-Silva, Tobi	6.0	Halifax	Thamesmead	27.03.95
Wilson, Donovan	5.11	Bath	Yate	14.03.97

SWINDON TOWN

Ground: County Ground, County Road, Swindon SN1 2ED. **Telephone:** 0871 423 6433. **Club nickname:** Robins. **Colours:** Red and white. **Capacity:** 15,728. **Record attendance:** 32,000 v Arsenal (FA Cup 3) Jan 15, 1972

Goalkeepers				
Wollacott, Jojo	6.3	Bristol City	Bristol	08.09.96
Defenders				
Baudry, Mathieu	6.2	MK Dons	Le Havre, Fr	24.02.88

Conroy, Dion	6.2	Chelsea	Redhill	11.12.95
Curran, Taylor	6.0	Southend	Redbridge	07.07.00
Grounds, Jonathan	6.1	Birmingham	Thornaby	02.02.88
Hunt, Rob	5.8	Oldham	Dagenham	07.07.95
Odimayo, Akin	6.0	Reading	Camden	28.11.99
Midfielders				
Iandolo, Ellis	5.10	–	Chatham	22.08.97
Lyden, Jordan	6.0	Aston Villa	Perth, Aus	30.01.96
Payne, Jack	5.7	Lincoln	Tower Hamlets	25.10.94
Forwards				
Pitman, Brett	6.0	Portsmouth	St Helier, Jer	03.01.88

TRANMERE ROVERS

Ground: Prenton Park, Prenton Road, West Birkenhead CH42 9PY. **Telephone:** 0871 221 2001. **Club nickname:** Rovers. **Colours:** White and blue. **Capacity:** 16,587. **Record attendance:** 24,424 v Stoke (FA Cup 4) Feb 5, 1972

Goalkeepers				
Davies, Scott	6.0	Fleetwood	Blackpool	27.02.87
Murphy, Joe	6.2	Shrewsbury	Dublin, Ire	21.08.81
Defenders				
Clarke, Peter	6.0	Fleetwood	Southport	03.01.82
Gogley, Josh	5.10	Birmingham	Coventry	12.03.96
Davies, Tom	5.11	Bristol Rov	Warrington	18.04.92
Knight-Percival, Nat	6.0	Morecambe	Cambridge	31.03.87
MacDonald, Calum	5.11	Blackpool	Norwich	18.12.97
Maguire, Joe	5.10	Accrington	Manchester	18.01.96
Midfielders				
Blackett-Taylor, Corey	5.8	Aston Villa	Erdington	23.09.97
Feeney, Liam	6.0	Blackpool	Hammersmith	21.01.87
Khan, Otis	5.9	Mansfield	Ashton-under-Lyme	05.09.95
McManaman, Callum	5.9	Melbourne	Huyton	25.04.91
Merrie, Chris	5.11	Wigan	Liverpool	02.11.98
Morris, Kieron	5.10	Walsall	Hereford	03.06.94
Spearing, Jay	5.8	Blackpool	Wallasey	25.11.88
Watson, Ryan	6.1	Northampton	Crewe	07.07.93
Forwards				
Dieseruvwe, Emmanuel	6.5	Salford	Leeds	20.02.95
Glatzel, Paul	–	Liverpool (loan)	Liverpool	20.02.01
Jolley, Charlie	5.10	Wigan	Liverpool	13.01.01

WALSALL

Ground: Banks's Stadium, Bescot Crescent, Walsall WS1 4SA. **Telephone:** 01922 622791. **Club nickname:** Saddlers. **Colours:** Red and white. **Capacity:** 11,300. **Record attendance:** Fellows Park: 25,453 v Newcastle (Div 2) Aug 29, 1961. Banks's Stadium: 11,049 v Rotherham (Div 1) May 10, 2004

Goalkeepers				
Rose, Jack	6.3	Southampton (loan)	Solihull	31.01.95
Defenders				
Mills, Zak	5.10	Port Vale	Peterborough	28.05.92
Monthe, Manny	6.1	Tranmere	Cameroon	26.01.95
Sadler, Mat	5.11	Shrewsbury	Birmingham	26.02.85
Taylor, Ash	6.1	Aberdeen	Bromborough	02.09.90

Ward, Stephen	5.11	Ipswich	Dublin, Ire	20.08.85
White, Hayden	6.1	Mansfield	Greenwich	15.04.95
Midfielders				
Bates, Alfie	5.7	Birmingham	Coventry	03.05.01
Earing, Jack	6.0	Halifax	Bury	21.09.99
Holden, Rory	5.7	Bristol City	Derry	23.08.97
Kiernan, Brendan	5.9	Harrogate	Lambeth	10.11.92
Kinsella, Liam	5.9	–	Colchester	23.02.96
Labadie, Joss	6.3	Newport	Croydon	30.08.90
Osadebe, Emmanuel	6.2	Macclesfield	Dundalk, Ire	01.10.96
Perry, Sam	6.0	Aston Villa	Walsall	29.12.01
Willis, Joe	5.11	–	Walsall	03.10.01
Forwards				
Phillips, Kieran	6.2	Huddersfield (loan)	Huddersfield	18.02.00
Wilkinson, Conor	6.3	Leyton Orient	Croydon	23.01.95

SCOTTISH PREMIERSHIP SQUADS 2021–22

(at time of going to press)

ABERDEEN

Ground: Pittodrie Stadium, Pittodrie Street, Aberdeen AB24 5QH. **Capacity:** 20,961.
Telephone: 01224 650400
Manager: Stephen Glass. **Colours:** Red and white. **Nickname:** Dons
Goalkeepers: Joe Lewis, Tom Ritchie, Gary Woods
Defenders: Andrew Considine, Michael Devlin, Declan Gallagher, Jack Gurr, Jonny Hayes, Jack Mackenzie, Ross McCrorie, Kieran Ngwenya, Calvin Ramsay
Midfielders: Scott Brown, Dean Campbell, Ryan Duncan, Lewis Ferguson, Ryan Hedges, Teddy Jenks (loan), Matty Kennedy, Dylan McGeouch, Funso Ojo, Miko Virtanen
Forwards: Jay Emmanuel-Thomas, Connor McLennan, Niall McGinn, Christian Ramirez

CELTIC

Ground: Celtic Park, Glasgow G40 3RE. **Capacity:** 60,832. **Telephone:** 0871 226 1888
Manager: Ange Postecoglu. **Colours:** Green and white. **Nickname:** Bhoys
Goalkeepers: Scott Bain, Vasilis Barkas, Conor Hazard
Defenders: Kristoffer Ajer, Boli Bolingoli, Christopher Jullien, Anthony Ralston, Greg Taylor, Osaze Urhoghide, Stephen Welch
Midfielders: Nir Bitton, Ryan Christie, Luca Connell, James Forrest, Ewan Henderson, Mikey Johnston, Callum McGregor, Olivier Ntcham, Scott Robertson, Tom Rogic, Liam Shaw, Ismaila Soro, David Turnbull
Forwards: Albian Ajeti, Odsonne Edouard, Joey Dawson, Leigh Griffiths

DUNDEE

Ground: Kilmac Stadium, Sandeman Street, Dundee DD3 7JY. **Capacity:** 11,850. **Telephone:** 01382 889966
Manager: James McPake. Colours: Dark blue and white. Nickname: Dark Blues
Goalkeepers: Adam Legzdins, Harrison Sharp
Defenders: Lee Ashcroft, Christie Elliott, Sam Fisher, Liam Fontaine, Cammy Kerr, Jordan Marshall, Jordan McGhee, Ewan Murray, Corey Panter (loan), Danny Strachan, Ryan Sweeney
Midfielders: Max Anderson, Charlie Adam, Shaun Byrne, Lyall Cameron, Declan McDaid, Paul McGowan, Paul McMullan, Callum Moore, Finlay Robertson, Luke Strachan
Forwards: Jason Cummings, Alex Jakubiak, Luke McCowan, Danny Mullen

DUNDEE UNITED

Ground: Tannadice Park, Tannadice Street, Dundee DD3 7JW. **Capacity:** 14,209. **Telephone:** 01382 833166
Manager: Tam Courts. **Colours:** Tangerine and black. **Nickname:** Terrors
Goalkeepers: Trevor Carson, Jack Newman, Benjamin Siegrist
Defenders: Mark Connolly, Nathan Cooney, Ryan Edwards, Kieran Freeman, Charlie Mulgrew, Lewis Neilson, Mark Reynolds, Jamie Robson, Liam Smith, Kerr Smith, Adrian Sporle
Midfielders: Louis Appere, Calum Butcher, Jeando Fuchs, Declan Glass, Ian Harkes, Florent Hoti, Archie Meekison, Chris Mochrie, Peter Pawlett
Forwards: Logan Chalmers, Nicky Clark, Kai Fotheringham, Lawrence Shankland, Darren Watson

HEART OF MIDLOTHIAN

Ground: Tynecastle Stadium, McLeod Street Edinburgh EH11 2NL. **Capacity:** 20,099. **Telephone:** 0871 663 1874.
Manager: Robbie Neilson. **Colours:** Maroon and white. **Nickname:** Jam Tarts
Goalkeepers: Craig Gordon, Ross Stewart
Defenders: Jamie Brandon, Alex Cochrane (loan), Craig Halkett, Stephen Kingsley, Cammy Logan, Michael Smith, Mihai Popescu, John Souttar
Midfielders: Loic Damour, Josh Ginnelly, Andy Halliday, Peter Haring, Gary Mackay-Steven, Aaron McEneff, Scott McGill, Connor Smith, Jamie Walker
Forwards: Liam Boyce, Armand Gnanduillet, Euan Henderson, Jordan Roberts

HIBERNIAN

Ground: Easter Road Stadium, Albion Place, Edinburgh EH7 5QG. **Capacity:** 20,451. **Telephone:** 0131 661 2159.
Manager: Jack Ross. **Colours:** Green and white. **Nickname:** Hibees
Goalkeepers: Kevin Dabrowski, Matt Macey
Defenders: Josh Day, Paul Hanlon, Tom James, Sean Mackie, Paul McGinn, Darren McGregor, Ryan Porteous, Lewis Stevenson
Midfielders: Scott Allan, Steven Bradley, Chris Cadden, Josh Campbell, Jake Doyle-Hayes, Alex Gogic, Melker Hallberg, Jackson Irvine, Daniel Mackay, Kyle Magennis, Stevie Mallan, Innes Murray, Joe Newell, Drey Wright
Forwards: Martin Boyle, Christian Doidge, Jamie Gullan, Jamie Murphy, Kevin Nisbet

LIVINGSTON

Ground: Tony Macaroni Arena, Alderstone Road, Livingston EH54 7DN. **Capacity:** 10,000. **Telephone:** 01506 417000
Manager: David Martindale. **Colours:** Gold and black. **Nickname:** Livvy's Lions
Goalkeepers: Daniel Barden (loan), Gary Maley, Max Stryjek
Defenders: Nicky Devlin, Jack Fitzwater, Adam Lewis (loan), Jackson Longridge, Jack McMillan, Ayo Obileye, Tom Parkes, James Penrice,
Midfielders: Marvin Bartley, Alan Forrest, Jason Holt, Keaghan Jacobs, Cristian Montano, Josh Mullin, Scott Pittman, Craig Sibbald, Ben Williamson
Forwards: Bruce Anderson, Jack Hamilton, Jaze Kabia, Gavin Reilly

MOTHERWELL

Ground: Fir Park, Firpark Street, Motherwell ML1 2QN. **Capacity:** 13,742. **Telephone:** 01698 333333
Manager: Graham Alexander. **Colours:** Claret and amber. **Nickname:** Well
Goalkeepers: Scott Fox, Liam Kelly, Peter Morrison

Defenders: Jake Carroll, David Devine, Liam Grimshaw, Max Johnston, Ricki Lamie, Nathan McGinley, Bevis Mugabi, Darragh O'Connor, Stephen O'Donnell
Midfielders: Dean Cornelius, Robbie Crawford, Liam Donnelly, Steven Lawless, Barry Maguire, Mark O'Hara
Forwards: Justin Amaluzor, Connor Shields, Kevin van Veen, Tony Watt, Kayne Woolery

RANGERS

Ground: Ibrox Park, Edmison Drive, Glasgow G51 2XD. **Capacity:** 50,411. **Telephone:** 0871 702 1972
Manager: Steven Gerrard. **Colours:** Blue. **Nickname:** Gers
Goalkeepers: Andy Firth, Allan McGregor, Jon McLaughlin
Defenders: Leon Balogun, Borna Barisic, Calvin Bassey, George Edmundson, Connor Goldson, Filip Helander, Nikola Katic, John Lundstram, Nathan Patterson, Jack Simpson, James Tavernier
Midfielders: Scott Arfield, Joe Aribo, Steven Davis, Ianis Hagi, Ryan Jack, Jordan Jones, Glen Kamara, Ryan Kent, Charlie Lindsay, Glen Middleton, Nnamdi Ofoborh
Forwards: Jermain Defoe, James Graham, Jake Hastie, Cedric Itten, Alfredo Morelos, Kemar Roofe, Fashion Sakala, Scott Wright

ROSS COUNTY

Ground: Global Energy Stadium, Victoria Park, Jubilee Road, Dingwall IV15 9QZ. **Capacity:** 6,541. **Telephone:** 01738 459090
Manager: Malky Mackay. **Colours:** Blue and white. **Nickname:** Staggies
Goalkeepers: Ross Laidlaw, Ross Munro, Logan Ross
Defenders: Coll Donaldson, Tom Grivosti, Alex Iacovitti, Connor Randall, Jake Vokins (loan), Keith Watson, Ben Williamson
Midfielders: Ross Callachan, Joe Chalmers, Regan Charles-Cook, Adam Mackinnon, Harry Paton, Alexander Robertson (loan), Blair Spittal, Jordan Tillson
Forwards: Dominic Samuel, Oli Shaw, Jordan White, Matthew Wright

ST JOHNSTONE

Ground: McDiarmid Park, Crieff Road, Perth PH1 2SJ. **Capacity:** 10,673. **Telephone:** 01738 459090
Manager: Callum Davidson. **Colours:** Blue and white. **Nickname:** Saints
Goalkeepers: Zander Clark, Elliot Parish, Ross Sinclair
Defenders: Callum Booth, James Brown, Reece Devine (loan), Liam Gordon, Jason Kerr, Jamie McCart, Hayden Muller (loan), Shaun Rooney
Midfielders: Cammy Ballantyne, Craig Bryson, Liam Craig, Murray Davidson, Charlie Gilmour, Ali McCann, David Wotherspoon
Forwards: Callum Hendry, Chris Kane, Stevie May, Michael O'Halloran, Jordan Northcott

ST MIRREN

Ground: Simple Digital Arena Greenhill Road, Paisley PA3 IRU. **Capacity:** 8,006. **Telephone:** 0141 889 2558
Manager: Jim Goodwin. **Colours:** Black and white. **Nickname:** Buddies
Goalkeepers: Jack Alnwick, Dean Lyness, Peter Urminsky
Defenders: Charles Dunne, Daniel Finlayson, Marcus Fraser, Conor McCarthy, Joe Shaughnessy, Richard Tait, Scott Tanser
Midfielders: Cameron Breadner, Ethan Erhahon, Ryan Flynn, Jay Henderson, Greg Kiltie, Cameron MacPherson, Kyle McAllister, Jamie McGrath, Alan Power, Dylan Reid
Forwards: Eamonn Brophy, Kristian Dennis, Lee Erwin, Josh Jack, Lewis Jamieson, Curtis Main

ENGLISH FIXTURES 2021–2022

Premier League and Football League

Friday 6 August
Championship
Bournemouth v WBA

Saturday 7 August
Championship
Blackburn v Swansea
Bristol City v Blackpool
Cardiff v Barnsley
Derby v Huddersfield
Luton v Peterborough
Preston v Hull
QPR v Millwall
Sheff Utd v Birmingham
Stoke v Reading

League One
Bolton v MK Dons
Cambridge v Oxford
Charlton v Sheff Wed
Crewe v Cheltenham
Doncaster v AFC Wimbledon
Fleetwood v Portsmouth
Gillingham v Lincoln
Ipswich v Morecambe
Rotherham v Plymouth
Shrewsbury v Burton
Sunderland v Wigan
Wycombe v Accrington

League Two
Carlisle v Colchester
Exeter v Bradford
Forest Green v Sutton
Harrogate v Rochdale
Hartlepool v Crawley
Mansfield v Bristol Rov
Northampton v Port Vale
Oldham v Newport
Salford v Leyton Orient
Scunthorpe v Swindon
Stevenage v Barrow
Tranmere v Walsall

Sunday 8 August
Championship
Coventry v Nottm Forest
Fulham v Middlesbrough

Friday 13 August
Premier League
Brentford v Arsenal

Saturday 14 August
Premier League
Man Utd v Leeds
Burnley v Brighton
Chelsea v Crystal Palace

Everton v Southampton
Leicester v Wolves
Watford v Aston Villa
Norwich v Liverpool

Championship
Barnsley v Coventry
Birmingham v Stoke
Blackpool v Cardiff
Huddersfield v Fulham
Hull v QPR
Middlesbrough v Bristol City
Millwall v Blackburn
Nottm Forest v Bournemouth
Peterborough v Derby
Reading v Preston
Swansea v Sheff Utd
WBA v Luton

League One
Accrington v Cambridge
AFC Wimbledon v Bolton
Burton v Ipswich
Cheltenham v Wycombe
Lincoln v Fleetwood
MK Dons v Sunderland
Morecambe v Shrewsbury
Oxford v Charlton
Plymouth v Gillingham
Portsmouth v Crewe
Sheff Wed v Doncaster
Wigan v Rotherham

League Two
Barrow v Hartlepool
Bradford v Oldham
Bristol Rov v Stevenage
Colchester v Northampton
Crawley v Harrogate
Leyton Orient v Exeter
Newport v Mansfield
Port Vale v Tranmere
Rochdale v Scunthorpe
Sutton v Salford
Swindon v Carlisle
Walsall v Forest Green

Sunday 15 August
Premier League
Newcastle v West Ham
Tottenham v Man City

Tuesday 17 August
Championship
Barnsley v Luton
Blackpool v Coventry
Huddersfield v Preston
Millwall v Fulham
Peterborough v Cardiff
Swansea v Stoke

League One
Accrington v Doncaster
AFC Wimbledon v Gillingham
Burton v Sunderland
Cheltenham v Ipswich
Lincoln v Bolton
MK Dons v Charlton
Morecambe v Rotherham
Oxford v Crewe
Plymouth v Cambridge
Portsmouth v Shrewsbury
Sheff Wed v Fleetwood
Wigan v Wycombe

League Two
Barrow v Exeter
Bradford v Stevenage
Bristol Rov v Oldham
Colchester v Mansfield
Crawley v Salford
Leyton Orient v Harrogate
Newport v Northampton
Port Vale v Carlisle
Rochdale v Forest Green
Sutton v Hartlepool
Swindon v Tranmere
Walsall v Scunthorpe

League One
Bolton v Oxford
Cambridge v Burton
Charlton v Wigan
Crewe v Accrington
Doncaster v Portsmouth
Fleetwood v Cheltenham
Gillingham v Morecambe
Ipswich v MK Dons
Rotherham v Sheff Wed
Shrewsbury v Plymouth
Sunderland v AFC Wimbledon
Wycombe v Lincoln

League Two
Carlisle v Leyton Orient
Exeter v Bristol Rov
Forest Green v Crawley
Harrogate v Barrow
Hartlepool v Walsall
Mansfield v Bradford
Northampton v Rochdale
Oldham v Colchester
Salford v Swindon
Scunthorpe v Sutton
Stevenage v Port Vale
Tranmere v Newport

Wednesday 18 August
Championship
Birmingham v Bournemouth
Hull v Derby
Middlesbrough v QPR
Nottm Forest v Blackburn
Reading v Bristol City
WBA v Sheff Utd

Friday 20 August
Championship
Bristol City v Swansea

Saturday 21 August
Premier League
Liverpool v Burnley
Aston Villa v Newcastle
Crystal Palace v Brentford
Leeds v Everton
Man City v Norwich
Brighton v Watford

Championship
Blackburn v WBA
Bournemouth v Blackpool
Cardiff v Millwall
Coventry v Reading
Derby v Middlesbrough
Fulham v Hull
Luton v Birmingham
Preston v Peterborough
QPR v Barnsley
Sheff Utd v Huddersfield
Stoke v Nottm Forest

Sunday 22 August
Premier League
Arsenal v Chelsea
Southampton v Man Utd
Wolves v Tottenham

Monday 23 August
Premier League
West Ham v Leicester

Friday 27 August
Championship
Peterborough v WBA

Saturday 28 August
Premier League
Man City v Arsenal
Aston Villa v Brentford
Brighton v Everton
Newcastle v Southampton
Norwich v Leicester
West Ham v Crystal Palace
Liverpool v Chelsea

Championship
Barnsley v Birmingham
Cardiff v Bristol City
Derby v Nottm Forest
Fulham v Stoke
Huddersfield v Reading
Hull v Bournemouth
Luton v Sheff Utd
Middlesbrough v Blackburn
Millwall v Blackpool

Preston v Swansea
QPR v Coventry

League One
Burton v Cheltenham
Cambridge v Bolton
Charlton v Crewe
Ipswich v AFC Wimbledon
MK Dons v Accrington
Morecambe v Sheff Wed
Oxford v Lincoln
Plymouth v Fleetwood
Rotherham v Doncaster
Shrewsbury v Gillingham
Sunderland v Wycombe
Wigan v Portsmouth

League Two
Barrow v Bristol Rov
Crawley v Northampton
Forest Green v Port Vale
Harrogate v Exeter
Hartlepool v Carlisle
Leyton Orient v Bradford
Rochdale v Colchester
Salford v Newport
Scunthorpe v Tranmere
Sutton v Oldham
Swindon v Mansfield
Walsall v Stevenage

Sunday 29 August
Premier League
Burnley v Leeds
Tottenham v Watford
Wolves v Man Utd

Saturday 4 September
League One
Accrington v Shrewsbury
AFC Wimbledon v Oxford
Bolton v Burton
Cheltenham v MK Dons
Crewe v Morecambe
Doncaster v Cambridge
Fleetwood v Wigan
Gillingham v Charlton
Lincoln v Rotherham
Portsmouth v Plymouth
Sheff Wed v Sunderland
Wycombe v Ipswich

League Two
Bradford v Walsall
Bristol Rov v Crawley
Carlisle v Salford
Colchester v Sutton
Exeter v Forest Green
Mansfield v Harrogate
Newport v Leyton Orient
Northampton v Scunthorpe
Oldham v Barrow
Port Vale v Rochdale

Stevenage v Swindon
Tranmere v Hartlepool

Friday 10 September
League Two
Harrogate v Newport

Saturday 11 September
Premier League
Arsenal v Norwich
Brentford v Brighton
Chelsea v Aston Villa
Crystal Palace v Tottenham
Leicester v Man City
Man Utd v Newcastle
Southampton v West Ham
Watford v Wolves

Championship
Birmingham v Derby
Blackburn v Luton
Blackpool v Fulham
Bournemouth v Barnsley
Bristol City v Preston
Coventry v Middlesbrough
Nottm Forest v Cardiff
Reading v QPR
Sheff Utd v Peterborough
Stoke v Huddersfield
Swansea v Hull
WBA v Millwall

League One
Burton v Gillingham
Cambridge v Lincoln
Charlton v Cheltenham
Ipswich v Bolton
MK Dons v Portsmouth
Morecambe v AFC Wimbledon
Oxford v Wycombe
Plymouth v Sheff Wed
Rotherham v Fleetwood
Shrewsbury v Crewe
Sunderland v Accrington
Wigan v Doncaster

League Two
Barrow v Colchester
Crawley v Carlisle
Forest Green v Northampton
Hartlepool v Bristol Rov
Leyton Orient v Oldham
Rochdale v Tranmere
Salford v Bradford
Scunthorpe v Exeter
Sutton v Stevenage
Swindon v Port Vale
Walsall v Mansfield

Sunday 12 September
Premier League
Leeds v Liverpool

Monday 13 September
Premier League
Everton v Burnley

Tuesday 14 September
Championship
Blackburn v Hull
Blackpool v Huddersfield
Bournemouth v QPR
Sheff Utd v Preston
Reading v Peterborough
WBA v Derby

Wednesday 15 September
Championship
Birmingham v Fulham
Bristol City v Luton
Coventry v Cardiff
Nottm Forest v Middlesbrough
Swansea v Millwall
Stoke v Barnsley

Friday 17 September
Premier League
Newcastle v Leeds

Saturday 18 September
Premier League
Aston Villa v Everton
Burnley v Arsenal
Liverpool v Crystal Palace
Man City v Southampton
Norwich v Watford
Wolves v Brentford

Championship
Barnsley v Blackburn
Cardiff v Bournemouth
Derby v Stoke
Fulham v Reading
Huddersfield v Nottm Forest
Hull v Sheff Utd
Luton v Swansea
Middlesbrough v Blackpool
Millwall v Coventry
Peterborough v Birmingham
Preston v WBA
QPR v Bristol City

League One
Accrington v Wigan
AFC Wimbledon v Plymouth
Bolton v Rotherham
Cheltenham v Oxford
Crewe v Burton
Doncaster v Morecambe
Fleetwood v Sunderland
Gillingham v MK Dons
Lincoln v Ipswich
Portsmouth v Cambridge
Sheff Wed v Shrewsbury
Wycombe v Charlton

League Two
Bradford v Barrow
Bristol Rov v Leyton Orient
Carlisle v Scunthorpe
Colchester v Crawley
Exeter v Sutton
Mansfield v Rochdale
Newport v Walsall
Northampton v Swindon
Oldham v Hartlepool
Port Vale v Harrogate
Stevenage v Forest Green
Tranmere v Salford

Sunday 19 September
Premier League
Brighton v Leicester
Tottenham v Chelsea
West Ham v Man Utd

Friday September 24
League Two
Barrow v Newport

Saturday 25 September
Premier League
Brentford v Liverpool
Chelsea v Man City
Everton v Norwich
Leeds v West Ham
Leicester v Burnley
Man Utd v Aston Villa
Watford v Newcastle

Championship
Birmingham v Preston
Blackburn v Cardiff
Blackpool v Barnsley
Bournemouth v Luton
Bristol City v Fulham
Coventry v Peterborough
Nottm Forest v Millwall
Reading v Middlesbrough
Sheff Utd v Derby
Stoke v Hull
Swansea v Huddersfield
WBA v QPR

League One
Burton v Lincoln
Cambridge v Fleetwood
Charlton v Portsmouth
Ipswich v Sheff Wed
MK Dons v Wycombe
Morecambe v Accrington
Oxford v Gillingham
Plymouth v Doncaster
Rotherham v Crewe
Shrewsbury v AFC Wimbledon
Sunderland v Bolton
Wigan v Cheltenham

League Two
Crawley v Bradford
Forest Green v Tranmere
Harrogate v Stevenage
Hartlepool v Exeter
Leyton Orient v Mansfield
Rochdale v Oldham
Salford v Northampton
Scunthorpe v Port Vale
Sutton v Carlisle
Swindon v Colchester
Walsall v Bristol Rov

Sunday 26 September
Premier League
Arsenal v Tottenham
Southampton v Wolves

Monday 27 September
Premier League
Crystal Palace v Brighton

Tuesday 28 September
Championship
Cardiff v WBA
Huddersfield v Blackburn
Hull v Blackpool
Middlesbrough v Sheff Utd
Preston v Stoke
QPR v Birmingham

League One
Burton v Portsmouth
Cambridge v Gillingham
Charlton v Bolton
Ipswich v Doncaster
MK Dons v Fleetwood
Morecambe v Lincoln
Oxford v Accrington
Plymouth v Crewe
Rotherham v AFC Wimbledon
Shrewsbury v Wycombe
Sunderland v Cheltenham
Wigan v Sheff Wed

League Two
Barrow v Newport
Crawley v Bradford
Forest Green v Tranmere
Harrogate v Stevenage
Hartlepool v Exeter
Leyton Orient v Mansfield
Rochdale v Oldham
Salford v Northampton
Scunthorpe v Port Vale
Sutton v Carlisle
Swindon v Colchester
Walsall v Bristol Rov

Wednesday 29 September
Championship
Barnsley v Nottm Forest
Derby v Reading
Fulham v Swansea
Luton v Coventry
Millwall v Bristol City
Peterborough v Bournemouth

Saturday 2 October
Premier League
Brighton v Arsenal
Burnley v Norwich
Chelsea v Southampton
Crystal Palace v Leicester
Leeds v Watford
Liverpool v Man City
Man Utd v Everton
Tottenham v Aston Villa
West Ham v Brentford
Wolves v Newcastle

Championship
Barnsley v Millwall
Birmingham v Nottm Forest
Blackpool v Blackburn
Bournemouth v Sheff Utd
Cardiff v Reading
Coventry v Fulham
Derby v Swansea
Hull v Middlesbrough
Luton v Huddersfield
Peterborough v Bristol City
QPR v Preston
Stoke v WBA

League One
Accrington v Ipswich
AFC Wimbledon v Burton
Bolton v Shrewsbury
Cheltenham v Rotherham
Crewe v Cambridge
Doncaster v MK Dons
Fleetwood v Charlton
Gillingham v Wigan
Lincoln v Plymouth
Portsmouth v Sunderland
Sheff Wed v Oxford
Wycombe v Morecambe

League Two
Bradford v Rochdale
Bristol Rov v Swindon
Carlisle v Forest Green
Colchester v Salford
Exeter v Walsall
Mansfield v Barrow
Newport v Scunthorpe
Northampton v Sutton
Oldham v Harrogate
Port Vale v Leyton Orient
Stevenage v Hartlepool
Tranmere v Crawley

Friday 8 October
League Two
Tranmere v Colchester

Saturday 9 October
League One
Accrington v Fleetwood
Charlton v Rotherham
Crewe v Doncaster
Ipswich v Shrewsbury
MK Dons v AFC Wimbledon
Morecambe v Cambridge
Plymouth v Burton
Portsmouth v Cheltenham
Sheff Wed v Bolton
Sunderland v Oxford
Wigan v Lincoln
Wycombe v Gillingham

League Two
Barrow v Leyton Orient
Bristol Rov v Carlisle
Forest Green v Swindon
Harrogate v Scunthorpe
Hartlepool v Northampton
Mansfield v Oldham
Newport v Bradford
Rochdale v Crawley
Stevenage v Exeter
Sutton v Port Vale
Walsall v Salford

Saturday 16 October
Premier League
Arsenal v Crystal Palace
Aston Villa v Wolves
Brentford v Chelsea
Everton v West Ham
Leicester v Man Utd
Man City v Burnley
Newcastle v Tottenham
Norwich v Brighton
Southampton v Leeds
Watford v Liverpool

Championship
Blackburn v Coventry
Bristol City v Bournemouth
Fulham v QPR
Huddersfield v Hull
Middlesbrough v Peterborough
Millwall v Luton
Nottm Forest v Blackpool
Preston v Derby
Reading v Barnsley
Sheff Utd v Stoke
Swansea v Cardiff
WBA v Birmingham

League One
AFC Wimbledon v Sheff Wed
Bolton v Wigan

Burton v Morecambe
Cambridge v Ipswich
Cheltenham v Accrington
Doncaster v Wycombe
Fleetwood v Crewe
Gillingham v Sunderland
Lincoln v Charlton
Oxford v Plymouth
Rotherham v Portsmouth
Shrewsbury v MK Dons

League Two
Bradford v Bristol Rov
Carlisle v Tranmere
Colchester v Harrogate
Crawley v Sutton
Exeter v Newport
Leyton Orient v Walsall
Northampton v Mansfield
Oldham v Stevenage
Port Vale v Barrow
Salford v Hartlepool
Scunthorpe v Forest Green
Swindon v Rochdale

Tuesday 19 October
Championship
Bristol City v Nottm Forest
Derby v Luton
Fulham v Cardiff
QPR v Blackburn
Sheff Utd v Millwall
Stoke v Bournemouth

League One
Cambridge v Sheff Wed
Charlton v Accrington
Cheltenham v Morecambe
Crewe v Sunderland
Fleetwood v Burton
Gillingham v Doncaster
Lincoln v AFC Wimbledon
Oxford v Shrewsbury
Plymouth v Bolton
Portsmouth v Ipswich
Rotherham v Wycombe
Wigan v MK Dons

League Two
Barrow v Scunthorpe
Bradford v Hartlepool
Colchester v Bristol Rov
Crawley v Exeter
Harrogate v Tranmere
Leyton Orient v Forest Green
Mansfield v Port Vale
Newport v Carlisle
Northampton v Stevenage
Oldham v Walsall
Salford v Rochdale
Sutton v Swindon

Wednesday 20 October
Championship
Huddersfield v Birmingham
Hull v Peterborough
Middlesbrough v Barnsley
Preston v Coventry
Swansea v WBA
Reading v Blackpool

Saturday 23 October
Premier League
Arsenal v Aston Villa
Brentford v Leicester
Brighton v Man City
Chelsea v Norwich
Crystal Palace v Newcastle
Everton v Watford
Leeds v Wolves
Man Utd v Liverpool
Southampton v Burnley
West Ham v Tottenham

Championship
Barnsley v Sheff Utd
Birmingham v Swansea
Blackburn v Reading
Blackpool v Preston
Bournemouth v Huddersfield
Cardiff v Middlesbrough
Coventry v Derby
Luton v Hull
Millwall v Stoke
Nottm Forest v Fulham
Peterborough v QPR
WBA v Bristol City

League One
Accrington v Portsmouth
AFC Wimbledon v Wigan
Bolton v Gillingham
Burton v Oxford
Doncaster v Cheltenham
Ipswich v Fleetwood
MK Dons v Rotherham
Morecambe v Plymouth
Sheff Wed v Lincoln
Shrewsbury v Cambridge
Sunderland v Charlton
Wycombe v Crewe

League Two
Bristol Rov v Newport
Carlisle v Oldham
Exeter v Mansfield
Forest Green v Salford
Hartlepool v Harrogate
Port Vale v Colchester
Rochdale v Sutton
Scunthorpe v Crawley
Stevenage v Leyton Orient
Swindon v Bradford
Tranmere v Northampton
Walsall v Barrow

Saturday 30 October
Premier League
Aston Villa v West Ham
Burnley v Brentford
Leicester v Arsenal
Liverpool v Brighton
Man City v Crystal Palace
Newcastle v Chelsea
Norwich v Leeds
Tottenham v Man Utd
Watford v Southampton
Wolves v Everton

Championship
Bristol City v Barnsley
Derby v Blackburn
Fulham v WBA
Huddersfield v Millwall
Hull v Coventry
Middlesbrough v Birmingham
Preston v Luton
QPR v Nottm Forest
Reading v Bournemouth
Sheff Utd v Blackpool
Stoke v Cardiff
Swansea v Peterborough

League One
Cambridge v AFC Wimbledon
Charlton v Doncaster
Cheltenham v Sheff Wed
Crewe v MK Dons
Fleetwood v Wycombe
Gillingham v Accrington
Lincoln v Shrewsbury
Oxford v Morecambe
Plymouth v Ipswich
Portsmouth v Bolton
Rotherham v Sunderland
Wigan v Burton

League Two
Barrow v Rochdale
Bradford v Forest Green
Colchester v Scunthorpe
Crawley v Port Vale
Harrogate v Bristol Rov
Leyton Orient v Hartlepool
Mansfield v Tranmere
Newport v Stevenage
Northampton v Carlisle
Oldham v Swindon
Salford v Exeter
Sutton v Walsall

Tuesday 2 November
Championship
Birmingham v Bristol City
Coventry v Swansea
Luton v Middlesbrough
Millwall v Reading
Nottm Forest v Sheff Utd
Peterborough v Huddersfield

Wednesday 3 November
Championship
Barnsley v Derby
Blackburn v Fulham
Blackpool v Stoke
Bournemouth v Preston
Cardiff v QPR
WBA v Hull

Saturday 6 November
Premier League
Arsenal v Watford
Brentford v Norwich
Brighton v Newcastle
Chelsea v Burnley
Crystal Palace v Wolves
Everton v Tottenham
Leeds v Leicester
Man Utd v Man City
Southampton v Aston Villa
West Ham v Liverpool

Championship
Barnsley v Hull
Birmingham v Reading
Blackburn v Sheff Utd
Blackpool v QPR
Bournemouth v Swansea
Cardiff v Huddersfield
Coventry v Bristol City
Luton v Stoke
Millwall v Derby
Nottm Forest v Preston
Peterborough v Fulham
WBA v Middlesbrough

Friday 12 November
League One
Bolton v Crewe

League Two
Hartlepool v Newport

Saturday 13 November
League One
Accrington v Plymouth
AFC Wimbledon v Cheltenham
Burton v Charlton
Doncaster v Fleetwood
Ipswich v Oxford
MK Dons v Cambridge
Morecambe v Wigan
Sheff Wed v Gillingham
Shrewsbury v Rotherham
Sunderland v Lincoln
Wycombe v Portsmouth

League Two
Bristol Rov v Northampton
Carlisle v Barrow
Exeter v Oldham

Forest Green v Colchester
Port Vale v Bradford
Rochdale v Leyton Orient
Scunthorpe v Salford
Stevenage v Mansfield
Swindon v Crawley
Tranmere v Sutton
Walsall v Harrogate

Friday 19 November
League Two
Bristol Rov v Tranmere

Saturday 20 November
Premier League
Aston Villa v Brighton
Burnley v Crystal Palace
Leicester v Chelsea
Liverpool v Arsenal
Man City v Everton
Newcastle v Brentford
Norwich v Southampton
Tottenham v Leeds
Watford v Man Utd
Wolves v West Ham

Championship
Bristol City v Blackburn
Derby v Bournemouth.
Fulham v Barnsley
Huddersfield v WBA
Hull v Birmingham
Middlesbrough v Millwall
Preston v Cardiff
QPR v Luton
Reading v Nottm Forest
Sheff Utd v Coventry
Stoke v Peterborough
Swansea v Blackpool

League One
Accrington v Sheff Wed
Charlton v Plymouth
Cheltenham v Shrewsbury
Crewe v Gillingham
Doncaster v Lincoln
Fleetwood v Morecambe
MK Dons v Burton
Portsmouth v AFC Wimbledon
Rotherham v Cambridge
Sunderland v Ipswich
Wigan v Oxford
Wycombe v Bolton

League Two
Barrow v Crawley
Bradford v Northampton
Exeter v Carlisle
Harrogate v Salford
Hartlepool v Forest Green
Leyton Orient v Sutton
Mansfield v Scunthorpe
Newport v Swindon

Oldham v Port Vale
Stevenage v Colchester
Walsall v Rochdale

Tuesday 23 November
Championship
Blackpool v WBA
Coventry v Birmingham
Fulham v Derby
Middlesbrough v Preston
Nottm Forest v Luton
Reading v Sheff Utd

League One
AFC Wimbledon v Crewe
Burton v Accrington
Cambridge v Wigan
Gillingham v Cheltenham
Ipswich v Rotherham
Lincoln v Portsmouth
Morecambe v Charlton
Oxford v Fleetwood
Plymouth v Wycombe
Sheff Wed v MK Dons
Shrewsbury v Sunderland
Bolton v Doncaster

League Two
Carlisle v Harrogate
Colchester v Exeter
Crawley v Newport
Forest Green v Barrow
Northampton v Oldham
Port Vale v Walsall
Rochdale v Stevenage
Salford v Bristol Rov
Scunthorpe v Leyton Orient
Sutton v Mansfield
Swindon v Hartlepool
Tranmere v Bradford

Wednesday 24 November
Championship
Barnsley v Swansea
Blackburn v Peterborough
Bristol City v Stoke
Cardiff v Hull
Millwall v Bournemouth
QPR v Huddersfield

Friday 26 November
League Two
Colchester v Newport

Saturday 27 November
Premier League
Arsenal v Newcastle
Brentford v Everton
Brighton v Leeds
Burnley v Tottenham
Chelsea v Man Utd
Crystal Palace v Aston Villa

Leicester v Watford
Liverpool v Southampton
Man City v West Ham
Norwich v Wolves

Championship
Birmingham v Blackpool
Bournemouth v Coventry
Derby v QPR
Huddersfield v Middlesbrough
Hull v Millwall
Luton v Cardiff
Peterborough v Barnsley
Preston v Fulham
Stoke v Blackburn
Swansea v Reading
WBA v Nottm Forest

League One
AFC Wimbledon v Fleetwood
Bolton v Cheltenham
Burton v Doncaster
Cambridge v Sunderland
Gillingham v Portsmouth
Lincoln v Accrington
Morecambe v MK Dons
Oxford v Rotherham
Plymouth v Wigan
Sheff Wed v Wycombe
Shrewsbury v Charlton

League Two
Carlisle v Walsall
Crawley v Mansfield
Forest Green v Bristol Rov
Northampton v Leyton Orient
Port Vale v Hartlepool
Rochdale v Exeter
Salford v Oldham
Scunthorpe v Bradford
Sutton v Barrow
Swindon v Harrogate
Tranmere v Stevenage

Sunday 28 November
Championship
Sheff Utd v Bristol City

League One
Ipswich v Crewe

Tuesday 30 November
Premier League
Aston Villa v Man City
Everton v Liverpool
Leeds v Crystal Palace
Watford v Chelsea
West Ham v Brighton
Wolves v Burnley
Man Utd v Arsenal

Wednesday 1 December
Premier League
Newcastle v Norwich
Southampton v Leicester
Tottenham v Brentford

Saturday 4 December
Premier League
Aston Villa v Leicester
Everton v Arsenal
Leeds v Brentford
Man Utd v Crystal Palace
Newcastle v Burnley
Southampton v Brighton
Tottenham v Norwich
Watford v Man City
West Ham v Chelsea
Wolves v Liverpool

Championship
Barnsley v Huddersfield
Blackburn v Preston
Blackpool v Luton
Bristol City v Derby
Cardiff v Sheff Utd
Coventry v WBA
Fulham v Bournemouth
Middlesbrough v Swansea
Millwall v Birmingham
Nottm Forest v Peterborough
QPR v Stoke
Reading v Hull

Tuesday 7 December
League One
Accrington v AFC Wimbledon
Charlton v Ipswich
Cheltenham v Cambridge
Crewe v Lincoln
Doncaster v Oxford
Fleetwood v Bolton
MK Dons v Plymouth
Portsmouth v Sheff Wed
Rotherham v Gillingham
Sunderland v Morecambe
Wigan v Shrewsbury
Wycombe v Burton

League Two
Barrow v Salford
Bradford v Colchester
Bristol Rov v Port Vale
Exeter v Northampton
Harrogate v Forest Green
Hartlepool v Rochdale
Leyton Orient v Swindon
Mansfield v Carlisle
Newport v Sutton
Oldham v Tranmere
Stevenage v Scunthorpe
Walsall v Crawley

Saturday 11 December
Premier League
Arsenal v Southampton
Brentford v Watford
Brighton v Tottenham
Burnley v West Ham
Chelsea v Leeds
Crystal Palace v Everton
Leicester v Newcastle
Liverpool v Aston Villa
Man City v Wolves
Norwich v Man Utd

Championship
Birmingham v Cardiff
Bournemouth v Blackburn
Derby v Blackpool
Huddersfield v Coventry
Hull v Bristol City
Luton v Fulham
Peterborough v Millwall
Preston v Barnsley
Sheff Utd v QPR
Stoke v Middlesbrough
Swansea v Nottm Forest
WBA v Reading

League One
Accrington v Bolton
Charlton v Cambridge
Cheltenham v Lincoln
Crewe v Sheff Wed
Doncaster v Shrewsbury
Fleetwood v Gillingham
MK Dons v Oxford
Portsmouth v Morecambe
Rotherham v Burton
Sunderland v Plymouth
Wigan v Ipswich
Wycombe v AFC Wimbledon

League Two
Barrow v Swindon
Bradford v Sutton
Bristol Rov v Rochdale
Exeter v Tranmere
Harrogate v Northampton
Hartlepool v Scunthorpe
Leyton Orient v Crawley
Mansfield v Salford
Newport v Port Vale
Oldham v Forest Green
Stevenage v Carlisle
Walsall v Colchester

Tuesday 14 December
Premier League
Arsenal v West Ham
Brentford v Man Utd
Brighton v Wolves
Burnley v Watford
Leicester v Tottenham

Norwich v Aston Villa
Crystal Palace v Southampton

Wednesday 15 December
Premier League
Chelsea v Everton
Liverpool v Newcastle
Man City v Leeds

Saturday 18 December
Premier League
Aston Villa v Burnley
Everton v Leicester
Leeds v Arsenal
Man Utd v Brighton
Newcastle v Man City
Southampton v Brentford
Tottenham v Liverpool
Watford v Crystal Palace
West Ham v Norwich
Wolves v Chelsea

Championship
Barnsley v WBA
Blackburn v Birmingham
Blackpool v Peterborough
Bristol City v Huddersfield
Cardiff v Derby
Coventry v Stoke
Fulham v Sheff Utd
Middlesbrough v Bournemouth
Millwall v Preston
Nottm Forest v Hull
QPR v Swansea
Reading v Luton

League One
AFC Wimbledon v Portsmouth
Bolton v Wycombe
Burton v MK Dons
Cambridge v Rotherham
Gillingham v Crewe
Ipswich v Sunderland
Lincoln v Doncaster
Morecambe v Fleetwood
Oxford v Wigan
Plymouth v Charlton
Sheff Wed v Accrington
Shrewsbury v Cheltenham

League Two
Carlisle v Bradford
Colchester v Hartlepool
Crawley v Oldham
Forest Green v Mansfield
Northampton v Barrow
Port Vale v Exeter
Rochdale v Newport
Salford v Stevenage
Scunthorpe v Bristol Rov
Sutton v Harrogate

Swindon v Walsall
Tranmere v Leyton Orient

Sunday 26 December
Premier League
Aston Villa v Chelsea
Brighton v Brentford
Burnley v Everton
Liverpool v Leeds
Man City v Leicester
Newcastle v Man Utd
Norwich v Arsenal
Tottenham v Crystal Palace
West Ham v Southampton
Wolves v Watford

Championship
Barnsley v Stoke
Cardiff v Coventry
Derby v WBA
Fulham v Birmingham
Huddersfield v Blackpool
Hull v Blackburn
Luton v Bristol City
Middlesbrough v Nottm Forest
Millwall v Swansea
Peterborough v Reading
Preston v Sheff Utd
QPR v Bournemouth

League One
Accrington v Rotherham
AFC Wimbledon v Charlton
Bolton v Morecambe
Cheltenham v Plymouth
Crewe v Wigan
Doncaster v Sunderland
Fleetwood v Shrewsbury
Gillingham v Ipswich
Lincoln v MK Dons
Portsmouth v Oxford
Sheff Wed v Burton
Wycombe v Cambridge

League Two
Bradford v Harrogate
Bristol Rov v Sutton
Carlisle v Rochdale
Colchester v Leyton Orient
Exeter v Swindon
Mansfield v Hartlepool
Newport v Forest Green
Northampton v Walsall
Oldham v Scunthorpe
Port Vale v Salford
Stevenage v Crawley
Tranmere v Barrow

Tuesday 28 December
Premier League
Arsenal v Wolves
Brentford v Man City
Chelsea v Brighton

Crystal Palace v Norwich
Everton v Newcastle
Leeds v Aston Villa
Leicester v Liverpool
Man Utd v Burnley
Southampton v Tottenham
Watford v West Ham

Wednesday 29 December
Championship
Birmingham v Peterborough
Blackburn v Barnsley
Blackpool v Middlesbrough
Bournemouth v Cardiff
Bristol City v QPR
Coventry v Millwall
Nottm Forest v Huddersfield
Sheff Utd v Hull
Swansea v Luton
Reading v Fulham
Stoke v Derby
WBA v Preston

League One
Burton v Bolton
Cambridge v Doncaster
Charlton v Gillingham
Ipswich v Wycombe
MK Dons v Cheltenham
Morecambe v Crewe
Oxford v AFC Wimbledon
Plymouth v Portsmouth
Rotherham v Lincoln
Shrewsbury v Accrington
Sunderland v Sheff Wed
Wigan v Fleetwood

League Two
Barrow v Oldham
Crawley v Bristol Rov
Forest Green v Exeter
Harrogate v Mansfield
Hartlepool v Tranmere
Leyton Orient v Newport
Rochdale v Port Vale
Salford v Carlisle
Scunthorpe v Northampton
Sutton v Colchester
Swindon v Stevenage
Walsall v Bradford

Saturday 1 January
Premier League
Arsenal v Man City
Brentford v Aston Villa
Chelsea v Liverpool
Crystal Palace v West Ham
Everton v Brighton
Leeds v Burnley
Leicester v Norwich
Man Utd v Wolves
Southampton v Newcastle
Watford v Tottenham

Championship
Birmingham v QPR
Blackburn v Huddersfield
Blackpool v Hull
Bournemouth v Peterborough
Coventry v Luton
Nottm Forest v Barnsley
Reading v Derby
Sheff Utd v Middlesbrough
Stoke v Preston
Swansea v Fulham
WBA v Cardiff

League One
Burton v Crewe
Cambridge v Portsmouth
Charlton v Wycombe
Ipswich v Lincoln
MK Dons v Gillingham
Morecambe v Doncaster
Oxford v Cheltenham
Plymouth v AFC Wimbledon
Rotherham v Bolton
Shrewsbury v Sheff Wed
Sunderland v Fleetwood
Wigan v Accrington

League Two
Barrow v Bradford
Crawley v Colchester
Forest Green v Stevenage
Harrogate v Port Vale
Hartlepool v Oldham
Leyton Orient v Bristol Rov
Rochdale v Mansfield
Salford v Tranmere
Scunthorpe v Carlisle
Sutton v Exeter
Swindon v Northampton
Walsall v Newport

Sunday 2 January
Championship
Bristol City v Millwall

Saturday 8 January
League One
Accrington v MK Dons
AFC Wimbledon v Ipswich
Bolton v Cambridge
Cheltenham v Burton
Crewe v Charlton
Doncaster v Rotherham
Fleetwood v Plymouth
Gillingham v Shrewsbury
Lincoln v Oxford
Portsmouth v Wigan
Sheff Wed v Morecambe
Wycombe v Sunderland

League Two
Bradford v Leyton Orient

Bristol Rov v Barrow
Carlisle v Hartlepool
Colchester v Rochdale
Exeter v Harrogate
Mansfield v Swindon
Newport v Salford
Northampton v Crawley
Oldham v Sutton
Port Vale v Forest Green
Stevenage v Walsall
Tranmere v Scunthorpe

Saturday 15 January
Premier League
Aston Villa v Man Utd
Brighton v Crystal Palace
Burnley v Leicester
Liverpool v Brentford
Man City v Chelsea
Newcastle v Watford
Norwich v Everton
Tottenham v Arsenal
West Ham v Leeds
Wolves v Southampton

Championship
Barnsley v Blackpool
Cardiff v Blackburn
Derby v Sheff Utd
Fulham v Bristol City
Huddersfield v Swansea
Hull v Stoke
Luton v Bournemouth
Middlesbrough v Reading
Millwall v Nottm Forest
Peterborough v Coventry
Preston v Birmingham
QPR v WBA

League One
Accrington v Sunderland
AFC Wimbledon v Morecambe
Bolton v Ipswich
Cheltenham v Charlton
Crewe v Shrewsbury
Doncaster v Wigan
Fleetwood v Rotherham
Gillingham v Burton
Lincoln v Cambridge
Portsmouth v MK Dons
Sheff Wed v Plymouth
Wycombe v Oxford

League Two
Bradford v Salford
Bristol Rov v Hartlepool
Carlisle v Crawley
Colchester v Barrow
Exeter v Scunthorpe
Mansfield v Walsall
Newport v Harrogate
Northampton v Forest Green
Oldham v Leyton Orient

Port Vale v Swindon
Stevenage v Sutton
Tranmere v Rochdale

Saturday 22 January
Premier League
Arsenal v Burnley
Brentford v Wolves
Chelsea v Tottenham
Crystal Palace v Liverpool
Everton v Aston Villa
Leeds v Newcastle
Leicester v Brighton
Man Utd v West Ham
Southampton v Man City
Watford v Norwich

Championship
Birmingham v Barnsley
Blackburn v Middlesbrough
Blackpool v Millwall
Bournemouth v Hull
Bristol City v Cardiff
Coventry v QPR
Nottm Forest v Derby
Reading v Huddersfield
Sheff Utd v Luton
Stoke v Fulham
Swansea v Preston
WBA v Peterborough

League One
Burton v AFC Wimbledon
Cambridge v Crewe
Charlton v Fleetwood
Ipswich v Accrington
MK Dons v Doncaster
Morecambe v Wycombe
Oxford v Sheff Wed
Plymouth v Lincoln
Rotherham v Cheltenham
Shrewsbury v Bolton
Sunderland v Portsmouth
Wigan v Gillingham

League Two
Barrow v Mansfield
Crawley v Tranmere
Forest Green v Carlisle
Harrogate v Oldham
Hartlepool v Stevenage
Leyton Orient v Port Vale
Rochdale v Bradford
Salford v Colchester
Scunthorpe v Newport
Sutton v Northampton
Swindon v Bristol Rov
Walsall v Exeter

Saturday 29 January
Championship
Barnsley v Bournemouth
Cardiff v Nottm Forest

Derby v Birmingham
Fulham v Blackpool
Huddersfield v Stoke
Hull v Swansea
Luton v Blackburn
Middlesbrough v Coventry
Millwall v WBA
Peterborough v Sheff Utd
Preston v Bristol City
QPR v Reading

League One
Accrington v Morecambe
AFC Wimbledon v Shrewsbury
Bolton v Sunderland
Cheltenham v Wigan
Crewe v Rotherham
Doncaster v Plymouth
Fleetwood v Cambridge
Gillingham v Oxford
Lincoln v Burton
Portsmouth v Charlton
Sheff Wed v Ipswich
Wycombe v MK Dons

League Two
Bradford v Crawley
Bristol Rov v Walsall
Carlisle v Sutton
Colchester v Swindon
Exeter v Hartlepool
Mansfield v Leyton Orient
Newport v Barrow
Northampton v Salford
Oldham v Rochdale
Port Vale v Scunthorpe
Stevenage v Harrogate
Tranmere v Forest Green

Saturday 5 February
Championship
Barnsley v Cardiff
Birmingham v Sheff Utd
Blackpool v Bristol City
Huddersfield v Derby
Hull v Preston
Middlesbrough v Fulham
Millwall v QPR
Nottm Forest v Coventry
Peterborough v Luton
Reading v Stoke
Swansea v Blackburn
WBA v Bournemouth

League One
Burton v Sheff Wed
Cambridge v Wycombe
Charlton v AFC Wimbledon
Ipswich v Gillingham
MK Dons v Lincoln
Morecambe v Bolton
Oxford v Portsmouth
Plymouth v Cheltenham
Rotherham v Accrington

Shrewsbury v Fleetwood
Sunderland v Doncaster
Wigan v Crewe

League Two
Barrow v Tranmere
Crawley v Stevenage
Forest Green v Newport
Harrogate v Bradford
Hartlepool v Mansfield
Leyton Orient v Colchester
Rochdale v Carlisle
Salford v Port Vale
Scunthorpe v Oldham
Sutton v Bristol Rov
Swindon v Exeter
Walsall v Northampton

Tuesday 8 February
Premier League
Aston Villa v Leeds
Brighton v Chelsea
Burnley v Man Utd
Norwich v Crystal Palace
West Ham v Watford
Wolves v Arsenal

Championship
Cardiff v Peterborough
Coventry v Blackpool
Derby v Hull
Fulham v Millwall
Luton v Barnsley
Stoke v Swansea

League One
Accrington v Oxford
AFC Wimbledon v Rotherham
Cheltenham v Sunderland
Crewe v Plymouth
Doncaster v Ipswich
Fleetwood v MK Dons
Gillingham v Cambridge
Lincoln v Morecambe
Portsmouth v Burton
Sheff Wed v Wigan
Wycombe v Shrewsbury
Bolton v Charlton

League Two
Carlisle v Port Vale
Exeter v Leyton Orient
Forest Green v Rochdale
Harrogate v Crawley
Hartlepool v Barrow
Mansfield v Colchester
Northampton v Newport
Oldham v Bristol Rov
Salford v Sutton
Scunthorpe v Walsall
Stevenage v Bradford
Tranmere v Swindon

Wednesday 9 February
Premier League
Newcastle v Everton
Tottenham v Southampton
Liverpool v Leicester
Man City v Brentford

Championship
Blackburn v Nottm Forest
Bournemouth v Birmingham
Bristol City v Reading
Preston v Huddersfield
QPR v Middlesbrough
Sheff Utd v WBA

Saturday 12 February
Premier League
Brentford v Crystal Palace
Burnley v Liverpool
Chelsea v Arsenal
Everton v Leeds
Leicester v West Ham
Man Utd v Southampton
Newcastle v Aston Villa
Norwich v Man City
Tottenham v Wolves
Watford v Brighton

Championship
Barnsley v QPR
Birmingham v Luton
Blackpool v Bournemouth
Huddersfield v Sheff Utd
Hull v Fulham
Middlesbrough v Derby
Millwall v Cardiff
Nottm Forest v Stoke
Peterborough v Preston
Reading v Coventry
Swansea v Bristol City
WBA v Blackburn

League One
Accrington v Crewe
AFC Wimbledon v Sunderland
Burton v Cambridge
Cheltenham v Fleetwood
Lincoln v Wycombe
MK Dons v Ipswich
Morecambe v Gillingham
Oxford v Bolton
Plymouth v Shrewsbury
Portsmouth v Doncaster
Sheff Wed v Rotherham
Wigan v Charlton

League Two
Barrow v Stevenage
Bradford v Exeter
Bristol Rov v Mansfield
Colchester v Carlisle
Crawley v Hartlepool

Leyton Orient v Salford
Newport v Oldham
Port Vale v Northampton
Rochdale v Harrogate
Sutton v Forest Green
Swindon v Scunthorpe
Walsall v Tranmere

Friday 18 February
League One
Rotherham v Wigan

Saturday 19 February
Premier League
Arsenal v Brentford
Aston Villa v Watford
Brighton v Burnley
Crystal Palace v Chelsea
Leeds v Man Utd
Liverpool v Norwich
Man City v Tottenham
Southampton v Everton
West Ham v Newcastle
Wolves v Leicester

Championship
Blackburn v Millwall
Bournemouth v Nottm Forest
Bristol City v Middlesbrough
Cardiff v Blackpool
Coventry v Barnsley
Derby v Peterborough
Fulham v Huddersfield
Luton v WBA
Preston v Reading
QPR v Hull
Sheff Utd v Swansea
Stoke v Birmingham

League One
Bolton v AFC Wimbledon
Cambridge v Accrington
Charlton v Oxford
Crewe v Portsmouth
Doncaster v Sheff Wed
Fleetwood v Lincoln
Gillingham v Plymouth
Ipswich v Burton
Shrewsbury v Morecambe
Sunderland v MK Dons
Wycombe v Cheltenham

League Two
Carlisle v Swindon
Exeter v Barrow
Forest Green v Walsall
Harrogate v Leyton Orient
Hartlepool v Sutton
Mansfield v Newport
Northampton v Colchester
Oldham v Bradford
Salford v Crawley

Scunthorpe v Rochdale
Stevenage v Bristol Rov
Tranmere v Port Vale

Tuesday 22 February
Championship
Bristol City v Coventry
Hull v Barnsley
Middlesbrough v WBA
Preston v Nottm Forest
Swansea v Bournemouth
Reading v Birmingham

League One
Cambridge v Plymouth
Charlton v MK Dons
Crewe v Oxford
Doncaster v Accrington
Fleetwood v Sheff Wed
Gillingham v AFC Wimbledon
Ipswich v Cheltenham
Rotherham v Morecambe
Shrewsbury v Portsmouth
Sunderland v Burton
Wycombe v Wigan
Bolton v Lincoln

Wednesday 23 February
Championship
Derby v Millwall
Fulham v Peterborough
Huddersfield v Cardiff
QPR v Blackpool
Sheff Utd v Blackburn
Stoke v Luton

Saturday 26 February
Premier League
Arsenal v Liverpool
Brentford v Newcastle
Brighton v Aston Villa
Chelsea v Leicester
Crystal Palace v Burnley
Everton v Man City
Leeds v Tottenham
Man Utd v Watford
Southampton v Norwich
West Ham v Wolves

Championship
Barnsley v Middlesbrough
Birmingham v Huddersfield
Blackburn v QPR
Blackpool v Reading
Bournemouth v Stoke
Cardiff v Fulham
Coventry v Preston
Luton v Derby
Millwall v Sheff Utd
Nottm Forest v Bristol City
Peterborough v Hull
WBA v Swansea

League One
Accrington v Wycombe
AFC Wimbledon v Doncaster
Burton v Shrewsbury
Cheltenham v Crewe
Lincoln v Gillingham
MK Dons v Bolton
Morecambe v Ipswich
Oxford v Cambridge
Plymouth v Rotherham
Portsmouth v Fleetwood
Sheff Wed v Charlton
Wigan v Sunderland

League Two
Barrow v Harrogate
Bradford v Mansfield
Bristol Rov v Exeter
Colchester v Oldham
Crawley v Forest Green
Leyton Orient v Carlisle
Newport v Tranmere
Port Vale v Stevenage
Rochdale v Northampton
Sutton v Scunthorpe
Swindon v Salford
Walsall v Hartlepool

Saturday 5 March
Premier League
Aston Villa v Southampton
Burnley v Chelsea
Leicester v Leeds
Liverpool v West Ham
Man City v Man Utd
Newcastle v Brighton
Norwich v Brentford
Tottenham v Everton
Watford v Arsenal
Wolves v Crystal Palace

Championship
Bristol City v Birmingham
Derby v Barnsley
Fulham v Blackburn
Huddersfield v Peterborough
Hull v WBA
Middlesbrough v Luton
Preston v Bournemouth
QPR v Cardiff
Reading v Millwall
Sheff Utd v Nottm Forest
Stoke v Blackpool
Swansea v Coventry

League One
Cambridge v Shrewsbury
Charlton v Sunderland
Cheltenham v Doncaster
Crewe v Wycombe
Fleetwood v Ipswich
Gillingham v Bolton
Lincoln v Sheff Wed

Oxford v Burton
Plymouth v Morecambe
Portsmouth v Accrington
Rotherham v MK Dons
Wigan v AFC Wimbledon

League Two
Barrow v Walsall
Bradford v Swindon
Colchester v Port Vale
Crawley v Scunthorpe
Harrogate v Hartlepool
Leyton Orient v Stevenage
Mansfield v Exeter
Newport v Bristol Rov
Northampton v Tranmere
Oldham v Carlisle
Salford v Forest Green
Sutton v Rochdale

Saturday 12 March
Premier League
Arsenal v Leicester
Brentford v Burnley
Brighton v Liverpool
Chelsea v Newcastle
Crystal Palace v Man City
Everton v Wolves
Leeds v Norwich
Man Utd v Tottenham
Southampton v Watford
West Ham v Aston Villa

Championship
Barnsley v Fulham
Birmingham v Hull
Blackburn v Bristol City
Blackpool v Swansea
Bournemouth v Derby
Cardiff v Preston
Coventry v Sheff Utd
Luton v QPR
Millwall v Middlesbrough
Nottm Forest v Reading
Peterborough v Stoke
WBA v Huddersfield

League One
Accrington v Charlton
AFC Wimbledon v Lincoln
Bolton v Plymouth
Burton v Fleetwood
Doncaster v Gillingham
Ipswich v Portsmouth
MK Dons v Wigan
Morecambe v Cheltenham
Sheff Wed v Cambridge
Shrewsbury v Oxford
Sunderland v Crewe
Wycombe v Rotherham

League Two
Bristol Rov v Harrogate

Carlisle v Northampton
Exeter v Salford
Forest Green v Bradford
Hartlepool v Leyton Orient
Port Vale v Crawley
Rochdale v Barrow
Scunthorpe v Colchester
Stevenage v Newport
Swindon v Oldham
Tranmere v Mansfield
Walsall v Sutton

Tuesday 15 March
Championship
Barnsley v Bristol City
Birmingham v Middlesbrough
Blackburn v Derby
Bournemouth v Reading
Nottm Forest v QPR
WBA v Fulham

League Two
Bristol Rov v Colchester
Carlisle v Newport
Exeter v Crawley
Forest Green v Leyton Orient
Hartlepool v Bradford
Port Vale v Mansfield
Rochdale v Salford
Scunthorpe v Barrow
Stevenage v Northampton
Swindon v Sutton
Tranmere v Harrogate
Walsall v Oldham

Wednesday 16 March
Championship
Blackpool v Sheff Utd
Cardiff v Stoke
Coventry v Hull
Luton v Preston
Millwall v Huddersfield
Peterborough v Swansea

Saturday 19 March
Premier League
Aston Villa v Arsenal
Burnley v Southampton
Leicester v Brentford
Liverpool v Man Utd
Man City v Brighton
Newcastle v Crystal Palace
Norwich v Chelsea
Tottenham v West Ham
Watford v Everton
Wolves v Leeds

Championship
Bristol City v WBA
Derby v Coventry
Fulham v Nottm Forest
Huddersfield v Bournemouth

Hull v Luton
Middlesbrough v Cardiff
Preston v Blackpool
QPR v Peterborough
Reading v Blackburn
Sheff Utd v Barnsley
Stoke v Millwall
Swansea v Birmingham

League One
Cambridge v MK Dons
Charlton v Burton
Cheltenham v AFC Wimbledon
Crewe v Bolton
Fleetwood v Doncaster
Gillingham v Sheff Wed
Lincoln v Sunderland
Oxford v Ipswich
Plymouth v Accrington
Portsmouth v Wycombe
Rotherham v Shrewsbury
Wigan v Morecambe

League Two
Barrow v Carlisle
Bradford v Port Vale
Colchester v Forest Green
Crawley v Swindon
Harrogate v Walsall
Leyton Orient v Rochdale
Mansfield v Stevenage
Newport v Hartlepool
Northampton v Bristol Rov
Oldham v Exeter
Salford v Scunthorpe
Sutton v Tranmere

Saturday 26 March
League One
Accrington v Gillingham
AFC Wimbledon v Cambridge
Bolton v Portsmouth
Burton v Wigan
Doncaster v Charlton
Ipswich v Plymouth
MK Dons v Crewe
Morecambe v Oxford
Sheff Wed v Cheltenham
Shrewsbury v Lincoln
Sunderland v Rotherham
Wycombe v Fleetwood

League Two
Bradford v Newport
Carlisle v Bristol Rov
Colchester v Tranmere
Crawley v Rochdale
Exeter v Stevenage
Leyton Orient v Barrow
Northampton v Hartlepool
Oldham v Mansfield
Port Vale v Sutton
Salford v Walsall

Scunthorpe v Harrogate
Swindon v Forest Green

Saturday 2 April
Premier League
Brighton v Norwich
Burnley v Man City
Chelsea v Brentford
Crystal Palace v Arsenal
Leeds v Southampton
Liverpool v Watford
Man Utd v Leicester
Tottenham v Newcastle
West Ham v Everton
Wolves v Aston Villa

Championship
Barnsley v Reading
Birmingham v WBA
Blackpool v Nottm Forest
Bournemouth v Bristol City
Cardiff v Swansea
Coventry v Blackburn
Derby v Preston
Hull v Huddersfield
Luton v Millwall
Peterborough v Middlesbrough
QPR v Fulham
Stoke v Sheff Utd

League One
Accrington v Cheltenham
Charlton v Lincoln
Crewe v Fleetwood
Ipswich v Cambridge
MK Dons v Shrewsbury
Morecambe v Burton
Plymouth v Oxford
Portsmouth v Rotherham
Sheff Wed v AFC Wimbledon
Sunderland v Gillingham
Wigan v Bolton
Wycombe v Doncaster

League Two
Barrow v Port Vale
Bristol Rov v Bradford
Forest Green v Scunthorpe
Harrogate v Colchester
Hartlepool v Salford
Mansfield v Northampton
Newport v Exeter
Rochdale v Swindon
Stevenage v Oldham
Sutton v Crawley
Tranmere v Carlisle
Walsall v Leyton Orient

Saturday 9 April
Premier League
Arsenal v Brighton
Aston Villa v Tottenham
Brentford v West Ham

Everton v Man Utd
Leicester v Crystal Palace
Man City v Liverpool
Newcastle v Wolves
Norwich v Burnley
Southampton v Chelsea
Watford v Leeds

Championship
Blackburn v Blackpool
Bristol City v Peterborough
Fulham v Coventry
Huddersfield v Luton
Middlesbrough v Hull
Millwall v Barnsley
Nottm Forest v Birmingham
Preston v QPR
Reading v Cardiff
Sheff Utd v Bournemouth
Swansea v Derby
WBA v Stoke

League One
AFC Wimbledon v MK Dons
Bolton v Sheff Wed
Burton v Plymouth
Cambridge v Morecambe
Cheltenham v Portsmouth
Doncaster v Crewe
Fleetwood v Accrington
Gillingham v Wycombe
Lincoln v Wigan
Oxford v Sunderland
Rotherham v Charlton
Shrewsbury v Ipswich

League Two
Carlisle v Exeter
Colchester v Stevenage
Crawley v Barrow
Forest Green v Hartlepool
Northampton v Bradford
Port Vale v Oldham
Rochdale v Walsall
Salford v Harrogate
Scunthorpe v Mansfield
Sutton v Leyton Orient
Swindon v Newport
Tranmere v Bristol Rov

Friday 15 April
Championship
Birmingham v Coventry
Bournemouth v Middlesbrough
Derby v Fulham
Huddersfield v QPR
Hull v Cardiff
Luton v Nottm Forest
Peterborough v Blackburn
Preston v Millwall
Sheff Utd v Reading
Stoke v Bristol City

Swansea v Barnsley
WBA v Blackpool

League One
Accrington v Burton
Charlton v Morecambe
Cheltenham v Gillingham
Crewe v AFC Wimbledon
Doncaster v Bolton
Fleetwood v Oxford
MK Dons v Sheff Wed
Portsmouth v Lincoln
Rotherham v Ipswich
Sunderland v Shrewsbury
Wigan v Cambridge
Wycombe v Plymouth

League Two
Barrow v Forest Green
Bradford v Tranmere
Bristol Rov v Salford
Exeter v Colchester
Harrogate v Swindon
Hartlepool v Port Vale
Leyton Orient v Scunthorpe
Mansfield v Sutton
Newport v Crawley
Oldham v Northampton
Stevenage v Rochdale
Walsall v Carlisle

Saturday 16 April
Premier League
Aston Villa v Liverpool
Everton v Crystal Palace
Leeds v Chelsea
Man Utd v Norwich
Newcastle v Leicester
Southampton v Arsenal
Tottenham v Brighton
Watford v Brentford
West Ham v Burnley
Wolves v Man City

Monday 18 April
Championship
Barnsley v Peterborough
Blackburn v Stoke
Blackpool v Birmingham
Bristol City v Sheff Utd
Cardiff v Luton
Coventry v Bournemouth
Fulham v Preston
Middlesbrough v Huddersfield
Millwall v Hull
Nottm Forest v WBA
QPR v Derby
Reading v Swansea

League One
AFC Wimbledon v Wycombe
Bolton v Accrington
Burton v Rotherham

Cambridge v Charlton
Gillingham v Fleetwood
Ipswich v Wigan
Lincoln v Cheltenham
Morecambe v Portsmouth
Oxford v MK Dons
Plymouth v Sunderland
Sheff Wed v Crewe
Shrewsbury v Doncaster

League Two
Carlisle v Mansfield
Colchester v Bradford
Crawley v Walsall
Forest Green v Oldham
Northampton v Harrogate
Port Vale v Bristol Rov
Rochdale v Hartlepool
Salford v Barrow
Scunthorpe v Stevenage
Sutton v Newport
Swindon v Leyton Orient
Tranmere v Exeter

Friday 22 April
League Two
Newport v Colchester

Saturday 23 April
Premier League
Arsenal v Man Utd
Brentford v Tottenham
Brighton v Southampton
Burnley v Wolves
Chelsea v West Ham
Crystal Palace v Leeds
Leicester v Aston Villa
Liverpool v Everton
Man City v Watford
Norwich v Newcastle

Championship
Birmingham v Millwall
Bournemouth v Fulham
Derby v Bristol City
Huddersfield v Barnsley
Hull v Reading
Luton v Blackpool
Peterborough v Nottm Forest
Preston v Blackburn
Sheff Utd v Cardiff
Stoke v QPR
Swansea v Middlesbrough
WBA v Coventry

League One
Accrington v Lincoln
Charlton v Shrewsbury
Cheltenham v Bolton
Crewe v Ipswich
Doncaster v Burton
Fleetwood v AFC Wimbledon

MK Dons v Morecambe
Portsmouth v Gillingham
Rotherham v Oxford
Sunderland v Cambridge
Wigan v Plymouth
Wycombe v Sheff Wed

League Two
Barrow v Sutton
Bradford v Scunthorpe
Bristol Rov v Forest Green
Exeter v Rochdale
Harrogate v Carlisle
Hartlepool v Swindon
Leyton Orient v Northampton
Mansfield v Crawley
Oldham v Salford
Stevenage v Tranmere
Walsall v Port Vale

Saturday 30 April
Premier League
Aston Villa v Norwich
Everton v Chelsea
Leeds v Man City
Man Utd v Brentford
Newcastle v Liverpool
Southampton v Crystal Palace
Tottenham v Leicester
Watford v Burnley
West Ham v Arsenal
Wolves v Brighton

Championship
Barnsley v Preston
Blackburn v Bournemouth
Blackpool v Derby
Bristol City v Hull
Cardiff v Birmingham
Coventry v Huddersfield
Fulham v Luton
Middlesbrough v Stoke
Millwall v Peterborough
Nottm Forest v Swansea
QPR v Sheff Utd
Reading v WBA

League One
AFC Wimbledon v Accrington
Bolton v Fleetwood
Burton v Wycombe
Cambridge v Cheltenham
Gillingham v Rotherham
Ipswich v Charlton
Lincoln v Crewe
Morecambe v Sunderland
Oxford v Doncaster
Plymouth v MK Dons
Sheff Wed v Portsmouth
Shrewsbury v Wigan

League Two
Carlisle v Stevenage

Colchester v Walsall
Crawley v Leyton Orient
Forest Green v Harrogate
Northampton v Exeter
Port Vale v Newport
Rochdale v Bristol Rov
Salford v Mansfield
Scunthorpe v Hartlepool
Sutton v Bradford
Swindon v Barrow
Tranmere v Oldham

Saturday 7 May
Premier League
Arsenal v Leeds
Brentford v Southampton
Brighton v Man Utd
Burnley v Aston Villa
Chelsea v Wolves
Crystal Palace v Watford
Leicester v Everton
Liverpool v Tottenham
Man City v Newcastle
Norwich v West Ham

Championship
Birmingham v Blackburn
Bournemouth v Millwall
Derby v Cardiff
Huddersfield v Bristol City
Hull v Nottm Forest
Luton v Reading
Peterborough v Blackpool
Preston v Middlesbrough
Sheff Utd v Fulham
Stoke v Coventry
Swansea v QPR
WBA v Barnsley

League Two
Barrow v Northampton
Bradford v Carlisle
Bristol Rov v Scunthorpe
Exeter v Port Vale
Harrogate v Sutton
Hartlepool v Colchester
Leyton Orient v Tranmere
Mansfield v Forest Green
Newport v Rochdale
Oldham v Crawley
Stevenage v Salford
Walsall v Swindon

Sunday 15 May
Premier League
Aston Villa v Crystal Palace
Everton v Brentford
Leeds v Brighton
Man Utd v Chelsea
Newcastle v Arsenal
Southampton v Liverpool
Tottenham v Burnley
Watford v Leicester
West Ham v Man City
Wolves v Norwich

Sunday 22 May
Premier League
Arsenal v Everton
Brentford v Leeds
Brighton v West Ham
Burnley v Newcastle
Chelsea v Watford
Crystal Palace v Man Utd
Leicester v Southampton
Liverpool v Wolves
Man City v Aston Villa
Norwich v Tottenham

SCOTTISH FIXTURES 2021–2022
Premiership Championship League One and League Two

Saturday 31 July
Premiership
Rangers v Livingston
Dundee v St Mirren
Ross Co v St Johnstone
Hearts v Celtic

Championship
Arbroath v Inverness
Morton v Dunfermline
Partick v Queen of South
Raith v Hamilton

League One
Airdrieonians v Montrose
Clyde v Dumbarton
Cove v Falkirk
East Fife v Queen's Park
Peterhead v Alloa

League Two
Albion Rovers v Edinburgh City
Annan v Forfar
Elgin v Stranraer
Kelty v Cowdenbeath
Stenhousemuir v Stirling

Sunday 1 August
Premiership
Aberdeen v Dundee Utd
Motherwell v Hibernian

Monday 2 August
Championship
Kilmarnock v Ayr

Saturday 7 August
Premiership
Celtic v Dundee
Dundee Utd v Rangers
Hibernian v Ross Co
Livingston v Aberdeen
St Mirren v Hearts

Championship
Ayr v Arbroath
Dunfermline v Partick
Hamilton v Morton
Inverness v Raith
Queen of South v Kilmarnock

League One
Alloa v East Fife
Dumbarton v Airdrieonians
Falkirk v Peterhead
Montrose v Clyde
Queen's Park v Cove

League Two
Albion Rovers v Stenhousemuir
Cowdenbeath v Elgin
Forfar v Edinburgh City
Stirling v Kelty
Stranraer v Annan

Sunday 8 August
Premiership
St Johnstone v Motherwell

Friday 13 August
League Two
Edinburgh City v Stenhousemuir

Saturday 14 August
League One
Airdrieonians v Falkirk
Clyde v Alloa
Cove v East Fife
Montrose v Peterhead
Queen's Park v Dumbarton

League Two
Annan v Stirling
Cowdenbeath v Stranraer
Elgin v Albion Rovers
Forfar v Kelty

Saturday 21 August
Premiership
Celtic v St Mirren
Hearts v Aberdeen
Livingston v Motherwell
Ross Co v Rangers
St Johnstone v Dundee Utd

Championship
Arbroath v Partick
Hamilton v Kilmarnock
Inverness v Ayr

Morton v Queen of South
Raith v Dunfermline

League One
Alloa v Queen's Park
Dumbarton v Cove
East Fife v Montrose
Falkirk v Clyde
Peterhead v Airdrieonians

League Two
Albion Rovers v Annan
Elgin v Forfar
Kelty v Edinburgh City
Stenhousemuir v Cowdenbeath
Stranraer v Stirling

Sunday 22 August
Premiership
Dundee v Hibernian

Friday 27 August
League Two
Edinburgh City v Elgin

Saturday 28 August
Premiership
Aberdeen v Ross Co
Dundee Utd v Hearts
Hibernian v Livingston
Motherwell v Dundee
St Mirren v St Johnstone

Championship
Ayr v Raith
Dunfermline v Arbroath
Kilmarnock v Inverness
Partick v Morton
Queen of South v Hamilton

League One
Airdrieonians v Alloa
Clyde v Cove
East Fife v Peterhead
Falkirk v Queen's Park
Montrose v Dumbarton

League Two
Cowdenbeath v Annan
Forfar v Stranraer
Stenhousemuir v Kelty
Stirling v Albion Rovers

Sunday 29 August
Premiership
Rangers v Celtic

Saturday 11 September
Premiership
Celtic v Ross Co
Dundee v Livingston
Hearts v Hibernian
Motherwell v Aberdeen

St Johnstone v Rangers
St Mirren v Dundee Utd

Championship
Arbroath v Hamilton
Ayr v Dunfermline
Inverness v Partick
Kilmarnock v Morton
Raith v Queen of South

League One
Alloa v Falkirk
Cove v Montrose
Dumbarton v East Fife
Peterhead v Clyde
Queen's Park v Airdrieonians

League Two
Albion Rovers v Cowdenbeath
Annan v Stenhousemuir
Kelty v Elgin
Stirling v Forfar
Stranraer v Edinburgh City

Friday 17 September
League Two
Edinburgh City v Stirling

Saturday 18 September
Premiership
Aberdeen v St Johnstone
Dundee Utd v Dundee
Hibernian v St Mirren
Livingston v Celtic
Rangers v Motherwell
Ross Co v Hearts

Championship
Dunfermline v Inverness
Hamilton v Ayr
Morton v Raith
Partick v Kilmarnock
Queen of South v Arbroath

League One
Airdrieonians v East Fife
Clyde v Queen's Park
Falkirk v Dumbarton
Montrose v Alloa
Peterhead v Cove

League Two
Albion Rovers v Kelty
Cowdenbeath v Forfar
Elgin v Annan
Stranraer v Stenhousemuir

Saturday 25 September
Premiership
Celtic v Dundee Utd
Dundee v Rangers
Hearts v Livingston

Hibernian v St Johnstone
Motherwell v Ross Co
St Mirren v Aberdeen

Championship
Arbroath v Kilmarnock
Ayr v Morton
Dunfermline v Hamilton
Inverness v Queen of South
Raith v Partick

League One
Cove v Airdrieonians
Dumbarton v Alloa
East Fife v Clyde
Montrose v Falkirk
Queen's Park v Peterhead

League Two
Annan v Edinburgh City
Forfar v Albion Rovers
Kelty v Stranraer
Stenhousemuir v Elgin
Stirling v Cowdenbeath

Friday 1 October
League Two
Edinburgh City v Cowdenbeath

Saturday 2 October
Premiership
Aberdeen v Celtic
Dundee Utd v Ross Co
Hearts v Motherwell
Livingston v St Mirren
Rangers v Hibernian
St Johnstone v Dundee

Championship
Hamilton v Inverness
Kilmarnock v Raith
Morton v Arbroath
Partick v Ayr
Queen of South v Dunfermline

League One
Airdrieonians v Clyde
Alloa v Cove
Falkirk v East Fife
Peterhead v Dumbarton
Queen's Park v Montrose

League Two
Elgin v Stirling
Kelty v Annan
Stenhousemuir v Forfar
Stranraer v Albion Rovers

Friday 15 October
League Two
Edinburgh City v Kelty

Saturday 16 October

Premiership
Dundee v Aberdeen
Hibernian v Dundee Utd
Motherwell v Celtic
Rangers v Hearts
Ross Co v St Mirren
St Johnstone v Livingston

Championship
Ayr v Queen of South
Dunfermline v Kilmarnock
Hamilton v Partick
Inverness v Morton
Raith v Arbroath

League One
Alloa v Peterhead
Clyde v Montrose
Dumbarton v Queen's Park
East Fife v Cove
Falkirk v Airdrieonians

League Two
Albion Rovers v Elgin
Cowdenbeath v Stenhousemuir
Forfar v Annan
Stirling v Stranraer

Saturday 23 October

Premiership
Aberdeen v Hibernian
Celtic v St Johnstone
Dundee Utd v Motherwell
Hearts v Dundee
Ross Co v Livingston
St Mirren v Rangers

Championship
Arbroath v Ayr
Kilmarnock v Hamilton
Partick v Dunfermline
Queen of South v Morton
Raith v Inverness

League One
Airdrieonians v Dumbarton
Cove v Clyde
Montrose v East Fife
Peterhead v Falkirk
Queen's Park v Alloa

Tuesday 26 October

Championship
Morton v Partick
Ayr v Kilmarnock
Dunfermline v Raith
Hamilton v Queen of South
Inverness v Arbroath

Wednesday 27 October

Premiership
Dundee v Ross Co

Hibernian v Celtic
Livingston v Dundee Utd
Motherwell v St Mirren
Rangers v Aberdeen
St Johnstone v Hearts

Saturday 30 October

Premiership
Aberdeen v Hearts
Celtic v Livingston
Dundee Utd v St Johnstone
Motherwell v Rangers
Ross Co v Hibernian
St Mirren v Dundee

Championship
Arbroath v Dunfermline
Kilmarnock v Queen of South
Morton v Hamilton
Partick v Inverness
Raith v Ayr

League One
Alloa v Airdrieonians
Clyde v Falkirk
Cove v Queen's Park
East Fife v Dumbarton
Peterhead v Montrose

League Two
Annan v Cowdenbeath
Elgin v Edinburgh City
Kelty v Stirling
Stenhousemuir v Albion Rovers
Stranraer v Forfar

Friday 5 November

League Two
Edinburgh City v Albion Rovers

Saturday 6 November

Premiership
Aberdeen v Motherwell
Dundee v Celtic
Hearts v Dundee Utd
Livingston v Hibernian
Rangers v Ross Co
St Johnstone v St Mirren

Championship
Ayr v Inverness
Dunfermline v Morton
Hamilton v Arbroath
Kilmarnock v Partick
Queen of South v Raith

League One
Airdrieonians v Peterhead
Dumbarton v Clyde
Falkirk v Alloa
Montrose v Cove
Queen's Park v East Fife

League Two
Annan v Stranraer
Cowdenbeath v Kelty
Forfar v Elgin
Stirling v Stenhousemuir

Friday 12 November
League Two
Edinburgh City v Stranraer

Saturday 13 November
Championship
Arbroath v Queen of South
Ayr v Partick
Hamilton v Raith
Inverness v Dunfermline
Morton v Kilmarnock

League One
Alloa v Montrose
Cove v Peterhead
Dumbarton v Falkirk
East Fife v Airdrieonians
Queen's Park v Clyde

League Two
Albion Rovers v Stirling
Elgin v Cowdenbeath
Kelty v Forfar
Stenhousemuir v Annan

Saturday 20 November
Premiership
Dundee Utd v Aberdeen
Hibernian v Dundee
Motherwell v Hearts
Rangers v St Johnstone
Ross Co v Celtic
St Mirren v Livingston

Championship
Dunfermline v Ayr
Kilmarnock v Arbroath
Partick v Hamilton
Queen of South v Inverness
Raith v Morton

League One
Airdrieonians v Cove
Alloa v Dumbarton
Clyde v East Fife
Falkirk v Montrose
Peterhead v Queen's Park

League Two
Annan v Albion Rovers
Forfar v Cowdenbeath
Kelty v Stenhousemuir
Stirling v Edinburgh City
Stranraer v Elgin

Saturday 27 November
Premiership
Celtic v Aberdeen
Dundee v Motherwell
Hearts v St Mirren
Livingston v Rangers
Ross Co v Dundee Utd
St Johnstone v Hibernian

Wednesday 1 December
Premiership
Aberdeen v Livingston
Celtic v Hearts
Dundee v St Johnstone
Hibernian v Rangers
Motherwell v Dundee Utd
St Mirren v Ross Co

Friday 3 December
League Two
Edinburgh City v Annan

Saturday 4 December
Premiership
Aberdeen v St Mirren
Dundee Utd v Celtic
Hibernian v Motherwell
Livingston v Hearts
Rangers v Dundee
St Johnstone v Ross Co

Championship
Arbroath v Raith
Hamilton v Dunfermline
Inverness v Kilmarnock
Morton v Ayr
Queen of South v Partick

League One
Clyde v Peterhead
Cove v Dumbarton
East Fife v Alloa
Montrose v Airdrieonians
Queen's Park v Falkirk

League Two
Albion Rovers v Forfar
Cowdenbeath v Stirling
Elgin v Kelty
Stenhousemuir v Stranraer

Saturday 11 December
Premiership
Celtic v Motherwell
Dundee Utd v Livingston
Hearts v Rangers
Ross Co v Dundee
St Johnstone v Aberdeen
St Mirren v Hibernian

Championship
Ayr v Hamilton
Dunfermline v Queen of South
Morton v Inverness
Partick v Arbroath
Raith v Kilmarnock

League One
Airdrieonians v Queen's Park
Alloa v Clyde
Dumbarton v Montrose
Falkirk v Cove
Peterhead v East Fife

League Two
Annan v Elgin
Forfar v Stirling
Kelty v Albion Rovers
Stenhousemuir v Edinburgh City
Stranraer v Cowdenbeath

Friday 17 December
League Two
Edinburgh City v Forfar

Saturday 18 December
Premiership
Dundee v Hearts
Hibernian v Aberdeen
Livingston v Ross Co
Motherwell v St Johnstone
Rangers v Dundee Utd
St Mirren v Celtic

Championship
Arbroath v Morton
Inverness v Hamilton
Kilmarnock v Dunfermline
Partick v Raith
Queen of South v Ayr

League One
Clyde v Airdrieonians
Cove v Alloa
Dumbarton v Peterhead
East Fife v Falkirk
Montrose v Queen's Park

League Two
Cowdenbeath v Albion Rovers
Elgin v Stenhousemuir
Stirling v Annan
Stranraer v Kelty

Sunday 26 December
Premiership
Aberdeen v Dundee
Dundee Utd v Hibernian
Hearts v Ross Co
Motherwell v Livingston
Rangers v St Mirren
St Johnstone v Celtic

Championship
Ayr v Raith
Dunfermline v Arbroath
Hamilton v Kilmarnock
Inverness v Partick
Morton v Queen of South

League One
Airdrieonians v Alloa
Cove v East Fife
Falkirk v Clyde
Montrose v Peterhead
Queen's Park v Dumbarton

League Two
Albion Rovers v Stranraer
Annan v Kelty
Cowdenbeath v Edinburgh City
Forfar v Stenhousemuir
Stirling v Elgin

Wednesday 29 December
Premiership
Aberdeen v Rangers
Celtic v Hibernian
Dundee Utd v St Mirren
Hearts v St Johnstone
Livingston v Dundee
Ross Co v Motherwell

Championship
Arbroath v Hamilton
Dunfermline v Inverness
Kilmarnock v Morton
Partick v Ayr
Raith v Queen of South

Sunday 2 January
Premiership
Celtic v Rangers
Dundee v Dundee Utd
Hibernian v Hearts
Livingston v St Johnstone
Ross Co v Aberdeen
St Mirren v Motherwell

Championship
Arbroath v Inverness
Kilmarnock v Ayr
Partick v Morton
Queen of South v Hamilton
Raith v Dunfermline

League One
Alloa v Falkirk
Clyde v Queen's Park
Dumbarton v Airdrieonians
East Fife v Montrose
Peterhead v Cove

League Two
Edinburgh City v Albion Rovers

Elgin v Forfar
Kelty v Cowdenbeath
Stenhousemuir v Stirling
Stranraer v Annan

Friday 7 January
League Two
Edinburgh City v Elgin

Saturday 8 January
Championship
Ayr v Arbroath
Hamilton v Partick
Inverness v Raith
Morton v Dunfermline
Queen of South v Kilmarnock

League One
Airdrieonians v East Fife
Clyde v Cove
Falkirk v Dumbarton
Montrose v Alloa
Queen's Park v Peterhead

League Two
Albion Rovers v Stenhousemuir
Cowdenbeath v Annan
Forfar v Stranraer
Stirling v Kelty

Saturday 15 January
Championship
Ayr v Morton
Dunfermline v Hamilton
Inverness v Queen of South
Partick v Kilmarnock
Raith v Arbroath

League One
Airdrieonians v Falkirk
Alloa v Queen's Park
Cove v Montrose
Dumbarton v East Fife
Peterhead v Clyde

League Two
Annan v Forfar
Elgin v Albion Rovers
Kelty v Edinburgh City
Stenhousemuir v Cowdenbeath
Stranraer v Stirling

Friday 21 January
League Two
Edinburgh City v Stenhousemuir

Saturday 22 January
League Two
Albion Rovers v Kelty
Cowdenbeath v Stranraer
Elgin v Annan
Stirling v Forfar

Wednesday 26 January
Premiership
Dundee Utd v Ross Co
Hearts v Celtic
Motherwell v Hibernian
Rangers v Livingston
St Johnstone v Dundee
St Mirren v Aberdeen

Saturday 29 January
Premiership
Aberdeen v St Johnstone
Celtic v Dundee Utd
Dundee v St Mirren
Hearts v Motherwell
Hibernian v Livingston
Ross Co v Rangers

Championship
Arbroath v Partick
Hamilton v Ayr
Kilmarnock v Inverness
Morton v Raith
Queen of South v Dunfermline

League One
Clyde v Alloa
Dumbarton v Cove
East Fife v Peterhead
Montrose v Falkirk
Queen's Park v Airdrieonians

League Two
Albion Rovers v Cowdenbeath
Annan v Stirling
Forfar v Edinburgh City
Kelty v Stranraer
Stenhousemuir v Elgin

Saturday 5 February
Premiership
Dundee v Ross Co
Hibernian v St Mirren
Livingston v Aberdeen
Motherwell v Celtic
Rangers v Hearts
St Johnstone v Dundee Utd

Championship
Arbroath v Kilmarnock
Ayr v Dunfermline
Inverness v Morton
Partick v Queen of South
Raith v Hamilton

League One
Cove v Airdrieonians
East Fife v Clyde
Falkirk v Queen's Park
Montrose v Dumbarton
Peterhead v Alloa

League Two
Annan v Stenhousemuir
Forfar v Albion Rovers
Kelty v Elgin
Stirling v Cowdenbeath
Stranraer v Edinburgh City

Wednesday 9 February
Premiership
Aberdeen v Celtic
Dundee Utd v Motherwell
Hearts v Dundee
Rangers v Hibernian
Ross Co v Livingston
St Mirren v St Johnstone

Friday 11 February
League Two
Edinburgh City v Stirling

Saturday 12 February
League One
Airdrieonians v Montrose
Alloa v East Fife
Clyde v Dumbarton
Falkirk v Peterhead
Queen's Park v Cove

League Two
Albion Rovers v Annan
Cowdenbeath v Forfar
Elgin v Stranraer
Stenhousemuir v Kelty

Saturday 19 February
Premiership
Celtic v Dundee
Dundee Utd v Rangers
Hibernian v Ross Co
Livingston v St Mirren
Motherwell v Aberdeen
St Johnstone v Hearts

Championship
Dunfermline v Partick
Hamilton v Morton
Inverness v Ayr
Kilmarnock v Raith
Queen of South v Arbroath

League One
Cove v Falkirk
Dumbarton v Alloa
East Fife v Queen's Park
Montrose v Clyde
Peterhead v Airdrieonians

League Two
Annan v Edinburgh City
Cowdenbeath v Elgin
Forfar v Kelty
Stirling v Albion Rovers
Stranraer v Stenhousemuir

Friday 25 February
League Two
Edinburgh City v Cowdenbeath

Saturday 26 February
Premiership
Aberdeen v Dundee Utd
Dundee v Livingston
Hibernian v Celtic
Rangers v Motherwell
Ross Co v St Johnstone
St Mirren v Hearts

Championship
Ayr v Queen of South
Dunfermline v Kilmarnock
Hamilton v Inverness
Morton v Arbroath
Raith v Partick

League One
Airdrieonians v Clyde
Alloa v Cove
Falkirk v East Fife
Peterhead v Dumbarton
Queen's Park v Montrose

League Two
Elgin v Stirling
Kelty v Annan
Stenhousemuir v Forfar
Stranraer v Albion Rovers

Wednesday 2 March
Premiership
Celtic v St Mirren
Dundee v Hibernian
Hearts v Aberdeen
Livingston v Dundee Utd
Motherwell v Ross Co
St Johnstone v Rangers

Saturday 5 March
Premiership
Dundee Utd v Hearts
Hibernian v St Johnstone
Livingston v Celtic
Motherwell v Dundee
Rangers v Aberdeen
Ross Co v St Mirren

Championship
Arbroath v Dunfermline
Kilmarnock v Hamilton
Partick v Inverness
Queen of South v Morton
Raith v Ayr

League One
Alloa v Airdrieonians
Clyde v Falkirk
Cove v Peterhead

Dumbarton v Queen's Park
Montrose v East Fife

League Two
Albion Rovers v Edinburgh City
Annan v Stranraer
Cowdenbeath v Kelty
Forfar v Elgin
Stirling v Stenhousemuir

Saturday 12 March
Championship
Ayr v Kilmarnock
Hamilton v Dunfermline
Inverness v Arbroath
Morton v Partick
Queen of South v Raith

League One
Cove v Clyde
East Fife v Dumbarton
Falkirk v Airdrieonians
Peterhead v Montrose
Queen's Park v Alloa

League Two
Annan v Elgin
Forfar v Stirling
Kelty v Albion Rovers
Stenhousemuir v Edinburgh City
Stranraer v Cowdenbeath

Friday 18 March
League Two
Edinburgh City v Stranraer

Saturday 19 March
Premiership
Aberdeen v Hibernian
Celtic v Ross Co
Dundee v Rangers
Hearts v Livingston
St Johnstone v Motherwell
St Mirren v Dundee Utd

Championship
Arbroath v Ayr
Dunfermline v Morton
Kilmarnock v Queen of South
Partick v Hamilton
Raith v Inverness

League One
Airdrieonians v Queen's Park
Alloa v Peterhead
Clyde v East Fife
Dumbarton v Falkirk
Montrose v Cove

League Two
Albion Rovers v Forfar
Cowdenbeath v Stenhousemuir

Elgin v Kelty
Stirling v Annan

Saturday 26 March
Championship
Arbroath v Raith
Hamilton v Queen of South
Inverness v Dunfermline
Kilmarnock v Partick
Morton v Ayr

League One
Airdrieonians v Cove
Dumbarton v Montrose
East Fife v Alloa
Peterhead v Falkirk
Queen's Park v Clyde

League Two
Annan v Albion Rovers
Elgin v Edinburgh City
Forfar v Cowdenbeath
Kelty v Stenhousemuir
Stirling v Stranraer

Friday 1 April
League Two
Edinburgh City v Kelty

Saturday 2 April
Premiership
Dundee v Aberdeen
Hibernian v Dundee Utd
Motherwell v St Mirren
Rangers v Celtic
Ross Co v Hearts
St Johnstone v Livingston

Championship
Ayr v Hamilton
Dunfermline v Raith
Morton v Kilmarnock
Partick v Arbroath
Queen of South v Inverness

League One
Alloa v Dumbarton
Clyde v Peterhead
Cove v Queen's Park
East Fife v Airdrieonians
Falkirk v Montrose

League Two
Albion Rovers v Elgin
Cowdenbeath v Stirling
Stenhousemuir v Annan
Stranraer v Forfar

Friday 8 April
League Two
Edinburgh City v Forfar

Saturday 9 April
Premiership
Aberdeen v Ross Co
Celtic v St Johnstone
Dundee Utd v Dundee
Hearts v Hibernian
Livingston v Motherwell
St Mirren v Rangers

Championship
Ayr v Inverness
Hamilton v Arbroath
Kilmarnock v Dunfermline
Queen of South v Partick
Raith v Morton

League One
Alloa v Clyde
Dumbarton v Peterhead
Falkirk v Cove
Montrose v Airdrieonians
Queen's Park v East Fife

League Two
Albion Rovers v Stranraer
Annan v Cowdenbeath
Elgin v Stenhousemuir
Kelty v Stirling

Saturday 16 April
Championship
Arbroath v Queen of South
Dunfermline v Ayr
Inverness v Kilmarnock
Morton v Hamilton
Partick v Raith

League One
Airdrieonians v Dumbarton
Clyde v Montrose
Cove v Alloa
East Fife v Falkirk
Peterhead v Queen's Park

League Two
Cowdenbeath v Edinburgh City
Forfar v Annan
Stenhousemuir v Albion Rovers
Stirling v Elgin
Stranraer v Kelty

Friday 22 April
League Two
Edinburgh City v Annan

Saturday 23 April
Championship
Hamilton v Raith
Kilmarnock v Arbroath
Morton v Inverness
Partick v Dunfermline
Queen of South v Ayr
League One
Clyde v Airdrieonians
Cove v Dumbarton
Falkirk v Alloa
Montrose v Queen's Park
Peterhead v East Fife

League Two
Albion Rovers v Stirling
Elgin v Cowdenbeath
Kelty v Forfar
Stenhousemuir v Stranraer

Friday 29 April
Championship
Arbroath v Morton
Ayr v Partick
Dunfermline v Queen of South
Inverness v Hamilton
Raith v Kilmarnock

League One
Airdrieonians v Peterhead
Alloa v Montrose
Dumbarton v Clyde
East Fife v Cove
Queen's Park v Falkirk

League Two
Annan v Kelty
Cowdenbeath v Albion Rovers
Forfar v Stenhousemuir
Stirling v Edinburgh City
Stranraer v Elgin

NATIONAL LEAGUE FIXTURES 2021–2022

Saturday 21 August
Aldershot v Chesterfield
Barnet v Notts Co
Bromley v Grimsby
Dover v Solihull
Halifax v Maidenhead
King's Lynn v Southend
Stockport v Dag & Red
Torquay v Altrincham
Wealdstone v Woking
Weymouth v Boreham Wood
Wrexham v Yeovil

Saturday 28 August
Boreham Wood v Aldershot
Chesterfield v Wealdstone
Dag & Red v Bromley
Eastleigh v Wrexham
Grimsby v Weymouth
Maidenhead v Dover
Notts Co v Torquay
Solihull v Barnet
Southend v Stockport
Woking v Halifax
Yeovil v King's Lynn

Monday 30 August
Aldershot v Yeovil
Barnet v Dag & Red
Bromley v Eastleigh
Dover v Boreham Wood
Halifax v Altrincham
King's Lynn v Chesterfield
Stockport v Grimsby
Torquay v Woking
Wealdstone v Southend
Weymouth v Maidenhead
Wrexham v Notts Co

Saturday 4 September
Altrincham v Dover
Boreham Wood v Stockport
Chesterfield v Bromley
Dag & Red v Wealdstone
Eastleigh v King's Lynn
Grimsby v Barnet
Maidenhead v Torquay
Notts Co v Aldershot
Solihull v Weymouth
Southend v Wrexham
Yeovil v Halifax

Saturday 11 September
Aldershot v Solihull
Barnet v Eastleigh
Bromley v Boreham Wood
Dover v Chesterfield
Halifax v Southend
King's Lynn v Dag & Red

Stockport v Yeovil
Torquay v Grimsby
Wealdstone v Altrincham
Weymouth v Notts Co
Wrexham v Woking

Tuesday 14 September
Altrincham v King's Lynn
Boreham Wood v Halifax
Chesterfield v Barnet
Dag & Red v Weymouth
Eastleigh v Dover
Grimsby v Wrexham
Maidenhead v Stockport
Notts Co v Wealdstone
Solihull v Torquay
Southend v Aldershot
Woking v Bromley

Saturday 18 September
Bromley v Barnet
Halifax v Stockport
Grimsby v Eastleigh
Notts Co v Maidenhead
Solihull v Boreham Wood
Torquay v Southend
Wealdstone v Aldershot
Weymouth v Dover
Woking v Chesterfield
Wrexham v Dag & Red
Yeovil v Altrincham

Saturday 25 September
Aldershot v Halifax
Altrincham v Notts Co
Barnet v Weymouth
Boreham Wood v Yeovil
Chesterfield v Torquay
Dag & Red v Solihull
Dover v Bromley
Eastleigh v Woking
King's Lynn v Wealdstone
Maidenhead v Grimsby
Stockport v Wrexham

Saturday 2 October
Aldershot v Wrexham
Barnet v Halifax
Chesterfield v Yeovil
Dag & Red v Altrincham
Eastleigh v Boreham Wood
Grimsby v Dover
Maidenhead v King's Lynn
Notts Co v Woking
Solihull v Southend
Torquay v Wealdstone
Weymouth v Stockport

Tuesday 5 October
Altrincham v Grimsby
Boreham Wood v Torquay
Bromley v Weymouth
Dover v Aldershot
Halifax v Notts Co
King's Lynn v Barnet
Southend v Eastleigh
Wealdstone v Solihull
Woking v Dag & Red
Wrexham v Chesterfield
Yeovil v Maidenhead

Saturday 9 October
Altrincham v Maidenhead
Boreham Wood v Dag & Red
Bromley v Torquay
Dover v Barnet
Halifax v Weymouth
King's Lynn v Solihull
Southend v Chesterfield
Stockport v Aldershot
Wealdstone v Eastleigh
Woking v Grimsby
Yeovil v Notts Co

Saturday 23 October
Aldershot v Bromley
Barnet v Wrexham
Chesterfield v Boreham Wood
Dag & Red v Southend
Eastleigh v Altrincham
Grimsby v Yeovil
Maidenhead v Woking
Notts Co v Stockport
Solihull v Halifax
Torquay v King's Lynn
Weymouth v Wealdstone

Tuesday 26 October
Aldershot v Weymouth
Altrincham v Solihull
Chesterfield v Eastleigh
Halifax v Dag & Red
King's Lynn v Boreham Wood
Maidenhead v Wrexham
Notts Co v Bromley
Southend v Dover
Stockport v Barnet
Wealdstone v Grimsby
Yeovil v Woking

Saturday 30 October
Barnet v Aldershot
Boreham Wood v Southend
Bromley v Halifax
Dag & Red v Chesterfield
Dover v Stockport
Eastleigh v Maidenhead
Grimsby v Notts Co
Solihull v Yeovil
Weymouth v King's Lynn

Woking v Altrincham
Wrexham v Torquay

Saturday 13 November
Aldershot v Grimsby
Altrincham v Boreham Wood
Chesterfield v Weymouth
King's Lynn v Wrexham
Maidenhead v Dag & Red
Notts Co v Solihull
Southend v Woking
Stockport v Bromley
Torquay v Dover
Wealdstone v Barnet
Yeovil v Eastleigh

Saturday 20 November
Barnet v Torquay
Boreham Wood v Maidenhead
Bromley v King's Lynn
Dag & Red v Yeovil
Dover v Halifax
Eastleigh v Notts Co
Grimsby v Southend
Solihull v Chesterfield
Weymouth v Altrincham
Woking v Stockport
Wrexham v Wealdstone

Tuesday 23 November
Aldershot v Torquay
Boreham Wood v Notts Co
Bromley v Yeovil
Chesterfield v Altrincham
Dag & Red v Eastleigh
Dover v Wealdstone
Halifax v Wrexham
Solihull v Grimsby
Southend v Maidenhead
Stockport v King's Lynn
Weymouth v Woking

Saturday 4 December
Aldershot v Altrincham
Barnet v Maidenhead
Bromley v Wealdstone
Chesterfield v Notts Co
Dag & Red v Grimsby
Dover v Wrexham
Halifax v King's Lynn
Solihull v Woking
Southend v Yeovil
Stockport v Eastleigh
Weymouth v Torquay

Saturday 11 December
Altrincham v Bromley
Eastleigh v Aldershot
Grimsby v Chesterfield
King's Lynn v Dover
Maidenhead v Solihull
Notts Co v Southend

Torquay v Stockport
Wealdstone v Halifax
Woking v Boreham Wood
Wrexham v Weymouth
Yeovil v Barnet

Sunday 26 December
Aldershot v Woking
Barnet v Boreham Wood
Bromley v Southend
Dover v Dag & Red
Halifax v Grimsby
King's Lynn v Notts Co
Stockport v Altrincham
Torquay v Yeovil
Wealdstone v Maidenhead
Weymouth v Eastleigh
Wrexham v Solihull

Tuesday 28 December
Altrincham v Wrexham
Boreham Wood v Wealdstone
Chesterfield v Halifax
Dag & Red v Aldershot
Eastleigh v Torquay
Grimsby v King's Lynn
Maidenhead v Bromley
Solihull v Stockport
Southend v Barnet
Woking v Dover
Yeovil v Weymouth

Sunday 2 January
Altrincham v Stockport
Boreham Wood v Barnet
Chesterfield v King's Lynn
Dag & Red v Dover
Eastleigh v Weymouth
Grimsby v Halifax
Maidenhead v Wealdstone
Notts Co v Wrexham
Southend v Bromley
Woking v Aldershot
Yeovil v Torquay

Saturday 8 January
Aldershot v Maidenhead
Barnet v Altrincham
Bromley v Solihull
Dover v Notts Co
Halifax v Eastleigh
King's Lynn v Woking
Stockport v Chesterfield
Torquay v Dag & Red
Wealdstone v Yeovil
Weymouth v Southend
Wrexham v Boreham Wood

Saturday 22 January
Altrincham v Torquay
Boreham Wood v Weymouth
Chesterfield v Aldershot

Dag & Red v Stockport
Grimsby v Bromley
Maidenhead v Halifax
Notts Co v Barnet
Solihull v Dover
Southend v King's Lynn
Woking v Wealdstone
Yeovil v Wrexham

Tuesday 25 January
Aldershot v Southend
Barnet v Chesterfield
Bromley v Woking
Dover v Eastleigh
Halifax v Boreham Wood
King's Lynn v Altrincham
Stockport v Maidenhead
Torquay v Solihull
Wealdstone v Notts Co
Weymouth v Dag & Red
Wrexham v Grimsby

Saturday 29 January
Barnet v Stockport
Boreham Wood v King's Lynn
Bromley v Notts Co
Dag & Red v Halifax
Dover v Southend
Eastleigh v Chesterfield
Grimsby v Wealdstone
Solihull v Altrincham
Weymouth v Aldershot
Woking v Yeovil
Wrexham v Maidenhead

Saturday 5 February
Aldershot v Barnet
Altrincham v Woking
Chesterfield v Dag & Red
Halifax v Bromley
King's Lynn v Weymouth
Maidenhead v Eastleigh
Notts Co v Grimsby
Southend v Boreham Wood
Stockport v Dover
Torquay v Wrexham
Yeovil v Solihull

Saturday 12 February
Barnet v Wealdstone
Boreham Wood v Altrincham
Bromley v Stockport
Dag & Red v Maidenhead
Dover v Torquay
Eastleigh v Yeovil
Grimsby v Aldershot
Solihull v Notts Co
Weymouth v Chesterfield
Woking v Southend
Wrexham v King's Lynn

urday 19 February

ncham v Weymouth
sterfield v Solihull
fax v Dover
g's Lynn v Bromley
denhead v Boreham Wood
tts Co v Eastleigh
thend v Grimsby
ckport v Woking
quay v Barnet
aldstone v Wrexham
vil v Dag & Red

esday 22 February

llershot v Dover
rnet v King's Lynn
esterfield v Wrexham
g & Red v Woking
stleigh v Southend
imsby v Altrincham
idenhead v Yeovil
tts County v Halifax
ihull v Wealdstone
quay v Boreham Wood
ymouth v Bromley

turday 26 February

rincham v Dag & Red
eham Wood v Eastleigh
er v Grimsby
ifax v Barnet
g's Lynn v Maidenhead
thend v Solihull
ckport v Weymouth
aldstone v Torquay
king v Notts Co
xham v Aldershot
vil v Chesterfield

turday 5 March

ershot v Stockport
net v Dover
sterfield v Southend
& Red v Boreham Wood
tleigh v Wealdstone
nsby v Woking
denhead v Altrincham
ts Co v Yeovil
hull v King's Lynn
quay v Bromley
mouth v Halifax

turday 12 March

ncham v Eastleigh
eham Wood v Chesterfield
mley v Aldershot
fax v Solihull
g's Lynn v Torquay
thend v Dag & Red
ckport v Notts Co
ldstone v Weymouth
ling v Maidenhead

Wrexham v Barnet
Yeovil v Grimsby

Saturday 19 March

Aldershot v King's Lynn
Barnet v Woking
Boreham Wood v Grimsby
Bromley v Wrexham
Chesterfield v Maidenhead
Dag & Red v Notts Co
Dover v Yeovil
Halifax v Torquay
Solihull v Eastleigh
Southend v Altrincham
Stockport v Wealdstone

Tuesday 22 March

Altrincham v Chesterfield
Eastleigh v Dag & Red
Grimsby v Solihull
King's Lynn v Stockport
Maidenhead v Southend
Notts Co v Boreham Wood
Torquay v Aldershot
Wealdstone v Dover
Woking v Weymouth
Wrexham v Halifax
Yeovil v Bromley

Saturday 26 March

Altrincham v Aldershot
Eastleigh v Stockport
Grimsby v Dag & Red
King's Lynn v Halifax
Maidenhead v Barnet
Notts Co v Chesterfield
Torquay v Weymouth
Wealdstone v Bromley
Woking v Solihull
Wrexham v Dover
Yeovil v Southend

Saturday 2 April

Aldershot v Eastleigh
Barnet v Yeovil
Boreham Wood v Woking
Bromley v Altrincham
Chesterfield v Grimsby
Dover v King's Lynn
Halifax v Wealdstone
Solihull v Maidenhead
Southend v Notts Co
Stockport v Torquay
Weymouth v Wrexham

Saturday 9 April

Aldershot v Boreham Wood
Barnet v Solihull
Bromley v Dag & Red
Dover v Maidenhead
Halifax v Woking
King's Lynn v Yeovil

Stockport v Southend
Torquay v Notts Co
Wealdstone v Chesterfield
Weymouth v Grimsby
Wrexham v Eastleigh

Friday 15 April
Altrincham v Halifax
Boreham Wood v Dover
Dag & Red v Barnet
Eastleigh v Bromley
Grimsby v Stockport
Maidenhead v Weymouth
Notts Co v King's Lynn
Solihull v Wrexham
Southend v Wealdstone
Woking v Torquay
Yeovil v Aldershot

Monday 18 April
Aldershot v Dag & Red
Barnet v Southend
Bromley v Maidenhead
Dover v Woking
Halifax v Chesterfield
King's Lynn v Grimsby
Stockport v Solihull
Torquay v Eastleigh
Wealdstone v Boreham Wood
Weymouth v Yeovil
Wrexham v Altrincham

Saturday 23 April
Altrincham v Wealdstone
Boreham Wood v Bromley
Chesterfield v Dover
Dag & Red v King's Lynn
Eastleigh v Barnet
Grimsby v Torquay
Notts Co v Weymouth
Solihull v Aldershot
Southend v Halifax
Woking v Wrexham
Yeovil v Stockport

Saturday 30 April
Aldershot v Notts Co
Barnet v Grimsby

Bromley v Chesterfield
Dover v Altrincham
Halifax v Yeovil
King's Lynn v Eastleigh
Stockport v Boreham Wood
Torquay v Maidenhead
Wealdstone v Dag & Red
Weymouth v Solihull
Wrexham v Southend

Monday 2 May
Altrincham v Barnet
Boreham Wood v Wrexham
Chesterfield v Stockport
Dag & Red v Torquay
Eastleigh v Halifax
Maidenhead v Aldershot
Notts Co v Dover
Solihull v Bromley
Southend v Weymouth
Woking v King's Lynn
Yeovil v Wealdstone

Saturday 7 May
Bromley v Dover
Halifax v Aldershot
Grimsby v Maidenhead
Notts Co v Altrincham
Solihull v Dag & Red
Torquay v Chesterfield
Wealdstone v King's Lynn
Weymouth v Barnet
Woking v Eastleigh
Wrexham v Stockport
Yeovil v Boreham Wood

Sunday 15 May
Aldershot v Wealdstone
Altrincham v Yeovil
Barnet v Bromley
Boreham Wood v Solihull
Chesterfield v Woking
Dag & Red v Wrexham
Dover v Weymouth
Eastleigh v Grimsby
Maidenhead v Notts Co
Southend v Torquay
Stockport v Halifax